March 3–5, 2014
San Antonio, Texas

I0028881

**Association for
Computing Machinery**

Advancing Computing as a Science & Profession

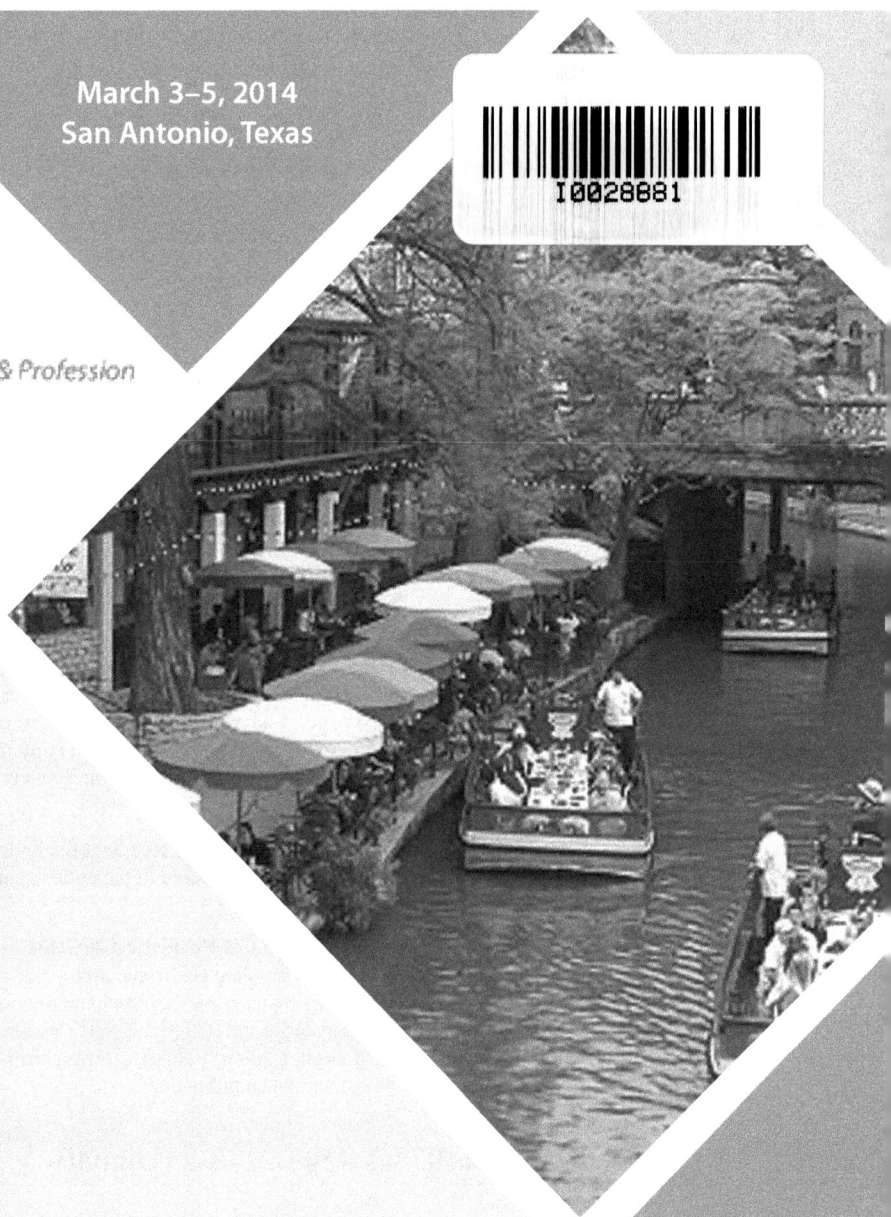

CODASPY'14

Proceedings of the 4th ACM Conference on

Data and Application Security and Privacy

Sponsored by:

ACM SIGSAC

Supported by:

ICS, CERIAS and Cyber Center

Association for
Computing Machinery

Advancing Computing as a Science & Profession

The Association for Computing Machinery
2 Penn Plaza, Suite 701
New York, New York 10121-0701

Notice to Past Authors of ACM-Published Articles
ACM intends to create a complete electronic archive of all articles and/or other material previously published by ACM. If you have written a work that has been previously published by ACM in any journal or conference proceedings prior to 1978, or any SIG Newsletter at any time, and you do NOT want this work to appear in the ACM Digital Library, please inform permissions@acm.org, stating the title of the work, the author(s), and where and when published.

ISBN: 978-1-4503-2278-2 (Digital)

ISBN: 978-1-4503-6101-2 (Print)

Additional copies may be ordered prepaid from:

ACM Order Department
PO Box 30777
New York, NY 10087-0777, USA

Phone: 1-800-342-6626 (USA and Canada)
+1-212-626-0500 (Global)
Fax: +1-212-944-1318
E-mail: acmhelp@acm.org
Hours of Operation: 8:30 am – 4:30 pm ET

Printed in the USA

Foreword

It is our great pleasure to welcome you to the fourth edition of the *ACM Conference on Data and Application Security and Privacy (CODASPY 2014)*, which follows the successful three editions held in February 2011, 2012 and 2013. This conference series has been founded to foster novel and exciting research in this arena and to help generate new directions for further research and development. The initial concept came up in a conversation between the two co-founders when both happened to be at the same meeting. This was followed by discussions with a number of fellow cyber security researchers. Their enthusiastic encouragement persuaded the co-founders to move ahead with the always daunting task of creating a high-quality conference.

Data and applications that manipulate data are crucial assets in today's information age. With the increasing drive towards availability of data and services anytime and anywhere, security and privacy risks have increased. Vast amounts of privacy-sensitive data are being collected today by organizations for a variety of reasons. Unauthorized disclosure, modification, usage or denial of access to these data and corresponding services may result in high human and financial costs. New applications such as social networking and social computing provide value by aggregating input from numerous individual users and the mobile devices they carry and computing new information of benefit to society and individuals. To achieve efficiency and effectiveness in traditional domains such as healthcare there is a drive to make these records electronic and highly available. The need for organizations to share information effectively is underscored by rapid innovations in the business world that require close collaboration across traditional boundaries. Security and privacy in these and other arenas can be meaningfully achieved only in context of the application domain. Data and applications security and privacy has rapidly expanded as a research field with many important challenges to be addressed.

In response to the call for papers of CODASPY 2014 a total of 119 papers were submitted from Africa, Asia, Australia, Europe, North America, and South America. The program committee selected 19 full-length research papers (less than 16% of acceptance rate). These papers cover a variety of topics, including privacy of social networks, novel privacy techniques and applications, and access control and security of smart appliances and mobile devices. The program committee also selected nine short papers for presentation. This year for the second time the program also includes a poster paper session presenting exciting work in progress. The program is complemented by keynote speeches by Dongyan Xu and by Jarret Raim, as well as a panel (topic not yet decided at press time).

The organization of a conference like CODASPY requires the collaboration of many individuals. First of all, we would like to thank the authors for submitting to the conference and the keynote speakers for graciously accepting our invitation. We express our gratitude to the program committee members and external reviewers for their efforts in reviewing the papers, engaging in active online discussion during the selection process and providing valuable feedback to authors. We also would like to thank the poster paper track chair, Gabriel Ghinita, and the committee of this track for an excellent job with soliciting and selecting poster papers. Our special thanks go to our local arrangement chair Suzanne Tanaka, to our Web master and publicity chair Ram Krishnan. Finally, we would like to thank our sponsor, ACM SIGSAC, for their support of this conference.

We hope that you will find this program interesting and that the conference will provide you with a valuable opportunity to interact with other researchers and practitioners from institutions around the world. Enjoy!

Jaehong Park
CODASPY'14 Program Chair
University of Texas at San
Antonio, USA

Elisa Bertino
CODASPY'14 General Chair
and co-founder
Purdue University, USA

Ravi Sandhu
CODASPY'14 General Chair
and co-founder
University of Texas at San
Antonio, USA

Table of Contents

Session Order 5: Poster Session

Session Chair: Gabriel Ghinita *(University of Massachusetts, Boston)*

Session Order 6: Mobile Security

Session Chair: Debin Gao *(Singapore Management University)*

Session Order 7: Novel Techniques for Data Security

Session Chair: Adam J. Lee *(University of Pittsburgh)*

Session Order 8: Keynote Address 2

Session Chair: Ravi Sandhu *(University of Texas at San Antonio)*

Session Order 9: Short Papers 1

Session Chair: Mohamed Shehab *(University of North Carolina at Charlotte)*

Session Order 10: Short Papers 2

Session Chair: Gabriel Ghinita *(University of Massachusetts, Boston)*

Session Order 11: Privacy Preserving Techniques

Session Chair: Murat Kantarcioglu *(University of Texas at Dallas)*

CODASPY 2014 Conference Organization

General Chairs: Elisa Bertino, *Purdue University, USA*
Ravi Sandhu, *University of Texas at San Antonio, USA*

Program/Publication Chair: Jaehong Park, *University of Texas at San Antonio, USA*

Local Arrangements Chair: Suzanne Tanaka, *University of Texas at San Antonio, USA*

Publicity/Web Chair: Ram Krishnan, *University of Texas at San Antonio, USA*

Poster Chair: Gabriel Ghinita, *University of Massachusetts at Boston, USA*

Program Committee: Gail-Joon Ahn, *Arizona State University, USA*
Barbara Carminati, *University of Insubria, Italy*
William Enck, *North Carolina State University, USA*
Elena Ferrari, *University of Insubria, Italy*
Philip W. L. Fong, *University of Calgary, Canada*
Debin Gao, *Singapore Management University, Singapore*
Gabriel Ghinita, *University of Massachusetts, Boston, USA*
Carl A. Gunter, *University of Illinois, USA*
Hannes Hartenstein, *KIT, Germany*
Murat Kantarcioglu, *University of Texas at Dallas, USA*
Guenter Karjoth, *Lucerne University of Applied Sciences, Switzerland*
Ram Krishnan, *University of Texas at San Antonio, USA*
Ashish Kundu, *IBM T J Watson Research Center, USA*
Adam J. Lee, *University of Pittsburgh, USA*
Qi Li, *ETH, Switzerland*
Fabio Martinelli, *IIT-CNR, Italy*
Jun Pang, *University of Luxembourg, Luxembourg*
Günther Pernul, *Universität Regensburg, Germany*
Alexander Pretschner, *Technische Universität München, Germany*
Indrajit Ray, *Colorado State University, USA*
Ahmad-Reza Sadeghi, *Technical University Darmstadt, Germany*
Seung-Hyun Seo, *Purdue University, USA*
Anna Squicciarini, *The Pennsylvania State University, USA*
Hassan Takabi, *University of North Texas, USA*
Mahesh Tripunitara, *The University of Waterloo, Canada*
Jaideep Vaidya, *Rutgers University, USA*
Vijay Varadharajan, *Macquarie University, Australia*
Danfeng Yao, *Virginia Tech, USA*
Chuan Yue, *University of Colorado Colorado Springs, USA*
Xinwen Zhang, *Samsung, USA*

CODASPY 2014 Conference Sponsor & Supporters

Sponsor:

Supporters:

On the Suitability of Dissemination-centric Access Control Systems for Group-centric Sharing

William C. Garrison III
bill@cs.pitt.edu

Yechen Qiao
yeq1@cs.pitt.edu

Adam J. Lee
adamlee@cs.pitt.edu

Department of Computer Science
University of Pittsburgh
Pittsburgh, Pennsylvania 15260

ABSTRACT

The Group-centric Secure Information Sharing (g-SIS) family of models has been proposed for modeling environments in which group dynamics dictate information-sharing policies and practices. This is in contrast to traditional, dissemination-centric sharing models, which focus on attaching policies to resources that limit their flow from producer to consumer. The creators of g-SIS speculate that it may not be strictly more expressive than dissemination-centric models, but that it nevertheless has pragmatic efficiency advantages in group-centric scenarios [12]. In this paper, we formally and systematically test these characteristics of an access control system's suitability for a scenario—expressiveness and cost—to evaluate the capabilities of dissemination-centric systems within group-centric workloads. We show that several common dissemination-centric systems lack the expressiveness to meet all security guarantees while implementing the wide range of behavior that is characteristic of the g-SIS models, except via impractical, convoluted encodings. Further, even more efficient implementations (admissible under relaxed security requirements) suffer from high storage and computational overheads. These observations support the practical and theoretical significance of the g-SIS models, and provide insight into techniques for evaluating and comparing access control systems in terms of both expressiveness and cost.

Categories and Subject Descriptors

D.4.6 [**Operating Systems**]: Security and Protection—*Access controls*; K.6.5 [**Management of Computing and Information Systems**]: Security and Protection

Keywords

Information sharing; Access control; Suitability analysis

1. INTRODUCTION

Group-centric Security Information Sharing (g-SIS) [11,12] is a modeling paradigm and class of access control models that has been proposed for sharing environments in which users and resources are brought together in groups to facilitate collaboration and efficient exchange of information. Its creators contrast it with the traditional, *dissemination-centric* modeling paradigms that are currently used in access control and information sharing. In dissemination-centric sharing, emphasis is placed on attaching policies (and/or attributes that determine policy) to resources as they are created or made available. These policies then restrict which consumers can access the resources. In g-SIS, on the other hand, users are granted access to resources based on their temporal membership in groups—e.g., if object o is added to a group that a user u is a member of, u will be granted access to o. The rules for users who join later, objects that are removed, and users who leave are determined by the particular parameterization of g-SIS used.

Although g-SIS seems to represent its motivating scenarios rather elegantly, there has, to date, been no fully-functional implementation of the g-SIS models. This may partially be due to the creators' hypothesis that group- and dissemination-centric techniques yield the same theoretical set of capabilities (i.e., that the set of dissemination-centric models is, collectively, equal in expressiveness to the set of group-centric models) [12]. Even assuming that this hypothesis holds, g-SIS seems pragmatically better-suited to group-centric workloads than systems such as role-based access control built with dissemination-centric uses in mind (in both ease of implementation and efficiency). Thus, in this work we evaluate the expressiveness hypothesis and other questions regarding the capabilities of dissemination-centric access control systems within the context of group-centric sharing workloads. Specifically, we investigate the following questions:

1. Which systems based on the g-SIS models can be *safely* implemented within, or simulated by, dissemination-centric access control systems?

2. How *strong* are the security properties that can be guaranteed by dissemination-centric systems when implementing workloads based on the g-SIS models?

3. How *efficiently* can dissemination-centric systems implement workloads based on the g-SIS models?

4. What practically-interesting instantiations of the g-SIS models *cannot* be safely and efficiently implemented by dissemination-centric systems?

While investigating these questions, we formalize several instantiations of the g-SIS models. Some are based on mathematical extrema in the space of g-SIS instantiations and are intended to represent a diverse cross-section of the capabilities of the g-SIS models. Others are based on realistic use cases to which g-SIS seems particularly well-suited. We then employ *parameterized expressiveness* [9]—a fine-grained, parameterized generalization of simulation-based expressiveness techniques—to answer questions #1 and #2. To evaluate question #3, we utilize a Monte Carlo simulation technique to generate traces of group-based sharing actions. These actions are then simulated in g-SIS systems, and they are translated into equivalent action sequences in dissemination-centric access control systems. The costs of executing these traces are recorded and compared. Finally, we address question #4 by interpreting and analyzing the results of questions #1–3, discussing the various failings of the use of dissemination-centric techniques in group-centric environments.

Our analysis provides new insights into the relationship between group-centric and dissemination-centric sharing, and represents the first in-depth analysis into the use of g-SIS. We support the notion that g-SIS is a practically significant proposal by demonstrating the inability of traditional systems to satisfy many of its models safely and efficiently. More fundamentally interesting, to the best of our knowledge, our analysis represents the first systematic examination and comparison of access control systems based on both their theoretical capabilities (i.e., relative expressive power) and more pragmatic notions of quantitative efficiency (i.e., implementation costs). We believe this style of analysis has the potential to answer many practical questions that arise when examining an application's access control needs, and that our demonstration of these techniques toward understanding the impact of g-SIS supports this claim by example.

The rest of this paper is structured as follows. In Section 2, we introduce g-SIS and expressiveness analysis. In Section 3, we describe the specific g-SIS instantiations that we will be analyzing. In Section 4, we explain our parameterized expressiveness analysis and interpret its results. In Section 5, we discuss our techniques for cost analysis via Monte Carlo simulation, and present the results of this analysis. We discuss our results and reason about the drawbacks of utilizing dissemination-centric techniques for group-centric workloads in Section 6. Finally, we discuss other related work in Section 7 and conclude in Section 8.

2. BACKGROUND AND PRIOR WORK

We now discuss the immediately relevant prior work. We first overview g-SIS, the group-centric secure information sharing paradigm that inspires our workloads. We then provide an overview of prior work on access control expressiveness analysis, with a particular focus on the technique used in this work: parameterized expressiveness. A discussion of other related work is deferred to Section 7.

2.1 The g-SIS Models

The g-SIS models encompass a wide range of access control systems and behavior, and seem to subsume other group- and role-based access control and information sharing systems [16, 18,21]. The motivating scenarios which inspired g-SIS include periodical subscriptions and secure message rooms. It is conceptually simpler to model such scenarios within g-SIS than by using dissemination-centric access control; that g-SIS

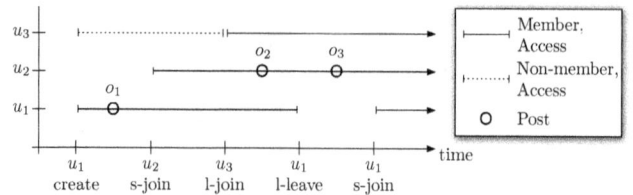

Figure 1: Example accesses in a single group in g-SIS

is inherently more capable of representing such scenarios is a claim that we make and support through the present work.

A major distinguishing feature of g-SIS is its preservation of a full membership record for groups. A graphical depiction of such a record is shown in Figure 1. Users can join and leave groups, and objects can be added and removed from groups. The log of these events is used to decide whether a user can access an object. The basic operations each have numerous variants, ranging from *strict* to *fully liberal*. The semantics of these variants depends on the type of action.

Users who perform a strict join to a group receive access only to objects added after they join, whereas a fully liberal join grants immediate access to all existing objects. Note that, in Figure 1, user u_2 performs a strict join whereas u_3 performs a liberal join, meaning that u_3 has access to o_1 while u_2 does not. A strict leave rescinds all of the user's accesses within the group; a liberal leave allows the user to retain access. Performing a strict add of a message to a group grants only current members access; a liberal add grants future members access as well. In Figure 1, if o_3 is added using strict add, then u_1 could not access it even after a liberal join. Finally, a strict remove rescinds access to the removed object from all users in the group, while a liberal remove allows users to retain access.

The application of these operations to the motivating scenarios (subscriptions, secure messaging) are, thus, fairly obvious. A subscription service can provide a base level of service with no access to back issues and no continued access after canceling. For an additional fee, users can access back issues (via liberal join) or maintain access to their issues after canceling (via liberal leave). Secure messaging can make various uses of combinations of strict and liberal actions: users can liberal leave before a discussion with which they have a conflict of interest and strict join at its conclusion; objects to which new members should not gain automatic access can be strict added while others are liberal added.

Restrictions on g-SIS in this paper. In this work, we primarily focus on strict and purely-liberal variants of actions, such as those described above. However, g-SIS also supports variants that lie between these extremes. For example, in some systems a liberal (but not *fully* liberal) leave might allow a user to retain only *some* of their accesses when leaving. The semantics of these variants are application-dependent. In this work, liberal actions are assumed to be fully liberal unless otherwise specified. Finally, g-SIS supports variants of join with different behavior for users who have left and re-joined a group. Lossy join may revoke some or all permissions retained from a past liberal leave; lossless join will not revoke any permissions. Restorative join may re-grant some or all permissions revoked by a past leave; nonrestorative join will not re-grant any permissions. In this work, we focus on lossless, nonrestorative joins unless otherwise specified.

2.2 Expressiveness Analysis

Prior Work. We first evaluate the ability of dissemination-centric approaches to implement group-centric workloads in terms of theoretical capability, or *expressiveness*. The expressiveness of an access control system describes the set of policies that it can represent. Many notions of expressiveness have been studied in the literature [1,3,5,7,9,13,14,17,19,20, 22], and today there is much ambiguity in saying simply, "$\mathcal{Y}$ is more expressive than $\mathcal{Z}$." Some notions only concern whether one system can represent all the same sets of authorizations as another [5], while others reduce a system's storage to an abstracted structure to show how one can subsume another structurally [1]. Somewhere in between, other notions of expressiveness define a set of queries (including authorizations) that must be preserved [9,22]. Some may only concern properties of the states [3], but most go further, enforcing preservation of state reachability [5,7,17,19]: i.e., "not only are all $\mathcal{Z}$'s states expressible in $\mathcal{Y}$, $\mathcal{Y}$'s mechanism for transforming states allows us to build them." Some notions even go so far as to enforce back-reachability, by requiring that any state in $\mathcal{Y}$ representing a state in $\mathcal{Z}$ should not be able to be transformed into a state that the original in $\mathcal{Z}$ could not be [1,22]. There are several other dimensions in which expressiveness notions differ, including the use of strong simulation (a state change in $\mathcal{Z}$ must be simulated in a single state change in $\mathcal{Y}$) vs. weak simulation (a state change in $\mathcal{Z}$ can be simulated in a number of changes in $\mathcal{Y}$).

Parameterized Expressiveness. Given this state of affairs, and our lack of tools for reconciling various notions of expressiveness, *parameterized expressiveness* is an attractive approach [9]. Parameterized expressiveness is an access control expressiveness framework created to generalize other expressiveness notions. This framework has much in common with other techniques, defining systems based on state machines and building various types of simulations between them. However, rather than commit to a single set of properties preserved by those simulations, the set of security guarantees to be preserved is a parameter of the analysis. This allows the notion of expressiveness used in a particular analysis to match the requirements of the application within which the systems are candidates for use.

This focus on expressiveness within the context of a particular application allows expressiveness to be defined with respect to *workloads*, which are descriptions of specific application environments. This allows an analyst to be more precise about expressiveness in a practical sense, with a focus on the capability to represent the policies that are needed by an application, rather than considering the ability to represent a superset of another system's policies. Whereas other expressiveness notions allow an analyst to make statements such as, "System $\mathcal{Y}$ admits a simulation of form S of $\mathcal{Z}$," parameterized expressiveness makes statements such as, "If system $\mathcal{Z}$ can implement workload $\mathcal{W}$ while preserving the set of properties $\mathcal{G}$, then $\mathcal{Y}$ can implement $\mathcal{W}$ while preserving $\mathcal{G}$," which is more closely aligned with the practical concerns associated with a system's expressiveness. For these reasons, parameterized expressiveness is a good fit for our goals.

PE Formalisms. We now summarize key structures used during parameterized expressiveness analyses. Interested readers can refer to [9] for full details.

- An access control *model* defines how protection state is encoded and interpreted. Given model $\mathcal{M} = \langle \mathcal{S}, \mathcal{R}, \mathcal{Q}, \vdash \rangle$, $\mathcal{S}$ is a set of states, $\mathcal{R}$ is a set of authorization requests, and $\mathcal{Q}$ is a set of queries. $\mathcal{Q}$ includes at least $auth(r)$ for each request r, and the entailment relation $\vdash: \mathcal{S} \times \mathcal{Q} \to \{\text{TRUE}, \text{FALSE}\}$ defines which queries are true in each state. We sometimes denote $\mathcal{S}$ as $States(\mathcal{M})$ and $\mathcal{Q}$ as $Queries(\mathcal{M})$. A *theory*, an assignment for each query in state x, is denoted $Th(\text{x})$. The subset of $Th(x)$ consisting of only $auth$ queries is $Auth(x)$. The set of all possible theories in $\mathcal{M}$ is denoted $Th(\mathcal{M})$.

- An access control *system* refines a model by defining methods for transforming the state. A system is thus a state machine $\langle \mathcal{M}, \mathcal{L}, next \rangle$ which defines its parent model $\mathcal{M}$, a set of labels $\mathcal{L}$ (representing access control commands), and the transition function $next : States(\mathcal{M}) \times \mathcal{L} \to States(\mathcal{M})$. We sometimes denote the set of states, theories, and queries in model $\mathcal{M}$ of system $\mathcal{Y}$ as $States(\mathcal{Y})$, $Th(\mathcal{Y})$, and $Queries(\mathcal{Y})$, respectively.

- An access control *workload* describes the access control demands of an application. This is accomplished by describing an idealized access control system encoding required functionality, and the set of allowable traces of labels through that system. A workload $\mathcal{W} = \langle \mathcal{A}, \mathcal{T} \rangle$ thus defines access control system $\mathcal{A}$ and set of traces $\mathcal{T}$. Each trace is a pair $\langle s_1, \tau \rangle$, where $s_0 \in States(\mathcal{A})$ is the initial state and $\tau = \ell_1 \circ \ell_2 \circ \cdots$ is a sequence of labels in $\mathcal{A}$: $\forall i, \ell_i \in Labels(\mathcal{A})$.

Given these formalisms, we now define the particular systems and workloads inspired by g-SIS, with respect to which we will evaluate dissemination-centric systems.

3. INSTANTIATIONS OF G-SIS

In this section, we describe the g-SIS systems and workloads that form the basis of our analyses in Sections 4 and 5. We describe these systems using the formalism described above to facilitate our analyses.

3.1 The g-SIS$_0$ Model

The g-SIS$_0$ model defines the state representation and queries for our g-SIS systems. It defines structures for storing the records for all combinations of the basic g-SIS strict and liberal actions (join, leave, add, remove). The authorization request is defined for non-restorative joins. In the g-SIS$_0$ model, states are comprised of the following fields.

- Sets $S, O, G,$ and T of subjects, objects, groups, and times
- $>_T$, the total order on T
- $Time \in T$, the current time
- $StrictJoin \subseteq S \times G \times T$, the record of strict joins
- $LiberalJoin \subseteq S \times G \times T$, the record of liberal joins
- $StrictLeave \subseteq S \times G \times T$, the record of strict leaves
- $LiberalLeave \subseteq S \times G \times T$, the record of liberal leaves
- $StrictAdd \subseteq O \times G \times T$, the record of strict adds
- $LiberalAdd \subseteq O \times G \times T$, the record of liberal adds
- $StrictRemove \subseteq O \times G \times T$, the record of strict removes
- $LiberalRemove \subseteq O \times G \times T$, the record of liberal removes

$$authForward(s, o, g) \triangleq \exists t_1, t_2.(\\
\quad Join(s, g, t_1) \land \\
\quad Add(o, g, t_2) \land \\
\quad t_2 > t_1 \land \\
\quad \forall t_3.(\\
\quad\quad Leave(s, g, t_3) \Rightarrow (t_1 > t_3 \lor t_3 > t_2) \land \\
\quad\quad StrictLeave(s, g, t_3) \Rightarrow t_2 > t_3 \land \\
\quad\quad StrictRemove(o, g, t_3) \Rightarrow t_2 > t_3 \\
\quad)\\
)$$

$$authBackward(s, o, g) \triangleq \exists t_1, t_2.(\\
\quad LiberalJoin(s, g, t_1) \land \\
\quad LiberalAdd(o, g, t_2) \land \\
\quad t_1 > t_2 \land \\
\quad \forall t_3.(\\
\quad\quad Remove(o, g, t_3) \Rightarrow (t_2 > t_3 \lor t_3 > t_1) \land \\
\quad\quad StrictLeave(s, g, t_3) \Rightarrow t_1 > t_3 \land \\
\quad\quad StrictRemove(o, g, t_3) \Rightarrow t_1 > t_3 \\
\quad)\\
)$$

$$auth(s, o, g) \triangleq authForward(s, o, g) \lor authForward(s, o, g)$$

Figure 2: The authorization procedure for g-SIS_0.

The g-SIS_0 model defines queries $Member(s, g)$ for whether subject s is currently a member of group g and $Assoc(o, g)$ for whether object o is currently associated with group g. These are answered in the obvious way. Authorization requests are answered as described in Figure 2. Here, $authForward$ applies in cases where the user joined the group before the object was added, and $authBackward$ applies when the user joined after the object was added.

3.2 Extrema Systems

Top, bottom, and role-like g-SIS are systems of the g-SIS_0 model. Each of these systems contains a subset of the full set of actions supported in g-SIS_0, and represents a different extreme in terms of resulting behavior.

Top g-SIS Top g-SIS contains only strict actions. Since all adds and joins are strict, there is no need for $authBackward$. Newer users to a group always have a subset of accesses of older users, users who leave retain no permissions to group-associated objects, and objects that are removed are no longer accessible by group members. We describe top g-SIS in full in Appendix A.

Bottom g-SIS Bottom g-SIS contains only liberal actions. Thus, a subject is granted access to an object as long as they belonged to a group at the same time at some point (currently or in the past), however briefly. Access to added objects is granted to current and new users, but once an object is removed no new users are granted access. Thus, new users tend to have fewer accesses than older users.

Role-like g-SIS Finally, role-like g-SIS is an approximation of a role-based access control system within g-SIS. It allows liberal join and add actions and strict leave and remove. Thus, all current members have access to all current objects, but users who leave lose all access, and objects that are removed are revoked from all users.

3.3 Workloads

In addition to the above extrema systems, we also study several more realistic parameterizations that reflect how g-SIS might be used in practice. Conceptually, these lie somewhere in the g-SIS spectrum between the extrema systems defined above, and represent real-world usages of group-centric techniques. We formalize these as workloads.

PC This is an instance of the "secure message room" example use case of g-SIS [11, 12] that is defined to model academic program committee discussions. It is also based on the g-SIS_0 model, and includes commands for liberal joining PC groups, as well as resigning via strict leave. The workload requires conflict-of-interest handling, so members can liberal leave before a discussion with which they have a COI, and strict join after it concludes. All discussion is liberal added. Traces restrict execution of this workload to sequential phases. In the creation phase, program chairs create PC groups. In the joining phase, PC members join PC groups. In the discussion phase, PC members discuss (add objects to groups) and execute COI patterns.

PSP The Playstation Plus premium gaming service [15] uses temporal constraints to decide accesses, and is thus a natural fit for modeling in g-SIS. PSP uses a g-SIS model with an extension over g-SIS_0: the $auth$ query supports *restorative* joins. Subscribers liberal join, and strict leave when canceling. If a user cancels and later joins again, she is re-granted access to all objects she had before leaving (except those which have been strict removed). Managers liberal add promotions (free games and discounts). When a promotion is complete, free games are liberal removed (users who are members at the time a free game is available may continue to access it as long as they are a member), while discounts are strict removed and thus become inaccessible to all users. Trace restrictions allow users to subscribe in 3-month increments. The managers add and remove several promotions each week, maintaining the same total number for each group.

4. EXPRESSIVENESS ANALYSIS

In this section, we describe the details of our expressiveness analysis using parameterized expressiveness and present a summary of the results. Full details, including full specifications of workloads, systems, implementations, and reductions, are deferred to a companion technical report [8].

A fundamental construction in parameterized expressiveness is the access control *implementation*, the set of mappings constructed to prove that a workload can be satisfied by a system. An implementation of $\mathcal{W}$ in $\mathcal{Y}$, $\langle \alpha, \sigma, \pi \rangle$, defines a state mapping $\sigma : States(\mathcal{W}) \to States(\mathcal{Y})$, a label mapping $\alpha : States(\mathcal{Y}) \times Labels(\mathcal{W}) \to Labels(\mathcal{Y})^*$, and a query mapping π which contains, for each $q \in Queries(\mathcal{W})$, a function $\pi_q : Th(\mathcal{Y}) \to \{\text{TRUE}, \text{FALSE}\}$ which maps a set of system query values to a value for the workload query q. Thus, each π_q is a procedure for answering workload query q given the value of each system query in the current state.

An access control *reduction*, then, is a set of mappings allowing us to prove that a system $\mathcal{Z}$ is at least as expressive as system $\mathcal{Y}$ with respect to a particular set of security guarantees $\mathcal{G}$. This is written $\mathcal{Y} \leq^{\mathcal{G}} \mathcal{Z}$, and indicates that any workload $\mathcal{W}$ that can be implemented in $\mathcal{Y}$ with guarantees

$\mathcal{G}$ can also be implemented in $\mathcal{Z}$ with $\mathcal{G}$. Making this type of statement is the goal of conducting parameterized expressiveness, and is a more precise and pragmatic view of a system's capabilities than other expressiveness techniques provide. A reduction from $\mathcal{Y}$ to $\mathcal{Z}$, $\langle \sigma, \pi \rangle$, defines a state mapping σ and a query mapping π where the state-mapping preserves the query-mapping $(\forall s \in States(\mathcal{Y})\ Th(s) = \pi(Th(\sigma(s))))$. The conditions put on the reduction differ based on the set of security guarantees it preserves.

4.1 Security Guarantees

In this work, we consider the following security guarantees.

Correctness Correctness is a bare minimum requirement for any implementation. Intuitively, correctness says the following: a workload state's image in a system answers mapped queries exactly as the original state answers the original queries; and the same resulting system state is reached by executing a workload action and mapping the result into the system as is reached by mapping the initial state and executing the action's image in the system. More precisely, given a workload, $\mathcal{W} = \langle \mathcal{A}, \mathcal{T} \rangle$, a system $\mathcal{Y}$, and an implementation $\langle \alpha, \sigma, \pi \rangle$, the implementation is correct if σ preserves π (i.e., for every workload state w, $Th(w) = \pi(Th(\sigma(w)))$ and α preserves σ (i.e., for every workload state w and label ℓ, $\sigma(next(w, \ell)) = terminal(\sigma(w), \alpha(\sigma(w), \ell)))$.

Weak AC-Preservation This guarantee is a weaker version of AC-preservation [9]. Intuitively, AC-preservation says that $\pi_{auth(r)}$ must map authorization request r from workload state w to system state $\sigma(w)$ directly, checking whether $\sigma(w) \vdash auth(r)$. This forces the workload and system to have the same format for requests. However, this is not the case with the workloads and systems we consider in this work. Specifically, g-SIS requests ask whether a subject has access to an object in a particular group, while, e.g., $RBAC_0$ requests ask whether a subject has access to a permission. We define weak AC-preservation which captures the spirit of AC-preservation (ensures the use of the authorization procedure of the system) but that allows us to answer a workload authorization using the system's authorization procedure, even if their requests use different formats. Thus, we allow the use of a *request transformation* function f, so we can ask $auth(f(r))$ for some function f. Formally, we require the following: For any workload state w and workload request r, $\pi_{auth(r)}(Th(\sigma(w))) = \text{TRUE} \Rightarrow \sigma(w) \vdash auth(f(r))$; and, for any workload state w and system request r', $\sigma(w) \vdash auth(r') \Rightarrow \exists r.(\pi_{auth(r)}(Th(\sigma(w))) = \text{TRUE} \land f(r) = r')$.

Homomorphism The homomorphic property eliminates implementations that abuse system state by encoding workload state in a way that is fragile to string substitutions. Without this requirement, an implementation can, e.g., store unbounded state in a single user name by encoding whole relations as a single string. A homomorphic mapping f is one in which $f(x)[v] = f(x[v])$ for any constant string substitution $[v]$. A homomorphic implementation is one in which each mapping is homomorphic. Intuitively, this requires that data elements be opaque, and that the symbol representing any element (e.g., user, object, role) can be substituted for any other without affecting the behavior of the system.

Safety A safe implementation is one that does not grant or revoke unnecessary permissions during the execution of the image of a single workload label. That is, if executing workload label ℓ in the implementing system yields

the state sequence $\langle s_1, \ldots, s_k \rangle$, then for all s_i in the sequence, $Auth(s_i) \setminus Auth(s_0) \subseteq Auth(s_k) \setminus Auth(s_0)$ and $Auth(s_0) \setminus Auth(s_i) \subseteq Auth(s_0) \setminus Auth(s_n)$. Intuitively, safety ensures that the intermediate states through which a system travels while implementing a single workload label do not add or remove granted requests except those that must be added or removed as determined by the start and end states. We consider safety for implementations only, as there is no known metatheorem for proving safety via reduction.

4.2 Dissemination-Centric Systems

We choose several dissemination-centric access control systems as candidates for implementing the group-centric workloads described in Section 3. In particular, we focus on role- and group-based models. While these access control models are dissemination-centric, they provide a level of indirection between subjects and objects that enables greater expressiveness than models based on the access matrix or access control lists [14, 16]. Comparing to group-enabled dissemination-centric access control systems enables our analysis to more directly compare the effect of the group-centric paradigm, whereas comparing to non-group-enabled systems would be more likely to highlight simply the advantage of the additional level of indirection provided by groups. Thus, we evaluate the following dissemination-centric systems.

RBAC $RBAC_0$ is the most basic role-based access control system proposed in the RBAC standard [18]. States contain the set of users U, set of roles R, and set of permissions P, as well as relations between them: $UR \subseteq U \times R$ describes users' membership in roles, and $PA \subseteq R \times P$ describes permissions' assignment to roles. A user u is authorized to permission p if $\exists r.(\langle u, r \rangle \in UR \land \langle r, p \rangle \in PA)$. Labels allow adding and removing from all of U, R, P, UR, and PA.

Hierarchical RBAC While $RBAC_0$ grants a level of indirection between users and permissions, $RBAC_1$ includes a hierarchical structure over roles to further extend this abstraction. $RBAC_1$ includes all state elements of $RBAC_0$ as well as the role hierarchy $RH \subseteq R \times R$, a binary relation over R whose transitive closure is the *Senior* partial order (we sometimes designate the transitive, reflexive closure $\geq$). In hierarchical RBAC, a user inherits all permissions from roles junior to roles she is explicitly assigned. That is, a user u is authorized to permission p if $\exists r_1, r_2.(\langle u, r_1 \rangle \in UR \land \langle r_2, p \rangle \in PA \land r_1 \geq r_2)$. Labels allow full manipulation of all state elements. We fully define $RBAC_1$ in Appendix A.

UNIX Permissions Finally, the *ugo* system is based on the *user, group, other* system of access control in UNIX. Thus, if $RBAC_0$ and $RBAC_1$ fill the need for a commonly-used industrial standard system, *ugo* fills the role of a common consumer system. In *ugo*, objects can be associated with an owner user and group, and permissions are then granted to the user, the group, or everyone else.

Thus, we evaluate standard, widely-deployed access control systems, in both the industrial and consumer spaces. These systems are likely candidates for a system administrator who desires to implement a group-centric workload using available and trusted access control mechanisms.

4.3 Expressiveness via System Reductions

We now present a summary of the system reductions proving expressiveness statements comparing the chosen

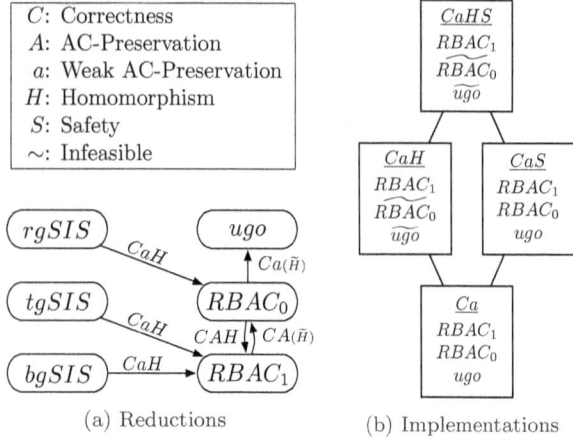

Figure 3: Expressiveness analysis results

dissemination-centric systems and the g-SIS extrema systems. A summary of the expressiveness reductions, including a key to our shorthand for denoting the guarantees a reduction satisfies, is shown in Figure 3a. We now describe the major results depicted in this figure. A sample proof is provided in Appendix A, with the remainder deferred to a companion technical report [8].

First, we note that it is simple to construct a reduction from role-like g-SIS ($rgSIS$) to $RBAC_0$ that satisfies all considered security guarantees (correctness, weak AC-preservation, homomorphism). Role-like g-SIS has only liberal add and join operations and strict leave and remove operations, and thus its $auth$ only depends on the current group members and associated documents. In this scenario, $RBAC_0$ can simply simulate groups using roles.

Theorem 1 $rgSIS \leq^{CaH} RBAC_0$.

Furthermore, $RBAC_1$ can trivially simulate $RBAC_0$ by ignoring the role hierarchy, yielding the following.

Lemma 2 $RBAC_0 \leq^{CAH} RBAC_1$.

Corollary 3 $rgSIS \leq^{CaH} RBAC_1$.

We are able to construct a reduction from top g-SIS ($tgSIS$) to $RBAC_1$ by identifying the pseudo-hierarchical structure of the authorization set in $tgSIS$: since all operations are strict, new members of a group will have a *subset* of the permissions of older members. The hierarchy is invoked by the fact that older members thus "inherit" access to all added objects, while new members only receive access to objects added after they joined. We simulate this structure in $RBAC_1$'s role hierarchy by creating a chain in RH for each group. When a g-SIS group g is created, the top of the chain, a role named g, is created in $RBAC_1$. Objects newly added to the group should be available to all users, and thus the corresponding permission in $RBAC_1$ is added to the bottom of the chain, ensuring all users in the chain will be authorized. Finally, when a new user joins group g, they create a new "view" of the g, since they are not authorized to any existing objects (due to strict join). Thus, we create in $RBAC_1$ a new role (named randomly) and link it to the bottom of g's chain.

Theorem 4 $tgSIS \leq^{CaH} RBAC_1$.

We provide a proof sketch for this theorem in Appendix A.

We build a reduction from bottom g-SIS ($bgSIS$) to $RBAC_1$ using a similar hierarchy-chain solution to $tgSIS$. Since $bgSIS$ contains all liberal actions, we still have a pseudo-hierarchy of $Auth(bgSIS)$. In this case, users who leave a group maintain access to objects from this group, so users who leave earlier have a subset of the authorizations of users who leave later (or are still members). An exception is made for removed objects, since these are not granted to new users after removal. Thus, we again create a hierarchy chain for each group. In this case, the chain grows upward. When a user is removed, a new role is created at the top of the chain and all users remaining in the group are added to this new role. Objects are added to this top role, granting access to all current members. Removed objects, being the exception to the hierarchy rule, are added to orphaned roles, along with all users who should maintain access to them.

Theorem 5 $bgSIS \leq^{CaH} RBAC_1$.

We utilize a non-homomorphic helper reduction from $RBAC_1$ to $RBAC_0$ (and expressiveness transitivity) to prove reductions from $tgSIS$ and $bgSIS$ to $RBAC_0$. This reduction, in order to store hierarchical accesses in a "flat" roleset, expands the set of roles to include a role named for every path through the hierarchy in the downward direction. Thus, if $RBAC_1$'s hierarchy says $A \geq B$, $B \geq C$, and $A \geq D$, then this is represented in $RBAC_0$ with roles $\{A, B, C, D, AB, ABC, AD, BC\}$. For every role r a user is assigned to in $RBAC_1$, she will be assigned to each role starting with r in $RBAC_0$. In the previous example, if $\langle u, A \rangle \in UR$ in $RBAC_1$, then in $RBAC_0$ this maps to $\{\langle u, A\rangle, \langle u, AB\rangle, \langle u, ABC\rangle, \langle u, AD\rangle\} \subset UR$ in $RBAC_0$.

Theorem 6 $RBAC_1 \leq^{CA} RBAC_0$.

Corollary 7 $tgSIS \leq^{Ca} RBAC_0$; $bgSIS \leq^{Ca} RBAC_0$.

We were also able to construct a *homomorphic* helper reduction from $RBAC_1$ to $RBAC_0$. This reduction makes use of an encoding technique which stores the information in the three binary relations (UR, PA, RH) of $RBAC_1$ in the two binary relations (UR, PA) of $RBAC_0$. Using this encoding, each tuple in $RBAC_1$ is stored using three to four tuples in $RBAC_0$. Thus, the resulting state encodes the required information in an unnatural, convoluted scheme which requires deeply nested looping to decode. For example, the originally straightforward authorization procedure of finding an r such that $\langle u, r\rangle \in UR$ and $\langle r, p\rangle \in PA$ must be carried out in this reduction by searching for a set of values r, v, x, y, z such that $\{\langle v, x\rangle, \langle u, v\rangle, \langle r, x\rangle\} \subseteq UR$ and $\{\langle y, z\rangle, \langle y, r\rangle, \langle z, p\rangle\} \subseteq PA$. These vast, compounding inefficiencies prevent this reduction from having any practical application. We conjecture that it is impossible to construct an asymptotically more efficient implementation than using this helper reduction while satisfying the given guarantees, which restricts us to storing the required workload state using only tuples in two relations, and using only existing constants (new constants must be information-less). We discuss this reduction further in Appendix B.

Finally, although ugo has the inherent disadvantage that each object is owned by only a *single* user and group, we can show $RBAC_0 \leq^{Ca} ugo$ since ugo can simulate $RBAC_0$ implementations by mapping a permission assigned to multiple roles to an object with a single group owner, which represents all roles with authorization and includes as members all users in the $RBAC_0$ roles. Though the implementation is weakly AC-preserving, it is not homomorphic since it requires the manipulation of strings for group names.

Theorem 8 $RBAC_0 \leq^{Ca} ugo.$

Corollary 9 $rgSIS \leq^{Ca} ugo; tgSIS \leq^{Ca} ugo; bgSIS \leq^{Ca} ugo.$

4.4 Expressiveness via Implementations

We now present a summary of the implementations of group-centric workloads in dissemination-centric systems. A summary of these implementations and their corresponding strengths is shown in Figure 3b. As in the previous section, we now describe the major results of these implementations.

The PC workload uses liberal join for users joining a program committee group and strict leave for resignation (permanent leave). Liberal leave is used for conflicts-of-interest (temporary leave), and strict join is used to re-join after a COI. We implement this workload in $RBAC_1$ using techniques from the reductions of both $tgSIS$ and $bgSIS$ in $RBAC_1$. Like in our reduction from $tgSIS$, each group uses a hierarchy chain building downward, adding a node (and thus a new "view" of the group) each time a user executes a strict join and assigning newly added objects to the bottom role of the chain. Like in the reduction from $bgSIS$, we use the orphan role concept, in this case for users who liberal leave; the departing user and permissions she should continue to be authorized to are added to a new role. We implement u strict leaving g by removing u from all roles connected to g, and u liberal joining g by assigning u directly to g (so she inherits permission to all current objects). This implementation is correct, weakly AC-preserving, homomorphic, and safe.

Theorem 10 *There exists a correct, weakly AC-preserving, homomorphic, and safe implementation of PC in $RBAC_1$.*

The PSP workload supports liberal (restorative) join, strict leave, liberal add, and both strict and liberal remove. Rather than use a role hierarchy chain, this reduction uses a single role for each group that is assigned to all current members and objects in the group. Two types of orphans are used, one for objects that are liberally removed (along with the users who should remain authorized to the object), and one for strict leave, to support the restorative join operation. On a strict leave of u from g, we create in $RBAC_1$ an orphan role pair r, s, where $s \geq r$, and assign u to r and all of u's permissions from g to s. Since u is in a role junior to the permissions, she is no longer authorized to them. On a re-join to the group, we simply assign u to s, re-enabling u's access to these permissions. This implementation is correct, weakly AC-preserving, homomorphic, and safe.

Theorem 11 *There exists a correct, weakly AC-preserving, homomorphic, and safe implementation of PSP in $RBAC_1$.*

We use helper reductions from the previous section to establish correct, weakly AC-preserving implementations of PC and PSP in $RBAC_0$ and ugo. We independently prove these implementations are safe, since there is no known meta-theorem for using reductions to prove safety.

Corollary 12 *There exist correct, weakly AC-preserving, and safe implementations of PC & PSP in $RBAC_0$ & ugo.*

4.5 Summary of Results

Observing the results of Figures 3a and 3b, it is clear that dissemination-centric systems are able to meet basic security guarantees when operating within group-centric scenarios. $RBAC_1$ is the most successful, simulating the extrema systems and workloads with all security guarantees. $RBAC_0$ was able to implement $rgSIS$ with strong guarantees, but for other g-SIS parameterizations (those with multiple "views" of a single group), $RBAC_0$ had to sacrifice homomorphism to admit feasible implementations. Finally, ugo was also able to satisfy all workloads and systems, but (due to each object being associated with only a single group) did not admit any homomorphic implementations.

We note that we also considered the π-system, a g-SIS system defined over the g-SIS$_0$ model with support for all action varieties [11], but were unable to construct a reduction from π-system to (or implementation of $\langle rgSIS, \mathcal{T}\rangle$ in) any dissemination-centric system that was AC-preserving. Thus, although there was some success among dissemination-centric systems in implementing *specific* parameterizations of group-centric workloads, these systems do not admit as readily implementations of the *fully expressive* form of g-SIS without the sacrifice of basic security guarantees.

5. COST ANALYSIS

Now that we have a clear picture of each dissemination-centric system's expressiveness with respect to group-centric scenarios (which, recall, reflects their theoretical capability), we investigate a second dimension of these systems' suitability to this set of workloads: efficiency and costs. To consider all of the candidate systems in practical contexts, we evaluate correct, weak AC-preservation implementations, disregarding the homomorphic requirement, which some systems can not always satisfy feasibly (see Section 4.3). We conduct cost analysis via Monte Carlo simulation driven by the structures built during expressiveness analysis.

5.1 Trace Generation

Recall from Section 2.2 that in a workload $\mathcal{W} = \langle \mathcal{A}, \mathcal{T}\rangle$, the set $\mathcal{T}$ describes the permissible traces through the ideal access control system $\mathcal{A}$. In cost analysis, we generate random traces from $\mathcal{T}$, execute these traces, and record various costs accrued during execution. Of course, just as it is infeasible to explicitly enumerate the set of all permissible traces, it is typically difficult to sample meaningful traces uniformly at random from this set. Thus, for the purpose of simulation, we specify a stochastic parameterization of this set of traces. In particular, we articulate distributions from which the components of the workload's initial state (e.g., number of users, number of objects, etc.) are drawn, and specify probabilistic models for the type and frequency of actions taken by active entities within the system.

During a simulation run, we first generate an initial state by sampling from the appropriate distributions. We then inspect this state to determine the set of *actors* that will execute labels on that state. Actors can be human users, daemons, or other entities that act on the access control system. We construct state machines that describe the order in which individual actors will execute labels and queries[1], and build

---

[1] Since queries can not alter the state, they are irrelevant to traces as they are used in expressiveness analysis. However, in cost analysis, we include both labels and queries in traces.

constrained workflows that describe actor cooperation. We execute all of the actors' state machines in parallel, with the constraints placed by the workflows and past actions, to generate traces of actions for each actor. The individual actor traces are then interleaved to produce global traces.

Once these traces are generated in terms of workload labels and queries, we translate them into traces of system actions for each of the implementing systems. This is made simple thanks to the expressiveness analysis described in Section 4. When simulating the implementation $\langle \alpha, \sigma, \pi \rangle$, we map initial workload states to system states with σ and workload labels to system labels with α. Finally, π acts as a set of procedures for answering queries using the mapped system state.

We generate initial states and traces to analyze each of our group-centric scenarios as follows.

Program Committee To simulate the PC workload, we select an initial state with 25–75 users. Traces are generated in three phases. First, PC groups are created. Next, PC members join groups. Finally, discussion occurs, and users post objects and execute conflict-of-interest workflows. Traces simulate an eight month cycle, overall.

Playstation Plus Initial states in PSP have 20–100 users and 2–5 regions (subscription groups), with 50–400 objects distributed between them, each representing a current promotion (free game or discount). Traces model users changing membership and administrators adding and removing objects to the regions. Each trace models a period of one year.

Extrema Systems To carry out cost analysis of top, bottom, and role-like g-SIS, we must define usage models from scratch, since these systems are not part of workloads. We generate initial states with 25–85 users, and a number of managers between 5 and 1/4 the number of regular users. In traces, managers create groups and sometimes delete posts (e.g., those that violate terms of service). Normal users join groups and share objects, both newly-created and existing (re-shares). Traces model three days to one week of heavy activity, with the average user posting multiple times per day and joining a new group every two days, on average.

5.2 Cost Measures

While the type of expressiveness analysis carried out by an analyst is defined by a set of security guarantees that must be upheld, the type of cost analysis is parameterized by the costs to be examined. There are numerous forms of cost measures, from the storage needed to maintain state, to the administrative overhead of executing labels, to the computational cost of evaluating queries. Some are named in a recent NIST report [10], which points out the need for a variety of "evaluation metrics" since no one measure answers what is necessary across all applications.

We investigate costs representing storage requirements (maximum state size during a run, number of roles); amount of data read/written (average I/O per label, proportion of state changed per label); degree to which atomicity of label execution is violated (number of stutter steps); and other application-specific measures of "misuse" of the implementing systems (average number of permission-assignments per role). To investigate the values of these measures, we plot them against properties of the trace (e.g., number of users, maximum number of objects) and against the workload's own performance within the scenario (e.g., workload I/O, maximum workload state size) for comparison purposes.

5.3 Selected Results

We carried out a comprehensive cost analysis of the implementations described in Section 4 using a purpose-built Monte Carlo simulator that our team developed. Our cost analysis uncovered a variety of clear drawbacks to implementing group-centric workloads with dissemination-centric systems. We present several demonstrative examples in Figure 4, but note that the remaining results do not inspire us to draw conclusions that are substantially different from those presented here. Note that each subfigure reports on the result of 200 runs of the workload being simulated.

Storage measures. Figure 4a shows that, in the PSP workload, the amount of storage required in each implementing system is superlinear in the size of the workload. This is mostly caused by the blow-up in number of roles/groups required to safely implement the group-centric workloads in systems without built-in temporal abilities. Although PSP is particularly inefficient to implement in dissemination-centric systems, only $rgSIS$ can be implemented using state size comparable to the original workload size even in ugo.

Figure 4b shows another aspect of storage, the proportion of the state that is changed on average per simulated (workload) action, again when implementing PSP. This figure shows that our implementation in ugo is particularly inefficient. This is largely due to the cached authorization table that must be maintained in ugo, making this system a poor choice in scenarios where writes are costly. This pattern is seen across all workloads, and implementations with lower state size generally have the highest proportion of state changing (up to 10% per action), indicating that even those with (relatively) low storage requirements are re-writing large amounts of data to simulate each action.

It is clear that, to support large numbers of users in groups with high object flux, not even hierarchical roles are an efficient replacement for time-aware groups.

I/O measures. Figure 4c shows the I/O cost (in number of state elements accessed) for simulating liberal add operations in $rgSIS$. Although $RBAC_0$ is able to simulate role-like g-SIS fairly naturally, ugo lacks the ability to natively grant multiple groups access to an object. This missing capability is necessary in group-centric workloads, and thus we must simulate it in ugo by assigning each object to a single group and assigning users to these special, semantics-less groups as needed. The extra overhead of iterating over the the Member relation to extract the information from $RBAC_0$'s UR and PA and rebuild the cached authorization table is evident in Figure 4c from the superlinear increase in I/O needed to add objects to groups as the number of total objects in the system increases. By comparison to $RBAC_0$'s simple lock-step implementation, ugo's is much more inefficient. The consumer-grade ugo system is not practical within even the most simple group-centric workloads.

Figure 4d demonstrates that high I/O is not restricted to implementations in ugo. This figure shows I/O for (liberal) joining groups in $bgSIS$. Recall that this is the operation that triggers the role hierarchy chain to expand in $RBAC_1$'s simulation of $bgSIS$, and thus as expected demands high I/O. Specifically, $RBAC_1$ I/O per join is about 1/4 the total I/O of all commands executed in $bgSIS$ in an average full simulation, and $RBAC_0$ regularly exceeds the workload's full I/O. Although $bgSIS$ in particular has expensive implementations of liberal join, each g-SIS workload (except $rgSIS$ which is

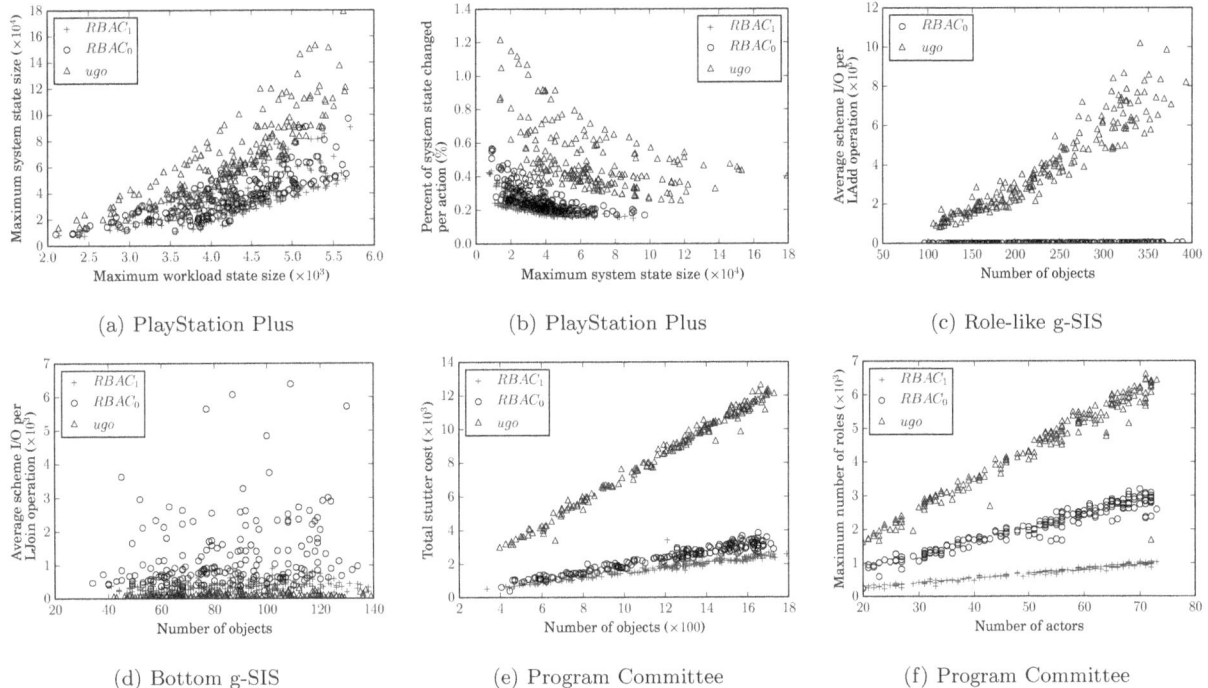

Figure 4: Group-centric cost analysis results

efficiently implemented in $RBAC_0$) has at least one action which causes this characteristically high I/O.

We study the amount of "stuttering" per trace in Figure 4e, which is a description of the number of extra operations that must be executed in implementing systems to simulate single workload actions. We see a drastic increase in stuttering while implementing PC, (especially in *ugo*) as more objects are added to the system. This quantifies the loss of atomicity of operations, and allows us to understand the increasing frequency with which the data structures must be locked to guarantee the desired security properties.

Role abuse. Finally, we measure the maximum number of roles created to accommodate the PC workload. It has been said that role-based systems lose their administrative value when the number of roles exceeds the number of users [23]. In Figure 4f, we compare the number of subjects in the PC workload to the number of roles (groups for *ugo*) in the corresponding state of the implementing systems. Roles vastly outnumber users, starting with $RBAC_1$'s role hierarchy chain for each group, and getting worse in both $RBAC_0$ and *ugo*, each requiring more roles than the previous in order to guarantee weak AC-preservation.

Summary. We have shown a number of measures for which dissemination-centric systems $RBAC_1$, $RBAC_0$, and *ugo* prove to be very inefficient in implementing group-centric workloads with strong security guarantees. Even the most space-efficient implementations use much more state storage than an equivalent g-SIS parameterization, and require much more I/O to operate. The number of roles created is often many times the number of users and several times the number of objects. With the exception of implementing role-like g-SIS in RBAC, all implementations also cause large amounts of stuttering, or non-atomic sequences of labels to simulate a

single workload action. Thus, it seems that in most practical scenarios one must heavily compromise security guarantees or suffer vastly inefficient implementations in order to utilize dissemination-centric systems in the group-centric context.

6. DISCUSSION AND FUTURE WORK

6.1 Dissemination-centric vs. Group-centric

We set out to evaluate the hypothesis stated by the creators of g-SIS [12]: that the group-centric class of models is equal in collective expressiveness to the dissemination-centric class, but that they are pragmatically different approaches and thus should complement, rather than substitute for, one another. We found in our experiments that these approaches do indeed yield pragmatically dissimilar systems, and that even on a theoretical expressiveness level may not be equivalent.

First, in expressiveness analysis, we displayed the reduction from $rgSIS$ to $RBAC_0$, the simplest role-based system. It was not surprising that the reduction achieved strong security guarantees ($rgSIS$ was, after all, modeled after role-based systems). However, when we noticed that $tgSIS$ (and, to a lesser extent, $bgSIS$) admitted a hierarchical set of authorizations within each group, and that this allowed the hierarchical $RBAC_1$ to implement it just as strongly, we realized that $rgSIS$ is not unique—other parameterizations of g-SIS could be safely implemented using dissemination-centric systems.

This pair of strong implementations shows that in some cases a g-SIS parameterization and a dissemination-centric system can provide the same theoretical capabilities, in part because of structural similarities between how the group- and dissemination-centric counterparts manage internal state. There does not seem to be anything special about these pairs that leads us to believe they are unique. However, in other cases we find the dissemination-centric system unable to fully match the g-SIS system, e.g. $RBAC_0$ and $tgSIS$. Thus, although we cannot count out the possibility that there is *some* traditional system with the same capabilities as a given g-SIS system, this is not a claim we can confirm based on our investigation of several commonly-used traditional systems and several natural g-SIS parametrizations.

To address the pragmatic differences between dissemination- and group-centric sharing, we carried out cost analyses of the implementations that we developed. Implementations that were bad fits in expressiveness analysis provided continuing evidence of their poor fit in cost analysis. State storage was much higher in these systems than in the ideal systems of the workloads. Executing workload actions often necessitated many stuttering steps in the implementing system, required higher I/O within the implementing system, and changed a high proportion of state for each action. However, these poorly-matched implementations were not alone—even the strongly secure, relatively simple implementation of $tgSIS$ in $RBAC_1$ had inefficiencies that became evident during cost analysis. Though $RBAC_0$ could not feasibly satisfy the homomorphic guarantee when implementing $tgSIS$ due to lacking a hierarchy, $RBAC_1$ required as much of a state space explosion as $RBAC_0$. Even though it had much lower I/O cost than $RBAC_0$, $RBAC_1$ required orders of magnitude greater I/O than in $tgSIS$ to execute its procedure for simulating a strict join.

Thus, we believe we have validated the second point in the hypothesis. Although certain dissemination-centric systems are *able* to implement group-centric workloads, it does not mean they *should*—even when they are theoretically capable, they are not necessarily pragmatically suitable.

6.2 Beyond Expressiveness

Although expressive power analysis has long been the measuring stick for understanding and ranking access control systems in the literature (e.g., [1, 3, 5, 7, 9, 13, 14, 17, 19, 20, 22]), the analysis conducted in this paper indicates that expressiveness alone does not always tell the whole story. For instance, recall that $RBAC_1$ was able to implement many interesting g-SIS workloads while maintaining strong security guarantees. However, the complexity required for these implementations to maintain this set of properties resulted in loss of atomicity when executing certain actions, increased state size and state management overheads, and (ultimately) a loss of the elegance of the original workload. From a theoretical perspective, $RBAC_1$ was expressive enough to encode a variety of group-centric workloads; from a practical perspective, these implementations are less than ideal.

We believe that this work represents the first comprehensive analysis of expressiveness and cost within the context of access control systems. Further, the results obtained by this analysis are significant in that they provide a concrete data point indicating the potential dangers of relying too heavily on any one measure of access control suitability when examining the needs of an application. It would be worthwhile to develop a generalized framework for carrying out the types of analysis conducted in this paper while supporting a wide variety of expressiveness and cost metrics.

6.3 Towards an Expressiveness Taxonomy

One goal of parameterized expressiveness [9] is to allow one to choose the notion of expressiveness that best matches the workload in question. Although it is often easy to decide whether to require a particular PE security guarantee, PE has not yet enabled the community to break down existing notions of expressiveness into their component properties. For example, it is not known whether there is any combination of parameterized expressiveness properties that yields expressiveness statements equivalent to those made by, e.g., the state matching reduction [22]. For this reason, we identify as another area of future work the continued investigation of PE techniques and guarantees, hoping to gain knowledge of both the properties of and relationships between expressiveness notions as well as deeper, more fundamental aspects of access control and state machine simulations.

7. OTHER RELATED WORK

The need for more general techniques for evaluating access control systems was discussed in a recent NIST report, which states that "when it comes to access control mechanisms, one size does not fit all" [10]. The report bemoans the lack of established quality metrics for access control systems and lists numerous possibilities. Several of these metrics relate to state size, number of actions committed, and other quantitative measures. The report stops short of explaining how one might choose between these metrics, or how to effectively evaluate systems with respect to these metrics. In this work, we perform what we believe is the first comprehensive access control evaluation using both expressiveness and quantitative measures, and thus make a first step toward realizing the evaluation mechanisms this NIST report hopes for.

For inspiration in generating access control traces (see Section 5.1), we turn to trace generation work in other domains. In the field of disk benchmarking, Ganger [6] observed that interleaved workloads provided the most accurate approximation of recorded traces. Thus, mechanisms for representing access control workloads must be capable of simulating the interleaved actions of multiple actors. This view is reinforced by the design of IBM's SWORD workload generator for stream processing systems [2, 4]. This work also points out that synthetic workloads need to replicate both volumetric and contextual properties of an execution environment in order to provide an accurate indication of a system's performance within that environment. Thus, we conjecture that access control workloads may also benefit from expressing not only volumetric statistics such as number of documents created, but also contextual statistics such as the type of content in created documents.

8. CONCLUSION

In this work, we examined the capabilities of popular dissemination-centric access control systems to operate within group-centric workloads. We formalized several group-centric workloads as instantiations of g-SIS, a family of information sharing models that has been formalized in temporal logic but not yet implemented. We then conducted a two-phase analysis that we believe to be the first of its kind. We first evaluated whether the dissemination-centric systems are expressive enough to implement the group-centric workloads, assessing the strength of these implementations by examining the security guarantees they can preserve. We then conducted a cost analysis, investigating more pragmatic metrics that provide insight into the efficiency of these systems when implementing group-centric workloads.

We found that while RBAC with role hierarchy was able to implement the workloads that we considered with strong security guarantees, a more basic variant of RBAC without role hierarchies could only implement one of our workloads without compromising the guarantees to be upheld. Further, we found that standard UNIX-style user-group-other permissions could not implement any of our group-centric workloads while upholding all required security guarantees. In cost analysis, we found that, with limited exceptions, even those implementations upholding strong security properties suffered from inefficiencies in state size, I/O, and atomicity of operations. These results indicate that g-SIS is a practically significant proposal that elegantly satisfies a class of workloads that existing access control techniques struggle with. More fundamentally, these results demonstrate the need for access control evaluation techniques and frameworks that allow not only theoretical expressiveness analysis but also the more pragmatic and quantitative cost analysis.

Acknowledgements. This work was supported in part by the National Science Foundation under awards CNS–0964295 and CNS–1228697. The authors also thank Timothy L. Hinrichs for insightful discussion during the development of our analysis techniques.

9. REFERENCES

[1] Paul Ammann, Richard J. Lipton, and Ravi S. Sandhu. The expressive power of multi-parent creation in monotonic access control models. *JCS*, 4(2/3), 1996.

[2] Kay S. Anderson, Joseph P. Bigus, Eric Bouillet, Parijat Dube, Nagui Halim, Zhen Liu, and Dimitrios E. Pendarakis. Sword: scalable and flexible workload generator for distributed data processing systems. In *Winter Simulation Conference*, 2006.

[3] Elisa Bertino, Barbara Catania, Elena Ferrari, and Paolo Perlasca. A logical framework for reasoning about access control models. *TISSEC*, 6(1), 2003.

[4] Eric Bouillet, Parijat Dube, David George, Zhen Liu, Dimitrios E. Pendarakis, and Li Zhang. Distributed multi-layered workload synthesis for testing stream processing systems. In *Winter Simulation Conference*, 2008.

[5] Ajay Chander, Drew Dean, and John C. Mitchell. A state-transition model of trust management and access control. In *CSFW*, 2001.

[6] Gregory R. Ganger. Generating representative synthetic workloads: An unsolved problem. In *International CMG Conference*, 1995.

[7] Srinivas Ganta. *Expressive Power of Access Control Models Based on Propagation of Rights*. PhD thesis, George Mason University, 1996.

[8] William C. Garrison III, Yechen Qiao, and Adam J. Lee. On the suitability of dissemination-centric access control systems for group-centric sharing: Full proofs. http://www.cs.pitt.edu/~adamlee/pubs/2014/garrison2014proofs.pdf, 2013.

[9] Timothy L. Hinrichs, Diego Martinoia, William C. Garrison III, Adam J. Lee, Alessandro Panebianco, and Lenore Zuck. Application-sensitive access control evaluation using parameterized expressiveness. In *CSF*, 2013.

[10] Vincent C. Hu, David F. Ferraiolo, and D. Rick Kuhn. *Assessment of Access Control Systems*. NIST, 2006.

[11] Ram Krishnan, Jianwei Niu, Ravi S. Sandhu, and William H. Winsborough. Group-centric secure information-sharing models for isolated groups. *TISSEC*, 14(3), 2011.

[12] Ram Krishnan, Ravi Sandhu, Jianwei Niu, and William H. Winsborough. A conceptual framework for group-centric secure information sharing. In *ASIACCS*, 2009.

[13] Qamar Munawer and Ravi S. Sandhu. Simulation of the augmented typed access matrix model (atam) using roles. In *INFOSECU99*, 1999.

[14] Sylvia L. Osborn, Ravi S. Sandhu, and Qamar Munawer. Configuring role-based access control to enforce mandatory and discretionary access control policies. *TISSEC*, 3(2), 2000.

[15] Playstation plus. http://us.playstation.com/psn/playstation-plus.

[16] Jerome H. Saltzer and Michael D. Schroeder. The protection of information in computer systems. *Proceedings of the IEEE*, 63(9), 1975.

[17] Ravi S. Sandhu. Expressive power of the schematic protection model. *Journal of Computer Security*, 1(1), 1992.

[18] Ravi S. Sandhu. Rationale for the RBAC96 family of access control models. In *ACM Workshop on Role-Based Access Control*, 1995.

[19] Ravi S. Sandhu and Srinivas Ganta. On testing for absence of rights in access control models. In *CSFW*, 1993.

[20] Ravi S. Sandhu and Qamar Munawer. How to do discretionary access control using roles. In *ACM Workshop on Role-Based Access Control*, 1998.

[21] Andrew Sciberras. Lightweight directory access protocol (LDAP): Schema for user applications. Technical Report RFC 4519, eB2Bcom, 2006. http://www.rfc-editor.org/rfc/rfc4519.txt.

[22] Mahesh V. Tripunitara and Ninghui Li. A theory for comparing the expressive power of access control models. *JCS*, 15(2), 2007.

[23] Dana Zhang, Kotagiri Ramamohanarao, Steven Versteeg, and Rui Zhang. RoleVAT: Visual assessment of practical need for role based access control. In *ACSAC*, 2009.

APPENDIX

A. EXAMPLE PROOF SKETCH

Here, we present an example proof sketch to demonstrate our techniques. Full definitions of systems, implementations, reductions, and proofs are deferred to a companion technical report [8].

First, we present $RBAC_1$, based on the system of the same name presented in [18]. States in $RBAC_1$ are comprised of the following.

- U, R, and P, the sets of users, roles, and permissions
- $UR \subseteq U \times R$, the user-role relation
- $PA \subseteq R \times P$, the role-permission relation
- $RH \subseteq R \times R$, a partially ordered role hierarchy

Requests are of the form u, p for whether user u has access to permission p. Queries include querying the relations $UR(u,r)$, $PA(r,p)$, and $RH(r_1,r_2)$, the transitive hierarchy relation $Senior(r_1,r_2) \triangleq RH(r_1,r_2) \vee \exists r_3.(Senior(r_1,r_3) \wedge Senior(r_3,r_2))$, and the authorizations $auth(u,p) \triangleq \exists r_1,r_2.(UR(u,r_1) \wedge PA(r_2,p) \wedge (r_1 = r_2 \vee Senior(r_1,r_2)))$.

Labels are included for managing the various data structures: $addU(u)$, $delU(u)$, $addR(r)$, $delR(r)$, $addP(p)$, $delP(p)$, $assignUser(u,r)$, $revokeUser(u,r)$, $assignPermission(r,p)$, $revokePermission(r,p)$, $addHierarchy(r_1,r_2)$, and $removeHierarchy(r_1,r_2)$.

Top g-SIS ($tgSIS$) uses the g-SIS$_0$ model, but utilizes only strict versions of state elements. It includes the following labels: $addS(s)$, $delS(s)$, $addG(g)$, $delG(g)$, $addO(o)$, $delO(o)$, $strictJoin(s,g)$, $strictLeave(s,g)$, $strictAdd(o,g)$, and $strictRemove(o,g)$.

Since $tgSIS$ contains only strict actions, we can utilize a simplified $auth$ definition:

$$
\begin{aligned}
auth(s,o,g) \triangleq \exists t_1, t_2.(\\
StrictJoin(s,g,t_1) \wedge \\
StrictAdd(o,g,t_2) \wedge \\
t_2 > t_1 \wedge \\
\forall t_3.(\\
StrictLeave(s,g,t_3) \Rightarrow t_1 > t_3 \wedge \\
StrictRemove(o,g,t_3) \Rightarrow t_2 > t_3 \\
) \\
)
\end{aligned}
$$

Theorem 13 *There exists a reduction from top g-SIS ($tgSIS$) to RBAC$_1$ where:*

- *σ preserves π, is pseudo-injective, preserves reachability, and is homomorphic*

- *π is homomorphic and weakly AC-preserving*

Thus, $tgSIS \leq^{CaH} RBAC_1$ (RBAC$_1$ is at least as expressive as top g-SIS with respect to correctness, weak AC-preservation and homomorphism).

PROOF (SKETCH) We prove the theorem by construction—we present the reduction $\langle \sigma, \pi \rangle$, and prove it satisfies each of the properties. The state mapping, σ, stores the $tgSIS$ state in RBAC$_1$ as follows. Subjects are stored as users, each group is stored as a role, and objects are stored as permissions. We process the records (strict variety of join, leave, add, and remove) in time order, and execute the mapped action for each one. Joins require creation of a new role added at the bottom of the group's role hierarchy chain (initially, directly below the group). Leaves require iterating over the group's role hierarchy chain, removing the user from each role. To add a document to a group, the corresponding permission is assigned to the bottom role in the group's role chain. To remove an object, similar to a user leaving, iterate over all roles below the group's role and remove the object's permission from each. We define this state mapping in HPL, a minimal programming language that can only implement homomorphic mappings [9].

The query mapping, π, is defined as follows.

$$\pi_{Member(s,g)}(T) = \exists r.(UR(s,r) \in T \wedge Senior(g,r) \in T)$$

$$\pi_{Assoc(o,g)}(T) = \exists r.(PA(r,o) \in T \wedge Senior(g,r) \in T)$$

$$
\begin{aligned}
\pi_{auth(s,o,g)}(T) = \exists r_1, r_2.(UR(s,r_1) \in T \wedge PA(r_2,o) \in T \wedge \\
(r_1 = r_2 \vee Senior(r_1,r_2) \in T) \wedge \\
Senior(g,r_1) \in T)
\end{aligned}
$$

This query mapping clearly contains no string manipulation, and is thus homomorphic.

We show that σ preserves π (for all $tgSIS$ states x, $Th(x) = \pi(Th(\sigma(x)))$) by contradiction. We assume that there is some $tgSIS$ state x and query q such that the value of q in x is the opposite of the value of $\pi(q)$ in $\sigma(x)$. We then show that, for each of the query forms of $tgSIS$, this assumption leads to contradiction, and thus that σ preserves π.

For all $tgSIS$ states x, x', if x' is reachable from x, then there exists a sequence of labels $\langle \ell_1, \ell_2, \ldots, \ell_n \rangle$ such that $terminal(x, \ell_1 \circ \ell_2 \circ \cdots \circ \ell_n) = x'$. We prove that σ preserves reachability by showing that, for any $tgSIS$ state x and label ℓ, $\sigma(next(x, \ell))$ is reachable from $\sigma(x)$ via RBAC$_1$ labels. By induction, this shows that for each intermediate $tgSIS$ state x_i between x and x', $\sigma(x_i)$ is reachable from $\sigma(x)$ and ultimately that $\sigma(x')$ is reachable from $\sigma(x)$. These actions are mapped in the same way as their corresponding records in the state mapping.

Finally, we show that σ is *pseudo-injective*, a property which allows us to show that the reduction preserves correctness. We do so by inspecting the state mapping, σ, and arguing that any two states in $tgSIS$ that map to the same RBAC$_1$ state can be treated identically by an implementation's label mapping—that is, we lose no meaningful information by mapping a $tgSIS$ state into RBAC$_1$. □

B. INFEASIBLE REDUCTION

Here, we describe the infeasible reduction from RBAC$_1$ to RBAC$_0$ mentioned in Section 4.3. The full reduction and proof are provided in the companion technical report [8].

In this reduction, we must store UR_1, PA_1, and RH_1 from RBAC$_1$ in only UR_0 and PA_0 in RBAC$_0$. We accomplish this using the following homomorphic encoding. For each $\langle u, r \rangle \in UR_1$, we generate two new constants a and b and store in UR_0 each of $\{\langle a,b \rangle, \langle u,a \rangle, \langle r,b \rangle\}$. For each $\langle r,p \rangle \in PA_1$, we generate two new constants c and d and store in PA_0 each of $\{\langle c,d \rangle, \langle c,r \rangle, \langle d,p \rangle\}$. Lastly, for each $\langle s,j \rangle \in RH_1$, we generate three new constants e, f, and g and store in PA_0 each of $\{\langle e,f \rangle, \langle f,g \rangle, \langle e,s \rangle, \langle g,j \rangle\}$.

Under this (partial) encoding, the second element of each tuple in UR_0 and the first element of each tuple in PA_0 are generated (information-less) constants. Since constants are generated to avoid collisions, there is no join over UR_0 and PA_0, which would violate AC-preservation. Finally, we add to the encoding the set of authorized requests, to fully satisfy AC-preservation. For each request $\langle u,p \rangle$ which is authorized (i.e., for each $\langle u,p \rangle$ such that $\exists s, j : \langle u,s \rangle \in UR_1 \wedge \langle j, p \rangle \in PA_1 \wedge \langle s,j \rangle \in RH_1$), we generate a new constant h and store $\langle u,h \rangle$ in UR_0 and $\langle h,p \rangle$ in PA_0.

The reduction answers queries (besides authorization requests) by extracting the relevent parts of UR_1, PA_1, and RH_1. Generated constants are identified by their positions in tuples. UR_1 tuples can be extracted from UR_0 by finding sets of three tuples which match the $\langle a,b \rangle$, $\langle u,a \rangle$, $\langle r, b \rangle$ pattern. Tuples from PA_1 and RH_1 can be extracted from PA_0 similarly.

Finally, the reduction must update the encoding after each command. For example, if user u is assigned role r, $\langle u, r \rangle$ is encoded and stored in UR_0, then each permission p_i which u gains must be determined and encoded in UR_0 and PA_0 to satisfy AC-preservation.

Streamforce: Outsourcing Access Control Enforcement for Stream Data to the Clouds

Dinh Tien Tuan Anh
School of Computing
National University of Singapore
13 Computing Drive, Singapore
dinhtta@comp.nus.edu.sg

Anwitaman Datta
School of Computer Engineering
Nanyang Technological University
50 Nanyang Avenue, Singapore
anwitaman@ntu.edu.sg

ABSTRACT

In this paper, we focus on the problem of data privacy on the cloud, particularly on access controls over stream data. The nature of stream data and the complexity of sharing data make access control a more challenging issue than in traditional archival databases. We present Streamforce — a system allowing data owners to securely outsource their data to an untrusted (curious-but-honest) cloud. The owner specifies fine-grained policies which are enforced by the cloud. The latter performs most of the heavy computations, while learning nothing about the data content. To this end, we employ a number of encryption schemes, including deterministic encryption, proxy-based attribute based encryption and sliding-window encryption. In Streamforce, access control policies are modeled as secure continuous queries, which entails minimal changes to existing stream processing engines, and allows for easy expression of a wide-range of policies. In particular, Streamforce comes with a number of secure query operators including Map, Filter, Join and Aggregate. Finally, we implement Streamforce over an open-source stream processing engine (Esper) and evaluate its performance on a cloud platform. The results demonstrate practical performance for many real-world applications, and although the security overhead is visible, Streamforce is highly scalable.

Categories and Subject Descriptors

H.2.0 [**Database Management**]: General—*Security, integrity and protection*

Keywords

access control, stream processing, outsourced databases, cloud computing

1. INTRODUCTION

An enormous amount of data is being generated everyday, and it has become increasingly common to process data as they arrive in continuous streams. Examples range from high-frequency streams such as generated from stock or network monitoring applications, to low-frequency streams originated from weather monitoring, social network or health monitoring applications. The variety and abundance of data, combined with the potential of social interactivity, mash-up services and data sciences, has brought data sharing into the foreground. A crucial problem with sharing data is security concerning the question of who gets access to which aspects of the data (fine-grained access control) and under which context (data privacy). This paper studies the former question, which we believe to be more challenging for stream data than for archival data because of three reasons. First, traditional archival data systems enforce access control by pre-computing views, which is not possible with stream data because of its infinite size. Second, access control over stream is inherently data-driven (triggered by arrival of specific data values) as opposed to user-driven, and it often involves temporal constraints (sliding windows). Third, many of the sharing activities take place in collaborative settings with large numbers of users and even larger numbers of policies.

At the same time, more businesses and individual users are leveraging the cloud for its instantly available and virtually unbounded computing resources provided by various vendors at competitive prices. Many enterprise systems are migrating their infrastructure to the cloud, while a plethora of small-to-medium size systems are being developed and deployed on the cloud regularly. In the context of stream data sharing, cloud computing emerges as an ideal platform for two reasons. First, data can be hosted and managed by a small number of cloud providers with unlimited resources, which is important since data streams are of infinite sizes. Second, data co-location makes it easy to share and to perform analytics. On the other hand, the cloud is a potential adversary since it may obtain unauthorized access to the data, or inadvertently leak data due to external attacks or software vulnerability. Thus, when considering the cloud for sharing data, it becomes imperative to design a mechanism which facilitates sharing while guaranteeing data confidentiality even from the cloud.

In this paper, we consider data streams being outsourced to untrusted (curious-but-honest) clouds. The challenge is then to protect data confidentiality from the cloud, while at the the same time leveraging the latter for fine-grained access control. We present *Streamforce* — a fine-grained access control system for stream data over untrusted clouds.

Streamforce is designed with three goals. First, it supports specification and enforcement of fine-grained access control policies. Second, data is outsourced to the cloud where access control policies are enforced, with the latter learning nothing about the data content. Third, the system is *efficient*, in the sense that the cloud handles most of the expensive computations. The last two goals require the cloud to be more active than being merely a storage and transit facility. To realize these goals, Streamforce uses a number of encryption schemes: deterministic encryption, proxy-based attribute based encryption, and a sliding-window based encryption. While encryption is necessary to protect data confidentiality against the cloud and against unauthorized access, we believe that directly exposing encryption details to the system entities (data owner, user and cloud) is not the ideal abstraction when it comes to access control. Instead, Streamforce models and enforces access control policies using secure query operators: secure Map, Filter, Join and Aggregate. These operators are at higher level and more human-friendly than raw encryption keys. Since existing stream processing engines are very efficient at executing continuous queries made from similar query operators, they can be leveraged by the cloud without major changes.

Streamforce occupies an unique position in the design space of outsourced access control. It considers untrusted (semi-honest) clouds, which is different to [4]. Systems such as Plutus [13] and CryptDb [17] assume untrusted clouds, but they support only coarse-grained policies over archival data. Recent systems utilizing attribute-based encryption [11, 19] achieve more fine-grained access control on untrusted clouds, but they do not support stream data. Furthermore, the cloud is not fully utilized as it is used mainly for storage and distribution. To the best of our knowledge, Streamforce is the first system that allows secure, efficient outsourcing of fine-grained access control for stream data to untrusted clouds. It is not catered for applications demanding high throughput, but it presents important first steps towards supporting them. Our contributions are summarized as follows:

- We present a system and formal security model for outsourcing access control of stream data to untrusted clouds. We discuss different security levels that query operators can achieve.

- We present details and analyze security properties of different encryption schemes used for enforcing fine-grained access control, including a new scheme supporting sliding window aggregation.

- We show how to combine these encryption schemes to construct secure query operators: secure Map, secure Filter, secure Join and secure Aggregate.

- We implement a prototype of Streamforce over Esper and benchmark it on Amazon EC2. The results indicate practical performance for many applications. Although the cost of security is evident, we show that it can be compensated by the system's high scalability.

Next we present the system and security model, followed by the constructions of the encryption schemes. We then describe how to construct secure query operators. Prototype implementation and evaluation is presented in Section 5. Related work follows in Section 6, before we draw conclusion and discuss future work.

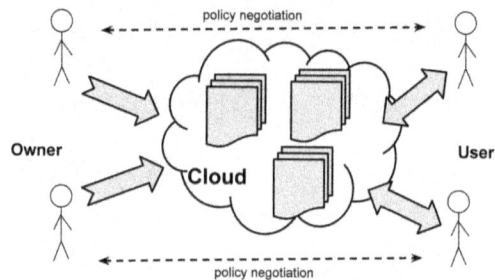

(a) Overview of Streamforce's deployment

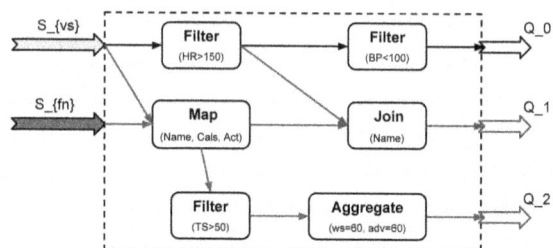

(b) Examples of access control policies via queries

Figure 1: System model and policy examples

2. SYSTEM AND SECURITY MODEL

2.1 System Model

2.1.1 Overview.

There are three types of entities: *data owners* (or owners), *data users* (or users) and a *cloud*. Their interactions are illustrated in Fig. 1[a]: the owners encrypt their data and relay them to the cloud, which performs transformation and forwards the results to the users for final decryption. We do not consider how the owner determines access control policies, and we assume that the negotiation process (in which the owner grants policies to the user) happens out-of-band. The system goals are three-folds:

1. The owner is able to express flexible, fine-grained access control policies.

2. The system ensures data confidentiality against untrusted cloud, and access control against unauthorized users (as elaborated later).

3. Access control enforcement is done by the cloud. Decryptions at the user are light-weight operations compared to the transformations at the cloud.

2.1.2 Data Model.

A data stream S has the following schema:

$$S = (TS, A_1, A_2, .., A_n)$$

where $TS = \mathbb{N}$ is the timestamp, and all data attributes A_i are of integer domains. A data tuple at time ts is written as $d_{ts} = (ts, v_{A_1}, .., v_{A_n})$. Queries over data streams are continuous, i.e. they are *triggered* when new data arrives. Each query is composed from one or more *query operators*, which take one or more streams as inputs and output another stream. We focus on four operators: Map, Filter, Join and Aggregate.

- *Map*: outputs only the specified attributes.

- *Filter*: outputs tuples satisfying a given predicate.

- *Join*: takes as inputs two streams (S_1, S_2), two integers (ws_1, ws_2) and a join attribute. Incoming data are added to the queues of size ws_1 and ws_2, from which they are joined together.

- *Aggregate*: outputs the averages over a sliding window. A sliding window is defined over the timestamp attribute, with a window size ws and an advance step *step*.

Note that the assumption of the data attributes being in the integer domain does not exclude data types such as float or string, since they can be converted to integer representation. Although our system falls short of supporting arbitrary type (some query operators may not make sense over some data types), the current data model nevertheless can cover a wide range of real-life applications.

2.1.3 Access Control via Queries.

As in traditional (relational) databases, access control in Streamforce is defined via *views* that are created by querying the database. This is facilitated by the use of the abstract operators, instead of exposing cumbersome encryption details to the system entities. Specifically, the access control process involves two steps. First, the owner specifies a policy by mapping it into a continuous query. Second, the query is registered to be executed by the cloud, whose outputs are then forwarded to authorized users.

The example depicted in Fig. 1[b] includes two streams: $S_{vs} = (TS, RTime, Name, HR, BP)$ and $S_{fn} = (TS, RTime, Name, Cals, Act, Loc)$. S_{vs} contains owner's vital signs as produced by health monitoring devices, where $RTime$, HR, BP are the real time, heart rate and blood pressure respectively. S_{fn} contains fitness information, where $Cals$, Act, Loc are the number of calories burned, the activity and the owner's location respectively. Data users could be friends from social network, research institutes or insurance companies. For a friend, the owner may want to share vitals data when they exceed a certain threshold (Q_0), or average fitness information every hour (Q_2). A research institute may be given a joined view from both streams in order to monitor the individual's vitals during exercises (Q_1).

2.2 Security Model

2.2.1 Adversary Model.

Streamforce is designed assuming that the cloud is not fully trusted, in that it may try to learn content of the outsourced data, however it still follows the protocol correctly. This curious-but-honest (semi-honest) adversary model is standard in the literature, since it reflects the cloud's incentives to gain benefits from user data while being bound by the service level agreements and market forces. We do not consider malicious cloud, which may try to break data integrity, launch denial of service attacks, or compute using stale data. Security against such attacks is crucial for many applications, but it is out of the scope of this paper. Data users are considered dishonest, in the sense that they may proactively try to access unauthorized data. To this end, they may collude with each other and also with the cloud.

2.2.2 Encryptions Model.

To meet both fine-grained access control and data confidentiality requirements, we use three different encryption schemes. Proxy attribute based encryption is used for Map and Filter operators. Second, Join operator is realized via deterministic encryption. Aggregate is supported by sliding-window encryption. This section provides formal definition of these schemes and their security properties. Detailed constructions and proofs of security are presented in Section 3.

Deterministic encryption scheme.

$\mathcal{E}_d = (\mathsf{Gen}, \mathsf{Enc}, \mathsf{Dec})$ is a private-key encryption scheme, where $\mathsf{Gen}(\kappa)$ generates secret key SK using security parameter κ, $\mathsf{Enc}(m, SK)$ encrypts message m with SK, and $\mathsf{Dec}(CT, SK)$ decrypts the ciphertext. Security of $\mathcal{E}_d$ (**Det-CPA**) is defined via the security game detailed in Appendix A.

Proxy Attribute-Based Encryption scheme.

Attribute-Based Encryption (ABE) is a public-key scheme that allows for fine-grained access control: ciphertexts can only be decrypted if the security credentials satisfy a certain predicate. Two types of ABE [11] exist: Key-Policy (KP-ABE) and Ciphertext-Policy (CP-ABE). We opt for the former, in which the predicate is embedded in user keys and the ciphertext contains a set of encryption attributes. KP-ABE and CP-ABE can be used interchangeably, but the former is more data-centric (who gets access to the given data), while the latter is more user-centric (which data the given user has access to).

ABE's encryption and decryption are expensive operations. Proxy Attribute Based Encryption [12] (or proxy ABE) is design to aid the decryption process by letting a third party *transform* the original ABE ciphertexts into a simpler form. It consists of five algorithms $\mathcal{E}_p = (\mathsf{Gen}, \mathsf{KeyGen}, \mathsf{Enc}, \mathsf{Trans}, \mathsf{Dec})$. $\mathsf{Gen}(\kappa)$ generates public parameters PK and master key MK. $\mathsf{KeyGen}(MK, P)$ creates a transformation key TK and a decryption key SK for the predicate P. $\mathsf{Enc}(m, PK, A)$ encrypts m with the set of encryption attributes A. $\mathsf{Trans}(TK, CT)$ partially decrypts the ciphertext using TK. Finally, $\mathsf{Dec}(SK, CT)$ decrypts the transformed ciphertext using the decryption key.

Security of $\mathcal{E}_p$ is defined in [12] via a game in the selective-set model. The highest level of security achievable is R-CCA, when the adversary is allowed to query the decryption oracles. In this paper, however, we use a lower level of security: CPA security in the selective model, achieved when the adversary has no access to the decryption oracle.

Sliding-window encryption scheme (SWE)..

The scheme consists of three algorithms: $\mathcal{E}_w = (\mathsf{Gen}, \mathsf{Enc}, \mathsf{Dec})$, which allows an user to decrypt only the aggregate of a window of ciphertexts, and not the individual ciphertexts. Let $s(M, ws)[i]$ and $p(M, ws)[i]$ be the sum and product of the ith window sliding windows (size ws and advance step $step = ws$) over a sequence M. $\mathsf{Gen}(\kappa)$ generates the public parameters and the private keys. $\mathsf{Enc}(M = \langle m_0, m_1, .., m_{n-1} \rangle, W)$ encrypts M using a set of window sizes W, whose result is $CT = \langle c_0, c_1, c_2, .. \rangle$. $\mathsf{Dec}(ws, CT, SK_{ws})$ decrypts CT for the window size ws using the private key SK_{ws}. The result is the aggregates of the sliding window, i.e. $s(M, ws)[i]$ for all i.

Security of $\mathcal{E}_w$ is defined via a *selective-window security game* consisting of four phases: *Setup, Corrupt, Challenge, Guess*.

- Setup: the challenger calls Gen(.) to setup public parameters. It chooses a value ws and sends it to the adversary.

- Corrupt: the adversary asks the challenger for the private key of a window size ws', provided that $gcd(ws, ws') = ws$.

- Challenge: the adversary picks two messages M_0, M_1 such that $M_0 = \langle m_{0,0}, m_{0,1}, .., m_{0,n-1} \rangle$, $M_1 = \langle m_{1,0}, m_{1,1}, .., m_{1,n-1} \rangle$ and $s(M_0, ws)[i] = s(M_1, ws)[i]$ for all i. The adversary sends (M_0, M_1) and a set of window sizes W to the challenger. The latter chooses $b \xleftarrow{R} \{0,1\}$, invokes Enc(M_b, W) and forwards the result to the adversary.

- Guess: the adversary outputs a guess $b' \in \{0,1\}$.

The adversary $\mathcal{A}$'s advantage is defined as $\mathsf{Adv}_{\mathcal{A}}^{\kappa}(ws) = |\Pr[b' = b] - \frac{1}{2}|$. $\mathcal{E}_w$ is said to be secure with respect to *restricted chosen encrypted window attacks* (or **Res-CEW secure**) in the selective-window model if the adversary's advantage is negligible. It is secure with respect to *chosen window attacks* (or **CW secure**) when the Corrupt phase is removed from the game.

2.2.3 Discussion

The encryption schemes above have different definitions of security with different assumptions about the adversary's capabilities. CPA security assumes a passive (eavesdropping) adversary who only tries to break the secrecy property of the ciphertext. It ensures confidentiality, while allowing meaningful changes to be made on the ciphertext (which is necessary for transformation to work). Det-CPA has a weaker security guarantee, as it protects data confidentiality only for unique messages.

Security of the sliding-window scheme $\mathcal{E}_w$ is related to that of secure multi-party computation, which ensures that no other information is leaked during the computation of a function except from the final output. Our model is similar, but stronger than the *aggregator oblivious* model proposed in [18], since the security game allows for more types of adversarial attacks. More specifically, [18] requires the two message sequences M_0 and M_1 to have the same aggregate, but our model requires only the windows (sub-sequences) of M_0 and M_1 to have the same aggregate. Both Res-CEW and CW security allow for meaningful computations (aggregate) over ciphertexts. Res-CEW is secure against a weak form of collusion (between users with access to window sizes which are multiples of each others), whereas CW is not.

2.2.4 Access control via Encryption.

Encryption plays two roles in our system: protecting data confidentiality against untrusted cloud, and providing access control against unauthorized users. Neither of cloud nor the unauthorized user have access to decryption keys, hence they cannot learn the plaintexts. In addition, Res-CEW and CW security ensure that given access to a window size ws, the user cannot learn information of other window sizes (except from what can be derived from its own window).

Res-CEW guarantees access control under weak collusion among dishonest users.

For access control to be enforced by the cloud, some information must be revealed to the latter. There exists a trade-off between security and functionality of the query operators that make up the policies. For Map and Filter policies, the cloud must be able to check if certain attributes are included in the ciphertexts, which is allowed by CPA security. For Join, the cloud needs to be able to compare if two ciphertexts are encryptions of the same message, which requires the encryption to be deterministic (or Det-CPA secure). For Aggregate, a homomorphic encryption is required, which in our case means the highest security level is Res-CEW.

3. ENCRYPTION SCHEMES

This section details the constructions of three encryption schemes defined in the previous section. Except for the proxy ABE construction which we take directly from the original work, the other encryption schemes are specifically designed for Streamforce. Detailed security proofs are omitted due to space constraint, and will be provided as an accompanying extended technical report if/when this paper is published.

3.1 Deterministic Encryption

Let $\mathbb{G}$ be a multiplicative group of prime order p and generator g. Let $F : \mathbb{Z}_p \times \{0,1\}^* \to \mathbb{G}$ be a pseudorandom permutation with outputs in $\mathbb{G}$. The scheme $\mathcal{E}_d$ is constructed as follows. Gen$(\kappa) \to SK = (k_1, k_2)$ where $k_1, k_2 \xleftarrow{R} \mathbb{Z}_p$. Enc$(m, SK) \to F(k_1, m)^{k_2}$. Finally, Dec$(CT, SK) \to F^{-1}(k_1, CT^{\frac{1}{k_2}})$.

Assuming that F is a pseudorandom permutation, $\mathcal{E}_d$ is Det-CPA secure.

3.2 Proxy ABE Construction

We use the CPA-secure construction as presented in [12]. Recall that $\mathcal{E}_p$ can actually achieve higher security level (R-CCA), but our system concerns confidentiality only, hence the CPA-secure construction suffices.

3.3 Sliding-Window Encryption

We propose three alternative constructions of the sliding-window encryption scheme: $\mathcal{E}_w^1, \mathcal{E}_w^2, \mathcal{E}_w^3$.

The naive construction, $\mathcal{E}_w^1$, masks the plaintext with random values whose sum over the sliding window is the user key. Encrypting a plaintext value produces $\mathcal{W}$ ciphertexts, where $\mathcal{W}$ is the set of all possible window sizes. The second construction, $\mathcal{E}_w^2$, employs an auxiliary scheme $\mathcal{E}_{aux}$ to encrypt the window aggregates directly. In particular, at timestamp ts, data owner computes and encrypts the aggregates of all windows ending at ts. Finally, $\mathcal{E}_w^3$ masks the plaintext with random values whose sum over the sliding window is encrypted with another scheme $\mathcal{E}_{aux}$. It can be considered as a generalized version of $\mathcal{E}_w^1$, but it places no restriction over the random values. As shown in Appendix C (Agg-3), one can select $\mathcal{E}_{aux}$ scheme to minimize space overhead. In the following, we present details of $\mathcal{E}_w^2$ (other constructions are described in Appendix C). We compare properties of $\mathcal{E}_w^1, \mathcal{E}_w^2, \mathcal{E}_w^3$ later in Section 4.4.

Let $\mathcal{W}$ be the set of all possible window sizes, $\mathcal{E}_{aux} = (\mathsf{Gen}, \mathsf{Enc}, \mathsf{Dec})$ be a CPA-secure public encryption scheme. $\mathcal{E}_w^2$ is implemented as follows:

- Gen(κ): let $\mathcal{E}_{aux} = (\mathsf{Gen}, \mathsf{Enc}, \mathsf{Dec})$ be a CPA-secure asymmetric encryption scheme. For all $ws \in \mathcal{W}$, invokes $\mathcal{E}_{aux}.\mathsf{Gen}(\kappa)$ to generate a key pair (PK_{ws}, SK_{ws}).

- Enc($M, \mathcal{W}$): $CT = \bigcup_{ws \in \mathcal{W}W} \mathcal{E}_{aux}.\mathsf{Enc}(PK_{ws}, s(M, ws)[i])$.

- Dec(ws, CT, SK_{ws}): extracts CT_{ws} from CT, then computes $s(M, ws)[i] = \mathcal{E}_{aux}.\mathsf{Dec}(SK_{ws}, CT_{ws}[i])$

We can prove that $\mathcal{E}_{ws}^1$ is Res-CEW secure, and given that $\mathcal{E}_{aux}$ is CPA-secure, both $\mathcal{E}_w^2$ and $\mathcal{E}_w^3$ are also Res-CEW secure.

4. SECURE QUERY OPERATORS

The encryption schemes discussed in previous sections provide the underlying security assurance for Streamforce. Using encryption directly, access control can be implemented by distributing decryption keys to the authorized users. Our system exposes a high-level abstraction, namely *secure query operators* which hide the complex and mundane cryptographic details. This section focuses on the implementation of the secure operators using the encryption schemes from previous sections. Many fine-grained policies can be constructed by using one of these operators directly. We also describe the design for combining these operators to support more complex policies. When implementing the operators, one must consider (1) how to map the corresponding policy to user decryption key, (2) how to encrypt the data at the owner, (3) how the transformation at the cloud is done.

4.1 Map

We use $\mathcal{E}_p$ (proxy ABE) to implement this operator, which returns data tuples containing attributes in a set $\mathbb{B}$. First, $\mathcal{E}_p.\mathsf{Gen}(.)$ is invoked to setup the public parameters and master key MK. The user decryption key is created by $\mathcal{E}_p.\mathsf{KeyGen}(MK, \mathsf{P\text{-}Map}(\mathbb{B}))$, where:

$$\mathsf{P\text{-}Map}(\mathbb{B}) = (`att = B_1\text{'} \cap `att = B_2\text{'} \cap ..)$$

The owner encrypts using:

$$\mathsf{Enc\text{-}Map}(d_{ts}) = (ts, \mathcal{E}_p.\mathsf{Enc}(v_{A_1}, \{`att = A_1\text{'}\}),$$
$$\mathcal{E}_p.\mathsf{Enc}(v_{A_2}, \{`att = A_2\text{'}\}), ..)$$

When the ciphertext CT arrives at the cloud, it is transformed using $\mathcal{E}_p.\mathsf{Trans}(TK, CT)$ and then forwarded to the user.

This operator has the same level of security as $\mathcal{E}_p$, i.e. CPA security in the selective set model. The storage cost is $O(|\mathbb{A}|.\log(p))$ bits per data tuple.

4.2 Filter

Let FA be the set of *filter attributes*. A filter *predicate* is defined by a tuple (A, k, op) in which $k \in \mathbb{Z}, A \in \mathbb{A}, op \in \{`='`, `\leq'`, `\geq'`, `mod\ p'\}$. The predicate returns true when $(A\ op\ k)$ returns true. Let $\lambda(A, v, b)$ be the bag-of-bit representation of v_A in base b, as explained in [11]. In particular, suppose $(v_0 v_1 v_2 v_3, ..,)_b$ is the value of v_A written in base b, then:

$$\lambda(A, v, b) = \{`A_{b,0} = v_0 * * * *..\text{'}, `A_{b,1} = *v_1 * * *..\text{'},$$
$$`A_{b,2} = * * v_2 * * *\text{'}, `A_{b,3} = * * * *v_3 * * *\text{'}..\}$$

Let $\mathbb{P}$ be a set of primes, and $AS(A, v) = \bigcup_{b \in \mathbb{P}} \lambda(A, v, b) \cup \{`att_A = \text{don't care}'\}$ be the set of encryption attributes representing the value v.

Denote $D(A, k, op)$ as the policy corresponding to the predicate (A, k, op). When $op \in \{=, \leq, \geq\}$, the policy is constructed as explained in [11]. When $op = `mod\ p'$, we consider three cases:

- $p \in \mathbb{P}$: $D(A, k, op)$ is the same as checking if the lowest-order bit v_A is equal to $k\ mod\ p$.

- $\exists t \in \mathbb{Z}, q \in \mathbb{P}. p = q^t$: the policy is the same as checking if the t lowest-order bits of $\lambda(A, v, q)$ is equal to $k\ mod\ p$.

- $\exists t_i \in \mathbb{Z}, q_i \in \mathbb{P}. p = (q_1^{t_1} q_2^{t_2}..)$: $D(A, k, `mod\ p') = \bigcap_i D(A, k\ mod\ q_i^{t_i}, mod\ q_i^{t_i})$.

The user decryption key is generated by $\mathcal{E}_p.\mathsf{KeyGen}\big(MK, \mathsf{P\text{-}Filter}(\{(A, k, op)\})\big)$, in which

$$\mathsf{P\text{-}Filter}(\{(A, k, op)\}) = \bigcap_{A \in FA} D(A, k, op)$$

The owner encrypts data using:

$$\mathsf{Enc\text{-}Filter}(d_{ts}) = \left(\{v_A \mid A \in FA\}, \mathcal{E}_p.\mathsf{Enc}\big(d, \bigcup_{A \in FA} AS(A, v_A)\big) \right)$$

When the ciphertext CT arrives at the cloud, the latter transforms it using $\mathcal{E}_p.\mathsf{Trans}(TK, CT)$ and forwards the result to the user.

Similar to Map, this operator uses proxy ABE scheme directly, hence it has CPA security in the selective set model. The storage cost per ciphertext is $O(|FA|.|\mathbb{P}|.\log(p))$ bits, which grows with the size of $\mathbb{P}$. The bigger the size of $\mathbb{P}$, the more policies of the type `mod p' can be supported, but at the expense of more storage overhead. Notice that values of filtering attributes are exposed to the cloud in the form of encryption attributes, thus the data owner should only use non-sensitive attributes, such as TS, for the set FA.

4.3 Join

Let J be the join attributes of two streams S_1, S_2. We assume that the join operator returns all data attributes (more complex cases are discussed in Section 4.5). We use a combination of proxy ABE scheme $\mathcal{E}_p$ and deterministic scheme $\mathcal{E}_d$. Initially, the two owners of S_1, S_2 invoke $\mathcal{E}_d.\mathsf{Gen}(.)$ in a way that satisfies two conditions: (1) both end up with the same group $\mathbb{G}$ and pseudorandom function F; (2) $SK_1 = (k_{1,1}, k_{1,2})$ and $SK_2 = (k_{2,1}, k_{2,2})$ are the two secret keys such that $k_{1,1} = k_{2,1}$. The user decryption for stream i is $(k_{i,2}, \mathcal{E}_p.\mathsf{KeyGen}(MK, \mathsf{P\text{-}Join}(J)))$, in which

$$\mathsf{P\text{-}Join}(J) = `att = J'$$

The owner encrypts using:

$$\mathsf{Enc\text{-}Join}(d_{ts}, J) = (U, V) = \big(\mathcal{E}_p.\mathsf{Enc}(d, `att = J'), \mathcal{E}_d.\mathsf{Enc}(v_J) \big)$$

The user who received both $k_{1,2}$ and $k_{2,2}$ computes $(z_1 = \frac{s}{k_{1,2}}, z_2 = \frac{s}{k_{2,2}})$ where $s \xleftarrow{R} \mathbb{Z}_p$ and sends it to the cloud. When two ciphertexts (U_1, V_1) and (U_2, V_2) arrive at the cloud, it checks if $V_1^{z_1} = V_2^{z_2}$. If true, the ciphertexts can be joined. The cloud then performs $\mathcal{E}_p.\mathsf{Trans}(TK_1, U_1)$, $\mathcal{E}_p.\mathsf{Trans}(TK_2, U_2)$ and forwards the results to the user.

Because $\mathcal{E}_d$ is Det-CPA secure, the cloud can learn if the encryption of v_J is the same as in both streams, but only

```
Enc-2(i, d, ℰ_p, 𝒲) :
    CT = ∅
    for all ws ∈ 𝒲
        if (i mod ws = ws − 1)
            CT = CT ∪ ℰ_p.Enc(s_ws, {'att = A_g', 'window = ws'})
            s_ws ← 0
    return CT
```

Figure 2: Implementation of aggregate operator (Agg-2)

if given the values z_1 and z_2. In other words, the cloud cannot perform joining unless requested by the user. Other attributes in d_{ts} are protected with CPA security by $\mathcal{E}_p$. The storage requirement is $O(\log(p))$ bits per data tuple, because $\mathcal{E}_d.\mathtt{Enc}(.)$ produces a group element and $\mathcal{E}_p$ encrypts the entire data tuple with only one encryption attribute.

4.4 Aggregate (Sliding Window)

In Streamforce, sliding windows are based on timestamp attribute TS, and they are non-overlapping, i.e. advance steps are the same as the window sizes. Let A_g be the aggregate attribute, over which the sums are computed. We propose three implementations based on three constructions of the sliding window encryption schemes, namely Agg-1, Agg-2, Agg-3. In Agg-1, the data is first encrypted with $\mathcal{E}_w^1$, then the result is encrypted with $\mathcal{E}_p$. In Agg-2, window aggregates are computed and encrypted with $\mathcal{E}_p$. In Agg-3, random values are added to the data which is then encrypted with $\mathcal{E}_p$, and the sum of the random values is also encrypted with $\mathcal{E}_p$. In this section, we describe Agg-2 which, as we later show, incurs low space and computation overhead in most cases. Other implementations are detailed in Appendix C.

Agg-2 uses $\mathcal{E}_w^2$ with $\mathcal{E}_p$ as the auxiliary encryption scheme. The owner itself computes the window aggregates and encrypts the result using $\mathcal{E}_p$. User decryption key is $\mathcal{E}_p.\mathtt{KeyGen}(MK, \mathtt{P\text{-}Agg2}(ws, A_g))$, where:

$$\mathtt{P\text{-}Agg2}(ws, A_g) = \text{'att = } A_g\text{'} \cap \text{'window = } ws\text{'}$$

To encrypt d_{ts}, the owner first executes $\mathtt{Enc\text{-}2}(ts, d_{ts}, \mathcal{E}_p, \mathcal{W}) \rightarrow CT$ as shown in Fig. 2, then the ciphertext is computed as:

$$\mathtt{Enc\text{-}Agg2}(d_{ts}) = \left(\mathcal{E}_p.\mathtt{Enc}(d_{ts}, \{'window = 1'\}), CT \right)$$

At the cloud, the ciphertexts for a window aggregate are of the same form as for a normal data tuple. The cloud simply invokes $\mathcal{E}_p.\mathtt{Trans}(CT_{ws}, TK_{ws})$ and forwards the results to the user.

Discussion.

Unlike Map, Filter and Join, the Aggregate operator requires more effort from the cloud, i.e. multiplication of ciphertexts. Since it uses $\mathcal{E}_p$ as the final layer of encryption, it achieves CPA security with respect to the cloud. In all three implementations, the transformed ciphertexts received by the user are data encrypted with $\mathcal{E}_w^1$, $\mathcal{E}_w^2$ or $\mathcal{E}_w^3$. As discussed in the previous section, these schemes achieve Res-CEW security, therefore the user learns nothing more than the aggregate values.

Agg-1 and Agg-2 support a fixed set of window sizes. Agg-3 is more flexible: it supports all window sizes whose prime factors are in $\mathbb{P}$, and it allows for arbitrary starting positions

of the sliding windows. The storage cost of Agg-1 and Agg-2 are $O(|W|.\log(p))$ bits per data tuple, but it is for the average case with Agg-1, and for the worst-case for Agg-2. For Agg-3, the average cost is $O(|\mathbb{P}|.\log(p))$. There is a trade-off between flexibility and storage overhead. When the owner wishes to support a small number of windows, Agg-2 is a better choice among the three. However, when more flexible windows are required, Agg-3 may have a better trade-off between flexibility and storage cost. Our experimentation with Streamforce in Section 5 suggests that this is indeed the case.

4.5 Combining Multiple Operators

Map and Filter.

The user decryption key is generated by combining the Map and Filter key,
i.e. $\mathcal{E}_p.\mathtt{Gen}\big(MK, \mathtt{P\text{-}Map}(\mathbb{B}), \mathtt{P\text{-}Filter}(\{A, k, op\})\big)$. The owner encrypts using:

$$\mathtt{MF\text{-}Enc}(d_{ts}) = \big(ts, \{v_A \mid A \in FA\}, \mathcal{E}_p.\mathtt{Enc}(v_{A_1}, A_1^*),$$
$$\mathcal{E}_p.\mathtt{Enc}(v_{A_2}, A_2^*), ..\big)$$

where $A_i^* = \{\text{'att = } A_1\text{'}\} \cup \bigcup_{A \in FA} AS(A, v_a)$ This operator is CPA secure, and the storage cost is $O(\mathbb{A}.|FA|.|\mathbb{P}|.\log(p))$ bits per data tuple.

Map, Filter and Join.

This operator allows the cloud to join two encrypted streams only when filter conditions on each stream are met. The user decryption key is made up of the Map-Filter key and the Join key, i.e:

$$\Big(k_{i,2}, \mathcal{E}_p.\mathtt{KeyGen}(MK, \mathtt{P\text{-}Join}(J)),$$
$$\mathcal{E}_p.\mathtt{Gen}\big(MK, \mathtt{P\text{-}Map}(\mathbb{B}), \mathtt{P\text{-}Filter}(\{A, k, op\})\big)\Big)$$

The data owner encrypts using:

$$\mathtt{MFJ\text{-}Enc}(d_{ts}) = \Big(\{v_A \mid A \in FA\}, \mathtt{MF\text{-}Enc}(d_{ts}), \mathcal{E}_p.\mathtt{Enc}\big(\mathcal{E}_d.\mathtt{Enc}(v_J)\big)\Big)$$

This operator is Det-CPA secure, and its storage cost is dominated by the cost of MF-Enc, which is $O(\mathbb{A}.|FA|.|\mathbb{P}|.\log(p))$ bits per data tuple.

Filter and Aggregate.

We assume that each sliding window contains only *continuous* elements,
i.e. $\{d_{ts}, d_{ts+1}, .., d_{ts+ws-1}\}$. Therefore, combining Filter and Aggregate only applies to filtering conditions of the form $(TS, k, \text{' } \geq \text{ '})$ for $k \in \mathbb{Z}$. Using Agg-2, the user decryption key is:

$$\Big(\mathcal{E}_p.\mathtt{KeyGen}\big(MK, \mathtt{P\text{-}Agg2}(ws, A_g)\big),$$
$$\mathcal{E}_p.\mathtt{KeyGen}\big(MK, \mathtt{P\text{-}Filter}(\{TS, k, \text{' } \geq \text{ '}\})\big)\Big)$$

To encrypt d_{ts}, the owner simply invokes $\mathtt{Enc\text{-}Agg2}(d_{ts})$. Thus, this operator has the same security level as that of Agg-2: CPA security against the cloud and Res-CEW security against users. The memory cost is $O(|\mathcal{W}|.\log(p))$ bits per data tuple.

4.6 Limitation

Streamforce does not support arbitrary combination of operators. For example, if a filter operator does not return continuous elements, it is not possible to link it with an aggregate operator. Another limitation is that the set of filter *FA* and join attributes *J* is pre-defined, hence filtering on attributes not in *FA* or joining on an attribute $J' \neq J$ is not allowed.

5. PROTOTYPE AND EVALUATION

5.1 Implementation and Benchmark

We implement a prototype of Streamforce over Esper[1] — an open source stream processing engine capable of processing millions of data items per second. One can register a continuous query to Esper, then implement a *listener* that processes the output stream. In Streamforce, policies are translated into queries (Table 1), and transformations for each policy are done at the corresponding listener. We leverage Esper to manage policies and data flow between operators, as well as to handle the complex join operation. We use OpenSSL's AES implementation for deterministic encryption scheme, while proxy ABE and sliding window schemes are implemented by extending the KP-ABE library [1].

We create a benchmark containing stock market data of the scheme:

$$StockEvent = (TS, hour, stockId, price, volume)$$

in which *hour* values are in $[0, 24)$ while *price, volume* values are in $[0, 100)$. Each stream is identified by its *stockId*. The benchmark data contains 1 million encrypted data tuples belonging to 100 streams[2]. We generate different types of policies, as listed in Table 1 which also shows how the policies are translated into Esper queries. Notice that when Agg-1 or Agg-3 implementation is used, the query involves Esper's window operator because we rely on Esper to maintain the window's buffer. In contrast, Agg-2 requires no window since the cloud only transforms individual ciphertexts. Join policies use Filter-Join operators (the Filter conditions are similar to those of T2, T3 and T4 policies), and involves two steps: the first transforms the input stream into *StockJoinEvent* stream containing the deterministic encryption of the join attribute, the second takes two StockJoinEvent streams and produces join outputs.

We first benchmark individual cost of various operations at the owner, the cloud and the user by measuring their execution time. Next, we evaluate system performance in terms of **throughput** and **latency**. Throughput is quantified by the number of unique data tuples processed by the system per second. For join policies, however, it is measured as the number of join outputs processed per second. Latency is determined from the time a data tuple enters Streamforce to the time it is sent to the user. This metric includes both queuing time and transformation time. Our experiments were carried out on Amazon's EC2 instances, with 8 window sizes ($\{2, 4, 8, .., 256\}$) and maximum of 100 policies (mixture of all different types) per stream.

5.2 Experiment Results

We start with a simple workload consisting of one stream and one T1 policy. We run the workload on different types of EC2 instances with different capacity, including (from small to large): *m1.large*, *m2.xlarge* and *m3.xlarge*. We vary the

[1] esper.codehause.org
[2] Our dataset is over 100GB in size and is available on request

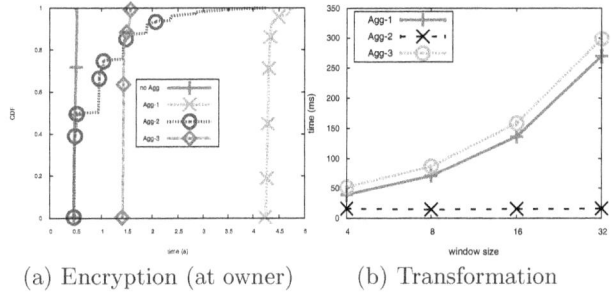

(a) Encryption (at owner)   (b) Transformation

Figure 3: Transformation for aggregate policies

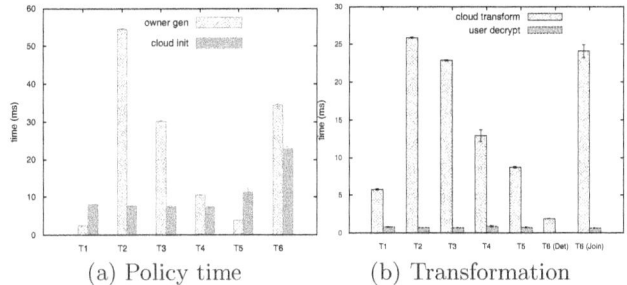

(a) Policy time   (b) Transformation

Figure 4: Cost incurred at the cloud

data rate, and observe the system performance at saturation point. *m3.xlarge* achieves the best performance, with throughput of 249 (tuples/sec) and latency of $567ms$ (at 99th percentile). In contrast, *m1.large* and *m2.xlarge* have lower throughputs at 125 and 160 (tuples/sec), and higher latency at $781ms$ and $628ms$. The results presented below are from experiments running on *m3.xlarge* instances. When the system first starts, the owners and users have to initialize the cryptographic sub-systems (running Gen(.), among other things). This one-off cost consists of a constant cost for pre-computing discrete logarithms, and a variable cost depending on the number of encryption attributes. Even with 1024 encryption attributes, this initialization process takes less than $3.5s$.

Fig. 3[a] shows the cost of encryption per data tuple at the owner. If the owner does not allow for aggregate policies, it is relatively constant at approximately $0.5s$. The cost for supporting Agg-1 is the largest (over $4s$), since the owner has to encrypt the data multiple times (one for each window size). Agg-3 is also more expensive, since two extra columns are encrypted for each tuple. The cost of Agg-2 stays low for most of the time (its maximum value is still as high as of that of Agg-1). This agrees with our analysis in Section 4, i.e. most of the time the owner incurs no extra encryption per tuple, but in the worst case it has to do 8 encryptions per tuple. Fig. 3[b] compares the transformation costs at the cloud for different implementations of the aggregate operator. It can be seen that for Agg-2 the cost is constant, whereas for others it is linear with the size of the window. This is because for Agg-1 and Agg-3, the cloud needs to transform many ciphertexts and multiply them to get the average.

The cost to generate and initialize different types of policies are depicted in Fig. 4[a]. Generating a new policy at the

Policy	Description	Esper query
T1	select certain stock	select * from StockEvent(stockId=x)
T2	stock within timestamp range	select * from StockEvent(stockId=x, $y < ts < z$)
T3	stock within time interval	select * from StockEvent(stockId=x, $y <$ hour $< z$)
T4	stock every fixed interval	select * from StockEvent(stockId=x, $ts\%x = y$)
T5	aggregate (Agg-1,3) aggregate (Agg-2)	select price('ws=l'), volume('ws=l') from StockEvent(stockId=x).win:length_batch(y) select price('ws=l'), volume('ws=l') from StockEvent(stockId=x)
T6	join price	select * from StockEvent(stockId=x, $y < ts < z$) //output StockJoinEvent stream select * from StockJoinEvent(policyId=p).win:length(l_1) as s_1, StockJoinEvent(policyId=p).win:length(l_2) as s_2 where s_1.price('det')=s_2.price('det')

Table 1: Access control policies

owner involves creating new transformation and decryption key for the corresponding predicate, which varies with the policy complexity. T2 policies, for example, contain many bag-of-bit attributes that make up complex predicates, and therefore they take longer. The cost of initializing policies at the cloud depends on key sizes, hence it is roughly the same for all types of policies, except for Join (which involves 2 keys from the two input streams). Fig. 4[b] shows the transformation cost at the cloud versus decryption cost at the user, in which the former is an order of magnitude bigger. This illustrates that heavy computations are being outsourced to the cloud. The highest throughput is for T1 policies, at 250 (tuples/sec). We remark that many current stream applications, such as fitness and weather monitoring, have very low data arrival rate (in order of minutes), therefore our throughput can sufficiently accommodate many streams at the same time.

Fig. 5 illustrates system throughputs for more complex workloads consisting of multiple policies, multiple streams and join policies. We create mixed workloads containing different types of policies. Fig. 5[a] shows that increasing the number of policies decreases the throughput, which is heavily influenced by the number of T2 policies (the workload of 2 and 4 policies contain only 1 T2 policy). This makes sense because each tuple has to be matched with (and transformed for) more policies, and because T2's transformation cost is the highest. When there are multiple streams but only one matching policy, communication overheads can reduce the throughput. But as Fig. 5[b] indicates, having more matching policies for every stream helps maintain the overall throughput (r, nP, nS are the data rate per stream, number of matching policies and number of streams respectively). The similar pattern is found for Join policies, as shown in Fig. 5[c]. It can be observed that throughput of join depends on the *similarity* of the two joining streams. Specifically, when two Filter conditions are of type T2 ($y < ts < z$), the output streams (for joining) have more matches and therefore are more similar (throughput of 60) than when one filter condition is of type T4 ($ts\%x = y$) where throughput is at 40 tuples/sec.

Finally, Fig. 6 illustrates how the system performance improves when more servers are utilized. We create a workload consisting of 16 streams and 320 policies. 4 of these streams incur expensive load with 4 T2 policies per stream. When there are more than one servers at the cloud, we consider two ways of distributing the workload: *simple* — each stream occupies one machine, and *balanced* — expensive policies are distributed evenly among the machine. The latter may result in one stream occupying multiple servers. Fig. 6[a] shows that the throughput increases linearly with the number of servers, which is as expected. Also, the balanced dis-

tribution achieves lower throughputs, because in the simple distribution the servers handling light workload gets very high throughputs, whereas with the balanced distribution all servers get low throughputs. However, at 16 servers, the balanced distribution outgrows the simple distribution, but this throughput is obtained over duplicate tuples. This is because at 8 and more servers, there are streams being processed by multiple servers. Fig. 6[b] shows the latency distributions which clearly demonstrates the benefit of having more servers. The maximum latency using 1 server is over $100s$, but is reduced to below $14s$ using 16 machines. The balanced distribution achieves lower maximum latency and lower variance, since all servers incur a similar load (as opposed to a few servers incurring much heavier loads than the others).

To understand this latency distribution, we examine the breakdown of execution time at the cloud. The latency per tuple consists of queueing time and processing time (transformation, or crypto time). Fig. 6[c] illustrates this breakdown for 16 servers. It can be seen that adding more servers does not benefit the crypto time. More importantly, the queuing time (overall time minus the crypto time) is an order of magnitude larger than crypto time. Adding more servers reduces the queue size at each node, therefore the queueing time and subsequently the overall execution time can be greatly improved.

Discussion.

Our experiments with a single cloud server showed that processing at the cloud (transformation of ciphertexts) achieves the highest throughput of only 250 tuples/sec. That this result compares poorly against Esper's reported performance of over 1 million tuples/sec may cause one to question the reason to outsource data to the cloud and subsequently the very practicability of Streamforce. However, we stress that our system model lends itself naturally to data outsourcing for two reasons. First, stream data is potentially infinite in size, hence the cost of storage and management can be greatly reduced by using the cloud. Second, our system follows the multi-client model (one stream is accessed by many different clients), and the stream processing can be computationally expensive. In such settings, the saving of network bandwidth and computation justify the moving of data to the cloud [6]. As demonstrated in Fig. 6, the overall throughput can be improved considerably by adding more servers at the cloud, so Streamforce is amenable to heavier workload by massive distribution and parallelization of the tasks. Finally, while there is room for improvement both in the set of features and functionalities, Streamforce makes an important first step in providing security assurance over streaming data outsourced to an untrusted cloud.

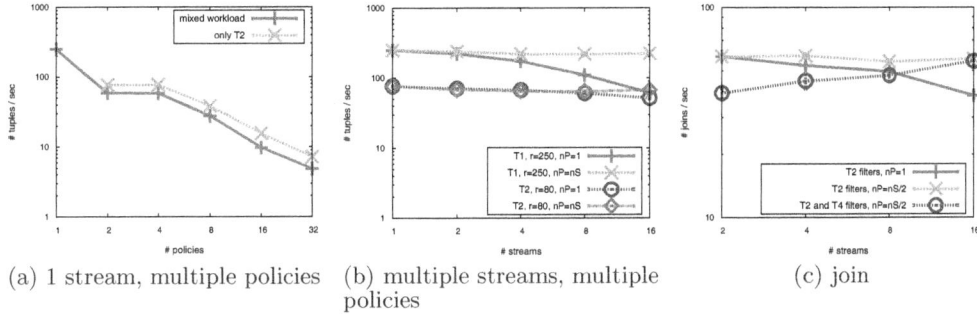

(a) 1 stream, multiple policies   (b) multiple streams, multiple policies   (c) join

Figure 5: System throughput for complex workloads

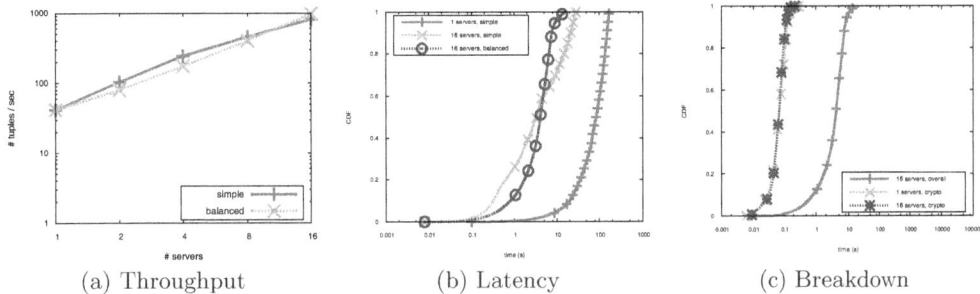

(a) Throughput   (b) Latency   (c) Breakdown

Figure 6: Workload distribution

6. RELATED WORK

The design space concerning access control enforcement on a cloud environment can be characterized using three properties [7]: policy *fine-grainedness*, cloud *trustworthiness* and cloud/client *work ratio*. The last property specifies how much work the cloud and user has to perform in relation to each other: the higher this value, the better it is to move to the cloud. When the cloud is trusted, it is equivalent to running a private infrastructure, thus the remaining concern is policy fine-grainedness. In this setting, [4] explores access control model on top of Aurora query model. Such systems achieve the highest level of fine-grainedness. When the cloud is untrusted, the security must be balanced against the fine-grainedness and work ratio property. CryptDb [17] ensures data confidentiality against the cloud for archival database, but it supports only coarse-grained access control policies. Systems such as [19] employ ABE schemes for more fine-grained policies, but the work ratio is low because the cloud only serves as a data storage and distribution facility.

Streamforce strikes an unique balance against all three properties. It considers untrusted cloud (same as in [17]) but it supports a wide range of policies (with more fine-grainedness than [19, 17]), and at the same time achieves high work ratio (the cloud shares a larger proportion of the workload than in the other systems).

7. CONCLUSIONS AND FUTURE WORK

In this paper, we have presented a system providing fine-grained access control for stream data over untrusted clouds. Our system — Streamforce — allows the owners to encrypt data before relaying them to the cloud. Encryption ensures both confidentiality against the cloud and access control against dishonest users. Streamforce uses combinations of three encryption schemes: a deterministic scheme, a proxy ABE scheme and a sliding-window scheme. We have showed how the cloud can enforce access control over ciphertexts by transforming them for authorized user, without learning the plaintexts. In Streamforce, the cloud handles most of the heavy computations, while the users are required to do only simple, inexpensive decryptions. We have implemented Streamforce on top of Esper, and carried out a benchmark study of the system. The security cost is large enough to hinder the system from achieving very high throughputs (as compared to the maximum throughput of Esper). However, we believe the current throughput is sufficient for many real-life applications in which data arrives at low rate. Furthermore, we have shown that employing more servers in the cloud can substantially improve the overall performance, since it is possible to a certain extent to parallelize the workload in Streamforce.

We believe that our work has put forth the first secure system for outsourcing the enforcement of fine-grained access control for stream data. Streamforce occupies an unique position in the design space, and also opens up a wide avenue for future work. There exists classes of applications that require much higher throughput than currently possible in Streamforce. We acknowledge that more effort is required to satisfy both security and demand for performance. However, Streamforce provides a crucial first step.

Our immediate plan is to make Streamforce scale better. To this end, we are investigating to implement Streamforce over cloud-based stream processing engines, such as Storm [14] and S4 [2]. These systems provide an easy way for users to specify how to process query graphs over a given number of servers. Supporting elasticity for Streamforce (spawning new servers to balance the load during runtime) is an interesting and challenging venue for future work, especially since processing states at the servers may not be partitionable [9]. At the current stage, getting the data into Streamforce is the main bottleneck: each ciphertext is over $100KB$ in size. We are exploring techniques to reduce the ciphertext sizes and to improve the (incoming) data throughput.

Although Streamforce supports a wide range of policies, this range can still be improved. As stated in [7], policies involving more complex functions such as granularity and similarity policies are useful in many applications. Supporting these functions over ciphertext requires more powerful homomorphic encryptions, such as [10]. However, one must be careful to strike the balance between security and performance. Our current encryption schemes do not support revocation, nor do they support negative and hidden attributes. In particular, hidden attributes are necessary when the owner wishes to hide more information from the cloud. We plan to explore if and how existing proposals for these features [3, 16, 15] can be implemented in our system. Furthermore, we would like to relax the current adversary model which is semi-honest. A malicious adversary may compromise data integrity, skip computation or compute using stale data. We believe that detecting and recovering from these attacks are important for outsourced database systems, but they may come at heavier cost of performance. Finally, in Streamforce we have assumed that owners know which data to share and under which policies. In reality, these decisions are not easy to make. Differential privacy [8] could help reasoning about which data to share, while recommendation techniques [5] can help determining the appropriate policies.

Acknowledgement

This work was supported by A*Star SERC grant no. 102 158 0038 for the project 'pCloud: Privacy in data value chains using peer-to-peer primitives', and by the Singapore NRF's CRP grant no. NFR-CRP8-2011-08 for the project 'Design and Development of a Comprehensive Information Technology Infrastructure for Data-Intensive Applications and Analysis'. The first author did part of this work while he was a research fellow at NTU Singapore.

8. REFERENCES

[1] Key-policy attribute-based encryption scheme implementation.
http://www.cnsr.ictas.vt.edu/resources.html.

[2] Apache. S4 - distributed stream computing platform.
incubator.apache.org/s4.

[3] N. Attrapadung. Revocation scheme for attribute-based encryption. RCIS Workshop, 2008.

[4] B. Carminati, E. Ferrari, J. Cao, and K. L. Tan. A framework to enforce access control over data streams. *ACM ToIS*, 2010.

[5] G. P. Cheek and M. Shehab. Policy-by-example for online social networks. In *SACMAT*, 2012.

[6] Yao Chen and Radu Sion. On securing untrusted clouds with cryptography. *DEB*, 2012.

[7] T. T. A. Dinh and A. Datta. The blind enforcer: on fine-grained access control enforcement on untrusted clouds. *DEB*, 2013.

[8] C. Dwork. Differential privacy. In *ICALP*, 2006.

[9] Rault Castro Fernandez, Metteo Migliavacca, Evangelia Kalyvianaki, and Peter Pietzuch. Integrating scale out and fault toelerance in stream processing using operator state management. In *SIGMOD*, 2013.

[10] C. Gentry. Fully homomorphic encryption using ideal lattices. In *SOTC*, 2009.

[11] V. Goyal, O. Pandey, A. Sahai, and B. Waters. Attribute-based encryption for fine-grained access control of encrypted data. In *CCS'06*, 2006.

[12] M. Green, S. Hohenberger, and B. Waters. Outsourcing the decryption of abe ciphertexts. In *USENIX Security*, 2011.

[13] M. Kallahalla, E. Riedel, R. Swaminathan, Q. Wang, and K. Fu. Plutus: scalable secure file sharing on untrusted storage. In *FAST*, pages 29–42, 2003.

[14] H. Lim, Y. Han, and S. Babu. How to fit when no one size fits. In *CIDR*, 2013.

[15] Y. Lu. Privacy-preserving logarithmic-time search on encrypted data in cloud. In *NDSS*, 2013.

[16] R. Ostrovsky, A. Sahai, and B. Waters. Attribute-based encryption with non-monotonic access structures. In *CCS'07*, 2007.

[17] R. A. Popa, N. Zeldovich, and H. Balakrishnan. Cryptdb: a practical encrypted relational dbms. Technical Report MIT-CSAIL-TR-2011-005, CSAIL, MIT, 2011.

[18] E. Shi, T. H. Chan, E. R. FxPal, R. Chow, and D. Song. Privacy-preserving aggregation of time-series data. In *NDSS*, 2011.

[19] S. Yu, C. Wang, K. Ren, and W. Lou. Achieving secure, scalable and fine-grained data access control in cloud computing. In *INFOCOM*, 2010.

APPENDIX

A. DET-CPA SECURITY DEFINITION

Security of $\mathcal{E}_d$ is defined via the security game consisting of three phases: *Setup, Challenge, Guess.*

- Setup: the challenger runs Gen(.).

- Challenge: the adversary sends to the challenger two messages: $M_0 = (m_{0,0}, m_{0,1}, ..)$ and $M_1 = (m_{1,0}, m_{1,1}, ..)$, such that $|M_0| = |M_1|$ and $m_{i,j}$ are all distinct. The challenger chooses $b \xleftarrow{R} \{0, 1\}$, runs $\mathsf{Enc}(M_b, SK)$ and returns the ciphertext to the adversary.

- Guess: the adversary outputs a guess $b' \in \{0, 1\}$.

$\mathcal{E}_d$ is said to be secure with respect to *deterministic chosen plaintext attacks*, or **Det-CPA secure**, if the adversary advantage, defined as $\mathsf{Adv}_{\mathcal{A}}^{\kappa} = |Pr[b = b'] - \frac{1}{2}|$, is negligible.

B. SLIDING-WINDOW ENCRYPTION

Let $\mathcal{W}$ be the set of all possible window sizes, $\mathbb{G}$ be a multiplicative group of prime order p and generator g. $dLog(x)$ computes the discrete log of x in $\mathbb{G}$ (we assumed that the plaintext domain is small).

B.1 Construction 1: $\mathcal{E}_w^1$

- Gen(κ): for all $ws \in \mathcal{W}$, $SK_{ws} \xleftarrow{R} \mathbb{Z}_p$.

```
Enc-1(i, d, W)
    for all ws ∈ W
        if (i mod ws < ws − 1) r ←ᴿ ℤₚ; else r ← SK_ws − s_ws
        CT_ws = g^(r+d.v_Ag); s_ws ← s_ws + r
    return {CT_ws}

Enc-2(i, d, ℰₚ, W):
    CT = ∅
    for all ws ∈ W
        if (i mod ws = ws − 1)
            CT = CT ∪ ℰₚ.Enc(s_ws, {'att = A_g', 'window = ws'})
            s_ws ← 0
    return CT

Enc-3(d):
    r ←ᴿ ℤₚ; s* ← s* + r
    return (g^(r+d.v_Ag), g^(s*))
```

Figure 7: Implementation of aggregate operator

- Enc(M, W): for each $ws \in W$, let $R = (r_0, r_1, .., r_{|M|})$ such that $r_i \xleftarrow{R} \mathbb{Z}_p$ and $s(R, ws)[i] = SK_{ws}$. The ciphertext is $CT = \bigcup_{ws} CT_{ws}$ where $CT_{ws} = (g^{m_0+r_0}, g^{m_1+r_1}, ..)$.

- Dec(ws, CT, SK_{ws}): extracts CT_{ws} from CT and compute: $s(M, \text{ws})[i] = dLog\left(\frac{p(CT_{ws}, ws)[i]}{g^{SK_{ws}}}\right)$

B.2   Construction 2: $\mathcal{E}_w^2$

- Gen(κ): let $\mathcal{E}_{aux} = (\text{Gen}, \text{Enc}, \text{Dec})$ be a CPA-secure asymmetric encryption scheme. For all $ws \in W$, invokes $\mathcal{E}_{aux}.\text{Gen}(\kappa)$ to generate a key pair (PK_{ws}, SK_{ws}).

- Enc(M, W): $CT = \bigcup_{ws \in W} \mathcal{E}_{aux}.\text{Enc}(PK_{ws}, s(M, ws)[i])$

- Dec(ws, CT, SK_{ws}): extracts CT_{ws} from CT, then computes $s(M, ws)[i] = \mathcal{E}_{aux}.\text{Dec}(SK_{ws}, CT_{ws}[i])$

B.3   Construction 3: $\mathcal{E}_w^3$

- Gen(κ): the same as in $\mathcal{E}_w^2$.

- Enc(M, W): let $R = (r_0, r_1, .., r_{|M|-1})$ where $r_i \xleftarrow{R} \mathbb{Z}_p$, let $CT_0 = (g^{m_0+r_0}, g^{m_1+r_1}, ..)$. For all $ws \in W$, let $CT_{ws}[i] = \mathcal{E}_{aux}.\text{Enc}(PK_{ws}, s(R, ws)[i])$. Finally, $CT = CT_0 \cup \bigcup_{ws \in W} CT_{ws}$.

- Dec(ws, CT, SK_{ws}): extracts CT_{ws} from CT, then computes $s(M, ws)[i] = dLog\left(\frac{p(CT_0, ws)[i]}{g^{\mathcal{E}_{aux}.\text{Dec}(SK_{ws}, CT_{ws}[i])}}\right)$

C.   AGGREGATE SECURE OPERATOR

Agg-1..
The owner first encrypts data using $\mathcal{E}_w^1$, the ciphertext is then encrypted with $\mathcal{E}_p$. The user decryption key is $(SK_{ws}, \mathcal{E}_p.\text{KeyGen}(MK, \text{P-Agg1}(ws, A_g)))$, where SK is the secret key generated by $\mathcal{E}_w^1.\text{Gen}(.)$, and

$$\text{P-Agg1}(ws, A_g) = \text{`att} = A_g' \cap \text{`window} = ws'$$

To encrypt d_{ts}, the owner first executes $\text{Enc-1}(ts, d_{ts}, W) \rightarrow \{CT_{ws}\}$ as shown in Fig. 7, then computes:

$$\text{Enc-Agg1}(d_{ts}, \{CT_{ws}\})$$
$$= \Big(\mathcal{E}_p.\text{Enc}(d, \{\text{`window} = 1'\}),$$
$$\bigcup_{ws \in W} \mathcal{E}_p.\text{Enc}(CT_{ws}, \{\text{`att} = A_g', \text{`window} = ws'\})\Big)$$

For every window size ws, the cloud maintains a buffer of size ws. The incoming ciphertext CT is transformed using $\mathcal{E}_p.\text{Trans}(.)$, and the result is added to the buffer. Once the buffer is filled, the cloud computes the product of its elements, sends the result to the user and clears the buffer.

Agg-2..
This implementation uses $\mathcal{E}_w^2$ with $\mathcal{E}_p$ as the auxiliary encryption scheme. The owner itself computes the window aggregates and encrypts the result using $\mathcal{E}_p$. User decryption key is $\mathcal{E}_p.\text{KeyGen}(MK, \text{P-Agg2}(ws, A_g))$, where:

$$\text{P-Agg2}(ws, A_g) = \text{`att} = A_g' \cap \text{`window} = ws'$$

To encrypt d_{ts}, the owner first executes $\text{Enc-2}(ts, d_{ts}, \mathcal{E}_p, \mathcal{A}) \rightarrow CT$ as shown in Fig. 7, then the ciphertext is computed as:

$$\text{Enc-Agg2}(d_{ts}) = \Big(\mathcal{E}_p.\text{Enc}(d_{ts}, \{\text{`window} = 1'\}), CT\Big)$$

At the cloud, the ciphertexts for a window aggregate are of the same form as for a normal data tuple. The cloud simply invokes $\mathcal{E}_p.\text{Trans}(CT_{ws}, TK_{ws})$ and forwards the results to the user.

Agg-3..
This implementation uses $\mathcal{E}_w^3$ with $\mathcal{E}_p$ as the auxiliary encryption scheme. The user key is $\mathcal{E}_p.\text{KeyGen}(MK, \text{P-Agg3}(ws, A_g))$, where:

$$\text{P-Agg3}(ws, A_g) = \text{`att} = A_g' \cup D(TS, ws - 1, \text{`mod } ws')$$

To encrypt d_{ts}, the owner first computes $\text{Enc-3}(d_{ts}) \rightarrow (U, V)$ as shown in Fig. 7 where $s^* \xleftarrow{R} \mathbb{Z}_p$ is a public parameter. The ciphertext is:

$$\text{Enc-Agg3}(d_{ts})$$
$$= \Big(ts, \mathcal{E}_p.\text{Enc}(v_{A_g}, \{\text{`window} = 1'\}),$$
$$\mathcal{E}_p.\text{Enc}(U, \{\text{`att} = A_g'\}), \mathcal{E}_p.\text{Enc}(V, \text{AS}(TS, i))\Big)$$

The cloud maintains a ws-size buffer, and a variable X whose initial value is $(g^{s^*}, 1)$. For the incoming ciphertext $CT = (ts, U, V, Z)$, the cloud performs $\mathcal{E}_p.\text{Trans}(TK, V)$ and adds the result to the buffer. Once the buffer is filled (at index ts), the cloud computes the product U' of the buffer elements and clears the buffer. Next, it computes $V' \leftarrow \frac{\mathcal{E}_p.\text{Trans}(TK, Z)}{X}$, and then assign $X \leftarrow V'$. Finally, it sends (U', V') to the user, at which the sum is decrypted as: $dLog\left(\frac{\mathcal{E}_p.\text{Dec}(SK, U')}{\mathcal{E}_p.\text{Dec}(SK, V')}\right)$

Compac: Enforce Component-Level Access Control in Android *

Yifei Wang, Srinivas Hariharan, Chenxi Zhao, Jiaming Liu, and Wenliang Du
Dept. of Electrical Engineering & Computer Science
Syracuse University, Syracuse, New York
{ywang123,srhariha,chzhao,jliu20,wedu}@syr.edu

ABSTRACT

In Android applications, third-party components may bring potential security problems, because they have the same privilege as the applications but cannot be fully trusted. It is desirable if their privileges can be restricted. To minimize the privilege of the third-party components, we develop Compac to achieve a fine-grained access control at application's component level. Compac allows developers and users to assign a subset of an application's permissions to some of the application's components. By leveraging the runtime Java package information, the system can acquire the component information that is running in the application. After that, the system makes decisions on privileged access requests according to the policy defined by the developer and user. We have implemented the prototype in Android 4.0.4, and have conducted a comprehensive evaluation. Our case studies show that Compac can effectively restrict the third-party components' permissions. Antutu benchmark shows that the overall score of our work achieves 97.4%, compared with the score of the original Android. In conclusion, Compac can mitigate the damage caused by third-party components with ignorable overhead.

Categories and Subject Descriptors

D.4.6 [**Operating Systems**]: Security and Protection—*Access Control*

General Terms

Security

Keywords

Android; dalvik; component permission; privilege separation

*This work is supported in part by NSF grants No. 1017771, No. 1318814, and by a Google research award.

1. INTRODUCTION

Android has become the most popular smartphone platform, taking more than 70 percent of the market shares [3]. Android uses permissions to restrict the behaviors of apps. An app (In the rest of the paper, apps are used for Android applications) needs to have specific permissions in order to access protected resources. The app declares permissions that it needs in `AndroidManifest.xml`. During app installation, users are asked to approve the declared permissions. Upon approval, the app will be installed.

In Android, permissions are assigned at the app level. When an app is installed, it is assigned a unique UID, and each UID is associated with a set of permissions. At runtime, access control uses the UID to find out the permissions of an app, regardless of what component of the app is making the access. Therefore, all the components in the same app have exactly the same permissions. This is not a problem if all these components come from the same developer. However, this is not the case in Android and most other mobile systems. In these systems, apps often include third-party components. In-app advertisement is the most representative example. When an app needs to display ads, it has to incorporate the advertisement code (e.g. Google's AdMob). Once incorporated, both the ads and the original app will have the same privilege. Other commonly used third-party components include social networking service APIs, Phone-Gap plug-ins, etc.

In most situations, apps need more permissions than what each component needs; when users grant the permissions to the apps, they also grant the same permissions to the components, leading to over-privileged components. In this case, some components in apps have more privilege than what they need. If they are malicious or have security flaws, they can cause problems. Previous work [45] indicates that several third-party components abuse apps' permissions to collect users' private information, without user consent.

Several ideas, such as AdDroid [34] and AdSplit [36], have been proposed to address the problem caused by a particular type of third-party component, namely, advertisement. AdSplit proposes to put ads in another process, isolating them from the app. AdDroid proposes to put ads into a service and assign a new ADVERTISING or LOCATION_ADVERTISING permission to this service. However, these solutions are mainly designed for advertisement; they are not general enough to extend to other types of third-party components.

In this paper, we propose COMPAC (COMPonent Access Control), a more generic solution, which extends Android's UID-based permission model [5] into UID- and component-based permission model. More specifically, several untrusted Java packages can be grouped into components, and an app can be divided into different components; app developer assign permission sets for the app and its components in AndroidManifest.xml. In such a case, both the app and components' permission sets are subject to Android system's control. To the best of our knowledge, this is the first time to propose a generic solution to limit part of app code's privileges in Android.

We have implemented Compac in Android 4.0.4, and have conducted a comprehensive evaluation on it, not only on its performance, but more importantly, on how Compac can be used to solve the over-privilege problems faced by today's apps when they use third-party components. Our results show that Compac is effective and applicable. We summarize the main contributions of this work as follows:

1. To restrict the privilege of third-party components, we propose a generic solution to contain in-app components' privileges by leveraging Java source code and extending the current Android permission model.

2. We implement the prototype called Compac and conduct comprehensive studies and performance evaluation to demonstrate that our approach can mitigate the damage caused by third-party code.

3. We provide app developers Compac APIs encapsulated in a customized SDK, which is compatible with the original Android SDK. We also develop a component permission manager to allow users to control app components' permissions on their devices.

2. BACKGROUND: ACCESS CONTROL IN ANDROID

In this section, we introduce the android sandbox protection for the system and data as well as the access control for non-privilege apps. At last, we define the reference monitors that will be used in our work.

2.1 Android Sandboxing

Generally speaking, Android has two types of resources that need to be protected. One is the app resources including the processes and files. The other is the system resources, such as camera, network, radio, GPS, and various sensors. To protect these resources, Android has developed a sandboxing mechanism that prevents apps from accessing the system resources or each other's resources. There are two aspects in this protection. First, each app is assigned a unique Linux UID, so Android can use Linux's UID-based DAC to restrict the privilege of apps. This naturally achieves the isolation among apps. Second, Android assigns most of the system resources to system UID, so they cannot be accessed directly by non-privilege apps.

2.2 The "Windows" on the Sandbox

Obviously, merely having such a sandbox is too restrictive. Apps should be allowed to access the system resources, as well as each other's resources. However, such accesses should be controlled, not arbitrary. The sandboxing mechanism eliminates the arbitrary accesses. To allow controlled accesses, "windows" have to be opened on the sandbox, but behind each window, there should be an access control.

System Calls. System calls are a typical way to allow user-level programs to access kernel-level resources. Android uses system calls to access some of the protected resources. For example, accessing the Internet is done through system calls, i.e., only apps with inet GID can directly access these resources by making the corresponding system calls. When an app invokes a system call to create an inet socket, the system call checks if the app has the inet GID; if it has, the app can get the socket and be able to access the Internet.

Android Permissions. Behind the GID check in privileged system calls, there are Android permissions, making sure that the authorized non-privilege apps can access the intended resources. Take the INTERNET permission as an example. When an app with the INTERNET permission is installed, Android will assign the inet GID to the app and its processes, as one of its additional GIDs. When the app accesses the Internet, request will be granted because of the inet GID; Unlike kernel resources, Android framework resources including services, content providers and broadcasts cannot be accessed directly by the system calls. These system resources provide an Android IPC interfaces as the "windows" to normal apps and Android permissions access control is built behind each window. When an app with the required permissions tries to access the intended system resources. The system resources call framework reference monitor to check the caller's permissions.

2.3 Reference Monitors

In the "windows" mentioned above, their access controls all have to get to one point: does the app have a particular permission? The windows themselves do not know the answer, they have to ask Android for its decision. In Android, this decision is only made in two places: at the framework level or at the kernel. We call them Framework Reference Monitor (FRM) or Kernel Reference Monitor (KRM).

FRM resides in the system_server process and it consists of two system services: Activity Manager Service (AMS) and Package Manager Service (PMS). Activities, content providers, services, and broadcasts check permissions using FRM. Whenever they need permission check, they send an IPC to AMS, which works together with PMS to conduct the check. In some cases, the caller is already in the system_server process, so the call will be a local one, not an IPC.

KRM resides in the kernel. Conceptually, the Linux Discretionary Access Control (DAC) is considered as KRM. When conducting permission check, KRM cannot reach out to AMS and PMS for the app's permission information. Pushing the permission information into the kernel can solve the problem, but can introduce significant kernel-level modification. Android chooses to utilize the Linux DAC by leveraging the UID and GIDs of a process to make the access control decisions in the kernel. For example, accesses to bluetooth, sdcard and the Internet need GIDs of net_bt, sdcard_r and inet respectively.

3. THE COMPAC DESIGN

3.1 The Overview

The main objective of Compac is to provide component-level access control. In Compac, each app consists of one

26

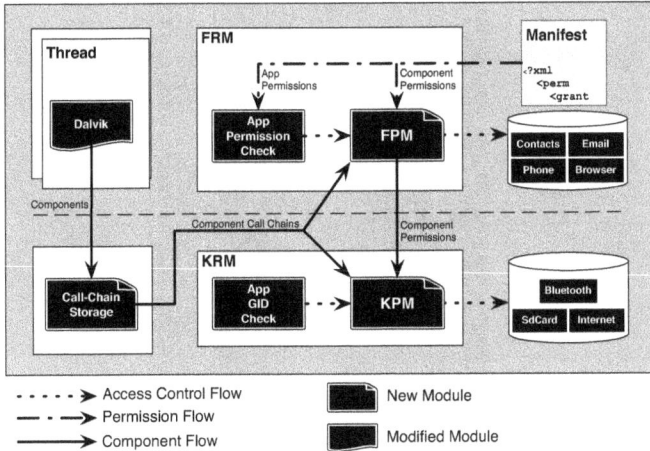

Figure 1: The Architecture of Compac

or more components[1]. App developers or device users can grant different permissions to components. For example, an app has two components, one for the main activity, and the other for advertisements. The app can give only one permission (INTERNET) to the advertisement components, while assigning several permissions (such as READ_PHONE_STATE, ACCESS_COARSE_LOCATION) to the rest of the app. Such a fine-grained access control is not possible in the existing Android system: each app can have one set of permissions; once granted by the users, all the components in the app will have the same privilege.

The architecture of our design is depicted in Figure 1. It is composed of three pieces. First, an app developer defines the app's permissions as well as the component permissions. When the app is installed, its app and component permissions are acquired by the reference monitors. As we mentioned in Section 2, Android has two permission-checking places: Framework Reference Monitor (FRM) and Kernel Reference Monitor (KRM). FRM still stores the app permissions as usual, and we do not modify the computing logic of the app permissions. To keep the best compatibility with current Android access control architecture, we extend the two RMs by adding two Policy Managers (PMs): Framework Policy Manager (FPM) and Kernel Policy Manager (KPM). The two PMs hold the component permissions that are obtained from the app's `AndroidManifest.xml`. Whenever permission update happens in Android framework, FPM synchronizes component permissions with KPM.

The second part is to extract the component information (Java package call chain) at runtime. We build hooks in Dalvik to trace the realtime Java method invocations. The trace is a call chain, which works like a call stack (FIFO). In order to make sure the component information is accurately recored, each thread of the app process has a call stack. If the thread is suspended, its call stack is locked. The thread's call stack follows the basic security rule. When a thread is forked from its parent, the parent's call stack status is inherited to avoid privilege escalation.

---

[1] Although Android platform has its own Android component definition, we use components to indicate Java packages. For example, Google Ads component means Google Ads related packages. Component is an abstract concept to facilitate the understanding of Compac.

The third piece is access control enforcement. The RMs make decisions based on app's UID permissions and component permissions. RMs first check if the app has the requested permissions. If it does, RMs ask PMs to check the component permissions. PMs consider a call chain as the principal in an access control. They have the privilege to request the call chain from Dalvik. After the PMs finish the computation of permissions, they check the component policy to return the result to RMs; If the app doesn't have the requested permission, the request is denied without any further component permission check.

3.2 Assumption & Trusted Computing Base

Most Android apps are written in Java, but for performance reasons, Android allows apps to include native code (compiled from C/C++ code) [4]. To distinguish this type of native code from that provided by the Android OS, we call it the app-specific native code. Since this native code runs in the same process space as Dalvik, if it is malicious, it can tamper with the process' stack and heap memory, including the memory used by Dalvik.

In Compac, Dalvik provides component call-stack information. If Dalvik's data memory can be changed by malicious components (through native code), there is no guarantee on the integrity of the runtime component information. In this paper, because of the lack of isolation between the app-specific native code and Dalvik, we block the invocation of app-specific native code in apps. The assumption is only temporary and has limited impact:

1. Based on the previous study [46], only 4.75% of benign apps have native code. Therefore, the majority of the apps will not be affected by this assumption.

2. Isolating the app-specific native code from the rest of the system is not impossible to implement. This goal is already achieved in the Chrome browser by the Native Client (NaCl) framework [43] using Software Fault Isolation (SFI) [40]. Robusta [37, 39] has successfully isolated the native code from Java Virtual Machine (JVM) in the traditional OSes. It will be just a matter of time before the isolation of the native code from Dalvik is achieved in Android.

3. If a component's permission set is the same as the app's permission set, i.e., there is no permission restriction on this component, we do allow the native code to be invoked by this component, because no extra privilege can be gained by this component even if it can modify Dalvik's memory. The blocking of native code is only enforced if a component has less permissions than the app.

It is quite tempting to enforce the component-level access control inside Dalvik, just like what the security manager does in the traditional JVM's security architecture [10]. In Android, the existing access control is not enforced inside Dalvik; instead, it is enforced either inside the kernel or in a privileged process (i.e., `system_server`). Android chooses to conduct access control in this way, rather than simply using the security architecture of JVM; this is mostly because Android itself uses a great deal of native code, in addition to the native code brought by apps. When an app invokes the native code, Dalvik will have no control. Thus we enforce the access control policy in Android framework not

Dalvik. However, in order to secure component boundaries and ensure the correct runtime component information, we do implement some auxiliary security rules (see section 4.2) in Dalivk. In general, we only use Dalvik to get the runtime component information, not for access control.

3.3 Component Permission Configuration

In the original Android platform, apps need to specify all the permissions they need in `AndroidManifest.xml`. During the installation, users will be asked whether they want to grant the requested permissions. Once granted the permissions, an app will have those permissions until it is uninstalled [25]. When the app requests protected resources, the corresponding permission will be checked.

To support component-level access control, we need to attach a separate permission set to different components. Consider all the participants involved in app management, We provide component permission configuration in two different ways. First, an app developer can specify what permissions each component needs. This is done by adding a special section in `AndroidManifest.xml`[2]:

```
<uses-permission android:name="READ_CONTACTS
    "/>
<uses-permission android:name="INTERNET"/>
<package-permission android:name="com.google.
    ads">
  <assign-permission android:name="INTERNET"/>
</package-permission>
```

In the above permission definition, the app's permissions are defined in Android's original `uses-permission` tag. The app has the INTERNET and READ_CONTACTS permissions. We call these permissions the app's default permissions. For the components that are not specifically mentioned in `AndroidManifest.xml`, they will have app's default permissions. If app developers want to restrict the permissions of some third-party components, they need to specify that using our new tag called `package-permission`. In the example, we have assigned only the INTERNET permission to the `com.google.ads` component. This component can use the Internet, but will not be able to read the user's contact data.

Second, experienced users have options to set their own security policies on a component, putting a restriction on what permissions it can have (see Figure 2), regardless of what are assigned to the component during the installation. This is very useful for users to control the popular components, such as advertising components, social networking service APIs, etc. Meanwhile, inexperienced users can keep apps' default settings configured by the developers. Users set component permissions per app. For example, if a user assigns only the INTERNET permission to the `AdMob` package in one app, then it will not affect the other apps' `AdMob` component permissions. This setting only overwrites the permissions assigned to the component in this app.

All the app permission definitions will be stored in framework reference monitor as what original Android does. However, all the component permission definitions will be acquired by framework policy manager. Once any component

---

[2]For formatting reasons, permission names in our examples are shortened by removing their prefix. For example, the full name of READ_CONTACTS should be android.permission.READ_CONTACTS.

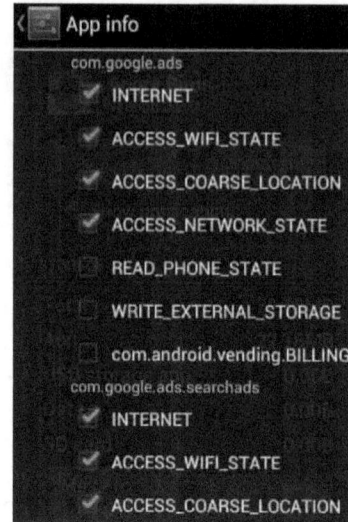

Figure 2: Permission Manager Interface for Users: third-party components with less permissions will be displayed in system settings, and experienced users have options to adjust component permissions in the app info section of system settings.

permission update happens, framework policy manager synchronizes the information of the component and its permissions with kernel policy manager. The synchronization is only done when the app is installed/updated, or when users modify the permissions assigned to a component.

3.4 Extracting Component Call Chains

To enforce component-level access control, Android needs to know what component initiates the access in addition to the UID information. However, that is not enough, as one component A can invoke another component B, and B then invokes C, which initiates the access. To make a correct access control decision, Android needs to know the entire call chain $A \rightarrow B \rightarrow C$, instead of C alone. This call chain is called the component call chain in this paper. Since Dalvik supports multi-thread, the call chain must be extracted at the thread level, one per thread. When a new thread is spawned, its initial call chain is inherited from the parent thread. The new thread has to keep the initial call chain during its lifetime to avoid escalating its privilege.

The component call chain needs to be extracted at runtime from inside Dalvik. Dalvik functions as the Java interpreter in Android; it converts Java bytecode in dex format into native code and executes the native code [23]. To extract the call chain, we put hooks in Dalvik.

3.4.1 Hooks

Dalvik's core interpreter is called `mterp` [42], which interprets the machine-independent bytecode to machine-dependent code. There are many opcodes in bytecode, such as conditional, mathematical, method operations, etc., but component transitions (i.e., from one component to another component) can only happen at the method invocation and return time, so we only focus on the opcodes related to method invocation and return. We have identified all these op-

28

(a) Policy Manager Structure

<UID, Components, Requested Permission>

UID
Components

INTERNET
READ_SMS
FINE_LOCATION

Component 1
Permissions

WRITE_SMS

Component 2
Permissions

INTERNET
READ_CONTACTS
COARSE_LOCATION

(b) Permission Checking Flow

App permission check

App requests permission RP

RP == APP_PERM ? — False / True

Component call-chain permission check

Get component call chain

Call chain is empty? — True / False

Remove one component, and get its permission list PERMs

RP ∈ PERMs ? — True / False

Deny   Grant

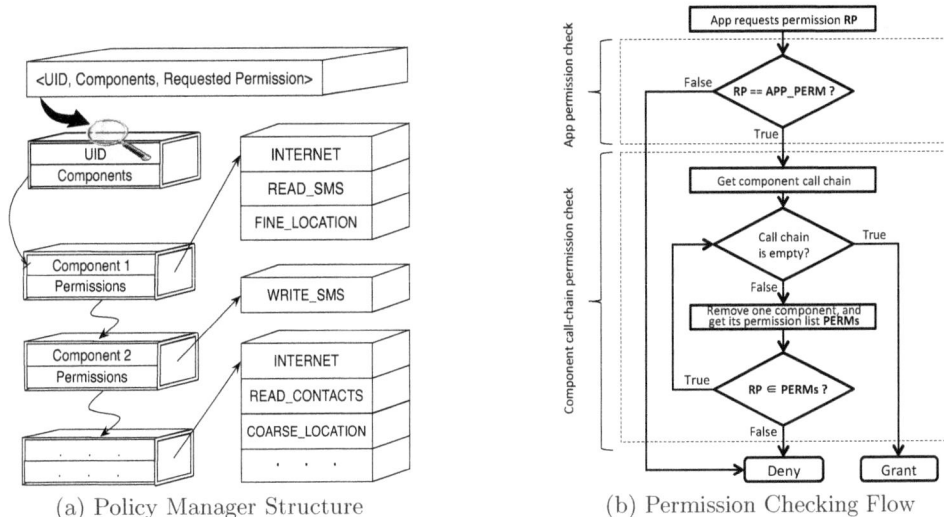

Figure 3: Policy Manager (PM) Structure & Permission Checking Flow

codes [3], and placed a corresponding hook in each of them. These hooks check whether there is a component transition; if so, record the transition to the call chain.

In addition to the hooks placed in mterp, we also place hooks in the Java reflection class and DexClassLoader to address implicit method invocation and code injection attacks. We will further discuss these two attacks in Section 4.

3.4.2 Call-chain storage

Once call chains are collected, the first question is where to store them. With respect to call chain extraction and permission enforcement, three candidate places are safe to store call chains: Dalvik, the kernel and the system_server process. From cost efficiency perspective, the kernel is the best place to store call chains. Suppose call chains are stored in Dalvik, every time system_server checks permissions, system_server needs to request call chain through IPCs. Similarly, if call chains are stored in system_server, whenever Dalvik updates a call chain, it has to talk to system_server via IPCs. These two operations are relatively frequent, and so many IPCs will lead to low performance. By storing call chains in the kernel, these two kinds of IPCs turn to system calls. According to our experiments, we find storing call chains in the kernel boosts the speed of call-chain update and permission checks.

Compac stores call chain based on thread. A process can have several threads running simultaneously, thus can have multiple component call chains, one for each thread. When Dalvik detects a component change, it sends the new component information into the kernel, or asks the kernel to remove one from its call chain, depending on whether it is an invocation or return.

Recording a call chain in Dalvik may introduce a high overhead if it is not properly handled. For performance rea-

sons, we optimize the design in three aspects: first, we do not record all component transitions. We only record transitions among the components specified in the AndroidManifest.xml and the user's settings, because only these components can cause permission changes. Second, we delay the call-chain synchronization at Java Native Interface (JNI). Dalvik does not synchronize call chain with the kernel every time when there is a component (package) transition. Instead, it does that in JNI. This is because the Java code will eventually be interpreted to native code provided by Android, and JNI is the only entry point where the transition from Java code to native code happens. Third, method invocation within the same component will not be recorded. For example, if a method in package A invokes another method in the same package, which in turns invokes a method in package B, the call chain will be "$A \rightarrow B$".

3.5 Access Control Enforcement Based on the Call Chain

Compac's permission model is composed of app permission check and component permission check (see Figure 3(b)). Compac keeps a clear and standalone design for the two permission checks. Compac remains the app permission check logic in RMs without modification, meanwhile, Compac has two new modules called *policy managers* and *kernel policy manager* to check the component permissions. The two Policy Managers (PMs) are built in the two Reference Monitors (RMs) separately. When a permission request comes to RMs, RMs first check app permissions. If the app does not have the specific permission, the request is denied immediately without going to PMs. Otherwise, RMs ask PMs to begin the component permission checking procedure. PMs send a privileged system call to call-chain storage in order to request component call chain. Once they receive the call chain, they calculate the call-chain permissions and check whether the caller's call chain have the requested permission. PMs return the result to RMs, no matter what the result is. After that, RMs handle the rest as what they do in original Android.

We name the permissions calculated from component call-chain permissions as the *effective permissions*. In the orig-

---

[3]We place hooks in the following opcodes: invoke-virtual, invoke-super, invoke-direct, invoke-static, invoke-interface, invoke-virtual/range,invoke-super/range, invoke-direct/range, invoke-static/range, invoke-interface-range, invoke-virtual-quick, invoke-virtual-quick/range, invoke-super-quick, invoke-super-quick/range, return-void, return vx, return-wide vx, and return-object vx.

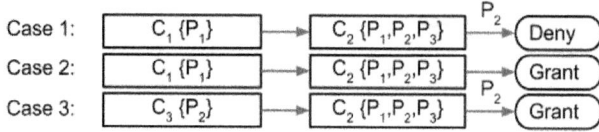

Figure 4: Component Intersection Cases

inal Android framework, there is no such call chain, so the effective permissions are the same as the app's permissions granted during the installation. In Compac, the effective permissions are calculated as the following definition:

Definition *Effective Permission.* Let $C_1, \ldots, C_n$ be components, and P_i be the permission set for the component C_i, where $i = 1, \ldots, n$. Assume that the current component call chain for a thread is $C_1 \rightarrow C_2 \rightarrow \ldots \rightarrow C_n$. The effective permission set eP of the current thread is defined as the following:

$$eP = P_1 \cap P_2 \cap \ldots \cap P_n.$$

If $P_{request} \in eP$, PMs allow the access request. In the actual enforcement, PMs do not calculate all the permissions, instead, PMs examine the call chain and just check each component to see if they have the requested permission.

The policy seems too restricted, however, it is effective and practical. First, all the components' permissions of an app are defined by one app developer. Consider the example in Figure 4, there are three components C_1, C_2, C_3, and they have permission sets $\{P_1\}$, $\{P_1, P_2, P_3\}$ and $\{P_2\}$. In case 1, when C_1 calls C_2 in order to use P_2, the access is denied. If the developer would like C_1 to use P_2, the developer will assign P_2 to C_1 just like C_3 in case 3. Otherwise, C_1 is trying to gain P_2 without user consent. So, the deny decision is correct. In case 2, we can see the policy allows the components with less privileges to call components with more privileges. As long as the privileged action is not requested, PMs will not check component permissions. Second, the call chain only records components (packages) that are specified with tag `package-permission` in `AndroidManifest.xml`. These are untrusted third-party libraries and there are not too many cross references among them. We conduct several experiments on Compac by recording third party components and logging the call chains. We never see the call chain having more than five components. We also evaluate 34 apps (downloaded from Google Play) by restricting all the third-party components, and we never experience false positives.

3.6 Policy Manager Implementation

Policy managers play a critical role in component call-chain access control. Thus, we take FPM as an example to illustrate the internal work flow in PMs. After app permission request is granted, the permission request comes to FPM and FPM begins to check component call-chain permissions. First, FPM gets the caller's identity from Binder IPC, In this case, the caller's identity is thread ID (TID). With the TID, FPM requests and gets the thread's component call chain from call-chain storage. Besides, FPM also has the caller's UID, so FPM can map out the app's components with their permissions from FPM's internal three-level hierarchical data structure, as shown in Figure 3(a). KPM

has a similar checking procedure except that KPM gets the call chain much easier, because there is no IPC and context switch involved.

During the FPM permission checking procedure, the most difficulty is how the FPM gets the caller's TID since there is no TID related support in original Android. It is much easier if the caller voluntarily sends the TID to FPM. However, such information cannot be trusted. We choose to let the kernel provide the caller's TID. We allow the FPM to call `getCallingTid` API, which is similar to the system's `getCallingUid` API. FPM can use `getCallingUid` to request UID from binder's kernel driver when FPM needs UID to check app permission. In our implementation, we add the `getCallingTid` API support in Binder's kernel driver by recording the caller's TID when IPC happens. We also build both the Java and native `getCallingTid` interfaces for any IPC that goes through binder. As a result, FPM can get the caller's TID through binder object for authorization.

4. POTENTIAL ATTACKS & DEFENSE

The traditional JVM has its own built-in access control [27], which is enforced through the security manager, access controller, and security packages in `java.security.*`. This access control in general falls into two categories: the access control on resources (such as file read/write, hardware access, etc.) and the access control on language properties (such as whether or not a program can use Java reflection or class loader).

To contain native code, Android relies on reference monitors to protect privileged resources and removes access control entirely from Dalvik. Without this kind of access control, it is difficult to achieve the isolation among components. For example, reflection can be used to inject code in another Java package, blurring the boundaries among components. Compac heavily relies on components, so we need to clearly identify component boundaries. In this section, we describe possible attacks on Compac and explain how we remedy these attacks in our design. In a nutshell, we need to compensate for the missing language security feature in Dalvik, in order to secure the component-level access control.

4.1 Implicit Invocation Attack

Attack. Reflection is a powerful Java language feature, which allows a piece of code to invoke any method of a class, including its private and protected methods, unless the method is marked as inaccessible for reflection. Based on our study (Table 1) [4], we can see that around 60% of benign apps use reflection to implicitly invoke other methods. Some usages are made by the advertisement code included in apps. After excluding that factor, about 42.49% of benign apps use reflection. The widely used reflection functionality drives the needs to handle this type of special invocations instead of simply blocking them.

Defense. Compac can easily solve the reflection problem. The Java code is interpreted in Dalvik and Dalvik can trace all the methods including reflection methods. So Dalvik knows which method will be invoked in a reflection invocation. Reflection's implicit invocation is implemented in the

---

[4] Benign apps are downloaded from Google Play, and most malware apps are collected from Android malware genome project [2].

Table 1: Implicit Invocation Usage (Total App Samples: Benign 16000, Malware 2566)

Implicit Invocation App Sample		Number	Percentage
Benign Apps	including Ads	9577	59.86%
	excluding Ads	6798	42.49%
Malware Apps	including Ads	1377	53.66%
	excluding Ads	989	38.54%

reflection_native() method, which resides in the core libraries of Dalvik. We place a hook in reflection_native to monitor which Java method will be invoked by reflection, and thus extract the Java package containing the real invoked method instead of reflection packages.

4.2 Inter-Component Code Injection Attacks

If a package can modify another package's code, it can break Compac, because a package with less privileges can simply inject its code into a package with more privileges. We call such an attack the *inter-component code injection attack*. The Java instrumentation class, java.lang.instrument [8], can be used to modify the contents of an existing class; fortunately, it has been disabled in Android SDK. Instead, Android develops its own instrumentation package, android.app.Instrumentation [11]. This package can be disabled in AndroidManifest.xml. It seems that we are safe, but unfortunately, in addition to instrumentation, there are two other ways to modify other class's code.

Attack 1. Reflection can be used to modify the field of a class object (see the following example):

```
import java.lang.reflect.Field;
Field field = classInstance.getClass().
    getDeclaredField(fieldName);
/* Allow modification on the field */
field.setAccessible(true);
/* Set the field to a new value */
field.set(classInstance, newValue);
```

The field itself can be an object of any type. If the object field is changed, the instance is modified. Moreover, if a class object is changed, the corresponding methods are changed accordingly. Initially, we decide to simply block set() method, but our study (Table 2) has shown that about 15.24% (12.03% if ads are excluded) of benign apps use the reflection in this way.

Table 2: Reflection for Code Injection Usage (Total App Samples: Benign 16000, Malware 2566)

Code Modification App Sample		Number	Percentage
Benign Apps	including Ads	2438	15.24%
	excluding Ads	1925	12.03%
Malware Apps	including Ads	56	2.18%
	excluding Ads	17	0.66%

Attack 2. The second attack is related to the class loader. If developers restrict an untrusted component's permissions, the untrusted component can escape the restriction using DexClassLoader. Using the class loader, an untrusted component can reload a class [28], and therefore can replace a more trustworthy component with its own malicious code. This completely defeats the component-level

access control. Class reloading is not possible in JVM, as special permissions need to be granted to an app before it can load classes. Since Android's Dalvik removes this access control, class reloading becomes possible.

When using class loader DexClassLoader in Dalvik, the protected method loadClass() in Dalvik does check whether the class is already loaded or not; if it is, it will not reload the same class. However, this is only enforced inside DexClassLoader, so if a malicious component extends DexClassLoader and overrides loadClass(), it can successfully reload a class.

Defense for attacks. For both attacks, we enforce the following policy in Dalvik: if code in package A tries to modify/reload a class in package B, this action is only allowed if $P_B \subseteq P_A$, where P_A and P_B are the permission sets of package A and B, respectively. In other words, a component with less privileges cannot modify/reload a class (component) with more privileges, and thus cannot gain privilege.

4.3 Package Forgery "Attack"

Since Compac identifies components using the Java package name, a potential attack is to forge the package name, so the restriction on the package can be circumvented. However, this is not a feasible attack. When developers intend to include a third-party package in their apps, they have the responsibility to ensure the integrity of the package. For example, if they plan to include Google advertisements in their apps, they need to ensure that the AdMob SDK they use is indeed from Google.

5. CASE STUDIES & EVALUATION

In this section, we conduct two types of evaluations. First, we use three case studies (Ads APIs, social networking service APIs, and web apps) to demonstrate how the privileges of components can be restricted using our component-level access control. In all the case studies, we focus on the most representative permissions, such as INTERNET, READ/WRITE/SEND_SMS, READ/WRITE_CONTACTS, READ_PHONE_STATE, ACCESS_COARSE/FINE_LOCATION. Second, we evaluate the performance of Compac.

5.1 Advertising APIs

We would like to evaluate how Compac works with various advertising packages. Certain advertising APIs (like InMobi) may use user's phone state or location information for displaying more relevant Ads to the user. To protect clients' privacy, a developer can prevent the advertising components from using these permissions without harming the app functionality and changing the app's permission set.

Figure 5: Angry Birds

We use the Angry Birds app [6] to demonstrate the aforementioned scenario. Angry Birds uses five advertisements including AdMob, InMobi, Millenial Media, JumpTap and

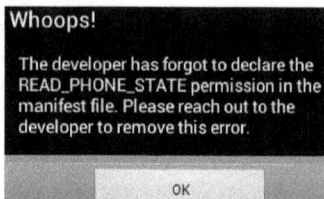

Figure 6: Angry Birds: No Permission Pop-up Window

```
D/dalvikvm( 663): DALVIKHOOK DEL pkg=com.jumptap.adtag; method=JtAdView.setAdViewListener|
StackSize=0
D/dalvikvm( 663): DALVIKHOOK ADD pkg=com.jumptap.adtag; method=JtAdView.loadUrlIfVisible|S
tackSize=1
D/PackageManager( 81): checkUidPermissionTid android.permission.INTERNET is granted, uid
=10037, tid=663
D/PackageManager( 81): checkUidPermissionTid android.permission.READ_PHONE_STATE is deni
ed, uid=10037, tid=663
E/JtAd ( 663): JtAdManager: Requires READ_PHONE_STATE permission
D/JtAd ( 663): Base url : http://a.jumptap.com/a/ads?textOnly=f&ua=Mozilla%2F5.0+%28Lin
uX%3B+U%3B+Android+4.0.4%3B+en-us%3B+Full+Android+on+Crespo%2FIMM76I%29+AppleWebKit%2F534.3
```

Figure 7: Ads in Angry Birds: Permission Deny Logcat

GreyStripe. In Angry Birds, advertisements display at the top of the screen (see Figure 5), and the app randomly chooses one advertisement from the five to display. We assign only two necessary permissions for the five Ads APIs, while the Angry Birds app has six default permissions. Component permission tags are defined in `AndroidManifest.xml` (to save space, we only show the tags for Google Ads).

```
<package-permission android:name="com.google.
    ads">
  <assign-permission android:name="INTERNET" />
  <assign-permission android:name="
      ACCESS_NETWORK_STATE" />
</package-permission>
```

We repackage app's APK file and run the Angry Birds game. As the game runs, we suddenly receive a pop-up window (Figure 6), indicating that the developer has not declared the READ_PHONE_STATE permission. From the logs (Figure 7), we can see that the JumpTap package throws an exception, but the game does not crash and continues running smoothly; this is because READ_PHONE_STATE is an optional permission and Ads handle it properly. Experienced users can achieve the same goal by modifying the package's permissions in the app setting.

Besides, we download 33 apps from Google Play and run the extreme experiments like giving empty permission set to an app' Ads. The results show that we can successfully restrict all the Ads in these apps. 29 apps handle the no-permission exception, so they continue to run without any problem, except that no advertisement is displayed. 4 apps display "no INTERNET permission" toast messages and then exit.

5.2 Social Networking Service APIs

Android apps use a number of social networking service (SNS) APIs, such as Facebook, Twitter, and Dropbox APIs. To use these APIs, apps can include the API packages in the program, and interact with the classes in the packages through the APIs. Once included, the API package will have the same privileges as the app. Unfortunately, some of the packages seem to abuse the privileges by collecting private

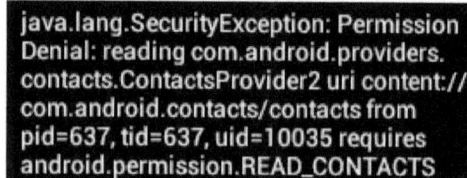

Figure 8: Facebook: Permission Deny Toast

```
D/ContentProvider( 231): enforceReadPermission uid=10035, tid=637
D/PackageManager( 79): checkUidPermissionTid android.permission.READ_CONTACTS is denied,
uid=10035, tid=637
E/DatabaseUtils( 231): java.lang.SecurityException: Permission Denial: reading com.androi
d.providers.contacts.ContactsProvider2 uri content://com.android.contacts/contacts from pi
d=637, tid=637, uid=10035 requires android.permission.READ_CONTACTS
```

Figure 9: Facebook: Permission Deny Logcat

information about users. It will be more desirable if apps can limit the privilege of these API packages.

The component-level access control in Compac can be used for this privilege-restriction purpose. To demonstrate that on SNS APIs, we emulate a scenario where a malicious SNS library attempts to read user contacts. We insert a small piece of malicious code in Facebook SDK. As long as the app that uses this API has the permission to read user's contacts, the inserted code can silently read the contacts from the phone and send them out, without user consent. We package the malicious Facebook SDK in a sample app. This app gets the information from the user's friend list (in Facebook), compares the list with the user's contacts (on the device), and sees whether any friend is on the contact list. This is a typical use of Facebook APIs. Without the protection from Compac, the privilege for reading contacts may be abused by the malicious Facebook APIs.

To block the READ_CONTACTS permission, we restrict the permissions of the Facebook SDK component to INTERNET only. When we run the app under Compac's protection, the app throws a "Permission Denial" toast for READ_CONTACTS (see Figure 8). As shown in Figure 9, the action (reading contacts from phone) has been blocked. The main app still has the READ_CONTACTS permission, so we can tell the blocked event is caused by the Facebook component.

5.3 Web Applications - PhoneGap

Compac can also protect web apps, although component hooks are not deployed in WebKit's JavaScript interpreter. To demonstrate that, we have conducted experiments on a popular cross-platform web app framework called Phone-Gap [9]. PhoneGap encapsulates a WebView, allowing developers use HTML5, JavaScript, and CSS to develop mobile apps. The JavaScript APIs provided by PhoneGap can access device resources through WebView's `addJavascriptInterface` API [26]. However, this API has caused many security problems [31] because it is exposed without control. A recent article [1] demonstrates that JavaScript code can use reflection to gain the Java object reference, thus can gain the app's privilege. The security problem is because WebView cannot contain the JavaScript code.

Compac easily fixes the above over-privilege problem by assigning only the INTERNET permission to WebView component. Every time the `addJavascriptInterface` API uses reflection to access privileged Java API, it is recorded in the call-chain. When the privileged Java API tries to perform

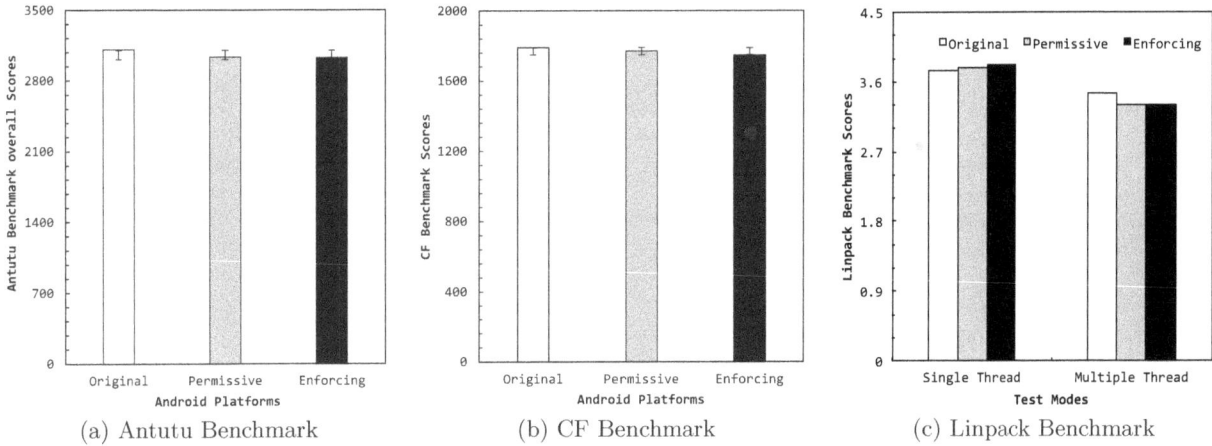

(a) Antutu Benchmark   (b) CF Benchmark   (c) Linpack Benchmark

Figure 10: Overall Performance: Benchmark Results

privileged actions on behalf of the JavaScript code, access is denied; If the Java API is called by the app's code and the `addJavascriptInterface` API is not in the call-chain, access is allowed.

Besides, Compac also provides a solution to enforce the principle of least privilege on PhoneGap plug-ins. In Phone-Gap, a plug-in usually conducts a particular functionality, such as reading/sending SMS, using camera, etc. All plug-ins are included as libraries. Once included, they have the same privilege as the app, leading to an over-privilege problem. Since all the plug-ins have their own unique packages, third-party plug-ins can be considered as components. Based on the functionalities of plug-ins, we evaluate six different plug-ins including `com.seltzlab.mobile`, `com.leafcut.ctrac`, `com.rearden`, `org.devgeeks`, `com.karq.gbackup`, `com.practicaldeveloper.phonegap.plugins`. According to their documents, they require permission GET_ACCOUNTS, CALL_LOG, READ_CONTACTS, READ_PHONE_STATE, READ_S-MS, SEND_SMS individually.

We conduct two experiments on these plug-ins. In the first experiment, we remove all the permissions from the plug-ins. We have observed that Compac is able to limit the behaviors of five plug-ins and their requests to access the device resources are all denied, The only exception is the Contact View plug-in (`com.rearden`), which needs no permission and does not perform privilege action directly. Instead, it displays the contacts by sending Intent to Android's built-in Contacts app. This is a privilege escalation problem [15] between apps and out of this paper's discussion. In our second experiment, we assign only the required permission as their documents describe to the six plug-ins. Our results show that all the plug-ins work properly. This indicates that they do not need extra permissions. By combining the two experiments, we have demonstrated that Compac can resolve the over-privilege problem associated with the PhoneGap plug-ins, without affecting their functionalities.

In conclusion, we demonstrate that Compac can successfully put access control on WebView and other web frameworks, and this is not easily done by previous work.

5.4 Performance

The overhead of Compac mainly comes from two sources. One is from the hooks that we insert in Dalvik, and the other is from the component permission checks (at both framework and kernel levels). Component permission checks are more complicated, as the effective permissions need to be calculated from the component call chain at runtime. Dalvik hooks just record the necessary Java packages. So, the cost from permission checks is far more than that from Dalvik hooks. We first evaluate the permission check overhead under an extreme condition, which provides a guideline on the upper boundary of Compac's performance. Then we evaluate the overall performance, which illustrates the overhead in normal situations. We employ a Nexus S phone as the evaluation platform. Our codebase is the `Android-4.0.4_r1.2` branch from the Android Open Source Project (AOSP). The original Android and Android with Compac are originally from the same copy of the source code.

5.4.1 Permission Checking Overhead

We first measure the overhead of Compac's permission checks. In Android, As we know, permissions are checked either in the kernel through system calls, or at the framework level through IPC (IPC permission checks). The cost of an IPC permission check is always higher than a kernel permission check, because an IPC involves several system calls. Therefore, we only perform evaluation on IPC permission checks to measure the upper boundary of overhead caused by Compac's access control. We use the following pseudo-code to show how we conduct the unit test.

```
time_start := System.currentTimeMillis
for i:=1 to 25000 do
    check random permission
time_end := System.currentTimeMillis
excute_time := time_end - time_start
```

We do the test by conducting the IPC permission checks on random permissions 25000 times. On the original Android, the test takes 38,153 ms, and on Android with Compac, it takes 46,614 ms. Therefore, Compac's overhead for IPC permission checks is 22.2%. Although this number seems high, it just provides the upper boundary of the Compac's performance and does not pose problems for the overall performance. Because the IPC permission check happens only when a privileged action is triggered. A normal app does not have many such IPC permission checks.

5.4.2 Overall Performance

To evaluate Compac's overall performance, we use three popular benchmark apps: Antutu, CF-bench, and Linpack. We plot the results in Figure 10. In the figure, "Original" means the AOSP Android; "Permissive" means Android with Compac will be in permissive mode, i.e. it will log access control denials but not enforce them; "Enforcing" means we restrict each package's permissions inside the benchmark apps and Android with Compac runs in enforcing mode.

The three benchmark apps show similar results that the overall performance of Compac is quite close to the original Android platform. A higher number is better in all the three benchmarks. Take the Antutu benchmark app as an example. Antutu produces an overall score based on the measures. The result shows that the original Android score is 3106, Compac in permissive mode scores 3033, and Compac in enforcing mode scores 3026. Taking the original Android score as the base, the performance of Compac in permissive mode is 97.6% and the performance of Compac in enforcing mode is 97.4%. One interesting thing is that for the single thread test with Linpack, Android with Compac has a higher score than original Android. We run the experiment several times and get similar results. Sometimes, Compac in permissive mode may score better than Compac in enforcing mode, but both always score better than original Android. The reason is we optimize Dalvik interpreter and related libraries when we implement Compac. According to Linpack for Android app's description [7], "the Dalvik VM has a huge impact on the Linpack number", and "this test is more a reflection of the state of the Android Dalvik Virtual Machine than of the floating point performance of the underlying processor. Software written for an Android device is written using Java code that the Dalvik VM interprets at run time".

6. RELATED WORK

Information Flow Tracking. To protect user privacy, the pioneering work TaintDroid [22] conducts taint analysis in Dalvik to trace information flows. It has the ability to trace when the sensitive information flows out of an app. TaintDroid taints data in Dalvik while our work builds hooks in Dalvik for system to make access control. AppFence [29] is built upon TaintDroid and can block unwanted data transmission.

Android Permission Control. A collection of work [19, 24, 32, 33, 35] adopt different policies to achieve fine-grained access control on app permissions in order to control an app's behaviors or make sure the app has the least privilege. Apex [32] and Kirin [24] allow users to accept a subset of the permissions declared by apps and enforce policies at installation-time. Saint [33] enforces policies at both installation-time and runtime, and the policies leverage the relationship between the caller app and the callee app. The user-driven work [35] considers certain user inputs as contexts. Upon occurrence of certain user actions in special UI components, the system grants corresponding permissions to the app. CRePE [19] uses environments as contexts to control the behavior of an app.

In-App Reference Monitor. Aurasium [41] and previous work [12, 20, 30] build a reference monitor within an app to achieve access control through code instrumentation or rewriting. They can flexibly enforce app level policies but may not enforce component-level policies. Because all the code as well as the reference monitor run in the same process. Without jumping out of Dalvik or the process, it is difficult for the reference monitor to recognize the running code. Besides, the current Android does not provide component information for access control either. However, Aurasium can still be used by app markets to protect users from malicious and untrusted apps if app markets wrap each app with a reference monitor and consider the whole app as the target.

Mandatory Access Control. Previous arts XManDroid [14], TrustDroid [16], IPC inspection [15] and Quire [21] deal with the privilege escalation problems across different apps, while Compac focuses on the components inside the same app (same process). They are the first work to propose mandatory access control concept in Android. SEDalvik [13] also intercepts the Java methods in Dalvik as Compac, but it enforces policy within Dalvik. SEDalvik can prevent some Java level malware, however, the system cannot be aware of the security contexts, and Dalvik cannot understand the contextual information of the code. So, SEDalvik turns to a language-level mandatory access control within apps.

SEAndroid [38] implements SELinux in Android kernel and builds middleware mandatory access control in both the kernel and Android framework. SEAndroid ports the core SELinux into Android's kernel and makes all the processes, files, sockets and other kernel resources under the control of the MAC. Thus, SEAndroid limits root and other users' privilege. SEAndroid's install-time MAC, intent MAC and content provider MAC provide a comprehensive protection to apps and Android middleware. SEAndroid and our work strictly follow the same design principle (least privilege principle). SEAndroid divides the privileges of the system, users and resources, while our work divides the privileges of the apps.

FlaskDroid [17, 18] extends the type enforcement policy language from SELinux to Android middleware and offers API-oriented MAC control for multiple stakeholders including app developers. FlaskDroid allows developers and users to have finer-grained access controls in services and content providers. For example, the content in content provider can be partially displayed according to the policy. FlaskDroid makes Android middleware be aware of the contextual information in services and content providers, and our work makes reference monitor get the component contexts of an app.

Component-level Access Control. AdDroid [34] isolates advertising components by encapsulating them as a service and creating ADVERTISING permission for the advertising service. AdSplit [36] enforces a fine-grained access control by putting the advertising component entirely in a separate process, which relies on the process-level isolation to achieve the protection. This solution implements a strong component isolation mainly for components like advertisements, which need less or no communication with other components. AFrame [44] provides a general approach to isolate third-party libraries into a separate process. It prefers libraries that need strong isolation and do not interact quite often with the main process while Compac is used for those libraries work tightly with other components.

7. CONCLUSION

To reduce the risks caused by the untrusted third-party code included in Android apps, we propose Compac, a generic approach to achieve component-level access control. Compac extends the existing Android security model. It uses Java package as component and enforces access control based on the UID and component. Using Compac, a component in an app can be given a subset of the app's permissions. We conduct case studies on various third-party APIs including advertising, social networking service, PhoneGap plug-ins, and WebView to demonstrate its effectiveness, usefulness and the compatibility with the existing Android architecture. We also evaluate its performance to show that the overhead is quite affordable. The source code is available at https://bitbucket.org/syr/compac.

8. REFERENCES

[1] Abusing webview javascript bridges.
http://50.56.33.56/blog/?m=201212.

[2] Android malware genome project.
http://www.malgenomeproject.org.

[3] Android marks fourth anniversary since launch with 75.0quarter, according to idc. https://www.idc.com/getdoc.jsp?containerId=prUS23771812.

[4] Android ndk. http://developer.android.com/tools/sdk/ndk/index.html.

[5] Android open source project. android security overview.
http://source.android.com/tech/security.

[6] Angry birds. http://www.angrybirds.com.

[7] Linpack for android - android apps on google play.
https://play.google.com/store/apps/details?id=com.greenecomputing.linpack&hl=en.

[8] Package java.lang.instrument.
http://docs.oracle.com/javase/6/docs/api/java/lang/instrument/package-summary.html.

[9] Phonegap. http://phonegap.com.

[10] The security manager.
http://docs.oracle.com/javase/tutorial/essential/environment/security.html.

[11] Testing fundamentals. http://developer.android.com/tools/testing/testing_android.html.

[12] BACKES, M., GERLING, S., HAMMER, C., MAFFEI, M., AND VON STYP-REKOWSKY, P. Appguard: enforcing user requirements on android apps. In *Proceedings of the 19th international conference on Tools and Algorithms for the Construction and Analysis of Systems* (Berlin, Heidelberg, 2013), TACAS'13, Springer-Verlag, pp. 543–548.

[13] BOUSQUET, A., BRIFFAUT, J., CLÉVY, L., TOINARD, C., AND VENELLE, B. Mandatory Access Control for the Android Dalvik Virtual Machine. In *Workshop on Embedded Self-Organizing Systems (ESOS)* (2013).

[14] BUGIEL, S., DAVI, L., DMITRIENKO, A., FISCHER, T., AND SADEGHI, A.-R. Xmandroid: A new android evolution to mitigate privilege escalation attacks. Technical Report TR-2011-04, Technische Universität Darmstadt, Apr. 2011.

[15] BUGIEL, S., DAVI, L., DMITRIENKO, A., FISCHER, T., SADEGHI, A.-R., AND SHASTRY, B. Towards taming privilege-escalation attacks on android. In *Proceedings of 19th Annual Network & Distributed System Security Symposium* (Feb 2012), NDSS '12.

[16] BUGIEL, S., DAVI, L., DMITRIENKO, A., HEUSER, S., SADEGHI, A.-R., AND SHASTRY, B. Practical and lightweight domain isolation on android. In *Proceedings of the 1st ACM workshop on Security and privacy in smartphones and mobile devices* (New York, NY, USA, 2011), SPSM '11, ACM, pp. 51–62.

[17] BUGIEL, S., HEUSER, S., AND SADEGHI, A.-R. Towards a framework for android security modules: Extending se android type enforcement to android middleware. Tech. Rep. TUD-CS-2012-0231, Center for Advanced Security Research Darmstadt, Nov. 2012.

[18] BUGIEL, S., HEUSER, S., AND SADEGHI, A.-R. Flexible and fine-grained mandatory access control on Android for diverse security and privacy policies. In *Proceedings of the 22nd USENIX conference on Security symposium* (2013), USENIX Security '13, USENIX.

[19] CONTI, M., NGUYEN, V. T. N., AND CRISPO, B. Crepe: context-related policy enforcement for android. In *Proceedings of the 13th international conference on Information security* (Berlin, Heidelberg, 2011), ISC '10, Springer-Verlag, pp. 331–345.

[20] DAVIS, B., SANDERS, B., KHODAVERDIAN, A., AND CHEN, H. I-arm-droid: A rewriting framework for in-app reference monitors for android applications. In *Proceedings of the Workshop on Mobile Security Technologies* (San Francisco, CA, May 2012), MOST '12.

[21] DIETZ, M., SHEKHAR, S., PISETSKY, Y., SHU, A., AND WALLACH, D. S. Quire: lightweight provenance for smart phone operating systems. In *Proceedings of the 20th USENIX conference on Security symposium* (Berkeley, CA, USA, 2011), USENIX Security '11, USENIX Association, pp. 23–23.

[22] ENCK, W., GILBERT, P., CHUN, B.-G., COX, L. P., JUNG, J., MCDANIEL, P., AND SHETH, A. N. Taintdroid: an information-flow tracking system for realtime privacy monitoring on smartphones. In *Proceedings of the 9th USENIX conference on Operating systems design and implementation* (Berkeley, CA, USA, 2010), OSDI '10, USENIX Association, pp. 1–6.

[23] ENCK, W., OCTEAU, D., MCDANIEL, P., AND CHAUDHURI, S. A study of android application security. In *Proceedings of the 20th USENIX conference on Security symposium* (Berkeley, CA, USA, 2011), USENIX Security '11, USENIX Association, pp. 21–21.

[24] ENCK, W., ONGTANG, M., AND MCDANIEL, P. On lightweight mobile phone application certification. In *Proceedings of the 16th ACM conference on Computer and communications security* (New York, NY, USA, 2009), CCS '09, ACM, pp. 235–245.

[25] FELT, A. P., CHIN, E., HANNA, S., SONG, D., AND WAGNER, D. Android permissions demystified. In *Proceedings of the 18th ACM conference on Computer and communications security* (New York, NY, USA, 2011), CCS '11, ACM, pp. 627–638.

[26] FELT, A. P., WANG, H. J., MOSHCHUK, A., HANNA, S., AND CHIN, E. Permission re-delegation: attacks and defenses. In *Proceedings of the 20th USENIX conference on Security symposium* (Berkeley, CA, USA, 2011), USENIX Security '11, USENIX Association, pp. 22–22.

[27] GONG, L. Java security architecture (jdk1.2). http://docs.oracle.com/javase/1.4.2/docs/guide/security/spec/security-spec.doc.html, 1998.

[28] HAO, H., SINGH, V., AND DU, W. On the effectiveness of api-level access control using bytecode rewriting in android. In *Proceedings of the 8th ACM Symposium on Information, Computer and Communications Security* (2013), AsiaCCS '13.

[29] HORNYACK, P., HAN, S., JUNG, J., SCHECHTER, S., AND WETHERALL, D. These aren't the droids you're looking for: retrofitting android to protect data from imperious applications. In *Proceedings of the 18th ACM conference on Computer and communications security* (New York, NY, USA, 2011), CCS '11, ACM, pp. 639–652.

[30] JEON, J., MICINSKI, K. K., VAUGHAN, J. A., FOGEL, A., REDDY, N., FOSTER, J. S., AND MILLSTEIN, T. Dr. android and mr. hide: fine-grained permissions in android applications. In *Proceedings of the second ACM workshop on Security and privacy in smartphones and mobile devices* (New York, NY, USA, 2012), SPSM '12, ACM, pp. 3–14.

[31] LUO, T., HAO, H., DU, W., WANG, Y., AND YIN, H. Attacks on webview in the android system. In *Proceedings of the 27th Annual Computer Security Applications Conference* (New York, NY, USA, 2011), ACSAC '11, ACM, pp. 343–352.

[32] NAUMAN, M., KHAN, S., AND ZHANG, X. Apex: extending android permission model and enforcement with user-defined runtime constraints. In *Proceedings of the 5th ACM Symposium on Information, Computer and Communications Security* (New York, NY, USA, 2010), AsiaCCS '10, ACM, pp. 328–332.

[33] ONGTANG, M., MCLAUGHLIN, S., ENCK, W., AND MCDANIEL, P. Semantically rich application-centric security in android. In *Proceedings of the 2009 Annual Computer Security Applications Conference* (Washington, DC, USA, 2009), ACSAC '09, IEEE Computer Society, pp. 340–349.

[34] PEARCE, P., FELT, A. P., NUNEZ, G., AND WAGNER, D. Addroid: Privilege separation for applications and advertisers in android. In *Proceedings of the 7th ACM Symposium on Information, Computer and Communications Security* (2012), AsiaCCS '12.

[35] ROESNER, F., KOHNO, T., MOSHCHUK, A., PARNO, B., WANG, H. J., AND COWAN, C. User-driven access control: Rethinking permission granting in modern operating systems. In *Proceedings of the 2012 IEEE Symposium on Security and Privacy* (may 2012), SP '12, pp. 224 –238.

[36] SHEKHAR, S., DIETZ, M., AND WALLACH, D. S. Adsplit: separating smartphone advertising from applications. In *Proceedings of the 21st USENIX conference on Security symposium* (Berkeley, CA, USA, 2012), USENIX Security '12, USENIX Association, pp. 28–28.

[37] SIEFERS, J., TAN, G., AND MORRISETT, G. Robusta: taming the native beast of the jvm. In *Proceedings of the 17th ACM conference on Computer and communications security* (New York, NY, USA, 2010), CCS '10, ACM, pp. 201–211.

[38] SMALLEY, S., AND CRAIG, R. Security enhanced (se) android: Bringing flexible mac to android. In *Proceedings of 20th Annual Network & Distributed System Security Symposium* (Feb 2013), NDSS '13.

[39] SUN, M., AND TAN, G. Jvm-portable sandboxing of java's native libraries. In *Proceedings of the 17th European Symposium on Research in Computer Security* (2012), vol. 7459 of *ESORICS '12*, pp. 842–858.

[40] WAHBE, R., LUCCO, S., ANDERSON, T. E., AND GRAHAM, S. L. Efficient software-based fault isolation. In *Proceedings of the 14th ACM symposium on Operating systems principles* (New York, NY, USA, 1993), SOSP '93, ACM, pp. 203–216.

[41] XU, R., SAÏDI, H., AND ANDERSON, R. Aurasium: practical policy enforcement for android applications. In *Proceedings of the 21st USENIX conference on Security symposium* (Berkeley, CA, USA, 2012), USENIX Security '12, USENIX Association, pp. 27–27.

[42] YAN, L. K., AND YIN, H. Droidscope: seamlessly reconstructing the os and dalvik semantic views for dynamic android malware analysis. In *Proceedings of the 21st USENIX conference on Security symposium* (Berkeley, CA, USA, 2012), USENIX Security '12, USENIX Association, pp. 29–29.

[43] YEE, B., SEHR, D., DARDYK, G., CHEN, J. B., MUTH, R., ORMANDY, T., OKASAKA, S., NARULA, N., AND FULLAGAR, N. Native client: A sandbox for portable, untrusted x86 native code. In *Proceedings of the 2009 30th IEEE Symposium on Security and Privacy* (Washington, DC, USA, 2009), SP '09, IEEE Computer Society, pp. 79–93.

[44] ZHANG, X., AHLAWAT, A., AND DU, W. AFrame: Isolating Advertisements from Mobile Applications in Android. In *Proceedings of the 29th Annual Computer Security Applications Conference (ACSAC)* (New Orleans, Louisiana, USA, December 9-13 2013).

[45] ZHOU, Y., AND JIANG, X. Dissecting android malware: Characterization and evolution. In *Proceedings of the 2012 IEEE Symposium on Security and Privacy* (Washington, DC, USA, 2012), SP '12, IEEE Computer Society, pp. 95–109.

[46] ZHOU, Y., WANG, Z., ZHOU, W., AND JIANG, X. Hey, you, get off of my market: Detecting malicious apps in official and alternative android markets. In *Proceedings of 19th Annual Network & Distributed System Security Symposium* (Feb 2012), NDSS '12.

KameleonFuzz:
Evolutionary Fuzzing for Black-Box XSS Detection

Fabien Duchene*
[lastname]@car-online.fr

Sanjay Rawat*
IIIT
Hyderabad, India
sanjayr@ymail.com

Jean-Luc Richier,
Roland Groz
LIG Lab
Grenoble F-38402, France
[first].[last]@imag.fr

ABSTRACT

Fuzz testing consists in automatically generating and sending malicious inputs to an application in order to hopefully trigger a vulnerability. Fuzzing entails such questions as: Where to fuzz? Which parameter to fuzz? Where to observe its effects? etc.

In this paper, we specifically address the questions: *How to fuzz a parameter? How to observe its effects?* To address these questions, we propose *KameleonFuzz*, a black-box Cross Site Scripting (XSS) fuzzer for web applications. KameleonFuzz can not only generate malicious inputs to exploit XSS, but also detect how close it is revealing a vulnerability. The malicious inputs generation and evolution is achieved with a genetic algorithm, guided by an attack grammar. A double taint inference, up to the browser parse tree, permits to detect precisely whether an exploitation attempt succeeded.

Our evaluation demonstrates no false positives and high XSS revealing capabilities: KameleonFuzz detects several vulnerabilities missed by other black-box scanners.

Categories and Subject Descriptors

[Security and privacy]: Systems security — *Vulnerability management, Vulnerability scanners*

General Terms

Security Testing

Keywords

Cross-Site Scripting, Fuzzing, Evolutionary Algorithm, Black-Box Security Testing, Taint Inference, Model Inference

---

*At the time of this work, Fabien and Sanjay were working at LIG, INP Grenoble, France.

1. INTRODUCTION

Context. Over the past years, XSS has, infamously, maintained its position in the top vulnerabilities[31]. Criminals use XSS for performing malicious activities e.g., spam, malware carrier, or user impersonation on websites like Paypal, Facebook, and eBay [25, 29, 53]. Due to the complexity and code size of such websites, automatic detection of XSS is a non-trivial problem. In case of access to the source code, white-box techniques range from static analysis to dynamic monitoring of instrumented code. If the binary or the code are inaccessible, black-box approaches generate inputs and observe responses. Such approaches are independent of the language used to create the application, and avoid a harness setup. As they mimic the behaviors of external attackers, they are useful for offensive security purposes, and may test defenses such as web application firewalls. Automated black-box security testing tools for web applications have long been around. However, even in 2012, the fault detection capability of such tools is low: the best ones only detect 40% of non-sanitized Type-2 XSS, and 1/3 do not detect any[3, 2]. This is due to an imprecise learned knowledge, approximate verdicts, and limited sets of attack values.

Automatic black-box detection of web vulnerabilities generally consists in first "crawling" to infer the *control flow* of the application (hereinafter referred as *macro-state* awareness), and then "fuzzing" to generate malicious inputs likely to exhibit vulnerabilities. As compared to scanners that are not macro-state aware, Doupé et al. increase vulnerability detection capabilities by inferring control flow models[10]. In LigRE, Duchène et al. extends such models with taint flow inference and guides a fuzzer to improve detection capabilities one step further[17]. XSS is a problem involving control+taint flows, and input sanitization. In presence of even basic sanitizers, many scanners have difficulties in creating appropriate inputs, and thus produce false negatives. In order to address aforementioned issues, we propose KameleonFuzz, a LigRE extension that mimics a human attacker by evolving and prioritizing the most promising malicious inputs and taint flows. We incorporate in KameleonFuzz a precise test verdict that relies on existing browser parsing and double taint inference.

Our Approach. KameleonFuzz is a black-box fuzzer which targets type-1 (reflected) and type-2 (stored) XSS and can generate full exploitation sequences. As illustrated in Figure 1, it consists of learning the model of the application and generating malicious inputs. We reuse the components A, B, C from [17]. The main contributions of this paper are the blocks *D1* and *D2*.

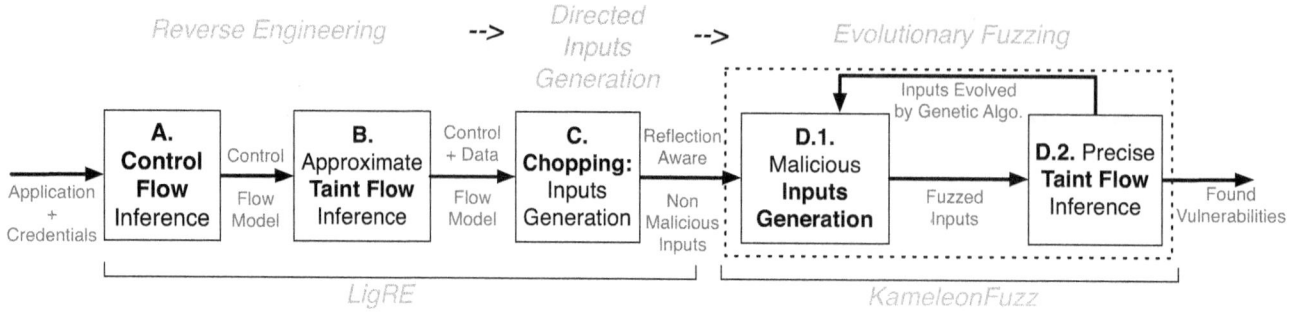

Figure 1: High Level Approach Overview

XSS involve a *taint flow* from a fuzzed value x_{src} on an HTTP request I_{src} to a vulnerable statement O_{dst} (HTML page). In a type-1 XSS, x_{src} directly appears (reflects) in the current output, whereas in a type-2, x_{src} is stored in an intermediate repository and reflected later.

Step A control flow inference learns how to navigate in the application. Given an interface and connection parameters(e.g., authentication credentials), a model is learnt in the form of an Extended Finite State Machine with instantiated parameter values, and a two level hierarchy (nodes and *macro-states*). The inferred model may not be complete.

Step B, approximate taint flow inference detects the possibility of XSS by observing reflections of a value x_{src}, sent in the request I_{src}, into an output O_{dst} (HTML page). It generates walks on the model, and approximatively infers the taint. A *substring matching* algorithm is used with a heuristic to avoid false negatives. Figure 2 illustrates a control+taint flow model.

Step C prunes the control+taint flow model by applying a specialized form of slicing, called *chopping*. This reduces the search space.

The blocks D.1 (malicious input generation) and D.2 (precise taint flow inference) are the main focus of this paper. A genetic algorithm (GA), parameterized by an *attack grammar*, evolves malicious inputs. The attack grammar reduces the search space and mimics the behavior of a human attacker by constraining the mutation and crossover operators which generate next generation inputs. We define a *fitness function* that favors most suitable inputs for XSS attacks. Since server sanitizers may alter the observed value at the reflection point O_{dst}, a naive substring match may not infer the taint precisely enough, which could lead to false negatives. To overcome such limitations, we perform a double taint inference. We detail these subcomponents in Section 3.

Contributions. The contributions of this paper are:

- the first black-box model-based GA driven fuzzer that detects type-1 and 2 XSS ;

- a combination of model inference and fuzzing ;

- an implementation of the approach and its evaluation.

The rest of the paper is organized as follows. Section 2 provides a walk-through of our approach over an example. Section 3 details how malicious inputs are generated and evolved. Section 5 evaluates KameleonFuzz on typical web applications. Finally, we discuss our approach in Section 6, survey related work in Section 7, and conclude in Section 8.

2. ILLUSTRATING EXAMPLE

P0wnMe is a vulnerable application. Once logged-in, a user can save a new note, view the saved notes, or logout.

KameleonFuzz Execution on P0wnMe In steps A and B of Figure 1, LigRE infers a control+taint flow model of which a simplified extract[1] is shown in Figure 2. The control flow is represented by plain arrows (transitions) and nodes. A taint flow originates from a bold text x_{src}, sent in I_{src}, and reflects(dotted arrows) in O_{dst}. For instance, the value egassem_ of the input parameter *msg* sent in the transition $7 \rightarrow 17$ is reflected in the output of the transition $18 \rightarrow 21$.

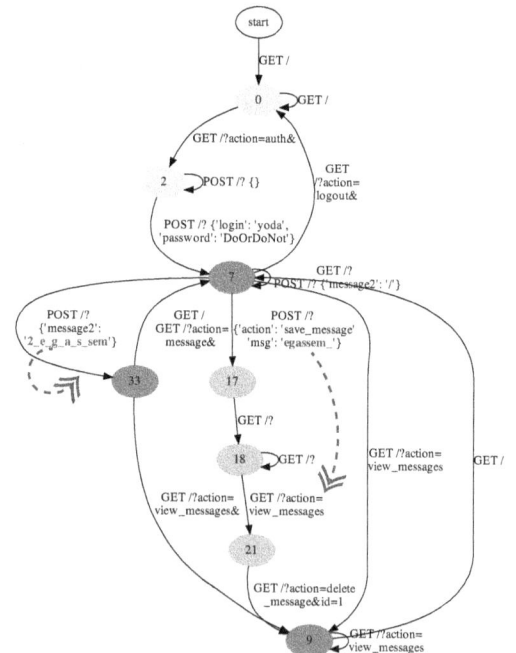

Figure 2: Inferred control+taint model (extract)

[1]For clarity sake, we only represent the inputs on the transitions, and the outputs correspond to colored nodes. Each color corresponds to a macro-state. The inputs are composed of an HTTP method(e.g., POST), a part of the URL (e.g., /?) and POST parameters (e.g., {'message2':'2_e_g_a_s_sem'}). [17] formalizes a control+taint flow model.

Figure 2 contains a reflection for the value 2_e_g_a_- s_sem of the parameter *message*2 sent in the transition $7 \rightarrow 33$. An extract of the output O_{dst} is `<input name=" message2" value=' 2_e_g_a_s_sem '/>` where we highlight the reflection. Here, the reflection *context* is inside a tag attribute value. The context influences how an attacker generates fuzzed values. Listing 1 shows the server sanitizer for this reflection. It blocks simple attacks. Attackers search a fuzzed value s.t. if passed through the sanitizer, then its reflection is not syntactically confined in the context[45] i.e., it spans over different levels in the parse tree.

```
1  <?php function webapp_filter($str) {
2      if(eregi('"|'|>|<|;|/',$str)) {
3          $filtered_str = "XSS attempt!";
4      } else {
5          $filtered_str = str_replace(" ","",$str);
6      }
7      return $filtered_str;
8  } ?>
```

Listing 1: A vulnerable sanitizer in P0wnMe

Table 1 shows fuzzed values sent by w3af[36], a black-box open source scanner, when testing WebApp. W3af iterates over a list of fuzzed values. It does not learn from previous requests, nor considers the reflection context.

Fuzzed Value (x_{src})	Reflection
SySlw	SySlw
uI<hf>hf"hf'hf(hf)uI	
</A/style="xss:exp/**/ression(fake_alert('XSS'))">	XSS attempt!
";!-"<klqn>=&{()}	
<IFRAME SRC="javascript:fake _alert('klqn');"></IFRAME>	

Table 1: w3af fuzzed values (extract)

In step D, KameleonFuzz generates individuals, i.e., normal input sequences in which it fuzzes the reflected value. The chopping (step C of LigRE) produces the input sequences. The attack grammar produces the fuzzed values. For each individual, the taint is precisely inferred. It is an input for the test verdict (did this individual trigger an XSS?) and the fitness score (how close is this individual of triggering an XSS?). The best individuals are mutually recombined according to the attack grammar to create the next generation: e.g., the individuals 3 and 4 of generation 1 produce the individual 1 of generation 2. This process is iterated until a tester defined stopping condition is satisfied (e.g., one XSS is found). Table 2 illustrates this evolution.

An extract of the output O_{dst} for the last individual is `<input name="message2" value=' WUkp'\t onload='alert(94478) '/>` Since the sanitizer in Listing 1 removes the space ␣, and not \t,\r or \n, the individual is a successful XSS exploit, as the syntactic confinement of the reflection of x_{src} is violated.

This example illustrates how evolutionary input generation can adapt to sanitizers. In the next section, we elaborate on the evolutionary nature of our fuzzing technique.

Fuzzed Value (x_{src})	Reflection	XSS Fit.	Gen.
T9nj1'><script>alert (18138)</script>	XSS␣Attempt!	3.1	1
oH1eqL'␣onload=" document.body.inner HTML+='<div␣id=90480> </div>'"␣fakeattr='	XSS␣Attempt!	3.2	1
ZuIa2'␣onload =alert(94478)	ZuIa2'onload =alert(94478)	13.3	1
WUkp'\tLgpRa	WUkp'\tLgpRa	9.1	1
WUkp'\t␣onload=' alert(94478)	WUkp'\tonload ='alert(94478)✓	18.5	2

Table 2: KameleonFuzz fuzzed values (extract)

3. EVOLUTIONARY FUZZING

The fuzzing (step D in Figure 1) generates a *population* of *individuals* (GA terminology). An individual is an input sequence generated by LigRE in which KameleonFuzz generates a fuzzed value x_{src} according to the attack grammar for the reflected parameter. As described in Algorithm 1, this population is evolved via the mutation and crossover operators (Section 3.6) w.r.t. the attack grammar (Section 3.2) and according to their fitness score (Section 3.5).

```
1               ▷ Create the first generation
2   for l ∈ [1..n] do
3       Popul[l] ← newIndividual(Chopping,
    Attack_Grammar)
4   end for
5                    ▷ Evolve the population
6   repeat
7       for all individual I(x) in Popul do
8           RESET the Application
9           O = SEND I(x) to Application
10          T = precise TAINT_INFERENCE(x,O,Parser)
11          Compute VERDICT(x,T,Patterns)
12          Compute FITNESS(I,x,O,T,Model)
13      end for
14      CROSSOVER: f fittest individuals to
    produce m Children
15      for all C in Children do
16          if random(0,1) ≤ MutationRate then
17              MUTATE(C,Attack_Grammar)
18          end if
19      end for
20      Popul ←   (n − m) fittest parents + m
    children
21  until stopCondition
```

Algorithm 1: Genetic Algorithm pseudo-code

3.1 Individual

An individual is an input sequence targeting a specific reflection. It contains a non-malicious input sequence extracted from the chopped model, and fuzzed value x_{src}. This sequence encompasses the originating transition I_{src}, and the transition where to observe the reflection O_{dst}.

3.2 Attack Grammar

In order to constrain the search space (subset of A^*, A being the alphabet for the targeted encoding), we use an attack grammar for generating fuzzed values. This grammar also constrains mutation and crossover operators (lines 3, 14, 16 of Algorithm 1). Attackers would attempt to send such fuzzed values to the application. As compared to a list of payloads as in w3af and skipfish, an attack grammar can generate more values, and is easier to maintain thanks to its hierarchical structure.

The knowledge used to build the attack grammar consists of the HTML grammar[49], string transformations in case of context change [51], known attacks vectors [38, 21].

We give a taste of **how to build the attack grammar**, as it is yet manually written and its automatic generation is a research direction. Figure 3 illustrates its structure. The first production rule consists of representation and context information. Inside an attribute value (`<input value=" reflection "/>`) and outside a tag(`<h1> reflection`) are examples of reflection contexts. The representation consists of encoding, charset, and special string transformation functions that we name anti-filter(e.g., PHP addslashes[32]).

In order to create the attack grammar, we assume the availability of S, a representative set of vulnerable web applications (different from the tested applications) and corresponding XSS exploits. For each reflection context, the analyst writes a generalization of the XSS exploits in the form of production rules with terminals and non-terminals. In case of production rules including the OR or REPEAT operators, she assigns weights on choices, depending on their frequency of use in the exploits of S. If no weights are assigned, all choices weigh equally. Once created, we use this attack grammar for fuzzing the tested applications.

We represent the grammar in an Extended Backus–Naur Form[40] with bounded number of repetitions. By construction, the attack grammar is acyclic. Thus it unfolds to a finite number of possibilities. Listing 3 of Appendix C contains an excerpt of the attack grammar.

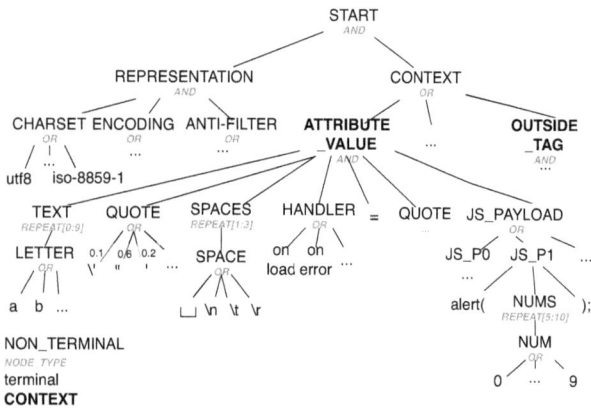

Figure 3: Structure of the attack grammar (extract)

Generating a fuzzed value consists in walking through its production rules and, if applicable, performing choices. Producing the corresponding string from a fuzzed value con-

sists in concatenating the strings obtained by a depth-first exploration of the context subtree, representing this string in a given charset, applying the anti-filter function, and applying an encoding function. For instance, the string that results from the fuzzed value of Figure 4 is `WUkp'␣\t onload='alert(94478)`, in UTF-8 charset, on which the `identity` function is applied as an anti-filter, and with no final encoding change (node `plain`).

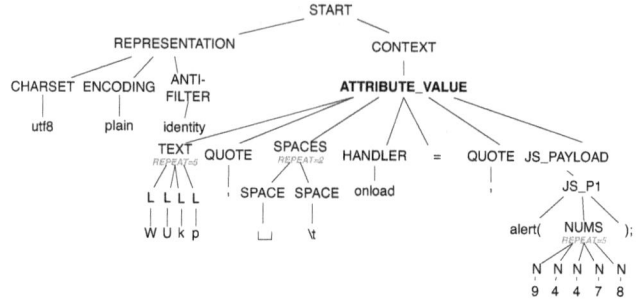

Figure 4: The Production Tree of a Fuzzed Value

3.3 Precise Taint Flow Inference (D.2)

The precise taint flow inference permits obtaining information about the context of a reflection. This later serves for computing a precise test verdict, and is an input for the fitness function.

The flow for producing the taint aware parse tree T_{dst} is illustrated in Figure 5. First, a string to string taint-

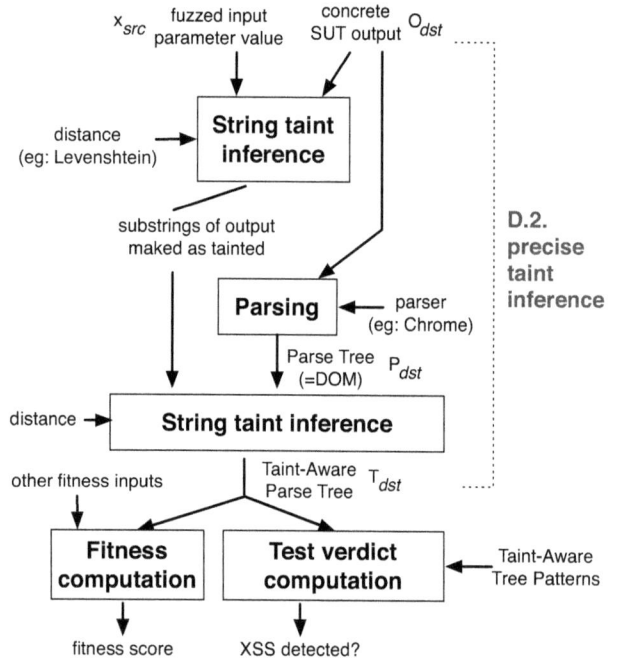

Figure 5: Precise Taint Inference ($I_{src} \to O_{dst} \to T_{dst}$)

inference algorithm (e.g., with Levenshtein edit distance [26]) is applied between the fuzzed value x_{src} and the output

O_{dst} in which it is reflected. In parallel, a parser (e.g., from Google Chrome) evaluates the application output O_{dst} and produces a parse tree P_{dst} (e.g., Document Object Model (DOM)). Then the taint is inferred between x_{src} and each node of P_{dst} to produce T_{dst}, a taint aware parse tree (see Figure 6), as follows.

For each node of an output parse tree P_{dst}, we compute a string distance between each tainted substring and the node textual value. Then we only keep the lowest distance score. If this score is lower than a tester defined threshold, then this node is marked as tainted. This taint condition may be slightly relaxed in case a cluster of neighbors nodes has a distance "close to the threshold". The inferred taint aware parse tree T_{dst} is an input for the fitness function and test verdict.

It is important to note that, instead of writing our own parser, as done in [41], we rely on a *real-world parser*. This has two advantages. First, we are flexible with respect to the parser (e.g., for XSS: Chrome, Firefox, IE ; for other vulnerabilities such as SQL injections, we could rely on a SQL parser). Secondly, we are certain about the real-world applicability of the detected vulnerabilities.

3.4 Test Verdict

The test verdict answers to the question "Did this individual trigger an XSS vulnerability?". The taint-aware parse tree T_{dst} (Figure 6) is matched against a set of *taint-aware tree patterns* (e.g., Figure 7). If at least one pattern matches, then the individual is an XSS exploit (i.e., the test verdict will output "yes, vulnerability detected"). A taint tree pattern is a tree containing regular expressions on its nodes. Those regular expressions may contain strings(e.g., `script`), taint markers , repetition operators($+,*$), or the match-all character($.$). The tester can provide its own patterns. We incorporate in KameleonFuzz default patterns for XSS vulnerabilities. Those all violate the syntactic confinement of tainted values. The second pattern illustrated in Figure 7 matches the parse tree represented in Figure 6.

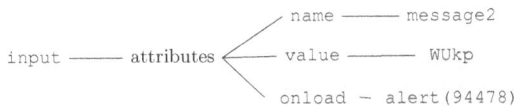

```
                         ╱ name ─────── message2
input ─────── attributes ◄─── value ─────── WUkp
                         ╲ onload ─ alert(94478)
```

Figure 6: A Taint -Aware Parse Tree T_{dst} (extract). The payload is a message box that displays 94478 (harmless).

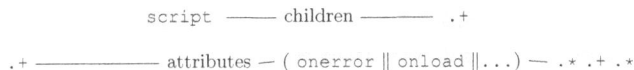

```
     script ─────── children ─────── .+

.+ ─────────── attributes ─ ( onerror ‖ onload ‖...) ─ .* .+ .*
```

Figure 7: Two Taint -Aware Tree Patterns, represented in a Linear Syntax (resp. a tainted script tag content and a tainted event handler attribute)

3.5 Fitness

The fitness function assesses "how close" is an individual to finding an XSS vulnerability. The higher its value, the more

weight	id	dimension
$+++$	1	successfully injected character classes
$+++$	2	tainted nodes in the parse tree T_{dst}
$++$	3	singularity
$++$	4	transitions from source I_{src} to reflection O_{dst}
$++$	5	new page discovered
$++$	6	new macro-state discovered
$+$	7	unexpected page seen
$+$	8	page correctly formed w.r.t. output grammar
$+$	9	unique nodes from the start node

Table 3: Dimensions of the `fitness` function

likely the GA evolution process will pick the genes of this individual for creating the next generation. The inputs of the fitness function are the individual I, the concrete output O_{dst} in which the fuzzed value x_{src}, sent in the transition I_{src}, is reflected, $T_{dst} = taint(parse(O_{dst}), x_{src})$ the taint-aware parse tree, and the application model M. The fitness dimensions are related to properties we observed between the fuzzed value and the reflection in case of successful XSS attacks. Those dimensions are listed in Table 3. In [13, 16], we drew a sketch of the currently used fitness function.

Those dimensions model several intuitions that a human penetration tester may have. The most significant ones are:

- **1: Percentage of Successfully Injected Character Classes**. Characters that compose leaves of individual fuzzed value tree (see Figure 4) are categorized into classes depending on their meaning in the grammar. This metric expresses the "injection power" for the considered reflection.

- **2: Number of Tainted Nodes in the Parse Tree**. Whereas injecting several character classes is important, it is however not a sufficient condition for an attacker to exert control on several parse tree nodes. Successful XSS injections are generally characterized by at least two neighbors tainted nodes (one which is supposed to confine the reflection, and the other(s) that contain the payload and a trigger for that payload). Thus, if an attacker is able to reflect on several nodes, we expect that it increases its chances to exploit a potential vulnerability.

- **3: Singularity of an individual w.r.t. its current generation**. A problem of GA is overspecialization that will limit the explored space and keep finding the same bugs [8]. To avoid this pitfall, we compute "how singular" an individual is from its current generation. This dimension uses the source transition I_{src}, the fuzzed value x_{src}, and the reflection context (i.e., the destination transition O_{dst} and the tainted nodes in the parse tree T_{dst}).

- 4: The higher the **Number of Transitions between the source transition I_{src} and its Reflection O_{dst}**, the more difficult it is to detect that vulnerability, because it expands the search tree.

- a **New Page (5) or Macro-State (6) discovered**: increases application coverage.

3.6 Mutation and Crossover Operators

A probability distribution decides wether an individual will be mutated or not. When a mutation will happen, an operator is applied either on the *fuzzed value* or on the *input sequence*.

The *fuzzed value* mutation operator works on the production tree of the fuzzed value x_{src} (see Figure 4). We implemented several strategies for choosing which node to mutate and how to mutate (e.g., uniform distribution, Least Recently Used, ...). The amplitude of the mutation is a decreasing function of the fitness score: if an individual has a high fitness score, the mutation will target nodes in the production tree that are close to leafs. Similarly, in case of low fitness score, the operator is more likely to mutate nodes close to the root. An example of fuzzed value mutation applied to Figure 4 consists in performing a different choice for the HANDLER non terminal (e.g., onmousover instead of onload).

The *input sequence* mutation operator works on the whole sequence I. It consists of either taking another path in the model from the source I_{src} to the destination O_{dst}, or targeting a different reflection.

The crossover operator works at the *fuzzed value* level, i.e., on the production tree. Its inputs are two individuals of high fitness scores. It produces two children.

4. IMPLEMENTATION

KameleonFuzz is a python3 program which targets Type-1 and 2 XSS. It is composed of 4500 lines of code. As shown in Figure 8, we instrument Google Chrome[18] with the Selenium library[24]. We use LigRE, a control+taint flow model inference tool and slicer.

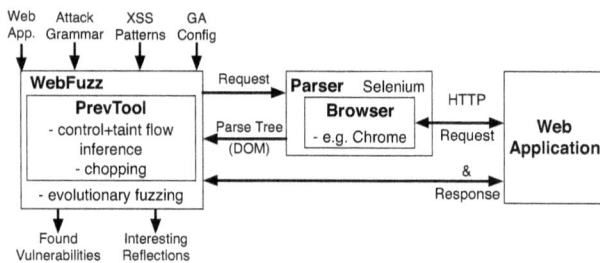

Figure 8: Architecture of KameleonFuzz

5. EMPIRICAL EVALUATION

Based on a prototype implementation, we evaluate KameleonFuzz against black-box open source XSS scanners, in terms of detection capabilities(RQ1) and detection efficiency(RQ2). In our experiments, KameleonFuzz detected most of the XSS detected by other scanners, several XSS missed by other scanners, and 3 previously unknown XSS.

5.1 Test Subjects

As described in Table 4, we select seven **web applications** of various complexity. In Appendix A, we detail our interest in them. KameleonFuzz detected at least one true XSS in all of them. We considered four **black-box XSS scanners** to compare with KameleonFuzz: Wapiti, w3af,

Application	Description	Version	Plugins
P0wnMe	Intentionally Vulnerable	0.3	
WebGoat		5.4	
Gruyere		1.0	
WordPress	Blog	3.2.1	Count-Per-Day 3.2.3
Elgg	Social Network	1.8.13	
phpBB	Forum	2.0	
e-Health	Medical	04/16/2013	

Table 4: Tested Web Applications

SkipFish and LigRE+w3af. Appendix B contains the configuration we used during the experiments. It is important to note that only LigRE and KameleonFuzz are macro-state aware.

5.2 Evaluation Setting

XSS Uniqueness: an XSS is uniquely characterized by its source transition I_{src}, its parameter name, its destination transition O_{dst} and the tainted nodes in the parse tree $T(P(O_{dst}), I_{src})$. Hence if a fuzzed value is reflected two times in O_{dst}, e.g., in two different nodes in the parse tree, and for each node, the scanner generated an exploitation sequence, then we count two distinct XSS. In our experiments, the only time we had to distinguish two XSS using the nodes in the parse tree was in the Gruyere application. We run the scanners on a Mac OS X 10.7.5 platform with a 64 Bit Intel Quad-Core i7 at 2.66GHz processor, and 4GB of RAM DDR3 at 1067MHz.

5.3 Research Questions

RQ1. (Fault Revealing): *Does evolutionary fuzzing find more true vulnerabilities than other scanners?*

To answer this question, we consider the number of true positives, the number of false positives, and the overlap of true positives. For the first two metrics, we compare all tools, whereas for the overlap, we compare LigRE+KameleonFuzz against the others(Wapiti, w3af, skipfish, LigRE+w3af). True positives are the number of XSS found by a scanner that actually are attacks, thus the higher, the better. If a scanner produces false positives, a tester will loose time, thus the lower the better. The overlap indicates vulnerabilities detected by several scanners. We denote as T_A the number of True XSS vulnerabilities found by the scanner A. We define the overlap as:

$$overlap(A, B) = \frac{T_A \cap T_B}{T_A \cup T_B}$$

A low overlap indicates that scanners are complementary. We also consider the vulnerabilities only detected by one scanner:

$$only\_by(A, B) = \frac{T_A}{T_A \cup T_B} - overlap(A, B)$$

A low only_by indicates that a given scanner does not find many XSS that the other missed.

For each scanner and application, we sequentially configure the scanner, reset the application, set a random seed to the scanner, run the scanner against the application, and retrieve the results. We repeat this process five times, using different seeds. Parameters have been adjusted so that each run lasts at most five hours. Beyond this period, we stop the scanner and analyze the produced results. The number of found vulnerabilities is the union of distinct true vulnerabilities found during the different runs. If possible, scanners are configured so that they only target XSS. We configure the scanners with the same information (e.g., authentication credentials). When a scanner does not handle this information correctly, we perform two sub-runs: one with the cookie of a logged-on user, and one without. Since all scanners, except LigRE and KameleonFuzz, are not macro-state aware we configure them to exclude requests that would irreversibly change the macro-state (e.g., logout when an authentication token is provided).

The **practicality of LigRE+KameleonFuzz** is illustrated in Table 5. This figure reports the number of potential reflections (i.e., potential sinks), found vulnerabilities (i.e., actual sinks for which a successful XSS exploit was generated), and generations to find all detected vulnerabilities during the fuzzing. The three columns in the middle report the length of created XSS exploits for the closest vulnerabilities from the start node.

True and False XSS Positives. We manually verify the XSS for each scanner. During our experiments, no scanner found a false positive XSS (Skipfish had other false positives). Figure 9 lists the results of the black-box scanners against each application. In our experiments, KameleonFuzz detected the highest number of XSS, and several XSS missed by others. The union of the distinct true XSS found by the scanners is 35. LigRE+w3af finds $\frac{23}{35} = 65.7\%$ of the known true XSS, whereas LigRE+KameleonFuzz finds $\frac{32}{35} = 91.4\%$. KameleonFuzz improves XSS detection capabilities. Since it is challenging to find reliable source (except our own human testing expertise) which provide an exhaustive list of the number of true XSS in the applications, we chose not to compute recall.

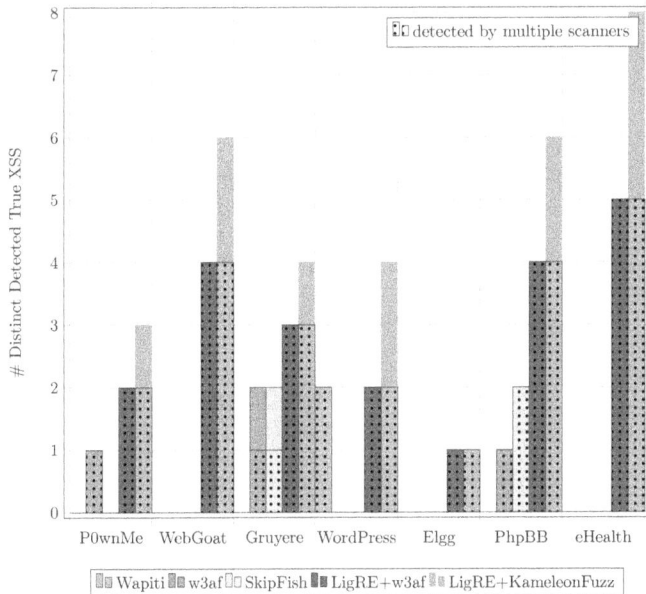

The **overlap and only_by** of true XSS found by LigRE+KameleonFuzz against other scanners are illustrated on Figure 10. KameleonFuzz finds the majority of known true XSS. W3af and SkipFish find the remaining ones. In the Gruyere application, Skipfish and w3af each found one vulnerability missed by all other scanners, including KameleonFuzz. Those consist of a not referenced 404 page containing a type-1 XSS, and of a type-2 XSS within the pseudo field when registering. It is harder to find the latter XSS than others: the application behaves differently as inferred when the scanner registers a new user with a fuzzed pseudo. Reusing the fuzzing learned knowledge in the inference may permit KameleonFuzz to detect this XSS. Additionally, SkipFish and w3af both detected one XSS in Gruyere that other scanners missed. Thus the only_by of SkipFish and w3af is two in Figure 10, whereas in Figure 9, one XSS is detected by both of them. Inferring the control flow for navigating to non-referenced pages may increase LigRE+KameleonFuzz XSS detection capabilities. If this is not an option, the tester should use LigRE+KameleonFuzz, SkipFish, and w3af.

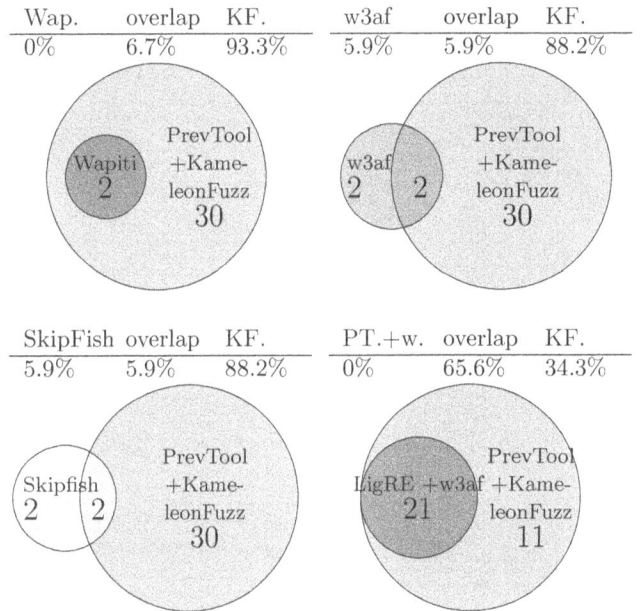

Wap.	overlap	KF.		w3af	overlap	KF.
0%	6.7%	93.3%		5.9%	5.9%	88.2%

SkipFish	overlap	KF.		PT.+w.	overlap	KF.
5.9%	5.9%	88.2%		0%	65.6%	34.3%

Figure 10: Number of True XSS found, only_by, and overlap of LigRE+KameleonFuzz and other scanners

> *LigRE+KameleonFuzz detects more true XSS than other scanners. It has no false positive.*
> *KameleonFuzz increases XSS detection capabilities.*
> *The non null only_by of w3af and Skipfish suggest they are complementary to KameleonFuzz.*

RQ2. (Efficiency): *How efficient are the scanners in terms of found vulnerabilities per number of tests?*

To answer this question, it is appropriate to observe the number of detected true XSS depending of the number of

Figure 9: Detection Capabilities of Black-Box XSS Scanners

43

Application	Potential Reflections	Generations to detect the found XSS	Transitions $start \rightarrow O_{dst}$			True XSS Found	False Positive
			1st	2nd	3rd		
P0wnMe	37	3	4	6	7	**3**	0
WebGoat	134	2	6	7	7	**6**	0
Gruyere	23	4	2	2	7	**4**	0
WordPress	52	2	2	2	5	**4**	0
Elgg	59	1	6			**1**	0
PhpBB	213	4	5	5	6	**6**	0
e-Health	12	1	4	4	4	**8**	0

Table 5: KameleonFuzz detection capabilities on the considered applications

HTTP requests. Thus, we set up a proxy between the scanner and the web application, and configure this proxy to limit the number of requests. We iteratively increase this limit, run the scanner, and retrieve the number of found distinct true XSS. We manually verify them. We run such a process five times per scanner, web application, and limit. For each number of requests, for each scanner, we sum the number of unique true XSS detected for all applications. The results are illustrated in Figure 11.

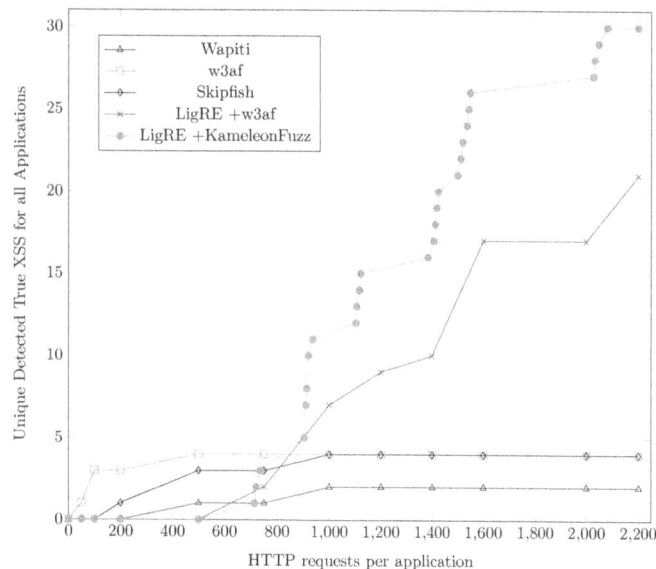

Figure 11: Detection Efficiency of Black-Box XSS Scanners

On considered applications, below approximatively 800 HTTP requests per application, w3af is the most efficient scanner. Thus we hypothesize that in applications with few macro-states, assuming it is able to navigate correctly, w3af is more efficient than other scanners at finding non filtered XSS. In our experiments, mainly happened in P0wnMe and Gruyere. In applications with more macro-states, assuming the cost of control+taint flow inference is acceptable, LigRE improves vulnerability detection. Starting from 900 HTTP requests, LigRE+KameleonFuzz detects more vulnerabilities per number of requests than LigRE+w3af. For instance, after 2200 requests per application, fuzzing with Kameleon-Fuzz detects 42.9% more XSS than fuzzing with w3af. On the LigRE+w3af and LigRE+KameleonFuzz curves, we can

observe several landings, which mostly correspond to the end of the LigRE control+taint flow inference for a given application.

> *If the cost of LigRE inference is acceptable, then*
> *LigRE+KameleonFuzz is more efficient than LigRE+w3af.*
> *Otherwise, w3af alone is of interest.*

6. DISCUSSION

6.1 Applicability to other Command Injection Vulnerabilities

Even though we only experimented with Type-1 and 2 XSS vulnerabilities, we are confident that the Kameleon-Fuzz approach can be applied to other types of interpreter injection vulnerabilities, with proper adaptations (e.g., attack grammar), as shown in Table 6. Such adaptation still

Vulnerability	Output Grammar	Where to Parse?
Cross Site Scripting	HTML	HTML page
HPP Param. Pollution	HTTP	Reply Headers
PHP Code Injection	PHP	argument of `eval`
SQL Injection	SQL	arg. of `sql_query`
Shell Injection	Shell	`...exec`, `system`

Table 6: Command Injections: Vulnerabilities, Output Grammars, and Observation Points

do not require access to the application source code, only the ability to intercept at run-time the arguments at the observation points. Thus for command injection vulnerabilities other than Type-1 and Type-2 XSS, one may consider our approach as having a grey-box harness. Using our approach for detecting Type-0 XSS and mutation-XSS is likely to require an adaptation of the attack grammar[19, 20].

6.2 Approach Limitations

Reset: We assume the ability to reset the application in its initial state, which may not always be practical (e.g., when testing a live application on which there are users connected ; we would work on a copy) or may take time. However, this does not break the black-box harness assumption: we do not need to be aware of how the macro-state is stored (e.g., database).

Generation of an Attack Grammar: Writing an attack grammar requires knowledge of the parameters mentioned in Section 3.2. This work is yet manual. The trade-off between the size of the language generated by this grammar and the fault detection capabilities is yet to be studied. A too narrow generated language (e.g., few produced fuzzed values for a given context, or very few contexts) may limit the fault detection capability, whereas a too important one may have limited efficiency. Moreover, the attack grammar is tied to the targeted injection sub-family (e.g., XSS, SQL injection, etc), thus the need for human input is a current limitation. There is room for research in automating this generation process[50].

XSS Model Hypothesis: We hypothesize that an XSS is the result of only one fuzzed value. Our current approach may have false negative on XSS involving the fuzzing of at least two fuzzed values at a time[7]. To our knowledge, no scanner handles such cases.

Limitations due to the use of LigRE: KameleonFuzz supports Ajax applications if they offer similar functionality when the client does not interpret JavaScript. LigRE requires to identify non deterministic values in the applications [15]. Hossen et al. automated this identification[23].

Encoding: The precision and efficiency of the taint flow inference is dependent of the considered encoding transformations. Plain, url and base64 encodings are implemented. LigRE and KameleonFuzz can be extended to support more.

6.3 Threats to Validity

External Comparison: We only compare to open source black-box web scanners and LigRE. We contacted several vendors of commercial products, but we did not receive a positive reply within a reasonable timeframe. Thus we were unaware to compare with commercial scanners. Those may obtain better results than the considered scanners.

Randomness: Scanners make extensive use of randomness. Since some XSS are not trivial to be found, their discovery may involve randomness and duration. We tried to limit such factors by running the scanners five times with different seeds and up to five hours. The chosen duration of the experiments may impact the results.

Considered Applications: Our comparison with other scanners is limited to the considered versions of scanners and applications. We cannot generalize results from those experiments. Running the scanners on other applications or scanners versions may produce different results.

KameleonFuzz Parameters: KameleonFuzz contains numerous adjustable parameters e.g., probabilities that drive the mutation and crossover operators during the fuzzing. In Appendix B, we provide significative parameters and their default values. Those are chosen empirically. Because the value domain of each parameter is quite wide, and it is time consuming to run the whole test suite, it was not feasible to evaluate the combination of all parameters values and their impact. Thus, we cannot guarantee that the chosen default values achieve the best detection capabilities and efficiency.

7. RELATED WORK

7.1 XSS Test Verdict in a Black-Box Approach

Confinement Based Approaches assume that malicious inputs break the structure at a given level (lexical or syntactical). As in Sekar's work[41], we rely on non-syntactical confinement and we use detection policies that are both syntax and taint aware. A key difference is that Sekar wrote his own parser to propagate the taint, whereas we use the parser of a browser (e.g., Google Chrome). Thus we infer the taint twice (see Figure 5). By doing so, we are sure about the real-world applicability of the found XSS exploits, and our implementation is flexible w.r.t. the browser. [45] relies on non-lexical confinement as a sufficient fault detection measure, which is more efficient than [41], but requires a correctly formed output (which is not an always valid assumption on HTML webpages[19]) and is prone to false negatives.

Regular-Expressions Based Approaches assume that the fuzzed value is reflected "as such" in the application output i.e., that the sanitizer is the identity function. In case of sanitizers this may lead to false negatives[36]. Moreover, most do not consider the reflection context, which can lead to false positive. IE8 [37] and NoScript [27] rely on regular expression on fuzzed values. XSSAuditor (Chrome XSS filter) performs exact string matching with JavaScript DOM nodes[1].

String Distance Based Approaches Sun[46] detects self-replicating XSS worms by computing a string distance between DOM nodes and requests performed at run-time by the browser.

IE8[37] and Chrome XSSAuditor[1] filters only work on Type-1 XSS. Whereas NoScript is able to block some Type-2 XSS, but is only available as a Firefox plugin.

7.2 Learning and Security Testing

In its basic form, **fuzzing** is an undirected black-box active testing technique[28]. [52, 48, 22, 39] mainly targets memory corruption vulnerabilities. Stock et al.'s recent work fuzzes and detects Type-0 XSS in a white-box harness[44]. Heiderich et al. detect in black-box mutation-based XSS caused by browser parser quirks[20]. LigRE+KameleonFuzz is a black-box fuzzer which targets Type-1 and 2 XSS.

GA for black-box security testing has been applied to evolve malwares[30] and attacker scripts[6]. *KameleonFuzz* is the first application of GA to the problem of black-box XSS search. Its fitness dimensions model the intuition of human security penetration testers.

An Attack Grammar produces fuzzed values for XSS as a composition of tokens. [50, 47] and KameleonFuzz share this view. In their recent work[47], Tripp et al. prune a grammar based on the test history to efficiently determine a valid XSS attack vector for a reflection. It would be interesting to compare KameleonFuzz to their approach, and to combine both. Wang et al. use a hidden Markov model to build a grammar from XSS vectors[50].

Model Inference for Security Testing Radamsa targets memory corruption vulnerabilities: it infers a grammar from known inputs then fuzzes to create new inputs[33]. Shu et al. passively infer a model from network traces, and actively fuzz inputs[42]. [34, 4, 5] infer the likelihood for specific inputs parts of triggering failures.

For command injection vulnerabilities(XSS, SQL injection, . . .), Dessiatnikoff et al. cluster pages according a specially crafted distance for SQL injections[9]. Sotirov iterates between reverse-engineering of XSS filters, local fuzzing, and remote fuzzing[43]. Doupé et al. showed that inferring macro-state aware control flow models increases vulnerability detection capabilities[10]. With LigRE, Duchène et al.

showed that enhancing such models with taint flows increases its capabilities even more[17].

KameleonFuzz extends LigRE and is a black-box fully active testing approach. It generates and evolves fuzzed inputs on the obtained reflections using an attack grammar and the control+taint flow model.

8. CONCLUSION AND FUTURE WORK

In this paper, we present KameleonFuzz, the first black-box GA driven fuzzer targeting Type-1 and 2 XSS. As compared to previous work, our precise double taint inference can reuse real-world parsers, our evolution is conformant to a tester defined attack grammar, and a fitness function drives the process by focusing on the most promising potential vulnerabilities. Our approach is of practical use to detect XSS, and outperforms state-of-the-art open source black-box scanners. It uncovered previously unknown XSS [11].

We consider the following directions interesting for future work: How to automatically create an attack grammar? How to combine our approach and [47] to increase the efficiency of XSS detection? How to improve the inferred model using additional knowledge gathered during the fuzzing? How to apply such a combination of model inference plus fuzzing to other class of vulnerabilities? [14, 12, 35]

Acknowledgments

This work was supported by the projects ITEA2 №09018 DIAMONDS "Development and Industrial Application of Multi-Domain Security Testing Technologies", FP7-ICT №257876 SPaCIoS "Secure Provision and Consumption in the Internet of Services" and ANR-INSE №0002-01 "BinSec BINary code analysis for SECurity".

References

[1] D. Bates, A. Barth, and C. Jackson. "Regular expressions considered harmful in client-side XSS filters". *WWW*. 2010, pp. 91–100.

[2] J. Bau et al. "State of the Art: Automated BlackBox Web Application Vulnerability Testing". *IEEE S&P*. 2010, pp. 332–345.

[3] J. Bau et al. *Vulnerability Factors in New Web Applications: Audit Tools, Developer Selection & Languages*. Tech. rep. Stanford, 2012.

[4] S. Bekrar et al. "A Taint Based Approach for Smart Fuzzing". *SECTEST with ICST*. 2012, pp. 818–825.

[5] S. Bekrar et al. "Finding Software Vulnerabilities by Smart Fuzzing". *International Conference on Software Testing, Verification, and Validation*. 2011, pp. 427–430.

[6] J. Budynek, E. Bonabeau, and B. Shargel. "Evolving computer intrusion scripts for vulnerability assessment and log analysis". *GECCO*. ACM, 2005.

[7] S. Dalili. *Browsers anti-XSS methods in ASP (classic) have been defeated!* 2012. URL: http://soroush.secproject.com/downloadable/Browsers_Anti-XSS_methods_in_ASP_(classic)_have_been_defeated.pdf.

[8] J. D. DeMott, R. J. Enbody, and W. F. Punch. "Revolutionizing the Field of Grey-box Attack Surface Testing with Evolutionary Fuzzing". *Black Hat USA* (2007).

[9] A. Dessiatnikoff et al. "A clustering approach for web vulnerabilities detection". *17th PRDC*. IEEE. 2011, pp. 194–203.

[10] A. Doupé et al. "Enemy of the State: A State-Aware Black-Box Web Vulnerability Scanner". *Usenix Sec* (2012).

[11] F. Duchene. *0-day XSS discovered with KameleonFuzz*. 2014. URL: http://car-online.fr/0_day_xss_kameleonfuzz.

[12] F. Duchene. "Harder, Better, Faster Fuzzer : Advances in BlackBox Evolutionary Fuzzing". *Hack In The Box (HITB)*. Amsterdam, Netherlands, 2014.

[13] F. Duchène et al. "XSS Vulnerability Detection Using Model Inference Assisted Evolutionary Fuzzing". *SECTEST with ICST*. 2012, pp. 815–817.

[14] F. Duchène. "Fuzz in the Dark: Genetic Algorithm for Black-Box Fuzzing". *Black-Hat*. São Paulo, Brazil, 2013.

[15] F. Duchène et al. "A Hesitation Step into the Black-box: Heuristic based Web Application Reverse Engineering". *NoSuchCon*. 2013.

[16] F. Duchène et al. "Fuzzing Intelligent de XSS Type-2 Filtrés selon Darwin: KameleonFuzz. Fuzzing Evolutionnaire de XSS Type-2 en Boîte Noire". *11th SSTIC*. 2013, pp. 289–311.

[17] F. Duchène et al. "LigRE : Reverse-Engineering of Control and Data Flow Models for Black-Box XSS Detection". *20th WCRE*. IEEE, 2013, pp. 252–261.

[18] Google. *Chrome*. URL: https://www.google.com/chrome/.

[19] M. Heiderich et al. *Web Application Obfuscation:'-/WAFs.. Evasion.. Filters//alert (/Obfuscation/)-'*. Syngress, 2010.

[20] M. Heiderich et al. "mXSS Attacks: Attacking well-secured Web-Applications by using innerHTML Mutations". *CCS*. ACM, 2013.

[21] G. Heyes et al. *Shazzer - Shared XSS Fuzzer*. 2012. URL: http://shazzer.co.uk.

[22] C. Holler, K. Herzig, and A. Zeller. "Fuzzing with Code Fragments". *21st Usenix Security*. 2012.

[23] K. Hossen, R. Groz, and J.-L. Richier. "Security Vulnerabilities Detection Using Model Inference for Applications and Security Protocols". *SECTEST with ICST*. IEEE, 2011, pp. 534–536.

[24] J. Huggins, P. Hammant, et al. *Selenium, Browser Automation Framework*. URL: http://code.google.com/p/selenium/.

[25] R. Kugler. *PayPal.com XSS Vulnerability*. 2013. URL: http://seclists.org/fulldisclosure/2013/May/163.

[26] V. Levenshtein. "Binary coors capable of correcting deletions, insertions, and reversals". *Soviet Physics-Doklady*. Vol. 10. 1966.

[27] G. Maone. *NoScript, Firefox plug-in*. 2006. URL: https://addons.mozilla.org/en-US/firefox/addon/noscript/.

[28] B. Miller, L. Fredriksen, and B. So. "An empirical study of the reliability of operating system utilities". *Communications of The ACM* (1989).

[29] Nirgoldshlager. *Stored XSS In Facebook*. 2013. URL: http://www.breaksec.com/?p=6129.

[30] S. Noreen et al. "Evolvable malware". *GECCO*. ACM, 2009, pp. 1569–1576.

[31] OWASP. *Top Ten Project*. 2013.

[32] PHP. *addslashes function*. URL: http://php.net/manual/en/function.addslashes.php.

[33] P. Pietikäinen et al. "Security Testing of Web Browsers". *Comm. of Cloud Software, vol. 1, no. 1, Dec. 23, ISSN 2242-5403* (2011).

[34] S. Rawat and L. Mounier. "An Evolutionary Computing Approach for Hunting Buffer Overflow Vulnerabilities: A Case of Aiming in Dim Light". *EC2ND*. 2010.

[35] S. Rawat et al. "Evolving Indigestible Codes: Fuzzing Interpreters with Genetic Programming". *CICS, with SSCI*. IEEE, 2013, pp. 37–39.

[36] A Riancho. *w3af - WebApp. Attack and Audit Framework*. URL: http://w3af.sourceforge.net.

[37] D. Ross. *IE 8 XSS Filter Implementation*. 2008. URL: http://blogs.technet.com/b/srd/archive/2008/08/19/ie-8-xss-filter-architecture-implementation.aspx.

[38] RSnake. *XSS Cheat Sheet Esp: for filter evasion*. 2007. URL: http://ha.ckers.org/xss.html.

[39] J. Ruderman. *Introducing jsfunfuzz*. 2007. URL: http://www.squarefree.com/2007/08/02/introducing-jsfunfuzz.

[40] R. S. Scowen. "Extended BNF — A generic base standard". *SESP*. 1993.

[41] R. Sekar. "An Efficient Blackbox Technique for Defeating Web Application Attacks". *NDSS*. 2009.

[42] G. Shu and D. Lee. "Testing Security Properties of Protocol Implementations - a Machine Learning Based Approach". *ICDCS*. IEEE, 2007.

[43] A. Sotirov. "Blackbox Reversing of XSS Filters". *ReCon*. 2008.

[44] B. Stock, S. Lekies, and M. Johns. "25 Million Flows Later - Large-scale Detection of DOM-based XSS". *20th CCS*. ACM, 2013.

[45] Z. Su and G. Wassermann. "The essence of command injection attacks in web applications". *POPL*. 2006.

[46] F. Sun, L. Xu, and Z. Su. "Client-Side Detection of XSS Worms by Monitoring Payload Propagation". *ESORICS* (2009), pp. 539–554.

[47] O. Tripp, O. Weisman, and L. Guy. "Finding your way in the testing jungle: a learning approach to web security testing". *ISSTA*. ACM, 2013, pp. 347–357.

[48] R. Valotta. "Fuzzing with DOM Level 2 and 3". *DeepSec*.

[49] W3C. *HTML5 Content Model*. 2012. URL: http://www.w3.org/TR/html5/content-models.html.

[50] Y.-H. Wang, C.-H. Mao, and H.-M. Lee. "Structural Learning of Attack Vectors for Generating Mutated XSS Attacks". *Computing Research Repository* (2010).

[51] J. Weinberger et al. "A systematic analysis of XSS sanitization in web application frameworks". *ESORICS*. Springer, 2011, pp. 150–171.

[52] M. Zalewski. *Announcing CrossFuzz*. 2011. URL: http://lcamtuf.blogspot.fr/2011/01/announcing-crossfuzz-potential-0-day-in.html.

[53] ZentrixPlus. *eBay Sec. Hall of Fame*. 2013. URL: http://zentrixplus.net/blog/ebay-security-researchers-hall-of-fame-hof/.

APPENDIX
A. WEB APPLICATIONS

P0wnMe v0.3 is an intentionally vulnerable web application for evaluating black-box XSS scanners. It contains XSS of various complexity (transitions, filters, structure).

WebGoat v5.4 is an intentionally vulnerable web application for educating developers and testers. Its multiple XSS lessons range from message book to human resources.

Gruyere v1.0 is an intentionally vulnerable web application for educating developers and testers. Users can update their profile, post and modify snippets, and view public ones.

Elgg v1.8.13 is a social network platform used by universities, governments. Users can post messages, create groups, update their profile. An XSS exists since several versions.

WordPress v3 is a blogging system: the blogger can create posts and tune parameters. Visitors can post comments, and search. The count-per-day plugin contains XSS.

PhpBB v2 is a forum platform. We include this version, as it is famous to contain several XSS[2].

e-Health 04/16/2013 is an extract of an industrial medical platform used by patients and practitioners.

B. WEB FUZZERS CONFIGURATION

We here list the main settings used during experiments. We also configure authentication credentials (cookie or username and login), but do not describe such settings here.

- **Wapiti 2.20**: `-m "-all,xss"`

- **w3af 1.2 kali 1.0**:

```
misc-settings
set maxThreads 1
set maxDepth 200
set maxDiscoveryTime 18000
back
plugins
discovery webSpider
discovery config webSpider
    set onlyForward True
    back
audit xss
audit config xss
    set numberOfChecks 3
    back
back
start
```

Listing 2: w3af configuration

- **SkipFish 2.10b**: `-Y -Z -m 10 -k 18000`

- **LigRE**:
  `taint_flow.min_length = 6 characters`
  `taint_flow.max_length = 8 HTTP requests`

- common parameters in **KameleonFuzz 2013-08-31** are mentioned in Table 7.

C. ATTACK GRAMMAR

Listing 3 contains an excerpt of the attack grammar. The fuzzed value in Figure 4 was generated using this grammar.

Parameter	Default Value
`LigRE.targeted_reflections` – The percentage of reflections that KameleonFuzz will focus on. LigRE orders them in descending order of potential interest[17].	0.8
`GA.population_size` – The size of the population i.e., the number of individuals. The actual amount is this value times the number of targeted LigRE reflections.	5
`GA.elitism` – Number of individuals having the highest fitness score that are kept for the next generation.	4
`GA.mutation_proba` – The probability to apply a mutation operator on a new child.	0.5
`GA.crossover_num_exchanges` – Number of exchanges performed by the crossover operator. One exchange means a two points crossover i.e., for the whole sub-tree of the exchanged grammar (non)-terminal.	1

Table 7: Common parameters in KameleonFuzz and their default values. See Section 6.3 on how we chose those default values.

```
1  START = REPRESENTATION CONTEXT
2  REPRESENTATION = CHARSET ENCODING
       ANTI_FILTER
3  CHARSET = ( "utf8" | "iso-8859-1" | ... )
4  ENCODING = ( "plain" | "base64_encode" |
       ... )
5  ANTI_FILTER = ( "identity" | "php_addslashes
       " | ... )
6  CONTEXT = ( ATTRIBUTE_VALUE | OUTSIDE_TAG |
       ... )
7  ATTRIBUTE_VALUE = TEXT QUOTE SPACES HANDLER
       "=" QUOTE JS_PAYLOAD QUOTE
8  HANDLER = ( "onload" | "onerror" | ... )
9  JS_PAYLOAD = ( JS_P0 | JS_P1 | ... )
10 JS_P1 = "alert(" NUMS ")"
11 NUMS = [5:10](NUM)
12 NUM = ("0" | "1" | "2" | ... | "9")
13 QUOTE = ("'" | "\"" | "" | "\\'" | ...)
14 SPACES = [1:3](SPACE)
15 SPACE = (" " | "\n" | "\t" | "\r")
16 TEXT = [0:9](LETTER)
17 LETTER = ("a" | "b" | ...)
```

Listing 3: attack grammar (excerpt)

Automated Black-box Detection of Access Control Vulnerabilities in Web Applications

Xiaowei Li
Google Inc.
Mountain View, CA USA
94043
xiaoweil@google.com *

Xujie Si
Department of Electrical
Engineering and Computer
Science
Vanderbilt University
Nashville, TN USA 37203
xujie.si@vanderbilt.edu

Yuan Xue
Department of Electrical
Engineering and Computer
Science
Vanderbilt University
Nashville, TN USA 37203
yuan.xue@vanderbilt.edu

ABSTRACT

Access control vulnerabilities within web applications pose serious security threats to the sensitive information stored at back-end databases. Existing approaches are limited from several aspects, including the coarse granularity at which the access control is modeled, the incapability of handling complex relationship between data entities and the requirement of source code and the specific application platform. In this paper, we present an automated black-box technique for identifying a broad range of access control vulnerabilities, which can be applied to applications that are developed using different languages and platforms. We model the access control policy based on a novel *virtual SQL query* concept, which captures both the database access operations (i.e., through SQL queries) and the post-processing filters within the web application. We leverage a crawler to automatically explore the application and collect execution traces. From the traces, we identify the set of database access operations that are allowed for each role (i.e., role-level policy inference) and extract the constraints over the operation parameters to characterize the relationship between the users and the accessed data (i.e., user-level policy inference). Based on the inferred policy, we construct test inputs to exploit the application for potential access control flaws. We implement a prototype system BATMAN and evaluate it over a set of PHP and JSP web applications. The experiment results demonstrate the effectiveness and accuracy of our approach.

Categories and Subject Descriptors

K.6.5 [**Management of Computing and Information Systems**]: Security and Protection—*Unauthorized access*; H.2.7 [**Database Management**]: Database Administration—*Security, integrity, and protection*

---

*This work was completed when the author was with Vanderbilt University.

Keywords

Access Control Vulnerability; Web Application Security; Black-box Detection; Role/User-level Policy Inference; Web Crawler

1. INTRODUCTION

Web applications have become the defacto platform for information and service delivery over the Internet. Users can access and manage a large amount of sensitive information stored at back-end databases via web applications. To protect the sensitive information, a web application implements access control mechanism, which restricts the data access privileges of different roles and users. When a web application has access control vulnerabilities, attackers can escalate their privileges to access unauthorized data. Access control vulnerabilities are perceived as one of the most serious security threats to the sensitive information managed by the web applications today. Three among top ten security risks for web applications [17][1] can be attributed to flawed access control within web applications.

Access control vulnerabilities stem from the discrepancies between the intended access control policy and the policy that is actually implemented within a web application. Observing the fact that an application implementation usually comes without an explicit specification of the access control policy, deriving the intended access control policy becomes the first critical step in identifying access control vulnerabilities. This is a very challenging task especially for database-backed web applications. First, access control policies are implemented jointly through the proper definition of database access operations (e.g., SQL queries) and the data processing and filtering functions within web applications. The policy enforcement may span multiple program blocks, files or web interactions. Second, complex data relationship within the databases may complicate the way how access control policies are manifested.

A few techniques (e.g., [25], [22], [2], [15], [12]) have been proposed in the existing works to automatically extract access control policies, as we will describe with greater details in Section 6. They are limited from several aspects. First, the techniques presented in [2, 3, 20] can only address specific types of vulnerabilities (i.e., form parameter tampering and Execution After Redirection). Second, the granularity

---

[1]Missing Functional Access Control (newly added in 2013), Insecure Direct Object Reference and Unvalidated Redirects and Forwards.

of the access control models in [25] and [22] and the data access operations considered in [22], [14] and [15] determine they can only identify a limited set of access control flaw types. For example, Sun et al [25] regard a web page as the basic unit for access control, which is too coarse to identify access control flaws within guarded pages. RoleCast [22] only considers a subset of SQL statements as sensitive operations and neglects SELECT statements when identifying missing checks on critical variables. In addition, many techniques require the availability of the source code (e.g., [12], [3], [25]), or access to server-side session information (e.g., [15],[14]), or can only be applied to specific web development languages and platforms (e.g., [12],[25]). Moreover, none of the existing approaches can model the complex data relationship that spans multiple program files and identify the access control flaws arising from it.

In this paper, we present a black-box technique, which can accurately identify a broad range of access control vulnerabilities, especially arising from complex data relationship. We present a virtual SQL query model, which captures both the database access action (i.e., SQL queries issued to the database) and the database access result (i.e., the actual information that is presented to the user through web responses). We model the access control policy at two levels – at the role level, as the mapping between roles and the virtual SQL queries; at the user level, as the constraints over virtual SQL query parameters which characterize the relationship between users and the data entities being accessed. Based on the observation that the access control policy is usually correctly implemented under normal user navigation, we employ a crawler to emulate normal users with different roles, explore the application's functionalities automatically, observe its interactions with users and the database and collect the execution traces for inferring the intended access control policy. Based on the inferred policy, we generate test inputs to exploit the application for potential access control flaws.

Our contributions can be summarized as follows.

- We introduce a virtual SQL query model to accurately represent the database access operations that a web application can perform. Based on this model, complex data relationship (i.e., first-order and second-order) between users and accessed data entities are formulated and considered in the inference of access control policies. This allows our approach to cover a broader range of vulnerabilities compared with existing approaches.

- We introduce a black-box technique that infers the access control policy of the web application at both the role and user level from collected execution traces and generates testing input to identify access control vulnerabilities based on the inferred policy. Our technique does not require application source code and server-side session information and thus is independent of the application development languages and platforms.

- We implement a prototype system BATMAN and evaluate it over a set of PHP and JSP web applications. The experiment results demonstrate that our approach is effective, accurate and applicable for applications developed in different languages. Our technique also provides detailed evidences to facilitate the manual analysis and the fix of the identified flaws.

The rest of paper is organized as follows. We describe and formalize the problem in Section 2. Our approach is illustrated in details in Section 3. Implementation details and evaluation results are presented in Section 4 and Section 5, respectively. Section 6 discusses related works. The paper is concluded in the final section.

2. PROBLEM DESCRIPTION

In this paper, we consider the following threat model: (1) the web application itself is benign (i.e., not hosted or owned for malicious purposes) and hosted on a trusted and hardened infrastructure (i.e., a trusted computing base, including OS, web server, interpreter, etc.); (2) when users follow the navigation links provided by the application, the information they are able to harvest are subject to the access control policy of the application; (3) the attacker is able to manipulate either the content or the sequence of web requests sent to the web application, but cannot directly compromise the infrastructure or the application code.

2.1 Database Access Model

Figure 1 illustrates a typical scenario where a user accesses the information stored at the back-end database through the front-end web application. In this scenario, a user's data access requests are carried in the web requests and processed by the web application. The application first validates the user identity, then grants the user access privilege based on his role by issuing the database access requests on the user's behalf. Based on the results received from the database, the application composes the web responses, which return the information to the user.

In this paper, we focus on relational database due to its popular deployment. In a web application, a user's privilege to access a relational database is granted through the issuance of SQL query, which specifies the operation and the set of data which the operation can be applied to. In the relational data model, data is represented as a set of n-ary relations, where each n-ary relation is an ordered set of attribute values. Visually, the basic data block can be represented as a table, which we refer to as *database view* in the paper. There are two types of operations that can be applied:

MODIFY operation, which is performed through SQL queries, including INSERT, UPDATE and DELETE statements. When a user performs a MODIFY operation, the operation immediately takes effect over the database view that is specified in the SQL query.

READ operation, which is achieved through SELECT statement. When a user performs a READ operation, the SQL response is first processed at the web application which filters and embeds the retrieved database view into the web response in the form of HTML. As a result, the actual data observed by the user, which we refer to as *web view*, could be different from the database view, since the application may only allow part of the information within the SQL response to flow into the web response. As shown in Figure 1, the returned SQL response (i.e., the database view) is structured as a table. Only selected relations of the table are used by the application for composing the web response (i.e., the web view). In this case, the database view specified in the original SQL query is not sufficient to model the user's data access privilege. The post-processing by the web application needs to be taken into account.

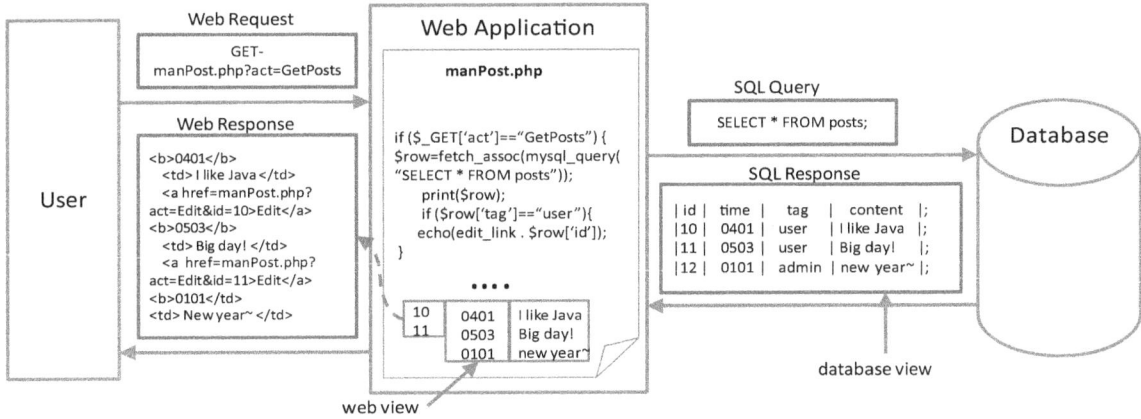

Figure 1: Example of Database Access via a Web Application

To establish a unified model to express the data access privilege for the above two operations, we introduce *virtual SQL query*. For a MODIFY operation, the virtual SQL query is the same as the original SQL query, as it directly captures the data access privilege. For a READ operation, the virtual SQL query supplements the original SQL query with additional filters to capture the post processing of the database view. The filters are constructed along two dimensions: *column-based filter*, which selects the attributes from the database view, and *row-based filter*, which selects the tuples from the database view. As shown in Figure 1, the application makes use of the *time*, *id* and *content* attributes to construct the web response, which we refer to as the *column-based filter*. Then two of the three rows of *id* values are used for composing the editing links, which we refer to as the *row-based filter*. The column-based filter can be represented by limiting the attributes in the SELECT statement (e.g., SELECT id FROM post) and the row-based filter can be represented by enhancing the SELECT statement of the column-based filter with WHERE clauses (e.g., SELECT id FROM post WHERE tag = 'user').

Formally, we represent a *virtual SQL query* using a skeleton structure and a set of query parameters. The skeleton structure is programmed in the source code, while the values of the parameters are dynamically fed by the application at runtime. For MODIFY operation, both the skeleton structure and the set of query parameters are derived from its original SQL query. For example, a virtual SQL query can be represented as: DELETE FROM user WHERE id = [p1], where p1 represents the value of the query parameter. For READ operation, the skeleton structure is composed of the skeleton structure of the original SQL query and the skeleton structures of the SQL queries that represent the post-processing filters. The set of parameters that are associated with both original SQL queries and the post-processing filter SQL queries collectively constitute the set of parameters for the virtual SQL query. Now we formalize our access control model as follows.

Database Access Operation: A database access operation represents the action performed by the web application on a behalf of users for retrieving or modifying data in the database. We model the database access operation through virtual SQL query. We use $o \in O$ to denote the skeleton of

the virtual SQL query and $\Phi(o)$ to denote the set of parameters associated with o.

Role: A role $r \in R$ represents a distinctive set of privileges. We assume the set of roles form a lattice ordering relationship. A less privileged role should not be able to access the data which are only allowed for more privileged roles.

User: A user $u \in U$ represents a concrete principal with one specific role (denoted by $r(u)$) that interacts with the web application. Each user who is registered with the application is identified through an entity defined in the database (e.g., a tuple in the *user* table). When a user u triggers an operation, the parameters passed into the operation are linked to the user's identity in the database, which are represented as user-based constraints. In this way, the access privileges of users under the same role can be differentiated.

Access Control (AC): The intended access control policy in a web application specifies the set of privileges for each user. It consists of two levels: role level and user level. The role-level access control policy is abstracted as the mapping from roles to the set of virtual SQL query skeletons $P : R \to 2^O$, where $P(r)$ represents the set of virtual SQL query skeletons that can be triggered under role r. The user-level access control policy attaches user-based constraints to each virtual SQL query skeleton that is accessible under $r(u)$.

2.2 Access Control Vulnerability

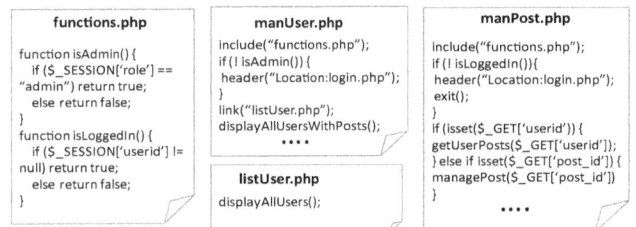

Figure 2: An Example Vulnerable Web Application

Access Control Vulnerability: A web application has an access control vulnerability if either of the following scenarios occurs: (1)at the role level, there exists a skeleton o, which is only allowed for role r, but can be triggered by a user with a less privileged role r'; (2)at the user level, there exists a skeleton o allowed for $r(u)$, which can be triggered by the user u while one of the constraints associated with o is violated.

Figure 2 shows an example application to demonstrate the access control flaws we focus on in this paper. It has three roles: guest user, regular user and admin user. *manUser.php* and *listUser.php* pages are only intended for admin users, since *manUser.php* page places *isAdmin()* function to check the user's role and the link to *listUser.php* page is only shown in *manUser.php* page. *manPost.php* page is intended for regular users to manage their own posts. This example application is specially crafted to contain several access control vulnerabilities that correspond to the above two scenarios: (1) an attacker, as a guest user, can trigger administrative operations within both *manUser.php* and *listUser.php* pages via forceful browsing. *listUser.php* page misses the *isAdmin()* function for checking the user's role, thus can be directly accessed and user list information can be collected by the attacker. Although the check function within *manUser.php* page redirects unauthorized users, it does not stop the application execution, so that the attacker's request is still processed and sensitive information is returned within the web response. This vulnerability is also referred to as Execution After Redirection (EAR) [9]; (2) an attacker, as a regular user, can retrieve and modify any post created by other users via parameter manipulation. *manPost.php* page fails to check whether the request parameter $_GET['userid'] really represents the current user when retrieving the posts for the user and whether the post with id $_GET['post_id'] belongs to the current user. The attacker can craft a web request pointing to *manPost.php* page with any valid user or post id to trigger the vulnerability.

3. APPROACH

3.1 High-level Overview

Our approach consists of three major phases: *Trace Collection*, *Policy Inference* and *Vulnerability Detection*. To identify access control vulnerabilities in web applications, we first infer the intended access control policy through observing the application normal execution where users follow the navigation links (including submitting forms) provided by the web application.

In the *Trace Collection* phase, we leverage a web crawler to emulate the behaviors of different users when they follow the navigation links. We note that the crawler is provided with user credentials, so that it can login to the web application and explore the web application like normal users with different roles. During crawling, we collect the web interactions between the crawler and the application (i.e., HTTP requests and responses), as well as the interactions between the application and the database (i.e., SQL queries and responses), as the application's execution traces. Figure 3 shows an overview of the trace structure. Each SQL sample is retrieved from the traces by including a pair of SQL query and response, as well as the web request and response in the interaction. In the *Policy Inference* phase, the collected traces are grouped into different sample sets for inferring the intended access control policy at two levels: role level and user level. In the *Vulnerability Detection* phase, test inputs are constructed based on the inferred access control policy and fed into the application to generate

a testing report of identified potential access control flaws. Finally, we manually analyze the testing report to confirm real vulnerabilities and false positives. Our approach regards the web application as a black-box and does not require the application source code.

We elaborate *Policy Inference* and *Vulnerability Detection* in the next two sections and describe the implementation details of the crawler in Section 4.1.

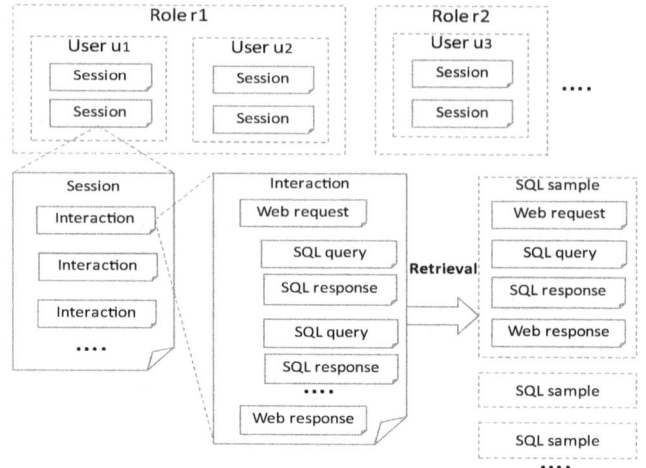

Figure 3: Trace Structure

3.2 Policy Inference

3.2.1 Role-level Policy Inference

At the role level, the access control policy is derived by identifying the set of virtual SQL query skeletons that are triggered by different roles (i.e., $P(r), r \in R$). Since this skeleton can be trivially constructed for the MODIFY operations from its original SQL queries, we focus on deriving the post-processing filters for constructing virtual SQL skeleton for READ operations. We first infer the column-based filters based on the database view presented in the SQL response and the web view embedded in the web response (i.e. HTML), then infer the row-based filters by leveraging the column-based filters.

Column-Based Filter Inference The key issue for inferring the column-based filter is to identify which attributes of the database view flow into the web response. There are two challenges here. First, database view is represented in a table structure, while the web response retains a tree-like DOM structure. Second, the columns in a database view can be represented through their attribute names, while this attribute information is usually removed when the data is embedded into the HTML page. Even worse, the data can be dispersed in the web page without a fixed representation. This structural and textual level mismatch prevents simple syntax-based filter construction. Thus we look for matching of the value domains between the data from database views and web responses. This is performed in three steps, as shown in Figure 4. First, we need to convert the data in HTML into a set of variables. We name these variables as web variables and denote them as $wv \in webResp$, where $webResp$ is a web response. In the second step, we match these web variables to the columns in the database view. Finally, we construct the column-based filter by choosing the columns that match web variables, which can be merged.

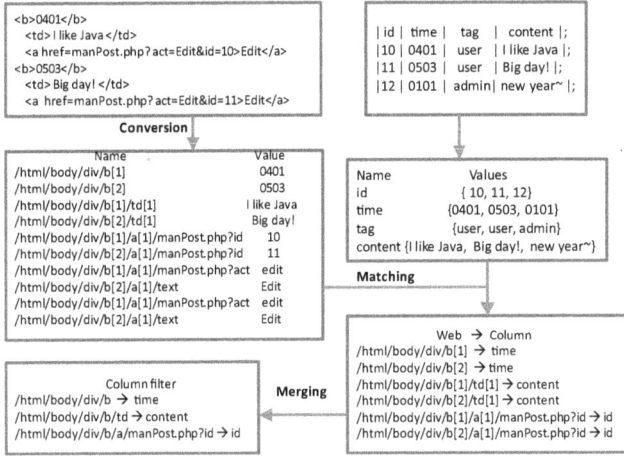

```
<b>0401</b>
  <td> I like Java </td>
    <a href=manPost.php?act=Edit&id=10>Edit</a>
<b>0503</b>
  <td> Big day! </td>
    <a href=manPost.php?act=Edit&id=11>Edit</a>
```

| id | time | tag | content |;
|10 | 0401 | user | I like Java |;
|11 | 0503 | user | Big day! |;
|12 | 0101 | admin| new year~ |;

Conversion

Name	Value
/html/body/div/b[1]	0401
/html/body/div/b[2]	0503
/html/body/div/b[1]/td[1]	I like Java
/html/body/div/b[2]/td[1]	Big day!
/html/body/div/b[1]/a[1]/manPost.php?id	10
/html/body/div/b[2]/a[1]/manPost.php?id	11
/html/body/div/b[1]/a[1]/manPost.php?act	edit
/html/body/div/b[1]/a[1]/text	Edit
/html/body/div/b[2]/a[1]/manPost.php?act	edit
/html/body/div/b[2]/a[1]/text	Edit

Name	Values
id	{ 10, 11, 12}
time	{0401, 0503, 0101}
tag	{user, user, admin}
content	{I like Java!, Big day!, new year~}

Matching

Web → Column
/html/body/div/b[1] → time
/html/body/div/b[2] → time
/html/body/div/b[1]/td[1] → content
/html/body/div/b[2]/td[1] → content
/html/body/div/b[1]/a[1]/manPost.php?id → id
/html/body/div/b[2]/a[1]/manPost.php?id → id

Column filter
/html/body/div/b → time
/html/body/div/td → content
/html/body/div/b/a/manPost.php?id → id

Merging

Figure 4: Column-based Filter Inference

HTML to variable conversion. To convert the data in HTML into a set of variables, we first identify the locations within web responses where dynamic information usually flows into (i.e. data sink). We observe that there are three types of data sinks: *text shown to the user*; *parameters in URL links*; and *form fields* (including select options, hidden fields, etc.). Each data sink is identified by the unique XPath leading to the sink from the DOM root. For the parameters in URL links, we also append the URL link and the parameter name. The unique XPath is constructed by appending the node along the general XPath (e.g., /html/body/div/b) with a sequence number (e.g., /html/body/div/b[1]).

Web-to-attribute matching. First, we group the SQL samples based on their original SQL query skeleton as well as their web request keys. The web request key is defined as the combination of HTTP method and the request URL (e.g., GET-manPost.php). The reason for grouping by web request key is that the post-processing is determined by the program block that is executed when the application composes the web response, while the web request key specifies the entry point of the execution. For convenience of presentation, we denote a column in the database view using a variable $sv \in sqlResp$, where $sqlResp$ is the database view carried in the SQL response. Let $V(v)$ represents the set of values of variable v. We identify a match between $sv \in sqlResp$ and $wv \in webResp$ if and only if $V(wv) \subseteq V(sv)$ holds for all $sqlResp$ and $webResp$ within the same sample group. To compare two values, we employ approximate string matching since the information from the database view can be manipulated by the application before it flows into the web response. We denote the *response propagation path* from sv to wv as $P_{resp} : sv \rightarrow wv$.

Web variable merging. We examine the web variables under the same general XPath. If they are matched with the same column, which means their values come from one single source, we recognize the attribute that flows into the web response as a column-based filter. The column filters in Figure 4 can be represented as: SELECT id, time, content FROM post.

Row-Based Filter Inference The row-based filter inference is performed in two steps. First, for each column selected from the column-based filter, we identify the rows whose values actually flow into the web response. Then, we observe the values of each attribute among the identified rows. If the values keep consistent for a certain attribute, we recognize it as one row-based filter and count the attribute as one operation parameter. In Figure 1, for the *time* and *content* attributes, all the rows flow into the web response and no attribute exists, whose values keep consistent. For the *id* attribute, the values of attribute *tag* keep consistent among the two rows that flow into the web response. Thus, we identify the *tag* attribute as an additional operation parameter and its value is "user".

3.2.2 User-level Policy Inference

The role-level policy specifies the set of database access operations that can be performed by all the users with the same role, while the user-level policy restricts the specific view the user is authorized to access through constraints over the operation parameters. Note that the operation parameters include the parameters from the original SQL queries and the parameters from the post-processing filters (for READ operations).

First-Order Constraint To differentiate the views among users, the operation parameters have to be linked with a user's identity, which reflect the relationship between the user and the view being accessed in the database. If the view being accessed is referenced by the user identity directly (e.g., through the primary key in the *user* table), we say there exists *First-Order Relationship* between the user and the view and the constraint on accessing this view is called *First-Order Constraint*. For example, if the application issues a SQL query: SELECT * FROM user WHERE id=5 to retrieve the information for the current user, the *id* parameter is subject to the first-order constraint.

We infer the first-order constraint in two steps. For each user u with role $r(u)$, let $o \in P(r(u))$ be a virtual SQL skeleton that is accessible based on the role-level access control policy and $\Phi(o)$ be the set of parameters associated with o. First, we identify the operation parameters $pv \subseteq \Phi(o)$ whose values are *consistent* for u. Then, from the consistent parameter set, we identify the parameters that are *unique* to each user of the same role by filtering out those whose values coincide across different users. In this way, the identified parameters are bounded to the user and directly linked to the user's identity.

Second-Order Constraint The operation parameters for accessing data may not always be linked with the user's identity directly. If the relationship between the data entity and the user's identity is reflected through foreign keys or a separate table, we say there exists *Second-Order Relationship* between the user and the data entity. As shown in Figure 5(1), the post entity is not directly linked with the user's identity, rather through the *author* table.

To compare with the first-order constraint which is imposed over the parameters of the virtual SQL query directly, the second-order constraint can be represented through a nested SQL query, e.g., DELETE FROM post WHERE id IN (SELECT post_id FROM author WHERE user_id = '6'). Here the parameter *id* does not directly link to the *user_id*, but is *bounded* to the database view that is subject to first-

Table: user

id	name	role
1	admin	admin
5	alice	user
6	bob	user

Table: author

id	post_id	user_id
1	10	6
2	11	6
3	12	5

Table: post

id	time	tag	content
10	0401	user	I like Java
11	0503	user	Big day!
12	0101	admin	new year~

(1) Database Schema

GET-manPost.php?act=DeleteAllPosts

```
<form action='POST'>
<input type='hidden' value='10'>
<input type='hidden' value='11'>
<input type='submit' name='act' value='confirmDelete'>
```

POST-manPost.php?act=ConfirmDelete&id=10&id=11

```
manPost.php
if ($_GET['act'] == "DeleteAllPosts") {
    mysql_query("SELECT post_id
FROM author WHERE user_id =".
$SESSION['userid'];
    return_confirmation();
}
....
if ($_POST['act'] == "ConfirmDelete")
{ for ($_POST as $id)
    mysql_query ("DELETE FROM
post WHERE id = " . $id );
}
```

SELECT post_id FROM author WHERE user_id = 6;

{ |id| ; |10| ; |11| ;}

DELETE FROM post WHERE id = '10'

DELETE FROM post WHERE id = '11'

(2) Second-Order Relationship Across Web Interactions

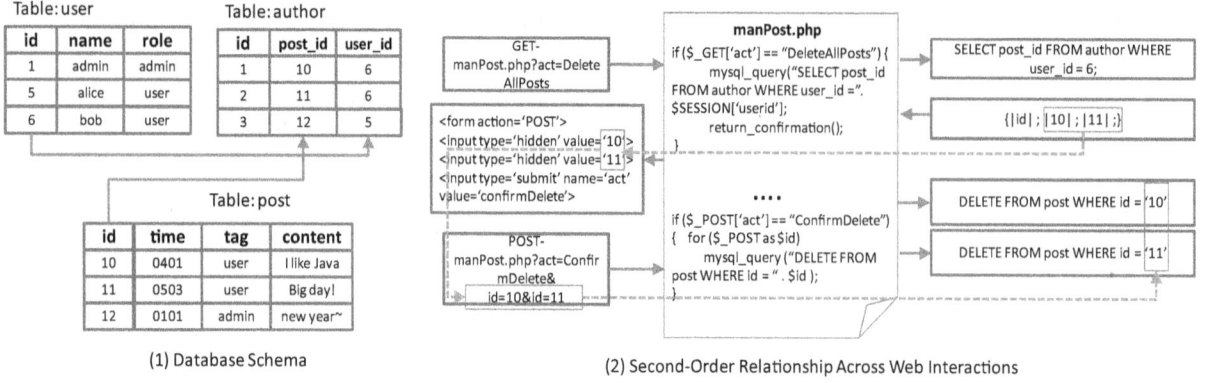

Figure 5: Second-Order Relationship Example

order constraint. If the second-order constraint is implemented in a nested SQL statement as the above example, it is reduced to a first-order constraint problem where the indirect relationship is automatically enforced.

However, in a web application the second-order constraint is usually implemented through two SQL statements within two web interactions, so that the users can be prompted with intermediate results. As shown in Figure 5(2), the application first retrieves all the posts created by the user, then the user can confirm the deletion. When this procedure is separated into more than one interactions, the user may violate this constraint by manipulating the web requests between interactions. As shown by dotted lines in Figure 5(2), this constraint actually reflects the value propagation chain across web interactions: the results returned by a previous operation are propagated through the web response, the web request parameters into a new operation. Since this constraint is manifested across interactions, in order to infer it we need to look back for previous web interactions. The number of web interactions we look back for depends on how long this value propagation chain lasts. We observe that this chain is usually no longer than three for most applications. Thus, we look back for two interactions in our inference.

We denote the operation in current interaction by o_{cur}, the operation from preceding interactions by o_{pre} and its result (i.e., SQL response) by $Re(o_{pre})$, the web (response) variables from preceding interactions by $webResp_{pre}$ and the web request parameters of current interaction by $webReq_{cur}$. We identify the second-order constraint if and only if the following rule holds for all the samples in the group:

Second-Order Relationship Rule: (1) o_{pre} is a READ operation; (2) $\exists v \in \Phi(o_{pre})$, v is subject to first-order constraint, since the returned result set should be specific to each user; (3) there exists a response propagation path from the SQL response to the web response in a preceding interaction, i.e., $\exists P_{resp} : sv \rightarrow wv$, where $sv \in Re(o_{pre})$, $wv \in webResp_{pre}$; (4) there exists a parameter propagation path from the web request to the operation in the current interaction i.e., $\exists P_{para} : rv \rightarrow pv$, where $rv \in webReq_{cur}$, $pv \in \Phi(o_{cur})$; (5) $V(rv) \subseteq V(wv)$, which means the request parameters come from the previous web response. The value propagation chain is $sv \rightarrow wv \rightarrow rv \rightarrow pv$.

Here the *parameter propagation path* $P_{para} : rv \rightarrow pv$, where $rv \in webReq_{cur}$, $pv \in \Phi(o_{cur})$ from web request parameters to virtual SQL query parameters can be inferred in a similar way as how we infer column-based filters. We

group the SQL samples by both virtual SQL query skeleton and web request key, since each request URL has a set of predefined request parameters. Within each sample group, we compare the values of web request parameters ($webReq$) against those of operation parameters (i.e., $\Phi(o)$). A parameter propagation path exists between a web request and an operation if and only if the following rule holds for all the samples: $\exists rv \in webReq$ and $\exists pv \in \Phi(o)$ and $V(rv) == V(pv)$.

3.3 Vulnerability Detection

3.3.1 Test Input Generation

We generate test inputs based on the inferred policy to check whether the policy is actually enforced by the application. Each test input is designed to examine whether a specific database access operation can be performed while the policy is violated. Concretely, two types of test inputs are generated through *differential analysis*: (1) role-based test, which examines whether a less privileged role can trigger a database access operation, which is only allowed for a more privileged role; (2) user-based test, which examines whether a user can trigger a database access operation with a parameter that is subject to the user-based constraint but takes a value that is linked to another user's identity.

To realistically emulate the attack inputs, our test inputs trigger the desired database access operations through web requests, since end users (including attackers) cannot directly trigger the database access operations. This can be nontrivial, since a random web request has a very low chance of triggering the desired operation. To address this challenge, we leverage the samples that are used for policy inference for constructing test inputs. For each test input, we select a seed sample from each sample group and manipulate the contents of the sample.

Role-based Test. For each pair of roles (r_1, $r_2 \in R$, assuming r_1 is less privileged than r_2) from the role set, we compare their sets of allowed virtual SQL query skeleton to identify the set of privileged operations (denoted by O_{test}), which should not be allowed for the less privileged role r_1 (i.e., $\forall o \in O_{test}, o \in P(r_2), o \notin P(r_1)$). To test each privileged operation, we first select a seed sample that is collected for users with role r_2, within which the operation under test has been triggered. Then, we change the user identity attached to the sample to be a user with role r_1, who should not be able to perform to this operation according to the inferred policy.

User-based Test. To test user-based constraints associated with the virtual SQL query skeleton, test inputs are constructed to violate such constraints and fed into the application to examine whether the operation can still be triggered. For test construction, we select a seed sample from each sample group and manipulate the value of the web request parameter that has a parameter propagation path leading to the operation parameter, which is subject to the constraint under test. Specifically, to violate the first-order constraint, we replace the parameter value with a value that is observed for a different user with the same role. We note that first-order constraints, which do not have parameter propagation paths from web request will not be tested, since their parameters can not be manipulated from web requests. To violate second-order constraints, test inputs need to contain a sequence of web requests. Such a test input is constructed in two steps. First, all the web requests, except the last one, from the sample are kept to trigger the READ operation that returns the set of data entities that are bound to the user. Next, we manipulate the parameter value of the last web request (i.e. test request) to fall beyond the above set.

3.3.2 Test Input Evaluation

Before a test input is fed into the application, if the user attached to the test input is required to log into the application, a login web request is first constructed with the user's login credentials and sent to the application to acquire the session cookie, so that subsequent web requests are recognized as the same user. If the test input is aimed at testing a second-order constraint, the sequence of web requests within the test input, except the test web request, are sent to the application. At the same time, all the SQL queries and responses are collected. The READ operation that returns the set of data entities will be identified and the test request is manipulated based on its operation results (i.e. web response). Then, the test web request is sent to the application. After the web response is received, we check the sequence of SQL queries and responses collected during this interaction to see whether the database access operation under the test has been triggered. Especially, for a READ operation, we need to analyze whether the information within the SQL response flows into the web response based on the filters. If the operation under test is identified, we flag the test input as a violation. After all the test inputs are evaluated, we manually analyze the reported violations and classify them as either true or false positive.

4. IMPLEMENTATION

We implement a prototype system BATMAN. Its architecture is shown in Figure 6. The crawler, web proxy and MySQL Proxy [16] are adapted from open source projects (i.e., Crawljax [7], WebScarab [18]) and cooperate with Sync Portal for exploring the web application and recording the interactions between the web application, the users and the database. The enhancements we make with the crawler are implemented in around 3000 LoC of Java. Inference Engine and Testing Engine are developed by ourselves in around 4600 LoC of Java for policy inference and vulnerability detection.

4.1 Crawler

The crawler is built upon Crawljax [7], an open-source crawler designed for exploring modern web applications. Crawljax leverages the web application testing framework Selenium [21] for instantiating browser instances and rending web pages. Crawljax iterates all the clickables on a web page and progressively constructs a graph of web pages for exploring application. Utilizing a crawler for trace collection allows for efficient exploration of a web application with high coverage. However, Crawjax (and most other open source crawlers) has several limitations and can not be directly applied for trace collection. Thus, we enhance Crawljax with two important functions, which are elaborated below.

Type-enhanced Form Filling. During crawling, whenever Crawljax encounters a web form, it will generate random inputs for filling the form. Since Crawljax is agnostics of the semantics of input fields, the randomly filled form is very likely to be rejected by the application, which prevents it from crawling the portion of the application behind form submission. For example, the user registration form usually checks the validity of user-provided email, password and etc.

To enhance Crawljax's capability of filling forms, we employ a two-round crawling strategy. In the first round, the crawler follows the identified links, fills random inputs and collects all the encountered input fields. We refer to this round as *form input discovery* phase. We define a set of commonly seen input data types, such as single-digit number, random string, email, phone number, etc. and manually attach the data type information to the input fields. For some input fields with special requirements, e.g., password, we directly specify a concrete value. In the second round, when the crawler encounters a form, it will generate a corresponding value based on the attached data type or take the concrete value and feed into the application. This two-round strategy cannot guarantee the crawler can successfully make through every form checking, but can greatly increase the crawling coverage. In particular, we implemented one plugin to enable the crawler to login to the web application like normal users with different roles, given user credentials, so that the crawler can explore the non-trivial functionalities of the web application.

Semantic-based Page Comparison. Crawljax employs a depth-first strategy for crawling and returns to the previous page when it encounters a web page that has been visited. The criteria for determining whether a web page has been visited is the exact DOM matching with any previously seen web page. Considering that the web application state is possibly changed during crawling (e.g., adding an item to the shopping cart), this stringent criteria can easily get the crawler stuck in a local loop (e.g., adding a different item every time), which prevents the crawler from exploring deeper and also diminishes the crawling efficiency.

To achieve both better coverage and efficiency, we relax this stringent criteria by modifying the underlying page representation and comparison within Crawljax. We observe that although some web pages are not identical to each other, their semantics can be the same, which means that the crawling paths starting from these pages are exactly the same. Thus, we can merge these pages with same semantics to stop crawling further beyond. To identify web pages with the same semantics, we leverage the intuition, pointed out in [10], that the links and forms within a web

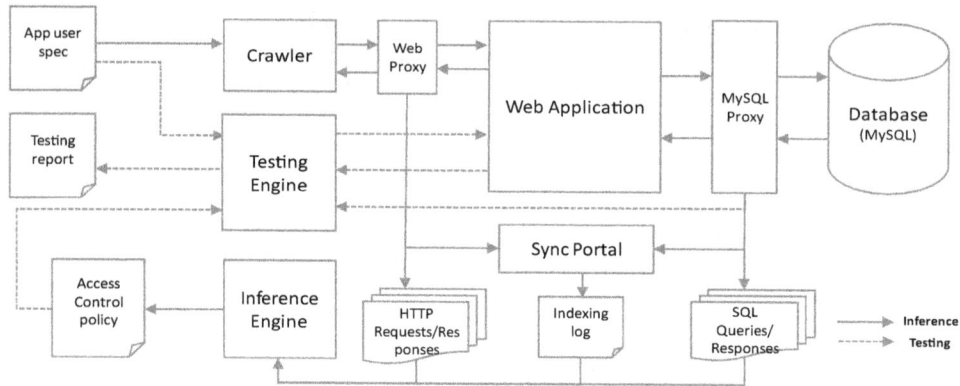

Figure 6: Prototype System Architecture

page determine where users can go from the current page. Thus, we represent a web page using the set of distinct link and form structures. To be more specific, we extract all the links and forms from the page, remove all the parameters and obtain their structure. An example link structure is */html/body/div/a/view.php?user_id=[p1]*, where [p1] is the place token for the parameter value. The web form is represented in a similar manner by combing the action URL with all input fields. An example form structure is */html/body/div/form/adduser.php?username=[p1]&password =[p2] &submit=[p3]*. In this way, the crawler identifies web pages with the same set of link/form structures, collapses them together and does backtracking from the current point.

4.2 Trace Collection

To collect traces, we leverage an open source web proxy WebScarab [18] to intercept HTTP requests/responses exchanged between the user and the application, and MySQL Proxy [16] to intercept SQL queries/response exchanged between the application and the database. Since MySQL Proxy is unaware of the HTTP interactions, we need to correlate the SQL queries and responses with the HTTP interactions during which they are collected. To do so, we implement Sync Portal, which is a web service running on Tomcat and can receive web requests coming from the web proxy and the MySQL proxy. We modify the WebScarab proxy, so that every time it intercepts a web request or response, it generates a unique index and sends the index to Sync Portal through a wrapping web request. An example web request is *http://127.0.0.1:8080/Portal? type=HTTP_REQUEST &index=10*. Similarly, MySQL proxy generates unique indexes for SQL queries and responses and send them to Sync Portal. This is implemented through writing a Lua script executed by MySQL Proxy. Sync Portal writes received indexes into an indexing file for synchronizing the SQL traffic with web interactions. This loosely couple structure enables us to deploy the components on different machines.

4.3 Inference & Testing

As shown by solid lines in Figure 6, Inference Engine takes the indexing file, collected web requests/responses, and SQL queries/responses together to generate the access control policy file. The dotted lines in Figure 6 show the testing workflow. Testing Engine generates test inputs based on the policy file, constructs test web requests and sends them to the application. At the same time, MySQL Proxy sends

SQL queries and responses observed during each interaction to Testing Engine. Testing Engine examines the web response and the sequence of SQL pairs received during the current interaction to identify if the data access operation under test has been executed. The application user specification is also utilized by Testing Engine to construct login requests.

5. EVALUATION

We select a set of open source web applications for evaluation, which include both PHP and JSP applications, to demonstrate the effectiveness of our approach across different platforms. We deploy all the applications on a 2.13GHz Core 2 Linux server with 2GB RAM, running Ubuntu 10.10, Apache web server (version 2.2.16), PHP (version 5.3.3) and Tomcat6 (version 6.0.28). Table 1 shows a summary of these applications with their programming language, the lines of executable code (LoC) and a brief description.

Table 1: Summary of Web Applications for Evaluation

Application	Lang.	Files	LoC	Description
Scarf (2007-0227)	PHP	19	797	conference system
Wackopicko	PHP	52	952	photo-sharing
EventsLister v2.03	PHP	27	837	event board
Bloggit v1.0	PHP	24	1071	blogging
minibloggie v2.1.6	PHP	11	838	blogging
JsForum v0.1	JSP	22	2224	web forum
JspBlog v0.2	JSP	17	1365	blogging

We first run the web crawler to collect execution traces. For each role, the crawler explores the application for several web sessions. For each session, the crawler randomly selects a user with the specific role. The maximum crawling depth is configured to 5, since most of the functionalities of a web application can be reached within five steps. To demonstrate that our crawler is able to cover most functionalities of the application, we show the percentage of the application's executable code that the crawler triggers (i.e., code coverage) in Table 2. PHP code coverage is measured using Spike PHPCoverage [24] and JSP code coverage is measured using Clover [5]. We also show the improvement of the code coverage achieved by our crawler compared to a baseline tool: wget. As pointed out in [10], code coverage is not an accurate metric for measuring the completeness of exploration and the performance of a crawler. This is because applications contain code used for installation, debugging, error-handling, and even dead code, which can never be reached by the crawler. We use code coverage as a metric and tool to assist the identification of the portion of the application which the crawler misses, and iteratively improve the crawling depth for better trace quality. The reason for why our crawler performs better than wget is that our crawler is enhanced with intelligent form filling, so that it can reach more web pages behind web forms.

Table 2: Summary of Code Coverage

Application	crawler coverage	wget coverage	crawler improvement
Scarf	64.74%	32.12%	101.56%
Wackopicko	64.02%	30.78%	107.99%
EventsLister	74.81%	42.53%	75.89%
Bloggit	81.87%	68.35%	19.78%
minibloggie	64.98%	42.12%	54.27%
JsForum	69.5%	37.9%	83.38%
JspBlog	58.7%	36.1%	62.60%

Inference Engine runs over the collected traces and generates the intended access control policy. Table 3 shows a summary of the policy inference results. For each application, we show the number of roles, web sessions, web requests and SQL queries being collected, along with the virtual SQL query skeletons (denote by skeleton) and two types of user-based constraints being identified.

Testing Engine generates test inputs based on the inferred policy and exploits the application. Table 4 shows a summary of the testing results. Three types of tests are evaluated: role-based test (denoted as R-Test), tests generated for first-order user-based constraint (denoted as FU-Test) and tests for second-order user-based constraint (denoted as SU-Test). For each type of test, we show the number of generated test inputs, flagged inputs (denoted by Flagged) and false positives (denoted by FP). We also report the number of real violations (true positives) in total (denoted by TP-Sum) and the number of access control vulnerabilities confirmed by manual analysis (denoted by Vuln). Note that these two numbers can be different, because one access control flaw within one check function allows all the operations that are guarded by the check to be triggered by unauthorized user, resulting in a number of violations. In the following, we describe the details of access control vulnerabilities we identify from each web application.

5.1 Details of Vulnerabilities

Scarf has three roles: guest user, regular user and admin user. Only admin users are allowed to manage papers, sessions and registered users. We identify one known authentication bypass vulnerability (CVE-2006-5909) within the *generaloptions.php* page, which misses the *require_admin()* function for authorization checks. This vulnerability allows an attacker, as a guest or regular user, to tamper the conference and user information.

Wackopicko is intentionally crafted with both input validation flaws and logic flaws. We identify two access control flaws within the application. The first one exists in the *users/view.php* page, which fails to check the intended first-order constraint on the parameter *userid*. This allows an attacker to access any user's information by tampering this pa-

rameter. The second one exists in the *highquality.php* page, which shows the high-quality pictures that are purchased by the user. This second-order constraint is implemented across two interactions. In the first interaction, the user visits the *purchased.php* page to retrieve a list of thumbnails and ids of the pictures being purchased. In the second interaction, the high-quality picture is requested via parameter *pic_id* whose value comes from the picture ids returned by the first interaction. The vulnerability within the *highquality.php* page fails to check this constraint on the parameter *pic_id*, which allows an attacker to view any high-quality pictures. The *highquality.php* page calls the same function to retrieve the picture information from the database as other pages, but presents the picture's high quality key value to the user. Our technique can accurately identify this sensitive operation by analyzing the post processing performed by the application.

Events Lister allows admin users to add new events, update or delete existing events, and manage users. We identify two access control flaws within the application. The first one exists in the *add_user.php* page, where the function for checking whether the current user is an admin (i.e., *checkUser()*) is missing. This allows an attacker to directly access this page and add new users. The second one is an Execution After Redirection vulnerability within the *checkUser()* function. All the PHP files that include this function for authorization checks are vulnerable and allow an attacker to trigger the database access operations within. Sun et al. [25] also study this application, but fail to identify the second vulnerability.

Bloggit only allows admin users to manage blogs and user information. We identify one known Execution After Redirection vulnerability (CVE-2006-7014) in the *session.inc.php* page. All of the files that include *session.inc.php* for authorization checks allow an attacker to trigger the database access operations even after being redirected. Our tool also generates two false positives. After investigation, we found out they result from spurious filtering rules where the values of two irrelevant variables coincide with each other, so that the same database access operation is identified as different ones for two roles.

Minibloggie only allows the admin user to manager posts and the regular user to edit or delete the posts created by himself. We identify one known access control flaw (CVE-2008-6650) within the *del.php* page, which misses the *verifyUser()* function for checking the user's role. This allows an attacker, as a guest user, to delete any posts. We also identify another previously unknown access control flaw, which allows the attacker, as a regular user, to delete other users' posts by tampering the parameter *post_id*, since the *del.php* page misses checking the second-order constraint on the parameter. This shows our technique can capture the data relationship between users and data entities across web interactions and identify access control flaws arising from it. RoleCast [22] also studies this application, but fail to identify the second vulnerability.

JsForum has three roles: guest user, regular user and admin user. Regular users can add threads and replies to the forum, while admin users can add new forum and moderate all threads and replies. We identify several access control flaws within this application. First, the application fails to check the current user's role. As a result, guest users can

Application	role	web session	web request	SQL query	skeleton	First-Order Constraint	Second-Order Constraint
Scarf	3	17	1931	14486	45	2	0
Wackopicko	2	7	4478	16074	26	14	1
EventsLister	2	9	2227	1857	12	0	0
Bloggit	2	13	416	934	22	0	0
minibloggie	2	9	466	655	12	10	9
JsForum	3	17	3666	29749	21	12	1
JspBlog	2	10	270	119	9	0	0

Table 4: Summary of Testing Results (#)

Application	R-Test	Flagged	FP	FU-Test	Flagged	FP	SU-Test	Flagged	FP	TP-sum	Vuln
Scarf	64	12	0	0	0	0	0	0	0	12	1
Wackopicko	24	0	0	1	1	0	1	1	0	2	2
EventsLister	9	9	0	0	0	0	0	0	0	9	2
Bloggit	19	16	2	0	0	0	0	0	0	14	1
minibloggie	16	1	0	0	0	0	9	2	0	3	2
JsForum	45	12	0	3	3	0	1	0	0	15	6
JspBlog	8	8	0	0	0	0	0	0	0	8	8
Summary	185	58	2	4	4	0	11	3	0	63	22

add new threads, replies and forums, and increase the view counters of certain threads without logging in. Second, the application fails to check the first-order constraint on the parameter within a hidden field *user* in the forms. This allows a regular user to add new threads or replies on behalf of other users by tampering this parameter. It is worth noting that second-order constraints are also identified for this application, where a user should only be able to edit his own replies. But testing results show that the application checks the relationship between the reply and the user. Thus no vulnerability is reported under the SU-test.

JspBlog only allows the admin user to manage the blogs and users. JspBlog implements the access control policy by hiding the links that lead to administrative pages from guest users. Vulnerabilities exist within administrative pages which fail to check the current user's role before any database access operations. Thus an attacker can forcefully access any administrative page and trigger those operations.

5.2 Discussion

We use dynamic analysis for policy inference and directed fuzzing for vulnerability detection. Here we discuss the intrinsic challenges and limits of these two techniques and how we address them in this work. First, dynamic analysis cannot guarantee the completeness of vulnerability discovery. Insufficient exploration of the web application may lead to false negatives. We enhance our crawler with two major functions, so that it can cover most functionalities of the application. During experiments, we measure the code coverage and use it as an assistance to determine the crawling depth so that we can make a sound tradeoff between the trace quality and the crawling time. Second, the accuracy of directed fuzzing is closely related with the database state. For example, when a test input of adding a new user is sent to the application, the test output may vary depending on whether the user already exists in the database. If it exists, the application will reject the request and the INSERT query cannot be triggered even the application contains a vulnerability of missing check. If the user does not exist in the database, then the vulnerability will be discovered. We

address this problem by ensure the consistency of database state between the inference phase and the testing phase. First we record the database state before crawling and leverage the collected traces for generating concrete test input values. Before testing, we restore the database state and feed test inputs that don't affect the database state before those which might change the state.

Albeit the merits, our work has several limitations, which can become future research directions. First, our inference technique extracts the invariants from collected traces as the access control policy, thus cannot handle dynamic access control scenario, where the access control policy can be changed or configured dynamically. How to incrementally infer the most updated access control policy is an interesting problem. Second, our web response analysis can be extended to handle AJAX web applications, where parts of the web pages get updated dynamically. Third, both our inference and testing techniques rely on the traces collected by the crawler, which may be either incomplete or inaccurate. Our technique can be combined with static analysis to achieve a better tradeoff between the completeness and the accuracy.

6. RELATED WORKS

Black-box Analysis. A number of black-box techniques are designed to discover various vulnerabilities within web applications [11, 4]. For example, both open-source and commercial scanners [11] are used to identify input validation vulnerabilities. [10] is similar to our work in the crawling stage to achieve better coverage. However, it aims to address input validation vulnerabilities by leveraging existing fuzzing techniques. To date, very few works (i.e., [2], [20], [14]) target at discovery of logic vulnerabilities. The main challenge is how to extract the application specification in a general and automated manner, without human efforts and the access of source code. NoTamper [2] targets one specific vulnerability: parameter tampering, which is introduced by the inconsistencies of web form checking between the client side and the server side. Payet et al. [20] discover Execution After Redirection (EAR) vulnerability by analyzing the information leaked through received redirection headers. In comparison, the access control vulnerabilities we focus on in this paper cover both parameter tampering and EAR. In addition, our technique not only covers the vulnerabilities behind web forms, but also the links that can be forcefully browsed. Though LogicScope [14] does not require the source code, it relies on the server-side session variables to construct the application specification. In addition, LogicScope cannot identify EAR. Since it only observes web requests and responses, tampering the integrity of the database is not necessarily reflected within web responses. In contrast, our technique does not require session variables and covers EAR. More importantly, our technique can address second-order data access constraint, which is not addressed in the above existing works.

White-box Analysis. Our work shares the same objective with several existing works targeting logic flaws through analyzing application source code (e.g., [1], [12], [3], [25]). Sun et al. [25] perform role-based analysis to identify missing security checks for accessing privileged files within PHP web applications. RoleCast [22] regards SQL statements that affect the database state (i.e., INSERT, DELETE, UPDATE) as sensitive operations and identifies missing access control checks on sensitive operations for each role. Their follow-up work FixMeUp [23] leverages a user-specified policy to generate candidate repairs. Doupe et al. [9] only target EAR vulnerability within Ruby web applications. Similar to No-Tamper, WAPTEC [3] focuses on the inconsistencies of web form checking between the client side and the server side. Waler [12] leverages model checking to identify the inconsistencies of invariant checks along different execution paths in JSP applications. Our work is significantly different from the above works from two aspects. First, most of the above techniques target only one specific vulnerability and cannot be easily extended to handle other forms of access control flaws. Our technique is designed to be general and cover a broad range of access control flaws. Specifically, we consider both READ and MODIFY operations on database objects as sensitive operations and design tests to cover both role-level and user-level authorization breaches, no matter they are caused by missing access control checks or futile reactions of failed checks (i.e., EAR). Second, all the above techniques are language-dependent, while our work does not require the application source code and can be applied to different development languages and platforms, as demonstrated in the evaluation section.

Runtime Detection. Our work is also related with several existing works (e.g., [8],[19], [6], [13], [15], [26]), which aim to detect attacks that exploit the application's access control mechanism at runtime. A key difference between our technique and all the above works is that all these runtime detection techniques require instrumenting the application infrastructure and introduce runtime performance overhead. Instead of detecting and stopping the attacks, our work aims to assist developers in discovering and fixing security flaws, so that the application can be immune to the exploits. This requires one additional challenging task beyond understanding the application specification, which is to construct concretes test inputs to exploit the application. Several of these works also perform specification inference (e.g., [6], [13], [15]). However, none of the specification inference techniques presented in these works can cover the range

of access control flaws in a purely black-box way. Specifically, BLOCK [13] can not cover MODIFY operation; SENTINEL [15] can not cover READ operation; and both of them require session variable information for specification inference.

7. CONCLUSION

In this paper, we present an automated black-box technique for inferring the access control policy and identifying access control flaws within web applications. We implement a prototype system BATMAN and evaluate it over a set of open source web applications. The experiment results demonstrate that our approach is accurate and effective and can be applied across different languages and platforms.

8. ACKNOWLEDGMENTS

This work was supported by NSF TRUST (The Team for Research in Ubiquitous Secure Technology) Science and Technology Center (CCF-0424422).

9. REFERENCES

[1] D. Balzarotti, M. Cova, V. Felmetsger, and G. Vigna. Multi-module vulnerability analysis of web-based applications. In *CCS'07: Proceedings of the 14th ACM conference on Computer and communications security*, pages 25–35, 2007.

[2] P. Bisht, T. Hinrichs, N. Skrupsky, R. Bobrowicz, and V. N. Venkatakrishnan. NoTamper: Automatic Blackbox Detection of Parameter Tampering Opportunities in Web Applications. In *CCS'10: Proceedings of the 17th ACM conference on Computer and communications security*, pages 607–618, 2010.

[3] P. Bisht, T. Hinrichs, N. Skrupsky, and V. Venkatakrishnan. WAPTEC: Whitebox Analysis of Web Applications for Parameter Tampering Exploit Construction. In *CCS'11: Proceedings of the 18th ACM conference on Computer and communications security*, pages 575–586, 2011.

[4] P. Chapman and D. Evans. Automated black-box detection of side-channel vulnerabilities in web applications. In *Proceedings of the 18th ACM conference on Computer and communications security*, CCS '11, pages 263–274, 2011.

[5] Clover. http://www.atlassian.com/software/clover/overview.

[6] M. Cova, D. Balzarotti, V. Felmetsger, and G. Vigna. Swaddler: An Approach for the Anomaly-based Detection of State Violations in Web Applications. In *RAID'07: Proceedings of the 10th International Symposium on Recent Advances in Intrusion Detection*, pages 63–86, 2007.

[7] Crawljax. http://crawljax.com/.

[8] M. Dalton, C. Kozyrakis, and N. Zeldovich. Nemesis: Preventing authentication and access control vulnerabilities in web applications. In *USENIX'09: Proceedings of the 18th conference on USENIX security symposium*, pages 267–282, 2009.

[9] A. Doupé, B. Boe, C. Kruegel, , and G. Vigna. Fear the EAR: Discovering and Mitigating Execution After Redirect Vulnerabilities. In *CCS'11: Proceeding of the 18th ACM Conference on Computer and Communications Security*, 2011.

[10] A. Doupé, L. Cavedon, C. Kruegel, and G. Vigna. Enemy of the state: A state-aware black-box web vulnerability scanner. In *Proceedings of the 21st USENIX conference on Security symposium*, Security'12, pages 26–26, 2012.

[11] A. Doupe, M. Cova, and G. Vigna. Why Johnny Can't Pentest: An Analysis of Black-box Web Vulnerability Scanners. In *DIMVA'10: Proceedings of the 7th Conference on Detection of Intrusions and Malware and Vulnerability Assessment*, pages 111–131, 2010.

[12] V. Felmetsger, L. Cavedon, C. Kruegel, and G. Vigna. Toward Automated Detection of Logic Vulnerabilities in Web Applications. In *USENIX'10: Proceedings of the 19th conference on USENIX Security Symposium*, pages 143–160, 2010.

[13] X. Li and Y. Xue. BLOCK: A Black-box Approach for Detection of State Violation Attacks Towards Web Applications. In *ACSAC'11: Proceedings of 27th Annual Computer Security Applications Conference*, pages 247–256, 2011.

[14] X. Li and Y. Xue. LogicScope: Automatic Discovery of Logic Vulnerabilities within Web Applications. In *ASIACCS '13: 8th ACM Symposium on Information, Computer and Communications Security*, 2013.

[15] X. Li, W. Yan, and Y. Xue. SENTINEL: Securing Database from Logic Flaws in Web Applications. In *CODASPY '12: Proceedings of the second ACM conference on Data and Application Security and Privacy*, pages 25–36, 2012.

[16] MySQL Proxy. http://dev.mysql.com/doc/refman/5.0/en/mysql-proxy.html.

[17] OWASP Top Ten Project 2013 Report. https://www.owasp.org/index.php/Top_10_2013-Top_10.

[18] OWASP WebScarab Project. https://www.owasp.org/index.php/category:owasp_webscarab_project.

[19] B. Parno, J. M. McCune, D. Wendlandt, D. G. Andersen, and A. Perrig. CLAMP: Practical prevention of large-scale data leaks. In *Oakland'09: Proceedings of the 30th IEEE Symposium on Security and Privacy*, 2009.

[20] P. Payet, A. Doupé, C. Kruegel, and G. Vigna. EARs in the Wild: Large-Scale Analysis of Execution After Redirect Vulnerabilities. In *Proceedings of the ACM Symposium on Applied Computing (SAC)*, Coimbra, Portugal, March 2013.

[21] SeleniumHQ: Web Application Testing System. http://seleniumhq.org/.

[22] S. Son, K. S. McKinley, and V. Shmatikov. Rolecast: Finding missing security checks when you do not know what checks are. In *OOPSLA '11: Proceedings of the 26th Annual ACM SIGPLAN Conference on Object-Oriented Programming, Systems, Languages, and Applications*, pages 1069–1084, 2011.

[23] S. Son, K. S. McKinley, and V. Shmatikov. Fix Me Up: Repairing Access-Control Bugs in Web Applications. In *NDSS'13: Proceedings of the 20th Annual Network and Distributed System Security Symposium*, 2013.

[24] Spike PHPCoverage. http://phpcoverage.sourceforge.net/.

[25] F. Sun, L. Xu, and Z. Su. Static Detection of Access Control Vulnerabilities in Web Applications. In *USENIX'11: Proceedings of the 20th USENIX Security Symposium*, pages 11–11, 2011.

[26] L. Xing, Y. Chen, X. Wang, and S. Chen. InteGuard: Toward Automatic Protection of Third-Party Web Service Integrations. In *NDSS'13: Proceedings of the 20th Annual Network and Distributed System Security Symposium*, 2013.

PhishSafe: Leveraging Modern JavaScript API's for Transparent and Robust Protection

Bastian Braun
ISL, University of Passau
Passau, Germany
bb@sec.uni-passau.de

Martin Johns
SAP Research
Karlsruhe, Germany
martin.johns@sap.com

Johannes Koestler
University of Passau
Passau, Germany
koestler@fim.uni-passau.de

Joachim Posegga
ISL, University of Passau
Passau, Germany
jp@sec.uni-passau.de

ABSTRACT

The term "phishing" describes a class of social engineering attacks on authentication systems, that aim to steal the victim's authentication credential, e.g., the username and password. The severity of phishing is recognized since the mid-1990's and a considerable amount of attention has been devoted to the topic. However, currently deployed or proposed countermeasures are either incomplete, cumbersome for the user, or incompatible with standard browser technology. In this paper, we show how modern JavaScript API's can be utilized to build PhishSafe, a robust authentication scheme, that is immune against phishing attacks, easily deployable using the current browser generation, and requires little change in the end-user's interaction with the application. We evaluate the implementation and find that it is applicable to web applications with low efforts and causes no tangible overhead.

Categories and Subject Descriptors

K.6.5 [**MANAGEMENT OF COMPUTING AND INFORMATION SYSTEMS**]: Security and Protection

Keywords

Web Security; Phishing; Protection

1. INTRODUCTION

From a security point of view, passwords are a terrible choice for authentication. They are easily stolen. Often, they are easy to guess, due to the fact that they were chosen in a fashion that allows the user to remember them (e.g., names of pets, children, or cars). And they are frequently

reused, causing the compromise of one server to probably affect several independent applications as well.

However, it is an unrealistic assumption, that we will reach a situation, in which password-based authentication looses its significance, even in the presence of well designed password-less techniques, such as client-side SSL authentication, and promising new developments, such as Mozilla Persona [30].

Unlike all alternatives, the user's requirements to utilize password authentication are extremely light-weight: All she needs to logon, is to remember her username and password. Password-less authentication systems either require preconfigured state on the device, such as installed client-side certificates, the presence of specific hardware, such as smart card readers, or the possession of additional items, e.g., a cell phone to obtain out-of-band credentials [15].

This characteristic of password authentication is even amplified in the presence of web applications: The only remaining software requirement is, that on the utilized computer a web browser is installed, something that can be taken for granted since several years. Hence, no matter in which situation a user is, as long as she remembers her password and has a networked device with a web browser at her disposal, she is able to access her applications. No other system for networked applications offers similar properties. It can even be argued that the ease of password authentication was one of the success-factors of the web.

However, the passwords' strength – their ease of use – is also their biggest weakness: As easily they are entered, as easily they are stolen, in case that a used password field is actually under the control of the attacker.

In variants, this class of attack, known under the term *phishing*, is probably as old as the discipline of password authentication itself, having its roots in social engineering attacks [29]. The severity of phishing is recognized since the mid-1990's and a considerable amount of attention has been devoted to the topic. However, as we will show in Section 2, currently deployed or proposed countermeasures are either incomplete, cumbersome for the user, or incompatible with standard browser technology.

In this paper, we present *PhishSafe,* a light-weight approach that provides robust security guarantees, even in case that the user's password was successfully stolen. The core of our approach is a transparent browser-personalization process, that is invisible to the user. This way, unlike the majority of existing anti-phishing approaches, *PhishSafe* does not burden the user with altered authentication interaction or additional burdens, such as recognizing security indicators or visual authenticity clues. On the contrary: As long as a user predominately uses only a single browser, she won't notice a difference to the currently established, insecure scheme.

Paper Organization

The remainder of this paper is structured as follows: The next section provides an in-depth discussion of phishing attack vectors, current solutions and their shortcomings, and the user as the weakest link in phishing protection as well as a definition of the attacker models considered in this paper. Section 3 presents the concept of PhishSafe, our authentication scheme to overcome phishing attacks. Section 4 describes the implementation of PhishSafe and provides technical details. The evaluation is given in Section 5. Section 6 discusses related work before Section 7 concludes.

2. PHISHING ATTACKS

While phishing attacks have a long history, phishing activity has not decreased over time (see Fig. 2). The attackers' strategy, however, has changed to counter the anti-phishing means in use, for instance, phishing sites move faster to prevent blacklisting (see Fig. 1). In this section, we describe modern phishing attack methods, model the attackers' capabilities, evaluate proposed anti-phishing solutions, and analyze why those solutions have not significantly reduced phishing activities.

2.1 Attack Method

The Anti-Phishing Working Group (APWG)[1] states that phishing schemes use "spoofed e-mails purporting to be from legitimate businesses and agencies, designed to lead consumers to counterfeit websites that trick recipients into divulging financial data such as usernames and passwords." [45] Attackers usually send emails or personal instant messages and put pressure on the recipients to perform actions intended by the attacker. For instance, recipients are told that their email quota is reached, their credit card is disabled, or an invoice has not been paid. Usually, to increase the pressure and omit a reconsideration, immediate steps are allegedly necessary. These steps require logging into an account on a website. In this scenario, attackers know the target business. All they need to do is copy the public design of the website and send bulk emails. In order to educate customers, anti-phishing campaigns published rules of conduct. For example, users are advised to not click on links embedded in emails if the link does not include the expected domain of the (seeming) sender. As another rule of thumb, reliable emails contain the recipient's name and maybe other personal information which is supposedly not known to a phisher.

The following attack vectors emerged in the past and illustrate the ongoing arms race between phishers and the anti-phishing community.

2.1.1 Concealing the Target Domain

In order to answer the anti-phishing suggestions, phishers took measures to make embedded links look familiar to the

---

[1] `http://www.apwg.org/`

user. These measures range from open redirects on the target website, over URLs featuring a target domain prefix and URL shorteners hiding the target, up to malicious relying parties in single sign-on protocols.

Open Redirects First of all, a phisher's chance is considerably higher if the link the victim is supposed to click appears to belong to the expected domain. In that sense, an attacker can succeed if he finds an open redirect function on the target web application. Web applications redirect their users for several reasons: when a requested web page is not found (HTTP 404), users are redirected to a landing page that explains what happened. Webmail providers redirect their customers via 'de-referrers' to avoid that the actual URL of the read email appears as a part of the subsequent request to the foreign domain (in the `Referrer` header). Open redirects do not sanitize their input, i.e., the redirect target and source. Given that the attacker prepared a phishing site for `example.com` that has an open redirect, he can send out emails asking users to click on `https://www.example.com/redirect?target=example-attack.com`. A better masking is possible by URL encoding the target parameter. Finally, the victim sees an `https` link to the expected domain and can eventually check the SSL lock on `https://www.example-attack.com` but is attacked, though.

Confusing URLs Second, it is often sufficient to make the URL appear innocent at a first glance.

Non-expert users can hardly distinguish between the host, domain, and path elements of a URL. Phishers exploit this weakness crafting links like `https://www.example.com.attacker-domain.com` which seem to contain the expect domain name `example.com`. Similar approaches include typos in the URL, e.g. `https://www.gooogle.com`.

A more sophisticated attack is known as international domain name (IDN) homograph attack [14]. This attack makes use of so-called homographs, characters from non-latin alphabets that are indistinguishable for humans but interpreted by browsers as different symbols.

URL Shorteners The emerging trend towards URL shorteners, that save characters on Twitter and prevent line breaks in emails, makes people familiar with short URLs and redirects to unpredictable URLs. Attackers exploit that people are more used to click on links from `bit.ly`, `tinyurl.com`, `is.gd`, or `goo.gl` than on links containing unknown domains. If the target website looks convincing enough, the user's focus is caught on the content [52].

Malicious Relying Parties Single sign-on (SSO) protocols require the user to log in once with her identity provider to obtain access to all related accounts. If the user first visits a relying party, she is redirected to her identity provider. A malicious relying party can redirect the user to a phishing identity provider to request the user's credentials.

2.1.2 Spear Phishing

Spear Phishing denotes a particular phishing attack vector that targets a set of victims the attacker has information about. While this attack is restricted to those users the attacker could gain knowledge about, it can still hit thousands of users. The first step in a common scenario is a data leak of a company's customer database. In most cases, there is a laxer security policy in place if the database does not contain critical data like passwords, social security numbers, or credit card information. Using the obtained data, however, an attacker can address his victims personally including the name, correct email address, and account number which used to be an indicator of a benign message.

2.1.3 Browser-less Phishing

A phisher can circumvent browser-based countermeasures if the user does not use her browser to follow his instructions. As a matter of fact, users regularly experience that colleagues or friends quickly ask for information by email or instant messenger. Phishers convey the notion of this scenario to make their victims reply with the credentials.

2.2 Attacker Models

In order to estimate a phishing attacker's capabilities, we define two attackers. These attackers define the scope of our work, i.e., we present existing approaches against these kinds of attackers in Section 2.3 and propose PhishSafe, our countermeasure, in Section 3.

We consider a *phishing attacker* as a remote web participant. He is able to set up websites and email accounts, can send emails and messages via instant messengers (IMs). He can obtain valid SSL certificates for his domains. We do not assume timing constraints, i.e., he can react immediately on any input at all time.

Moreover, we consider an *XSS attacker*. He has all capabilities of the phishing attacker but can also inject JavaScript code into vulnerable web pages.

Neither of both has control over the user's platform nor over the network. We neglect browser vulnerabilities and respective exploits. Also, they can not break cryptography.

2.3 Current Solutions

Several approaches have been applied so far to mitigate phishing attacks. In this section, we name them and explain their strengths and weaknesses. We find that they are either incomplete, cumbersome for the user, or incompatible with standard browser technology.

2.3.1 Incomplete Countermeasures

One class of countermeasures suffers from incompleteness in terms of false positives and false negatives, i.e., they do not protect against phishing on some sites and prevent access to genuine sites suspected to phishing.

Browser vendors, e.g. Microsoft[2] and Google[3], as well as third parties, e.g. PhishTank[4], provide lists of malicious and genuine websites. Browsers query their list upon accessing a website and check whether this site is known for phishing. The blacklists suffer from a window of vulnerability between the setup of a phishing site and its listing [43]. This window can be decreased by real-time queries towards the list providers for each unknown domain. The additional online query slows down page loading and reveals almost the complete browsing history to the list providers. List providers went over to classify websites automatically to capture phishing sites earlier [51], however, at the expense of accuracy, i.e., more false positives and false negatives [25]. The extraction of features from phishing sites provoked an arms race between phishers, who have a financial interest

[2] http://windows.microsoft.com/en-US/windows-vista/
Phishing-Filter-frequently-asked-questions
[3] https://support.google.com/chrome/answer/99020?
hl=en
[4] http://www.phishtank.com/

in passing those filters, and the blacklist providers. Among other features, phishers reduce the uptimes of their sites (see Figure 1) to make the blacklists come to nothing. The trend lasts and led to an average uptime of one day in 2012 leaving only very short reaction time to blacklist providers [44].

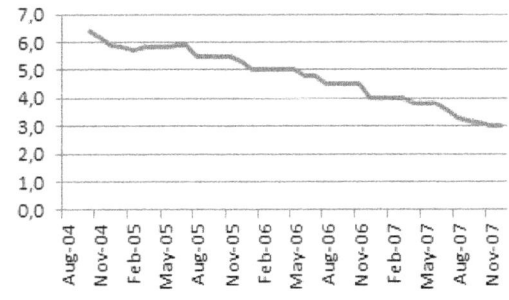

Figure 1: The Average Online Time of Phishing Sites in Days Between Oct '04 and Dec '07, the Time of Acquisition by the APWG, *src: Regular APWG Phishing Attack Trends Reports [46]*

2.3.2 Countermeasures Cumbersome for the User

Another class of approaches makes use of the increasing propagation of mobile devices. Users need to enter a second credential that is either received or generated by their mobile device in order to login or perform critical actions. This breaks their ongoing workflow as they need to switch to a different device. Example implementations include Google Authenticator [15] and one-time passwords sent to cell phones. Beside the fact that malware now also targets mobile devices to intercept received tokens [8], both approaches can not help against our attacker models (see above) because the attacker only needs to wait for the victim to enter her credentials and relay all gathered user data to the actual web application in real time. This way, the user serves as an oracle that provides the needed information. In this scenario, the attacker plays the role of a man in the middle without manipulation on the network layer.

Client-side SSL aims at replacing username/password-based logins. Though SSL could overcome most of currently known weaknesses in knowledge-based authentication, it has not become popular probably due to its setup complexity for non-expert users. Finally, SSL certificates are hardly portable. A user can login to web accounts from every device using an off-the-shelf browser and her password. It is rather difficult to store, carry, and use an SSL certificate securely on an untrusted computer.

2.3.3 Countermeasures Incompatible with Standard Browser Technology

A family of approaches extends the user's browser [21, 39, 56, 6, 55, 53, 37, 17, 47, 3, 38, 27, 2, 57, 41] (see Section 6 for details). Browser extensions and toolbars share a number of drawbacks:

- They provide no protection by default but only protect risk-aware users after installation.
- They are inherently incompatible with standard browser technology and can only protect users of supported browsers while porting them to other browsers is hard. [35]

- The majority of browser-based solutions aims at detecting phishing websites while accessed. However, most users ignore issued warnings and more rely on the web content to estimate a website's authenticity. [52]
- Browser toolbars, that classify websites into phishing and harmless, are susceptible to false positives and false negatives, i.e. letting phishing sites pass while warning of genuine sites. Case studies showed that a high detection rate often comes with a high false positive rate. [59]
- Phishing is a particular problem on mobile devices while existing approaches are hard to port because of the limited screen size. [12]
- Phishers can evade most browser-based protection approaches by asking victims to reply by email to their inquiry.

2.3.4 Summary

We can conclude that the existing approaches still leave room for phishing attacks. None of the current solutions offers thorough protection for all users. The volatile number of active phishing sites reflect the ongoing arms race between phishers and anti-phishing blacklist providers (see Figure 2). The more stable number of phishing campaigns shows the unabated activity of phishers over a long period. Matters are complicated by more targeted spear phishing attacks which are harder to detect by generic features than common large-scale attacks.

Emerging consumer-oriented SSO protocols like Mozilla Persona [30], OpenID [36], and OAuth [33] decrease the user's attack surface. Nevertheless, they still require user logins with the identity provider and, thus, cannot remedy phishing attacks. SAML [24] and Shibboleth [20] target business environments and require a higher level of coordination between participants, thus, are more suitable for closed application scenarios. We provide more details in Section 6.3.

2.4 The Weakest Link: The User

After analyzing existing countermeasures and modern attack vectors, we identify the user as the weakest link. We find that phishing attacks abuse the user's misconception concerning her communication partner in the World Wide Web. Transferred to the physical world, a phishing attacker would set up a storefront that looks familiar to many people. In the virtual world of the World Wide Web, the attacker can succeed much easier for several reasons: First of all, the user has no personal reference point in terms of location. Informally speaking, she does not know where she actually is. Most users are not familiar with domains and URLs, and even if they were, they could still be misled by exploiting weaknesses in the Domain Name System (DNS spoofing, pharming). The international domain name (IDN) homograph attack [14] even deceived skilled security experts.

Second, users learned to assess a person's trustworthiness. While this assessment can be manipulated, there is hardly any natural feeling of trustworthiness with respect to programs and machines nor do reliable indicators help. Existing approaches focus on proving an email's (e.g. DKIM [4], SenderID [28]) or a website's (e.g. https) trustworthiness but not the opposite, i.e. in an attack scenario, they do not provide any helpful hint. Teaching users to check SSL indicators inspired phishing attackers to spoof those indicators or ob-

tain valid certificates for similar domains, e.g. `gooogle.com`. Such indicators are missing on most mobile devices due to the limited screen size [32]. The opposite approach – warning users instead of indicating trustworthiness – made users being annoyed and ignore such warnings [9], because users want to make things happen and not think about security, so they do whatever is asked for in even unusual emails [7]. Attackers increase their chances by threatening their victims, for example, announcing bad consequences like blocking an email account or disabling the credit card. This strategy prevents that users contemplate on the message's reliability.

Third, automation allows large-scale attacks making the efforts worthwhile. The intention to classify phishing attempts led to an arms race meaning that attacks evolve and require new features to detect phishing [13].

To sum up, we conclude that the user must not play a decisive role in phishing protection nor can the user behavior be supposed to change. An algorithmic approach is needed to rule out phishing attacks.

3. PHISHSAFE

In this section, we describe the idea of our authentication scheme, named PhishSafe, that avoids the drawbacks identified in Sec. 2. Section 4 gives details of the implementation.

3.1 Design Goals

Following the lessons learned from previous approaches and current phishing techniques (see Sec. 2), we phrase the following design goals for PhishSafe: It

- sidesteps the arms race between phishers and the anti-phishing community,
- reduces reliance on the user,
- avoids dependence on the browser's interface,
- waives the need for additional devices and the installation of protective tools, and
- withstands the attackers defined in Section 2.2.

Our design goals are in parts inspired by Parno et al. [34] (see Section 6). In the remainder of this section, we motivate our design goals in more detail.

Sidestep the arms race between phishers and the anti-phishing community It is important to quit the arms race with financially motivated phishers that are always one step ahead. The anti-phishing community can only react on new phishing techniques while phishers update their features again.

Reduce reliance on the user We showed in Section 2.4 that the user is the weakest link in phishing scenarios. Hence, a reliable countermeasure must not rely on the user. Instead, it must tolerate that the user can be tricked and gives away all credentials she knows.

Avoid dependence on the browser's interface Approaches relying on the browser's interface either require the installation of additional software (e.g., toolbars or extension, thus, excluding users of not supported browsers or platforms) or can be spoofed using JavaScript or a favicon (e.g., simulating an SSL lock symbol). The interface is even hidden on mobile devices due to the limited screen size.

Waive the need for additional devices and the installation of protective tools The need for second devices makes processes more complex and requires considerable changes of the used logon procedure. Those devices must be always at hand, secure, and have a direct connection to the browser to transfer control. Obtaining passcodes

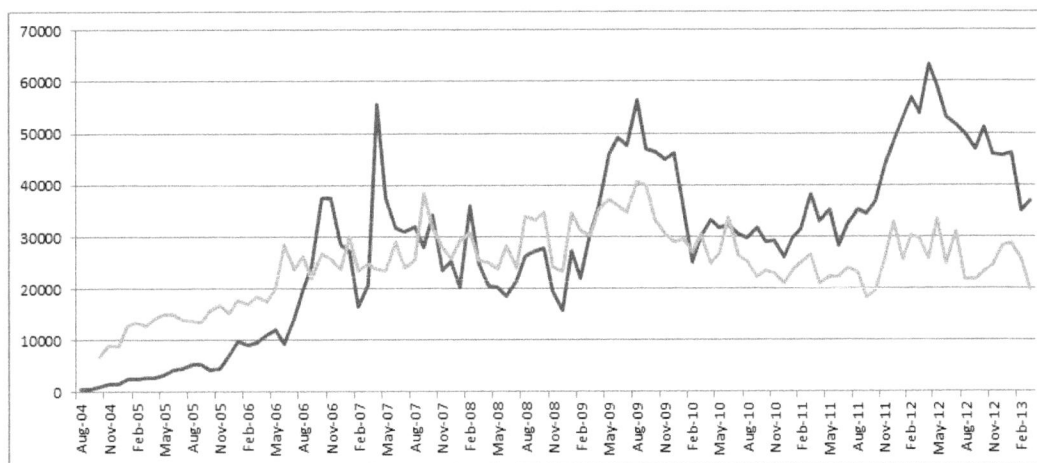

Figure 2: Phishing Statistics Since Aug. 2004 in Terms of Active Phishing Sites (dark grey) and Email Phishing Campaigns (pale grey), *src: Anti-Phishing Working Group (APWG) Reports [46]*

from a second device is not an option because these can be phished and exploited.

The usage of protective software is always limited to risk-aware users utilizing a supported platform.

Withstand the attackers defined in Section 2.2 We modeled the attackers according to realistic assumptions. So, a reliable approach must provide protection against their attacks.

3.2   High-Level Overview

The main idea of PhishSafe is to release the user from responsibility: she neither needs to perform special actions nor check security indicators nor keep a secret other than her password. Instead, she will use a second factor she does not know and, thus, can not disclose to a phisher. This factor is stored in her browser and attached to logins towards the genuine web application. The web application prohibits logins without proper second factor authentication. An attacker luring his victim on a phishing site can obtain her password but not the second factor credential. However, the password alone is not enough to login. The second factor is established during account setup and, if necessary, restored after visiting a URL sent by email.

3.3   Detailed Authentication Process

As emphasized above, the authentication scheme implements two-factor authentication without the user knowing about it. In order to apply our authentication scheme, the website stores a secret token in the persistent web storage of the user's browser (see Sec. 3.4 for details). The user does not have to be aware of this token nor does she have to care. The important point is that this token is subject to the same-origin policy (SOP) [58] and not accessible to web applications on foreign domains.

When the user accesses the login page, a challenge string is invisibly included in the HTML form beside the username and password input fields. The page also embeds JavaScript code that computes the second factor credential from the challenge and the secret browser token using an HMAC function [23]. The second factor is then appended to the HTML form and transmitted to the web application together with the username and password. The web application verifies

the second factor by performing the same computation that happened in the browser. It denies access to the user account if the verification fails.

A phisher could lure the user into visiting his prepared page. Given that the user does not detect the attack, she enters her username and password and sends them to the attacker's site. Then, the attacker tries to log into the user's account exploiting the phished credentials. The web application, however, denies access because the necessary browser token is not available to compute the valid second factor.

There are scenarios where a browser is not only used by one user but at least two where both have an account on the same web application respectively, e.g., a family sharing one laptop (and OS account) or tablet PC. In this case, they would share the same browser token. This is also true for guests accessing the web application via this browser just once. We prevent such unintended sharing of the browser token by assigning it to the respective user account in the browser's storage, i.e., the second factor can only be computed if a browser token associated with the given username is found.

3.4   Browser Enrollment

The idea how PhishSafe proceeds has been described above. What remains is PhishSafe's bootstrapping, i.e., the process that establishes the token in the user's browser. There are two options when the token is stored: during account setup or, afterwards, whenever the user logs in from a previously unknown browser.

The web application can set a token during the registration process unless the user opts out, e.g., because she uses a friend's device. After the user chooses username and password, the token is stored in the browser's web storage.

3.4.1   Restoring the Browser Token

We assume that account information includes the user's email address and leverage this as a second channel for token installation. Given that the user uses more than one device to access the web application, changes her browser, reinstalls her operating system or firmware, or just deletes the browser's web storage for privacy reasons, she needs an opportunity to restore her browser token. The password

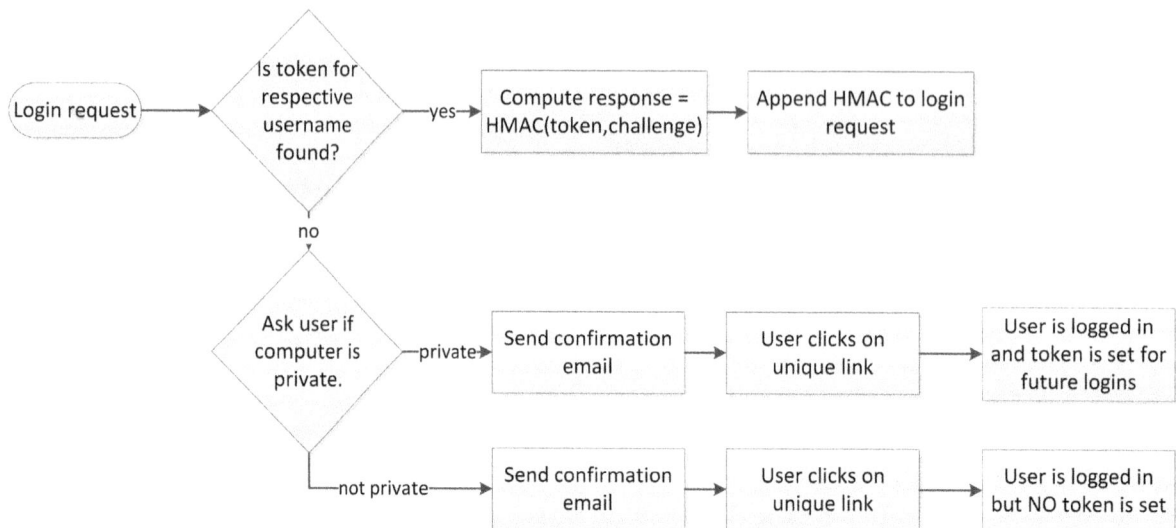

Figure 3: Authentication Token Logic

alone is insufficient because the attacker can learn it and so use it to equip his browser with a valid token.

Usual second authentication tokens are not sufficient, either. Examples for this class are apps or devices that issue two-step verification numbers, e.g. Google Authenticator [15] and RSA SecurID [10], as well as one-time passcodes sent to the cell phone or by email. A phishing attacker could lure the victim on his page and at the same time request the original login page. When the victim provides her password, he forwards it and is prompted with an input field for the second authentication step. Then, he leads his victim to believe that her browser token needs to be reset and requests the same authentication credential that he is supposed to enter. Finally, he only needs to forward the user's second factor credential to finally own the password and the browser token. Note that this attack even works with passcodes sent to the user's cell phone because the application indeed sends such a code to the user (upon the attacker's request). We believe that receiving the code makes the actual phishing attack even more credible. The attacker acts as a man in the middle.

Our authentication scheme uses complete URLs that must be clicked (or copied and pasted to the browser) by the user. When the user enters her username and password on the login page but no respective browser token is found, the web application sends a confirmation email to her account. The email contains a unique URL that must be accessed within the same session context as the login request. In the attack scenario described above, the attacker's login attempt triggers the email confirmation. However, if the user clicks on the provided link, she accesses the real web application but not the phishing page. At that point, the attack becomes detectable for the web application because the session context does not match. The attacker never obtains the necessary input to obtain a valid browser token.

3.4.2 One-Time Account Access

Finally, the user might use a public computer to access the web application. So, a persistent credential in the browser's web storage is not appropriate. For this reason, Phish-Safe also provides one-time access. The only difference to

the above described browser token reset is that no token is stored. After the user enters her username and password and no browser token for this username is found, she is asked if she is using a public computer or if she trusts all users of this computer and uses it regularly. In both cases, the web application sends an email with a unique URL. However, if the user requests the URL from a public computer, no browser token is set and access to the account is granted only once. The token handling logic is given in Fig. 3.

3.5 Protection against the XSS Attacker

The authentication process described above perfectly protects against the phishing attacker (see Sec. 2.2). The XSS attacker, however, could inject JavaScript code that is executed within the same domain context as the web application. This allows him to read the browser's web storage and obtain the secret browser token. For this reason, we move the token and all related computations to a secure subdomain. Given that the actual web application runs on `www.example.com`, a subdomain, e.g., `auth.example.com`, is responsible to handle and store the secure browser token. This subdomain only contains static JavaScript dedicated to this task and nothing else. Based on this, we consider well audited and XSS-free code to be feasible. An HTML document served from the subdomain and embedded into the main web application as an invisible iframe contains the JavaScript code. This way, we leverage the guarantees provided by the same-origin policy [58] and the postMessage API [50] to prohibit access by the XSS attacker to the browser token while enabling controlled interaction between the web application and the secure subdomain.

Hence, the challenge appended to the login form is submitted to the secure subdomain via JavaScript and the postMessage API. The code of the subdomain computes the HMAC of the challenge using the browser token. The HMAC is then sent back to the original document and attached to the subsequent login request (see Fig. 4). Please note that all this communication happens within the browser.

4. IMPLEMENTATION

The implementation of our proposed authentication scheme comprises three interacting components: the *TokenManager* handles the browser token in the secure subdomain, the *Authenticator* assembles necessary input for the login, and the server-side *AccountManager* fits into legacy or new web applications in order to handle browser challenges and responses.

4.1 Client-side Components

We first describe the client-side components, the TokenManager that is loaded in the iframe from the secure subdomain and the Authenticator that delivers the web application's challenge to the TokenManager and appends the retrieved response to the HTML login form.

4.1.1 The TokenManager

The TokenManager implements the necessary functions to fetch the browser token, compute the HMAC of the token and the web application's challenge, and return an error message if no token is found. It runs in the domain context of a secure subdomain. We use the CryptoJS[5] library as an implementation of the cryptographic functions.

The TokenManager uses the browser's `localStorage` part of the web storage [18]. Web storage is supported by all major browsers on mobile and desktop platforms which makes our authentication scheme platform and browser independent. The localStorage is persistent, i.e., it is not cleared on a regular basis as the `sessionStorage` is. The storage is limited in size per origin between 5 and 25 Mbytes depending on the browser which, however, is far more than necessary for our purposes. Web storage is meant for pairs of identifiers and values where both must be strings. More complex data structures can be stored as JSON objects [5] that are easily converted to string and back. The TokenManager uses JSON to store the username and the associated browser token.

The communication interface of the TokenManager is restricted to a function that expects a challenge and a username as input and provides an HMAC as the output (see Fig. 4). The Authenticator's direct access to the subdomain's localStorage is prohibited by the same-origin policy [58]. So, the Authenticator needs to use the JavaScript `postMessage` API [50] that enables two web documents in a browser to communicate across origin boundaries in a secure manner. A `postMessage(msg, target)` call expects a message string and the target origin as parameters. The receiving document needs to register an event handler to receive a message. The triggered event comes with additional metadata provided by the browser, e.g., the origin of the sender. This allows the receiver,i.e., the TokenManager, to carefully check the sender's authenticity.

4.1.2 The Authenticator

The HTML login form contains two additional hidden fields for PhishSafe: `AuthChallenge` and `AuthResponse`. The first contains the web application's challenge, the second is initially blank. The Authenticator reads the challenge and the user's username from the input field. It passes both arguments to the TokenManager and reads back the answer. The answer either contains the computed HMAC or an error. In

---

[5] http://code.google.com/p/crypto-js/

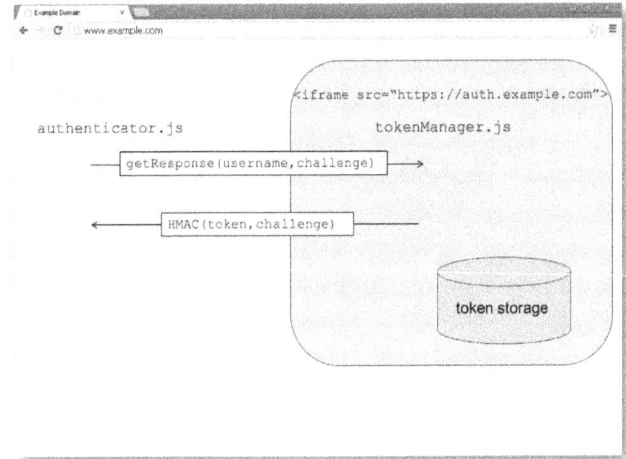

Figure 4: Domain-Isolated Token Storage

the success case, the Authenticator rewrites the login form's `AuthResponse` field to append the response. It prompts the user if the TokenManager reported that no browser token was found (see Fig. 5).

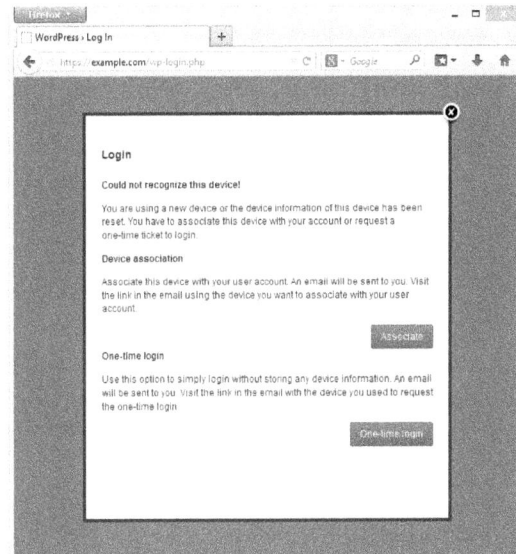

Figure 5: User Prompt If No Browser Token Is Found

4.2 Server-side Component

The server-side part of PhishSafe consists of a single component, the AccountManager.

4.2.1 The AccountManager

The AccountManager implements the server-side part of our authentication scheme. We equipped WordPress with the AccountManager as a plugin. The integration required only reasonable efforts and no changes of the application code due to the modular architecture of WordPress together with the hooking feature. We consider the integration into modular or new web applications as an easy task while necessary efforts might be bigger for non-modular legacy applications.

The AccountManager issues the user's browser token and adds the invisible iframe and the Authenticator to the web application's login page. It generates a new challenge for every user login, adds the `AuthChallenge` and `AuthResponse` fields to the HTML login form, and checks incoming login requests for valid responses.

The XSS attacker could inject a payload that reads the user's username, password, and the returned HMAC for authentication. Having all this information, he can log into the web application without a valid browser token. For this reason, the AccountManager sets a cookie in the user's browser. This cookie has a random value that is saved by the AccountManager together with the user's current challenge. Only login requests that carry this cookie and the valid response are processed. The cookie has the `HttpOnly` and the `Secure` flags set to prevent it from being read by the attacker's payload or during plain `http` transport.

4.2.2 Security Configuration

Though it is not part of our attacker model, we leverage two more modern security features to shelter from SSL stripping [26] and pharming [49] attacks. A man-in-the-middle attacker performing an SSL stripping attack could prevent the user's browser from using `https` and then read transmitted information or even inject code into the document loaded in the invisible iframe. A pharming attacker could serve own code on behalf of the abused web application and so bypass the same-origin policy. Both attackers could hijack the secure browser token.

To overcome these attacks, the AccountManager adds HTTP Strict Transport Security (HSTS) [19] and Public Key Pinning (PKP) [11] policy headers to the web application's HTTP responses. HSTS makes sure that the browser only contacts the website using `https`. There is an inherent bootstrapping problem before the first request, i.e., the website must ensure that the browser eventually receives the HSTS header. Google Chromium and Mozilla Firefox overcome this problem using a static list of pre-defined domains[6]. The PKP policy prevents that a pharming attacker presents his own certificate. After receiving the policy header, the browser only accepts SSL certificates with the pinned public key.

5. EVALUATION

We evaluate the security properties of our authentication scheme and validate our design goals from Section 3.1.

5.1 Security Evaluation

We first explain how far PhishSafe protects users against the attackers defined in Section 2.2. Then, we give details of further security properties, and finally, we identify open issues of the proposed scheme.

5.1.1 The Phishing Attacker

The phishing attacker counterfeits the design of a web application in scope and lures victims. The latter can be done either by email or by links and ads on other websites. In any case, our proposed authentication scheme does not prevent a victim from accessing the phishing page. However,

the information the phisher can obtain is not sufficient to abuse the user's account because the web application denies access if no valid response is appended to the login request.

5.1.2 The XSS Attacker

The XSS attacker differs from the phishing attacker in his ability to execute JavaScript code on vulnerable domains. For instance, the XSS attacker could perform a reflected XSS attack by sending a specially crafted link via email or IM. The injected payload can read the username, password, the current challenge for login and the respective response if a browser token is stored in the browser. However, we assumed that the attacker can not break cryptography, thus, he can not compute the browser token from the challenge and the response. The captured data is still insufficient because it lacks the related cookie which is inaccessible to JavaScript. Finally, we consider the task to develop invulnerable static code for the secure subdomain feasible such that there is no attack vector for the XSS attacker.

5.1.3 Further Security Advantages

The proposed authentication approach comes with additional security features.

First of all, though running purely in the browser, the scheme thwarts email-based phishing attempts. Phishers try to evade browser-based protection by asking the victims to reply to their phishing emails and give credentials in the email. The obtained username and password, however, do not give an attacker access to the user's web account. We consider phishing for the browser token to be infeasible as it requires major efforts and advanced knowledge of a user to read the token from the browser's web storage.

Phishing attacks rely on unprepared users that disclose credentials. This general observation holds true for any kind of credentials a user may know. So, second authentication factors that must be entered by the user in a web form are inherently susceptible to phishing attacks, too. Examples include one-time passcodes sent to the user's cellphone or generated by apps. Our approach utilizes complete URLs to overcome second factor phishing. A user clicking on a link not only proves access and knowledge but is also directed to the right web application.

5.1.4 Open Issues

Next, we emphasize on potential attacks on our authentication scheme.

Our approach relies on the security of the user's email account. The attacker can request and read the confirmation URL sent to the user if he has access to the email account and the user's credentials to the target web application. We are here in line with today's best practices for password reset as virtually all web applications offer email-based processes at least if no cell phone number is given or the attacker pretends the cell phone is stolen.

An email account can not be protected if the confirmation URL is sent to the same address. There are two options to make sure that the user can always access the confirmation URL: First, the user can provide an alternative email account where the confirmation URL is sent to. Second, the email provider can offer application-specific passwords[7]. These passwords are chosen by the provider and not remembered by the user. Instead, they are stored by client appli-

---

[6]http://www.chromium.org/sts

[7]https://support.google.com/accounts/answer/185833

cations to obtain access to the user's account. Given an application-specific password and an email client on a PC or mobile device, access to the confirmation URL is assured.

An attacker can try to acquire the confirmation URL sent to the user by making the user enter it into a prepared input field on the phishing site. The easiest way to avoid this is to make the user click on the link. Moreover, a highlighted warning in the email reduces the attacker's chances.

A window of vulnerability towards a pharming attacker remains before the first PKP header is received by the user's browser (see Section 4.2.1). As long as the browser did not pin the server's public key, a pharming attacker can present a spoofed certificate and submit malicious content. In the future, a similar pre-defined list of certificates might be implemented as it happened for HSTS.

Finally, though completely out of scope of our authentication scheme, fully fledged spyware can read and transmit the browser token. Less elaborate keyloggers, however, are ineffective because the browser token is never entered via the keyboard.

5.2 Validation of Design Goals

In this section, we evaluate the compliance of PhishSafe with the design goals given in Section 3.1.

Sidestep the arms race between phishers and the anti-phishing blacklist community: Our approach does not exploit features of phishing sites or emails for classification. So, there is no motivation for actions and reactions. In fact, we do not consider phishing activities at all but only hide some piece of information from phishers. We argued in the section above that phishers can hardly learn the browser token.

Reduce reliance on the user: The security of the approach barely relies on the user. She neither needs to enter her credentials only when a dedicated indicator is shown, nor does she need to remember additional credentials. In fact, the only change compared to her used workflow is the decision if a computer is trusted or not and the click on the confirmation link. The actual login procedure does not change at all on regularly used browsers.

Avoid dependence on the browser's interface: Phish-Safe does not depend on the browser's interface, nor does it change the browser's appearance. This feature not only avoids confusing the user but is one important aspect of cross-platform applicability (see below).

Waive the need for additional devices and the installation of protective tools PhishSafe only needs an off-the-shelf browser and neither relies on extensions, nor toolbars, nor third-party plug-ins, like Flash or Silverlight. A second device is also not necessary.

Withstand the attackers defined in Section 2.2 We showed in Section 5.1 that PhishSafe resists attacks by the phishing attacker and the XSS attacker.

Further points: PhishSafe runs on mobile as well as desktop browsers because all modern browsers support the WebStorage and postMessage APIs. It does not rely on visual indicators which makes it applicable on mobile devices with limited screen size.

PhishSafe can easily complement other approaches. If the browser maintains a blacklist of phishing sites, it can prevent that the user reveals her credentials. Approaches leveraging a secure password entry field to some degree also work to-

gether with PhishSafe even though details need to be sorted out.

6. RELATED WORK

There is a long history of approaches to overcome phishing attacks. We classify the existing body of work into three categories: approaches that augment the visible user interface with trust indicators (Sec. 6.1), approaches leveraging sophisticated authentication protocols to prevent that the real password is sent to the attacker (Sec. 6.2), single sign-on protocols (Sec. 6.3), and approaches aiming to distinguish between reliable and phishing sites (Sec. 6.4).

6.1 Augmenting the User Interface

A number of approaches tries to protect the user from phishing attempts using individual authenticity features. The overall goal is to ensure that the user enters her password only if a pre-shared symbol indicates trustworthiness. Basic approaches just embed personalized images in the login page [40, 48].

Other approaches require the installation of client-side extensions to tune the browser's user interface. They display custom names, logos, and the certification authority (CA) of the visited website [17], open personalized windows including user-defined pictures [6], combine images with custom names of websites [56], or use colored frames to indicate the website's trust level [53, 55].

This class of approaches burdens the user with challenging tasks, including

- remembering a visual authenticity feature [40, 48, 17, 56],
- tolerating adverse impacts on usability and browsing experience [53],
- passing complex setup processes, for instance, choosing site labels, master passwords, appropriate protection service providers, and finally start the protection feature by hand [56],
- manually maintaining a list of supporting sites and compare two displayed pictures to authenticate the server before login [6], and
- install a dedicated browser [55].

Finally, these approaches are not portable and require support by the server and the client, thus being subject to a chicken-and-egg problem.

6.2 Sophisticated Authentication Protocols

The second class of phishing mitigation approaches applies changes to the common username and password based authentication. The main goal is to not submit the password in plaintext to an unauthenticated remote server but mutually authenticate client and server [16, 42, 47], utilize a zero-knowledge protocol to avoid transmitting confidential information [22], check for user-specific knowledge that changes over time [31], use trusted second devices to establish an authenticated session [34], generate site-specific passwords from a seed [39], or use bookmarks as a secure entry point [1].

The implementation of non-standard authentication protocols by design requires effort on both communication parties for support. The user either needs to store and maintain a particular bookmark for every protected website [1], remember to activate protection before entering her credentials [39], install a plugin [47] or a browser toolbar and regularly verify that it is not spoofed [42], use a dedicated browser [22] or a second device that must be trustworthy but also able to establish a direct connection with the browser [34], or remember every past action with respect to this account [31], while some approaches are not implemented or practically evaluated [16].

6.3 Single Sign-On

A set of so-called single sign-on protocols aims at releasing the user from maintaining one unique password for each web account respectively, among them OpenID [36], Mozilla Persona [30] (aka BrowserID), SAML [24], and Shibboleth [20]. They allow a user to login once with a single authority in order to access several accounts at different providers.

The distributed authorization protocol OAuth [33] is used in some cases to log into third party web applications, too. A previous login with the provider, usually a social network, is required.

These protocols decrease credential management overhead caused by the trend of an increasing number of web accounts. Nevertheless, the user must log in once in order to apply such a protocol. In this respect, PhishSafe complements those approaches to secure the one remaining login.

6.4 Detecting Phishing Sites

This class of approaches tries to identify phishing sites in order to warn the user and prevent information leakage. There are three main vectors for site classification: First, approaches use web crawlers to check websites for phishing features [51, 54, 13]. These approaches utilize machine learning algorithms to update their classification criteria. They generate blacklists of suspicious domains. Browsers can download those blacklists and warn the user whenever she accesses a listed site. The delay between the setup of a phishing site and the time it is listed in the browsers grants phishers a temporal advance.

Approaches of the second vector attempt to classify visited websites in real time [21, 37, 3, 38, 27]. These approaches do not suffer the time delay the blacklisting approaches have. However, they create an overhead for examination for every page access.

Finally, some approaches feed suspicious websites with bogus credentials and observe the reaction on those spoofed login requests [2, 57, 41]. The point is that phishing sites supposedly accept all combinations of username and password or always answer with an error message.

All described vectors for classification of phishing sites are part of an arms race with phishers. The approaches rely on features that can be easily changed by phishers to circumvent classification. In a next step, the classification criteria can be adjusted and so on. Moreover, classification is always prone to mistakes, i.e., genuine websites may be classified as phishing attempts while phishing sites are treated as genuine. Nevertheless, phishing detection approaches can serve as a first line of defense and complement PhishSafe to prevent leakage of username and password.

7. CONCLUSION

In the course of this paper, we analyzed the root causes for the continuing prevalence of phishing attempts and classified existing solutions into three main categories: incomplete countermeasures prone to false positives and false negatives, countermeasures cumbersome for the user compared to common logon processes, and countermeasures relying on browser extensions or toolbars, thus, expecting risk-awareness by the user and excluding users of not supported browsers and platforms.

Then, we identified the user as the weakest link when it comes to phishing protection. She can neither be expected to apply cumbersome countermeasures, nor install protective tools, nor take care of security indicators. We presented PhishSafe, a reliable approach to overcome phishing attacks, that runs in browsers out of the box and barely changes known logon processes. The user must only decide if she uses her private browser or not. This way, PhishSafe implements a two-factor authentication scheme where the second factor is only accessible to the genuine web application but not to the phisher nor to the user. Without knowing the second factor, the user cannot disclose the necessary information for account access to an attacker.

PhishSafe can be easily deployed by web application providers and is not susceptible to the chicken-and-egg problem. Moreover, it complements SSO protocols and anti-phishing blacklists.

Acknowledgments

This work was in parts supported by the EU Project Web-Sand (FP7-256964), https://www.websand.eu. The support is gratefully acknowledged.

8. REFERENCES

[1] B. Adida. BeamAuth: Two-Factor Web Authentication with a Bookmark. In *Proceedings of the 14th ACM Conference on Computer and Communications Security (CCS '07)*, 2007.

[2] M. Chandrasekaran and R. Chinchani. PHONEY: Mimicking User Response to Detect Phishing Attacks. In *International Symposium on a World of Wireless Mobile and Multimedia Networks (WoWMoM 2006)*, 2006.

[3] N. Chou, R. Ledesma, Y. Teraguchi, D. Boneh, and J. C. Mitchell. Client-Side Defense against Web-based Identity Theft. In *Proceedings of the 11th Annual Network and Distributed System Security Symposium (NDSS '04)*, 2004.

[4] D. Crocker, T. Hansen, and M. Kucherawy. DomainKeys Identified Mail (DKIM) Signatures. RFC 6376, http://tools.ietf.org/html/rfc6376, (09/03/13).

[5] D. Crockford. The application/json Media Type for JavaScript Object Notation (JSON). RFC 4627, http://tools.ietf.org/html/rfc4627, (09/03/13).

[6] R. Dhamija and J. D. Tygar. The Battle Against Phishing: Dynamic Security Skins. In *Proceedings of the 2005 Symposium on Usable Privacy and Security (SOUPS '05)*, 2005.

[7] J. S. Downs, M. B. Holbrook, and L. F. Cranor. Decision Strategies and Susceptibility to Phishing. In *Symposium On Usable Privacy and Security (SOUPS)*, 2006.

[8] Dr. Web. New Trojan steals short messages. [online], http://news.drweb.com/show/?i=3549, (09/12/13).

[9] S. Egelman, L. F. Cranor, and J. Hong. You've Been Warned: An Empirical Study of the Effectiveness of

Web Browser Phishing Warnings. In *Proceedings of the SIGCHI Conference on Human Factors in Computing Systems (CHI '08)*, 2008.

[10] EMC Corporation. RSASecurID. [online], `http://www.emc.com/security/rsa-securid.htm`, (09/12/13).

[11] C. Evans, C. Palmer, and R. Sleevi. Public Key Pinning Extension for HTTP. Internet-Draft, `http://tools.ietf.org/html/draft-ietf-websec-key-pinning-08`, (09/10/13).

[12] A. P. Felt and D. Wagner. Phishing on Mobile Devices. In *Web 2.0 Security and Privacy (W2SP)*, 2011.

[13] I. Fette, N. Sadeh, and A. Tomasic. Learning to Detect Phishing Emails. In *Proceedings of the 16th international conference on World Wide Web (WWW '07)*, 2007.

[14] E. Gabrilovich and A. Gontmakher. The Homograph Attack. *Communications of the ACM*, 45, 2002.

[15] Google. Authenticator. [online], `http://code.google.com/p/google-authenticator/`, (09/12/13).

[16] M. G. Gouda, A. X. Liu, L. M. Leung, and M. A. Alam. SPP: An anti-phishing single password protocol. *Computer Networks*, 51(13):3715 – 3726, 2007.

[17] A. Herzberg and A. Jbara. Security and identification indicators for browsers against spoofing and phishing attacks. *ACM Transactions on Internet Technology (TOIT)*, 2008.

[18] I. Hickson. Web Storage. [online], `http://www.w3.org/TR/webstorage/`, (09/10/13).

[19] J. Hodges, C. Jackson, and A. Barth. HTTP Strict Transport Security (HSTS). RFC 6797, `http://tools.ietf.org/html/rfc6797`, (09/10/13).

[20] Internet2. Shibboleth. [online], `http://shibboleth.net/`.

[21] E. Kirda and C. Kruegel. Protecting Users agains Phishing Attacks with AntiPhish. In *29th Annual International Computer Software and Applications Conference (COMPSAC 2005)*, 2005.

[22] P. Knickerbocker. Combating Phishing through Zero-Knowledge Authentication. Master's thesis, Graduate School of the University of Oregon, 2008.

[23] H. Krawczyk, M. Bellare, and R. Canetti. HMAC: Keyed-Hashing for Message Authentication. RFC 2104, `https://tools.ietf.org/html/rfc2104`, (09/03/13).

[24] H. Lockhart and B. Campbell. SAML V2.0. `https://www.oasis-open.org/committees/download.php/27819/sstc-saml-tech-overview-2.0-cd-02.pdf`, March 2008.

[25] C. Ludl, S. McAllister, E. Kirda, and C. Kruegel. On the Effectiveness of Techniques to Detect Phishing Sites. In *Proceedings of the 4th international conference on Detection of Intrusions and Malware, and Vulnerability Assessment (DIMVA '07)*, 2007.

[26] M. Marlinspike. New Tricks For Defeating SSL In Practice. Talk at BlackHat '09, `http://www.blackhat.com/presentations/bh-dc-09/Marlinspike/BlackHat-DC-09-Marlinspike-Defeating-SSL.pdf`, (09/10/13).

[27] E. Medvet, E. Kirda, and C. Kruegel. Visual-Similarity-Based Phishing Detection. In *Proceedings of the 4th International Conference on Security and Privacy in Communication Networks (SecureComm '08)*, 2008.

[28] Microsoft. SenderID. [online], `http://www.microsoft.com/senderid`, (09/03/13).

[29] K. D. Mitnick and W. L. Simon. *The Art of Deception: Controlling the Human Element of Security*. John Wiley & Sons, 2002.

[30] Mozilla. Persona. [online], `https://developer.mozilla.org/en-US/docs/Mozilla/Persona`, (09/03/13).

[31] N. Nikiforakis, A. Makridakis, E. Athanasopoulos, and E. P. Markatos. Alice, What Did You Do Last Time? Fighting Phishing Using Past Activity Tests. In *Proceedings of the 3rd European Conference on Computer Network Defense*, 2009.

[32] Y. Niu, F. Hsu, and H. Chen. iPhish: Phishing Vulnerabilities on Consumer Electronics. In *Proceedings of the 1st Conference on Usability, Psychology, and Security (UPSEC '08)*, 2008.

[33] OAuth. [online], `http://oauth.net/`, (09/03/13).

[34] B. Parno, C. Kuo, and A. Perrig. Phoolproof Phishing Prevention. In *Proceedings of the 10th International Conference on Financial Cryptography and Data Security (FC'06)*, 2006.

[35] T. Raffetseder, E. Kirda, and C. Kruegel. Building Anti-Phishing Browser Plug-Ins: An Experience Report. In *Proceedings of the Third International Workshop on Software Engineering for Secure Systems (SESS '07)*, 2007.

[36] D. Recordon and D. Reed. OpenID 2.0: a platform for user-centric identity management. In *DIM*, 2006.

[37] V. P. Reddy, V. Radha, and M. Jindal. Client Side Protection from Phishing Attack. *International Journal of Advanced Engineering Sciences and Technologies (IJAEST)*, pages 39–45, 2011.

[38] A. P. E. Rosiello, E. Kirda, C. Kruegel, and F. Ferrandi. A Layout-Similarity-Based Approach for Detecting Phishing Pages. In *Proceedings of the third International Conference on Security and Privacy in Communication Networks (SecureComm 2007)*, 2007.

[39] B. Ross, C. Jackson, N. Miyake, D. Boneh, and J. C. Mitchell. Stronger Password Authentication Using Browser Extensions. In *Proceedings of the 14th Usenix Security Symposium (USENIX 2005)*, 2005.

[40] RSA Data Security. SiteKey. [Hosted at Bank of America], `https://www.bankofamerica.com/privacy/online-mobile-banking-privacy/sitekey.go`, (08/01/13).

[41] H. Shahriar and M. Zulkernine. PhishTester: Automatic Testing of Phishing Attacks. In *Fourth International Conference on Secure Software Integration and Reliability Improvement (SSIRI)*, 2010.

[42] M. Sharifi, A. Saberi, M. Vahidi, and M. Zorufi. A Zero Knowledge Password Proof Mutual Authentication Technique Against Real-Time Phishing Attacks. In *Third International Conference on Information Systems Security (ICISS 2007)*, 2007.

[43] S. Sheng, B. Wardman, G. Warner, L. F. Cranor, J. Hong, and C. Zhang. An Empirical Analysis of Phishing Blacklists. In *Sixth Conference on Email and AntiSpam (CEAS 2009)*, 2009.

[44] The Anti-Phishing Working Group (APWG). Global Phishing Survey: Domain Name Use and Trends in 2H2012. [online], `http://docs.apwg.org/reports/APWG_GlobalPhishingSurvey_2H2012.pdf`, (09/03/13).

[45] The Anti-Phishing Working Group (APWG). Phishing Activity Trends Report, 1st Quarter 2013. [online], `http://docs.apwg.org/reports/apwg_trends_report_q1_2013.pdf`, (09/03/13).

[46] The Anti-Phishing Working Group (APWG). Phishing Attack Trends Reports. [online], `http://www.apwg.org/resources/apwg-reports/`, (09/03/13).

[47] H. Tout and W. Hafner. Phishpin: An Identity-Based Anti-Phishing Approach. In *International Conference on Computational Science and Engineering (CSE '09)*, 2009.

[48] L. Varteressian. Yahoo! Sign-In Seal. [online], `http://security.yahoo.com/sign-seal-000000996.html`, (08/01/13).

[49] B. Violino. After Phishing? Pharming! [online], `http://www.csoonline.com/article/220629/after-phishing-pharming-`, (09/10/13).

[50] WHATWG. Cross-document messaging. [online], `http://www.whatwg.org/specs/web-apps/current-work/multipage/web-messaging.html`, (09/06/13).

[51] C. Whittaker, B. Ryner, and M. Nazif. Large-Scale Automatic Classification of Phishing Pages. In *Proceedings of the 17th Annual Network and Distributed System Security Symposium (NDSS '10)*, 2010.

[52] M. Wu, R. C. Miller, and S. L. Garfinkel. Do Security Toolbars Actually Prevent Phishing Attacks? In *Proceedings of the SIGCHI Conference on Human Factors in Computing Systems (CHI '06)*, 2006.

[53] M. Wu, R. C. Miller, and G. Little. Web Wallet: Preventing Phishing Attacks by Revealing User Intentions. In *Proceedings of the Second Symposium on Usable Privacy and Security (SOUPS '06)*, 2006.

[54] G. Xiang, J. Hong, C. P. Rose, and L. Cranor. CANTINA+: A Feature-rich Machine Learning Framework for Detecting Phishing Web Sites. *ACM Transactions on Information and System Security (TISSEC)*, 2011.

[55] Z. E. Ye and S. Smith. Trusted Paths for Browsers. In *Proceedings of the 11th USENIX Security Symposium (USENIX 2002)*, 2002.

[56] K.-P. Yee and K. Sitaker. Passpet: Convenient Password Management and Phishing Protection. In *Proceedings of the Second Symposium on Usable Privacy and Security (SOUPS '06)*, 2006.

[57] C. Yue and H. Wang. Anti-Phishing in Offense and Defense. In *Annual Computer Security Applications Conference (ACSAC 2008)*, 2008.

[58] M. Zalewski. Browser Security Handbook, part 2. [online], `http://code.google.com/p/browsersec/wiki/Part2#Same-origin_policy`, (09/03/13).

[59] Y. Zhang, S. Egelman, L. Cranor, and J. Hong. Phinding Phish: Evaluating Anti-Phishing Tools. In *Proceedings of the 14th Annual Network and Distributed System Security Symposium (NDSS 2007)*, 2007.

Virtualization and Security: Happily Ever After?

Dongyan Xu
Department of Computer Science and
CERIAS
Purdue University
dxu@cs.purdue.edu

ABSTRACT

Virtualization has been a major enabling technology for improving trustworthiness and tamper-resistance of computer security functions. In the past decade, we have witnessed the development of virtualization-based techniques for attack/malware monitoring, detection, prevention, and profiling. Virtual platforms have been widely adopted for system security experimentation and evaluation, because of their strong isolation, maneuverability, and scalability properties. Conversely, the demand from security research has led to significant advances in virtualization technology itself, for example, in the aspects of virtual machine introspection, check-pointing, and replay. In this talk, I will present an overview of research efforts (including our own) in virtualization-based security and security-driven virtualization. I will also discuss a number of challenges and opportunities in maintaining and elevating the synergies between virtualization and security.

Categories and Subject Descriptors

D.4.6 [**Security and Protection**]: invasive software, unauthorized access.

Keywords

Virtualization, System and Network Security, Trusted Computing.

Speaker Bio

Dongyan Xu is a professor of computer science and University Faculty Scholar at Purdue University. His research interests include virtualization technologies, computer security and forensics, and cloud computing. He has been on the faculty at Purdue University since 2001, when he received his Ph.D. in computer science from the University of Illinois at Urbana-Champaign. Together with his colleagues and students, he received the Best Paper Award from the 11th International Symposium on Recent Advances in Intrusion Detection (RAID'08), a Paper of Distinction award from the 2nd ACM Symposium on Cloud Computing (SoCC'11), and an ACM SIGSOFT Distinguished Paper Award from the 28th IEEE/ACM International Conference on Automated Software Engineering (ASE'13).

CODASPY'14, March 3–5, 2014, San Antonio, Texas, USA.
ACM 978-1-4503-2278-2/14/03.
http://dx.doi.org/10.1145/2557547.2557590

On Protection in Federated Social Computing Systems

Ebrahim Tarameshloo   Philip W. L. Fong   Payman Mohassel
Department of Computer Science
University of Calgary
Calgary, Alberta, Canada
{etarames, pwlfong, pmohasse}@ucalgary.ca

ABSTRACT

Nowadays, a user may belong to multiple social computing systems (SCSs) in order to benefit from a variety of services that each SCS may provide. To facilitate the sharing of contents across the system boundary, some SCSs provide a mechanism by which a user may "connect" his accounts on two SCSs. The effect is that contents from one SCS can now be shared to another SCS. Although such a connection feature delivers clear usability advantages for users, it also generates a host of privacy challenges. A notable challenge is that the access control policy of the SCS from which the content originates may not be honoured by the SCS to which the content migrates, because the latter fails to faithfully replicate the protection model of the former.

In this paper we formulate a protection model for a federation of SCSs that support content sharing via account connection. A core feature of the model is that sharable contents are protected by access control policies that transcend system boundary — they are enforced even after contents are migrated from one SCS to another. To ensure faithful interpretation of access control policies, their evaluation involves querying the protection states of various SCSs, using Secure Multiparty Computation (SMC). An important contribution of this work is that we carefully formulate the conditions under which policy evaluation using SMC does not lead to the leakage of information about the protection states of the SCSs. We also study the computational problem of statically checking if an access control policy can be evaluated without information leakage. Lastly, we identify useful policy idioms.

Categories and Subject Descriptors

D.4.6 [**Security and Protection**]: Access Controls

General Terms

Security

Keywords

Protection Model, Federated Social Computing Systems, Account Connection, Secure Content Sharing, Secure Multiparty Computation, Safe Function Evaluation, Composite Policy, Policy Language

1. INTRODUCTION

Although a social computing system (SCS) provides a wide variety of services for its members, users may prefer to be members of different SCSs to benefit from unique services of these SCSs, or socialize differently on different SCSs. For instance, a user could be a member of Facebook, Google+ or Path to be connected with her friends or family, and share pictures and postings in order to socialize. In Yelp or Foursquare, members locate local deals and restaurants, and share their experiences with friends. Banjo or Sonar users generally try to explore new people and events nearby, and share their feeds and photos with them. To benefit from each of these services, a user usually ends up with accounts on multiple SCSs [19, 26].

To facilitate the sharing of contents across the system boundary, some SCSs provide a mechanism by which a user may "connect" her accounts on two SCSs [20, 30]. The effect is that contents from one SCS can now be shared to another SCS. For instance, by connecting Banjo to Foursquare, a user can read her friends' Foursquare feeds in Banjo, and can post her current location to Foursquare from within Banjo.

Although such a connection feature delivers clear usability advantages for users, it also generates a host of privacy challenges. A notable challenge is that the access control policy of the SCS from which the content originates may not be honoured by the SCS to which the content migrates, because the latter fails to faithfully replicate the access control policy and/or the protection model of the former. As a case in point, a member may declare her location in Foursquare, and share it on her Facebook account through Foursquare's connection service. Facebook treats her declared location information as its own resource so the user's Facebook policy (instead of her Foursquare policy) will be applied on the shared content. On closer examination, three protection challenges make this research problem nontrivial.

1. *Policy Fidelity.* The access control policy of a shared content prior to migration is not communicated to the destination site. As a result, the policy to be enforced on the destination site need not be consistent with the user's privacy expectation as expressed in the origin policy. This ambiguity in terms of what policy to be

used for protecting shared contents is a first protection challenge.

2. **Mechanism Fidelity.** Even if the origin policy (e.g., "friends" in Facebook) is known to the destination site (e.g., Foursquare), the latter may not be able to enforce it. A reason is that the destination site has to emulate the authorization mechanism of the origin site in order to enforce the origin policy. One can do so by reverse engineering, but the protection model of a typical SCS (e.g., Facebook) is a moving target (consider how often Facebook "upgrades" its protection model), and thus tracking the protection model of the origin site with fidelity is a tremendous software engineering challenge.

3. **State Fidelity.** Another reason for the destination site not to be able to enforce the origin policy is that the access control policies of an SCS usually depends on user information not available to the destination site. In a traditional information system, the protection state and the application state of the system do not intersect. A characteristic of SCSs is that user-contributed information is used for authorization. For example, friendship information or location claims (i.e., "check in") are used for authorization purposes. Consequently, to evaluate the "friends" policy of Facebook, one needs to know the social network of Facebook. If the destination site (e.g., Foursquare) attempts to "approximate" this proprietary knowledge (e.g., by consulting the Foursquare friend list of the user), then emulation fidelity is compromised.

To the best of our knowledge, the need of a privacy policy for shared data across social network systems were first identified by Ko *et al.* [20]. We are aware of two lines of previous work that have considered protection of shared data across distributed systems [19, 26, 28]. In their pioneering work [19, 26], Shehad *et al.* proposed the formulation of cross-site policies for shared contents, in order to address the challenge of Policy Fidelity. They advocated also the adoption of a trusted third party, *x-mngr*, for managing cross-site policies and arbitrating accesses. Their work, however, considers policies in the form of access control lists. Consequently, the considered policies do not reflect the kind of policies that are actually used in the context of social computing (e.g., colocation and friendship). The rationale is understandable: adoption of social computing policies would result in the challenge of State Fidelity that to date has no obvious solution.

A second line of related work is that of Squicciarini *et al.* [28]. This ambitious work deals with the general problem of protecting shared data in distributed systems, and thus its scope is not restricted to that of content sharing in social computing. They introduced the idea of a self-controlling object (SCO), which encapsulates the shared data object, the access control policy, mobile code that specifies the semantics of the policy (i.e., the procedure for evaluating the policy), as well as ways to synchronizing the policy to its latest version. This framework clearly addresses the challenges of Policy and Mechanism Fidelity. Yet, again, the type of policies considered in this work is not the kind typical in social computing. The protection states of the SCSs simply cannot be encapsulated in such a package. Apply their

framework to protect shared contents in SCSs does not address the challenge of State Fidelity.

This paper proposes a protection model for shared contents in a confederation of SCSs, with the goal of supporting access control policies commonly found in social computing (e.g., friends, co-location, etc), while tackling the challenge of State Fidelity head on (as well as Policy and Mechanism Fidelity). Our contributions are the following:

1. A novel protection model for controlling access to shared contents in SCSs is proposed in §2. To ensure Policy Fidelity, we allow users to formulate explicit shared access policies for protecting shared accesses. Two key features of the policy language are: (a) Atomic policies come from the policy vocabulary of the SCSs in the confederation, thereby supporting social computing policies; (b) The atomic policies are interpreted according the authorization mechanisms of explicitly named SCSs. Atomic policies can be combined into composite policies. To ensure Mechanism Fidelity, such a composite policy is evaluated using distributed computing: each atomic policy is evaluated by a query to the SCS who knows how to interpret that query. Such SCS also has access to the protection state needed for evaluating the atomic policy, so State Fidelity is guaranteed.

2. Distributed evaluation of shared access policies may disclose part of the protection states (and thus user information) of SCSs to one another. Prevention of such information leak is a novel privacy goal that has not been studied in the context of SCS content sharing before. In §3, we describe how to employ a variant of Secure Multi-party Computation (SMC), known as Private Function Evaluation (PFE), for achieving such a privacy goal.

3. Motivated by the need of default policies to ease policy administration, we notice that the PFE solution may not be applicable in the presence of default policies. We therefore articulate another means to achieve the privacy goal using regular SMC. In §4, we formally characterize policies that do not leak information about protection states of the SCSs when it is evaluated using SCM, and do so via the classical notion of nondeducibility [29]. We also characterize the computational complexity of deciding if a policy leaks information (i.e., Π_2^p-complete). Lastly, we discuss policy idioms that are useful in practice.

2. FEDERATED SCSs

We present a protection model for shared resources among a confederation of SCSs, in which member SCSs collaborate to offer protection. We begin with detailing the assumptions we make of the member SCSs as they participate in the confederation (§2.1). We then outline the features offered by this protection model (§2.2). After that, the protection model itself will be described in details (§2.3, §2.4, §2.5).

2.1 Assumptions

Suppose a user has the user name u_1 on SCS i_1, and user name u_2 on SCS i_2. When she "connects" her account on i_2 to her account on i_1, she is essentially claiming that the identity u_1 on i_1 is equivalent to the identity u_2 on i_2. Typically, she does so by presenting to i_1 the user name u_2 as well as the corresponding password. Then, SCS i_1 attempts to use the credential to log on to SCS i_2, success of which will be taken as a proof that the claim of identity mapping is trustworthy. In short, account connection is a manual identity mapping process. We make the following assumption.

ASSUMPTION 1 (USER IDENTITY). *The manual identity mapping process is (a) consistent and (b) applied whenever needed.*

Technically, part (a) of the assumption requires that the establishment of the "is equivalent to" relation among identities of different SCSs result in an equivalence relation (i.e., reflexive, symmetric and transitive), such that no two identities within the same equivalence class come from the same SCS. This is not necessarily true with current technology. For example a user may claim to Google+ that his Facebook identity is "James White," while at the same time claiming to Foursquare that his Facebook identity is "Jim White." We assume that, collaboration within the confederation will regulate such inconsistencies (e.g., by identifying cases of account hijacking and duplicate identities). Part (b) of the assumption requires that, as our proposed model is adopted by a confederation of SCSs, the latter will faithfully impose manual identity mapping whenever our model demands it. In existing implementations, manual identity mapping is only imposed under two scenarios. First, when a user attempts to "push" information from SCS i_1 to SCS i_2, she does so by presenting to i_1 her credential in i_2. Second, when a user attempts to "pull" information from SCS i_1 to SCS i_2, she will do so by presenting to i_2 her credential in i_1. In short, manual identity mapping is performed when resources are shared. In our protection model, we also require manual identity mapping when a user accesses a resource that has been shared to an SCS. That is, manual identity mapping predicates access to shared resources. Part (b) assumes this will be enforced by member SCSs of the confederation.

A major corollary of Assumption 1 is that users across all SCSs are uniquely identifiable. From now on, we will bypass the differentiation of user identities in different SCSs. This does not mean that the confederation needs to have a universal identifier for each user (e.g., a single sign-on mechanism). Each SCS will continue to feature its own identity management system, and identity mapping is still performed manually, on demand, via account connection. All that we assume is that the equivalence classes of user identities can uniquely identify users within the confederation.

Next, we assume that when a resource created in SCS i_1 by a user u is shared to SCS i_2, the destination SCS will retain all information regarding the origin of the resource, its identity in the originating SCS, as well as which user created that resource.

ASSUMPTION 2 (RESOURCE IDENTITY). *Every shared resource retains its identity, its originating SCS as well as ownership. Other auxiliary information regarding a shared resource that is needed for protection will also be retained after sharing*

Consequently, we can uniquely identify a shared resource across all SCSs in the confederation.

The third assumption is concerned with the Policy Decision Points (PDPs) of the federated SCSs.

ASSUMPTION 3 (AUTHORIZATION SERVICE). *The member SCSs of the confederation open up their PDPs (or part of them) as services that other member SCSs can query.*

While current implementations do not yet support this assumption, we believe that the assumption is in line with current trend, in which the authentication mechanisms of popular SCSs are turned into services that other web applications may reuse (e.g., logging in via Facebook or Google+). This is an architectural price to be paid for participating in the confederation. Privacy enhancing technologies are devised in §3 and §4 to ensure that, by turning its PDP into a queriable service, an SCS will not compromise privacy.

Lastly, we assume that the members of the confederation are cooperative in implementing the protection model.

ASSUMPTION 4 (CURIOUS MEMBER). *The member SCSs of the confederation are curious but not malicious.*

We are aware that SCSs are curious in that they may gather information about other SCSs as they participate in the protection model. As we shall make explicit in §3, our privacy goal is to ensure that, by opening the authorization procedure as a queriable service, an SCS does not disclose information about its protection state to other SCSs.

2.2 Feature Overview

Our proposed protection model for federated SCSs offers four key features: (1) protection of shared resources, (2) shared access policies, (3) distributed evaluation of situated queries, and (4) policy composition.

2.2.1 Protection of Shared Resources

Suppose u and v are both users of an SCS i_1 (e.g., Facebook). Suppose u is the owner of a resource r (e.g., a photo) that she created on i_1. When v attempts to access r within i_1, this is called a ***native access***. Such an access is mediated by the protection model of i_1, and thus it is *not* the focus of this work.

Now suppose u shares r to a different SCS i_2 (e.g., Banjo), on which she also has an account (Assumption 1). Suppose v also has an account on i_2. When v attempts to access r from within i_2, this is called a ***shared access***. Such an access is the focus of this work. In current implementations, there is no guarantee that a shared access is properly mediated. Even if the developer of i_2 attempts to emulate the protection model of i_1, limitations of reverse engineering may affect the fidelity of emulation. The goal of this work is to articulate a rational protection model for shared accesses.

2.2.2 Shared Access Policies

In the proposed model, u, who is the owner of the shared resource r, may specify a ***shared access policy*** for controlling shared accesses to r (but not native accesses). This shared access policy is assumed to be known within the confederation of SCSs (Assumption 2), so that wherever shared access is requested, the SCS to which r is shared will honor this policy (Assumption 4). This feature addresses the need for Policy Fidelity.

2.2.3 Distributed Evaluation of Situated Queries

The shared access policy may take the form of ***situated queries***. For example, u may demand that r be accessible only to her friends on Facebook, no matter where r has been shared. The shared access policy for r will then be "friends@*Facebook*," meaning that u and the requestor shall satisfy the query "friends" at the SCS *Facebook*.

In our running example, when v requests a shared access to r on i_2, the latter will not attempt to emulate friendship testing. Instead, it will query the authorization service of *Facebook* to ascertain if u and v are friends of one another (Assumption 3). Distributed evaluation ensures Mechanism and State Fidelity.

2.2.4 Policy Composition

To make the protection model more flexible, users may formulate composite policies made up of boolean combinations of situated queries. For example, consider the composite policy below:

$$\text{friends@}\textit{Facebook} \vee \text{friends@}\textit{Google+}$$

The policy grants shared access to either friends in Facebook or friends in Google+. Note that a requestor may be known to be a friend of the owner on Google+ but not on Facebook. Essentially, the query term friends has different semantics on different SCSs.

2.3 Schema, Configuration and State

Our formal model of federated SCSs is composed of three layers — schema, configuration and state. The schema of a confederation (§2.3.1) specifies the basic entities that exist in the confederation. Components of the schema remain constant unless the membership of the confederation changes (e.g., a new SCS joining the confederation) or when the protection model of a member SCS evolves. A privacy configuration (§2.3.2) of the confederation specifies the current privacy settings of the users. Components of a configuration may change as a result of administrative actions, such as the introduction of new users, creation of new resources, or the change of privacy settings. A protection state (§2.3.3) of the confederation tracks the current protection states of member SCSs within the confederation, as well as the whereabout of shared resources. Change of protection state occurs during the normal operation of the confederation. Configuration and state transitions are not modelled in this work.

2.3.1 Confederation Schema

The **schema** of a confederation is a 6-tuple $\mathcal{F} = \langle Id, \{\Sigma_i\}_{i \in Id}, \mathcal{U}, \mathcal{R}, Q, \mathcal{I}\rangle$, where:

- Id is a finite set of **system identifiers**. Each identifier uniquely identifies an SCS in the confederation. A typical member of Id is denoted by i.

- $\{\Sigma_i\}_{i \in Id}$ is a family of countable sets, indexed by system identifiers. Each Σ_i is the set of all possible **protection states** for the SCS i. The sets are assumed to be pairwise disjoint (i.e., they don't intersect with one another). We write Σ for $\bigcup_{i \in Id} \Sigma_i$. A typical member of Σ is denoted by σ.

- $\mathcal{U}$ is a countable set of **user identifiers**. By Assumption 1, we do not differentiate the different user names of the same user in different SCSs. We are not suggesting that actual implementation of this model needs to have a centralized identity management infrastructure. The global user identifiers are but a mathematical abstraction of users within the model.

- $\mathcal{R}$ is a countable set of **resource identifiers**. Again, this is but a mathematical abstraction of resources within the confederation (Assumption 2).

- Q is the universe of **atomic queries** (or simply **queries**). For instance, friends, friends-of-friends, and acquaintances are queries known to Facebook, and friends, co-located, in, nearby are queries known to Foursquare. Because the same query may be known across multiple systems (e.g., friends), we postulate that there is a common universe of queries. A typical member of Q is denoted by q.

- The **interpretation function** $\mathcal{I} : \Sigma \times \mathcal{U} \times \mathcal{U} \times Q \rightarrow \textit{Bool}$ defines the semantics of atomic queries. Suppose $\sigma \in \Sigma_i$. That $\mathcal{I}(\sigma, u, v, q) = 1$ signifies that query q is satisfied by owner u and requestor v in protection state σ of system i. Otherwise, q is not satisfied by u and v when i is in state σ, or q is not supported by system i, or one of u and v does not have a corresponding identity in system i, or q is not applicable when system i is in state σ.

2.3.2 Privacy Configuration

A confederation can be configured with different privacy settings over its life cycle. A **privacy configuration** (or simply **configuration**) is an abstraction of such settings. Intuitively, a configuration specifies (a) the access control policies of user resources and (b) static properties of a resource such as the SCS in which the resource is created (Assumption 2). Formally, given a schema $\mathcal{F} = \langle Id, \{\Sigma_i\}_{i \in Id}, \mathcal{U}, \mathcal{R}, Q, \mathcal{I}\rangle$, a configuration is a tuple $\mathcal{C} = \langle U, R, org, own, pol\rangle$, in which:

- $U \subseteq \mathcal{U}$ is a finite set of **active users**.

- $R \subseteq \mathcal{R}$ is a finite set of **active resources** that is currently being protected by the systems.

- Every resource is assumed to have been created in exactly one system. The function $org : R \rightarrow Id$ identifies the **origin** of each resource.

- The function $own : R \rightarrow U$ identifies the **owner** of every resource in the confederation.

- The function $pol : R \rightarrow \mathcal{PO}(Q, Id)$ assigns a shared access policy to each resource. Note that this policy is not used for protecting a resource against native accesses. This policy controls shared accesses after a resource is shared to another SCS. Lastly, $\mathcal{PO}(Q, Id)$ is the set of all policies. The syntax and semantics of policies are described in §2.4.

2.3.3 Protection State

The **protection state** (or simply **state**) of a confederation is a pair $\mathcal{S} = \langle sta, cur\rangle$, such that:

- The function $sta : Id \rightarrow \Sigma$ assigns a protection state to each system identifier such that $sta(i) \in \Sigma_i$.

- The binary relation $cur \subseteq R \times Id$ records the SCSs to which each resource has been shared. A resource may have been shared to multiple systems at one time. An additional requirement is that $(r, org(r)) \notin cur$. That is, a resource is never "shared" to its origin.

2.4 Policy Language

We present a policy language (i.e., the set $\mathcal{PO}(Q, Id)$ in §2.3.2) for expressing shared access policies in federated SCSs. The most distinctive feature of the policy language is that one can specify policies as atomic queries to be interpreted at specific SCSs, thereby ensuring that their SCS-specific semantics are honoured. Such atomic queries can then be composed into composite policies via boolean connectives. To simplify discussion (especially in §4), we use propositional logic for policy composition. We could have adopted, for example, the Belnap Logic [5] as our policy composition framework, but such an extension is trivial.

2.4.1 Syntax

A policy is a propositional formula with the following abstract syntax:

$$\phi, \psi ::= \top \mid q@t \mid \phi \vee \phi \mid \neg\phi$$
$$t ::= i \mid \mathsf{org} \mid \mathsf{cur}$$

where $q \in Q$ and $i \in Id$. A **situated query** $q@t$ is an atomic query q that will be evaluated at the SCS represented by the **location tag** t (Assumption 3). A location tag t can be either **absolute** (i.e., a system identifier i) or **relative** (i.e., org or cur). The relative location tag org means that the tagged query is to be evaluated at the originating SCS of the resource that the policy is protecting. The relative location tag cur means that the tagged query is to be evaluated at the SCS in which the resource is being accessed. We write $\mathcal{PO}(Q, Id)$ for the set of all policies.

Standard derived forms can be defined as follows:

$$\bot = \neg\top \qquad\qquad \phi \wedge \psi = \neg(\neg\phi \vee \neg\psi)$$

2.4.2 Semantics

The semantics of the policy language is defined with respect to a schema $\mathcal{F} = \langle Id, \{\Sigma_i\}_{i \in Id}, \mathcal{U}, \mathcal{R}, Q, \mathcal{I} \rangle$, a configuration $\mathcal{C} = \langle U, R, org, own, pol \rangle$, and a $\mathcal{S} = \langle sta, cur \rangle$. In particular, the semantics is defined via a preprocessing function and a satisfaction relation.

First, the preprocessing function translates all occurrences of relative location tags to absolute ones. Suppose the system identifiers i_o and i_c are the SCSs to which org and cur respectively represent, and ϕ is a policy formula. Then $\mathsf{preproc}_{i_o, i_c}(\phi)$ is obtained from ϕ by replacing occurrences of org and cur by i_o and i_c respectively. The preprocessed formula contains only absolute location tags.

Second, the following satisfaction relation specifies the meaning of a formula ϕ with only absolute location tags:

$$\mathcal{I}, sta, u, v \models \phi$$

in which $u, v \in U$ are the owner and requestor respectively. The satisfaction relation is defined inductively as follows:

- $\mathcal{I}, sta, u, v \models \top$ always hold.

- $\mathcal{I}, sta, u, v \models q@i$ iff $\mathcal{I}(sta(i), u, v, q) = 1$.

- $\mathcal{I}, sta, u, v \models \neg\phi$ iff $\mathcal{I}, sta, u, v \not\models \phi$.

- $\mathcal{I}, sta, u, v \models \phi \vee \psi$ iff either $\mathcal{I}, sta, u, v \models \phi$ or $\mathcal{I}, sta, u, v \models \psi$.

2.5 Access Requests and their Authorization

A user v working in an SCS with system identifier i may request to access a resource r that has been shared to i. Such a request is characterized by the triple (v, r, i), and is authorized when both of the following two tests succeed:

$$(r, i) \in cur \tag{1}$$
$$\mathcal{I}, sta, u, v \models \phi \tag{2}$$

where $u = own(r)$, $\phi = \mathsf{preproc}_{i_o, i}(\psi)$, $i_o = org(r)$, and $\psi = pol(r)$. Test (1) is simply a sanity check, while test (2) evaluates the preprocessed policy against the owner of the resource.

3. PRIVACY VIA PFE

According to Assumption 3, each SCS opens up part of its authorization mechanism as a queriable service in order to support the distributed evaluation of shared access policies. This results in the disclosure of their protection states and thus user information. As a case in point, since interpersonal relationships are part of the Facebook protection state and user location claims are part of the Foursquare protection state, evaluating the situated queries friends@*Facebook* and nearby@*Foursquare* leads to disclosure of user information. If no further measures are imposed, then this could breach user privacy or compromise the SCSs' competitive advantages (i.e., competitors harvesting your business data).

Preserving the privacy of the SCSs' protection states during the evaluation of shared access policies is therefore an important privacy goal. To this end, we adopt **secure multiparty computation (SMC)** to carry out policy evaluation in a secure manner. In particular, this section focuses on the application of a variant of SMC known as **private function evaluation (PFE)**.

In this section, we first review basic backgrounds on SMC and PFE (§3.1). We then survey a number of architectures in which the distributed evaluation of shared access policies is conducted in a secure manner with the help of PFE (§3.2).

3.1 Secure Multiparty Computation

Secure Multiparty Computation (SMC) allows a group of parties $P_1, \ldots, P_n$ each with their own private inputs $x_1, \ldots, x_n$ to collectively compute a function f of their inputs without revealing any additional information. SMC is a fundamental problem in cryptography and distributed computing and has been studied for over thirty years with seminal results on its feasibility in various settings [31, 15, 7, 3]. Recent work on *practical* SMC has even led to the design and implementation of several SFE/MPC frameworks [22], VIFF [10], Sharemind [4], Tasty [16], and many more.

The two most common guarantees provided by SMC protocols are *privacy* and *correctness*. Loosely speaking, privacy means that no "admissible" collusion of dishonest parties are able to learn any information about the honest parties' inputs besides what is derived from their own input and output. Correctness means that a similar collusion of dishonest parties, cannot trick the honest parties to learn and/or reveal an incorrect function f' of their input. Additional guarantees not discussed here but provided by some SMC protocols include output delivery, input independence, and fairness. Dishonest parties are allowed to behave in two different ways, i.e., semi-honest or malicious. Semi-honest parties follow the steps of the protocol but try to learn more information by looking at the transcripts. Malicious parties, on the other hand, are not restricted in any way and can behave arbitrarily. In this paper we only need SMC with security against semi-honest adversaries (Assumption 4).

The above security guarantees for an SMC protocol π_f computing a function f are usually formalized by comparing the actual execution of π_f in the real world (the real execution), with an ideal execution wherein each party sends his input to a trusted third party (TTP) through a secure channel, and receives an honestly computed output in return. One then declares π_f "secure" if for any adversary corrupting a subset of parties in the real execution, there exists a simulator corrupting the same parties in the ideal execution where the final output of the real-execution adversary and the ideal-execution simulator are indistinguishable. Given that the extent of the simulator's cheating is very limited in the ideal-execution, security of π_f implies that the real-world adversary cannot do much better either. We refer the reader to [14], for a more formal presentation of the above intuition. An important benefit of proving protocols secure in this fashion is that once we prove π_f secure, we can treat it as an ideal functionality, and when describing larger systems that use π_f as a building block, replace π_f with this ideal functionality that simply receives each parties' input and returns to him the portion of the output that belongs to him.

3.1.1 Private Function Evaluation

In the above discussion, we assumed that the function f is publicly known to all the participants in the SMC. But this is not always the case in practice. The function may be proprietary, or may otherwise contain private and sensitive information. Private Function Evaluation (PFE) is a variant of SMC that tries to address this problem. In a PFE protocol, unlike SMC, we assume that f is the private input of one of the parties (say P_1), while each party P_i also holds a private input x_i of its own. The protocol then computes P_1's private function on parties input in a secure manner. The security definitions for PFE are essentially identical to SMC, as PFE can be seen as an SMC protocol where the description of f is part of P_1's private input. The description of the ideal functionality can also be adjust to take as P_1's input not only x_1 but also the function f.

Several implementations of PFE protocols have been considered in the literature [21, 18, 25]. We also note while it is usually assumed that f is known by a single party in PFE, many of the existing constructions can be naturally extended to consider the case where f is secretly shared between a subset or all the parties but no individual party knows the function itself.

3.1.2 Safe Functions for SMC

In SMC protocols, traditionally, we assume that parties have agreed on a function f and are willing to reveal to others anything that can be derived from its output. In other words, SMC does not try to determine which functions are "safe" and delegates this to the participants of the SMC. To see why some functions are not "safe," and knowledge of its output allows one to infer its inputs (even if SMC protocols are used for function evaluation), consider the following boolean function: $f(x, y) = x \wedge y$. If one learns that the output of f is 0, then one can infer that x and y are both 0.

3.2 Three PFE-based Architectures

When a shared access to resource r is requested in an SCS i, i will need to evaluate policy $\phi = pol(r)$ to reach an authorization decision. To do so, it requires the truth values of the situated queries that appear in ϕ. In the interest of privacy, the SCSs that are referenced in the location tags of the situated queries cannot simply send those truth values to i. Instead, the evaluation of ϕ will be conducted using SMC, and the output is made available to i.

A potential hole in this scheme is that ϕ may not be a safe function (§3.1.2). By reading the output of ϕ, a curious i may still infer information about the truth values of some of the situated queries that appear in ϕ.

In this work we employ two approaches to address this issue. A first approach is to hide $pol(r)$ from the SCSs, so that they do not know what function the SMC protocol is computing. In that way, simply learning the output of an unknown function does not allow i to infer the truth values of the situated queries. This requires the deployment of PFE protocols (§3.1.1).

The advantage of this approach is that there is almost no restriction on what ϕ can be. The core challenge is to ensure that the shared access policies are hidden from the SCSs involved. The assumption behind this approach is that SCSs are semi-honest (Assumption 4).

We will examine a number of architectures that are the natural starting points for realizing this approach. Our goal is not to advocate PFE as the optimal solution, but to carefully examine the design forces at play in the problem, so as to motivate the second approach (formulation of safe functions) that we advocate in §4.

In the following, we will first describe the three architectures without passing value judgement (§3.2.1, §3.2.2, §3.2.3), and then assess them in §3.2.4. We conclude this section by pointing out the fundamental limitation of achieving our privacy goal via PFE (§3.2.5), thereby paving the way to the next section.

3.2.1 Origin Tracks Policy (ORIGIN)

In the ORIGIN architecture, each SCS keeps track of the shared access policies for resources that originate from that SCS: i.e., SCS i stores $pol(r)$ whenever $org(r) = i$.

When a user v requests to access a shared resource r on SCS i_c, site i_c will contact the originating SCS $i_o = org(r)$ to initiate the computation of authorization decision. The originating SCS i_o will then look up the shared access policy $\phi = pol(r)$, and compute $\psi = \mathsf{preproc}_{i_o, i_c}(\phi)$ (i.e., replacing relative location tags by absolute ones). Based on the policy formula ψ, i_o identifies the parties that should participate in PFE, and then initiate π_ψ. The participants include i_o (who contributes the formula ψ), the SCSs who appear in the situated queries in ψ (if the situated query $q@i$ appears in ψ, then SCS i will contribute the input that corresponds to the truth value of $q@i$), and i_c (who reads the output of ϕ). The output of the PFE protocol will be visible only to i_c, the SCS from which the request was first raised.

3.2.2 User Tracks Policy (USER)

In the USER architecture, each user stores the shared access policies of the resources that she owns, on a user-owned storage. For example, a user can save her shared access policies on a network attached storage, or in her cloud storage account. Whenever an access to a shared resource is requested, the storage site will have to participate in the PFE protocol as the party to contribute the function as an input to the protocol. The rest is similar to the ORIGIN architecture. The architectural price is that the storage service that tracks the user's policies must now need to understand the confederation architecture as well as the PFE protocol.

3.2.3 Third Party Tracks All Policies (TP)

In the TP architecture, rather than having a vast number of storage services involved, as in the case of the USER architecture, we postulate the existence of a centralized policy storage service, who is an honest third party denoted by $\hat{T}$. We assume that the SCSs may collude with each other except with $\hat{T}$.

The centralized policy storage service will be contacted when a shared access is to be authorized, and it will be the party to contribute policy formulas as inputs to the PFE protocol. The policies are hidden from all SCSs except for $\hat{T}$. The architectural price is much lower in this case: only one additional party other than the SCSs need to understand the confederation architecture and the PFE protocol.

3.2.4 Assessment

We analyze the pros and cons of the three architectures.

Privacy.

Can the three architectures achieve the core privacy goal by keeping the policies hidden from the SCSs in the confederation?

Consider the ORIGIN architecture. Suppose the policy contains the relative location tag org, or an absolute location tag that is identical to $org(r)$, then the originating SCS will be contributing both the function to be evaluated as well as one of the inputs to the function when it participates in the PFE protocol. As a result, the originating SCS may end up learning something about the protection states of the other SCSs who are named in the situated queries of the policy. One way to prevent this issue is to ban the use of the relative location tag org, or the mentioning of the originating SCS in situated queries. Such a restriction reduces the flexibility of the architecture.

The USER architecture can effectively hide the policies from the SCSs in the confederation. Yet, practical considerations suggest that the SCSs are likely to be the cloud storage service providers adopted by the users. For example, Google+ belongs to the confederation, and a user stores his shared access policies in Google Drive. In such a case, it is difficult to convince the other SCSs that Google Drive (being aware of the confederation architecture) will not leak the policy to Google+, thereby compromising the privacy of the other confederation members.

The TP architecture meets the privacy goal by hiding the policies from the SCSs, so long as the assumptions in §3.2.3 are met.

Knowledge of Query Vocabulary.

In order to participate in the PFE protocol, the party who stores the policy and contributes the function to be evaluated must understand the query vocabulary of all the SCSs in the confederation. In the ORIGIN architecture, this means that *every* SCS in the confederation must understand the full query vocabulary of all the other confederation members. This is a rather high price to pay. The same objection

can be said of the USER architecture, only that the situation is even worse: the storage services outside of the confederation are involved. In comparison, only one party ($\hat{T}$) needs to have such knowledge in the TP architecture.

Fault Tolerance.

With a centralized storage service, TP presents a single point of failure. If $\hat{T}$ is not available, the entire confederation is rendered dysfunctional. With the ORIGIN architecture, the failing of one SCS in the confederation affects the policy lookup of all resources originating from that SCS. This is actually not bad as native accesses would not be possible either if the originating SCS is down. The USER architecture appears to be the most fault tolerant: the failing of a policy storage provider will affect only the shared resources of the users who use that provider for storing policies. The situation will be worsen if there is an oligopoly in the cloud storage service industry.

Final Assessment.

Balancing various considerations, TP appears to be a viable foundational architecture on which future work can be built. ORIGIN can be considered a compromise if one is willing to live with syntactic restrictions on the policy language. USER does not seem to be viable as storage services outside of the confederation are required to participate in PFE.

3.2.5 The Challenge of Policy Administration

Implicit in the presentation of the protection model and the three architectures above is the assumption that every user must specify a shared access policy for every resource that she might want to share to other SCSs in the future. It is unlikely that a user will bother to go through such a tedious exercise. An obvious way to alleviate this problem is to allow the specification of **default policies** for various categories of resources. For example, a user can specify friends@org ∨ co-located@cur as the default shared access policy for *all* her photo albums across all the SCSs in the confederation. In fact, the provision of relative location tags has exactly this application in mind.

With default policies, keeping policies hidden from the SCSs becomes an unrealistic assumption. As default policies are shared by multiple resources, and different users tend to end up adopting similar default policies, curious SCSs can make educated guesses of what policies are involved in the PFE protocol[1]. Consequently, adoption of PFE for policy evaluation is not sufficient for guaranteeing privacy.

4. PRIVACY VIA SAFE FUNCTIONS

Rather than hiding the shared access policies from the SCSs in the confederation, in this section we consider a solution in which all shared access policies are allowed to be publicly known, thereby accommodating the use of default policies. In particular, we ensure that the policies are "safe," in the sense that even if a party obtains the output of the SMC protocol, it will not be able to deduce any information regarding the inputs to the function.

This approach employs regular SMC rather than PFE. At the centre of the approach is the static analysis of the shared access policies to detect if they are safe. When a

---

[1]That Facebook takes "friends-of-friends" as the default policy is a widely discussed and well documented issue.

shared access policy is detected to be unsafe by an SCS who needs to supply the truth values of situated queries, that SCS can refrain from participating in the SMC protocol, thereby preserving its privacy.

We begin our discussion by fixing some notations (§4.1). We then offer offer a novel formalization of safety (§4.2) and its application to the distributed evaluation of shared access policies (§4.3). We then study the time complexity of the static analysis for determining if a give policy is safe (§4.4). Lastly, we will look at useful policy idioms (§4.5).

4.1 Preliminaries

Let $f : A \to B$ be a function. We write $ran(f)$ for the range of f: i.e., the set $\{y \in B \mid \exists x \in A \, . \, f(x) = y\}$. We write $pre_f(y)$ for the preimage of f at y, which is the set $\{x \in A \mid f(x) = y\}$.

In the following, we use the term boolean functions to refer to functions with type signature $\mathbb{B}^n \to \mathbb{B}$, where $\mathbb{B} = \{0, 1\}$. We are not particularly concerned with the representation of the functions (i.e., whether they are represented as propositional formulas, circuits, or binary decision diagrams, etc). We simply assume that the evaluation of the function can be performed in time polynomial to the size of the input and the size of the representation of the function.

Given a bit vector $\vec{u} \in \mathbb{B}^n$, and a set $I = \{i_1, i_2, \ldots, i_k\}$ such that $1 \le i_1 < i_2 < \ldots < i_k \le n$, we write $\mathsf{proj}_I(\vec{u})$ to denote the bit vector $u_{i_1} u_{i_2} \cdots u_{i_k}$. We also write proj_i as a shorthand for $\mathsf{proj}_{\{i\}}$.

Given two bit vectors $\vec{u}, \vec{v} \in \mathbb{B}^n$, we write $\vec{u} =_I \vec{v}$ whenever $\mathsf{proj}_I(\vec{u}) = \mathsf{proj}_I(\vec{v})$.

4.2 Input Nondeducibility

Our formal definition of "safe" functions is based on Sutherland's classical definition of information flow via the notion of deducibility [29, §2], which we reproduce here.

DEFINITION 5 (INFORMATION FLOW). *Given a set of possible worlds W and two functions f_1 and f_2 with domain W, we say that information flows from f_1 to f_2 if and only if there exists some possible world w and some element z in the range of f_2 such that z is achieved by f_2 in some possible world but in every possible world w' such that $f_1(w') = f_1(w)$, $f_2(w')$ is not equal to z.*

The intuition behind this definition is the following. Suppose the world is in the state w. There is an observer O_2 who does not know that the world is in state w. Yet O_2 observes the world state indirectly through an information function f_2. His observation is $z = f_2(w)$. So O_2 is aware that the actual world state must be among the set $pre_{f_2}(z)$. In the meantime, O_2 is also aware of the existence of another observer O_1, as well as the fact that O_1 observes the world state through the information function f_1. Now O_2 wants to infer something about the observation of O_1. O_2 knows the following: (a) y is a potential observation of O_1 (i.e., $y \in ran(f_1)$); (b) for every possible world state $w' \in pre_{f_1}(y)$ that produces observation y, $f_2(w') \neq z$ (in other words, $pre_{f_1}(y) \cap pre_{f_2}(z) = \emptyset$). With this, O_2 can safely conclude that $f_1(w)$ cannot be y, and thus O_1 is not observing y, even though O_1 does not know that w is the current world state. Since such a deduction is possible, we say that information flows from f_1 to f_2.

Sutherland observed that information flow in the above sense is symmetric [29, §2]: i.e., information flows from f_1

to f_2 if and only if it flows from f_2 to f_1. So we only need to say that there is information flow between f_1 and f_2.

In our application, we are particularly concerned with the inference of input values from output values.

EXAMPLE 6. *Suppose $f(x, y) = \neg x \vee y$. If we know that $f(x, y) = 0$, then we can infer that $x = 1$. However, if we know that $f(x, y) = 1$, then we cannot infer any information about x, for both $f(1, 1) = 1$ and $f(0, 1) = 1$.*

This notion of inference can be captured by the definition of Sutherland, by observing that the value of an input is simply the output of a projection function. Suppose we are dealing with a boolean function $f : \mathbb{B}^n \to \mathbb{B}$. The set of possible worlds here is $\mathbb{B}^n$. Let proj_i be the projection function for the i'th argument: that is, $\mathsf{proj}_i(x_1, \ldots, x_n) = x_i$. According to Sutherland's definition, one can deduce information about the i'th input from examining the output of f whenever information flows from proj_i to f.

DEFINITION 7. *A function $f : \mathbb{B}^n \to \mathbb{B}$ is input nondeducible for a non-empty set I of size k, where $I \subseteq \{1, \ldots, n\}$, if and only if for every $b \in \mathbb{B}$, if there exists $\vec{w} \in \mathbb{B}^n$ for which $f(\vec{w}) = b$, then for every $\vec{v} \in \mathbb{B}^k$, there exists $\vec{u} \in \mathbb{B}^n$ such that $\mathsf{proj}_I(\vec{u}) = \vec{v}$ and $f(\vec{u}) = b$.*

If I is a singleton set $\{i\}$, then we simply say f is i'th input nondeducible.

In short, f is input nondeducible for I if and only if there is no information flow between proj_I and f, and f is i'th input nondeducible if and only if there is no information flow between proj_i and f.

4.3 Application and Generalization

To see how input nondeducibility captures the notion of safe function, consider this scenario. Suppose a shared access to resource r is requested in SCS i_c, and the shared access policy is $\phi = pol(r)$. Suppose further that ϕ is the boolean function $f(x_1, \ldots, x_n)$, where each input of f is the truth value of a situated query. Say the input x_j is the situated query $q@i$, for some $i \neq i_c$. Assume for the time being that i_c does not contribute any input to the SMC protocol π_f. In order for SCS i to be convinced that participating in π_f will not leak information about x_j to i_c, i will check that f is j'th input nondeducible. In fact, SCS i will repeat this check for every x_j that it contributes.

Now the above scenario has an assumption, that i_c, the SCS who obtains the authorization decision (the output of f), does not contribute any input to π_f. That is, ϕ does not contain situated queries that refers to i_c. We know that this may not be avoidable, especially when the relative location tag cur is involved. This situation requires special attention.

DEFINITION 8. *Given a function $f : \mathbb{B}^n \to \mathbb{B}$, suppose $I, J \subseteq \{1, \ldots, n\}$ such that $I \neq \emptyset$ and $I \cap J = \emptyset$. Let $k = |I|$ and $m = |J|$. Function f is input nondeducible for I despite J if and only if for every $\vec{a} \in \mathbb{B}^m$ and $b \in \mathbb{B}$, if there exists $\vec{w} \in \mathbb{B}^n$ such that $\mathsf{proj}_J(\vec{w}) = \vec{a}$ and $f(\vec{w}) = b$, then for every $\vec{v} \in \mathbb{B}^k$, there exists $\vec{u} \in \mathbb{B}^n$ such that $\mathsf{proj}_I(\vec{u}) = \vec{v}$, $\mathsf{proj}_J(\vec{u}) = \vec{a}$, and $f(\vec{u}) = b$.*

If I is a singleton set $\{i\}$, then we simply say f is i'th input nondeducible despite J.

Note that Definition 7 is a special case of the definition above (when $J = \emptyset$). The set J is essentially the set of inputs contributed by the reader of the output (i_c). If a function f is i'th input nondeducible despite J, then even though the reader of the output knows the inputs in J, he still cannot infer the value of the i'th input. Therefore, in the general case, an SCS must ensure that f is i'th input nondeducible for J, for every input i that it contributes, with J being the set of inputs contributed by the SCS who reads the output. In summary, an SCS determines the safety of participating in an SMC protocol by deciding input nondeducibility.

4.4 Deciding Input Nondeducibility

We examine the computational complexity of deciding input nondeducibility. We begin with defining two corresponding decision problems.

DEFINITION 9. IND_0 is the set of all pairs (f, I) for which f is input nondeducible for I. IND is the set of all triples (f, I, J) for which f is input nondeducible for I despite J.

The following result shows that IND_0 and IND are in the second level of the polynomial hierarchy [1]. We begin with an upper bound for the time complexity of IND (consult Appendix A for a proof).

PROPOSITION 10. IND is in Π_2^p.

The following proposition gives a lower bound for the time complexity of IND_0 (see Appendix B for a proof).

PROPOSITION 11. IND_0 is Π_2^p-hard.

Since there is a trivial polynomial-time reduction from IND_0 to IND, the following is a corollary of the above results.

COROLLARY 12. Both IND_0 and IND are Π_2^p-complete.

To implement the static analysis, one can encode the IND instance as a Quantified Boolean Formula (QBF), along the line of formula (3) in Appendix A, and then use an existing QBF solver to test the satisfiability of the QBF.[2] As (3) is a 2QBF (i.e., a QBF with two alternations of quantifiers), one can employ dedicated 2QBF solvers [17, 2] for better efficiency.[3] As we shall see in §4.5, safe policies are relatively small in practice, and thus present no performance challenge to these solvers.

4.5 Policy Idioms

To facilitate discussion, we adopt the following convention.

CONVENTION 13. Suppose the inputs of a function $f(\vec{x})$ is named by variables $\vec{x}$ (e.g., f is represented by a propositional formula). When we assert that f is input nondeducible for I, the set I may be specified as a subset of $\{\vec{x}\}$.

The following example demonstrates the rarity of input nondeducible functions.

EXAMPLE 14. Of the $2^{2^2} = 16$ boolean functions with two inputs, only XOR and its negation are i'th input nondeducible for $i \in \{1, 2\}$. That means the usual boolean combinations such as conjunction and disjunction do not guarantee input nondeducibility.

---

[2] Examples of QBF solvers are Quantor, NanoFlex, DepQBD and Bloqqer by Armin Biere and Florian Lonsing, and Cirqit by Alexandra Goultiaeva and Fahiem Bacchus.

[3] Efficient implementations of 2QBF solvers include Mini2QBF and Free2QBF by Sam Bayless (www.sambayless.ca).

While XOR appears not to be particularly useful for composing policies, there are indeed boolean functions that are both useful and input nondeducible, so long as we are willing to consider boolean functions of higher arities.

EXAMPLE 15 (THRESHOLD FUNCTION). Define the threshold function $\tau_{m/n}(x_1, \ldots, x_n)$ such that 1 is returned if at least m of the inputs are 1, and 0 is returned otherwise. Note that $\tau_{m/n}$ is i'th input nondeducible for each of the inputs x_i if $1 < m < n$.

Observe that boolean disjunction and conjunction are respectively $\tau_{1/n}$ and $\tau_{n/n}$. They do not satisfy the requirement of $1 < m < n$, and thus it is no surprise that they are not input nondeducible. The smallest m and n to satisfy $1 < m < n$ are 2 and 3 respectively.

More generally, $\tau_{m/n}$ is i'th input nondeducible despite J, for a set J of size k, if it can be guaranteed that $1 + k < m < n - k$. If $k = 1$, then the smallest m and n to satisfy the above requirement are respectively 3 and 5. That is, for $\tau_{3/5}$, if the adversary knows the output as well as one of the inputs, it still cannot infer any of the other 4 inputs.

EXAMPLE 16 (CONDITIONAL FUNCTION). Consider the boolean function if:

$$\mathsf{if}(x_1, x_2, x_3) = (x_1 \wedge x_2) \vee (\neg x_1 \wedge x_3)$$

Function if is i'th input nondeducible for each $i \in \{1, 2, 3\}$. Intuitively, the input x_1 "confuses" the adversary who learns of the output, making it impossible for it to infer which of x_2 or x_3 that it is observing through the output.

Note, however, function if is not i'th input nondeducible despite J for $J \neq \emptyset$. If an adversary knows of the output and at least one other input, it may be able to infer the value of input x_i.

A generalization of if is the following function:

$$\mathsf{switch}(x_1, \ldots, x_n; y_0, \ldots, y_{2^n})$$

Depending on which of the 2^n values in $\mathbb{B}^n$ that the bit vector $x_1 \cdots x_n$ assumes, one of the y_i's will be selected as output. The function $\mathsf{if}(x_1, x_2, x_3)$ is equivalent to $\mathsf{switch}(x_1; x_3, x_2)$.

The input x_1 in if and the inputs $x_1, \ldots, x_n$ in switch are called **condition inputs**. The inputs x_2 and x_3 in if and the inputs $y_1, \ldots, y_{2^n}$ are called **branch inputs**.

When $|J| < n$, function switch is i'th input nondeduciable despite J. If J is a singleton set, then the smallest n that meets the above precondition is 2.

The two functions in Examples 15 and 16 offer us replacements for boolean disjunction and conjunction. Specifically, conjunction is used in policy formulation in strengthening the authorization condition, so that multiple criteria need to be met before access can be granted. The threshold function can be used in a similar way. So long as m of the n criteria are met, authorization will succeed. The adversary is "confused" by the surplus of n criteria, not know which of the m-subsets of the n criteria had been used for establishing access. On the other hand, disjunction is used in policy formulation by providing alternatives to justify access. The conditional function switch can be used as a replacement. The criteria are passed as y_is, and n additional x_is are passed as "confusion factors."

Input nondeducible functions have limited composability, as the following result shows.

PROPOSITION 17 (LIMITED COMPOSABILITY). *If a function is input nondeducible for I, then so is its negation.*

Suppose $\vec{x}$ and $\vec{y}$ are two disjoint lists of boolean variables, and $f(\vec{x})$ and $g(\vec{y})$ are input nondeducible for I_f and I_g respectively (where $I_f \subseteq \{\vec{x}\}$ and $I_g \subseteq \{\vec{y}\}$). Then $h_\vee(\vec{x}, \vec{y}) = f(\vec{x}) \vee g(\vec{y})$ and $h_\wedge(\vec{x}, \vec{y}) = f(\vec{x}) \wedge g(\vec{y})$ are input nondeducible for $I_f \cup I_g$.

Considering the rarity of functions that are provably input nondeducible, and the limited composibility that input nondeducible functions have, it is unwise to leave it to the users to formulate their own shared access policies that can be safely evaluated by SMC. Instead the users are presented with templates of policies that are known to be "safe," and given guidance on how to instantiate the templates. This is an acceptable practice in the industry: even though there is a vast space of policies for Facebook-style Social Network Systems (FSNSs) [13, 12], Facebook offers a standard vocabulary of common policies for users to choose from (e.g., me-only, friends-only, friends-of-friends, everyone). In the following, we describe two safe policy templates that are based on threshold and conditional functions.

POLICY TEMPLATE 18 (THRESHOLD POLICIES). *This policy template guides a user into formulating a threshold policy ($\tau_{m/n}$). The user will be asked to specify five (5) situated queries, with the following restrictions: (a) each of cur and org can be referenced in at most one of the situated queries, and (b) each system identifier can be referenced as an absolute location tag in at most one situated query.*

After preprocessing, no system identifier appears more than twice (remember org and cur must refer to two distinct system identifiers, as we are only concerned with shared accesses). If the identifier of the SCS to read the output appears twice, then the function to be evaluated by SMC will be $\tau_{2/3}$ with the remaining three (3) situated queries as arguments. This is safe (i.e., i'th input nondeducible) according to Example 15, as the three situated queries do not refer to the SCS to read the output. Otherwise, the identifier of the SCS to read the output appears no more than once, and the function to be evaluated will be $\tau_{3/5}$, with all the five (5) situated queries as arguments. According to Example 15, this is safe (i.e., i'th input nondeducible despite J, for $|J| \leq 1$).

POLICY TEMPLATE 19 (CONDITIONAL POLICIES). *This template guides a user in formulating a conditional policy (switch). The user will be asked to specify four (4) situated queries called branch queries, plus two (2) situated queries called condition queries. The following requirements apply: (a) the system identifiers that appear as absolute location tags in the condition queries must be distinct, (b) the system identifiers that appear as absolute location tags in the branch queries must be distinct, and (c) each of org and cur must appear at most once, as a relative location tag in a branch query.*

After preprocessing, no system identifier appears twice in the branch queries (recall that org and cur must refer to two distinct system identifiers, since we are only concerned with shared accesses). Denote by i_c the system identifier of the SCS to read the output of policy evaluation. If i_c appears at most once among all the situated queries, then the function to be evaluated will be switch, with the branch queries as branch inputs, and the condition queries as condition inputs. According to Example 16, this switch policy is i'th input nondeducible despite J, since $|J| = 1 < 2$.

Otherwise, in the worst case, i_c appears in two branch queries and one condition query. That is, there are at least one condition query and at least two branch queries for which i_c does not appear as location tags. Call these "clean" queries. In that case, the function to be evaluated will be if, with two clean branch queries as branch inputs, and one clean condition query as the condition input. (When there are more clean queries than is needed, break ties randomly.) According to Example 16, this if policy is i'th input nondeducible.

5. RELATED WORK

In recent years, a great deal of attention has been invested on access control models for social computing applications [6, 13, 27, 8]. Although a protection model has been proposed in each of the above works, none of them deals with the protection of contents shared to other social computing systems.

The privacy problem of shared contents in SCSs was first identified by Ko *et al.* [20]. We are aware of two lines of previous work that address this problem. The first is the pioneering work of Ko *et al.* [19] and its follow-up work [26]. They proposed a cross-site interaction framework, *x-mngr*, which features cross-site policies (i.e., what we call shared access policy) for protecting shared contents. They proposed the use of a trusted third party for managing cross-site policies and arbitrating accesses. Another distinctive feature is their identity mapping feature, which is based on machine learning technologies.

We learned from their work the use of shared access policies, as well as the need of trusted third party for policy tracking (in the TP architecture). Our work differs from theirs in the following respects. First, the policies they considered are in the form of access control lists, and thus they do not represent typical policies found in social computing. Our policies are boolean combinations of atomic policies defined in the policy vocabulary of individual SCSs. This allows us to directly confront the issue of State Fidelity. Second, we see the account connection feature not only as a content migration mechanism, but also as a manual, on-demand identity mapping mechanism. Third, we consider not only a centralized architecture (TP) for policy tracking, but also other alternatives (ORIGIN and USER).

In the ambitious work of [28], Squicciarini *et al.* proposed a policy enforcement mechanism for content sharing across a distributed system based on *self-controlling objects* (SCO). An SCO is a movable data container, composed of *Content*, *Application* and *Network* components. The Content component encapsulates a shared data and its security policy. Application and Network sections are responsible for policy enforcement and synchronization between SCOs. Policy enforcement can be done at the time of access by each SCO itself, since the core security modules are embedded in the Application section. For preserving consistency of SCOs, modification to an SCO's content will be propagated to all the SCO copies with the help of a synchronization algorithm.

Their work has a much wider scope than the current one (i.e., content sharing in SCSs). As we pointed out in the introduction, their work considers policies that are not typical for social computing, and thus they do not have to consider the problem of State Fidelity, which our work is targeting to address.

A novel aspect of our work is the formalization of "safe" functions for SMC, together with static analysis for detecting safe functions, as well as the enumeration of idiomatic safe functions. The problem of defining "safe" functions and determining which functions are indeed safe, is an important and open research direction in the study of SMC protocols. We are aware of two lines of work that attempt to answer this question, yielding very different notions of "safe" functions. *Differential privacy* [11], when considered in the context of SMC [24], tries to add randomized noise to the output the function being computed in order to guarantee that any party's decision to participate in the protocol does not change the probability of any observable event except with a small probability (for all possible inputs). The definitions are strong and independent of the input distributions but also quite hard to achieve and often require adding significant noise to the desired output. *Belief tracking* [9], when considered in the context of SMC (e.g., see [23]), tries to reason for each party, whether it is beneficial to take part in the protocol or not. This is done by tracking the other participants' *believes* about the value of the party's input before and after the protocol takes place. Our definition of "safe" functions is the first one that is deterministic and non-probabilistic.

6. CONCLUSION AND FUTURE WORK

We proposed a protection model for shared contents in a confederation of SCS. The model allows the formulation of policies that are typical in social computing, and achieves all of Policy Fidelity, Mechanism Fidelity and State Fidelity through distributed evaluation of policies. We considered two approaches to achieve privacy in policy evaluation, one based on PFE, the other based on the novel characterization of "safe" functions.

Future directions include the following: (a) a framework for administrating shared access policies in our model, (b) supporting the resharing of contents, (c) extending the model so that it is resilient to the breaking down of part of Assumption 1 (i.e., when manual identity mapping through account connection is not consistent), and (d) supporting third-party applications.

7. ACKNOWLEDGMENTS

We thank Fahiem Bacchus (University of Toronto) and Vijay Ganesh (University of Waterloo) for introducing us to QBF and QBF2 solvers. This work is supported in part by the NSERC Discovery Grants of Fong and Mohassel.

8. REFERENCES

[1] S. Arora and B. Barak. *Computational Complexity: A Modern Approach*. Cambridge, 2009.

[2] S. Bayless and A. J. Hu. Single-solver algorithms for 2qbf. In *Proceedings of the 15th International Conference on Theory and Applications of Satisfiability Testing (SAT'2012)*, volume 7317 of *LNCS*, Trento, Italy, June 2012. Springer.

[3] M. Ben-Or, S. Goldwasser, and A. Wigderson. Completeness Theorems for Fault-tolerant Distributed Computing. In *Proceeding of ACM Symposium on the Theory of Computation (STOC'88)*, pages 1–10, 1988.

[4] D. Bogdanov, S. Laur, and J. Willemson. Sharemind: A Framework for Fast Privacy-Preserving Computations. In *ESORICS'08*, pages 192–206, Berlin, Heidelberg, 2008. Springer.

[5] G. Bruns and M. Huth. Access Control via Belnap Logic: Intuitive, Expressive and Analyzable Policy Composition. *ACM Transactions on Information and System Security*, 14(1), 2011.

[6] B. Carminati, E. Ferrari, and A. Perego. Enforcing Access Control in Web-based Social Networks. *ACM Transactions on Information and System Security*, 13(1), Nov. 2009.

[7] D. Chaum, C. Crépeau, and I. Damgard. Multiparty Unconditionally Secure Protocols. In *ACM symposium on Theory of computing (STOC '88)*, pages 11–19. ACM, 1988.

[8] Y. Cheng, J. Park, and R. Sandhu. Relationship-Based Access Control for Online Social Networks: Beyond User-to-User Relationships. In *Proceeding of SOCIALCOM-PASSAT'12*, pages 646–655. IEEE, 2012.

[9] M. R. Clarkson, A. C. Myers, and F. B. Schneider. Quantifying Information Flow with Beliefs. *Journal of Computer Security*, 17(5):655–701, 2009.

[10] I. Damgard, M. Geisler, M. Krøigaard, and J.-B. Nielsen. Asynchronous Multiparty Computation: Theory and Implementation. In *Proceedings of the 12th International Conference on Practice and Theory in Public Key Cryptography*, PKC'09, pages 160–179. Springer, 2009.

[11] C. Dwork. Differential Privacy. In *Automata, languages and programming*, ICALP (2), pages 1–12. Springer Berlin Heidelberg, 2006.

[12] P. W. L. Fong. Preventing Sybil attacks by privilege attenuation: A design principle for social network systems. In *Proceedings of the 2011 IEEE Symposium on Security and Privacy (S&P'11)*, pages 263–278, Oakland, CA, USA, May 2011.

[13] P. W. L. Fong, M. Anwar, and Z. Zhao. A Privacy Preservation Model for Facebook-style Social Network Systems. In *Proceedings of the 14th European conference on Research in computer security*, ESORICS'09, pages 303–320, Berlin, Heidelberg, 2009.

[14] O. Goldreich. *The Foundations of Cryptography – Volume 2*. Cambridge University Press, 2004.

[15] O. Goldreich, S. Micali, and A. Wigderson. How to Play ANY Mental Game. In *ACM Symposium on the Theory of Computation (STOC '87)*, pages 218–229, 1987.

[16] W. Henecka, S. Kogl, A.-R. Sadeghi, T. Schneider, and I. Wehrenberg. TASTY: Tool for Automating Secure Two-party Computations. In *ACM CCS'07*, 2010.

[17] M. Jonota and J. Marques-Silva. Abstraction-based algorithm for 2qbf. In *Proceedings of the 14th International Conference on Theory and Applications of Satisfiability Testing (SAT'2011)*, volume 6695 of *LNCS*, Ann Arbor, MI, USA, June 2011. Springer.

[18] J. Katz and L. Malka. Constant-Round Private Function Evaluation with Linear Complexity. In *Advances in Cryptology ASIACRYPT*, volume 7073, pages 556–571. Springer, 2011.

[19] M. Ko, H. Touati, and M. Shehab. Enabling Cross-Site Content Sharing between Social Networks. In *Privacy, Security, Risk and Trust*, PASSAT'11, pages 493–496, 2011.

[20] M. N. Ko, G. P. Cheek, M. Shehab, and R. Sandhu. Social-networks connect services. *IEEE Computer*, 43(8):37–43, Aug. 2010.

[21] V. Kolesnikov and T. Schneider. A Practical Universal Circuit Construction and Secure Evaluation of Private Functions. In *Financial Cryptography and Data Security*, volume 5143 of *LNCS*, pages 83–97. Springer Berlin Heidelberg, 2008.

[22] D. Malkhi, N. Nisan, B. Pinkas, and Y. Sella. Fairplay–A Secure Two-party Computation System. In *Proceedings of the 13th conference on USENIX Security Symposium - Volume 13*, SSYM'04, pages 20–20, Berkeley, CA, USA, 2004.

[23] P. Mardziel, M. Hicks, J. Katz, and M. Srivatsa. Knowledge-oriented Secure Multiparty Computation. In *Proceedings of the 7th ACM Workshop on Programming Languages and Analysis for Security*, PLAS'12, pages 1–12, New York, NY, USA, 2012.

[24] I. Mironov. Differential Privacy as a Protocol Constraint. In *Information Theory Workshop (ITW)*, pages 81–83. IEEE, 2012.

[25] P. Mohassel and S. Sadeghian. How to Hide Circuits in MPC an Efficient Framework for Private Function Evaluation. In *Advances in Cryptology EUROCRYPT 2013*.

[26] M. Shehab, M. Ko, and H. Touati. Enabling Cross-site Interactions in Social Networks. *Social Network Analysis and Mining*, 3(1):93–106, 2013.

[27] A. Squicciarini, F. Paci, and S. Sundareswaran. PriMa: An Effective Privacy Protection Mechanism for Social Networks. In *Proceedings of the 5th ACM Symposium on Information, Computer and Communications Security*, ASIACCS'10, pages 320–323, New York, NY, USA, 2010.

[28] A. C. Squicciarini, G. Petracca, and E. Bertino. Adaptive Data Protection in Distributed Systems. In *Proceedings of the third ACM Conference on Data and Application Security and Privacy*, CODASPY'13, pages 365–376, New York, NY, USA, 2013.

[29] D. Sutherland. A model of information. In *Proceedings of the 9th National Computer Security Conference*, pages 175–183, Gaithersburg, MD, Sept. 1986.

[30] A. Tapiador, V. Sánchez, and J. Salvachúa. An Analysis of Social Network Connect Services. *CoRR*, 1207, 2012.

[31] A. Yao. Protocols for Secure Computations. In *IEEE Symposium on Foundations of Computer Science (FOCS'82)*, pages 160–164, 1982.

APPENDIX

A. MEMBERSHIP OF IND IN Π_2^P

PROOF. To demonstrate that IND is in Π_2^p, we note that the complement of IND is in Σ_2^p, as every triple (f, I, J) that does not belong to IND satisfies the following:

$$\exists \vec{a} \in \mathbb{B}^m . \exists b \in \mathbb{B} . \exists \vec{v} \in \mathbb{B}^k . \exists \vec{w} \in \mathbb{B}^n . \forall \vec{u} \in \mathbb{B}^n .$$
$$P(\vec{a}, b, \vec{u}, \vec{v}, \vec{w}) \quad (3)$$

where $P(\vec{a}, b, \vec{u}, \vec{v}, \vec{w})$ holds whenever:

$$(\mathsf{proj}_J(\vec{w}) = \vec{a}) \wedge (f(\vec{w}) = b) \wedge$$
$$((\mathsf{proj}_I(\vec{u}) \neq \vec{v}) \vee (\mathsf{proj}_J(\vec{u}) \neq \vec{a}) \vee (f(\vec{u}) \neq b))$$

Predicate P is obviously checkable in polynomial time. $\square$

B. Π_2^P-HARDNESS OF IND_0

PROOF. To demonstrate that IND_0 is Π_2^p-hard, we reduce a known Π_2^p-complete problem to IND_0. The specific Π_2^p-complete problem we will use is $\Pi_2\mathsf{SAT}$ [1, Example 5.6].

Problem: $\Pi_2\mathsf{SAT}$

Input: a boolean formula $\phi(\vec{x}, \vec{y})$, where $\vec{x}$ and $\vec{y}$ are disjoint lists of variables in ϕ

Question: Is it the case that $\forall \vec{x} . \exists \vec{y} . \phi$?

Let $\phi(\vec{x}, \vec{y})$ be a propositional formula. We specify below the construction of a pair (ψ, I).

- Let z_1 and z_2 be boolean variables that do not belong to $\{\vec{x}, \vec{y}\}$.
- Let $\psi = z_1 \rightarrow (\neg\phi \wedge z_2)$.
- Let $I = \{\vec{x}, z_2\}$.

We claim that $\phi(\vec{x}, \vec{y})$ is in $\Pi_2\mathsf{SAT}$ if and only if (ψ, I) is in IND_0.

Suppose $\forall \vec{x} . \exists \vec{y} . \phi$. Note that $\psi = 1$ is realizable by setting $z_1 = 0$. In that case, $\vec{x}$ and z_2 can assume any value and ψ would remain 1. Note also that $\psi = 0$ is realized when $z_1 = 1$ and $\phi = 1$. The supposition above guarantees that for every setting of $\vec{x}$, ϕ can be turned to 1. The value of z_2 does not matter. In summary, $(\psi, I) \in \mathsf{IND}_0$.

Suppose $\exists \vec{x} . \forall \vec{y} . \neg\phi$. Note that $\psi = 0$ is realizable by setting $z_1 = 1$ and $z_2 = 0$. For $\psi = 0$, it must not be the case that $(\neg\phi \wedge z_2) = 1$. Yet the above supposition guarantees there exists some $\vec{u}$ such that if $\vec{x} = \vec{u}$ then $\neg\phi = 1$ no matter what $\vec{y}$ is. Further setting $z_2 = 1$ renders $(\neg\phi \wedge z_2) = 1$. Therefore, $(\vec{x}, z_2)$ must not be $(\vec{u}, 1)$ when $\psi = 0$ is realized. In summary, $(\psi, I) \notin \mathsf{IND}_0$. $\square$

COMPARS: Toward An Empirical Approach for Comparing the Resilience of Reputation Systems

Euijin Choo
North Carolina State
University
echoo@ncsu.edu

Jianchun Jiang
Institute of Software Chinese
Academy of Science
jianchun@nfs.iscas.ac.cn

Ting Yu
North Carolina State
University
Qatar Computing Research
Institute
tyu@ncsu.edu
tyu@qf.org.qa

ABSTRACT

Reputation is a primary mechanism for trust management in decentralized systems. Many reputation-based trust functions have been proposed in the literature. However, picking the right trust function for a given decentralized system is a non-trivial task. One has to consider and balance a variety of factors, including computation and communication costs, scalability and resilience to manipulations by attackers. Although the former two are relatively easy to evaluate, the evaluation of resilience of trust functions is challenging. Most existing work bases evaluation on static attack models, which is unrealistic as it fails to reflect the adaptive nature of adversaries (who are often real human users rather than simple computing agents).

In this paper, we highlight the importance of the modeling of adaptive attackers when evaluating reputation-based trust functions, and propose an adaptive framework—called COMPARS—for the evaluation of resilience of reputation systems. Given the complexity of reputation systems, it is often difficult, if not impossible, to exactly derive the optimal strategy of an attacker. Therefore, COMPARS takes a practical approach that attempts to capture the reasoning process of an attacker as it decides its next action in a reputation system. Specifically, given a trust function and an attack goal, COMPARS generates an attack tree to estimate the possible outcomes of an attacker's action sequences up to certain points in the future. Through attack trees, COMPARS simulates the optimal attack strategy for a specific reputation function f, which will be used to evaluate the resilience of f. By doing so, COMPARS allows one to conduct a fair and consistent comparison of different reputation functions.

Categories and Subject Descriptors

C.2.4 [**Computer Communication Networks**]: Distributed Systems-Distributed applications; K.4.4 [**Computer and Society**]: Electronic Commerce—*Security*

Keywords

Reputation system; resilience; evaluation framework;trust functions

1. INTRODUCTION

Large-scale decentralized systems, such as peer-to-peer systems, online auction communities and ad hoc mobile networks, often involve transactions between strangers from different security domains with no pre-existing knowledge of each other. Although such systems offer great benefits in terms of service diversity, flexibility and scalability, they also give malicious parties the opportunity to cheat during transactions without being identified or punished [28, 31]. Inspired by social interactions between human beings, reputation mechanisms have emerged as a major technique for trust establishment in decentralized systems. In a reputation system, upon completion of a transaction, the involved parties issue feedback to evaluate one another's service or behavior during the transaction. Before a new transaction starts, one may first assess a party's trustworthiness based on the feedback on its previous transactions. This process can be viewed as the application of a *trust function*, which conceptually takes as input the feedback for a party's past transactions (or that of other parties, when necessary), and outputs a trust value to indicate its trustworthiness.

Many trust functions have been proposed in the literature (e.g., [1, 3, 12, 13, 29, 30, 33]). However, when building a decentralized system, it is non-trivial to pick the right trust function. One has to consider and balance a variety of factors, including computation and communication costs, scalability and resilience to manipulation. While many other factors are relatively straightforward to evaluate, the evaluation of resilience can be challenging. Resilience refers to how accurately a computed trust value reflects a party's true trustworthiness in the presence of malicious manipulation. Malicious manipulation includes selectively and strategically providing good or bad transactions, or issuing dishonest positive or negative feedback. We emphasize that the evaluation of resilience has to consider adaptive attackers who are aware of how a trust function works and adapt their behavior accordingly to maximize their gain in a system.

Unfortunately, though a large amount of work has been done on the design of trust functions, very few studies are devoted to systematic evaluation of their resilience [11, 14, 20]. Most existing efforts focus on performance evaluation [9, 28], while efforts on resilience evaluation are rather limited and are often built on the assumption that attackers are likely to behave within a fixed set of strategies that can be described by static models [3, 9, 14, 20, 26, 28]. This assumption is unrealistic, as it does not consider the adaptive nature of adversaries. Furthermore, evaluations based on fixed strategies do not offer a fair comparison of different trust functions. A particular trust function may be resilient to one type of attack yet vulnerable to another. Hence, comparing two trust functions using a fixed attack strategy may only offer a biased and incomplete view of their strength against manipulation. To be fair, one has to compare the worst cases of two trust functions. That is, it is necessary to compare their resilience against the *most effective attacks*, which are likely to be different for different trust functions.

In this paper, we propose an evaluation platform for the COMParison of Reputation Systems (COMPARS) that specifically takes into consideration the adaptiveness of adversaries. Essentially, an adversary tries to game a reputation system to achieve maximum profits, while normal users behave more or less consistently. Therefore, from an attacker's point of view, a reputation system sets up a single-player game. The trust function along with the behavior of normal users forms the environment and rules of the game (i.e., how the system will evolve when certain actions are taken), and the goal of the attacker is to carefully choose its actions to maximize certain profit measures (e.g., to meet a profit goal in the shortest time, or obtain the maximum profit in a given period of time).

Theoretically, given a trust function and a model of normal user behavior, there exists an optimal strategy for an attacker to game the system (i.e., the most effective attack). However, in practice, it is often hard to derive such optimal strategies. A system's state is determined by the behavior of a large number of users. Further, although normal users follow some behavior models more or less consistently, they are non-deterministic in nature (e.g., even if an honest user strives to provide good service, unsatisfactory transactions may happen from time to time due to uncontrollable factors such as network delays or interruption of delivery services, which have to be captured through probabilistic models). Therefore, it is very difficult, if not impossible, to purely rely on theoretical analysis to reason about the ultimate future state of a system and derive the optimal strategy directly.

We adopt an empirical approach that approximates the optimal strategy of an attacker. Specifically, COMPARS explores the future system states after an attacker takes up to k actions, similar to the idea of MiniMax [21]. Among these future states, COMPARS picks the one that is most beneficial to the attacker, and uses it to determine the attacker's next action. When doing so, we use a probabilistic reasoning method to deal with the non-deterministic nature of other users, which we will detail in sections 4 and 5.

Our main contributions are summarized as follows.

• We propose a general methodology to unbiasly and practically evaluate the resilience of trust functions by considering the adaptive nature of realistic attackers. The essential principle is to compare different trust functions based on their worst cases, i.e., to examine their vulnerability to manipulation when attackers adopt the optimal strategy specific for each trust function.

• We present the design of a highly configurable platform for trust function resilience evaluation. Through a set of well-defined interfaces, the platform allows us to plug in key modules of a reputation system, including honest user behavior models, initial system environment parameters, attack objectives and trust functions, so that we can study the resilience of a reputation system under various configurations. Once these basic modules are provided, the platform will automatically approximate the optimal strategies for an attacker to reflect the true resilience of the system (i.e., the worst case scenario).

• As a case study, we use COMPARS to compare several influential trust functions, including EigenTrust [13], PeerTrust [29] and TNA-SL [12], and observe their differences in terms of resilience to malicious manipulations.

The remainder of the paper is organized as follows. We start by discussing related works in Section 2. In Section 3 we present an abstract model of reputation systems, and introduce some basic concepts and notations used throughout this paper. Section 5 presents the proposed analysis framework, COMPARS. We provide a detailed description about four functional components of COMPARS in this section. Moreover, we discuss the evaluation criteria of COMPARS that considers the adaptive nature of attackers. Section 6 presents experimental results and analysis of existing reputation systems with the COMPARS framework. Finally, Section 7 concludes the paper.

2. RELATED WORK

A number of reputation systems have been proposed with the goals of ensuring trustworthy transactions between participants [1, 3, 5, 12, 13, 24, 29, 30, 33]. Most research efforts focus primarily on the design of trust functions. For example, some reputation systems utilize a few power (trustworthy) nodes to compute trust values [13, 33]. PeerTrust[29] employs similar ideas, but is built in a decentralized system. Some systems utilize additional information such as relationships between participants (e.g., transitive chains/paths) [12]. These reputation systems have shown their applicability in different application domains, and their effectiveness has been analyzed under a few scenarios in which malicious users attempt to exploit the systems. However, these systems are designed for specific application domains, and are evaluated only on those targeted domains, making general comparison difficult.

In order to facilitate a systematic analysis, several papers discuss design issues of reputation systems [9, 17, 26] and classify trust functions into a few categories [4, 16, 23, 27, 32]. Some of them further discuss attacks and defenses related to design issues [9]. Papers that deal with design issues can offer a clear view on different dimensions of reputation systems with a common criteria [9, 17, 23, 26, 27, 32]. Also, existing reputation systems can be theoretically analyzed with the proposed criteria[2]. A theoretic analysis, however, has the limitation that it does not take a practical perspective into account. Indeed, Jøsang *et al.* address that a reputation system, which is considered theoretically robust, can be nevertheless vulnerable in realistic environments [11]. Unlike theoretical approaches, we construct an evaluation framework that can generate quantitative assessment so that the different systems can be compared in a fair and consistent manner.

A few studies have attempted to address and evaluate the resilience of trust functions [2, 4, 7, 15, 28]. Jøsang *et al.* and Hoffman *et al.* discuss a set of properties to evaluate reputation systems [9, 11]. Although they mention resilience, they do not provide an analysis of resilience, instead focusing on algorithm analysis including how to compute trustworthiness. Zunping *et al.*[4] classify trust-based recommender systems into three categories and pick a representative system in each category to analyze their resilience. Through experiments, the authors prove vulnerabilities in trust-based recommender systems. However, their evaluations are limited to a few specific recommender models and specific attacks.

Fullam *et al.*[7] propose a testbed to evaluate reputation systems, called *ART*. Unfortunately, ART can only be used in a few specific applications and it only allows a small number of participants. Consequently, ART can deal with only simple and static user/attack behavior scenarios, which is unrealistic. For example, every participant is assumed to behave in exactly the same way, attackers do not change their behavior, and no participant can enter/leave during evaluation. Instead, we employ a probabilistic reasoning method to handle a large number of users' behavior.

Kerr*et al.*[15] propose a more general platform, TREET, to analyze reputation systems. Although TREET is more flexible than ART, supporting both centralized and decentralized systems, it can only handle marketplace scenarios and specific attacks in the marketplace. Our COMPARS framework, on the other hand, is general and domain-independent.

West et al.[28] and Irissappane et al.[10] propose evaluation frameworks based on empirical approaches. West et al. define possible user/attacker behavior models and implements a simulator with a static trace. Irissappane et al. simulate reputation systems with static user behavior models and fixed attack models. Static behavior models and traces, however, make systems vulnerable by nature, since attackers may be well-aware of how a trust function works and intentionally change their behavior to exploit a reputation system. Further, both [28] and [10] do not take users' non-deterministic nature into consideration. Hence, it is hard to handle real scenarios where each user may have their own behavioral pattern in [28] and [10]. In contrast, we employ a probabilistic user behavior model to capture the non-deterministic nature of other users.

Considerable research on evaluation frameworks lies in the classification of reputation systems and attacks/defenses in reputation systems [2, 9, 10, 18, 26, 28]. These works try to classify reputation systems considering their resilience against a few static attack models [2, 4, 6, 10, 11, 14, 24, 25, 28]. In contrast, we believe an evaluation based on static attack models is not sufficient to reflect the true resilience of a reputation system. Instead, we propose an evaluation framework that captures the adaptive nature of attackers who can exploit the properties of specific trust functions and behave accordingly to maximize their profits.

3. REPUTATION SYSTEM

Reputation systems help users estimate the trustworthiness of other parties in a decentralized system. By decentralized, we mean that entities are autonomous; there is no single centralized authority that asserts the trustworthiness of entities, or makes decisions on the appropriate actions of an entitie. This concept is orthogonal to the underlying exchange structures of a system including centralized (e.g., e-commerce systems) or decentralized (e.g., a peer-to-peer file sharing systems). We assume that entities in a decentralized system interact with each other through transactions. Transactions are not limited to monetary interactions; they also include activities such as retrieving information from a website, downloading files from a peer, and etc. We assume that a transaction is unidirectional, i.e., given a transaction, there is a clear distinction between a service provider and a service consumer.

In general, reputation systems share a common structure[9], typically modeled as a 5-tuple (C, P, R, F, A), where C is a set of service consumers, P is a set of service providers, R is a set of feedbacks, F is a trust function, and A is a set of actions. We describe the five components in detail below.

Service consumers. A service consumer is an entity who seeks services from a decentralized system, such as a buyer in an e-commerce market and a downloader in a file-sharing system. Each consumer is associated with a profile, which is a set of properties that are relevant to reputation management. For example, a profile may include the time a consumer joins the system and demographic information. A service consumer may have a set of services that it would like to get from the system at a certain time, but such information is not likely to be publicly known. Hence, we do not explicitly model it as a part of a consumer's profile. Instead, it is modeled by a consumer behavior model, which is essential to reason about the evolution of a reputation system.

Service providers. A service provider is an entity who offers a set of services that may be requested by consumers (e.g. sellers in an e-commerce market and uploaders in file-sharing applications). Usually, the set of services offered by a provider is public (e.g., in

ebay we can see all the items a seller is selling, but we do not know what items a buyer may need). Therefore, the services offered by a provider is a part of its profile. Its profile may also have other similar properties to that of consumers. Note that the set of consumers and providers may not be disjoint; an entity may be a consumer in one transaction and a provider in another.

Feedbacks. A feedback γ for a transaction takes the form (c, p, i, r, t), meaning that consumer c received service i from provider p at time t, and its rating is r. We leave the format of the rating opaque as it is application specific. In many systems, it is a single numerical/categorical value (e.g., 0 to 5 stars, or from poor to excellent). In others, it may instead be a vector that reflects a transaction's quality from multiple aspects, e.g., price, product quality, and responsiveness of customer service.

Trust function. If an entity a wants to evaluate the trustworthiness of another entity b, then we call a and b the source and target of the trust evaluation, respectively. A trust function takes a source, a target and a set of feedbacks, and returns the target entity's trust score. Similar to feedbacks, the format of a trust score is also opaque, and depends on the specific trust function. Most trust functions return a single numerical value as a trust score, while some others advocate returning a vector of numerical values [32], each corresponding to an aspect of the target.

Most trust functions in the literature are subjective (i.e., from the point of view of different sources, the same target may have different trust scores). Some other functions are objective (or global), meaning the trust score of an entity does not depend on the source. Nevertheless, the above modeling of trust functions is general enough to capture both types of functions.

Actions. An entity can take many different actions in a reputation system. For example, a provider may list a set of services that are available to others; a consumer may choose to start a transaction with a provider; a consumer may post a positive or negative feedback regarding a transaction; a provider may provide good or poor transactions intentionally or unintentionally, etc.

The set of actions essentially defines the capabilities with which an attacker can manipulate a system, and is highly system-specific. For instance, many e-commerce systems have mechanisms to ensure that an entity cannot post a feedback unless it was indeed a consumer in a transaction. Other systems, such as online rating systems, cannot verify whether an entity has direct experience with a service before rating it. As another example, some systems require a user to present some real-world credentials (e.g., credit cards) before creating an account, to circumvent Sybil attacks[3]. Many other systems however allow free entry. Therefore, attackers may create multiple accounts and launch coordinated manipulation through these accounts.

As discussed earlier, an adaptive attacker does not stick with a fixed strategy to game a reputation system. Instead, it would evaluate the possible consequences of actions available at any given time, and decide which action is the best to achieve its goal. Note that the consequence considered might not be just the immediate ones. Instead, it is often desirable to consider an action's long term impact to identify the best action at present. For example, cheating in a transaction at present might give the attacker an immediate payoff, but it may dramatically hurt its trust score such that consumers are much less likely to come to the attacker for service in the future, which is not desirable for achieving its goal (e.g., get a certain amount of profits in the shortest time). Thus, in terms of the overall long-term payoff, it may not be the best action to cheat immediately at present. To model this reasoning process, we introduce the concept of the state of a reputation system and its transition.

The *state* of a reputation system is a 3-tuple (C, P, R), consisting of the set of consumers, the set of providers, and the set of feedbacks in the system. When an action occurs in a system, its state will change accordingly. For instance, when a new user joins the system, C is updated; when a provider lists a new service, its profile is updated; R is updated when a new feedback is issued. Let S_t be the system state at time t_0. After an action a happens at time t_1, the system state *transitions* to S_{t_1}, denoted $S_t \xrightarrow{(a,t_1)} S_{t_1}$. Given a sequence of actions $X = (a_1, t_1), \ldots, (a_i, t_i)$, we denote the transition as $S_{t_0} \xrightarrow{X} S_{t_e}$.

4. OPTIMAL ATTACK STRATEGIES

The attackers' goal is to manipulate a reputation system to gain advantages (e.g., money payoff, free downloading, or spreading of malware). To do so, attackers often change their behavior according to the change of system states. Hence, it is important to model attackers' adaptive behavior to evaluate the resilience of trust functions. Attackers essentially try to find and perform the *most effective attack* for a specific trust function. Clearly, the most effective attack will be different for different trust functions; and attackers should have *an optimal strategy* to perform the most effective attack for the trust function. We model a reputation system as a game, in which players are either normal users or attackers. In Section 4.1, we first explain our model of a game in reputation system, and we describe how to find the optimal strategy in sections 4.2 and 4.3

4.1 Games in Reputation Systems

Generally, there are multiple players in a game whose type can be normal users and attackers in a reputation system. Depending on the setting, a player may join or leave during the game. Each player has multiple choices of actions in each turn and a system state transitions to the next system state depending on each player's action.

For a reputation system to reflect a user's true trustworthiness, users are expected to behave in a way that the system wants them to (i.e., to behave in a predictable manner). For example, a reputation system requires consumers to give a high (low) rating to a good (bad) service[31]. However, each user may behave in its own way, not the same way as other users. For instance, one user may tend to give relatively low ratings habitually, even when it is satisfied with a service; an honest user strives to provide good service, but unsatisfactory transactions may still occur due to unreliable delivery from third-party. Hence, the behavior of normal users is predictable yet non-deterministic, and each normal user has its own behavior model.

An attacker, on the other hand, tries to game a reputation system to achieve its goal. Therefore, from an attacker's point of view, a reputation system sets up a single-player game. The trust function along with the behavior models of normal users forms the environment and rules of the game. The goal of an attacker is to carefully choose its actions to maximize its profit. To choose an action in each turn, an attacker considers the consequence of the action. That is, the attacker needs not only to examine a current system state, but also to estimate a future system state. For example, an attacker will choose a certain action, if it estimates the action will bring a profit; an attacker will not choose a certain action, if it estimates the action will punish itself.

Theoretically, given a trust function and models of normal user behavior, there exists an optimal strategy for an attacker to achieve its goal. Unlike classical games such as chess, however, there are a large number of users whose behavior is non-deterministic in a reputation system. Also, the design of reputation systems is more

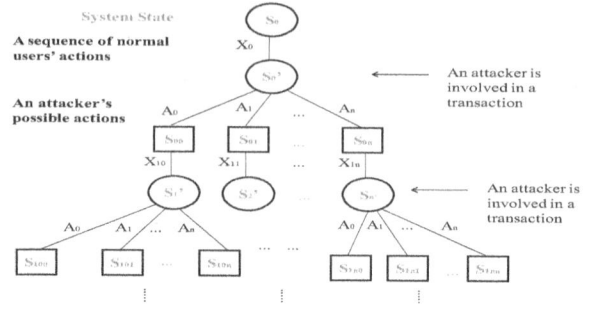

Figure 1: An attack tree

complicated. Therefore, purely using a theoretical analysis to pick the optimal attack strategy can be very difficult. We thus employ an empirical approach to explore future system states after an attacker takes a sequence of actions and approximate the optimal strategy of the attacker. Similar to the idea of MiniMax[21], we represent possible system states as a tree, called *an attack tree*, but only in an attacker's point of view. In the following subsections, we delineate how we generate an attack tree.

4.2 Attack Tree

A conceptual view of an attack tree is shown in Fig.1. The formal definition of an attack tree is given as follows.

Definition 1. *An attack tree is a rooted tree given by <S, X, A>, where*
- *S is the set of nodes, each of which ($S_i = (C_i, P_i, R_i)$) represents a system state at a certain time point.*
- *X is the set of edges, each of which ($X_i = \{(a_1, t_1), \ldots, (a_m, t_m)\}$) represents a sequence of normal users' actions.*
- *A is the set of edges, each of which ($A_i = (a_i, t_i)$) represents one of an attacker's possible actions.*

As discussed in Section 3, a system state transitions into the next system state, whenever an action occurs. The action may be performed by attackers or normal users. The attack tree, however, is employed to derive the attackers' optimal strategy, while estimating future system states from an attacker's point of view. Accordingly, we do not represent every possible system state that evolves depending on a normal user's action as a node. Instead, we represent system states as nodes only when an attacker is involved in the transactions. In order to differentiate a system state right after an attacker's single action A_i from a system state after a sequence of normal users' actions X_i, we represent the former as a square node and the latter as a round node. Each round node (except the root node) has n square child nodes, each of which corresponds to a system state after an attacker's action A_i occurs. Each square node and the root node have one round child node corresponding to a system state after a sequence of normal users' actions X_i occurs.

We assume that an attacker is involved in a transaction at time $t_{j'}(j = 0, \ldots, n)$. And $S_{j'}(j = 0, \ldots, n)$ are the system states at time $t_{j'}(j = 0, \ldots, n)$. As shown in Fig.1, when an attacker tries to estimate a system state, a sequence of normal users' actions is generated first by randomly choosing users and their actions according to the users' behavior models. Each action results in a transition into a new system state. A node S_0 *transitions* to a node S_0' after a sequence of normal users' actions X_0 happens, as shown in Fig.1. At time $t_{0'}$ when an attacker is involved in a transaction, the attacker has a set of choices A_i's, i.e. the attacker's possible actions. After taking one of the actions, an attacker will estimate its next system state. Depending on which ac-

90

AttackBehavior()
1: $S \leftarrow S_0$
2: $r \leftarrow 0$
3: $Gen\_AttackTree(S, r)$

Add_Node(Parent S_p, Child S_c)
1: Add S_c as one of S_p's children into an attack tree.

Gen_AttackTree(System state S_p, r)
1: $r \leftarrow r + 1$
2: $S_c \leftarrow Normal\_Sequence(S_p)$
3: $Add\_Node(S_p, S_c)$
4: **for** $k = 0$ **to** N_A **do**
5:     // Do an action a_k
6:     $S_k \leftarrow Get\_SystemState(S_c, a_k)$
7:     $Add\_Node(S_c, S_k)$
8:     **if** $r < M_T$ **then**
9:        $Gen\_AttackTree(S_k, r)$
10:     **end if**
11: **end for**

Get_SystemState(System state S_p, Action a)
1: $S_p \xrightarrow{a} S_c$
2: S_p transitions to S_c after a happens.
3: **return** S_c;

Normal_Sequence(S_p)
1: **for** $k=0$ **to** L_S **do**
2:     Randomly pick a user and its action, ω.
3:     $S_p \leftarrow Get\_SystemState(S_p, \omega)$
4: **end for**
5: **return** S_p;

S_0: an initial system state
S_i: System states at time i
M_T: Maximum height of an attack tree.
r: A counter for the height of an attack tree
A: The set of attackers' possible actions to achieve their goals.
a_k: An attacker's one possible action at a certain time point. ($\in A$)
N_A: The number of attackers' possible actions at a certain time point.
Ω: The set of normal users' possible actions.
ω: One of normal users' actions. ($\in \Omega$)
L_S: Chosen length of one sequence of normal users' actions.

Figure 2: The pseudocode for generation of an attack tree

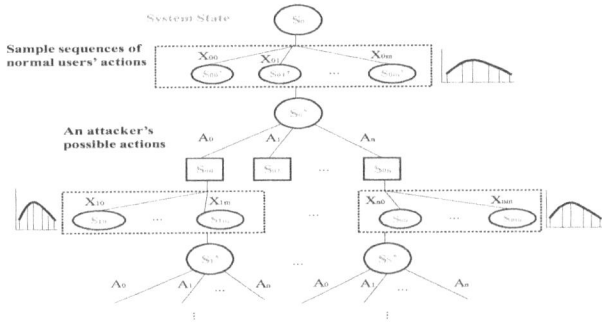

Figure 3: An attack tree with sample sequences

tion is taken by the attacker, a node S_0' *transitions* to its n child nodes, $S_{0i}(i = 1, \ldots, n)$.

An attacker repeats this *reasoning process*, until the number of the attacker's transactions exceeds a certain number, which is defined by the attacker. We call the number of the attacker's transactions in an attack tree as the *height* of the attack tree, which is the same as the depth of a tree only considering round nodes. For example, the height of the attack tree in Fig.1 is two. Ideally, if we can explore all possible system states, we can get the most accurate estimate of an attacker's optimal strategy. In practice, it would be computationally infeasible to explore the whole space of state transition. We thus limit the maximum height of an attack tree so that attackers can predict future system states with a reasonable computation. Fig. 2 shows the pseudocode to generate an attack tree.

4.3 Attack Tree with Sample Sequences

A system state is determined by the behavior of a large number of users, which is likely to be probabilistic, as discussed earlier. Since the generation of an attack tree is an estimation process of the attackers, only one sequence of normal users' actions would not be representative to reflect a large number of users' probabilistic behavior. We thus sample the users' actions to make better estimation of system states. That is, we generate sample sequences of normal users' actions, instead of one single sequence of normal users' ac-

tions. We now describe how we generate an attack tree with sample sequences of normal users' actions.

Fig.3 depicts an example of an attack tree with sample sequences of normal users' actions. Similar to Fig.1, we assume that an attacker is involved in a transaction at time $t_{j'}(j = 0, \ldots, n)$ and $S_{j'}(j = 0, \ldots, n)$ are system states at time $t_{j'}(j = 0, \ldots, n)$. Whenever an attacker tries to estimate a system state, m sample sequences of normal users' actions $X_{jk}(k = 0, \ldots, m)$ are generated first. Each sequence X_{jk} is generated by randomly choosing users and their actions according to the users' behavior models. Although each action results in a transition into the next system state, we only represent system states after the last action in the sequence X_{jk} occurs as nodes in an attack tree. Hence, a node S_0 *transitions* to nodes $S_{0k}'(i = 0, \ldots, m)$ after sequences of normal users' actions $X_{0k}(k = 0, \ldots, m)$ happen, as shown in Fig.3.

To estimate a system state at $t_{j'}(j = 0, \ldots, n)$, we need to analyze the distribution of system states $S_{jk}'(k = 0, \ldots, m)$. Then, the attacker picks a *representative system state*, S_j', among $S_{jk}'(k = 0, \ldots, m)$'s for the time, $t_{j'}(j = 0, \ldots, n)$. The representative system state can be defined by the attacker. For example, let $v_{jk}'(k = 0, \ldots, m)$ be the trust score of an attacker at each system state, $S_{jk}'(i = 0, \ldots, m)$. Then, the attacker may choose a system state $S_{j,avg}'$, at which an attacker's trust score $v_{j,avg}'$ is the average of trust scores $v_{jk}'(i = 0, \ldots, m)$, as a representative system state for the time, $t_{j'}(j = 0, \ldots, n)$.

Similar to Fig.1, the attacker has a set of choices A_i's, i.e. attackers' possible actions, at time $t_{j'}$ when an attacker is involved in a transaction. After taking one of the actions, an attacker will estimate its next system state. Depending on which action is taken by the attacker, a node S_j' *transitions* to its n child nodes, $S_{ji}(j = 1, \ldots, n)$. An attacker repeats this reasoning process, until the number of the attacker's transactions exceeds a certain number, which is defined by the attacker.

5. COMPARS: A FRAMEWORK FOR COMPARISON OF REPUTATION SYSTEMS

The goal of the proposed approach is to evaluate trust functions in the presence of adaptive attack behavior. In Section 5.1, we first

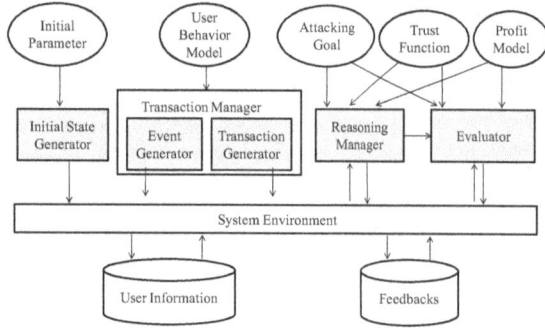

Figure 4: The architecture of COMPARS

give a brief overview of the proposed framework, called *COMPARS* (COMParison of Reputation Systems). In sections 5.2, 5.3, 5.4, and 5.5, we discuss four major functional components of COMPARS and the evaluation criteria of COMPARS.

5.1 Overview of COMPARS

COMPARS simulates the evolution of a reputation system. The framework is built with basic components common to reputation systems so that any reputation system can be easily integrated into COMPARS and so that different trust functions can be evaluated with COMPARS. Fig.4 shows the architecture of COMPARS, which consists of four functional components: *initial state generator, transaction manager, reasoning manager*, and *evaluator*.

As noted before, strategic attackers often change their behavior, depending on specific properties of trust functions and of normal users. In order to reflect an attacker's adaptive strategy, COMPARS considers a reputation system from the attacker's point of view. Essentially, given the initial system state, the goal of an attacker is to carefully choose its behavior to maximize its profits. COMPARS thus derives an attacker's optimal strategy to achieve its goal. First, the *initial state generator* generates an initial system state, which is defined by basic user information (e.g., the list of consumers, providers, and items each user has). Given the initial system state, *the transaction manager* controls who will be involved in each transaction. In general, normal users will not change their behavior much. Along with this observation, *the transaction manager* takes user behavior models as input. *The transaction manager* consists of *an event generator* and *a transaction generator. The event generator* controls who will be a consumer, c, based on a current system state and user behavior models. Depending on the user behavior models, *the transaction generator* decides who will be chosen as a provider, p by a consumer, c. In Section 5.3, we discuss how we define behavior models for normal users in detail.

Given a trust function and a system state, attackers attempt to game a reputation system to achieve their goals. Different from normal users, attackers are adaptive so that they are able to choose the optimal strategy under a specific system state. For attackers to derive their optimal strategy, COMPARS explores the future system states after an attacker takes up to k actions. COMPARS represents possible system states with different attacking actions as an attack tree, as illustrated in Section 4.

The *reasoning manager* handles the reasoning process of attackers, generating attack trees to reason about the attackers' future actions. By monitoring a generated tree, COMPARS picks the most beneficial action to the attacker and uses it to determine the next action that the attacker should take. Given the optimal strategy, the *evaluator* carries out the optimal strategy and evaluates the resilience of the reputation systems.

In the following sections, we describe each component in detail.

c: A consumer who wants to get a service
S_t, S_{t_1}, S_{t_2}: System states at given time t, t_1, and t_2, respectively
Σ_c: The set of consumers' strategies to pick service providers
σ_c: c's strategy to pick service providers ($\in \Sigma_c$)
γ : A feedback from a single transaction

ConsumerBehavior()
1: Pick a service provider p who meets the requirements of σ_c.
2: Do a transaction with p.
3: $S_t \xrightarrow{c \ gets \ a \ service} S_{t_1}$
4: Issue a feedback, γ.
5: $S_{t_1} \xrightarrow{c \ issues \ a \ feedback \ \gamma} S_{t_2}$

Figure 5: A consumer's behavior and the evolution of system states

5.2 The Initial State Generator

An initial system state is the system state before an attacker's action. Note that COMPARS simulates the evolution of a reputation system in an attacker's point of view. Hence, the initial state does not mean no transactions ever happen in the system. An attacker may join in the middle of a system; or, normal users can be compromised by attackers and start to behave maliciously. To generate the initial system state, the *initial state generator* takes initial parameters as input, including basic information (e.g., the list of consumers, providers, and services offered by providers). With the given parameters, the *initial state generator* generates the initial system state $S_0 = (C, P, R)$, where C is a set of service consumers, P is a set of service providers, and R is a set of feedbacks.

5.3 The Transaction Manager

Given the initial system state, the *transaction manager* controls who will be involved in each transaction. As mentioned earlier, normal users in reputation systems are likely to behave consistently. The *transaction manager* takes user behavior models as input. Our abstract model of normal user behavior is as follows. Note that the abstract model is not fixed, but is flexible and able to accommodate different user behavior model.

A. A Consumer Behavior Model: A consumer seeks services from a decentralized system. While doing so, a consumer needs to choose a set of services it would like to get as well as a provider from whom it would like to get the services. Given a trust function, a consumer's *strategy* for choosing a provider may vary depending on a current system state. For example, one consumer may choose a provider whose trust value is over certain threshold, whereas another may only choose the top-ranked providers in the system. Based on its own strategy at a given system state, consumer c chooses provider p and starts a transaction with p. After c gets service i, c issues feedback γ. Fig.5 describes how a system state evolves depending on a consumer's action.

B. A Provider Behavior Model: A provider offers a set of services, which is usually publicly known. Therefore, provider p's set of services should be a part of its profile, as discussed previously. However, even if a provider offers the same services at different time, the quality of transactions may vary due to uncontrollable factors such as network delays or interruption of delivery services. Also, a provider may want to change the quality of transactions for the same services depending on the trust function and consumers' strategies. For example, uploaders in file-sharing applications may publish normal quality files rather than high quality files to save their resources. As another example, sellers in e-commerce markets who do not have a good transaction history may try to post

p: A provider who wants to provide a service
c: A consumer who wants to get a service
S_t, S_{t_1}, S_{t_2}: System states at given time t, t_1, and t_2
Σ_p: The set of providers' strategies
σ_p: p's strategy to provide a service ($\in \Sigma_p$)

ProviderBehavior()
1: **while** p is not chosen by any consumer **do**
2:     p checks a current system state.
3:     p picks a strategy σ_p.
4:     p lists a set of services, which meet requirements of σ_p.
5:     $S_t \xrightarrow{\ p\ lists\ a\ set\ of\ services\ } S_{t_1}$
6: **end while**
7: **if** p is chosen by a consumer c **then**
8:     $S_{t_1} \xrightarrow{\ p\ offers\ a\ service\ to\ c\ } S_{t_2}$
9: **end if**

Figure 6: A provider's behavior and the evolution of system states

only best items to repair their reputations. Note that this is different from the attackers' behavior, in which an attacker intentionally provides good or bad services to maximize its profits. To capture such factors, we use a provider behavior model in addition to a provider's profile. Fig. 6 shows a provider's behavior and how a system state evolves depending on a provider's action.

Provider p lists a set of services and waits until it is chosen by a consumer. If p is not chosen within a certain time, p checks the current system state and changes its *strategy* to offer the services. For instance, p may offer the same quality of services at a lower price or p may offer a better quality of services at the same price.

Given the initial system state and user behavior models, the *transaction manager* controls who will be involved in each transaction. The transaction manager consists of the *event generator* and the *transaction generator*. Based on the current system state and user behavior model, the event generator picks a consumer who will be involved in each transaction. For example, the event generator may pick a user as a consumer only when its trust value is over a certain threshold. Once the event generator picks consumer c, the transaction generator selects provider p depending on c's strategy to pick a service provider. The quality of each transaction is decided depending on a specific system configuration. In some reputation systems, one provider may explicitly mention (advertise) a service quality; or, a reputation system may have its own measure to judge a service quality [28].

5.4 The Reasoning Manager

As described in Section 4, sophisticated attackers often change their behavior intentionally based on the trust functions. If a framework evaluates trust functions based on a set of pre-defined strategies, this always leaves chances for attackers to exploit trust functions by using different strategies that are not adopted in the evaluation. COMPARS thus employs an empirical approach to model attackers' adaptive behavior, which is delineated in Section 4.

A reasoning process begins when an attacker is chosen for a transaction, generated by the transaction manager. An attacker can be a consumer or a provider. The *reasoning manager* takes an attacker's goal as input. The attacking goal can be defined with a few parameters, which may include, but are not limited to a trust score, a profit, and a time period. For example, an attacker may want to achieve its profit goal within a certain time period, while maintaining a trust score above a certain value; or, an attacker may want to demote a competing provider's trust score so as to prevent

the provider from being chosen by consumers. To compute profits from a given action, the reasoning manager takes *a profit model* as input. A profit model is a method to compute profits resulting from a single action at a specific system state.

Depending on a specific reputation system, the attacker may have different choices of actions at each system state to achieve its goal. For example, if allowed by a system, an attacker may also create a new account, so that it can control multiple accounts in one reputation system. Accordingly, the reasoning manager takes into account the attacker's capabilities in a given reputation system and handles the attacker's reasoning process in the system, so that COMPARS can accurately predict the optimal action at present.

The reasoning process continues until the maximum reasoning step (i.e., the maximum height of an attack tree) is reached. More reasoning will lead to better estimation. The amount of reasoning performed, however, will impact computation overhead. Therefore, we limit the maximum number of reasoning steps so that COMPARS can predict future system states with a reasonable amount of computation.

5.5 The Evaluator

A good trust function will restrict the chances for an attacker to exploit a system. In other words, if an attacker can achieve its goal early, it is expected that the trust function is vulnerable to manipulation. Hence, the *evaluator* observes how many transactions are required for an attacker to achieve its goal with its optimal strategy.

6. EXPERIMENTAL RESULTS AND ANALYSIS

This section describes an analysis of reputation systems using COMPARS. Many reputation systems have been developed in different application domains[32]. To show the validity of COMPARS, three influential reputation systems—EigenTrust [13], PeerTrust [29], and TNA-SL [12]—have been integrated into the COMPARS framework. Note that COMPARS is general and domain-independent, so that there are many ways to materialize COMPARS depending on which reputation system will be evaluated. For example, different user behavior models and profit models can be used to evaluate different reputation systems. Here, we provide a few case studies with the three reputation systems in an eBay-like e-commerce system; and show how COMPARS can be used to observe the resilience of different reputation systems with adaptive attackers.

We implemented EigenTrust and PeerTrust ourselves, and modified and adjusted the TNA-SL code by Andrew G. West *et al* [28]. As discussed in Section 2, EigenTrust is designed for peer to peer file sharing applications with the assumption that there are peers who always behave in an honest way and can thus be pre-trusted. PeerTrust is implemented in a decentralized P2P environment without any pre-trusted users. TNA-SL utilizes a theoretical approach with a greater emphasis on prior direct interaction. Details of the three reputation systems can be found in their respective papers [12, 13, 29]. Considering the fundamental differences between these three systems, we believe other reputation systems can be integrated easily into COMPARS and evaluated as well. We first present the parameters used for our experiments in Section 6.1 and we present experimental results in Section 6.2.

6.1 Materialization

Table.1 summarizes the notation for the parameters used in our experiments. Except for experiments where we needed to change some parameter values, we used the default values listed in the table.

Normal user behavior model: As mentioned earlier, the behavior of normal users in e-commerce markets (e.g., eBay) is typi-

Parameter	Description	Default
N_U	the number of users in our network	100
N_S	the number of samples for reasoning	15
H_i	feedback reliability rate of a consumer i	1.0
Q_i	service quality rate of a provider i	1.0
σ_c	consumers' strategy to choose a provider	OVER TRUST
G	an attacking goal (the amount of profit that an attacker wants to get)	60
M_T	the maximum height of an attack tree for reasoning	1
T_{avg}	the average of trust values	*
α	a range value to calculate profits	0.01
δ_T	threshold to be selected as a provider with "OVER TRUST" strategy	T_{avg}
δ_R	threshold to be selected as a provider with "OVER RANK" strategy	$N_U \times \frac{50}{100}$

Table 1: List of parameters for experiments

Reputation	Profit (Cheating)	Profit (No cheating)
$> T_{avg} + 5 * \alpha$	20	10
$> T_{avg} + 4 * \alpha$	18	9
$> T_{avg} + 3 * \alpha$	16	8
$> T_{avg} + 2 * \alpha$	14	7
$> T_{avg} + \alpha$	12	6
$> T_{avg}$	10	5
$> T_{avg} - \alpha$	8	4
$> T_{avg} - 2 * \alpha$	6	3
$> T_{avg} - 3 * \alpha$	4	2
$> T_{avg} - 4 * \alpha$	2	1

Table 2: Profit setting

cally predictable, but non-deterministic. Such nature can be captured by probabilistic models [28, 31]. We thus employed two parameters-*feedback reliability rate* H_i and *service quality rate* Q_i, each of which was defined for consumers and providers, respectively. Feedback reliability rate H_i is the probability that consumer i gives feedbacks consistent with true service quality; service quality rate Q_i is the probability that provider i offers good services.

The value for H_i ranges from 0.0 to 1.0, where consumers whose H_i is close to 0.0 are untrustworthy and those whose H_i is close to 1.0 are trustworthy. Although normal consumers' H_i should usually be close to 1.0, 0.0 does not necessarily mean the consumer is an attacker. This is because it is possible that one consumer may keep offering bad feedbacks for good services unintentionally, because of uncontrollable factors (e.g., a consumer is under a bad network condition or a bad delivery service); or, a consumer may accidentally give good feedbacks for bad services. We used a default value of 1.0 for H_i.

The value for Q_i also ranges from 0.0 to 1.0, where providers whose Q_i is close to 0.0 are untrustworthy and those whose Q_i is close to 1.0 are trustworthy. Similar to H_i, 0.0 does not necessarily mean the provider is an attacker, because uncontrollable factors (e.g., a provider is under a bad network condition or a bad delivery service) may affect the provider's service quality. We used a default value of 1.0 for Q_i.

Each trust function in three reputation systems (i.e., EigenTrust, PeerTrust, TNA-SL) returns a single trust score for each user reflecting their trustworthiness. In many reputation systems, the trust score is often represented as either a trust value that ranges from 0.0 to 1.0 (i.e., a trust value-based approach) or a rank among users (i.e., a rank-based approach) [9, 32]. We thus defined two strategies for a consumer to choose a provider. One is "OVER TRUST" with which a consumer will choose a provider whose trust value is over a certain threshold. A consumer can choose a threshold δ_T to pick a provider when the "OVER TRUST" is selected. Another is "OVER RANK" with which a consumer will choose a provider who is in the set of top-ranked providers. A consumer can choose a threshold δ_R to define top-ranked providers so that a user will be chosen as a provider if its rank is higher than δ_R. If a consumer does not have any strategy, a provider will be chosen randomly. Most reputation systems employ a trust value-based approach. We thus assumed that users choose "OVER TRUST", except when we compare trust value-based with rank-based approaches.

Although each user may behave in its own way, we assumed in this experiment that every user follows the same behavior model

for simplicity. That is, every user was assumed to share the same feedback reliability rate, the same service quality rate, and the same strategy to choose a provider. Also, normal users are often expected to behave consistently regardless of reputation systems. Accordingly, we plugged in the same normal consumer/provider behavior models to COMPARS for a fair evaluation of three reputation systems. That is, if a consumer whose feedback reliability rate is 1.0 has a transaction with a provider whose service quality rate is 1.0 , the consumer's feedback about the transaction is the highest value in each system.

Attacker: An attacker can be a consumer or a provider. In this experiment, however, we assumed that the attacker is a malicious provider who wants to increase its profit in e-commerce markets so as to clearly show the attacker's profits while it carries out the best actions. For simplicity, we assumed that there is a single attacker in the system who has two possible actions at each system state, i.e. provide a bad service (*cheating*) and provide a good service (*not cheating*). Note that we can add more choices of actions to deal with various types of attacks. For example, we may allow creating a new account as one of an attacker's possible actions to capture Sybil attacks.

Reasoning: When an attacker reasons, COMPARS should decide the maximum height M_T of an attack tree for a reasoning process, i.e. the maximum number of reasoning steps. We used 1 as default value of M_T.

While generating an attack tree, we produced 15 sample sequences of normal users' actions based on their behavior models, resulting in transitions to 15 system states at each timepoint. Although an attacker is not involved in the transactions, the attacker's trust score at each system state may or may not be different, because of global aggregations in some reputation systems [13]. For simplicity, we picked a system state as representative for the given time at which an attacker's trust value is the average of an attacker's trust values at 15 system states.

Attacking goal and profit model: We assumed the goal of the attacker is to get an amount of profits G with a default value 60 by gaming the system. Table 2 shows how we calculated an attacker's profits at each system state, whose rationale is explained below.

Although it is hard to define a definite relation, a number of studies have found that in e-commerce markets, the provider's reputation has impacts on the profits it can get in each transaction [19, 22] . Also, Hazard *et al.* [8] and Melnik *et al.* [19] have found that the reputation and profits have a multiplicative relationship on e-commerce markets such as eBay. Along with previous studies, we allocated different amounts of profits that an attacker gains from a single action, depending on an attacker's reputation. Since we used "OVER TRUST" as the default strategy for normal users to pick providers, we assumed that an attacker gains profits depending on its trust value.

An attacker will essentially try to look like normal users so that it will try to maintain its trust value similar to that of normal users. If the attacker's trust value is too low compared to that of normal users, it would be easily identified as untrustworthy and avoided by others; therefore, the attacker will not be able to make profits [19, 22]. We thus assumed that an attacker's profit will depend on how far its trust value is from the the average trust value of users. We divided users into 10 groups according to how far a user's trust value is from the average trust value. Depending on the range of users' trust values, we set a value α. Let T_{avg} and T_{max} denote the average and maximum trust value of users, respectively. Then,

$$\alpha = \frac{T_{max} - T_{avg}}{5}$$

We generated 100 sequences of normal users' actions to compute T_{avg} and T_{max} for the three trust functions.

An attacker in e-commerce markets attempts to make more profits by cheating [9, 14]. Clearly, if an attacker can gain a large profits without cheating, it does not need to cheat. Therefore, we assumed that an attacker makes more profits by cheating, and set a larger value of profit when an attacker is cheating at a specific state.

The entries of Table 2 indicate that if an attacker's trust value is over a defined trust value in the column, *Reputation*, it will get profits depending on its action, cheating or no cheating. The first entry, for instance, means that if an attacker's trust value is larger than $T_{avg} + 5 * \alpha$, it will get 20 profits if it cheats; 10 profits if it does not cheat.

Even though an attacker may gain more profits by cheating at a specific system state, it does not mean that the attacker's best strategy is to keep cheating all the time. That is because its trust value will change depending on its actions and the profit at a given system state is affected by its trust value. The relationship between attack goals and optimal strategies will be discussed in Section 6.2.

Since an attacker is a malicious provider in our experiments, we assumed for simplicity that normal providers' Q_i is 1.0. Note that a consumer chooses a provider whose trust value is over a certain threshold. Therefore, the attacker can still be chosen by a consumer as long as it maintains its trust value over the threshold.

6.2 Analysis of Existing Reputation Systems with COMPARS

In this section, we present our experimental results and analysis of the three reputation systems by plugging in parameters discussed in Section 6.1 to COMPARS. Note that different conclusions can be drawn from evaluations with different user behavior models, profit models and attack goals. In other words, our results do not mean an absolute conclusion that one reputation system is more or less resilient than another regardless of parameters.

Clearly, an attacker will try to choose the optimal strategy with which it obtains large profits within a small amount of time. That is, an attacker's goal is to reduce the number of transactions to satisfy a given profit goal G; whereas, the goal of trust functions is to increase the number of the attacker's transactions. We thus evaluated the number of the attacker' transactions N_{trans} to satisfy a given profit goal with different normal user behavior models (Section 6.2.1) and different number of reasoning steps (Section 6.2.2).

6.2.1 Analysis with Normal User Behavior Models

As mentioned before, we used consumers' feedback reliability rate and provider's service quality rate to handle non-deterministic nature. Since an attacker in our experiments is assumed to be a malicious provider, we assumed service quality rates of normal providers are 1.0 for simplicity.

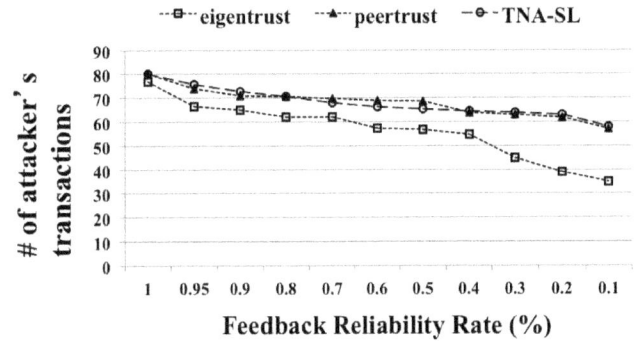

Figure 7: The required number of an attacker's transactions with change in consumers' feedback reliability rate

Fig. 7 shows the required number of an attacker's transactions N_{trans} (Y-axis) with varying consumers' feedback reliability rates H_i (X-axis). Even though each user can have different feedback reliability rates, we assumed that every consumer shares the same feedback reliability rate for simplicity.

A low feedback reliability rate of a consumer means that the consumer's feedback is not consistent with true service quality. Therefore, a consumer with a low feedback reliability rate has a high probability of giving a good feedback for an attacker's bad service (i.e., cheating). In other words, the attacker's misbehavior will not be punished under a given trust function, if most users have low feedback reliability rates. In such a case, the attacker's optimal strategy is cheating continuously to achieve its profit goal early, because the attacker obtains more profits by cheating at each system state and cheating will not damage the attacker's reputation much. Consequently, the required number of an attacker's transactions N_{Trans} decreases as consumers' feedback reliability rate H_i decreases, as shown in Fig. 7.

EigenTrust uses the weighted sum of each user's local trust value to compute global trust values and pre-trusted peers are responsible for a big part of the computation because of their large weight. Although pre-trusted peers should have a high H_i, it is possible for pre-trusted peers to issue bad feedbacks because of uncontrollable factors as discussed in Section 3. We thus assumed even pre-trusted peers share the same H_i with other users. Hence, a low H_i of pre-trusted peers allows an attacker to manipulate a system easily. That is, the resilience of EigenTrust greatly depends on the feedback reliability rate of normal users (especially that of pre-trusted peers), compared with PeerTrust and TNA-SL. Accordingly, N_{Trans} under EigenTrust greatly decreases (i.e., less resilient than PeerTrust and TNA-SL), as the feedback reliability rate gets lower.

We considered two typical strategies (i.e., OVER TRUST and OVER RANK) for consumers to choose a provider. To compare the resilience of trust functions under different consumers' strategies, we thus assessed the number of an attacker's transactions N_{Trans} with those two strategies as shown in Fig. 8.

PeerTrust takes 1.0 as a trust value for every user at an initial state. An attacker thus has a high trust value for a while from the beginning of transactions under PeerTrust, because of its initial parameters. An attacker under PeerTrust can thus reach a goal early (i.e., less resilient) with a high trust value compared to EigenTrust and TNA-SL; because the trust value of an attacker is still relatively high, even though it continues to cheat in the first several steps. Since an attacker can get more profits by cheating at one specific state, an attacker's optimal strategy under PeerTrust is to cheat continuously for a while from a initial state. However, the attacker will not have a high trust value if a lot of continuous cheat-

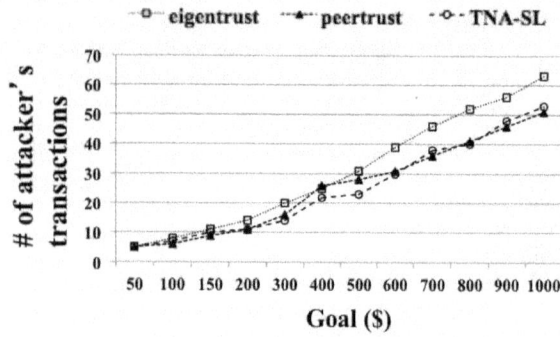

(a) A trust value-based approach (OVER TRUST)

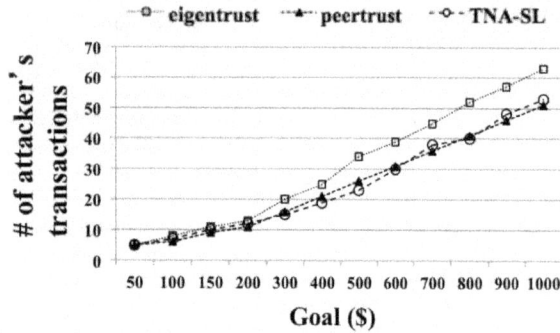

(b) A rank-based approach (OVER RANK)

Figure 8: The number of required transactions to reach a goal with two strategies

ing actions are performed. Hence, N_{Trans} increases gradually, as G increases as shown in Fig. 8.

Similar to PeerTrust, the curve of N_{Trans} shows a gradual increase under TNA-SL, as the goal G increases as shown in Fig. 8; because TNA-SL weighs information from direct interaction. As the number of transactions increases, more direct information will be collected. Hence, the trust values under TNA-SL reflect more accurate information with more direct information, as the number of transactions increases. However, EigenTrust utilizes normalized global trust values so that the difference between an attacker's trust values with more or fewer transactions is relatively small [13]. Therefore, N_{Trans} increases in almost direct proportion to the G under EigenTrust as shown in Fig. 8.

When "OVER TRUST" is employed, a consumer should choose δ_T that defines the minimum trust value required for a provider to be selected. If "OVER RANK" is employed, a consumer should choose δ_R to define the maximum rank for a provider to be selected. To compare the resilience of trust functions under different thresholds, we evaluated the required number of an attacker's transactions N_{Trans} with different values for δ_T and δ_R.

Fig. 9 represents the required number of an attacker's transactions with different values for a threshold δ_T in trust value-based reputation systems. Initially, we used the average trust value T_{avg} of users for δ_T and increased by $p\%$ with the following equation until an attacker does not satisfy the required threshold.

$$\delta_T = T_{avg} + (1 - T_{avg}) * p$$

A large value of δ_T implies that consumers set high standards for providers' reputations. As δ_T increases, the attacker should have more honest transactions (more actions with no cheating) to build a reputation and to be selected as a provider. At each system state, an attacker's profits from not cheating are smaller than the profits from cheating. Hence, the required number N_{Trans} of the attacker's

transactions increases gradually, as δ_T increases. And, N_{Trans} increases dramatically, when δ_T increases by 40 % over T_{avg}.

Fig. 10 illustrates the required number of an attacker's transactions with different values for a threshold δ_R in rank-based reputation systems. Initially, we used the top 50 % for δ_R and decrease by p % with following equation until an attacker does not satisfy the required threshold.

$$\delta_R = N_U \times \frac{50 - p}{100}$$

A small value of δ_R means that consumers set high standards of providers' reputations. As δ_R decreases, an attacker should behave honestly in more transactions (more actions with no cheating) to build a reputation and to meet consumers' requirements. As mentioned above, an attacker's profits from not cheating are smaller than the attacker's profits from cheating at each system state. Hence, N_{Trans} increases incrementally, as δ_R decreases.

6.2.2 Effect of Different Number of Reasoning Steps

COMPARS can choose different number of reasoning steps to make more or less accurate estimation of the attacker's optimal strategy. Therefore, we evaluated the number of the attacker' transactions N_{trans} to satisfy a given profit goal with changes in the number of reasoning steps as shown in Fig. 11.

As shown in Fig. 11, N_{trans} (Y-axis) decreased as the attacker performs more reasoning steps (X-axis). This indicates that the attacker can achieve its goal much more efficiently with more reasoning steps. The number of reasoning steps essentially mean that the attacker behaves more or less adaptively (i.e., 0 reasoning step means static behavior and more reasoning steps mean more adaptive behavior). Accordingly, Fig. 11 shows that highly adaptive attackers can indeed better game the system, compared to less adaptive attackers.

EigenTrust assumes that there exist pre-trusted peers who are the most trustworthy and computes trust values with a weighted sum of each user's local trust value. Pre-trusted peers are thus assumed to follow static behavior model and the weight of them is much greater than that of other normal users. If an attacker acts badly to pre-trusted peers, it will greatly damage the attacker's trust value, because of their weight. Consequently, it is relatively easy (i.e., less reasoning is needed) for an attacker to guess how a system works and to estimate its optimal strategy (i.e., no cheating, if a pre-trusted peer is involved in a transaction; otherwise, behave depending on each user's behavior). In other words, the attacker can save its time in satisfying a given profit goal G with a small number of reasoning steps. As shown in Fig. 11, an attacker can greatly reduce N_{trans} with only three reasoning steps under EigenTrust.

PeerTrust assumes that every user has the highest trust value at an initial state, so that an attacker's first few actions will not have significant impacts on the attacker's trust value. That is, it will be hard for the attacker to guess how a system works within a few reasoning steps. Hence, more reasoning is needed to reach a goal sooner. As shown in Fig.11, an attacker will begin to reduce the number of transactions greatly with reasoning steps more than three.

TNA-SL weighs information from direct interaction. As more transactions have done in the system, users who have relatively many direct interactions may appear under TNA-SL. In such a case, the feedback of those users will have bigger impact on others. In other words, those users who had a lot of direct interactions under TNA-SL can be considered to play a similar role to pre-trusted peers under EigenTrust. Similar to EigenTrust, it will greatly damage the attacker's trust value for an attacker to act badly to those users. It is thus relatively easy (i.e. needs less reasoning) for an

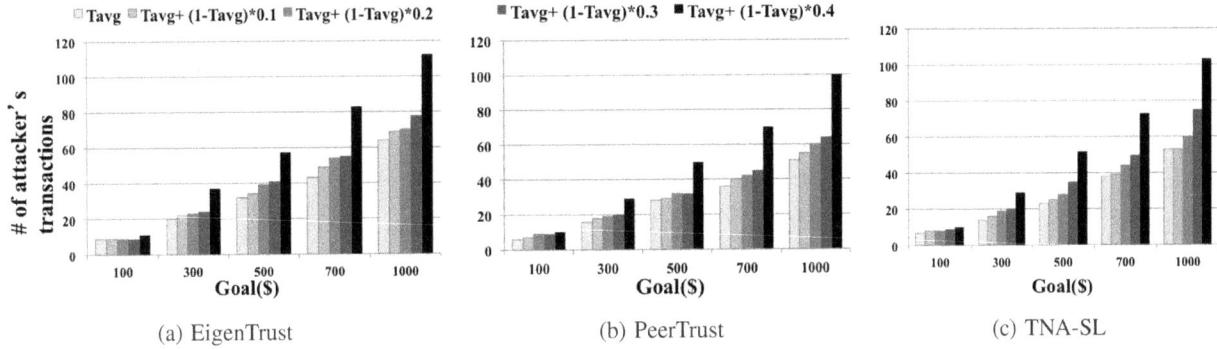

Figure 9: The required number of an attacker's transactions with different δ_T

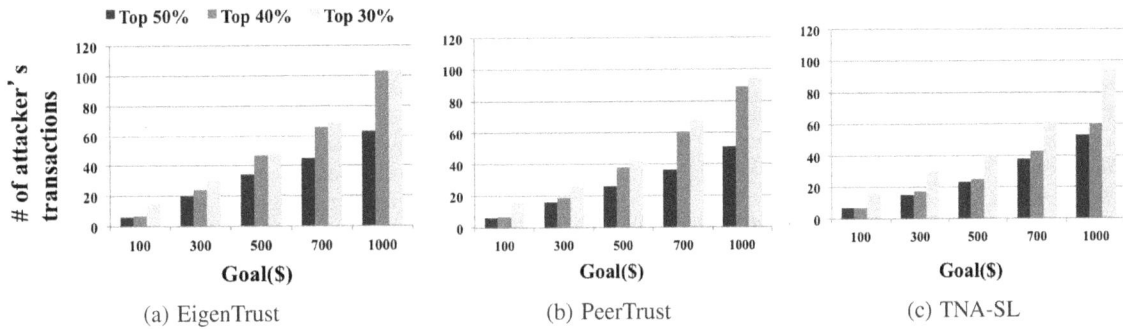

Figure 10: The required number of an attacker's transactions with different δ_R

attacker to guess how a system works. As shown in Fig. 11, an attacker can greatly reduce the number of transactions with only three reasoning steps under TNA-SL.

An interesting finding in Fig. 11 was that with 1 reasoning step, EigenTrust was much more resilient than PeerTrust and TNA-SL; but with 5 reasoning steps, EigenTrust and TNA-SL offer similar resilience. This corroborates that the evaluation of resilience with less reasoning (i.e., static or less adaptive attack) do not reflect the true resilience of a trust function.

7. CONCLUSION

The adaptive nature of strategic attackers presents challenging issues for the evaluation of resilience of trust functions. Specifically, reputation systems based on static user models leave opportunities for malicious parties to exploit systems easily by changing behavior arbitrarily with knowledge of trust functions. This paper presents an evaluation framework for the COMPArison of Reputation Systems (COMPARS), which models adaptive attackers. COMPARS simulates attackers' optimal strategies with an attack tree. We evaluated the resilience of trust functions against attacks by observing how many transactions are required for attackers to achieve their goal based on assumption that a good trust function will restrict the opportunities for attackers to exploit a system,

Acknowledgement

This work is supported in part by the National Science Foundation under the awards CNS-0747247, CCF-0914946 and CNS-1314229, and by an NSA Science of Security Lablet grant at North Carolina State University. We would also like to thank the anonymous reviewers for their valuable feedback.

References

[1] R. Aringhieri, E. Damiani, S. D. C. D. Vimercati, S. Paraboschi, and P. Samarati. Fuzzy techniques for trust and reputation management in anonymous peer-to-peer systems. *J. Am. Soc. Inf. Sci. Technol.*, 57(4):528–537, 2006.

[2] P. Chandrasekaran and B. Esfandiari. A model for a testbed for evaluating reputation systems. In *Trust, Security and Privacy in Computing and Communications (TrustCom), 2011 IEEE 10th International Conference on*, pages 296–303. IEEE, 2011.

[3] A. Cheng and E. Friedman. Sybilproof reputation mechanisms. In *Proceedings of the 2005 ACM SIGCOMM workshop on Economics of peer-to-peer systems*, pages 128–132. ACM, 2005.

[4] Z. Cheng and N. Hurley. Analysis of robustness in trust-based recommender systems. In *Adaptivity, Personalization and Fusion of Heterogeneous Information*, pages 114–121. LE CENTRE DE HAUTES ETUDES INTERNATIONALES D'INFORMATIQUE DOCUMENTAIRE, 2010.

[5] M. Fan, Y. Tan, and A. B. Whinston. Evaluation and design of online cooperative feedback mechanisms for reputation management. *IEEE Transactions on Knowledge and Data Engineering*, 17:244–254, 2005.

[6] J. Feng, Y. Zhang, S. Chen, and A. Fu. Rephi: A novel attack against p2p reputation systems. In *Computer Communications Workshops (INFOCOM WKSHPS), 2011 IEEE Conference on*, pages 1088–1092. IEEE, 2011.

[7] K. K. Fullam, T. Klos, G. Muller, J. Sabater-Mir, K. S. Barber, and L. Vercouter. The agent reputation and trust (art) testbed. In *Trust Management*, pages 439–442. Springer, 2006.

[8] C. J. Hazard and M. P. Singh. Reputation dynamics and convergence: A basis for evaluating reputation systems. 2009.

[9] K. Hoffman, D. Zage, and C. Nita-Rotaru. A survey of attack and defense techniques for reputation systems. *ACM*

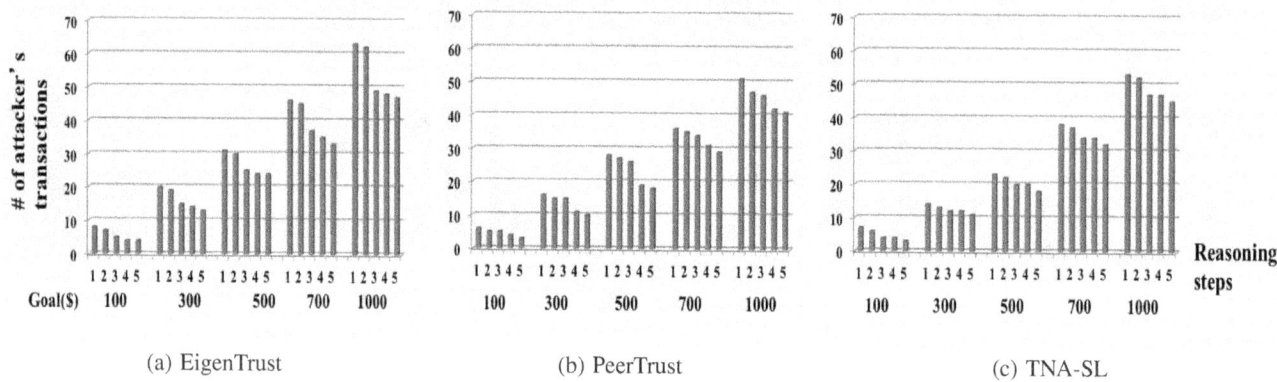

(a) EigenTrust   (b) PeerTrust   (c) TNA-SL

Figure 11: The effect of the number of reasoning steps

Comput. Surv., 42(1):1–31, 2009.

[10] A. A. Irissappane, S. Jiang, and J. Zhang. Towards a comprehensive testbed to evaluate the robustness of reputation systems against unfair rating attack. In *UMAP Workshops*, volume 12, 2012.

[11] A. Jøsang and J. Golbeck. Challenges for Robust of Trust and Reputation Systems. In *Proceedings of the 5th International Workshop on Security and Trust Management.* Elsevier Science B. V., 2009.

[12] A. Jøsang, R. Hayward, and S. Pope. Trust network analysis with subjective logic. In *ACSC '06: Proceedings of the 29th Australasian Computer Science Conference*, pages 85–94. Australian Computer Society, Inc., 2006.

[13] S. D. Kamvar, M. T. Schlosser, and H. Garcia-Molina. The eigentrust algorithm for reputation management in p2p networks. In *WWW '03: Proceedings of the 12th international conference on World Wide Web*, pages 640–651. ACM, 2003.

[14] R. Kerr and R. Cohen. Smart cheaters do prosper: defeating trust and reputation systems. In *Proceedings of The 8th International Conference on Autonomous Agents and Multiagent Systems*, volume 2, pages 993–1000. International Foundation for Autonomous Agents and Multiagent Systems, 2009.

[15] R. Kerr and R. Cohen. Treet: the trust and reputation experimentation and evaluation testbed. *Electronic Commerce Research*, 10(3-4):271–290, 2010.

[16] H. Li and M. Singhal. Trust management in distributed systems. *Computer*, 40:45 –53, 2007.

[17] S. Marti and H. Garcia-Molina. Taxonomy of trust: Categorizing p2p reputation systems. *Computer Networks*, 50(4):472 – 484, 2006.

[18] K. McNally, M. P. O'Mahony, and B. Smyth. A comparative study of collaboration-based reputation models for social recommender systems. *User Modeling and User-Adapted Interaction*, pages 1–42, 2013.

[19] M. I. Melnik and J. Alm. Does a seller's ecommerce reputation matter? evidence from ebay auctions. *The Journal of Industrial Economics*, 50(3):337–349, 2002.

[20] J. Mundinger and J. Le Boudec. Analysis of a reputation system for mobile ad-hoc networks with liars. In *Third International Symposium on Modeling and Optimization in Mobile, Ad Hoc, and Wireless Networks*, pages 41 – 46, 2005.

[21] N. J. Nilsson. *Problem-Solving Methods in Artificial Intelligence.* McGraw-Hill Pub. Co., 1971.

[22] P. Resnick, R. Zeckhauser, J. Swanson, and K. Lockwood. The value of reputation on ebay: A controlled experiment. *Experimental Economics*, 9:79–101, 2006.

[23] J. Sabater and C. Sierra. Review on computational trust and reputation models. *Artificial Intelligence Review*, 24:33–60, 2005.

[24] A. Selcuk, E. Uzun, and M. Pariente. A reputation-based trust management system for p2p networks. In *IEEE International Symposium on Cluster Computing and the Grid*, pages 251 – 258, 2004.

[25] Y. Sun and Y. Liu. Security of online reputation systems: The evolution of attacks and defenses. *Signal Processing Magazine, IEEE*, 29(2):87–97, 2012.

[26] Y. L. Sun, Z. Han, W. Yu, and K. J. R. Liu. A trust evaluation framework in distributed networks: Vulnerability analysis and defense against attacks. In *IEEE INFOCOM*, pages 230–236, 2006.

[27] G. Suryanarayana and R. N. Taylor. A survey of trust management and resource discovery technologies in peer-to-peer applications, 2004.

[28] A. G. West, S. Kannan, I. Lee, and O. Sokolsky. An evaluation framework for reputation management systems. 2009.

[29] L. Xiong and L. Liu. Peertrust: Supporting reputation-based trust for peer-to-peer electronic communities. *IEEE Transactions on Knowledge and Data Engineering*, 16:843–857, 2004.

[30] Y. Yanchao Zhang and Y. Yuguang Fang. A fine-grained reputation system for reliable service selection in peer-to-peer networks. *IEEE Transactions on Parallel and Distributed Systems*, 18(8):1134 –1145, 2007.

[31] Q. Zhang, W. Wei, and T. Yu. On the modeling of honest players in reputation systems. *Journal of Computer Science and Technology*, 24:808–819, 2009.

[32] Q. Zhang, T. Yu, and K. Irwin. A classification scheme for trust functions in reputation-based trust management. In *International Workshop on Trust, Security, and Reputation on the Semantic Web.* Australian Computer Society, Inc., 2004.

[33] R. Zhou and K. Hwang. Powertrust: A robust and scalable reputation system for trusted peer-to-peer computing. *IEEE Transactions on Parallel and Distributed Systems*, 18:460–473, 2007.

RISKMON: Continuous and Automated Risk Assessment of Mobile Applications

Yiming Jing[†], Gail-Joon Ahn[†], Ziming Zhao[†], and Hongxin Hu[‡]

[†]Arizona State University   [‡]Delaware State University

{ymjing,gahn,zzhao30}@asu.edu, hhu@desu.edu

ABSTRACT

Mobile operating systems, such as Apple's iOS and Google's Android, have supported a ballooning market of feature-rich mobile applications. However, helping users understand security risks of mobile applications is still an ongoing challenge. While recent work has developed various techniques to reveal suspicious behaviors of mobile applications, there exists little work to answer the following question: *are those behaviors necessarily inappropriate?* In this paper, we seek an approach to cope with such a challenge and present a continuous and automated risk assessment framework called RISKMON that uses machine-learned ranking to assess risks incurred by users' mobile applications, especially Android applications. RISKMON combines users' coarse expectations and runtime behaviors of trusted applications to generate a risk assessment baseline that captures appropriate behaviors of applications. With the baseline, RISKMON assigns a risk score on every access attempt on sensitive information and ranks applications by their cumulative risk scores. We also discuss a proof-of-concept implementation of RISK-MON as an extension of the Android mobile platform and provide both system evaluation and usability study of our methodology.

Categories and Subject Descriptors

C.4 [**Performance of Systems**]: Measurement techniques; D.4.6 [**Operating Systems**]: Security and Protection—*Access controls, Information flow controls*

Keywords

Smartphones; Android; Risk Assessment

1. INTRODUCTION

Mobile operating systems, such as Android and iOS, have tremendously supported an application market over the last few years. Google Play announced 48 billion app downloads in May 2013 [27]. Almost at the same time, Apple's AppStore reached 50 billion downloads [31]. Such a new paradigm drives developers to produce feature-rich applications that seamlessly cater towards users' growing needs of processing their personal information such as contacts, locations and other credentials on their mobile devices. Unfortunately, the large installed base has also attracted attention of unscrupulous developers who are interested in users' sensitive information for a variety of purposes. For example, spyware tracks users' locations and reports to remote controllers, and adware collects users' identities for enforcing an aggressive directed marketing.

To defend against such rogue applications, Android assists users to review them at install time. Primarily, Android relies on permissions to help users understand the security and privacy risks of applications. In Android, an application must request permissions to be allowed to access sensitive resources. In other words, it is mandatory for Android applications to present its expected behaviors to users. Even though permissions outline the resources that an application attempts to access, they do not provide fine-grained information about how and when such resources will be used. Suppose a user installs an application and allows it to access her location information. It is hard for her to determine whether the application accesses her locations on her demand or periodically without asking for her explicit consent. Therefore, it is imperative to continuously monitor the installed applications so that a user could be informed when rogue applications abuse her sensitive information. Previous work has proposed real-time monitoring to reveal potential misbehaviors of third-party applications [14, 22, 30, 38, 39]. Specifically, TaintDroid [14] and Aurasium [38] inspect an application's behaviors at variable and syscall level, respectively. While these techniques partially provide valuable insights into a user's installed applications, it is still critical to answer the following challenge: *are the behaviors in mobile applications necessarily inappropriate?*

To answer this question, it is an end-user's responsibility to conduct risk assessment and make decisions based on her disposition and perception. Risk assessment is not a trivial task since it requires the user to digest diverse contextual and technical information. In addition, the user needs to apprehend *expected behaviors* of applications under different contexts prior to addressing her risk assessment baseline.

However, it is impractical for the normal users to distill such a baseline. Instead, it is essential to develop an automated approach to continuously monitor applications and effectively alert users upon security and privacy violations.

In this paper, we propose an automated and continuous risk assessment framework for mobile platforms, called RISKMON. RISKMON requires a user's coarse expectations for different types of applications while user intervention is not required for the subsequent risk assessment. The user needs to provide her selection of trusted applications from the installed applications on her device and her ranking of permission groups in terms of their relevancy to the corresponding application. Then, RISKMON builds the user's risk assessment baseline for different application categories by leveraging API traces of her selected applications. RISKMON continuously monitors the installed applications' behaviors, including their interactions with other applications and system services. The risk of each interaction is measured by how much it deviates from the risk assessment baseline. For a better risk perception, RISKMON ranks installed applications based on the risk assessment results in a real-time manner. Intuitively, the user can deem an application as safe if it is less risky than any of her trusted applications.

As RISKMON interposes and assesses API calls before an application gets the results, we foresee the possibility of integrating RISKMON into an automated permission granting process as discussed in [18] and [32]. Furthermore, while we implement RISKMON on the Android platform, RISKMON is equally applicable to other platforms (e.g. Apple iOS and Microsoft Windows Phone) in assisting security experts to discover high-risk applications. Tools like RISKMON would practically help raise awareness of security and privacy problems and lower the sophistication required for concerned users to better understand the risks of third-party mobile applications.

This paper makes the following contributions:

- We propose a methodology for establishing a risk assessment baseline from a user's trusted applications and her coarse expectations. Our approach lowers the required sophistication to conduct effective risk assessment for end-users;

- We propose a machine-learned ranking based framework that continuously monitors the runtime behaviors of mobile applications, automatically measures their risks, and intuitively presents the risks;

- We implement a proof-of-concept prototype of RISKMON and demonstrate how it can be seamlessly deployed in Android; and

- We evaluate RISKMON with comprehensive experiments, case studies, and crowd-sourced user surveys. Our experimental results demonstrate the feasibility and practicality of RISKMON.

The remainder of this paper proceeds as follows. Section 2 provides the motivation and problem description of this paper. Section 3 provides a high-level overview of the RISKMON framework and system design by illustrating each stage of automated risk assessment. Section 4 presents prototype implementation and evaluation of our framework. Section 5 discusses the limitations of our approach. Section 6 describes related work. Section 7 concludes the paper.

2. MOTIVATION AND BACKGROUND TECHNOLOGIES

Users are concerned about security and privacy issues on mobile devices. However, in most cases they are not aware of the issues unless highlighted. Although Apple's mandatory application review process [1] and Google Bouncer [25] strive to mitigate misbehaving applications, users are still responsible for defending themselves.

2.1 Use Cases and Threat Model

A continuous and automated risk assessment framework enhances a number of use cases in the current mobile application ecosystems. In general, such a framework improves user experience of security features and promotes understanding about risks of mobile applications. This enables more users to discover misbehaving applications and possibly write negative reviews, thereby alerting and protecting other users. In addition, it complements static and dynamic analysis in ensuring appropriateness justifications by security analysts. This could be applied in both official and alternative application markets as a pre-screening mechanism to select suspicious applications for further analysis. Alternatively, a developer can evaluate her applications against those of her competitors and improve security practices if necessary. For the purposes of this paper we consider the generic scenario where a user assesses her installed applications.

Applications, as long as they are not on users' devices, do not incur any substantial risk. Once an application is installed, it starts interacting with the operating system and other applications. While the application accesses sensitive resources, it gradually builds a big picture of the system as well as the user. Each access, such as calling an API, returns a tiny fraction of the picture and incurs a small amount of risk. Once the picture is finished, it may contain a user's personal identities (e.g. contacts), device identities (e.g. manufacturer) and context identities (e.g. locations, WiFi SSIDs). Since risk assessment at the pre-installation stage does not address such threats on users' devices, we aim to provide continuous risk assessment for normal users.

2.2 Risk Assessment of Mobile Applications

Recent work has proposed mechanisms to extract risk signals from meta information on application markets such as permissions [16, 28, 33, 36], ratings [9, 10], and application descriptions [26]. Their limitation is that such information is fuzzy and fails to provide fine-grained information about how and when sensitive resources are used. For example, an application may stay in the background and keep probing a user's locations and surroundings. Moreover, a malicious application with split personalities [5] can evade screening mechanisms of application markets. We argue that users deserve the rights to understand what is happening on their own devices. Thus, continuously revealing runtime behaviors plays a vital role as a necessary defense line against rogue applications.

Previous research concerning applications' runtime behaviors specifies a set of risk assessment heuristics tailored to their specific problems. For example, TaintDroid [14] considers a case in which sensitive data is transmitted over the network. DroidRanger [40] and RiskRanker [20] assume that dynamically loaded code is a potential sign of malware. While these techniques provide valuable insights about runtime behaviors of mobile applications, they do not justify the appropriateness of the revealed behaviors. We argue that runtime behaviors are not the only factor to determine appropriateness. Another important factor is the contextual properties. For example, a location-based application has good reason to upload a user's locations for discovering nearby restaurants. In contrast, it does not make sense for a video player to use the locations. Also, a user's expectations are another critical factor. Even though an application is allowed to use a user's sensitive information, the user should have the capability to specify preferences for determining accesses to her own sensitive information. However, we cannot assume that all users are able to digest contextual information and system-level expectations, which is necessary for establishing a risk assessment baseline that captures appropriate behaviors. The absence of such a baseline renders current risk assessment process ineffective. Therefore, it is imperative to automate risk assessment for seamlessly helping users accommodate their preferences without requiring additional intervention.

2.3 Android Platform

Android is a computing platform for mobile devices. It implements a security architecture that adopts a sandbox and a permission framework. While system services and installed applications are isolated and confined in their respective sandboxes, they can interact and collaborate via APIs. Each permission protects a set of APIs that access some sensitive resources. A user can approve permission requests of an application at install time so that the application is allowed to use the corresponding APIs.

Permission groups: Permission group is a logical grouping of related permissions. For example, `SOCIAL_INFO` includes permissions that access a user's contacts and call logs. Given Android API level 18, Android provides 31 permission groups to cover 134 permissions. Most permission groups are self-descriptive, such as `LOCATION` and `CAMERA`. Android also provides a short description for each permission group to elaborate its corresponding resources.

API and direction of control flow: A typical Android application's execution is orchestrated by API calls and callbacks with opposite directions of control flows. An API call initiates a synchronous control flow so that the caller application gets results immediately after the API returns. API callbacks are designed for asynchronous control flows which enable a system service to notify an application when an event occurs or a result is ready. Both API calls and callbacks are frequently used in accessing sensitive resources, such as getting a contact entry and receiving location updates.

Binder IPC framework: While APIs enable applications to interact with each other and system services in their respective process sandboxes, they are implemented based on an underlying inter-process communication framework called *Binder*. Binder includes a kernel driver and a userspace library. It serializes data objects as *parcels* for sender process, and de-serialize parcels for recipient process. Binder also manages IPC transactions in which parcels are processed and delivered. Binder identifies a transaction with the UIDs and PIDs of sender and recipient processes as well as a command code that specifies the action to be performed in the receipt process.

3. RISKMON: OVERVIEW AND SYSTEM DESIGN

In this section, we describe our risk assessment framework that lowers the required intervention and sophistication in risk assessment of mobile applications.

IT risk assessment guidelines, such as NIST SP 800-30 [35] and CERT OCTAVE [2], illustrate general methodologies that enable organizations to understand, assess and address their information risks. For example, OCTAVE covers the following critical tasks [3]:

1. Identify critical information assets and their security requirements;
2. Consider the activities that can expose the identified assets to threats due to organizational and/or technological vulnerabilities;
3. Define risk evaluation criteria that captures operational context and organization's tolerance; and
4. Create practice-based protection strategies and risk mitigation plans.

While these guidelines deal with the infrastructure and organizational risks by security experts, our framework attempts to adapt and automate the sophisticated risk assessment tasks for general users. Several existing state-of-the-art frameworks attempt to automatically extract a universal risk assessment baseline by mining the meta information of a large number of mobile applications (e.g. Peng et al. [28]). Compared with their approaches, RISKMON adheres to general risk assessment methodologies and considers user's security requirements and operational contexts as indispensable inputs. This design choice enables our framework to accurately capture user's expected appropriate behaviors rather than average practices of developers.

An underlying assumption of RISKMON is that a user's trusted applications could define her expected appropriate behaviors. Recent empirical analysis showed that applications of similar categories normally request a similar set of permissions [6], implying similar core functionalities. Hence, each of the user's trusted applications can be used as a reference point of appropriate behaviors for applications of similar categories. For example, Netflix application is under "Entertainment" category, and Pandora's Internet Radio application is under "Music & Audio" category. Even though they are not in the same category, each application similarly uses one of core functionalities such as the streaming service of personalized media contents from remote servers. If a user trusts Netflix application, it implicitly affirms that Pandora application may also incur commensurate risks caused by Netflix application. Thus, using Netflix application as a reference point, the deviation or "distance" of runtime behaviors between Netflix and Pandora applications indicates Pandora's additional inherent risks.

We now summarize the design goals for a continuous and automated risk assessment framework:

Continuous and fine-grained behavior monitoring: Applications access sensitive resources by calling APIs to communicate with each other and system services. To ensure continuous monitoring on API calls, RISKMON interposes Binder IPC on a user's device. The risks incurred by API calls are determined by the caller, the callee, and the data. To capture such information, RISKMON opts for a fine-grained

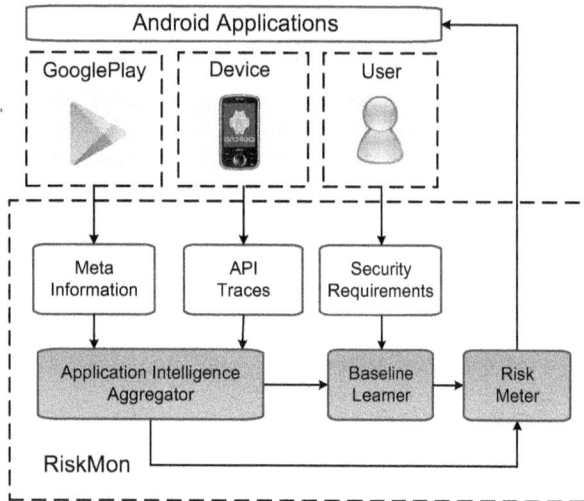

Figure 1: RiskMon Architecture for Android

scheme to capture various intelligences about applications. This provides a well-founded base for measuring the "distance" between two API calls in the space of runtime behaviors.

Simplified security requirement communication: It is a challenging task for users to specify security requirements for security tools. To tackle this problem, RISKMON adopts a simple heuristic that allows users to communicate security requirements through their coarse expectations. Although this reduces the burden on the user, we cannot entirely eliminate it. We note that acquiring a user's expectations is necessary since each user has diverse preferences on the same application. For instance, all users of Facebook application may have disparate expectations for controlling their location and camera utilities.

Intuitive risk representation: The way in which risk is presented significantly influences a user's perception and decision upon risky applications. A counterexample would be standalone risk scores, such as a risk indicator saying "Facebook incurs 90 units of risk" without proper explanation. As Peng et al. noted in [28], "it is more effective to present comparative risk information". Inspired by their approach, RISKMON presents a ranking of applications so that a user can compare the potential loss of using an application with other applications. In addition, the user can view the risk composition of an application for supporting evidences.

Iterative risk management: Risk assessment is an ongoing iterative process. As applications get upgraded and bring more functionalities, they introduce new risks that should be measured. To this end, the risk assessment baseline should evolve to continuously monitor installed applications and update the risk assessment baseline periodically. Moreover, users need to provide their feedbacks to RISKMON by adding or revising their security requirements.

We now present our risk assessment framework. Figure 1 depicts the RISKMON architecture for Android. Our framework consists of three components: an application intelligence aggregator, a baseline learner, and a risk meter.

The application intelligence aggregator compiles a dataset from API traces collected on a user's device and meta infor-

mation crawled from application markets. API traces cover an application's interactions with other parts of the system via API calls and callbacks. To complement API traces with contextual information, RISKMON uses meta information on application markets such as ratings, number of downloads and category which provide a quantitative representation of applications' reputation and intended core functionalities. The baseline learner combines a user's coarse expectations and aggregated intelligences of her trusted applications to generate a training set. Afterwards, the baseline learner applies a machine-learned ranking algorithm to learn a risk assessment baseline. Then the risk meter measures how much an application's behaviors deviate from the baseline. Using the deviation to provide risk information, risk meter ranks a user's installed applications by their cumulative risks and presents the ranking to the user in an intuitive way. The remainder of this section describes each component in detail.

3.1 Application Intelligence Aggregator

This component aggregates intelligences about a user's installed applications, including their runtime behaviors and contextual information. As RISKMON monitors runtime behaviors by interposing Binder IPC, we propose a set of features for API traces tailored to the peculiarity of Binder. Also, we seek contextual information from application markets and propose corresponding features to represent and characterize them. The proposed features build a space of application intelligences and enables subsequent baseline generation and risk measurement. Unless explicitly specified, all features are normalized to [0,1] so that each of them contributes proportionally.

3.1.1 Features for API Traces

Android applications frequently use APIs to interact with system services. Considering that using most APIs does not require any permission, we assume that resources protected by at least one permission are a user's assets.

We are interested in runtime behaviors, i.e. Binder transactions, that are used by APIs to reach the assets. However, APIs do not carry information about Binder transactions. To bridge this gap, we adopt existing work [4, 17] to provide mappings from permissions to APIs. Meanwhile, we analyzed the interface definitions of Android system services and core libraries to generate a mapping from APIs to Binder transactions. As a result, we extracted 1,003 permission-protected APIs, of which each corresponds to a type of Binder transactions. Each type of Binder transaction is identified by the corresponding system service, direction of control flow, and a command code unique to the service. For example, an API named `requestLocationUpdate` is identified as Binder IPC transaction (`LocationManager`, `callback, 1`).

We attempt to represent a Binder transaction with its internal properties and contents. For a specific Binder transaction between an application and a system service, we are interested in its type so as to identify the corresponding asset. Also we need to know the direction of control flow for determining who initiates the transaction. As users trust the system services more than applications, RISKMON should differentiate Binder transactions initiated by applications and system services. Thus, internal properties are represented with the following features:

- **Type of Binder transaction**: 1,003 boolean features as a bit array, where one bit is set to 1 for the corresponding transaction type and others are 0; and

- **Direction of control flow**: another boolean feature: 0 for transactions initiated from applications (API calls), 1 for transactions initiated from system services (API callbacks).

Note that we use 1,003 boolean features to represent the type of Binder transactions instead of using one integer value. This is because Binder transactions are independent from each other, and the Binder command codes are simply nominal values. By using the array of 1,003 boolean values, the distances between any two Binder transaction types are set to the same value, which is important for our learning algorithm (Section 3.2.3).

In terms of contents, parcels in Binder transactions are unstructured and highly optimized, and it is hard to restore the original data objects without implementation details of the sender and recipient. Therefore, we use length as one representative feature of parcel. A motivating example is accesses on contacts. From the length of a parcel we can infer whether an application is reading a single entry or dumping the entire contacts database. Thus, we propose the following two features for parcels:

- **Length of received parcel**: length of the parcel received by an application in bytes; and

- **Length of sent parcel**: length of the parcel sent by an application in bytes.

3.1.2 Features for Meta Information

Although meta information on application markets cannot describe applications' runtime behaviors, it is still viable to use such information as contextual properties that capture users' and developers' opinions and complement runtime behavior information.

In terms of representing the opinions of users, we use the following features in correspondence with their counterparts of meta information on application markets:

- **Number of installs**: a range of total number of installs since the first release[1]. We use logarithmic value of the lower bound, i.e., *log(1+lower bound of #installs)*;

- **Number of reviews**: a number of reviews written by unique users. We use the logarithmic value, i.e. *log(1+#reviews)*; and

- **Rating score**: a number indicating the user-rated quality of the application ranged from 1.0 to 5.0.

These three features capture an application's popularity and reputation. The first two features are similar to number of views and comments in online social networks. Recent studies [37] demonstrated that online social networks and crowd-sourcing systems expose a long-tailed distribution. Therefore, we assume they follow the same distribution and use the logarithmic values.

We emphasize that we do not attempt to extract risk signals from these features. Instead, we adopt these features

---

[1] Number of installs is specified with exponentially increasing ranges: 1+, 5+, ..., 1K+, 5K+, ..., 1M+, 5M+.

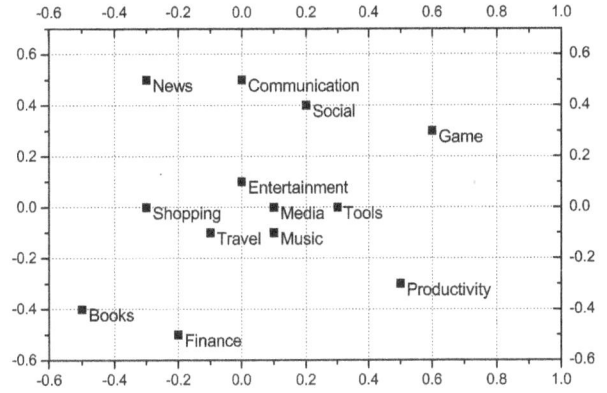

Figure 2: SOM Representation of 13 Categories

to capture the underlying patterns of a user's trusted applications as specified by the user and apply the patterns for the subsequent risk assessment.

Next, we propose a feature to capture the developer's opinion:

- **Category:** a tuple of two numerical values normalized to [-0.5, 0.5].

Google Play uses an application's category to describe its core functionalities (e.g. "Communication"). As of this writing, Google Play provides 27 category types. We choose Self-Organizing Map (SOM) to give a 2-dimension representation of categories. Barrera et al. [6] demonstrated that SOM can produce a 2-dimensional, discretized representation of permissions requested by different categories of Android applications. Categories in which applications request similar permissions are clustered together. Therefore we use the x and y coordinates in the map to represent categories. Figure 2 depicts the coordinates of 13 categories as an example. It is clear to see that some categories bear underlying similarities, such as "Entertainment", "Media and Video" and "Music and Audio" in the center of the figure[2].

Clearly an unscrupulous developer can claim an irrelevant category to disguise an application's intended core functionalities. However, a user can easily notice the inconsistencies and remove such applications. In addition, falsifying an application's meta information violates the terms of application market's developer policies and may lead to immediate takedown.

Finally, based on the scheme defined by these features, the application intelligence aggregator generates a dataset consisted of feature vectors extracted from API traces and meta information of each installed application.

3.2 Baseline Learner

The baseline learner is the core module of RISKMON. It takes two types of inputs, which are a user's expectations and feature vectors extracted by the application intelligence aggregator. Then the baseline learner generates a risk assessment baseline which is represented as a predictive model.

3.2.1 Acquiring Security Requirements

It is challenging for most users to express their security requirements accurately. We aim to find an approach that

---

[2] For more details on SOM, please refer to [6].

could be mostly acceptable by users. Krosnick and Alwin's dual path model [24] demonstrated that a *satisficing* user would rely on salient cues to make a decision. Based on this model we develop a simple heuristic:

> *For a specific application, accesses on resources that are more irrelevant of a user's expected core functionalities incur more risks.*

This heuristic captures a user's expectations as security requirements by risk aversion, which implies the reluctance of a user to use a functionality with an unknown marginal utility [29]. For example, a user may consider that, microphone is necessary to a VoIP application such as Skype. But location seems not because she does not understand the underlying correlation between disclosing her location and making a phone call. Thus, microphone is more relevant and less risky than location in her perception.

Base on this, the risk learner asks a user to specify a relevancy level for each permission group requested by her trusted applications. We choose permission groups to represent resources because it is much easier for general users to learn 20+ permission groups than 140+ permissions. And recent usability studies demonstrated the ineffectiveness of permissions due to limited comprehension [12,19]. Although users tend to overestimate the scope and risk of permission groups, they are more intuitive and reduce warning fatigue [19].

The process for users to communicate their security requirements with RISKMON is similar to a short questionnaire. Each permission group requested by a user's trusted applications corresponds to a five-point Likert item. The user specifies the level of relevancy on a symmetric bipolar scale, namely *relevant, probably relevant, neutral, probably irrelevant* or *irrelevant*. Figure 3 shows an example of relevancy of permission groups for Facebook and Skype. Permission groups are represented by self-descriptive icons, which are identical to those shown in Android Settings. CAMERA preceding LOCATION for Facebook is possibly due to the user's preference to photo sharing compared to check-ins.

Note that the relevancy levels specified by users are *subjective*. With that said, users' biased perception of applications and resources may affect their specified relevancy levels. From our user study, a user told us that PHONE_CALLS is relevant to Google Maps because he tapped a phone number shown in Google Map and then the dialer appeared. Although the dialer rather than Google Map has the capability to make phone calls, the baseline learner considers it as the security requirements for inter-application communication.

We next formalize the problem of acquiring security requirements. $PG = \{pg_1, pg_2, \cdots, pg_m\}$ is a set of permission groups available in a mobile operating system. $A = \{a_1, a_2, \cdots, a_n\}$ is a set of a user's installed applications. TA is a set of a user's trusted and installed applications and $TA \subseteq A$. $RequestedPG : A \to 2^{PG}$ is a function that maps an application to its requested permission groups. A user's security requirement Req is a mapping $Req : TA \times PG \to R$. $R = \{1, 2, 3, 4, 5\}$ is a set of relevancy levels, where a larger value indicates higher relevancy and less risk and vice versa.

3.2.2 Compiling Training Set

Next we describe how the baseline learner compiles a training set from the aggregated application intelligences and user-specified relevancy levels. For brevity, we apply the

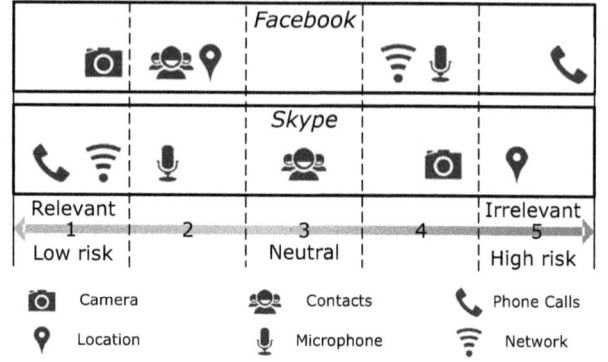

Figure 3: An Example of Specifying Relevancy for Permission Groups

relevancy levels onto the feature vectors generated by the application intelligence aggregator to generate a set of vectors annotated with relevancy levels.

To bridge the gap between permission groups and feature vectors, we extract mappings of permission groups and permissions from the source code of Android. Meanwhile, existing work has provided mappings between permissions and APIs [4,17]. Therefore, we can assign the relevancy level on feature vectors because each vector represents an API call or callback.

We formalize the problem of compiling a training set as follows. Algorithm 1 illustrates the process to compile the training set T.

- X is a space of features as defined by the scheme discussed in Section 3.1, $X = \{\vec{x}_1, \vec{x}_2, \cdots, \vec{x}_l\}$, $X \in \mathbb{R}^i$, where i denotes the number of features;
- $DS = \{D_{a1}, D_{a2}, \cdots, D_{am}\}$ is a collection of sets of feature vectors, where $D_{aj} \subseteq X$ and D_{aj} corresponds to an application a_j;
- $Apd : A \times PG \to DS$ is a function that maps an application and one of its requested permission groups to a set of feature vectors; and
- $T = \{(\vec{x}_1, r_1), (\vec{x}_2, r_2), \cdots, (\vec{x}_n, r_n)\}$ is a training set consisted of annotated vectors, $r_k \in R$, $\vec{x}_k \in X$.

Algorithm 1: Compiling Training Set

Data: DS, TA, Req
Result: T
$T \gets \emptyset$;
for $a \in TA$ **do**
    $pg \gets RequestedPG(a)$;
    $r \gets Req(a, pg)$;
    $D \gets Apd(a, pg)$;
    for $\vec{x} \in D$ **do**
        add $(\vec{x}, r)$ to T;
    end
end
return T

3.2.3 Generating Risk Assessment Baseline

Ranking Support Vector Machine (RSVM) [21,23] is a pair-wise ranking method. Generally it utilizes a regular

Support Vector Machine (SVM) solver to classify the order of *pairs of objects*. Next we explain how we apply RSVM to learn a risk assessment baseline.

We assume that a set of ranking functions $f \in F$ exists and satisfies the following:

$$\vec{x}_i \prec \vec{x}_j \iff f(\vec{x}_i) < f(\vec{x}_j), \qquad (1)$$

where $\prec$ denotes a preferential relationship of risks.

In the simplest form of RSVM, we assume that f is a linear function:

$$f_{\vec{w}}(\vec{x}) = \langle \vec{w}, \vec{x} \rangle, \qquad (2)$$

where $\vec{w}$ is a weight vector, and $\langle \cdot, \cdot \rangle$ denotes inner product.

Combing (1) and (2), we have the following:

$$\vec{x}_i \prec \vec{x}_j \iff \langle \vec{w}, \vec{x}_i - \vec{x}_j \rangle < 0, \qquad (3)$$

Note that $\vec{x}_i - \vec{x}_j$ is a new vector that expresses the relation $\vec{x}_i \prec \vec{x}_j$ between $\vec{x}_i$ and $\vec{x}_j$. Given the training set T, we create a new training set T' by assigning either a positive label $z = +1$ or a negative label $z = -1$ to each pair $(\vec{x}_i, \vec{x}_j)$.

$$(\vec{x}_i, \vec{x}_j) : z_{i,j} = \begin{cases} +1 & \text{if } r_i > r_j \\ -1 & \text{if } r_i < r_j \end{cases} \qquad (4)$$
$$\forall (\vec{x}_i, r_i), (\vec{x}_j, r_j) \in T$$

In order to select a ranking function f that fits the training set T', we construct the SVM model to solve the following quadratic optimization problem:

$$\begin{aligned} \underset{\vec{w}}{\text{minimize}} \quad & \frac{1}{2}\vec{w} \cdot \vec{w} + C \sum \xi_{i,j} \\ \text{subject to} \quad & \forall (\vec{x}_i, \vec{x}_j) \in T' : z_{i,j}\langle \vec{w}, \vec{x}_i - \vec{x}_j \rangle \geq 1 - \xi_{i,j} \\ & \forall i \forall j : \xi_{i,j} > 0 \end{aligned} \qquad (5)$$

Denoting $\vec{w}^*$ as the weight vector generated by solving (5), we define the risk scoring function $f_{\vec{w}^*}$, for assigning risk scores to the feature vectors in the application intelligence dataset:

$$f_{\vec{w}^*} = \langle \vec{w}^*, \vec{x} \rangle \qquad (6)$$

For any $\vec{x} \in X$, the risk scoring function measures its projection onto $\vec{w}^*$, or the distance to a hyperplane whose normal vector is $\vec{w}^*$. Thus, the hyperplane is indeed the risk assessment baseline.

3.3 Risk Meter

Risk meter measures the risks incurred by each installed application including those are trusted by the user. Note that (6) gives a signed distance. We use the absolute value to represent the deviation and risk. The risks incurred by an application a_i are the cumulative risks of its runtime behaviors:

$$\sum_{\vec{x} \in D_{a_i}} |f_{\vec{w}^*}(\vec{x})| \qquad (7)$$

Another goal of the risk meter is to provide supporting evidences to end-users. To this end, it presents the measured risks at three levels of granularities.

Application: In the simplest form, the risk meter presents a ranking of installed applications by their risks as a bar chart. The X axis indicates the applications and the Y axis indicates the risks. A user can trust an application if it is less risky than her trusted ones. In contrast, an application that is significantly risky can also draw a user's attention. Note that the risk meter does not provide any technical explanation at this level.

Permission group: The ranking of applications may seem unconvincing sometimes for users. In such a case, the risk meter can provide risk composition by permission groups which is represented as a pie chart. The pie chart intuitively reveals the proportion of the risks incurred by the core functionalities of an application. As users have basic knowledge of permission groups when they specify security requirements, they should be able to interpret the risk composition correctly.

API calls and callbacks: The evidences presented at this level are intended for experienced security analysts who are familiar with the security mechanisms under the hood of Android. This is the raw data generated by the risk scoring function. An analyst can inspect values of features to reconstruct the semantic view of runtime behaviors.

Moreover, RISKMON allows a user to establish and revise her security requirements iteratively. RISKMON may generate biased or unconvincing evidences as a user may not have clear and accurate security requirements at the very beginning of using RISKMON. Thus, a user can provide her feedback by adjusting her security requirements and/or adding more trusted applications. RISKMON also periodically updates the security assessment baseline for observed new runtime behaviors. All of these enable RISKMON to approximate an optimum risk assessment baseline to help users make better decisions.

4. IMPLEMENTATION AND EVALUATION

In this section we first discuss a proof-of-concept implementation of RISKMON. Then, we present the results of our online user study followed by two case studies. We conclude our evaluation with the usability and performance of our system.

4.1 Implementation and Experimental Setup

We implemented a proof-of-concept prototype of RISK-MON on the Android mobile platform. In terms of continuous monitoring, we implemented a reference monitor for Binder IPC by placing hooks inside the Binder userspace library. The hooks tap into Binder transactions and log the parcels with zlog[3] which is a high-performance logging library. In addition, we implemented automated risk assessment based on SVMLight[4] and its built-in Gaussian radial basis function kernel.

We designed and conducted a user study to evaluate the practicality and usability of RISKMON. We hand-picked 10 applications (Table 2) that were mostly downloaded from Google Play in their respective categories. We assumed that all the participants trust them. Then we used participants' security requirements for the 10 applications and their application intelligences to generate the baselines. We also randomly selected 4 target applications from the Top Charts of Google Play to calculate their risks based on the generated baselines, including: *a*) CNN App for Android Phones (abbreviated as CNN); *b*) MXPlayer; *c*) Pandora Internet Radio (abbreviated as Pandora); and *d*) Walmart. For both trusted

---

[3]https://github.com/HardySimpson/zlog
[4]http://svmlight.joachims.org/

Table 1: Demographics of the Participants

	Category	# of users
Gender	Male	29 (87.9%)
	Female	4 (12.1%)
Age	18-24	15 (45.5%)
	25-34	16 (48.5%)
	35-54	2 (6.1%)
Education	Graduated high school or equivalent	3 (9.1%)
	Some college, no degree	6 (18.2%)
	Associate degree	1 (3.0%)
	Bachelor's degree	11 (33.3%)
	Post-graduate degree	12 (36.4%)

Table 2: Applications Assumed to be Trusted by the Participants in the User Study

Application	Category
AmazonMobile	Shopping
BejeweledBlitz	Game
ChaseMobile	Finance
Dictionary.com	Books & Reference
Dropbox	Productivity
Google+	Social
GooglePlayMovies&TV	Media & Video
Hangouts(replacesTalk)	Communication
MoviesbyFlixster	Entertainment
Yelp	Travel & Local

(a) Chase Mobile

(b) Dropbox

Figure 4: Average Relevancy Levels Specified by the Participants for Chase Mobile and Dropbox

(10) and target (4) applications, we collected their one-day runtime behaviors on a Samsung Galaxy Nexus phone. In addition, we developed a web-based system that acquires a participant's security requirements, feeds them to RISK-MON and presents the results calculated by RISKMON to the participant. A participant was first presented with a tutorial page that explains how to specify relevancy levels as her security requirements. Then she was required to set relevance levels for each permission group requested by each trusted application after reading the application's descriptions on Google Play. Afterwards, RISKMON generated a risk assessment baseline for the participant based on her inputs and runtime behaviors of the 10 trusted applications. Then RISKMON applied the baseline on each of the 14 applications, and displayed a bar chart that illustrates a ranking of 14 applications by their measured cumulative risks. Finally, an exit survey was presented to collect the participant's perceived usability of RISKMON. Our study protocol was reviewed by our institution's IRB. And we recruited participants through university mailing lists and Amazon MTurk. 33 users participated in the study and Table 1 lists the demographics of them.

4.2 Empirical Results

4.2.1 Security Requirements

From our user study shown in Table 2, we highlight the results of Chase Mobile and Dropbox because they both request some ambiguous permission groups that are hard to justify for users. Figure 4 demonstrates the average relevancy levels set by the participants for each permission group requested by Chase Mobile and Dropbox. The error bars indicate the standard deviation.

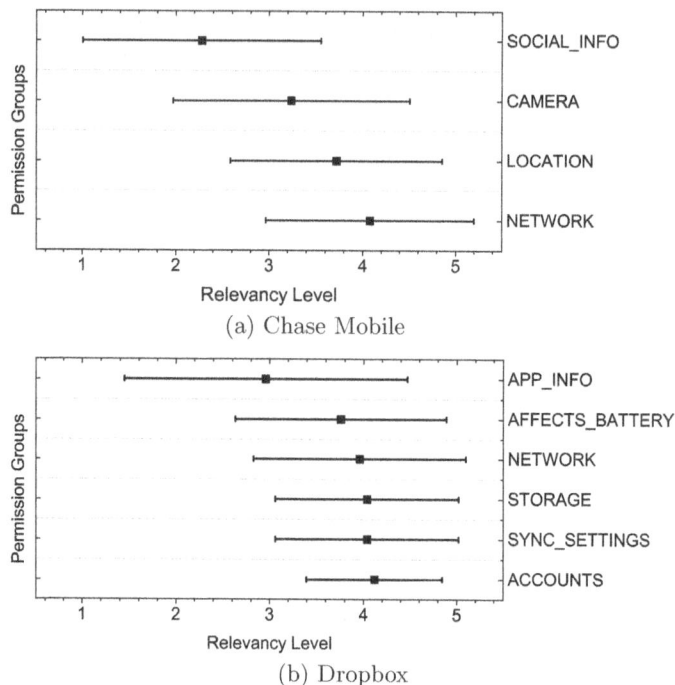

Chase Mobile is a banking application with functionalities like depositing a check by taking a picture and locating nearest branches. Apparently NETWORK is more relevant than others as participants agree that Chase Mobile needs to access the Internet. Even though Chase Mobile uses LOCATION to find nearby bank branches and CAMERA to deposit checks, both LOCATION and CAMERA have lower relevancy levels than NETWORK. We believe it is because some participants do not have the experiences of using such functionalities, but the averages are still higher than neutral. We can also observe that SOCIAL_INFO falls below "neutral", showing participants' concerns of why Chase Mobile uses such information.

Dropbox is an online file storage and synchronization service. From its results, we identified an interesting permission group, APP_INFO, whose description in Android's official document is: *group of permissions that are related to the other applications installed on the system.* This authoritative description does not provide any cue of negative impacts, which leads to user confusion as we can see that APP_INFO has the largest standard deviation. STORAGE, SYNC_SETTINGS and ACCOUNTS are all above "probably relevant" possibly due to their self-descriptive names that are semantically close to Dropbox's core functionalities.

Moreover, we noticed that the participants tend to set higher relevancy levels for self-descriptive permission groups, while they tend to be conservative for other permission groups. We note that this does not affect RISKMON in acquiring a user's security requirements, because RISKMON captures the precedence of one permission group over another. Thus, the least relevant permission group (e.g. SOCIAL_INFO of Chase Mobile) always gets the highest risk scores for both trusted and distrusted applications.

4.2.2 Application Risk Ranking

Figure 5 illustrates the ranking of 14 applications by their average cumulative risk scores as measured by 33 risk assessment baselines generated for the participants. We can see that MXPlayer (2.55) and Walmart (12.72) fall within the trusted applications, while CNN (54.15) and Pandora (69.22) are ranked with highest risk scores.

Note that both Pandora and CNN are renowned applications developed by well-trained developers. Seemingly, they should use sensitive information appropriately. Hence, we verified them by manually dissecting their API traces. We found that they both stayed in the background and attempted to keep connected to remote servers. To this end, they kept polling ConnectivityManager for a fine-grained state of the current network connection. This is an unexpected practice for both privacy and performance perspectives and the official Android documents suggest developers register CONNECTIVITY_CHANGE broadcasts[5] to get connectivity updates accordingly instead of polling. On the contrary, Hangouts incurred almost imperceptible amount of risks, although it has similar requirements for connectivity. Therefore, RISKMON showed that even popular applications might use sensitive information in a way that incurs potential risks for users.

4.3 Case Studies

In this section we evaluate the effectiveness of our approach. Note that there is no ground truth of user's expected appropriate behaviors. Thus, we opt for two case studies on two applications, SogouInput and PPS.TV. We specified the relevancy levels for 10 trusted applications and generated a risk assessment baseline. Then, we verified their identified risk composition with manual analysis.

SogouInput is an input method based on the pinyin method of romanization, and PPS.TV is a video streaming application similar to its counterparts such as Hulu and Netflix. Both of them are feature-rich, free and have accumulated over 5,000,000 installs on Google Play. We note that PPS.TV and SogouInput request 22 and 29 permissions, respectively. The numbers of requested permissions make them suspicious over-privileged or privacy-infringing applications.

The measured cumulative risk scores are 179.0 for SogouInput and 366.9 for PPS.TV. Table 3 demonstrates the risk composition of SogouInput and PPS.TV by their requested permission groups. First, the unusually large portion of PHONE_CALLS indicates significant use of capabilities related to making phone calls and reading unique identifiers. We verified the corresponding API traces and revealed that it attempted to read a user's subscriber ID and device ID. Second and more notably, SOCIAL_INFO contributed 4.02% of the total risks incurred by SogouInput. We verified the corresponding API traces and found that SogouInput accessed content://com.android.contacts and received a parcel of 384 bytes. Usually an Android application queries the contact application and receives only the entries a user picks, which is several bytes long. On the contrary, SogouInput attempted to dump the whole contacts data repository. Similar to SogouInput, PPS.TV utilized permissions related to PHONE_CALL. In addition to reading a user's device ID and

[5] http://developer.android.com/training/monitoring-device-state/connectivity-monitoring.html

Table 3: Risk Composition by Permission Groups of Applications in Case Studies

Application	Permission Group	Risk Score
SogouInput	LOCATION	5.6 (3.13%)
	NETWORK	104.4 (58.29%)
	PHONE_CALLS	61.8 (34.56%)
	SOCIAL_INFO	7.2 (4.02%)
	Total:	179.0 (100%)
PPS.TV	LOCATION	26.0 (7.09%)
	NETWORK	108.3 (29.52%)
	PHONE_CALLS	232.6 (63.40%)
	Total:	366.9 (100%)

Table 4: Usability Evaluation Results

Metric	Average	Lower bound on 95% confidence interval
Likeability	0.811	0.797
Simplicity	0.674	0.645
Risk perception	0.758	0.751

subscriber ID, it also registered a callback to receive events of call states. We note that this allows PPS.TV to read the number of incoming calls.

The results leave much room for imagination: how come an input method and a video streaming application need capabilities related to PHONE_CALLS, LOCATION and SOCIAL_INFO? Possibly users get personalized services by disclosing these information. However it comes with a price of privacy. RISKMON highlights the risks so that users can weigh the benefit and relevant cost by themselves.

4.4 System Usability

The criteria for usability were split into three areas: *likeability*, *simplicity* and *risk perception*. Likeability is a measure of a user's basic opinion towards automated risk assessment. This identifies whether users would like to accept the proposed mechanism. Simplicity is a measure of how intuitive the concepts and procedures are, which is useful in evaluating the burden placed on users. Risk perception is a measure of a user's perceived awareness of risks through risk assessment, which evaluates how users interpret the risks as presented by RISKMON.

After using RISKMON, an exit survey was presented to collect users' perceived usability of RISKMON. In the survey we asked users questions on *likeability* (e.g. "indicate how much you like using your trusted apps to set a baseline"), *simplicity* (e.g. "do you agree that RISKMON requires less mental efforts in risk assessment"), and *risk perception* (e.g. "do you feel the increased awareness of the risks of your installed applications"). Questions were measured with a five-point Likert scale. A higher score indicates a positive opinion or agreement, while a lower score indicates a negative one or disagreement. Then scores were adjusted to [0,1] for numerical analysis.

We analyzed a 95% confidence interval for users' answers. Specifically we are interested in determining the average user's minimum positive opinions. Hence, we looked at the lower bound of the confidence interval. Table 4 shows that an average user asserts 79.7% positively on likeability, 64.5% on simplicity and 75.1% on risk perception. The results show usability of RISKMON with the above-average feedback.

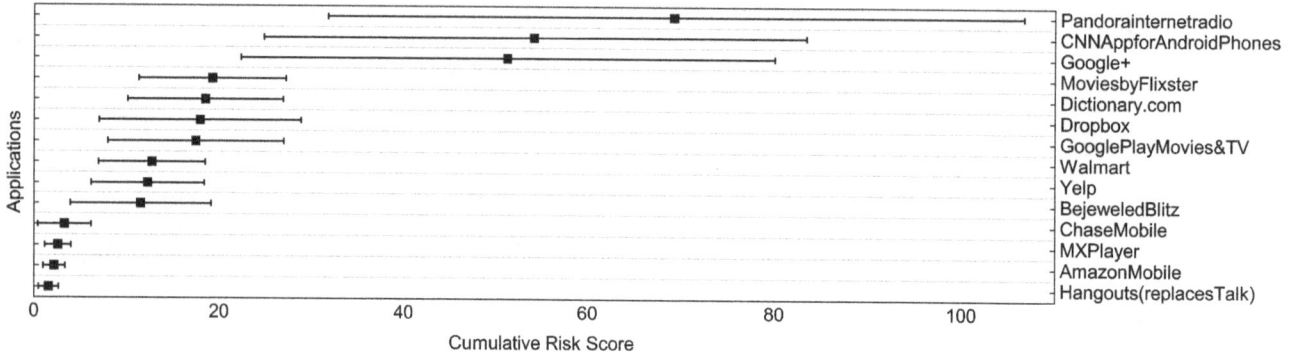

Figure 5: Average Cumulative Risk Scores Measured by the Participants' Risk Assessment Baselines

Table 5: Microbenchmark Results

Benchmark	Average (s)	Standard Deviation (s)
Feature extraction	8.27	0.07
Baseline generation (10 apps)	289.56	235.88
Risk measurement (per app)	0.55	0.17

4.5 System Overhead

To understand the performance overhead of RISKMON, we performed several microbenchmarks. The experiments were performed on a Samsung Galaxy Nexus phone with a 1.2GHz dual-core ARM CPU. The phone runs Android v4.2.2 and RISKMON built on the same version. Table 5 shows the average results.

Feature extraction: The application intelligence aggregator extracted feature vectors from the raw API traces of 33,368,458 IPC transactions generated by 14 applications in one day. We measured the CPU-time used by parsing the API traces and generating the feature vectors. The average time is 8.27 seconds, which is acceptable on a resource-constrained mobile device.

Baseline generation: We ran baseline generation based on the input acquired in the online user study. The processing time varies for different participants, while the average time is approximately 289.56 seconds due to the computation complexity of the radial basis function kernel of SVM-Light.

Risk measurement: Applying the risk assessment baseline is much faster than baseline generation. We measured the time taken to apply a risk assessment baseline on 14 applications. The average time per application is 0.55 seconds, which is imperceptible and demonstrates the feasibility of repeated risk assessment.

Finally, we anecdotally observed that it took 5-10 minutes for the participants to set relevancy levels for 10 applications. This usability overhead is acceptable compared to the lifetime of a risk assessment baseline.

5. DISCUSSION

To capture actual risks incurred by applications used by a user, RISKMON fundamentally requires running them on the user's device. We note that 48.5% of the respondents in our user study claimed that they often test drive applications on their devices. RISKMON itself does not detect or prevent sensitive data from leaving users' devices. We would

recommend users use on-device isolation mechanisms (e.g. Samsung KNOX[6]) or data shadowing (e.g. [22]). However, it is far from perfect for running untrusted applications on trusted operating systems.

RISKMON requires users to specify security requirements through permission groups. While most of the frequently requested permission groups are self-descriptive (e.g. LOCATION and CAMERA), some are ambiguous (e.g. APP_INFO) and contain low-level APIs only known to developers. Although we identify permission groups as an appropriate trade-off between granularity and usability, we admit that permission groups are still a partial artifact in representing sensitive resources for users. Note that we choose permission groups only to demonstrate the feasibility of our approach of security requirement communication. As our future work, we plan to develop a systematic and intuitive taxonomy of sensitive resources on mobile devices to facilitate more effective requirement communication. Moreover, generating a risk assessment baseline is a compute-intensive task that does not quite fit resource-constrained mobile devices. Thus, we plan to offload such a task to trusted third-parties or users' public or private clouds in the future.

Regarding our current implementation of RISKMON, it does not address: (1) interactions between third-party applications; and (2) interactions that do not utilize Binder. This indeed illustrates potential attack vectors that can bypass RISKMON. Unauthorized accesses on resources of third-party applications [11] might be possible because such resources are not protected by system permissions. Also, two or more malicious applications can collude via local sockets or covert channels and evade the Binder-centric reference monitor in RISKMON. For our future work, we will extend our framework to maximize the coverage of attack vectors in our approach.

6. RELATED WORK

Analysis of meta information: Meta information available on application markets provides general descriptions of applications. Recent work has proposed techniques to distill risk signals from them. Kirin [16] provides a conservative certification technique that enforces policies to mitigate applications with risky permission combinations at install time. Sarma et al. [33] propose to analyze permissions alongside with application categories in two large application

---

[6] http://www.samsung.com/global/business/mobile/solution/security/samsung-knox#con02

datasets. Peng et al. [28] use probabilistic generative models to generate risk scoring schemes that assign comparative risk scores on applications based on their requested permissions. In addition to analysis on permissions, Chia et al. [10] and Chen et al. [9] performed large-scale studies on application popularity, user ratings and external community ratings. In particular, Pandita et al. proposed WHYPER [26] which automatically infers an application's necessary permissions from its description in natural languages. However, meta information does not accurately describe the actual behaviors of applications. RISKMON uses meta information to provide contextual information so as to complement the analysis on the runtime behaviors for risk assessment.

Static and dynamic analysis: Analysis on execution semantics of applications, such as static analysis of code and dynamic analysis of runtime behaviors, can reveal how applications use sensitive information. Stowaway [17] extracts API calls from a compiled Android application and reveals its least privilege set of permissions. Enck et al. [15] developed a decompiler to uncover usage of phone identifiers and locations. Pegasus [8] checks temporal properties of API calls and detects API calls made without explicit user consent. TaintDroid [14] uses dynamic information flow tracking to detect sensitive data leaking to the network. Regarding malware analysis, DroidRanger [40] and RiskRanker [20] are systematic and comprehensive approaches that combine both static and dynamic analysis to detect dangerous behaviors. DroidScope [39] reconstructs semantic views to collect detailed execution traces of applications. These work focuses on fundamental challenges for assessing actual risks incurred by applications. However, they do not provide a baseline to capture the appropriate behaviors under diverse contexts of different applications. Thus, their approaches are more intended for security analysts rather than end users.

Mandatory access control frameworks: RISKMON includes a lightweight reference monitor for Binder IPC. While it monitors IPC transactions for risk assessment, several frameworks mediate IPC channels as part of their approaches to support enhanced mandatory access control (MAC). SEAndroid [34] brings SELinux kernel-level MAC to Android. It adds new hooks in the Binder device driver to address Binder IPC. Quire [13] provides IPC provenance by propagating verifiable signatures along IPC chains so as to mitigate confused deputy attacks. Aurasium [38] uses libc interposition to efficiently monitor IPC transactions without modifying the Android platform. FlaskDroid [7] provides flexible MAC on multiple layers, which is tailored the peculiarity of the Android system. Along these lines, RISKMON captures Binder transactions with a fine-grained scheme to facilitate risk assessment on applications' runtime behaviors.

7. CONCLUSION

In this paper, we have presented RISKMON that continuously and automatically measures risks incurred by a user's installed applications. RISKMON has leveraged machine-learned ranking to generate a risk assessment baseline from a user's coarse expectations and runtime behaviors of her trusted applications. Also we have described a proof-of-concept implementation of RISKMON, along with the extensive evaluation results of our approach.

8. ACKNOWLEDGEMENTS

This work was supported in part by the NSF grant (CNS-0916688). Any opinions, findings, and conclusions or recommendations expressed in this material are those of the authors and do not necessarily reflect the views of the funding agencies. We would also like to thank the anonymous reviewers for their valuable comments that helped improve the presentation of this paper.

9. REFERENCES

[1] App review - apple developer. https://developer.apple.com/support/appstore/app-review/, 2013.

[2] C. Alberts, A. Dorofee, J. Stevens, and C. Woody. Introduction to the octave approach. *Pittsburgh, PA, Carnegie Mellon University*, 2003.

[3] C. J. Alberts and A. Dorofee. *Managing information security risks: the OCTAVE approach*. Addison-Wesley Longman Publishing Co., Inc., 2002.

[4] K. W. Y. Au, Y. F. Zhou, Z. Huang, and D. Lie. Pscout: analyzing the android permission specification. In *Proceedings of the 2012 ACM conference on Computer and communications security*, pages 217–228. ACM, 2012.

[5] D. Balzarotti, M. Cova, C. Karlberger, E. Kirda, C. Kruegel, and G. Vigna. Efficient detection of split personalities in malware. In *Proceedings of the 19th Annual Network and Distributed System Security Symposium*, 2010.

[6] D. Barrera, H. G. Kayacik, P. C. van Oorschot, and A. Somayaji. A methodology for empirical analysis of permission-based security models and its application to android. In *Proceedings of the 17th ACM conference on Computer and communications security*, pages 73–84. ACM, 2010.

[7] S. Bugiel, S. Heuser, and A.-R. Sadeghi. Flexible and fine-grained mandatory access control on android for diverse security and privacy policies. In *22nd USENIX Security Symposium (USENIX Security 2013)*. USENIX, 2013.

[8] K. Z. Chen, N. Johnson, V. D'Silva, S. Dai, K. MacNamara, T. Magrino, E. Wu, M. Rinard, and D. Song. Contextual policy enforcement in android applications with permission event graphs. 2013.

[9] Y. Chen, H. Xu, Y. Zhou, and S. Zhu. Is this app safe for children?: a comparison study of maturity ratings on android and ios applications. In *Proceedings of the 22nd international conference on World Wide Web*, pages 201–212. International World Wide Web Conferences Steering Committee, 2013.

[10] P. H. Chia, Y. Yamamoto, and N. Asokan. Is this app safe?: a large scale study on application permissions and risk signals. In *Proceedings of the 21st international conference on World Wide Web*, pages 311–320. ACM, 2012.

[11] E. Chin, A. P. Felt, K. Greenwood, and D. Wagner. Analyzing inter-application communication in android. In *Proceedings of the 9th international conference on Mobile systems, applications, and services*, pages 239–252. ACM, 2011.

[12] E. Chin, A. P. Felt, V. Sekar, and D. Wagner. Measuring user confidence in smartphone security and

privacy. In *Proceedings of the Eighth Symposium on Usable Privacy and Security*, page 1. ACM, 2012.

[13] M. Dietz, S. Shekhar, Y. Pisetsky, A. Shu, and D. S. Wallach. Quire: Lightweight provenance for smart phone operating systems. In *USENIX Security Symposium*, 2011.

[14] W. Enck, P. Gilbert, B.-G. Chun, L. P. Cox, J. Jung, P. McDaniel, and A. Sheth. Taintdroid: An information-flow tracking system for realtime privacy monitoring on smartphones. In *OSDI*, volume 10, pages 255–270, 2010.

[15] W. Enck, D. Octeau, P. McDaniel, and S. Chaudhuri. A study of android application security. In *Proceedings of the 20th USENIX conference on Security*, SEC'11, pages 21–21, Berkeley, CA, USA, 2011. USENIX Association.

[16] W. Enck, M. Ongtang, and P. McDaniel. On lightweight mobile phone application certification. In *Proceedings of the 16th ACM conference on Computer and communications security*, pages 235–245. ACM, 2009.

[17] A. P. Felt, E. Chin, S. Hanna, D. Song, and D. Wagner. Android permissions demystified. In *Proceedings of the 18th ACM conference on Computer and communications security*, pages 627–638. ACM, 2011.

[18] A. P. Felt, S. Egelman, M. Finifter, D. Akhawe, D. Wagner, et al. How to ask for permission. In *Proc. USENIX Workshop on Hot Topics in Security*, 2012.

[19] A. P. Felt, E. Ha, S. Egelman, A. Haney, E. Chin, and D. Wagner. Android permissions: User attention, comprehension, and behavior. In *Proceedings of the Eighth Symposium on Usable Privacy and Security*, page 3. ACM, 2012.

[20] M. Grace, Y. Zhou, Q. Zhang, S. Zou, and X. Jiang. Riskranker: scalable and accurate zero-day android malware detection. In *Proceedings of the 10th international conference on Mobile systems, applications, and services*, pages 281–294. ACM, 2012.

[21] R. Herbrich, T. Graepel, and K. Obermayer. Large margin rank boundaries for ordinal regression. *Advances in Neural Information Processing Systems*, pages 115–132, 1999.

[22] P. Hornyack, S. Han, J. Jung, S. Schechter, and D. Wetherall. These aren't the droids you're looking for: retrofitting android to protect data from imperious applications. In *Proceedings of the 18th ACM conference on Computer and communications security*, pages 639–652. ACM, 2011.

[23] T. Joachims. Optimizing search engines using clickthrough data. In *Proceedings of the eighth ACM SIGKDD international conference on Knowledge discovery and data mining*, pages 133–142. ACM, 2002.

[24] J. A. Krosnick and D. F. Alwin. An evaluation of a cognitive theory of response-order effects in survey measurement. *Public Opinion Quarterly*, 51(2):201–219, 1987.

[25] H. Lockheimer. Android and security - official google mobile blog. http://googlemobile.blogspot.com/2012/02/android-and-security.html, 2012.

[26] R. Pandita, X. Xiao, W. Yang, W. Enck, and T. Xie. Whyper: Towards automating risk assessment of mobile applications. In *Proceedings of the 22nd USENIX conference on Security symposium*. USENIX Association, 2013.

[27] M. Panzarino. Google announces 900 million android activations, 48 billion apps downloaded, 2013.

[28] H. Peng, C. Gates, B. Sarma, N. Li, Y. Qi, R. Potharaju, C. Nita-Rotaru, and I. Molloy. Using probabilistic generative models for ranking risks of android apps. In *Proceedings of the 2012 ACM conference on Computer and communications security*, pages 241–252. ACM, 2012.

[29] M. Rabin. Risk aversion and expected-utility theory: A calibration theorem. *Econometrica*, 68(5):1281–1292, 2000.

[30] V. Rastogi, Y. Chen, and W. Enck. Appsplayground: automatic security analysis of smartphone applications. In *Proceedings of the third ACM conference on Data and application security and privacy*, pages 209–220. ACM, 2013.

[31] A. Robertson. Apple passes 50 billion app store downloads, 2013.

[32] F. Roesner, T. Kohno, A. Moshchuk, B. Parno, H. J. Wang, and C. Cowan. User-driven access control: Rethinking permission granting in modern operating systems. In *Security and Privacy (SP), 2012 IEEE Symposium on*, pages 224–238. IEEE, 2012.

[33] B. P. Sarma, N. Li, C. Gates, R. Potharaju, C. Nita-Rotaru, and I. Molloy. Android permissions: a perspective combining risks and benefits. In *Proceedings of the 17th ACM symposium on Access Control Models and Technologies*, pages 13–22. ACM, 2012.

[34] S. Smalley and R. Craig. Security enhanced (se) android: Bringing flexible mac to android. In *Proc. of the 20th Network and Distributed System Security Symposium (NDSS 2013), San Diego, CA*, 2013.

[35] G. Stoneburner, A. Goguen, and A. Feringa. Risk management guide for information technology systems. *Nist special publication*, 800(30):800–30, 2002.

[36] Y. Wang, J. Zheng, C. Sun, and S. Mukkamala. Quantitative security risk assessment of android permissions and applications. In *Data and Applications Security and Privacy XXVII*, pages 226–241. Springer, 2013.

[37] D. M. Wilkinson. Strong regularities in online peer production. In *Proceedings of the 9th ACM conference on Electronic commerce*, pages 302–309. ACM, 2008.

[38] R. Xu, H. Saïdi, and R. Anderson. Aurasium: Practical policy enforcement for android applications. In *Proceedings of the 21st USENIX Security Symposium*, 2012.

[39] L. K. Yan and H. Yin. Droidscope: seamlessly reconstructing the os and dalvik semantic views for dynamic android malware analysis. In *Proceedings of the 21st USENIX Security Symposium*, 2012.

[40] Y. Zhou, Z. Wang, W. Zhou, and X. Jiang. Hey, you, get off of my market: Detecting malicious apps in official and alternative android markets. In *Proceedings of the 19th Annual Network and Distributed System Security Symposium*, 2012.

Situational Awareness through Reasoning on Network Incidents

Anna Cinzia Squicciarini
College of Information
Sciences and Technology
Pennsylvania State University
asquicciarini@ist.psu.edu
University Park, PA
United States

Giuseppe Petracca
Computer Science and
Engineering
Pennsylvania State University
gxp18@psu.edu
University Park, PA
United States

William Horne
Hewlett-Packard Research
Lab
bill.horne@hp.com
Princeton, NJ
United States

Aurnob Nath
Computer Science and
Engineering
Pennsylvania State University
axn218@cse.psu.edu
University Park, PA
United States

ABSTRACT

Corporations worldwide work with teams of often dedicated system administrators to maintain, detect and prevent network infringements. This is a highly user-driven process that consumes hundreds (if not thousands) of man hours yearly. User reporting, the basis of most of these incident detection systems suffers from various biases and leads to below-par security measures. In the paper, we provide an approach for near real-time analysis of ongoing events on controlled networks, while requiring no end-user interaction and saving on system administrator's effort. Our proposed solution, ReasONets, a lightweight, distributed system, provides situational awareness in case of network incidents. ReasONets combines aspects of anomaly detection with Case-Based Reasoning (CBR) methodologies to reason about ongoing security events in a network, including their nature, severity and sources. We build a fully running prototype of ReasONets, to demonstrate the accuracy of the system, in doing reasoning and inference on the network status by exploiting events and network features. To the best of our knowledge, ReasONets is the first of its kind system combining detection and classification of network events with real-time reasoning while being capable of scaling up to large network sizes.

Categories and Subject Descriptors

H.3.3 [**Information Search and Retrieval**]: Search process; C.3 [**Computer Systems Organization**]: SPECIAL-PURPOSE AND APPLICATION-BASED SYSTEMS

Keywords

Situational awareness,Incident detection, Case-base reasoning

1. INTRODUCTION

Detection is just one step in an overall plan to handle security incidents. Once detected, security incidents are typically forwarded to a Security Operation Center (SOC) and to Computer Security Incident Response Team (CSIRT), where security analysts triage and investigate incidents and formulate a response [33]. This work is labor intensive and relies on extensive domain expertise. Further, user reporting, the basis of most of these incident detection systems, suffers from various biases and leads to below-par security measures. To this date, despite large amount of work in intrusion and anomaly detection (e.g. [34, 9, 8]), there is a great need to improve situational awareness upon incident detection [26], as current incident detection systems are often complex, rigid, and provide limited feedback on the incidents being detected. The objective of our work is to tackle these issues by means of an approach for deep and real-time understanding of ongoing events in a controlled network. In particular, we aim to provide in-depth reasoning of reported anomalies to determine the nature and severity of occurring security events, by using only a small amount of network information.

We propose ReasONets, an effective and lightweight system, able to process and reason about anomalies and incidents observed in closed networks. ReasONets leverages anomaly detection components with Case-Based Reasoning (CBR) methodologies [10, 16], in order to provide situational awareness in case of network incidents. Underlying the Case-Based Reasoning process deployed within ReasONets is the understanding that no security event will ever be identical to previously experienced incidents in absolute terms, but should show enough similarities to be qualified as an event of a certain type. The understanding of anomalous events is not gathered from rules or general statistics, but by the analysis of *cases*. Each case represents a specific type of event which is already analyzed and described by means of a flexible set of metrics collected on-the-fly. Furthermore, we control the uncertain and inaccurate information collected in real-time, by exploiting the Fuzzy Logic Theory [27]. In particular, we use a Fuzzy Clustering Algorithm, as well as a Fuzzy-based Ranking for disambiguating incidents, in case a clear mapping to known cases cannot be determined.

As a result, rather than acting as a log-based network intrusion detection system which simply raises alerts or labels an incident that matches static signatures, ReasONets leverages information *from* an anomaly detection system to achieve a more accurate understanding of network specific incidents. Not only does it specifically locate an incident, but it also determines whether multiple machines were involved, whether they were affected by the same incident, what type of incident it was, whether it was human-driven, accidental, malware-driven etc. Further, it provides in-depth information about the machines connected to the incident, their behavior and (for certain cases) the incident cause.

Our system is also highly adaptive to real-time traffic events: if no previous case matches an observed event, we determine when new cases are to be adapted and, possibly, merge existing previous cases.

The detection of a machine accessing malicious domains is a simple yet effective example demonstrating how ReasONets differs from common Security Event Management (SEM) systems. SEM systems usually rely on Black Lists and White Lists, through which it is difficult to infer if a "new" domain is a good one or not [8]. ReasONets combines to this basic information a set of metrics that allow us to infer the nature of a domain on-the-fly. In details, our system measures the content type (i.e. mature, political, sport), and the geographical distance of the domain with respect to the closest known malicious domain. Further, we check if the registrant is an organization that owns other malicious domains, and if the domain is in the same network of a well-known malicious domain. The added value of our system is the capability to do inference on completely unknown domains, allowing us to obtain early identification of malicious domains, and their relationship (if any) with existing ones.

We deployed a fully running prototype of ReasONets, and carried out extensive experimental evaluation in actual networks of various sizes, using a real-world dataset. Our experiments demonstrate good accuracy and reasonable performance, even when the system is posed under great stress with a large number of incidents.

To the best of our knowledge, ReasONets is a first of its kind system combining detection and classification of network events with real-time reasoning while being capable of scaling up to to large network sizes. Our approach is however inline with current industry and government efforts for systematic classification of network incidents to increase situational awareness by means of new metrics to supplement current measures of detection [22]. In particular, our cases may be considered instances of classified threats, which can be deployed under the STIX format promoted by Mitre [21].

The rest of the paper is organized as follows. In Section 2, we compare this work with related projects. Next, we provide an overview of the ReasONets system. We then present the main components of our architecture, and discuss their functionality. In Section 5, we describe the ReasONets pro-totype. Section 6 is devoted to experimental evaluation. We conclude in Section 7.

2. RELATED WORK

Several host-based and network-based approaches to incident (and intrusion) detection have been proposed in literature [34, 30, 9, 10, 4]. Some of these approaches are anomaly-based, and rely on models based on traffic or events generated during a normal operation of the system [13, 32, 12, 6]. Others are based on matching observed events with predefined signatures of known incidents [15, 31]. ReasONets leverages these well-known paradigms to provide more fine-grained analysis of new and well-known incidents. Without resorting to either complex statistics or static signatures, ReasONets enables processing and reasoning of conventional anomaly detection input toward accurate and customized incident analysis.

Within the extensive body of work on anomaly detection, the closest approaches to ours are from Guha and colleagues [10] and Esmaili [7]. Guha and colleagues develop an incident detection system for wireless networks, with an underlying CBR. The system architecture and capability are however fundamentally different from that of ReasONets. In Guha, the CBR is distributed, and the main focus is on computational and network performance, rather than accuracy. The authors provide no specific discussion on how the cases are built, the similarity metric used and achieved accuracy. The level of adaptiveness achieved by the approach is unclear, given the lack of empirical evaluation. Esmaili and colleagues [7] discuss a high level model for integrating case-based reasoning techniques in intrusion detection systems. The authors highlight the benefit of introducing CBR in such systems and provide important insights on the challenges of integrating CBR in a real-time detection system. However, their focus is purely on intrusions and therefore on the analysis of audit trails, which is very different from our approach. Further, they do not develop any sensitive metrics for cases similarity and indexes nor do they provide any working prototype. Other loosely related approaches exploit the modeling of network traffic, by analyzing the packet payload [8]. These approaches are often inefficient due to the high amount of data to process, and the difficulty in analyzing encrypted packets.

Some of the recent works on incident and intrusion detection focus on the problem of false detection rate [36], in that false positive rates continue to be a significant problem in most current intrusion detection systems [2]. An interesting approach is proposed by Zomlot and colleagues, who present an efficient algorithm for carrying out Dempster-Shefer belief calculation on an intrusion detection alert correlation graph, to reduce false positives based on computed belief scores. The problem of false positive rates is also elegantly tackled in Disclosure [3], wherein Bilge and colleagues also studied a botnet detection system that uses NetFlow records to distinguish C&C channels from benign traffic. To reduce false positive rate, authors incorporate a number of external reputation scores into their system's detection procedure. As shown in our experimental evaluation (Section 6), in ReasONets, fine tuning and careful configuration are needed to control false positives. Hence, it is part of our future work to study how to adopt approaches such as the one proposed by Zomlot et al. or Bilge to reduce the false positive rate.

3. OVERVIEW OF THE REASONETS SYSTEM

The ReasONets system provides a knowledge-based reasoner system for detection and analysis of real time incidents in controlled networks. Specifically, ReasONets relies on a layered architecture, which consists of adopting anomaly detection first, and reasoning afterward. In order to function effectively, anomaly detection is based on the preliminary analysis of patterns of ordinary network activities within the local network, through the definition of standard network traffic patterns, or signatures, generated by means of network metrics. The anomalies identified using the standard patterns as reference represent the starting point of case-based reasoning (CBR).

In general, the idea of using CBR is to dynamically solve complex questions by comparing observed events with similar cases, whereby each case describes a known significant event [16], and is described using symbolic descriptors. In our context, reasoning not only provides indications about the severity of the anomaly, but also it provides large amount of information about the incident being experienced. This information includes, for example, the type of malware being used to attack the network or whether an insider is suspected. Each case is described by a set of relevant network features, collected during an initial training and adapted to the observed incidents over time. Case mapping is achieved by means of fuzzy logic operations, so as to control and abstract away from the coarse network data collected by the loggers. In particular, we use a fuzzy clustering algorithm, as well as a fuzzy-based ranking to determine the degree of similarity between incidents and classify an observed incident in a known or newly experienced case.

From an architectural standpoint, ReasONets may be deployed either as a fully centralized system or in a distributed fashion. In either deployment, the main actors are the monitored machines and a standalone network administrator machine. In the distributed settings, on monitored machines, network traffic logs are generated and optimized. The network traffic logs provide data about the machines' network activities, the amount of data being transmitted from these foreign locations, type of requests being made (GET, POST, DELETE) and how long a connection to a foreign address lasts. The network logs are kept along with local statistics at the machines level, to provide information about the network activities of the machine during these sessions with external locations. In case of centralized deployment, some of the functionality at the client is moved to network proxies or log collectors, that can process and store the data, and produce the statistics required for analysis.

On the main system, the administrator's machine, the ReasONets is in charge of aggregating all these logs from the participating monitored machines, gathering additional information, and analyze these enriched logs. This additional information takes the form of metrics related to unknown domains, traffic comparison with malware clusters, etc. It is also required for creating and dispersing traffic rules to the monitored machines to safeguard against future incidents.

We report the overall flow of execution of the ReasONets system in Figure 1. The input parameters are represented by the data and the network logs obtained from monitored computers connected to the network, whereas the output parameters are detailed indications about the suspected na-

ture of the incident, its severity, and the confidence associated with this assessment. Further, feedback on possible actions to be completed to address the incident is provided to the ReasONets user.

4. THE REASONETS CORE COMPONENTS

The ReasONets is organized into two key layers: anomaly detection and reasoning. We begin this section with a discussion of the anomaly detection component. Reasoning, which is the core of our solution, is discussed next.

4.1 Anomaly-Detection Component

Similar to many anomaly-based systems, the ReasONets Anomaly Detection Component (ADC) operates in two different modes: training mode and monitoring mode. As we discuss next, ReasONets's ADC merely focuses on anomaly discovery, rather than incidents and intrusions analysis. Therefore, it purposely lacks sophisticated metrics and anomaly models, in that incident analysis is performed by the additional layers of the system. This component is currently deployed by leveraging the SNORT intrusion detection system, as we discuss in Section 5.

4.1.1 Training mode

The first step of the ReasONets ADC aims at defining baseline network patterns of the controlled network, to later on search for network events that do not meet these observed and ordinary patterns. Hence, during training ReaSOnets collects patterns of regular traffic of both portions of the monitored network as well as of each individual machine within the monitored network. The normal behavior of a machine is measured in terms of network traffic and application (HTTP) traffic generated, plus performance metrics that measure the average usage of the CPU and RAM, over a certain time interval.

We specifically log incident-free network activities of each monitored machine, by using a simple and lightweight representation of the traffic. A single entry in a log file has information stripped from packet headers, and specifically include the following basic elements:

`< TimeStamp, Protocol, SourceIP, SourcePort, DestIP, DestPort >`

To extract patterns of groups of machines, the generated logs of all systems in the network are simultaneously processed by the ReasONets. By means of pattern matching methods, ReaSOnets then generates and stores network "signatures" indicative of groups of machines displaying the same traffic [17]. In general, two or more machines belong to the same group if in the generated logs at least two entries among `Protocol, SourceIP` or `DestIP, SourcePort` and `DestPort` match.[1]

At the end of the training phase all the regular traffic is stored in traffic "clusters". Starting from these clusters, the ReasONets generates new logging rules that are sent to the logger running on the monitored machine, to exclude regular traffic from future logged activities. Intuitively, machines belonging to the same cluster receive the same set of logging rules. In particular, we generate a new `pass` rule for each cluster generated, which allows to discard the traffic belonging to it from log activities. For example, a `pass` rule in the SNORT rules file has the following form:

---

[1]Only one of the IP (destination or source) needs to match, due to the fact that the other IP refers to the IP of the monitored machine.

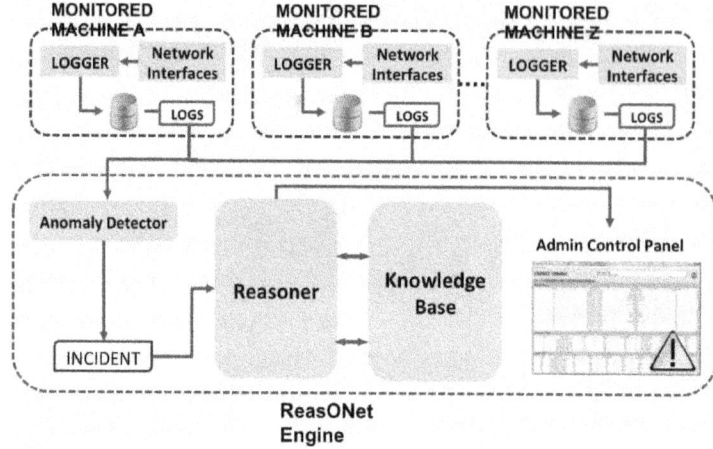

Figure 1: Overall Approach

pass IP 130.203.157.23 80 − > 123.55.1.140 2134

This rule states that all the IP traffic going from the machine with IP equals to 130.203.157.23 by using the port number 80, and going toward the machine with IP equals to 123.55.1.140 by using the port number 2134, must be ignored by SNORT.

4.1.2 Monitoring mode

The ADC, upon filtering out the ordinary traffic by training the model, is in charge of implementing a two-variate model to check whether the reported suspicious traffic is in fact representative of anomalies. Two types of anomaly are detected: (1) single machines that open connection toward unknown domains/machines, or toward known domains/machines but using unusual protocols or port numbers; (2) subset of machines with same sequence of connections toward specific unknown domains/ machines, not necessarily in the same order. Here, as unknown domain/machine we mean a web domain or machine external to the monitored network, never visited/contacted before by any internal machines.

The focus on these two basic anomalies, as a first level of detection, is motivated by the assumption that malicious activities most likely exhibit some specific communication pattern that is different from the norm, i.e. contacting destination that the internal hosts would not have contacted otherwise, misusing protocols, or using uncommon port number that internal host have never used before [24]. In fact, in an ordinary operation of the network, the IP addresses with which a group of hosts communicates exhibit stability over time. We specifically group the machines' behavior in clusters, since one of the most common cause of network failure, and security issues, is malware. Since malware often infects multiple machines within a large network, then the infected machines should have closely similar characteristic behaviors [24]. With the first type of anomaly we address any other case in witch only one machine is involved, for example clumsy actions performed by a user that is operating on a monitored machine.

In order to detect the above anomalies, we employ a set of metrics for machine profiling. The metrics (details are reported in Appendix A, for each class of metric) include:

- **Network Level Metrics**, aiming to measure network traffic activity. Examples of metrics in this category

are: *Average Flow Packet Count* and *Ratio Flow Count per Average Package Size*, that allow to measure the machine network activity.

- **Application Level Metrics**, to approximate the HTTP traffic generated by each monitored machine, during its interaction with external machines and the Internet. Table 6 in Appendix reports additional examples of Network and Application Level metrics, respectively.

- **Machine Performance Metrics** aiming to measure the work load of monitored machine in term of CPU and RAM, metrics collected directly from the machine involved in our analysis.

Whenever an anomaly is detected in the traffic generated by the monitored machines, an additional set of metrics is gathered for each visited domain. The objective of this new set of metrics is to investigate whether the visited domain may be the source of the incident, and therefore related to the machines anomalous behavior. These metrics are then combined to derive the *maliciousness level* of a particular domain among all the domains involved in a suspect incident. Below we include simple descriptives for the metrics generated, which are normalized before computation.

- *Same Network (sn)* indicates if the suspicious domain is in the same network of a well-known malicious domain

- *Spatial Distance (sd)* between the suspicious domain and its closest well-known malicious domain

- *Bad Owner (reg)* indicates if the domain registrant is the owner of a well-known malicious domain

- *Blacklisted (b)* states if the domain is Blacklisted

- *Whitelisted (w)* states if the domain is Whitelisted

The state of a domain is determined to be blacklisted through comparison with an exhaustive database available from ShallaList [29], integrated with few other well-known lists [28, 35]. Starting from the above metrics, the domain's maliciousness level is calculated simply as follow:

$$dml = \sum_{i=\{sn,sd,reg,c,b,w\}} w_i * i \qquad (1)$$

114

where $i = \{sn, sd, reg, c, b, w\}$ denotes the metrics and their corresponding weight w_i, calculated in order to reflect the relevance of the feature for the overall domain maliciousness level (dml) value. The vector of weights $\overline{w}$ can be computed by training with a number of known malicious domains.

Note that dml is only useful for certain classes of incidents, and it is considered as an add-on, rather than a core metric. It is therefore disregarded in case of a suspect event where no malicious domain might have been visited.

4.2 Reasoning

The core of our architecture consists of Case-Based Reasoner (CBR) [10] on the events detected by the higher system layers. A case represents a known incident or security event, which has been experienced in the system and addressed by administrators. Each case is represented by a vector of significant features, each feature denoting a metric and the corresponding value range. For the purpose of our analysis we adopt a knowledge base (KB) which currently collects and models two classes of cases. First is the set of cases which represent the most common network spread malware (e.g., DoS, Virus, Botnet, Worms, Keylogger and Spyware). Second is the set of non-malware related incidents, that can be observed through network analysis. For example, voluntary access to a domain with adult-only content, as well as cases of unauthorized access to a monitored machine from a remote one. The cases are obtained using a hybrid approach that combines empirical evaluations and analysis of well-known security incidents affecting small enterprise networks. Additional cases are dynamically added to the KB as they are experienced, according to a set of adaptation rules within the model.

Previous attempts have used threshold-based approaches to detect incidents, with and without the aid of a CBR system. However, using simple thresholds may not provide sufficient knowledge about the event, and would fail in case of hybrid events, that appear similar to more than one incident [14]. To cope with these issues, we have designed our reasoner by adopting a multi-layer approach that builds on *Fuzzy Logic* and on *ad hoc-case Fuzzy Ranking*.

The goal is to develop appropriate similarity metric for cases analysis that are defined as a collection of feature comparison results, and use fuzzy rules to specify how these intermediate results are combined. Although each case feature may require a different type of comparison, using fuzzy, the result of the comparison is a similarity assessment between the same case feature of the problem specification and of a case from the case archive. In addition, fuzzy logic handles situations where no-crisp answers can be found, which often occurs when one needs to determine to what degree an incident is related to a known case. Beside fuzzy-based analysis, we compare selected and weighted features of relevant cases for any potential new input, in order to check for relevant information that is most indicative of a case, and therefore can help discern the nature of the incident.

4.2.1 Case Representation

ReasONets models a case c as follows:

$$< cid, \{m_1, ..., m_k, dml\}, r_c, p_c, \overline{w}^c > \qquad (2)$$

where cid is the case identifier, $\{m_1, ..., m_k\}$ represents a set of triplets $m_i = \langle min(f_i), mid(f_i), max(f_i) \rangle$ for each collected metric $f_i \in [1, k]$. dml represents the domain mali-

ciousness level, per the discussion in Section 4.1.2. r_c represents the risk level associated to the case, p_c represents the likelihood of the case. The latter two metrics can be derived either by gathering local statistics collected within the organization or through public data associated to the frequency and the impact of the incidents described by the case. Finally, $\overline{w}^c$ is the vector of weights associated to the case's metrics. Weights model how representative certain metrics are for the case they are associated with. For example, network flow metrics are of great relevance during denial of service attacks, but may matter little in case of access to prohibited domains. We discuss in detail the use of the last three components in our discussion of the case analysis.

Instances of a case c are stored in analogous way as the original case they belong to:

$$inst = < iid, \{m_1, ..., m_k, dml\}, c, deg(c) > \qquad (3)$$

Here, $deg(c)$ denotes the membership degree of the instance to the case c which it is assigned to. This information is added upon incident assignment.

4.2.2 Case Retrieval and Ranking

We propose a multi-step ranking algorithm for identifying the best match among possible candidate cases. The algorithm allows us to ascertain not only to what extent the incident belongs to a given case, but also whether a new ad hoc case should be generated.

Given an observed incident inc, the first task consists of computing its membership degree with all possible cases in the knowledge base. This value, denoted as $deg_{inc}(c)$, for case c is to determine how "similar" inc is to the profiled cases. We provide two computations of deg_{inc}, depending on whether the system already has record of observed instances for the case or not. The intuition for both formulae is that membership is computed as a function of the metrics vector's distance from other occurrences of the case, and these occurrences' memberships.

Specifically, let $|m|$ denote the cardinality of the set of triplets $\{m_1, ..., m_k\}$ with $m_i = \langle min(f_i), mid(f_i), max(f_i) \rangle$ of Equation 2, representing the values stored for each case's metric f_i. Let $diff(f) = max(f) - min(f)$. If there are recorded instances (denoted as $inst$) of a case c, $deg_{inc}(c)$ leverages the information collected for each previous incident of the case, and it is computed as follows:

$$\frac{\sum^{inst \in c} \left[deg_{inst}(c) \times \sum^{|m|} \left(diff(f) - \left\| \frac{inc(mid(f))}{\left(\frac{max(f)}{diff(f)} \right)} - \frac{inst(mid(f)}{\left(\frac{max(f)}{diff(f)} \right)} \right\| \right) \right]}{\sum^{|f|} \left(diff(f) - \left\| \frac{inc(mid(f))}{\left(\frac{max(f)}{diff(f)} \right)} - \frac{inst(mid(f))}{\left(\frac{max(f)}{diff(f)} \right)} \right\| \right)}$$
$$(4)$$

Here, $max(f)$ and $diff(f)$ are used for normalization, whereas $inc(f)$ and $inst(f)$ represent respectively the measured value of f for the current incident inc and the instance $inst \in c$. Finally, $deg_{inst}(c)$ is the membership degree of a previously experienced incident associated with case c, and therefore labeled as instance ($inst$). Note that in Equation 4, we use all the instances of case c stored in the KB, so as to increase the accuracy of the detection algorithm.

As seen in Equation 4, the assigned memberships are influenced by the inverse of the distances from the existing instances of the case and their class memberships. The inverse distance serves to weigh a vector's membership more if it is closer and less if it is farther from the vector under consideration.

If the case has no recorded instances, the membership degree is instead computed in a similar manner, by relating the metrics of the incident directly with the case record, as follows:

$$\sum^{|m|} \left(diff(f) - \left|\left| \frac{inst(mid(f))}{\left(\frac{\max(f)}{diff(f)}\right)} - \frac{c(mid(f))}{\left(\frac{\max(f)}{diff(f)}\right)} \right|\right| \right) \quad (5)$$

In the above equation, $c(mid(f))$ represents the value of the metric f that is associated with the case c.

Next, given the cases $C=[c_1,\ldots c_n]$ ordered according to the corresponding membership degree (per Equation 4) for incident inc $[deg_{inc}(c_1),\ldots,deg_{inc}(c_n)]$ such that $deg_{inc}(c) > 0.1 \ \forall c \in C$, we compute K-NN clustering algorithm among all incident instances recorded for $c_1,..,c_n$. Note that this step is particularly useful for large KBs with a rich history of incidents, since the computed membership degrees represent an average of the incident similarity with the case, but these values may vary greatly even within incidents of a same case. Hence, they may not represent crisp indicators of similarity. This step is instead omitted or less relevant if few cases' instances are recorded. In the latter case, the incident may simply be assigned to the case with the highest membership degree. If the majority of the close neighbors in the K-NN set belong to a same case c_i with a degree above a system defined threshold β (set to 0.65 on our experiments), we model the incident as an instance of c_i.

If no dominant case is found, that is

$$deg_{inc}(c_1) - deg_{inc}(c_2) < \epsilon$$

where ϵ is a small threshold, we compute an additional ranking for the cases in C. The additional ranking algorithm requires recomputing a refined membership degree $deg_{inc}(c)$, determined using fuzzyfied feature values, to control the noise introduced by comparing empirically collected values which may be coarse or not accurate. At the core of the algorithm is the following computation of membership degree to replace $deg_{inst}(c)$ in Equation 4. This is again computed for every case the incident may be associated with - given the crisp membership degree values obtained in the previous step of the algorithm. We first compute the distance among weighted metrics of previous instances:

$$\alpha = \sum^{|m|} \left(w_c(f) \times Defuzzy\left[diff(f) - ||Fuzzy(inc(f)) - Fuzzy(c(f))||\right]\right) \quad (6)$$

Then, we compute the actual membership degree as follows:

$$deg_{fuz\_inc}(c) = r_c \times p_c \times \alpha \quad (7)$$

Note that $deg_{fuz\_inc}(c)$ differs from $deg_{inst}(c)$ in two ways. First, in computing α we assign a different weight $w_c(f)$ to each specific feature. Further, risk parameter r_c and a likelihood parameter p_c from the case representation in (2), are also taken into account, to classify the incident with a greater accuracy. Finally, α includes fuzzification and defuzzification steps of the measured features, represented in the equation 6 by means of $Fuzzy$ and $Defuzzy$ functions - in accordance with the Fuzzy Theory [27].

If even fuzzy ranking does not reveal a dominant case, ReasONets classifies the incident as new case by starting the case profiling process and stores it in the KB.

Also note that the KB is periodically optimized: If several incidents with same features are mapped on the same subset of cases, we execute a merge operation that allows the creation of a single case representing all the cases in the subset.

5. REASONETS PROTOTYPE

ReasONets was built to be an Operating System (OS) independent incident-detection solution. The system includes multiple monitored client machines in the network, and one federated administrative server machine.

Each client machine is equipped with 3 major components in addition to the ReasONets client. First, each monitored machine hosts and runs SNORT[1], a lightweight network packet sniffer and logger, which generates and stores network traffic logs. Second, each machine also runs "TypePerf" [19], which helps capture client system statistics like processor usage by various processes. TypePerf is pre-installed program in Windows 7 and requires no additional plugins for its usage. Analogous performance loggers are available for Unix and Macintosh OS. The third component is a database where all the network and machine performance logs, once captured, can be stored and appropriately accessed by the admin console machine (e.g. MySQL, or Microsoft SQL Server). All client programs including the client version of ReasONets are designed to be non-intrusive and create minimal interference for the user. Note that in principle, the three client programs could be offloaded to a network appliance that monitors a local subnet. This approach would deploy a decentralized model of ReasoNets, with the following advantages: (1) it would make the management of endpoints easier, (2) it might be more secure since if malware gets on an endpoint it could disable these services, while it is more difficult to compromise an appliance, and (3) it might be more scalable.

The administrative machine is equipped with a MySQL database and the server version of ReasONets. The ReasONets houses the main logic for incident detection, reasoning and learning and is known as the *engine*. The engine is responsible for all database interactions across the machines, for data gathering and network traffic policy dispersal. The engine is configured to retrieve logs from remote clients using an encrypted connection. The input is given by the data obtained from monitoring computers connected to the network, whereas the output are detailed indications about the suspected nature of the incident, its severity, and the confidence associated with this assessment. Feedback and possible actions to complete in order to address the incident are provided to the network administrator, as shown by the interface presented in Figure 2. The admin console is a multi-tab GUI which displays synthesized data on the experienced incidents and their types. In the main control panel, the top half of the GUI displays a processed log of recent network incidents, including creation time, case, and clients involved. The middle window visualizes anomalous patterns of behavior across multiple machines, along with detailed information on the specific of the behavior, including traffic type, direction, external IPs etc. Finally, the bottom window displays unusual traffic originated by individual machines, and that is yet to be processed and assigned to

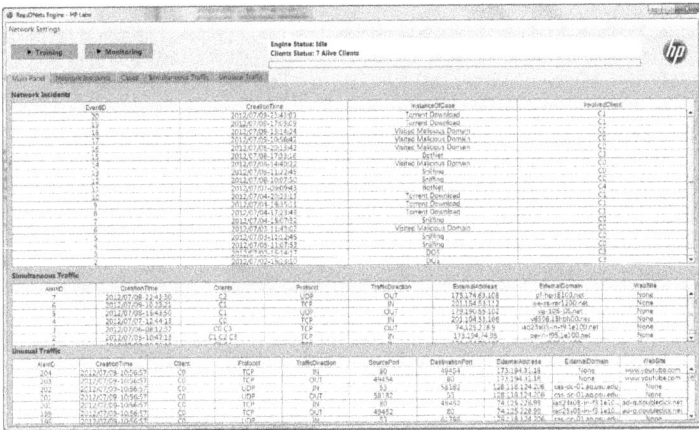

Figure 2: ReasONets console

cases. Other tabs (not shown in Figure) report expanded information on the above data, including a description of the incident and its association with alike cases, possible overlapping cases and feedback for future action.

6. EXPERIMENTAL EVALUATION

In this section, we discuss our experimental evaluation. We first present the datasets used for our analysis, and the experiments we focused on. Next, we discuss our system setup. Finally, we present the results of our experiments.

6.1 Test Data

For the purpose of the experiments, the client prototype, described in the previous section, was modified by discarding the packet sniffing tool SNORT and replacing it with a dataset (DITL_I2-20080317 from PREDICT [25]) which contains 48 hours worth of clean, real traffic IP packet headers collected from an academic ISP. This dataset allows us to generate a constant and varied stream of traffic, in absence of incidents. The data was parsed and fed into the client databases so that each client machine acted as a concentrator and stored data from up to 5 different IP addresses. To this clean traffic data, various traffic records were injected, so as to introduce/replicate/emulate various network incidents.

We generated malicious traffic to specify baseline cases for our tests. To ensure real-world (or at least, realistic) traces, we leveraged existing specialized datasets or generated the actual traffic as ground-truth. When generating malicious traffic, test machines were used, which were first formatted with a clean image of Microsoft Windows (Xp or 7), configured to run a packet sniffer (SNORT) followed

Table 1: Core Cases

Case Id	Case Type
1	REGULAR - No Browsing
2	REGULAR - Browsing
3	Torrent Download
4	Bot Net
5	DOS (Denial of Service)
6	Sniffing
7	Visited Malicious Domain

by running the programs related to that certain test case (the machines were promptly re-formatted afterwards). A detailed example of the adopted methodology for case generation is reported in Appendix B.

On average, we observed about 50 incidents per generated case. We report examples of our approach for developing some interesting cases below.

Torrent traffic was studied and replicated by running the actual torrent programs, uTorrent[23] and BitTorrent[5]. Each program was used to download 2 hours worth of data during which, all incoming and outgoing IP headers were recorded. Similarly, BotNet attacks were simulated by accessing/running known malware [18] while sniffing and recording all incoming and outgoing IP headers.

"Visited Malicious Domains" corresponds to the case of users accessing blacklisted or prohibited sites. This case was instantiated by performing browsing sessions of various duration to sites listed on the ShallaList's blacklist [29], a downloadable, regularly updated list of blacklisted websites which is freely available online. Likewise, denial of service attacks (DoS) were studied by analyzing multiple datasets available online for researchers. The first dataset downloaded from CAIDA[11] provided 1 hour worth of anonymized trace data for a DDoS attack which occurred on Aug 4,2007. The other two datasets from PREDICT ("iperf_emulated_attacks-20090621" and "DoS_traces-20020629")[25] provide trace data for DoS related traffic captured from 4 different attacks.

Like for the former cases, the CAIDA dataset too was passed onto the ReasONets system for case-based metric generation and classification. Studying the traffic records from the PREDICT database (4 different attacks lasting for up to 10 minutes), allowed us to specifically isolate the traffic responsible for the DoS attacks. As this contained both single source to destination machine based attack and multiple source to single destination attacks, we simply replicated the same traffic during our testing for simulating an attack on one of our client machines, when required.

Furthermore, in order to model network issues that are not strictly related to the actions of malware but are instead due to the actions of a malicious user, we generated two additional cases. The first involved voluntary access to "restricted" domain; these domains were restricted due to either its mature (e.g. pornographic) nature or malicious content (e.g. malware repository). The second one was the unauthorized access to a monitored machine over a remote connection.

Upon having obtained the desired traces for each case, we stored each of them along with the network metrics of Expression (2). Some of the representative cases are reported in Table 1. Additional cases were subsequently added for testing purposes, inspired by the analysis of patterns of common attacks described in [20]. Subsequently, to generate testing data, we designed ad-hoc scripts that modified the original incidents logs to reflect the same pattern of behavior with customized and disguised dimensions.

6.2 Experiments

We completed several experiments, to check for scalability, performance and accuracy of ReasONets. We briefly introduce each set of experiments below.

- **Performance and Accuracy.** The first set of experiments consisted of 5 rounds for each of the 5 network size configurations. The purpose of this set of experi-

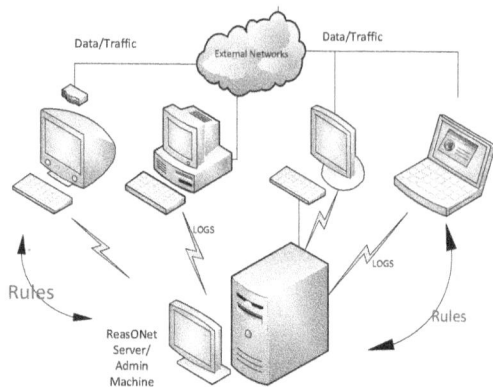

Figure 3: Network layout

ments was to assess the performance and accuracy of the system against 5 types of cases when tested against increasing number of client machines plugged into the system. In addition, we tested the accuracy achieved when varying the weights' feature vector for the tested cases, and studied how features' weights of representative cases can be configured for best results.

- **Stress Test.** We tested the detection rate in case of an increasingly high number of incidents, and in case of a large KB.

- **Comparison with baseline approach.** We aim to compare the accuracy of our system against a standard baseline system which provides basic traffic classification.

- **Scalability.** We complete scalability tests to determine the efficiency and scalability of the system over larger network sizes. Networks of up to 80 machines, with traffic from about 450 distinct IP addresses, were considered.

6.3 Setup

The experiments were run in an environment having a client-server architecture, with one dedicated machine acting as the central server (our admin console) and multiple remote clients connected to the admin machine via an ethernet based L2 (data link layer) network (see Figure 3). Each client machine was running Windows 7 on a 2.5 Ghz Intel-based dual core processors with at least 4 GB of RAM.

The server was kept in the same subnet as the rest of the client machines. This achieves two goals: It simulates a pure point-to-point client-server interaction and it lowers network latency. The central admin console periodically polls (every 5 minutes) the remote clients to look for new traffic data in their database(s), which are then filtered, moved in a compressed manner over the network and processed to be analyzed. Incidents are displayed to the system admin through the engine's graphical interface, shown in Figure 2.

At the start of every experiment, all client and server databases were erased. Next, approximately 6 to 10 hours worth of clean traffic data was introduced from the LANDER dataset, succeeded by injection of traffic data related to

the test being conducted. The ratio of incident-to-clean data was kept between 10%-15%. Scalability tests had around 4 hours worth of clean data introduced along with 10% worth of malicious traffic. Our incident data also included "false" incidents. True incidents were real traffic representations of the case whereas false incidents were traffic data with patterns similar to either a) some other case b) random behavior resembling other incidents.

To handle a larger set of machines while having a workable network performance, the outgoing traffic from the client databases was compressed. It was observed that, for every poll made by the admin console for new data from the client machines approximately 3,000 to 4,500 traffic records were transferred per machine. Average size of each traffic record was i) for Uncompressed data (before transmission) about 16 Kb; ii) For Compressed data (during network transmission), about 10-12 Kb. Note that a large number of traffic records together comprise an incident. For example, the DDoS attack required at least 3000-4000 records from multiple machines to be identified as an incident. Torrent required a lower number, of around 500 records[2].

Except for the scalability tests, all the experiments were conducted under cold start conditions. This means that before performing an experiment, we did not perform any training, so as to test the worse possible setting for our system. The content of the KB varied according to the experiment type. As the training phase is responsible for weeding out all the regular/ safe traffic, not running the training phase leads to presence of several 100's or even 1000's of traffic logs which should otherwise have been filtered out. Note that running a scalability test in such a scenario leads to a potential distributed DoS attack on our admin machine.

Thus, to reduce the chances of clogging the engine, for the scalability test only we reduced the number of records being sent over from the remote clients, while still injecting 10-15% of incident data into the system. The rate of traffic flow was pre-determined by running the training phase of ReasONets for 40 clients over a time span of 7 days, followed by observation of the average number of traffic records being sent over a 6 hours time interval.

6.4 Results

Accuracy The first experiment involved varying the number of test (client) machines from a range of 7 to 15 while evaluating the system on the basis of its time performance, CPU utilization, false positive (FP) and precision values. We kept the network small for this experiment to better focus on the accuracy of specific cases. As we show in our scalability test, the results with larger networks are comparable. The FP ratio for a system is important in assessing the accuracy of the system, as a high FP ratio has the ability to drown out legitimate incident detection alerts. False negative FN are also relevant, but we note that our system has consistently less than 1% FN rates. Hence, we do not discuss it here.

The expected trend for change of values of precision and FP ratio for a learning based system is an increasing curve for precision and a decreasing curve for FP ratio. This is because, as the system gains more information, it should able to take more informed decisions. This trend is confirmed

---

[2]Generally, we observe a range of 0-25 or more traffic records for a Source and Destination IP pair within the time span of a second.

experimentally. Figure 4 reports the overall precision values recorded during this experiment. Recall that precision values express the ability of the system to correctly identify and tag an incident. This pattern is observed consistently in all of the cases. We notice that for DoS (Case 5), precision is consistently increasing, except for the transition from 9 to 11 machines, where the precision remains constant. This transition can be speculated as the minimum threshold of network configuration size for the critical/ stable functionality of the system. In other words, it is the minimum network size required for the system to gather sufficient data for a specific kind of incident.

Further, for all cases, we observed a false positive rate (not reported in the graphs) ranging from 6.4% to about 3.7%, with a notable improvement when the number of machines increases. Higher FP rates were always observed with smaller network configurations. For instance, for case 3 (DoS), we find the FP rates for configurations under 7 machines to be at 6.67% from where it linearly decreases to 5.13% for 11 machines succeeded by no visible change over the next size configuration of 13 machines, after which it promptly decreases to 3.67% over the final size configuration of 15 machines (corresponding to over 60 distinct IP addresses).

The decrease in FP ratio as the network size configuration increases follows the expected decreasing pattern except for transition from 11 to 13 machines. During this transition, the evaluations show no change in performance rate. Given the randomized distribution of incidents over its timeline across multiple machines and the interval between each poll by the server, we speculate that it is not un-realistic to see the system learning the same amount of information in both configurations (11 and 13 machines), hence leading to no change in output. Concerning the output for Botnet (case 4), here too we find a decreasing trend, with a non changing transition over 9 to 11 machines, before and after which the graph plots are always decreasing. The same trend is seen for the rest of the three cases, which lends more credibility to the explanation that the randomized distribution of incidents over the timeline leads to unpredictable jumps in increase in learning.

To further investigate whether the accuracy can be improved, we repeated the same tests on a network counting 20 hosts (78 IP addresses) and 20 cases (8 cases were variations of the original cases in Table 1), and varied uniformly weights for some of the features. We particularly focused on the aggregate feature dml, and the weights used for the "spatial distance" (sd) metric. Recall that spatial distance aims at measuring the distance between the domain observed during the incident and its closest well-known malicious domain. This metric was chosen for our analysis as it is the least intuitive to be interpreted as compared to the other ones forming dml. Variations on other metrics (e.g. black list, white list etc) also reported less notable results.

We study the changes in accuracy upon changing in the same way dml for all cases. This test was executed for 24 hours, and the machine's data included 200 true and actual incidents per case. 100 of these incidents were of DoS type, the remaining were randomly distributed across the other cases. We report the most interesting results in Table 2. In

Table 2: Weights influence on detection accuracy - weights are changed for for sd in dml

Setting	Case	FP	TP	Prec.
Baseline	DoS	6	94	94.059
	Other cases	5	94	94.949
Increasing $\overline{w}$	Dos	1.8	91	97.849
	Other cases	9	98	91.588
Decreasing $\overline{w}$	Dos	11	97	89.814
	Other cases	2.4	89	96.739

the table, we highlight the performance achieved with DoS detection, as compared to other cases. This is to highlight the distinct pattern observed in the DoS versus other cases. As reported, varying dml has a great influence on the overall accuracy and can bring our precision close to 98% and a false positive rate to 1.8% for DoS and of 96.7% precision (about 2% FP) for the other cases, respectively. When we increased weight to the sd metric used to compute dml, and in specifics we gave it a stronger weight in case of farther distances, a better accuracy was achieved for DoS and the performance suffered on the other cases. The reverse pattern was observed for the other cases. We speculate that, since during a DoS attack multiple source machine tend to attack a single destination machine, our study shows (roughly) that the machines tend to be spatially apart from each other so as to prevent early detection.

Stress Testing. In the second set of experiments we tested *how the system performs when an increasing number of incidents occur*. The number of incidents were varied from 5 to 500, with an increase of 10 incidents for every round of experiment. Each round was executed for over 16 hours. The results are reported in Figure 5. Except for the initial rounds where the system has apparently not gathered enough knowledge (5 to 50 incidents) and therefore results in higher FP, overall we consistently observed a decreasing FP ratio. The exact reverse is seen for precision metrics, which decreases initially, and after 50 incidents it gradually increases.

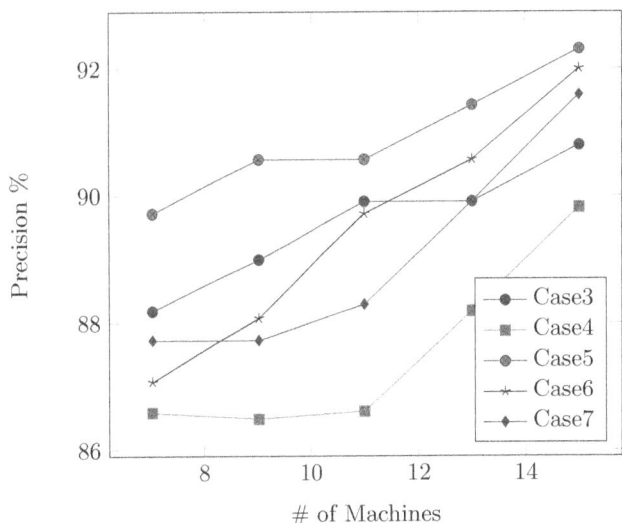

Figure 4: Case-wise Precision % Rates

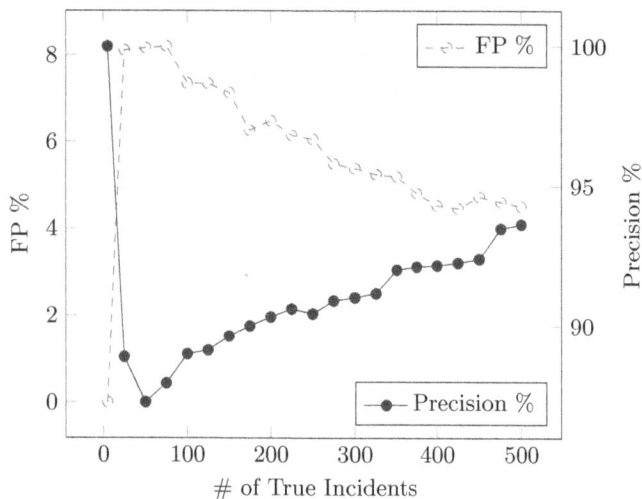

Figure 5: Stress Precision Rates

Table 3: Advantage of Fuzzy'ification (accuracy)

Settings	FP	TP	FN	TN	Prec.
Basic	16.66	61.5	5.2	16.66	78.163
ReasONets	4.36	64.93	2.6	26.66	93.55

Table 4: Scalability Test; Accuracy

#	FP	TP	FN	TN	Prec.
40	7.123	64.86	2	26	89.97
90	4.146	65.33	1.2	29.36	90.74

As part of our experiments on stress testing, we also tested the *performance of the reasoner with an increasing number of cases* in the system. The number of cases ranged from 7 to 90. The system's performance does not appear affected by the number of cases in the system. The traffic data included 320 incidents with around 200 true incidents over 45 client machines with worth 10 hours of clean traffic. Overall, our experiments show a false positive rate of average 3.9% (with a lowest performance at 5.3% for 50 cases), a false negative rate below 1% and an overall precision of 93.33%.

Comparison with baseline approach. The next test was to gauge the overall accuracy performance of ReasONets when compared to a generic traffic classification system. We calculated precision, FP, FN, TN and TP rates under two different scenarios; a) Under normal functionality of the system b) After disabling the fuzzy logic reasoning part of ReasONets and replacing with a simple detection logic, based on standard cluster analysis (through crisp K-nn). Table 3, showcases the decrease in FP and increase in precision under ReasONets. This is expected as ordinary data classification based systems cannot properly serve the numerous borderline cases which fall under more than one category, which is where our ranking algorithm based on fuzzy performs at its best.

Scalability. Scalability tests allow us to observe the ability of the system to incorporate an ever growing network size and measure the hit/drop in performance that comes with it. The CPU usage was found to be relatively high in previous

Table 5: Scalability Test; Performance Metrics (seconds)

#	Server Poll	Process time	Avg. CPU
40	400	109	71.3
90	800	124	82.7

tests due to the un-naturally high number of records (data) being transferred from the client machines, we reduced the number of records being transferred to a more realistic number, as described in Section 6.3. This allowed us to test the system in near real-world conditions. Results from these tests are reported in Tables 4 and 5. As explained earlier, under normal functionality of a learning based system, the system should show trends of lowering of FP ratio and increasing in precision. This is exactly what is seen across 40 (corresponding to about 185 distinct IP addresses) and 90 machines (corresponding to about 450 distinct IPs).

7. CONCLUSION

Incident detection is an ongoing issue among corporations worldwide, as highlighted by recent industry and government efforts for classifying and addressing network threats [21, 20]. Though many approaches to incident and intrusion detection exist, they seem too strict to provide real-time situational awareness to system administrators.

To address this shortcoming, in this paper, we presented ReasONets, a novel approach for situational awareness of network incidents. ReasONets aims to leverage input from classic anomaly detection tools to learn about ongoing incidents and notable events within a closed network. Through extended experiments, we demonstrate the performance of the system against several system and network parameters. To date, this is the first system offering a concrete incident reasoner for increased awareness in controlled networks.

Our next step consists of integrating our case representation with the Structured Threat Information eXpression (STIX) format promoted by Mitre [21]. We will deploy the KB in an extended STIX format, and characterize each case by means of observables and STIX indicators. Further, we will refine our case processing for improved accuracy. We also plan to conduct tests on very large networks, of over 1,000 hosts. The ability of our system to scale seamlessly to over 400 IP addresses with no significant performance delay is a strong indicator of the capability of ReasONets. Nevertheless, a slight architectural re-design may be required, wherein the functionality of the engine may be replicated among collaborating systems managed by a set of network administrators.

8. ACKNOWLEDGEMENTS

Portions of this work from Squicciarini, Petracca and Nath was supported by a Hewlett-Packard Innovation Research Program Award: "Analytics for Situational Awareness", 2011. The work from Squicciarini was partially supported by National Science Foundation under award No. 1250319.

9. REFERENCES

[1] Snort, a lightweight network intrusion detection system. http://www.snort.org/.

[2] Stefan Axelsson. The base-rate fallacy and the difficulty of intrusion detection. *ACM Trans. Inf. Syst. Secur.*, 3(3):186–205, August 2000.

[3] Leyla Bilge, Davide Balzarotti, William Robertson, Engin Kirda, and Christopher Kruegel. Disclosure: detecting botnet command and control servers through large-scale netflow analysis. In *Proceedings of the 28th Annual Computer Security Applications Conference*, pages 129–138. ACM, 2012.

[4] Leyla Bilge, Engin Kirda, Christopher Kruegel, and Marco Balduzzi. Exposure: Finding malicious domains using passive dns analysis. In *Proceedings of the 21st Network and Distributed System Security Symposium (NDSS)*, 2011.

[5] BitTorrent. Official website for bittorrent. http://www.bittorrent.com.

[6] Eleazar Eskin. Anomaly detection over noisy data using learned probability distributions. 2000. http://academiccommons.columbia.edu/item/ac:125813.

[7] Mansour Esmaili, Bala Balachandran, Reihaneh Safavi-Naini, and Josef Pieprzyk. Case-based reasoning for intrusion detection. In *12th Annual Computer Security Applications Conference*, pages 214–223. 1996.

[8] Juan M. Estévez-Tapiador, Pedro Garcia-Teodoro, and Jesús E. Díaz-Verdejo. Measuring normality in http traffic for anomaly-based intrusion detection. *Computer Networks*, 45(2):175–193, 2004.

[9] P. García-Teodoro, J. Díaz-Verdejo, G. Maciá-Fernández, and E. Vázquez. Anomaly-based network intrusion detection: Techniques, systems and challenges. *Computers & Security*, 28(1–2):18–28, 2009.

[10] R. Guha, O. Kachirski, D. Schwartz, S. Stoecklin, and Y. Yilmaz. Case-based agents for packet-level intrusion detection in ad hoc networks. In *Proceedings of the 17th International Symposium on Computer and Information Sciences*, pages 315 – 320. CRC Press, October 2002.

[11] Paul Hick. The CAIDA DDoS Attack 2007 Dataset (collection). http://imdc.datcat.org/collection/1-06Y1-W=The+CAIDA+DDoS+Attack+2007+Dataset (accessed on August 2013).

[12] Xuan Dau Hoang, Jiankun Hu, and Peter Bertok. A multi-layer model for anomaly intrusion detection using program sequences of system calls. In *Proceedingi of the 11th IEEE IntÖl. Conference on Networks (ICON)*, 2003.

[13] Steven A. Hofmeyr, Stephanie Forrest, and Anil Somayaji. Intrusion detection using sequences of system calls. *Journal of Computer Security*, 6(3):151–180, 01 1998.

[14] Eyke Hüllermeier, Didier Dubois, Henri Prade, De Toulouse, and Universit'e Paul Sabatier. Fuzzy rules in case-based reasoning. In *in Conf. AFIA99 Raisonnement à Partir de Cas*, pages 45–54, 1999.

[15] Christopher Kruegel and Thomas Toth. Using decision trees to improve signature-based intrusion detection. In *Proceedings of Recent Advances in Intrusion Detection (RAID)*, pages 173–191. Springer, 2003.

[16] David B. Leake. Case-based reasoning. *The Knowledge Engineering Review*, 9(01):61–64, 1994.

[17] Wenke Lee, S.J. Stolfo, and K.W. Mok. A data mining framework for building intrusion detection models. In *Proceedings of the 1999 IEEE Symposium on Security and Privacy*, pages 120–132, 1999.

[18] Malware Domain List. http://www.malwaredomainlist.com.

[19] Microsoft. Windows based performance counter data logger. http://technet.microsoft.com/en-us/library/bb490960.aspx.

[20] Mitre. Common attack pattern enumeration and classification. http://capec.mitre.org/data/definitions/113.html.

[21] Mitre. Structured threat information expression. http://stix.mitre.org/.

[22] Soumyo D. Moitra. Situational awareness metrics from flow and other data sources. 2013.

[23] Official Website for uTorrent. http://www.utorrent.com.

[24] Roberto Perdisci, Wenke Lee, and Nick Feamster. Behavioral clustering of http-based malware and signature generation using malicious network traces. In *Proceedings of the 7th USENIX conference on Networked systems design and implementation*, NSDI'10, pages 26–26, Berkeley, CA, USA, 2010. USENIX Association.

[25] Predict. Protected repository for the defense of infrastructure against cyberthreats. http://www.predict.org.

[26] J. Reason. Too little and too late: A commentary on accident and incident reporting systems. 1991.

[27] Timothy J. Ross. *Fuzzy Logic*, pages i–xxi. John Wiley & Sons, Ltd, 2010.

[28] Sans Education. https://isc.sans.edu/feeds/suspiciousdomains_high.txt.

[29] Shalla Secure Services KG. Shalla list website blacklist database. http://www.shallalist.de/Downloads/shallalist.tar.gz.

[30] Jessica Steinberger, Lisa Schehlmann, Sebastian Abt, and Harald Baier. Anomaly detection and mitigation at internet scale: A survey. In *Emerging Management Mechanisms for the Future Internet*, pages 49–60. Springer, 2013.

[31] Vimal Vaidya. Dynamic signature inspection-based network intrusion detection, August 21 2001. US Patent 6,279,113.

[32] Christina Warrender, Stephanie Forrest, and Barak Pearlmutter. Detecting intrusions using system calls: Alternative data models. In *Security and Privacy, 1999. Proceedings of the 1999 IEEE Symposium on*, pages 133–145. IEEE, 1999.

[33] M. West-Brown, D. Stikvoort, K.-P. Kossakowski, G. Killcrece, R. Ruefle, and M. Zajicek. Handbook for computer security incident response teams (csirts), 2003. Technical Report CMU/SEI-2003-HB-002.

[34] Dit-Yan Yeung and Yuxin Ding. Host-based intrusion detection using dynamic and static behavioral models. *Pattern Recognition*, 36(1):229 – 243, 2003.

[35] Zeus Tracker Domain Blocklist. https://secure.mayhemiclabs.com/malhosts/malhosts.txt.

Table 6: Application Metrics

Metric name	Description
# HTTP requests	Level of machine activity in the network
# GET requests	Number of GET requests for retrieving data from specific resources
# POST requests	Number of POST requests sent to an identified resource
# PUT requests	Number of requests for uploading a representation of a specified resource
# DELETE requests	Number of requests for deleting a specified resource
Avg. URLs length	Avg number of character in the URL
Avg. parameters in request	Avg number of parameters in the URL
Avg. data sent by POST requests	Avg size of POST requests received
Avg. responses length	Helps identify change in the traffic behavior, should remain constant over time
Avg. re-directions	Occurrences of the class of status code 3xx (further action needs to be taken by the user agent in order to fulfill the HTTP request)
Avg. client errors	Occurrences of class of status code 4xx (client seems to have erred)
Avg. server errors	Occurrences of class of status code 5xx (server failed to fulfill an apparently valid request)

Table 7: Network Metrics

Metric name	Description
Flow count	A flow is identified by: sourceIP, sourcePort, destinationIP, destinationPort, and Protocol
Avg. flow packet count	average number of packets in a flow
Avg. flow byte count	average number of bytes in a flow
Avg. packet size	Average of bytes per packet in a flow
Flow Behavior	Ratio of the flow count and the average packet size

[36] Loai Zomlot, Sathya Chandran Sundaramurthy, Kui Luo, Xinming Ou, and S. Raj Rajagopalan. Prioritizing intrusion analysis using dempster-shafer theory. In *Proceedings of the 4th ACM workshop on Security and artificial intelligence*, AISec '11, pages 59–70, 2011.

APPENDIX

A. APPLICATION METRICS

In tables 6 and 7 we report examples of application and network metrics, respectively.

B. TRAFFIC GENERATION

Below is a brief description of the approach taken to generate network traffic for our case base. We provide an example of the DoS case.

- We inspected the data set available to us (i.e. Caida and Predict, as discussed in Section 6.1) to identify the smallest unit of traffic (minimal set of traffic records) which would constitute (be detected) an incident (say a DoS attack). This was achieved by running all the traffic records through ReasONets, so as to recognize the machine(s) and time it came under attack.

- After identifying the machine and time, we segregated all the traffic records reflecting traffic coming in or going out from the victim machine until the time of the attack.

- We then filtered records which were too far apart (time-wise) to reduce the traffic records being considered and tested whether ReasONet would still recognize the reduced traffic record set as an attack. In this way, we obtained a *minimal traffic set identifiable as a DoS attack* which we would re-use later to create multiple attacks.

- To create the synthetic attacks, the script changed the IP address of the machine which was attacked to that of the client machine which we wanted to simulate an attack on. The script also changed the source of the attacks (the external IP addresses from which the attacks had originated) to random values from a lookup table maintained by us. It also updated the timestamp and attack distribution, to ensure it was not a perfect replica of the original attack.

Example 1. *Assume the Src IP = 130.203.157.12 (the machine inside the network which got attacked in the Predict data set)*
New Src IP = local client Machine's IP address
Old Dest IP = 69.203.157.12
New Dest IP = 145.10.1.1

- Every occurrence of the old Dest IP was changed to the above new value and the association stored in a table for convenience and consistency.

Measuring the Robustness of Source Program Obfuscation

Studying the Impact of Compiler Optimizations on the Obfuscation of C Programs

Sandrine Blazy
IRISA
University of Rennes 1
Sandrine.Blazy@irisa.fr

Stephanie Riaud
DGA-MI
INRIA
Stephanie.Riaud@inria.fr

ABSTRACT

Obfuscation is a commonly used technique to protect software from the reverse engineering process. Advanced obfuscations usually rely on semantic properties of programs and thus may be performed on source programs. This raises the question of how to be sure that the binary code (that is effectively running) is still obfuscated.

This paper presents a data obfuscation of C programs and a methodology to evaluate how the obfuscation resists to the GCC compiler. Information generated by the compiler (including effects of relevant optimizations that could deobfuscate programs) and a study of the disassembled binary code, as well as a dynamic analysis of the performances of binary code show that our obfuscation is worthwhile.

Categories and Subject Descriptors

D.2.0 [**Software Engineering**]: General—*Protection mechanisms*

Keywords

obfuscation, compiler optimization, anti-reverse engineering

1. INTRODUCTION

A well-known way of attacking a software is to start by reverse engineering it in order to reconstruct the memory layout using static or dynamic analysis tools operating over disassembled or binary code. Software reverse engineering is an active field of research and new reverse engineering techniques are regularly published. Obfuscating a program consists in transforming it into an equivalent program that is more difficult to understand or to analyze. Among the applications of obfuscation is the protection of software from reverse engineering. The numerous obfuscation techniques range from elementary syntactic techniques such as inserting opaque predicates to more sophisticated semantics-based techniques such as complicating control flows [3].

CODASPY'14, March 3–5, 2014, San Antonio, Texas, USA.
ACM 978-1-4503-2278-2/14/03.
http://dx.doi.org/10.1145/2557547.2557577.

Improvements in reverse engineering call for improvements in obfuscation. Obfuscation can be performed at different levels of program representation: at the source level, on any intermediate language or at the assembly or binary level. On the one hand, many obfuscations are performed directly at the binary or assembly level. It ensures that the code that is running is obfuscated. On the other hand, obfuscating a source program facilitates the design of advanced obfuscations relying on semantic properties of source programs.

Obfuscating a source program raises the question of how to be sure that the binary code (that is effectively running) is still obfuscated. Obfuscations can be classified according to two main categories, depending whether they mainly transform the control flow of a program or its data [3]. Many obfuscations related to control flow exist in the literature. Data obfuscations mainly hide data in memory and can also complicate the reverse engineering process.

This paper presents a data obfuscation of C programs and a methodology to evaluate how the obfuscation resists to the GCC compiler (including optimizations). This obfuscation is an example of obfuscation that is easier to design at the C level than at the assembly level. The obfuscation is hiding data structure fields at the source level, so that it will become much more difficult to reverse engineer the memory layout from a corresponding binary code. A detailed study of the information generated by the compiler (including effects of relevant optimizations that could deobfuscate programs) and of the disassembled binary code, as well as a dynamic analysis of the performances of obfuscated code show that our obfuscation is worthwhile.

2. BACKGROUND

We now present our data obfuscation and explain how the GCC compiler could possibly deobfuscate C programs.

2.1 A Data Obfuscation

Data obfuscations are usually classified according to the transformation they perform [3]. A data obfuscation aims at modifying the encoding of data, or the way data are stored, or the aggregation of data or the ordering of data. Our data obfuscation performs these four transformations.

It is detailed in Fig. 1 and replaces each field access having a scalar type (*e.g.* `t.a` in the example program of Fig. 1) by an address storing the current field value[1]. This address is computed by a function called `access` (that is added to the source program and detailed in Fig. 1). For instance,

---

[1] By default, all fields of C structures are replaced, but it is also possible to obfuscate only some selected fields.

the field `t.a` is replaced by the address `*access()`. Thus, the address of the current field is hidden in an array (called `access_array` in Fig. 1) that is accessed from the auxiliary function `access`. This access array groups together the whole field accesses of the program (*e.g.* its size is 4 in Fig. 1). Moreover, a new indirection is added. The access array is used to calculate indices of another array (called `address_array` in Fig. 1) storing the different field values.

Furthermore, the function `access` is exchanging the field values and updates accordingly the access array: at each function call (*i.e.* each field access in the original program) two field values are randomly chosen to be permutated.

```
struct test {int a;int b;};
int main (void){  /* Initial example program */
   struct test t;           int c;
   t.a =10;   t.b =20;   c = t.a;   return c + t.b;
}  /*------------------------------------------------------------*/
int access_counter;                      /* Obfuscated code */
int access_array[4] = { 0, 1, 0, 1, };
int *address_array[2];
int rand_a_b(int a, int b) { ... }  /* Returns an int in [a;b] */
int *access(){
   int nb_elem = 2, id1, id2, t, *ptr;
   id2 = rand_a_b(0, nb_elem);
   id1 = rand_a_b(0, nb_elem);
   t = **(address_array + id1);
   **(address_array + id1) = **(address_array + id2);
   **(address_array + id2) = t;
   ptr = *(address_array + id1);
   *(address_array + id1) = *(address_array + id2);
   *(address_array + id2) = ptr;
   access_counter = access_counter + 1;
   return *(address_array + *(access_array + (access_counter-1)));
}
int main(void)                    /* Obfuscated main function */
   struct test t;
   int c;
   access_counter = 0;
   *(address_array + 1) = &t.b;  *(address_array + 0) = &t.a;
   *access()= 10;                *access()= 20;
   c = *access();                return (c + *access());     }
```

Figure 1: An example of obfuscated program

Finding all field accesses in a given C program is more complex to perform at the assembly level, where the data flow is more difficult to interpret. It requires to consider all possible accesses via the registers, the stack and the rest of the memory. Thus, we designed our obfuscation at the C level that is better adapted than the assembly level.

2.2 Compiler Optimizations

Our obfuscation operates over C programs and we want to be sure that the corresponding binary code is as obfuscated as the source program. Consequently, we study the impact of the compilation on our obfuscation. We focus on the GCC compiler, as it is a widely used open compiler.

Among the great deal of compiler optimizations, we only study the relevant ones performing inverse transformations w.r.t. our obfuscation. As our obfuscation transforms scalar field accesses, we chose to study two kinds of optimizations: scalar reduction of aggregates (SRA) and scalar optimizations. SRA is the most relevant optimization as it transforms all the fields of a structure into different independent variables. Scalar optimizations rely on three basic optimizations: constant propagation, copy propagation and dead code elimination. We want to be sure that they neither transform the fields we obfuscate nor the statements that our obfuscation adds in the original program.

As other optimizations do, SRA selects candidate fields and rejects other fields of the program (*e.g.* a scalar field belonging to a structure having a pointer field). Then, among the candidate fields, SRA selects fields that will be changed and disqualifies the others (*e.g.* a field that is never accessed during program execution). Thus, only some of the field accesses are optimized by SRA. We then need to compare these fields with those of the original program. This impact analysis of SRA is also performed for scalar optimizations.

3. EVALUATION PROCESS

Our goal is to check that a binary obfuscated code is more difficult to reverse engineer than its corresponding initial program. Our method is general enough to be applied on other obfuscations operating over source programs. It follows the three main steps that are detailed in this section.

3.1 Impact Analysis of the Compilation

We compile separately the original program and the obfuscated program. Each compilation is performed twice: without any compiler optimization, as well as at the highest level of optimization. Then, we study the impact of each optimization on our obfuscation. Each optimization consists in different compiler passes (at least an intraprocedural and an interprocedural pass for the optimizations we have studied). For each pass, we analyze the optimization details generated by the compiler, in order to distinguish between the fields remaining obfuscated after the pass from the other optimized fields. For scalar optimizations, we also track the optimized expressions. Then, we compare these results with those of the original program. Our global measure is the conservation rate of field accesses in the obfuscated program.

3.2 Analysis of Disassembled Binaries

The next analysis takes into account the assembling and linking steps occurring after compilation, and checks that all the transformations added by the obfuscation (*e.g.* the permutation of values in an array) are still performed in the binary code. Using the interactive dynamic analysis of IDA Pro, the analysis compares the memory layout of the original and the obfuscated programs. We chose the IDA Pro tool because it is one of the most used tools for reverse engineering binary files.

The BinDiff tool built on IDA Pro is also used to compare two binary files and generate a similarity rate between both files [5]. We use it to study separately the effects of the optimization and the obfuscation, as well as the effects of the optimization on the obfuscation. Thus, we perform three comparisons with BinDiff: between the original program and the optimized program, between the original program and the obfuscated program, and between the obfuscated program and the optimized and obfuscated program.

3.3 Dynamic Binary Analysis

Instead of analyzing statically the impact of the compilation, we could perform a dynamic binary analysis. A static analysis is done once for each program, but a dynamic analysis is easier to implement, provided it scales to real-size source programs and does not generate huge execution traces that become impossible to interpret.

We used the Pin tool [10] to instrument obfuscated binaries and check whether the compiler has compiled away the obfuscation. Our Pin tool aims at collecting memory access to the access array added by our obfuscation, as well as the calls to the `access` function. Moreover, we also observed that the obfuscated binaries cannot be easily reverse engineered by such a dynamic binary instrumentation tool.

In addition, we reused our Pin tool to check that our obfuscation resists to a different compiler. We chose the Intel ICC compiler that is performing interprocedural optimizations that could modify obfuscated programs more than GCC can. The only difference we observed is the inlining of functions added by our obfuscation. But, the data structures remain the same in the obfuscated code, thus showing that compiled programs are still obfuscated.

Last, we also measured the increase of the execution time when obfuscating programs. Even if the main goal of an obfuscation is to have it resist reverse engineering analyses, the loss in performance cannot be completely neglected [1]. When the execution time of the obfuscated binary is much slower, the obfuscation is considered as unsatisfactory. Then, we chose to obfuscate less fields and we obfuscated again the initial program. This process was repeated until the execution times of the original and obfuscated programs become close. When the execution trace is small enough to be interpreted, another solution to update the obfuscation is to use the Pin tool in order to understand the discrepancy in the execution times of both programs and select the fields that will be obfuscated.

4. EXPERIMENTAL EVALUATION

Our benchmark for the impact analysis of the compilation is the GCC testsuite devoted to optimizations. Our results show that when a field is optimized in the original program, it is never optimized in the obfuscated program.

Next, the analysis of disassembled binaries shows that all the structure fields still exist in the obfuscated binary codes (even if the program was optimized), as well as the auxiliary variables and functions added by the obfuscation.

Last, we used the latest stable version of the GNU coreutils utility suite as input to our performance analysis. The size of programs ranges between 500 and 4800 lines. The execution times of all obfuscated programs were similar to those of their original programs, except for one program. We then used Pin to help us improving our obfuscation.

5. RELATED WORK

There is an abundant literature on control flow obfuscations. Data obfuscations were also designed mainly either to hide specific data by encrypting them (*e.g.* see [4]) or to diversify software by generating different binaries from a same source program [2, 9, 8]. Data obfuscations operate over C programs or over lower levels. For instance, the obfuscation defined in [9] randomizes the ordering of fields in C structures and inserts unused fields between them. Our obfuscation shares similarities with the obfuscation described in [1] that obfuscates both data location and data usage in order to protect against malware detectors. However, the transformations performed by their obfuscation differs from ours as the obfuscation operates directly over binary code.

Since the general criteria (*e.g.* resilience) defined in [3] for evaluating obfuscations, there is still no standard way of evaluating the effectiveness of an obfuscation. Evaluations based on static analysis exist [11, 6]. They rely on more advanced static analysis techniques than those of IDA Pro

that we used, but to the best of our knowledge it is not clear that they scale on large programs such as those we tested.

6. CONCLUSION

We have presented a data obfuscation that hides field accesses in an array that is modified at each field access and hidden in a function. Indirect accesses to this array generate many pointers in obfuscated programs. Our obfuscation operates over C programs. We have showed that it is robust against compilation and very useful for programs manipulating structure fields storing information that need to be protected against reverse engineering tools.

Our experiments showed that reverse engineering of our obfuscated programs is very hard because of the code that is added by our obfuscation. It requires to analyze step by step a great deal of array accesses in order to replace many function calls by semantically equivalent array accesses.

We intend to conduct more experiments to test our obfuscation against some automatic deobfuscators relying on compiler optimizations such as those we have studied [7]. We also intend to design a program analyzer that will be able to automate some of the tedious tasks required to reverse engineer obfuscated programs.

7. REFERENCES

[1] A.Moser, C.Kruegel, and E.Kirda. Limits of static analysis for malware detection. In *Computer Security Applications Conf.*, pages 421–430, 2007.

[2] E. Bhatkar, D. C. Duvarney, and R. Sekar. Address obfuscation: an efficient approach to combat a broad range of memory error exploits. In *Proc. of USENIX Security Symp.*, pages 105–120, 2003.

[3] C. Collberg, C. Thomborson, and D. Low. A taxonomy of obfuscating transformations. Technical Report 148, University of Auckland, New Zeland, 1997.

[4] E. Damiani, S. De, C. Vimercati, and al. Computing range queries on obfuscated data. In *Proc. of the Information Processing and Management of Uncertainty in Knowledge-Based Systems*, 2004.

[5] H. Flake. Structural comparison of executable objects. In *Proc. of the Conf. DIMVA*, pages 161–173, 2004.

[6] R. Giacobazzi and I. Mastroeni. Making abstract interpretation incomplete: Modeling the potency of obfuscation. In *Static Analysis Symposium*, volume 7460 of *LNCS*, pages 129–145. 2012.

[7] Y. Guillot and A. Gazet. Automatic binary deobfuscation. *Journal in Computer Virology*, 6(3):261–276, 2010.

[8] T. Hagog. Cache aware data layout reorganization optimization in GCC. In *Proc. of the GCC Developers' Summit*, 2005.

[9] Z. Lin, R. D. Riley, and D. Xu. Polymorphing software by randomizing data structure layout. In *Proc. of the Conf. DIMVA*, pages 107–126, 2009.

[10] C.-K. Luk, R. Cohn, R. Muth, and al. Pin: building customized program analysis tools with dynamic instrumentation. *SIGPLAN Not.*, 40(6):190–200, 2005.

[11] A. Majumdar, A. Monsifrot, and C. Thomborson. On evaluating obfuscatory strength of alias-based transforms using static analysis. In *Conf. on Advanced Computing and Comms.*, pages 605–610, 2006.

Interaction Provenance Model for Unified Authentication Factors in Service Oriented Computing

Ragib Hasan and Rasib Khan
SECRETLab, Department of Computer and Information Sciences
University of Alabama at Birmingham, AL, USA
{ragib, rasib}@cis.uab.edu

ABSTRACT

Authentication is one of the most fundamental security problems. To date, various distinct authentication factors such as passwords, tokens, certificates, and biometrics have been designed for authentication. In this paper, we propose using the history or provenance of previous interactions and events as the generic platform for all authentication challenges. In this paradigm, provenance of past interactions with the authenticating principle or a third party is used to authenticate a user. We show that the interaction provenance paradigm is generic and can be used to represent existing authentication factors, yet allow the use of newer methods. We also discuss how authentication based on interactions can allow very flexible but complex authentication and access control policies that are not easily possible with current authentication models.

Categories and Subject Descriptors

K.6.5 [**MANAGEMENT OF COMPUTING AND INFORMA-TION SYSTEMS**]: Security and Protection (D.4.6, K.4.2): Authentication

Keywords

Authentication, Events, Interaction, Provenance, Security

1. INTRODUCTION

In our everyday lives, we frequently face the need to prove our identities to others. A valid claim of identity allows a service provider to link the claimed user to the available services. In service oriented computing, authentication refers to proving one's identity to a challenging authority, and subsequently, avail the offered services from the provider. Authentication is the most critical part in ensuring security in any service oriented architecture. Service providers incorporate different authentication mechanisms according to their need and purpose. Usually, authentication services are dependent on three prime factors, that is, what the user knows, what the user has, and what the user is. However, most authentication mechanisms still remain proprietary and pose as a challenge in ensuring a completely secure process.

We have identified an inherent similarity among all the authentication factors, in their singular form or in any combination of fac-

tors. A system can authenticate a user only based on past events where the user interacted with the system. For example, a password can be used for authentication to a system only if the user has registered an account in the system and created (or was assigned) a password before. This is similar to authentication in social contexts. People recognize each other based on their previous interactions, events, and actions. Additionally, this information is not presented only at the time of recognition, but rather exists as a string of events over the particular subject's timeline.

Based on this observation, we believe that these apparently disjoint authentication factors can be fundamentally merged under a common root. In this paper, we use this notion to propose a model to unify all existing authentication factors into a single interaction provenance verification scheme. Our proposed model delivers a concept of using past interactions between various entities to validate the entities involved in authentication. We refer to the term interaction provenance to represent the set of events in a user's history of interactions with various systems. We claim that all authentication factors can be represented in terms of interaction provenance.

2. MOTIVATION

In everyday practices, the more secure a system is, the less usable it becomes for its users. For authentication, three major factors have been developed and deployed over the years [2]. Authentication challenges are considered to be fundamentally designed around one or more of the following factors:

Knowledge: In this case, authentication is done by the subject by presenting a secret shared between the subject and the system at an earlier time. This can be a password, which the subject has established when setting up her account with the system. This can also be a shared knowledge about the user (e.g., the amount of a few transactions posted to a user's bank account in the last week). This factor is perhaps the most commonly used factor in authentication, yet the most attacked. Passwords are vulnerable to simple guessing attacks using a dictionary-based or a brute force approach. Strong passwords that are hard to break are also hard to remember, making them difficult to enforce in practice.

Possession: Here, authentication is done by presenting a physical or digital object that the subject holds. For example, it can be a badge or a token or a X.509 digital certificate held by the subject. There are also hardware devices which a user must use to generate one-time-pads and present to the provider. The system can verify the token and therefore the identity of the subject. In each of these cases, the authentication in dependent on a certain possession of the user at the time of validation, and has been registered as a valid item.

Biometrics: The physical characteristics of the subject are also used for authentication. The most common and widely used biometric authentication schemes include fingerprints, voice recognition, iris recognition, and face recognition. Bodily attributes can be considered as the most unique authentication features. However, in case biometric information, such as fingerprints, is forged, the subject loses the ability to use fingerprints ever again for authentication purposes.

Contextual Information: There can be other authentication factors used in the validation process. In general, they are referred to as contextual information, and include the location of the subject, background or network oriented data, and recommendation chains from other users [3]. However, this information is not secure and self-sufficient, and therefore, acts as a reinforcement factor for other authentication mechanisms.

Therefore, we can see that each of the factors is prone to multiple vulnerabilities when considered on their own. Multi-factor authentication mechanisms have been incorporated into systems which require higher security. However, the usability of such multi-factor authentication mechanisms are greatly reduced, as users are required to memorize passwords, save certificates, and carry around one-time-pad generating devices. Another problem with all existing authentication mechanisms is that they rely on credentials presented at only the given time. As a result, any lost credential (username/password, certificate) results in authentication fraud and identity theft. Identity thefts as such are very easy, since an attacker only needs to provide the information (knowledge, possession, or biometrics) only at the time of authentication.

Access control and authorization of resources are also complicated in terms of such authentication credentials. The main security problem is to determine the rights (e.g., read, read-write, etc.) a user has over a given resource or object [2]. However, common access control mechanisms are unable to impose such policies based on authentication credentials. Furthermore, cross-platform compatibility of authentication and authorization are always a critical problem among service providers, when it comes to agreeing on a common protocol for supporting user transition from one provider to the other.

3. UNIFICATION OF AUTHENTICATION FACTORS

In this section, we present the concept of interaction provenance, and its applicability for authentication and other security domains.

3.1 Interaction Provenance

An interaction is an event or a record of a user action with one or more other entities. Therefore, an interaction entry is a log of the protocol execution, and is maintained in an ordered set of messages or actions performed by two or more entities. A principal is a participant in an interaction provenance entry, if it had sent or received at least one message, or had initiated at least one action. We define an event as a particular action or a record of a protocol execution that has taken place in the past. Interaction provenance of a principal is a chronologically ordered sequence of interaction entries, in each of which, the principal was a participant for a particular event.

From the definition of interaction, it immediately follows that interactions are always about events. Since time is linear, interactions for a user form a chronologically ordered chain, with no cycles. Interactions are strongly attached to the user and cannot be transferred. Interactions are also considered mutual. That is, both parties in an interaction will always have a record of the same event. For example, when Alice registers an account with a ser-

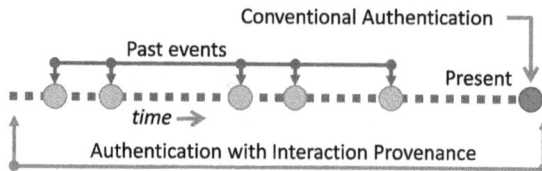

Figure 1: Interaction Provenance for Authentication

vice provider, she interacts with it by following its new account registration protocol, accessing the system, and then setting a user name and a password. The provider also sees Alice's actions and is a participant in the registration protocol. Later, whenever Alice logs into the service, she runs different protocols and has various interactions with the system and/or other external or internal users.

Additionally, ordering of the interaction entries are chained, such that, the chronological sequence cannot be altered with respect to each other. To use interaction provenance for authenticating users, it is essential that the data can be verified and any tampering should be detected. We can adapt techniques from secure data provenance for designing tamper-proof individual interactions and the order of interaction provenance chains [8, 9].

3.2 Interaction Provenance for Authentication

The various conventional authentication factors depend on some previous events or interactions that the user had with the server, or some other entity trusted by the server. Authentication is dependent on a past event when the user created or registered the secure credentials with the provider. From this perspective, we can say that all the authentication factors can simply be represented as the use of past interactions. Based on this observation, we propose using interaction provenance as the only generic authentication factor, and thus unifying all the conventional authentication factors. Users can prove k out of n recorded past events and corresponding interactions, and authenticate themselves to a system. The provider verifies that the claimed interaction indeed occurred and satisfies the authentication policy of the system. Upon successful validation, the system can verify the identity of the principal subject in the interaction, and map that to a known user in the system. Therefore, as shown in Figure 1, authentication using interaction provenance enforces a validity check on the timeline of past events. On the contrary, conventional authentication procedures only rely on presenting authentication credentials at the present time.

We used certain models of data block composition to represent events and interactions, and also for user-provider interaction at later times, as shown below:

Interaction [UserID, ProviderID, EventType [Key|Value, ..]]

To illustrate how current authentication factors can be represented in the form of events and interactions, we can consider the individual authentication types. In the case of password or shared-secret based authentication systems, we can model a 'registration' event as a past interaction. Therefore, this event is presented by the user during authentication at a later time as follows:

Sender: *UserA*, **Receiver**: *ProviderB*
Interaction: [*UserA*, *ProviderB*, Registration [UserID: *UserA*,
    ProviderID: *ProviderB*, Password: *password*,
    RegTime: *timestamp*]]

Authentication systems based on certificate or token possession can also be modeled as above. According to our scheme of interaction provenance, we can consider the issuance of the token by a trusted certification authority as an event. Therefore, the user can present this interaction to any other provider for the purpose of authentication as follows:

Sender: *UserA*, **Receiver**: *ProviderB*
Interaction: [*UserA*, *TrustedPartyID*, Issue_Credential [
      UserID: *UserA*, ProviderID: *TrustedPartyID*,
      Credential: *token*, CreateTime: *timestamp*]]

In the same way shown for the above cases, biometric authentication can also be represented using interaction provenance. As we know that the user had a past event when the biometric information was registered with the provider, this interaction can be presented during authentication as follows:

Sender: *UserA*, **Receiver**: *ProviderB*
Interaction: [*UserA*, *ProviderB*, Register [UserID: *UserA*,
      ProviderID: *ProviderB*, Biometric: *data*,
      CreateTime: *timestamp*]]

Additional factors, such as, contextual information and recommendation chains can also be presented using interaction provenance [3]. The representation of information may vary based on the type of factor in use. All authentication factors represented as past events can thus be unified under a single paradigm of authentication using interaction provenance items.

3.3 Extension of Interaction Provenance in Secure Systems

Interaction provenance can be extended to serve other security services. We can augment access control and authorization to make it more flexible and dynamic via the use of interaction provenance. Access policies can be written in terms of past interactions and events. Therefore, a user will be allowed access to a resource if a specific type of interaction provenance can be presented. In an example scenario, an airline traveler will require to present interaction records with the ticketing system, which implies that, a successful purchase of tickets. Next, the passenger is required to present successful verification of documents and passing through the airport security checkpoints. Another example can be to share contents on social network, only with people who had previous interactions with the user. Interaction provenance can be used to implement path-based access control, where access to a resource depends on the physical (or logical) path of the user or data item. Past interactions with secure systems and other users can be used to leverage assertion and contextual information based admission to resources.

4. MODEL ANALYSIS

Unifying different authentication factors into a single authentication paradigm based on provenance is beneficial in many respects. First, the proposed model unifies all existing authentication factors into a common representation model. This unification can be leveraged to implement cross-platform and common authentication mechanism among service providers. Second, interaction provenance can be used to enforce authentication mechanisms based on a string of past events, in contrary to only presenting credentials at the present moment. This allows an improved level of security for the domain of service oriented computing. Third, the proposed model allows newer methods or factors of authentication, such as, knowledge belonging to group interactions. This also introduces increased flexibility in authentication and brings the authentication process closer to real life trust establishment. Fourth, interaction provenance can allow mutual authentication of users and providers, where both of which should present a previous record of interaction. Fifth, we can utilize interactions to allow anonymous authentications by creating an authentication event the first time, and validating the provenance in the subsequent occasions. Finally, extending the idea of interaction provenance to other security problems introduces significant benefits. Authorization and access control can be defined using richer and simpler semantics, which will allow writing complex and innovative security policies based on past interactions.

5. RELATED WORK

A lot of research in recent years has focused on securing provenance information against illicit tampering and confidentiality or information flow violations [2, 4–6]. However, our proposed primitive looks at the opposite problem: how provenance can be used to solve security problems such as authentication and access control. New innovative methods of authentication such as using recommendations from other validated users have been proposed recently [3]. However, to the best of our knowledge, no attempts have been made to unify all authentication factors. In this work, we propose using interaction provenance as the only generalized authentication factor. The use of the history of a user or an application for access control has been explored by some researchers. Edjlali et al. discussed the use of the history of mobile code to determine access control [7]. Abadi et al. presented an access control model based on application execution history [1]. Krukow et al. extended the idea to provide a logical framework for history based access control [10]. In our paper, we propose making history or provenance of interactions as the only factor in access control.

6. CONCLUSION

This paper introduces interaction provenance as a generalized factor for authentication. We showed that existing authentication factors can be represented via interactions, and new authentication methods can be introduced through the use of interactions. We posit that the notion of interaction provenance as a fundamental security primitive can be successfully used in many areas of security and has the potential of bringing flexibility and introducing novel applications that are not currently possible with existing approaches.

Acknowledgment

This research was supported by a Google Faculty Research Award, the Office of Naval Research Grant #N000141210217, the DHS Grant #FA8750-12-2- 0254, and under NSF Grant #0937060 to the Computing Research Association for the CIFellows Project.

References

[1] M. Abadi and C. Fournet. Access control based on execution history. In *Proceedings of the 10th Annual Network and Distributed System Security Symposium*, pages 107–121, 2003.

[2] M. A. Bishop. *The Art and Science of Computer Security*. Addison-Wesley Longman Publishing Co., Inc., Boston, MA, USA, 2002.

[3] J. Brainard, A. Juels, R. L. Rivest, M. Szydlo, and M. Yung. Fourth-factor authentication: somebody you know. In *Proceedings of the 13th ACM conference on Computer and Communications Security*, CCS '06, pages 168–178, New York, NY, USA, 2006. ACM.

[4] U. Braun, A. Shinnar, and M. Seltzer. Securing provenance. In *Proceedings of The 3rd USENIX Workshop on Hot Topics in Security (HotSec)*, July 2008.

[5] J. Cheney. A formal framework for provenance security. In *Computer Security Foundations Symposium (CSF), 2011 IEEE 24th*, pages 281–293, 2011.

[6] S. Chong. Towards semantics for provenance security. In *First workshop on on Theory and practice of provenance*, TAPP'09, pages 2:1–2:5, Berkeley, CA, USA, 2009. USENIX Association.

[7] G. Edjlali, A. Acharya, and V. Chaudhary. History-based access control for mobile code. In *Proceedings of The 5th ACM Conference on Computer and Communications Security*, CCS '98, pages 38–48, New York, NY, USA, 1998. ACM.

[8] R. Hasan, R. Sion, and M. Winslett. Introducing secure provenance: problems and challenges. In *Proceedings of The ACM Workshop on Storage security and survivability (StorageSS)*, pages 13–18, New York, NY, USA, 2007. ACM.

[9] R. Hasan, R. Sion, and M. Winslett. Preventing history forgery with secure provenance. *ACM Transactions on Storage (TOS)*, 5(4):12:1–12:43, Dec. 2009.

[10] K. Krukow, M. Nielsen, and V. Sassone. A logical framework for history-based access control and reputation systems. *Journal of Computer Security*, 16(1):63–101, Jan. 2008.

Detecting Man-in-the-Middle Attacks on Non-Mobile Systems

Visa Vallivaara
VTT,
Technical Research Center of
Finland
visa.vallivaara@vtt.fi

Mirko Sailio
VTT,
Technical Research Center of
Finland
mirko.sailio@vtt.fi

Kimmo Halunen
VTT,
Technical Research Center of
Finland
kimmo.halunen@vtt.fi

ABSTRACT

In this paper we propose a method for detecting man-in-the-middle attacks using the timestamps of TCP packet headers. From these timestamps, the delays can be calculated and by comparing the mean of the delays in the current connection to data gathered from previous sessions it is possible to detect if the packets have unusually long delays. We show that in our small case study we can find and set a threshold parameter that accurately detects man-in-the-middle attacks with a low probability of false positives. Thus, it may be used as a simple precautionary measure against malicious attacks. The method in its current form is limited to non-mobile systems, where the variations in the delay are fairly low and uniform.

Categories and Subject Descriptors

C.2.5 [**Computer Systems Organization**]: Computer-Communication Networks —*Local and Wide-Area Networks*

Keywords

Man-in-the-Middle attack, network monitoring

1. INTRODUCTION

Man-in-the-Middle (MitM) attacks are an old and yet challenging threat for networked computing systems. MitM attack is an attack, where the attackers intrude into an existing connection to intercept the exchanged data and inject false information. It involves eavesdropping on a connection, intruding into a connection, intercepting messages, and selectively modifying data. The problem has been extensively researched and there are many variations to the basic attack [7]. Different subsets of techniques have been offered to mitigate some specific subsections of the problem.

Despite the old age of MitM attacks they are still one of the favorite tools for Internet cyber criminals. Attacks are usually directed at client-server communications with the purpose of either obtaining authentication credentials or performing tasks, such as money transfers, in the client's name. While two-way authenticated encryption can be used to prevent unauthorized persons from affecting communications, most of the problems arise from the fact that the security measures required for protection are hard to deploy or may seem inconvenient, especially when usability comes into question. They can be often circumvented when the user of a service is not technically savvy.

1.1 Related work

Most successful strategies for preventing MitM attacks are currently relying either on strong authentication or two-way authenticated encryption. Both of these strategies have their downsides, which affect their usability. The first one requires the users to carry a physical device for authentication and the second one requires all the devices that connect to the server have encryption certificates. History has it that even with the assumption of ideal cryptography, one can not be assured that the messages will be safely delivered to the intended recipient [6]. This is because even though a security protocol is designed perfectly, security vulnerabilities in the implementation do not cease to exist. Additionally, the ability of users to assure the security of a connection is lacking, due to the complexity of modern networked systems.

Ordean and Giurgiu have presented a design concept for an authentication string that makes use of the server's public key and provides client's authenticity through its password without the need of a client side certificate or a second channel [8]. Alicherry and Keromytis have published a solution which detects the MitM attack by retrieving the certificate from a remote host using multiple alternate paths [1]. Belenguer and Calafate have introduced low-cost embedded Intrusion Detection Systems which, when plugged into a switch or hub, are able to detect and/or prevent MitM attacks automatically and efficiently [2]. Choi *et al.* have performed a detailed analysis of point-to-point packet delay in an operational tier 4 network [3].

1.2 Our contribution

In this paper we analyze the ability to detect MitM attacks at a timely fashion when connecting to familiar websites in non-mobile systems. We propose a solution which uses the timestamps of TCP packets to calculate the delay of sequential packets. By comparing the mean of the delays in the current session to reference data from old sessions, we can detect packets that have unusually long delays and thus suspect a MitM-attack. We use the timing information alone without requiring any form of authentication.

CODASPY'14, March 3–5, 2014, San Antonio, Texas, USA.
ACM 978-1-4503-2278-2/14/03.
http://dx.doi.org/10.1145/2557547.2557579 .

The rest of the paper is constructed in a following way. In the next section we give the details of our proposed solution and describe our test setup. In Section 3 we give an analysis of our solution and the results of our tests. In Section 4 we present our conclusions.

2. SOLUTION OVERVIEW

2.1 Example

Consider the following scenario: Alice starts a connection to the Boogle website at the time t_s from her home PC. The connection is intercepted by Eve and altered before being forwarded to Boogle. This action takes some time t_1. Boogle receives the TCP packets and sends a response to Alice. Again Eve intercepts the connection before forwarding packets to Alice and this takes time t_2. Finally, Alice receives the response from Boogle at the time t_r. The delay of this connection is $\tau = t_s - t_r$. From the data of previous connections we can calculate the mean μ and estimate the minimum delay caused by Eves interception $min(t_1 + t_2) = \delta$ and choose a detection threshold $\theta > \mu$ such that $\tau_i + \delta_i > \theta > \tau_i$ $\forall i = 1, 2...$.

Our hypothesis is that by collecting and analyzing packet delays of safe connections, we can estimate a detection threshold θ which will detect MitM attack and not trigger false alarms from normal connections. Since it is hard to estimate δ for testing purposes, we choose the threshold as low as possible and test it against false positives. So we have our null hypothesis $H_0 : \tau_i \geq \theta$ and our alternative hypothesis is $H_1 : \tau_i < \theta \ \forall \ i = 1, 2, ...$.

Since we are using only the timestamps of TCP packets to detect attackers, we need some assumptions related to the network traffic and timing. We assume that the two endpoints do not move and that in the absence of an attacker, the round-trip time between the endpoints does not differ massively. This also implies that the speed of the channel between the endpoint does not change significantly over time. Additionally, we assume that at least once we have gotten a safe connection, which has given us some mean value of delays. Lastly, we must assume that neither endpoint is malicious and that we have the capability to accurately timestamp incoming and outgoing packets.

2.2 Test environment

Our test setup comprised of a prototype made with *Python 2.6* which uses *pcapy* and *impacket* modules for packet sniffing. *Squid 3* was configured appropriately and is used as the MitM attacker for our tests. Data was collected by a script that loads the website with the *Mozilla Firefox* browser every two minutes. The program sniffs TCP packets and converts the source and destination IP addresses to URLs. If the destination URL is on our list, then the timestamp, sequence number and acknowledgment numbers are saved. If the same packet data exists, the older one is removed.

If the source URL is on our list, sniffed acknowledgment number minus one is compared to saved sequence numbers. If a match is found, the delay is calculated from the timestamps and added to a list of delays with the mean of current delays. At the same time, all data with delays greater than one second are removed, for optimal performance of the prototype.

Sometimes anomalous behavior of individual routers or the network can introduce unpredictable factors that affect

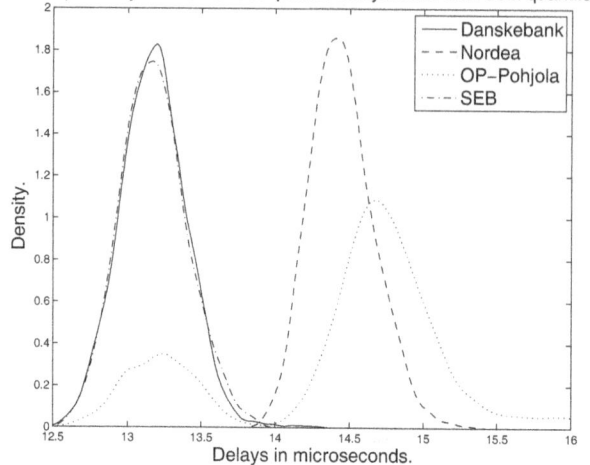

Figure 1: Round-trip delay can often be approximated by a truncated normal distribution.

point-to-point packets delays [3]. Such large delays can be caused by a router performing other functions such as routing and forwarding table updates, etc [9]. In addition, during the routing protocol convergence, transient forwarding loops may occur, and packets caught in such loops will suffer unusually long delays [5]. These very large delays are obviously not representative of the typical delay performance of a network and thus should be considered as outliers in the delay measurement.

The prototype keeps track of the mean delay of the current session μ_0 and makes warnings when $\mu_0 > \theta$, where θ is the detection threshold. If the connection is safe, the collected data is saved with an updated mean and standard deviation.

3. ANALYSIS

We want our detection threshold to be as small as possible to ensure maximal MitM attack detection rate. A few false positives are not a problem since the warnings are given only when the current mean crosses the detection threshold, so keeping 99% of the normal delays τ_i under the threshold should be enough to minimize false alarms. We should also include some precautions against the effect of the variance σ^2 in the Internet traffic. Best way to handle all this would be to use a simple detection threshold $\theta = \mu + \sigma$, where μ and σ are the mean and the standard deviation from previous connections. This should be able to detect all MitM attacks without a risk of many false positives.

Our null hypothesis thus becomes: $H_0 : \tau_i \geq \mu + \sigma$ while our alternative hypothesis is $H_1 : \tau_i < \mu + \sigma$.

To test our hypothesis for optimal θ, data was collected with systematic sampling from four big Nordic financial companies: Nordea, SEB, Danske Bank and OP-Pohjola Group. Test does not include banks whose homepages contain big data streams.

Sampling was done by sniffing TCP packets for 24 hours as our script made connection to target website every two minutes. Then a second test was conducted towards the same website with the connections routed through a proxy to imitate a MitM attack.

Table 1: Statistical parameters from test results.

URL	Frequency	σ	Min.	μ	99th percentile	θ=threshold	Max.	$\tau_i > \theta$	Min.Proxy
www.danskebank.com	12600	3.163	12.48	13.28	14.30	16.44	200.2	0.29%	22.65
www.nordea.com	13570	2.465	13.48	14.58	15.40	17.04	220.6	0.73%	22.79
www.op.fi	5644	2.036	12.53	14.53	16.21	16.57	74.63	0.46%	23.20
www.sebgroup.com	5921	2.234	12.55	13.31	13.90	15.54	94.37	0.54%	23.21

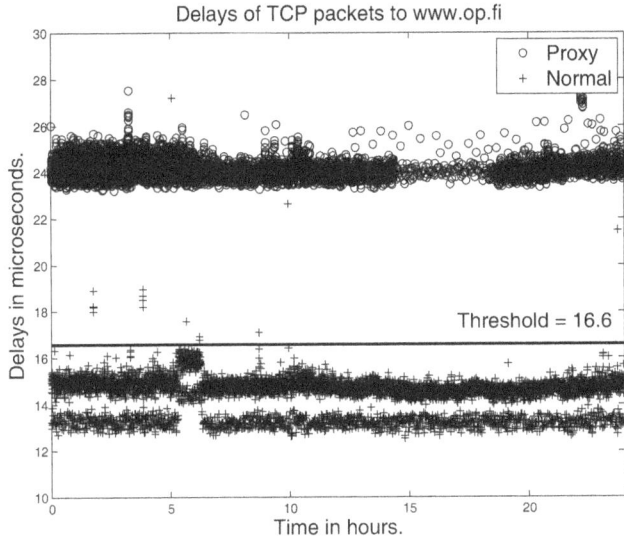

Figure 2: If this was an actual MitM attack, the prototype would notice it with a 100% accuracy.

3.1 Test Results

Statistical parameters from our test results we can be seen in the Table 1. All delays from the proxy connections were significantly larger than threshold formed from normal connections. The difference between the minimum delay from the proxy and the threshold is more than 6 ms in every data set.

In Figure 1 we can see probability density functions of packet delays lower than 99th quantile point. Though the difference between the minimum and the 99th percentile delay is less than 5 ms in every connection, the maximum delay is significantly larger than the 99th percentile. As the number of packets with such extreme delay is very small, they represent very rare events in the network [3]. Most of the delays are concentrated near the mean with truncated left tail and long right tail. Exception are delays from www.op.fi which form two peaks, this is probably caused by the packets coming from two different locations. As previous research done by Elteto and Molnar also indicates, the round-trip delay can often be approximated by a truncated normal distribution [4]. Truncation point of the distribution is the smallest possible round-trip delay.

Figure 2 has the delays under 30 microseconds from www.op.fi arranged by their arrival time. The minimum delay through the proxy is 23.20 milliseconds, detection threshold is 16.57 milliseconds and the false positive rate of single delays is 0.46%. If this was an actual MitM attack, the prototype would notice it with a 100% accuracy.

4. CONCLUSIONS

In this paper we have shown a method for detecting MitM attacks. The test results show that our method can detect MitM attacks. And as our test results indicate, there will be no false alarms unless a rare event has occurred. Our solution has limited uses because it requires non-mobile systems and highly reliable internet connections. However, it is excellent for monitoring a limited amount of critical destinations, e.g. bank URL:s, for all users in a commercial ISP or a company network. Luckily, the majority of connections are not interesting from a normal attackers point of view.

5. REFERENCES

[1] M. Alicherry and A. Keromytis. Doublecheck multi-path verification against man-in-the-middle attacks. *Computers and Communications*, pages 557 – 563, July 2009.

[2] J. Belenguer and C. Calafate. A low-cost embedded ids to monitor and prevent man-in-the-middle attacks on wired lan environments. *Emerging Security Information, Systems and Technologies*, pages 122 – 127, Oct. 2007.

[3] B.-Y. Choi, S. Moon, Z.-L. Zhang, K. Papagiannaki, and C. Diot. Analysis of point-to-point packet delay in an operational network. *Twenty-third AnnualJoint Conference of the IEEE Computer and Communications Societies*, 3:1797 – 1807, March 2004.

[4] T. Elteto and S. Molnar. On the distribution of round-trip delays in tcp/ip networks. *Local Computer Networks*, pages 172–181, Oct. 1999.

[5] U. Hengartner, S. Moon, R. Mortier, and C. Diot. Detection and analysis of routing loops in packet traces. *ACM Sigcomm Internet Measurement Workshop*, pages 107–112, Nov. 2002.

[6] C. Meadows. Formal methods for cryptographic protocol analysis: emerging issues and trends. *Selected Areas in Communications*, 21(1):44–54, Jan. 2003.

[7] G. Nayak and S. Samaddar. Different flavours of man-in-the-middle attack, consequences and feasible solutions. *Computer Science and Information Technology*, 5:491 – 495, July 2010.

[8] M. Ordean and M. Giurgiu. Towards securing client-server connections against man-in-the-middle attacks. *Electronics and Telecommunications*, pages 127 – 130, Nov. 2012.

[9] K. Papgirnoaki, S. Moon, C. Fraleigh, P. Thiran, and C. Diot. Measurement and analysis of single-hop delay on an ip backbone network. *Selected Areas in Communications*, 21(6):908 – 921, Aug. 2003.

A Modular Multi-Location Anonymized Traffic Monitoring Tool for a WiFi Network

Justin Hummel, Andrew McDonald, Vatsal Shah, Riju Singh, Bradford D. Boyle,
Tingshan Huang, Nagarajan Kandasamy, Harish Sethu, and Steven Weber
Department of Electrical Engineering and Computer Engineering
Drexel University, Philadelphia, PA, 19104
{jch59,awm32,vbs27,rs557,bdb24,th423,nk78,hs42,spw26}@drexel.edu

ABSTRACT

Network traffic anomaly detection is now considered a surer approach to early detection of malware than signature-based approaches and is best accomplished with traffic data collected from multiple locations. Existing open-source tools are primarily signature-based, or do not facilitate integration of traffic data from multiple locations for real-time analysis, or are insufficiently modular for incorporation of newly proposed approaches to anomaly detection. In this paper, we describe *DataMap*, a new modular open-source tool for the collection and real-time analysis of sampled, anonymized, and filtered traffic data from multiple WiFi locations in a network and an example of its use in anomaly detection.

1. INTRODUCTION

A typical piece of new malware today uses a variety of obfuscation techniques to avoid detection, especially signature-based detection typical of antivirus products currently on the market [13]. Such increasing sophistication of viruses, worms and other malware has made their early detection immediately after launch significantly harder. Some reported success rates with signature-based detection have been as low as 5% [9]. Many security professionals argue that real-time monitoring for anomalous behavior in the traffic data over a network, as opposed to signature-based detection, offers a surer approach to protecting networks [6,7].

Real-time monitoring for anomalous behavior, however, offers its own challenges. One challenge is the matter of minimizing false positives and false negatives in the detection of patterns that deviate from the normal after the data is gathered and stored [5]. The other challenge is gathering and storing the data in real-time to enable the immediate use of detection algorithms on it. This challenge stems primarily from the fact that traffic data collected at a single location is usually insufficient to infer an anomaly; one requires traffic data from multiple locations to be able to conclude that an anomalous behavior is ongoing.

CODASPY'14, March 3–5, 2014, San Antonio, Texas, USA.
ACM 978-1-4503-2278-2/14/03.
http://dx.doi.org/10.1145/2557547.2557580.

While data from multiple locations is helpful to anomaly detection, the volume of data can be prohibitively large. One approach is to allow the transfer of only a statistical sample of the data, such as histograms constructed over slices of time [4], as opposed to individualized packet data. In this paper, we describe an open-source tool, called *DataMap*, developed as part of a project to facilitate real-time analysis of traffic data from multiple locations in a large-scale WiFi network. The DataMap tool is designed for adaptation to a variety of statistical sampling and aggregation techniques. It is also intended to provide a means for empirical estimation of fundamental trade-offs such as between the sampling rate of traffic data and the accuracy of inferences on anomalies possible from it.

2. RELATED WORK

There are a number of open-source tools available for data collection to monitor network traffic and detect intrusions. Most of these are primarily targeted for detecting known types of intrusions (as opposed to detecting an anomalous pattern of behavior) using signature-based approaches, the most widely used of these being *Snort* [11]. Snort is a lightweight sniffer, packet logger and an intrusion detection system which can generate alerts when it observes specific types of probes or attacks that indicate a potential intrusion attempt. The detection can be based on a rule set included in the snort download and updated daily or on custom rules written by the user of snort. An installation of snort runs on a single machine and it takes a complementary set of tools to gather traffic data from multiple locations and detect in real-time a gradually spreading worm such as that described in Section 1. Also, being signature-based, Snort is not able to detect anomalies whose signature is not yet known.

Open-source software tools that come closest to some of the functionality of the DataMap tool include *Security Onion* [10] and *OpenWIPS-ng* [8]. While these tools are also based on signature detection—sometimes based on tools such as Snort—they do allow data collection from multiple locations to facilitate an integrated analysis of the full network-level context. While these very useful tools are close in some functionality to the DataMap tool, they are all largely built on a foundation of signature-based detection and are not ideal for an academic study of approaches to anomaly detection when signatures are not known.

DataMap can be employed in conjunction with approaches that use any combination of signature-based algorithms to detect known patterns (with rule sets) and anomaly-based

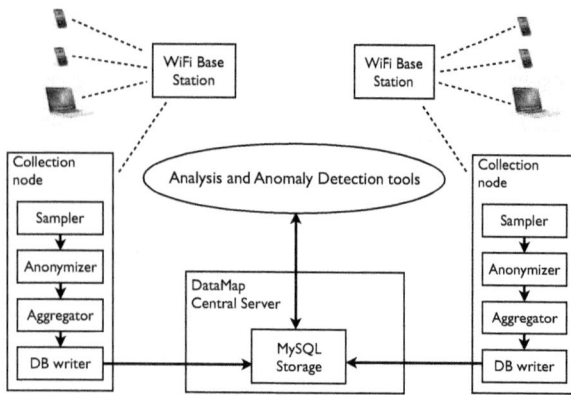

Figure 1: A DataMap traffic monitoring system showing two collection nodes (also called traffic sensors) and the central server.

algorithms to detect patterns not seen before (without predetermined rule sets). DataMap's modular design facilitates the sampling, aggregation, and transfer of data from multiple locations (sensors) to a central server for real-time analysis. Built on replaceable modules, the DataMap tool is intended to facilitate the study of newer techniques for anomaly detection, such as those based on compressive sampling, histogram construction, or information-theoretic metrics. While we have only reviewed the dominant open-source tools in this section, the tools that require paid licenses are even less adaptable to modification for academic research on new approaches to anomaly detection.

3. OVERVIEW OF THE DATAMAP COMPONENTS

The DataMap tool, a pre-release version of which is available on Github [2], utilizes a series of collection nodes and a central server to collect traffic data from a set of WiFi access points at multiple locations. The collected data is aggregated into a single database hosted on the central server. DataMap builds upon existing open-source software and, in contrast to other currently available tools, is open-source, offers concurrent multi-location traffic monitoring, enables integrated analysis on the multi-location aggregated data, and is modular to allow easy modification for academic research in anomaly detection. DataMap is designed to facilitate experiments on sampling rates and both time-domain and space-domain data aggregation strategies. It can be used with unencrypted WiFi networks or on encrypted networks with administrative authority.

Figure 1 shows a high-level block diagram of the DataMap infrastructure. The collection node consists of four primary components: the sampler module, the aggregator module, the anonymizer module and the DbWriter module. These components on the collection nodes work as part of a node daemon which is managed by the central server. The central server hosts the database which serves as the data repository and manages the collection nodes by way of a server daemon. A web interface, provided with the DataMap tool, can be used to keep track of the state of all the collection nodes and to start or stop them all at once.

The *sampler module* uses Vermont (Versatile Monitoring

Toolkit [12]) to capture traffic with the desired sampling algorithm and the desired filtering strategy. It is the modular nature of Vermont that enables the DataMap project to create replaceable and independent components in the DataMap tool. The wireless network interface on a collection node is placed into monitor mode in order to collect all packets from access points on a given channel. A node can be configured to identify and channel hop to capture traffic data from multiple wireless networks in a location.

The *anonymizer module* uses Crypto-PAn (Cryptography-based Prefix-preserving Anonymization [3]) to anonymize individual IP addresses in a way that protects individual network users' privacy while preserving topological information about the network. Other identifying information such as MAC address and application-layer data is discarded in this module. Sophisticated data mining even on anonymized data can identify individuals and patterns of individual actors and privacy is preserved in the use of the DataMap tool only if it is used exclusively for the intended purpose.

The *aggregator module* summarizes the raw data gathered by the node for each pre-programmed slice of time. The aggregation can be based on any combination of packet header fields specified in an XML file. Data is passed from the sampler through the anonymizer to the aggregation module via shared memory such that the anonymization occurs before the collected data is transmitted across the network.

Finally, the *DbWriter module* sends the aggregated, filtered, and anonymized data to the central server. Data is labelled with a unique identifier corresponding to the location of the collection node and entered into the database.

These components on the collection nodes work as part of a node daemon which, upon start-up, sends a *Hello* message to the central server with its id and location. The daemon then waits for instructions from a server deamon on the central server, which keeps track of all the nodes and periodically pings them with a *Heartbeat* message to retrieve their latest state. A web interface, provided with the DataMap tool, can be used to keep track of the state of all the collection nodes and to start or stop them all at once.

Our experience and other research suggests that patterns of data across multiple locations are best analyzed based on the statistical distribution (e.g., a histogram) of features of interest [4]. The pattern of changes in correlations over time between these distributions at different locations is not sensitive to time skews between the collection nodes (even if the correlations themselves fluctuate from one time slice to the next). This allows DataMap to dispense with clock synchronization between collection nodes and the associated overhead.

4. AN EXAMPLE OF DATAMAP USAGE

We present a simple example of data collection across multiple nodes and how it can be helpful in traffic monitoring and, potentially, the detection of an Internet worm in its early stages. A typical worm begins its life by first scanning for vulnerabilities on open ports at as many different IP addresses as possible in as short a time as possible using any of a number of sophisticated approaches. The distribution of the destination IP addresses of IP packets emerging from a worm-infected node is likely very different from that of an uninfected node. Detection of a wider range of anomalies in this or other features is made possible by constructing histograms of these features as described in [4].

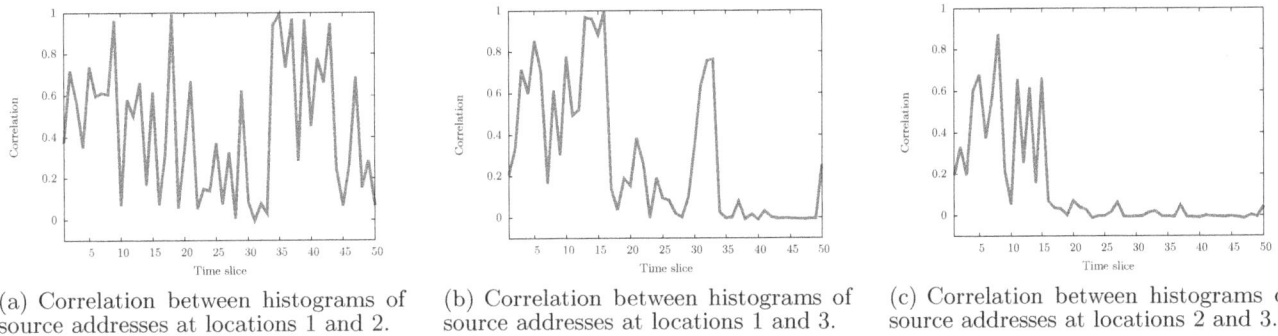

(a) Correlation between histograms of source addresses at locations 1 and 2.

(b) Correlation between histograms of source addresses at locations 1 and 3.

(c) Correlation between histograms of source addresses at locations 2 and 3.

Figure 2: An example of data collected at three locations on the Drexel University campus. The plots show correlations between the histograms computed on the traffic at these locations for source addresses.

However, for the same reasons mentioned in Section 1, it is ideal to not rely entirely on a signature-based assessment of normal vs. anomalous histograms. A more effective approach is one that also uses a real-time assessment of deviations between the histograms computed at different nodes. Past research has shown that an analysis of correlations between traffic features through techniques such as Principal Component Analysis can achieve effective anomaly detection [1]. The DataMap tool allows precisely this kind of analysis. These correlations will likely fluctuate from one time slice to the next, but the pattern of fluctuations itself can serve as an indication of what is "normal". A sustained shift in the pattern of changes/fluctuations in the correlation between the histograms computed at two different but equally busy nodes indicates one of these nodes as a potential candidate for further examination by a system administrator. Such a sustained shift can be observed by dividing time into slices and computing the correlation between histograms at each slice.

Figure 2 presents data collected over a period of 30 minutes (or 50 time slices of 36 seconds each) from three nodes at different locations within the Drexel University campus network using the DataMap tool. Plotted is the correlation between histograms of the source IP addresses at two different locations, with each data point in a graph representing the correlation computed over a 36-second period.

The figure shows a sustained shift in the pattern of correlations between traffic at location 3 and the traffic at the other two locations beginning sometime between time slice 15 and time slice 20. This can be an indication of something anomalous or it could be a normal event in which location 3 is exhibiting some deviation for legitimate reasons. A deeper analysis using correlations between histograms of other features can complete a determination of whether or not this event deserves to be flagged with an alert.

5. CONCLUDING REMARKS

In this paper, we have briefly described a pre-release version of the DataMap tool for multi-location traffic monitoring and analysis. While DataMap helps detect malware threats, it does not take action to neutralize threats. It is a modular tool intended to serve as a framework for research and development of new approaches to traffic sampling, data aggregation, and analysis for effective network traffic anomaly detection.

Acknowledgment

This work was partially funded by the National Science Foundation Award #1228847.

6. REFERENCES

[1] D. Brauckhoff, K. Salamatian, and M. May. Applying PCA for traffic anomaly detection: Problems and solutions. In *Proc. IEEE INFOCOM*, 2009.

[2] DataMap. https://github.com/DataMap13/DataMap/. Accessed: August 8, 2013.

[3] J. Fan, J. Xu, M. H. Ammar, and S. B. Moon. Prefix-preserving IP address anonymization: measurement-based security evaluation and a new cryptography-based scheme. *Computer Networks*, 46(2):253–272, 2004.

[4] A. Kind, M. P. Stoecklin, and X. Dimitropoulos. Histogram-based traffic anomaly detection. *IEEE Trans. Netw. Service Manag.*, 6:110–121, June 2009.

[5] A. Lakhina, M. Crovella, and C. Diot. Mining anomalies using traffic feature distributions. In *Proc. ACM SIGCOMM*, 2005.

[6] P. Li, M. Salour, and X. Su. A survey of Internet worm detection and containment. *IEEE Communications Surveys and Tutorials*, 10:20–35, 2008.

[7] D. Moore, C. Shannon, G. M. Voelker, and S. Savage. Internet quarantine: Requirements for containing self-propagating code. In *Proc. IEEE INFOCOM*, pages 1901–1910, 2003.

[8] OpenWIPS-ng. http://www.openwips-ng.org/. Accessed: August 8, 2013.

[9] N. Perlroth. Outmaneuvered at their own game, antivirus makers struggle to adapt. *The New York Times*, December 31, 2012.

[10] Security Onion. https://code.google.com/p/security-onion/. Accessed: August 8, 2013.

[11] Snort. http://www.snort.org/. Accessed: August 8, 2013.

[12] Vermont (VERsatile MONitoring Toolkit). https://github.com/constcast/vermont/wiki. Accessed: August 8, 2013.

[13] C.-H. Wu and J. D. Irwin. *Introduction to Computer Networks and Cybersecurity*. CRC Press, 2013.

Consistency Checking in Access Control

Anja Remshagen
University of West Georgia
Department of Computer Science
Carrollton, GA 30118
+1-678-839-6657
anja@westga.edu

Li Yang
University of West Georgia
Department of Computer Science
Carrollton, GA 30118
+1-678-839-6656
lyang@westga.edu

ABSTRACT
As access control models have become more complex, tools should be developed to support the maintenance of policies. We have adapted a powerful privacy-aware role-based access control model to incorporate a context-restriction component to alleviate the policy maintenance complexity issue. We discuss how the process of entering policies and user-specified rules can be guided by a system that evaluates permission assignments when they are entered.

Categories and Subject Descriptors
C.2.0 [**Computer Communication Networks**]: General – *security and protection;* D.4.6 [**Operating Systems**]: Security and Protection—*Access Controls*; K.6.5 [**Management of Computing and Information Systems**]: Security and Protection

General Terms: Management, Security, Theory.

Keywords: Policy maintenance; P-RBAC; context awareness.

1. INTRODUCTION
As regulations (like HIPAA, SOX, or PCI) need to be met and new technologies and corporate policies (like Bring Your Own Device) facilitate new access options to data, access control models have become more complex. For example, the widely used RBAC model [4, 7] has been expanded to include obligations, purposes, and conditions. See [3, 5, 6] to name only a few. The increase in granularity of these models comes at a cost. Specifying and maintaining consistent policies, for example, is more complex, and the chance of human error increases. Tools need to be developed to support the maintenance of policies. We have adapted the powerful Privacy-aware Role-Based Access Control model (P-RBAC) by Ni et al. [5, 6] to incorporate a context-restriction component to alleviate the policy maintenance complexity issue. We investigate possible inconsistencies among policies and design an algorithm that checks for conflicts and redundancies when policies are added and modified.

P-RBAC extends the traditional Role-Based Access Control model to include the components: users, roles, actions, objects, purposes, obligations, and conditions. The condition component specifies a "regular" condition and a contextual condition. For example, a policy might say that parent consent is necessary if the data owner is less than 13 years old. In other words, only if AGE<13 holds, the condition PC=Yes needs to be fulfilled in

order to access the data of that person. In P-RBAC, a *permission assignment (PA)* with the condition AGE<13 ∧ PC=Yes will be added. The requirement AGE<13 is not a condition that necessarily needs to be fulfilled in order to grant access to data, but a condition that limits the privacy policy to apply only in a specific scenario. In P-RBAC [5], the variable AGE is considered to be a *context splitting variable*, while PC is a *context variable*. PAs can be connected by AND or OR in P-RBAC [6], which enables great flexibility of representing any kind of complex conditions, but at the cost of more complex policy maintenance and consistency checking. We suggest instead to connect PAs by AND only and to introduce a separate component, the so-called *context restriction*. In the example above, the predicate AGE<13 would be modeled as a context restriction in our model, while PC=Yes would be in the condition. When an access request comes in, only the policies whose context restriction components evaluate to true are relevant to the request, thus only the conditions in those polices should be evaluated to determine whether or not to grant the request. One can show that our model has the same expressive power as P-RBAC even though our model connects PAs by AND only.

There are a variety of other contextual access control models. The idea of most models is to activate a policy only if a context-related condition is fulfilled. Analogous conflict scenarios as the one discussed here can be carved out. Ni et al. have implemented a system to help policy officers write and manage human readable privacy policies [5]. However consistency checking is limited to checking if any pair of PAs is inconsistent. Using the normalized PAs in [6], criteria for inconsistencies and solution methods are pointed out. We propose here an algorithm that checks for inconsistencies among all PAs.

2. THE MODEL
Due to space limitations we omit a formal definition of our model. A *permission assignment (PA)* is defined to be a 7-tuple

$$(sbj, act, dta, pur, obl, cnd, cxt)$$

where *sbj* is a subject, *act* is an action, *dta* is a data object, *pur* is a purpose, *obl* is an obligation, *cnd* is a predicate specifying a condition, and *cxt* is a predicate specifying a *context restriction*.

The following variables may appear in the *context restriction* component:

(1) Variables representing data owner's property, like age or sex, for example, whose values partition data items into disjoint sets [5]

(2) In the absence of variables satisfying (1), any contextual variables such as location and time, or variables representing consent.

Note that the condition and context component may include predicates over the same variables in different PAs. An *access control system* consists of a set of PAs.

CODASPY'14, March 03–05, 2014, San Antonio, TX, USA
ACM 978-1-4503-2278-2/14/03.
http://dx.doi.org/10.1145/2557547.2557581

Consider, for example, a scenario where read access to the grade of a student for research purpose may be granted to instructors if the data owner has given consent and is at least 18 years old, the following PA pa_1 can be added to the system.

pa_1: (instructor, read, grade, research, none, OC=Yes, AGE≥18)
In another case, the access is granted to the instructor for a student under 18 years only if parental consent is given. The following PA can be added:

pa_2: (instructor, read, grade, research, none, PC=Yes, AGE<18)
Our model does not limit the logic operators in the context and condition component. But the model is limited to the AND operation among PAs to ease the maintenance of policies. Nevertheless, our model can represent the same complex conditions as P-RBAC, which allows for the OR and AND operation. For instance, assume the following two PAs are connected by OR in P-RBAC:

(instructor, read, grade, research, none, PC=Yes and AGE<=18)

(instructor, read, grade, research, none, AGE>18 and OC=Yes)
where AGE is a context-splitting variable and OC and PC are context variables. Our model can represent the PAs as:

(instructor, read, grade, research, none, PC=Yes, AGE<=18)

(instructor, read, grade, research, none, OC=Yes , AGE>18)
In general, any two PAs of P-RBAC connected by OR or AND can be represented in our model. Inductively, one can show that any set of PAs can be modeled, and thus our model has the same expressive power as P-RBAC.

A user usr is granted the action act to access data dta for the purpose pur iff ALL PAs $(sbj, act, dta, pur, obl, cnd, cxt)$, where (a) $sbj=usr$ or sbj is a role associated with usr and (b) the context requirement cxt holds, fulfill the condition component cnd. In addition, at least one such PA must exist. For instance, consider an access control system with the condition variable OC (owner consent) and PC (parent consent) and the context variables AGE and PAs pa_1-pa_4 where pa_1 and pa_2 are defined as above and pa_3 and pa_4 are:

pa_3: (456, read, grade, research, none, OC=Yes, true)

pa_4: (instructor, read, grade, advising, none, true, true)
Assume the user with ID 123 and role instructor wants to read the grade of the student with ID 020 for research purpose. Further assume that the OC=Yes and PC=No holds for the requested data and that the age of the student with ID 020 is 20. The PA pa_2 is irrelevant since the context restriction is false. The PA pa_3 and pa_4 are irrelevant since at least one of the components subject, action, data, or purpose does not match the corresponding component of the access request. Since pa_1 is relevant and its condition is satisfied, the access is granted.

Consider a similar read request by the user with id 456 and role instructor for the grade of student with ID 017. Further assume the student with id 017 is 17 years old and OC=Yes and PC=No holds for that student. Then pa_2 and pa_3 are relevant PAs. However, the condition of pa_2 is violated and therefore the access request is not granted.

3. INCONSISTENCIES

Whenever a new PA is added, the set of PAs may not be consistent with the modeled privacy policies. Let $pa* = (sbj*, act*, dta*, pur*, obl*, cnd*, cxt*)$ be a new PA that is added to an access control system. The new PA can only conflict with PAs that possibly are relevant for the same access request. We call a set of PAs *overlapping* iff they have the same subject, action, data, and purpose component and if the conjunction of their context components is satisfiable. In the following, we discuss three scenarios that may arise. We describe an algorithm to detect each scenario in Section 4.

(1) $pa*$ is redundant and can be dropped from the access control system without changing it. In this case, there is a set S of overlapping PAs with $pa* \in S$ such that $(\bigwedge_{(sbj*, act*, dta*, pur*, obl , cnd, cxt) \in S \setminus \{pa*\}} cnd) \rightarrow cnd*$ holds.

For example, this scenario occurs if a PA is added twice. The scenario could also point to a possible error in the set of PAs. The administrator added $pa*$. However, it was redundant because the previous PAs were too restrictive. For example, the access control system may contain the PA (sales, write, order, update, SEND_EMAIL, OC_PHONE=Yes, true) to allow a sales person to write to the order of a customer for update purpose if the owner has given consent over the phone, and once the write is complete, an email should be sent to the data owner. A change in policies allows now that the owner's consent may be retrieved by email as well. Thus the new PA (sales, write, order, update, SEND_EMAIL, OC_PHONE=Yes ∨ OC_EMAIL=Yes, true) is added. In this case the old PA (sales, write, order, update, SEND_EMAIL, OC_MAIL=Yes, true) should be removed.

(2) An existing PA $pa' = (sbj*, act*, dta*, pur*, obl', cnd', cxt')$ becomes redundant when $pa*$ is added. The new PA $pa*$ limits access and pa' can be removed without changing the access control system. In this case, there is a set S of overlapping PAs with $pa*$, $pa' \in S$ such that $(\bigwedge_{(sbj*, act*, dta*, pur*, obl , cnd, cxt) \in S \setminus \{pa'\}} cnd) \rightarrow cnd'$ holds.

To illustrate this scenario, we can use the reverse of the example shown in (1). Suppose there is an existing PA $pa' = $ (sales, write, order, update, SEND_EMAIL, OC_PHONE=Yes ∨ OC_EMAIL=Yes, true), and now a new and more restrictive PA $pa* = $ (sales, write, order, update, SEND_EMAIL, OC_PHONE=Yes, true) is to be added. If the policy maker indeed intends to make the permission more restrictive, the existing PA pa' should be removed.

However, this scenario may also occur due to an unintentional error. For example, assume that access is allowed if the data owner's age is at least 13 due to the PA (staff, read, portrait, advertising, inform_owner, AGE≥13, true). A new policy says that parent consent is required if the age is between 13 and 18. The new PA (staff, read, portrait, advertising, inform_parent, AGE≥13 ∧ AGE<18 ∧ PC=Y, true) is added. However, now access cannot be granted if the age is greater than or equal to 18. Here the age limitations should be moved to the context restriction. The two PAs $pa*$ and pa' should be replaced by (staff, read, portrait, advertising, inform_owner, true, AGE≥13) and (staff, read, portrait, advertising, inform_parent, PC=Yes, AGE≥13 ∧ AGE<18).

(3) $pa*$ causes a conflict so that access cannot be granted. In this case, there is a set S of overlapping PAs with $pa* \in S$ such that the conjunction $(\bigwedge_{(sbj*, act*, dta*, pur*, cnd, obl, cxt) \in S} cnd)$ is a contradiction.

This scenario may point to an unintentional conflict. For example, assume a PA allows access if the age is greater than or equal to 18: (instructor, read, grade, research, obl, AGE≥18, true). A new policy allows access if the age is less than 18 and parent have consented, and the new PA (instructor, read, grade, research, obl*, AGE<18 ∧ PC=Yes, true) is added to the access control system. But then the conditions cause the conflict AGE≥18 ∧ AGE<18. As in the previous example, the age restriction should be part of the context limitation. The corrected PAs are (instructor, read, grade, research, obl, true, AGE≥18) and (instructor, read, grade, research, obl*, PC=Yes, AGE<18). A conflict in the conditions may be intentional, and access should not be granted in that context.

4. DETECTING INCONSISTENCIES

If for a set S of overlapping PAs one of the three conditions

(1) $(\bigwedge_{(sbj, act, dta, pur, obl, cnd, cxt) \in S \setminus \{pa^*\}} cnd) \rightarrow cnd^*$

(2) $(\bigwedge_{(sbj, act, dta, pur, obl, cnd, cxt) \in S \setminus \{pa'\}} cnd) \rightarrow cnd'$

(3) $\neg \bigwedge_{(sbj, act, dta, pur, cnd, obl, cxt) \in S} cnd$

holds, then the same condition holds also for a maximal set of overlapping PAs that contains set S. Thus, when a new PA is entered, it is sufficient to evaluate maximal sets of overlapping PAs in order to check for the above scenarios.

Let $pa^* = (sbj^*, act^*, dta^*, pur^*, obl^*, cnd^*, cxt^*)$ be a new PA that is added to an access control system, and let $S^* = \{pa \mid pa = (sbj^*, act^*, dta^*, pur^*, obl, cnd, cxt)\}$ be the set of all PAs in the access control system with subject sbj^*, action act^*, data dta^*, and purpose pur^*. The maximal overlapping sets contained in S^* can be computed through a tree search employing a branch-and-bound approach. In real-world applications, we can expect that S^* contains only few permission assignments, and therefore the number of maximal overlapping sets is anticipated to be small. In order to check whether a conjunction of predicates is satisfiable, we can reduce the problem to the satisfiability problem (SAT) and then apply a SAT solver. We outline a transformation of a predicate into a CNF formula below. Even though the SAT problem is well known to be NP-complete, state-of-the-art SAT solvers can solve even huge instances, particularly of practical problems, very effectively [1, 2].

Input:
$pa^* = (sbj^*, act^*, dta^*, pur^*, obl^*, cnd^*, cxt^*)$
set S_{ACS} of permission assignments

Algorithm:
Set $S^* = \{pa \mid pa \in S_{ACS} \land pa = (sbj, act, dta, pur, obl, cnd, cxt) \land$
     $sbj = sbj^* \land act = act^* \land dta = dta^* \land pur = pur^*\}$
foreach maximal set S of overlapping permission assignments
     with $S \subseteq S^*$ **do**

  if $((\bigwedge_{(sbj, act, dta, pur, obl, cnd, cxt) \in S \setminus \{pa^*\}} cnd) \rightarrow cnd^*)$ **then**
     output "pa^* is redundant"
  endif
  foreach $pa' = (sbj', act', dta', pur', obl', cnd', cxt') \in S$ **do**
    if $(\bigwedge_{(sbj, act, dta, pur, obl, cnd, cxt) \in S \setminus \{pa'\}} cnd) \rightarrow cnd')$ **then**
      output "pa' is redundant"
    endif
  endfor
  if $(\neg \bigwedge_{(sbj, act, dta, pur, cnd, obl, cxt) \in S} cnd)$ **then**
    output "pa^* conflicts with the assignments in S"
  endif
endfor

Figure 1: Algorithm to detect inconsistencies

For each maximal overlapping set S, we need to check whether the formula specified in the conditions (1)-(3) as discussed in the previous section is true under every value of the underlying domain. In other words, the negation of the condition has to be checked for unsatisfiability. We reduce each condition to a SAT instance as follows. The reduction transforms the predicate first into an equivalent Boolean formula. For example, assume that there are two PAs in S with the conditions OC=Yes ∧ AGE<21 and AGE>18, respectively. The variable OC can be represented by a single Boolean variable, say OC^b, where OC^b=true is equivalent to OC=Yes. The variable AGE can be represented by two variables AGE^b_1 and AGE^b_2 by splitting the

domain of AGE into the three disjoint sets $\{age \mid age \leq 18\}$, $\{age \mid age > 18 \land age < 21\}$, and $\{age \mid age \geq 21\}$. Then AGE^b_1=true represents the scenario AGE≤18 and AGE^b_2=true represents AGE>18 ∧ AGE<21. In order to model only valid values of AGE, we need to exclude the case where both, AGE^b_1 and AGE^b_2, are true. Hence the proposition $p_{AGE} = \neg AGE^b_1 \lor \neg AGE^b_2$ has to hold. Then the predicate OC=Yes ∧ AGE<21 is equivalent to $p_{AGE} \land OC^b \land (AGE^b_1 \lor AGE^b_2)$, and AGE>18 is equivalent to $p_{AGE} \land \neg AGE^b_1$. The resulting Boolean formula is negated and further reduced to a CNF formula using the Tseitin transformation [8]. In general, the reduction will increase the number of variables and the size of the underlying Boolean formula. However, the increase is linear in the size of the formula, and successful SAT solvers are expected to solve these instances effectively.

A system that detects inconsistencies in the PAs should point out potential errors for each of the conditions (1)-(3) that is met as discussed in Section 3. The system possibly suggests modifications for each scenario. Then the administrator can decide whether the new PA is correct or whether the PAs need to be changed. An outline of the algorithm is given in Figure 1.

5. CONCLUSION AND FUTURE WORK

In this paper, we have presented a model that allows a policy writer to write and maintain PAs modeling complex policies. The model introduces a component called *context restriction*, which separates policies that are relevant for the current request from the ones that are not, thus alleviating the difficulty in evaluating PAs that are connected by different operators in other models.

Moving forward, we would like to investigate further the issues involved in a system that allows maintaining PAs as we envisioned in Section 4, and implement such a system. In addition, we intend to explore possible inconsistencies that may arise from the obligation component of PAs.

6. REFERENCES

[1] Balint, A., Belov, A., Diepold, D., Gerber, S., Järvisalo, M., Sinz, C. (eds). 2012. *Proceedings of SAT Challenge 2012: Solver and Benchmark Descriptions*, Department of Computer Science Series of Publications B, vol. B-2012-2, University of Helsinki, Helsinki.

[2] Biere, A., Heule, M., Van Maaren, H., Walsh, T. 2009. *Handbook of Satisfiability*. Frontiers in Artificial Intelligence and Applications 185. IOS Press.

[3] Byun, J., Li, N. 2008. Purpose based access control for privacy protection in the relational database systems. *The VLDB Journal*. 17, 4 (July 2008), 603-619.

[4] Ferraiolo, D. F., Sandhu, R., Serban G., Kuhn, D. R., Chandramouli, R. 2003. Proposed NIST standard for role-based access control. *ACM Trans. on Information and System Security (TISSEC)* 4, 3 (Aug. 2001), 224-274.

[5] Ni, Q., Bertino, E., Lobo, J., Brodie, C., Karat, C., Karat, J., Trombetta, A. 2010. Privacy-aware role-based access control. *ACM Trans. Inf. Syst. Secur.* 13,3 (July 2010), 1-31.

[6] Ni, Q., Lin, D., Bertino, E., and Lobo, J. 2007. Conditional privacy-aware role based access control. *12th European Symposium On Research In Computer Security*, (Dresden, Germany, September 24 - 26, 2007). ESORICS 2007. 72-89.

[7] Sandhu, R. S., Coyne, E. J., Feinstein, H. L., Youman, C. E. 1996. Role-based access control models. *IEEE Computer Society* 29, 2 (Feb. 1996), 38-47.

[8] Tseitin, G. S. 1968. On the complexity of derivation in propositional calculus. In Studies in Constructive Mathematics and Mathematical Logic, Part II, 115–125.

POSTER: A Pairing-free Certificateless Hybrid Sign-Cryption Scheme for Advanced Metering Infrastructures

Seung-Hyun Seo, Jongho Won, Elisa Bertino
Purdue University
305 N. University Street,
West Lafayette, IN, 47907
{seo29, won12, bertino}@purdue.edu

ABSTRACT

CertificateLess Hybrid SignCryption (CL-HSC) scheme is useful for efficiently encapsulating symmetric keys for secure communications. It solves the key escrow problem and the certificate management problem. However, the existing scheme is not suitable for Advanced Metering Infrastructure (AMI) networks because of the utilization of expensive pairing operations. As smart meter devices have limited computing power, we need efficient algorithms for AMI networks. In this poster, we propose a novel CL-HSC scheme without pairing operations. In order to evaluate its performance, we implemented our CL-HSC scheme and conventional hybrid encryption approaches. The experimental results show that our CL-HSC scheme is efficient and suitable for secure communications in AMI networks.

Categories and Subject Descriptors

E.3 [**Data**]: Data Encryption—*Public key cryptosystems*

General Terms

Theory, Implementation

Keywords

Key Management, Certificateless cryptography, Advanced Metering Infrastructure

1. INTRODUCTION

The smart grid is an intelligent power grid in which the different components are interconnected by a two-way communications network with the goal of optimizing and enhancing power distribution and management. The Advanced Metering Infrastructure (AMI) is a system that collects, measures, and analyzes energy usage data through smart meters deployed within the smart grid. Even though the AMI is a key component for the overall goals of the smart grid, its deployment raises security and privacy concerns[5]. In order to

guarantee data confidentiality and integrity, an efficient encryption approach must be utilized for the AMI. The ANSI C12.22[1] standard recommends that smart meters utilize an authenticated symmetric encryption algorithm. For using the symmetric encryption in the AMI, an efficient key management approach which deals with secret keys of numerous smart meters is required. Moreover, in a case that smart meters' secret keys are compromised or there are security vulnerabilities at the level of the smart meters, a large scale re-key operation must be performed. Thus, an efficient and scalable approach to transmitting new symmetric keys is crucial. A hybrid encryption approach can be utilized to efficiently encapsulate new keys and securely transmit data for the AMI. In hybrid encryption, the Key Encapsulation Mechanism (KEM) is used to encrypt a one-time symmetric key. In contrast, the symmetric key encryption is used as the Data Encapsulation Mechanism (DEM) to encrypt actual data. We can consider two kinds of conventional hybrid encryption approaches based on both traditional PKI (Public Key Infrastructure), using ECC to generate an authenticated symmetric key, and the symmetric encryption algorithm, to encrypt data. The Approach I combines a key agreement approach based on the Elliptic Curve Digital Signature Algorithm (ECDSA) and Elliptic Curve Diffie-Hellman (ECDH) protocol with AES encryption algorithm. The Approach II combines a key transport approach based on Elliptic Curve Integrated Encryption Scheme (ECIES) and ECDSA with AES encryption algorithm. However, since these approaches rely on traditional PKI using a certificate trusted by CA, they require managing certificates. Although Identity-base Public Key Cryptography (ID-PKC)[4] was introduced to eliminate the dependency from explicit certificates, it has a key escrow problem because the Key Generation Center (KGC) stores the private keys of all users. Thus, we apply the concept of Certificateless Public Key Cryptography (CL-PKC)[2] to resolve those drawbacks for the AMI. CL-PKC does not require certificates and each user has a complete private key which is a combination of a partial private key generated by the KGC and the user's own secret value. CL-PKC can overcome the key escrow problem, because the KGC does not have access to the user's secret value. Recently, Li et al.[3] first constructed a hybrid signcryption scheme which was truly certificateless by using certificateless signcryption tag-KEM and a DEM. However, such schemes are based on bilinear pairings. Compared with standard operations, the computation of pairing is extremely taxing.

CODASPY'14, March 3–5, 2014, San Antonio, Texas, USA.
ACM 978-1-4503-2278-2/14/03.
http://dx.doi.org/10.1145/2557547.2557582.

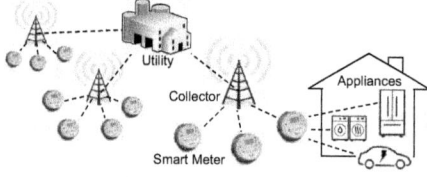

Figure 1: AMI overview

In our poster, we propose a novel CertificateLess Hybrid SignCryption (CL-HSC) scheme that does not utilize pairing operations and is thus appropriate for use in AMI networks. Our scheme can be used as the basis for efficiently encapsulating symmetric keys and for securing communications between the utility and the smart meters within an AMI network. Furthermore, we implemented our scheme, Approach I and Approach II, to evaluate the performance of our CL-HSC scheme. As shown by experimental results, our scheme is more efficient than the ECC-based conventional hybrid encryption approaches. The remainder of this paper is organized as follows. Section 2 introduces our CL-HSC scheme without pairing. Section 3 reports the results from the experimental evaluation of our scheme and its comparison. Finally, Section 4 concludes the paper.

2. CL-HSC SCHEME WITHOUT PAIRING

In this section, we provide a simplified overview of an AMI network and present the CL-HSC scheme.

2.1 AMI Overview

As shown in Figure 1, an AMI typically consists of a utility, several collectors, smart meters, and electronic home appliances. The utility transmits requests and commands to the smart meters while also gathering and analyzing power usage data sent by each smart meter. The collector gathers data from a group of smart meters and then transfers the data in bulk to the utility. All data exchanged between the utility and smart meters typically reach their destination through multiple communication paths. However, the link-level security supported by communication protocols in each path is not sufficient to guarantee the required data integrity and confidentiality. In the event that intermediate nodes are compromised, the link-level security provided would be inadequate. Thus, the AMI must provide end-to-end security by establishing secure communication channels between the communicating entities by utilizing an encryption mechanism. In order to deploy encryption mechanisms in the AMI, an efficient and scalable approach is required for managing symmetric keys.

2.2 Details of the CL-HSC Scheme

Our scheme consists of the following probabilistic polynomial time algorithms:

- SetUp: The Key Generation Center (KGC) runs this algorithm, which takes a security parameter $k \in \mathbb{Z}^+$ as input, and returns a list of system parameter Ω and KGC's master private key msk. Given k, KGC performs the following steps:

    1. Choose a k-bit prime q and determine the tuple $\{F_q, E/F_q, G_q, P\}$, where the point P is the generator of G_q.

    2. Choose the master key $x \in \mathbb{Z}_q^*$ uniformly at random and computes the system public key $P_{pub} = xP$.

    3. Choose cryptographic hash functions $H_0 : \{0,1\}^* \times G_q^2 \to \mathbb{Z}_q^*$, $H_1 : \{0,1\}^* \times G_q^2 \to \mathbb{Z}_q^*$ and $H_2 : \{0,1\}^* \times G_q^2 \to \mathbb{Z}_q^*$.

    4. Publish $\Omega = \{F_q, E/F_q, G_q, P, P_{pub}, H_0, H_1, H_2\}$ as the system's parameter and keeps the master key x is secret.

- SetSecretValue: The entity **A** with an identity ID_A chooses $x_A \in \mathbb{Z}_q^*$ uniformly at random as its secret value and generates the corresponding public key as $P_A = x_A P$.

- PartialPrivateKeyExtract: The KGC runs this algorithm to generate the partial private key of the entities. It takes KGC's master secret key, identity of an entity and the system parameter as input. Then, it returns the partial private key of the entity. In order to obtain the partial private key, the entity **A** sends (ID_A, P_A) to the KGC and then KGC executes the following steps:

    1. Choose $r_A \in \mathbb{Z}_q^*$ uniformly at random and compute $R_A = r_A P$.

    2. Compute $d_A = r_A + x H_0(ID_A, R_A, P_A) \bmod q$.

The partial private key of the entity **A** is d_A. The entity can validate its private key by checking whether $d_A P = R_A + H_0(ID_A, R_A, P_A)P_{pub}$ holds.

- SetPrivateKey: The entity **A** takes the pair $sk_A = (d_A, x_A)$ as its full private key.

- SetPublicKey: The entity **A** takes the pair $pk_A = (P_A, R_A)$ as its full public key.

- SymmetricKeyGen: This symmetric key generation algorithm is run by the sender A to obtain the symmetric key K and an internal state information ω, which is not known to a receiver B. Given the sender(entity **A**)'s identity ID_A, pk_A, sk_A, the receiver's identity ID_B and pk_B as input, the sender executes this symmetric key generation algorithm to obtain the symmetric key K as follows:

    1. Choose $l_A \in \mathbb{Z}_q^*$ uniformly at random and compute $U = l_A P$.

    2. Compute $T = l_A \cdot H_0(ID_B, R_B, P_B)P_{pub} + l_A \cdot R_B \bmod q$ and $K = H_1(U, T, l_A \cdot P_B, ID_B, P_B)$.

    3. Output K and the intermediate information $\omega = (l_A, U, T, ID_A, pk_A, sk_A, ID_B, pk_B)$.

- Encapsulation: This key encapsulation algorithm is executed by the sender A. Given a state information ω and an arbitrary tag τ, the sender **A** obtains the encapsulation φ by performing the following steps:

    1. Compute $H = H_2(U, \tau, T, ID_A, P_A, ID_B, P_B)$, $H' = H_3(U, \tau, T, ID_A, P_A, ID_B, P_B)$ and $W = d_A + l_A \cdot H + x_A \cdot H'$

    2. Output $\varphi = (U, W)$.

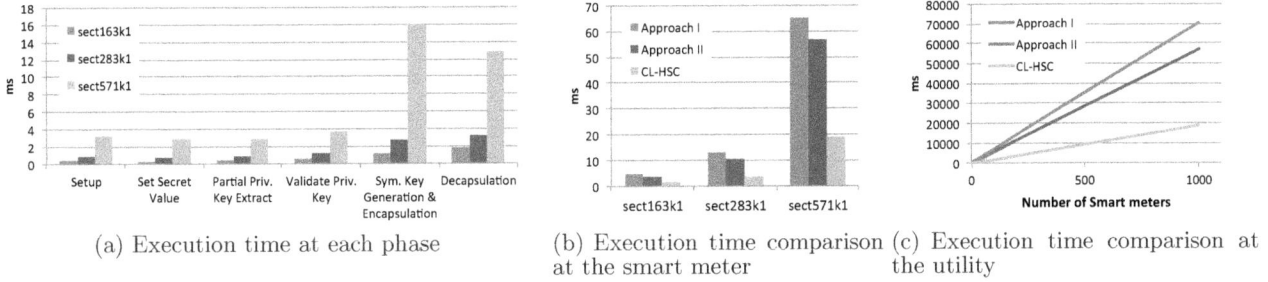

(a) Execution time at each phase

(b) Execution time comparison at the smart meter

(c) Execution time comparison at the utility

Figure 2: Experimental results

- Decapsulation: This key decapsulation algorithm is executed by the receiver B to obtain the key K. Given the encapsulation φ, a tag τ, ID_A, pk_A, ID_B, pk_B and sk_B, the key K is computed as follows:

  1. Compute $T = d_B \cdot U$ ($= (r_B + x H_0(ID_B, R_B, P_B)) \cdot l_A P \bmod q = l_A \cdot H_0(ID_B, R_B, P_B) P_{pub} + l_A \cdot R_B \bmod q)$.
  2. Compute $H = H_2(U, \tau, T, ID_A, P_A, ID_B, P_B)$ and $H' = H_3(U, \tau, T, ID_A, P_A, ID_B, P_B)$.
  3. If $W \cdot P = R_A + H_0(ID_A, R_A, P_A) \cdot P_{pub} + H \cdot U + H' \cdot P_A$, output $K = H_1(U, T, x_B \cdot U, ID_B, P_B)$. Otherwise, output invalid.

If we apply our CL-HSC scheme for the authenticated symmetric key generation for the AMI, the entity A corresponds to the smart meter and the entity B corresponds to the utility. The security of our CL-HSC scheme is based on the assumed intractability of the Computational Diffie-Hellman (CDH) problem, which is defined as follows: Given $(P, aP, bP) \in \mathbb{G}^3$ for unknown $a, b \in \mathbb{Z}_q^*$, the CDH problem in G is to compute abP. For CL-HSC, we assume that there are two kinds of adversary: a normal third party adversary and a malicious KGC. Those adversaries can access to key encapsulation oracle and decapsulation oracle. If the adversary can break our CL-HSC scheme, it means that the adversary can solve the CDH problem. Due to space limit, we omit the detailed security proofs.

3. EXPERIMENTAL RESULTS

In this section, we present the experimental results for our proposed scheme and compare its performance with the performance of Approach I and Approach II. We implemented three schemes using OpenSSL and used the VMware Fusion running on Mac OS X with Intel Core i5 and 4GB memory. The experiments were performed on a Linux guest machine running 64-bit GNU Linux kernel version 3.5.0-23. We utilized three different elliptic curves which were recommend by NIST: sect163k1, sect283k1 and sect571k1. They are curves over a 163 bit, 283 bit and 571 bit binary fields, respectively. Fig. 2(a) shows the time required to execute each phase of our scheme. sect283k1 approximately requires the double of the time than sect163k1, and sect571k1 approximately requires four times the time of sect283k1. Considering that a typical smart meter has limited resources and the utility must deal with large numbers of meters, an appropriate elliptic curve must be selected. In addition, these experimental results confirm that the execution time of each phase mainly depends from the number of elliptic curve point multiplications rather than from other operations such as elliptic curve point additions, hash functions or scalar multiplications.

Fig. 2(b) compares the execution times required for a smart meter to generate an authenticated symmetric key for each of the three schemes. To measure the exact computation time required to execute the algorithms, network delays were excluded. When sect571k1 is used, our scheme is 2.9 times faster than Approach I and 3.4 times faster than Approach II. Fig. 2(c) shows the execution time at the utility side for the authenticated symmetric key exchange when sect571k1 is used for the elliptic curve. When 1,000 smart meters send requests for the previously discussed three operations simultaneously, the utility takes 71 seconds and 57 seconds to process all requests under Approach I and Approach II, respectively. Whereas the utility only takes 19 seconds to execute our scheme which is 3.7 times and 3 times faster than Approach I and Approach II, respectively.

4. CONCLUSIONS

In this paper, we have proposed the first Certificateless Hybrid SignCryption scheme without pairing operations. Our CL-HSC scheme solves both the key escrow problem and certificate management problem. As our experimental results show, our CL-HSC scheme is much more efficient than conventional approaches and it is thus suitable for large scale environments with limited resource devices, such as an AMI.

5. ACKNOWLEDGMENT

The work reported in this paper has been partially funded by the US Department of energy under the project "Cryptographic Key Management Systems" through a subcontract by Sypris Electronics.

6. REFERENCES

[1] In *ANSI C 12 smart grid meter package*.
[2] S. Al-Riyami and K. Paterson. Certificateless public key cryptography. In C.-S. Laih, editor, *ASIACRYPT '03*, volume 2894, pages 452–473. 2003.
[3] F. Li, M. Shirase, and T. Takagi. Certificateless hybrid signcryption. In *Proceedings of the 5th International Conference on Information Security Practice and Experience*, ISPEC '09, pages 112–123, Berlin, Heidelberg, 2009. Springer-Verlag.
[4] A. Shamir. Identity-based cryptosystems and signature schemes. In *Proceedings of CRYPTO 84 on Advances in cryptology*, pages 47–53, New York, NY, USA, 1985. Springer-Verlag New York, Inc.
[5] W. Yang, N. Li, Y. Qi, W. Qardaji, S. McLaughlin, and P. McDaniel. Minimizing private data disclosures in the smart grid. In *Proceedings of the 2012 ACM conference on Computer and communications security*, CCS '12, pages 415–427, New York, NY, USA, 2012. ACM.

Spoilt for Choice: Graph-based Assessment of Key Management Protocols to Share Encrypted Data

Holger Kuehner
Karlsruhe Institute of Technology (KIT)
Steinbuch Centre for Computing (SCC)
Karlsruhe, Germany
holger.kuehner@kit.edu

Hannes Hartenstein
Karlsruhe Institute of Technology (KIT)
Steinbuch Centre for Computing (SCC)
Karlsruhe, Germany
hartenstein@kit.edu

ABSTRACT

Sharing data with client-side encryption requires key management. Selecting an appropriate key management protocol for a given scenario is hard, since the interdependency between scenario parameters and the resource consumption of a protocol is often only known for artificial, simplified scenarios. In this paper, we explore the resource consumption of systems that offer sharing of encrypted data within real-world scenarios, which are typically complex and determined by many parameters. For this purpose, we first collect empirical data that represents real-world scenarios by monitoring large-scale services within our organization. We then use this data to parameterize a resource consumption model that is based on the key graph generated by each key management protocol. The preliminary simulation runs we did so far indicate that this key-graph based model can be used to estimate the resource consumption of real-world systems for sharing encrypted data.

Categories and Subject Descriptors

H.3.5 [**Information Storage and Retrieval**]: Online Information Services—*Data sharing*; E.1 [**Data Structures**]: [Graphs and networks]

General Terms

Performance, Security

Keywords

key management protocols, workloads

1. INTRODUCTION

A lot of services nowadays offer data sharing between users as core functionality, e.g., photo sharing communities like Flickr or Picasa, but also sync-and-share services like Dropbox. Typically, the service provider itself is able to get insight into the data that is shared. However, there may be a need for hiding shared data from the service provider, driven by the sensitivity of the data on the one hand, and the compromisability of the service provider on the other hand.

The most obvious approach to hide shared data from the service provider is to encrypt the data before uploading it and to provide each intended reader of the data with the cryptographic keys necessary for decryption. The latter is achieved by key management protocols. Lots of key management protocols have been proposed in the last decades [1], and finding an appropriate protocol for a given data sharing service is hard: The protocols differ in the access control model they support, the level of security they ensure, and implementation details, and all these factors affect the resources a protocol requires in terms of computing power, storage and network traffic. The resource consumption of a protocol further depends on the scenario it is applied to, i.e., the uploading and sharing behavior of the users, and has a major impact on the scalability of the whole system. So far, the interdependency between scenario and resource consumption is only known for simplified scenarios, often comprising only one set of data, where each user is either allowed to read the whole data set or no data at all. However, real-world scenarios are usually far more complex: different users may have access to different data sets, and for ease of access management, users and data may be grouped, and these groups may be hierarchically ordered, allowing to employ inheritance of permissions along these hierarchies. In consequence, a real-world scenario is determined by many parameters, and it is unclear which of these parameters have a major impact on the resource consumption of the key management protocol and, therefore, the system as a whole.

We propose to identify scenario parameters that are relevant for the resource consumption of key management protocols by a simulation approach: we simulate systems for sharing encrypted data and then infer relevant scenario parameters from the simulation results. This methodology, however, brings up some challenges:

i) A model parametrization has to be found which is representative for real-world scenarios. Data describing such scenarios is, to the best of our knowledge, not published. Furthermore, collecting this data is hard since it is individual-related and, therefore, typically protected.

ii) A model that represents systems for sharing encrypted data has to be built that is at the same time general enough to comprise a large set of protocols and detailed enough to yield useful estimations of the resource consumption.

CODASPY'14, March 3–5, 2014, San Antonio, Texas, USA.
ACM 978-1-4503-2278-2/14/03.
http://dx.doi.org/10.1145/2557547.2557583 .

iii) From the large set of parameters that describes a real-world scenario, the parameters have to be determined that are relevant for the resource consumption of the system.

Our contributions in this poster paper are as follows:

1. We monitor large-scale services within our organization to obtain data that represents real-world scenarios (see Section 2). While we use the collected data to parameterize our simulation model, we claim that this data is useful in a far broader context, as it builds a basis for performance assessments of access management strategies in general.

2. We present a simulation model for resource consumption estimation that supports a broad range of key management protocols. Our model facilitates the concept of a "key graph" that was already introduced in literature, but not used for resource consumption estimations before (see Section 3).

In Section 4, we give an outlook on how our simulation model can be leveraged to get a generalized resource consumption model for systems that offer sharing of encrypted data.

2. REAL-WORLD SERVICES AND THEIR SHARING DYNAMICS

To be able to realistically parameterize our simulation model, we need information about the aspects of real-world user data sharing behavior that influence the resource consumption of key management protocols. Essentially, each change in the sharing permissions and each data upload operation may cause the key management protocol to create and publish new keys, thereby consuming resources like computing power, storage and network traffic. Therefore, we need information about changes in the permission structure and about upload operations.

It is challenging to collect data concerning the permission structure or upload operations from real-world services: Since this data allows conclusions to be drawn about user behavior and interests, many services do not make it publically available. Therefore, we leverage large-scale collaboration services available within our organization to retrieve pseudonymized usage information. As a starting point, we collect this information from our group collaboration portal based on Microsoft Sharepoint and from our e-learning platform based on ILIAS. We chose these services as both allow the data owner to grant and deny data access, opposed to a system-wide administrator. Furthermore, we wanted to cover services with different expected sharing behaviors, ranging from sharing in a publisher-subscriber fashion within our e-learning platform to a rather homogenous sharing between peers within the group collaboration portal.

By monitoring these services, we get what we call *scenario*. A scenario consists of users and resources, which can be linked either directly or by group memberships. These links may change over time, and the sequence of link changes makes up a *workload*. An access control model based on "Group-Centric Secure Information Sharing" (g-SIS) [3] allows to infer a user's current access permissions from the history of link changes. g-SIS can be parameterized in some aspects, for example, whether a user joining a group is allowed to access resources that were added to the group before. Additionally, our access control model allows to order resources hierarchically to support permission inheritance,

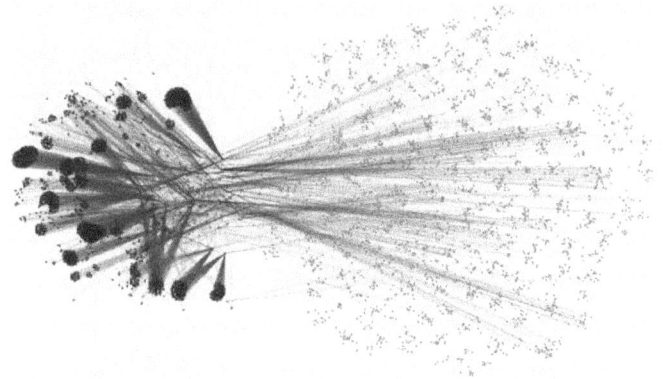

Figure 1: An exemplary scenario representing a part of our e-learning platform. The blue nodes (left) represent users, the red nodes (middle) groups and the green nodes (right) resources. Edges from users to groups indicate group membership, edges from groups to resources indicate access permissions. Users with the same group memberships are clustered. Resources are organized as a tree, with the central node as root.

i.e., a user allowed to access the parent resource can access all child resources. Finally, a workload specifies which resources were read or written by which user.

The scenarios we collected so far exhibit a complexity and heterogeneity that go far beyond simplified access-all-or-nothing structures: For example, a snapshot of our e-learning platform that implements RBAC includes 35 593 users, 35 666 groups and 143 936 resources. A user is a member of 13 groups on average. Groups are permitted to read two resources and all their child resources on average, ranging from only one up to 477 resources that a group is allowed to read. Figure 1 shows a graph visualization of a part of this snapshot. The complexity and heterogeneity we found make it essential to parameterize our simulation with real-world scenarios.

3. PREDICTION OF RESOURCE CONSUMPTION

To build a simulation model for calculating the resource consumption of key management protocols is challenging as available descriptions of these protocols differ in their abstraction level, ranging from mere descriptions of approaches to completely and formally specified protocols. A model based on the key graph each protocol generates can be applied to a broad range of key management protocols at the one hand, but yields more exact results than existing high-level models on the other hand.

Key graphs have already been introduced in literature [4]. Basically, a key graph is a directed acyclic graph made up of user, key and resource nodes. Edges from users to keys or resources indicate that a user knows or possesses a key or a resource, whereas key-resource edges represent a resource encrypted with a key. Key management protocols typically facilitate a multitude of keys, where a user can use a key she already knows to derive a key she needs. Edges between keys indicate that the edge target key can be derived by everyone knowing the edge source key.

Systems for sharing encrypted data implicitly generate and manipulate key graphs. Changes in the key graph reflect the major resource-consuming actions, e.g., a new edge from

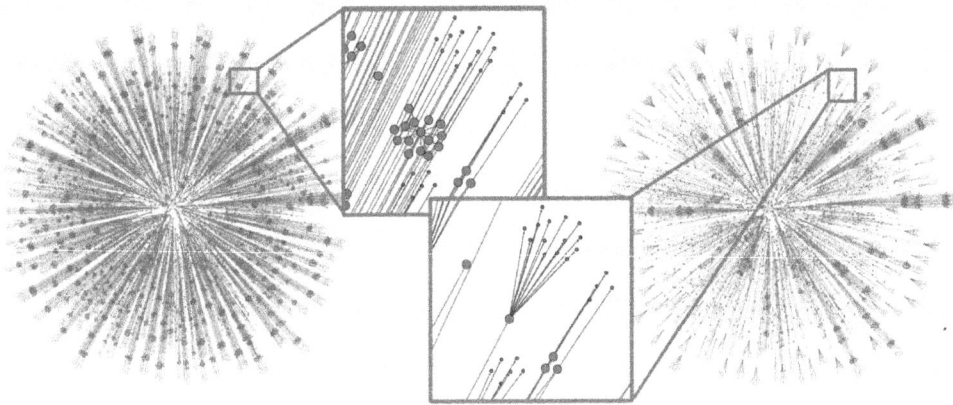

Figure 2: Key graph generated by unmodified (left) and modified (right) Cryptree protocol. Green nodes represent resources and red nodes keys. For the sake of clarity, user nodes are omitted. In Cryptree, the key structure is based on the resource tree (central node as root).

	Key Manager		
	comp (ms)	stor (KB)	net (KB)
unmodified Cryptree	14803	6319	13540
modified Cryptree	5181	2755	4630

Table 1: Resource consumption of key manager as result of simulating unmodified and modified Cryptree. Computing power abbreviated by *comp*, storage by *stor*, and network traffic by *net*.

a user to a resource indicates that the user has downloaded and decrypted the resource, thereby requiring network traffic for the download, computing power for the decryption, and memory for the storage of the resource. We model a system for encrypted sharing as a set of rules that explicitly describe the key graph manipulations carried out in reaction to a certain event. For example, a *UserUploadsResource* event may cause a protocol to insert into the key graph a resource node, an edge from the user to the resource and an edge from the encryption key to the resource. Furthermore, we assign certain network, computing and storage costs to each type of key graph manipulation. The cost are based on preliminary measurements, e.g., adding a key node - which indicates that a key was generated - incurs $200\,\mu s$ of computing time. By "replaying" a scenario as a sequence of events and tracking the costs caused by the key graph manipulations, we get an estimation for the resource consumption of the system.

To evaluate this approach, we have already modeled the Cryptree protocol described in [2] and ran simulations based on the partial e-learning scenario described in Section 2, which comprises 26 734 read access grants and 2 053 upload events. Cryptree builds on a hierarchically organized file system; a dedicated key manager assigns a set of keys to each file and folder. We also implemented a modification to Cryptree, which generates a key set for a file only if there are dedicated access permissions assigned to this file. Since in the e-learning scenario, access permissions are rather granted on folders than on files, we expect our modification to decrease the number of required keys and, therefore, the resource consumption for the key manager. The simulation of both unmodified and modified Cryptree yields results that met our expectations: The visualization of the key graphs (cf. Fig. 2) shows that unmodified Cryptree generates more file keys, visible as red key nodes on the border of the visuali-

zed graph. Consequently, the simulation shows considerable differences in the resource consumption (cf. Table 1) for the key manager, while the differences in the resource consumption for the users and the storage provider are negligible. Note that our test scenario does not include access revocations; if, e.g., all access permissions of 10% of the users would be revoked, about 41 GB of data had to be re-encrypted to make sure these users lose access immediately after revocation. In general, we expect the resource consumption to be significantly higher with key management protocols that re-encrypt data immediately after an access revocation.

4. NEXT STEPS

We will continue collecting empirical data that represents real-world scenarios. Since we see a great potential in this data as a basis for assessing access management strategies in general, we encourage the community to collect, anonymize and contribute such data. Furthermore, we will model and simulate more key management protocols, based on the different scenarios we collected so far. In addition, we will validate our simulation model against measurements taken from a system that implements sharing of encrypted data. Thereafter, we plan to analyze real-world scenario parameters and simulation results to derive a generalized resource consumption model for systems that offer sharing of encrypted data.

5. REFERENCES

[1] Y. Challal. Group Key Management Protocols: A Novel Taxonomy. *International Journal of Information Technology*, 2(2):105–118, 2005.

[2] D. Grolimund, L. Meisser, S. Schmid, and R. Wattenhofer. Cryptree: A Folder Tree Structure for Cryptographic File Systems. In *25th IEEE Symposium on Reliable Distributed Systems - SRDS '06*, pages 189–198, 2006.

[3] R. Krishnan, R. Sandhu, J. Niu, and W. H. Winsborough. Foundations For Group-Centric Secure Information Sharing Models. In *Proceedings of the 14th ACM Symposium on Access Control Models and Technologies - SACMAT '09*, page 115, 2009.

[4] C. K. Wong, M. Gouda, and S. S. Lam. Secure Group Communications Using Key Graphs. *ACM SIGCOMM Computer Communication Review*, 28(4):68–79, Oct. 1998.

Trust Ranking of Medical Websites

Haruna Kibirige
Department of Computer Science
Texas Southern University
3100 Cleburne Street
Houston Texas
1-832-387-1963
Kibirigeh@yahoo.com

Lila Ghemri
Department of Computer Science
Texas Southern University
3100 Cleburne Street
Houston, Texas
1-713-313-7936
Ghemri_lx@tsu.edu

ABSTRACT

The use of the Web as a reference to locate and validate medical information has been growing. A recent report shows that more than 77% of internet users use general purpose search engines, such as Google or Bing, to look up specific diseases, treatments or procedures and that 67% of them believe that the online health information is reliable and trustworthy. However the internet has also become a worrisome source for the propagation of fake online pharmacies, sham hospitals and medical schools. We present a novel method for re-ranking webpages based on the website names in order to not only increase their precision but also their trustworthiness. Our re-ranking approach aims at capturing and returning only those websites that are consistently retrieved across search engines and takes advantage of the fact that the life span of fake websites is relatively short compared to legitimate ones.

Categories and Subject Descriptors

H4.3 [**Communication Applications**]: Information browsers
H3.3 [**information Search and Retrieval**]: Selection process; information filtering

Keyword

Link re-ranking; WordNet; trust; e-health.

1. INTRODUCTION

A recent report by the Pew Research Center showed that 72% of internet users have searched for medical information on the Internet [1]. The report adds that 77% of online health seekers used general purpose search engines such as Google [2], Bing [3], or Yahoo [4] to look for the health information, while only 13% said they began their search at a site that specializes in health information, such as WebMD [5]. The most commonly researched topics are specific diseases or conditions; treatments or procedures. In another study by the same center, more than 67% of all Americans thought that online health information was reliable and trusted it. Of these, more than half act upon the information they read; typically by deciding to seek professional care to address their health concern [6]. Furthermore, studies have also shown that most information seekers do not look beyond the top

* This work was partially funded by NSF Grant # 1241626. Any opinions, findings, and conclusions or recommendations expressed in this material are those of the author(s) and do not necessarily reflect the views of the National Science Foundation.

few web links displayed to them. This situation brings about the question on how to direct the user to the most relevant and most trustworthy medical websites.

2. SYSTEM DESIGN

We present a novel method to web link re-ranking which solely uses the website name and its associated Meta information. Most re-ranking approaches explore the content of websites by analyzing its pages [7]. However this approach can be costly and lengthy for a visitor querying a search engine. Our method uses two criteria to re-rank webpages:

2.1 Website Popularity Criterion (C1)

The popularity of a website is strongly related to the way the search engine defines it. In Google, the PageRank algorithm weights, among other things, external link references and their own popularity. We assume that if a website is returned in the search results of the majority of search engines, this indicates a higher relevance to the topic being searched than a website which is only retrieved by fewer search engines.

2.2 Website Meta Tags Criterion (C2)

Some reliable medical websites are general in nature, although they maybe the best source of information about the topic being looked up. This generality could impact their ranking when results to the user query are returned. The use of Meta tags for ranking purposes is not new and has been used to "trick" search engines to increase the relevance of websites beyond their actual one. In our approach, Meta data is only used for the purpose of re-ranking after a first step has ranked the pages based on their popularity.

2.3 System Description:

There are approximately 15 major search engines available to end users for browsing the Web and searching millions of webpages. However a recent study showed that only two search engines are primarily used by most web visitors. These are Google and Bing, with Yahoo coming as a close third. Both Google and Bing provide developers with free REST API's that allow the gathering of results of hundreds of queries per month for research purposes. For these reasons; wide use and free access; these two search engines have been selected for our system.

The system designed takes a user query such as "skin cancer" and runs the query and returns the top one-hundred links from Google and Bing. Each link is represented by its name and its rank

<Link Name, Retrieval Position>. The re-ranking algorithm comprises two steps:

Step 1: The retrieved links are put in a list and a new list is built with only those links common to both result pages. The rank of each element of this new list is calculated by averaging their ranks in the original list. This first step was useful in eliminating about 68% of the websites; however it also brought about the problem of transient web links. Every so often, newspaper articles related to some medical scandal or story might rank as one of the top websites on the topic. Usually this high ranking will not last and will diminish as the news story fades away. We dubbed these links as "transient links". Our system is affected by these links, since they tend to be ranked high and be present in the results returned by both engines. Step 2 remedies this situation.

Step 2: After this first re-ranking is performed in the newly formed list, Meta tags in each link are extracted. This information is useful because it contains data about the actual content of a website regardless of what words make up its name. For example MD Anderson is one of the most respected US institutions for cancer treatment, however no words in its link www.mdanderson.org indicates a relationship to cancer or its treatment. However its Meta tags indicate clearly this relationship. Example:

Site Name= www.mdanderson.org
Meta title= {*Cancer Treatment and Cancer Research | MD Anderson Cancer Center*}
Meta Keywords= {*cancer treatment, cancer prevention, eliminate cancer, cancer research, cancer clinical trials*}
Meta Description= {*Receive your cancer treatment and learn about cancer prevention at MD Anderson Cancer Center. Appointments Available. 1-877-632-6789.*}

In order to retrieve this information, from the web links, several processing steps are performed using OpenNLP [8]. First, a tokenizer is used to split the Meta tags into tokens and a Part of Speech tagger is used to tag each token with their lexical information. For the purpose of our work, we only keep tokens tagged as nouns. Both the user query and the Meta data go through this process. The final strings are used in the similarity functions.

2.4 WordNet Similarity Functions:

WordNet [9] is a lexical database that organizes entries into sets of synonyms. There are several similarity algorithms that are readily available. We compared several similarity measures algorithms to assess the distance between words in the user query and the website Meta tags and selected the best similarity measures. Eventually, we decided to re-rank our list based on averaging distances obtained from the following algorithms: Resnik, Path, Leacock-Chodorow, and WuPalmer [10] (Figure 1). We implemented this portion of the system using the Apache OpenNLP library. This is a machine learning based toolkit for the processing of natural language text. It supports the most common NLP tasks, such as tokenization, sentence segmentation, part-of-speech tagging, named entity extraction, chunking, parsing, and co-reference resolution. These tasks are usually required to build more advanced text processing tasks.

3. PRELIMINARY RESULTS

We tested our system on four queries: "*Skin Cancer*", "*Yellow Fever*", "*Growing taller*", and "*Impotence*." The two last topics were selected in order to elicit retrieval of many "dubious" websites and assess the performance of our system on the results.

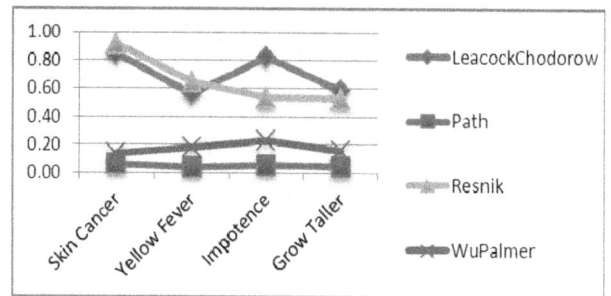

Figure 1: User query/Web link similarity

3.1 Results using the Web Popularity Criterion (C1):

The purpose of this first step is to collect only those websites that are retrieved by both search engines and re-rank them by averaging their original ranks. The average number of links that both search engines have in common is 26 (38 highest and 8 lowest). This first step would allow health information seekers to focus on the most important of these links. Table1 and Table 2 show the results:

Table 1: C1 Re-ranking for user query "Skin Cancer"

Link Name	Bing	Google	C1
www.skincancer.org	1	1	1
www.webmd.com	2	3	2.5
www.cancer.org	9	5	7
www.cancer.gov	12	9	10.5
www.cdc.gov	14	10	12
www.cancercenter.com	10	22	16
skincancer.com	28	12	20
www.emedicinehealth.com	4	43	23.5
www.mskcc.org	44	13	28.5
www.everydayhealth.com	45	37	41

Table 2:C1 Re-Ranking for user query "Impotence"

Link Name	Bing	Google	C1
www.medicinenet.com	2	1	1.5
en.wikipedia.org	3	2	2.5
www.webmd.com	6	5	5.5
dictionary.reference.com	4	13	8.5
www.thefreedictionary.com	17	3	10
www.merriam-webster.com	16	9	12.5
www.onhealth.com	13	12	12.5
menshealth.about.com	21	11	16
thesaurus.com	19	14	16.5
www.emedicinehealth.com	9	28	18.5

3.2 Re-Ranking Results Using the Similarity measures:

We define the semantic similarity measure as:

$$Similarity(W, Q_T) = \left(\sum_{i=0}^{N} similarity(M_i, Q_T) \right) \Big/ N, \text{ where:}$$

- *Q is a user query describing a topic T*
- *W is a Web link.*
- *M be the set of tokens with part of speech* **noun** *in the W's Meta information*
- *N is |M|*

We obtained the following results for the two strings "Skin Cancer" and "Impotence"

Table 3: C2 Re-ranking of query "Skin Cancer"

Link Name	Bing	Google	C1	C2
www.cancer.gov	12	9	10.5	1.17
skincancer.com	28	12	20	1.02
www.cdc.gov	14	10	12	0.76
www.mskcc.org	44	13	28.5	0.72
www.everydayhealth.com	45	37	41	0.70
www.naturalnews.com	83	34	58.5	0.70
www.webmd.com	2	3	2.5	0.70
www.cancer.org	9	5	7	0.69
www.skincancer.org	1	1	1	0.61
www.emedicinehealth.com	4	43	23.5	0.58

Table 4: C2 Re-Ranking of query "Impotence"

Link Name	Bing	Google	C1	C2
www.webmd.com	6	5	5.5	0.69
menshealth.about.com	21	11	16	0.68
www.emedicinehealth.com	9	28	18.5	0.65
www.medicalnewstoday.com	44	87	65.5	0.64
www.levitra.com	12	71	41.5	0.61
www.netdoctor.co.uk	36	7	21.5	0.58
www.healthcommunities.com	31	59	45	0.54
adam.about.net	71	85	78	0.51
www.medicinenet.com	2	1	1.5	0.47
health.nytimes.com	82	38	60	0.47

4. CONCLUSION AND FUTURE WORK

Establishing the credibility of a medical website is difficult because of the constant proliferation of e-health outlets and their increasing sophistication. Most current approaches to establishing trust in medical websites rely on user feedback [11, 12, 13]. Our approach on the other hand, is mostly dependent on refining results returned by search engines and uses the semantic Meta information contained in those websites to determine trustworthiness. Preliminary results of our method show that there is an improvement in the ranking of medical websites. Further confirmation of these findings is planned with users.

One important criterion that has not been included in our system is the sponsor information. Information about a website sponsor can be obtained by looking up the registered domain. The website sponsorship plays an important role in ascertaining the validity of information in the website. Indeed, it is generally accepted that websites that are sponsored by government agencies and not-for-profit health or medical organizations and university medical centers will present the most reliable and non-biased information about a given medical matter.

Websites sponsored by for-profit organizations, such as drug or insurance companies on the other hand, may want to advertise their product and hence may be less trustworthy.

A third type of websites are the fake websites whose purpose is either to defraud health information seekers of their money by selling them miracle cures or are used as an outlet for identity theft. These "quack" websites are a constant threat to credulous patients and a big concern to authorities. Knowing who the website sponsor is can greatly help in detecting these fake websites and closing them down [14] [15].

5. REFERENCES

[1] Fox, S. PEW Internet: Health DOI= http://www.pewinternet.org/Commentary/2011/November/Pew-Internet-Health.aspx

[2] Google. DOI= http://www.google.com/

[3] Bing. DOI= http://www.bing.com/

[4] Yahoo. DOI= http://www.yahoo.com

[5] WebMD. DOI= http://www.webmed.com

[6] Fox, S Duggan, M. Health Online 2013. DOI= http://www.pewinternet.org/Reports/2013/Health-online.aspx

[7] Abbasi, A., Zahedi, F. M., and Kaza, S. 2012. Detecting Fake Medical Websites using Recursive Trust Labeling. ACM Trans. Info. Syst. 9, 4, Article 39 (March 2012). DOI= http://doi.acm.org/10.1145/0000000.0000000

[8] APACHE OpenNLP. DOI= http://opennlp.apache.org/

[9] WordNet a lexical database for English. DOI= http://wordnet.princeton.edu/

[10] WordNet Similarity. DOI= https://code.google.com/p/ws4j/

[11] McNally, S. et al. Can Consumers Trust Web-Based Information about Celiac Disease? Accuracy, Comprehensiveness, Transparency, and Readability of Information on the Internet. Interact J Med Res (2012) vol. 1 issue 1. DOI= http://www.i-jmr.org/2012/1/e1/

[12] Sillence, E., Hardy, C., Briggs, P. Why don't we trust health websites that help us help each other? An analysis of online peer-to-peer healthcare. *Proceedings of the ACM Web Science* 2013 (Paris, France, May 02 - 04, 2013). 1-9

[13] Vydiswaran V.G., Zhai, C., Roth D., Gauging the Internet Doctor: Ranking Medical Claims based on Community Knowledge. *Proceeding of KDD-DMH '11,* (San Diego, California, USA, August 21, 2011).42-51

[14] FDA Cracks Down on Fake Medical Websites. DOI=http://www.nationofchange.org/fda-cracks-down-fake-medical-websites-1349364892

[15] Quackwatch. DOI= http://www.quackwatch.com/

A Cloud Architecture for Protecting Guest's Information from Malicious Operators with Memory Management

Koki Murakami, Tsuyoshi Yamada,
Rie Shigetomi Yamaguchi, Masahiro Goshima, Shuichi Sakai
Graduate School of Information Science and Technology
The University of Tokyo
7-3-1, Hongo, Bunkyoku, Tokyo, Japan
{murakami, yamada, rie.yamaguchi, goshima, sakai}@mtl.t.u-tokyo.ac.jp

ABSTRACT

We introduce a novel cloud computing architecture that ensure s privacy for guest's information and computation. In conventional cloud architecture, a security policy proposed by a provider only ensured the protection of guest's information. This enabled malicious operators to steal or modify guest's information. Our architecture protects guest's information with novel memory management function of hypervisor from malicious operators. Cloud computing generally relies on virtualization, and VMM or hypervisor maintains page table for interfering VM's memory accesses, which is called shadow page table. Our hypervisor regulates memory accesses by management VM by adding a authority bit to shadow page table entry. Our architecture also prohibits a theft of guest's information when it is stored in storage by encrypting data when they leave memory.

Categories and Subject Descriptors

D.4.6 [Operating Systems]: Security and Protection

Keywords

Cloud computing; Security; Memory protection; Virtualization

1. INTRODUCTION

Cloud computing is a model for enabling on-demand assignment of computer resources and application based on the Internet. This technology is one of the fastest growing segments of the IT industry. NIST defines three kinds of service model of cloud computing, Software as a Service (SaaS), Platform as a Service (PaaS) and Infrastructure as a Service (IaaS)[6].

Owe to cloud computing, companies as well as individuals have become able to gain fast access to variable applications or boost their IT infrastructure without heavy cost for management. On the other hand, clients, especially companies concern security to store critical information in cloud. According to Intel's survey on IT professionals[4], 28 percent of professionals have experienced a public cloud-related security breach. For heavily regulated industries such as banking, finance and healthcare, 83 percent of professionals concern the estrangement of legal responsibilities between legal-sensitive companies and cloud providers.

Cloud providers guarantee with their security policies that there is no leakage of clients' data nor computations. If a operator of provider or data center is malicious, however, they may steal or modify the data or computations of clients with their authority. Security policy cannot prevent these operators from illegal behavior.

We propose a novel cloud computing architecture of IaaS cloud environment. Our architecture ensures the privacy of data owned by clients on memory and storage even if provider's operator is malicious.

Cloud computing normally bases on virtualization. Virtual Machine Monitor(VMM) or Hypervisor has special page table for converting true physical memory space to virtual machine's virtual memory space and showing it to Virtual Machine(VM) as physical memory space. The data protection method of our architecture is based on additional privilege information to entries of shadow page table, which is owned by hypervisor, and encryption of data when they are swapped out to storage.

Our hypervisor prohibits accesses executed by malicious operators to memory which is assigned to clients. The data swapped out to storage is always encrypted and cannot be read by attackers. As far as our architecture is adopted in cloud provider's infrastructure, the privacy of clients' data is ensured.

The rest of the paper is organized as follows. Section 2 shows related work. Section 3 presents our assumptions, general description of hypervisor and the design of our architecture. Section 4 discusses the security of our architecture. Finally, we conclude in Section 5.

2. RELATED WORK

In virtualized environment, a malicious guest may attack the vulnerability of hypervisor and gain a privilege. Once the malicious guest does that, it may run the illegal processes or steal their secret information. There are many studies[1, 7, 8] for preventing it. Those studies focused on the limitation of malicious guests' processes, thus the malicious operator is not limited on his/her privilege.

Dealing with a malicious operator's illegal behavior is also studied. CertiKOS[3] is an architecture for preventing information leakage on cloud environment by extending the general method of certification. CertiKOS hides the function of resource assignment in hypervisor and does not give its function to management VM. Assigned resources are tagged and ownership record is owned by hypervisor. The granularity of CPU allocation on CertiKOS is a CPU core, since tagging resource allocation method. Time slicing allocation, however, cannot be performed.

NoHype[5] protects a guest operating system by extending CPU architecture and removing hypervisor. The address space conversion, which is normally performed by hypervisor, is implemented in special CPU. This means that No-Hype cannot be applied on current commercial CPUs.

3. OVERVIEW AND DESIGN OF HYPERVISOR

The challenge of our architecture is how to protect guest's data from malicious operators without preventing the operation of innocent ones. Clients should manage the guest OSes in the completely same way as conventional environment. Operators should have a privilege required to manage VMs as well as be prohibited from stealing client's data and computations. The rest of this section is design details.

3.1 Assumptions

We assume that a provider offers IaaS cloud service and use a data center as a storage. The provider authorizes its operator enough to do his/her operation; otherwise he/she does not obey the security policy which is presented by provider. A client puts its data to assigned storage, which may contain critical information. The provider adopts Type 1 hypervisor.

3.2 Paging

Paging is a mechanism of memory allocation performed by OS. OS divides address space in a fixed size (normally 4KiB) called pages, and assign them to each processes. The physical memory is partitioned into the same size, and their fragments are called frames. Processes refer their virtual address space and OS converts it to physical address space with a structure named page table.

This conversion is one of reasons of overhead. Most CPUs relieve overhead by caching its conversion information in its memory management unit(MMU). Some of these kinds of CPUs defines the structure of page table entry(PTE) having access permission bit and regulates accesses of processes. User processes, which have lower authority than kernel processes, are prohibited accessing physical address with PTEs whose bit is not set available for user processes.

3.3 Virtualization

3.3.1 Architecture

Virtualization is a technology for abstraction of physical resources of computer. This enables to manage plural computers as one VM or to run variable VMs in the same time.

The host software of virtualization, which is called hypervisor or Virtual Machine Monitor(VMM), manages the VMs as guests. Hypervisors are classified under two types (shown in fig1), Type 1(bare metal) and Type 2(hosted). Type 1

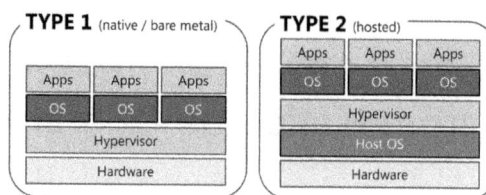

Figure 1: A classification of hypervisors.

hypervisor runs directly on hardware and all guest OS do on hypervisor. Type 2 hypervisor runs on host OS as an application.

Type 1 hypervisor interrupts some kinds of critical instructions of guest, and other kinds of ones are computed in the same as physical environment. This means the guest OS runs fast. Type 2 hypervisor, otherwise, simulates VM's hardware. This means the guest OS runs slower than one of Type 1. Due to the faster computation, almost public cloud services consist on Type 1 environment. Our architecture also assumes that a hypervisor is Type 1.

3.3.2 Management VM

In cloud environment, provider has authority for managing it and can access to management interface. Since there is no host OS in Type 1 hypervisor-environment, management interface is equipped to unique VM. Xen[2], which is microkernel-type hypervisor, has the same architecture. The first-launched VM of Xen environment is named dom0 and operator controls it as management interface. All accesses to hardware applies dom0's device driver and a guest OS on dom0 can directly access all kinds of physical hardware.

In our architecture, a hypervisor limits management VM's authority of accessing physical hardware for protecting malicious operator to steal guest's information.

Frame table contains the information about occupation of frames. Advanced systems store which PTE is correlated to those frames, statistics, etc. Minimal paging system consists of PTE and frame table.

3.3.3 Shadow Page Table

When a guest OS accesses to memory, ordinary OS directory refers certain physical address. In virtualized environment, however, direct accesses to physical address performed by guest OS makes encroachment of memory assigned to host or other guests. Shadow page table (SPT) avoid this by converting system's physical address to guest's address. Fig. 2 is the relationship between address and page table. Hypervisor informs guest OS of virtual address as physical address referring SPT. Since this physical address is actually virtual address, hypervisor can isolate each assigned addresses for guests.

3.4 Kernel Design

3.4.1 Authority Bit of Shadow Page Table Entry

Our architecture adds a novel authority information to shadow page table entry (SPTE). Certain bit of SPTE presents whether management VM can access the address related to SPTE or not. When hypervisor generates new instance of VM except for management VM, hypervisor assigns demanded amount of physical memory. This physical

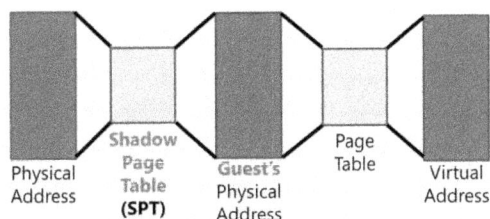

Figure 2: Address conversion of shadow page table.

memory is converted to guest's physical memory space with SPTE, and its permission bit is set true.

When a management OS tries to map certain physical address, hypervisor refers frame table and checks if its frame has been already occupied. If so, hypervisor searches a correlated entry for SPT. Hypervisor prohibits the access when a permission bit of its SPTE is set true, otherwise allows it.

Note that the guest OS cannot distinguish a physical environment and virtualized environment. The novel permission bit does not violate all processes of VMs of clients.

3.4.2 Storage Encryption

Our architecture protects a clients' information when data exists on memory from attacks of management VM ordered by malicious operators. On the other hand, when clients' information leaves memory and is stored to storage, such as swapping out and suspend, it is easily stolen by malicious operators of data centers. Our architecture encrypts all information when they left memory. Encryption keys are unique to each clients.

Guest OSes do not need to be informed of encryption keys. Both encryption on swap out and decryption on swap in are performed on hypervisor layer.

3.4.3 Key Management

A method of managing cryptograph keys is critical problem. Leaving client a duty of generating private key and public key pair and requiring public key does not solve this problem. This is because VM must handle the plaintext and it needs private keys. Our hypervisor has key-generating function and shares a generated key with client by the private pass such as Virtual Private Network (VPN). On second or later logging on the VM, hypervisor requires a client to send it. Encryption keys are managed by hypervisor when they are on memory. The area of physical memory where keys are stored as well as SPT is not allowed to be mapped by VMs.

4. DISCUSSION

- The safety of Cache Most commonly, an OS manages the plural processes by performing context switch. the OS saves the value of registers and cache of the information of address conversion(a general processor retains it in Translation Lookaside Buffer(TLB)) to memory when the OS changes the running processes. Hypervisor, likewise, saves value when it changes a running VM. Accesses on memory performed by posterior VM do not result in accesses to cache TLB is cleared. This means that conventional hypervisor does not allow the leakage of cached data from a VM to another VM.

- Protection of Memory According to section 4.1, all accesses on memory after context switch lead accesses to memory. They are always accompanied by address conversion from guest's physical address to system's physical address. This means that hypervisor can interrupt all memory accesses performed by VMs and validate a permission bit we added. Therefore a malicious operator cannot map the memory domain which is assigned to client and steal contents of it.

- Protection of Storage Saving data from memory to storage is always followed by encryption. As far as the encryption key does not be exposed, the privacy of stored information is ensured. Encryption key is protected both on communication path and on memory by VPN and access limitation, respectively.

5. CONCLUSION

We have proposed and presented a novel cloud architecture, which ensured the privacy of clients' information even if provider's operator was malicious. Our architecture is focused especially when those kinds of information are in memory, but can protect them when they are in storage. This protection consists on additional access permission bit of SPTE and storage encryption.

Acknowledgements

This work is supported by Secom Science and Technology Foundation and Mitsubishi UFJ NICOS Co., Ltd. We would like to thank anonymous reviewers who give valuable suggestions and acknowledge the support from our colleges and staffs of our laboratory.

6. REFERENCES

[1] A. M. Azab, P. Ning, Z. Wang, X. Jiang, X. Zhang, and N. C. Skalsky. Hypersentry: enabling stealthy in-context measurement of hypervisor integrity. In Proceedings of the 17th ACM conference on Computer and communications security, CCS '10, pages 38–49, New York, NY, USA, 2010. ACM.

[2] P. Barham, B. Dragovic, K. Fraser, S. Hand, T. Harris, A. Ho. R. Neugebauer, I. Pratt, and A. Warfield. Xen and the art of virtualization. In Proceedings of the nineteenth ACM symposium on Operating systems principles, SOSP '03, pages 164–177, New York, NY, USA, 2003. ACM.

[3] L. Gu. A. Vaynberg, B. Ford, Z. Shao, and D. Costanzo. Certikos: a certified kernel for secure cloud computing. In Proceedings of the Second Asia-Pacific Workshop on Systems, APSys '11, pages 3:1–3:5, New York. NY, USA, 2011. ACM.

[4] Intel. What's holding back the cloud? http://www.intel.com/content/dam/www/public/us/en/documents/reports/whats-holding-back-the-cloud-peer-research-report2.pdf.

[5] E. Keller, J. Szefer, J. Rexford, and R. B. Lee. Nohype: virtualized cloud infrastructure without the virtualization. In Proceedings of the 37th annual international symposium on Computer architecture, ISCA '10, pages 350–361, New York, NY, USA, 2010. ACM.

[6] P. Mell and T. Grance. The NIST definition of cloud computing (draft). NIST special publication, 800(145):7, 2011.

[7] R. Sailer, T. Jaeger, E. Valdez, R. Caceres, R. Perez, S. Berger, J. L. Griffin, and L. van Doorn. Building a MAC-based security architecture for the Xen open-source hypervisor. In Proceedings of the 2005 Annual Computer Security Applications Conference, ACS '05, pages 276–285, 2005.

[8] Z. Wang and X. Jiang. Hypersafe: A lightweight approach to provide lifetime hypervisor control-flow integrity. In Security and Privacy (SP), 2010 IEEE Symposium on, SP, '10, pages 380–395, 2010.

Privacy-Preserving Publication of Provenance Workflows

Mihai Maruseac
UMass Boston
mmarusea@cs.umb.edu

Gabriel Ghinita
UMass Boston
gabriel.ghinita@umb.edu

Razvan Rughinis
Politehnica Univ., Bucharest
razvan.rughinis@cs.pub.ro

ABSTRACT

Provenance workflows capture the data movement and the operations changing the data in complex applications such as scientific computations, document management in large organizations, content generation in social media, etc. Provenance is essential to understand the processes and operations that data undergo, and many research efforts focused on modeling, capturing and analyzing provenance information. Sharing provenance brings numerous benefits, but may also disclose sensitive information, such as secret processes of synthesizing chemical substances, confidential business practices and private details about social media participants' lives. In this paper, we study privacy-preserving provenance workflow publication using differential privacy. We adapt techniques designed for sanitization of multi-dimensional spatial data to the problem of provenance workflows. Experimental results show that such an approach is feasible to protect provenance workflows, while at the same time retaining a significant amount of utility for queries. In addition, we identify influential factors and trade-offs that emerge when sanitizing provenance workflows.

Categories and Subject Descriptors

H.2.0 [**Database Management**]: Security, integrity, and protection

General Terms

Security, Experimentation

1. INTRODUCTION

Provenance workflows capture the movement of data, as well as the operations performed on them, in complex applications such as scientific computation, document management in large organizations, content generation in social media, etc. Provenance is essential in understanding the processes and operations that data undergo, and numerous research efforts in recent years have focused on capturing and analyzing provenance workflows information [1]. Data provenance is modeled using directed acyclic graphs (DAGs), where a node represents an entity that accesses or changes the data (e.g., a scientific computation software module, a department in an enterprise, etc.) and an edge captures the transfer of data between entities. In complex applications, the size and diameter of such graphs can become very large, leading to challenges in storing, processing and sharing provenance.

Sharing and publication of provenance brings numerous benefits to researchers and practitioners alike. Researchers that work on similar problems can share some of their processes used in synthesizing new drugs for incurable diseases. Two companies that

CODASPY'14, March 3–5, 2014, San Antonio, Texas, USA.
ACM 978-1-4503-2278-2/14/03.
http://dx.doi.org/10.1145/2557547.2557586.

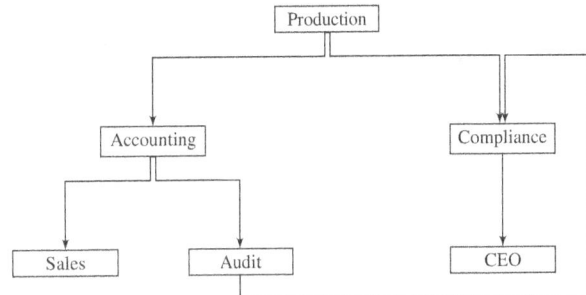

Figure 1: Document Workflows in an Organization

are operating in similar market segments may want to share information about their business workflows, in order to determine the cost/benefit of a potential merger. In social media applications, releasing information about how content is generated and propagated may lead to new insights into how humans interact online.

However, uncontrolled disclosure of provenance can lead to privacy breaches. For instance, within a workflow for developing a drug, there may be a confidential process for synthesizing a secret chemical. For social media participants, knowing that a certain individual had contributed to a specific content item may disclose details about health status, political orientation, etc. Therefore, it is necessary to sanitize provenance before release.

Differential privacy [2] is widely accepted as the de-facto standard for privacy-preserving data publication. It allows release of aggregate information, while at the same time preventing an adversary from inferring whether any particular data item is present in the original dataset. For instance, it is impossible to learn whether a certain individual contributed to social media contents, or whether a single document with a certain provenance has been created in an organization. Figure 1 shows several document flows between departments in a company. Most documents will travel from *Production* to *Accounting* and then to *Sales*. However, a single document may follow an alternate path going through *Audit*, then through *Compliance* and finally to the *CEO*. The existence of such a document may reveal an unusual reporting event. Releasing publicly such provenance may lead to shareholders believing that there is a serious problem with the company, and the company's stock price will plummet. If provenance is first sanitized, then the release will allow some aggregate query answering, but will not allow an adversary to learn whether any particular document workflow exists in the original dataset.

In this paper, we model provenance paths as sets of points in a multi-dimensional spatial domain, and we identify mappings between typical provenance queries and corresponding spatial patterns. We adapt two existing private publication methods that employ *private spatial decompositions* [3] and *ngram* based sanitization [4]. Experimental evaluation results show that our approach is feasible to protect provenance workflows, while at the same time retaining a significant amount of utility in the data. We also identify important trade-offs that emerge when sanitizing provenance workflows with the two considered approaches.

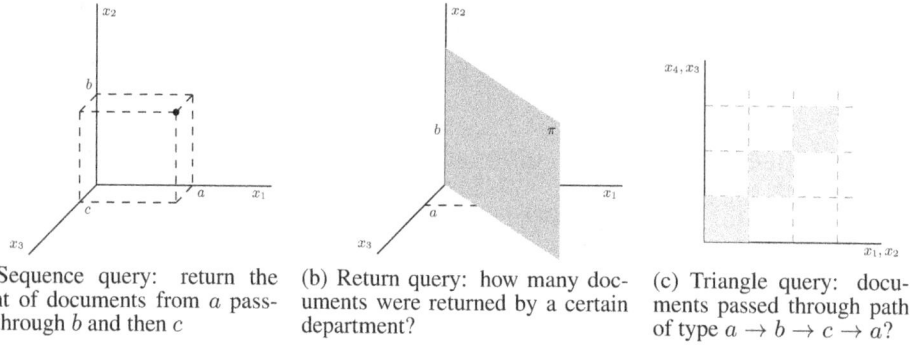

(a) Sequence query: return the count of documents from a passing through b and then c

(b) Return query: how many documents were returned by a certain department?

(c) Triangle query: documents passed through path of type $a \rightarrow b \rightarrow c \rightarrow a$?

Figure 2: Provenance queries representation as subdomains of the $\mathbb{N}^d$ space

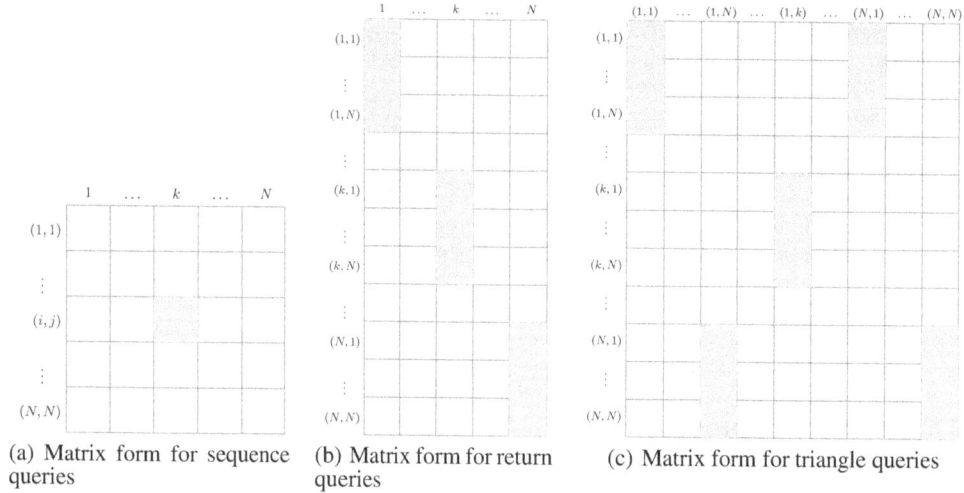

(a) Matrix form for sequence queries

(b) Matrix form for return queries

(c) Matrix form for triangle queries

Figure 3: Queries from Figure 2 represented in matrix form

2. PROPOSED APPROACH

Provenance and Privacy Model. Provenance workflows are modeled as directed graphs, where a node represents an entity that generates/modifies/forwards data (e.g., department of an organization, user of a social network, etc.), and an edge captures data movement between two entities. Denote by *provenance metagraph* $\mathbb{G} = (\mathbb{V}, \mathbb{E})$ a graph where $\mathbb{V}$ is the set of all entities, and $\mathbb{E}$ is the set of connections between entities. If two entities are not connected in the metagraph (e.g., two users in a social network that are not friends), then there can be no data flow between them. A provenance graph of a *document* is a subgraph $G = (V, E)$, where $V \subset \mathbb{V}$ and $E \subset \mathbb{E}$. For example, in Figure 1 the paths $Production \rightarrow Accounting \rightarrow Sales$ and $Production \rightarrow Accounting \rightarrow Audit \rightarrow Compliance \rightarrow CEO$ represent the provenance workflows of two documents. For simplicity, we label graph vertices with natural numbers from set $\mathbb{N}$ and edges drawn from $\mathbb{N}^2$. A provenance workflow is an element of $\mathbb{N}^d$ where d is the node count of a document path. A *provenance query* is an element of $\mathbb{N}^{d'}$ where d' is the *query length* defined as the number of nodes in the query. Our objective is to answer *count* queries such as *"find how many documents contain path $a \rightarrow b \rightarrow c$"* where $a, b, c \in \mathbb{V}$ and $\{(a,b),(b,c)\} \subset \mathbb{E}$.

Differential privacy [2] is a statistical model that releases results to aggregate queries. Given a privacy threshold $\epsilon > 0$ and two *sibling* datasets D_1, D_2 that differ in a single graph G, differential privacy returns noisy query answers that prevent an adversary from learning which one of D_1 and D_2 is the queried dataset. Effectively, the presence in the dataset of any individual provenance

workflow is hidden. The ratio between the occurrence probabilities of the two datasets is bounded by e^ϵ. To achieve this amount of protection, random noise drawn from a Laplace distribution with mean $\lambda = S/\epsilon$ is added to each answered count query, where S is the *sensitivity* parameter that in our case equals the length of the longest workflow document path.

We study how common types of provenance queries are mapped using the spatial representation. The simplest type is that of *sequence* queries, shown in Figure 2(a), which counts the number of occurrences of a given node sequence. A query with length of three nodes is represented by the value of a point in the three-dimensional space. Another interesting query is to find how many documents follow the reverse path to the originator, i.e., *return* queries. For length three queries, this boils down to finding the sum of counts of all point in the plane π in Figure 2(b). Similar representations can be devised for longer queries, of the form $a_1 \rightarrow a_2 \rightarrow \ldots \rightarrow a_{n-1} \rightarrow a_n \rightarrow a_{n-1} \rightarrow \ldots \rightarrow a_2 \rightarrow a_1$. Finally, *triangle* queries find how many documents were returned to the originator after passing through two other steps in the workflow: queries of type $a_1 \rightarrow a_2 \rightarrow a_3 \rightarrow a_1$. The multi-dimensional representation in Figure 2(c) maps the four-dimensional space $(x_1 x_2 x_3 x_4)$ into a two-dimensional one by grouping together two consecutive axes. The answer to this query is the sum of counts for all points inside the shaded squares in Figure 2(c), where each of the dashed grid line is drawn at a changing value of the x_1 coordinate (the requirement being that $x_4 = x_1$).

Multi-dimensional Grid Approach. Since the node labels are natural numbers, we are concerned with discrete spatial domains, i.e., all non-zero counts are concentrated in several points at the

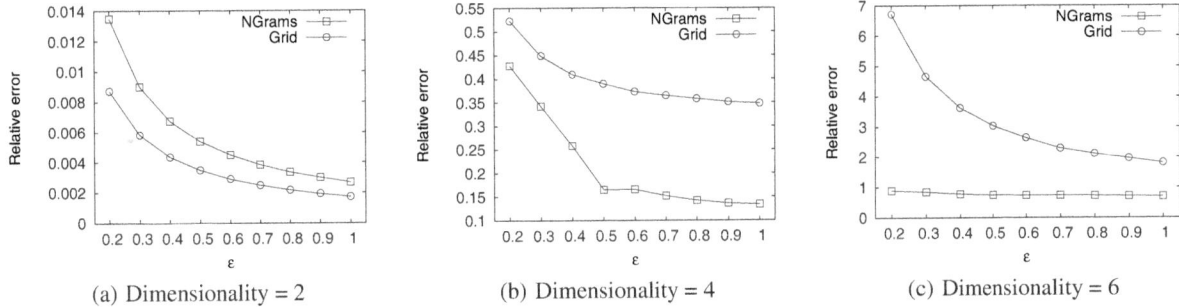

(a) Dimensionality = 2   (b) Dimensionality = 4   (c) Dimensionality = 6

Figure 4: Accuracy of Queries on Sanitized Data

intersection of integer-coordinates axes. This is similar to the representation of multi-dimensional matrices. We provide the matrix form representation for considered queries in Figure 2. Rows and columns of the matrix are labeled with tuples of elements instead of only with labels of nodes. For instance, in order to answer triangle queries we need to sum counts from all shaded elements of the matrix from Figure 3(c).

The matrix representation corresponds to a regular discrete grid space-partitioning approach. Private spatial decompositions with differential privacy have been considered before in [3]. We adopt a similar sanitization technique, where we publish a counter for each matrix element. Since each two matrix cells are disjoint, the maximum number of cells affected by the addition/removal of a single workflow is equal to the maximum workflow length, denoted by l_{max}. Each element count will be added with random noise of magnitude l_{max}/ϵ before publication. Although such an approach is likely to do well for short-length queries, as the dimensionality increases the accuracy is likely to deteriorate, so we consider also an alternative approach that is designed for trajectory publication.

N-gram Tree Approach. To deal with high-dimensionality queries, we also consider an adaptation of the method from [4] which is designed for private publication of trajectories. Each provenance workflow can be considered as a trajectory in the multi-dimensional space of representation. A hierarchical structure is constructed to index sub-trajectories of various lengths. A sub-trajectory of length N is denoted as a *N-gram*. The resulting N-gram tree also has sensitivity l_{max}, due to the fact that all paths in a tree are disjoint. However, some of the privacy budget ϵ must be spent to protect the index structure as well, which is data dependent. Hence, at lower query dimensionality, the N-gram approach may perform worse than its grid counterpart.

3. EXPERIMENTAL EVALUATION

We implemented a Python prototype of the two proposed techniques for provenance sanitization, namely the grid-based partitioning method (label *Grid*) and the sequence protection techniques from [4] (label *NGrams*). We consider an organization with 10 departments, and a number of 10, 000 documents with provenance path length uniformly distributed between 3 and 7. Each department is connected on average to 5 other departments (i.e., there exists at least one document that traveled between that specific source and destination department). We consider as workload 10, 000 queries, asking for the number of paths that match a given query path with length ranging from 2 (i.e., single-edge count queries) to 6 (path length of up to 5 edges). We denote the path length using *query dimensionality* parameter $d = 2, \ldots, 6$. For each dimensionality, we generate 10, 000 sequence queries with length uniformly distributed in the range $[\lfloor d/2 \rfloor, d]$. We vary the privacy requirement parameter ϵ from 0.2 (tight privacy constraint) up to 1.0 (relaxed privacy constraint). We use as performance met-

ric the relative error of count queries compared to the non-private case. All results are averaged over 10 random seeds. The experimental testbed consists of an Intel Core i7-3770 3.4 GHz CPU machine with 8 cores with 16 GB of RAM, running Linux OS.

Figure 4 (a)-(c) shows the relative error obtained for each setting of query dimensionality. As expected, in all cases the relative error decreases as the privacy requirement is relaxed (i.e., ϵ increases). For the lowest $d = 2$ setting, the grid method returns very accurate results, with less than 1% relative error, outperforming $NGrams$. However, as dimensionality increases, the grid-based method is adversely effected by the decrease of data density. For the $d = 4$ case, the $NGrams$ method always outperforms $Grid$, and it better utilizes the available budget, as the error decreases sharply when ϵ increases, whereas for $Grid$ the decrease is less significant.

As dimensionality grows further, the performance of the $Grid$ method deteriorates significantly, with relative errors well in excess of 100% for $d = 6$. $NGrams$ obtains relative errors up to an order of magnitude better than $Grid$. However, at the highest dimensionality, the error levels of $NGrams$ approach 100%, which will provide poor utility. Although $NGrams$ is clearly better for higher query dimensionality, further research is necessary to identify improved techniques with higher utility.

4. CONCLUSION

We proposed methods for provenance graphs sanitization using mapping to a multi-dimensional spatial domain. In the mapped space, we considered two alternative techniques for differentially private publication, namely using a multi-dimensional grid partitioning, and N-gram based sanitization. Experimental results show that the considered approach is feasible in practice, and there is an inherent trade-off between the two methods as query dimensionality varies. In future work, we will customize further sanitization techniques for spatial data to improve query accuracy. We will consider multi-level grids and balanced index structures (e.g., kd-trees [3]), as well as alternative budget allocation strategies for N-grams.

Acknowledgments. This work has been supported by NSF award CNS-1111512.

5. REFERENCES

[1] Y. L. Simmhan, B. Plale, and D. Gannon, "A survey of data provenance in e-science," *SIGMOD Rec.*, vol. 34, no. 3, pp. 31–36, Sep. 2005.

[2] C. Dwork, F. McSherry, K. Nissim, and A. Smith, "Calibrating noise to sensitivity in private data analysis," in *TCC*, 2006, pp. 265–284.

[3] G. Cormode, C. Procopiuc, E. Shen, D. Srivastava, and T. Yu, "Differentially private spatial decompositions," in *ICDE*, 2012, pp. 20–31.

[4] R. Chen, G. Acs, and C. Castelluccia, "Differentially private sequential data publication via variable-length n-grams," in *ACM CCS*, 2012, pp. 638–649.

Large-Scale Machine Learning-based Malware Detection: Confronting the "10-Fold Cross Validation" Scheme with Reality

Kevin Allix, Tegawendé F. Bissyandé, Quentin Jérome, Jacques Klein, Radu State,
Yves Le Traon
University of Luxembourg
4 rue Alphonse Weicker
L-2721 Luxembourg, Luxembourg
{firstname.lastname}@uni.lu

ABSTRACT

To address the issue of malware detection, researchers have recently started to investigate the capabilities of machine-learning techniques for proposing effective approaches. Several promising results were recorded in the literature, many approaches being assessed with the common "10-Fold cross validation" scheme. This paper revisits the purpose of malware detection to discuss the adequacy of the "10-Fold" scheme for validating techniques that may not perform well in reality. To this end, we have devised several Machine Learning classifiers that rely on a novel set of features built from applications' CFGs. We use a sizeable dataset of over 50,000 Android applications collected from sources where state-of-the art approaches have selected their data. We show that our approach outperforms existing machine learning-based approaches. However, this high performance on usual-size datasets does not translate in high performance in the wild.

Categories and Subject Descriptors

D.4.6 [**Operating Systems**]: Security and Protection—*Invasive software (e.g., viruses, worms, Trojan horses)*

Keywords

Machine Learning, Ten-Fold, Malware, Android

1. INTRODUCTION

The increasing adoption of smartphones and electronic tablets has created unprecedented opportunities of damages by malicious software which are hidden among the millions of mobile apps available, often for free, on application markets [1]. Malware pose various threats that range from simple user tracking and leakage of personal information [2], to unwarranted premium-rate subscription of SMS services, advanced fraud, and even damaging participation to botnets.

CODASPY'14, March 3–5, 2014, San Antonio, Texas, USA.
ACM 978-1-4503-2278-2/14/03.
http://dx.doi.org/10.1145/2557547.2557587.

Machine learning techniques, by allowing to sift through large sets of applications to detect malicious applications based on measures of similarity of features, appear to be promising for large-scale malware detection. Unfortunately, measuring the quality of a malware detection scheme has always been a challenge, especially in the case of malware detectors whose authors claim that they work "in the wild".

In this paper: a) We propose a novel feature set for machine-learning classifiers for malware detection, based on abstract basic blocks extracted from the Control-Flow Graph; b) We show that our implemented classifiers yield a high malware discrimating power when evaluated with the 10-fold cross validation scheme; c) We show that 10-fold validation on the usual sizes of datasets presented in the literature is not a reliable performance indicator for realistic malware detectors.

We introduce in section 2 our datasets. Section 3 describes our approach of malware detection. Section 4 presents the assessment of our approach. Related work is discussed, and section 6 concludes and enumerates future work.

2. DATASETS

In this section, we present the datasets that are used to build and assess our classifiers.

We have used two sources of Android applications that are often used by researchers and practitioners of machine learning-based malware detection for Android.

Building an Android market dataset.

Google Play is the main Android applications market available. We have built a tool that automatically crawls and downloads free applications available in this source. In the course of six months, we have collected a dataset of nearly 52 000 unique applications.

Collecting known malware.

For training needs, we must have access to a reliable set of Android malware. To this end, we leverage a dataset released in the course of the Genome project [3]. The *Genome dataset* contains over 1 200 Android malware samples.

Malware labeling.

In order to construct a reference classification to which we can compare the predictions of our approaches, we collected from VirusTotal[1] the analysis report of each application in

---

[1] https://www.virustotal.com

our datasets. VirusTotal is a service that allows to readily obtain information on antivirus products which have identified a given application sample as malware.

3. OUR APPROACH

In this paper we propose a novel approach to extract, from an application program, elements of applications' Control Flow Graphs which should capture, in a more meaningful way than n-grams, the implementation of a malicious behavior inside program code.

3.1 Novel Feature Set for Malware Detection

We perform static analysis of Android applications' byte-code to extract a representation of the program control-flow graph (CFG). The extracted CFG is expressed as character strings using a method devised by Pouik *et al.* [1]. This method is based on a grammar proposed by Cesare and Xiang [5].

Given the abstract representation of an application's CFG, we collect all the basic blocks and refer to them as the features of the application. A basic block is a sequence of instructions in the CFG with only one entry point and one exit point.

For reproducibility purposes, the feature matrices that we have computed are publicly available for download[2].

3.2 Classification Model

We now discuss the different steps, illustrated in Figure 1, for building the classification model.

Step 0: Set composition. Our complete dataset contains over $50\,000$ applications that we divide into two distinct sets, one significantly smaller than the other, for the purpose of assessment. The first set, Set_α, contains all known malware, i.e., all items in the *Genome* dataset. To complete this set, we randomly select a subset of the *Google Play* dataset to add as the goodware portion of the dataset. The second set, Set_δ, is then composed of the remaining subset of the Google Play dataset. Set_δ is always used as a testing set, whereas Set_α can be used as training set (in the wild) or as the entire universe (10-Fold).

Step 1: Feature Evaluation. Once the sets of an experiment are defined, a feature evaluation step is performed to measure the discriminating power of every feature.

Step 2: Feature Selection. For practical reasons, given the large number of features to process, we only retain, after the evaluation step, the best N features, i.e. those with the highest InfoGain values.

Step 3: Classification validation scenarios. We propose to use two distinct scenarios to validate our malware detection approach.

10-Fold cross validation. For assessing our malware detection approach with the 10-fold cross validation scheme we consider Set_α as the dataset where both training and testing data will be drawn.

Validation in the wild. We perform large-scale experiments where the training is performed on Set_α. The trained classifier is then used to predict the class of every single application from Set_δ. Those predictions are compared to our reference classification obtained from VirusTotal.

[2]https://github.com/malwaredetector/malware-detect

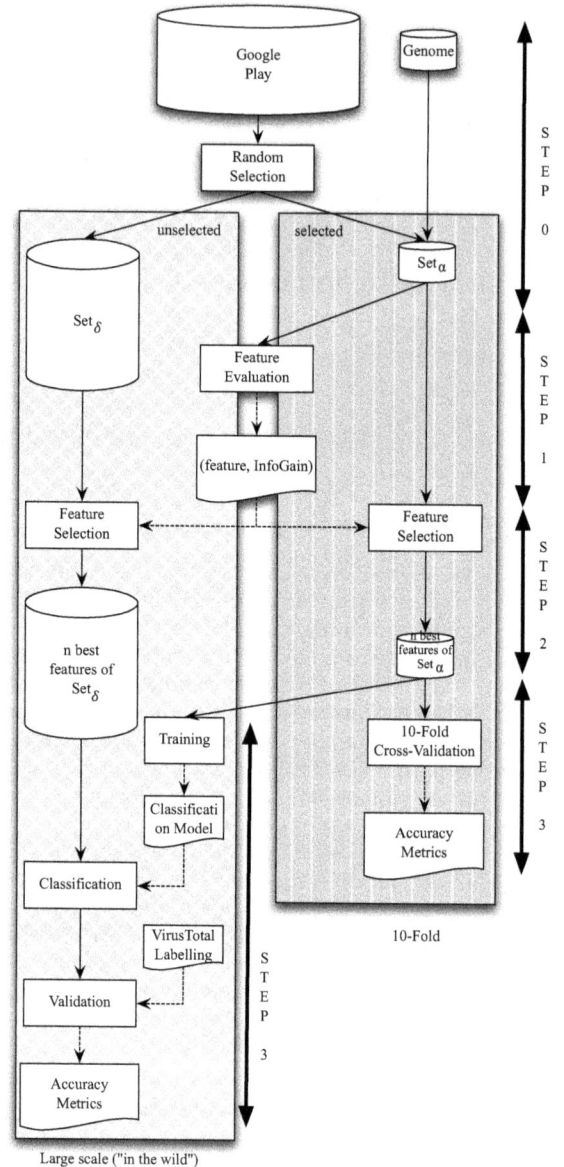

Figure 1: The steps in our approach

3.3 Varying & Tuning the Experiments

We now succinctly describe the parameters that are used in our experiments.

Goodware/Malware ratio. We performed various experiments tuning the ratio value to 1/2, 1, 2 and up to 3, representing respectively 620, $1\,247$, $2\,500$ and $3\,500$ Android applications selected in the goodware set.

Volume of processed features. Our experiments were done with different numbers of selected features: 50, 250, 500, $1\,000$, $1\,500$, $5\,000$.

Classification algorithm. Our malware detectors are implemented using 4 well-known machine learning algorithms, namely RandomForest, J48, JRip and LibSVM,

Since the selection of Goodware performed in Step 1 is performed randomly, we repeat 10 times each experiment with a given triplet of parameter values. In total, 4 (values for number of Goodware) ×6 (values for number of features) ×4 (number of algorithms) ×10 = 960 runs were processed for our experiments.

4. ASSESSMENT

Figure 2 depicts the distribution of *precision, recall* and *F-measure* that the 960 10-fold cross validation tests have yielded.

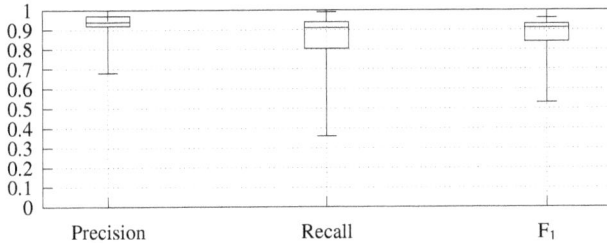

Figure 2: Distribution of precision, recall and F-measure for the *malware* class yielded by all 960 10-fold cross validation experiments

The results indicate that the vast majority of our 960 built classifiers exhibit a very high precision rate with a median value of 0.94. Although recall values are lower than precision values, a large portion of our classifiers exhibit a high recall rate. The F-measure values obtained are high, going from 0.53 to 0.96, with a median value of 0.91.

Figure 3 illustrates the distribution of precision, recall and F-measure values for the 960 large-scale experiments. Those classifiers exhibit a very low precision rate with a median value of 0.11. The global performance of the classifiers is very in large-scale experiments, with F-measure values close to 0.

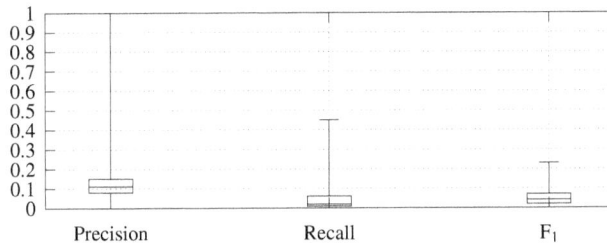

Figure 3: Distribution of precision, recall and F-measure values in "in the wild" experiments

5. RELATED WORK

None of the approaches introduced by the literature discussed in this section provide a large scale evaluation of their approach.

Android malware detection.

Using permissions and API calls as features, Wu et al. [6] performed their experiments on a dataset of 1 500 goodware and 238 malware. In 2013, Amos et al. [7] leveraged dynamic application profiling in their malware detector. Demme et al. [8] also used dynamic application analysis to perform malware detection with a dataset of 210 goodware and 503 malware. Yerima et al. [9] built classifiers based on API calls, external program execution and permissions. Their dataset consists in 1 000 goodware and 1 000 malware. Canfora et al. [10] experimented feature sets based on SysCalls and permissions. Their classifiers were evaluated on a dataset of 200 goodware and 200 malware.

6. CONCLUSION

We have discussed in this paper the validation of machine-learning malware detection with 10-fold cross validation and in the wild with realistic datasets. We proposed a novel Feature set that yield high performance measures in 10-Fold cross validation. Beyond this validation, we have assessed the actual ability of our classifiers to detect Malware in a large dataset. The recorded poor performance has provided us with new insights regarding the validity of 10-fold cross validation. In future work, we plan to investigate under what conditions 10-fold cross validation could be a reliable indicator of realistic malware detectors accuracy.

7. REFERENCES

[1] Felt, A.P., Finifter, M., Chin, E., Hanna, S., Wagner, D.: A survey of mobile malware in the wild. In: Proceedings of the 1st ACM workshop on Security and privacy in smartphones and mobile devices. SPSM '11, New York, NY, USA, ACM (2011) 3–14

[2] Enck, W., Octeau, D., McDaniel, P., Chaudhuri, S.: A study of android application security. In: Proceedings of the 20th USENIX conference on Security. SEC'11, Berkeley, CA, USA, USENIX Association (2011) 21–21

[3] Zhou, Y., Jiang, X.: Dissecting android malware: Characterization and evolution. In: Proceedings of the 2012 IEEE Symposium on Security and Privacy. SP '12, Washington, DC, USA, IEEE Computer Society (2012) 95–109

[4] Pouik, G0rfi3ld: Similarities for fun & profit. Phrack **14**(68) (April 2012) http://www.phrack.org/issues.html?id=15&issue=68.

[5] Cesare, S., Xiang, Y.: Classification of malware using structured control flow. In: Proceedings of the Eighth Australasian Symposium on Parallel and Distributed Computing - Volume 107. AusPDC '10, Darlinghurst, Australia, Australia, Australian Computer Society, Inc. (2010) 61–70

[6] Wu, D.J., Mao, C.H., Wei, T.E., Lee, H.M., Wu, K.P.: Droidmat: Android malware detection through manifest and api calls tracing. In: Information Security (Asia JCIS), 2012 Seventh Asia Joint Conference on. (2012) 62–69

[7] Amos, B., Turner, H., White, J.: Applying machine learning classifiers to dynamic android malware detection at scale. In: Wireless Communications and Mobile Computing Conference (IWCMC), 2013 9th International. (2013) 1666–1671

[8] Demme, J., Maycock, M., Schmitz, J., Tang, A., Waksman, A., Sethumadhavan, S., Stolfo, S.: On the feasibility of online malware detection with performance counters. In: Proceedings of the 40th Annual International Symposium on Computer Architecture. ISCA '13, New York, NY, USA, ACM (2013) 559–570

[9] Yerima, S., Sezer, S., McWilliams, G., Muttik, I.: A new android malware detection approach using bayesian classification. In: Advanced Information Networking and Applications (AINA), 2013 IEEE 27th International Conference on. (2013) 121–128

[10] Canfora, G., Mercaldo, F., Visaggio, C.A.: A classifier of malicious android applications. In: Availability, Reliability and Security (ARES), 2013 eight International Conference on. (2013)

Securing OAuth Implementations In Smart Phones

Mohamed Shehab, Fadi Mohsen
Department of Software and Information Systems
University of North Carolina at Charlotte
Charlotte, NC, USA
{mshehab, fmohsen}@uncc.edu

ABSTRACT

With the roaring growth and wide adoption of smart mobile devices, users are continuously integrating with culture of the mobile applications (apps). These apps are not only gaining access to information on the smartphone but they are also able gain users' authorization to access remote servers on their behalf. The Open standard for Authorization (OAuth) is widely used in mobile apps for gaining access to user's resources on remote service providers. In this work, we analyze the different OAuth implementations adopted by some SDKs of the popular resource providers on smartphones and identify possible attacks on most OAuth implementations. We give some statistics on the trends followed by the service providers and by mobile applications developers. In addition, we propose an application-based *OAuth Manager* framework, that provides a secure OAuth flow in smartphones that is based on the concept of privilege separation and does not require high overhead.

Categories and Subject Descriptors

D.4.6 [**Security and Protection**]: Authentication; K.6.5 [**Security and Protection**]: Authentication

Keywords

Authentication, OAuth, Smart Phones

1. INTRODUCTION

Smartphones and tables are continuously transforming the lives of millions of people, which is mainly supported by the astonishing growth in mobile applications (apps). For example, in the first quarter of 2013, Apple customers have downloaded more than 40 billion apps, the developers have created more than 775,000 apps, and generating billions in revenue. Developing mobile apps is becoming more accessible to developers, and plenty of development resources and support are available. As a result, thousands of applications are now available in the market, some of them are free, others are not. Moreover, these applications are so diverse, one could almost find an application for every aspect in life, such as, applications for mail, chat, text, bank, social web sites, etc. However, the majority of these applications require permissions to access the phone resources: phone book, camera, sensors, etc. Therefore, many concerns have arise regarding data privacy. The risk is even higher in the case of some applications that require users authorization to access remote servers on their behalf. For instance, the social networking sites (e.g. Facebook and Twitter) and cloud storage services (e.g. Dropbox and Box) allow their users to connect to their services via mobile applications. Popular social networking services are also now being used as identity providers by other web sites and services. Secure authentication and authorization standards are adopted to enable authenticated users to grant authorizations to third party apps to access the users' resources.

Open standards such as Open Authorization (OAuth), allow the resource owner (user) to grant permissions to a third-party (mobile app) access to their information hosted on a resource provider (Facebook). With the OAuth technology, the users are no longer required to share their credentials to third party apps in order to grant them authorizations. In addition, OAuth allows different access granularity, where users are able to grant access to specific resources, and there are provisions for revoking access at any time. Other related authorization approaches include Google AuthSub [2], Microsoft Live ID [3], OpenID [1], and Yahoo BBAuth [5]. OAuth is the most adopted with over one billion OAuth-based user accounts supported by the major online service providers. Major services providers offer software development kits (SDK) that can be included in apps to enable the apps to seamlessly integrated with their services. However, if other parties choose to develop their owns libraries they are required to follow the standards required by the service providers. Through the SDKS, service providers offer their own implementations of the authentication and authorization protocols. For example, the different OAuth implementations adopted by popular mobile SDKs vary in their security assumptions and guarantees. Several mobile SDKs rely on embedded web components to execute the OAuth authentication and authorization stages, which does not provide the required isolation and can easily be exploited by malicious apps.

In this work, we analyze the different OAuth implementations adopted by the SDKs of the popular resource providers on smartphones, for instance Facebook. We identify some

CODASPY'14, March 3–5, 2014, San Antonio, Texas, USA.
ACM 978-1-4503-2278-2/14/03.
http://dx.doi.org/10.1145/2557547.2557588.

attacks and problems with the different implementations that can affect the trustworthiness of the OAuth flow. To the best of our knowledge, this is the first study that focuses on investigating the security of the different OAuth implementations in smartphone SDKs. We provide some statistics on the current OAuth implementation trends followed by some service providers and by the mobile application developers. In addition, we propose an application-based *OAuth Manager* framework, that provides a secure OAuth flow in smartphones that is based on the concept of privilege separation. The solution overcomes the security and practicality issues identified by our work.

2. OAUTH AND MOBILE APPLICATIONS

Several of the OAuth authorization flow steps require a user-agent, which is usually a web browser. On desktops, the web browser's isolation mechanisms, such as the same origin policy, provides the required separation between the user-agent, client and authorization server. The user-agent presents the resource owner with the authentication and authorization information, and the user-agent is used to redirect and pass tokens between the client and the authorization server. In mobile applications, the user agent is implemented using one of the following approaches:

- Using a web component embedded in the client app. The web browser component is a UI view component that can be embedded in a mobile app to display online contents within the hosting app. This component is available in the different mobile frameworks, WebView in Android platform, UIWebView in iOS, and WebBrowser in Windows Phone.

- Using the resource provider's native mobile app. This OAuth flow requires an installed resource provider native app as part of the authorization flow.

- Using the system's native browser. Several service providers rely on the system native web browser for both the user authentication and the app authorization, where the native browser is used to play the role of the user-agent in the OAuth flow.

Each user agent implementation offers different security and isolation guarantees. The details of each approach will be discussed in the complete paper. There are several attacks and problems that are possible due to weaknesses in current user agents and authentication element, which include, stealing of user credentials, modifying the authorization interface (see Figure 1(a) and Figure 1(b)), hijacking the access token, and inconvenience in user's experience.

2.1 Case Study

We conducted an empirical study on the current OAuth implementation trends followed by the service providers and by the OAuth development choices made by application developers. Figure 2, shows the summary of our findings.

3. PROPOSED APPROACH

In this section we discuss the design and implementation of our proposed *OAuth Manager* approach. Based not on the previous section, the design objectives of the proposed OAuth approach should include:

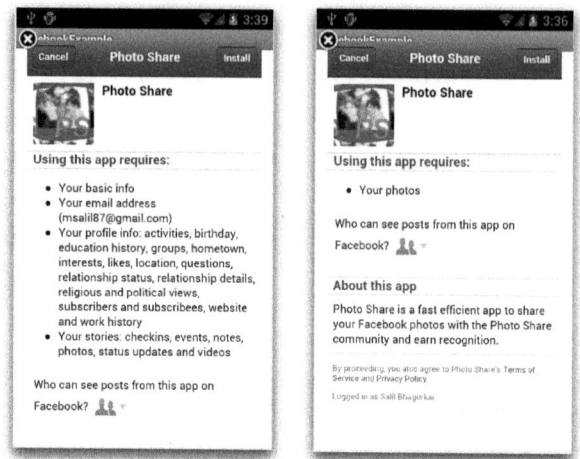

(a) Authorization Page   (b) Manipulated Page

Figure 1: Manipulating the Authorization Page

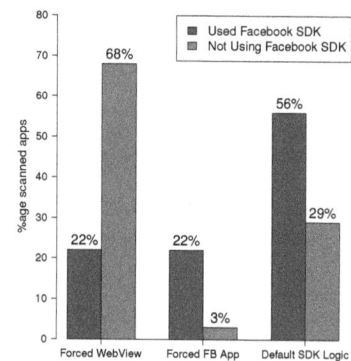

Figure 2: Facebook OAuth Implementations

- **Deterrent:** should prevent malicious apps from interfering with the OAuth flow and provide the required isolation to ensure the protection of the user's sensitive authentication information.

- **Adoptable:** the proposed approach should require minimum changes to the online resource providers SDKs, otherwise, developers and SDK providers will be reluctant in adopting the proposed approach.

- **Transparent:** this particularly desirable in mobile environment where users are diverse and usually are confused when confronted with new user interfaces. The proposed approach should provide a seamless experience similar to the original experience provided by original SDK.

We propose to use the privilege separation [4] concept to ensure that the client application has no access to the user-agent. We removed the critical OAuth components and implemented it in a separate application (secure sandbox), which we refer to as the *OAuth Manager*. While many aspects of the proposed solution is applicable for other smart phone platforms (iOS, and Windows Phone), we focus our discussion on Android platform. The user-agent used is a WebView embedded in the trusted *OAuth Manager* app, which isolates it from the client application and can be accessed only through the secured channel that is managed by the system (intent manager).

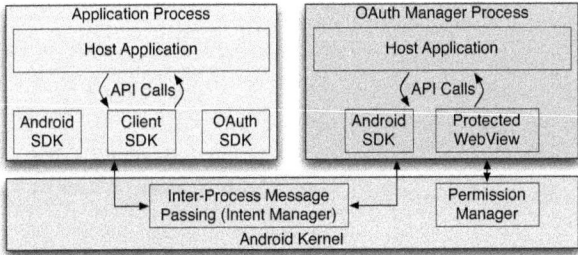

Figure 3: OAuth Manager running on a separate application and communicating with the client apps via the intents

Figure 3, shows the OAuth Manager framework. The OAuth Manager is implemented as a separate application, and is responsible for displaying the authorization and authentication in an embedded web component hosted in the OAuth manager and is accessible to the client app. The flow starts when the client application sends an intent to the intent manager requesting to start the OAuth Manager application and passes it the required OAuth parameters such as the client app id, secret, and requested permissions (scope). The OAuth manger app is started and passed the required parameters. The OAuth manager ensures that the client application is a signed application and has the required permission such that the internet permission `android.permission.INTERNET`, which avoids the privilege escalation scenario. The OAuth flow terminates if the client application is not granted the internet permission, otherwise the authentication and authorization steps are completed, and the auth code is retrieved in the web component embedded in the OAuth manager. This form of isolation will ensure that the client application is not able to manipulate and control the authentication and authorization WebViews. Moreover, OAuth Manager accepts only explicit intents which prevents impersonation attacks similar to the attacks mentioned in the previous section. As the final step, the OAuth manager sends the retrieved OAuth access code to the client application through the intent manager as a result to the requested intent result. Then the OAuth manager automatically finishes and destroys its process. To the user the the execution is transparent and is very similar to the WebView experience. To the developer the SDK can be easily updated to open the OAuth manager instead of opening an embedded WebView, which is a very minor change to the original resource provider SDK.

4. PERFORMANCE

For the purpose of comparing our proposed *OAuth Manager* approach with the other OAuth flow implementations, we conducted a performance study based on memory consumption and response time.

4.1 Response time

We performed benchmarking to estimate the overhead of OAuth manager on displaying the authentication page. It is the required by the OAuth flow implementation to com-

plete the loading of the authentication page after the user authentications. The Facebook OAuth flow was used for this experiment. Table 1 shows the time in millisecond required by the different OAuth flow implementations.

Method	Response(milliseconds)
System Browser	3429
Embedded WebView	8077
Facebook App	1879
OAuth Manager	1892

Table 1: Comparison of response time (milliseconds)

4.2 Memory overhead

We recorded the memory consumption for each method. Table 2 shows the memory required in kB by the different OAuth flow implementations.

Method	Memory (kB)
System Browser	41386
Embedded WebView	5525
Facebook App	22114
OAuth Manager	13518

Table 2: Comparison of memory consumption (kB)

5. CONCLUSION

The different OAuth implementations adopted by popular mobile SDKs vary in their security assumptions and guarantees. In this work, we identified some problems and security concerns for each of the main OAuth flows in mobile apps, such as using an embedded web component, native web browser, and using a provider installed app. We describe some attacks that can be performed on the different implementations and discussed the effect of these attacks on the trustworthiness of the OAuth flow. We analyzed the SDKs of some resource providers. We provide some statistics on the OAuth implementation trends followed by these service providers and by mobile applications developers. Finally, we propose an application-based *OAuth Manager* framework, that provides a secure OAuth flow in smartphones that is based on the concept of privilege separation. We show that our approach offers rapid response and doesn't require extensive memory usage.

6. REFERENCES

[1] D. Recordon and B. Fitzpatrick. OpenID Authentication 2.0. "http://openid.net/specs/openid-authentication-2_0.html", 2007.

[2] Google. Google's AuthSub authentication. "http://code.google.com/apis/accounts/docs/AuthSub.html", 2008.

[3] Microsoft. Microsoft Live Connect. "http://msdn.microsoft.com/en-us/windowslive/default.aspx", 2010.

[4] N. Provos, M. Friedl, and P. Honeyman. Preventing privilege escalation. In *Proceedings of the 12th conference on USENIX Security Symposium - Volume 12*, SSYM'03, Berkeley, CA, USA, 2003. USENIX Association.

[5] Yahoo. Yahoo Browser-based Authentication. "http://developer.yahoo.com/auth", 2008.

Minimizing Lifetime of Sensitive Data in Concurrent Programs

Kalpana Gondi, A. Prasad Sistla and V.N. Venkatakrishnan
Department of Computer Science, University of Illinois, Chicago, USA
{kgondi, sistla, venkat}@cs.uic.edu

ABSTRACT

The prolonged lifetime of sensitive data (such as passwords) in applications gives rise to several security risks. A promising approach is to erase sensitive data in an "eager fashion", i.e., as soon as its use is no longer required in the application. This approach of minimizing the lifetime of sensitive data has been applied to sequential programs. In this short paper, we present an extension of the this approach to concurrent programs where the interleaving of threads makes such eager erasures a challenging research problem.

Categories and Subject Descriptors

K.6.5 [**Security and Protection**]: Unauthorized access; H.2.4 [**Systems**]: Concurrency; D.4.6 [**Security and Protection**]: Verification

General Terms

Security, Confidentiality, Verification

Keywords

Data Lifetime Minimization, Static Analysis, Concurrency, Privacy

1. INTRODUCTION

Confidentiality of sensitive data is an important concern for modern enterprise organizations as well as end users. While a number of enterprise solutions have been proposed for protecting data residing in databases and permanent storage, the issue of addressing data confidentiality in running programs has received relatively less attention. In this paper, we look at this issue of data confidentiality in the context of programs that operate on sensitive data residing in memory. In particular, we focus our efforts on programs that are written in C, a widely used systems programming language.

The risk of not handling data properly in applications can lead to its disclosure to unauthorized principals. Sensitive data can be stolen by attackers who can employ various low-level attacks in order to steal such data from C programs. For instance, a format string attack can be employed to read any piece of sensitive data in program memory. In [13], the authors describe a mimicry attack

that exploits an overflow attack to steal credit-card numbers and keys from a web server application. Another vulnerability (CVE-2011-0992) [1] allows remote attackers to obtain sensitive information from Mono (an implementation of Silverlight for Linux). Threads in Mono were not properly cleaned up upon finalization, so if one thread was resurrected, it would be possible to observe the pointer to freed memory, leading to unintended information disclosure. Recently, there were various vulnerabilities identified in the Linux kernel, where certain data structures were not initialized properly leading to obtain sensitive information from kernel heap and stack memory (CVE-2013-3222 to CVE-2013-3237) [1]. In the above examples, sensitive data was made available in the program's memory well beyond its **lifetime** in the program. The memory should have been erased of its contents before returning the location for other use.

Prior work: In [9], the authors proposed an approach to minimize the lifetime of data in applications written in C. The approach employed an eager strategy to aggressively reduce the lifetime of sensitive data in legacy applications. This work also provided a detailed analysis of threats involved in longer data lifetimes and implement a tool SWIPE which transforms C applications with erase instructions for sensitive data. The approach in [9] is based on static analysis techniques. The main idea is to locate the "first no use" point (First-No-Use) for any piece of sensitive data and erase it immediately before those points. The implementation of their approach was tested on several C programs and was demonstrated to work on large applications. One main limitation of the SWIPE approach is that it cannot handle concurrent applications, which is a large and important class of applications being developed today.

In this paper, we extend approach of SWIPE to handle concurrent applications. Concurrency has become a natural phenomenon in the computing environment with the advent of graphical interfaces, smartphone applications and other hardware-software interfaces. However implementing and understanding a concurrent application is relatively more difficult for a programmer due to the added complexity of programming such applications. In order to develop concurrent applications, programmers often require to keep track of various concurrency constructs to ensure correct implementation. While following such disciplines, it is possible that a programmer may ignore other security considerations such as keeping track of usage of sensitive data in the program, and erase at the end of its lifetime. Therefore, this paper considers the problem of retrofitting a concurrent program with additional instructions that minimizes the lifetime of sensitive data used by that application.

To the best of our knowledge, this is the first known analysis in the literature to bring data lifetime reduction techniques to the realm of concurrent programs.

CODASPY'14, March 3–5, 2014, San Antonio, Texas, USA.
ACM 978-1-4503-2278-2/14/03.
http://dx.doi.org/10.1145/2557547.2557589.

2. PROBLEM ANALYSIS

We start with an example to highlight the problem of data exposure in the context of concurrent applications. We use an abstract version of famous *producer-consumer* model implemented using threads. There are many real-world scenarios that implement the producer-consumer pattern. For example, a web service (producer) receives http requests for data, places the request into an internal queue. A worker thread (consumer) pulls the request from the queue and performs the work. Another scenario involves packet processing in networking applications. One thread polls the network and retrieves the packets and puts them in a buffer, and another thread picks packets from buffer and analyzes them.

```
1   DEFINE LNTH 20;          14   int consumer(){
2   char *data;               15   lock(&lockv);
3   mutex type lockv;         16   if (data != NULL)
4                             17   consume(data);
5   int producer( ){          18   unlock(&lockv);
6   char *lcldata ;           19   }
7   lock(&lockv);             20
8   data = makeData(LNTH);    21   int main(){
9    lcldata  = produce ();   22   mutex init (&lockv);
10  strncpy ( data , lcldata ,LNTH);  23   thread  create ( producer );
11  unlock(&lockv);           24   thread  create (consumer);
12  }                         25   // other work lines  25−35 }
13
```
Figure 1: Example to show the need for data lifetime minimization

Example: Figure 1 gives a version of producer-consumer example implemented using threads. In this program, a Producer produces data which is consumed by a Consumer. In real scenario, there will be a cyclic list of a buffer which would be used as a common buffer to produce and consume the data by both the methods. We use only one instance of buffer to explain the concept. The program is implemented using threads with producer and consumer running as threads in parallel to the main thread.

Threads are created by the *main* function(which is the main thread) at lines 23 and 24 and all the three threads run in parallel starting from line 25. Shared data, *data* (defined at line 2) is used by producer and consumer threads and it is protected by a lock variable *lockv* for synchronization purpose. Producer thread, puts some value in *data* at line 10. Consumer thread, reads the same data on line 17. After the use of *data* on line 17, it is no longer required in the program, but remains available in the rest of the consumer thread as well as in other threads (lines 18, 19 and lines 25-35). Please note that the actual execution at line 17 will depend on thread interleavings in general. We explain the challenges involved in our analysis to minimize lifetime of shared data.

2.1 Challenges

In order to minimize data lifetime, one must analyze the lifetime of sensitive data in concurrent programs. There are various challenges involved in analyzing the concurrent applications. The major challenge is to track the use of sensitive data in a concurrent application. The non-determinism involved in thread interleavings leaves a challenge for a static analysis to precisely reason the order of shared memory accesses by different threads. In general, programmers try to make use of locks to access any shared data to avoid conflicts in updating and accessing the data. Thus, any analysis should also keep track of all such synchronization constructs used in the program while accessing any shared data (i.e., the number of locks used for accessing a shared data). In addition, our analysis should also consider function invocations from threads as they may change the behavior of lock regions inside a thread. The

erase instructions that would be introduced by our analysis should also be well guarded by such locks.

The number of threads that may access a shared data could be dynamic in nature. Often, it is not feasible to assume the number of threads statically. For example, if a thread is invoked within a loop, our analysis should also consider a possible interleaving of a thread with itself.

3. APPROACH OVERVIEW

Our approach is to transform concurrent applications with a mechanism to erase shared data so that the exposure of data is minimized. For this, all the potential parallel executions of threads need to be considered before erasing data. This is to ensure that we do not erase a shared data before its access by any parallel thread (and thereby changing its original intended behavior). We apply static analysis methods to minimize runtime performance overheads. Using our approach, we exclusively handle shared data and minimize its lifetime by inserting erase instructions in a conservative way. By conservative we mean that any piece of shared data may not be erased by our approach if there can be a potential access by some thread in the program.

For the running example given in figure 1, once the consumer consumes the data at line 17, it is no longer required in consumer thread. Furthermore, the data is not accessed/required in producer or main threads. Thus, it is safe to introduce erasure for the data in consumer thread immediately after line 17 as shown below -

```
14   int consumer(){
15   lock(&lockv);
16   if ( data != NULL)
17   consume(data);
     Erase ( data );
18   unlock(&lockv);
19   }
```

However, in general it is not always the case that, the data is accessed only once. For example, consider another version of producer-consumer example given in figure 2, producer thread accesses the data at a later point at line 15 after producing the data at line 10. In this case, if we introduce erasure after line 21 in consumer thread, the access at line 15 in producer thread may get a wrong value. Hence we can not erase data in this case. Therefore, our analysis should capture all potential accesses before actually erasing it. For this, we capture all accesses made by threads and use this information to decide whether to erase certain shared data. Furthermore, even if there are accesses made to the shared data, our analysis should identify that, whether those accesses will be actually influenced by the erasures we introduce for the shared data.

```
5   int producer(){          18   int consumer(){
6   char * lcldata ;          19   lock(&lockv);
7   lock(&lockv);             20   if ( data != NULL)
8   data = makeData(LNTH);    21   consume(data);
9   lcldata  = produce ();    22   unlock(&lockv);
10  strncpy ( data , lcldata ,LNTH);  23   }
11  unlock(&lockv);           24
12  ... // some code          25   int main(){
13  ...                       26   mutex init (&lockv);
14  lock(&lockv);             27   thread  create ( producer );
15  access ( data );          28   thread  create (consumer);
16  unlock(&lockv);           29   // other work lines  28−38 }
17  }
```
Figure 2: Data can not be erased in consumer thread

In summary, our approach is to identify potential locations where the shared data can be erased. To identify potential locations, we

Application	no. of globals	no. of threads	no. of erasures for globals
pfscan	18	2	11
knot	43	6	10

Table 1: Scope for shared data erasure

adopt the approach of SWIPE [9], to identify last use points for each definition of shared data. For this, we treat each shared variable as a formal variable to each thread. Similar to SWIPE, we compute the reachability set for each definition of the shared data. The reachability set consists of all the nodes of the control flow graph where the definition is available. We split the reachability set into two sets called use and no-use set. The transition between use and no-use set is the First-No-Use set before which the data can be erased. Once the locations of erasure are identified, our analysis should confirm if the erasure at those potential locations actually influence any of the accesses made by other threads running in parallel. If the erasures for the shared data at potential locations do not influence any other accesses, our analysis safely introduces erasures at those locations.

4. PRELIMINARY EVALUATION

Using our approach we manually analyzed two small applications implemented using threads (less than 2500 lines of code). First application is *pfscan* [2], a file scanner utility. It uses worker threads to search through files simultaneously for a given input string. Second application we analyzed is *knot* [3], which is a small webserver implemented using cappricco threads package.

Table 1 shows the number of locations we identified to erase the shared data in column 4. Table also presents the minimum number of threads required (column 3) to run each application and total number of global variables present in each application (column 2).

We observed that the shared variables in *knot* application hold the statistics information about the data between server and clients. For commercial applications which use a webserver such as *knot*, this data is sensitive and its lifetime as minimized by our approach is useful. Similarly, for the *pfscan*, the search string and the directory locations can be sensitive. For example an SSN could be searched in a private directory, thus the minimized lifetime of such data would be beneficial.

5. RELATED WORK

There have been various works in the literature to minimize the data lifetime [10, 4, 5]. . Similarly, various static analysis tools to analyze concurrent applications were proposed [12, 8, 14, 7, 6]. However, none of them focus exclusively on data lifetime minimization in the realm of concurrent applications. Our approach is close to garbage collection approaches [11]. The key difference is that our approach is aimed at erasing data, whereas garbage collector reclaims the memory allocated to objects. As a consequence, an object, during its lifetime can hold more than one piece of data and may be erased multiple times, whereas the garbage collector will aim to reclaim the memory only once.

6. CONCLUSION AND FUTURE WORK

In this paper, we have proposed an idea to minimize data lifetime in concurrent applications. We have shown that the shared data in applications is available beyond its ideal lifetime and our approach is useful in reducing the exposure. As part of our future work, we will evaluate more applications using our approach and demonstrate that it is sound.

7. ACKNOWLEDGMENT

This work is partially supported by National Science Foundation grants CCF-0916438, CNS-1035914, CCF-1319754, CNS-1314485, CNS-0845894, DGE-1069311, CNS-1065537, CNS-1141863, CNS-0917229, and NSF-1018836. Finally, we thank Dr. Lenore Zuck for her suggestions on improving the draft.

8. REFERENCES

[1] Common vulnerability exposures. https://cve.mitre.org/.

[2] Pfscan. http://freecode.com/projects/pfscan.

[3] BEHREN, R. V., CONDIT, J., ZHOU, F., MCCLOSKEY, B., BREWER, E., AND NECULA, G. Knot. http://capriccio.cs.berkeley.edu/.

[4] BOEHM, H.-J. A Garbage Collector for C and C++. http://www.hpl.hp.com/personal/Hans_Boehm/gc, 2002.

[5] CHOW, J., PFAFF, B., GARFINKEL, T., AND ROSENBLUM, M. Shredding Your Garbage: Reducing Data Lifetime through Secure Deallocation. In *USENIX Security Symposium* (Baltimore, MD, 2005).

[6] CHUGH, R., VOUNG, J. W., JHALA, R., AND LERNER, S. Dataflow analysis for concurrent programs using datarace detection. In *Proceedings of the 2008 ACM SIGPLAN conference on Programming language design and implementation* (New York, NY, USA, 2008), PLDI '08, ACM, pp. 316–326.

[7] DE, A., D'SOUZA, D., AND NASRE, R. Dataflow analysis for datarace-free programs. In *Proceedings of the 20th European conference on Programming languages and systems: part of the joint European conferences on theory and practice of software* (Berlin, Heidelberg, 2011), ESOP'11/ETAPS'11, Springer-Verlag, pp. 196–215.

[8] DWYER, M. B., AND CLARKE, L. A. Data flow analysis for verifying properties of concurrent programs. In *Proceedings of the 2nd ACM SIGSOFT symposium on Foundations of software engineering* (New York, NY, USA, 1994), SIGSOFT '94, ACM, pp. 62–75.

[9] GONDI, K., BISHT, P., VENKATACHARI, P., SISTLA, A. P., AND VENKATAKRISHNAN, V. N. Swipe: eager erasure of sensitive data in large scale systems software. In *Proceedings of the second ACM conference on Data and Application Security and Privacy* (New York, NY, USA, 2012), CODASPY '12, ACM, pp. 295–306.

[10] GUTMANN, P. Data Remanence in Semiconductor Devices. In *USENIX Security Symposium* (Washington, DC, 2001).

[11] JONES, R. *Garbage Collection: Algorithms for Automatic Dynamic Memory Management*. John Wiley and Sons, July 1996. With a chapter on Distributed Garbage Collection by Rafael Lins. Reprinted 1997 (twice), 1999, 2000.

[12] LEE, J., PADUA, D. A., AND MIDKIFF, S. P. Basic compiler algorithms for parallel programs. In *Proceedings of the seventh ACM SIGPLAN symposium on Principles and practice of parallel programming* (New York, NY, USA, 1999), PPoPP '99, ACM, pp. 1–12.

[13] PARAMPALLI, C., SEKAR, R., AND JOHNSON, R. A practical mimicry attack against powerful system-call monitors. In *ASIACCS* (2008), pp. 156–167.

[14] SINHA, N., AND WANG, C. Staged concurrent program analysis. In *Proceedings of the eighteenth ACM SIGSOFT international symposium on Foundations of software engineering* (New York, NY, USA, 2010), FSE '10, ACM, pp. 47–56.

Systematic Audit of Third-Party Android Phones

Michael Mitchell, Guanyu Tian, Zhi Wang
Florida State University
{mitchell, tian, zwang}@cs.fsu.edu

ABSTRACT

Android has become the leading smartphone platform with hundreds of devices from various manufacturers available on the market today. All these phones closely resemble each other with similar hardware and software features. Manufacturers must therefore customize the official Android system to differentiate their devices. Unfortunately, such heavily customization by third-party manufacturers often leads to serious vulnerabilities that do *not* exist in the official Android system. In this paper, we propose a comparative approach to systematically audit software in third-party phones by comparing them side-by-side to the official system. Specifically, we first retrieve pre-loaded apps and libraries from the phone and build a matching base system from the Android open source project repository. We then compare corresponding apps and libraries for potential vulnerabilities. To facilitate this process, we have designed and implemented DexDiff, a system that can pinpoint fine structural differences between two Android binaries and also present the changes in their surrounding contexts. Our experiments show that DexDiff is efficient and scalable. For example, it spends less than two and half minutes to process two 16.5MB (in total) files. DexDiff is also able to reveal a new vulnerability and details of the invasive CIQ mobile intelligence software.

Categories and Subject Descriptors

D.4.6 [**Security and Protection**]: Information flow controls; D.2.5 [**Software Engineering**]: Testing and Debugging—*Code inspections and walk-throughs*

Keywords

Android; DexDiff; BinDiff; Security Audit; Static Analysis

1. INTRODUCTION

Recent years have witnessed the increasing adoption of smartphones. According to a recent report by Gartner [22], there were more than 150 million smartphones sold to end users in the second quarter of 2012, an increase of 42.7% year over year. Android-based smartphones lead the market share with nearly 99 million

(64.1%) units sold, surpassing the second market leader (iOS) by 45.3%. The vast popularity of Android can be partially attributed to the wide variety of Android-based smartphones from many manufacturers (or vendors) such as Samsung, LG, and HTC. Currently, there are more than 210 Android smartphones from 24 well-known manufacturers being sold worldwide. Among them, 75 Android phones from 16 manufacturers are available in the US market as of September 2013 [25]. Many of these phones closely resemble each other as they all follow the same hardware design guideline and run the similar Android-based software. This lack of product differentiation may lead to competitive disadvantages. As such, third-party manufacturers heavily customize the official Android system to differentiate their products from others. Major Android manufacturers all have their own distinct flavors of Android such as HTC Sense and Samsung TouchWiz.

Unfortunately, deep customization by third-party manufacturers often introduces vulnerabilities that do *not* exist in the official Android system. For example, the HTCLoggers application [50] in many HTC phones was found to collect lots of sensitive information, and provide it over a local network port accessible to any application with the INTERNET permission. Also, researchers found that many Android phones sold by the major US operators are pre-installed with "rootkit-like" software from CarrierIQ [13], which can remotely collect "a vast array of metrics" including the received calls and locations, posing serious threats to user privacy. Moreover, design flaws vulnerable to the confused deputy attack [32] were identified in pre-installed apps. These flaws can be leveraged to indirectly break the Android permission model [19, 29]. In light of these serious vulnerabilities, there is a pressing need to systematically audit the third-party customization in these commercial off-the-shelf Android smartphones.

In this paper, we propose to audit third-party Android phones by comparing them side-by-side to the official Android system based on the key observation that design flaws often creep in through the vendor customization [13, 29, 50]. This comparative approach allows us to quickly locate the manufacturer's modifications to the original system and further assess their security impacts. Specifically, we first need to obtain a copy of the pre-installed apps and libraries from the phone, and build a matching system from the Android open-source project [26] (for brevity, we call it "the base"), then compare corresponding apps and libraries from the phone being assessed with and the base for potential vulnerabilities. To facilitate this process, we built DexDiff, a tool that can automatically pinpoint fine differences between two Android binaries. Although Android consists of both Java and native code that may be customized by a vendor, DexDiff focuses on the Java-based Android binaries. Previous systems target only native binaries [20,21]. Thus, with the help of DexDiff, an external security analyst, who has no access to the source code, can focus their efforts on modifications where vulnerabilities are most likely to be introduced, thereby significantly reducing the time and efforts needed to audit a phone.

However, providing such functionality is a challenge. First, manufacturers almost always keep user-space apps and libraries close-sourced, as permitted by their liberal licenses (core Android libraries and apps usually are licensed with the three clause BSD or the Apache license, unlike the Linux kernel which has a GPL license.) Therefore, it is not feasible to directly use existing source code diffing tools such as the UNIX `diff`. Instead, we need to directly compare Android binaries. Second, it is also infeasible to simply disassemble the binaries [1] and then compare the resulting assembly code with `diff` or a similar tool because the compiler uses complex algorithms to achieve an optimal layout for the binary. Possibly, even simple insertion or deletion of instructions can lead to dramatic changes to the instruction layout. It is thus necessary to structurally compare these two binaries (i.e., to compare their control flow graphs [3]). Structural comparison also brings the benefit of putting these modifications into the surrounding context to help the analyst assess their impacts. Third, the solution should be able to scale to the size of commodity Android binaries, which could contain tens of thousands of methods. For example, the `framework.dex` file in our test phone consists of $5,423$ classes and $52,566$ methods with a file size of 9.9MB, while its corresponding base binary has $3,924$ classes and $38,283$ methods in a 6.6MB file. Large files pose significant challenge to DexDiff because algorithms for graph comparison usually have limited scalability. By applying a series optimization, DexDiff can handle the aforementioned files in about two and half minutes.

To address these challenges, we design a tool called DexDiff that can pinpoint fine differences between two Android binaries. Unlike other tools [11, 58] [1] that linearly compare disassembled Android instructions, DexDiff structurally compares the control flow graphs (CFG) [3] of two Android apps. Given two Android binaries, DexDiff works in two phases. In the first parse, it parses the binaries into classes and methods, and uses a fast but coarse-grained similarity comparison algorithm to find an assignment of classes and methods (one from each file), in which each assigned class or method is sufficiently similar to its peer; In the second phase, DexDiff constructs the control flow graphs of each pair of matched methods, and performs a fine-grained graph-based comparison of their CFGs using an approximation of the maximum common sub-graph isomorphism problem [2]. By doing so, we can heavily reduce the workload for the more expensive graph-based comparison, thus making DexDiff scalable to commodity Android binaries. We have implemented a prototype of DexDiff and used it to audit a popular Android phone to demonstrate the effectiveness of our approach. Through examining the manufacturer's modifications of the Android framework, we discovered a vulnerable device management app that accepts commands from a local network port without authenticating the connection first. This particular app is loaded with Android permissions, and willingly provides private information obtained through these permissions to any app with the Internet access permission. Moreover, we verified that the phone has the CarrierIQ software embedded [13]. With the help of DexDiff, we further systematically report metrics collected by the software, especially in the stock Android browser. To summarize, this paper makes the following contributions: ,

- Based on the observation that vulnerabilities often are introduced by vendor customization, we propose an approach to systematically audit third-party Android phones by comparing them side-to-side against the official Android system.

- To facilitate the audit of third-party phones, we have designed DexDiff, a tool that can pinpoint modifications to Android binaries and highlight these changes in their surrounding context, allowing security analysts to focus their efforts to locations that are most likely to cause problems. Although each individual algorithm of DexDiff has been applied in security before, the overall design of DexDiff is efficient and scalable.

- We have implemented a prototype of DexDiff. Our evaluation shows that DexDiff is efficient and scalable. It is also effective in leading to the discovery of new vulnerabilities in our test phone.

The rest of this paper is organized as follows: we first describe the design and implementation of DexDiff in Section 2, and then evaluate the system performance and effectiveness in Section 3. Afterward, we discuss possible limitations and future improvements in Section 4, and present related work in Section 5. Finally, we conclude the paper in Section 6.

2. DEXDIFF DESIGN

2.1 Overview

DexDiff is designed to help (external) security analysts to assess security impacts of vendor customization to the official Android system. It structurally compares two Android binaries and highlights the changes in their surrounding context, i.e., the control flow graphs [3]. To use DexDiff, the analyst first obtains a copy of the pre-install Android apps and libraries from the phone, and builds their corresponding base binaries from the release branch in AOSP [26] on which the phone is based. Then, the analyst uses DexDiff to compare each pair of the Android binaries and evaluate the security impacts of individual modifications. Although the security evaluation still requires human expertise (probably no automated systems can eliminate such a need), DexDiff can significantly reduce the time and effort required by directing them to locations where problems are most likely to occur. To this end, we have three design goals for DexDiff:

- *Accuracy*: DexDiff should accurately locate changes to an Android binary and present them in the right context. In particular, it should be able to tolerate common mechanical changes, for example, to the instruction layout by an optimizer, or to the class names that are often targeted by trivial obfuscators [43]. The former requires a non-linear comparison (e.g., graph-based), while the latter prevents any exact matching.

- *Scalability*: Our solution should scale to commodity Android binaries, which could consist of hundreds of thousands methods even for pre-loaded apps and libraries. However, algorithms for graph-based comparison (i.e., isomorphism) usually have high resource demands. Therefore, it is necessary to pre-process the binaries with a faster (but less precise) algorithm to reduce the workload for graph comparison.

- *Efficiency*: The third requirement is closely related the second one. Our solution should not only scale to large inputs, but also process them quickly because, as an aid to the analyst, DexDiff will be used interactively.

---

[1] Our tool is not related to [58], which is incomplete and inactive. Both projects were started at roughly the same time.

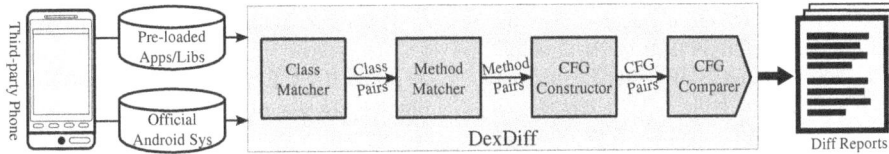

Figure 1: Overview of DexDiff

Figure 1 shows a high level overview of DexDiff. Given two Android binary files, DexDiff produces a diff report in two phases. In the first phase, DexDiff uses a fast but coarse-grained similarity algorithm to quickly match classes and methods. Specifically, it parses the binary files into Java classes, and uses code similarity to find for each class its match in the peer binary, if there is any (*Class Matcher*). For every pair of matched classes, DexDiff applies the same technique to find for each method its match in the peer class (*Method Matcher*). In the second phase, DexDiff leverages a slower but more precise algorithm to compare the control-flow graphs for each pair of matched methods. Specifically, it breaks the pair of matched methods into basic blocks and constructs the control flow graph for each method (*CFG Constructor*). It further uses a graph isomorphism engine to find a maximum matching of these basic blocks. The resulting matched basic blocks consist of unchanged or modified basic blocks, while unmatched basic blocks are basic blocks that have been deleted or inserted, depending on which file they belong to (*CFG Comparer*). To facilitate the auditor, DexDiff lays out the CFGs of each pair of matched methods side-by-side in a graph (using dot [6]), and visually highlights their differences. Figure 3 shows an example output of DexDiff. In the following subsections, we will give more details of each step.

2.2 Matching Classes

We rephrase class matching as an assignment problem [55]: given two disjoint set of classes from two Android binaries, DexDiff tries to find an optimal assignment of classes in which each class is assigned to a resembling class in the other file (if there is any). To solve this problem, DexDiff first parses the input files into classes, and performs a pair-wise comparison of these classes (one from each input file) to calculate their similarity. This generates a matrix of similarity scores. It then leverages the *Hungarian algorithm* [57] to find an optimal assignment of these classes that maximizes the overall similarity between the two files.

Parsing Android Binary Given two Android binaries, DexDiff first parses them into classes. Android's Dalvik class file has a different format than the standard Java class file: the definition for each class in the standard Java is contained in a separate file; while in Android, a single class file (the `classes.dex` file in an `apk` file) includes definitions for all the classes of an app or library. For example, `framework.dex`, the Android framework file, in the official Gingerbread firmware (Android version 2.3.3) contains 3,924 classes, while the same file in the HTC's Gingerbread firmware for HTC EVO 4G has 5,423 classes, or a 38.2% increase over the official firmware. Encapsulating all classes in a single file allows Android to reduce the binary size by maximizing shared identifiers and values.

Calculating Similarity After parsing the inputs into classes, DexDiff performs a pair-wise comparison of classes (one from each input) to calculate their similarity. This amounts to $p \times q$ comparisons if the inputs have p and q classes, respectively. For example, it would requires 21,279,852 comparisons for the two previously mentioned `framework.dex` files. It is thus critical to construct an efficient algorithm for each comparison. To this end, DexDiff first converts each class into its string representation and further leverages feature-hashing [56] to reduce the overhead of n-gram based similarity.

Specifically, DexDiff computes class similarity in two steps. It first converts each class into its string representation for easy similarity calculation. The string representation of a class is a concatenation of its name, super class name, implemented interfaces, class and member fields, and methods. Particularly, a method consists of its signature (i.e., parameters, return value, and exceptions it may throw), name, and disassembled instructions. To tolerate differences in compiler's register allocation, DexDiff ignores registers in instructions but leaves other references intact. This is an improvement over previous system designs that rely (almost) solely on opcodes [31, 59] because rich type information is encoded in the Dalvik bytecode and retained in DexDiff. For example, the `new-array vA, vB, type@CCCC` instruction [27] constructs a new array of size `vB` and puts the result into register `vA`. `type@CCCC` is a reference to a type in the symbol table. If only opcode is considered, this instruction will be abbreviated as `new-array`, losing the type information. In DexDiff, we resolve all the references such as types, method prototypes, and strings, and append them to the opcode of the instructions. For instance, the `new-array v0, v1 [Ljava/lang/String` instruction that creates a string array will be reduced to `new-array [Ljava/lang/String` in DexDiff. Similarly, method invocation instructions in DexDiff (i.e., `invoke-kind`) keep the method prototypes to be called, such as the `invoke-virtual Lcom/android/browser/WebDialog->findViewById(I)Landroid/view/View` instruction. It is clear from these examples that disassembled instructions in DexDiff keep rich semantic information about the original program.

After converting classes into strings, DexDiff uses n-gram to calculate their similarity. Previous research [37, 38] has shown that n-gram based similarity is reliable against reordering, insertion, and deletion. To measure similarity between classes, DexDiff slides a window of length n over the strings for the class, advancing the window one string at a time. Each n-gram of strings is considered as a unit for comparison. We then calculate the similarity as the percentage of common n-grams out of the total unique n-grams. That is, the similarity of two classes c_a and c_b can be expressed as the Jaccard index of:

$$Similarity(c_a, c_b) = \frac{|c_a \cap c_b|}{|c_a \cup c_b|} \quad (1)$$

As mentioned earlier, DexDiff performs a pair-wise comparison of classes to generate a p-by-q matrix of similarity scores. However, string comparison used by n-gram similarity is an expensive operation, especially when implemented naively. For example, the number of string comparison operations if we compute Equation (1) by pair-wise string comparison is: $\sum_{\substack{1 \le i \le p \\ 1 \le j \le q}} |c_i| \times |c_j|$ which is prohibitively expensive for large Android binaries. To improve the efficiency in calculating similarity, we adopt an algorithm called *feature hashing*, which has been shown to closely approximate the true similarity if the hash function uniformly distributes its output in a large value space [38]. More specifically, we compute the hash (a 32-bit number) for each n-gram, and replace the n-grams with their hashes in Equation (1). As such, set operations in strings in Equation (1) are substituted by set operations in integers. However, unlike Juxtapp [31] and ReDeBug [37] that encode hash values in a large bit-vector (e.g., $128K$ bits), we directly use dynamic arrays to save hash values. This design is chosen because n-gram sets for many Android classes are very sparse if encoded in bit-vectors. Performing $2p \times q$ set operations on these sparse bit-vectors (as required by pair-wise similarity comparison) is prohibitively time-consuming. Therefore, in DexDiff, we store the hashes in a dynamic array, and normalize the array by sorting it and removing duplicates before set operations. The set operations thus can be efficiently implemented as the intersection and merging of two sorted arrays.

Matching Classes Given the matrix of similarity scores calculated in the previous step, we can rephrase class matching as the assignment problem [55]. Specifically, we can view classes in one input file as workers, and classes in the other input file as tasks. Each similarity score can then be interpreted as the gain for a worker to complete a task. The assignment problem looks for an optimal assignment of the workers to the tasks so that the total gain is maximized. The Hungarian algorithm [57] is a well-known algorithm to solve the assignment problem in polynomial time. In DexDiff, we apply this algorithm to find an optimal assignment of classes that maximizes the overall similarity for the input files. The outputs of this step are pairs of assigned (or matched) classes.

2.3 Matching Methods

Given a pair of matched classes, DexDiff further refines the result by finding an assignment of methods between each pair of classes. The approach is the same as that used to match classes. More specifically, DexDiff first converts these methods into their string representations, and calculates a matrix of similarity scores between each pair of the methods using n-gram based similarity. It then finds an optimal assignment of methods that maximizes the overall similarity for these two classes. The output of this step is pairs of matched methods, which will be further processed to structurally compare their differences.

2.4 Constructing Control Flow Graphs

DexDiff compares two Android binaries in two phases. In the first phase, it uses a faster but coarse-grained algorithm to find a matching between classes and methods. Each pair of matched methods will be further processed in the second phase to reveal their structural differences. Specifically, DexDiff first constructs the control-flow graph for each method, and then uses an approximation algorithm for the maximum common subgraph isomorphism problem [2] to structurally compare these two graphs. The resulting subgraph contains basic blocks shared between these two methods, while an unmatched basic block is either deleted or newly inserted, depending on the graph to which it belongs.

DexDiff uses a traditional algorithm [3] to construct CFG for a method. It first goes through all the instructions to identify basic blocks. A basic block is a straight-line sequence of instructions with only one entry and one exit. Any instruction that may change control flow is an exit, including unconditional jump (e.g., goto), conditional branch (e.g., if-eqz), method invocation (e.g., invoke-virtual) and return, as well as any instructions that may throw an exception. However, a large number of Dalvik instructions [27] may cause exceptions (103 out of 246 defined bytecode,

or 41.9%), including some frequently used ones such as iget and iput to access a field in an object, and aget and aput to access an array. If we allow these instructions to terminate a basic block, the average size of basic blocks becomes too small, usually containing one or two instructions. This will increase the overhead of our graph isomorphism engine because there are many more basic blocks to consider and more basic blocks are similar to each other. Therefore, we do not terminate a basic block with this kind of instructions unless it also belongs to an earlier type such as method invocation or it is the throw instruction. After identifying basic blocks, DexDiff goes through the list of basic blocks and connects them together to form the CFG for the method.

2.5 Comparing Control Flow Graphs

DexDiff compares CFGs of each pair of matched methods to locate code modifications, i.e., which basic blocks have been changed, inserted, or deleted. This problem can be rephrased as the *maximum common subgraph isomorphism* problem, which seeks to find the largest common isomorphic subgraph of two input graphs. Each node (basic block) in the resulting common subgraph is shared by these methods and its counterpart in the other method is also given. Meanwhile, a node outside of the common subgraph is not matched, i.e., the basic block is inserted or deleted. More formally, given two graphs $\mathcal{G}_1 = (V_1, E_1)$ and $\mathcal{G}_2 = (V_2, E_2)$, their maximum common subgraph is the largest subgraph $\mathcal{H}_1 = (\bar{V}_1, \bar{E}_1)$ of $\mathcal{G}_1$ that is isomorphic to a subgraph $\mathcal{H}_2 = (\bar{V}_2, \bar{E}_2)$ of $\mathcal{G}_2$. Therefore, subgraph $\mathcal{H}_1$ and $\mathcal{H}_2$ are of equal size and satisfy the structural requirements of isomorphism. That is, there is a bijective mapping from $\bar{V}_1$ to $\bar{V}_2$ that preserves the connectivity between these nodes.

In applications of the maximum common subgraph problem, there are often additional requirements regarding nodes and edges. In DexDiff, the inputs to the problem are two CFGs with basic blocks being their nodes. The format and semantics of basic blocks can vary significantly from one to another. DexDiff thus allows only similar basic blocks to be matched. Two basic blocks BB_1 and BB_2 are considered to be similar if $Similarity(BB_1, BB_2) > \theta$, in which θ is a configurable threshold (DexDiff uses 80% for θ). DexDiff uses the same n-gram based similarity for basic blocks. However, it is not feasible to use the Hungarian algorithm to match basic blocks (like what we have done in matching classes and methods) because many basic blocks are exactly the same or very similar to each other. It is necessary to use the connectivity between basic blocks to get an accurate result. Meanwhile, edges in a CFG represent control flow between basic blocks. They can be categorized according to their types of control flow, such as conditional jump, unconditional jump, fall through, and return [3]. However, it might be too restrictive to require matched edges in the common subgraph to have the same type because it is common to change control flow type, for example, by adding a conditional test. Therefore, DexDiff does not impose additional requirements on edges.

Maximum common subgraph isomorphism is a NP-complete problem [2]. However, efficient approximation algorithms exist for two similar graphs. In DexDiff, the class and method matching ensure that two CFGs to be compared reasonably reassemble each other. We adopt such an algorithm called backtracking [42]. Intuitively, the backtracking algorithm explores all possible assignments of nodes for the input graphs. Its efficiency lies in aggressively pruning dead branches during the exploration. This algorithm fits for comparison of CFGs, in which most nodes have a relatively small number of incoming and outgoing edges. Backtracking has been applied before to binary diffing for native programs [21]. We refine the same algorithm for Android apps.

```
 1: procedure BACKTRACK(𝒟)
 2:     if EXTENDABLE(𝒟) then
 3:         v = PICKNODE(𝒟)
 4:         𝒵 = GETMAPPABLENODES(v, 𝒟)
 5:         for all w ∈ 𝒵 do
 6:             ℳ = ℳ + {(v, w)}
 7:             𝒟′ = REFINE(𝒟)
 8:             BACKTRACK(𝒟′)
 9:             ℳ = ℳ − {(v, w)}
10:         end for
11:         𝒱 = 𝒱 − {v}
12:         BACKTRACK(𝒟)
13:         𝒱 = 𝒱 + {v}
14:     else if |ℳ| > |ℛ| then
15:         ℛ = ℳ
16:     end if
17: end procedure
```

Figure 2: Backtracking algorithm

The backtracking algorithm (Figure 2) provides a framework to solve the subgraph isomorphism problem by enumerating all possible assignments. The inputs to this algorithm, CFG $\mathcal{G}_1$ and CFG $\mathcal{G}_2$, are global variables (as well as $\mathcal{V}$, $\mathcal{M}$, and $\mathcal{R}$). $\mathcal{V}$ is the node set of $\mathcal{G}_1$. Set $\mathcal{D}$ contains all the pairs of basic blocks that remain to be matched. $\mathcal{D}$ initially consists of all the basic block pairs that satisfy the similarity requirement, i.e., $Similarity(BB_1, BB_2) > \theta$. Set $\mathcal{M}$ contains node pairs that have already been matched so far. The algorithm first checks whether $\mathcal{M}$ can still be extended by $\mathcal{D}$ (line 2). If not (line 14-16), $\mathcal{M}$ is maximal and thus a candidate for the maximum common subgraph. It is then compared to $\mathcal{R}$, the temporary result so far (Line 14), and replace it if $\mathcal{M}$ is larger (Line 15). When Backtrack returns, $\mathcal{R}$ contains the final result. If $\mathcal{M}$ is extendable (Line 3-13), Backtrack performs a depth-first search for larger subgraphs (Line 3 to 10). Specifically, it first selects a still unmatched node v (Line 3) from $\mathcal{G}_1$, and gets the set of nodes in $\mathcal{G}_2$ that can be matched to v (Line 4), i.e., nodes that are similar to v and do not violate the structural requirement of graph isomorphism. Next, it performs a depth-first search (Line 6 to 9) for each possible match (Line 5): in Line 6, it extends $\mathcal{M}$ by (v, w). However, adding (v, w) to $\mathcal{M}$ may render some potential matches in $\mathcal{D}$ invalid. For example, any matches involving v or w are no longer necessary and should be removed. The pruning of invalid matches in $\mathcal{D}$ is performed at Line 7. In the next Line, Backtrack recursively extends $\mathcal{M}$. This recursion returns when $\mathcal{M}$ cannot be further extended (Line 2). Line 9 restores $\mathcal{M}$ for the next potential match of v. Moreover, it is possible that the maximum common subgraph might not contain v at all. This possibility is explored in Line 11 and 12 by temporarily removing node v from consideration, and recursively computing a subgraph without v. Line 13 returns v to $\mathcal{G}_1$'s node set for future consideration.

The backtracking algorithm in Figure 2 provides a framework to solve the maximum common subgraph problem by exhaustive search. Its efficiency (or even feasibility) depends on how aggressively dead branches can be trimmed. Each application of the algorithm needs to implement as effectively as possible for these four sub-routines: Extendable, PickNode, GetMappableNodes, and Refine. (1) DexDiff returns true for Extendable if there are still unmapped nodes, and it is possible to find a larger subgraph than the current one ($\mathcal{R}$) with the remaining nodes. In other words, DexDiff stops searching the branch as soon as there are not enough nodes for $\mathcal{M}$ to have more nodes than $\mathcal{R}$. (2) It picks the node

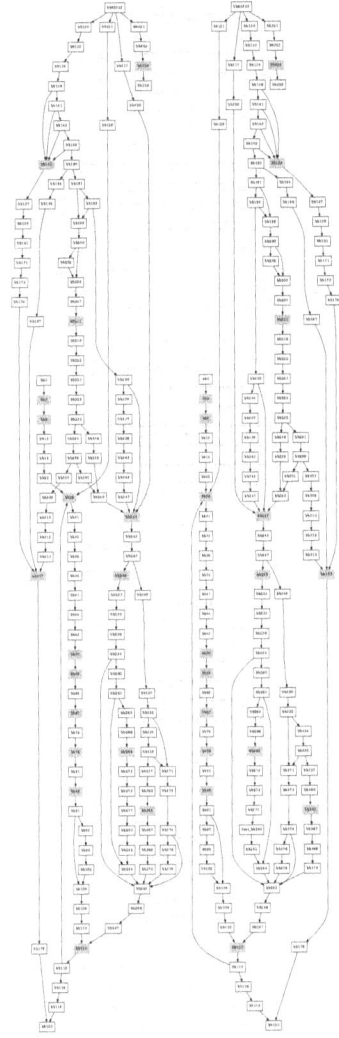

Figure 3: DexDiff example output

with the highest similarity score and the smallest number of candidates in PickNode. It is beneficial to try good matches first because Extendable will reject a larger number of smaller-sized matching faster. (3) GetMappableNodes returns all the nodes in $\mathcal{G}_2$ that are similar to node v and satisfy the structural requirements. These nodes are ordered by their similarity to node v for the same reason to try good matches first; (4) Refine prunes set $\mathcal{D}$ by removing any candidates that involve v or w because v and w have already been matched. It also removes any candidates that are structurally incompatible with node v and w. Because CFG is a directed graph, we require structural compatibility in both incoming and outgoing directions. More precisely, we remove any match (n_1, n_2) having

$$e(v, n_1) \neq e(w, n_2) \quad or \quad e(n_1, v) \neq e(n_2, w)$$

$e(a, b)$ is a function returning whether edge (a, b) exists in their graph. For example, $e(v, n_1)$ returns true if edge (v, n_1) exists in graph $\mathcal{G}_1$ and false otherwise.

By eagerly pruning dead branches, the backtracking algorithm converges quickly for most inputs. However, there still exist cases that require too much time or memory to complete. To address this problem, we introduce timeout into the algorithm to limit the total number and depth of the recursive calls. The timeout is only acti-

Item		Configuration/Version
Desktop	System	Dell Optiplex 9010
	Distribution	Ubuntu 12.04 LTS 64-bit
	Kernel	Linux 3.2.0-33 x86_64 SMP
	graphviz (dot)	2.26.3
Phone	Model	HTC Evo 4G (Sprint)
	Firmware	4.54.651.1
	Android	2.3.3
	Radio	2.15.00.0808
	Kernel	Linux 2.6.35.10-g13578ee

Table 1: Configuration for the evaluation

vated after the algorithm has already found at least one assignment (i.e., $\mathcal{R} \neq \emptyset$). With these customization and optimization of the algorithm, DexDiff can handle all the tested binaries in less than three minutes.

2.6 Prototype

We have built a prototype of DexDiff in the C programming language. The prototype has about 13,600 lines of source code in total, of which about two third (9,200 SLOC) is a library to parse the Dex file format [27]. Each component of DexDiff (Figure 1) is multi-threaded. For example, class matcher calculates a matrix of similarity scores for two binaries. It first parses the binary into classes and further converts them into hashes of strings. It then uses multiple threads to calculate the pair-wise similarity between these classes with each thread handling roughly equal number of the class pairs. Other components are similarly multi-threaded.

To facilitate the analyst, outputs of DexDiff are visualized using "dot" [6] to highlight differences between methods and their surrounding context. Figure 3 shows an example output of DexDiff. In this figure, each rectangle represents a basic block, labeled with the index of its first instruction [2]. Matched basic blocks are linked by dotted (red) lines. Filled (blue) basic blocks are different for the two methods. Given the size of the methods (much larger samples exist in our test), it would be highly difficult and error-prone to manual locate these changes, let alone putting them into the correct context.

3. EVALUATION

DexDiff uses an approximation algorithm to solve the NP-complete maximum common subgraph isomorphism problem (Section 2.5). In this section, we first measure the performance of DexDiff to demonstrate its practicality, and then evaluate its effectiveness by systematically studying HTC EVO 4G [34] (for brevity, we will refer to this phone as "the phone" subsequently in this section.)

3.1 Performance Evaluation

To measure the performance of DexDiff, we extracted the sixteen Android files under the /system/framework directory of the phone and built their corresponding counterparts from the Android open source project repository. We use the Linux time command to measure how long it takes for DexDiff to process each pair of these binaries. We repeat each experiment three times and report the average time. The variations between these executions are negligible as the approach is deterministic except for the scheduling of

---

[2]Due to the space constraint, simplified labels are used in Figure 3. The actual labels also include the complete disassembled instructions of the basic block.

policy:	2	javax:	1
core:	3	service:	12
framework:	38	sqlite-jdbc:	1

Table 3: Number of timeouts

multi-threads. All the experiments use eight threads, the same number as the CPU threads. As shown in Table 1, all the experiments were conducted on a desktop machine with a 3.4GHz quad-core Intel Core i7-3770 CPU and 16GB memory. The processor has four (real) cores and each core has two hyper-threads [36], which are treated by Linux as real CPU cores. The results are summarized in Table 2.

These sixteen pairs of Android binaries cover a wide range of file sizes (from a few kilo-bytes to about ten mega-bytes) and numbers of classes (from one to more than five thousands). The execution time accordingly varies from less than 0.01 seconds to about 160 seconds. Notice that the time used by DexDiff is not directly correlated to the binary file size. For example, it takes DexDiff 7.5 times longer to handle framework.dex than core.dex even though the former is only about 30% larger than the latter. This uncertainty is caused by the backtracking algorithm [42], which exhaustively searches for the maximum common isomorphic subgraphs (the n-gram string similarity algorithm and the Hungarian algorithm [57] are both polynomial.) Execution time of backtracking depends heavily on how effective it can eliminate dead branches. To quantify its impact, we run the experiments twice with and without graph comparison. The latter only calculates similarity between two binaries, while the former also compares their structural differences. Their difference roughly equals to the time consumed by graph comparison. The results are shown in Figure 4. For experiments like android.policy.dex and service.dex that have relatively small input files but long processing time, graph comparison monopolies the execution time at around 99%. Also, graph comparison for core.dex takes only a short period because its methods are relatively small and, more importantly, do not have complicated control flows. The last column of Figure 4 shows the average percentages of similarity calculation (29%) and graph comparison (71%).

As mentioned earlier, we set a timeout on the backtracking algorithm (Section 2.5) to limit the total number of recursive calls. We empirically choose one million as the threshold. Larger thresholds fail to effectively reduce timeouts, but also considerably increase the process time. The number of timeouts provides an indication to the relative complexity of the corresponding CFG. For example, service.dex timeouts 12 times during graph comparison, and in total it requires about 160 seconds to complete. Table 3 lists the number of timeouts for all the tests with timeouts. We further examine these 38 cases in framework.dex. The leading causes of timeouts are: (1) large methods with many basic blocks that do not belong to the common subgraph, i.e., many new or deleted basic blocks. These basic blocks may cause discontinuity in the partial result ($\mathcal{M}$), leading the algorithm to hunt for the next continuous part of the subgraph. (2) many identical basic blocks. Some methods repeatedly use the same instruction sequence to perform a series of similar operations (e.g., to initialize a HashMap). These instruction sequences become identical after we remove register references. The algorithm slows down because the possible matches returned by GetMappableNodes contain many equally good choices. (3) nodes with large ingress and egress degrees. In CFG, most basic blocks have 1 or 2 outgoing edges determined by the exit instructions (fall-through, unconditional, or

Name	Base			Phone			Modified		New		Time
	Size	Class#	Method#	Size	Class#	Method#	Class#	Method#	Class#	Method#	
am	25KB	6	38	26K	6	39	1	1	0	1	0.10
policy	179KB	96	833	258K	140	1,200	29	105	44	368	10.23
test.runner	172KB	105	1,001	172K	105	1,002	2	1	0	1	0.17
bmgr	12KB	2	25	14K	2	27	1	2	0	2	0.05
bouncycastle	678KB	507	3,186	677K	507	3,186	31	47	0	0	1.37
location	6.3KB	4	56	6.3K	4	56	0	0	0	0	0.01
core	4.1MB	3,009	27,952	4.1M	3,017	28,093	353	1264	8	141	17.04
core-junit	21KB	19	142	21K	19	142	0	0	0	0	0.05
ext	1.2MB	960	6,896	1.2M	960	6896	209	468	0	0	40.01
framework	6.6MB	3,924	38,283	9.9M	5,423	52,566	1,198	4,556	1,504	14,290	144.70
ime	5.6KB	1	10	5.6K	1	10	0	0	0	0	0.03
input	3.6KB	1	7	3.6K	1	7	0	0	0	0	0.01
javax	53KB	24	164	53K	24	164	2	9	0	0	6.55
monkey	79KB	50	237	76K	50	237	1	1	0	0	0.17
pm	25KB	7	43	25K	7	43	1	2	0	0	0.09
services	1.3MB	437	4,014	1.7M	531	5,153	124	384	95	1,139	159.86
sqlite-jdbc	130KB	29	858	130K	29	858	3	16	0	0	2.49
svc	7KB	6	26	7.3K	6	26	1	1	0	0	0.03

Table 2: **Processing time for files under /system/framework. Note that: (1)the size columns specify the size of the uncompressed** classes.dex **file in the apps. (2) The time reported here is the wall clock time (in seconds) to execute the command. (3) As expected, almost no classes or method are removed from the base.**

conditional) except the switch instruction. However, the number of incoming edges to a basic block is not limited. To make it even worse, the proceeding (or succeeding) nodes to this kind of nodes are likely similar to each other. For example, exception handlers tender to start with a move-exception instruction followed by a goto instruction to jump to a common handler. The backtracking algorithm cannot quickly converge because its dead branch pruning (Line 7) is ineffective in this case.

In addition to limit numbers of recursion, we also constrain its depth to prevent memory depletion because extra memory is allocated for each call. This rule only affects one method during our test, org.ccil.cowan.tagsoup.HTMLSchema.<init>) in ext.dex, which uses 2,859 sequential basic blocks to initialize the HTML schema. Without this rule, the method causes DexDiff to nest too many times because DexDiff performs depth-first search and eventually depletes the memory. We did not encounter any other cases that cause the problem.

3.2 Effectiveness Evaluation

In this section, we demonstrate the effectiveness of our method by reporting the results of auditing the phone. During our audit, we systematically compare the common Android framework files (under /system/framework) and pre-loaded apps (under /system/app) of the phone and its base. The framework should be carefully audited because many of its libraries are loaded into every Dalvik virtual machine and thus accessible to all the apps. Moreover, APIs for propriety services provided by the vendor likely are exposed in one of the framework libraries as well. Table 2 summarizes the vendor's modifications to the framework. Even though these files are about 33 MB in total, one of the authors spent *less than 5 days* to process all of them because DexDiff allows analysts to focus on changes presented in their surrounding context.

Using DexDiff, we find that the vendor's modifications to the framework concentrate on five binaries: android.policy.dex enforces the device security policies such as mandatory screen lock. The vendor customizes this file to change the look and feel of the screen lock and to support its proprietary touch-based stylus;

core.dex contains the core Java language public APIs and other popular Java libraries such as the Apache Harmony library [5]. DexDiff shows that changes to this file are minor and sporadic. Most of these changes seem to come from Google rather than introduced by the vendor. This is possible because DexDiff builds the base according to the Android version reported by the phone. Therefore, our base is likely to be slightly different from the actual base. This difference introduces noise into the system. In Section 4, we will discuss methods to locate or closely approximate the actual base; Changes to ext.dex have the same nature as core.dex. A few new Java libraries are added to ext.dex, such as the open-source NIST SIP stack, Apache logger, and the Apache HTTP library. The vendor extensively customizes framework.dex (the core library of the framework), and services.dex (the host of a number of services such as window manager and activity manager). For example, it adds the 4G and WiMax wireless network support, a proprietary logging facility [50], HTC Pen support, USB-based networking, HDMI and Bluetooth support etc to these files. In the following of this section, we report a number of representative unsafe customization revealed by DexDiff.

Case Study 1: Broadcast Input Services framework.dex is the core library of the Android framework (also the largest one). It is loaded into every Android app, and thus accessible to all the running apps. With DexDiff, we find that three new APIs have been added to android.view.IWindowManager. Their names indicate that they can enable broadcast of input events of the keyboard, touch screen, and trackball:

```
void broadcastKeyinEvent     (boolean);
void broadcastMotionEvent    (boolean);
void broadcastTrackballEvent(boolean);
```

android.view.IWindowManager defines a Java interface to access the Android window manager [24] defined in services. dex. At runtime, all the services in services.dex are hosted in the system_server process thus unreachable to apps directly. Instead, apps need to use inter-process communication (IPC) to access these services. The corresponding implemen-

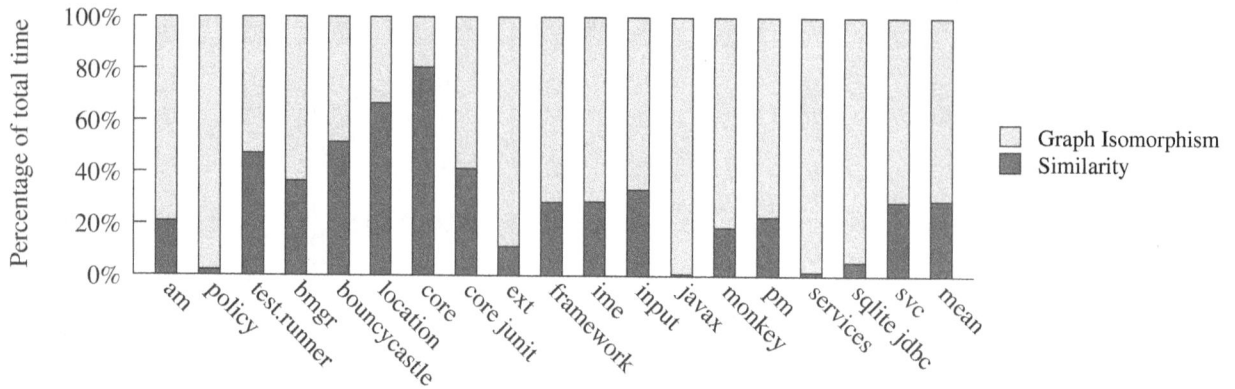

Figure 4: Distribution of processing time between class/method matching and CFG comparison

tation of the `IWindowManager` interface uses IPC to remotely invoke these three methods. Following the leads, DexDiff reveals that three new methods are added to `com.android.server.WindowManagerService` in `services.dex` that will actually enable the broadcast of these input events. If these methods are not guarded by proper permissions, it is a serious security issue since any apps can log user inputs. In the following, we describe how we try to exploit these potentially "rewarding" services and how it leads to the discovery of another vulnerability.

Since these APIs are a part of `framework.dex` and accessible to normal apps, we first try to call them directly. However, these APIs are adequately protected by the vendor-specific permissions, for example, the `com.htc.Manifest.permission.BROADCAST_KEYIN_EVENT` permission is required to call `broadcastKeyinEvent`. In addition, these permissions have the "SIGNATURE" protection level, and thus can only be granted to apps signed by the vendor. Normal apps cannot be granted these permissions. Again, following the leads, we try to audit pre-loaded apps that have these permissions. In this phone, these permissions are only granted to the `com.htc.android.omadm.service` package (/system/app/HtcDm.apk), a proprietary app without a counterpart in the base. Further inspection shows that this app has a plethora of dangerous permissions, for example, `INSTALL_PACKAGES` and `DELETE_PACKAGES` to install and delete apps, `MASTER_CLEAR` to factory-reset the phone, and `HTC_FOTA_UPDATE` to update the firmware. It can also access the Internet with its `INTERNET` permission. We further use DexDiff to generate its CFGs to study its internal. Supposedly, the app is designed to perform remote device management tasks such as wiping the phone in case it is lost or stolen. As such, it can read and execute commands from the IPC interface or the Internet [3]. However, the app has *no* authentication at all on the input. It blindly accepts and executes any commands received from these interfaces. Fortunately (and somewhat ironically), the most dangerous commands such as remotely bricking the phone have not been completely implemented yet. When triggered by our test app, these commands write a log to `logcat` and return an OK status. Nevertheless, we are able to retrieve some private information about the phone such as its device ID and software configuration by exploiting this app. Our

inspection of the app shows that the input broadcast services (e.g., `broadcastKeyinEvent`) are used by the app to intercept user inputs during the firmware update. With the help of DexDiff, we are able to quickly identify this *new* vulnerability.

Case Study 2: CarrierIQ CarrierIQ is a piece of monitoring software tightly integrated into many smartphones. It can be instructed by the manufacturer or the service provider to gather, store, and retrieve diagnostic information (also call metrics) about the phone. The software can provide valuable information to the service provider about user experiences and software reliability. However, the vast array of metrics collected by the software leads to serious privacy concerns [13].

Our test phone is also loaded with the CarrierIQ software. The CarrierIQ agent resides in the `com.htc.android.iqrd` package (/system/app/IQRD.apk). With the help of DexDiff, we find that the base Android system has been extensively modified by the vendor to insert numerous hooks which will notify the agent of interested events. The captured metrics are forwarded to the agent through targeted intents. The phone defines 41 such intents, whose names follow the common pattern of `com.htc.android.iqagent.action.*`. For example, there are 11 UI-related metrics named such as `com.htc.android.iqagent.action.ui01`. The metrics collected by the software are thus meticulously categorized and fine-grained.

The vendor has strategically implanted hooks for the agent all over the phone to capture "a vast array of metrics". As mentioned earlier, the Android framework libraries are loaded into every app or manage data for them(e.g., `services.dex`). Inserting hooks in these libraries allows the vendor to log events for both pre-loaded apps and apps downloaded from the online app store. For example, in `services.dex`, DexDiff uncovers a hook inserted into the `reportLocation` method of `GpsLocationProvider` that can log detailed location information such as longitude, altitude, and heading; another three UI-related metrics are found in `ActivityManagerService` to log events such as process creation, process errors, and process termination. In total, we uncover 6 different types of metrics in `services.dex`, and 19 in `framework.dex`. In addition to general hooks in the framework, specialized hooks are also found in pre-loaded apps as well, particularly, the browser, the dialer, and (surprisingly) the calculator [4].

---

[3]In this version of firmware, the socket interface is disabled by default. But it can easily be enabled by restarting the service and passing it a parameter of `EnableSocket`. A recent firmware update from the vendor enables the socket interface by default.

[4]A hook is inserted into the `com.android.calculator2.CalculatorImageButton.onTouch` method to capture key press events. We suspect this hook is used just for testing.

Hook	Methods (Hooking Points)
callBrowserStopLoading	BrowserActivity.stopLoading
callOnPageStarted	Tab$2.onPageStarted
callOnProgressChanged	Tab$3.onProgressChanged
callOnReceivedError	Tab$2.onReceivedError
callOnReceivedTitle	Tab$3.onReceivedTitle
callReloadPage	BrowserActivity.onOptionsItemSelected BrowserActivity.resumeBrowser BrowserActivity$StopLoadingPageTimer.ResumeLoadingPage htc.ui.HtcTitleBar.onClick
callUserCancel	BrowserActivity.onKeyUp BrowserActivity.onOptionsItemSelected

Table 4: CarrierIQ hooks in the browser (to save space, we omit the common prefix of com.android.browser.htc.util. HTCBrowserIQAgent for the hooks, and com.android.browser for the methods.)

Table 4 lists the Carrier IQ hooks inserted into the browser to log many internal events. This information shows that the Carrier IQ software is intrusive and poses a serious threat to user privacy.

Case Study 3: Firmware Update During our experiments, the phone receives a firmware update that contains "important security updates". To locate what vulnerabilities are patched in this release, we upgrade the phone to the new release and compare it to the old one with DexDiff. The major change turns out to be the removal of the Carrier IQ software from the phone. Using DexDiff, we confirm that the agent and most of the hooks have been deleted from the phone. However, the hook in Calculator.apk has been missed and remains in the file. Also, vulnerabilities we discovered in HtcDm.apk have not been fixed while new functionality is added to it (hence more information can be leaked). The new firmware is based on a newer version of Android, which contains several security fixes. For example, the firmware adds the previously-missing capability to validate certificates against the PKI revocation list in org.bouncycastle.jce.provider. PKIXCertPathValidatorSpi.engineValidate.

3.3 Side-loaded App Verification

In a recent update to Android Jelly Bean (4.2.0), Google introduces the capability to scan side-loaded apps (i.e., apps installed from places other than the official app store) for malware. We use DexDiff to study how the side-loaded app verification is implemented. We find out that before side-loading an app, the app installer broadcasts an android.intent.action.PACKAGE_ NEEDS_VERIFICATION intent to any apps providing the app verification service (e.g., the Google play app). To understand how the apps are verified by Google play, we use DexDiff to compare two versions of the app: version 3.8.17 from Jelly Bean 4.1.2, and version 3.9.16 from Jelly Bean 4.2.0. In the latter version of the app, a new Java package (com.google.android.vending.verifier) has been added. Instead of scanning the app locally, the verifier sends the identifying information of the app (e.g., package name, SHA256 hash, and origin, etc) to a remote server, and then receives a verdict from the server, similar to virustotal [54].

4. DISCUSSION

In this section, we discuss potential improvements to our system. First, DexDiff assumes that the official Android system is relatively safe and thus focuses on studying security of vendor customization. As demonstrated by previous and our own research, vendors tend to introduce subtle but serious vulnerabilities into the system through aggressive customization [13,19,29]. In this case, DexDiff provides

a valuable comparative approach to audit the vendor customization. Nevertheless, the official Android could be vulnerable as well [40]. There have been a long stream of research that can be applied to improve security of Android [7, 10, 15, 17, 29, 31, 45, 59]. These systems and DexDiff have difference focuses and complement each other. For example, they can be used to scrutinize pre-loaded apps and libraries that do not have a counterpart in the official system. Moreover, although our experiment used a relatively old phone to demonstrate the effectiveness of our approach, the approach itself is generic and can be readily applied to newer phones and phones made by other manufacturers.

Second, like other similar systems, DexDiff makes various trade-offs between accuracy and in the design that may affect its effectiveness in some specific cases. For example, DexDiff ignores registers in the bytecode. This mitigates the impact of register allocation of the Java and Dex compiler. However, some basic blocks can only be distinguished by registers. Ignoring registers makes these basic blocks indistinguishable. Similarly, DexDiff does not take edge labels into consideration when comparing two CFGs. This improves the system's tolerance to control flow type changes, but may be less accurate for some structures (e.g., the switch statement). Moreover, DexDiff utilizes Hungarian algorithm [57] to find an optimal assignment of classes and methods that maximizes the overall similarity. This optimizes global similarity but might not produce best-match for individual classes or methods. For example, assuming we have two binary files with classes A, B and A', B', the similarity between AA', AB', BA' and BB' are 100%, 80%, 80%, and 50%, respectively. With Hungarian algorithm, DexDiff will assign A to B', and B to A' (a total of 160%). However, the best match for A is instead A' (100%). In addition, DexDiff uses n-gram similarity to match classes and methods before comparing CFGs. This improves the scalability and efficiency of DexDiff by avoiding pairwise graph comparison for all the CFGs, but it might be less flexible if methods are "cut-and-pasted" across classes. Although we did not encounter such cases during our experiment, the issue can be mitigated by comparing a class to several most similar classes, instead of the only class returned by class matching.

Third, DexDiff compares two Android binary files at the bytecode level. We choose this approach because most of pre-loaded apps in a third-party phone are close-sourced due to their liberal license models (except for the GPL-licensed Linux kernel). Alternatively, we could first de-compile the apps/libraries and compare them against the base [16]. The same technologies in our paper (similarity and graph isomorphism) can be easily adapted to compare the de-compiled Java source code. On the other hand, the usefulness of our system is not constrained by it because Dalvik bytecode contains adequate semantic information about the app.

Fourth, in its current form, DexDiff uses a simple method to locate the phone's base. Differences between the located and the actual base introduce noise into the system. It is desirable for the located base to be as close to the actual base as possible. We can use the fingerprinting technique to improve the accuracy in locating the base. Specifically, for each possible base (i.e., tags in the AOSP repository near the phone's reported version), we select a few unique changes as its fingerprint, and then try to locate (part of) the fingerprint in the phone. The phone's closest base is the most recent possible base whose fingerprint exists in the phone's software. Binary search can be used to accelerate the process.

Finally, DexDiff is a tool to pinpoint differences between two Android binary files. It can provide valuable inputs to (external) security analysts. However, it does not understand semantics of these differences. Much of the vulnerability identification still relies on human efforts and experiences. In the future, we plan to extend DexDiff with (some) automatic vulnerability detection capabilities to further reduce manual efforts.

5. RELATED WORK

Smartphone Security: the first area of related work is recent efforts in understanding and protecting security and privacy in mobile phones. Many systems have focused on detecting threats on the smartphone platforms. For example, TaintDroid [15] and PiOS [14] apply dynamic taint tracking [52] and static data-flow analysis to identify privacy leaks in Android and iOS apps, respectively. Stowaway [17] uses automated testing tools to map Android APIs to permissions, and then detects permission over-privilege for apps. PScout [7] analyzes the design and implementation of the Android permission systems. DexDiff focuses on analyzing security of customization made by the third-party manufacturers. ComDroid [10], Felt *et al.* [19], Woodpecker [29], and CHEX [45] employ static program analysis to detect confused-deputy [32] problems (or capability leaks) in Android apps. We also identified a similar problem in a pre-loaded system app with the help of DexDiff. Both Woodpecker [29] and DexDiff target pre-loaded apps and libraries, but have different focuses and approaches. Droid-MOSS [59] and Juxtapp [31] are two closely related systems. They apply fuzzy-hashing and feature-hashing, respectively, based code similarity to detect repackaged Android apps. In addition to leveraging code similarity to match classes and methods, DexDiff further reveals structural differences between matched methods by comparing their control flow graphs. Our system thus provides more fine-grained differences of two apps, which benefits security audit more than a binary verdict of similar or not. Moreover, WHY-PER [47] uses natural language processing to automatically assess the risk of mobile applications.

There are also various works focusing on malware detection of individual apps or the Android markets [16,18,23,30,60,61]. Enck *et al.* [16] decompile Android apps and applies Java-based program analysis to detect security issues in Android apps. DexDiff instead works directly on the Android binaries. However, our solution is not constrained by this because Dalvik bytecode contains rich type information. Moreover, the same techniques in DexDiff can be applied to compare Java source code. The MalGenome project [60] characterizes existing Android malware families to study their evolving trend. DroidRanger [61] applies behavioral pattern matching to detect malware in Android markets.

From another perspective, many works propose effective ways to enhance security of Android systems: QUIRE [12] and Felt *et al.* [19] allow apps to inspect the IPC call chain and, if necessary,

drop privileges that the caller lacks to prevent the confused-deputy attack; AdDroid [48], AdSplit [53], APEX [46], AppFence [33], and TISSA [62] extend the Android system to fine-tune app's access to private information. For example, AdDroid [48] and Ad-Split [53] separate the in-app advertisement libraries from the host app so privileges can be granted differently for them. Cells [4] and L4Android [44] build efficient virtualization platforms for Android, allowing multiple virtual phones to securely run on a single physical device, isolated from each other. While all these systems enhance the Android system security, DexDiff has a different goal of detecting unsafe manufacturer customization. They can be naturally combined to provide defense-in-depth.

Code Similarity and Binary Diff: the second area of related work includes systems to detect code similarity and compare binary files. Code similarity has been employed in various security applications such as malware classification [35,38], code plagiarism detection [8,51], (unpatched) code clone detection [37,39,41], and Android repackaged app detection [31,59]. For example, Bit-Shred [38] leverages feature hashing based code similarity analysis to enable large-scale malware triage and clustering. ReDeBug [37] uses feature hashing to quickly detect unpatched code clones in large code bases. MOSS proposes a technique called winnowing based on fuzzy hashing to generate fingerprints for documents (including source code). MOSS is a popular tool to detect plagiarism in programming assignments. In comparison, DexDiff additionally provides structural differences for two Android binaries as required by our goal.

Binary diff has been used widely to analyze malware, vulnerabilities, and improve (or exploit) patches. For example, BinDiff [20] compares two binaries by using heuristics to identity a common isomorphic subgraph. In comparison, DexDiff extends the backtracking algorithm to construct more reliable maximum common subgraphs. BinHunt [21] is a closely related system. It uniquely leverages symbolic execution to semantically compare basic blocks and then uses the backtracking framework to compare two x86 binaries. DexDiff instead targets the Android binaries. It applies code similarity to first coarsely classify classes and methods, saving the expensive graph isomorphism only for CFG comparison. We adapt backtracking for Android binaries as well to make the exhaustive algorithm practical for even large Android binaries. Given a vulnerable program and its patched version, Brumley *et al.* [9] propose to automatically generate exploits that target essential differences between these two versions of the program. There are also binary update tools (e.g., bsdiff & bspatch [49] and Courgette [28]) that generate and apply patches in binary differences. Patches produced by these tools have substantially smaller size, thus improving efficiency and timeliness of patch distribution. Courgette (also known as Google update) is more efficient than bsdiff by first transforming the programs into an intermediate format in which binary diffing is more effective. However, these tools do not provide capabilities required by Android binary auditing.

6. SUMMARY

Android has become the leading mobile platform due to the wide availability of third-party Android phones. To differentiate their products, vendors often deeply customize their phones, leading to vulnerabilities that do not exist in the official Android system. In this paper, we propose to systematically audit vendor customization by comparing the phone side-by-side to its base. To facilitate these efforts, we designed DexDiff, a system that can pinpoint fine structural differences of two Android binaries and further present them in the surrounding context. DexDiff allows external security analysts (without source code access) to focus on modifications that are more likely to introduce vulnerabilities. It first coarsely matches classes and methods in the input Android binaries with n-gram based code similarity, and then generates fine-grained structural comparisons by identifying the maximum common isomorphic subgraphs of the CFGs for each pair of matched methods. We have built a prototype of DexDiff and applied it to a popular commodity Android phone. Our evaluation demonstrates that DexDiff is efficient, scalable, and effective in identifying unsafe vendor customization.

7. ACKNOWLEDGEMENTS

We would like to thank the anonymous reviewers for their insightful comments that helped to improve the presentation of this paper. We also want to thank Yajin Zhou, Gary Tyson, and Xuxian Jiang for the helpful discussion. This work was supported in part by the First Year Assistant Professor award of Florida State University. Any opinions, findings, and conclusions or recommendations expressed in this material are those of the authors and do not necessarily reflect the views of FSU.

8. REFERENCES

[1] An Assembler/Disassembler for Android's dex Format. http://code.google.com/p/smali/.

[2] Subgraph Isomorphism Problem. http://en.wikipedia.org/wiki/Subgraph_isomorphism_problem.

[3] Alfred V. Aho, Monica S. Lam, Ravi Sethi, and Jeffrey D. Ullman. *Compilers: Principles, Techniques, and Tools*. Prentice Hall, 2006.

[4] Jeremy Andrus, Christoffer Dall, Alexander Van't Hof, Oren Laadan, and Jason Nieh. Cells: a Virtual Mobile Smartphone Architecture. In *Proceedings of the 23rd SOSP*, 2011.

[5] Apache. Apache Harmony: Open Source Java Platform. http://harmony.apache.org/.

[6] AT&T. Graphviz - Graph Visualization Software. http://www.graphviz.org/.

[7] Kathy Wain Yee Au, Yi Fan Zhou, Zhen Huang, and David Lie. PScout: Analyzing the Android Permission Specification. In *Proceedings of the 19th ACM CCS*, 2012.

[8] Brenda S. Baker. Deducing Similarities in Java Sources from Bytecodes. In *Proceedings of the 1998 USENIX ATC*, 1998.

[9] David Brumley, Pongsin Poosankam, Dawn Song, and Jiang Zheng. Automatic Patch-Based Exploit Generation is Possible: Techniques and Implications. In *Proceedings of the 29th IEEE S&P*, 2008.

[10] Erika Chin, Adrienne Porter Felt, Kate Greenwood, and David Wagner. Analyzing Inter-Application Communication in Android. In *Proceedings of the 9th ACM MobiSys*, 2011.

[11] Anthony Desnos. androguard:Reverse engineering, Malware and goodware analysis of Android applications ... and more (ninja !). https://code.google.com/p/androguard/.

[12] Michael Dietz, Shashi Shekhar, Yuliy Pisetsky, Anhei Shu, and Dan S. Wallach. QUIRE: Lightweight Provenance for Smart Phone Operating Systems. In *Proceedings of the 20th USENIX Security Symposium*, 2011.

[13] Trevor Eckhart. CarrierIQ. http://androidsecuritytest.com/features/logs-and-services/loggers/carrieriq/.

[14] Manuel Egele, Christopher Kruegel, Engin Kirda, and Giovanni Vigna. PiOS: Detecting Privacy Leaks in iOS Applications. In *Proceedings of the 18th NDSS*, 2011.

[15] William Enck, Peter Gilbert, Byung-Gon Chun, Landon P. Cox, Jaeyeon Jung, Patrick McDaniel, and Anmol N. Sheth. TaintDroid: an Information-flow Tracking System for Realtime Privacy Monitoring on Smartphones. In *Proceedings of 9th USENIX OSDI*, 2010.

[16] William Enck, Damien Octeau, Patrick McDaniel, and Swarat Chaudhuri. A Study of Android Application Security. In *Proceedings of the 20th USENIX Security Symposium*, 2011.

[17] Adrienne Porter Felt, Erika Chin, Steve Hanna, Dawn Song, and David Wagner. Android Permissions Demystified. In *Proceedings of the 18th ACM CCS*, 2011.

[18] Adrienne Porter Felt, Matthew Finifter, Erika Chin, Steve Hanna, and David Wagner. A Survey of Mobile Malware in the Wild. In *Proceedings of the 1st ACM SPSM*, 2011.

[19] Adrienne Porter Felt, Helen J. Wang, Alexander Moshchuk, Steven Hanna, and Erika Chin. Permission Re-Delegation: Attacks and Defenses. In *Proceedings of the 20th USENIX Security Symposium*, 2011.

[20] Halvar Flake. Structural Comparison of Executable Objects. In *Proceedings of the 1st DIMVA*, 2004.

[21] Debin Gao, Michael K. Reiter, and Dawn Song. BinHunt: Automatically Finding Semantic Differences in Binary Programs. In *Proceedings of the 10th ICICS*, 2008.

[22] Gartner. Gartner Says Worldwide Sales of Mobile Phones Declined 2.3 Percent in Second Quarter of 2012. http://www.gartner.com/it/page.jsp?id=2120015.

[23] Peter Gilbert, Byung-Gon Chun, Landon P. Cox, and Jaeyeon Jung. Vision: Automated Security Validation of Mobile Apps at App Markets. In *Proceedings of the second international workshop on Mobile cloud computing and services*, 2011.

[24] Google. Android Developers. http://developer.android.com.

[25] Google. Android Device Gallery. http://www.android.com/devices/?f=phone.

[26] Google. Android Open Source Project. http://source.android.com.

[27] Google. Dalvik Technical Information. http://source.android.com/tech/dalvik/.

[28] Google. Software Updates: Courgette. http://dev.chromium.org/developers/design-documents/software-updates-courgette.

[29] Michael Grace, Yajin Zhou, Zhi Wang, and Xuxian Jiang. Systematic Detection of Capability Leaks in Stock Android Smartphones. In *Proceedings of the 19th NDSS*, 2012.

[30] Michael Grace, Yajin Zhou, Qiang Zhang, Shihong Zou, and Xuxian Jiang. RiskRanker: Scalable and Accurate Zero-day Android Malware Detection. In *Proceedings of the 10th ACM MobiSys*, 2012.

[31] Steve Hanna, Ling Huang, Edward Wu, Saung Li, Charles Chen, and Dawn Song. Juxtapp: A Scalable System for Detecting Code Reuse Among Android Applications. In *Proceedings of the 9th DIMVA*, 2012.

[32] Norman Hardy. The Confused Deputy: (or why capabilities might have been invented). *ACM SIGOPS Operating Systems Review*, 22, October 1998.

[33] Peter Hornyack, Seungyeop Han, Jaeyeon Jung, Stuart Schechter, and David Wetherall. These Aren't the Droids You're Looking For: Retrofitting Android to Protect Data from Imperious Applications. In *Proceedings of the 18th ACM CCS*, 2011.

[34] HTC. HTC EVO 4G. http://www.htc.com/us/smartphones/htc-evo-4g-sprint/.

[35] Xin Hu, Tzi cker Chiueh, and Kang G. Shin. Large-Scale Malware Indexing Using Function-Call Graphs. In *Proceedings of the 16th ACM CCS*, 2009.

[36] Intel. Intel 64 and IA-32 Architectures Software Developer Manuals. August 2012.

[37] Jiyong Jang, Abeer Agrawal, and David Brumley. ReDeBug: Finding Unpatched Code Clones in Entire OS Distributions. In *Proceedings of the 33rd IEEE S&P*, 2012.

[38] Jiyong Jang, David Brumley, and Shobha Venkataraman. BitShred: Feature Hashing Malware for Scalable Triage and Semantic Analysis. In *Proceedings of the 18th ACM CCS*, 2011.

[39] Lingxiao Jiang, Ghassan Misherghi, Zhendong Su, and Stephane Glondu. DECKARD: Scalable and Accurate Tree-Based Detection of Code Clones. In *Proceedings of the 29th ICSE*, 2007.

[40] Xuxian Jiang. SEND_SMS Capability Leak in Android Open Source Project (AOSP), Affecting Gingerbread, Ice Cream Sandwich, and Jelly Bean. `http://www.cs.ncsu.edu/faculty/jiang/send_sms_leak.html`.

[41] Toshihiro Kamiya, Shinji Kusumoto, and Katsuro Inoue. CCFinder: a Multilinguistic Token-based Code Clone Detection System for Large Scale Source Code. *IEEE Transactions on Software Engineering*, 2002.

[42] Evgeny B. Krissinel and Kim Henrick. Common Subgraph Isomorphism Detection by Backtracking Search. *Software–Practice & Experience*, 2004.

[43] Eric Lafortune. ProGuard. `http://proguard.sourceforge.net/`.

[44] Matthias Lange, Steffen Liebergeld, Adam Lackorzynski, Alexander Warg, and Michael Peter. L4Android: A Generic Operating System Framework for Secure Smartphones. In *Proceedings of the 1st ACM SPSM*, 2011.

[45] Long Lu, Zhichun Li, Zhenyu Wu, Wenke Lee, and Guofei Jiang. CHEX: Statically Vetting Android Apps for Component Hijacking Vulnerabilities. In *Proceedings of the 19th ACM CCS*, 2012.

[46] Mohammad Nauman, Sohail Khan, and Xinwen Zhang. Apex: Extending Android Permission Model and Enforcement with User-Defined Runtime Constraints. In *Proceedings of the 5th ACM ASIACCS*, 2010.

[47] Rahul Pandita, Xusheng Xiao, Wei Yang, William Enck, and Tao Xie. WHYPER: Towards Automating Risk Assessment of Mobile Applications. In *Proceedings of the 22th USENIX Security Symposium*, 2013.

[48] Paul Pearce, Adrienne Porter Felt, Gabriel Nunez, and David Wagner. AdDroid: Privilege Separation for Applications and Advertisers in Android. In *Proceedings of the 7th ACM ASIACCS*, 2012.

[49] Colin Percival. Naive Differences of Executable Code. `http://www.daemonology.net/bsdiff/`.

[50] Artem Russakovskii. Massive Security Vulnerability In HTC Android Devices (EVO 3D, 4G, Thunderbolt, Others) Exposes Phone Numbers, GPS, SMS, Emails Addresses, Much More. `http://www.androidpolice.com/2011/10/01/massive-security-vulnerability-in-htc-android-devices-evo-3d-4g-thunderbolt-others-exposes-phone-numbers-gps-sms-emails-addresses-much-more`.

[51] Saul Schleimer, Daniel S. Wilkerson, and Alex Aiken. Winnowing: Local Algorithms for Document Fingerprinting. In *Proceedings of the 2003 ACM SIGMOD*, 2003.

[52] Edward J. Schwartz, Thanassis Avgerinos, and David Brumley. All You Ever Wanted to Know About Dynamic Taint Analysis and Forward Symbolic Execution (but might have been afraid to ask). In *Proceedings of the 31rd IEEE S&P*, 2010.

[53] Shashi Shekhar, Michael Dietz, and Dan S. Wallach. AdSplit: Separating smartphone advertising from applications. In *Proceedings of the 21th USENIX Security Symposium*, 2012.

[54] VirusTotal. VirusTotal - Free Online Virus, Malware and URL Scanner. `http://www.virustotal.com/`.

[55] Wikipedia. Assignment Problem. `http://en.wikipedia.org/wiki/Assignment_problem`.

[56] Wikipedia. Feature Hashing. `http://en.wikipedia.org/wiki/Feature_hashing`.

[57] Wikipedia. Hungarian algorithm. `http://en.wikipedia.org/wiki/Hungarian_algorithm`.

[58] Allan Wojciechowski. DexDiff. `https://github.com/allanwoj/DexDiff`.

[59] Wu Zhou, Yajin Zhou, Xuxian Jiang, and Peng Ning. DroidMOSS: Detecting Repackaged Smartphone Applications in Third-Party Android Marketplaces. In *Proceedings of the 2nd ACM CODASPY*, 2012.

[60] Yajin Zhou and Xuxian Jiang. Dissecting Android Malware: Characterization and Evolution. In *Proceedings of the 33rd IEEE S&P*, 2012.

[61] Yajin Zhou, Zhi Wang, Wu Zhou, and Xuxian Jiang. Hey, You, Get off of My Market: Detecting Malicious Apps in Official and Alternative Android Markets. In *Proceedings of the 19th NDSS*, 2012.

[62] Yajin Zhou, Xinwen Zhang, Xuxian Jiang, and Vincent W. Freeh. Taming Information-Stealing Smartphone Applications (on Android). In *Proceedings of the 4th International Conference on Trust and Trustworthy Computing*, 2011.

PREC: Practical Root Exploit Containment for Android Devices

Tsung-Hsuan Ho, Daniel Dean, Xiaohui Gu, William Enck
Department of Computer Science
North Carolina State University
{tho,djdean2}@ncsu.edu, {gu,enck}@cs.ncsu.edu

ABSTRACT

Application markets such as the Google Play Store and the Apple App Store have become the *de facto* method of distributing software to mobile devices. While official markets dedicate significant resources to detecting malware, state-of-the-art malware detection can be easily circumvented using logic bombs or checks for an emulated environment. We present a Practical Root Exploit Containment (PREC) framework that protects users from such conditional malicious behavior. PREC can dynamically identify system calls from high-risk components (e.g., third-party native libraries) and execute those system calls within isolated threads. Hence, PREC can detect and stop root exploits with high accuracy while imposing low interference to benign applications. We have implemented PREC and evaluated our methodology on 140 most popular benign applications and 10 root exploit malicious applications. Our results show that PREC can successfully detect and stop all the tested malware while reducing the false alarm rates by more than one order of magnitude over traditional malware detection algorithms. PREC is light-weight, which makes it practical for runtime on-device root exploit detection and containment.

Categories and Subject Descriptors

D.4.6 [**Operating Systems**]: Security and Protection—*Invasive software (e.g., viruses, worms, Trojan horses)*; D.2.5 [**Software Engineering**]: Testing and Debugging

Keywords

Android, Host Intrusion Detection, Dynamic Analysis, Malware, Root Exploit

1. INTRODUCTION

Popular application markets (e.g., Apple's App Store, and the Google Play Store) [13, 54] have become a boon for users and developers, but they also provide a distribution point for malware. While markets perform malware analysis

(e.g., Bouncer [39]), dynamic analysis environments can be easily detected by malware or avoided using logic bombs and checks for emulation [20, 24, 44]. Thus, it is necessary to provide on-device malware containment that can detect and stop the malware during runtime.

We observe that the dynamic malware analysis performed by application markets provides an opportunity to obtain a *normal behavior model* for an application. In effect, this forces malware authors to *commit* to a behavior during market malware analysis. Therefore, we can use online anomaly detection and malware containment to protect the user from the malware that uses logic bombs or attempts to change execution based on an emulated environment.

The primary challenges in making runtime root exploit containment practical are achieving a low false alarm rate [18] and imposing low interference to benign applications. We address those challenges using two novel techniques. First, we propose a *classified system call monitoring* scheme that can separate system calls based on their origins (e.g., the library that initiates the system call). Thus, we can dynamically identify system calls originated from high-risk components such as third-party native libraries (i.e., native libraries that are not included in the Android system libraries but are downloaded with applications from the app market). Since less than 10% of benign applications include third-party native code [31], the majority of benign applications will have zero false alarms using our scheme. Second, we propose a *delay-based fine-grained containment* mechanism that executes the anomalous system calls using a pool of separate threads, and slows them down exponentially to defeat the attack. The rationale behind our approach is that address space layout randomization (ASLR) in Android [6] forces exploits to repeat the attack sequence many times in order to guess the right stack address. Moreover, most existing root exploits (e.g., Rage Against the Cage) use resource exhaustion attacks (e.g., continuously forking). By slowing down the malicious activity, the exploit becomes unsuccessful and often results in an Application Not Responding (ANR) status, which causes the Android system to kill the malicious application.

In this paper, we present the Practical Root Exploit Containment (PREC) framework to achieve on-device malware containment. We specifically focus on malware that exploits root privilege escalation vulnerabilities. This type of malware represents the highest risk for smartphones, because root access enables the greatest amount of malicious functionality, allows for hiding its existence, and makes the malware difficult to remove [31]. Figure 1 depicts the overall

PREC architecture. PREC operates in two phases: 1) offline learning when a developer submits an app into the market; and 2) online enforcement when the user downloads and installs the app.

When a developer submits an app into the market, the market server (e.g., Google's Bouncer) runs the app within a controlled emulator, performing comprehensive malware detection using a combination of signature detection and dynamic analysis. If the application contains malicious functionality, the market dynamic analysis will detect it and reject the malicious application. However, as mentioned earlier, malware authors often attempt to evade the malware detection system using logic bombs or by not executing malicious code when running in a dynamic analysis environment. This is where PREC provides contribution by forcing the app to commit to a normal behavior.

During dynamic malware analysis, PREC records and labels a system call trace based on our classified monitoring criteria. For this work, PREC labels each system call as originating either from third-party native code or from Java code. We use the third-party native code as the classifying criteria, because it is more risky than Java code or system libraries: 1) all existing malware that exploits root privilege escalation vulnerabilities uses third-party native code; 2) low-level system APIs required by the root exploits are often not available to Java code; and 3) program analysis of third-party native code is significantly more difficult than Java code or system libraries, therefore most malware analysis tools to date ignore third-party native code.

Once system calls are labeled by PREC, it creates a normal behavior model for the app. The normal behavior model is sent to the PREC service that could be hosted within a computing cloud. When choosing a model to represent the normal behavior of an application, we considered several factors such as accuracy, overhead, and robustness to mimicry attacks. After examining several common models such as the hidden Markov model (HMM) and finite state automata (FSA), we developed a new lightweight and robust behavior learning scheme based on the self-organizing map (SOM) technique [35, 23]. SOM is robust to noise in system calls by projecting a high dimensional space (noisy system call sequences) into a two-dimensional map that still captures the principal normal patterns. Moreover, SOM is significantly less computation-intensive than most other learning methods such as HMM.

Ideally, the normal behavior model should be comprehensive in order to avoid false alarms. PREC currently uses a random input fuzz testing tool [11] to create the per-app normal behavior model. Alternatively, app developers can submit an input trace for PREC if a more precise model is desired. Note that PREC is a general behavior learning framework, which can work with any input testing tools or user provided input traces. Our experiments show that using the simple input fuzz testing tool, PREC can already produce high quality behavior models for most of the real Android apps.

The enforcement phase uses the normal behavior model from the PREC service to perform on-device anomaly detection and malware containment. Therefore, PREC dynamically identifies system calls from the third-party native code and performs anomaly detection only on system calls that originate in third-party native code. Monitoring only

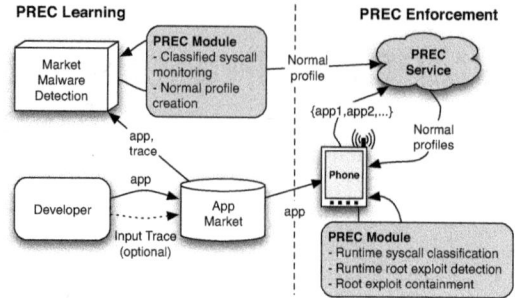

Figure 1: **Overview of the PREC architecture. When the developer submits an app to the app market, the market performs extensive malware detection in a controlled emulator. If the app is detected as malware, it is rejected. If not, a normal execution profile is saved and forwarded to the PREC service. When a smartphone user downloads an app, the normal execution profile is retrieved. PREC then monitors operation and contains root exploits on the phone.**

third-party native code significantly reduces false alarms of runtime root privilege escalation attack detection.

This paper makes the following contributions:

- We present an architecture for mitigating root exploit malware that hides its existence during dynamic analysis. Our approach forces malware to commit to a normal behavior during market dynamic analysis and malicious attacks are detected and stopped at runtime.

- We describe a runtime, kernel-level, system call origin identification mechanism that allows us to build *fine-grained* behavior models (i.e., third-party native code behaviors v.s. java code behaviors) for higher anomaly detection accuracy and practical malware containment.

- We provide a scalable and robust behavior learning and anomaly detection scheme using the self-organizing map (SOM) learning algorithm [35] that can achieve both high accuracy and low overhead.

We have implemented PREC and evaluated our methodology on 140 most popular benign applications (80 with native code and 60 without native code) covering all different application categories and 10 root exploit malware (4 known root exploit applications from the Malware Genome project [59] and 6 repackaged root exploit applications). Our experiments show that PREC can successfully detect and stop all the tested root exploits. More importantly, PREC achieves practicability by 1) raising 0 false alarm on the benign applications without native code. In contrast, traditional schemes without our classified system call monitoring raise 67-92% per-app false alarms; and 2) reducing the false alarm rate on the benign applications with native code by more than one orders of magnitude over traditional anomaly detection algorithms: from 100% per-app false alarm rate (FSA) and 78% per-app false alarm rate (HMM) to 3.75% per-app false alarm rate (PREC). Since less than 10% apps over the whole market have third-party native code [31], we expect the false alarm rate for PREC will be very low in practice. Our delay-based fine-grained containment scheme can not only defeat all the tested root exploit attacks but also minimize the false alarm impact to the benign applications. Our experiments show that PREC imposes noticeable false alarm impact to

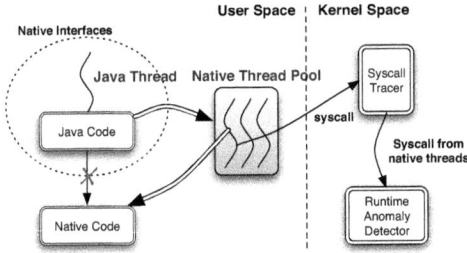

Figure 2: Thread-based system call origin identification. When a third-party native function is called, we dynamically choose a thread from a pool of special "native threads" to execute the function.

only 1 out of 140 tested popular benign applications. PREC is light-weight, which only imposes less than 3% runtime execution overhead on the smartphone device.

2. DESIGN AND IMPLEMENTATION

In this section, we present the design and implementation details of the PREC system. We first describe the system call origin identification scheme. We then describe our on-device root exploit detection schemes. Finally, we present our automatic root exploit containment scheme.

2.1 System Call Origin Identification

PREC performs *classified* system call monitoring by separating the system calls originated from high risk third-party native code from the system calls issued by the less dangerous Java code. However, we cannot simply look at the return address of the code that invokes the system call, because both Java code and third-party native code use system-provided native libraries (e.g., libc) to invoke system calls.

Performing user-space stack unwinding from the kernel is one option to understand program components on the call path. However, such backtrace information resides in the user-space and therefore, needs to be well protected. Furthermore, most system libraries do not include debug information (e.g., DWARF [4] or EXIDX [5]) that is needed to unwind the stack.

Another simple approach is to have the Dalvik VM notify the kernel when a thread switches to third-party native code. The kernel can then maintain a flag in the corresponding thread structure in the kernel space. Then, when the native function returns, the Dalvik VM notifies the kernel to clear the flag. This approach makes labeling easy; however it is vulnerable to a confused deputy attack. That is, the kernel cannot determine if it is the Dalvik VM that requested the flag to be unset or a malicious third-party native code.

In light of these limitations, we propose a thread-based approach to identify the system call origins. The basic idea is to maintain a pool of special threads called *native threads* and execute all the third-party native functions using those native threads as shown in Figure 2. Functions executed in these threads are monitored without exception. Malicious code cannot change a native thread to a normal thread. No direct communication is needed between the Dalvik VM and kernel since the pool of native threads are created by PREC at application launch time. Thus, our approach is not vulnerable to the confused deputy attack. Furthermore, the code logic for determining the switching between native

threads and java threads is in Dalvik VM which Android ensures is read-only to the application process [1]. Thus, the malicious attacker cannot bypass the switching from java threads to native threads in order to execute the third-party native code.

We build our system call tracer as a Linux kernel module on top of kprobes. Kprobes are a set of Linux interfaces that allow us to implant probes and register corresponding handlers. Compared to user space system call tracers (e.g., ptrace [7]) that can introduce over 20% overhead due to frequent context switches, our kernel tracer only incurs less than 2% overhead. PREC could also use other kernel space system call tracing tools such as SystemTap [10], DTrace [3], or Linux Trace Toolkit - next generation (LTTng) [8] that are orthogonal to our approach.

Our system call origin identification scheme leverages the natural boundary between Java code and native code. Android allows Java components to access native binaries (including both libraries and executables) in three different ways. First, Java components can use the JNI Bridge to call native functions. The JNI Bridge is the aggregation point that maps Java abstract native function names (i.e., static native function appeared in Java code) to real native function addresses. Second, when the Java code requires a native library to be loaded, System.loadLibrary() will load the native library to the memory and then call the JNI_OnLoad() callback in the library. Since JNI_OnLoad() is defined by the developer of the native library, it can be used by an adversary to execute native code. Lastly, Java allows applications to use System.Runtime.exec() to execute native executables. This function is the best place for attackers to apply root privilege escalation attacks because most exploits are released as native executables. For the rest of this paper, we use *native interfaces* to represent different ways to invoke third-party native functions.

When a Java thread needs to invoke a third-party native function through one of the aforementioned native interfaces, PREC is triggered to suspend the Java thread and use a native thread to execute the native function instead. One brute force implementation is to create a new native thread each time the native function is invoked. However, this simple implementation suffers from high performance overhead when the application frequently invokes native functions. Instead, PREC creates a pool of native threads at application launch. When a Java thread needs to execute a third-party native function, we suspend the Java thread and dynamically select an idle native thread to execute the native function. The native function sometimes calls back to the Java code (e.g., NewStringUTF(), which is a function that creates a Java string inside the Java heap). Under those circumstances, we continue use the native thread to execute the Java function because it might be a potential attack to Java components. When the native function exits, we resume the Java thread and recycle the native thread.

Our thread-based system call origin identification scheme has several advantages over other alternatives. First, the kernel tracer can easily identify the system call origins (i.e., from Java or native components) by checking whether the thread belongs to the native thread pool. Second, the thread-based approach allows us to isolate a small portion of the application rather than kill the whole application. This allows us to reduce the disturbance to the user by minimizing the containment scope. We will describe our containment

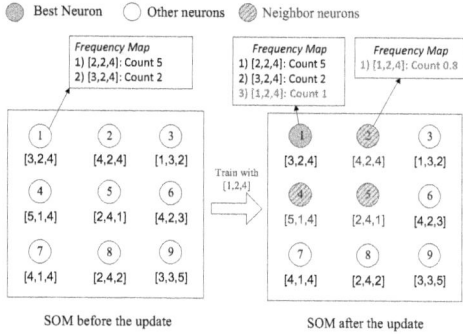

Figure 3: SOM update example using the input vector [1,2,4].

scheme in Section 2.3. Third, PREC can easily incorporate other execution sandboxing mechanisms (e.g., software fault isolation [57]) to provide additional security isolations between Java code and malicious native code.

2.2 On-Device Root Exploit Detection

After we extract the system calls from the high-risk native code, we need to build a normal behavior model for the app before it is released to the market. The behavior model is then transferred to the smartphone device for runtime root exploit detection.

Normal app behavior learning. We capture the normal behavior of each application during the market dynamic malware analysis. As mentioned in the Introduction, we develop a new lightweight and robust behavior learning scheme based on the self-organizing map (SOM) technique [35]. Our previous work [23] has used SOM to train a system behavior model using system-level metrics such as CPU usage and memory consumption. To the best of our knowledge, this work makes the first step in applying SOM to system call sequences.

SOM is a type of artificial neural network that is trained using unsupervised learning to map the input space of the training data into a low dimensional (usually two dimensions) map space. Each map consists of $n \times m$ nodes called *neurons* arranged in a grid, illustrated by Figure 3. Each neuron is associated with a *weight vector* that has the same length as the input vector. In our case, both input vectors and weight vectors are sequences of system call identifiers (ids) of length k (i.e., k-grams). Both n, m, and k are configurable parameters that can be dynamically set during map creation. At map creation time, each weight vector element is initialized randomly to be a value i such that $1 \le i \le S$, S equals to the largest system call id. In order to handle applications with different behaviors, PREC builds a SOM for each individual application and only uses the system calls originated by high-risk third-party native code to train the SOM.

The traditional SOM learning algorithm updates weight vectors continuously. However we cannot use this method directly, since two system calls with similar ids do not necessarily have similar actions. For example, system call id 12 (sys_chdir) is completely different than system call id 13 (sys_time). To address these issues, we have made two modifications to the traditional SOM learning algorithm. First, we use the string edit distance instead of Euclidean or Manhattan distance as a measure of similarity when mapping input vectors to neurons. This is because graph edit dis-

tance only considers if two items are exactly the same in the weight vector. Second, to address the continuous update problem, we have developed a frequency-based weight vector update scheme, which we describe next.

Each SOM model training occurs in three iterative steps, illustrated by Figure 3. First, we form an input vector of length k by reading k system calls from the training data. Second, we examine the string edit distance from that input vector to the weight vectors of all neurons in the map. Whichever neuron has the smallest distance is selected as the winning neuron to be trained. We break ties using Euclidean distance. Third, we add 1 to the count for the input vector in the *frequency map* of the winner neuron. At this point we also update the frequency maps of all neighbor neurons. In this example, we define our neighborhood to be the neurons in a radius of $r = 1$. The count value added to the neighbor neuron is reduced based on a neighborhood function (e.g., Gaussian function) which depends on the grid distance from the winning neuron to the neighbor neuron. For example, in Figure 3, the input vector $[1, 2, 4]$ is added into the frequency map of the winning neuron 1 with a count 1 and is also added into the frequency map of the neighbor neuron 2 with a reduced count 0.8.

The frequency map keeps track of how many times each particular system call sequence has been mapped to that neuron. For example, in Figure 3, the frequency map of neuron 1 shows that the sequence $[2, 2, 4]$ is mapped to the neuron 1 five times, the sequence $[3, 2, 4]$ is mapped to neuron 1 two times, and the sequence $[1, 2, 4]$ is mapped to neuron 1 just once. We repeat the above three steps for all the system call sequences recorded in the training data. After training is complete, we use the sequence with the highest count in the frequency map to denote the weight vector of the neuron. We sum the count values of all the sequences in the frequency map to denote the frequency count value for this neuron.

Use of system call arguments. System call arguments provide finer-grained information to system call anomaly detections. In PREC, we selected two types of arguments to help detect root exploits: file paths and socket arguments. We divide each file and socket related system call into multiple subgroups based on the arguments it contains. Specifically, we classify file paths into two types: application accessible directories and system directories. We divide socket system calls into three different groups based on its protocol type: 1) the socket call that connects to a remote server on the network, 2) a local server on the device, and 3) a kernel component with the NETLINK socket. Each file or socket system call is assigned with different identifiers based on the argument type. For example, the system call open is assigned with an identifier 5 for accessing its home directory or SD card partition and a different identifier (e.g., 300) for accessing the system directories.

Some system calls (e.g., symlink, rename) include two file paths in their arguments. If the two file paths belong to the same type, we can assign the system call identifier in a similar way as single file path ones. However, if the two file paths belong to different types, we assign a unique identifier to the system call. The intuition behind our approach is that we observe that benign applications do not simultaneously access files in the application home directory and the system directory. For example, benign applications do not move files from its home directory to system partitions and vice versa. In contrast, we observe that most malicious applications try to access home directories and system directories at the same time (e.g., symlink a system file to a local directory).

Runtime root exploit detection. When a user purchases an app from the market, its normal behavior model represented by SOM is downloaded to the user's smartphone. After the application starts, PREC performs runtime system call origin identification to form the sequences of system calls originated by the third-party native code. We then match the system call sequences against the SOM model. If a root exploit begins to execute, PREC identifies system call sequences that are mapped to rarely trained neurons. Thus, if we map the collected system call sequence to a neuron whose frequency count is less than a pre-defined threshold (e.g., 0 represents never trained), the current sequence is considered to be malicious. The threshold allows users to control the tradeoff between malware detection rate and false alarm rate. The map size and the sequence length are other configuration parameters that might contribute to the malware detection accuracy tradeoff. We will quantify such tradeoffs in the experimental evaluation section.

2.3 Automatic Root Exploit Containment

When a root exploit is detected, PREC automatically responds to the alarm by containing the malicious execution. A brute force response to the malware alarm would be killing the entire application to protect the device from the root compromise. However, this brute force approach might cause a lot of undesired disturbances to the user, especially when the anomaly detector raises a false alarm. To address the challenge, PREC provides fine-grained containment by stopping or slowing down the malicious activities only instead of the whole application.

As mentioned in Section 2.1, PREC executes system calls from the third-party native code within the special native threads. When a malicious system call sequence is detected, PREC sends a predefined signal to the malicious native thread to terminate the thread. To process the signal, we also insert a signal handler inside the native thread before the native function is called. In our current prototype implementation, we use `SIGSYS` (signal 31) to trigger the native thread termination. We confirm that `SIGSYS` is not used by any other Android system components. Furthermore, PREC disallows applications from sending or registering handlers for `SIGSYS`.

Although killing native threads can effectively stop the attack, it might still break the normal application execution when the anomaly detector raises a false alarm. Thus, PREC provides a second containment option that is less intrusive: slowing down the malicious native thread by inserting a delay during its execution. Our experiments show that most root exploits become ineffective after we slow down the malicious native thread to a certain point. The delay-based approach can handle the false alarms more gracefully since the benign application will not suffer from crashing or termination due to transient false alarms.

To insert delay into the malicious thread, we force the kernel to call our sleep function before each system call is dispatched to the corresponding handler. After the anomaly detection module raises an alarm, it sets a delay value in the `task_struct` of the malicious native thread. Note that the `task_struct` is ready-only to the user process. Thus,

PREC pauses the native thread based on the delay specified by PREC. The delay time is applied to all subsequent system calls in the thread, and exponentially increases for each new alarm in order to stop the malicious activities in a timely way. Our prototype starts at 1 ms and doubles per alarm. For each normal system call sequence, we exponentially decrease (halves) the delay. There are other possible policies for increasing or decreasing the delay, which can be used as tuning knobs for controlling the false alarm sensitivity. For example, we also tested a linear decrease policy, but found exponential decrease can tolerate more false alarms.

3. EXPERIMENTAL EVALUATION

We implement PREC and evaluate our approach using real world root exploits and applications. We evaluate PREC in terms of detection accuracy, malware containment effectiveness, and overhead.

3.1 Evaluation Methodology

Benign application selection: We first test PREC with a variety of popular benign apps to evaluate the false alarm rate of PREC. We select our benign apps as follows. We downloaded top 10 popular free apps from all different application categories (Android Market includes 34 application categories). We then test those applications from the most popular ones to less popular ones and check whether we can run them successfully on the emulator and our Samsung Galaxy Nexus device. We find 80 popular apps include third-party native code and can be correctly executed on our test devices. The majority of them are games and multimedia applications. We also test 60 popular apps without any third-party native code. We use more benign apps with third-party native code than without third-party native code in order to estimate the worst-case false alarm rate of PREC since PREC will not raise any false alarm for benign apps without any third-party native code. In contrast, other alternative schemes without our classified monitoring techniques will still raise false alarms on those benign apps without third-party native code. We evaluated all the benign apps using a Samsung Galaxy Nexus device with Android 4.2, which is equipped with 1.2 GHz Dual-Core cortex A9 processor, and 1GB RAM.

Malware selection: To evaluate the root exploit containment capability of PREC, we extensively studied all the existing real root exploits. Table 1 shows the 10 malicious applications used in our experiments that covers four real root exploits. We first used four real malware samples reported by the Malware Genome project [59]. To evaluate PREC under more challenging cases, we repackage existing root privilege escalation attacks into a popular application (AngryBirds), which contains a lot of native code.

We first studied all the six root exploit malware families (DroidDream, DroidKungFu1, DroidKungFu2, Ginger Master, BaseBridge, DroidKungFuSapp) reported by the Malware Genome Project [59]. Our experiments covered the first four malware families. The BaseBridge malware only attacks Sony and Motorola devices, which cannot be triggered on our Nexus phones. The DroidKungFuSapp performs attacks by connecting to a remote command and control server. However, the server was inaccessible at the time of our testing, which did not allow us to trigger the root exploit.

Table 1: Malware samples tested in the experiments. The first 4 malware samples are existing malware and the last 6 malware samples are repackaged AngryBirds applications with existing root exploits.

Malware Sample	Application Package	Root Exploits	Description
DroidDream	com.beauty.leg	Exploid, **RATC**	Plaintext root exploits which are triggered once the infected application has been launched
DroidKungFu1	com.sansec	Exploid, **RATC**	Encrypt Exploid and RATC root attacks and is triggered when a specific event is received at a predefined time condition.
DroidKungFu2	com.allen.txtdbwshs	Exploid, **RATC**	Encrypt the RATC root attack and is triggered when a specific event is received at a predefined time condition.
GingerMaster	com.igamepower.appmaster	**GingerBreak**	Hides shell code suffix and is triggered during the next reboot.
RATC-1	AngryBirds	**RATC**	Attack is triggered when the application receives BOOT_COMPLETED broadcast intent.
RATC-2	AngryBirds	**RATC**	Attack is triggered ten seconds after the application is launched.
ZimperLich-1	AngryBirds	**ZimperLich**	Attack is triggered when the application receives BOOT_COMPLETED broadcast intent.
ZimperLich-2	AngryBirds	**ZimperLich**	Attack is triggered ten seconds after the application is launched.
GingerBreak-1	AngryBirds	**GingerBreak**	Attack is triggered when the application receives BOOT_COMPLETED broadcast intent.
GingerBreak-2	AngryBirds	**GingerBreak**	Attack is triggered ten seconds after the application is launched.

The RiskRanker project [31] and the X-ray project [12] reported 9 root exploits in total. Our experiments covered four of them (Exploid, RATC, GingerBreak, ZimperLich). We did not cover the other five root exploits for the following reasons. Three reported root exploits (Ashmem, zergRush, Mempodroid) are not found in real Android applications. Ashmem uses a vulnerability that Android failed to protect *Android Share Memory* so unprivileged process can change the value of `ro.secure` arbitrarily. This variable is used by the Android Debug Bridge Daemon (ADBD) to determine whether developer can login as *root*. However, attackers cannot embed this exploit into applications because Android applications cannot access ADBD. Similarly, *zergRush* requires several information in ADBD and *Mempodroid* executes `run-as` inside the Android Debug Bridge shell. Therefore, it is infeasible for attackers to use those exploits in applications. The remaining two root exploits (*Asroot*, which is named *Wunderbar* in X-ray, and *Levitator*) are not tested due to lack of software or hardware: *Asroot* targets on Linux kernel version prior 2.6.30-4, and the earliest available version that we can use for Nexus One device is 2.6.32. *Levitator* targets PowerVR driver and our Nexus One device uses Adreno 200 GPU. However, we also studied the source code of *Asroot* and *Levitator* and confirmed that PREC can detect those two root exploits if they are triggered. The reasons are that they either use some system calls that should never be used by normal applications (e.g., syscall 187 in *Asroot*) or need to repeatedly execute certain system calls (similar to GingerBreak) to achieve success.

We tested all the root exploit malware on a Google Nexus One device with Android 2.2 with 1GHz single core cortex A8 processor and 512MB RAM. Although the latest root exploit in our data set targets Android 2.3, root privilege escalation attacks are an increasing concern in Android. For example, Google introduced SELinux in Android 4.3 to mitigate the damage of root escalation attacks [9]. PREC provides a complementary first-line defense to detect and contain the root escalation attacks.

Model learning data collection in emulator: All the application behavior model learning data were collected on the Android emulator enhanced with our classified system call monitoring scheme. We used the Android Monkey [11] tool to generate random inputs to simulate user behaviors. We chose Monkey in this work because it is the best publicly available fuzz input generation tool we could find at the time of writing. Previous work [52] also shows that Monkey can provide similar coverage as manual collection given sufficient rounds of testing. We note that using Monkey input generation is a limitation in our current implementation, which will be discussed in detail in Section 4. However, our experiments show that PREC can achieve high accuracy even by using such a simple tool. We expect PREC can achieve even more accurate malware detection given a more powerful input generation tool or using developer provided input traces. Although previous work [58, 56, 49, 41] proposed to automate the trace collection process by analyzing decompiled Java source code and standard Android user interface (UI) components, those approaches cannot be applied to PREC for two main reasons. First, PREC focuses on third-party native code which is very difficult, if not totally impossible, to decompile. Second, most applications that contain native code do not use standard UI components. Rather, they often draw UI components themselves.

Each application learning data collection lasted 10 minutes. For benign applications, trace collection was performed on a modified Android 4.2 emulator (API level 17). We collected traces for malicious applications on a modified Android 2.2 emulator (API level 8) because they require Android 2.2 to trigger the exploits. Note there is no root exploit triggered in the training data collection phase since we assume that malware try to hide themselves in the dynamic analysis environment using logic bombs or detecting emulation. If the root exploit is triggered, the malicious activities will be detected by the market malware analysis and the application will be rejected.

On-device real application testing data collection: To evaluate the on-device benign application false alarm rates and malware detection accuracy of PREC, we use real users to run all the 140 benign applications on our Samsung Galaxy Nexus device with Android 4.2 for collecting realistic user behaviors. For each app, the user is asked to play the app for about three minutes. Although we could also use the same dynamic testing tool to collect the testing data automatically, we chose not do so to avoid producing biased results using the same tool for both learning and testing. For those 10 malicious applications listed in Table 1, we run them on a Google Nexus One device with Android 2.2 and make sure those root exploits are triggered during our testing phase.

Alternative algorithms for comparison: In addition to PREC, we also implement a set of different anomaly detection schemes for comparison: 1) *SOM (full)* that applies the SOM learning algorithm over *all* system calls to create normal application behavior models; 2) *HMM (native)* that applies the hidden Markov model [53] over the system calls from the third-party native code only, which learn normal system call sequence transition probabilities and raises an alarm if the observed tradition probability is below a threshold; 3) *HMM (full)* that uses the hidden Markov model over all system calls; 4) *FSA (native)* [42] that uses the finite state automaton over the system calls from the third-party native code only, which learns normal system call sequence patterns and raises an alarm if the observed system call sequence transition probability is below a pre-defined threshold; and 5) *FSA (full)* that uses a finite state automaton over all system calls. Note that we only compare PREC with common *unsupervised* learning methods since supervised learning methods (e.g., support vector machine [32]) cannot be applied to PREC as they require malware data during the learning phase and cannot detect unknown malware.

Evaluation metrics: We evaluate the malware detection accuracy using the standard *receiver operating characteristic* (ROC) curves. ROC curves can effectively show the tradeoff between the true positive rate (A_T) and the false positive rate (A_F) for an anomaly detection model. We use standard *true positive rate* A_T and *false positive rate* A_F metrics, as shown in Equation 1. N_{tp}, N_{fn}, N_{fp}, and N_{tn} denote the true positive number, false negative number, false positive number, and true negative number, respectively.

$$A_T = \frac{N_{tp}}{N_{tp} + N_{fn}}, \quad A_F = \frac{N_{fp}}{N_{fp} + N_{tn}} \quad (1)$$

A false positive means that our anomaly detection system raises an alarm for a benign application. A false negative means that we fail to raise any alarm for a malware sample. In our results, we report both per-sequence (i.e., system call sequence) and per-app true positive rates and false positive rates.

3.2 Results and Analysis

Runtime classified system call monitoring: We first evaluate the effectiveness of our runtime classified system call monitoring module that serves as the foundation for PREC. Figures 4(a) shows the percentage of the system calls originated from the third-party native code for the 80 benign apps that include third-party native code. Although all those 80 apps contain native code, we observe that over 50% of the apps execute less than 10% third-party native code. Thus, PREC can still filter out a large number of system calls for those benign applications with third-party native code during model creation and malware detection.

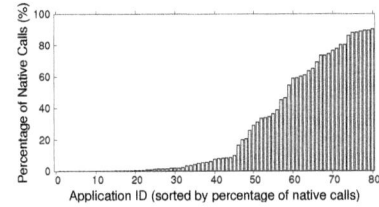

(a) 80 benign apps with native code

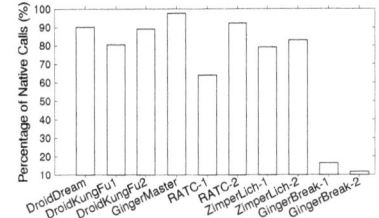

(b) 10 Malicious apps

Figure 4: Percentage of system calls originated from native code for 80 apps with third-party native code and 10 malicious apps.

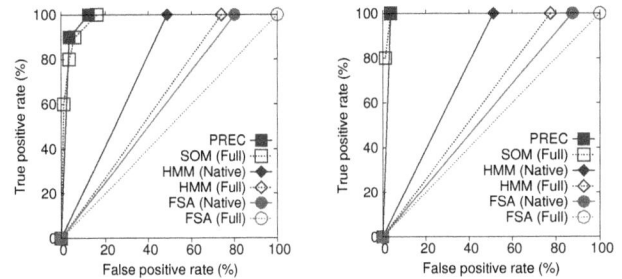

(a) Without arguments   (b) With arguments

Figure 5: Per-app malware detection accuracy comparison results for 80 apps that include third-party native code.

We also observe that PREC never misclassifies a system call from Java as a system call from third-party native code. Thus, PREC will not raise any false alarm for those benign applications that do not include any third-party native code. Figure 4(b) shows that the classified monitoring results for the 10 malware samples used in our experiments. We can see most malware applications contain a large portion of system calls from the third-party native code. This also validates our hypothesis: malware exploits root privilege escalation vulnerabilities using third-party native code. Thus, our classified monitoring scheme will not reduce the root exploit detection capability.

Runtime on-device detection accuracy: We now evaluate the runtime on-device detection accuracy of the PREC system. Figure 5 shows the per-app true positive and false positive rate using different anomaly detection algorithms for the 80 benign apps that include third-party native code. Figure 5(a) shows the results without considering system call arguments while Figure 5(b) shows the results of including system call arguments. We adjust different parameters in each anomaly detection algorithm to obtain the ROC curves. For SOM algorithms, we adjusted the map size, the length of the system call sequences, the anomalous frequency thresh-

(a) Without arguments (b) With arguments

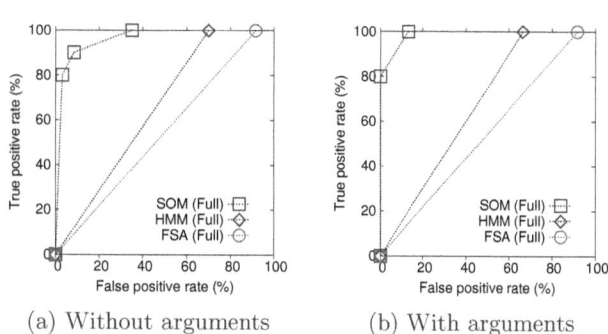

Figure 6: Per-app malware detection accuracy comparison results for 60 apps that do not have any native code.

old, and the neighborhood area size. For HMM and FSA algorithms, we adjusted the number of states, the system call sequence length, and the anomalous probability threshold. Each point on the ROC curve represents one accuracy result under a certain configuration setting and we use the configuration for all the 80 apps. If two configurations produce the same true positive rate but different false positive rates, we only plot the point with the smaller false positive rate to show the best accuracy result of each scheme. The results show that all algorithms can easily achieve 100% true positive rate but their false positive rates vary a lot. HMM and FSA can achieve 49% and 80% false positive rate at their best, respectively. In contrast, PREC can significantly reduce the false positive rate to 3.75%. This validates our choice of SOM since it is much more robust to noise in system calls than HMM and FSA by projecting the original noisy input space (noisy system call sequences) into a two-dimensional map without losing principal patterns.

We believe that the user perceived false positive rate of PREC will be even lower since most popular benign apps do not include third-party native code and PREC will not raise any false alarm on them with the help of classified system call monitoring. However, without performing classified system call monitoring, any anomaly detection algorithm might still raise false alarms on those apps without third-party native code. Figure 6 shows the anomaly detection accuracy results of different algorithms without using the classified system call monitoring scheme for 60 benign apps without third-party native code. We observe that SOM (full), HMM (full), and FSA (full) raise 13%, 67%, and 92% per-app false alarms at their best under 100% true positive rate. This validates our hypothesis that classified monitoring can greatly reduce the false alarms in practice during runtime root exploit detection.

We further compare different anomaly detection algorithms at fine granularity by measuring per-sequence false positive rates. Figure 7 shows the per-sequence false positive rates at 85-99 percentile achieved by different schemes for the 80 benign apps that include third-party native code. For fair comparison, we pick the configuration for each algorithm that yields the best per-app anomaly detection accuracy result for the algorithm. We observe that SOM algorithms can reduce the per-sequence false positive rates by more than one order of magnitude compared to HMM and FSA. Figure 8 shows the per-sequence false positive rate comparison for the benign apps without any third-party native code. We also

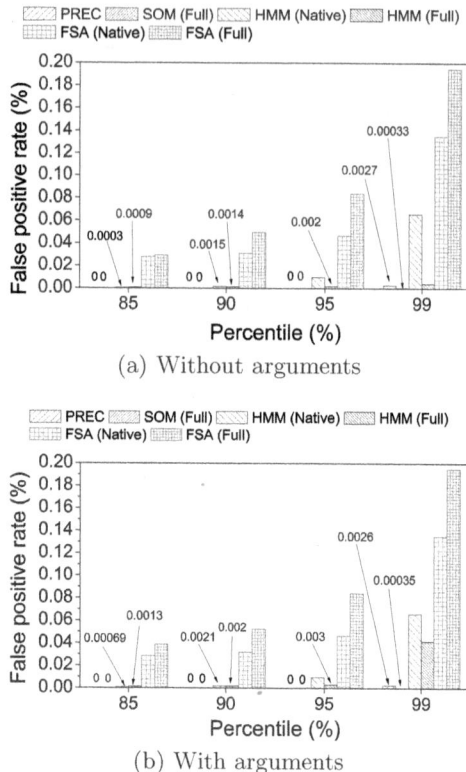

(a) Without arguments

(b) With arguments

Figure 7: Per-sequence false positive rate comparison for 80 apps that include third-party native code.

observe that SOM can significantly reduce the false positive rate by orders of magnitude.

Malware containment results: We now evaluate the malware containment effectiveness of PREC. We trigger each malicious app on the smartphone and run the PREC system on the phone to see whether it can stop the root exploit attack. Table 2 summarizes our malware containment results. As mentioned in Section 2.3, PREC provides two different containment mechanisms: 1) *termination-based containment* that stops the root exploit attack by killing the malicious native threads and 2) *delay-based containment* that stops the root exploit attack by inserting exponentially increasing delays in anomalous system calls. The results show that our anomaly detection can successfully detect and stop all the root exploit attacks before they succeed. We measure the alarm lead time as the time elapsed between the when root exploit is detected and when the root exploit is successful if no containment scheme is taken. For the repackaged malicious applications (RATC-1, RATC-2, ZimperLich-1, ZimperLich-2, GingerBreak-1, GingerBreak-2), we can terminate the malicious native threads only and continue to run the AngryBirds application normally.

We further analyze which system call sequences first cause our anomaly detector to raise alarms. For the GingerBreak and both repackaged RATC malware samples, PREC detects the abnormal sequence [execve, execve, execve, execve, close, getpid, sigaction, sigaction, sigaction]. This is consistent with the behaviors of those root exploits which first copy exploit files to a given directory and execute chmod executable to change permission to 0755 for later execution. Because different devices place chmod in different

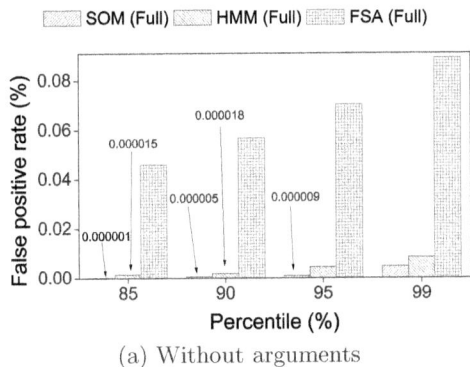

(a) Without arguments

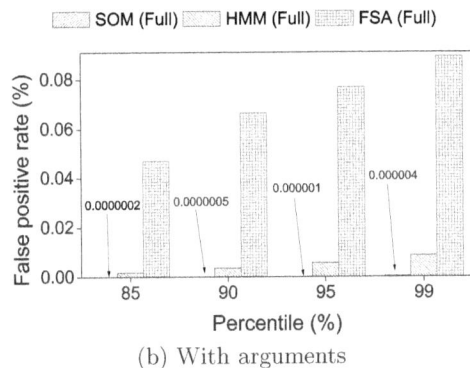

(b) With arguments

Figure 8: Per-sequence false positive rate comparison for 60 apps that do not include any third-party native code.

Table 2: Malware detection and containment results.

Malware Samples	Alarm lead time	Termination-based containment	Delay-based containment
DroidDream	20.7 sec	success	success
DroidKungFu1	16.1 sec	success	success
DroidKungFu2	96.5 sec	success	success
GingerMaster	318.3 sec	success	success
RATC-1	26.6 sec	success	success
RATC-2	17.1 sec	success	success
ZimperLich-1	14.1 sec	success	success
ZimperLich-2	20.9 sec	success	success
GingerBreak-1	35 sec	success	success
GingerBreak-2	34.6 sec	success	success

Table 3: Anomaly detection model training and runtime detection time comparison. For HMM, "$S = i$" means the number of states is configured to be i in HMM. "$S = max$" means the number of states equal to the number of distinctive system calls in the trace. The average per-app system call sequence number is 244K under all system call monitoring and 106K under native thread system call monitoring.

Scheme	Per-app training time	Per-sequence detection time
PREC	39.7 ± 59.3s	0.07 ± 0.03ms
SOM (full)	131.3 ± 88.6s	0.12 ± 0.00001ms
HMM (S= 10, native)	11.8 ± 15.9s	1.1 ± 2.7ms
HMM (S= 10, full)	32.3 ± 22s	0.2 ± 0.3ms
HMM (S= 20, native)	72.5 ± 107.7s	8.8 ± 20.4ms
HMM (S= 20, full)	140.8 ± 121.8s	1.8 ± 2.7ms
HMM (S = max, native)	1040 ± 2123s	7.7 ± 13ms
HMM (S = max, full)	2449 ± 1834.2s	105.9 ± 143.2ms
FSA (native)	0.6 ± 1s	0.05 ± 0.26ms
FSA (full)	1.1 ± 0.7s	0.01 ± 0ms

directories, the root exploit must try several locations to find the right directory. We omit the detailed malicious system call sequence results for other malware samples due to space limitation. In summary, our sequence analysis results show that PREC can accurately catch the malicious behaviors of those malware samples.

False alarm impact results: We now evaluate the false alarm impact of our system using different containment schemes. As shown in Figure 5 and 6, PREC only raises false alarms in 3 (out of 140 tested) benign apps (Forthblue.pool, TalkingTom2Free, CamScanner). We first tried the *termination-based containment* over those three benign applications. We found that those applications crashed even if we only killed the malicious native threads. We then tested our *delay-based containment scheme* over these three apps. If we only insert delays in malicious native threads, we observed that our containment scheme incurs negligible impact (0.1-0.25 second total delay during 3 minutes run) to the two benign applications, TalkingTom2Free and CamScanner. Forthblue.pool hangs after the delay-based containment is triggered. To summarize, PREC only incurs significant false alarm impact to 1 out of 140 benign popular apps tested in our experiments.

PREC overhead results: We first evaluate our anomaly detection overhead. Table 3 shows the per-app model training time and per-sequence anomaly detection time comparison among different algorithms. We can see both SOM and FSA algorithms are light-weight. However, FSA tends to raise a large number of false alarms, which makes it impractical for runtime malware detection. HMM is sensitive

to the number of states configured in the model. As we increase the number of states to its maximum value (i.e., the number of distinctive system calls used in the training trace), the overhead of HMM becomes too large to be practical. Although we see increased detection accuracy as we increase the number of states, the best case of HMM is still much worse than SOM, as shown in our detection accuracy results. To quantify the runtime overhead of PREC, we run PREC on a Galaxy Nexus phone with Andriod 4.2 using Antutu benchmarks [2]. Figure 9 shows the benchmark performance results. We observe that our classified monitoring scheme imposes less than 1% overhead and the SOM anomaly detection algorithm imposes up to 2% overhead. Overall, PREC is light-weight, which makes it practical for smartphone devices.

4. LIMITATION DISCUSSION

Our current trace collection prototype implementation has two limitations. First, simple fuzz-testing tools such as the Monkey tool are not guaranteed to produce sufficient behavioral coverage. However, our experiments show that this simple tool works fine for the apps tested in our experiments. One method of overcoming this limitation is to perform the trace collection with a more fine-tuned automation process such as event triggering and intelligent execution [49]. Developers can also provide application input traces, which

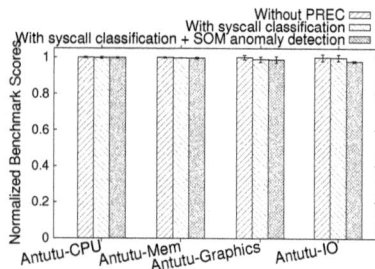

Figure 9: PREC runtime performance overhead under different benchmark apps on Galaxy Nexus running Andriod 4.2.

allow us to collect training data based on the developer-provided input trace for sufficient coverage. Second, a few applications use different libraries (e.g., OpenGL library) when the application runs in the real device and in the emulator due to the hardware difference between the real device and the emulator host. To eliminate the impact of this library difference to our results, we exclude those applications that use OpenGL library in our experiments. One solution to this limitation is to collect the training data for those applications using special libraries on real devices offline to eliminate the issue of platform difference [47].

PREC currently only monitors system calls from the third-party native code. Thus, it is possible to have false negatives if the attacker performs root exploits from the Java code. While it is theoretically possible for the root exploit to originate from Java code, root exploits require access to low-level APIs that are difficult to execute purely in Java. Thus, our approach raises the bar for attackers. However, we note this as a limitation and topic of future research.

Any system call based anomaly detection schemes is susceptible to mimicry attacks. SOM includes randomization as part of its learning, which makes it potentially more robust to mimicry attacks. We can initialize the map with different random seeds for different users. The resultant normal profiles will look similar, but not exactly the same. Therefore, our approach makes it harder for attackers to infer the exact normal model for each user and succeed in hiding the malicious system call sequences in normal behaviors on all the attacked devices.

5. RELATED WORK

Forrest et al. [26] first proposed the system call malware detection schemes by building a database of *normal* system call sequences. Warrender et al. [53] extended this idea by using hidden Markov models (HMMs) to model sequences of normal system calls. Other researchers [16, 34, 22] adapted artificial neural network to perform intrusion detection. Kruegel et al. [37] proposed to use system call arguments to improve the performance of host-based intrusion detection. Maggi et al. [40] proposed to cluster similar system calls or similar system call arguments to further improve the accuracy. Previous work [30, 38] also used SOM for network intrusion detection by clustering system call arguments such as user name, connection type, and connection time. Gao et al. [28, 27] perform real-time anomaly detection based on differences between execution graphs and the replica graphs constructed using system call traces and runtime information (e.g., return addresses).Traditional system

call based intrusion detection approaches have to collect *all* system calls made by the target process, as there is no clear boundary to reduce the collection scope. This increases both noise and design complexity of intrusion detection. In contrast, PREC leverages the natural component boundary in the Android system to perform *classified* system call monitoring. As a result, PREC can achieve more accurate and practical malware detection.

Crowdroid [17] collects system calls on smartphones and sends system call statistics to a centralized server. Based on the theory of crowdsourcing, symptoms that are shared by a small number of devices are treated as abnormal. Similarly, Paranoid Android [48] runs a daemon on the phone to collect behaviors and a virtual replica of the phone in the cloud. The daemon transmits collected behaviors to the cloud and the virtual phone replays the actions happening on the smartphone based on the collected behaviors. Both Crowdroid and Paranoid Android incur 15-30% overhead to smartphone devices. In contrast, PREC imposes less than 3% overhead to the smartphone device, which makes it practical for runtime smartphone malware containment. Smart-Siren [21] gathers and reports communication information to a proxy for anomaly detection. Besides the runtime overhead, propagating sensitive communication data to a public server might be a privacy concern for users. In contrast, PREC does not require any smartphone data to be sent to remote servers.

Recent work has explored using specific subsets of system calls for smartphone security. Isohara et al. [33] monitor a *pre-defined* subset of system calls such as `open` on smartphones. pBMDS [55] hooks input-event related functions (e.g., `sys_read()` for keyboard events, specific drivers for touch events) to collect system calls related to user interaction behaviors (e.g., GUI events). It then performs malware detection using HMMs. In contrast, PREC selects system calls based on their origins rather than pre-defined system call types. To the best of our knowledge, PREC makes the first step in classifying system calls based on their origins to significantly reduce the false alarms during runtime malware detection.

Moser et al. [43] monitor system calls executed when a program tries to terminate, with the intention of understanding how malware evades detection in virtualized test environments. Bayer et al. [15] create malicious application behavioral profiles by combining system call traces with system call dependency and operation information. Kolbitsch et al. [36] generate hard to obfuscate models that track the dependencies of system calls in known malware, which they then can use to detect malware. CloudAV [45] intercepts every `open` system call and extracts the target file. It compares this signature with signatures of abnormal files maintained in the cloud to detect the access of malicious files. DroidRanger [60] utilizes a signature-based algorithm to detect known malware from markets and monitors sensitive API accesses to discover zero-day malware. In contrast, PREC does not train on malware and can detect zero-day malware that hides itself during market malware analysis. Several researchers have also applied machine learning to statically detect malicious applications based on their permissions [50, 46, 19]; however, the root exploit malware addressed by PREC does not require permissions.

Previous work has been done to automatically respond to malicious attacks on networked hosts. For example, Somayaji et al. [51] delay anomalous system calls with increasing delay durations to prevent security violations such as a buffer overflow. Feinstein et al. [25] dynamically apply filtering rules when a DDoS attack is detected. Balepin et al. [14] use a cost model to compare predefined exploit costs with various predefined benefits to select the best response to a compromised system resource. Garfinkel et al. [29] sandbox applications by using user defined policies to control access to system resources by blocking certain system calls. Additionally, their tool emulates access to these resources to prevent applications from crashing. In contrast, our approach implements a fine-grained attack containment scheme that can reduce the disturbance to the user from the anomaly responses without using user defined detection or response rules.

6. CONCLUSION

In this paper, we have presented PREC, a novel classified system call monitoring and root exploit containment system for Android. PREC provides an on-device malware detection and containment solution to stop those malicious applications that hide themselves during market dynamic malware analysis using logic bombs or checks for an emulated environment. PREC achieves high detection accuracy and low false alarm impact by 1) classifying system calls by origin (e.g., third-party native library), 2) adapting SOM learning algorithm to detect root exploit activities, and 3) inserting exponentially increasing delays to malicious threads. We have implemented a prototype of PREC and evaluated it on 140 most popular benign applications and 10 malicious applications. Our experiments show that PREC successfully detected and stopped all the tested root exploit attacks. Compared to other anomaly detection algorithms, PREC reduces the false alarm rate by more than one order of magnitude. Our delay-based containment scheme only impose noticeable impact to 1 out of 140 popular benign applications. PREC is light-weight, which makes it practical for runtime malware containment on smartphone devices.

Acknowledgements

This work was supported in part by an NSA Science of Security Lablet grant at North Carolina State University, U.S. Army Research Office (ARO) under grant W911NF-10-1-0273, NSF CAREER Award CNS-1149445, NSF CAREER Award CNS-1253346, NSF grant CNS-1222680, IBM Faculty Awards, and Google Research Awards. Any opinions, findings, and conclusions or recommendations expressed in this material are those of the authors and do not necessarily reflect the views of the funding agencies. We would also like to thank Adwait Nadkarni, Ashwin Shashidharan, Vasant Tendulkar, Hiep Nguyen, and the anonymous reviewers for their valuable feedback during the writing of this paper.

7. REFERENCES

[1] Android Security Overview. Android Source. http://source.android.com/devices/tech/security/.

[2] Antutu Benchmark. https://play.google.com/store/apps/details?id=com.antutu.ABenchMark.

[3] DTrace. http://docs.oracle.com/javase/6/docs/technotes/guides/vm/dtrace.html.

[4] DWARF Debugging Standard. http://www.dwarfstd.org/.

[5] Exception Handling ABI for ARM Architecture. http://infocenter.arm.com/help/topic/com.arm.doc.ihi0038a/IHI0038A_ehabi.pdf.

[6] Ice Cream Sandwich. Android Developer. http://developer.android.com/about/versions/android-4.0-highlights.html.

[7] Linux man page - pTrace - process trace. http://linux.die.net/man/2/ptrace.

[8] Linux Trace Toolkit - next generation. https://lttng.org.

[9] Security-Enhanced Linux. Android Developer. http://source.android.com/devices/tech/security/se-linux.html.

[10] SystemTap. http://sourceware.org/systemtap/.

[11] UI/Application Exerciser Mokey. http://developer.android.com/tools/help/monkey.html.

[12] Vulnerabilities. X-Ray. http://www.xray.io/#vulnerabilities.

[13] Apple. Apple Updates iOS to 6.1. Apple. http://www.apple.com/pr/library/2013/01/28Apple-Updates-iOS-to-6-1.html.

[14] I. Balepin, S. Maltsev, J. Rowe, and K. Levitt. Using specification-based intrusion detection for automated response. In *Proc. of RAID*, 2003.

[15] U. Bayer, P. Milani, C. Hlauschek, C. Kruegel, and E. Kirda. Scalable, Behavior-Based Malware Clustering. In *Proc. of NDSS*, 2009.

[16] C. M. Bishop. *Neural Networks for Pattern Recognition*. Oxford University Press, Inc., New York, NY, USA, 1995.

[17] I. Burguera, U. Zurutuza, and S. Nadjm-Tehrani. Crowdroid: Behavior-Based Malware Detection System for Android. In *Proc. of CCS-SPSM*, 2011.

[18] D. Canali, A. Lanzi, D. Balzarotti, C. Kruegel, M. Christodorescu, and E. Kirda. A Quantitative Study of Accuracy in System Call-Based Malware Detection. In *Proc. of ISSTA*, 2012.

[19] S. Chakradeo, B. Reaves, P. Traynor, and W. Enck. MAST: Triage for Market-scale Mobile Malware Analysis. In *Proc. of WiSec*, 2013.

[20] X. Chen, J. Andersen, Z. M. Mao, M. Bailey, and J. Nazario. Towards an Understanding of Anti-virtualization and Anti-debugging Behavior in Modern Malware. In *Proc. of DSN*, 2008.

[21] J. Cheng, S. H. Wong, H. Yang, and S. Lu. SmartSiren: Virus Detection and Alert for Smartphones. In *Proc. of MobiSys*, 2007.

[22] G. Creech and J. Hu. A Semantic Approach to Host-based Intrusion Detection Systems Using Contiguous and Discontiguous System Call Patterns. *IEEE Transactions on Computers*, 2013.

[23] D. Dean, H. Nguyen, and X. Gu. UBL: Unsupervised behavior learning for predicting performance anomalies in virtualized cloud systems. In *Proc. of ICAC*, 2012.

[24] M. Egele, T. Scholte, E. Kirda, and C. Kruegel. A Survey on Automated Dyanmic Malware-Analysis Techniques and Tools. *ACM Computing Surveys*, 44(2), Feb. 2012.

[25] L. Feinstein, D. Schnackenberg, R. Balupari, and D. Kindred. Statistical approaches to ddos attack detection and response. In *Proc. of the DARPA Information Survivability Conference and Exposition*, 2003.

[26] S. Forrest, S. A. Hofmeyr, A. Somayaji, and T. A. Longstaff. A Sense of Self for Unix Processes. In *Proc. of IEEE Symposium on Security and Privacy*, 1996.

[27] D. Gao, M. K. Reiter, and D. Song. Gray-box extraction of execution graphs for anomaly detection. In *Proc. of CCS*, 2004.

[28] D. Gao, M. K. Reiter, and D. Song. Behavioral Distance for Intrusion Detection. In *Proc. of RAID*, 2005.

[29] T. Garfinkel. Traps and pitfalls: Practical problems in system call interposition based security tools. In *Proc. of NDSS*, 2003.

[30] L. Girardin and D. Brodbeck. A visual approach for monitoring logs. In *Proc. of LISA*, 1998.

[31] M. Grace, Y. Zhou, Q. Zhang, S. Zou, and X. Jiang. RiskRanker: Scalable and Accurate Zero-day Android Malware Detection. In *Proc. of MobiSys*, 2012.

[32] W. Hu, Y. Liao, and V. R. Vemuri. Robust anomaly detection using support vector machines. In *Proc. of ICML*, 2003.

[33] T. Isohara, K. Takemori, and A. Kubota. Kernel-based Behavior Analysis for Android Malware Detection. In *Proc. of CIS*, 2011.

[34] H. Jiang and J. Ruan. The application of genetic neural network in network intrusion detection. *Journal of Computers*, 2009.

[35] T. Kohonen, J. Tan, and T. Huang. *Self-Organizing Maps*. Springer, 3rd edition, 2001.

[36] C. Kolbitsch, P. M. Comparetti, C. Kruegel, E. Kirda, X. Zhou, and X. Wang. Effective and Efficient Malware Detection at the End Host. In *Proc. of USENIX Security*, 2009.

[37] C. Kruegel, D. Mutz, F. Valeur, and G. Vigna. On the detection of anomalous system call arguments. In *Proc. of ESORICS*, 2003.

[38] P. Lichodzijewski, A. Nur Zincir-Heywood, and M. Heywood. Host-based intrusion detection using self-organizing maps. In *Proc. of IJCNN*, 2002.

[39] H. Lockheimer. Android and Security. Google Mobile Blog. http://googlemobile.blogspot.com/2012/02/android-and-security.html.

[40] F. Maggi, M. Matteucci, and S. Zanero. Detecting intrusions through system call sequence and argument analysis. *IEEE TODS*, 2008.

[41] R. Mahmood, N. Esfahani, T. Kacem, N. Mirzaei, S. Malek, and A. Stavrou. A whitebox approach for automated security testing of android applications on the cloud. In *Proc. of AST*, 2013.

[42] C. Michael and A. Ghosh. Using Finite Automata to Mine Execution Data for Intrusion Detection: A Preliminary Report. In *Proc. of RAID*, 2000.

[43] A. Moser, C. Kruegel, and E. Kirda. Exploring Multiple Execution Paths for Malware Analysis. In *Proc. of IEEE Symposium on Security and Privacy*, 2007.

[44] J. Oberheide. Dissecting Android's Bouncer. The Duo Bulletin. https://blog.duosecurity.com/2012/06/dissecting-androids-bouncer/.

[45] J. Oberheide, E. Cooke, and F. Jahanian. CloudAV: N-Version Antivirus in the Network Cloud. In *Proc. of USENIX Security*, 2008.

[46] C. Peng, C. yu Li, G. hua Tu, S. Lu, and L. Zhang. Mobile Data Charging: New Attacks and Countermeasures. In *Proc. of CCS*, 2012.

[47] H. Pilz. Building a Test Environment for Android Anti-malware Tests. In *Proc. of VB*, 2012.

[48] G. Portokalidis, P. Homburg, K. Anagnostakis, and H. Bos. Paranoid Android: Versatile Protection For Smartphones. In *Proc. of ACSAC*, 2010.

[49] V. Rastogi, Y. Chen, and W. Enck. Appsplayground: automatic security analysis of smartphone applications. In *Proc. of CODASPY*, 2013.

[50] B. P. Sarma, N. Li, C. Gates, R. Potharaju, C. Nita-Rotaru, and I. Molloy. Android permissions: a perspective combining risks and benefits. In *Proc. of SACMAT*, 2012.

[51] A. Somayaji and S. Forrest. Automated response using system-call delays. In *Proc. of the USENIX Security*, 2000.

[52] A. M. R. Tahiliani and M. Naik. Dynodroid: An input generation system for android apps. Technical report, Georgia Institute of Technology, 2012.

[53] C. Warrender, S. Forrest, and B. Pearlmutter. Detecting Intrusions Using System Calls: Alternative Data Models. In *Proc. of IEEE Symposium on Security and Privacy*, 1999.

[54] B. Womack. Google Says 700,000 Applications Available for Android. Bloomberg Businessweek, Oct. 2012. http://www.businessweek.com/news/2012-10-29/google-says-700-000-applications-available-for-android-devices.

[55] L. Xie, X. Zhang, J.-P. Seifert, and S. Zhu. pBMDS: A Behavior-based Malware Detection System for Cellphone Devices. In *Proc. of WiSec*, 2010.

[56] W. Yang, M. Prasad, and T. Xie. A Grey-box Approach for Automated GUI-Model Generation of Mobile Applications. In *Proc. of FASE*, 2013.

[57] B. Yee, D. Sehr, G. Dardyk, J. B. Chen, R. Muth, T. Ormandy, S. Okasaka, N. Narula, and N. Fullagar. Native Client: A Sandbox for Portable, Untrusted x86 Native Code. In *Proc. of IEEE Symposium on Security and Privacy*, 2009.

[58] C. Zheng, S. Zhu, S. Dai, G. Gu, X. Gong, X. Han, and W. Zou. SmartDroid: an Automatic System for Revealing UI-based Trigger Conditions in Android Applications. In *Proc. of CCS-SPSM*, 2012.

[59] Y. Zhou and X. Jiang. Dissecting Android Malware: Characterization and Evolution. In *Proc. of IEEE Symposium on Security and Privacy*, 2012.

[60] Y. Zhou, Z. Wang, W. Zhou, and X. Jiang. Hey, You, Get Off of My Market: Detecting Malicious Apps in Official and Alternative Android Markets. In *Proc. of NDSS*, 2012.

DIVILAR: Diversifying Intermediate Language for Anti-Repackaging on Android Platform

Wu Zhou *, Zhi Wang †, Yajin Zhou *, Xuxian Jiang *
*North Carolina State University   †Florida State University
wzhou2@ncsu.edu   zwang@cs.fsu.edu   yajin_zhou@ncsu.edu   jiang@cs.ncsu.edu

ABSTRACT

App repackaging remains a serious threat to the emerging mobile app ecosystem. Previous solutions have mostly focused on the postmortem detection of repackaged apps by measuring similarity among apps. In this paper, we propose DIVILAR, a virtualization-based protection scheme to enable self-defense of Android apps against app repackaging. Specifically, it re-encodes an Android app in a diversified virtual instruction set and uses a specialized execute engine for these virtual instructions to run the protected app. However, this extra layer of execution may cause significant performance overhead, rendering the solution unacceptable for daily use. To address this challenge, we leverage a lightweight hooking mechanism to hook into Dalvik VM, the execution engine for Dalvik bytecode, and piggy-back the decoding of virtual instructions to that of Dalvik bytecode. By compositing virtual and Dalvik instruction execution, we can effectively eliminate this extra layer of execution and significantly reduce the performance overhead. We have implemented a prototype of DIVILAR. Our evaluation shows that DIVILAR is resilient against existing static and dynamic analysis, including these specific to VM-based protection. Further performance evaluation demonstrates its efficiency for daily use (an average of 16.2% and 8.9% increase to the start time and run time, respectively).

Categories and Subject Descriptors

K.5.1 [**Hardware/Software Protection**]: Copyrights

Keywords

Android; Anti-Repackaging; Virtual Machine

1. INTRODUCTION

In recent years, mobile apps have gained unprecedented adoption due to the increasing popularity of smartphones and other mobile devices. For example, recent data shows that Google and Apple have accumulated more than 48 billion and 50 billion app downloads from their online app store, respectively [8, 25]. Online app store provides many effective ways for developers

```
const-string v0, "content://com.example.notepad.provider.NotePad/notes"
invoke-static {v0}, Landroid/net/Uri;->parse(Ljava/lang/String;)Landroid/net/Uri;
move-result-object v0
sput-object v0, Lcom/example/android/notepad/e;->a:Landroid/net/Uri;
```

Figure 1: Snip of code processed by Proguard (only app's class names are changed).

to monetize their apps, such as paid apps, in-app purchase, and ads. Unfortunately, app repackaging, in which legitimate apps are repackaged and sold without the knowledge or consent of their rightful owners, poses serious threats to this new economy model since its inception: app repackaging can lead to proliferation of app piracy, causing monetary lose for developers [12,22,29,53,73,74]; even worse, repackaged apps are often used as the media for stealthy malware [73–75]. Recent research shows that repackaged apps have mostly plagued third-party app stores, which are virtually unregulated in the distribution of those apps [29, 74]. With little help available from the operators of those stores, app developers have to resort to technologies that can enable *self-defense* for their apps.

In light of these serious threats, researchers have proposed different approaches to address the problem. For example, a number of systems aim at detecting repackaged apps by measuring similarity among a large set of apps, particularly between third-party stores and the official store [12, 29, 53, 73, 74]. They are designed to provide postmortem detection and jurisdiction, and thus cannot prevent apps from being repackaged at the first place. To thwart app piracy, Google and others introduced server-side license verification [32, 52] that can be employed by linking to provided libraries. However, plain deployment of these libraries can be easily bypassed. There even exist automated tools just for that purpose [43–45]. Server-side verification is thus advised to be deployed with other protections such as obfuscation to make it difficult to be bypassed [32]. Existing Android-based obfuscators [36,41] are relatively easy to bypass due to the fact that Dalvik bytecode contains rich semantics of an app. Figure 1 shows a short snip of code processed by Proguard [41], arguably the most popular obfuscator for Android due to its inclusion in the official Android developer's guide. Notice that calls to the Android framework APIs are virtually not changed, providing "valuable" information to the repackager of where and how to make modifications (although it is technically viable to obfuscate these calls with Java reflection and string transformation, it likely will lead to unacceptable overhead because such calls are highly frequent.) In this paper, we propose DIVILAR(DIVersified Intermediate Language for Anti-Repackaging), an Android protection scheme that diversifies the Dalvik bytecode to significantly raise the bar against app repackaging.

DIVILAR draws its inspiration from an effective and reliable technology on the traditional desktop systems: virtual machine(VM) based protection, in which the target binary is re-encoded in a randomized virtual instruction set and packed together with a specialized interpreter for the instruction set. At run-time, the interpreter translates and executes the protected app (for brevity, we call it the guest app). By encoding the guest app in an unknown instruction set, VM-based protection immediately disables existing tools that expect the original instruction set as input. It thus becomes necessary for the attackers to first reverse-engineer the VM interpreter in order to recover and manipulate the guest app. However, an interpreter could be implemented in a highly convoluted and obscure way. For example, the original QEMU (before TCG) [6] demonstrates how complicated a *benign* emulator (a type of virtualization) could be. Moreover, virtual instructions can be readily randomized and customized for individual software (or software revisions), further increasing the reverse-engineering efforts. As such, VM-based protection has been successfully applied by both malware authors and developers to protect their "intellectual property" from being analyzed and reverse-engineered [21, 46, 61, 62, 65].

Successful deployments of VM-based protection have been largely limited to native binaries, but not for managed code such as Java Bytecode or Microsoft Intermediate Language (MSIL) [21, 46, 61, 62, 65]: performance overhead caused by the extra layer of instruction interpretation is prohibitive for an interpreter in the managed code, but has little effect over a native interpreter. A native interpreter not only executes faster (because it is executed natively), but also can employ mature technologies such as fast binary translation [4] and just-in-time compilation [40] to improve performance. In contrast, managed code already requires a layer of interpretation/translation. The additional layer of execution can further significantly slow down the system. For example, Proteus [2], a VM-based protection system designed for MSIL, reports from $50\times$ to $3500\times$ performance overhead. Such an overhead is even more prohibitive on a mobile platform due to its limited computation power and battery life.

To address this challenge, we observe that Android already has a mature and efficient interpreter for its apps, Dalvik VM. Dalvik VM is loaded as a native library into each app's address space, which is shared with the app's own native libraries. The latter thus can freely access and manipulate Dalvik VM at run-time. DIVILAR leverages this accessibility to dynamically hook into Dalvik VM and decode the virtual instructions right before they are loaded for execution. By doing so, the interpreter for the virtual instructions is merged into the existing execution engine of Dalvik bytecode. This not only significantly reduces overhead of the extra layer of execution, but also allows DIVILAR to be much harder to reverse-engineer: compared to interpreters implemented in managed code [2], DIVILAR's interpreter is implemented as a native binary. Therefore, many coding/obfuscation techniques not available to managed code (e.g., direct memory manipulation) can be employed and a large body of existing obfuscation tools can be directly applied to it.

We have implemented a prototype of DIVILAR. It accepts an Android app as input, transforms its Dalvik bytecode into a randomly generated intermediate language, and wraps the resulting binary together with a lightweight virtual instruction interpreter. DIVILAR is intended to be used by app developers at the last stage of development before releasing the app into public online app stores. DIVILAR-protected apps need no special treatment from Android or the app store. They can be released, installed, and executed in the same way as normal Android apps. Our evaluation demonstrates that DIVILAR is robust against common countermeasures, including existing static and dynamic analysis,

and even these specific to VM-based protection. DIVILAR also has a small and acceptable performance overhead with an average of 16% increase to app start time and 8.9% to run time.

In summary, this paper makes the following contributions:

- First, we propose a diversified virtualization-based protection for Android to thwart app repackaging. DIVILAR-protected apps are compatible with the existing Android ecosystem. To the best of our knowledge, it is the first VM-base protection system for Android.

- Second, we design a lightweight in-app hooking mechanism for DIVILAR's interpreter to composite virtual instruction and Dalvik bytecode execution. Evaluation shows that our prototype interpreter is robust and incurs small performance overhead.

- Third, we have implemented a prototype of DIVILAR. Our evaluation demonstrates that DIVILAR is effective against common countermeasures, including static analysis, dynamic analysis, and particularly these specific to VM-based protection or obfuscation.

The rest of the paper is organized as the follows: we give background information and state the app repackaging problem in Section 2, and describe the DIVILAR design and implementation in Section 3 and Section 4, respectively. After that, we present the robustness analysis and evaluate its performance in Section 5. In Section 6, we discuss the system's limitations and suggest some possible improvements. Lastly, we present related work in Section 7 and conclude the paper in Section 8.

2. PROBLEM STATEMENT

In this section, we introduce key concepts of Dalvik VM, the execution engine for Android apps, and the widespread issue of app repackaging in the Android platform.

2.1 Android App and Dalvik VM

Most Android apps are written in the Java programming language with some components optionally implemented as native libraries. At compiling time, the Java source code is compiled into Dalvik bytecode, which are then assembled into a single Dalvik executable (the .dex file). Each Android app can optionally load native libraries and interact with them through the JNI interface [14]. To release an app, all files of the app are compressed into an apk file that is subsequently signed with the developer's private key. The developer's key is usually self-certified without involvement of a central certificate authority. The signature of an app therefore cannot be used as an indication of trustworthiness of the developer, or that the signer is the rightful owner of the app. Instead, Android security model uses the signature to safely allow apps of the same developer to share certain privileges.

Android apps are executed by Dalvik VM, a register-based Java virtual machine designed by Google. Figure 2 shows the high-level architecture of Dalvik VM. There are two major components: class loader and execution engine. Class loader is responsible for loading Dalvik classes for execution. Specifically, when a new class needs to be executed, class loader reads its definition from either the app's dex file which contains all the classes of the app, or from system libraries. The class definition includes information such as fields, methods, and bytecode for each method (except abstract method). For safety, class loader needs to perform a fairly complicated verification to make sure the class is well-formed and does not violate constrains set by the Java specification [42].

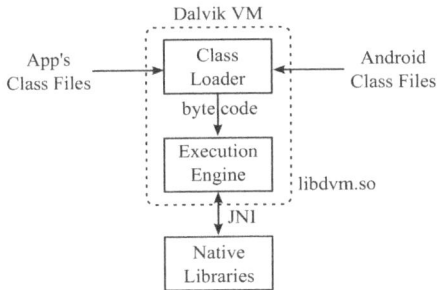

Figure 2: Architecture of Dalvik Virtual Machine

Since DIVILAR uses a completely different instruction encoding than Dalvik bytecode, it is necessary for DIVILAR to bypass the verification of class loader.

Execution engine of Dalvik VM decodes and executes the byte-code of Java methods. Dalvik bytecode has a different encoding scheme than the standard Java bytecode: it is register-based (the standard Java bytecode is stack-based) and has variable lengths (1, 2, 3, or 5 code units, each code unit is 16-bit). For example, the add-int instruction has an opcode of $90h$ and three register operands encoded in 2 code units. By re-encoding an app in a virtual instruction set, DIVILAR will lead existing Android analysis tools (e.g., the baksmali disassembler [19]) to misinterpret the instruction boundaries and thus fail to decode the instruction stream. The original implementation of Dalvik VM executes byte-code through opcode-dispatching, in which it fetches and decodes the bytecode into opcode and operands, and dispatches execution to the corresponding handler for the opcode. Recent versions of Dalvik VM speed up the execution by supporting just-in-time compilation, where frequently-executed bytecode is compiled into native code and executed natively.

Dalvik VM is shipped as a native library (libdvm.so) and loaded into each app's address space, which it shares with other app-provided native libraries. The virtual instruction interpreter of DIVILAR is also a native library (libhook.so). At run-time, libhook.so hooks into Dalvik VM and manipulates its internal data structure for its own purposes.

2.2 App Repackaging in Android Platform

App repackaging has plagued the Android platform. For example, a recent survey of top 100 paid and free apps on the Android (and iOS) platform shows that most of these popular apps suffer from app repackaging [64]. App developers are also finding their apps pirated, leading to considerable revenue loss [16,22,60]. Even worse, researchers found that 86% of Android malware samples are distributed to their victims through repackaged apps [75]. A few reasons contribute to the proliferation of app repackaging in the Android platform: first, most Android apps are written in Java whose bytecode retains rich semantics of the apps. This makes Android apps relatively easy to understand and modify without source code. Second, as mentioned earlier, Android apps are signed with self-certified keys. The signature of an app does not establish integrity or ownership of the app. Third, Android apps can be distributed through non-official channels such as third-party app stores where virtually no regulation or vetting process exists. Android users are also free to install apps of unknown origin (e.g., downloaded off the web).

With the help of publicly-available tools such as smali/baks-mali [19], repackaging an Android app is straightforward: the attacker only needs to disassemble the app to locate points of modification. The modification can be as simple as changing the

ad client ID (in order to redirect ad revenues to the attacker) or as complicated as tweaking of internals of the app [1]. After that, the attacker can reassemble the app and sign it with *his or her* own key. The repackaged app can now be distributed in (third-party) online app stores. This process is so well-defined that automated tools have been designed to repackage apps [70]. Given the easiness of this process, there is a pressing need to prevent app repackaging in the first place, in addition to the postmortem detection and jurisdiction [12,29,53,72–74]. To this end, DIVILAR applies the effective VM-based protection to Android apps. It aims to significantly increase the efforts needed to reverse-engineer and modify the app. By encoding apps in a different virtual instruction set, it immediately disables all existing tools that are based on Dalvik bytecode. The attacker has to reverse-engineer the DIVILAR execution engine for virtual instructions in order to manipulate the app.

3. DESIGN

3.1 DIVILAR Overview

DIVILAR aims at protecting Android apps from being repackaged by re-encoding them in a diversified virtual instruction set. We have three design goals for DIVILAR:

Robustness: although fundamentally it is an arms race, we expect DIVILAR to be robust against existing countermeasures, including commonly available static analysis, dynamic analysis, and these specific to VM-based protection. DIVILAR should also be architecturally flexible to accommodate new countermeasures.

Compatibility: DIVILAR-protected apps should be compatible with the current Android ecosystem. Specifically, the developers should be able to release their protected apps in the official Google play store or any third-party app stores, and users can download, install, and execute these apps just like normal apps. Compatibility is the key to the adoption of DIVILAR. Any requirements to change the Android framework will significantly limit the usability of such solutions.

Performance: DIVILAR introduces an extra layer of execution to managed code. With a straightforward design (e.g., implementing DIVILAR in the managed code), such a system will lead to prohibitive overhead [2]. Excessive performance overhead will render DIVILAR unsuitable for everyday use. As such, we design a lightweight hooking mechanism to merge virtual instruction execution into Dalvik VM to minimize its performance overhead.

Figure 3 shows the overall architecture of DIVILAR. It has four components: virtual instruction selector, bytecode transformer, virtual instruction interpreter, and Apk packager. Virtual instruction selector decides a virtual instruction set and produces a transforming rules (and its inverse) to describe how to translate Dalvik bytecode into virtual instructions (and vice versa). These two rules are used by the second and third components to guide conversion between Dalvik and virtual instructions. Specifically, bytecode transformer applies the transforming rule to an Android app to convert its classes from Dalvik bytecode to the selected virtual instruction set. The interpreter is an execution engine for the virtual instruction set. It is customized by the inverse transforming rule so that it can reverse virtual instructions back to Dalvik bytecode. Moreover, the interpreter is a native library to be bundled together with the guest app. At run-time, it will be loaded into the app's address space to execute the guest app. The last component, apk packager, packs the guest app and its interpreter inside a shell

---

[1]Java's late-binding makes this process considerably easier than native binary as symbols are dynamically resolved.

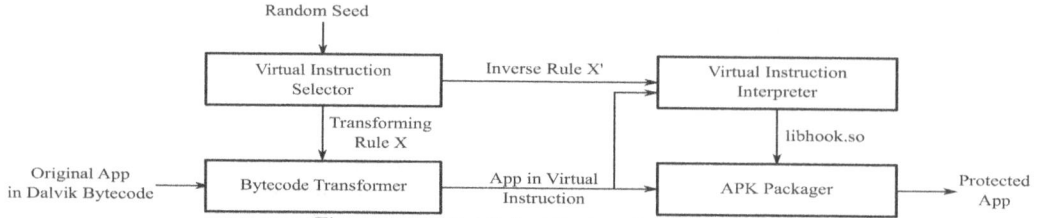

Figure 3: DIVILAR Architecture Overview

app. The shell acts as a proxy for the guest app (it is needed because the guest app is no longer recognizable by Android.) It is responsible for preparing the running environment for the guest app such as loading the interpreter. The shell also creates a custom class loader for the guest app, and uses it to load the guest's classes for execution. From Android's point of view, the shell is a well-formed app, while the guest app and its interpreter are just resources loaded by the shell. As such, a DIVILAR-protected app can pass the verification and be released, downloaded, and installed in the same way as a regular app.

DIVILAR is architecturally flexible. Various components can have varying levels of design and implementation. For example, the selector defines the conversion between Dalvik bytecode and virtual instructions. It could use a straightforward one-on-one mapping or implement complicated transformation by mixing cryptography algorithms as long as the process is reversible. Similarly, the interpreter can decode virtual instructions in different granularity: one method at a time, one basic block at a time, or one instruction at a time. Different granularity leads to different trade-off between performance (finer granularity has higher overhead) and information leakage (finer granularity leaks less information to an adversary who can monitor memory of the running app). In the rest of this section we will give more details about these four components of DIVILAR.

3.2 Virtual Instruction Selector

DIVILAR transforms an app encoded in Dalvik bytecode to that in a diversified virtual instruction set. Consequently, attackers are forced to first reverse-engineer virtual instructions as implemented by the interpreter, a native binary that can readily be obfuscated. In DIVILAR, each protected app is encoded in an unique set of virtual instructions decided by virtual instruction selector. The selector produces two rules: a transforming rule X to convert Dalvik bytecode to virtual instructions, and its inverse X' to reverse the process. DIVILAR does not pose any restrictions on the selector as long as the conversion is reversible. For example, it is possible to choose fixed or variable instruction length, apply different encoding scheme for opcodes and operands, or even use different styles of bytecode (stack-based v.s. register-based). Different choices of virtual instructions will affect DIVILAR's capability in resisting attacks that intend to reverse-engineer the interpreter.

Dalvik bytecode	Original opcode	Target opcode	Transforming rule	Inverse rule
add-int	90	7101	$90 \rightarrow 7101$	$7101 \rightarrow 90$
invoke-static	71	3202	$71 \rightarrow 3202$	$3202 \rightarrow 71$
if-eq	32	9003	$32 \rightarrow 9003$	$9003 \rightarrow 32$

Table 1: Example Mapping Rules for Opcode (in hex)

In our prototype, the selector is designed as a plugin of DIVILAR so that selectors with different levels of sophistication can be readily used and new selector can be created in response to unforeseen attacks. Our prototype implements a linear mapping between Dalvik opcode and virtual opcode. For easy of use by the other modules, the selector generates two mapping rules $X = \{R_1, R_2, ..., R_n\}$ and its inverse X' to formally describe how to translate from and to the Dalvik bytecode. Specifically, each member of X defines how the original Dalvik bytecode is transformed into a randomized virtual instruction. Table 1 gives some examples of the mappings for opcode. For example, Dalvik opcode $90h$, an add-int instruction, will be replaced by a two-byte opcode $7101h$. A tool that expects Dalvik bytecode will interpret this two-byte opcode as the invoke-static instruction (opcode $71h$) with $01h$ being the first byte of the operand [56]. Semantically, this "instruction" tries to invoke a static function (specified by 2 following bytes) with zero parameter. This mapping will also shift the instruction boundary around because $90h$ (add-int) has 4 bytes while $71h$ (invoke-static) has 6 bytes instead. Our evaluation shows that even this linear mapping can disable existing dynamic and static analysis tools, including these specific to VM-based protection. The produced set of rules will be used in bytecode transformer and virtual instruction interpreter to guide conversion between Dalvik bytecode and virtual instructions.

3.3 Bytecode Transformer

Bytecode transformer converts an Android app (an apk file) encoded in Dalvik bytecode to the instruction set decided by the selector. It first extracts from the app its Dalvik executable file (classes.dex), which contains definitions of all the app's classes. The transformer then decomposes the dex file into a list of classes and further parses them into fields and methods. A method consists of a method prototype and its associated Dalvik bytecode. At this point, the transformer converts the Dalvik instructions (including its opcode and operands) into virtual instructions guided by the transforming rule X. For example, in our linear mapping rule, opcode $90h$ will be converted to $7101h$, and opcode $71h$ will be converted to $3202h$ and so on. As an example of more sophisticated transformation, our prototype also supports an opcode chaining mode in which (the first byte of) the last virtual opcode is xor'ed with the next Dalvik opcode to get the input to the transforming rule X. For example, if the last target virtual opcode is $9003h$ (Table 1) and the next Dalvik opcode is $E1h$. The input to X is $71h$ ($90h \oplus E1h$), and the target opcode will be $3202h$. Such small tweaks are effortless to implement but will make the interpreter harder to reverse-engineer. After transformation, the resulting classes will be re-assembled into a DIVILAR-executable file. This file will be packaged into the final app as a data asset to be loaded and executed by the interpreter, described in the next section.

3.4 Virtual Instruction Interpreter

Using virtualization to protect apps is in general an expensive operation. For example, even in the native $x86$ mode, simple implementations could incur tens of times of overhead [17]. When an extra layer of virtualization is added to managed code, the performance simply becomes unacceptable for any real-world use [2], especially for mobile platforms where computation power and battery life are severely limited. Most Android apps consist of

202

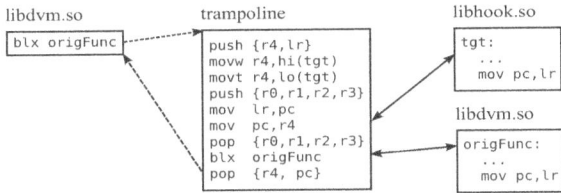

Figure 4: Function hooking in DIVILAR

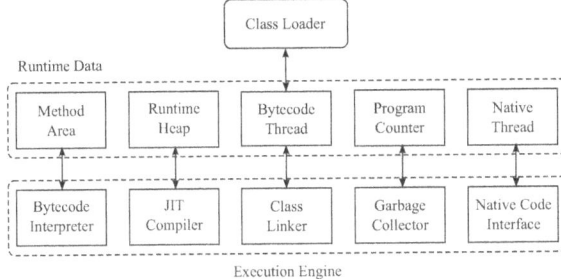

Figure 5: Components of Dalvik VM

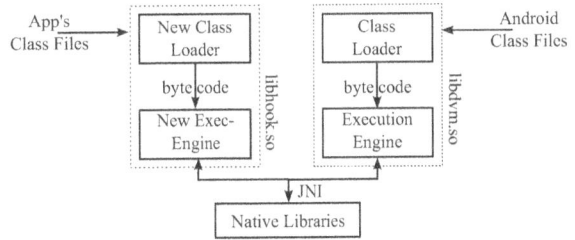

Figure 6: Architecture of Dalvik VM after DIVILAR loaded

managed code and run on mobile devices such as smartphone or tablets. Therefore, it is critical for DIVILAR to minimize performance overhead. The overhead comes mainly from the extra layer of bytecode execution. Observing that Android already contains a mature execution engine for Dalvik bytecode (Dalvik VM), DIVILAR tackles this problem by merging its interpreter into Dalvik VM, thus eliminating one layer of execution. More specifically, Android provides a Java virtual machine called Dalvik VM to execute the bytecode of apps. Dalvik VM is a mature intermediate language execution engine with rich features such as just-in-time compilation. Over the years, Dalvik VM has gradually stabilized with few updates [2]. In Android, it is shipped as a native library (libdvm.so) and loaded into the address space of every Android app, where it co-exists with other user-supplied native libraries (Android apps are free to load native binaries.) There exist no security boundary to isolate them (Figure 2). Therefore, it is feasible for DIVILAR to load its interpreter as a native library into the protected app, and manipulate Dalvik VM to piggy-back the execution of virtual instructions. The interpreter needs to be written in native code so it can directly operate on Dalvik VM's memory and issue system calls such as mprotect to change memory attributes.

To facilitate manipulation of Dalivk VM, DIVILAR provides a light-weight hooking mechanism (Figure 4) similar to Detours [31]. In DIVILAR, hooking points are function calls whose functionality needs to be extended or intercepted (blx origFunc in the figure). The call instruction will be overwritten with another instruction to redirected control flow to a trampoline. The trampoline is a short sequence of ARM instructions. It first saves the current CPU states (caller-saved registers $r_0 - r_4$ and the link register lr that contains the return address) to the stack, and loads the address of the extending function (tgt function in libhook.so) into one of the available registers (r_4) for execution. After tgt returns, the trampoline calls the original function so the call's functionality can be maintained and augmented. Finally, the trampoline restores the CPU state and returns back to the call site. Alternatively, we can insert a detour at the beginning of the original function (instead of the call site) to hook the function. We choose the current design because it provides more fine-grained control over when and where to hook a function.

---

[2]This alleviates the concern that DIVILAR is too dependent on the internals of Dalvik VM and thus is less compatible.

With this light-weight hooking mechanism, DIVILAR can hook into Dalvik VM to intercept and modify its execution in order to composite execution of virtual instructions and Dalvik bytecode. Manipulation of VM states at run-time requires clear understanding of its internals and careful planning. Figure 5 shows the major components of Dalvik VM: class loader and execution engine. Both components can operate on the shared run-time data such as method definitions and the heap. Execution engine has a number of components itself such as the bytecode interpreter (to execute bytecode), JIT compiler (to compile hot spots into native instructions), and class linker (to link classes from different Java libraries). Architecturally, DIVILAR can accommodate different designs of virtual instruction execution. For example, an implementation can provide a complete execution engine (possibly based on the Dalvik VM source code) and totally bypass Dalvik VM. Our prototype implements a pre-execution decoding scheme. More specifically, it hooks into functions that execute a method and decodes the method by reversing the opcode and operand mapping before its execution. In addition to these functions, we also need to modify class loader (so it knows how to load the guest app) as well as the meta-data in the method area. Section 4 contains details about our prototype. Figure 6 shows the logical architecture of Dalvik VM after the interpreter (libhook.so) is loaded. In the figure, Libhook.so is responsible for the loading of the guest app's classes because these classes are encoded in virtual instructions and cannot pass the sanity check of Dalvik's class loader. DIVILAR's execution engine hooks into and leverages Dalvik's execute engine to run the app. Technically, the interpreter contains complete information required to recover the original app. It is thus important to prevent it from being reverse-engineered. To this end, various obfuscation technologies for native binaries can be readily applied to libhook.so, such as packer/unpacker [28,48].

3.5 APK Packager

One of our design goal for DIVILAR is compatibility so that DIVILAR-protected apps do not require special install-time processing or modifications to the Android framework. As such, APK packager, the last component of DIVILAR, wraps all components necessary to execute the guest app into a single shell app. The interpreter (libhook.so) and the guest app are both contained in the shell as data assets. The shell app is a simple wrapper of the guest app, synthesized by APK packager. From Android's point of view, the shell app *is* the main body of the final app. Therefore, it can pass the install-time and run-time verification by the Android system. The shell app inherits the permissions required by the guest app so it can execute the guest app with enough permissions. It also needs to provide a wrapper for every entry point in the guest app, such as activities, content providers, and services defined in the guest app's manifest file [35]. These entry points are automatically loaded by Dalvik VM when starting an app. At run-time, when the shell's entry points are called, they simply load the corresponding guest app classes into memory and

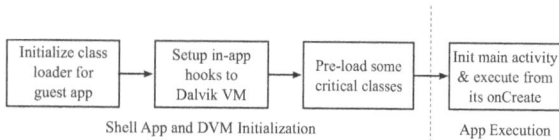

Figure 7: Execution Flow of the Protected App

dispatch them for execution. Note that this loading process does not decode virtual instructions. Instead, they are decoded only when necessary by `libhook.so`. After collecting all the required components, APK packager reassembles them into a single `apk` file which can be released, downloaded, and installed as a normal app.

The final app produced by DIVILAR consists of the shell, the guest app, and the interpreter. Figure 7 shows the run-time execution flow of the app. The shell first initializes the execution environments for the guest app. Specifically, it creates a custom class loader for the guest app's classes, loads the interpreter in the memory and hooks it to Dalvik VM, and finally pre-loads some critical classes of the guest app because Android expects these classes to be loaded upon returning from initialization. These steps need to be performed before executing the first instruction of the guest app. For this purpose, the shell app extends a special Android class called `android.os.Application`. This class (or its subclass) is guaranteed to be executed just after the (*shell*) app's classes are loaded and before the first bytecode of the main activity is executed.

4. IMPLEMENTATION

We have implemented a prototype of DIVILAR based on Android 4.0.4. Our prototype is a standalone Java application. It accepts an existing app as the input and generates an functionally-equivalent protected app. DIVILAR is intended to be used at the last stage of app development. The resulting app can be released in the online app stores for users to download and install. As mentioned earlier, the DIVILAR architecture can accommodate different levels of sophistication in the implementation. In this section, we describe details of our prototype in the order of DIVILAR's four components: instruction selector, bytecode transformer, the interpreter, and apk packager.

Our prototype adopts a linear mapping for Dalvik bytecode's opcodes and operands (Section 3.2). To guarantee that each protected app is encoded differently, the instruction selector uses a random number to permute the opcode/operand mapping. This generates two rules: the transforming rule X and its inverse. For example, $X =< 7503, 83, ... >$ specifies that opcode $01h$ will be converted to $7503h$, opcode $02h$ will be converted to $83h$, and so on. These rules are subsequently used to guide conversion between Dalvik and virtual instructions for the second and third components, bytecode transformer and the interpreter.

Bytecode transformer re-encodes the guest app in the virtual instruction set as specified by the transforming rule X. Our implementation utilizes the library of baksmali/smali [19], an open-source Dalvik disassembler/assembler. Specifically, the guest app is first parsed into a list of classes with their methods disassembled to the string format. Bytecode transformer then reassembles these classes into a `dex` file except that the opcode/operands have been adjusted according to rule X (file `org/jf/dexlib/Code/Opcode.java` of the baksmali library is changed to write out the custom opcode and operands). For example, the bytecode $01h$ is first parsed into its readable format (`move` in this case). DIVILAR then converts `move` to the new opcode of $7503h$ when

assembling the file. All classes of the guest app will be assembled together into a single `dex` file, and further packed into the final app as a data asset for the interpreter to execute.

The next step of the prototype generates a virtual instruction interpreter customized by rule X'. At run-time, the interpreter hooks into Dalvik VM in order to composite the virtual and Dalvik instruction execution. The interpreter is a native binary written in the C++ programming language. When loaded for execution, it first uses system call `mprotect` to make Dalvik VM writable so that it can be hooked. It then searches the code section of Dalvik VM for call sites of some specific functions, as determined by the hooking strategy. Each of these call sites will then be replaced by a call to the corresponding trampoline, as shown in Figure 4. A wide range of hooking schemes can be employed. In our prototype, we choose to extend the class initialization module, which is responsible for bytecode loading and method initialization (in file `vm/oo/Class.cpp` and `vm/oo/Object.cpp`). We add to it the pre-execution conversion of virtual instructions to Dalvik bytecode. To reduce the risk of the decoded methods being extracted from memory, our prototype flushes the Dalvik code cache randomly from time to time.

At the last step, APK packager assembles the guest app and the interpreter into a final app that can be publicly released later. It first parses the manifest file (`AndroidManifest.xml`) of the original app to get the list of requested permissions, entry points, and other resource files. It then synthesizes a wrapper (the shell) for the guest app. The shell inherits the requested permissions from the original app, and has a wrapper class for each entry point. It is also responsible for loading and executing of the guest app, a task performed in its subclass of `android.os.Application` because it is guaranteed to be executed before any other classes.

5. EVALUATION

DIVILAR aims to protect Android apps from being repackaged by applying VM-based protection. In this section, we first analyze DIVILAR's robustness against existing static and dynamic analysis, and countermeasures specific to VM-based protection in particular [11, 20, 57, 59]. We also evaluate the performance overhead introduced by DIVILAR.

5.1 General Analysis

DIVILAR re-encodes Android apps in a secret and diversified virtual instruction set. The guest app is wrapped as a data asset in the resulting app together with the interpreter for these virtual instructions. The interpreter hooks into the complicated Dalvik VM to composite execution of virtual and Dalvik instructions. By introducing this additional layer of indirection, existing tools that expect Dalvik bytecode will immediately be disabled. Attackers have to shift their focus from understanding Dalvik bytecode into reverse-engineering the interpreter first (presumably, the interpreter contains adequate information about the virtual instructions). In this sub-section, we will analyze DIVILAR's protection strength against app repackaging.

Rooted in native code: managed code is in general harder to obfuscate than native code because it contains rich semantics of the app. For example, intermediate languages like Java bytecode often use late binding, in which the target of a call is resolved at run-time *by name*. As such, call instructions in an intermediate language normally contain a reference to the method name as shown in Figure 1. Moreover, managed code has numerous run-time and compile-time checks to ensure program safety. This significantly limits the operations that can be performed by the program. Operations such as complex pointer arithmetic or direct memory access

```
unknown opcode encountered - 73. Treating as nop.

UNEXPECTED TOP-LEVEL EXCEPTION:
org.jf.dexlib.Util.ExceptionWithContext: 72
  at org.jf.dexlib.Util.ExceptionWithContext(ExceptionWithContext.java:54)
  ......
  at org.jf.dexlib.Section.readFrom(Section.java:143)
  at org.jf.dexlib.DexFile.<init>(DexFile.java:431)
  at org.jf.baksmali.main.main(main.java:280)
Caused by: java.lang.ArrayIndexOutOfBoundsException:72
  ......
  ... 6 more
Error occured at code address 140
code_item @0x784
```

Figure 8: Exception when applying *baksmali* on a transformed app

are almost always disallowed. Native code instead runs directly on the physical machine and has few restrictions in operations and program structures. Native code thus has more freedom in the support of obfuscation. Particularly, in native code, code and data can be mixed together; instructions can directly access any memory mapped in the program; a program can also mutate itself with the self-modifying code. Obfuscation in native code can leverage these features to make it more reliable. For example, Giffin et al. [23] propose to strengthen software self-checksumming using self-modifying code; Jacob et al. [37] leverage overlapped instructions in the x86 architecture to implement a stronger tamper-proof solution. These technologies make obfuscated native binaries more difficult to reverse-engineer, usually requiring laborious human efforts.

DIVILAR has its robustness rooted in the native code. Instead of implementing the interpreter in Dalvik bytecode, the interpreter is a native executable. This not only reduces the overhead, but also allows advanced obfuscation technologies [23, 37] to be applied, making the interpreter hard to reverse-engineer.

Varied virtual instruction selections: architecturally, DIVILAR can accommodate a wide range of virtual instruction selections as long as it can be reversed. The instruction selector works as a plugin of DIVILAR to support different encoding schemes, such as fixed-length v.s variable-length instructions, stack-based v.s register-based instructions, or even overlapped instructions [37]. Moreover, DIVILAR randomizes the virtual instruction set for each individual app. Breaking one protected app thus does not necessarily lead to compromise of other protected apps. In our prototype, we choose a linear mapping for virtual instructions. The combination of such a mapping is sufficiently large so that the brutal-force attack (to try every possible combinations) is simply infeasible. Meanwhile, our prototype can confuse a parser of Dalvik bytecode with shifted instruction boundaries. This makes frequency analysis ineffective because it relies on a parser to decode the app first (Section 5.4). Therefore, even with this simplified virtual instruction selection, our prototype provides a strong protection against existing countermeasures.

Diverse interpreter design: to reduce overhead, DIVILAR hooks into Dalvik VM in order to composite virtual and Dalvik instruction execution. A wide range of interpreter design (hence hooking schemes) can be supported. For example, it is possible to even write a standalone interpreter and completely bypass Dalvik VM. Different interpreter design needs to modify different components of Dalvik VM (Figure 5). Our prototype implements a pre-execute decode scheme in which virtual instructions are reverted back to Dalvik bytecode before execution. An adversary monitoring the memory of the app might be able to extract the recovered bytecode. To reduce the time window of possible exposure, our prototype will randomly flush the code cache. To further reduce the window, we may hook into code that execute instructions in a finer granularity, such as basic block level or instruction level.

To protect the interpreter from reverse-engineering, the interpreter should be obfuscated as mentioned before. A large number of existing obfuscation schemes for native binaries can be applied.

In addition, with the interpreter implemented in native code, performance overhead will not be a concern for DIVILAR as a variety of optimization techniques can be applied [1, 3, 9, 67], such as ahead-of-time compilation or adaptive optimization.

Compatible with other schemes: DIVILAR encodes the guest app in a diversified virtual instruction set. This kind of transformation is compatible with a wide variety of other protection mechanisms. For example, AppInk [72] embeds watermarks into an app to identify the source of an app. DIVILAR can be applied to the app after watermarks are embedded. Obfuscation techniques can also be applied before or after DIVILAR. For example, Java based obfuscation can be attempted first, and then DIVILAR is applied, or DIVILAR is used first and native code obfuscation can be used to obfuscate the interpreter in the resulting app. Moreover, DIVILAR aims to provide a strong preventive mechanism for apps. It does not provide services such as integrity check in itself. These services can also be combined with DIVILAR. For example, self-checksumming is often used to ensure program integrity. Due to various constrains of managed code, self-checksumming is challenging to implement in managed code. With DIVILAR, it can be implemented in the native code and be used at various stages of Dalvik VM execution. This would make self-checksumming for Android not only feasible but also more reliable against adversaries.

In the following of this section, we analyze DIVILAR's robustness against various specific static and dynamic analysis, including experiments with popular tools frequently used in Android app repackaging.

5.2 Static Analysis

To repackage an app, attackers often apply some form of static analysis to understand how the app is organized and where to make necessary modifications. All these tools include some form of disassembler to parse the app into machine- or human-readable format, such as the mnemonic representation of Dalvik bytecode. Baksmali [19] probably is the most popular disassembler for Android apps. Its source code has been embedded in many other Android analysis/reverse-engineering tools [24, 55]. Meanwhile, many static analysis tools for Android, such as Dare [51] and smali2java [24], re-target Android apps to Java bytecode (Java bytecode is stack-based while Dalvik bytecode is register-based) in order to leverage a rich set of existing Java analysis tools [66]. In this subsection, we will evaluate DIVILAR's resilience against two representative static analysis tools: baksmali [19] and Dare [51]. Specifically, we encode seven Android apps into virtual instructions, and apply these two tools on the resulting apps to observe their behaviors.

Baksmali is an open-source Android disassembler. Its companion project, Smali, is a corresponding assembler. Baksmali and Smali are frequently used to manually repackage apps [39]. Baksmali provides a library that can reliably parse Dalvik execute files [56] and further disassemble them into the mnemonic format. The source code of Baksmali has since been embedded in many other tools (including DIVILAR). For all these seven apps, Baksmali reports an error message of "unknown opcode encountered - nn. Treating as nop" and throws an unexpected top-level exception. Figure 8 shows an encountered exception when we apply Baksmali to one of the guest app. Baksmali and other Android analysis tools expect Dalvik bytecode as inputs. By re-encoding Android apps in virtual instructions, DIVILAR has changed the semantic of opcode

```
W/dalvikvm( 6997): Can't decode unexpected format 0 (op=115)
GLITCH: zero-width instruction at idx=0x0000
W/dalvikvm( 6997): Can't decode unexpected format 0 (op=115)
GLITCH: zero-width instruction at idx=0x0000
```

Figure 9: Error message when applying Dare on a transformed app

seen by these tools and shifted instruction boundaries around. However, these tools still interpreter the guest app according to the Dalvik bytecode format. This usually leads to unknown opcodes, as shown in Figure 8.

To leverage a wide variety of existing static analysis tools for Java bytecode, some analysis tools opt to re-target Android apps into Java bytecode. Dare [51] is one of the most effective tools for this purpose, which is reported to work correctly on more than 99.99% of 262,110 Dalvik classes. Since the very first step of Dare is also to parse the `dex` file, it fails with a similar symptom as Baksmali. Figure 9 shows the error message reported by Dare on the same guest app.

The above experiments show that DIVILAR can immediately render these existing Android disassemblers and analysis tools ineffective because they all depend on parsing the well-formed Dalvik bytecode. These tools include decompiler, slicer, control flow analyzer, data flow and data dependency analyzer [19,51,55, 66]. For these tools to function correctly, it is necessary to first recover the original Dalvik bytecode by reverse-engineering the interpreter.

5.3 Dynamic Analysis

Dynamic analysis executes the app under investigation in a monitored environment, such as a virtual machine or an emulator, to observe its behaviors. Dynamic analysis has been widely used in malware analysis and program development. In dynamic analysis, the monitor can be placed either inside or out of the run-time environment of the target app. The former has the advantage of direct access to system/app states, but its result may be disturbed or even tampered with by the target app. While the latter gains the tamper-resistance, but faces the "semantic gap" challenge [10,38], in which the monitor has to *deduce* app states given only externally observable data such as a memory dump [38,69]. It is challenging to apply this out-of-box approach to analyze Android apps because we need to reconstruct both operating system states and Dalvik VM states due to the two layers of virtualization [69]. DIVILAR makes the problem even more challenging by adding another layer of indirection: the monitor needs to infer states of the operating system, the virtual instruction interpreter, and Dalvik VM.

Our current prototype adopts a pre-execution decoding scheme. An adversary who *continuously* monitors the app's memory might be able to extract the bytecode of the original app. Such powerful attacks can be (partially) addressed by either limiting the amount of restored bytecode (e.g., from method to basic block) and shortening the time window of exposure, or by detecting whether the app is run in a virtual environment (the Android emulator) and refusing to run if so.

5.4 Virtualization Specific Analysis

Virtualization-based protection/obfuscation has been long employed by malware to hide its malicious behavior. A number of countermeasures have been proposed to detect or prevent such malware. For example, some systems aim to reverse-engineer the VM and use this information to infer semantics of individual virtual instructions [57,59]. Coogan et al. propose an inside-out approach [11], which intends to identify instructions that may affect the observable behavior of the wrapped code (i.e., system calls) .

Ghosh et al. propose to replace the protecting VM with an attacking VM in order to render the application amicable to analysis and modification [20]. Frequency analysis [68] is often used to break classical ciphers by studying the frequency of letters or groups of letters to disclose the mapping between plaintext and ciphertext. It may potentially be used to infer the mapping between Dalvik bytecode and virtual instructions. In the rest of this sub-section, we discusses DIVILAR's robustness against these virtualization-specific attacks.

Reverse-engineering VM: a few approaches are proposed to automatically reverse-engineer the virtual machine, and then use the recovered semantics of virtual instruction to understand the original app [57,59]. Automatic reverse-engineering a virtual machine, in general, is an unsolvable problem. As such, existing approaches limit the scope by, for example, assuming that the VM works in the loop of fetch-decode-dispatch. In case of DIVILAR, these assumptions do not hold, thus making these approaches ineffective: Dalvik VM has a complex structure with about 104,000 lines of C++ code and 99,000 lines of assembly code. Moreover, Dalvik VM supports many different execution modes, including portable, fast, and JIT modes. These execution modes can also be extended by DIVILAR in many possible ways as discussed earlier.

Inside-out approach: a recent work proposes an inside-out approach [11] that complements the VM reverse-engineering approach. Instead of recovering all instructions of the wrapped app, this approach aims at identifying instructions that interact with the operating system and instructions that may affect these instructions. It is assumed that these instructions together approximate the behavior of the original code, while other instructions are considered to be uninteresting. This approach can help malware analysts to gain better understanding of the malware under examination without being overwhelmed by details of all the instructions. However, partial understanding of virtual instructions is not enough to make meaningful modifications to the guest app and repackage it. In particular, any executable additions to the guest app need to be encoded in the same virtual instructions as the app. This is not possible without a complete understanding of the virtual instruction set first.

VM replacement attack: VM replacement attack is proposed to subvert virtualization-protected apps by replacing the protecting VM with an attacking VM, within which the app's execution can be monitored and analyzed. However, this attack is not effective against systems where virtual machine is sufficiently anchored to the execution environment [20]. DIVILAR's in-app hooking mechanism allows it to deeply hook into Dalvik VM and merge the execution of virtual and Dalvik instructions. This tight coupling with the underlying execution environment makes VM replacement attacks ineffective against DIVILAR. In addition, DIVILAR can identify whether the underlying VM has been modified or whether an attacking VM (specifically, its code introspection framework) has been loaded into the app's address space. Essentially, VM replacement attack in this case becomes an in-VM monitor and thus subjects to tampering [38].

Frequency analysis Frequency analysis is often used to break classic cipher where a plaintext letter is mapped to one ciphertext letter. By studying the frequency of letters or groups of letters, the analyst can deduce the mappings between the plaintext letters and ciphertext letters [68]. Our prototype of DIVILAR also uses a mapping table to convert Dalvik bytecode into virtual instructions. However, our system is not susceptible to frequency analysis. Specifically, by simply replacing one letter with another, a counting tool can easily count the frequency of plain-text and cipher-text in a classic cipher. However, it does not know how

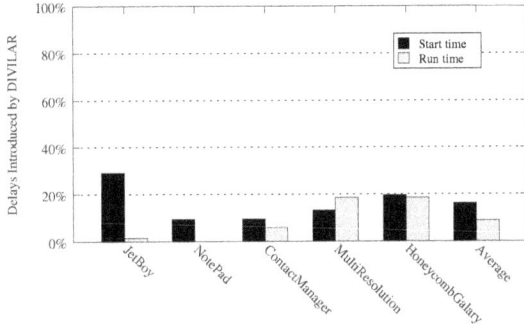

Figure 10: Performance overhead introduced by DIVILAR

to count the instruction frequency for virtual instructions without the knowledge of the virtual instruction set first. In fact, such tools would require a parser to decode instructions, which has been shown to be ineffective against DIVILAR (Section 5.2).

5.5 Performance Evaluation

In this section we evaluate the performance overhead introduced by DIVILAR. We measure both start-time and run-time overheads, two overheads that matter most to end users. We choose five sample apps from the Android SDK as our target apps: jet boy, notepad, contact manager, multi-resolution, and honeycomb gallery. We select these apps because their source code are freely available so that we can insert probing points into the apps to measure time required to execute certain operations.

We first measure how DIVILAR affects the app start up, from launching the app to the appearance of the main activity on-screen. To prepare an app for execution, the Android framework performs a series of steps such as loading Dalvik VM. DIVILAR adds to the start-time in order to prepare execution of virtual instructions. Specifically, the guest app is wrapped in a shell app. Android launches the shell first which in turn loads the guest app. To measure the start time, we use the `logcat` command [34] of Android Debug Bridge [33]. The verbose logging level of `logcat` is used so that it shows the elapsed time from app launching to the appearance of the first app view. All the experiments were executed three times with the average reported. Figure 10 shows the percentage of delays introduced by DIVILAR. They range from 9.4% to 29.2% with an average of 16.2%. Considering that all these test apps start in less than half-second even under DIVILAR's protection, the extra delay to start time caused by DIVILAR likely will not be perceived by end users at all.

Next, we measure the overhead of DIVILAR to a running app by adding probe points to log its execution time. Specifically, we first examine their source code to select code ranges where no user interaction is required (so as to exclude the impact of uncontrollable user interaction), and manually insert a call to `android.util.Log` before and after each of these selected code ranges. We then rebuild these apps and use DIVILAR to generated their corresponding protected apps. Figure 10 reports the percentage of overhead caused by DIVILAR to parts of these running apps. They range from 0% to 18.6% with an average of 8.9%. DIVILAR has fixed overhead for each method, i.e., the time to translate the method from virtual instructions to Dalvik bytecode. The run-time of a method, on the other hand, is determined by dynamic program states such as branch conditions and loops. For example, a method could execute only a failed branch in one run and execute hundreds of times in a loop in another run. Overall, our interpreter design is efficient and end users will not perceive any delays or stuttering.

6. DISCUSSION

In this section, we discuss implications and possible improvements of DIVILAR and , in particular, our prototype.

In essence, DIVILAR is an obfuscation technology used to protect the Android app from repackaging. Although the technology itself is neutral, obfuscation has long been used by malware authors to evade detection by anti-malware software. Many security researchers and practitioners share the opinion that benign software (Android apps in this case) should not use obfuscation so that its behaviors can be easily analyzed or even formally verified. Unfortunately, it is not an option for anti-repackaging. Most apps are repackaged and distributed in third-party online app stores [74]. These stores often lack regulations against app piracy (some even benefit from it), and many are located in other countries. It is thus difficult for developers to resolve the issue through jurisdiction. Instead, the developers have to enforce their apps for self-defense. App repackagers would try to defeat or bypass these defense mechanisms. It becomes an arms race between developers and app repackagers. For example, Google suggests to use string and other obfuscation techniques to prevent its server-side license verification from being disabled or bypassed [32]. In addition, VM-based protection has been previously proposed to protect applications [21, 46, 61, 62, 65].

Although not an architectural limitation, our prototype has a relatively simple design: a linear mapping of opcode/operand is used to select virtual instructions, and the interpreter implements a pre-execution decoding mode. Our initial experiments and analysis show that this design works reliably against existing static and dynamic countermeasures, including these specific to virtualization-base protection. Nevertheless, the design can be enhanced by additional techniques to thwart analysis. In the future, we will study ways to fortify our current design, particularly, how to formally measure the strength of obfuscation technologies and how to maximize its strength given certain performance overhead.

In its current operation model, developers use DIVILAR to process their apps before releasing them to the online app store. All installations of the app thus are the same across all its users (although different apps will have a different virtual instruction set). In the future, we will study methods to securely perform per-installation obfuscation, for example, to re-encode the app at its first run. In this way, each installation will have a different encoding, possibly tied to the user's device. This would provide a stronger protection because every installation of the app is different.

DIVILAR hooks into Dalvik VM to composite execution of virtual and Dalvik instructions. Like other such software [30], compatibility with different revisions of the host software is a concern. Dalvik VM, the host of DIVILAR , has become relatively stable since Honeycomb (Android 3.0). Our prototype further alleviates the problem by avoiding hard-coding any specific hooking points and locating them through pattern matching instead. Under the unlike circumvents that Dalvik VM is changed significantly and frequently, we could implement a self-contained execution engine (possibly based on the source code of Dalvik VM) and completely bypass Dalvik VM. This will improve the compatibility but may lose the benefit of updates made by Google.

Lastly, DIVILAR implements the VM-based protection for Android apps. From another point of view, VM-base protection can be considered as a generation of instruction set randomization [5]. For example, in addition to randomizing instruction set, VM-base protection can provide a randomized view of memory. Our current prototype focuses on the randomization of Dalvik bytecode. In the future, we will experiment randomization of other components in VM-based protection as well.

7. RELATED WORK

In this section, we present related work in the following category: diversification for security, virtualization-based protection, and Android app protection.

Diversification for security: the first category of related work includes researches that apply the principle of diversity to enhance security. For example, address space layout randomization is a defense mechanism to prevent low-level memory-base exploits such as buffer overflow [58]. It randomizes locations of a program's code or data so that an exploit cannot (easily) locate the vulnerability. It has since been ubiquitously deployed in Linux [63], Windows [49], Android [54], and Mac OS X [13]. Instruction-set randomization is a closely related work. It diversifies a program's instruction set to render injected attacking code ineffective (because they are encoded in a different instruction set) [5]. DIVILAR and other virtualization-based protection systems [2] adopt a similar idea to obfuscate a program in order to protect it from reverse-engineering. As software diversity becomes more popular, automated tools have been proposed to improve its performance. For example, Franz et al. use profile-guided optimization to reduce the overhead of software diversity [18]. This line of researches is orthogonal to our study and thus can be leveraged by DIVILAR to further reduce the overhead.

Virtualization-base protection: the second category of related work consists of systems that employ virtualization-based protection. Virtualization has long been applied to protect native code from reverse-engineering [21,61,62,65]. Malware authors are also found to use virtualization to thwart detection or analysis. Meanwhile, countermeasures have been proposed to detect or reverse-engineer virtualization-based malware. For example, Rotalume can automatically reverse-engineer virtualization-based malware that employs a virtual machine with a fetch-decode-execute model [59]. To allow malware analyst to focus on the critical behaviors of malware, an inside-out approach is proposed to identify instructions that interact with the underlying operating system and other instructions that may affect those instructions [11]. Moreover, Ghosh et al. propose to use an attacking VM to replace the protecting VM to subject the protected software to analysis. It assumes that the protecting VM is not tightly bound to the execution environment [20]. DIVILAR leverages virtualization to protect Android apps from repackaging. An adversary of DIVILAR could apply these techniques against DIVILAR. In section 5.4, we have analyzed DIVILAR's resilience against these approaches. Virtualization-based protection has also been applied to protect managed code as well (specifically MSIL) [2]. Their interpreters are implemented in managed code, causing performance overhead as high as 50 times to 3500 times. DIVILAR, also targeting managed code, achieves much better performance (Section 5) by combining virtual instruction and Dalvik bytecode execution.

Android app security: the last category of related work includes a long stream of research in Android app security, particularly these related to app repackaging. For example, a few systems aim to detect repackaged apps by measuring similarity among a large number of apps [12,29,53,73,74]. DIVILAR instead enables self-defense of Android apps using virtualize-based protection. It intends to prevent app repackaging at the first place. Recently, Google and other mobile platform providers introduced different flavors of server-side license verification solutions [32,52]. These solutions and DIVILAR complement each other: DIVILAR

can prevent these mechanisms from being circumvented, while they provide license verification. Similarly, Android app watermark [72] and software integrity check [23] can also be combined with DIVILAR to provide a more complete protection. There are also obfuscation technologies for Android [36, 41]. However, they tend to keep high-level semantic information of the app intact. Also, a new app installation mechanism is proposed to perform pre-installation verification and app encryption to protect app from repackaging [71]. However, it requires the app installation mechanism, a fundamental process of the Android platform, to be changed, hampering its adoption. DIVILAR has better compatibility with existing Android systems.

There are also a series of research on other aspects of Android app security. For example, TaintDroid [15] applies information flow tracking to monitor privacy leak in Android apps. Apex [50] and MockDroid [7] intend to address the privacy leak problem caused by invasive Android apps by modifying the Android framework. DroidRanger [76] and RiskRanker [27] propose different approaches to detect malicious Android apps in (third-party) online app stores. Woodpecker [26] and CHEX [47] try to discover capability leak and component hijacking vulnerabilities in Android apps. DIVILAR differs from them by introducing the self-defense capability into Android apps to protect themselves from being repackaged.

8. CONCLUSION

App repackaging remains a serious threat to the Android ecosystem and the emerging mobile economy model. To thwart repackaging, we adopt virtualization-based protection to enable the app's self-defense. To this end, we design an effective solution called DIVILAR which hooks into Dalvik VM to efficiently composite the virtual instruction and Dalvik bytecode execution. Our evaluation demonstrates that DIVILAR is robust against existing static and dynamic analysis including these specific to virtualization-based protection or obfuscation. Our prototype incurs a small performance overhead that likely is not perceivable to end users. In conclusion, DIVILAR is an effective and promising technology to enable app self-defense and prevent app repackaging in particular.

9. REFERENCES

[1] J. Absar and D. Shekhar. Eliminating Partially-Redundant Array-Bounds Check in the Android Dalvik JIT Compiler. In *Proceedings of the 9th International Conference on Principles and Practice of Programming in Java*, PPPJ '11, pages 121–128, New York, NY, USA, 2011. ACM.

[2] B. Anckaert, M. Jakubowski, and R. Venkatesan. Proteus: Virtualization for Diversified Tamper-Resistance. In *Proceedings of the Sixth ACM Workshop on Digital Rights Management*, pages 47–57, 2006.

[3] M. Arnold, S. J. Fink, D. Grove, M. Hind, and P. F. Sweeney. A Survey of Adaptive Optimization in Virtual Machines. In *Proceedings of the IEEE, 93(2), 2005. Special Issue on Program Generation, Optimization, and Adaptation*, 2004.

[4] S. Bansal and A. Aiken. Binary translation using peephole superoptimizers. In *Proceedings of the 8th USENIX conference on Operating systems design and implementation*, OSDI'08, pages 177–192, Berkeley, CA, USA, 2008. USENIX Association.

[5] E. G. Barrantes, D. H. Ackley, T. S. Palmer, D. Stefanovic, and D. D. Zovi. Randomized Instruction Set Emulation to Disrupt Binary Code Injection Attacks. In *Proceedings of the 10th ACM conference on Computer and communications security*, CCS '03, pages 281–289, New York, NY, USA, 2003. ACM.

[6] F. Bellard. Qemu, a fast and portable dynamic translator. In *Proceedings of the annual conference on USENIX Annual Technical Conference*, ATEC '05, pages 41–41, Berkeley, CA, USA, 2005. USENIX Association.

[7] A. Beresford, A. Rice, N. Skehin, and R. Sohan. MockDroid: Trading Privacy for Application Functionality on Smartphones. In *Proceedings of the 12th Workshop on Mobile Computing Systems and Applications*, HotMobile '11, 2011.

[8] A. D. Blog. Android at Google I/O 2013: Keynote Wrapup. http://android-developers.blogspot.com/2013/05/android-at-google-io-2013-keynote-wrapup.html.

[9] S. Brunthaler. Virtual-Machine Abstraction and Optimization Techniques. *Electron. Notes Theor. Comput. Sci.*, 253(5):3–14, Dec. 2009.

[10] P. M. Chen and B. D. Noble. When virtual is better than real. In *Proceedings of the Eighth Workshop on Hot Topics in Operating Systems*, HOTOS '01, pages 133–, Washington, DC, USA, 2001. IEEE Computer Society.

[11] K. Coogan, G. Lu, and S. Debray. Deobfuscation of Virtualization-Obfuscated Software: a Semantics-Based Approach. In *Proceedings of the 18th ACM conference on Computer and communications security*, CCS '11, pages 275–284, New York, NY, USA, 2011. ACM.

[12] J. Crussell, C. Gibler, and H. Chen. Attack of the Clones: Detecting Cloned Applications on Android Markets. In *17th European Symposium on Research in Computer Security*, ESORICS 2012, September 2012.

[13] O. X. Developer. Mac OS X Lion Security Enhancements – Improved ASLR. http://osxdeveloper.wordpress.com/2011/07/28/mac-os-x-lion-security-enhancements-improved-aslr/.

[14] A. Developers. Android NDK. http://developer.android.com/tools/sdk/ndk/index.html. Online; accessed at June 30, 2013.

[15] W. Enck, P. Gilbert, B.-g. Chun, L. Cox, J. Jung, P. McDaniel, and A. Sheth. TaintDroid: An Information-Flow Tracking System for Realtime Privacy Monitoring on Smartphones. In *Proceedings of the 9th USENIX Symposium on Operating Systems Design and Implementation*, USENIX OSDI '11, 2011.

[16] T. A. Entrepreneur. Android App Piracy Is A Huge Problem! http://theappentrepreneur.com/android-app-piracy-is-huge-problem.

[17] H. Fang, Y. Wu, S. Wang, and Y. Huang. Multi-stage Binary Code Obfuscation Using Improved Virtual Machine. In X. Lai, J. Zhou, and H. Li, editors, *Information Security*, volume 7001 of *Lecture Notes in Computer Science*, pages 168–181. Springer Berlin Heidelberg, 2011.

[18] M. Franz, S. Brunthaler, P. Larsen, A. Homescu, and S. Neisius. Profile-Guided Automated Software Diversity. In *Proceedings of the 2013 IEEE/ACM International Symposium on Code Generation and Optimization (CGO)*, CGO '13, pages 1–11, Washington, DC, USA, 2013. IEEE Computer Society.

[19] J. Freke. Smali - An Assembler/Disassembler for Android's dex Format. http://code.google.com/p/smali/. Online; accessed at Jun 30, 2013.

[20] S. Ghosh, J. Hiser, and J. W. Davidson. Replacement Attacks against VM-Protected Applications. In *Proceedings of the 8th ACM SIGPLAN/SIGOPS conference on Virtual Execution Environments*, VEE '12, pages 203–214, New York, NY, USA, 2012. ACM.

[21] S. Ghosh, J. D. Hiser, and J. W. Davidson. A Secure and Robust Approach to Software Tamper Resistance. In *Proceedings of the 12th international conference on Information hiding*, IH'10, pages 33–47, Berlin, Heidelberg, 2010. Springer-Verlag.

[22] C. Gibler, R. Stevens, J. Crussell, H. Chen, H. Zang, and H. Choi. AdRob: Examining the Landscape and Impact of Android Application Plagiarism. In *Proceedings of 11th International Conference on Mobile Systems, Applications and Services*, 2013.

[23] J. T. Giffin, M. Christodorescu, and L. Kruger. Strengthening Software Self-checksumming via Self-Modifying Code. In *The 21st Annual Computer Security Applications Conference*, pages 23–32. IEEE Computer Society, 2005.

[24] GitHub. Smali 2 Java Conversion Tool. https://github.com/demitsuri/smali2java. Online; accessed at Jun 30, 2013.

[25] R. Goodwin. WWDC 2013: Apple's App Store Numbers are Insane - 50 Billion App Downloads, $10 Billion Paid to Devs. http://

www.knowyourmobile.com/apple/20409/wwdc-2013-apples-app-store-numbers-are-insane-50-billion-app-downloads.

[26] M. Grace, Y. Zhou, Z. Wang, and X. Jiang. Systematic Detection of Capability Leaks in Stock Android Smartphones. In *Proceedings of the 19th Annual Network and Distributed System Security Symposium*, NDSS '12, February 2012.

[27] M. Grace, Y. Zhou, Q. Zhang, S. Zou, and X. Jiang. Riskranker: scalable and accurate zero-day android malware detection. In *Proceedings of the 10th international conference on Mobile systems, applications, and services*, MobiSys '12, pages 281–294, New York, NY, USA, 2012. ACM.

[28] F. Guo, P. Ferrie, and T.-C. Chiueh. A study of the packer problem and its solutions. In *Proceedings of the 11th international symposium on Recent Advances in Intrusion Detection*, RAID '08, pages 98–115, Berlin, Heidelberg, 2008. Springer-Verlag.

[29] S. Hanna, L. Huang, S. Li, C. Chen, and D. Song. Juxtapp: A Scalable System for Detecting Code Reuse Among Android Applications. In *9th Conference on Detection of Intrusions and Malware & Vulnerability Assessment*, DIMVA 2012, July 2012.

[30] G. Hoglund and J. Butler. *Rootkits: Subverting the Windows Kernel*. Addison-Wesley Professional, 2005.

[31] G. Hunt and D. Brubacher. Detours: binary interception of win32 functions. In *Proceedings of the 3rd conference on USENIX Windows NT Symposium - Volume 3*, WINSYM'99, pages 14–14, Berkeley, CA, USA, 1999. USENIX Association.

[32] G. Inc. Android Application Licensing. http://developer.android.com/guide/google/play/licensing/index.html. Online; accessed at Jun 30, 2013.

[33] G. Inc. Android Debug Bridge. http://developer.android.com/tools/help/adb.html. Online; accessed at Jun 30, 2013.

[34] G. Inc. Android Logcat. http://developer.android.com/tools/help/logcat.html. Online; accessed at Jun 30, 2013.

[35] G. Inc. The AndroidManifest.xml File. http://developer.android.com/guide/topics/manifest/manifest-intro.html. Online; accessed at Jun 30, 2013.

[36] S. Inc. A Specialized Optimizer and Obfuscator for Android. http://www.saikoa.com/dexguard. Online; accessed at Jun 30, 2013.

[37] M. Jacob, M. H. Jakubowski, and R. Venkatesan. Towards Integral Binary Execution: Implementing Oblivious Hashing Using Overlapped Instruction Encodings. In *Proceedings of the 9th workshop on Multimedia & security*, pages 129–140, New York, NY, USA, 2007. ACM.

[38] X. Jiang, X. Wang, and D. Xu. Stealthy malware detection through vmm-based "out-of-the-box" semantic view reconstruction. In *Proceedings of the 14th ACM conference on Computer and communications security*, CCS '07, pages 128–138, New York, NY, USA, 2007. ACM.

[39] S. Joo and C. Hwang. Mobile Banking Vulnerability: Android Repackaging Threat. Virus Bulletin, May 2012.

[40] A. Krall. Efficient javavm just-in-time compilation. In *Parallel Architectures and Compilation Techniques, 1998. Proceedings. 1998 International Conference on*, pages 205–212, 1998.

[41] E. Lafortune. ProGuard. http://proguard.sourceforge.net/. Online; accessed at Jun 30, 2013.

[42] T. Lindholm and F. Yellin. *Java Virtual Machine Specification*. Addison-Wesley Longman Publishing Co., Inc., Boston, MA, USA, 2nd edition, 1999.

[43] Lohan+. AntiLVL - Android License Verification Library Subversion. http://androidcracking.blogspot.com/p/antilvl_01.html. Online; accessed at Jun 30, 2013.

[44] Lohan+. Cracking Amazon DRM. http://androidcracking.blogspot.com/2011/04/cracking-amazon-drm.html. Online; accessed at Jun 30, 2013.

[45] Lohan+. Cracking Verizon's V Cast Apps DRM. http://androidcracking.blogspot.com/2011/06/cracking-verizons-v-cast-apps-drm.html. Online; accessed at Jun 30, 2013.

[46] S. T. Ltd. StarForce - Reliable Copy Protection for Software, Content, CD/DVD/USB. http://www.star-force.com/.

[47] L. Lu, Z. Li, Z. Wu, W. Lee, and G. Jiang. Chex: statically vetting android apps for component hijacking vulnerabilities. In *Proceedings of the 2012 ACM conference on Computer and communications security*, CCS '12, pages 229–240, New York, NY, USA, 2012. ACM.

[48] L. Martignoni, M. Christodorescu, and S. Jha. Omniunpack: Fast, generic, and safe unpacking of malware. In *Computer Security Applications Conference, 2007. ACSAC 2007. Twenty-Third Annual*, pages 431–441, 2007.

[49] MSDN. Address Space Layout Randomization for Windows Vista. http://blogs.msdn.com/b/michael_howard/archive/2006/05/26/608315.aspx. Online; accessed at Jun 24th, 2013.

[50] M. Nauman, S. Khan, and X. Zhang. Apex: Extending Android Permission Model and Enforcement with User-Defined Runtime Constraints. In *Proceedings of the 5th ACM Symposium on Information, Computer and Communications Security*, ASIACCS '10, 2010.

[51] D. Octeau, S. Jha, and P. McDaniel. Retargeting Android Applications to Java Bytecode. In *Proceedings of the ACM SIGSOFT 20th International Symposium on the Foundations of Software Engineering*, FSE '12, pages 6:1–6:11, New York, NY, USA, 2012. ACM.

[52] A. Police. [Updated: Amazon Provides Clarifications] Amazon App Store's DRM To Be More Restrictive Than Google's? http://www.androidpolice.com/2011/03/07/amazon-app-stores-drm-to-be-more-restrictive-than-googles/. Online; accessed at Jun 30, 2013.

[53] R. Potharaju, A. Newell, C. Nita-Rotaru, and X. Zhang. Plagiarizing Smartphone Applications: Attack Strategies and Defense Techniques. In *Proceedings of the 4th International Conference on Engineering Secure Software and Systems*, ESSoS'12, pages 106–120, Berlin, Heidelberg, 2012. Springer-Verlag.

[54] A. O. S. Project. Android Security Overview. http://source.android.com/tech/security/index.html#memory-management-security-enhancements. Online; accessed at Jun 24th, 2013.

[55] G. C. Project. Android-Apktool - Tool for Reengineering Android apk Files. http://code.google.com/p/android-apktool/. Online; accessed at Jun 30, 2013.

[56] T. A. O. S. Project. Bytecode for the Dalvik VM. http://source.android.com/tech/dalvik/dalvik-bytecode.html. Online; accessed at Jun. 23, 2013.

[57] R. Rolles. Unpacking Virtualization Obfuscators. In *Proceedings of the 3rd USENIX conference on Offensive technologies*, WOOT'09, pages 1–1, Berkeley, CA, USA, 2009. USENIX Association.

[58] H. Shacham, M. Page, B. Pfaff, E.-J. Goh, N. Modadugu, and D. Boneh. On the Effectiveness of Address-Space Randomization. In *Proceedings of the 11th ACM conference on Computer and communications security*, CCS '04, pages 298–307, New York, NY, USA, 2004. ACM.

[59] M. Sharif, A. Lanzi, J. Giffin, and W. Lee. Automatic Reverse Engineering of Malware Emulators. In *Security and Privacy, 2009 30th IEEE Symposium on*, pages 94–109, 2009.

[60] Slashgear. 95% Android Game Piracy Experience Highlights App Theft Challenge. http://www.slashgear.com/95-android-game-piracy-experience-highlights-app-theft-challenge-15282064/.

[61] A. Software. ASProtect - Software Protection Tools for Software Developers. http://www.aspack.com/asprotect.html.

[62] V. Software. VMProtect Software Protection. http://vmpsoft.com/.

[63] P. Team. Pax Document for Linux ASLR. http://pax.grsecurity.net/docs/aslr.txt. Online; accessed at Jun 24th, 2013.

[64] A. Technologies. State of Security in the App Economy: Mobile Apps Under Attack. http://www.arxan.com/assets/1/7/state-of-security-app-economy.pdf, 2012.

[65] O. Technologies. Code Virtualizer Overview. http://www.oreans.com/codevirtualizer.php.

[66] R. Vallée-Rai, P. Co, E. Gagnon, L. Hendren, P. Lam, and V. Sundaresan. Soot - a java bytecode optimization framework. In *Proceedings of the 1999 conference of the Centre for Advanced Studies on Collaborative research*, CASCON '99, pages 13–. IBM Press, 1999.

[67] C.-S. Wang, G. Perez, Y.-C. Chung, W.-C. Hsu, W.-K. Shih, and H.-R. Hsu. A Method-based Ahead-of-Time Compiler for Android Applications. In *Proceedings of the 14th international conference on Compilers, architectures and synthesis for embedded systems*, CASES '11, pages 15–24, New York, NY, USA, 2011. ACM.

[68] WikiPedia. Frequency analysis. http://en.wikipedia.org/wiki/Frequency_analysis. Online; accessed at Jun 24th, 2013.

[69] L. K. Yan and H. Yin. Droidscope: seamlessly reconstructing the os and dalvik semantic views for dynamic android malware analysis. In *Proceedings of the 21st USENIX conference on Security symposium*, Security'12, pages 29–29, Berkeley, CA, USA, 2012. USENIX Association.

[70] M. Zheng, P. P. Lee, and J. C. Lui. ADAM: An Automatic and Extensible Platform to Stress Test Android Anti-Virus Systems . In *Proceedings of the 9th Conference on Detection of Intrusions and Malware & Vulnerability Assessment*, 2012.

[71] M. Zheng, M. Sun, and J. Lui. Reboot the Android Third-party Markets:The Way to Defend Against Cracking and Malware Repackaging on Android Application. In *Internet Security Forum*, 2012.

[72] W. Zhou, X. Zhang, and X. Jiang. AppInk: Watermarking Android Apps for Repackaging Deterrence. In *Proceedings of the 8th ACM SIGSAC symposium on Information, computer and communications security*, ASIA CCS '13, pages 1–12, New York, NY, USA, 2013. ACM.

[73] W. Zhou, Y. Zhou, M. Grace, X. Jiang, and S. Zou. Fast, Scalable Detection of Piggybacked Mobile Applications. In *Proceedings of the 3nd ACM Conference on Data and Application Security and Privacy*, CODASPY '13, February 2013.

[74] W. Zhou, Y. Zhou, X. Jiang, and P. Ning. DroidMOSS: Detecting Repackaged Smartphone Applications in Third-Party Android Marketplaces. In *Proceedings of the 2nd ACM Conference on Data and Application Security and Privacy*, CODASPY '12, February 2012.

[75] Y. Zhou and X. Jiang. Dissecting Android Malware: Characterization and Evolution. In *Proceedings of the 33rd IEEE Symposium on Security and Privacy*, Oakland 2012, May 2012.

[76] Y. Zhou, Z. Wang, W. Zhou, and X. Jiang. Hey, You, Get off of My Market: Detecting Malicious Apps in Official and Alternative Android Markets. In *Proceedings of the 19th Annual Network and Distributed System Security Symposium*, NDSS '12, February 2012.

On Quantitative Dynamic Data Flow Tracking

Enrico Lovat, Johan Oudinet, Alexander Pretschner
Technische Universität München, Germany
{lovat,oudinet,pretschn}@in.tum.de

ABSTRACT

We present a non-probabilistic model for dynamic quantitative data flow tracking. Estimations of the amount of data stored in a particular representation at runtime — a file, a window, a network packet — enable the adoption of fine-grained policies which authorize or prohibit partial leaks of data. We prove the correctness of the estimations, provide an implementation that we evaluate w.r.t. precision and performance, and analyze one instantiation at the OS level.

Categories and Subject Descriptors

H.4 [**Information Systems Applications**]: Miscellaneous

Keywords

Information flow; runtime monitoring; usage control

1. INTRODUCTION

Information flow tracking can be used to support access and usage control [29]. In order to enforce real-world usage control requirements on data, one must take into account that data exist in multiple representations. This requires tracking the data flow from one representation to another within and across different abstraction layers [29]. For example, a picture to be protected may be at the same time a file on the disk (operating system (OS) level), a browser object (application level) and/or a set of pixels on the screen (window manager level). It is therefore convenient to distinguish between abstract data (e.g., a picture) and concrete representations of data at different levels of abstraction, which we also call *containers* (e.g., a file at the OS level, a record at the database level, a set of pixels at the windowing level). Using this model, one can track the distribution of data among different containers in the system at any time and, using such information, enforce advanced usage control requirements such as "every copy of this data item must be deleted in 30 days." However, the information this model can offer about a certain container c and a certain datum d

is binary: either c potentially contains (possibly partially) d, or it does not, similarly to the notion of *tainting* in information flow analyses.

We propose a refinement of this model that keeps track of the (estimated) *amount* of data that flows to a container. We do not limit our analysis to whether or not data flowed, but answer the question of *how much data flowed?*

The benefit of this extension is the ability to express and enforce *quantity-based policies*, such as *if more than 5% of customer data is stored in a file, then that file must not leave the system and must be deleted on log out.*

Quantitative measurements are useful for preventive enforcement but also for *a posteriori* analyses. Consider a company's software querying a customer database and the policy *access to these data allowed during opening hours only*. Without preventive enforcement mechanisms, employees might take home sensitive data. Often, this is the only way to get the job done in time, in violation of the policy. For auditing purposes, it should then at least be recorded how much sensitive data have been disclosed. An auditor spotting a policy violation that concerns only 0.01% of customer data once a month may decide to ignore it, while daily disclosure, or disclosure of 30% of data, must be sanctioned.

This concept of *acceptable exception* is very important in security in practice. Even though confidential data should never be disclosed, this restriction is occasionally circumvented to accomplish specific tasks. While quantifying the threshold between an acceptable exception and a violation to report depends on the context-specific security goal (e.g., cost in case of disclosure), thanks to Quantitative Data Flow Tracking (QDFT) it is possible to measure quantitative flows of data and to enforce rules on them.

Research problem We study how to perform quantitative data flow measurements and how to incorporate these measurements into a data usage control framework.

Solution and contribution We define a formal model for dynamic quantitative information flow measurements; implement it; and integrate it into a usage control framework, thus allowing the specification and enforcement of *quantity-based* policies. We see our contribution in a generic model for quantitative data flows that can be instantiated to different layers of abstraction and that uses a non-probabilistic layer-specific quantitative measure for data (*units*). We provide an exemplary instantiation at the OS level.

Structure After an introduction to measuring data in § 2, § 3 presents our model for measuring data flow quantities. § 4 sketches quantitative policies. § 5 describes an experimental evaluation. § 6 puts our work in context. We discuss the underlying assumptions and some perspectives in § 7. Future work and conclusions are left to § 8.

Running example Alice works as an analyst for a smartphone manufacturer. All sensitive projects are stored in a central repository, which is accessible by each client machine, like Alice's. She regularly requires information about new models under development. Her job includes combining it with data from field experiments and from various public sources into reports for suppliers and for other departments. To prevent leakage of sensitive data, each enterprise machine implements measures such as forbidding the installation of third-party software. However, too restrictive measures, such as preventing sensitive data from being saved locally, proved not to be very effective in the past. This is because they slow down the business process too much and sometimes were circumvented on a regular basis. For this reason, each machine is equipped with an OS-level monitor that tracks the amount of sensitive data that is processed by each system call. This system aims at the enforcement of policies such as: *if a file contains more than 1MB of sensitive data, then it must be saved in encrypted form and may not be emailed.* Such a policy allows Alice to send to a supplier some details about a specific smartphone, like for example size, weight or screen resolution, but prevents her from disclosing too many details such as a high-resolution pictures of the circuit board. In order to prevent violations of the policy by splitting data in multiple different files and mails, the aggregated number of chunks mailed to the same destination is recorded and stored for a reasonable amount of time, e.g., until the phone is publicly released.

2. MEASURING DATA QUANTITIES

In the rest of this paper we use the following terminology: a *data item* is a representation-independent abstract content that we want to protect (e.g., a phone specification). Data (items) are abstract concepts that exist in the system only in the form of layer-specific representations, called *containers* (e.g., a file, a window, a database record). For example, if picture P is stored in file F, then we say that F is a (partial) representation of P or equivalently that container F (partially) contains data item P. Note that one container may contain more than one data item (e.g., one single file may contain the specifications of two phones).

With our model, we want to track the distribution of *data* across different *containers*. If we know that data are stored in one particular container, and an action (e.g., a copy command or a query) transfers half of the content of the container into a new one, intuition suggests that also half of the data is stored in the new representation. Thus, our model refines the so-called *tainting approach* (yes, data are stored in this container / no, they are not) by the notion of *quantity* (50% of data are stored in this representation). Given a specific container, such as a file or a database, we want to know *how much* different sensitive data are stored in it. We can then enforce policies such as *if more than 1MB of data related to a phone specification are stored in a file, then that file must be encrypted and deleted on log out.*

We define as *data unit* the smallest part of a container that can be addressed by an event of the system, like a system call or a query, and as *size* of a container the number of units that compose it. The size of an event is the number of units the event processes. Units may differ depending on the level of instantiation. For example, at the database level, records (or cells) are units ("database d.db contains 14 sensitive records") whereas at the file system level, containers are measured in bytes or blocks, depending on the granularity of the events that operate on them ("file f.doc contains 150KB of sensitive data"). If data flow across different layers, units at one layer must be converted into units of the other layer. We get back to conversion in § 7.

The goal of this work is to *estimate how many different* units of sensitive data are stored in a specific container. Multiple copies of the same unit stored in the same container do not make the container more sensitive than a single copy: if a document contains the same paragraph twice, it contains as much information as a document with only one instance of this paragraph. Given a data source (the initial representation), we want to know how many different units of this data item are stored in each container of the system at a specific moment in time. If a container c contains q units of data d, then, by looking at c, one may come to know up to q different units of (the initial representation of) d.

We assume each unit to be as informative as any other unit, i.e., no unit is more important than another. If this assumption cannot be justified, then we may assume that the data items are structured into parts of different informative value, and we separately cater to the different parts of the structure. We do not consider covert or side-channels (e.g., knowing whether a unit has been copied or not does not leak any information about its actual value). Compression and/or different encoding schemas conflict with the assumption of informative equality of units. However, in closed or semi-closed environments as in our example, it is reasonable to assume the behavior of every single event or process in the system to be known, and therefore also knowledge of where compression takes place. For simplicity's sake, we do not consider this case in our solution but discuss it in § 7.

Knowing *how many* data units are stored in a container does not necessarily imply knowledge of *which* data units. Knowing exactly which units of data are transferred requires monitoring and storage capabilities that may not be available in every scenario. For example, in a database system, it may be reasonable to log the *number* of records retrieved by a query (size of the result table), but not to log the *complete content* of each query (values in the result table).

The precision of our quantitative approach is in-between coarse-grained and fine-grained tainting approaches. Coarse-grained tainting tracks data at the level of containers: if one data unit flows to a container, the whole container is considered as sensitive as if the complete data item had been transferred to this container. Fine-grained tainting tracks each data unit independently and computes exactly which data unit is stored in each container. Our quantitative method records the size of each event and infers that the destination container of a transfer operation of size n contains at most n different data units, *but not which ones*. If tracking every data unit is not possible or requires too many storage or computational resources, the quantitative approach can be a good compromise between security and usability.

3. QDFT MODEL

We now describe how to compute for every container, at each moment in time, an upper bound for the number of different units of a sensitive data item in this container. This is done on the grounds of a quantitative data flow model.

The model relies on three abstractions: data, containers, and events. Three types of events affect the amount of data in a container: container initializations, transfers of data units from one container to another (e.g., copying or appending parts of a file), and deletion of data from a container (e.g., deleting some records from a database table). These abstract events need to be instantiated according to the instantiation of the model (e.g., system calls for an OS, queries for a database).

Initially, each container in the system contains no unit of sensitive data. If a new sensitive data item is introduced into the system, this event is modeled by mapping the number of sensitive units in this data item to its initial representation(s). Usually, the initial amount of sensitive data corresponds to the size of the initial representation, but we allow for the case where a data item is only partially sensitive, i.e., the number of sensitive units may be strictly smaller than the size of the initial representation.

After the initialization of a data item d, every event in the system that corresponds to a transfer or deletion of units of d in some container is monitored. We will show how different events lead to different upper bounds for the number of sensitive units in each container.

The amount of sensitive data transferred by an event is bounded by the amount of sensitive data stored in the source container. This bound can sometimes be improved. Consider two transfers of 6 units each from a container A of size 10 to a new container B. Simply adding units to the destination after every transfer would assign to B an upper bound of 12, even though A is bounded by 10 (hence no more than 10 different units could have flowed from A to B).

A similar observation can be made if a container receives data from multiple related sources. Consider a scenario where 6 units are transferred from A of size 10 to B. An additional transfer of 6 units from A to C and a subsequent transfer of 6 units from C to B would lead to the same result of B containing 12 different units—but all the units in B originate in A of size 10. To increase precision, we hence need to keep track of previous transfers. This historic information is stored in a *provenance graph*.

Provenance graphs For simplicity's sake, we assume that there is only one data item d in this section. If there is more than one item, we need more than one provenance graph, which we discuss in § 4. Data provenance is recorded by a flow graph $\mathcal{G} = (\mathcal{N}, \mathcal{E})$. Each node $n \in \mathcal{N}$ in this graph represents a container at a specific moment in time, encoded by a natural number: $\mathcal{N} \subseteq C \times \mathbb{N}$, where C is the set of containers. We assume the existence of a special external source node $(S, 0) \in \mathcal{N}$ for the data item for which the graph is built. Edges $\mathcal{E} \subseteq \mathcal{N} \times \mathbb{N} \times \mathcal{N}$ represent events that add data to or remove data from containers. The label of an edge is the actual amount (number of units) of data that flowed from the source container to the destination container in the considered event. As a consequence, it also is an upper bound for the amount of *sensitive* data units that flowed from the source node's container to the destination node's container. Its precise value is determined by the event, e.g., 100 bytes or 10 records have been copied.

Goal We want to compute an upper bound for the number of different sensitive units of data item d in each container in the system. For reasons that will become apparent in step 6 of the example below, we do this on the grounds of a provenance graph. We will define a function κ that com-

putes such an upper bound for those nodes of the provenance graph that correspond to the containers in the current (that is, latest) time step.

Construction at runtime A provenance graph is incrementally built at runtime. This gives rise to a sequence of graphs $\mathcal{G}_0, \ldots, \mathcal{G}_t$ for each moment in time, t. Let $\mathcal{G}_t = (\mathcal{N}_t, \mathcal{E}_t)$ for all t. For a node $n \in \mathcal{N}_t$, let $\kappa(n)$ be the above mentioned upper bound for the maximum number of sensitive units in the container that corresponds to the node (the computation of κ will be discussed below). For every event at time t, at most one new node as well as one or two new edges are created. This evolves $\mathcal{G}_{t-1}$ into $\mathcal{G}_t$ where $\mathcal{G}_{t-1}$ is a subgraph of $\mathcal{G}_t$. Possible graph evolutions are the following:

I step The *initialization* of data is modeled by copying all data from the data source node to an initial container c_i. Assuming the event at time t is the initialization, we add a node (c_i, t) to $\mathcal{N}_{t-1}$ and, for m units of sensitive data contained in data item d, an edge $((S, 0), m, (c_i, t))$ to $\mathcal{E}_{t-1}$, which yields $\mathcal{G}_t = (\mathcal{N}_t, \mathcal{E}_t)$.

C steps If, at time t, container c_1 may contain some sensitive units and the event *copies*, without knowledge of whether or not they are sensitive, ℓ units of data from container c_1 to c_2, then we add a node (c_2, t) and the first or both of the following two edges to $\mathcal{G}_{t-1}$:

C1 step $((c_1, t'), \ell, (c_2, t))$ for the node $(c_1, t') \in \mathcal{N}_{t-1}$ with $t' < t$ such that there is no $(c_1, t'') \in \mathcal{N}_{t-1}$ with $t' < t'' < t$ (this ensures that we copy data from the "latest representation" of container c_1).

C2 step If c_2 already exists (copying then is appending), we also need to consider its content at time $t - 1$. In this case, there is a $t' < t$ such that $(c_2, t') \in \mathcal{N}_{t-1}$ and there is no t'' with $t' < t'' < t$ such that $(c_2, t'') \in \mathcal{N}_{t-1}$. To make sure that the sensitive content of c_2 at time t' (which is the same as at $t - 1$) is not forgotten at time t, we add the edge $((c_2, t'), \kappa((c_2, t')), (c_2, t))$ to $\mathcal{E}_{t-1}$. Replacing the label $\kappa((c_2, t'))$ by ∞ would not impact correctness nor precision; our choice of $\kappa((c_2, t'))$ is motivated by presentation concerns. See the introductory remark in the appendix.[1]

T step If the event at time t is a *truncation* of c, we need to compare the amount of sensitive data in c (i.e., $\kappa((c, t'))$ such that $(c, t') \in \mathcal{N}_{t-1}$ and $(c, t'') \in \mathcal{N}_{t-1} \Rightarrow t'' \leq t'$) to the new size of c, m. Since a container cannot store more sensitive data than its actual size, if $\kappa((c, t')) > m$, we add a node (c, t) and an edge $((c, t'), m, (c, t))$ to $\mathcal{G}_{t-1}$. Otherwise, no new node is added.

Example Before we explain how to compute κ, consider the example in Figure 1.

1. First, container A is initialized with the content from the external data source (an I step). This yields node $(A, 1)$ as well as the edge labelled 20 from $(S, 0)$ to $(A, 1)$, indicating that the data item in question contains 20 units of sensitive data (and possibly more non-sensitive data). The only useful estimation is $\kappa((A, 1)) = 20$. Note that this only measures the number of sensitive units; similar to S, A may well contain more non-sensitive units of data.

---

[1] Note that a C step can be performed with more than one source container. This is modeled as a C1 step for each source container and only one C2 step if the destination container already exists.

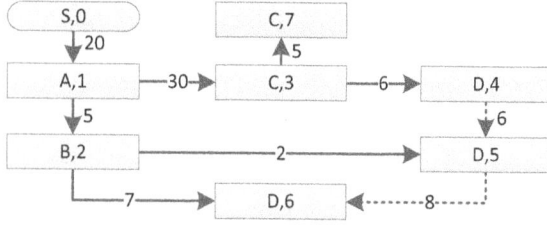

Figure 1: Example provenance graph at time $t = 6$. Dashed arrows are C2 steps.

2. In the second step, 5 units of data are copied from A to B, which results in node $(B, 2)$ and the edge labelled 5 from $(A, 1)$ to $(B, 2)$ (a C1 step). Since only five units of data have been moved, $\kappa((B, 2)) = 5$ is reasonable.

3. The third event copies 30 units of data from container A to container C (another C1 step), resulting in an edge with label 30 from node $(A, 1)$ to a newly created node $(C, 3)$. Note that it is possible to copy 30 units because the size of A may well exceed the number of sensitive units. Still, since A contains at most 20 units of sensitive data, 20 is also an upper bound for the number of sensitive units in C, yielding $\kappa((C, 3)) = 20$.

4. The fourth event copies 6 units from C to D (another C1 step). This yields a new node $(D, 4)$ and an edge labelled 6 from node $(C, 3)$ to $(D, 4)$. We know that C contains at most 20 sensitive units and have hence to assume that all data copied from C to D is sensitive. We estimate $\kappa((D, 4)) = 6$.

5. The fifth event copies 2 units from B to D (a C1&C2 step). This results in a new node $(D, 5)$, an edge labelled 2 from $(B, 2)$ to $(D, 5)$ and, in order to reflect the content previously contained in D, another new edge from $(D, 4)$ to $(D, 5)$ labelled 6 (which is the κ value of $(D, 4)$). The maximum number of sensitive units in D now is $\kappa((D, 5)) = 8$, the sum of at most 2 units from B and at most 6 units from the earlier instance of D.

6. The sixth event copies another 7 units from B to D (another C1&C2 step). We create a new edge labelled 7 from $(B, 2)$ to a new node $(D, 6)$, and an edge labelled $\kappa((D, 5)) = 8$ from $(D, 5)$ to $(D, 6)$. This is where the computation of a precise value for κ becomes non-trivial. A first estimate for the upper bound is $\kappa((D, 6)) = 8 + 7$, a result of the flows from B and an earlier version of D to D, similar to what happened in step 5. However, we know that the actual flows are upper bounds for flows of sensitive data, and since $\kappa((B, 2)) = 5$ and $\kappa((D, 5)) = 8$, it is impossible to have more than 13 distinct sensitive units in D. A better estimate is hence $\kappa((D, 6)) = 5 + 8$. Yet, it is impossible that 13 *different* units flowed from A to D: The upper bound of $\kappa((D, 5)) = 8$ units of sensitive data includes 2 units received from B (step 5). Since we do not need to count these units twice, D cannot contain more than $\kappa((D, 6)) = 5 + 6$ different sensitive units.

7. The seventh event truncates the size of container C to the new size of 5. This results in a new node $(C, 7)$ and an edge labelled 5 from $(C, 3)$ to $(C, 7)$. $\kappa((C, 7)) = 5$, because C is now composed of 5 units only, i.e. C contains at most 5 different sensitive units.

Motivation for provenance graphs Step 6 of the example motivates the use of provenance graphs: The fact that

$(D, 6)$ necessarily contains duplicates of two units of sensitive data is something that we can know only by considering the *history* of data flows (in this case, step 5 that appended two units of data to container D—and the transfer of sensitive data in step 5 depends on steps 2 and 4, as we will see below). It is this historical knowledge that allows us to reduce the upper bound $\kappa((D, 6))$ from 13 to 11 units.

Motivation for max-flow/min-cut In fact, *the number of units transferred from $(B, 2)$ to $(D, 5)$ (i.e., the 6th event) is not the only relevant influence for the computation of $\kappa((D, 6))$*; regardless of the number of units that had been transferred from B to D in step 5, we would still have an upper bound of at most $\kappa((D, 6)) = 11$. From this perspective, the provenance graph now reveals that $(B, 2)$ and $(D, 5)$ together cannot contain more than 5+6 units of sensitive data: historically, B received 5 units in step 2 and D received 6 units in step 4. *This information is stored in the form of the edge labels.* This motivates the computation of κ via the max-flow/min-cut theorem rather than via recursive computations on predecessors or dominators of the newly created nodes as follows. Remember that the *actual* flows of possibly non-sensitive data in-between containers (the edge labels) are *upper bounds* for the flow of *sensitive* data. We can hence interpret them as *capacities for sensitive data* in the flow graph. Then, the upper bound for the amount of different sensitive data in each container (corresponding to a node n) equals the maximum flow of sensitive data from the source node to this node n. In our example, the max flow to D in step 6 is determined by steps 2 and 4, corresponding to the edges from $(A, 1)$ to $(B, 2)$ and from $(C, 3)$ to $(D, 4)$.

Computation of κ The definition of κ then is simple: if $n \in \mathcal{N}_t$ is the new node created in time step t, then $\kappa(n) = maxflow_{\mathcal{G}_t}((S, 0), n)$. Since every container can be the destination of a copying event in the next step (a C step), we always need to know the current κ value of all nodes.

Algorithmically, we need to compute at most one maxflow/min-cut on a directed acyclic graph per event for the new node. This is because we never add incoming edges to existing nodes; their κ value is constant over time.

Correctness Our model is correct if, at each moment in time, the number of different units of a sensitive data item actually contained in a container is not greater than the κ value we have computed. We assume a function φ that provides this actual amount for a node (i.e., container and a moment in time). We do not say how to compute φ, we just assume its existence.

We need to assume that all events in the system are adequately reflected in the construction of the flow graph. Whenever an event moves data in-between containers, this event is used to construct the provenance graph as described above. Conversely, no edge or node is added if there is no corresponding event. This assumption connects the model (provenance graph) to the real system. Note that κ denotes a property of the model and φ a property of the real world.

The proof that $\forall t \in \mathbb{N} \, \forall c \in C : \varphi(c, t) \leq \kappa((c, t))$ indeed holds is provided in Appendix A.

Simplification Because the complexity of the computation of maximum flows depends on the size of the graph, it is desirable to keep graphs small. We are hence interested in reducing their size while maintaining correctness and precision of the algorithm presented above. Our simplification rules are motivated by the observation that a sequence of event can sometimes be shortened to another sequence that leads to a smaller provenance graph that provides the same upper bounds for every current and future container.

Intuitively, provenance graphs $\mathcal{G}_t$ and $\mathcal{G}'_t$ are equivalent if (i) for each container c, if n and n' are the most recent nodes created for c in $\mathcal{G}_t$ and $\mathcal{G}'_t$ respectively, then $\kappa(n) = \kappa'(n')$ where $\kappa'(n') = maxflow_{\mathcal{G}'_t}((S,0), n')$; and (ii) if the content of any set of containers (i.e., most recent nodes) is copied to a (possibly new) container after time t, then the evolutions of the two graphs yield the same upper bounds for the amount of sensitive data in this container. (i) stipulates that the two graphs yield identical upper bounds for every container. Since future evolutions of a provenance graph add edges to the respective most recent nodes only, (ii) stipulates that independently of the events that connect such nodes in the future, the maximum flows from the source to the new nodes must be identical in both graphs.

Formally, let $cn_\mathcal{G}(X)$, the *current nodes*, be the nodes in $\mathcal{G}$ that are the latest representation of each container in $X \subseteq C$: $\forall \mathcal{G} = (\mathcal{N}, \mathcal{E}), X \subseteq C : cn_\mathcal{G}(X) = \{(c,t) \mid c \in X \wedge (c,t) \in \mathcal{N} \wedge \forall t' : (c,t') \in \mathcal{N} \Rightarrow t' \leq t\}$. Assuming a set of containers X, $\mathcal{G}_{t,X}$ denotes the graph in which every node in $cn_{\mathcal{G}_t}(X)$ is connected to a dummy node dn that represents a virtual sink of all future operations on the nodes in $cn_{\mathcal{G}_t}(X)$ (and therefore all future evolutions of $\mathcal{G}_t$ on every possible set of containers): $\mathcal{G}_{t,X} = (\mathcal{N}_t \cup \{dn\}, \mathcal{E}_t \cup \bigcup_{n \in cn_{\mathcal{G}_t}(X)} \{(n, \infty, dn)\})$. For a node n, let $\kappa_{t,X}(n) = maxflow_{\mathcal{G}_{t,X}}((S,0), n)$ and, similarly, $\kappa'_{t,X}(n) = maxflow_{\mathcal{G}'_{t,X}}((S,0), n)$. *Equivalence of provenance graphs* then reads as $\mathcal{G}_t \sim \mathcal{G}'_t \Leftrightarrow \forall X \subseteq C : \kappa_{t,X}(dn) = \kappa'_{t,X}(dn)$.

We now describe several cases where we can obtain a smaller but equivalent provenance graph that will considerably increase performance in the experiments of § 5.3. We believe these to be the interesting cases but make no claim of completeness. The proof that these simplifications are *correct* in that the original provenance graph, $\mathcal{G}_t$, is equivalent to the modified graph, $\mathcal{G}'_t$ (i.e., $\forall t \in \mathbb{N} : \mathcal{G}_t \sim \mathcal{G}'_t$), is provided in Appendix B.

Removal of a truncation. If at time k there is a copying action of size q from c_a to a new container c_b, and a truncation of c_b to size m occurs at time $t > k$, and, between these two events, there is no other truncation or transfer to c_b, and the sum of transfers from c_b is lower than $q - m$, then this sequence leads to a provenance graph equivalent to the one yielded by the sequence that transfers exactly m data units to c_b at time k, copies data from c_a instead of c_b from time $k+1$ to $t-1$, and does not contain the truncation of c_b at time t. We hence modify the edge label of the copying step at time k, replace any further copying action from c_b by a copying action from c_a, and remove the final truncation.

Removal of a copy (case 1). If a copying action from c_a to c_b of size s_1 takes place at time k, and another copying action from c_c to c_b of size s_2 occurs at time $t > k$, and in between these two events there is no truncation or transfer to c_a or to/from c_b, then this sequence leads to a provenance graph that is equivalent to the one yielded by the sequence that directly transfers s_1 and s_2 data units at time k from c_a and c_c, respectively. We hence add c_c to the source containers of the copying at time k and remove the last copying step.

Removal of a copy (case 2). If at time k there is a copying action from c_a to a new container c_b of size s_1, and another copying action also from c_a to c_b of size s_2 occurs at time $t > k$, and in between these two events there is no truncation

or transfer to c_a or c_b, and the sizes of all transfers from c_b after time k sum to a value that is below s_1, then this sequence leads to a provenance graph that is equivalent to the one yielded by the sequence that copies $s_1 + s_2$ data units at time k and does not contain the final transfer.

4. QUANTITATIVE POLICIES

Semantic Model We now use provenance graphs to generalize the model presented in [29] to combine QDFT with data usage control. In that model, possibilistic data flows are captured by sequences of states that map data items to their representations, i.e. containers. The considered systems are modeled as tuples $(P, Data, Event, C, \Sigma, \sigma_i, \varrho)$, where P are principals, $Data$ are data items, $Event$ are events happening in the system that are triggered by principals' actions, C are data containers, Σ are the states of the system with σ_i being the initial state ($\varnothing$), and ϱ is the state transition function. We first show how to compute a provenance graph for each data item at each moment in time and then use this definition for the specification of usage control policies that restrict a provenance graph's evolution.

States $\Sigma = Data \rightarrow Graph$ associate each data item with a provenance graph. Provenance graphs consist of nodes, $Nodes \subseteq C \times \mathbb{N}$, i.e., container-timestamp pairs. We require $Nodes$ to contain a reserved identifier $(S, 0)$ that stands for the external source of data. Provenance graphs are modeled as a (partial) function of type $Graph = Nodes \times Nodes \rightarrow \mathbb{N}$ which associates each edge with the corresponding event's size, i.e., the number of flowed data items.

Given a provenance graph and an event, function $step : (Graph \times Event) \rightarrow Graph$ updates the graph according to the rules presented in § 3. We hence assume that each concrete event in the system is (1) mapped to one of the abstract events and therefore possible graph evolutions (init, transfer, truncation) and (2) associated with a size, possibly 0. Then, $\varrho : (\Sigma \times Event) \rightarrow \Sigma$ where $\varrho(\sigma, e) = \sigma'$ and $\sigma'(d) = step(\sigma(d), e)$ for each data item $d \in dom(\sigma)$.

Quantitative usage control policies are defined over traces that map abstract time points to events. For simplicity's sake, we assume it is always possible to linearly sort events chronologically, and therefore only one event per timestep: $Trace : \mathbb{N} \rightarrow Event$. Then, given a trace tr, function $states_q : (Trace \times \mathbb{N}) \rightarrow \Sigma$ computes the information state at a given moment in time t via $states_q(tr, 0) = \sigma_i$ and $t > 0 \Rightarrow states_q(tr, t) = \varrho(states_q(tr, t-1), tr(t-1))$.

Policies Policies describe situations to be avoided or enforced. In usage control contexts, this is often specified by sequences of allowed/disallowed events or states (mappings from data to containers) using temporal logic formulae. We do not discuss general usage control policies here, since this has been done elsewhere [40, 29], but concentrate on one possible way of restricting data quantities. To this end, we need to capture function κ introduced in § 3. Given a graph $\mathcal{G}_t$ and a container c, function $K : (Graph \times C) \rightarrow \mathbb{N}$ returns the maximum amount of different sensitive units stored in c according to the provenance graph $\mathcal{G}_t$. K corresponds to the application of $\kappa()$ to the most recent version of c in $\mathcal{G}_t$. We then define one *state-based operator* ($\Phi_q ::= atMostInSet(Data, \mathbb{N}, \mathbb{P}(C))$) to specify quantitative policies: `atMostInSet(d, q, Cs)` limits the combined capacity of a set of containers. For example, the policy "No more than 1MB of customer data can be saved on a removable device" could be checked by the proposition `at-`

`MostInSet(d,1MB, REMOVABLE)`, where `REMOVABLE` is the set of containers that represent files on removable devices. The policy "no more than 10MB may be sent over the network" is specified as `atMostInSet(d,10MB,CNET)` where `CNET` is the set of all network sockets. Lack of space prevents us from presenting other operators in Φ_q here, for instance, `atMostInEach(d, q, Cs)` with its intuitive semantics. Given a trace and a time point, we define the semantics $\models_q \subseteq (Trace \times \mathbb{N}) \times \Phi_q$ of this quantitative data usage operator by $\forall tr \in Trace, \forall t \in \mathbb{N}, \forall \phi \in \Phi_q, \forall \sigma \in \Sigma \bullet (tr, t) \models_q \phi \Leftrightarrow$ $\sigma = states_q(tr, t) \wedge \exists d \in Data, Cs \subseteq C, Q \in \mathbb{N} \bullet$
$\phi = atMostInSet(d, Q, Cs) \wedge \sum_{c \in Cs} K(\sigma(d), c) \leq Q.$

Using Φ_q we can specify simple information flow policies only. In order to express more complex policies like those presented in our reference scenario in § 1, we need a more expressive policy language. For reasons of space, we do not describe here how to embed Φ_q into a full temporal logic language such as the ones defined in [29, 40]. However, by leveraging $\models_q$ and $states_q$, it is possible to define the semantics of a new language $\Phi \supset \Phi_q$ for the specification of quantitative policies that capture temporal and propositional operators as well. Using this language Φ, it is then possible to specify policies such as $always(\neg atMostInSet(d, q, Cs) \Rightarrow notify)$ that issue a notification whenever the amount of data d stored in the specified set of containers Cs exceeds q. This kind of policies will be used in § 5.

5. EXPERIMENTAL RESULTS

We conducted two experiments to evaluate the adequacy of the QDFT model in terms of the scenario in § 1. First, we measured precision and performance of the model alone, i.e., at an abstract level. Then, we instantiated the model to the OS level, extending previous work [19] and refining the abstract events from the first experiment to system calls.

5.1 Implementation and methodology

Remember that Alice performs a sequence of report generation/ update actions in the phone scenario presented in § 1 and that she is subjected to a set of policies of the kind $always(\neg atMostInSet(d, 1MB, MAIL) \Rightarrow notify)$ as introduced in § 4. An action is a transfer of some units of data from a specification or from an existing report to another (possibly new) report. We generated random sequences of actions of different lengths, and observed the evolution of our model during their execution. In each step, Alice can choose between creating a new and updating an existing report with probability PN. We ran 100 sequences for each length and used average and median values for the analyses in the remainder of this section.

In the first set of experiments (*atomic*, denoted by **A**), we modeled each action after the initialization as one single abstract event, either a T or a C step (see § 3), where specifications and reports are containers. In the second set of experiments (*syscalls*, denoted by **S**), we instantiated the model to the OS level and performed QDFT at this level. In this refined context, events are system calls, and containers are files, pipes, memory locations, and message queues. Specifically, the MAIL set from the above policy is a set of sockets for email communication. Specifications and reports are modeled as files, and each abstract action from the first set of experiments corresponds to one system call or a sequence of system calls: initialization is done in the beginning by extracting the data item d to be protected from the pol-

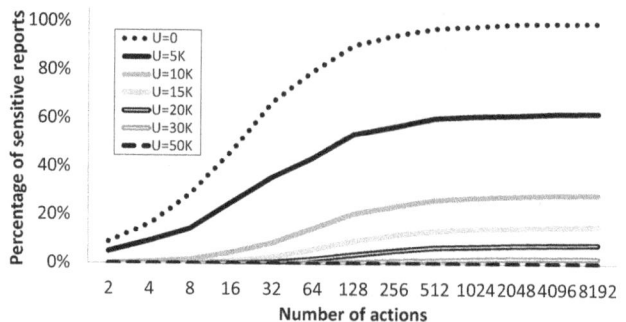

Figure 2: Percentage of reports considered sensitive by a quantitative policy vs. number of actions (PN=50%)

icy and mapping it to the initial representation; truncation is modeled as `open()` with the overwrite flag set, as `truncate()`, `ftruncate()`, or `unlink()`; transfer is modeled by `mmap()`, as `read()` from file to process, and as `write()` from process to file or socket. These are the concrete events used to define the ϱ relation in § 4. They also refine, by disjunction, the abstract events specified in the above policy.

The length of an event sequence depends on the size of the files and of the transfers involved. In our tests, one abstract action corresponds, on average, to 40 system calls. We started each experiment from the same arbitrary yet fixed amount of (sensitive) specifications and (initially nonsensitive) reports. For both experiments, we evaluate our model with (denoted **s**) and without (denoted **n**) simplification. For the *syscalls* tests without simplification (i.e., the Sn configuration), we considered sequences of at most 1024 actions because the time required to perform 100 executions longer than 1024 is prohibitive without simplification.

For the second set of experiments, we extended an existing usage-control framework for system call interposition based on the Systrace tool [30]. The amount of bytes that a process tries to read/write from/to a file corresponds to the event size used by our tracking framework. If any of the defined policies does not allow the respective system call to be executed, the system call is denied. Otherwise, the system call is dispatched to the kernel and executed as usual.

We study the following questions: **(i)** How precise is our model (i.e., how far is the estimated value from the exact amount of different sensitive data units)? **(ii)** What is the overhead of QDFT w.r.t native execution?

5.2 Precision

One problem with possibilistic data flow tracking is usability: because of the involved over-approximations, systems quickly become unusable because very many data items are quickly tainted ("label creep"). For a typical run of the system, Figure 2 shows the relative number of reports considered sensitive (tainted) for the policy "do not distribute a report if it contains more than U units of sensitive data," for varying U (50K is the number of sensitive units in the system), as a function of the number of hitherto executed actions. The figure suggests that usability may indeed be increased because reports are considered sensitive less quickly and thus not blocked when sent, depending on the value of U. Note that all curves are well below the uppermost reference line $U = 0$ (possibilistic estimation).

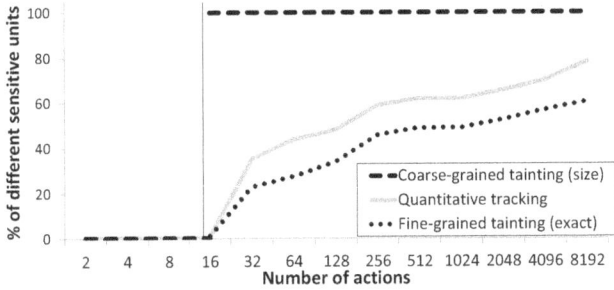

Figure 3: Estimation of different sensitive units in an exemplary container during one execution (PN=50%). Before the 16th action, no sensitive data is stored in the container.

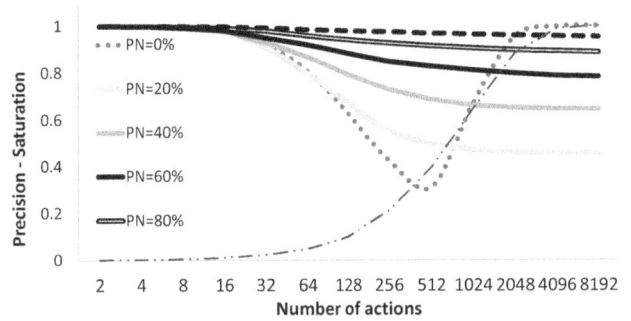

Figure 4: Median precision vs. number of events and percentage of new reports for *syscalls* tests

A second perspective is provided by Figure 3, which shows how many units are considered sensitive according to different tracking methods for one typical container. As expected, the quantitative estimation is in-between coarse-grained and fine-grained tainting.

To more precisely answer the first research question we want to know in general how close the quantitative tracking curve is to the fined-grained tainting curve; the smaller this gap is, the more precise our model is. We therefore empirically measure the precision of our model, for a container c at a specific moment in time, by letting $Prec(c) = (Size(c) - Estim(c))/(Size(c) - Exact(c))$ if $Size(c) \neq Exact(c)$, and 1 otherwise, where $Size(c)$ is the total number of data units in c (including non-sensitive data and duplicates), $Exact(c)$ is the precise number of different sensitive units in c, and $Estim(c)$ is the number computed by our model, i.e., the value of κ. Thus, $Exact(c) \leq Estim(c) \leq Size(c)$. The estimation is most accurate if $Estim(c) = Exact(c)$ (i.e., $Prec(c) = 1$), and the worst case ($Prec(c) = 0$) is $Estim(c) = Size(c)$. In the special case $Size(c) = Exact(c)$, our estimation is still correct (i.e., $Prec(c) = 1$). The proportion of non-sensitive units (or duplicates of sensitive units) in a container c that are incorrectly considered additional different sensitive units by our model corresponds to $1 - Prec(c)$.

Precision obviously depends on the sequence of actions considered. For instance, if the user always copies the complete content of one container to another, then the quantity-based approach will not be more precise than any coarse-grained tainting approach. Similarly, if the user always copies the same few specific units from a container that contains a lot of other sensitive units, the quantity-based approach will be significantly less precise than a fine-grained tainting approach. However, it is interesting to see how the precision evolves in scenarios in-between these two extremes.

Figure 4 shows the median precision for all containers after Alice performed a number of transfers. Since she can choose between creating a new report or updating an existing one, we varied the probability PN that she creates a new report in each step from 0, where no new report is created but only existing ones are updated, to 1, where every action creates a new report. Precision monotonically decreases for each value of PN but 0. For $PN = 0$, only updates of existing reports are possible: Alice keeps transferring data to and in-between the same fixed set of reports, with the consequence that after a while all data in the specifications is transferred to every report. Let max be the maximum

number of different sensitive units in the specifications (and thus, in the system). If a report contains all specification data ($Exact(c) = max$), we call it *saturated*. Considering that max is an upper bound for our estimation, precision for saturated containers is equal to 1 ($max = Exact(c) \leq Estim(c) \leq max \Rightarrow Exact(c) = Estim(c)$), and the closer to saturation a container is, the higher its precision will be. Figure 4 shows the positive correlation, after some time, between the median precision (dotted line) and the average report saturation (average ($Exact(c)/max$) over every report container c, dashed line) for $PN = 0$. For other values of PN, median precision asymptotically decreases to a limit that depends on PN: the higher PN, the higher precision.

5.3 Simplification

Without simplification (§ 3), the provenance graph grows by one node and one or two edges per event on a sensitive container. Memory and also time consumption may then become critical because max-flow computation time is quadratic in the size of the graph. In particular, monitoring Alice's behavior at the OS level requires observing many events (~ 40 system calls per action), which significantly impacts the size of the provenance graph.

Figure 5 shows the growth of the provenance graph as the number of actions increases. We compare the monitoring of each action as an atomic transfer (1 action = 1 event) with the instantiation at the OS level (1 action ~ 40 events), with and without simplification. By construction, the graphs grow by at most one node after each event. As expected, monitoring a fourty-fold number of events is reflected in a graph fourty times larger (Sn). However, simplification (Ss) made the graph as small as the atomic one (As), with direct implications in terms of time required to capture a new event, as explained in the next section. After 336248 events, Ss contains 5460 nodes only, which is less than 2% of the non-simplified graph's size.

5.4 Performance

In addition to precision, we are also interested in evaluating the storage and the time required to update our model when receiving an event. As for the graph's size, performance depends on the sequence of actions performed by the user. Our implementation requires a fixed amount of $\sim$12Mb of RAM plus $\sim$285 bytes per node and $\sim$110 bytes per edge, i.e. less than 17Mb in total for traces of more than 330K

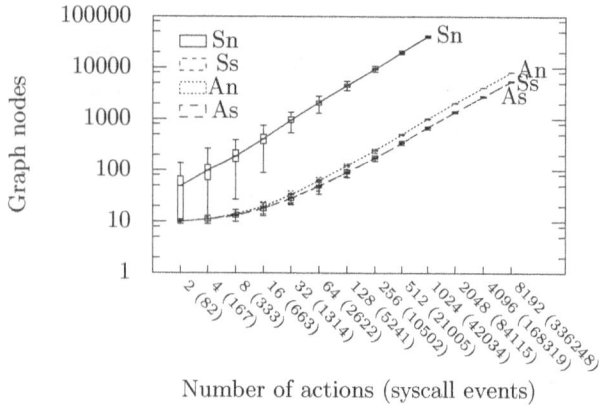

Figure 5: Graph size vs. number of actions (PN=50%), level of abstraction (**A**tomic/**S**yscall), with (**s**) and without (**n**) simplification. Note As and Ss overlap.

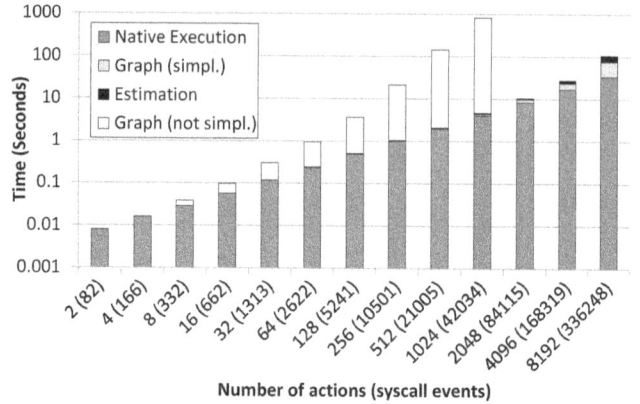

Figure 6: Time overhead for the *syscalls* tests (PN=50%) with and without QDFT, with and without optimizations.

events. Because these numbers are negligible on modern machines, we focus our analysis on the dimension of time.
Worst-case scenario We observe that it is possible for every **C2** step to replace the edge's capacity by ∞ without impacting correctness or precision. This allows us to build a provenance graph at runtime *without* computing max-flow: only if a usage event (i.e. an event whose execution is constrained by a quantitative policy) addressing a container c is observed, max-flow from source to c is computed (*lazy evaluation*). Concretely, in our scenario this means computing max-flow only if we observe a `write()` system call to one of the containers in *MAILS*, and not for every `read()` and `write()` in the trace. For instance, if only 1 in every 10 reports is actually sent via email (the rest is sent to other departments), then the median overhead after 8192 actions (336248 events) is 43 seconds instead of 72 (124% vs 211%).

To answer the second research question, we measure the performance overhead of maintaining our provenance graph with and without applying optimizations (simplification rules and lazy evaluation). Figure 6 shows the median performance overhead compared to the native execution time. For the optimized case, we distinguish between the minimum overhead, introduced by the pure creation of the graph, without any max-flow computation (Graph (simpl.)) and the maximum overhead, required to compute max-flow after the execution of each event (Estimation). Although the time to maintain the non-simplified graph grows very quickly (13700% of the native execution time for 1024 actions), the overhead remains quite small for the optimized version (43 seconds, 124%, two orders of magnitude less than before for traces 8 times longer). In this example, a max-flow computation on such graphs always requires less than 115 msec.
Average-case scenario The numbers obtained from the previous experiments make scalability a concern in the worst case. However, these experiments were *designed* to stress this particular aspect. In order to test whether or not scalability is an issue *in an average real-world scenario*, we conducted another experiment: we instantiated the model at the level of MS Windows, where events are API calls (`WriteFile()`, `ReadFile()`, `CreateFile()`, etc.) and containers are files, pipes and memory locations. As in the previous experiments, we considered a set of sensitive source files and the creation of 64 reports with PN=50%. In this scenario, we simulated a user opening two files with a text

editor (notepad or wordpad) and copy-pasting some content from each source to a third file, possibly adding some (non-sensitive) content before saving it. Note that the destination could be either a new report or an existing one.

In this scenario we noted two important differences: a) in addition to the API calls generated by the user interaction, we considered every other API call in the system, including those generated by background processes; b) some processes in Windows read/write files using many API calls with blocks of fixed size (e.g. 4KB for notepad), whilst other transfer large amounts of data in a single call, similar to the behaviors of, respectively, the *syscalls* experiment and the *atomic* experiment described before.

We observed a total of $60K$ API calls, out of which $48K$ were filtered using trivial heuristics (like ignoring certain system services). The remaining 12K were ca. 10% related to sensitive data and 90% unrelated "noise" calls created by other processes. All the 12K calls were sent to our model and translated into respective **I**, **C** or **T** actions, updating the graph and requiring for each event an estimation of the sensitive data in its target container. The total time needed by our model to handle all the updates was ca. 40msec, less than 17% of the native execution time of the 12K API calls. With respect to the total time required by a fast user to perform the task (at least 5 seconds per report), this overhead is not perceptible. This further instantiation of our model shows that it is indeed usable in a realistic scenario.

5.5 Discussion

The experimental results confirm that the precision of our QDFT lies in-between a coarse-grained and a fine-grained tainting approach. Although highly dependent on the properties of the sequences of actions analyzed, the precision of our quantitative estimation is usually quite good (i.e., the estimated amount of different sensitive units is close to the exact amount). In terms of performance, without the application of simplification rules we notice the expected quadratic dependence between time required to perform an operation on the graph and its size (which, in turn, is linearly growing with the number of actions performed). With the introduction of simplification and lazy evaluation, the size of the graph decreases by more than one order of magnitude and the performance of our model improves significantly.

The quadratic complexity of the max-flow algorithm will always be a limit to the scalability of this approach; however, in an average-case scenario the overhead introduced by our model may remain negligible. In several contexts, moreover, sensitivity of data is *time-bounded*, e.g., a phone specification may be sensitive only until the phone is released, hence no need to maintain a provenance graph afterward.

Finally, if our traces represent real-world documents creation, it is unlikely that Alice would anyway notice an overall overhead of 72 seconds during the preparation of more than 8000 reports ($\sim 9ms$ per report). Though this overhead does not take into account the delay introduced by the system call interposition framework (up to 270% [19], and 1-3 orders of magnitude for other levels of abstraction), note that the delay introduced by our model is absolute, i.e. *independent* of the time required to *perform* or *intercept* any action. This means that, for instance, $1ms$ to update the provenance graph may be an intolerable overhead if we are modeling the execution of a system call, but may at the same time be a negligible delay for a BPEL or ESB event [26].

6. RELATED WORK

Information flow tracking, in the context of security policy enforcement [32], is at least thirty years old [16]. The two main approaches are *static* [13, 25, 18] and *runtime* checking, based on dynamic tainting analysis. In terms of static checking, Denning [14] first proposed to quantitatively measure information flow, defining the amount of information transferred in a flow as "the reduction in uncertainty (entropy) of a random variable". Solutions in this area (e.g., [7, 8]) rely on a specific input distribution's entropy or universally quantify over all input distributions. In contrast, our analysis applies to runtime systems and is independent of any stochastic notion of input data distribution.

Approaches more similar to ours perform dynamic taint analysis (DTA). Several techniques have been proposed for DTA, mainly for detecting malware and unknown vulnerabilities in software [10, 34, 4], checking integrity (tainted data should not affect normal behavior of the program, where tainted means "possibly bad") [10, 11] and confidentiality (public output should not be influenced by tainted data, where tainted stands for "possibly secret") [6, 23, 38]. However, most of them are "hybrid" approaches, because they rely on static annotations to account for implicit flows [13, 36]. In contrast, our approach does not require any static annotation to perform the analysis. A common pattern in all these solutions is the idea that monitoring should be done "as close to the hardware as possible" [38]. We hence find solutions based on binary rewriting [5, 10, 9, 21, 27, 23], memory and pointer analysis [33, 34], partial- or full-system emulation [20, 24, 38, 6, 12] or on making information flow a first-class OS abstraction [15, 39, 22]. In contrast, we believe that high-level events such as "print" or "play" or "screenshot" are handled more conveniently at higher levels of abstraction because they can directly been observed there. For this reason, our abstract model is deliberately not bound to one specific architecture or platform.

Our work is inspired by [23] which introduces the idea of measuring information flow as a network flow capacity. Their tool estimates the amount of information flowing from inputs to outputs of a particular program for one (or some) specific executions. Our work generalizes the idea to a generic model that can be instantiated to multiple layers of abstraction, including the level of code considered by McCamant et al. We have commented on the benefits of data flow tracking at levels different from the machine code level above. Since our model is based on the observation of events and therefore does not consider control flow dependencies, it does not measure implicit flows. At the cost of manual instrumentation, these are, in contrast, considered in [23].

The idea of measuring information flows by considering information as an incompressible fluid flowing through a network appears also in [37], where it has been applied to the socio-information networks domain. This model uses dataflow risk estimations for access control purposes, assuming likelihood of information leakages (e.g., in-between subjects) to be given. Our work, in contrast, is domain-agnostic and relies only on the size of actions that actually took place.

Data provenance tracking has been thoroughly investigated, in particular in the context of databases [3]. A recent work of Demsky [12] relies on data provenance tracking to perform basic usage control enforcement, similar to what our system does. In addition to the more advanced types of policies our system can enforce, the goal of our provenance tracking is different: we use provenance to determine *how much* data comes from *where*, whereas Demsky's and other approaches in literature track *what* data comes from *where*.

Our model is a *quantitative* extension of the data-flow tracking model for usage control presented in [29], which makes the distinction between data and representations of data, in contrast to other usage control models (e.g., [31, 35, 28]). Since this model has been instantiated at different levels of abstraction, such as OS, X11, Java-bytecode, and Android mobile devices, it makes our extension suitable for all these environments.

7. DISCUSSION

We start by making the assumptions of our model explicit. First of all, data must be *quantifiable* with respect to a *data unit*. Choosing the appropriate unit for each level of abstraction is not a trivial task, especially in presence of heterogeneous representations (e.g., an OS handles both files and windows). Furthermore, converting a type of units into another type is usually not possible. For example, two records of a database, containing ten characters each, may have the same size in bytes as a single record containing twenty characters. How could a monitor using bytes as data units distinguish between the two cases?

Additionally, we also assume the absence of *data compression*. Otherwise, an event may transfer more data than the size of the event itself or transferring a single data unit from one representation could mean transferring the whole data. This assumption can be removed if an upper bound for the compression ratio of each event is known. An event of compression ratio r ($0 < r \leq 1$) that transfers t units of data will be considered of size $s = t/r$.

Next, we assume a *fixed size for the initial representation*. If such size changes over time, a policy like *no more than 5% of customer data can be stored in an unencrypted file* can be interpreted in different ways: 5% of the amount of customer data when the policy is activated (static), 5% according to the current amount of customer data (current), or 5% according to the total amount of different customers (max). For example, if at time t_1 the customer database contains 1000 records, at time t_2 it contains 200 records and at time t_3 it contains 2000 records, the maximal amount of data that can be stored in an unencrypted file at time t_3 without violating the property can be either: 50 (static), 100 (current), or 140 (max). To handle these various interpretations, the roots of each provenance graph need some adjustments whenever the size of an initial representation changes. We implemented all these different interpretations but do not include them in this paper due to space limitations.

A common problem in data-flow tracking solutions is the *over-tainting* issue. Quantitative estimations can be used as declassification criterion to mitigate the problem by constraining the application of a policy to only those containers containing at least a certain amount of sensitive data (cf. Figure 2). However, if a small amount of data is allowed for disclosure, we also need to make sure that such disclosures cannot be channeled to the same recipient via unknown ways. For example, in our scenario, we need to make sure that the same supplier cannot receive mails on more than one account. Otherwise she could receive 10KB of different data on each email address, and with enough addresses (and Alice cooperation) she could possibly obtain all the phone specifications and test results via mail. For this reason, usage control usually requires a fully controlled environment.

Our QDFT maintains a flow graph per data item. Assuming D sensitive data items and at most V representations per item, linked by at most E edges, the memory overhead is in $\mathcal{O}(D(V+E)) = \mathcal{O}(DE)$. We use a maxflow algorithm [2] which gives the best performance on graphs with less than 10^6 nodes [17]. The augmenting paths algorithm is based on a residual graph that is reused for subsequent maxflow computations. It is hence particularly suitable for our problem because the provenance graph is built incrementally.

The existence of one independent provenance graph per data item introduces an overapproximation. Consider a container c_a containing units of data items d_1 and d_2. A transfer of size l from c_a to c_b would be modeled as a transfer of l units from c_a to c_b in the provenance graph of d_1, and as a transfer of l units from c_a to c_b in the graph of d_2. However, in a single transfer of size l, it is not possible to transfer both, l units of data d_1 and l units of data d_2. This overapproximation can be reduced by modifying the analysis, but the task must be done carefully, in order to preserve soundness (e.g., multiple data may share capacity via coding [1]).

As a final remark, quantitative measurements, in themselves, do not always reflect the usefulness of data. For example, consider a group picture: removing every second pixel or taking only the bottom half of the picture reduces in both cases the size of 50%. But the reduction in terms of information content may be very different in the two cases for someone who wants to identify people in the picture. In general, quantitative measurements make sense only if combined with the interpretation of data.

8. CONCLUSION

In this paper, we presented a model for quantitatively tracking flows of sensitive data. This model works in a dynamic context of runtime monitors. We proved the correctness of this model and assessed its precision and performance by embedding it in a usage control infrastructure.

Depending on the specific actions performed by a user, our model's precision can be as good as a fine-grained approach, which knows exactly how many different data units are in every container, or as bad as a coarse-grained approach, which knows only if a data item could be in a container but not exactly how many data units are in it. Usually, our model precision lies somewhere in between because it knows that not every data unit in a container is sensitive but over-approximates the exact amount of sensitive units.

Our model is embodied in a usage control infrastructure, similarly to what has been done in [29], and used to enforce, preventively or detectively, usage control policies. A valuable use of our system is to support the notion of acceptable exceptions, i.e. quantitative policies defined *a posteriori*. For example, in case of a data leakage, analyzing the logs of the actions with our model may establish that only 0.1% of sensitive data have been leaked. At this point, an auditor may decide that this violation is still acceptable, whereas it is unlikely that a policy defines a leakage of 0.1% to be acceptable in advance, i.e., before the leakage happens.

In terms of future work, we want to extend our model to cope with compression, model sources of data of variable sizes and investigate the problem of measuring data across different layers of abstraction (i.e., converting units of data).

Acknowledgments This work was done as part of the DFG's Priority Program SPP 1496 "Reliably Secure Software Systems," ref. numbers PR-1266/1-2. Fabio Massacci suggested to present the results as done in Figure 2.

9. REFERENCES

[1] R. Ahlswede, N. Cai, S.-Y. R. Li, and R. W. Yeung. Network information flow. *IEEE Transactions on information theory*, pages 1204–1216, 2000.

[2] Y. Boykov and V. Kolmogorov. An experimental comparison of min-cut/max-flow algorithms for energy minimization in vision. *TPAMI*, pages 1124–1137, 2004.

[3] P. Buneman, S. Khanna, and T. Wang-Chiew. Why and Where: A Characterization of Data Provenance. In *ICDT*, pages 316–330, 2001.

[4] L. Cavallaro, P. Saxena, and R. Sekar. On the limits of information flow techniques for malware analysis. In *DIMVA*, pages 143–163, 2008.

[5] W. Cheng, Q. Zhao, B. Yu, and S. Hiroshige. Tainttrace: Efficient flow tracing with dynamic binary rewriting. In *ISCC*, pages 749–754, 2006.

[6] J. Chow, B. Pfaff, T. Garfinkel, K. Christopher, and M. Rosenblum. Understanding Data Lifetime via Whole System Simulation. In *SSYM*, pages 321–336, 2004.

[7] D. Clark, S. Hunt, and P. Malacaria. Quantitative Analysis of the Leakage of Confidential Data. *ENTCS*, 59:238–251, 2002.

[8] M. Clarkson, A. Myers, and F. Schneider. Belief in information flow. In *CSFW*, pages 31–45, 2005.

[9] J. A. Clause, W. Li, and A. Orso. Dytan: a generic dynamic taint analysis framework. In *ISSTA*, pages 196–206, 2007.

[10] M. Costa, J. Crowcroft, M. Castro, A. Rowstron, L. Zhou, L. Zhang, and P. Barham. Vigilante: End-to-end containment of internet worm epidemics. *TOCS*, pages 1–68, 2008.

[11] J. R. Crandall and F. T. Chong. Minos: Control Data Attack Prevention Orthogonal to Memory Model. In *MICRO-37*, pages 221–232. IEEE, 2004.

[12] B. Demsky. Cross-application data provenance and policy enforcement. *TISSEC*, pages 1–22, 2011.

[13] D. E. Denning. A lattice model of secure information flow. *Commun. ACM*, pages 236–243, May 1976.

[14] R. Denning and D. Elizabeth. *Cryptography and data security*. Addison-Wesley, 1982.

[15] P. Efstathopoulos and E. Kohler. Manageable fine-grained information flow. In *SIGOPS*, pages 301–313, 2008.

[16] J. S. Fenton. Memoryless subsystems. *The Computer Journal*, 17(2):143–147, Feb. 1974.

[17] B. Fishbain, D. S. Hochbaum, and S. Mueller. Competitive analysis of min-cut max-flow algorithms in vision problems. Technical report, UC Berkeley, 2010.

[18] J. W. Gray. Toward a mathematical foundation for information flow security. In *SP*, pages 21–34, 1991.

[19] M. Harvan and A. Pretschner. State-based Usage Control Enforcement with Data Flow Tracking using System Call Interposition. In *NSS*, pages 373–380, 2009.

[20] A. Ho, M. Fetterman, C. Clark, A. Warfield, and S. Hand. Practical taint-based protection using demand emulation. *EuroSys 06*, 40(4):29, 2006.

[21] M. G. Kang, S. McCamant, P. Poosankam, and D. Song. DTA++: Dynamic taint analysis with targeted control-flow propagation. In *NDSS*, 2011.

[22] M. Krohn, A. Yip, M. Brodsky, N. Cliffer, M. F. Kaashoek, E. Kohler, and R. Morris. Information flow control for standard OS abstractions. In *SOSP*, pages 321–334, 2007.

[23] S. McCamant and M. D. Ernst. Quantitative information flow as network flow capacity. In *PLDI*, pages 193–205, 2008.

[24] J. Mccullough, M. Vrable, A. C. Snoeren, G. M. Voelker, and S. Savage. Neon: system support for derived data management. *VEE*, pages 63–74, 2010.

[25] J. K. Millen. Covert channel capacity. In *SP*, pages 60–66, 1987.

[26] R. Neisse, A. Pretschner, and V. D. Giacomo. A trustworthy usage control enforcement framework. In *ARES*, pages 230–235. IEEE, 2011.

[27] N. Nethercote and J. Seward. Valgrind: a framework for heavyweight dynamic binary instrumentation. *ACM Sigplan Notices*, 42(6):89–100, 2007.

[28] J. Park and R. Sandhu. The ucon abc usage control model. *TISSEC*, pages 128–174, 2004.

[29] A. Pretschner, E. Lovat, and M. Büchler. Representation-independent data usage control. In *Proc. SETOP/DPM*, pages 122–140, 2011.

[30] N. Provos. Improving host security with system call policies. In *Proc. SSYM*, pages 257–272, 2003.

[31] E. Rissanen. Extensible access control markup language v3.0, 2010.

[32] A. Sabelfeld and A. C. Myers. Language-based information-flow security. *IEEE Journal on Selected Areas in Communications*, 21(1):5–19, 2003.

[33] A. Slowinska and H. Bos. Pointless tainting?: evaluating the practicality of pointer tainting. In *Proc. EuroSys '09*, pages 61–74. ACM, 2009.

[34] G. E. Suh, J. W. Lee, D. Zhang, and S. Devadas. Secure program execution via dynamic information flow tracking. In *ASPLOS*, pages 85–96, 2004.

[35] K. Twidle, N. Dulay, E. Lupu, and M. Sloman. Ponder2: A Policy System for Autonomous Pervasive Environments. In *ICAS*, ICAS, pages 330–335, 2009.

[36] N. Vachharajani, M. J. Bridges, J. Chang, R. Rangan, G. Ottoni, J. A. Blome, G. Reis, M. Vachharajani, and D. August. Rifle: An architectural framework for user-centric information-flow security. *MICRO 37*, 2004.

[37] T. Wang, M. Srivatsa, D. Agrawal, and L. Liu. Modeling data flow in socio-information networks: a risk estimation approach. In *SACMAT*, pages 113–122, 2011.

[38] H. Yin, D. Song, M. Egele, C. Kruegel, and E. Kirda. Panorama: capturing system-wide information flow for malware detection and analysis. *ACM CCS*, 2007.

[39] N. Zeldovich, S. Boyd-Wickizer, E. Kohler, and D. Mazi. Making Information Flow Explicit in HiStar. In *OSDI*, pages 263–278, 2006.

[40] X. Zhang, J. Park, F. Parisi-Presicce, and R. S. Sandhu. A logical specification for usage control. In *SACMAT*, pages 1–10, 2004.

APPENDIX

The two correctness proofs assume that the label of edges corresponding to C2 steps are ∞ rather than $\kappa((c_2, t'))$ for the source container c_2 and a time $t' \in \mathbb{N}$. Since $\kappa((c_2, t')) < \infty$, this does not impact correctness. Precision also is not impacted because the edge can, in any case, not transfer more than $\kappa((c_2, t'))$ units. The reason for not using ∞ in the definition of the C2 step is that, throughout the paper, this would have obscured the dual nature of edge labels as capacities and actual flows — actual flows are never infinite.

A. CORRECTNESS OF TRACKING

To show correctness of the model in the sense of § 3, we need to prove $\forall t \in \mathbb{N} \forall c \in C : \varphi(c, t) \leq \kappa((c, t))$.

The proof is by induction. It is trivial for the empty provenance graph (PG) of the base case. In terms of the inductive step, we assume that correctness has been established for all $\mathcal{G}_{t'}$ with $t' < t$: The induction hypothesis $(*)$ is $\forall c \in C \forall t' \in \mathbb{N} : t' < t \Rightarrow \varphi(c, t') \leq \kappa((c, t'))$.

I step: The only edge from $(S_d, 0)$ to (c_i, t) is the newly created one with label m. Consequently, $\kappa((c_i, t)) = m$. There are exactly m different units in c_i by assumption, and hence $\varphi(c_i, t) = m \leq \kappa((c_i, t))$.

T step: A container c (most recent node with time stamp $t' < t$) is reduced to size m. If $m \geq \kappa((c, t'))$, the PG is not modified, thus $\mathcal{G}_t = \mathcal{G}_{t-1}$. This implies $\kappa((c, t)) = \kappa((c, t'))$ which, by induction hypothesis $(*)$ was a correct estimation for $\varphi(c, t')$. Since truncating actions remove data from a container, the amount of sensitive data in c can be either the same of or less than before. Therefore, $\kappa((c, t'))$ is still a correct estimation, and we have $\varphi(c, t) \leq \kappa((c, t))$.

If, instead, $m < \kappa((c, t'))$, then node (c, t) is added as a successor of (c, t') with an edge labeled m. Because (c, t') is the only predecessor of (c, t), the min cut will now contain exactly this edge, hence $\kappa((c, t)) = m$. This estimation is also correct, because if the new size of c is m, then c cannot contain more than m different units of sensitive data. We have $\varphi(c, t) \leq \kappa((c, t))$.

C1 step: ℓ units of data are to be copied from c_A to a c_B that does not exist at time $t - 1$. We introduce a new edge e_ℓ with label ℓ from (c_A, t') to the newly created (c_B, t) where t' is the most recent timestamp for c_A. Because c_B cannot contain more different units of sensitive data than c_A, we know $\varphi(c_B, t) \leq \min(\ell, \varphi(c_A, t'))$. Let $\alpha = \kappa((c_A, t'))$. By induction hypothesis $(*)$, $\varphi(c_A, t') \leq \alpha$. Hence $\varphi(c_B, t) \leq \min(\ell, \alpha)$. If $\ell < \alpha$, $\{e_\ell\}$ is the only edge crossing the minimal cut, and we have $\kappa((c_B, t)) = \ell$. If $\ell \geq \alpha$, then $\kappa((c_B, t)) = \kappa((c_A, t')) = \alpha$. In both cases $\varphi(c_B, t) \leq \kappa((c_B, t))$.

C1 step immediately followed by a C2 step: Assume we copy ℓ units of data from container c_A to the existing container c_B. By construction of the PG, there are $t' < t$ and $t'' < t$ and nodes $(c_A, t'), (c_B, t'') \in \mathcal{N}_{t-1}$, a new node $(c_B, t) \in \mathcal{N}_t$, and two edges $e_\ell = ((c_A, t'), \ell, (c_B, t))$ and $e_k = ((c_B, t''), \infty, (c_B, t)) \in \mathcal{E}_t$.

We note that by construction in every $\mathcal{E}_\tau$ $(\tau < t)$, all labels corresponding to I, C1, and T steps measure *actual* flows of data (sensitive and non-sensitive units) in-between containers and are determined by the action corresponding to the step. We can interpret these edge labels as upper bounds for the flow of *sensitive* units: For each edge (action), it is impossible that more sensitive than overall units flow.

We then observe that all edges $((c, t'''), \infty, (c, \tau)) \in \mathcal{E}_\tau$ for all $\tau < t$ corresponding to C2 steps also provide (trivial) upper bounds for the flow of sensitive units. By induction hypothesis $(*)$, $\varphi(c_A, t') \leq \kappa((c_A, t'))$ and $\varphi(c_B, t'') \leq \kappa((c_B, t''))$. The same argumentation as for the edge labels in $\mathcal{E}_\tau$ applies to the newly created labels in $\mathcal{E}_t$: The label ℓ of e_ℓ is an upper bound for the flow of sensitive units from (c_A, t') because it is impossible that more sensitive units flow than overall units flow. The label ∞ is an upper bound for the number of sensitive units in (c_B, t''), $\varphi(c_B, t'')$, which by induction hypothesis is bounded from above by $\kappa((c_B, t''))$.

In sum, all edge labels in $\mathcal{E}_t$ are upper bounds for the flow of *sensitive* units for all kinds of steps. Edge labels can hence be seen as capacities for flows of sensitive data units.

Then, every cut of the PG between $(S_d, 0)$ and (c_B, t) partitions the nodes in two sets: the source set containing $(S_d, 0)$ and the destination set containing (c_B, t). Since labels are capacities for flows of different sensitive units, the size of every cut between $(S_d, 0)$ and (c_B, t) is an upper bound for the amount of different sensitive units that flowed to any node in the destination set. Specifically, for every cut between $(S_d, 0)$ and (c_B, t), $\varphi(c_B, t)$ can't exceed the size of this cut.

Finally, by definition, $\kappa((c_B, t))$ is the maximum flow between $(S_d, 0)$ and (c_B, t). By the max-flow/min-cut theorem, this is equivalent to the value of a minimal cut that separates (c_B, t) from $(S_d, 0)$. $\kappa((c_B, t))$ hence necessarily is an upper bound for $\varphi(c_B, t)$. $\square$

Note that the proof's structure also shows that the max-flow must be computed explicitly for combined C1&C2 steps only—for the others, κ values can directly be determined.

B. CORRECTNESS OF OPTIMIZATIONS

We prove equivalence $\sim$ of a graph $\mathcal{G}_t$ with its optimized version $\mathcal{G}'_t$ according to the rules presented in § 3.

Let $I(a, q)$ denote actions that initialize a container a with q units of sensitive data, $C(a_1, q_1, a_2, q_2, \ldots, b)$ actions that transfer q_1 units and q_2 units from container a_1 and a_2 to b, respectively, and $T(a, q)$ truncations of container a to q units. C is the set of containers. While function $maxflow$ returns a number, let $mincut$ returns the cut.

Removal of Truncation. For a sequence of events $tr = (\varepsilon_0, \ldots, \varepsilon_k, \ldots, \varepsilon_t)$ such that $\exists k \in \mathbb{N} \, \forall c_a, c_b, c \in C, q, x \in \mathbb{N}, i \in [k+1..t-1], j \in [0..k-1]: \varepsilon_k = C(c_a, q, c_b) \wedge \varepsilon_t = T(c_b, m) \wedge \varepsilon_j \neq I(c_b, x) \wedge \varepsilon_j \neq C(c, x, c_b) \wedge \varepsilon_i \neq T(c_b, x) \wedge \varepsilon_i \neq C(c, x, c_b) \wedge \kappa((c_b, k)) > m \wedge s_Y + m \leq q$ where $s_Y = \sum_{\varepsilon_i = C(c_b, x, c) \in tr} x$, we construct a new sequence $tr' = (\varepsilon_0, \ldots, \varepsilon_{k-1}, C(c_a, m, c_b), \varepsilon'_{k+1} \ldots, \varepsilon'_{t-1})$ with $\varepsilon'_i = C(c_a, q_i, c_i)$ if $\varepsilon_i = C(c_b, q_i, c_i)$ or $\varepsilon'_i = \varepsilon_i$ otherwise, for every $i \in [k+1..t-1]$. tr' results in a simpler (i.e. *smaller*), yet equivalent graph. Let (c_a, u) be the source node of the copy action at time k and, because there is no truncation or transfer to c_b in between times $k+1$ and $t-1$, (c_b, k) the source node of the truncation action at time t. We define $\mathcal{N}'_t = \mathcal{N}_t \setminus \{(c_b, t)\}$ and
$$\mathcal{E}'_t = \Big(\mathcal{E}_t \setminus \big(\{((c_b, k), m, (c_b, t)), ((c_a, u), q, (c_b, k))\} \cup$$
$$\bigcup_{\varepsilon_i = C(c_b, q_i, c_i)}\{((c_b, k), q_i, (c_i, i))\}\big)\Big) \cup \big(\{((c_a, u), m, (c_b, t))\} \cup$$
$$\bigcup_{\varepsilon_i = C(c_b, q_i, c_i)}\{((c_a, u), q_i, (c_i, i))\}\big).$$ Let $X \subseteq C$ be a set of containers. $\kappa_{t,X}(d) \neq \kappa'_{t,X}(d) \Rightarrow ((c_a, u), q, (c_b, k)) \in mincut_{\mathcal{G}_{t,X}}((S, 0), d)$ because any other edge has the same value in both graphs, but this is impossible (i.e. it is not a minimum cut) since $q \geq m + s_Y$. Hence $\mathcal{G}'_t \sim \mathcal{G}_t$.

Removal of Copy (case 1). For a sequence of events $tr = (\varepsilon_0, \ldots, \varepsilon_k, \ldots, \varepsilon_t)$ such that $\exists k \in \mathbb{N} \, \forall c, c_a \in C, q \in \mathbb{N}, i \in [k+1..t-1], x \in \mathbb{N}: \varepsilon_k = C(c_a, s_1, c_b) \wedge \varepsilon_t = C(c_c, s_2, c_b) \wedge \varepsilon_i \neq T(c_b, x) \wedge \varepsilon_i \neq C(c, x, c_b) \wedge \varepsilon_i \neq C(c_b, x, c) \wedge \varepsilon_i \neq T(c_a, x) \wedge \varepsilon_i \neq C(c, x, c_a)$, we construct a new sequence $tr' = (\varepsilon_0, \ldots, \varepsilon_{k-1}, C(c_a, s_1, c_c, s_2, c_b), \ldots, \varepsilon_{t-1})$ that results in a simpler, yet equivalent graph. Let (c_a, u) be the source node of the copy action at time k, (c_b, v) the current node for c_b (if any) at time $k-1$, and (c_c, w) the source node of the copy action at time t. We define $\mathcal{N}'_t = \mathcal{N}_t \setminus \{(c_b, t)\}$ and $\mathcal{E}'_t = (\mathcal{E}_t \setminus \{((c_b, k), \infty, (c_b, t)), ((c_c, w), s_2, (c_b, t))\}) \cup \{((c_c, w), s_2, (c_b, k))\}$. Let $X \subseteq C$ be a set of containers. If $c_b \notin X$, then $\kappa_{t,X}(d) = \kappa'_{t,X}(d)$ because no flow would go through the modified part. If $c_b \in X$, $\kappa_{t,X}(d) \neq \kappa'_{t,X}(d) \Rightarrow \big(((c_c, w), s_2, (c_b, k)) \in mincut_{\mathcal{G}'_{t,X}}((S, 0), d) \wedge ((c_c, w), s_2, (c_b, t)) \notin mincut_{\mathcal{G}_{t,X}}((S, 0), d)\big)$. This is impossible since the node (c_b, t) must be separated from $(S, 0)$ by the cut and $s_2 < \infty$. Therefore, having $((c_c, w), s_2, (c_b, k))$ in the cut in $\mathcal{G}'_t$ implies that $((c_c, w), s_2, (c_b, t))$ is in the cut in $\mathcal{G}_t$. Hence $\mathcal{G}'_t \sim \mathcal{G}_t$.

Removal of Copy (case 2). For a sequence of events $tr = (\varepsilon_0, \ldots, \varepsilon_k, \ldots, \varepsilon_t)$ such that $\exists k \in \mathbb{N} \, \forall c_a, c \in C, q, x \in \mathbb{N}, i \in [k+1..t-1], j \in [0..k-1]: \varepsilon_k = C(c_a, s_1, c_b) \wedge \varepsilon_t = C(c_a, s_2, c_b) \wedge \varepsilon_j \neq I(c_b, x) \wedge \varepsilon_j \neq C(c, x, c_b) \wedge \varepsilon_i \neq T(c_b, x) \wedge \varepsilon_i \neq C(c, x, c_b) \wedge \varepsilon_i \neq T(c_a, x) \wedge \varepsilon_i \neq C(c, x, c_a) \wedge s_1 > \sum_{\varepsilon_i = C(c_b, x, c)} x$, we construct a new sequence $tr' = (\varepsilon_0, \ldots, \varepsilon_{k-1}, C(c_a, s_1 + s_2, c_b), \ldots, \varepsilon_{t-1})$ that results in a simpler, yet equivalent graph. Let (c_a, u) be the source node of the copy action at time k and $Y = \{((c_b, k), q_i, (c_i, i)) \mid i \in [k+1..t-1], c_i \in \mathcal{C}, q_i \in \mathbb{N}, \varepsilon_i = C(c_b, q_i, c_i) \in tr\}$ the destination nodes of the copy steps from c_b between time $k+1$ and time $t-1$, and s_Y the sum of those edges' capacities. We define $\mathcal{N}'_t = \mathcal{N}_t \setminus \{(c_b, t)\}$ and $\mathcal{E}'_t = (\mathcal{E}_t \setminus \{((c_b, k), \infty, (c_b, t)), ((c_a, u), s_1, (c_b, k)), ((c_a, u), s_2, (c_b, t))\}) \cup \{((c_a, u), s_1 + s_2, (c_b, k))\}$. Let $X \subseteq C$ be a set of containers. $\kappa_{t,X}(d) \neq \kappa'_{t,X}(d) \Rightarrow Y \cap mincut_{\mathcal{G}_{t,X}}((S, 0), d) \neq \varnothing$. Let s_X be the sum of those edges' capacities. Since $\kappa_{t,X}(d) \neq \kappa'_{t,X}(d)$, it means $s_1 < s_X$. This is impossible since $s_X \leq s_Y \leq s_1$. Hence $\mathcal{G}'_t \sim \mathcal{G}_t$.

Security of Graph Data: Hashing Schemes and Definitions

Muhammad U. Arshad[†1], Ashish Kundu[‡2] , Elisa Bertino[†3], Krishna Madhavan[†4], Arif Ghafoor[†5]

[†]Purdue University
West Lafayette, Indiana, USA
{[1]marshad, [3]bertino, [4]cm, [5]ghafoor}@purdue.edu

[‡]IBM T J Watson Research Center
Yorktown Heights, New York, USA
[2]akundu@us.ibm.com

ABSTRACT

Use of graph-structured data models is on the rise – in graph databases, in representing biological and healthcare data as well as geographical data. In order to secure graph-structured data, and develop cryptographically secure schemes for graph databases, it is essential to formally define and develop suitable collision resistant one-way hashing schemes and show them they are efficient. The widely used Merkle hash technique is not suitable as it is, because graphs may be directed acyclic ones or cyclic ones. In this paper, we are addressing this problem. Our contributions are: (1) define the practical and formal security model of hashing schemes for graphs, (2) define the formal security model of perfectly secure hashing schemes, (3) describe constructions of hashing and perfectly secure hashing of graphs, and (4) performance results for the constructions. Our constructions use graph traversal techniques, and are highly efficient for hashing, redaction, and verification of hashes graphs. We have implemented the proposed schemes, and our performance analysis on both real and synthetic graph data sets support our claims.

Categories and Subject Descriptors

D.4.6 [**Security and Protection**]: *Cryptographic controls*

Keywords

Integrity; Hash Functions; Perfectly Secure Hash Functions; Graphs; Privacy

1. INTRODUCTION

One of the fundamental building blocks of modern cryptography is hash function. Hash functions are used towards verification of data integrity as well as message authentication codes and digital signature schemes. Traditional hash functions handle messages as bit strings. $\mathcal{H} : \{0, 1\}^* \to \{0,$

$1\}^n$ defines a hash function that takes a bitstring of any size as input and outputs a hash-value of size n-bits. Integrity protection of data includes not only data objects that are bit strings but also data objects that are graphs.

Some of the several contexts where graph-structured data models are widely used are healthcare, biological, geographical and location data as well as financial databases [6, 18]. Often it is required to check if a given graph has been updated or not or whether two graphs are identical[1]. Hashing is used to carry out these operations [12]. The problem of hashing graphs is of great immediate practical value and just not of conceptual value – programmers are looking for techniques that they can implement in order to compute hash values of directed graphs[2]. Moreover, authenticating graph-structured data is often a crucial security requirement for databases [17]. Hashing is used as a basic building block for authentication schemes based on hash-and-sign paradigm. In this paper, we have focused on hashing schemes (integrity) and not on authenticity.

In case of hashing schemes such as SHA-1, SHA-2, a message is either shared completely or not shared at all with the user. In contrast, when graphs are used, a user may receive part(s) of a graph (subgraph(s)). Graph models are often used for representing sensitive data as well (such as healthcare, biological data). Traditional hashing schemes leak information (for SHA1 and SHA2 leak information about the length of the plaintext [2]). The challenge is how to hash graphs so that no information is leaked at least in the context of probabilistic polynomial adversaries [8]. The Merkle hash technique (MHT) has been proposed as an approach for computing hashes for trees [15] and has been extended for directed acyclic graphs [14].

Cryptographic hashing techniques for cyclic graphs have not been well-studied in the existing literature. There are schemes for hashing trees and directed acyclic graphs: Merkle hash technique, and Search DAG, which is based on MHT. Existing schemes rely on the fact that updates do not change a tree into a non-tree graph and a DAG to a cyclic graph. That restriction is quite strong – it limits the operations that can be carried out on a graph database. Moreover, it is desireable to have one hashing scheme that is applicable to any type of graph, which helps simplifying security of graph

---

[1]Identical graphs are isomorphic graphs, but the reverse is not true [4].

[2]http://stackoverflow.com/questions/14532164/hash-value-for-directed-acyclic-graph

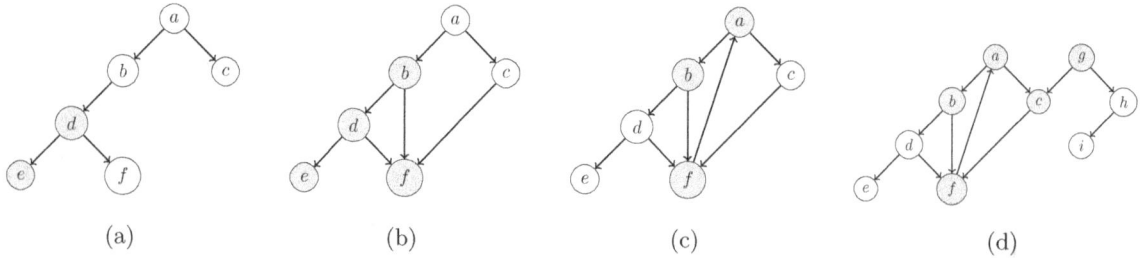

Figure 1: Graphs: (a) Tree, (b) DAG, (c) Graph with cycles, (d) Graph with multiple sources (vertices with no incoming edge). The shadowed with dotted boundary are the subgraphs that a user may receive.

databases; without such a generic yet efficient scheme, graph security technqiques need to determine the type of the graph being hashed and then determine which scheme would be applicable. Such a process would not only add cost of software engineering and maintenance for such additional schemes and logic, but also add cost in terms for performance and latency to the security schemes using hashing.

In many application domains, such as health care and military, an additional requirement is to maintain the secrecy of the content from which its hash value: by secrecy, we mean that the hash value of a content does not leak any information of the content. Canetti et al. [3] refer to this as perfectly secure hashing. As in the MHT, when a subtree is shared with a user, the user also receives a set of Merkle hash values for some of the nodes that are not in the shared subtree. If the hash function used is not perfectly collision-resistant , the hash values could lead to leakage of information about the unshared nodes, which needs to be prevented. In addition the user may learn the existence of nodes that he/she is not allowed to access; such knowledge may lead to inferences that may then result in privacy or confidentiality breaches [11]. Encryption is too heavyweight and has different security properties than the properties required for hash functions.

Therefore, in case of graph data, there is a need to define the formal notions of hashing and perfectly secure hashing schemes, and develop constructions for such definitions that are efficient and practical to be used by real-world graph database systems. In addition, the formalization of such secure hashing schemes for graphs is essential towards analyzing different constructions with respect to their security.

In this paper, we make the following contributions: (1) we define the formal security model of hashing schemes for graphs, (2) we define the formal security model of perfectly secure hashing schemes, (3) we have proposed efficient generic constructions of hashing and perfectly secure hashing schemes that can be applied to any types of graphs, and (4) we have carried out experiments, and our performance results for the constructions corroborate that our schemes are highly efficient and can be used in real-world graph databases and graph security schemes.

2. RELATED WORK AND BACKGROUND

There are two techniques in the literature that come closest to the constructions presented in this paper: The Merkle hash technique [15] (MHT) and the Search-DAG technique [14] (SDAG).

Integrity assurance of tree-structured data is primarily carried by the Merkle hash technique [15]. We would describe the issues associated with MHT in the next section. Martel et al. [14] proposed SDAG – an authentication technique for directed acyclic graphs referred to as "Search DAGs" in third party distribution frameworks. Their technique uses MHT. The SDAG technique only covers DAGs, not the general directed graphs, which is of greater interest in this paper. Martel et al. do not define security of hashing of directed graphs nor they address perfectly secure hashing of graphs. Kundu et al. [10] have defined the security of leakage-free signatures for graphs, which however does not cover the hashing schemes.

Throughout the paper, we have cited other related works as and when needed.

2.1 Hashing Trees with Merkle Hash Technique

The Merkle hash technique [15] works bottom-up. For a node x in tree $T(V, E)$, it computes a Merkle hash (MH) $mh(x)$ as follows: if x is a leaf node, then $mh(x) = \mathcal{H}(c_x)$; else $mh(x) = \mathcal{H}(mh(y_1)\|mh(y_2)\| \dots \|mh(y_m))^3$, where y_1, y_2, ...,y_m are the m children of x in T in that order from left to right. For example, consider the tree in Figure 1(a). The MH for this tree is computed as follows. The MH of e and f are computed as $\mathcal{H}(c_e)$ and $\mathcal{H}(c_f)$, respectively, which are then used to compute the MH of d as $mh(d) = \mathcal{H}(mh(e) \| mh(f))$. The MH of b is computed as $\mathcal{H}(mh(d))$. Similarly, the MH of c and a are computed as $\mathcal{H}(c_c)$ and $\mathcal{H}(mh(b) \| mh(c))$, respectively.

By using such a technique, only the contents of the leaf nodes can be authenticated. In case the non-leaf (intermediate or root) nodes have contents, the computation of the MH of non-leaf nodes x involves the MH of all of its children, and either (a) the content of x, or (b) hash of the content of x (used in 1(a)). Suppose x to be a non-leaf node in T. The MH of x is defined as follows: $mh(x) = \mathcal{H}(\mathcal{H}(c_x) \| mh(y_1) \| mh(y_2) \| \dots \| mh(y_m))$.

Consider again the tree in Figure 1(a). MH of d, b and a are computed respectively as $\mathcal{H}(\mathcal{H}(c_d) \| mh(e) \| mh(f))$, $\mathcal{H}(\mathcal{H}(c_b) \| mh(d))$, and $\mathcal{H}(\mathcal{H}(c_a) \| mh(b) \| mh(c))$.

2.1.1 Integrity Verification

Let T_δ be a subtree of tree T as shown shadowed to be shared with a user. The following set of verification objects $\mathcal{VO}$ is also sent to the user, for integrity verification of T_δ.

---
[3]Henceforth, $\mathcal{H}$ denotes a one-way, collision-resistant hash function, and $\|$ stands for concatenation

Such *auxiliary information* constitutes the information leakages by MHT (Figure 1). The user then computes the MH of the whole tree using such information (the subtree and auxiliary information) and verifies the hash of the original tree using using this MH.

1. Let x be a node is T_δ. The MH of each sibling of x the is in T but not in T_δ. (e.g., $mh(f)$ w.r.t. e)

2. The MH of each sibling y of each ancestor x, such that y is not in T_δ. (e.g., $mh(c)$ and $mh(f)$ w.r.t. e)

3. The hash of the content of each ancestor of x. (e.g., $\mathcal{H}(c_a)$ and $\mathcal{H}(c_b)$ w.r.t. x)

4. (i) The structural order between a node x in T_δ and its sibling(s) that are not in T_δ, and (ii) the structural order between the sibling nodes that are not in T_δ. (e.g., (i) the order between e and f, and (ii) the order between b and c.)

5. (i) Parent-child/ancestor-descendant relationship(s) between a node in T_δ and another node not in T_δ and (ii) those between the nodes that are not in T_δ . (e.g., the relationships (i) between b and d, (ii) between a and b, and between a and c.)

6. The fact that a given node is the root of T (even if it is the root of T_δ).

The user then computes the MH of the whole tree using such information (the subtree and $\mathcal{VO}$) and compares it with the received signed MH of the root. If they are equal, the integrity of the subtree is validated. Moreover, this process verifies the integrity of the subtree against the original tree.

2.2 Hashing Graphs

In graphs, nodes may have multiple incoming edges, there maybe no roots or source nodes; perhaps, there maybe a number of roots or source nodes. The major challenges in hashing graphs arise out of the fact that (i) a graph may have cycles, (ii) changes to the nodes affect hashes of multiple other nodes, and (iii) a graph can be shared with a user in parts or in terms of subgraphs. For example, in Figure 1, subgraphs that are shared are shown as shadowed regions on each of the graphs.

Consider the DAG in Figure 1(b). Node f has three incoming edges. If we use the SDAG technique, then the hash of node f influences the hashes of three other nodes from which these nodes originate: d, b, and c. While that is acceptable, any update to f affects the hashes of all nodes other than e. In general in the SDAG technique, an update to a node in a DAG affects $|V| + |E|$ nodes.

Hashing graphs with cycles is more complex because such graphs cannot be ordered topologically [4]. For the graphs in Figure 1 (c) and (d), the cycles involve nodes a, b, c and f. The issue is then how to hash such graphs so that the cyclic structure is also preserved in the hash – dissimilar structures should not have the same hash even if the contents maybe identical.

2.3 Formal Security Models

Existing approaches [15, 14] do not formally define the notion of graph hashing, nor they define how to construct perfectly collision-resistant graph hash functions. Canetti et

al. [2, 3] developed the notion of perfectly collision-resistant hash functions for messages that are bit-strings and are not graphs nor any structured/semi-structured objects. Canetti et al. [3] also proposed that the *verify* method should be included in the definition of random oracles. In this paper, we also propose a similar *hash-verify* method as well as a *hash-redact* method that is specific for structured/semi-structured data.

3. TERMINOLOGY

Trees and Graphs: A directed graph $G(V, E)$ is a set of nodes (or vertices) V and a set of edges E between these nodes: $e(x, y)$ is an edge from x to y, $(x, y) \in V \times V$. Undirected graphs can be represented as directed graphs. Therefore, in what follows we consider only the case of directed graphs and we will use the term graph with the meaning of directed graph. A node x represents an atomic unit of data, which is always shared as a whole or is not shared at all. A source is a node that does not have any incoming edge. A node x is called the ancestor of a node y iff there exists a path consisting of one or more edges from x to y. Node x is an immediate ancestor, also called parent, of y in G iff there exists an edge $e(x, y)$ in E. Nodes having a common immediate ancestor are called siblings. Let $G(V, E)$ and $G_\delta(V_\delta, E_\delta)$ be two graphs. We say that $G_\delta(V_\delta, E_\delta)$ is a *redacted subgraph* of $G(V, E)$ if $G_\delta(V_\delta, E_\delta) \subseteq G(V, E)$. $G_\delta(V_\delta, E_\delta) \subseteq G(V, E)$ if an only if $V_\delta \subseteq V$ and $E_\delta \subseteq E$. Also $G_\delta(V_\delta, E_\delta) \subset G(V, E)$ if and only if $V_\delta \cup E_\delta \subset V \cup E$. A redacted subgraph $G_\delta(V_\delta, E_\delta)$ is derived from the graph $G(V, E)$ by redacting the set of nodes $V \setminus V_\delta$ and the set of edges $E \setminus E_\delta$ from G. A directed tree $T(V, E)$ is a directed graph with the following constraint: removal of any edge $e(x, y)$ from E leads to two disconnected trees with no edge or path between nodes x and y. As in the case of graphs, a redacted subtree of tree $T(V, E)$ denoted by $T_\delta(V_\delta, E_\delta)$ is such that $T_\delta(V_\delta, E_\delta) \subseteq T(V, E)$. $T_\delta(V_\delta, E_\delta) \subseteq T(V, E)$ denotes that $V_\delta \subseteq V$ and $E_\delta \subseteq E$. Redacted subgraph $T_\delta(V_\delta, E_\delta)$ is derived from the tree $T(V, E)$ by redacting the set of nodes $V \setminus V_\delta$ and the set of edges $E \setminus E_\delta$ from T. Two trees/graphs/forests with the same nodes and edges, but *different ordering* between at least one pair of siblings are different trees/graphs/forests.

4. REVIEW OF STANDARD HASHING SCHEMES

In this section, we review the standard definition of hashing schemes (adopted from [8]). A standard hashing scheme Π is a tuple $(\texttt{Gen}, \mathcal{H})$. ($\texttt{s}$ is not a secret key in standard cryptographic sense.)

Definition 1. (**Standard hashing scheme**) A hashing scheme Π consists of two probabilistic polynomial-time algorithms $\Pi = (\texttt{Gen}, \mathcal{H})$ satisfying the following requirements:

KEY GENERATION: The probabilistic key generation algorithm $\texttt{Gen}$ takes as input a security parameter 1^λ and outputs a key $\texttt{s}$: $\texttt{s} \leftarrow \texttt{Gen}(1^\lambda)$.

HASH: There exists a polynomial l such that $\mathcal{H}$ takes a key $\texttt{s}$ and a string $x \in \{0, 1\}^*$ and outputs a string $\mathcal{H}^\texttt{s}(x) \in \{0, 1\}^{l(\lambda)}$ (where λ is the value of the security parameter implicit in $\texttt{s}$).

If $\mathcal{H}^s$ is defined only for inputs $x \in \{0,1\}^{l'(\lambda)}$ and $l'(\lambda) > l(\lambda)$, then we say that $(\text{Gen}, \mathcal{H})$ is a fixed-length hash function for inputs of length $l'(\lambda)$.

4.1 Security of Hash Functions

The strongest form of security for hash functions include three properties: (1) collision resistance, (2) second pre-image resistance, and (3) pre-image resistance. Collision resistance is the strongest notion and subsumes second pre-image resistance, which in turn subsumes pre-image resistance [8]. In other words, any hash function that satisfies (2) satisfies also (3) but the reverse is not true; and any hash function that satisfies (1) satisfies also (2) (and transitively (3)) but the reverse is not true. In the rest of the paper, security of hash functions refer to the strongest property, i.e., collision resistance.

For the traditional hash functions defined in the previous section, we are now reviewing the collision-finding experiment (adapted from [8]). In the rest of the paper, $\mathcal{A}$ is a probabilistic polynomial-time (PPT) adversary.

Collision-finding Experiment: $\text{H-Coll}_{\mathcal{A},\Pi}(\lambda)$

1. Key $s \leftarrow \text{Gen}(1^\lambda)$

2. $\mathcal{A}$ is given s and outputs x and x'. (If Π is a fixed-length hash function for inputs of length $l'(\lambda)$ then $x, x' \in \{0,1\}^{l'(\lambda)}$)

3. The output of the experiment is 1 if and only if $x \neq x'$ and $\mathcal{H}^s(x) = \mathcal{H}^s(x')$. In such a case, we say that $\mathcal{A}$ has found a collision for $\mathcal{H}^s$; else the output of the experiment is 0.

Definition 2. A hash function $\Pi = (\text{Gen}, \mathcal{H})$ is collision-resistant if for all PPT adversaries $\mathcal{A}$ there exists a negligible function[4] negl such that

$$\Pr[\text{H-Coll}_{\mathcal{A},\Pi}(\lambda)] \leq \text{negl}(\lambda)$$

5. COLLISION-RESISTANT HASHING OF GRAPHS

The standard definition of hashing schemes cannot be applied directly to graphs because the standard definition operates on messages $x \in \{0,1\}^*$ and each message is shared either fully or not shared at all with a user. In contrast, a graph $G(V,E)$ is a set of nodes and edges, where each node may be represented by x, and a user may have access to one or more subgraphs instead of the complete graph.

As discussed earlier, a hashing scheme for graphs requires a key generation algorithm and a hash function algorithm. We would also need a method to verify hashes for a graph as well as its subgraphs. We refer to this algorithm as the "hash-verification" method. This is because as mentioned earlier, users may receive entire graphs or subgraphs, and need to verify their integrity. To that end, if the hash function used to compute the hash of a graph is a collision-resistant hash function, then the user would need certain extra information along with the proper subgraphs. Otherwise, the hash value computed by the user for the received

---

[4]A function $\epsilon(k)$ is negligible in cryptography if for every polynomial $p(.)$, there exists an N such that for all integers $k > N$ it holds that $\epsilon(k) < \frac{1}{p(k)}$ ([8]:Definition 3.4).

subgraphs would not match the hash value of the graph unless there is a contradiction to the premise that the hash function is collision-resistant. We refer to this extra information as "verification objects" $\mathcal{VO}$??. Computation of the $\mathcal{VO}$ for a subgraph with respect to a graph is carried out by another algorithm also part of the definition of the hashing scheme for graphs. We call this algorithm as "hash-redaction" of graphs.

The conceptualization of these two algorithms for verification and redaction described in the previous paragraph is already in use by schemes such as the MHT, but have not been formalized. As essential components of our formalization of the notion of graph hashes, we need to formalize these methods. Such formalization is also essential for a correct design and rigorous analysis of the protocols that realize these definitions. The definition of the graph hashing schemes is as follows.

Definition 3. (**Collision-resistant graph hashing scheme**) A hashing scheme $g\Pi$ consists of three PPT algorithms and one deterministic algorithm $g\Pi = (\text{gGen}, g\mathcal{H}, \text{ghRedact}, \text{ghVrfy})$ satisfying the following requirements:

KEY GENERATION: The probabilistic key generation algorithm gGen takes as input a security parameter 1^λ and outputs a key s: $s \leftarrow \text{gGen}(1^\lambda)$.

HASHING: The hash algorithm $g\mathcal{H}$ takes a key s and a graph $G(V,E)$ and outputs a string $g\mathcal{H}^s(G(V,E)) \in \{0,1\}^{l(\lambda)}$, where l a polynomial, and λ is the value of the security parameter implicit in s.

HASH-REDACTION: The redaction algorithm ghRedact is a probabilistic algorithm that takes $G(V,E)$ and a set of subgraphs $\mathcal{G}_\delta$ (such that each $G_\delta \in \mathcal{G}_\delta$, $G_\delta \subseteq G(V,E)$) as inputs and outputs a set $\mathcal{VO}_{\mathcal{G}_\delta, G(V,E)}$ of verification objects for those nodes and edges that are in $G(V,E)$ but not in any of the subgraphs in $\mathcal{G}_\delta$.

$$\mathcal{VO}_{\mathcal{G}_\delta, G(V,E)} \leftarrow \text{ghRedact}(\mathcal{G}_\delta, G(V,E))$$

HASH-VERIFY: ghVrfy is a deterministic algorithm that takes a hash value gH, a set of graphs $\mathcal{G}$, and a set of verification objects $\mathcal{VO}$, and returns a bit b, where $b = 1$ if the hash value gH is a valid hash for $\mathcal{G}$ and $\mathcal{VO}$, and $b = 0$ otherwise: $b \leftarrow \text{ghVrfy}^s(gH, \mathcal{G}, \mathcal{VO})$

5.1 Correctness

A hashing scheme for graphs is correct if the following properties hold.

Hashing Correctness (Empty redaction): For any graph $G(V,E)$, any positive integer value of λ, any key $s \leftarrow \text{gGen}(\lambda)$, and any $gH \leftarrow g\mathcal{H}^s(G(V,E))$, $\mathcal{VO} \leftarrow \text{ghRedact}(\{G\}, G)$, $\text{ghVrfy}^s(gH, \{G(V,E)\}, \mathcal{VO})$ always outputs 1.

Hash-Redaction Correctness: For any graph $G(V,E)$, any positive integer value of λ, any key $s \leftarrow \text{gGen}(\lambda)$, any set $\mathcal{G}_\delta$ of subgraphs $G_\delta(V_\delta, E_\delta) \subseteq G(V,E)$ such that the union of all the subgraphs in $\mathcal{G}_\delta$ results in a graph that is a proper subgraph of G, and $gH \leftarrow g\mathcal{H}^s(G)$, $\mathcal{VO} \leftarrow \text{ghRedact}(\mathcal{G}_\delta, G)$, $\text{ghVrfy}^s(gH, \mathcal{G}_\delta, \mathcal{VO})$ always outputs 1.

5.2 Security of Hash Functions

The strongest form of security for hash functions for graphs also includes three properties: (1) collision resistance, (2) second pre-image resistance, and (3) pre-image resistance. As earlier, collision resistance is the strongest notion and subsumes second pre-image resistance, which in turn subsumes pre-image resistance.

Collision-finding Experiment: $\texttt{GH-Coll}_{\mathcal{A},g\Pi}(\lambda)$

1. Key $\mathbf{s} \leftarrow \texttt{gGen}(1^\lambda)$

2. $\mathcal{A}$ is given $\mathbf{s}$ and outputs (a) $G(V,E)$ and $G'(V',E')$, and (b) $\mathcal{VO}_{\mathcal{G}_\delta,G(V,E)} \leftarrow \texttt{ghRedact}(\mathcal{G}_\delta, G(V,E))$ and $\mathcal{VO}'_{\mathcal{G}'_\delta,G'(V',E')} \leftarrow \texttt{ghRedact}(\mathcal{G}'_\delta, G'(V',E'))$

3. The output of the experiment is 1 if and only if any of the following is true: in such a case, we say that $\mathcal{A}$ has found a collision for $\mathcal{H}^\mathbf{s}$; else the output of the experiment is 0.

   (a) $G(V,E) \neq G'(V',E')$ and $gH = gH'$, where $gH \leftarrow g\mathcal{H}^\mathbf{s}(G)$, and $gH' \leftarrow g\mathcal{H}^\mathbf{s}(G'(V',E'))$.

   (b) $G(V,E) \neq G'(V',E')$ and $\texttt{ghVrfy}^\mathbf{s}(gH', \mathcal{G}_\delta, \mathcal{VO}) = g\mathcal{H}^\mathbf{s}(gH, \mathcal{G}'_\delta, \mathcal{VO}')$.

Definition 4. A hash function $g\Pi = (\texttt{gGen}, g\mathcal{H}, \texttt{ghRedact}, \texttt{ghVrfy})$ is collision-resistant if for all PPT adversaries $\mathcal{A}$ there exists a negligible function $\texttt{negl}$ such that

$$\Pr[\texttt{GH-Coll}_{\mathcal{A},g\Pi}(\lambda) = 1] \leq \texttt{negl}(\lambda)$$

6. PERFECTLY COLLISION-RESISTANT HASHING SCHEME FOR GRAPHS

In this section, we formalize the notion of perfectly one-way (i.e., collision-resistant) hash functions for graphs.

Hash functions used in practice do not hide information about the message being hashed. Canetti [2] showed that there is the need for a hash function that is perfectly one-way, i.e., for which it is hard to find a collision. SHA1, MD5 do not satisfy the "perfectly one-way" property. In this paper, we refer to "perfectly one-way" hash functions as "perfectly collision-resistant" hash functions. Before we define what perfectly collision-resistant hash functions are for graphs, we discuss why such a notion is necessary and what the leakages are.

Standard hashing schemes may leak information about the image being hashed. Even though such schemes are one-way in a computational sense (informally speaking, to find a collision one needs to solve a hard problem or do intractable amount of work), the hash value $\mathcal{H}(x)$ of image x reveals some information about x. Such information leaks in the reverse direction – $\mathcal{H}(x)$ to x makes this function "not perfectly one way"; such leakage may allow the attacker to construct pre-images and second-preimages with less work than what was defined by the random oracle model. In the case of sensitive data, such leakages via hash values lead to another security issue: leakage of sensitive information. As Canetti et al. describe in [3], if x represents a confidential information, $\mathcal{H}(x)$ may leak the length of x and bits of x, which is a serious security breach.

The formal definition of hashing schemes does not capture the requirement of non-leakage of information about pre-images. Canetti has introduced a formal definition for $x \in$ $\{0,1\}^*$ and several constructions for perfectly one-way hash functions [3].

However, for graphs no such notion has been defined. Graphs are often used to represent sensitive data, and it is thus essential to hide all the information contained in the nodes. There is another reason for the need of perfectly collision-resistant hash functions: the standard definition operates on messages $x \in \{0,1\}^*$ and each message is either fully shared or not shared at all with a user. In contrast, a graph $G(V,E)$ is a set of nodes and edges, where each node may be represented by x, and a user may have access to one or more subgraphs instead of the complete graph. As in the MHT, when a subtree is shared with a user, the user also receives a set of MH values for some of the nodes that are not in the shared subtree. If the hash function used is not perfectly collision-resistant, then the hash values could lead to leakage of information about the unshared nodes, which needs to be prevented. Encryption is too heavyweight and has different security properties than those required for hash functions. We thus need perfectly collision-resistant hash functions for graphs.

In the previous section, we formally defined the notion of collision-resistant graph hashing schemes. The definition of a perfectly collision-resistant graph hash function is identical to this definition but includes an extra element: a key that is used towards making the scheme perfectly collision-resistant (as well as hiding).

Definition 5. (**Perfectly collision-resistant graph hashing scheme**) A hashing scheme $pg\Pi$ consists of three probabilistic polynomial-time algorithms and one deterministic algorithm $pg\Pi = (\texttt{pgGen}, pg\mathcal{H}, \texttt{pghRedact}, \texttt{pghVerify})$ satisfying the following requirements:

KEY GENERATION: The probabilistic key generation algorithm $\texttt{pgGen}$ takes as input security parameter 1^λ and outputs a key $\mathbf{s}$.

$$\mathbf{s} \leftarrow \texttt{pgGen}(1^\lambda).$$

RANDOMIZER GENERATION: The probabilistic randomizer generation algorithm $\texttt{pgRandom}$ takes as input security parameter 1^{λ_r} and outputs a uniformly chosen random $\mathbf{r} \in \{0,1\}^{\lambda_r}$.

$$\mathbf{r} \leftarrow \texttt{pgRandom}(1^{\lambda_r}).$$

HASHING: There exists a polynomial l such that the hash algorithm $\texttt{pg}\mathcal{H}$ takes keys $\mathbf{s}$ and $\mathbf{r}$ along with a graph $G(V,E)$ as input and outputs a string pgH.

$$pgH \leftarrow pg\mathcal{H}^{\mathbf{s},\mathbf{r}}(G(V,E)) \in \{0,1\}^{l(\lambda,\lambda_r)}.$$

HASH-REDACTION: The redaction algorithm $\texttt{ghRedact}$ is a probabilistic algorithm that takes $G(V,E)$ and a set of subgraphs $\mathcal{G}_\delta$ (such that each $G_\delta \in \mathcal{G}_\delta$, $G_\delta \subseteq G(V,E)$) as inputs and outputs a set $\mathcal{VO}_{\mathcal{G}_\delta,G(V,E)}$ of verification objects for those nodes and edges that are in $G(V,E)$ but not in any of the subgraphs in $\mathcal{G}_\delta$.

$$\mathcal{VO}_{\mathcal{G}_\delta,G(V,E)} \leftarrow \texttt{pghRedact}(\mathcal{G}_\delta, G(V,E)).$$

HASH-VERIFY: $\texttt{pghVerify}$ is a deterministic algorithm that takes a hash value $pg\mathcal{H}$, a set of graphs $\mathcal{G}$, and a set of verification objects $\mathcal{VO}$, and returns a bit b, where $b = 1$ meaning valid if the hash value pgH is a

227

valid hash for $\mathcal{G}$ and $\mathcal{VO}$, and $b = 0$ meaning invalid hash value.

$$b \leftarrow \texttt{pghVerify}^{\texttt{s,r}}(pgH, \mathcal{G}, \mathcal{VO})$$

6.1 Correctness

A perfectly collision-resistant hashing scheme for graphs is correct if the following properties hold: Hashing Correctness (Empty redaction) and Hash-Redaction Correctness. These two properties have definitions similar to the definitions of such properties for the collision-resistant hash function for graphs in section 5.1.

6.2 Security

There are two security requirements: (1) collision-resistance, and (2) semantically perfect one-wayness of graph hash functions. The collision-resistance experiment is similar to the one defined earlier in Section 5.2.

Collision-finding Experiment: $\texttt{PGH-Coll}_{\mathcal{A},pg\Pi}(\lambda, \lambda_r)$

1. Key $\texttt{s} \leftarrow \texttt{pgGen}(1^\lambda)$

2. Randomizer $\texttt{r} \leftarrow \texttt{pgRandom}(1^{\lambda_r})$

3. $\mathcal{A}$ is given $\texttt{s}$, $\texttt{r}$; $\mathcal{A}$ outputs (a) $G(V,E)$ and $G'(V',E')$, and (b) $\mathcal{VO}_{\mathcal{G}_\delta, G(V,E)} \leftarrow \texttt{pghRedact}(\mathcal{G}_\delta, G(V,E))$ and $\mathcal{VO}'_{\mathcal{G}'_\delta, G'(V',E')} \leftarrow \texttt{pghRedact}(\mathcal{G}'_\delta, G'(V',E'))$

4. The output of the experiment is 1 if and only if any of the following is true: in such a case, we say that $\mathcal{A}$ has found a collision for $\mathcal{H}^{\texttt{s,r}}$; else the output of the experiment is 0.

    (a) $G(V,E) \neq G'(V',E')$ and $pgH = pgH'$, where $pgH \leftarrow pg\mathcal{H}^{\texttt{s,r}}(G)$, and $pgH' \leftarrow pg\mathcal{H}^{\texttt{s,r}}(G'(V',E'))$.

    (b) $G(V,E) \neq G'(V',E')$ and $\texttt{pghVerify}^{\texttt{s,r}}(pgH', \mathcal{G}_\delta, \mathcal{VO}) = pg\mathcal{H}^{\texttt{s,r}}(pgH, \mathcal{G}'_\delta, \mathcal{VO}')$.

The following experiment involves the adversary who can learn information about the graphs applied with hash. In the first game, the adversary is challenged to determine the graph that has been hashed without the knowledge of the graphs themselves. The adversary is given two hash values computed either for the same graph or for two distinct graphs. Iff the hash function is not perfectly collision-resistant hash function then the adversary can determine whether the two hash values correspond to one graph or the two graphs with a probability non-negligibly greater than $\frac{1}{2}$.

Privacy experiment-1: $\texttt{PGH-Priv1}_{\mathcal{A},pg\Pi}(\lambda, \lambda_r)$

1. Key $\texttt{s} \leftarrow \texttt{pgGen}(1^\lambda)$

2. Randomizers $\texttt{r}_1, \texttt{r}_2 \leftarrow \texttt{pgRandom}(1^{\lambda_r})$

3. Any two random graphs $G_0(V_0, E_0)$, and $G_1(V_1, E_1)$ that differ only at the contents of one or more nodes, drawn uniformly from $\mathcal{G}$.

4. Toss an unbiased coin; if it returns head then bit $b = 1$, else $b = 0$.

5. Compute the following: $pgH_0 \leftarrow pg\mathcal{H}(\texttt{r}_0, G_0(V_0, E_0))$ and $pgH_1 \leftarrow pg\mathcal{H}(\texttt{r}_1, G_1(V_1, E_1))$.

6. $\mathcal{A}$ is given $\texttt{s}$, $\texttt{r}$, pgH_0 and pgH_1; $\mathcal{A}$ outputs a bit b'.

7. The output of the experiment is 1 if and only if any of $b = b'$.

The following experiment is for privacy, but is with respect to the hash-redaction algorithm.

Privacy experiment-2: $\texttt{PGH-Priv2}_{\mathcal{A},pg\Pi}(\lambda, \lambda_r)$

1. Compute Key $\texttt{s} \leftarrow \texttt{pgGen}(1^\lambda)$

2. Compute randomizer $\texttt{r} \leftarrow \texttt{pgRandom}(1^{\lambda_r})$

3. Draw a random graph $G(V,E)$. Determine any two sets of subgraphs $\mathcal{G}_{\delta 0}, \mathcal{G}_{\delta 1} \subseteq G(V,E)$. Compute the hash of $G(V,E)$: $pgH \leftarrow pg\mathcal{H}^{\texttt{s,r}}(G(V,E))$.

4. Toss an unbiased coin; if it returns head then bit $b = 1$, else $b = 0$.

5. Compute the following: $\mathcal{VO}_0 \leftarrow \texttt{pghRedact}(\mathcal{G}_{\delta 0}, G(V,E))$ and $\mathcal{VO}_1 \leftarrow \texttt{pghRedact}(\mathcal{G}_{\delta 1}, G(V,E))$

6. $\mathcal{A}$ is given $\texttt{s}$, $\texttt{r}$, pgH, $\mathcal{VO}_0$ and $\mathcal{VO}_1$; $\mathcal{A}$ outputs a bit b'.

7. The output of the experiment is 1 if and only if any of $b = b'$.

Definition 6. A hash function $pg\Pi = (\texttt{pgGen}, ph\mathcal{H},$ $\texttt{phgRedact}, \texttt{pghVerify})$ is collision-resistant if for all PPT adversaries $\mathcal{A}$ there exists a negligible function $\texttt{negl}$ such that

$$\Pr[\texttt{PGH-Coll}_{\mathcal{A},pg\Pi}(\lambda, \lambda_r) = 1] \leq \texttt{negl}(\lambda, \lambda_r)$$

Definition 7. A hash function $pg\Pi = (\texttt{pgGen}, ph\mathcal{H},$ $\texttt{phgRedact}, \texttt{pghVerify})$ is perfectly collision-resistant if for all PPT adversaries $\mathcal{A}$ there exists a negligible function $\texttt{negl}$ such that

$$\Pr[(\texttt{PGH-Priv1}_{\mathcal{A},pg\Pi}(\lambda, \lambda_r) = 1)$$
$$\vee (\texttt{PGH-Priv2}_{\mathcal{A},pg\Pi}(\lambda, \lambda_r) = 1)] \leq \frac{1}{2} + \texttt{negl}(\lambda, \lambda_r)$$

7. CONSTRUCTION OF HASHING SCHEME FOR GRAPHS

In this section, we propose a construction of collision-resistant hashing scheme for general graphs that is applicable to trees, DAGs and graphs with cycles. The scheme is secure with respect to $g\Pi$. Our construction exploits a specific property of graph traversals, and defines a new type of trees "efficient-tree" that are used to represent graphs.

7.1 Graph Traversal

A graph $G(V,E)$ can be traversed in a depth-first manner or breadth-first manner [4]. Post-order, pre-order, and in-order graph traversals are defined in [9, 4]. While post-order and pre-order traversals are defined for all types of trees, in-order traversal is defined only for binary trees. In each of these traversals, the first node visited is assigned 1 as its *visit count*. For every subsequent vertex visited, the *visit count* is incremented by 1 and is assigned to the vertex. This sequence of numbers is called the sequence of post-order (PON), pre-order (RON), or in-order (ION) numbers for the tree T, depending on the particular type of traversal. Figure 2 shows the traversal numbers and the DFT for a graph.

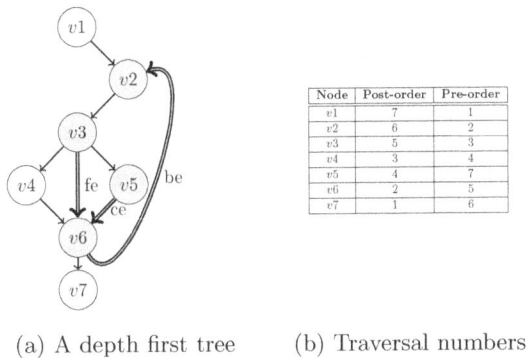

(a) A depth first tree   (b) Traversal numbers

Node	Post-order	Pre-order
v1	7	1
v2	6	2
v3	5	3
v4	3	4
v5	4	7
v6	2	5
v7	1	6

Figure 2: A graph with depth-first tree.

Properties of traversal numbers: The post-order number of a node is smaller than that of its parent. The pre-order number of a node is greater than that of its parent. The in-order number of a node in a binary tree is greater than that of its left child and smaller than that of its right child. A specific traversal number of a node is always smaller than that of its right sibling. The following lemma provides the basis for using traversal numbers in hash computation.

LEMMA 1. *The pair of post-order and pre-order number for a node in a non-binary tree correctly and uniquely determines the position of the node in the structure of the tree, where the position of a node is defined by its parent and its status as the left or right child of that parent.*

PROOF. From the post-order and pre-order traversal sequences of the vertices, it is possible to *uniquely* re-construct a non-binary tree [5] [7]. Thus from these sequences or from their counterparts, for a node, it is possible to correctly identify its parent and its status as left or right child of that parent in the tree. □

7.2 Graphs

In our scheme we are going to use the notion of post-order and pre-order numbers. However, in order to do that, we need to represent the graph as a tree. To that end, what we do is: we carry out a depth-first search (DFS) of the graph $G(V, E)$, which gives us one or more depth-first trees (DFT).

The various types of edges in a graph are defined below using the notion of traversal numbers. An example of depth-first tree and types of its edges is given in Figure 2 with the post- and pre-order numbers for each node being given in the table in the figure. Edge $e(v_3, v_6)$ is a forward-edge, edge $e(v_5, v_6)$ is a cross-edge and edge $e(v_6, v_2)$ is a back-edge. However, DFTs do not capture the edges that are called forward-edges, cross-edges and back-edges.

Definition 8. Let τ be the depth-first tree (DFT) of a directed graph $G = (V, E)$. Let $x, y \in V$, and $e(x, y) \in E$. Let p_x and r_x refer to post-order number and pre-order number of node x, respectively. With respect to the DFT τ, $e(x, y)$ is a (1) tree-edge, iff $p_x > p_y$, and $r_x < r_y$; (2) forward-edge, iff there is a path from x to y consisting of more than one tree-edges, $p_x > p_y$, and $r_x < r_y$; (3) cross-edge, iff $p_x > p_y$, and $r_x > r_y$; (4) back-edge, iff $p_x < p_y$, and $r_x > r_y$.

Efficient-Tree Representation of a Graph: In the efficient tree representation of a graph, $G(V, E)$ we represent forward-, cross-, and back-edges by a special node called edge-node which contains information about both the source and target vertex pre- and post-processing numbers (for that specific edge). Moreover, edge-node has an incoming edge from the node the specific edge originates from. The edge-nodes do not have any outgoing edges. Once the post-order and pre-order numbers have been assigned to the nodes, we can dismantle the structure of the DFT, because the traversal numbers can be used to re-construct the DFT again (Lemma 1 and Definition 8). Figure 3 shows such tree-representations of graphs.

7.3 Construction of Collision-resistant Hashing Scheme for Graphs

The construction of the collision-resistant hash functions for graphs $g\Pi$ is given below. $\mathcal{H}$ refers to a standard hash function as defined by Π. The last statement in $g\mathcal{H}$ computes the hash of a tree as shown in Figure 3 (b-efficient) and (c-efficient).

Using the proposed schemes different hash values are generated for isomorphic graphs [4] i.e., if the origin or DFS-tree changes the resulting hash value also changes.

$g\mathcal{H}$: *Input*: a graph $G(V, E)$.

1. Sort the source nodes of the graphs in the non-decreasing order of their contents or label.

2. Let x be the first source node in the sorted order. If there are no source nodes in $G(V, E)$ choose x randomly.

3. Carry out the depth-first traversal of the graph $G(V, E)$ from source node x as follows.

   (a) If node y is visited in DFS, assign its (post-order, pre-order) numbers to it: (p_y, r_y).

   (b) Let there be an edge $e(y, z)$ such that $e(y, z) \in E$ and $z \in V$. If $e(y, z)$ is not a tree-edge, then create an edge-node yz having the following content:
      - If cross-edge: $ce((p_y, r_y), (p_z, r_z))$;
      - If forward-edge: $fe((p_y, r_y), (p_z, r_z))$;
      - If back-edge: $be((p_y, r_y), (p_z, r_z))$.

   (c) Add an edge from y to the new node yz, and remove the edge $e(y, z)$.

4. Remove x from the sorted order of source nodes if exists.

5. If there are nodes in $G(V, E)$ that are not yet visited, then repeat from 2.

6. Compute hash of each node y as follows:

$$H_y \leftarrow \mathcal{H}((p_y, r_y)\|y).$$

7. To each edge-node yz, assign $H_{yz} \leftarrow \mathcal{H}(H_y\|H_z)$.

8. Compute the hash of graph $gH_{G(V,E)}$ as follows:

$$gH_{G(V,E)} \leftarrow \mathcal{H}(H_{y_1}\|H_{y_2}\|\ldots\|H_{y_m})$$

where y_i refers to the i'th node in the increasing order of the post-order numbers of the nodes, and of the

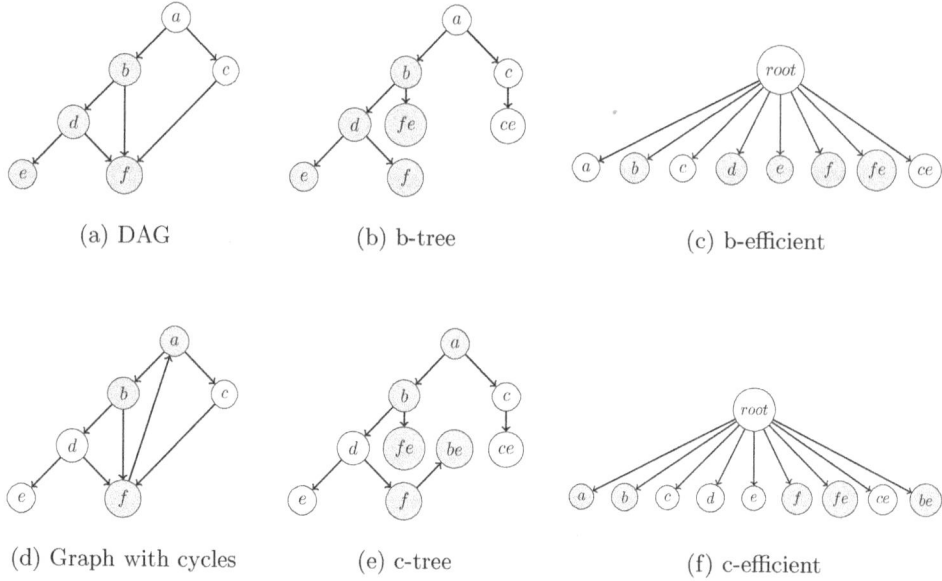

(a) DAG   (b) b-tree   (c) b-efficient

(d) Graph with cycles   (e) c-tree   (f) c-efficient

Figure 3: Tree representation of the running examples from Figure 1: (b-tree) and (c-tree) are tree-representations of the graphs in (a) and (d) – each node contains its (post-order, pre-order) number. (b, c-efficient) are one-level tree representations of the graphs exploiting the post-order and pre-order numbers of graph traversals. Each node contains their numbers. *fe*, *ce*, and *be* represent forward-edges, cross-edges and back-edges, respectively. Each of these nodes contain the post- and pre-order numbers of the origin and target of the edges and the hashes of their contents.

originating nodes of the edge-nodes, and m is the total number of nodes in the efficient-tree including original nodes and the edge-nodes.

`ghRedact`:

1. Input: a set of subgraphs $\mathcal{G}_\delta$ that contains the efficient tree representations of the subgraphs, and the efficient tree-representation of graph $G(V, E)$.

2. Given $\mathcal{G}_\delta$, and $G(V, E)$, determine the set $V \backslash excluded$ and $E \backslash excluded$ consisting of excluded nodes and edge-nodes, respectively, in the efficient tree-representation of the graph.

3. $\mathcal{VO} \leftarrow \emptyset$

4. $\mathcal{VO} \leftarrow \mathcal{VO} \cup ((p_y, r_y), H_y)$, where $y \in V \backslash excluded$.

5. $\mathcal{VO} \leftarrow \mathcal{VO} \cup (\tau((p_y, r_y), (p_z, r_z)), H_{yz})$, where τ defines the type of the edge-node: *fe*, *ce*, and *be*, and $yz \in E \backslash excluded$.

`ghVrfy`:

1. Input: a set of subgraphs $\mathcal{G}'_\delta$ that contains the efficient tree representation of the subgraphs, a set of verification objects $\mathcal{VO}$, and the hash of the complete graph gH.

2. Sort the received nodes, edge-nodes in the increasing order of the post-order numbers of the nodes or origins of the edge-nodes.

3. For each node x that is in a subgraph $G_\delta \in \mathcal{G}'_\delta$, compute H_x.

4. For each edge-node xy that is in a subgraph $G_\delta \in \mathcal{G}'_\delta$, compute H_{xy}.

5. Compute the hash $gH' \leftarrow \mathcal{H}(H_{x1} || H_{x2} || \ldots || H_{xm'})$, where x_i refers to the i'th node in the increasing order of the post-order numbers of the nodes, and of the originating nodes of the edge-nodes, and m' is the total number of nodes in the efficient-tree including original nodes and the edge-nodes.

6. Iff $gH' = gH$, return 1, else return 0.

7.4 Construction of Perfectly Collision-resistant Hashing Scheme for Graphs

In order to construct perfectly collision-resistant hash functions for graphs, we need to handle two cases of use of hashes: (1) redaction is not necessary, and (2) redaction is necessary. The reason is: redaction leads to use of non-empty verification objects that contain post-order and pre-order numbers, which would leak information (as shown in previous Section). When redaction is to be supported, the verification object needs to protect the information about the graph, and should not leak it to the verifier via the hash value. As in standard hashing for graphs described earlier, the verification object contains the post-order and pre-order number of each node that is not in the redacted graph and its hash. Post-order and pre-order numbers leak information about the number of nodes in the graph, and other information such as cycles or whether there are different types of edges in the graph. In order to make the hash scheme perfectly collision-resistant one, then it has to prevent leakage of such information.

There are use-cases that do not need redaction, and there are other use-cases that need redaction. If redaction is not essential for hashing, then the computation of hash has to make sure that the hash value $pgH_{G(V,E)}$ does not leak any information about the graph $G(V,E)$, which is defined in the Section 6.2; it should be secure against the Privacy Experiment - 1 in Section 6.2. If redaction is necessary, in order to prevent any leakage by the redacted hash value of a subgraph $G_\delta(V_\delta, E_\delta)$, the verification object must also not leak any information; the hash function should be secure against both privacy experiments: Privacy Experiment - 1 and 2.

7.5 Perfectly Collision-resistant Hashing Without Redaction

In this section, we would discuss what changes we would make to the hashing scheme described in the previous section in order to make it perfectly-secure without supporting redaction. In what follows, we have referred to the steps of the previous section 7.

For hashing:

1. In Step 3(a), generate a unique random number $\mu(x)$ for each node/edge-node x.

2. In Step 6 for computing hash of a node, use the random number: compute hash

$$H_y \leftarrow \mathcal{H}((p_y, r_y)||\mu(y)||y).$$

3. In Step 7 for computing hash of an edge-node yz, compute hash

$$H_{yz} \leftarrow \mathcal{H}(\mu(yz)||H_y||H_z).$$

4. Hash-value of the graph is: $(H_{G(V,E)}, \sigma)$, where σ is an ordered list of the random numbers computed during the process of hashing, and the order is the order in which the nodes are sorted for hashing.

For verification:

1. A verifier receiver the hash value that has $H_{G(V,E)}$, and σ;

2. Verifier sorts the nodes as in Step 2, and computes the hash of each of the node by using the random number for that node in σ: it concatenates the random value while computing the hash.

Use of the random numbers help this updated scheme support the Privacy Experiment - 1.

7.6 Perfectly Collision-resistant Hashing With Redaction

In order to develop a hashing scheme for graphs that supports both Privacy Experiment - 1 and 2, we need to ensure that the post-order and pre-order numbers do not leak any information. In that case, we recommend use of order-preserving encryption to encrypt the post-order numbers and pre-order numbers, and use the encrypted values in place of the corresponding plaintext values [16] [1]. Use of such encrypted values have been supported in the notion of randomized traversal numbers [13].

Computation of hash of a graph and redacted graph would use encrypted randomized traversal numbers, and the random numbers, which support Privacy Experiments - 1 and 2, respectively. The rest of the scheme is as described in the previous section 7.5.

7.7 Security

The following lemma states the security of the proposed constructions for $g\Pi$ and $pg\Pi$.

LEMMA 2. *Under the random-oracle model, the $g\Pi$ is a collision-resistant hash function for graphs.*

LEMMA 3. *Under the random-oracle model, the $pg\Pi$ is a perfectly collision-resistant hash function for graphs.*

Due to space constraints we are unable to provide detailed proofs, which will be added in a technical report as an extension of this paper. However, the proof of Lemma 2 follows from the properties of post-order and pre-order numbers and the random oracle hypothesis. Post-order and pre-order numbers prevent collision for graphs that have same set of nodes and edges but having the possibility that the order between siblings may have been changed, which would be invalidated by these numbers. The hash function being used to hash nodes and edge-nodes implement the random oracle and thus they are collision resistant. Any collision found by $g\Pi$ implies that our claims about the post-order and pre-order numbers and the hash functions are invalid.

Similarly, for Lemma 3, security depends on the security of (1) traversal numbers, (3) order-preserving encryption and (2) random oracle premise. In fact collision resistance is dependent on 1 and 3, while privacy properties of the hash values depend on the security properties of the encryption function. We would specify the proofs in a technical report.

8. PERFORMANCE RESULTS

In the following sections, we analyze the complexity and performance of the proposed schemes.

Cost: Each of the schemes gℋ, ghRedact, and ghVrfy, performs a traversal on the graph in the worst case (when the graph is shared as it is with no redaction). The cost of such traversal and each of these methods is: $O(|V| + |E|)$.

We have implemented the two schemes in Java 1.6 using JGraphT 0.8.3 (a free Java Graph Library) APIs. The experiments were carried out on a machine with following specification: Dell PowerEdge 2950, 64-bit Linux (Gentoo 2.6.32.20) running on dual 3.0GHz Intel Xeon E5450 processors with 32GB of RAM. We provided JVM with the following parameters: -Xss1024m, -Xms2048m, and -Xmx4096m to set the thread stack size and min/mix values for buffer space. For our experiments, we generated synthetic graph data sets using JGraphT's RandomGraphGenerator class and used real world directed graph data sets available at Stanford Large Network Dataset Collection[5]. Table 1 shows the specification of real world data sets as we used in our simulations. We ran all our simulations 10 times - per input instance - and report the average computation time for the results.

In our experiments, we have implemented the hashing scheme for graphs as in Section 7, and the perfectly collision-resistant hashing scheme without redaction as in Section 7.5.

---

[5] http://snap.stanford.edu/data/

Table 1: Different graph data sets

Table 1: Different graph data sets

Graph	$|V|$	$|E|$	Description
soc-Epinions1	75,879	508,837	Who-trusts-whom network of Epinions.com
soc-Slashdot0902	82,168	870,161	Slashdot social network from February 2009
email-Enron	265,214	418,956	Email communication network from Enron
web-NorteDame	325,729	1,469,679	Web graph of Notre Dame
web-Google	875,713	5,105,039	Web graph from Google

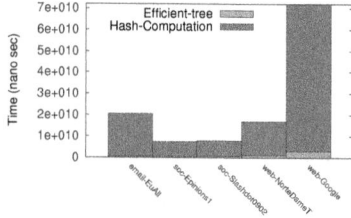

(a) Hash computation   (b) Perfectly collision-resistant hash computation (128-bit key)   (c) Perfectly collision-resistant hash computation (256-bit key)

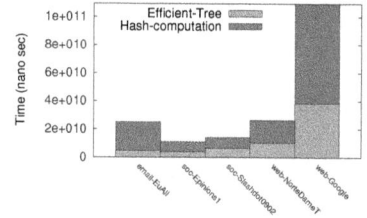

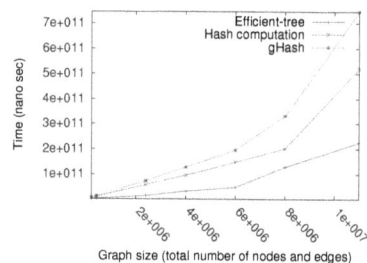

Figure 4: Time taken to compute hash of the graph using $g\mathcal{H}$ scheme; Efficient-tree represents the time to build the efficient-tree; and the Hash computation represents the time to compute the $gH_{G(V,E)}$ value using efficient-tree.

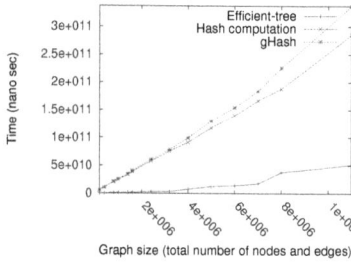

(a) Hash computation   (b) Perfectly collision-resistant hash computation (128-bit key)   (c) Perfectly collision-resistant hash computation (256-bit key)

Figure 5: Time taken to compute the hash of graph end-to-end; Efficient-tree represents the time to build the efficient-tree; Hash computation represents the time to compute the $gH_{G(V,E)}$ value using efficient-tree; and gHash represents the total time to compute the graph hash i.e., efficient-tree and hash computation combined.

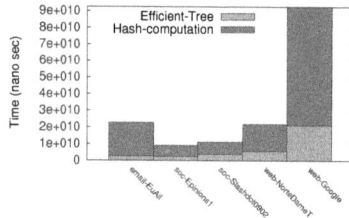

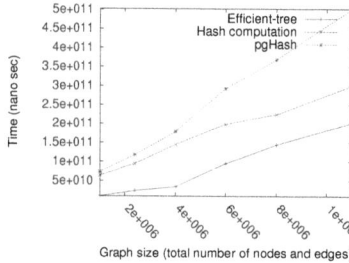

Our simulation results report three different kind of results:

- For $g\mathcal{H}$ function we report (a) the time to construct Efficient-tree from input graph and (b) the graph hash value computation, $gH_{G(V,E)}$, time for the two proposed hashing schemes.

- For `ghRedact` we report the time to compute the redacted graph vs number of nodes requested for `ghRedact`. Besides computing the redacted graph this process also involves generating the set of verification objects, $\mathcal{VO}$ for both original nodes and edge-nodes in the redacted graph.

- In the final set of experimental results we plot `ghVrfy` computation time vs number of nodes requested by the user.

Time taken to build Efficient-tree: This process involves running the Depth First Search (DFS) traversal algorithm on the input directed graph to assign both the pre- and post-processing numbers to nodes (i.e., determining the structural positions of nodes in a directed graph) and based-on these numbers classifying the graph edges as tree, forward, cross, and back edges. Additionally, this process also involves making the edge-node set for forward-, cross-, and back-edges. This is part of the one-time process of computing graph hash value, $gH_{G(V,E)}$.

Time taken to compute $gH_{G(V,E)}$ value: This process requires computing the hash value of all the nodes in the Efficient-tree representation of $G(V,E)$ by traversing the nodes in post-order fashion. Our implementation uses `TreeMap()` to keep a sorted listing of all the nodes (original nodes and edge-nodes) by post-order number. We use Java's **String-**

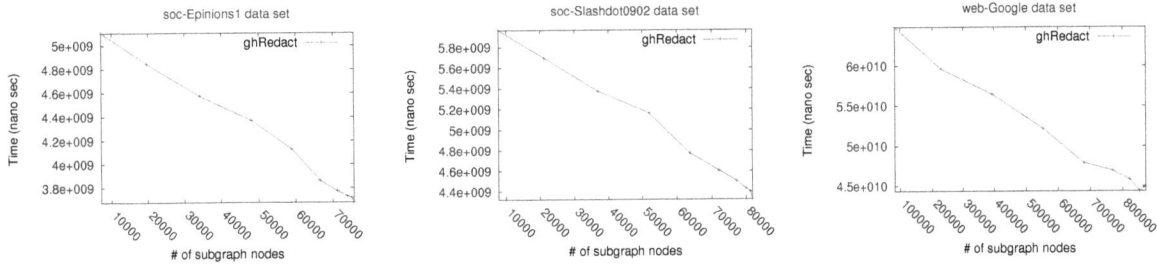

(a) Redaction time for soc-Epinions1 (b) Redaction time for soc- (c) Redaction time for web-Google data set Slashdot0902 data set data set

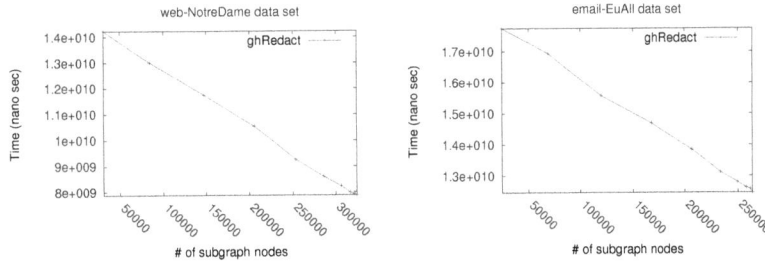

(d) Redaction time for web- (e) Redaction time for email-EuAll NotreDame data set data set

Figure 6: `ghRedact`/`pghRedact` function computation time vs number of requested subgraph nodes

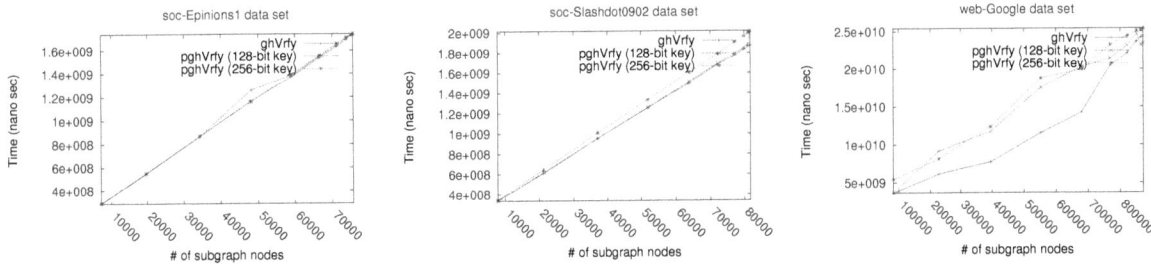

(a) Verification time for soc- (b) Verification time for soc- (c) Verification time for web-Google Epinions1 data set Slashdot0902 data set data set

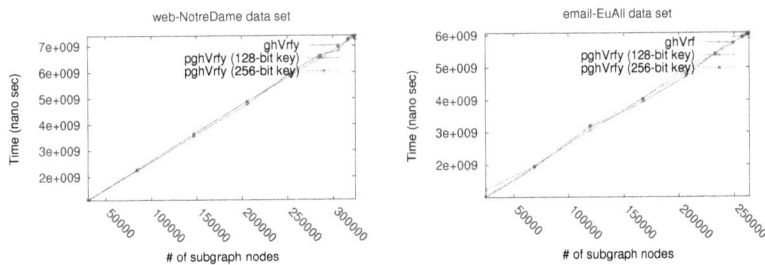

(d) Verification time for web- (e) Verification time for email-EuAll NotreDame data set data set

Figure 7: `ghVrfy`/`pghVrfy` function computation time vs number of requested subgraph nodes

`Buffer` class to maintain a running concatenation of hash values for all the nodes in the Efficient-tree.

From Figure 4 (a) we can see that the time to construct Efficient-tree is significantly less than the time to compute $gH_{G(V,E)}$ value whereas it is less than the time to compute

$pgH_{G(V,E)}$ value (Figure 4 (b) and (c)); We can also infer that the time to compute $pgH_{G(V,E)}$ value with 128/256-bit key is more than the time to compute $gH_{G(V,E)}$ value, as this process now involves generating a random key with 128/256-bit length. The results depict that the overall time to compute $g\mathcal{H}$ is between 70-100 seconds for web-Google data set with approximately six million nodes and edges combined signifying that our scheme is highly efficient. In fact we can make this more-efficient by by-passing $O(n \log n)$ the sorting phase by placing the nodes in sorted-order during the DFS traversal once a node is finally visited. Figure 5 shows the end-to-end computation time for calculating the hash of graph for synthetic data.

Time taken to compute `ghRedact`: This operation is performed either by the data owner itself or by a third party data distributor on behalf of the user. From Figure 6 (a), (b), (c), (d), and (e) we can see that for all the graphs the `ghRedact` computation time decreases as we increase the number of nodes requested from the original graph. This is understandable that as we increase the size of the number of nodes requested the redacted graph size decreases and hence the computation required to generate the $\mathcal{VO}$ set.

Time taken to compute `ghVrfy`: This function takes as input three parameters the original graph hash value $gH_{G(V,E)}$, the requested subgraph and the $\mathcal{VO}$ set. Figure 7 (a), (b), (c), (d) and (e) shows the graph verification time vs the number of subgraph nodes returned. This function also incorporates computing the H_x and H_{xy} values for each node x and for each edge-node xy. We can see that as we increase the subgraph size the time to compute `ghVrfy` also increases; this is owing to the fact that this function has to compute the hash values for node and edge-nodes in the returned subgraph. Moreover, the time taken is more for the case of perfect graph hashing scheme when compared to the scheme $g\mathcal{H}$.

9. CONCLUSION AND FUTURE WORK

Graphs are widely used to specify and represent data. Verifications of integrity and whether two graphs are identical or not are often required by applications that involve graphs such as graph databases. Collision resistant one-way hashing schemes are the basic building blocks of almost all crypto-systems. In this paper, we studied the problem of hashing graphs with respect to crypto-systems and proposed two constructions for two notions of collision-resistant hash functions for graphs. We defined the formal security models of hashing schemes for graphs, and perfectly collision-resistant hashing schemes for graphs. We proposed the first constructions for general graphs that includes not only trees and graphs but also graphs with cycles and forests. Our constructions use graph traversal techniques and are highly efficient for hashing, redaction, and verification of graphs. Moreover, our proposed schemes require only a single traversal on the graph. To the best of our knowledge this is the first perfectly collision-resistant hashing schemes for graphs that are practical and are highly efficient for hashing, redaction, and verification of hashes graphs.

As a future work, we plan to take updates into consideration, parts of graph maybe updated and other parts may not be updated; the challenge is how to recompute hash of the updated graph with $O(1)$ cost, which is currently logarithmic to linear (Merkle hash technique for trees requires $O(n)$ – linear cost).

10. ACKNOWLEDGMENTS

This work is partially supported by NSF Grants IIS-0964639 and TUES-1123108.

11. REFERENCES

[1] A. Boldyreva, N. Chenette, Y. Lee, and A. OŠneill. Order-preserving symmetric encryption. In *Advances in Cryptology-EUROCRYPT 2009*, pages 224–241. Springer, 2009.

[2] R. Canetti. Towards realizing random oracles: Hash functions that hide all partial information. In *CRYPTO*, pages 455–469, 1997.

[3] R. Canetti, D. Micciancio, and O. Reingold. Perfectly one-way probabilistic hash functions (preliminary version). In *STOC*, pages 131–140, 1998.

[4] T. H. Cormen, C. E. Leiserson, R. L. Rivest, and C. Stein. *Introduction to Algorithms*. MIT Press, 2001.

[5] S. K. Das, K. B. Min, and R. H. Halverson. Efficient parallel algorithms for tree-related problems using the parentheses matching strategy. In *IPPS*, pages 362–367, Washington, DC, USA, 1994.

[6] H. V. Jagadish and F. Olken. Database management for life sciences research. *SIGMOD Rec.*, 33(2):15–20, June 2004.

[7] V. Kamakoti and C. P. Rangan. An optimal algorithm for reconstructing a binary tree. *Inf. Process. Lett.*, 42(2):113–115, 1992.

[8] J. Katz and Y. Lindell. *Introduction to Modern Cryptography: Principles and Protocols*. Chapman & Hall/CRC, 2007.

[9] D. E. Knuth. *The Art of Computer Programming*, volume 1. Pearson Education Asia, third edition, 2002.

[10] A. Kundu, M. J. Atallah, and E. Bertino. Leakage-free redactable signatures. In *Proceedings of the Second ACM Conference on Data and Application Security and Privacy*, CODASPY '12, pages 307–316, New York, NY, USA, 2012. ACM.

[11] A. Kundu and E. Bertino. Structural signatures for tree data structures. *PVLDB*, 1(1):138–150, 2008.

[12] A. Kundu and E. Bertino. On hashing graphs. *IACR Cryptology ePrint Archive*, 2012:352, 2012.

[13] A. Kundu and E. Bertino. Privacy-preserving authentication of trees and graphs. *International Journal of Information Security*, pages 1–28, 2013.

[14] C. Martel, G. Nuckolls, P. Devanbu, M. Gertz, A. Kwong, and S. G. Stubblebine. A general model for authenticated data structures. *Algorithmica*, 39:21–41.

[15] R. C. Merkle. A certified digital signature. In *CRYPTO*, 1989.

[16] R. A. Popa, F. H. Li, and N. Zeldovich. An ideal-security protocol for order-preserving encoding. *IACR Cryptology ePrint Archive*, 2013:129, 2013.

[17] M. L. Yiu, E. Lo, and D. Yung. Authentication of moving knn queries. In *Proceedings of the 2011 IEEE 27th International Conference on Data Engineering*, ICDE '11, pages 565–576, Washington, DC, USA, 2011. IEEE Computer Society.

[18] Y. Zhou, H. Cheng, and J. X. Yu. Graph clustering based on structural/attribute similarities. *Proc. VLDB Endow.*, 2(1):718–729, Aug. 2009.

Inference Attack against Encrypted Range Queries on Outsourced Databases

Mohammad Saiful Islam
Computer Science
Department
University of Texas at Dallas
saiful@utdallas.edu

Mehmet Kuzu
Computer Science
Department
University of Texas at Dallas
mehmet.kuzu@utdallas.edu

Murat Kantarcioglu
Computer Science
Department
University of Texas at Dallas
muratk@utdallas.edu

ABSTRACT

To mitigate security concerns of outsourced databases, quite a few protocols have been proposed that outsource data in encrypted format and allow encrypted query execution on the server side. Among the more practical protocols, the "bucketization" approach facilitates query execution at the cost of reduced efficiency by allowing some false positives in the query results. *Precise Query Protocols* (PQPs), on the other hand, enable the server to execute queries without incurring any false positives. Even though these protocols do not reveal the underlying data, they reveal query access pattern to an adversary. In this paper, we introduce a general attack on PQPs based on access pattern disclosure in the context of secure range queries. Our empirical analysis on several real world datasets shows that the proposed attack is able to disclose significant amount of sensitive data with high accuracy provided that the attacker has reasonable amount of background knowledge. We further demonstrate that a slight variation of such an attack can also be used on imprecise protocols (e.g., *bucketization*) to disclose significant amount of sensitive information.

Categories and Subject Descriptors

K.6.5 [**Management of Computing and Information Systems**]: Security and Protection—*Unauthorized access*; H.2.0 [**Database Management**]: General—*Security, integrity, and protection*

Keywords

Encrypted Range Query; Inference Attack; Database-as-a-service

1. INTRODUCTION

Database-as-a-service (DAS) model has been considered as an emerging technology over the last few years. New web services such as *Google Bigquery* [1] are introduced to provide SQL-like capabilities to analyze massive datasets on the cloud. Outsourcing databases to the remote servers paves the way of sharing expertise of database professionals among different organizations at a lower cost. But, executing queries effectively on an encrypted database has been a very challenging issue in the database community. Hacigümüş et al. [15] were the first to propose a notion of encrypted database which supports a limited execution of SQL queries in the remote server without requiring to decrypt the data elements. Since then, a lot of research (e.g., [4–6, 12, 16, 23]) has been conducted in this context to enhance the basic solution proposed in [10, 15]. Most of these protocols, however, focuses only on range queries (e.g., [4–7, 16, 23]).

The basic DAS paradigm proposed in the literature consists of three entities: the users, the clients and the server. Each row in the outsourced database is encrypted individually and called as *etuple*. The remote server in DAS model is assumed to be 'honest but curious'. That is, the server does not deviate from the protocol, however she wants to learn as much knowledge about the encrypted data as possible. A *user* in this model submits queries to the *client*. The *server* is the remote machine that hosts the database physically in encrypted form and handles queries received from various *clients*. Client transforms a user-query to an appropriate encrypted server-query and sends it to the server. The server executes this query on the encrypted database and sends back the appropriate etuples to the client. Upon receiving the set of etuples, the client decrypts them and returns it to the user.

There are two mainstream approaches to implement the DAS model that supports range queries. The *Precise Query Protocols* (PQPs) (e.g., [4–7, 23, 29]) use sophisticated encryption techniques that enables the server to execute range queries without incurring any false positives. That is, for any given encrypted range query, the server returns the exact set of etuples that satisfies the given query. The second approach, known as the *bucketization* approach (e.g., [15, 16]), facilitates range query execution at the cost of reduced efficiency in terms of the number of false positives. In fact, in bucketization approach, each query attribute is divided into some contiguous buckets based on a bucketization strategy. During the execution of queries, all the etuples in a bucket is included in the resultset if this bucket overlaps with the range specified in the query. Needless to mention, this may introduce a reasonable amount of false positives in the resultset depending on the bucket width. The client, in this case, does some post processing to get rid of the false positives before presenting the result to the user.

Although cryptography researchers are taking significant strides in designing efficient Oblivious RAM (e.g., [25, 27]) solutions that allow all the basic operations to be applied directly on outsourced data without revealing any information to the server, the performance overhead of such systems is still significant. In fact, it has been shown in [18] that it is extremely difficult for a remote database server to provide cryptography-style security, and yet be efficient enough to be practical. Therefore, all the practical DAS protocols intentionally allow some information to be leaked to the remote server in exchange of greater efficiency. In essence, all the precise protocols disclose Query Access Pattern (QAP) to an adversary. Informally, we say that a DAS model leaks QAP if for a given query Q, the adversary can see the list of etuples $\langle e_1, \cdots, e_k \rangle$, but does not learn the content of these *encrypted tuples*.

To illustrate how QAP leakage can be exploited to launch an attack, consider two encrypted range queries of the form $[s_1, f_1]$ and $[s_2, f_2]$. Furthermore, let E_1 and E_2 be the respective set of etuples returned as a response to these queries. An attacker can extract valuable information about $[s_1, f_1]$ and $[s_2, f_2]$ by analyzing E_1 and E_2. For example, if $E_1 \subset E_2$, then an adversary can tentatively assume the range $[s_1, f_1]$ is completely contained within the range $[s_2, f_2]$. That is, the condition $(s_1 \geq s_2) \wedge (f_1 \leq f_2)$ holds. In fact, we show that if an attacker has a reasonable estimate of the data distribution of the query attribute (e.g., from publicly available databases), these inferences can lead to very accurate estimates of the range queries, and thereby violates the security of the underlying DAS model.

Since imprecise protocols (i.e., the bucketization approach) do not reveal true access pattern due to the presence of false positives, they are much more resistant to the access pattern based inference attacks. However, bucketization approach reveals the bucket identifiers to an attacker. In fact, we show how a slight variation of our attack can be used to successfully reveal the bucket boundaries in §4.

In recent years, complete database solutions (e.g., Monomi [26], CryptDB [22]) have been proposed in the literature that can run almost any queries on encrypted data. These solutions use the existing practical DAS models outlined earlier and incur a very reasonable amount of added overhead. In fact, the reported median overhead of Monomi is only 1.24 for the TPC-H benchmark [26]. Therefore, it is very likely that there would be commercially available encrypted databases for general use in the near future. The main objective of this paper is to raise awareness to the users before using a database system that leaks QAP. We argue that the DAS models and their vulnerabilities (e.g., QAP leakage) should be thoroughly studied before they can be used in a secure encrypted database system. However, we do not claim that our work presents a worst case exploitation of QAP disclosure. In fact, there is a possibility that future studies may suggest that more information can be inferred exploiting QAP using lesser amount of prior knowledge. In that regard, we consider this work as a stepping stone towards a series of future works in this area of research. The main contributions of this paper are summarized as follows.

1. We present an attack model which exploits access pattern disclosure to reveal range boundaries of encrypted range queries on DAS model.

2. We also propose a variation of such an attack to disclose the bucket boundaries in the bucketization approach.

3. Finally, we empirically demonstrate the efficacy of our model using publicly available real datasets.

The rest of the paper is organized as follows. We present the motivation behind this work in §2. We outline our basic attack model in §3. In §4, we show how a slight variation of our basic model can still be applied to attack imprecise protocols such as "bucketization". We propose a new prediction metric in §5. A thorough empirical evaluation of our attack model is presented in §6. We present a brief survey of the contemporary literature related to this work in §7. Finally, we conclude this paper with §8.

2. MOTIVATION

Access pattern disclosure alone does not pose any significant threat to the overall data security of a DAS model. However, when combined with reasonable amount of background knowledge, access pattern disclosure may cause substantial privacy breach. We like to highlight this claim further by considering the following hypothetical scenario.

Let us assume that a bank is outsourcing its database to a remote server for reduced database management cost. Now, let us consider the account holder table in the outsourced database. Since the names of the account holders may not be considered as sensitive information, we may assume that the remote server (e.g., *Mallory*) has obtained the list of account holder's names through some covert channel. For example, *Mallory* can monitor the recipients of postal mails sent from the bank to find out the customers of this bank. Quite naturally, the bank wants to keep more sensitive account information (e.g., account balance etc.) safe. Therefore, all the tuples in the account table is kept encrypted in the remote database. However, since *Mallory* has the plaintext distribution of names, she can monitor queries and responses to estimate a mapping from the individual names to their corresponding etuples by applying **a similar attack such as ours** with reasonable accuracy. Since the tuples are encrypted, *Mallory* still does not learn any useful information form the etuples yet.

However, suppose the bank is investigating a case of money laundering and keeps a list of suspects incorporated in the account table. Naturally, the information whether an account holder belongs to this list is considered to be highly sensitive and disclosure of such information may very well lead to lawsuits. Now, further assume that an investigating authority is making a query to the remote database to pull the list of suspects. However, if *Mallory* observes the set of etuples accessed by the investigating authority, she can ascertain this sensitive list with reasonable accuracy by using her estimate of the *name-to-etuple* mapping.

Quite clearly, neither the list of the account holder's names nor the encrypted tuples are detrimental to the overall data security. However, it is the association between these two sets of information that can lead to a significant privacy breach. For example, the information that 'John has an account in this bank' does not seem sensitive. Again, an adversary (e.g., the remote database server) may see all the etuples in the encrypted table and still learns no useful information. However, as soon as the adversary has a way to link the name 'John' with a particular etuple, she can use

Table 1: Notations

Notation	Meaning
$|x|$	The cardinality of the set x.
R	The relation on which queries are executed.
A	An attribute on *Relation R*.
$\mathcal{D}$	A positive, discrete, ordered domain of A.
$\mathcal{D}_{low}$	The lowest value of the domain $\mathcal{D}$.
$\mathcal{D}_{high}$	The highest value of the domain $\mathcal{D}$.
n	The number of distinct elements in $\mathcal{D}$. That is, $n = |\mathcal{D}|$.
m	The number of queries in the query set.
$[s, f]$	A query with left end s and right end f. That is, $[s, f] = \{x | (x \geq s) \wedge (x \leq f)\}$.
β, γ	*Real* valued constants.
B_{size}	Individual batch size.

this to gain sensitive information. For example, she can easily find out whether the person named 'John' is a suspect of the money laundering scheme or not. Therefore, attack such as ours may cause significant privacy breach by establishing a mapping from attribute values to their corresponding etuples.

In this paper, we show that if a DAS model reveals access pattern, an adversary can use plaintext data distribution to ascertain the encrypted queries. This ultimately reveals the association of the range query attribute with their corresponding etuples. Quite naturally, using such DAS models naively may cause significant security breach. Therefore, we strongly argue that these protocols should only be used in controlled settings where an adversary is guaranteed not to possess any background knowledge on the plaintext data distribution.

3. THE PROPOSED MODEL

In this section, we describe an attack model that exploits query access pattern to identify sensitive data. For the sake of simplicity, we focus our attention to one dimensional range queries. *Range Queries* are perhaps one of the most important queries and most of the existing techniques supports range queries on one dimension anyway. Since any *equality* query can be equivalently replaced by a range query, all the discussions in this paper is implicitly applicable to *equality queries* as well. Let us assume R is a relation with a sensitive attribute A. We assume A has a finite ordered discrete domain (e.g., the set of all the non-negative integers less than t, where $t \in \mathcal{N}$). We denote the domain of A by $\mathcal{D}$ such that $|\mathcal{D}| = n$. That is, the domain $\mathcal{D}$ has n discrete elements[1]. A comprehensive list of notations used in this paper has been presented by *Tab.* 1. We define most of these notations as needed, but we encourage the readers to use *Tab.* 1 as a reference throughout the paper.

3.1 Threat Model

In our attack model, we assume an attacker (e.g., *Mallory*) has access to a sequence of m range queries of the form $\mathcal{Q} = \langle [s_1, f_1], [s_2, f_2], \cdots [s_m, f_m] \rangle$ and their corresponding result sets $\langle E_1, E_2, \cdots E_m \rangle$. Ideally, we assume an 'honest but curious' server as our adversary. Furthermore, we assume that

---

[1] This assumption does not limit the applicability of our approach. An adversary can still apply our attack model to a continuous domain by discretizing the domain.

Mallory has access to the following background knowledge on data distribution to facilitate an attack.

1. The attacker knows the plaintext distribution (exact or approximate) of the column A in the original database. That is, for any domain value x, the attacker knows how many tuples in the table contains x as the attribute value of A. Let, $S_{i,j}$ denotes the set of elements in A that falls into the range $[i, j]$. Therefore, we can assume that the adversary knows how to calculate $S_{i,j}$ values for any value of i and j.

2. Finally, the attacker knows the true ranges of k queries in $\mathcal{Q}$, where k can be 0. Let $\langle \langle a_1, b_1 \rangle \cdots \langle a_m, b_m \rangle \rangle$ be the sequence of true values for the observed sequence of range queries. That is, $\forall i, (s_i = a_i) \wedge (f_i = b_i)$ holds. Then, for some sequence of k values s.t. $k < m$, $\langle c_1 \cdots c_k \rangle$, the adversary knows the right assignments for each of the c_i queries. That is, for all $i \in [1, k]$, the adversary knows the sequence $\langle \langle a_{c_1}, b_{c_1} \rangle \cdots \langle a_{c_k}, b_{c_k} \rangle \rangle$.

The first assumption has been adopted in some notable previous works in this area (e.g., [8, 10]). Also, many different data distributions can be obtained from publicly available databases. For example, there is a publicly available database, namely the *North Carolina Voter Database* [21] that presents many key personnel information about the voters in the state of *North Carolina*. Again, in a bank account database, the list of account holder's names can be fully known beforehand [10]. The *ZIP* codes of the account holders, on the other hand, can be approximated from population data [10]. In fact, we empirically show that an attacker can obtain a very reasonable amount of sensitive information by attacking range queries on *NC Voter Dataset* using the age statistics of NC census data [2] in §6.2.4. Therefore, we argue that the first assumption is reasonable in this context. Finally, we see it appropriate to add the second assumption for the following reasons. First of all, we believe that revelation of a few queries should not compromise the secrecy of other queries in a secure system (e.g., [14]). Secondly, this assumption may be true for scenarios where an inside attacker has restricted permission to execute a very few queries, and therefore can use his limited privilege to compromise many other queries. Finally, the required number of known queries is extremely small. In fact, our empirical analysis indicates that a very few known queries, e.g., 2, is sufficient for a large query set of over hundred queries.

3.2 The Attack Model

We formalize the attack model to a *Constrained Optimization* problem. The adversary has a sequence of range queries $\mathcal{Q}$ of the form $\langle [s_1, f_1], [s_2, f_2], \cdots [s_m, f_m] \rangle$ and their corresponding result set $\langle E_1, E_2, \cdots E_m \rangle$. The goal of the adversary is to estimate the values of $s_1, \cdots, s_m, f_1, \cdots, f_m$ from the domain $\mathcal{D}$ as accurately as possible with the help of her prior knowledge. We model this problem as a *constrained optimization* problem in the following way.

$$\underset{\langle [s_1,f_1], \cdots [s_m,f_m] \rangle}{\operatorname{argmin}} \sum_{[s_i,f_i],[s_j,f_j]} \left(\left| S_{s_i,f_i} \cap S_{s_j,f_j} \right| - |E_i \cap E_j| \right)^2 \tag{1}$$

Subject To : T

Here, T is the set of constraints. It should be noted that this optimization problem trivially incorporates individual cardinalities of the etuple sets when $i = j$. We describe the constraint generation process in great detail in the following section.

3.3 Generating Constraints.

The first set of trivial constraints that the optimization problem has to respect is that the known queries has to be assigned to their known values. Therefore, we have k such trivial constraints. But, the set of *etuples* reveal many other constraints in the following way.

Let us assume that $[s_1, f_1]$ and $[s_2, f_2]$ be any two range queries. Also, let E_1 and E_2 be the set of corresponding etuples for these queries. Regardless of the underlying data distribution, one of the following four scenarios should hold for these two queries.

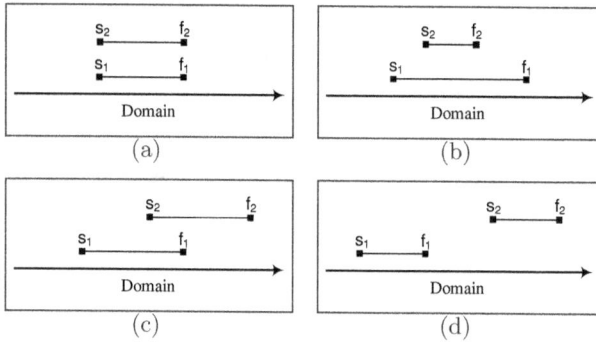

Figure 1: **Possible relationships between two** *range* *queries.* **(a) Two queries are equal. (b) One of the queries is a proper subset of the other. (c) Queries are overlapping. (d) Queries are mutually exclusive.**

1. These two queries represent the same range.

2. One of the ranges is completely subsumed by the other.

3. The ranges are overlapping.

4. The ranges are non-overlapping, i.e., they are disjoint.

These four different scenarios are pictorially depicted in Fig. 1. It should be noted that in Fig. 1(b), it has been arbitrarily assumed that the first range contains the second one. But, the other possibility can also occur where the second range contains the first one. Similarly, alternate considerations also exist for cases (c) & (d).

Interestingly enough, an attacker can tentatively ascertain which one of the above mentioned four scenarios holds for a given pair of queries by using their corresponding set of etuples E_1 and E_2. For example, *if $E_1 = E_2$, then* the given queries are assumed to represent the same range and hence falls into the first scenario. This fact can be further expressed into a succinct logical expression of the form: $(s_1 = s_2) \wedge (f_1 = f_2)$. An attacker can use this expression as a constraint to the optimization problem presented in (1) to limit the search space of feasible solutions. Similarly, if $E_2 \subset E_1$, then case (b) holds and the expression $(s_2 \geq s_1) \wedge (f_1 \geq f_2)$ can be used as a constraint.

Therefore, if *Mallory* observes a sequence of m queries and their respective set of *etuples* $\langle E_1, E_2, \cdots E_m \rangle$, she can

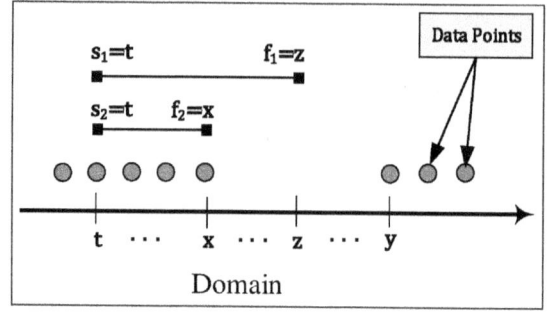

Figure 2: **Imperfect constraints due to absence of data points.**

take any two set of *etuples* E_i and E_j, and generate a new constraint involving the corresponding start and end variables, namely, s_i, f_i, s_j and f_j. Thus, an adversary can generate $\binom{m}{2} = \frac{1}{2}m(m-1)$ different non-trivial constraints from m different range queries. Additionally, any given query $[s_i, f_i]$ trivially satisfies the constraint $s_i \leq f_i$. So, given the query response of m queries, an adversary can generate $m + \frac{1}{2}m(m-1) + k$ constraints to the optimization problem presented in (1).

However, caution must be exercised in generating constraints when some of the domain values of the attribute A are devoid of any data points. To further illustrate this point, let us consider the scenario depicted in Fig. 2. Here, no tuple in the relation R contains an element from the range (x, y) as a value of the attribute A. Furthermore, let z be a point such that $z \in (x, y)$ holds. It is quite apparent from the figure that the etuple sets for the queries $[s_1, f_1]$ and $[s_2, f_2]$ contain the same set of etuples. Therefore, an attacker may erroneously conclude that these two queries fall to the first category and thus generate the constraint $(s_1 = s_2) \wedge (f_1 = f_2)$. But, even a cursory examination of the figure tells us that these queries belong to the second category and thus the afore-mentioned constraint is wrong. The main reason behind this error is that there is no data point between x and z. Even the existence of a single data point between x and z would make E_2 a proper subset of E_1. In that case, the attacker could successfully identify that these queries fall into the second scenario and generate the correct constraint: $(s_2 \geq s_1) \wedge (f_1 \geq f_2)$.

Definition 1. For a given domain $\mathcal{D}$ of an attribute A and an instance distribution D, τ is defined to be the maximum number of consecutive domain values for which there is no data point in D.

Example 1. (τ) Let us consider a domain $\mathcal{D} = [1, 10]$ and a given distribution $\{1, 1, 3, 7, 8, 10\}$. Here, the maximum number of consecutive domain values where there is no data points is 3 (no data points in $4, 5$ and 6). Therefore, the value of τ for this distribution is 3.

It should be noted that an attacker can efficiently calculate τ from a given data distribution with an $O(n)$ algorithm. An attacker can use τ to model the amount of error in the constraints. In essence, an attacker just relaxes the constraints by τ to compensate the errors generated by the lack of data points in some domain values. *Lemma $1 - 4$* outline how much relaxation is necessary under different scenarios.

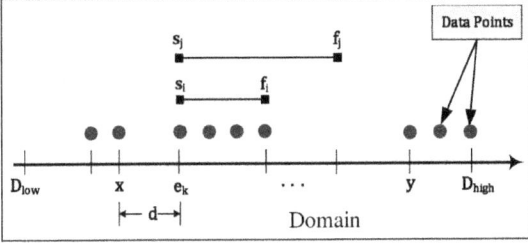

Figure 3: Generating constraints when $E_i = E_j$.

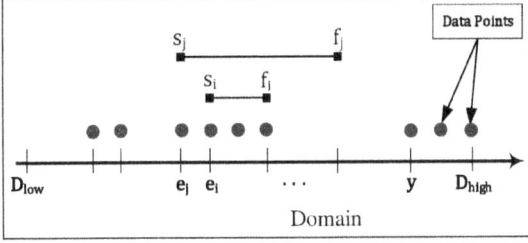

Figure 4: Illustrating case $e_j < e_i$ when generating constraints for $E_i \subset E_j$.

Throughout the proofs of Lemma $1-4$, we assume an ordered discrete attribute A on which the range queries are performed. We further assume $\mathcal{D} = [\mathcal{D}_{low}, \mathcal{D}_{high}]$ be the domain of A and D be an instance data distribution. Furthermore, throughout the proofs, we adopt some notational abuses for the sake of simplicity. That is, we informally use encrypted tuples as arguments of comparison operators (e.g., $=, <, >, \geq, \leq$) and arithmetic operators (e.g., $+, -$) to mean that the actual operation is to be performed on the attribute value of A of the argument etuples. For example, we simply write $e_1 = e_2$ to mean that both these etuples has the same attribute value of A. It should be noted that this slight abuse simplifies the notations in the proofs significantly.

LEMMA 1. *If $[s_i, f_i]$ and $[s_j, f_j]$ be a given pair of queries and E_i and E_j be their corresponding set of etuples s.t. $E_i = E_j$, then the following constraint holds.*

$$(|s_i - s_j| \leq \tau) \wedge (|f_i - f_j| \leq \tau)$$

PROOF. Let us assume, without loss of generality, $e_k \in E_i, E_j$ be the lowest data point in E_i and E_j. If D is the data distribution of attribute A, let us assume $x \in D$ be the maximum data point s.t. $x < e_k$ if such x exists, $x = \mathcal{D}_{low}$ otherwise. This scenario is depicted in Fig. 3. Since e_k is the lowest data point in E_i and E_j, x can not be a member of either E_i and E_j, i.e., $x \notin E_i, E_j$. Since both E_i, E_j contains e_k, but not x, it is obvious that the condition $x \leq s_i, s_j \leq e_k$ holds.

Therefore, if $d = e_k - x$ is the distance between x and e_k, then the inequality $|s_i - s_j| \leq d$ holds. But, by the definition of τ, we have $d \leq \tau$. Therefore, the inequality $|s_i - s_j| \leq d \leq \tau$ holds. That is, $|s_i - s_j| \leq \tau$ holds. By a similar way, we can show that the inequality $|f_i - f_j| \leq \tau$ holds. This concludes the proof. $\square$

LEMMA 2. *If $[s_i, f_i]$ and $[s_j, f_j]$ be a given pair of queries and E_i and E_j be their corresponding set of etuples s.t. E_i*

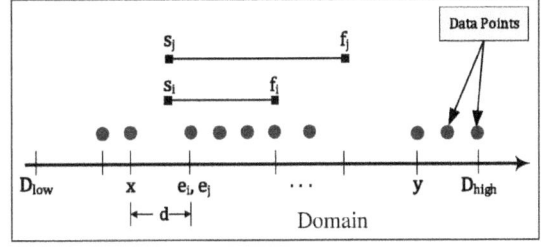

Figure 5: Case $e_j = e_i$ when generating constraints for $E_i \subset E_j$.

is a proper subset of E_j, i.e., $(E_i \subset E_j)$, then the following constraint holds.

$$(s_j \leq (s_i + \tau)) \wedge (f_i \leq (f_j + \tau)).$$

PROOF. Expressions $(s_j \leq (s_i + \tau))$ and $(f_i \leq (f_k + \tau))$ are connected by conjunction in this constraint. Therefore, it is sufficient to show that both these expressions hold independently of each other. At first, let us prove that the expression $(s_j \leq (s_i + \tau))$ holds.

Let $e_i \in E_i$ and $e_j \in E_j$ be the lowest elements in E_i and E_j respectively. Since $E_i \subset E_j$, e_i can not be strictly less than e_j. Therefore, one of the following two conditions must hold.

(a) $e_j < e_i$. This scenario is depicted in Fig. 4. In this case, since $e_i \in E_i$ and $e_j \notin E_i$, the inequality $e_j < s_i \leq e_i$ holds. Again, since $e_j \in E_j$, we have $s_j \leq e_j$. Combining these two inequalities, we can say that the inequality $s_j \leq e_j < s_i$ holds.

Again, since $\tau \geq 0$ and $s_j < s_i$, s_j is less than $s_i + \tau$. Therefore, the inequality $s_j \leq s_i + \tau$ holds.

(b) $e_j = e_i$. This scenario is depicted in Fig. 5. Since $e_i = e_j$, we can interchangeably use e_i and e_j to denote the lowest point of E_i and E_j without loss of generality. Let us assume $x < e_i, e_j$ be the highest data point in D such that $x \notin E_i, E_j$. According to the definition of x, there exists no data point y such that $x < y < e_i$. If such an y exists, then y becomes the maximum data point such that $y < e_i$ and $y \notin E_i, E_j$, contradicting the definition of x. Let d be the distance between x and e_i. That is, $d = e_i - x$. Since x and e_i are two consecutive data points in D, the inequality $d \leq \tau$ must hold according to the definition of τ.

On the other hand, since $x < e_i$ and x does not belong to E_i, E_j, the inequality $x < s_i, s_j \leq e_i, e_j$ holds. Since both s_i and s_j are located between the points x and e_i, the difference between s_i and s_j can not possibly be greater than the distance between x and e_j. Therefore, the constraint $|(s_j - s_i)| \leq d$ holds. That is, s_i can not be less than s_j by more than d. Therefore, the inequality $s_j \leq (s_i + d)$ holds.

Since $d \leq \tau$ and $s_j \leq (s_i + d)$ holds, we can conclude that the inequality $s_j \leq (s_i + \tau)$ holds.

In the same way, we can show that $f_i \leq (f_j + \tau)$. This concludes the proof. $\square$

LEMMA 3. *If $[s_i, f_i]$ and $[s_j, f_j]$ be a given pair of queries and E_i and F_j be their corresponding set of etuples s.t. $(((E_i \cap E_j) \neq \phi) \wedge ((E_i - E_j) \neq \phi) \wedge ((E_j - E_i) \neq \phi))$, then the following constraint holds.*

$$(((s_i < s_j) \wedge (f_i < f_j)) \vee ((s_j < s_i) \wedge (f_j < f_i)))$$

PROOF. Let us assume $[s_i, f_i]$ and $[s_j, f_j]$ be a given pair of queries and E_i and E_j be their corresponding set of *etuples*

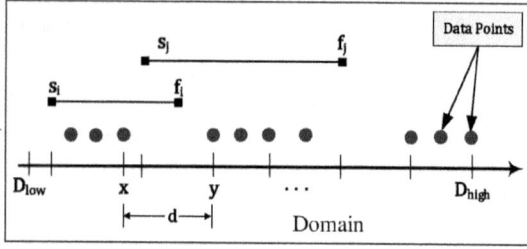

Figure 6: Generating constraints when $E_i \cap E_j = \phi$

s.t. $(((E_i \cap E_j) \neq \phi) \wedge ((E_i - E_j) \neq \phi) \wedge ((E_j - E_i) \neq \phi))$. It should be noted that for this given pair of queries, the equality $s_i = s_j$ can not hold. Because, if $s_i = s_j$ holds, then either E_i is a subset of E_j if $f_i \leq f_j$, or E_j is a subset of E_i if $f_j \leq f_i$. Therefore, either one of the following two conditions must hold.

(a) $s_i < s_j$. According to a similar argument presented in the preceding paragraph, the equality $f_i = f_j$ can not hold under the premises of this lemma. Again, since $s_i < s_j$, f_i can not possibly be greater than f_j. This is because, $((s_i < s_j) \wedge (f_i > f_j)) \Rightarrow (E_j \subset E_i)$ holds. But, this contradicts the premise $(E_j - E_i) \neq \phi$. Therefore, $(f_i < f_j)$ holds. Therefore, in this case, $(s_i < s_j) \wedge (f_i < f_j)$ holds.

(b) $s_j < s_i$. If we interchange the indices i and j and follow a similar argument as presented in the previous paragraph, we can conclude that the constraint $(s_j < s_i) \wedge (f_j < f_i)$ holds.

Since one of the two conditions depicted above always holds, we can conclude that the constraint holds. This concludes the proof. □

LEMMA 4. *If $[s_i, f_i]$ and $[s_j, f_j]$ be a given pair of queries and E_i and E_j be their corresponding set of etuples s.t. $(E_i \cap E_j) = \phi$, then the following constraint holds.*

$$(f_i \leq (s_j + \tau)) \vee (f_j \leq (s_i + \tau)).$$

PROOF. Let us assume $[s_i, f_i]$ and $[s_j, f_j]$ be a given of queries and E_i and E_j be their corresponding set of etuples s.t. $(E_i \cap E_j) = \phi$. Now, at least one of the following conditions must hold.

(a) $s_i \leq s_j$. This scenario is depicted in Fig. 6. It should be noted that although the condition $(E_i \cap E_j) = \phi$ holds in Fig. 6, interestingly enough, the ranges $[s_i, f_i]$ and $[s_j, f_j]$ are overlapping with each other. Now, let $y \in E_j$ be the lowest data point. Quite naturally, the condition $s_j \leq y \leq f_j$ holds. Again, let $x \in D$ be the maximum data point such that $y < s_j$. Since $y < s_j$ holds, y can not be a member of E_j.

On the other hand, according to the definition of x and y, there can be no more data point $z \in D$ s.t. $x \leq z \leq y$ holds. That means, x and y are two consecutive data points in D. Therefore, if d be the distance between x and y, the inequality $d \leq \tau$ would always hold according to the definition of τ. Now, there can be one of the two possibilities.

1. $x \leq f_i$. Since $E_i \cap E_j = \phi$, the inequality $y \notin E_i$ holds. Therefore, both s_j and f_i fall belongs to the range $[x, y]$. Therefore, the value of $f_i - s_j$ can not be larger than the distance between x and y. That is, $(f_i - s_j) \leq d$ holds. Since $d \leq \tau$ holds, the inequality $f_i - s_j \leq \tau$ also holds. Therefore, we can conclude that $f_i \leq s_j + \tau$ holds.

2. $x > f_i$. In this case, since $x < s_j$ holds, the inequality $f_i < s_j$ trivially holds. Therefore, the inequality $f_i \leq s_j + \tau$ also holds.

Therefore, we can conclude that if $s_i \leq s_j$ holds, the inequality $f_i \leq s_j + \tau$ would also hold.

(b) $s_j \leq s_i$. By interchanging the indices i and j and following the similar arguments as presented above, we can conclude that if $s_j \leq s_j$ holds, the inequality $f_j \leq s_i + \tau$ would also hold.

Since at least one of the conditions always holds, the constraint $(f_i \leq (s_j + \tau)) \vee (f_j \leq (s_i + \tau))$ holds. □

Using *Lemma* $1 - 4$, the set of constraints T can be generated using Alg. 1.

Algorithm 1 Building Constraint Set: T

$T \leftarrow \emptyset$
for all $i \in [1, m]$ **do**
　$T \leftarrow T \cup \{s_i \leq f_i\}$
end for
for all $i \in [1, k]$ **do**
　$T \leftarrow T \cup \{(s_{c_i} = a_{c_i}), (f_{c_i} = b_{c_i})\}$
end for
for all $\langle [s_i, f_i], [s_j, f_j] \rangle$ **do**
　if $(E_i = E_j)$ **then**
　　$T \leftarrow T \cup \{(|s_1 - s_2| \leq \tau) \wedge (|f_1 - f_2| \leq \tau)\}$
　end if
　if $(E_i \subset E_j)$ **then**
　　$T \leftarrow T \cup \{(s_j \leq (s_i + \tau)) \wedge (f_i \leq (f_j + \tau))\}$
　end if
　if $(E_j \subset E_i)$ **then**
　　$T \leftarrow T \cup \{(s_i \leq (s_j + \tau)) \wedge (f_j \leq (f_i + \tau))\}$
　end if
　if $((E_i \cap E_j) = \emptyset)$ **then**
　　$T \leftarrow T \cup \{(f_i \leq (s_j + \tau)) \vee (f_j \leq (s_i + \tau))\}$
　end if
　if $(((E_i \cap E_j) \neq \emptyset) \wedge ((E_i - E_j) \neq \emptyset) \wedge ((E_j - E_i) \neq \emptyset))$
　then
　　$T \leftarrow T \cup$
　　　$\{((s_i < s_j) \wedge (f_i < f_j)) \vee ((s_j < s_i) \wedge (f_j < f_i))\}$
　end if
end for
return T

---

4. ATTACK AGAINST BUCKETIZATION

In this section, we carry out an inference attack against the "bucketization" approach. Intuitively speaking, the bucketization approach is more resistant to access pattern based attacks. Partitioning data values into buckets can be viewed as a way of adding noise to the query access patterns. Therefore, attack techniques like the one described in §3.2 are ill-suited to attack the bucketization approach.

Interestingly, if we slightly modify our attack goal, we may still be able to discover some useful information from the bucketization approach. First of all, we notice that from an adversary's point of view, each data point inside a bucket is indistinguishable from the other points in the same bucket. Secondly, the $bucket - ids$ in the queries are sent in plaintext to the server in the bucketization method. Therefore, an adversary can easily identify the set of etuples that belongs to a set of buckets that appear in a query. Therefore, instead of predicting range query values, we look to identify bucket boundaries in the bucketization approach. In essence, an attacker generates assignments of domain values to bucket

240

boundaries such that the number of data points returned in response to a list of bucket identifiers matches with the number of elements in the buckets according to the assignment for each query in the observed query set.

In bucketization, each range query is converted into a list of buckets and the bucket identifiers are sent to the server in plaintext. Therefore, the attacker sees a set of bucket identifiers and the set of etuples returned for this bucket set. Let $\beta_1, \beta_2, \cdots, \beta_p$ be the set of buckets. Let l_{β_i} and h_{β_i} be the low and high boundaries of bucket β_i assigned by the attacker where $\forall_i,\ l_{\beta_i}, h_{\beta_i} \in [\mathcal{D}_{low}, \mathcal{D}_{high}]$. Let $\mathcal{Q} = \{q_i\}$ be the set of observed queries and E_i be the corresponding set of etuples for each query q_i. Let $B_i = \{\beta_t\}$ be the set of bucket identifiers for each query q_i. Since, B_i is sent to the server in plaintext, an adversary (e.g., the untrusted server) can see B_i. In our model, an adversary tries to assign values to l_{β_i} and h_{β_i} for all i s.t. the observed set of response matches the actual data distribution D. More specifically, the adversary tries to optimize the following expression.

$$\operatorname*{argmin}_{\langle [l_{\beta_1}, h_{\beta_1}], \cdots [l_{\beta_p}, h_{\beta_p}] \rangle} \sum_{i=1}^{|\mathcal{Q}|} \left(\left| \bigcup_{\beta \in B_i} [l_\beta, h_\beta] \right| - |E_i| \right)^2 \quad (2)$$

It should be noted that an attacker does not need to know the values of any query beforehand for this attack. Again, the solution to the problem above is an approximation of the bucket boundaries. Therefore, it does not guarantee the revelation of the range queries exactly. However, if the buckets are small enough, an attacker can still get a very good approximation of the actual query values.

5. QUERY EVALUATION METRIC

In this section, we propose a new metric to evaluate range query prediction. Of course, we can use an exact right/wrong approach as our evaluation metric. Under this approach, for a given range query $[s, f]$, we evaluate a prediction $[s', f']$ as right if and only if the predicted query is exactly similar to the original query (i.e., $s = s' \land f = f'$). Unfortunately, such a simple approach does not do justice to the predictions which are almost accurate but not exactly right. Therefore, we need another metric to evaluate query predictions more accurately.

As a first step towards designing a rigorous evaluation metric, we intuitively identify the following factors which affect the quality of a given prediction.

1. *Absolute Error.* We define *absolute error* to be the difference between a given query and its prediction. That is, given a query $[s, f]$ and its predicted value $[s', f']$, we define *absolute error* $= |s - s'| + |f - f'|$. Quite naturally, a lower value of the absolute error should indicate a better prediction under a reasonable evaluation metric.

2. *Domain Interval.* The second key factor is the *domain interval*, i.e., $(\mathcal{D}_{high} - \mathcal{D}_{low})$. A given query prediction seems more accurate under a larger domain than a smaller domain if *absolute error* is kept constant.

3. *Query Interval.* We define *query interval* to be the value $(f - s)$. Intuitively, higher values of *query interval* indicates more accurate prediction when all the other

factors are kept constant. For example, let $[20, 20]$ and $[30, 80]$ be any two given queries in the domain $[0, 100]$. Let $[19, 21]$ and $[29, 81]$ be the predictions for these two queries. Intuitively the second prediction ($[29, 81]$) appears to be more accurate than the first one ($[19, 21]$) even though the other factors are same for both these queries. Therefore, a good evaluation metric should take into account the *query interval*.

Definition 2. For a given domain $\mathcal{D} = [\mathcal{D}_{low}, \mathcal{D}_{high}]$, if a given query $Q = [s, f]$ is predicted as $Q' = [s', f']$, we define the prediction error $Err_{Q,Q'}$ in the following way.

$$Err_{Q,Q'} = \frac{|s - s'| + |f - f'|}{\beta \times (\mathcal{D}_{high} - \mathcal{D}_{low}) + \gamma \times (f - s)}$$

Here, β and γ are two real valued constants such that $0 < \beta \le 1$ and $0 \le \gamma \le 1$. we purposefully do not allow β to be equal to *zero* in order to prevent the denominator in *Definition 2* from going to *zero*. Since we implicitly assume a non-empty domain (i.e., $|\mathcal{D}| > 0$), the denominator will always be greater than *zero* as long as $\beta > 0$.

It should be noted that β and γ are placed to restrict the influence of *Domain Interval* and *Query Interval* over the prediction error. For example, without these constants in place, a very large *Domain Interval* can utterly dominate a batch of queries with smaller intervals in the error measure. But, putting control parameters such as β and γ can prevent this domination under the current error definition.

Definition 3. A prediction Q' of a given query Q is *Correct* under the ϵ-*tolerant metric if and only if* the following condition holds.

$$Err_{Q,Q'} \le \epsilon$$

Interestingly, according to Def. 3, a prediction $[s', f']$ of a given query $[s, f]$ is *correct* under the *0-tolerant metric if and only if* the condition $(s = s') \land (f = f')$ holds. Using different values of ϵ, we get a family of error measures which can be used to evaluate an attack mechanism such as ours.

6. EXPERIMENTS & RESULTS

6.1 Experimental Setup

We use two publicly available real datasets in our experiments. First of these datasets is the *Adult Dataset* [3] from the *UCI Machine Learning Repository*. We choose the *North Carolina Voter Dataset* [21] as our second real dataset. The Adult Dataset is a well used personnel dataset with 48842 data instances. The North Carolina Voter Dataset, on the other hand, is a publicly available dataset of real personal identifiers that contains 6190504 instances. Furthermore, we use age demographic statistics [2] of North Carolina to attack range queries on *North Carolina Voter Dataset* to demonstrate the efficacy of our attack model under a more real life settings.

In all these datasets, we choose *age* as our query attribute. Even though all these domains are around $[0, 100]$, our attack approach is equally applicable to attributes with larger domain such as *salary*. A larger domain (e.g., $[0, 100000]$) can easily be discretized into a smaller domain like that of *age*. For example, an attribute *salary* with Domain $\mathcal{D} = [0, 100000]$ can be converted to a shorter domain by dividing each domain value by 1000 and rounding up to the closest integer value. This way, an adversary can attack the converted domain to get a reasonable estimate of the range queries on the larger domain. Of course, this method inherently contains an error margin (in this case, ±500), but for a larger domain size, this error margin seems quite reasonable. Therefore, we argue that **our attack approach is equally applicable to attributes with larger domain size**.

6.1.1 Query Generation.

In our experiments, we use two different query generation methods. For most of the experiments reported in this paper, we generate queries uniformly from the attribute domain. For a discrete domain of size n, there can be $\frac{1}{2}n(n+1)$ number of distinct queries. To generate a uniform query set, we uniformly choose two distinct values s and t from the domain and add a *range query* of the form $[min(s,t), max(s,t)]$ in our query set.

In §6.2.5, we investigate how a non-uniform query load affects the prediction accuracy of our proposed model. Furthermore, we devote §6.2.5 to explain how we generate non-uniform query sets. It should be noted that the query generation process is implicitly assumed to be uniform in all our experiments unless otherwise stated.

6.1.2 Simulated Annealing.

The attack model described in §3 is a hard one to solve. In fact, a simpler version of this problem has been shown to be $NP - Complete$ in [17]. The brute-force approach seems extremely inefficient in solving this optimization problem. Therefore, we alternatively seek to solve an approximation of the given problem using *Simulated Annealing* [19]. We justify our choice by empirically showing that *Simulated Annealing* is able to produce a reasonable solution very efficiently.

6.1.3 Batch Mode Execution.

As we have already mentioned in §3.3, a query set of size m has a constraint set size of $m + \frac{1}{2}m(m-1) + k$. *Simulated Annealing* generates a valid candidate solution at each round that respects each of these constraints. Therefore, generating a valid candidate solution may prove to be extremely inefficient for large values of m. On the other hand, a naive execution approach requires $10 - 20\%$ of the total queries to be known beforehand (*known query set*) to obtain a reasonable query prediction accuracy. Again, knowing this many queries beforehand may turn out to be quite impractical.

To circumvent both these problems, we solve the optimization problem in batches instead of a single execution. If we have a query set of size m with k known queries, we divide the $(m-k)$ unknown queries into l equi-size batches. Finally, we add the k known queries to each of these individual batches. We denote the size of each individual batch by B_{size}. Finally, we run each of these individual batches independently and agglomerate their results after their executions to get the prediction for the overall query load. Since both k and $Batch_{size}$ are user defined parameters and are intended to respect the inequality $k < B_{size} << m$, this batch mode execution paves the way to run unlimited number of queries with a very small constant number of known queries very efficiently. Furthermore, the individual batches can be run in parallel to improve the overall execution efficiency. It should be noted that the number of individual batches l is defined by (3).

$$l = \left\lceil \frac{(m-k)}{(B_{size} - k)} \right\rceil \qquad (3)$$

Finally, to summarize the above discussion on batch execution, we list the following two important advantages that batch mode operation has to offer.

(a) As the size of each batch is kept to a smaller value, *Simulated Annealing* can run extremely fast for each individual batch.

(b) Since we are reusing the known queries, a very few number of known queries can be used to successfully predict a large set of unknown queries.

To further underscore the fact that batch mode execution reduces the number of known queries required, we like to mention that most of the experiments reported in this paper use **only 2 known queries for an overall query set size of 100. In fact, our model could ascertain a query set of size** 150 **with more than** 70% **accuracy using only 2 known queries** (please see Fig. 7). Therefore, it is quite apparent that because of batch mode execution, an extremely few number of known queries (e.g., 2) are required to ascertain even a very large set of queries.

6.1.4 Known Query Generation.

As mentioned earlier, our model requires a few queries to be known beforehand. These known queries work as pivot elements in assigning correct values to other queries. Therefore, the choice of known query set can largely affect the accuracy of our model. Unfortunately, we did not find any publicly available real query sets to use in our experiments. However, we argue that an adversary might not have any control to the set of known queries. That is, it is most likely that an adversary does not get to choose the set of known queries himself. With this argument in mind, we generate the known query set uniformly from the query set in all our experiments.

6.1.5 Execution Time.

We do not use any parallel processing in any of the experiments noted in this paper. All the experiments mentioned in this paper were run in a AMD Phenom II $X6$ $1045T$ Windows 7 machine clocked at 2.70 GHz with 8 GB of system memory. Each of the individual executions took no more than 1 hour to finish. Therefore, we argue that even a reasonable serial implementation of our attack model is quite efficient. However, the *Batch Mode Execution* leaves us adequate room to improve the efficiency even further by running the batches in parallel.

6.1.6 Evaluation Metric

In this paper, we evaluate our proposed attack model using three such evaluation metrics, namely 0-tolerant metric, 0.1-tolerant metric and finally, 0.2-tolerant metric as defined in §5. Furthermore, Since we use age as the query attribute, the domain interval does not dominate the query interval in our experiments. Therefore, we use a value of 1 for both β and γ in all our experiments. However, we strongly advise a bigger value of γ and a relatively smaller value of β for large domains.

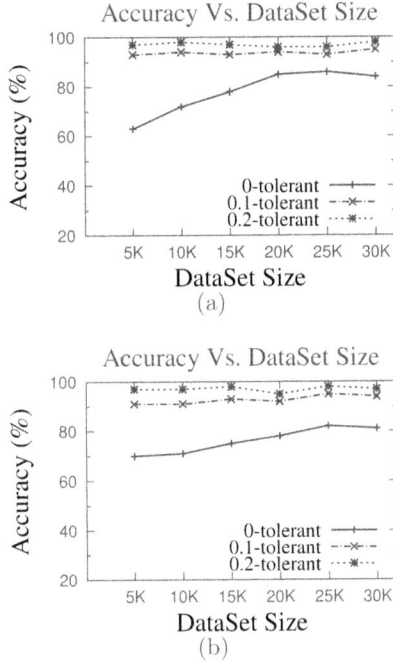

Figure 7: Accuracy for various dataset size. a) Adult dataset. b) North Carolina Voter dataset.

6.2 Experimental Results

In this section, we present a thorough empirical evaluation of our attack approach. Default parameters for all these experiments are as follows. Query set size: 100, known query set size: 2. Our empirical evaluation suggests that the batch size value of 5 is an ideal choice considering the overall accuracy and efficiency (see §6.2.3). These default values mentioned above are implicitly assumed to be used in all the experiments unless otherwise mentioned.

6.2.1 Accuracy on Different Datasets

In this section, we describe the accuracy of our attack model on different datasets. For these experiments, we choose datasets of different size uniformly from the *Adult Dataset* and *North Carolina Dataset*. We present the prediction accuracy of our model for various dataset size in Fig. 7. As is evident from Fig. 7, initially the prediction accuracy rises as the dataset size is increased. However, the accuracy does not rise significantly when the dataset size reaches to 10000 mark. Beyond that, any subsequent increase to the dataset size hardly improves the prediction accuracy. It is quite apparent from the figure that our model is able to predict around 80% of the queries correctly even under the *0-tolerant metric* with a reasonable dataset size. The performance is around high 90 percentile when we consider *0.1 − tolerant* and *0.2 − tolerant* metrics. Since most of the real-world database consists of thousands of tuples, our proposed model is likely to succeed with very high probability.

6.2.2 Changing Known Query Set Size

In these set of experiments, we choose known query set of different size and investigate its effect on query prediction accuracy. As Fig. 8 (a) & (b) suggests, prediction accuracy quickly rises as we increase the known query set size from

Table 2: Discrepancies in Age Distribution between NC Voter Dataset and NC Census Data

Age Range	NC Voter Data (thousands)	NC Census Data (thousands)
20-24	570	661
25-29	626	627
30-34	637	619
35-39	620	660
40-44	684	667
45-49	669	699
50-54	678	670
55-59	631	601
60-64	567	538
65-69	478	403
70-74	345	295
74-79	264	224
80-85	214	165

0 to 2. After that point, the model has enough information it needs and the accuracy does not improve significantly. This is why, we use 2 as our default known query set size parameter. Again, it should be noted that since our query load consists of 100 queries, we only need 2% of them to be known beforehand. Furthermore, if we increase the query set size, we need even a less percent of queries to be known beforehand.

6.2.3 Effect of Batch Size

In this section, we report the effect of various batch size on the adult dataset and the North Carolina voter dataset. We run our attack on both these datasets with batch size varying from 5 to 10. It can be readily seen from Fig. 8 (c) & (d) that changing batch size only affects the accuracy very insignificantly. However, as the batch size increases, the execution time of the attack also increases. For this reason, we have chosen 5 as the default batch size for all the other experiments in this paper to favor better execution time.

6.2.4 Imperfect Background Information

All the experiments reported so far have been conducted under the assumption that the attacker has access to an exact plaintext distribution. In this section, we relax such an assumption by restricting an attacker's possession of perfect background information. In this section, we present two experiments where an attacker possesses two different kinds of imperfect background information. In the first experiment, we assume that an attacker is attacking range queries on North Carolina voter dataset. However, we assume that the attacker is completely unaware of the plaintext data distribution of this dataset. Rather, he uses the North Carolina demographic age statistics [2] to formulate his attack. In the second experiment, we assume that the attacker has a noisy version of the plaintext distribution at his disposal.

Using a different age distribution. In this experiment, we present a very practical attack using real world datasets to showcase the efficacy of our attack model. Here, we assume that an attacker is attacking range queries performed on the *age* attribute of the North Carolina voter dataset [21]. Again, we assume that he is completely unaware of the age distribution of this voter dataset. However, we show that an attacker can still launch a reasonably successful attack

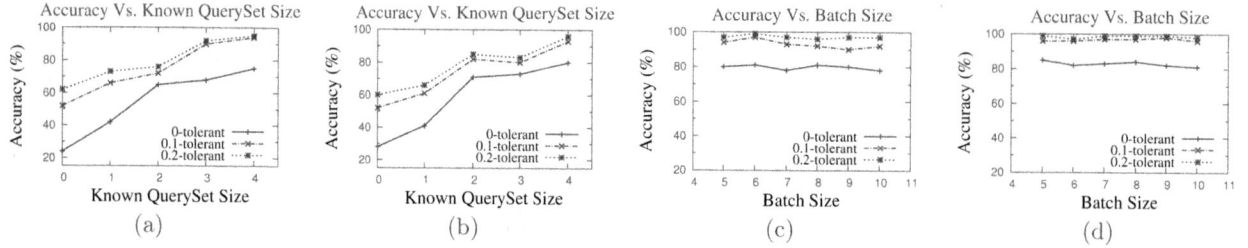

Figure 8: a) Effect of known query size on NC Voter dataset. b) Effect of known query size on adult dataset. c) Effect of batch size on NC voter dataset. d) Effect of batch size on adult dataset.

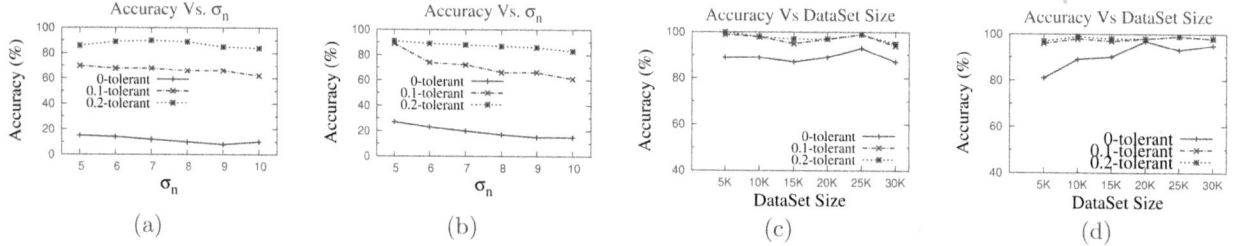

Figure 9: a) Noisy background knowledge on NC voter dataset. b) Noisy background knowledge on adult dataset. c) Zipfian query distribution on NC voter data. d) Zipfian query distribution on adult data.

Table 3: Accuracy for Imperfect Background Information

Query Set	0-Tolerant (%)	.1-Tolerant (%)	.2-Tolerant (%)
1	33	81	93
2	30	77	89
3	34	78	91

by using the age distribution of the people of North Carolina from the U.S. Census Bureau [2]. Before we present the empirical results, we like to point out that although both these datasets are focused on the inhabitants of North Carolina, there is a significant amount of discrepancy between the age statistics presented in these two datasets which is presented in *Table 2*.

However, our empirical results show that an attacker can still launch a successful attack regardless of this discrepancy. We present the accuracy of such attacks on three different uniform query loads of size 100 in Table 3. It should be noted that the entire NC voter dataset has been used for this attack. Because of the discrepancies between the datasets, the $0 - tolerant$ accuracy of the attack model lies around 30%. However, considering the fact that an attacker uses a completely different dataset to approximate the real age distribution, the attack seems reasonably effective. Again, high accuracy values for $0.1 - tolerant$ and $0.2 - tolerant$ measure further indicates that a very high percentage of queries are reasonably approximated by the attack.

Using noisy background information. In this experiment, we assume that the attacker has a noisy version of the plaintext distribution of the query attribute. More specifically, we change the actual $|S_{i,j}|$ values by adding a noise term $\mathcal{N}(0, \sigma_n^2)$. More specifically, for a given value of $|S_{i,j}|$, we generate a noisy version $|S'_{i,j}|$ in the following way:

$$|S'_{i,j}| = |S_{i,j}| \left(1 + \frac{\mathcal{N}(0, \sigma_n^2)}{100}\right)$$

Here, σ_n is the *Standard Deviation* that determines the amount of noise. Fig. 9 (a) & (b) shows the prediction accuracy under noisy background information for three different datasets. Although the accuracy suffers under the *0-tolerant metric*, our model still does quite well under the *0.1-metric* and *0.2-metric*. Therefore, we argue that our approach is capable of inferring a reasonable amount of sensitive information for a noisy version of the background information.

6.2.5 Non-Uniform Query Load

All the experiments discussed so far assume an uniform query generation process. But, this assumption of uniform query load may not hold for all practical applications. Therefore, the question arise, how a non-uniform query load affects the prediction accuracy of our proposed model? In this section, we answer this question by generating different query loads using *Zipfian Distribution* and conducting several experiments using such query loads on different datasets.

To use the *Zipfian Distribution*, we choose a total ordering among all the possible queries uniformly. That is, we uniformly assign a rank to each of the $\frac{n(n+1)}{2}$ possible queries. Finally, we use *Zipfian Distribution* to choose queries in our query load. That is, if a particular query has a rank j in the ordering, we choose this query in our query set with probability $P_j = \frac{\frac{1}{j}}{N}$, where $N = \sum_{i=1}^{t} \frac{1}{i}$ is the *Normalization Factor* and $t = \frac{n(n+1)}{2}$ is the total number of all possible queries.

Fig. 9 depicts the prediction accuracy of our model for *Zipfian Query Distribution* on the real datasets, namely the *Adult* dataset and the *North Carolina Voter* dataset. The prediction accuracy of *non-uniform query load* on these two datasets is very high even under the rigorous $0 - tolerant$

metric. Therefore, Fig. 9 (c) & (d) indicates that our approach is capable of exhibiting reasonable accuracy under any given queryload.

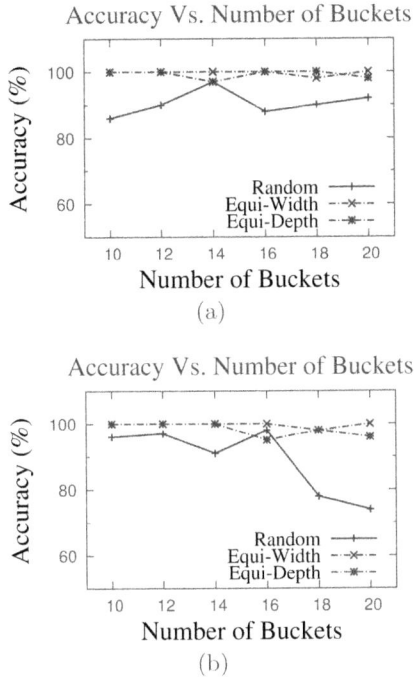

Accuracy Vs. Number of Buckets

(a)

Accuracy Vs. Number of Buckets

(b)

Figure 10: a) NC voter data. b) Adult Data.

6.3 Attack Against Bucketization

Figure 10 reports the accuracy of attacks against bucketization on different datasets for various bucket size. The metric used to evaluate these results is very similar to the one we defined for the range queries. However, we replace the *query interval* parameter with the *bucket interval* in this evaluation metric. Furthermore, the empirical results presented in this section have been evaluated under the $0 - tolerant$ metric only. In these experiments, we consider three bucketization approaches, namely the *random bucketization*, the *equi-width bucketization* and the *equi-depth bucketization* [20]. Our empirical results show that our approach can successfully ascertain the bucket boundaries for all these three bucketization methods with very high accuracy even under the $0 - tolerant$ metric. Although protocols like [15,16] favors equi-width or equi-depth bucketization, our empirical results show that an adversary has higher probability of success for these two approaches than that of the *Random* bucketization. Therefore, we conclude that *random* bucketization approach is more resistant to access pattern based inference attacks than the *equi-width* and *equi-depth* ones.

7. RELATED WORK

Search Over Encrypted Text. Goldreich et al. proposed their oblivious RAM model in [14]. Unfortunately, even the most efficient variant of the oblivious RAM model is impractical for real world applications. Vimercati et al. proposed a secure B+-tree based shuffle index technique in [12]. A similar technique has been also proposed in [28]. Song et al. were the first to propose an efficient encryption scheme

in [24] that allows keyword search over a remote encrypted document set. Following their footsteps, many new schemes were proposed with different levels of security guarantees (e.g., [9, 13]).

DAS Model. Hacigümüş et al. are the first to propose a notion of encrypted database in [15], which supports a limited execution of SQL queries in the remote server. Damiani et al. proposed a metric called *inference exposure* to quantitatively measure the extent of information an adversary can gain probabilistically about the sensitive data [8,10]. Again, Hore et al. proposed a privacy-preserving index for range query in [16]. Even though all these techniques shares the same basic structure, they significantly differ in the bucket construction.

There are quite a few schemes that use encryption techniques to support range query execution(e.g., [4–6,23]). The most notable among these techniques is the one proposed by E. Shi et al. in [23]. Their protocol can handle multi dimensional range queries. Again, there are several techniques in the literature [4–6] that use *Order Preserving Encryption* to facilitate range queries on *encrypted data*. None of these techniques allow any false positives, and therefore are quite efficient. In [22], Popa et al. presented CryptDB, a comprehensive DBMS that supports SQL query execution in encrypted database incurring a very modest overhead. The *order preserving encryption* presented in [5] has been used in this work to facilitate the range query execution. Also, Stephen Tu et al. [26] proposed a complete encrypted database for executing analytical workloads. Since both Monomi and CryptDB uses precise query protocols to facilitate range query, they are vulnerable to our attack.

Attacks on outsourced database. Islam et al. proposed a new attack model in [17] which leverages access pattern leakage to disclose significant amounts of sensitive information. Although the basic attack approach of [17] is similar to this attack, the context as well as the methodologies used are quite different. Again, the model described in [17] is only applicable to keyword search. Our work, on the other hand, is tailored towards the more general concept of range queries. Again, Dautrich et al. presented an attack on precise query protocols to ascertain the order of the query attribute values in [11]. However, their attack can not be applied to imprecise protocols such as bucketization. Furthermore, the objective of [11] is to obtain the ordering of etuples based on the query attribute. The objective of our approach is to ascertain the encrypted range queries. Again, their attack does not guarantee a solution for any given range query load and may require a very large number of queries to ascertain a complete ordering. Our approach, on the other hand, is able to disclose encrypted range queries with reasonable accuracy for query load with size as low as 5.

8. CONCLUSIONS

In this paper, we propose an attack model that leverages query access pattern to disclose significant amount of sensitive information about the encrypted range queries on outsourced databases. We empirically show the efficacy of our model by applying it to several real world datasets. Our empirical results suggest that the proposed model can predict encrypted range queries with high accuracy under a rigorous evaluation metric. Furthermore, we also show that a variation of this attack can be used on the bucketization approach to disclose the bucket boundaries with high accuracy.

Therefore, we argue that in cases where data security is the primary concern, it is better to use secure, albeit inefficient protocols like that of *Oblivious RAM*. However, in controlled settings where an adversary is guaranteed not to possess significant amount of prior knowledge about the plaintext data distribution, a user may prefer to use sophisticated and efficient protocols.

9. ACKNOWLEDGMENTS

This work was partially supported by Air Force Office of Scientific Research FA9550-12-1-0082,National Institutes of Health Grants 1R0-1LM009989 and 1R01HG006844, National Science Foundation (NSF) Grants Career-CNS-0845803, CNS-0964350, CNS-1016343, CNS-1111529, CNS-1228198 and Army Research Office Grant W911NF-12-1-0558.

10. REFERENCES

[1] Google BigQuery.
    http://code.google.com/apis/bigquery/.

[2] Profile of general population and housing characteristics: 2010 demographic profile data.
    http://factfinder2.census.gov/bkmk/table/1.0/en/DEC/10_DP/DPDP1/0400000US37.

[3] Adult Data Set. Uci machine learning repository.
    http://archive.ics.uci.edu/ml/datasets/Adult.

[4] R. Agrawal, J. Kiernan, R. Srikant, and Y. Xu. Order-preserving encryption for numeric data. In *SIGMOD 2004*, pages 563–574. ACM, 2004.

[5] A. Boldyreva, N. Chenette, Y. Lee, and A. O'Neill. Order-preserving symmetric encryption. In *EUROCRYPT 2009*, volume 5479, pages 224–241, 2009.

[6] A. Boldyreva, N. Chenette, and A. O'Neill. Order-preserving encryption revisited: Improved security analysis and alternative solutions. In *CRYPTO 2011*, volume 6841, pages 578–595. Springer, 2011.

[7] D. Boneh and B. Waters. Conjunctive, subset, and range queries on encrypted data. In *TCC 2007*, volume 4392, pages 535–554. Springer, 2007.

[8] Ceselli, Damiani, di Vimercati, Jajodia, Paraboschi, and Samarati. Modeling and assessing inference exposure in encrypted databases. *ACMTISS: ACM Transactions on Information and System Security*, 8, 2005.

[9] R. Curtmola, J. Garay, S. Kamara, and R. Ostrovsky. Searchable symmetric encryption: improved definitions and efficient constructions. In *CCS*, pages 79–88, 2006.

[10] E. Damiani, S. De Capitani di Vimercati, S. Jajodia, S. Paraboschi, and P. Samarati. Balancing confidentiality and efficiency in untrusted relational DBMSs. In *CCS 2003*, pages 93–102. ACM Press, 2003.

[11] J. L. Dautrich Jr and C. V. Ravishankar. Compromising privacy in precise query protocols. In *EDBT*, pages 155–166. ACM, 2013.

[12] S. D. C. di Vimercati, S. Foresti, S. Paraboschi, G. Pelosi, and P. Samarati. Efficient and private access to outsourced data. In *ICDCS*, pages 710–719. IEEE Computer Society, 2011.

[13] E. Goh. Secure indexes. *Cryptology ePrint Archive*, (Report 2003/216), 2003.

[14] O. Goldreich and R. Ostrovsky. Software protection and simulation on oblivious RAMs. *JACM: Journal of the ACM*, 43, 1996.

[15] H. Hacigümüş, B. Iyer, C. Li, and S. Mehrotra. Executing SQL over encrypted data in the database-service-provider model. In *SIGMOD*, pages 216–227, 2002.

[16] B. Hore, S. Mehrotra, and G. Tsudik. A privacy-preserving index for range queries. In *VLDB 2004*. Morgan Kaufmann Publishers, 2004.

[17] M. S. Islam, M. Kuzu, and M. Kantarcioglu. Access pattern disclosure on searchable encryption: Ramification, attack and mitigation. In *NDSS 2012*. ISOC, 2012.

[18] M. Kantarcioglu and C. Clifton. Security issues in querying encrypted data. In *DBSec*, 2005.

[19] S. Kirkpatrick, C. Gelatt, and M. Vecchi. Optimization by simulated annealing. *Science*, 220:671–679, 1983.

[20] E. Mykletun and G. Tsudik. Aggregation queries in the database-as-a-service model. In *20th Annual IFIP WG 11.3 Working Conference on Data and Applications Security*, pages 89–103. Springer, 2006.

[21] North Carolina Voter Data.
    ftp://www.app.sboe.state.nc.us/data.

[22] R. A. Popa, C. M. S. Redfield, N. Zeldovich, and H. Balakrishnan. CryptDB: protecting confidentiality with encrypted query processing. In *SOSP*, 2011.

[23] E. Shi, J. Bethencourt, H. T.-H. Chan, D. X. Song, and A. Perrig. Multi-dimensional range query over encrypted data. In *IEEE Symposium on Security and Privacy*, pages 350–364. IEEE Computer Society, 2007.

[24] D. Song, D. Wagner, and A. Perrig. Practical techniques for searches on encrypted data. In *IEEE Symposium on Security and Privacy*, 2000.

[25] E. Stefanov and E. Shi. Oblivistore: High performance oblivious cloud storage. In *Proc. of IEEE Symposium on Security and Privacy*, 2013.

[26] S. Tu, M. F. Kaashoek, S. Madden, and N. Zeldovich. Processing analytical queries over encrypted data. In *PVLDB*, pages 289–300, 2013.

[27] P. Williams, R. Sion, and B. Carbunar. Building castles out of mud: practical access pattern privacy and correctness on untrusted storage. In *CCS*, pages 139–148. ACM, 2008.

[28] K. Yang, J. Zhang, W. Zhang, and D. Qiao. A light-weight solution to preservation of access pattern privacy in un-trusted clouds. In *ESORICS*, volume 6879, pages 528–547. Springer, 2011.

[29] Z. Yang, S. Zhong, and R. N. Wright. Privacy-preserving queries on encrypted data. In *ESORICS 2006*, pages 479–495. Springer, 2006.

Shared Responsibility is Better than No Responsibility

Federated Encryption in the Cloud

Jarret Raim
Rackspace
San Antonio, Texas
dxu@cs.purdue.edu

ABSTRACT

The process of encrypting data for Cloud services is usually presented two ways. The data owner can encrypt it themselves or rely on the service provider to do so. On one hand, we have significant security, but high-complexity. On the other, we have ease of use, but limited protection. This false choice leads to data going unprotected as customers throw up their hands. There is a better way. In this keynote, we'll discuss a middle ground that improves upon the standard use cases using Barbican, an open-source key manager created by Rackspace for the OpenStack Cloud.

Categories and Subject Descriptors

D.4.6 [**Data**]: Data Encryption - *public key cryptosystems*

Keywords

barbican; openstack; open-source; federation; encryption; security; compliance.

Speaker Bio

CODASPY'14, March 3–5, 2014, San Antonio, Texas, USA.
ACM 978-1-4503-2278-2/14/03.
http://dx.doi.org/10.1145/2557547.2557591

Efficient Privacy-Aware Search over Encrypted Databases

Mehmet Kuzu
Department of Computer
Science
University of Texas at Dallas
Richardson, TX, USA
mehmet.kuzu@utdallas.edu

Mohammad Saiful Islam
Department of Computer
Science
University of Texas at Dallas
Richardson, TX, USA
saiful@utdallas.edu

Murat Kantarcioglu
Department of Computer
Science
University of Texas at Dallas
Richardson, TX, USA
muratk@utdallas.edu

ABSTRACT

In recent years, database as a service (DAS) model where data management is outsourced to cloud service providers has become more prevalent. Although DAS model offers lower cost and flexibility, it necessitates the transfer of potentially sensitive data to untrusted cloud servers. To ensure the confidentiality, encryption of sensitive data before its transfer to the cloud emerges as an important option. Encrypted storage provides protection but it complicates data processing including crucial selective record retrieval. To achieve selective retrieval over encrypted collection, considerable amount of searchable encryption schemes have been proposed in the literature with distinct privacy guarantees. Among the available approaches, oblivious RAM based ones offer optimal privacy. However, they are computationally intensive and do not scale well to very large databases. On the other hand, almost all efficient schemes leak some information, especially data access pattern to the remote servers. Unfortunately, recent evidence on access pattern leakage indicates that adversary's background knowledge could be used to infer the contents of the encrypted data and may potentially endanger individual privacy.

In this paper, we introduce a novel construction for practical and privacy-aware selective record retrieval over encrypted databases. Our approach leaks obfuscated access pattern to enable efficient retrieval while ensuring individual privacy. Applied obfuscation is based on differential privacy which provides rigorous individual privacy guarantees against adversaries with arbitrary background knowledge.

Categories and Subject Descriptors

H.2.7 [**Database Administration**]: Security, integrity and protection; H.3.3 [**Information Search and Retrieval**]: Information filtering

General Terms

Security, Experimentation, Performance

Keywords

Security, Searchable encryption, Differential privacy

1. INTRODUCTION

Modern computation environment faces rapid change in the data management and storage with the advances in cloud computing. Cloud based services such as database as a service (DAS) model removes the burden of large scale data management in a cost effective manner. Hence, huge amount of potentially sensitive data is increasingly outsourced to the cloud. At the same time, transfer of sensitive records to untrusted cloud servers leads to concerns about their privacy. To alleviate such concerns, encrypted remote storage emerges as an important risk mitigation option. Although encryption protects outsourced records, it complicates the computation on them including the important selective record retrieval. Still, this fundamental operation could be achieved with the utilization of searchable encryption schemes [2, 3, 14]. In fact, such schemes have enabled secure DAS models [13, 17].

Available searchable encryption schemes offer various privacy and efficiency guarantees. Among available approaches, oblivious RAM (ORAM) model [8] does not leak any information including access pattern to the cloud. However, it does not scale well for real world data sources due to the excessive computational costs. Even the improved versions of ORAM (e.g., [12, 15]) incur logarithmic overhead in the number of outsourced records for a single record request. On the other hand, more efficient protocols selectively leak information to the server while protecting record contents [2, 3, 7, 14, 17]. Although the leaked information slightly varies among protocols, almost all of them leak access pattern. That is, untrusted server learns which records are included in the result set of an issued query without observing their contents. Unfortunately, statistical information that is revealed by access pattern may be dangerous if adversary has some background knowledge. In fact, a recent attack [10] demonstrates that privacy of individuals can be compromised through statistical analysis on the access pattern.

The fundamental question that we try to answer in this paper is, "Do we need the optimal protection of ORAM during the record retrieval to ensure individual privacy or could we allow some information leakage for efficiency?". In this study, we address this question with a novel construction. Proposed approach leaks obfuscated access pattern to enable practical search while ensuring individual privacy. Applied obfuscation relies on the rigorous definition of differential privacy (DP) [5, 6]. Specifically, with very high probability, it prevents an adversary from learning a new information about a particular individual due to the inclusion of his/her record in the outsourced database. To our knowledge, this is the first study that relaxes ORAM style protection against access pattern disclosure for more practical constructions. Our DP based approach focuses on protecting individual privacy instead of hiding access pattern completely.

To satisfy DP, some fake records are injected into the outsourced database and limited number of records are kept in the local cache. Consider the common access leakage approach presented in Figure 1-A. Although the record and query contents are computationally indistinguishable from server perspective due to the applied secure encryption, server observes the real counts of the records that are in the result set of a particular query. On the other hand, proposed approach leaks only differentially private counts to the untrusted server as depicted in Figure 1-B. In this example, differentially private count for the query 'education = masters' is three. In fact, server observes retrieval of three encrypted records instead of two against the corresponding query trapdoor. Additional observation is due to the injected fake record for DP which is eliminated on the client side after its decryption.

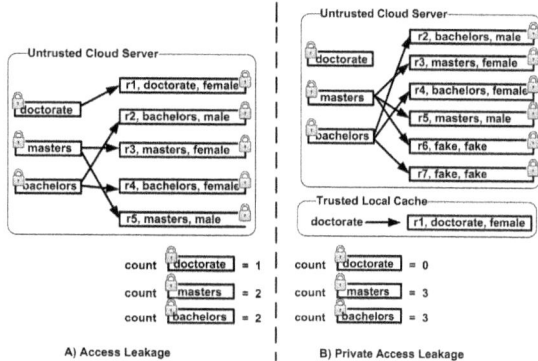

Figure 1: Server Memory Access Obfuscation

Contributions of this paper can be summarized as follows:

Differentially Private Access Pattern : The main information leakage of almost all efficient protocols that enable search over encrypted databases is data access pattern. In the context of this study, we propose obfuscated access pattern leakage which provides privacy guarantees of DP while enabling efficient retrieval over encrypted records.

Efficient Private Search Protocol : We propose an efficient search protocol over encrypted databases through private indexes. These indexes obfuscate physical memory accesses of the server to hide real accesses for the retrieval.

Capacity Oriented Mean Shift : Most solutions involving DP use a Laplace distribution with mean zero for noise addition to the real statistics. In the context of our protocol, noise with negative magnitude necessitates record placement into the local cache with limited capacity. To satisfy the capacity constraint, we propose mean shift on the positive axis of the distribution.

2. PROBLEM FORMULATION

Suppose Alice owns a set of sensitive records (e.g., electronic medical records) and she needs to provide access on them for the permitted users (e.g., medical researchers).

However, she has limited computational resources that is insufficient to manage large amount of data. Hence, she stores the records in their encrypted form on the cloud. In this setting, permitted users should be able to selectively retrieve records from the remote servers using the query interfaces provided by Alice. This capability is provided through private indexes that are built on the subsets of the available attributes.

We assume that cloud service provider is honest but curious. As such, he follows the record retrieval protocol as it is defined. However, he may try to infer private information about the records he hosts based on his background knowledge and any leaked information. In this setting, we assume that communication channels between the protocol participants are secure. The main privacy goal of our scheme is to ensure individual privacy instead of hiding any leakage completely. To achieve this goal, proposed construction employs differential privacy (DP). With high probability, DP guarantees that adversary (e.g., cloud provider) infers almost the same information about the outsourced records whether a specific record is included or not in the dataset [5].

3. BACKGROUND

Differential Privacy: Many privacy protection mechanisms are vulnerable to some type of background knowledge known to a hypothetical adversary [5]. As a result, undesirable disclosures for an individual can occur regardless of whether or not the corresponding individual is included in the attacked database. Thus, it has been recommended that, instead of tailoring privacy definitions against different types of background knowledge, a data owner should minimize the risk of disclosure that arises from participation in a database. This notion is captured by the differential privacy protection mechanism [5]. To protect privacy, DP adds random noise to each query result. The magnitude of the noise depends on a privacy parameter ϵ and sensitivity of the query set Q. Denoting the response to query Q over dataset D with Q^D, sensitivity [6] is defined as follows:

L_1-sensitivity : Over any neighbor datasets D_1, D_2 that differ by at most one row such that $|(D_1 - D_2) \cup (D_2 - D_1)| = 1$, the L_1-sensitivity of query set, $Q = \{Q_1, \ldots, Q_v\}$, is measured as:

$$S(Q) = \max_{\forall D_1, D_2} \sum_{i=1}^{v} |Q_i^{D_1} - Q_i^{D_2}|.$$

Theorem 3.1 provides a sufficient condition to satisfy ϵ-differential privacy [6].

THEOREM 3.1. *Let Q be a set of queries and $S(Q)$ be the L_1-sensitivity of Q. Then, ϵ-differential privacy can be achieved by adding random noise X to each query result, i.e., $Q_i^D \leftarrow Q_i^D + X$, where X is a random, i.i.d. variable drawn from a Laplace distribution with magnitude $\lambda \geq S(Q)/\epsilon$.*

4. PROPOSED SOLUTION

In this section, we present the proposed private searchable symmetric encryption scheme. We discuss its building blocks in Section 4.1. In Section 4.2, we present the privacy protection mechanism against access pattern leakage. Then, in Section 4.3, we present a replication strategy to reduce the computational overhead of the scheme. Finally, in Section 4.4, we describe the private index construction mechanism.

4.1 Private Search Scheme

Overview of the proposed scheme is depicted in Figure 2. Initially, data owner builds private indexes on the desired subsets of the attributes. Then, it outsources them to the cloud along with the encrypted records. In this setting, access statistics leaked by the indexes are obfuscated according to differential privacy (DP). To satisfy the requirements of DP, data owner keeps limited amount of records in its local cache and injects some fake records into the outsourced set. Prior to outsourcing, data owner forms multiple replicas of the encrypted records in such a way that distinct query types are served by distinct replicas. Query space splitting through replication reduces the number of intersecting query regions. This results in less L_1-sensitivity for DP which implies less amount of noise and overhead in the system.

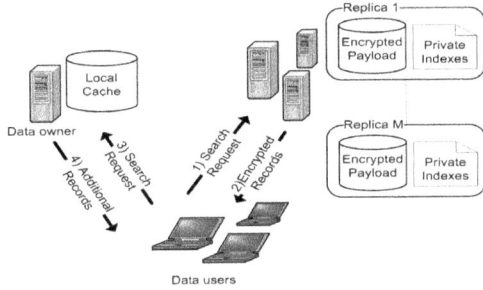

Figure 2: Search Scheme

After the construction of private indexes, permitted users could perform search through the provided query interfaces. The building blocks of the search scheme is as follows:

1. Key Generation : Initially, data owner generates secret keys $K_{R_1}, ..., K_{R_M}$ for the payload encryption of distinct replicas, K_{cell} and K_{loc} for the index encryption.

2. Index Construction : Data owner forms replicas $R_1, ..., R_M$ on the data source. Each replica has its own encrypted payload and associated private indexes. In this setting, each query interface $\Delta_i \in \Delta$ is served by a particular index of a particular replica where Δ_i corresponds to subset of available attributes (e.g., {gender, education}). The entries of a private index are in the form of $[\pi_{c_k}, \pi_{locs(c_k)}]$ where π_{c_k} and $\pi_{locs(c_k)}$ represent the encrypted versions of identifier c_k and the payload addresses of the records that contain c_k respectively.

After the transfer of the replicas into the cloud server along with the mapping between the query interfaces and private indexes, data owner shares the secret keys and available query interfaces with data users.

3. Trapdoor Construction : Suppose a user would like to issue a query using interface $\Delta_k \in \Delta$ where Δ_k consists of attributes $\{A_{k_1}, ..., A_{k_\ell}\}$ in the listed order. To form query q_x, she initially assigns values to attributes such that $\{A_{k_1} = v_i, ..., A_{k_\ell} = v_j\}$. Then she encrypts identifier $(v_i, ..., v_j)$. Specifically, she forms $F_{K_{cell}}(v_i, ..., v_j)$ and $F_{K_{loc}}(v_i, ..., v_j)$ where $F_{K_{cell}}$ and $F_{K_{loc}}$ are pseudo-random functions with keys K_{cell} and K_{loc}. Finally, trapdoor for q_x denoted as $T_{q_x} = \{F_{K_{cell}}(v_i, ..., v_j), F_{K_{loc}}(v_i, ..., v_j), \Delta_k\}$ is formed.

4. Search : Once server receives T_{q_x}, it locates replica R_i and index $PInd_{R_i}^j$ corresponding to query interface Δ_k. If $[F_{K_{cell}}(v_i, ..., v_j), \pi_{locs(q_k)}] \in PInd_{R_i}^j$, server identifies the payload addresses of the records that satisfy the issued query using $\pi_{locs(q_k)}$ and $F_{K_{loc}}(v_i, ..., v_j)$ (details of address identification is presented in Section 4.4.3). Then, encrypted records that are located in the corresponding payload addresses are sent to the user.

5. Data Decryption : Once the encrypted records corresponding to the search request are retrieved, user decrypts them to obtain their plain versions.

6. Local Cache Retrieval : Data owner keeps limited amount of records in her local cache due to the applied obfuscation mechanism. Hence, user may not receive all the records that she is interested in after communication with the server. To obtain any missing record, user sends her query to the data owner as well[1].

4.2 Differentially Private Access Pattern

Almost all efficient searchable encryption schemes [2, 3, 7, 11, 14, 17]) leak access pattern which is defined as follows:

Definition 4.2.1 Access Pattern (A_p) : Suppose $M(q_i)$ denotes memory addresses of the encrypted records that match with query q_i on dataset D. Then, access pattern for n consecutive queries is defined as $\{M(q_1), ..., M(q_n)\}$.

A_p leakage provides efficiency for retrieval. However, statistical information that is observable from it may be dangerous (e.g., frequency distribution of the retrieved records against distinct queries). Specifically, service provider may infer private information about the individual records even if they are stored in encrypted form. In fact, recent evidence on A_p leakage [10] indicates that an adversary can compromise individual privacy if he has some background knowledge. To ensure strong individual privacy guarantees against A_p leakage, we propose a protection mechanism that relies on differential privacy.

According to the proposed search scheme, data users issue queries of types $\Delta_1, ..., \Delta_k$ through provided query interfaces. To generate a query of type Δ_i, a particular value is assigned to all attributes in it from their respective domains. For instance, suppose $\Delta_i = \{gender, maritalstatus\}$. Then (gender = male, maritalstatus = married) is a query for Δ_i. In this setting, access statistics are collected from the physical memory access logs during the record retrieval. Hence, it is necessary to obfuscate these accesses.

Prior to the obfuscation, it is critical to consider the interactions between the interfaces in Δ. Such interactions may lead to implicit interfaces that are not explicitly provided by Δ. For instance, suppose $\Delta = \{\{age, gender\}, \{city\}\}$, $M(q_1) = \{m_1, m_2, m_4\}$ and $M(q_2) = \{m_2, m_5\}$ represent the accessed memory locations on the server when the trapdoors for queries (age = 20, gender = male) and (city = Boston) are issued respectively. Note that, memory locations to respond query (age = 20, gender = male, city = Boston) denoted as $M(q_3)$ can be obtained from $M(q_1)$ and $M(q_2)$ such that $M(q_3) = M(q_1) \cap M(q_2) = \{m_2\}$. Although the initial query interface set does not contain a member with attributes {age, gender, city}, the interaction leads to another observable interface. In this setting, accessed memory locations contain encrypted records which are computationally indistinguishable from the server perspective. However, server can collect statistical information about the accesses during the retrieval.

Access Pattern Statistics: Suppose Δ is the initial

---

[1]In the context of local cache retrieval, all operations can be done in plain text since communication channel is secure.

query interface set provided by the data owner, $subsets(\Delta)$ represents the subsets of Δ and $s_k = \{\Delta_i, ..., \Delta_j\}$ is a member of $subsets(\Delta)$. Then $A_{s_k} = \Delta_i \cup ... \cup \Delta_j$ is the attribute collection for s_k and final query interface set denoted as Δ^F consists of all distinct A_{s_k} for any $s_k \in subsets(\Delta)$ (e.g., $\Delta = \{\{age\}, \{gender, city\}\}$, $\Delta^F = \{\{age\}, \{gender, city\}, \{age, gender, city\}\}$). Note that, Δ^F contains all possible query interfaces that are observable from Δ including the implicit ones. In this setting, let q_i be any query of any type in Δ^F and D be the dataset. Then access pattern statistics correspond to issuing count queries of the following form:

select count(*) from D where q_i is true

Given a set of queries $Q = \{q_1, ..., q_n\}$, differential privacy adds Laplace noise with magnitude λ to the true response. λ is determined by privacy parameter ϵ and query set sensitivity $S(Q)$. Here, ϵ is assumed to be set by the data owner and sensitivity depends on the cardinality of Δ^F such that $S(Q) = |\Delta^F|$. To satisfy DP on the access statistics, they should be perturbed with random noise drawn from $Lap(\mu, \lambda = |\Delta^F|/\epsilon)$.

4.3 Data Replication

The goal of replication is to reduce the overhead of the protocol resulting from the obfuscation on the memory accesses through differential privacy (DP). To achieve this goal, it is critical to keep the number of final query interfaces (i.e., $|\Delta^F|$) small for less query-set sensitivity and less noise due to DP. It is clear that $|\Delta^F| \geq |\Delta|$ since $|\Delta^F|$ consists of all interfaces in $|\Delta|$ as well as the new interfaces resulting from the interactions among the initial interfaces. The minimum $|\Delta^F|$ can be obtained by eliminating all interactions and this is achievable through data replication. Specifically, suppose P_i is a random permutation, K_{R_i} is a secret key, $P_i(D)[j]$ is the jth record of the permuted data source D and $Enc_K(r_j)$ is the encryption of r_j with key K. Then i^{th} replication of D denoted as R_i is a collection with encrypted records $R_i[1], ..., R_i[|D|]$ such that $R_i[j] = Enc_{K_{R_i}}(P_i(D)[j])$ for $1 \leq j \leq |D|$.

Note that, interactions between the members of Δ can be eliminated by responding the queries of distinct query interfaces from distinct replicas. In such a case, accessed memory locations for queries of type Δ_i and Δ_j will be independent from the server perspective. This is because, same records in distinct replicas are encrypted with distinct keys and placed into distinct locations by the applied permutation.

Although replica generation for each member of Δ implies the equality of Δ and Δ^F, it brings additional storage cost. To minimize the overall cost resulting from the increase in sensitivity (i.e., $|\Delta^F| - |\Delta|$) and additional replica generation, some replicas should be shared by multiple members of Δ. For instance, suppose $\Delta = \{\{age, gender\}, \{age\}\}$. Then it is clear that union of the attributes among interfaces $\{age, gender\}$ and $\{age\}$ will not result in a new interface. In this scenario, distinct replica generation for both interfaces will not provide any gain in terms of sensitivity but leads to additional storage cost. Hence, both interfaces should share the same replica for lower cost.

More formally, suppose I_{R_i} represents the set of query interfaces that share replica R_i, $subsets(I_{R_i})$ represents subsets of I_{R_i} and $s_k = \{\Delta_i, ..., \Delta_j\}$ is a member of $subsets(I_{R_i})$. Then $A_{s_k} = \Delta_i \cup ... \cup \Delta_j$ is the attribute set for s_k and constitutes an observable query interface for replica R_i. Fi-

nal interfaces of R_i denoted as $\Delta_{R_i}^F$ consists of all distinct A_{s_k} for any $s_k \in subsets(I_{R_i})$. In this setting, obfuscation cost is defined as follows:

Definition 4.3.2 (Obfuscation Cost) : Let replica-Cost(z) and sensitivityCost(y) be the costs due to the generation of z replicas and query-set sensitivity of magnitude y respectively, $R = \{R_1, ..., R_M\}$ be the set of replicas such that each member of Δ is distributed among them and Δ^F be the final interfaces such that $\Delta^F = \bigcup_{i=1}^{M} \Delta_{R_i}^F$. Then, the obfuscation cost is defined as the sum of $replicaCost(M)$ and $sensitivityCost(|\Delta^F| + 1)$.

Here, 'replicaCost' is due to the storage of M replicas each with n_D records[2] where n_D represents the number of records in dataset D. 'sensitivityCost' is due to the both additional storage and bandwidth requirement for the fake records that will be injected into the outsourced set for access obfuscation. This is because, amount of such fake records depends on the sensitivity (details of fake record generation is presented in Section 4.4). In this context, suppose sI and bI represents the relative importance of the storage and bandwidth consumption, Q represents all distinct queries that are provided by the final query interfaces, $E(fR, y)$ is the amount of expected fake records that are in the result set of a single query under sensitivity y, $n_{\widetilde{D}}$ is the noisy count of the records in D and $qLoad$ is the expected number of queries that will be issued against the server. Then costs are formulated as follows:

$$replicaCost(z) = sI \cdot z \cdot n_{\widetilde{D}}$$

$$sensitivityCost(y) = (sI \cdot |Q| + bI \cdot qLoad) \cdot E(fR, y)$$

To reduce overall obfuscation cost by distributing initial query interfaces among distinct replicas is an instance of a clustering problem. In fact, our replication strategy is based on a common clustering technique, known as agglomerative hierarchical clustering [18]. Initially, a distinct cluster is formed for each query interface in Δ which implies the generation of $|\Delta|$ replicas without any implicit interfaces. After initial construction, clusters are successively combined until no improvement is achieved on the obfuscation cost. Finally, a replica R_i is formed for each final cluster C_i in such a way that query interfaces in C_i are served by replica R_i. Once final query interfaces and associated replicas are identified, private indexes are formed on them.

4.4 Private Index Construction

The goal of the private indexes is to provide privacy aware search capability over encrypted databases. They are constructed through the steps that are presented through Sections 4.4.1 to 4.4.3.

4.4.1 Mean Shift

Private indexes enforce obfuscation on the access pattern in addition to the content protection. To satisfy the necessary obfuscation according to differential privacy (DP), data

---

[2]To learn the number of records (n_D) while satisfying DP, an additional count query that asks for n_D can be added to the initial query set Q. It is clear that additional query is distinct from any query in Q and its result can change by at most one between neighbor datasets. Hence, sensitivity increases by 1 such that it becomes ($|\Delta^F| + 1$).

owner keeps some records in its local cache and adds some fake records to the outsourced database. The amount of fake record injection and local cache placement depends on the parameters of the Laplace mechanism. As explained in Section 3, DP is satisfied if the observable statistics are perturbed with noise drawn from a Laplace distribution with magnitude $\lambda = S(Q)/\epsilon$. It should be noted that Laplace noise can take on positive and negative values and is not necessarily integral. Integrality can be addressed by rounding-up to the closest integer value. In our context, positive noise is incorporated by adding fake records to the dataset, while negative noise requires placement of the original records in a local cache. For instance, in Figure 3, r_1 is placed to the local cache because random noise is equal to -1 for query (gender = Male). On the other hand, fake records f_1 and f_2 are placed to the cloud bucket which will be sent to the cloud server after its content is encrypted. This is because, noise is equal to 2 for query (gender = Female).

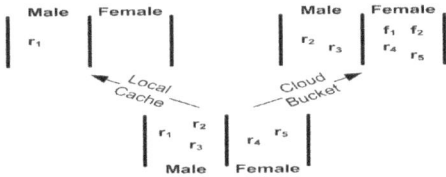

Figure 3: Index on Gender Attribute

In this setting, it is important to recognize that the effect of positive and negative noise is different. Consider, for each unit of positive noise, an additional fake record is sent to the cloud. On the other hand, negative noise requires the placement of a record to local cache with limited capacity. To satisfy the limited capacity constraint, it is necessary to decrease the amount of negative noise. Fortunately, this is achievable through the mean shift on the positive axis of the distribution as shown in Figure 4. Although Laplace mechanism does not have any restriction on the mean selection, it is critical to keep it closer to zero. This is because, zero mean offers less perturbation if we do not have any constraint and it is widely used as the default value in the literature. Hence, our goal is to keep mean closer to zero while satisfying the capacity constraint.

Figure 4: Mean Shift

More formally, let Q be the set of distinct queries that can be issued against the index, C be the capacity parameter which indicates the number of records that can be placed to cache, λ be the scale of the Laplace distribution and $E(N)$ be the expected amount of negative noise for a single query $q_i \in Q$. Here, $E(N)$ records are expected to be hosted by the cache for q_i. Accordingly, the mean shift that identifies mean closest to zero under the capacity constraint can be estimated according to the following equation:

$$|E(N)| \cdot |Q| \leq C \implies |\frac{1}{2\lambda} \int_{-\infty}^{0} x \cdot e^{-|x-\mu|/\lambda} \, dx| \cdot |Q| \leq C \quad (1)$$

THEOREM 4.1. *Estimated mean for Laplace distribution that is closest to zero under the constraint of Equation 1 is:*

$$\mu = max(-\lambda \cdot \ln(\frac{2C}{\lambda \cdot |Q|}), \ 0)$$

PROOF.

$$|E(N)| \cdot |Q| \leq C \implies e^{-\mu/\lambda} \leq \frac{2C}{\lambda \cdot |Q|}$$

$$\implies \mu \geq -\lambda \cdot \ln(\frac{2C}{\lambda \cdot |Q|}) \implies \mu = max(0, \ -\lambda \cdot \ln(\frac{2C}{\lambda \cdot |Q|}))$$

□

In this setting, expected number of fake records for a single query denoted as $E(fR)$ depends on the mean and scale of the distribution and can be computed as follows:

$$E(fR) = \frac{1}{2\lambda} \int_{0}^{+\infty} x \cdot e^{-|x-\mu|/\lambda} dx = \mu + \lambda/2 \cdot e^{-\mu/\lambda}$$

Note that, formulation considers only the positive axis of Laplace distribution. This is because, fake records are generated if the injected Laplace noise is positive. Accordingly, the expected amount of fake records is equal to the expected magnitude of positive noise for a single query.

4.4.2 Noisy Statistics Generation

The goal of the noisy statistics generation phase is to identify the amount of necessary fake record injection and local cache placement for each possible query. Suppose R_i is a replica with query interface set $I_{R_i} = \{\Delta_i, ..., \Delta_j\}$. Here, each query interface consists of some attributes such that $\Delta_k = \{A_{k_1}, ..., A_{k_\ell}\}$. Then, to construct observable statistics for the queries of type Δ_k, a count query is issued against data source D for each possible value $(v_i, ..., v_j)$ where $v_i \in dom(A_{k_1}), ..., v_j \in dom(A_{k_\ell})$. Finally, each output is perturbed with noise drawn from $Laplace(\mu, \lambda)$.

Example 4.4.1: Suppose $I_{R_i} = \{\{gender\}, \{gender, maritalstatus\}\}$ such that dom(gender) = {male, female} and dom(maritalstatus) = {single, married}. Then, count queries are issued against the interfaces {gender} and {gender, maritalstatus} for all possible values such that Q_g= {(male), (female)} and $Q_{g,m}$ = {(male, single), (male, married), (female, single), (female, married)}. Finally, each output for the issued queries is perturbed as shown in Figure 5.

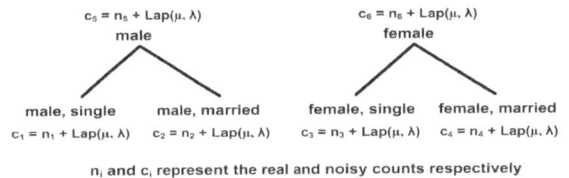

Figure 5: Noisy Statistics Generation

Note that, generated statistics are not necessarily consistent. Consider the example in Figure 5, $c_5 = c_1 + c_2$ is expected to hold true but it may not be the case due to the involved randomness. Fortunately, an efficient algorithm [4] is available to satisfy the consistency among the noisy statistics. The main idea is to estimate the statistics of base cells that consist of all possible values for the joint attribute set of $I_{R_i} = \{\Delta_i, ..., \Delta_j\}$ denoted as $Attributes(I_{R_i}) = \Delta_i \cup ... \cup \Delta_j$. Once base cell statistics are generated, all remaining statistics are derived from them. Consider the Example 4.4.1, base cells consists of all possible values for {gender, maritalstatus} such as {(male, single), (male, married), (female, single), (female, married)}. This is because, {gender, maritalstatus} contains all attributes of interfaces {gender} and {gender, maritalstatus}. In this context, base cells of a specific query q_j denoted as $base(q_j)$ is defined as follows:

Definition 4.4.1 Query Base (base(q_j)) : Suppose $Attributes(I_{R_i})$ represents all attributes in I_{R_i} and q_j is a query on a particular interface $\Delta_k = \{A_{k_1}, ..., A_{k_\ell}\}$ such that $\Delta_k \subseteq Attributes(I_{R_i})$. Then base cells of query q_j denoted as $base(q_j)$ is a set of all possible queries on $Attributes(I_{R_i})$ with the same assignments as q_j on the attributes of Δ_k.

Consider the Example 4.4.1, base cells of query (gender = male) are (male, single) and (male, married). This is because, base(gender = male) should contain all possible base cells with assignment 'male' on the gender attribute.

To estimate the base cell counts, least square estimator is utilized as in [4]. More formally, suppose Q_{R_i} represents all possible queries that can be issued using the interfaces in I_{R_i}, $c(q_i)$ represents the noisy count for the result set size of query $q_i \in Q_{R_i}$ and $base(q_i)$ represents the base cells corresponding to q_i. Then least square estimation of any base cell b_j denoted as $\omega(b_j)$ is formulated as follows:

$$minimize \sum_{q_i \in Q_{R_i}} (\sum_{b_j \in base(q_i)} \omega(b_j) - c(q_i))^2 \quad (2)$$

Fortunately Equation 2 has an efficient closed form solution to find optimal $\omega(b_j)$ for each base cell b_j. The closed form solution is devised in [4] in the context of differentially private data cube release.

Once the estimated counts of the base cells are identified, real base cells are obfuscated accordingly. Specifically, suppose b_j is a base cell, $cnt(b_j)$ and $\omega(b_j)$ represent the real and noisy counts of the records in b_j respectively, $rnd(\omega(b_j))$ is the closest integer to $\omega(b_j)$ and $diff_{b_j}$ is the difference between noisy and real counts such that $diff_{b_j} = rnd(\omega(b_j)) - cnt(b_j)$. Then, if $diff_{b_j} > 0$, $diff_{b_j}$ fake records are formed and added to the cell b_j. Otherwise, $|diff_{b_j}|$ real records of b_j are placed into the local cache. In this setting, a fake record is formed by assigning values to its attributes such that assigned values are not members of their attribute domains (e.g., gender='fake', maritalstatus='fake').

After fake record injection and local cache placement on base cells, obfuscated indexes are formed for each query interface $\Delta_k \in I_{R_i}$. Specifically, obfuscated index for $\Delta_k = \{A_{k_1}, ..., A_{k_\ell}\}$ denoted as $Ind_{R_i}^k$ is obtained by applying roll-up on the dimensions $Attributes(I_{R_i}) - \Delta_k$ of the base cells.

Example 4.4.2: Suppose $I_{R_i} = \{\{gender\}, \{gender, maritalstatus\}\}$ and corresponding base cells along with their real records and noisy counts are as depicted in Figure 6-A. Then obfuscated indexes are formed as in Figure 6-B. Here, r_i and f_j represent the real and fake records respectively.

After obfuscated index construction, suppose $R_i[cache]$ represents records placed into the local cache and $R_i[server]$ represent the remaining records including both fake and real ones. Then records in $R_i[cache]$ along with their index structure are stored in the local cache. Records in $R_i[server]$ and their associated indexes are subject to *encryption*.

4.4.3 Record Encryption

Once records that will be transferred to the cloud along with the associated indexes are identified, a secure encryption should be applied on them to hide their content. Suppose $\{Ind_{R_i}^1, ..., Ind_{R_i}^z\}$ is the set of obfuscated indexes for replica R_i, $R_i[server]$ is the set of records that will be stored

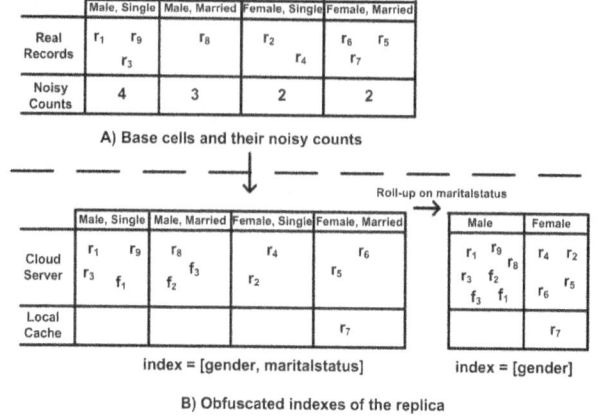

A) Base cells and their noisy counts

Roll-up on maritalstatus

B) Obfuscated indexes of the replica

Figure 6: Obfuscated Index Construction

in the payload of R_i. Then, both records in $R_i[server]$ and index cells (e.g., (male,married) is a cell for index [gender, maritalstatus]) are encrypted as follows:

1. Records in $R_i[server]$ are shuffled with a random permutation P_i such that $P_i(R_i[server])$ is formed. The goal of this step is to break up the relation between the memory locations of the records for distinct replicas.

2. Each record in $P_i(R_i[server])$ is encrypted with a secure encryption scheme (e.g., AES in CTR mode of operation [9]). Let K_{R_i} be a secret key, Enc_K be a secure encryption with key K and $maxRecordSize$ be the size of the largest record in $P_i(R_i[server])$. Then, each record $r_j \in P_i(R_i[server])$ is initially padded to $maxRecordSize$. After padding, encrypted version of r_j (π_{r_j}) is formed such that $\pi_{r_j} = Enc_{K_{R_i}}(r_j)$. Once records are encrypted, they are outsourced as the payload of R_i in the order of their location in $P_i(R_i[server])$.

3. Note that cells of any index $Ind_{R_i}^j$ are filled with records of $R_i[server]$ during the obfuscated index construction phase (see Section 4.4.2). To form private indexes, these records are initially replaced by their location in $P_i(R_i[server])$. For instance, suppose {male} is a cell in $Ind_{R_i}^j$ with associated records $\{r_3, f_1\}$ and $P_i(R_i[server]) = \{r_2, f_2, r_3, r_1, f_1\}$. Then content of cell {male} becomes $\{3, 5\}$ since $loc(r_3) = 3$ and $loc(f_1) = 5$ where $loc(r_i)$ represents the location of r_i in $P_i(R_i[server])$. After content replacement, each cell and associated locations are encrypted with a secure encryption scheme. Finally encrypted cell, location pairs are outsourced to the server as private index $PInd_{R_i}^j$.

Specifically, let c_k be a cell in $Ind_{R_i}^j$ with records $\{c_k^1, ..., c_k^z\}$, $locs_{c_k} = \{loc(c_k^1), ..., loc(c_k^z)\}$ be the location set for the records that contain c_k where $loc(x)$ represents the location of x in $P_i(R_i[server])$, K_{cell} and K_{loc} be secret keys for the index, $F_{K_{cell}}$ and $F_{K_{loc}}$ be pseudo-random functions, H_K be a random oracle with key K, α_i be a k-bit random string and $\oplus$ be the xor operator. Then, encryption for c_k ($[\pi_{c_k}, \pi_{locs(c_k)}]$) is formed as follows[3]:

---

[3]This encryption construct is derived from the random oracle based searchable encryption construction of [11]. Cryptographic keyed hash functions such as HMAC-SHA256 could be utilized as a random oracle for the implementation.

$$\pi_{c_k} = F_{K_{cell}}(c_k), \; key(c_k) = F_{K_{loc}}(c_k)$$

$$\pi_{locs(c_k)} = [\pi_{loc(c_k^1)}, ..., \pi_{loc(c_k^z)}]$$

$$\pi_{loc(c_k^i)} = (H_{key(c_k)}(\alpha_i) \; \oplus \; loc(c_k^i), \; \alpha_i)$$

Encrypted cell, location pairs constitute a private index $PInd_{R_i}^j$ such that $[\pi_{c_k}, \pi_{locs(c_k)}] \in PInd_{R_i}^j$. In this setting, suppose a user issues a trapdoor $T_{c_k} = \{F_{K_{cell}}(c_k), F_{K_{loc}}(c_k), \Delta_\iota\}$ where Δ_ι is mapped to $PInd_{R_i}^j$ and $[F_{K_{cell}}(c_k), \pi_{locs(c_k)}] \in PInd_{R_i}^j$. Then the following decryption is applied to extract the locations of the requested records:

$$key(c_k) = F_{K_{loc}}(c_k)$$

$$loc(c_k^i) = H_{key(c_k)}(\alpha_i) \; \oplus \; \pi_{loc(c_k^i)}$$

Note that decrypted payload locations point both fake and real encrypted records. Although server accesses to the physical memory that are pointed by the decrypted addresses, it observes only differentially private counts of the records that satisfy the query. Encrypted records will be decrypted by the client after their retrieval and fake ones will be eliminated.

5. EXPERIMENTAL ANALYSIS

5.1 Experimental Design

To perform the evaluation, we selected a publicly available dataset of real personal identifiers, namely Census-Income dataset [1] from UCI Machine Learning Repository. Dataset consists of 48842 individual records and each record has 14 attributes. Among all attributes, 8 are categorical and remaining ones are numerical. We built private indexes on the categorical ones. During the index construction, noise is added to each index cell (e.g., [male, single]) regardless of the dataset and these cells are further filled with real records.

The default parameters for the index construction is as follows: privacy parameter $\epsilon = 0.5$, capacity parameter $C = 2500$, relative importance of bandwidth and storage consumption $bI/sI = 100$, the expected number of queries $qLoad = 1000$ and the default initial interface size ($|\Delta|$) is 7. We randomly selected $|\Delta|$ query interfaces from all possible interfaces to build private indexes. To generate queries against the constructed indexes, we initially formed all possible queries that can be issued using available query interfaces. Then we randomly selected 1000 queries from them and sent the corresponding trapdoor to the server for the record retrieval.

In all experimental settings, index setup and a single search can be performed quite efficiently since efficient symmetric encryption schemes are utilized for the construction. The main bottleneck of the protocol is bandwidth consumption during the retrieval. Hence, we utilize the bandwidth consumption of the cloud server and local cache as a main evaluation metric. We reported the average results over 10 executions for all experiments.

5.2 Effect of Parameters

To investigate the effect of distinct parameters on the protocol, we modified a single parameter at a time and used the default values for the others. Reported results are the average retrieval results over issued 1000 queries.

In differential privacy formulation, ϵ is a parameter specified by data-owner. Lower ϵ implies higher privacy with

ϵ	Server Overhead (%)	Cache Overhead (%)
0.3	6.62	1.60
0.4	4.88	1.32
0.5	3.93	1.12
0.6	3.25	0.97
0.7	2.78	0.87

Table 1: Protocol Overhead

the cost of more noise. Figure 7 demonstrates the influence of ϵ on the efficiency. Here, real(KB) and fake(KB) represent the amount of real and fake records retrieved from the cloud respectively, and local(KB) represents the amount of records retrieved from the local cache in terms of kilobytes. With increasing ϵ, both fake record and local cache retrieval decreases. This is because, both of them result from the perturbation through Laplace mechanism and the amount of perturbation becomes less for higher ϵ. Note that, decrease in fake record retrieval is more sharper than decrease in local cache retrieval. This is due to the additional influence of ϵ on the mean of the Laplace distribution. To satisfy the capacity constraint of the cache, mean of the distribution is shifted on positive axis which results in more fake records. Higher ϵ enables less mean shift and less fake records. It is clear that sum of the real records retrieved from cloud and local cache is constant for all ϵ since they constitute the correct result set. Hence, decrease in cache retrieval leads to increase in the real record retrieval from the server.

Table 1 summarizes the overhead of the proposed scheme on the server and cache with distinct privacy levels. Here server overhead is $100 \cdot fake_{\epsilon_i} / (real_{\epsilon_i} + local_{\epsilon_i})$ and cache overhead is $100 \cdot local_{\epsilon_i} / (real_{\epsilon_i} + local_{\epsilon_i})$ where $fake_{\epsilon_i}$ and $real_{\epsilon_i}$ represents the amount of fake and real data retrieved from the server and $local_{\epsilon_i}$ is the amount of data retrieved from the cache for privacy parameter ϵ_i. When ϵ_i was set to 0.3, 1.6% of the query results were retrieved from the cache. Approximately 6.6% of the records that were downloaded from the server were fake.

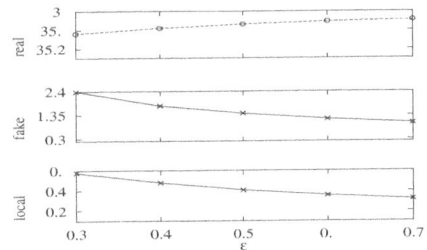

Figure 7: Effect of ϵ on Retrieval

Figure 8 demonstrates the influence of the number of initial query interfaces ($|\Delta|$). Note that, query set sensitivity for Laplace mechanism is proportional to the number of provided query interfaces. Hence, sensitivity increases with increasing $|\Delta|$ which results in more noise. This leads to increase in the number of fake records on the server and records that are placed into the cache. Note that, there is slight decrease on the fake records from $|\Delta| = 7$ to $|\Delta| = 9$. This is due to the influence of the applied least square estimator. Estimator considers the constraints among the interfaces in addition to the their noisy statistics. Although addition of more interface increments the sensitivity, it may also add more constraints. Such constraints enables some reduction in the noise. For instance, consider the interfaces $\Delta_1 = \{gender\}$ and $\Delta_2 = \{gender, marital\,status\}$. Since $\Delta_1 \subset \Delta_2$, there is a constraint among them (e.g., $count_{male,married} + count_{male,single} = count_{male}$).

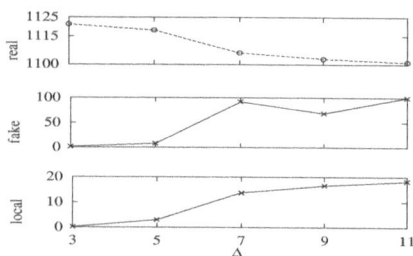

Figure 8: Effect of $|\Delta|$ on Retrieval

6. RELATED WORK

Over the years, various protocols were proposed for searchable encryption. ORAM model of Goldreich et al. [8] enables selective retrieval over encrypted data without revealing access pattern (A_p). However, it is too costly to be practical on real data sources. Even the more efficient versions of ORAM [12, 15, 16] incur logarithmic overhead in the number of outsourced records for each single record request. In contrast to approaches that hide A_p, our approach leaks obfuscated A_p to offer more efficient retrieval while ensuring individual privacy. The overhead of our approach is independent of the dataset size while fully secure solutions depend on it at least logarithmically.

As an alternative to fully secure solutions, there are approaches ([2, 3, 7, 11, 14]) that selectively leak information, especially access pattern, for efficiency. The first of such practical approaches was provided in [14]. Later on, Goh et al. proposed a security definition to formalize the security requirements of SSE in [7]. Similarly, Chang et al. introduced a slightly stronger definition in [2]. However, both definitions do not consider adaptive adversaries. This shortcoming was addressed in [3] with an adaptive security definition. Considerable amount of protocols based on SSE schemes were proposed for database as a service model. In [17], a protocol that enable conjunctive search over encrypted databases was proposed. Later, a system known as CryptDB [13] was designed to enable execution of different query types over encrypted databases. However, these approaches do not provide any guarantee about access pattern leakage.

7. CONCLUSION

In this paper, we propose a protocol for efficient and private selective record retrieval over encrypted databases that are hosted on the cloud servers. The proposed scheme leaks obfuscated access statistics to enable efficient retrieval while ensuring the privacy of individuals whose records are included in the database. Applied obfuscation mechanism relies on differential privacy which offers strong privacy guarantees against adversaries with arbitrary background knowledge. To investigate the efficiency of the proposed scheme, we conduct empirical analysis on real personal records. Empirical evaluations indicates the practical nature of the proposed scheme.

8. ACKNOWLEDGEMENTS

This work was partially supported by Air Force Office of Scientific Research FA9550-12-1-0082, National Institutes of Health Grants 1R0-1LM009989 and 1R01HG006844, National Science Foundation (NSF) Grants Career-CNS-0845803, CNS-0964350, CNS-1016343, CNS-1111529, CNS-1228198 and Army Research Office Grant W911NF-12-1-0558.

9. REFERENCES

[1] Census income dataset. archive.ics.uci.edu/ml/datasets/census+ income, 2013.

[2] CHANG, Y., AND MITZENMACHER, M. Privacy preserving keyword searches on remote encrypted data. In *Proc. of ACNS'05* (2005), pp. 442–455.

[3] CURTMOLA, R., GARAY, J., KAMARA, S., AND OSTROVSKY, R. Searchable symmetric encryption: Improved definitions and efficient constructions. *Journal of Computer Security 19*, 5 (2011), 895–934.

[4] DING, B., WINSLETT, M., HAN, J., AND LI, Z. Differentially private data cubes: Optimizing noise sources and consistency. In *SIGMOD'11* (2011).

[5] DWORK, C. Differential privacy. In *ICALP (2)* (2006).

[6] DWORK, C., MCSHERRY, F.AND NISSIM, K., AND SMITH, A. Calibrating noise to sensitivity in private data analysis. In *TCC* (2006), pp. 265–284.

[7] GOH, E. Secure indexes. In *Cryptology ePrint Archive, Report 2003/216* (2003).

[8] GOLDREICH, O., AND OSTROVSKY, R. Software protection and simulation on oblivious rams. *Journal of the ACM 43* (1996), 431–473.

[9] GOLDWASSER, S., AND BELLARE, M. *Lecture Notes on Cryptography.* http://cseweb.ucsd.edu/ mihir/papers/gb.html, 2008.

[10] ISLAM, M. S., KUZU, M., AND KANTARCIOGLU, M. Access pattern disclosure on searchable encryption: Ramification, attack and mitigation. In *NDSS'12* (2012).

[11] KAMARA, S., PAPAMANTHOU, C., AND ROEDER, T. Dynamic searchable symmetric encryption. In *CCS'12* (2012), pp. 965–976.

[12] PINKAS, B., AND REINMAN, T. Oblivious ram revisited. In *CRYPTO'10* (2010), pp. 502–519.

[13] POPA, R., REDFIELD, C., ZELDOVICH, N., AND BALAKRISHNAN, H. Cryptdb: protecting confidentiality with encrypted query processing. In *SOSP'11* (2011), pp. 85–100.

[14] SONG, D., WAGNER, D., AND PERRIG, A. Practical techniques for searches on encrypted data. In *Proc. of the IEEE S&P'00* (2000), pp. 44–55.

[15] STEFANOV, E., SHI, E., AND SONG, D. Towards practical oblivious ram. In *NDSS'12* (2012).

[16] WILLIAMS, P., SION, R., AND CARBUNAR, B. Building castles out of mud: Practical access pattern privacy and correctness on untrusted storage. In *CCS'08* (2008), pp. 139–148.

[17] YANG, Z., ZHONG, S., AND WRIGHT, R. Privacy preserving queries on encrypted data. In *ESORICS'06* (2006).

[18] ZAIANE, O. R., FOSS, A., LEE, C., AND WANG, W. On data clustering analysis: Scalability, constraints and validation. In *PAKDD'00* (2000).

DroidBarrier: Know What is Executing on Your Android [*]

Hussain M. J. Almohri
almohri@cs.ku.edu.kw
Department of Computer
Science
Kuwait University, Kuwait

Danfeng (Daphne) Yao
danfeng@cs.vt.edu
Department of Computer
Science
Virginia Tech
Blacksburg, VA 24061

Denis Kafura
kafura@cs.vt.edu
Department of Computer
Science
Virginia Tech
Blacksburg, VA 24061

ABSTRACT

Many Android vulnerabilities share a root cause of malicious unauthorized applications executing without user's consent. In this paper, we propose the use of a technique called process authentication for Android applications to overcome the shortcomings of current Android security practices. We demonstrate the process authentication model for Android by designing and implementing our runtime authentication and detection system referred to as DroidBarrier. Our malware analysis shows that DroidBarrier is capable of detecting real Android malware at the time of creating independent processes. A performance evaluation of DroidBarrier unveils its low performance penalties.

Categories and Subject Descriptors

D.4.6 [**Operating Systems**]: Security and Protection—
Authentication, Access controls

Keywords

Android system security, authentication, malicious processes, Android malware

1. INTRODUCTION

An important feature of the Android operating system is that it relies on mature technologies such as the Linux kernel. In particular, Android's Dalvik runtime system relies on Linux process creation when launching an application or a service, making the runtime system as the parent process of all user application processes in Android.

With the assistance of the Linux kernel, Android implements a fundamental security feature called application sandboxes. Android's approach is to install each application

[*]This work has been supported in part by Kuwait University, and, NSF grant CAREER CNS-0953638 and ONR grant N00014-13-1-0016.

with an isolated sandbox to protect its data from unauthorized accesses by other applications, by means of file system permissions and creating independent processes for each application at runtime. Similar to other Linux-base systems, Android suffers from numerous vulnerabilities that cause the Android's application sandboxes to fail. For example, the `Gingerbreak` exploit affected the popular Android 2.3 enabled a malicious application to gain `root` privileges and completely bypass Android's application sandboxes. This privilege escalation is used to establish attacks on various system and user resources. Malicious applications can then exploit other vulnerabilities above the Linux kernel level such as the ones in Android's inter-component communications [6, 12]. A malicious application may launch attacks to misuse system resources with the goal of spying on users, stealing private user data, and causing financial loss [13].

To combat the security vulnerabilities in Android, current state of the art focuses on a wide range of approaches. For example, previous work such as SELinux for Android [5] provide a runtime protection mechanism to disable exploits by leveraging a rich policy specification framework originally developed as part of SELinux. Further, FlaskDroid [24], inspired by SELinux also provides a comprehensive framework for specifying access control for policies in Android. There have been proposals for behavioral analysis of malware [27], the use of virtual layers to separate execution domains [3], data-provenance verification [28], using control-flow to limit access to data [10], and protecting inter-component communications in Android's Binder [8]. Despite Android's heavy reliance on its Linux-based security sandboxes, with a few exceptions (e.g., [19]), existing security solutions barely attempt to enhance the security capabilities of the Linux kernel in Android. Prior work specifically targeting traditional Linux-based systems (e.g., [2, 17, 22]) are not directly applicable to Android. This limitation of security solutions for Linux-based systems is because of major differences in the system architecture, application and security models used in Android, despite the reliance on a modified Linux kernel.

In this paper, we present a technique, referred to as *process authentication for Android applications*, that complements the Android's sandbox mechanism and provides strong protection for system resources against malicious and unauthorized applications. The concept of authentication has been previously applied and used by (i) Quire [8] for providing provenance proof on inter-component communications in Android, (ii) A2 [2, 1] for authenticating native Linux applications, and (iii) the authenticated system calls [21] for preventing misuse of system calls. However, developing an authentication model for Android applications imposes unique technical challenges since the Android framework primarily runs Java applications running in virtual machines and makes use of features such as application services that run in background. These and other Android features require rethinking application and process authentication, which is the subject of our work.

Our key observation is that critical vulnerabilities in Android share a root cause: *malicious applications that are installed and executed without the user's consent.* Our process authentication model addresses the problem by regarding application processes as individuals that must be authenticated before using system resources. In this model, legitimate applications are given credentials that are used for authentication at runtime. When enforcing process authentication, unauthorized processes that do not possess credentials fail to authenticate. This failure results in denying access to critical system services provided by the kernel.

The main property of our process authentication model is enabling the detection of unauthorized processes at runtime. To demonstrate this property, we design and implement DroidBarrier, a runtime system, that enforces a mandatory authentication on all processes for any application in Android. Using this mandatory authentication enforcement, DroidBarrier *guarantees* the detection of processes that fail to authenticate and prevents their subsequent attacks. Our technical contributions are summarized below.

1. *Process authentication model.* We present a process authentication model and discuss the security requirements and guarantees of our model. We discuss a general set of operations needed to implement our model at runtime.

2. *Runtime system.* We design a runtime system called DroidBarrier that is capable of detecting unauthorized processes. Our runtime system mediates the authentication between a process and the kernel. Our design does not require modification of existing applications or Android's Dalvik runtime system.

3. *Implementation.* We implemented and tested DroidBarrier for a physical Android device. Our implementation consists of patches to the kernel, a set of tools for process monitoring, authentication, and a lightweight access control system in the kernel.

Per our evaluation, DroidBarrier detects and stops malicious processes of three major Android malware categories with hundreds of instances. According to our performance experiments on a physical Android tablet, DroidBarrier has negligible performance penalties in process creation. It also shows a maximum and a minimum I/O performance penalty of 12.92% and 3.76%, respectively.

The rest of this paper is organized as follows. In Section 2, we present a motivating example, followed by our security analysis and the description of the process authentication model. Section 3 describes the details of DroidBarrier and its functions. We describe the implementation of DroidBarrier and our experiments in Sections 4 and 5, respectively. Finally, we discuss the related work in Section 6 and conclude in Section 7.

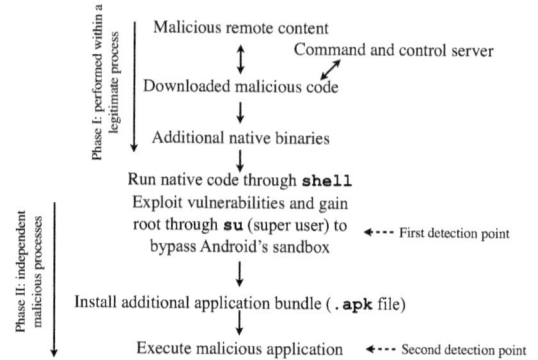

Figure 2.1: A remote attack sequence to bypass Android's sandbox and install malicious applications without user's permissions.

2. OVERVIEW

We address the problem of *preventing stealthy installation and execution of malicious applications in Android-enabled devices.* This is a root cause of many malicious attacks that exploit other vulnerabilities in Android, with attack goals such as stealing private data and incurring financial loss.

Motivating example attack. We conducted a runtime analysis of three sets of Android malware DroidKungFu, BaseBridge, and AnserverBot. Each of these malware sets have a number of variants with nearly identical malicious activities with differences in their user interface elements. According to our findings, and the results in [29] and [30], these malware sets rely on malicious shell scripts (running in independent processes) to perform a privilege escalation exploit. In Section 5.1, we discuss that our runtime system, DroidBarrier, is capable of detecting and stopping these applications at the time of creating processes that fail to authenticate.

To demonstrate the problem, we construct an example attack scenario that is common to these (and other) malware categories. As depicted in Figure 2.1, the remote attack exploits two vulnerabilities that result in execution of malicious applications without the user's permission. In the first phase of the attack, a vulnerable client is exploited to execute a payload that downloads a native malicious executable. In the second phase, the downloaded native binary exploits a vulnerability in a system task (e.g., Android debugging bridge daemon) to gain root privileges. Having root privileges, the native binary bypasses Android's sandbox and installs applications on the file system without asking for the user's permission.

Once the malicious application is installed with all the requested permissions defined in its manifest file, it can conduct further attacks. The key element to this attack strategy is the ability to install applications without the user's explicit authorization. DroidBarrier does not directly detect the payload that is downloaded to install malicious applications. However, DroidBarrier is designed to prevent such installations by means of detecting their unauthenticated processes, thereby foiling this form of attack.

Challenges and Goals. To develop a solution for protecting the system from execution of unauthorized malicious applications, we face two technical challenges:

- The kernel only enforces file system permissions, and provides memory isolation for processes. In Android, the kernel lacks advanced capabilities to detect possible misuse of `root` privileges.

- Because Android application processes execute in virtual machines and are managed by the Android runtime, monitoring application processes inside the kernel, without modifying the runtime, faces a semantic gap.

To address these challenges and develop a mechanism that can detect installation and execution of unauthorized applications, this work

- provides a mechanism for the kernel to authenticate processes and unveil the existence of malicious applications, and

- aims to detect malicious processes at runtime with high confidence about their origins. In our detection, we reconstruct the semantics between the kernel and Android's runtime by monitoring process forks and the runtime's subsequent loading of application class files into the newly created processes.

2.1 Security Model

Security assumptions and trust model. We trust the kernel's code and the isolation of memory provided by the kernel used in Android. We assume that the integrity and confidentiality of kernel's memory are preserved. Further, we assume that Android's system software and processes do not intentionally contain malicious functionality.

Attack model. We target the following methods of attacks. We first categorize the attacks according to their installation approach.

- **Remote attacks.** As shown in the example attack in Figure 2.1, remote exploitation attacks start by remotely exploiting a vulnerability in an application. For example, attackers can exploit the many vulnerabilities in Android's WebView API (that applications use to show specific web pages) to trigger drive-by-downloads [18] and install malicious applications. These attacks can download the application and use system vulnerabilities to bypass user's permission for installing the application.

- **Physical attacks.** Using a physical communication channel such as Android Debug Bridge (adb) daemon to install malicious applications [26]. In this case, the attacker has physical access to the device and the attack goal is to install malicious applications without the user's knowledge. These attacks either require that the device is not password protected or existence of a system vulnerability to bypass the password protection.

According to their execution dependencies attacks are further categorized into two main classes:

- **Dependent attacks.** The malicious code runs in a compromised application's processes. Thus, the malicious code depends on another legitimate application to continue execution. For example, the malicious code may run within a hijacked trusted process.

- **Independent attacks.** The malicious code needs to run in at least one independent process that is created by a native code or a Dalvik application.

In this paper, we specifically target independent (physical or remote) attacks that require installation of *independent* malicious applications with full capabilities.

3. SYSTEM DETAILS

In this section we first describe an abstract *process authentication model* followed by the design of our runtime system DroidBarrier.

3.1 Process Authentication Model

To achieve our goals for protecting Android from malicious applications that could be installed without the user's consent, we develop a process authentication model that can detect malicious application executions. Our process authentication model (also referred to as authentication model in this paper) regards application processes as individual principals that must be authenticated at runtime. Our mandatory authentication provides legitimate applications with valid *application credentials*, and, detects malicious applications that lack such credentials. We define an application credential as follows:

DEFINITION 1. *A secure application credential (SAC) is a unique secret issued to an application by a trusted process. Each SAC is associated with exactly one installed Dalvik or native application. A SAC is computationally hard to regenerate and must not be accessible by any unauthorized user process.*

To perform authentication using application credentials as proofs of applications' identities, we define two special processes:

DEFINITION 2. *The verifier process π is a trusted process that has the authority of authenticating other processes.*

DEFINITION 3. *The registrar process ρ is authorized to perform the registration of an application by associating an application bundle with a unique SAC. The registration of the application is performed at install time with explicit user permission.*

The operating system is responsible for using application credentials to authenticate processes. The rationale behind our authentication model is determined by the following *Process Authentication (PA)* properties:

1. User processes (other than π and ρ) may not create or modify credentials, or, assign credentials to other processes and applications.

2. If a process fails to authenticate itself with a valid secure application credential, then the process is potentially malicious.

3. A process may not be authenticated with more than one credential.

4. A process may not inherit its *authentication status* from parent processes or any other process. Sibling processes are authenticated with a shared application credential.

5. A Dalvik application process is always a child of the `zygote` process. Native processes must either be a child of an Android system process or a Dalvik application process.

The PA properties ensure that processes are bound to proper application credentials such that a malicious process (under our attack model in Section 2.1) does not bypass the authentication, or, spoof other legitimate processes.

Operations. Our authentication model has three core operations (discussed in Section 3.2.1): credential registration, process authentication, and runtime detection. These operations ensure proper authentication of all processes and detection of unauthorized ones. In the following section, we present the design of DroidBarrier that implements these operations in the Android operating system.

3.2 Design of DroidBarrier

We design *DroidBarrier* to realize our process authentication model. In the following sections, we present the core components of DroidBarrier and discuss some of the alternative design approaches.

We follow a proactive approach in DroidBarrier by registering the applications that the user desires to run. This registration enables the user to control which applications are legitimate and allowed to run. Also, we include a detection capability in DroidBarrier to monitor process creations and activities and authenticate processes at runtime. In the following sections, we present the core components of DroidBarrier for implementing the operations of our authentication model described in Section 3.

3.2.1 Credential Registration and Protection

To perform the registration of credentials, DroidBarrier includes a component referred to as the *credential registrar* (also referred to as the registrar in this paper). As depicted in Figure 3.1, credential registrar's task is to generate credentials for applications that the user designates as legitimate.

Establishing the trustworthiness of applications is an important procedure that can be executed before registering an application with a valid credential. To establish this trustworthiness, there exists a number of classification techniques using static analysis [9, 11, 14], dynamic analysis [29] of the application, or based on experts' knowledge. In this work, we do not explicitly address this problem.

Credential generation. The registrar generates a credential that is computationally hard to guess. Among many ways to generate a credential, the registrar can use a strong pseudo random number generator.

There are two alternative approaches to our authentication mechanism based on secret credentials. First, registering a public checksum (e.g., a hash of application's class file) of an application bundle, and, recomputing the checksum at runtime to establish the authenticity and integrity of the application. Our approach is to use a *secret* credential, which eliminates the need for recomputing the checksum. Although by checking the checksum one can determine if the application bundle's integrity was violated, we choose to protect application bundles (as described below) for verifying and *preserving* their integrity and disabling possible denial of service. The second alternative approach is to use developer signatures to establish trust. In fact, Android uses developer signatures, but without an actual verification of

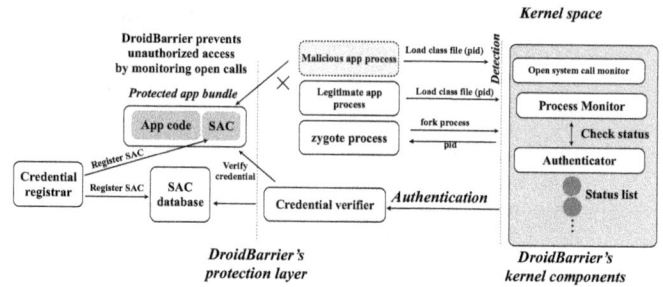

Figure 3.1: DroidBarrier performs three operations: credential storage and protection, runtime monitoring, and authentication of processes. Applications with valid credentials are allowed normal execution.

the signature. Our design eliminates the need for third party certifications and verifications of public keys yet delivers the required level of trust.

To correctly establish the authenticity of an application, the registrar uses a two-way registration method. First, the registrar generates and stores a credential γ in A's bundle, forming a new application bundle A^*. We refer to an application bundle with an embedded credential, as a *protected application bundle*. This design choice is important to bind processes to specific executables in our runtime detection system, and, to protect the credential γ from attacks (described below). Second, the registrar stores a copy of γ in a *SAC database*. The SAC database implements the unique set Γ, which is the set of reference for validating any credential. Maintaining a copy of γ in the SAC database prevents forgery and replay attacks on the credentials. Note that an application's credential γ is invalidated if γ is removed from Γ and if the application is reinstalled or deleted.

Credential protection. To fulfill the specification of credentials (Section 3) and the PA properties (Section 3.1), our design must fully protect the credentials generated by the registrar to preserve their integrity, without relying on file system permissions. Our approach to this problem is to enforce access restrictions on the protected application bundles and the SAC database. To maintain integrity and confidentiality, we disable any process, other than the verifier process and the registrar, from read/write access to protected application bundles and the SAC database. We enforce this protection using DroidBarrier's kernel-side components by intercepting all open system calls and preventing unauthorized access to the SAC database (Section 4).

3.2.2 Runtime System

DroidBarrier includes a *process monitor* (Figure 3.1) to track the creation of processes by the Android's runtime. The process monitor relies on the authentication decision by DroidBarrier's *authenticator*. To maintain compatibility, we design these components as part of the Linux kernel without modifying Android's runtime. Our design strategy is to detect process creations, bind them to specific application bundles, and authenticate the processes according to registered credentials.

Process Monitoring and Runtime detection. The process monitor's policy is to regard every new process as unauthorized until it is authenticated. The detection strategy of the process monitor is to check the authentication status of applications at the time of creation. A process's status is either authenticated or unauthenticated.

The technical challenge in the design of DroidBarrier's runtime system is the semantic gap between the kernel and Dalvik virtual machine, which runs Android applications. Android's runtime system process, `zygote`, forks a new process when the user wants to run an application. At this point, it is not clear to the kernel which application is loaded in the newly created process. To reconstruct the semantics, in addition to monitoring process creations, the process monitor keeps track of file accesses by `zygote` to bind the loaded class file of the application to the newly forked process. When the newly forked process is bound to a Dalvik class file, the process monitor's runtime detection is complete and the process's identifier (PID) is sent for authenticator to proceed with the authentication.

Process authentication. DroidBarrier needs a reliable mechanism for authentication to prevent stealing credentials and spoofing legitimate processes. We follow a design choice to mediate the authentication between DroidBarrier and user applications. Using our authentication mediation strategy, DroidBarrier performs the process authentication operation in three stages:

1. *Kernel-side checking.* As shown in Figure 3.1, a kernel-side component, authenticator (denote as AT), receives an authentication request from process monitor (denote as PM) for a process P. AT maintains a *status list* L, which records the authentication status for each process, *authenticated*, or, *unauthenticated*. If P's status is unauthenticated, AT sends an authentication verification request to the verifier process π. The format of the request is $(P.PID, P.path)$, where $P.PID$ is P's process ID and $P.path$ is the file path for the Dalvik class file that created P.

2. *Verification of credentials.* π loads the credential c from the protected application bundle on $P.path$ and the corresponding credential c' from the SAC database. If $c = c'$, then π sends a success response message back to AT.

3. *Status update.* When AT receives the response message from π, AT updates P's authentication status in L, accordingly.

3.3 Security Analysis

Security guarantees. DroidBarrier guarantees that all processes are authenticated. This property ensures that stealthy applications that were installed without the user's consent are detected. Independent remote or physical attacks described in Section 2.1 are detected as soon as a process with no valid credential is created. However, DroidBarrier does not guarantee the isolation of hijacked processes described under dependent attacks in Section 2.1.

Security of credentials. To secure application credentials, we study various attacks that can occur on the credentials and provide solutions accordingly. An important attack on DroidBarrier is to steal or corrupt application credentials. DroidBarrier protects the credentials from being exposed to attackers by denying access to application bundles at the user processes level. In order to prevent fake credentials, DroidBarrier registers all valid credentials and checks this validity at runtime.

Protecting DroidBarrier code and data. DroidBarrier's process monitor and authenticator execute in kernel mode. This guarantees the isolation of process monitor and authenticator data from user space attacks under the reasonable assumption of a trusted Linux kernel (Section 2.1).

Limitations of DroidBarrier. DroidBarrier specifically targets processes that are created by malicious applications. This is a critical category of attacks that is used by modern Android malware [30]. However, embedded attacks that run entirely within the boundaries of a legitimate process cannot be detected by our current mechanism. In general, any malicious application that possesses valid credentials (by hijacking legitimate applications, or granted by mistake) bypasses our security guarantees.

DroidBarrier's code and data may be subject to kernel-based attacks either by rootkits or malicious kernel modules. In principle, rootkit attacks (such as return-oriented rootkits [16] and system call obfuscation [25]) can cause kernel integrity and confidentiality violations. Although DroidBarrier is not designed to specially prevent rootkits, assuming that the kernel is initially free of malicious code, DroidBarrier prevents further malicious code executions.

4. IMPLEMENTATION

We describe a prototype of DroidBarrier implemented in C using Android's native APIs. Our implementation involves an extension to the Linux kernel for process monitor and authenticator (described in Section 3.2.2). We use Android Honeycomb 3.2 with the Linux kernel version 2.6.36.4 for our implementation platform.

Credential registrar. We implemented a credential registrar that installs application credentials for an Android application bundle. The registrar uses a random number generation function to generate a credential and labels the application bundle (with the `apk` extension) with the newly created credential. The registrar also records the new credential in a sequential database of keys and application names for reference at authentication time. Our labeling of the `apk` bundle does not alter the functionality of the application in any way. The label only includes an additional header and the credential in a format that DroidBarrier can recognize.

Credential protection. We protect credentials (Section 3.2.1) by implementing a light-weight access control system in the kernel. We place checkpoints in the beginning of `do_sys_open`, which enables us to intercept all open system calls. Before returning a file descriptor `fd` to the requesting process, we check for two conditions. First, we check if the requested file path is a protected application bundle, by reconstructing the full file path from the process's current directory. Then, we verify if the requested file path is an executable. If the condition is true, we check if the requesting process is the registrar, the credential verifier or `zygote`. According to our policies (Section 3.1), DroidBarrier denies access to executables for all other processes. Second, we check the file path against our credential database. For the credential database, we only return an `fd`, if the calling process is either the credential verifier or the registrar.

Process monitor. We implement the process monitor by inserting check points in specific kernel functions. To maintain performance, we avoid using existing Linux APIs to trace kernel functions (such as `kprobe` or `ptrace`). To monitor the creation of processes by the Android's runtime, we insert check points in `do_fork`, for Android's Dalvik applications, and `do_execve`, for native applications loaded directly by the kernel. The `zygote` process calls `fork()` to create a new process and load a Dalvik class in it. We record the generated `pid` in `do_fork` and track `zygote`'s subsequent system calls so that we bind the new `pid` to its application bundle.

DroidBarrier tracks the loading of Dalvik class files through our check point in the `do_sys_open` function. When the process `pid` (that must be the child of `zygote`) loads a class file from the file system, the authentication operation can proceed to verify `pid`'s credentials. Since the authentication is asynchronous and waits for the open system call, DroidBarrier maintains a dynamic pool of awaiting authentication processes (an array `requests` of type `struct auth_request`) to perform the authentication.

5. EVALUATION

We evaluate DroidBarrier by testing its detection capabilities against Android malware samples. Also, we present experiments for evaluating the performance of DroidBarrier.

5.1 Detection of Malicious Applications

According to Android's application model, every application bundle must run in at least one process independent of other applications. Thus, to detect malicious Android applications, we design DroidBarrier to detect malicious applications based on their process creations. According to the analysis performed in [30], about 36.7% of the applications (in a collection of 1260 malware instances) contained embedded privilege escalation exploits that execute through hidden shell scripts requiring their own independent processes.

We analyzed three chosen sets of Android malware `DroidKungFu`, `BaseBridge`, and `AnserverBot`. These malware (provided by Android genome project[1]) have 96, 122, and 187 variants, respectively. Our chosen malware categories use sophisticated social engineering, root vulnerability exploitation, and financial attacks, found in many other similar malware sets [30]. Nevertheless, our malware analysis is not limited to the chosen sets and is applicable to all malware with privilege escalation attacks as described in [30]. The three analyzed malicious applications share a core functionality that results in their detection by DroidBarrier. That is, they try to gain escalated privileges by running an exploit and subsequently calling the `su` utility. The `su` utility is not included in Android by default, but the malicious application can install it after gaining installation privileges that bypass user's permissions.

DroidBarrier successfully detected all the samples that we tested from these three sets. All the samples tried to run `su`, which resulted in processes that failed to authenticate. `DroidKungFu` tried to run other unknown executables that were also immediately detected at the time of process creation.

5.2 Performance Evaluation

We evaluate the performance of our implementation prototype described in Section 4. Our performance evaluation investigates the effect of DroidBarrier on I/O performance, process creation, and Dalvik applications.

In the rest of this section, we describe our experimental setup followed by three sets of experiments for I/O and process creation. Our results show efficient performance of

[1]http://www.malgenomeproject.org/

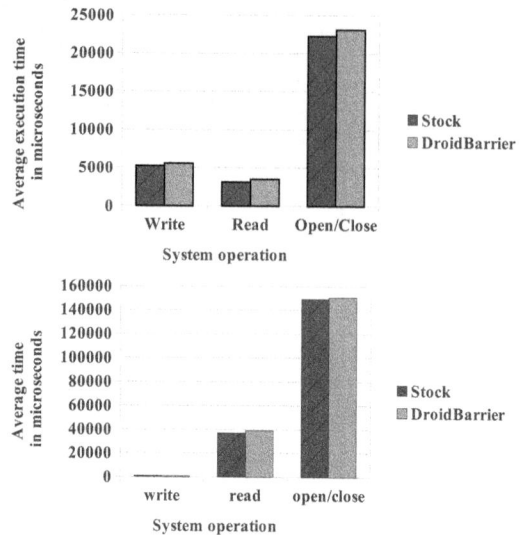

Figure 5.1: I/O operations write, read, open, and close for (a) native, and (b) Dalvik applications.

DroidBarrier with low extra overhead in I/O performance, and, negligible performance penalty in process creation.

Experimental setup. Our evaluation focuses on the effect of DroidBarrier on the performance of the Linux kernel in Android. We run all the experiments on a Samsung Galaxy Tab 10 (with model number P7510) running Android Honeycomb 3.2 with the Linux kernel version 2.6.36.4. For our evaluations, we port the benchmarking suites lmbench[2] and UnixBench[3] to Android.

For our evaluations we needed a benchmarking suite that can accurately measure I/O and process creation. There are existing suites such as lmbench[4] and UnixBench[5] that conveniently run on Linux distributions for x86 machines. Per our research, these suites have not been ported to embedded Linux running on the ARM architecture. Thus, we modified some of the existing code in lmbench and UnixBench for compatibility with the ARM Linux.

When running the modified kernel with DroidBarrier, we periodically simulate the authentication of processes as if a user is consistently launching new applications. When performing experiments, there was about a total of 130–150 running Linux processes.

I/O performance. I/O performance experiments show a consistently efficient performance of DroidBarrier with the performance penalty not exceeding 13%. We experimented with read, write, open and close calls with a measurement of the total time for 10,000 iterations. We performed 250 runs of each loop to collect an average performance value. In the results of our experiments (depicted in Figure 5.2), we have an average maximum of 12.92% performance penalty for the read calls, an average minimum of 3.76% performance penalty for open/close, and for write calls there is an average of 6.01%.

To examine the performance of Dalvik applications under DroidBarrier, we conducted an I/O experiment by making

[2]http://www.bitmover.com/lmbench/
[3]http://code.google.com/p/byte-unixbench/
[4]http://www.bitmover.com/lmbench/
[5]http://code.google.com/p/byte-unixbench/

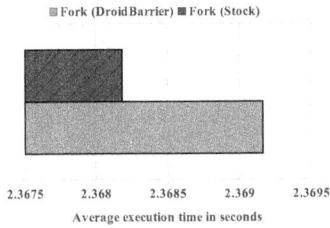

■ Fork (DroidBarrier) ■ Fork (Stock)

2.3675   2.368   2.3685   2.369   2.3695

Average execution time in seconds

Figure 5.2: Performance of fork system call evaluated in loops of 1000 iterations.

file writes, reads, open and close using the `BufferedWriter` and `BufferedReader`. The open and close calls involve opening a file using `FileWriter`, which is used to create a `BufferedWriter` and we close the `BufferedWriter` subsequently. We developed an application to perform 1000 iterations of each I/O operation (we call open and close calls together in one iteration). The results of Figure 5.2 shows the average performance for 200 runs of all experiments.

Process creation performance. We measure the fork system call in loops of 1000 iterations. In each iteration we fork a child, and, a child exits immediately, and, we perform a total of 100 runs of the experiments. Android heavily uses fork for process creations. Since DroidBarrier performs the authentication asynchronously, we do not see major performance downgrade for forking a process. The average performance penalty is 0.041% (depicted in Figure 5.2), which is insignificant.

6. RELATED WORK

Quire is a cryptographic solution that annotates interprocess communications (IPC) in Android to provide provenance assurance to the receivers of the IPC messages [8]. Our work differs from Quire by authenticating Linux processes in Android as one unit and also restricting access to system resources to authorized process.

A2 [2], uses a challenge-response protocol to authenticate applications. A2 [2] is designed to work with Linux processes created for native C applications. DroidBarrier authenticates Android's interpreted applications by reconstructing the semantics between the Linux kernel and Android's runtime (Section 3.2.2). DroidBarrier substantially improves and advances the techniques discussed in A2 by (i) an authentication model that specifically addresses the challenges for authenticating Dalvik applications, (ii) an authentication mediation strategy that reconstructs the semantic gap between the Dalvik runtime and the kernel, and (iii) a runtime system that monitors Android's `zygote` for process creation and enforcing authentication.

VMWare Mobile Virtualization Platform (MVP) [3] is a type 2 hypervisor and is capable of isolating restricted and normal execution environments. Bare Metal Hypervisor [15] runs security sensitive applications in trusted and isolated environments. Also, Cells [7] runs multiple virtual phones using a shared underlying physical phone to provide isolation. Other systems such as TrustDroid [4] isolate applications in isolated logical domains. In DroidBarrier, we do not use virtualization to provide isolation at runtime. This helps in achieving better compatibility.

Mandatory access control (MAC) systems complement DroidBarrier to provide fine-grained authorization. An-

droid's SELinux [23], for example, can benefit from DroidBarrier's strong authentication guarantees. More recent implementations of SELinux for Android [24] provide a more comprehensive framework to achieve fine-grained control on applications. Paranoid [20] is a system that takes a novel direction by delivering a cloud-based security solution for Android.

Finally, general static analysis techniques such as [9] can also be used to provide information on installing applications.

7. CONCLUSIONS

We presented a general model for providing high assurance authentication for application processes running on an Android-enabled device. We achieve the high assurance by developing an authentication model that uses secure application credentials, maintained and protected by our runtime system, to authenticate processes and bind their identity to legitimate applications installed on the device. Our authentication approach guarantees protecting the system from execution of malicious applications that may exploit the many system and application vulnerabilities to be installed on the device. Our future work will focus on authenticating interprocess communications and authenticating access to applications' assets.

8. REFERENCES

[1] H. Almohri, D. Yao, and D. Kafura. Process authentication for high system assurance. *IEEE Transactions on Dependable and Secure Computing*, PP(99), 2013.

[2] H. M. Almohri, D. Yao, and D. Kafura. Identifying native applications with high assurance. In *Proceedings of the second ACM conference on Data and Application Security and Privacy*, pages 275–282, New York, NY, USA, 2012. ACM.

[3] K. Barr, P. Bungale, S. Deasy, V. Gyuris, P. Hung, C. Newell, H. Tuch, and B. Zoppis. The VMware mobile virtualization platform: is that a hypervisor in your pocket? *ACM SIGOPS Operating Systems Review*, 44(4):124–135, Dec. 2010.

[4] S. Bugiel, L. Davi, A. Dmitrienko, S. Heuser, A.-R. Sadeghi, and B. Shastry. Practical and lightweight domain isolation on Android. In *Proceedings of the 1st ACM Workshop on Security and Privacy in Smartphones and Mobile Devices*, SPSM'11, pages 51–62, New York, NY, USA, 2011. ACM.

[5] S. Bugiel, S. Heuser, and A.-R. Sadeghi. Flexible and fine-grained mandatory access control on android for diverse security and privacy policies. In *22nd USENIX Security Symposium (USENIX Security '13)*. USENIX, Aug. 2013.

[6] E. Chin, A. P. Felt, K. Greenwood, and D. Wagner. Analyzing inter-application communication in Android. In *Proceedings of the 9th International Conference on Mobile Systems, Applications, and Services*, MobiSys '11, pages 239–252, New York, NY, USA, 2011. ACM.

[7] C. Dall, J. Andrus, A. Van't Hof, O. Laadan, and J. Nieh. The design, implementation, and evaluation of cells: A virtual smartphone architecture. *ACM Trans. Comput. Syst.*, 30(3):9:1–9:31, Aug. 2012.

[8] M. Dietz, S. Shekhar, Y. Pisetsky, A. Shu, and D. S. Wallach. Quire: lightweight provenance for smart phone operating systems. In *Proceedings of the 20th USENIX Conference on Security*, SEC'11, pages 23–23, Berkeley, CA, USA, 2011. USENIX Association.

[9] K. O. Elish, D. Yao, and B. G. Ryder. User-centric dependence analysis for identifying malicious mobile apps. In *Proceedings of the Workshop on Mobile Security Technologies (MoST)*, May 2012. In conjunction with the IEEE Symposium on Security and Privacy.

[10] W. Enck, P. Gilbert, B.-G. Chun, L. P. Cox, J. Jung, P. McDaniel, and A. N. Sheth. Taintdroid: an information-flow tracking system for realtime privacy monitoring on smartphones. In *Proceedings of the 9th USENIX conference on Operating systems design and implementation*, OSDI'10, pages 1–6, Berkeley, CA, USA, 2010. USENIX Association.

[11] W. Enck, M. Ongtang, and P. McDaniel. On lightweight mobile phone application certification. In *Proceedings of the 16th ACM Conference on Computer and Communications Security*, CCS '09, pages 235–245, New York, NY, USA, 2009. ACM.

[12] W. Enck, M. Ongtang, and P. McDaniel. Understanding Android Security. *IEEE Security and Privacy*, 7(1):50–57, Jan. 2009.

[13] A. P. Felt, M. Finifter, E. Chin, S. Hanna, and D. Wagner. A survey of mobile malware in the wild. In *Proceedings of the 1st ACM workshop on Security and privacy in smartphones and mobile devices*, SPSM '11, pages 3–14, New York, NY, USA, 2011. ACM.

[14] M. Grace, Y. Zhou, Q. Zhang, S. Zou, and X. Jiang. RiskRanker: scalable and accurate zero-day Android malware detection. In *Proceedings of the 10th international conference on Mobile systems, applications, and services*, MobiSys '12, pages 281–294, New York, NY, USA, 2012. ACM.

[15] K. Gudeth, M. Pirretti, K. Hoeper, and R. Buskey. Delivering secure applications on commercial mobile devices: the case for bare metal hypervisors. In *Proceedings of the 1st ACM Workshop on Security and Privacy in Smartphones and Mobile Devices*, SPSM '11, pages 33–38, New York, NY, USA, 2011. ACM.

[16] R. Hund, T. Holz, and F. C. Freiling. Return-oriented rootkits: bypassing kernel code integrity protection mechanisms. In *Proceedings of the 18th conference on USENIX security symposium*, SSYM'09, pages 383–398, Berkeley, CA, USA, 2009. USENIX Association.

[17] T. Jaeger, R. Sailer, and U. Shankar. PRIMA: policy-reduced integrity measurement architecture. In *Proceedings of the 11th ACM symposium on Access control models and technologies*, SACMAT '06, pages 19–28, New York, NY, USA, 2006. ACM.

[18] T. Luo, H. Hao, W. Du, Y. Wang, and H. Yin. Attacks on webview in the Android system. In *Proceedings of the 27th Annual Computer Security Applications Conference*, ACSAC '11, pages 343–352, New York, NY, USA, 2011. ACM.

[19] Y. Park, C. Lee, C. Lee, J. Lim, S. Han, M. Park, and S.-J. Cho. RGBDroid: a novel response-based approach to Android privilege escalation attacks. In *Proceedings of the 5th USENIX conference on Large-Scale Exploits and Emergent Threats*, LEET'12, pages 9–9, Berkeley, CA, USA, 2012. USENIX Association.

[20] G. Portokalidis, P. Homburg, K. Anagnostakis, and H. Bos. Paranoid Android: versatile protection for smartphones. In *Proceedings of the 26th Annual Computer Security Applications Conference*, ACSAC '10, pages 347–356, New York, NY, USA, 2010. ACM.

[21] M. Rajagopalan, M. Hiltunen, T. Jim, and R. Schlichting. Authenticated system calls. In *Proceedings of the 2005 International Conference on Dependable Systems and Networks*, pages 358–367, June 2005.

[22] R. Sailer, X. Zhang, T. Jaeger, and L. van Doorn. Design and implementation of a TCG-based integrity measurement architecture. In *Proceedings of the 13th conference on USENIX Security Symposium - Volume 13*, SSYM'04, pages 16–16, Berkeley, CA, USA, 2004. USENIX Association.

[23] A. Shabtai, Y. Fledel, and Y. Elovici. Securing Android-powered mobile devices using SELinux. *Security Privacy, IEEE*, 8(3):36–44, may-june 2010.

[24] S. Smalley and R. Craig. Security enhanced (se) android: Bringing flexible mac to android. In *NDSS*, 2013.

[25] A. Srivastava, A. Lanzi, J. Giffin, and D. Balzarotti. Operating system interface obfuscation and the revealing of hidden operations. In *Proceedings of the 8th international conference on Detection of intrusions and malware, and vulnerability assessment*, DIMVA'11, pages 214–233, Berlin, Heidelberg, 2011. Springer-Verlag.

[26] T. Vidas, D. Votipka, and N. Christin. All your droid are belong to us: a survey of current Android attacks. In *Proceedings of the 5th USENIX conference on Offensive technologies*, WOOT'11, pages 10–10, Berkeley, CA, USA, 2011. USENIX Association.

[27] K. Xu, D. Yao, Q. Ma, and A. Crowell. Detecting infection onset with behavior-based policies. In *5th International Conference on Network and System Security (NSS)*, pages 57–64, 2011.

[28] R. Xu, H. Saïdi, and R. Anderson. Aurasium: practical policy enforcement for Android applications. In *Proceedings of the 21st USENIX conference on Security symposium*, Security'12, pages 27–27, Berkeley, CA, USA, 2012. USENIX Association.

[29] L. K. Yan and H. Yin. DroidScope: seamlessly reconstructing the os and dalvik semantic views for dynamic Android malware analysis. In *Proceedings of the 21st USENIX conference on Security symposium*, Security'12, pages 29–29, Berkeley, CA, USA, 2012. USENIX Association.

[30] Y. Zhou and X. Jiang. Dissecting Android malware: Characterization and evolution. In *2012 IEEE Symposium on Security and Privacy (SP)*, pages 95–109, may 2012.

RopSteg: Program Steganography with Return Oriented Programming

Kangjie Lu
Georgia Institute of
Technology
kjlu@gatech.edu

Siyang Xiong
D'crypt Pte Ltd
xiong_siyang@d-
crypt.com

Debin Gao
Singapore Management
University
dbgao@smu.edu.sg

ABSTRACT

Many software obfuscation techniques have been proposed to hide program instructions or logic and to make reverse engineering hard. In this paper, we introduce a new property in software obfuscation, namely *program steganography*, where certain instructions are "diffused" in others in such a way that they are non-existent until program execution. Program steganography does not raise suspicion in program analysis, and conforms to the $W \oplus X$ and mandatory code signing security mechanisms. We further implement RopSteg, a novel software obfuscation system, to provide (to a certain degree) program steganography using return-oriented programming. We apply RopSteg to eight Windows executables and evaluate the program steganography property in the corresponding obfuscated programs. Results show that RopSteg achieves program steganography with a small overhead in program size and execution time. RopSteg is the first attempt of driving return-oriented programming from the "dark side", i.e., using return-oriented programming in a non-attack application. We further discuss limitations of RopSteg in achieving program steganography.

Categories and Subject Descriptors

D.4.6 [**OPERATING SYSTEMS**]: Security and Protection

Keywords

Code obfuscation, watermarking, program steganography, return-oriented programming

1. INTRODUCTION

Many software program obfuscation techniques have been proposed to deliberately conceal various aspects of an executable to make reverse engineering hard [7, 11, 20, 15, 26]. These techniques are powerful in terms of their robustness, semantic-preservation, obscurity, resilience, stealth, and other properties [7, 11, 15]. However, most existing techniques

raise suspicion in program analysis, and may violate the $W \oplus X$ or mandatory code signing security mechanisms [14].

Software watermarking [6], on the other hand, tries to embed a secret message into a cover program, which is very similar to the concept of steganography, the art and science of hiding information. Although both software obfuscation and software watermarking are forms of security through obscurity, a notable difference in them are 1) software obfuscation tries to *transform* something while software watermarking tries to *hide* something; 2) target of software obfuscation is usually executable code in the original program, while that of software watermarking is usually additional secret message (data) that is not part of the original program.

This paper introduces a new property in software obfuscation, which, in some sense, combines the ideas of traditional software obfuscation and watermarking, namely *program steganography*. Program steganography refers to an interesting property that part of the executable code is hidden. It differs from existing software obfuscation in that the instructions are hidden instead of being transformed. It also differs from existing software watermarking in that part of the executable code in the original program, instead of some additional information, is hidden.

We do not introduce program steganography just for the sake of combining the ideas of existing obfuscation and watermarking techniques. Program steganography has some specific and useful properties absent from existing approaches, out of which the most important ones being not attracting attention to itself, a well documented advantage of steganography over cryptography. Even the strongest existing software obfuscation, in which instructions are encrypted to make static analysis next to impossible (e.g., [26, 20]), cannot hide the existence of the instruction sequence and leaves suspicion to program analysis. Program steganography, on the other hand, completely hides the existence of certain instructions from static analysis and raises no suspicion or attention. This is also different from self-generating code where instructions to be executed are generated by the program itself on the fly, which violates the $W \oplus X$ security mechanism and is not suitable in mandatory code signing environments (e.g., iOS). Note that we do not include resistance to *dynamic* analysis as a necessary property of program steganography, as the hidden instructions are intended to be executed in a dynamic run.

One of the reasons why program steganography has not been widely studied is its difficulty. It was not clear how some instructions to be executed could be completely hidden in an executable. However, steganography has been well studied to embed secret into documents, images, audio and video files, and so thidehe concept behind it and the techniques to achieve it are well known. The gap lies in the availability of a special technique to achieve program steganography. We propose that using return-oriented programming [3, 4, 17, 19, 12] could be a good way to close this gap.

Return-oriented programming (ROP) [19] has attracted a lot of research attention in the last few years. The idea of using unintended gadgets (unintended instruction sequences ending with `ret`) in ROP is to disassemble instructions from the middle of some inhidetended instruction to perform attacks. Such instructions are "hidden" in the sense that they were not intended to exist when the binary was created, and therefore a disassembler would never pick them up. If we could *intentionally* "diffuse" some instructions into such an unintended form, they will be hidden and therefore non-existent until program execution.

We design and implement *RopSteg*, a novel software obfuscation technique that hides the existence of program instructions while providing (to a certain degree) program steganography. More specifically, RopSteg hides instructions from static analysis while conforming to the $W \oplus X$ and mandatory code signing security mechanisms with minimal suspicions raised. We additionally evaluate RopSteg by applying it to different Windows executables, including desktop application, server program, and malware. Results show that RopSteg achieves program steganography with a small overhead in program size and execution time.

Note that RopSteg applies the concept of ROP in a completely new way. Return-oriented programming had always been considered as an attacking technique in previous research, where an attacker locates and uses unintended gadgets found in a given and vulnerable program. RopSteg, on the other hand, turns instructions into unintended form and embeds the ROP code into a program. In this respect, RopSteg is the first proposal of driving return-oriented programming from the "dark side", i.e., using return-oriented programming in a non-attack application[1].

In summary, our paper makes the following contributions.

- Introducing a new property in software obfuscation, namely, program steganography, to hide the existence of program instructions.

- Designing and implementing RopSteg, a novel technique for providing program steganography using return-oriented programming.

- Evaluating RopSteg by applying it to different Windows programs.

- First proposal of driving return-oriented programming from the "dark side".

2. PROGRAM STEGANOGRAPHY AND RELATED WORK

In this section, we first introduce the new property in software obfuscation, namely, *program steganography*. Due to its close relationship with a few previously proposed concepts, we also present a summary of these related works as well as their differences from program steganography.

Given a piece of executable code, program steganography refers to the result of hiding part of the program's functionality and the corresponding instructions such that they are non-existent till the point of execution. Figure 1 shows a simple example of a program segment that exhibits program steganography. Static analysis of this code segment reveals 100% disassembled instructions (see bottom of Figure 1). These instructions are prepared by a normal compiler and can be easily disassembled. However, the exact same byte sequence could also be interpreted in a different way to obtain completely different instructions (see top of Figure 1). A normal disassembler would not be able to pick up these instructions. They are hidden till the point of execution.

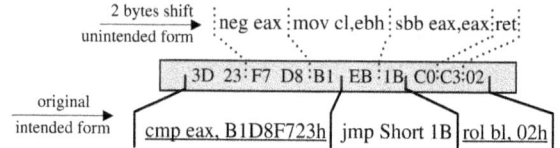

Figure 1: Program steganography example

Software watermarking.

Software watermarking is the closest to our property of program steganography. In software watermarking, some information is embedded in the software program to be reliably located and extracted [9, 8]. This is similar to program steganography in the sense that something is hidden in a program. The main difference is on the target of hiding — software watermarking usually hides a piece of information, e.g., the author's identity, which is a foreign object to the program; program steganography, on the other hand, hides some of its own instructions. The information hidden by software watermarking needs to be extracted via some special means, while instructions hidden by program steganography will be executed during program's normal runs.

Software obfuscation.

Many software program obfuscation techniques have been proposed to deliberately conceal various aspects of an executable to make reverse engineering hard. These techniques are powerful in terms of their robustness, semantic preservation, obscurity, resilience, stealth, etc [7, 11, 15, 26], most of which are designed to transform readable code into obfuscated code that is hard to understand or reverse engineer.

Two types of software obfuscation techniques are worth noting due to their close relationship with program steganography. One is to make disassembling of machine code difficult [11, 20, 15] so that only a small portion gets disassembled. Although in some sense program steganography also tries to hide information from the disassembler, it does it in such a way that the disassembler believes that it succeeds in disassembling 100% of the binary code, although the fact is that there are still instructions hidden.

Another work in software obfuscation technique applies encryption to some of the instructions so that they are hidden without a key. Encryption provides very strong protection; however, it always leaves suspicion to program analysis and attracts attention. Program steganography has a very similar objective, but tries to achieve it without attracting attention from the analyzer by hiding the existence of the instructions from static analysis. Program steganography could be considered a new property in software obfuscation.

---

[1]RopSteg could also be used by malware writers to hide malicious instructions to evade detection.

Self-generating code.

Executable code can be generated on the fly before they are executed, hiding themselves from static analysis of the program binary [20]. The difference between self-generating code and program steganography is subtle, in that self-generating code comes to live (e.g., code placed on writable and executable memory) before they are executed, while instructions hidden by program steganography never come to live. Even if program analysis is performed right before, during, or after the execution, the hidden instruction in program steganography never "exists" in any noticeable form and no self-modifying is introduced. This makes program steganography suitable in mandatory code signing environments, e.g., iOS, where self-generating code is not allowed.

Document, image, audio, and video steganography.

Steganography [2, 23] is a well studied technology widely applied to documents, images, audio, and video files. Steganography refers to hiding information in these files, while the information to be hidden is usually a foreign object, just like that in software watermarking. Program steganography, on the other hand, tries to hide part of itself.

Deniable encryption.

Analyzing the example in Figure 1, one may notice that the bytes in code segment are interpreted two times in two different ways, a concept similar to deniable encryption [16, 13]. Deniable encryption provides multiple ways of explaining a single ciphertext so that the creator of the message could deny having produced it. Inspired by deniable encryption, one way to provide program steganography is to prepare multiple ways of explaining some binary code, out of which one is given to the disassembler to make it believe that the code segment has been 100% disassembled, and others are used to execute the hidden instructions. Unfortunately, encryption is not a solution because we do not want to attract attention or to generate new code upon decryption.

Return-oriented programming.

Return-oriented programming (ROP) had been proposed as an attacking technique to perform arbitrary computation without injected code [3, 4, 5, 17]. The idea behind ROP is to disassemble the program under attack at different offsets and to execute the new instructions to perform arbitrary computation. This idea matches with the example shown in Figure 1 in that the hidden instructions could be those disassembled at a new offset. Our proposed system, RopSteg, actually applies the idea of ROP to achieve program steganography; see the next section for an overview.

3. OVERVIEW OF RopSteg

Having introduced the concept of program steganography, we now turn to our novel system RopSteg that provides the property of program steganography. RopSteg takes as input the binary instructions of a program P and some sequence of instructions I from P to be hidden. RopSteg tries to hide these instructions in a way that they are non-existent until being executed, i.e., I is hidden from static analysis but visible in a dynamic run. Note that as discussed in Section 2, RopSteg does not use encryption or dynamic code generation, and thus conforms to the $W \oplus X$ and mandatory code signing security mechanisms.

Figure 2 shows an overview of RopSteg and the four steps in which the obfuscated program executes. Code block 2 (ending at `addr2`) denotes I, which is the instruction sequence to be hidden. RopSteg modifies Code block 3 (starting at `addr1`) such that I is embedded in unintended form. RopSteg then replaces I with an *ROP board* which performs the control transfer. When the ROP code embedded at `addr1` finishes execution, control returns to `addr2`. To combat static analysis of finding values of `addr1` and `addr2`, RopSteg uses an *ROP generator* to dynamically calculate the values of them and to store them in memory.

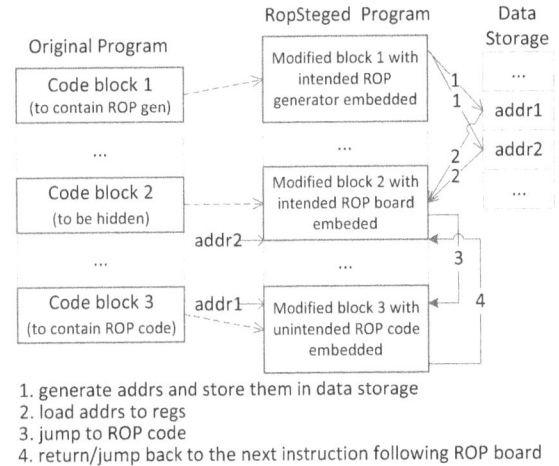

1. generate addrs and store them in data storage
2. load addrs to regs
3. jump to ROP code
4. return/jump back to the next instruction following ROP board

Figure 2: An overview of RopSteg

Figure 3 shows an example where I = `<neg eax; sbb eax, eax; ret>`[2]. RopSteg first finds an unintended form of I. This could be easy when I is short and when P is large, but it could also be impossible unless we insert additional instructions into P, as shown in Figure 3b at `addr1`. After the unintended form of I is located, RopSteg replaces the original I with an ROP board (see Figure 3c), which loads `addr1` into `eax`, stores `addr2` on the stack, and jumps to `addr1`. In the end, RopSteg inserts an ROP generator (see Figure 3d) to dynamically calculate and store `addr1` and `addr2`.

4. DESIGN OF RopSteg

As explained in Section 3, RopSteg performs three main modifications on P, namely the embedded I in the form of ROP code, the ROP board to facilitate control transfers, and the ROP generator to dynamically generate ROP gadgets. In this section, we present details of these three parts and outline the binary rewriting to perform the modification.

4.1 Finding and constructing unintended ROP code

Previous work on ROP has demonstrated that gadgets and unintended code can be found efficiently and automatically [19, 18]. However, RopSteg uses ROP in a different setting in which the execution of ROP is legitimate and planned. RopSteg could modify P to plant seeds for ROP execution. Therefore, the algorithm to find and construct unintended ROP code is different from any previous work.

---

[2]The return or return-like instruction was inserted at the end to facility a return after I finishes execution.

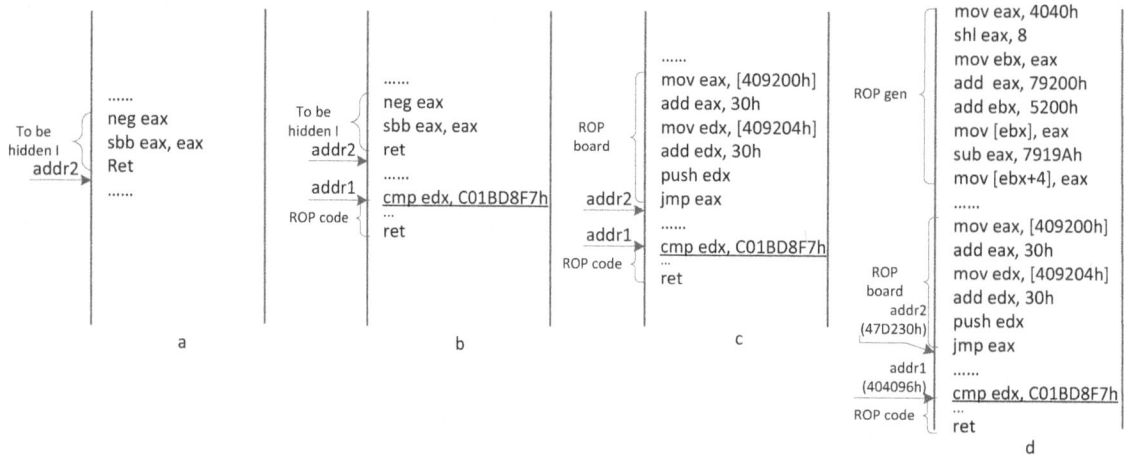

Figure 3: Using ROP for program steganography

RopSteg first removes I from P to obtain P^-. It then uses a modified Galileo algorithm G to find a sequence of candidate instructions C that fully or partially match with I. For each $c \in C$ that does not fully match with I, RopSteg looks for I' that is semantically equivalent with I and P' that is semantically equivalent with P^- such that the resulting c' fully matches with I'.

4.1.1 A modified Galileo algorithm G

Unlike the original Galileo algorithm presented when return-oriented programming was first introduced [19], our modified algorithm G is flexible enough to be able to find *partial matches* of the unintended form of I. Refer to an example shown in Figure 4 c-i where I = <F7 D8 1B C0 C3>. Upon searching for I in P^-, we realized that no exact match exists, and therefore G output a partial match c = <EB 1B> (a one-byte match). G then inserts three instructions into P^- to form P' such that I' = <F7 D8 B1 EB 1B C0 C3> is semantically equivalent with I and has an exact match in P'.

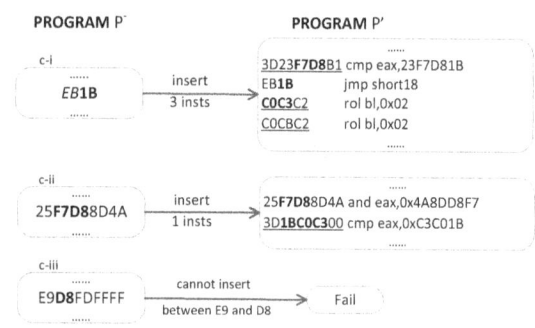

Figure 4: Partial matches found by G

It may sound simple, but G is much more complicated than a substring search to maximize matches. For example, G might consider a partial match c = <E9 D8 FD FF FF>. However, no matter how we insert additional instructions into P^- to produce a semantically equivalent P', the byte immediately proceeding the matching byte D8 can never change, which means that the resulting c' will always have E9 proceeding the matching byte D8. This happens because the matching byte D8 appears in the middle of an instruction instead of locating at the beginning as in c-i in Figure 4.

Note that here we only insert instructions when transforming from P^- to P' and from I to I' (additions). G rules out a candidate match c containing a matching byte b if

- $!\text{isLast}(b, P^-) \cap !\text{isLast}(b, I) \cap \lhd(b, P^-) \neq \lhd(b, I)$, and;

- $!\text{isFirst}(b, P^-) \cap !\text{isFirst}(b, I) \cap \rhd(b, P^-) \neq \rhd(b, I)$.

where $\text{isFirst}(b, X)$ and $\text{isLast}(b, X)$ denote that b is the first or the last byte in the corresponding instruction in context X, respectively; and $\lhd(b, X)$ and $\rhd(b, X)$ denote the byte proceeding or following b in context X, respectively. In Figure 4, c-iii is filtered out because we cannot insert bytes between E9 and D8. After finding the valid candidates, RopSteg arranges them in a sequence C according to the following considerations (in order of importance).

1. number of instructions c covers;

2. number of matching bytes c covers;

3. number of matching bytes that satisfy $\text{isFirst}(b, P^-)$;

4. number of matching bytes that satisfy $!\text{isFirst}(b, P^-) \cap !\text{isLast}(b, P^-)$;

5. number of matching bytes that satisfy $\text{isLast}(b, P^-)$.

It it easier to construct I' when b is the first byte in an instruction in P^-, and that is why the last three counts are in the order in which they are presented above. We explain this in more detail in the next subsection. In the examples presented in Figure 4, c-ii ranks higher than c-i because c-ii matches one more byte than c-i. With all the candidate matches found and arranged in a ranking sequence, RopSteg proceeds to construct I' and P' such that there exists a corresponding c' that fully matches I'.

4.1.2 Constructing equivalent versions of I by inserting ineffective instructions

RopSteg constructs semantically equivalent P' and I' by inserting *ineffective instructions*, which have no effect in the semantics of the corresponding execution context.

Context Insensitive	Context Sensitive	
Instructions	Instructions	Context
mov edi, edi	add eax,????	CF
	sub ebx,????	
or eax, eax	cmp ebx,????	CF/ZF/SF/OF/AF/PF
push ebp; pop ebp	test eax,????	CF/ZF/SF/OF/AF/PF
xchg eax, ebx; xchg eax, ebx	mov eax,????	eax not in use

Table 1: Two types of ineffective instructions

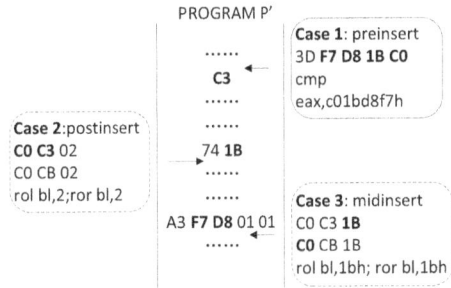

Figure 5: Locations of the matching/unmatching bytes in c

Ineffective instructions.

RopSteg uses two types of ineffective instructions, context insensitive ones and context sensitive ones. Table 1 shows some examples of ineffective instructions RopSteg uses (where ? denotes a "don't care" byte).

Ineffective instructions that are context insensitive never change anything regardless of the execution context, e.g., <mov eax,eax>. On the other hand, context sensitive ones only possess the ineffectiveness property in some particular execution context, e.g., <add eax,????; sub eax,????> is ineffective when flag CF is not in use.

The use of ineffective instructions is a well-studied area, and they have been widely used in previous research work to produce polymorphic and metamorphic malware [21, 10, 1]. RopSteg takes advantage of the existing work in this area and constructs a database of ineffective instructions, which currently contains 230 entries (still evolving though). It is our future work to explore other types of ineffective instructions, and to experiment inserting more context sensitive ones to P^-. Expanding the search space of ineffective instruction will result in higher success rates of RopSteg in providing program steganography.

Inserting ineffective instructions into P^-.

Inserting ineffective instructions into P^- is one of the most complicated tasks in RopSteg. Here we first discuss the sensitive context check, and then explain the different types of instructions to be inserted.

RopSteg performs the context sensitive analysis with the classical *def-use* chain analysis [24]. First, we delineate the context from the insertion point to the end of the function (taking direct jumps into consideration). If there is any use of the resources (e.g., the flags) or an indirect jump instruction before a re-def of the resources, we consider the resources is sensitive in the context; otherwise insensitive.

To explain the different types of ineffective instructions to be inserted, we consider three cases shown in Figure 5 where I = F7 D8 1B C0 C3, i.e., <neg eax; sbb eax, eax; ret>.

The first case is when a matched byte is the first in an instruction in P^- before which an unmatched byte exists, i.e., $\triangleleft(b, P^-) \neq \triangleleft(b, I) \cap \text{isFirst}(b, P^-)$. To increase the matching between P^- and I, we insert an instruction right before the matched one in P^- where the last byte of the instruction inserted is $\triangleleft(b, I)$. As shown in case 1 in Figure 5, C3 is the original matching byte. RopSteg inserts an instruction ending with <F7 D8 1B> to increase matching with I.

In this first case, we always manage to find such an instruction from our database of ineffective instructions. The catch here is that our requirement on the instruction is at its last (few) byte(s), and there exists ineffective instructions

where the last few bytes are "don't cares". With our def-use chain analysis, RopSteg selects (context insensitive or sensitive) ineffective instructions, e.g., mov ebx, ????, where ebx is not in use in the context. Note that this case also corresponds to the third criteria when ordering the candidate matches (see Section 4.1.1).

The second case is an exact opposite, i.e., when a matched byte is the last byte in an instruction in P^-, after which an unmatched byte exists ($\triangleright(b, P^-) \neq \triangleright(b, I) \cap \text{isLast}(b, P^-)$). In this case, RopSteg tries to insert an ineffective instruction right after the matched instruction; however, such an ineffective instruction is the most difficult to find because its first byte is given as $\triangleright(b, I)$ (e.g., C0 in case 2 in Figure 5). The database of ineffective instructions we have right now does not contain one for every possible initial byte, and therefore the success rate in this case is about 36% (our ineffective instruction database covers about 36% opcode). Note that this case corresponds to the fifth criteria when ordering the candidate matches (see Section 4.1.1).

The third case deals with a more general scenario where a matched byte appears in the middle of an instruction ($\triangleright(b, P^-) \neq \triangleright(b, I) \cap \text{!isFirst}(b, P^-) \cap \text{!isLast}(b, P^-)$). The successful rate of this case varies a lot depending on the actual scenario, and it usually takes the longest time to search for an ineffective instruction. That is why we give it the second lowest ranking as discussed in Section 4.1.1. In case 3 of Figure 5, we could not find a single ineffective instruction that meets all the requirements.

We also exercise care during the insertion process to minimize suspicions for steganalysis. For example, we only insert ineffective instructions that are commonly used in normal programs (e.g., jecxz is not used), we insert additional instructions to make instruction sequences look normal (e.g., instead of having <push ebp; pop ebp>, we change it to <push ebp; pop eax; mov ebp, eax>). The insertions usually result in additional unmatched bytes in I and c. We perform additional check to make sure the newly inserted unmatched bytes constitute an ineffective instruction in I.

4.2 ROP Board

After constructing I' and its unintended form, the next step is to transfer control to the unintended gadgets. As shown in Figure 3, ROP board performs this assuming addr1 (address of the unintended code) and addr2 (address of the instruction after the original I) are already stored in memory (what the ROP generator is supposed to do, see Section 4.3). To make it difficult for static analysis to detect the ROP board, RopSteg has multiple ways of accessing data storage in order to load them into registers. For example, the address of memory storage is indirectly calculated rather than an immediate as shown in Figure 3. After loading the addresses into registers, ROP board makes an indirect jump to `addr1`. `addr2` might be loaded onto the stack if the ROP code ends with a `ret` instead of an indirect jump.

4.3 ROP Generator

With I' constructed and ROP board connecting P' with I', RopSteg manages to hide I in unintended form. However, `addr1` and `addr2` could raise suspicion in steganalysis; therefore, RopSteg introduces ROP generator to make such analysis difficult. As shown in Figure 3, ROP generator dynamically calculates the address of the ROP code and the address to which ROP code returns, and stores them in the data segment. In the ASLR environment, the address of data segment is randomized. RopSteg adopts a common way, i.e., `call-pop` instruction sequence, used in position-independent executable (`PIE`) to load the value of the current `eip` into `eax`. By adding the offset to `eax`, we can get the randomized address of the data segment.

4.4 Binary Rewriting

After successfully constructing I and connecting I' and its original context, RopSteg constructs the new binary via binary rewriting. Although we envision that RopSteg could be integrated with a compiler to produce the new executable from source code directly, for the purpose of finer-grained performance evaluation, we implemented RopSteg as a standalone component using binary rewriting in the current version and leave the integration with a compiler as future work.

As shown in Figure 3, existing code section needs to be expanded to make room for new instructions. Operands of jump and call instructions, direct or relative, need to be relocated. When the expansion goes beyond the original code section, other sections after it have to be moved backward.

If the program is ASLR-enabled with relocation tables, the binary rewriting would be much easier as the positions of the code blocks could be changed by simply adjusting the addresses in direct call/jump instructions and modifying the entries in the relocation table. Similarly, in a PIE-enabled program, we can simply identify the program counter related instructions and adjust the relative addresses in them to address the offset problem. The binary rewriting for these two scenarios is easy and we will not elaborate it here. When the program strips the relocation information or disables PIE, further adjustments are required to the following code, which is challenging.

In order to handle such case, accurate disassembling would be the most important part. We use IDA Pro (together with NDISASM[3]) to obtain function boundary information and the set of potential targets of branch instructions. And then we use *binary sled*, inspired by binary stirring [25], to address the offset problem of binary rewriting. The basic idea in binary stirring is to put the extended blocks in a new `.text` segment. When control is transferred to the original code (with lookup table), it redirects control to the corresponding code in the new `.text` segment.

In order not to raise suspicion for steganalysis, we perform three additional steps. First, our inserted code block could be put either in the old `.text` or the new one. Second, RopSteg gathers the "innocent blocks" that are relatively large (e.g., greater than 100 bytes) but don't contain any

jump instructions (the locality of jump instruction might raise suspicions) and put them in the new `.text` segment. After that, the original innocent blocks in the old `.text` can be used as a container to put our inserted code. Lastly, the indirect binary sled makes use of indirect jump/call instructions to transfer control to the corresponding block in the new `.text` segment. In this way, every code block could potentially be the block that contains our inserted code, and steganalysis is difficult.

5. EXPERIMENTS AND EVALUATION

In this section, we evaluate the effectiveness of RopSteg in providing program steganography in a few scenarios, one in hiding a secret algorithm, one in hiding some malicious code, and others in hiding random instructions. In addition, we analyze the overhead of the resulting binary in both program size and execution time.

Our experiments were performed with Microsoft Windows 7 ultimate on a desktop computer with AMD Phenom II X6 1090T CPU at 3.21GHz and 4GB of RAM. We implement RopSteg in C/C++ with around 7000 LOC.

5.1 Experiments

5.1.1 Protecting a secret algorithm

In this experiment, we apply RopSteg to hide the quicksort algorithm in `searchcand.exe` (a program we developed as part of RopSteg to search for unintended gadgets).

The original quick sort in `searchcand.exe` corresponds to 90 instructions or 266 bytes. We choose five critical instruction sequences (core variable calculation, control flow prediction, function calls, etc.) each containing one to three instructions for hiding, see Figure 6.

5.1.2 Hiding malicious code

Another use of RopSteg could be to hide malicious code. We select `trojan.dll` (the main malicious module of malware GhOst) as the example, whose functionality includes FileManagement, ScreenMonitor, KeyMonitor, RemoteShell, and SystemManager, and use RopSteg to hide virus signatures in it. The signature of `trojan.dll` was located with MyCCL (a tool used to identify malicious feature) and is shown in Table 2[4].

Location	Instructions	Machine code
0x000000DB	mov eax,[ebp-118h]; push eax	8B85E8FEFFFF 50
0x00000CA4	mov edx,[ebp+8]; call [edx]	8B5508 FF12
0x00000800	and [esi+0Dh], 0EEh;	80660DEE
0x00006980	mov edx,[ebp+8]; mov eax,[ecx*4+edx+4]; add eax, 1	8B5508 8B448A04 83C010

Table 2: Signature of trojan

5.1.3 Hiding random instruction sequences

We pick six more common x86 Windows programs (see Table 3) and randomly select 100 different instruction sequences in each of the eight programs to hide. The instruc-

---

[3]http://www.nasm.us/doc/nasmdoca.html

[4]Here we focus on the signature in code section only and ignore that in the data segment.

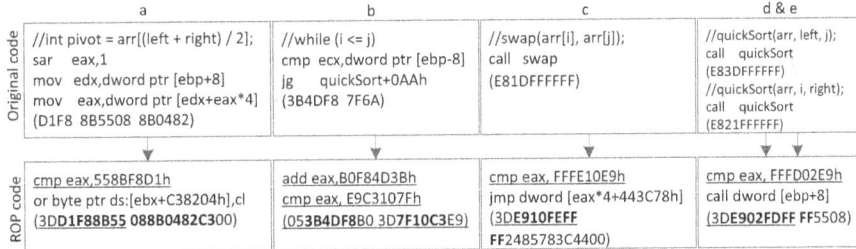

	a	b	c	d & e

Original code	//int pivot = arr[(left + right) / 2];
	sar eax,1
	mov edx,dword ptr [ebp+8]
	mov eax,dword ptr [edx+eax*4]
	(D1F8 8B5508 8B0482)
		//while (i <= j)
		cmp ecx,dword ptr [ebp-8]
		jg quickSort+0AAh
		(3B4DF8 7F6A)
			//swap(arr[i], arr[j]);
			call swap
			(E81DFFFFFF)
				//quickSort(arr, left, j);
				call quickSort
				(E83DFFFFFF)
				//quickSort(arr, i, right);
				call quickSort
				(E821FFFFFF)

ROP code	cmp eax,558BF8D1h
	or byte ptr ds:[ebx+C38204h],cl
	(3DD1F88B55 088B0482C300)
		add eax,B0F84D3Bh
		cmp eax, E9C3107Fh
		(053B4DF8B0 3D7F10C3E9)
			cmp eax, FFFE10E9h
			jmp dword [eax*4+443C78h]
			(3DE910FEFF FF2485783C4400)
				cmp eax, FFFD02E9h
				call dword [ebp+8]
				(3DE902FDFF FF5508)

Figure 6: RopSteg on quick-sort

tion sequences ranges from 2 to 13 bytes in length and cover different types of instructions including load/store, arithmetic, conditional branch, function call, system call, etc. Results are shown in 5.2.

5.2 Results and evaluation

All instruction sequences were successfully hidden by RopSteg. We use a linear sweep disassembler, objdump (Windows version), and a recursive disassembler, IDA pro, to disassemble the obfuscated programs. Neither could locate any of the hidden instruction sequences.

For the experiment of Section 5.1.2, we use Kaspersky, Macfee, and 360 Anti-Virus to scan the resulting binaries. Results show that none of them could identify any of the signatures. This also confirms our intuition that ROP generator and ROP board use very common instructions (e.g., load, store, and arithmetic operations) which, at least, does not raise suspicions on existing anti-virus engines.

In the following sections, we show more detailed results and our analysis on the results of these experiments.

5.2.1 Short I

One interesting finding is that the shorter I is, the more likely RopSteg succeeds in hiding it. This is intuitive as the shorter I is, the more likely that G finds relatively long candidate matches, making it easier to find P' and I'.

Figure 6 shows the five instruction sequences from search-cand.exe that were successfully hidden and their corresponding ROP code in unintended form (bold face). We also show the corresponding machine code in square brackets. Instructions underlined are ineffective instructions RopSteg inserts.

It shows that longer I (cases A and B) results in fewer matching candidates (less than 100 for case A and zero for case B), while short ones (cases C, D, and E) result in more than 500 matching candidates. Therefore, a useful strategy RopSteg uses is to divide I into short sequences (usually fewer than 5 bytes long) that only have one or two instructions to obtain high succeed rate (100% in our experiments).

5.2.2 Size and runtime overhead

The insertion of ROP generator, ROP board, and ROP code are the main contributors to the increase in program size, which usually add about 30 bytes, 25 bytes, and fewer than 10 bytes, respectively. Table 3 presents the increase in size of the program when 100 instruction sequences are hidden (without reusing the ROP generator). We find that the increase in bytes remains more or less a constant, which translates to a small percentage for relatively large programs (except one in our experiments).

Program	Original size (bytes)	Size increment (bytes)	Size increment (percentage)
AcroRd32.exe	806941	5613	0.70%
iexplore.exe	13129	6410	48.80 %
java.exe	93240	5836	6.26%
calc.exe	75440	5890	7.80%
ftpsvc2.dll	100475	5717	5.69%
trojan.dll	100864	5712	5.66%
searchcand.exe	1335472	5507	0.41%
shell32.dll	2075888	4887	0.24%

Table 3: Size increment

We monitor the overhead of specific operations performed by trojan.dll to get an idea of the runtime overhead. Table 4 shows the time to execute five different operations (average taken on 100 runs) before and after applying RopSteg. We notice that the runtime overhead resulted from our modification to the Trojan is small.

Operation	Original (ms)	Modified (ms)
FileManagement	5313	5344
ScreenMonitor	62	62
KeyMonitor	31	40
RemoteShell	281	319
SystemManager	78	94

Table 4: Runtime overhead

6. CONCLUSION AND LIMITATION

In this paper, we design and implement RopSteg to make program steganography using return-oriented programming. We show that RopSteg successfully hide program instructions such that they are hidden from static analysis. Here we discuss the potential limitations of RopSteg.

Dynamic analysis.

As discussed in Section 1, program steganography does not intend to hide instructions from dynamic analysis. The hidden instructions will eventually get executed, and dynamic analysis could reveal their existence. There have been proposed methods [22, 20] to resist dynamic analysis, and we consider combining them with RopSteg a potential future direction of our research.

Compatibility with ROP defenses.

In the past several years, many ROP defense and detection techniques have been proposed. As RopSteg makes use of ROP to achieve steganography, it is incompatible with ROP defense and could be detected as malicious at run time. We argue that this is mainly due to the fact that ROP has always been considered in the "dark side" in the literature, which is no longer true with the introduction of RopSteg. Future ROP defenses would then need to carefully differentiate between ROP in attack and ROP in program steganography.

7. REFERENCES

[1] K. G. Anagnostakis and E. P. Markatos. An empirical study of real-world polymorphic code injection attacks. In *In USENIX Workshop on Large-Scale Exploits and Emergent Threats*, 2009.

[2] D. C. B. Anckaert, B. De Sutter and K. D. Bosschere. Steganography for executables and code transformation signatures. *Lecture Notes in Computer Science*, pages 425–439, 2005.

[3] E. Buchanan, R. Roemer, H. Shacham, and S. Savage. When good instructions go bad: generalizing return-oriented programming to risc. In *Proceedings of the 15th ACM conference on Computer and communications security (CCS 2008)*, Alexandria, VA, USA, Oct.27-31, 2008.

[4] S. Checkoway, L. Davi, A. Dmitrienko, A.-R. Sadeghi, H. Shacham, and M. Winandy. Return-oriented programming without returns. In *Proceedings of the 17th ACM conference on Computer and Communications Security (CCS 2010)*, Chicago, IL, USA, Oct 4-8, 2010.

[5] S. Checkoway, A. J. Feldman, B. Kantor, J. A. Halderman, E. W. Felten, and H. Shacham. Can dres provide long-lasting security the case of return-oriented programming and the avc advantage. In *Proceedings of the 2009 Electronic Voting Technology Workshop/Workshop on Trustworthy Elections (EVT/WOTE09)*, Montreal, Canada, Aug. 10-11, 2009.

[6] C. T. Christian Collberg. Software watermarking: models and dynamic embeddings. In *Proceedings of the 26th ACM SIGPLAN-SIGACT Symposium on Principles of Programming Languages (POPL 99)*, San Antonio, Texas, USA, Jan. 20-22, 1999.

[7] C. Collberg, C. Thomborson, and D. Low. A taxonomy of obfuscating transformations. 1997.

[8] C. S. Collberg and C. Thomborson. Watermarking, tamper-proofing, and obfuscation - tools for software protection. *IEEE Transactions on Software Engineering*, 28:735–746, 2002.

[9] P. COUSOT and R. COUSOT. An abstract interpretation-based framework for software watermarking. In *Proceedings of the 31st ACM SIGPLAN-SIGACT symposium on Principles of programming languages (POPL 2004)*, 2004.

[10] T. Detristan, T. Ulenspiegel, Y. Malcom, and M. S. V. Underduk. Polymorphic shellcode engine using spectrum analysis. *Phrack magazine, 9(61)*, Aug. 2003. http: //www.phrack.org/issues.html?issue=61&id=9.

[11] C. Linn and S. Debray. Obfuscation of executable code to improve resistance to static disassembly. In *Proceedings of 10ththe ACM Conference on Computer and Communications Security (CCS 2003)*, Washington, DC, USA, Oct. 27-30,2003.

[12] K. Lu, D. Zou, W. Wen, and D. Gao. Packed, printable, and polymorphic return-oriented programming. In *Proceedings of the 14th International Symposium on Recent Advances in Intrusion Detection (RAID 2011)*, Menlo Park, California, USA, September 2011.

[13] M. K. M. Klonowski, P. Kubiak. Practical deniable encryption. *LNCS, Springer*, 4910:599–609, 2008.

[14] C. Miller, D. Blazakis, D. DaiZovi, S. Esser, V. Iozzo, and R.-P. Weinmann. *iOS Hacker's Handbook*. Wiley, May 8, 2012.

[15] I. V. Popov, S. K. Debray, and G. R. Andrews. bi obfuscation using signals. In *Proceedings of the 16th USENIX Security Symposium (Security 2007)*, Boston, MA, USA, Aug 6-10,2007.

[16] M. N. R. Canetti, C. Dwork and R. Ostrovsky. Deniable encryption. In *Proceedings of the 17th Annual International Cryptology Conference (CRYPTO 1997)*, Santa Barbara, California, USA, August, 1997.

[17] R. Roemer, E. Buchanan, H. Shacham, and S. Savagm. Return-oriented programming: Systems,languages, and applications, 2009.

[18] E. J. Schwartz, T. Avgerinos, and D. Brumley. Q: exploit hardening made easy. In *Proceedings of the 20th USENIX conference on Security (Security'11)*, San Francisco, CA, USA, August, 2011.

[19] H. Shacham. The geometry of innocent flesh on the bone: return-into-libc without function calls (on the x86). In *Proceedings of the 14th ACM conference on Computer and Communications Security (CCS 2007)*, Alexandria, VA, USA, Oct. 29-Nov. 2,2007.

[20] M. Sharif, A. Lanzi, and W. Lee. Impeding malware analysis using conditional code obfuscation. In *Proceedings of the 16th Network and Distributed System Security Symposium (NDSS 2008)*, San Diego, CA, USA, Feb. 8-11, 2008.

[21] F. Skulason. 1260-the variable virus. 1990. Virus Bulletin.

[22] C. Song, P. Royal, and W. Lee. Impeding automated malware analysis with environment-sensitive malware. In *Proceedings of The 7th USENIX conference on Hot topics in Security (HotSec 2012)*, Bellevue, WA, USA, August 2012.

[23] G. R. Tadiparthi and T. Sueyoshi. A novel steganographic algorithm using animations as cover. *Information Technology and Systems in the Internet-Era*, 45:937–948, Nov, 2008.

[24] F. Tip. A survey of program slicing techniques. *JOURNAL OF PROGRAMMING LANGUAGES*, 3:121–189, 1995.

[25] R. Wartell, V. Mohan, K. W. Hamlen, and Z. Lin. Binary stirring: self-randomizing instruction addresses of legacy x86 binary code. In *Proceedings of the 2012 ACM conference on Computer and communications security (CCS 2012)*, Raleigh, NC, USA, Oct, 2012.

[26] Z. Wu, S. Gianvecchio, M. Xie, and H. Wang. Mimimorphism: A new approach to binary code obfuscation. In *Proceedings of the 17th ACM conference on Computer and Communications Security (CCS 2010)*, Chicago, IL, USA, Oct 4-8, 2010.

SobTrA: A Software-based Trust Anchor for ARM Cortex Application Processors

Julian Horsch, Sascha Wessel, Frederic Stumpf, and Claudia Eckert
Fraunhofer AISEC
Garching near Munich, Germany
{firstname.lastname}@aisec.fraunhofer.de

ABSTRACT

In this paper, we present SobTrA, a Software-based Trust Anchor for ARM Cortex-A processors to protect systems against software-based attacks. SobTrA enables the implementation of a software-based secure boot controlled by a third party independent from the manufacturer. Compared to hardware-based trust anchors, our concept provides some other advantages like being updateable and also usable on legacy hardware. The presented software-based trust anchor involves a trusted third party device, the verifier, locally connected to the untrusted device, e.g., via the microSD card slot of a smartphone. The verifier is verifying the integrity of the untrusted device by making sure that a piece of code is executed untampered on it using a timing-based approach. This code can then act as an anchor for a chain of trust similar to a hardware-based secure boot. Tests on our prototype showed that tampered and untampered execution of SobTrA can be clearly and reliably distinguished.

Categories and Subject Descriptors: D.4.6 [Operating Systems]: Security and Protection

Keywords: Software-based Trust Anchor; Self-checksumming Code; Smartphone; Mobile Security; ARM Architecture; Secure Boot

1. INTRODUCTION

A widely used technique to improve embedded devices security and especially smartphone security is a *secure boot process* [1], which can be used to enforce that only signed code can be executed on the smartphone. Core of a *hardware-based secure boot* is the software stored in the Read-Only Memory (ROM) of the device. This first stage of the boot process, called *root of trust* or *trust anchor*, is the first code to be executed at system start. The main task of this trust anchor is to *measure* the next stage, i.e., to verify its signature, and to load it if the verification was successful, building the basis for a *chain of trust* controlled by the manufacturer. The hardware-based secure boot approach has some downsides. First, it can only be utilized by the authority that has control over the ROM of the device. Second, the secure boot may not be added to legacy devices. Finally, if the trust anchor code has a vulnerability or the key is compromised, there is no way to restore the security properties on the affected devices.

To overcome the aforementioned disadvantages, we propose the concept of a Software-based Trust Anchor (SobTrA) as the basis for a *software-based secure boot*. The concept is developed for the ARM architecture. SobTrA provides the guarantee that a piece of code runs untampered on the booting platform. With that, the software-based secure boot can establish a chain of trust on the *initially* untrusted platform. In contrast to the hardware-based concept, the guarantee is not provided to the manufacturer but to a trusted device, the *verifier*, which is connected to the untrusted platform. The verifier could, for example, be realized as microSD card issued by a trusted third party (e.g., a company) and connected via Secure Digital Input Output (SDIO) or Serial Peripheral Interface (SPI) to the untrusted platform. Figure 1 shows our concept for a software-based secure boot process. The software-based secure boot can conceptually be initialized at any point during runtime of the system. The basic idea is to let the verifier measure the time the untrusted platform needs to perform a self-checksumming calculation initialized by some challenge. If the verifier receives the correct result in a timeframe which does not exceed some previously determined upper bound, the untrusted platform is verified successfully. Because of the strong hardware dependency, existing primitives for *software-based externally verifiable untampered execution* cannot be simply used to realize SobTrA on ARM.

This paper is organized as follows. In Section 2, we describe our attacker model and assumptions. In Section 3, we give an overview of existing research. Section 4 introduces the basic concept and protocol of SobTrA. The ARM

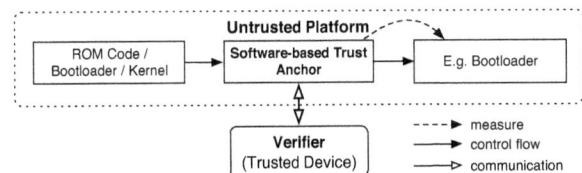

Figure 1: Software-based secure boot process

Cortex-A8 specific design and implementation of the SobTrA checksum function is presented in Section 5. Section 6 discusses the secure execution environment to be established in SobTrA. Finally, we present the experimental results on our prototype in Section 7 and conclude in Section 8.

2. ATTACKER MODEL & ASSUMPTIONS

The main goal of SobTrA is to prevent remote attacks, e.g., via the internet. Therefore, in our attacker model, the attacker has complete control over the software on the untrusted platform, but is not allowed to do hardware modifications or use hardware-based debug facilities (JTAG). Furthermore, DMA-based attacks are out-of-scope for this paper since they require platform specific countermeasures. Our assumptions for the execution of SobTrA are:

- The exact hardware configuration of the untrusted platform must be known to the verifier, including CPU type (e.g. ARM Cortex-A8) and clock speed.

- The verifier can be sure that the messages it receives are coming from the untrusted platform, excluding Man-In-The-Middle (MITM) attacks.

- No proxy or relay attack is possible. These are attacks where the untrusted platform uses the help of another device to fulfill the challenge from the verifier.

Especially in the context of a smartphone with a fixed, low-latency connection to the verifier and not allowing hardware modifications, these assumptions can be considered quite reasonable.

3. RELATED WORK

The first approach for externally-verifiable execution was proposed by Kennell and Jamieson in 2003 [9] for an x86 architecture platform. Their primitive, called *Genuinity*, is a *self-checksumming* function that additionally to its own memory layout includes performance counters, into the checksum. Unfortunately, the approach suffers from some serious problems as Shankar et al. describe in [17] (*substitution attacks*, see Section 4.2.1).

The first concept targeting embedded devices was SWATT, proposed in 2004 by Seshadri et al. [16] for an Atmel 8-bit microcontroller. SWATT tries to reduce the time needed for one iteration of the underlying checksum function main loop to a minimum, while still including some fast accessible CPU state inputs like the *program counter* and *status register*. This enables the verifier to measure even very small overheads introduced by attacker's code trying to circumvent the self-checksumming property. Another crucial advantage is that the execution time is only dependent on the number of iterations and not on the challenge itself. Therefore, it is *not* necessary to measure the "correct" time for a response from the untrusted platform for every challenge-response pair on a trusted device incorporating the target hardware. Later publications by Seshadri et al. refine the approach and adapt it to other architectures, namely x86 with *Pioneer* [15, 13] and TI MSP430 with *ICE* [14].

Newer publications introduce other concepts to implement checksum functions with similar properties. Either by generating the checksum function itself as the challenge [11] or by introducing a memory bottleneck during the checksum calculation to slow down the attacker's code [5, 7]. Downside

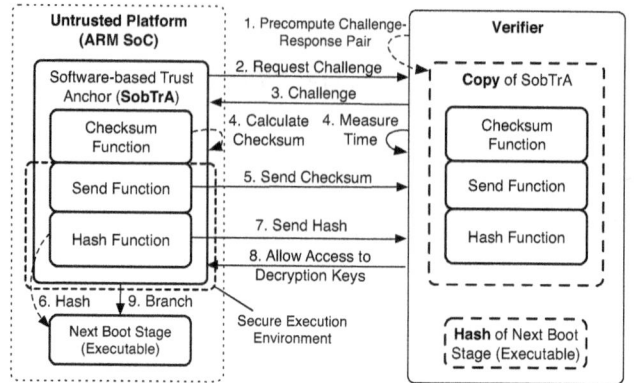

Figure 2: Basic concept of SobTrA and the software-based secure boot process

of the first approach is that it reintroduces a higher variance for the checksum function execution time. Downsides of the latter approach are that it takes more time to execute and is harder to be used at system runtime, requiring massive memory swapping.

SobTrA is based on the concepts by Seshadri et al. [16, 15, 14, 13] but presents a new secure boot use case and, most importantly, is designed and implemented on a different processor architecture, ARMv7-A, resulting in substantial changes to the underlying algorithm design and implementation.

4. SOBTRA CONCEPT

The typical hardware architecture for the SobTrA secure boot concept consists of a ARM System on a Chip (SoC) device as the *untrusted platform*, e.g., a smartphone, and a low performance device of arbitrary architecture as the *verifier*. Both are interconnected via a local, low-latency physical interface, such as SPI or SDIO. The core of the proposed software-based secure boot, as shown in Figure 1, is the software-based trust anchor SobTrA. An overview of the SobTrA functionality is depicted in Figure 2.

4.1 Basic Structure and Protocol

SobTrA on the untrusted platform consists of three main parts. First, there is the *checksum function*, which is the core of the software primitive. In the first communication step, SobTrA requests a challenge (2.). The verifier either pre-computes (1.) challenge-response pairs to accelerate the protocol or computes one on demand directly before sending the challenge back to the untrusted platform (3.). SobTrA uses the challenge to initialize the checksum function which then calculates a checksum (4.) over itself and the other two main parts of SobTrA while the verifier measures the time. Afterwards, SobTrA initializes a *secure execution environment* for the rest of the trust anchor to run in, preventing an attacker from gaining control via exceptions (see Section 6). The second part of SobTrA is the *send function* which is responsible for sending the result checksum back to the verifier (5.). The last part inside the checksummed region is the *hash function*, which computes (6.) a hash digest of the next stage in the boot process. The following steps depend on the application scenario. In our secure boot, the untrusted platform sends the hash digest to the verifier (7.) who checks if the hash is correct and only allows access to decryption keys/functionality (8.) if the verification is successful. The keys could, for example, protect the root file system and therefore prevent a further boot. All parts of SobTrA must be self-contained, i.e., they must *not* call code outside the checksummed region and must not cause exceptions.

The verifier contains an exact copy of the SobTrA binary image. It is therefore able to calculate the correct checksum to validate the checksum received from the untrusted platform. Besides the challenge, the verifier also sends the number of loop iterations for the checksum function which determines the maximum time the untrusted platform is allowed to take for returning the correct checksum. This maximum time must be pre-measured *once* on a trusted device identical to the untrusted platform and is valid for *all* challenges with the same iteration number. After receiving the checksum result from the untrusted platform, the verifier checks if the time taken is below the pre-measured threshold and whether the checksum is correct. If both conditions are met, the secure boot can succeed.

4.2 Checksum Function Design

The checksum function must provide the following *basic property*: A *tampered* checksum function either yields a *wrong checksum* or causes a *measurable* execution time *overhead*. Figure 3 shows the basic structure of the checksum function in the context of the other SobTrA parts. The first step towards the basic property is to make the checksum function *self-checksumming*, incorporating itself and all other parts of SobTrA into the checksum. This forces an attacker, trying to modify a part of SobTrA, to manipulate accesses to these memory regions to avoid yielding a wrong checksum. This increases computation time and therefore generates a measurable overhead. The function mainly consists of one main loop, in which a word from memory is read, transformed and included into the checksum together with CPU state input. An attacker trying to circumvent the self-checksumming property always introduces overhead inside this main loop. Therefore, even very small overheads can be made measurable by simply increasing the number of loop iterations. The epilogue code is mainly responsible for initializing the secure execution environment for the rest of the trust anchor (discussed in Section 6).

4.2.1 Common Attack Types

There are two basic types of attacks against such a checksum function: Substitution attacks and memory copy attacks. In a *substitution attack*, the attacker replaces parts of the trust anchor code, for which he then tries to circumvent the self-checksumming property specifically. Figure 4 visualizes an example. In a *memory copy attack*, the attacker modifies the code but still keeps an untampered version somewhere in memory. The attacker's tampered code then computes the checksum by redirecting all memory reads

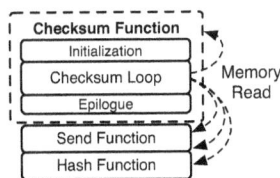

Figure 3: Checksum function structural overview

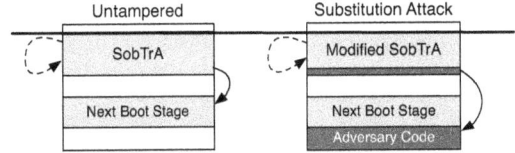

Figure 4: Substitution attack example: The final branch is substituted to redirect the flow to adversary code.

performed in the context of the self-checksumming functionality to the untampered image. Figure 5 illustrates the two basic forms of memory copy attacks.

4.2.2 Desired Properties

Seshadri et al. [16, 15] postulated some properties which should be fulfilled by a checksum function to provide the aforementioned basic property of either producing a wrong checksum or causing a measurable overhead when tampered. These are the basis for the SobTrA checksum function properties explained in the following: (1.) The memory which is getting checksummed should be *traversed in a pseudo-random manner* to prevent substitution attacks. (2.) The checksum function should include *CPU state inputs*, e.g., Program Counter (PC) and Status Register (SR), into the checksum, mainly to prevent memory copy attacks. (3.) The checksum function should be as *strongly-ordered and non-parallelizable* as possible to prevent addition of malicious instructions without overhead. (4.) Iterative parts, i.e., the main loop, of the checksum function should be *as small as possible* to allow the measurement of even very small attacker overheads and to reduce complexity for the code optimization. (5.) The checksum function implementation should be *time optimal*. The optimality could be made sure in the future using tools like Denali [8]. (6.) The checksum function execution time should have a *low variance*, i.e., only depend on the number of loop iterations to be able to do a verification for random challenges. (7.) To prevent precomputation of the checksum, the checksum function should be *initialized by a random challenge*. (8.) To slow down code added by an adversary (register spilling), the checksum function should *use all available CPU registers*.

5. CORTEX-A8 CHECKSUM FUNCTION

A checksum function implementation *must* be designed very specifically for a processor architecture to provide the introduced properties. SobTrA is designed and implemented for the ARMv7-A architecture and, currently, even more specifically for Cortex-A8 processors. Despite this specifity, SobTrA provides the basis for an implementation on other ARM cores. For multi-core processors SobTrA could be combined with the generic approach by Yan et al. [19]. The ARMv7-A architecture has some specialties which must

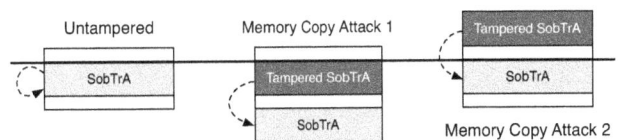

Figure 5: Two forms of memory copy attacks

Input:
    y: number of iterations of the function
    challenge initializing C, *rand* and $r13$

Output: Checksum C

Variables:
    $[start_code, end_code]$: checksummed memory area
    daddr: address of current memory access
    rand: current pseudorandom number
    $r13$: intermediate result from previous iteration
    t: variable to save parallel processing results
    j: index of current checksum part
    l: loop counter
    SR: status (flags) register
    PC: program counter

for $l = y$ to 0 **do**
    // T-Function [10] updates *rand*
    $rand \leftarrow rand + (rand^2 \vee 5) \bmod 2^{32}$
    // Update memory address with *rand*
    $daddr \leftarrow ((C_{j-1} \oplus rand) \wedge MASK) + start$
    // Update checksum part with index j
    $C_j \leftarrow C_j + PC$
    $t \leftarrow mem[daddr]$
    $C_j \leftarrow t \oplus rotate(C_j)$
    $t \leftarrow t + r13$
    $r13 \leftarrow r13 + C_j$
    $t \leftarrow t \oplus l + C_{j-1} \oplus rand + daddr \oplus C_{j-2}$
    $C_j \leftarrow C_j + PC \oplus l +_c C_{j-1} \oplus rand +_c daddr \oplus C_{j-2} +_c t$
    $C_j \leftarrow SR \oplus rotate(C_j)$
    // Update index j
    $j \leftarrow (j + 1) \bmod 10$
end for

Figure 6: SobTrA checksum function algorithm

be considered in the checksum function design: First, the Program Counter (PC) is represented as an explicit register while the Status Register (SR) is *not* accessible like a normal register and flags must be set explicitly. Second, memory accesses are always done by dedicated instructions (load/store architecture). Third, many instructions allow the second operand to be rotated/shifted without an additional instruction (and without costs at least on Cortex-A8). Finally, there are two different instruction sets with different instruction encodings: ARM and Thumb–2. The latter mixes 16 and 32 bit wide instructions for higher code density.

It is crucial that the hardware is configured to provide the maximum possible performance for running the checksum function. Every unused optimization could potentially be abused by an attacker to hide latencies introduced by his code. So, the CPU must be configured to run the highest possible clock speed available in software and branch prediction as well as all caches must be activated. Latter requires the Memory Management Unit (MMU) to be *enabled* [3].

Besides these performance initializations, it is also necessary to temporarily disable all *interrupts* to prevent an attacker from gaining control during or shortly after the checksum function. Our implementation includes all these initializations. An attacker cannot change these settings without reducing performance and therefore failing a verification.

5.1 Basic Algorithm

Figure 6 shows pseudocode for the SobTrA checksum function main loop. The loop body can be structured into three parts:

1. Calculation of the next pseudorandom number, i.e., the *pseudorandom update* (Line 6).

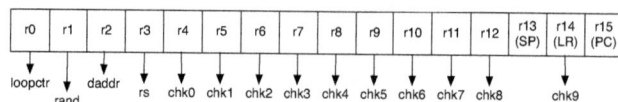

Figure 7: Mapping of ARM registers to their names in the SobTrA checksum function

2. Calculation of the address of the next memory word to be incorporated into the checksum, i.e., the *data address update* (Line 8).

3. Update of the current checksum part (Lines 10 to 17).

Together with a final loop counter decrementation, these three parts are called *basic block* or *block* in the following. The checksum is split into several parts to fill the available registers. Part 2 and 3 of the algorithm are specific to the checksum part updated in the current iteration. The checksum update algorithm part is highly architecture specific and the design ideas will therefore be explained later together with the implementation. Most of the previously introduced checksum function properties, for example the pseudorandom memory traversal and CPU state inputs (PC and SR), are fulfilled obviously. The function is strongly ordered and non-parallelizable by making blocks dependent on previous results, interdependencies between subparts of the loop body and by interleaving add $+$, add-with-carry $+_c$ and xor $\oplus$ operations for updating the checksum parts.

5.2 Main Loop Implementation

The checksum function implementation runs in Supervisor Mode. The presented assembler code uses named registers, as specified in Figure 7, to increase readability. There is one dedicated register for each running variable in the algorithm and an additional scratch register named `rs` to hold different values, especially the t variable, during a loop iteration. Ten registers (`chk0` to `chk9`) store the checksum parts resulting in a 320 bit wide checksum. To make most efficient use of available registers, the algorithm loop is *unrolled* in ten checksum part specific blocks, so the index j in the pseudocode has no equivalent in the actual implementation. The SobTrA checksum function implementation must be encoded using the Thumb–2 instruction set because the checksum function leverages the mixed instruction size (16 and 32 bits) to prevent a specific form of memory copy attack (discussed in Section 5.3.2). In Thumb–2 encoding, the registers `r13` (Stack Pointer) and `r15` (PC) are restricted to be usable only in some instructions. Register `r13` can therefore not be used as a checksum register or working register. To fulfill the property of using all registers, `r13` is occupied by saving an intermediate result to be included into the checksum in the next block. So it maps directly to the identically named variable in the algorithm pseudocode. To reduce the possibilities for an attacker to insert instructions without overhead, we did a manual cycle-exact analysis of the checksum function implementation for the Cortex-A8 dual-issue, in-order pipeline using information provided by [2]. Based on the analysis (verified by performance counters) we made sure that the presented implementation makes highly efficient use of the pipeline features, so that a basic block executes in only 31 processor cycles. The branch instruction at the end of the unrolled loop and the self-modification sequence added in Section 5.3.3 account for another 0.1 and 0.42 cycles per block.

```
1  mul  rs, rand, rand            @ x²
2  orr  rs, rs, 0x5               @ x² ∨ 5
3  add  rand, rs, rand            @ (x² ∨ 5) + x
```

Figure 8: Pseudorandom generator update sequence

The checksum function is **initialized** with a 320 bit wide challenge filling all checksum registers with a starting value. The seed for the random number generator is derived from the challenge by xoring their parts. Besides that, also `r13` is initialized with some value derived from `rand`.

Like other concepts [16, 11, 15], SobTrA uses a T-Function [10] for the **pseudorandom update** (Figure 6, Line 6), mainly because it can be implemented with only few instructions as shown in Figure 8. Therefore, an optimal implementation can be ensured more easily. The calculation only depends on the previous value of `rand` and uses the scratch register `rs` to hold intermediate results.

The SobTrA **data address update** implementation for the first checksum function block is shown in Figure 9. For optimal performance, only word-aligned addresses are generated. Eight KiB beginning at the `start_code` label are checksummed, which is enough to include all SobTrA parts. The `start_code` label address is generated PC-relative using the `adr` instruction.

Figure 10 shows the SobTrA implementation of the **checksum update sequence**. The code updates the first checksum part register and is therefore specific to the first checksum function block of the unrolled loop. To keep the scratch register `rs`, used for loading the memory value (Line 10), alive and unavailable to an attacker, SobTrA processes it with a sequence of operations parallel to the checksum register and incorporates it into the checksum just before it is needed again to load the Current Program Status Register (CPSR) (the ARM status register). These operations fill the Cortex-A8 dual-issue pipeline optimally and therefore cause nearly no overhead. Some operations are used in their flag-setting variants (mnemonic suffixed with "s") to impede the forgery of the CPSR. This is particularly important for the addition immediately before the `mrs` instruction, which reads the CPSR, since it prevents reordering of this instruction to an upper position. The `mrs` instruction is quite expensive, costing about eight CPU execution cycles on the Cortex-A8 [2]. Nevertheless, it is not possible to forge the CPSR in the same or less time since an attacker would have to forge the dynamically set flags. To keep register `r13` unavailable to an attacker, SobTrA uses two instructions (Lines 12 and 13) which incorporate an intermediate result from the previous block into the checksum. To reduce the overhead, to maintain the order of the **add**/**eor** sequence and to harden against certain memory copy attacks (discussed later), this is done via an indirection over the scratch register (i.e., variable t) which is included into the checksum near the end of the sequence (Line 25). Further details of the implementation are discussed in the next section with regard to the specific attacks they prevent.

```
4  eors  daddr, chk9, rand        @ derive random value
5  ldr   rs, =0x7ff<<2            @ load mask in scratch register
6  and   daddr, daddr, rs         @ mask random to get an offset
7  adr   rs, start_code           @ gen. start address PC-relative
8  add   daddr, daddr, rs         @ add offset to start address
```

Figure 9: SobTrA data address update implementation for the first block

```
9   add   chk0, chk0, pc          @ C₀ ← C₀ + PC
10  ldr   rs, [daddr]             @ t ← mem[daddr]
11  eor   chk0, rs, chk0, ror 1   @ C₀ ← t ⊕ rotate(C₀)
12  add   rs, rs, r13             @ t ← t + r13
13  add   r13, chk0               @ r13 ← r13 + C₀
14  add   chk0, chk0, pc          @ C₀ ← C₀ + PC
15  eors  rs, rs, loopctr         @ t ← t ⊕ l
16  eors  chk0, chk0, loopctr     @ C₀ ← C₀ ⊕ l
17  add   rs, rs, chk9            @ t ← t + C₉
18  adcs  chk0, chk0, chk9        @ C₀ ← C₀ +_c C₉
19  eors  rs, rs, rand            @ t ← t ⊕ rand
20  eors  chk0, chk0, rand        @ C₀ ← C₀ ⊕ rand
21  add   rs, rs, daddr           @ t ← t + daddr
22  adcs  chk0, chk0, daddr       @ C₀ ← C₀ +_c daddr
23  eors  rs, rs, chk8           @ t ← t ⊕ C₈
24  eors  chk0, chk0, chk8        @ C₀ ← C₀ ⊕ C₈
25  adcs  chk0, chk0, rs          @ C₀ ← C₀ +_c t
26  mrs   rs, cpsr                @ load the SR
27  eor   chk0, rs, chk0, ror 1   @ C₀ ← SR ⊕ rotate(C₀)
28  sub   loopctr, loopctr, 1     @ decrement l
```

Figure 10: SobTrA checksum update sequence (first block)

5.3 Attack Prevention

In the following, attacks on the checksum function are discussed and how SobTrA prevents them. With one block taking 31.52 cycles to execute, an overhead of only one CPU cycle per block ($^{32.52}/_{31.52}-1 = 3.17\%$) is enough to be easily measurable (see Section 7). Therefore, it is sufficient to show that an attack generates an overhead of at least one cycle to be prevented successfully.

5.3.1 Substitution Attacks

A successful substitution attack replaces parts of the checksummed memory region without changing the resulting checksum or causing an execution time overhead. The most basic forms of substitution attacks are prevented by the pseudorandom memory traversal of the algorithm, which forces an attacker to insert, at least, a basic conditional (**if**-like) statement into the checksum loop to check if a location previously modified by him is read and to hide the modification accordingly. This easily causes an overhead of at least one cycle. Like Seshadri et al. [14] we use the *Coupon Collector's Problem* to calculate the number of iterations needed to include every memory word at least once with high probability. For 8 KiB (equaling 2048 32-bit words) this results in $2048 \ln 2048 + 2048 \approx 17663$ iterations.

Castelluccia et al. introduced an attack [4] which exploits the fact that the Most Significant Bit (MSB) is treated the exact same way by an addition as by a bitwise exclusive-or. Therefore, a sequence of alternating additions and exclusive-ors, like it is the basis for updating the checksum, yields the same result if the MSB is inverted in an even number of operands. In order to prevent such attacks, SobTrA implements, like other concepts [12], flag-setting add-with-carry (**adcs**) operations instead of simple additions.

Unfortunately, Thumb-2 does not allow the PC as operand to any add-with-carry operation. This results in an attack where the MSBs of the PC in the two PC incorporating instructions, in the following called *PC inclusions* (Figure 10, Lines 9 and 14), cancel each other out. So a SobTrA execution from a location with inverted MSBs would result in the same checksum. SobTrA prevents such an attack by rotating the checksum between both PC inclusions (Line 11). Since the rotation is piggybacked by the **eor** instruction, it does not cost additional cycles on the Cortex-A8 processor.

277

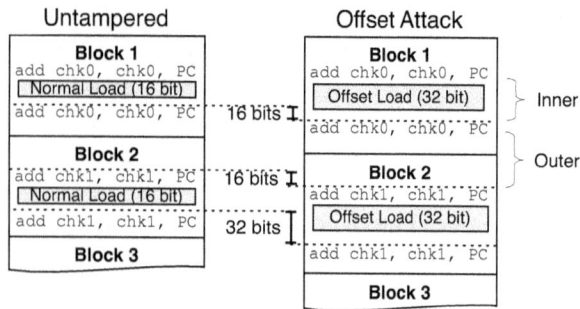

Figure 11: PC corruption for the offset attack on the checksum function

Furthermore, SobTrA prevents MSB attacks spanning over multiple iterations of the unrolled loop with a rotation at the end of every block (Line 27) and the address update being dependent on previous block's checksum register.

5.3.2 Memory Copy Attacks Type 1

In memory copy attacks of this type, the attacker runs his malicious checksum function in the originally intended place, but computes the checksum over an untampered image stored somewhere else in memory (see Figure 5 in the middle). Since the ARM architecture allows a load instruction to have a fixed offset without additional costs, such an attack could be realized quite easily by replacing the load instruction with an offset variant. For a successful *offset attack*, the untampered image has to be in range of the load offset. This range is different depending on the used instruction encoding. To prevent the offset attack, the SobTrA checksum function leverages the fact that there are different size encodings of the load (`ldr`) instruction in the Thumb–2 instruction set. There is only one 16-bit encoding (T1), which allows loads with the `daddr` base register. For this encoding, the range of offsets is 0-124 in multiples of four. This is *not* sufficient for a successful attack since the unrolled checksum function loop itself is about 1 KiB in size and can therefore not be passed. If the attacker uses a 32-bit instruction encoding which allows offsets to be big enough, he implicitly changes the position of the following PC inclusions and therefore corrupts the checksum. The deviation of the PC inclusions from their original position cumulates for the following blocks in the unrolled loop. Figure 11 illustrates the situation for the attacker. To repair the corrupted PC inclusions, the attacker may either forge the PCs, which in fact leads to a type 2 memory copy attack, or try to balance the bigger offset load instruction by encoding other instructions shorter. To prevent such attacks, we examined the SobTrA code to use the smallest possible encoding (e.g. use `eors` instead of `eor`). Especially in the *inner* region (see Figure 11) this is important since there only 16 bits must be saved for a successful attack. Saving 16 bits in the *outer* region is *not* enough as the distance between the two PC inclusions must be correct as well. Many instructions can only be encoded in their short form (16 bits) if the operands are from the lower half of the register bank (registers 0-7) so SobTrA maps the frequently used variables to lower register.

5.3.3 Memory Copy Attacks Type 2

In this type of memory copy attacks, the untampered SobTrA image is kept in its originally intended position and the attacker checksums it from another position. There are three spots in the checksum function which have to be considered for such an attack because of their PC usage:

- The base address is generated PC-relative (Figure 9, Line 7) and the `adr` instruction must therefore be in range of the untampered code start.

- The **two** PC inclusions (Figure 10, Lines 9 and 14) must be forged. For the first forgery, the scratch register `rs` is available, for the second it is *not*.

The attacker is free in terms of code size and encoding because he forges the PC inclusions anyway. He is even free to use the ARM instruction set instead of Thumb–2 because the `mrs` instruction does *not* read the actual values of the processor state bits, encoding if the processor runs in ARM or Thumb mode [3]. We identified two different type 2 memory copy attacks to be discussed in the following.

Basic PC Forgery. An attacker might try to replace the PC register operand with immediates, i.e., static values to be encoded directly into the instruction. Because of the restrictions on immediates in the ARM architecture, such an attack would be only possible for unrealistic simple addresses. As the place for the checksum function is specified by the verifier, this does not pose a problem.

An attacker might try to forge the PC values with basic arithmetic operations on his own PC. This is only possible if the attacker's code is in range of the untampered code. The first PC inclusion can then be forged using the free scratch register `rs`. The second PC inclusion *cannot* be forged like this because there is no spare register available. So, forging the second PC value forces the attacker to spill a register, i.e., store it to memory and restore it afterwards, easily causing an overhead of at least one cycle. Besides the additional store and load instruction, spilling a register in the most cases incurs overhead for an extra address generation.

Shifting Attack. This attack is based on the idea to forge the original PC only by shifting the actual attacker's PC, exploiting free shifts on Cortex-A8 CPUs. The malicious checksum function is positioned in a way so that its base address equals the base address of the untampered checksum function logically left-shifted by one. Thumb–2 does not allow shifts/rotates on the PC, but the attacker is free to use ARM encoding which allows shifting and adding of the PC in the same instruction. The attacker has to align its code (e.g., by inserting NOPs) so that its shifting PC inclusions are in positions where they yield the correct PC just by right-shifting.

The SobTrA checksum function prevents such an attack by running from addresses which cannot be generated by a simple logical or arithmetic right-shift (possibly configuring the MMU accordingly). The key characteristic of such an address is that its two most significant bits are "10". Furthermore, the attack is prevented because of the PC-relative base address generation in the data address update sequence, requiring the attacker to either do a shift to get in range and subtract an offset (always two instructions), or to do a memory load, both causing at least a one cycle overhead.

5.3.4 TLB Desynchronization Attack

Wurster et al. in 2005 introduced [18] a technique which exploits Harvard-style Translation Lookaside Buffers (TLBs) to attack self-checksumming code. The basic idea of the attack is to desynchronize the TLBs in a way that the same Virtual Address (VA) is mapped to a malicious copy of the checksum function in the Instruction Translation Lookaside Buffer (ITLB) and to an untampered image in the Data Translation Lookaside Buffer (DTLB). Then, all instructions are fetched from the malicious checksum function in physical memory, but the load instructions, used to checksum the code, access the untampered copy in physical memory, resulting in a quasi hardware-accelerated memory copy attack. We successfully implemented the attack on ARM Cortex-A8 in a less generic but much easier way than described by Wurster et al. leveraging the explicit DTLB invalidation operations available on ARM.

Giffin et al. [6] in 2005 proposed a technique using self-modifying code to strengthen self-checksumming code against TLB desynchronization attacks. Self-modifying code accesses its code via the DTLB, and therefore corrupts the checksum in case of a TLB desynchronization. Like some related work concepts [11, 13] for x86 SobTrA uses self-modifying code to prevent such attacks but employs a different approach since, in contrast to x86, the ARM architecture requires explicit and expensive cache maintenance operations when implementing self-modifying code, mainly to propagate the changes from the data cache to the instruction cache. SobTrA optimizes the self-modification sequence by configuring the level 1 cache to be write-through and the level 2 cache to be write-back and by removing unnecessary barriers. Still, The necessary instruction cache invalidation costs about 60 cycles, which is too long in comparison to a block's execution time of 31 cycles to do a self-modification in every block. Therefore, SobTrA reduces the per-block overhead by doing a self-modification only every n-th block. The self-modification code is executed every $n/10$-th unrolled loop iteration. It randomly picks one block and changes the rotation immediate of a specific instruction (Figure 10, Line 11) in the block to a random value. An attacker who simulates the self-modification functionality in a static way, has to do the same computations every n-th block to update his untampered image with the modified instructions. He saves 60 cycles ($60/n$ per block) from not having to issue the cache line flush, but for the simulation additional instructions are required in *every* attacker's block (e.g., load number of rotations and rotate by register). This simulation causes at least one cycle overhead per block since there is no spare register available and additional instructions corrupt the PC inclusions, especially in the inner region where the simulation has to be done (see Section 5.3.2).

6. SECURE EXECUTION ENVIRONMENT

SobTrA must ensure that an attacker *cannot* gain control after the successful computation of the checksum. Otherwise, such an attacker could use the valid checksum to obtain the trust of the verifier and run arbitrary code afterwards.

Assuming that the checksum function has finished successfully, it is ensured that only checksummed and untampered code is executed afterwards. Therefore, the only possible way for an attacker to gain control of the execution is to trigger an exception. The ARM literature uses the term *exception* to denote all kinds of interrupts or traps and the term *interrupt* to denote only asynchronous interrupts. SobTrA establishes a secure execution environment by replacing the exception vector table with an own table (containing dead

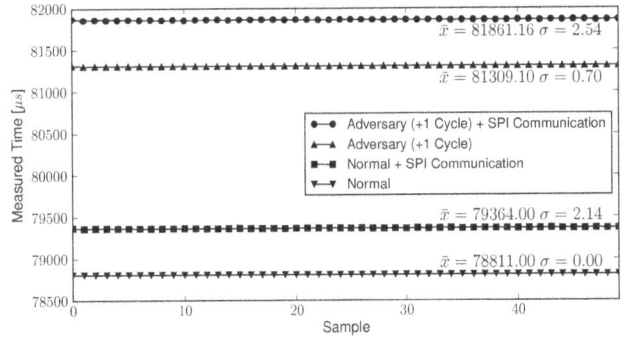

Figure 12: Consecutive measurements of execution time for 1.5 million iterations

loops) stored *inside* the checksummed region immediately after the checksum calculation and *before* sending the result. Code inside the checksummed-region may *not* cause any exceptions or call unmeasured and unchecksummed code.

It must also be ensured that an attacker cannot gain control *before* the secure execution environment is established, i.e., during and shortly after the checksum function execution. For that, we analyzed the different exception types regarding their attack potential. As shown before, it can be assumed that there are no successful attacks on the checksum function itself, i.e., it is guaranteed that the SobTrA code runs untampered:

Undefined Instruction and Supervisor Call. Synchronous exceptions are caused explicitly by instructions. Since the SobTrA code runs untampered and does not trigger any of these, they do not pose a threat.

IRQ, FIQ and external Abort. External interrupts are disabled by SobTrA and their status is incorporated into the checksum via the CPSR.

Prefetch Abort. These are triggered by the MMU when fetching instructions from invalid memory addresses. The checksum function and secure execution environment establishment code reside on the same minimal page, which prevents Prefetch Aborts.

Data Abort. These are triggered by the MMU when accessing invalid data addresses. Since the checksummed region is about 8 KiB in size, a Data Abort might be caused by an attacker *during* the checksum calculation. As the calculation is not yet finished when such an exception might occur and every execution of the exception takes long in relation to one checksum function block, it cannot be abused by an attacker.

7. EXPERIMENTAL RESULTS

We implemented a prototype, which is able to run a complete software-based secure boot using the SobTrA primitive. The prototype hardware consists of a Beagleboard (Rev. C3, Cortex-A8, 600 MHz) as the untrusted platform and a mbed LPC1768 microcontroller as verifier, interconnected via SPI. SobTrA on the Beagleboard is implemented as bare-metal, standalone binary image containing the checksum function, an SPI driver for the communication protocol and a minimal ARM Linux kernel bootloader as well as a

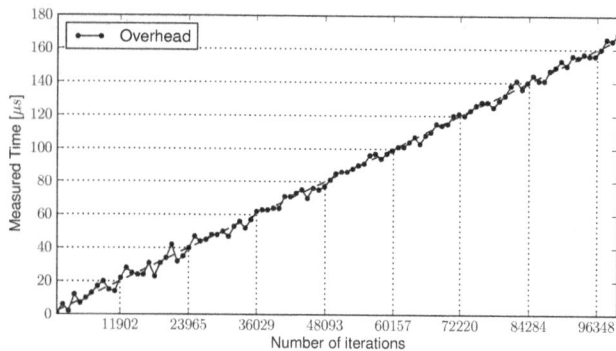

Figure 13: Measured attacker overhead for 1000 to 100000 iterations

minimal SHA-1 implementation to hash and start a trusted kernel. To support arbitrary hardware as verifier, we implemented a SobTrA simulator in C which is used to compute challenge-response pairs on the mbed LPC1768.

First, we measured the SobTrA execution time several times with the same number of iterations in the untampered case and in case of a minimal attack causing a *one* cycle overhead per checksum function block. For each case, we differentiated pure execution time and time measured by the verifier via SPI at 3 MHz. The resulting plot is depicted in Figure 12 with mean value ($\bar{x}$) and standard deviation (σ). With an overhead of $^{81861}/_{79364} - 1 \approx 3.15\%$ for the communication including case and the low latency of the SPI bus, even attacker overheads smaller than one cycle are measurable quite well.

In a second step, we measured the execution time, including communication overheads, for an increasing number of iterations. Figure 13 shows the overhead generated by the attacker (one cycle overhead), i.e., the difference between normal and tampered execution time. On the average, about 24000 iterations are needed to generate 40 μs overhead for the attacking case, sufficient to be reliably measured. The 24000 iterations are also sufficient to cover SobTrA's 8 KiB in the random memory traversal (see Section 5.3.1). The SobTrA execution time in this case is about 1.8 ms.

8. CONCLUSION

In this paper, we introduced SobTrA, a software-based trust anchor for ARM Cortex-A processors. As our main application scenario, the concept of a software-based secure boot for embedded devices, e.g., smartphones without usable hardware-based secure boot, was presented. In this concept, a verifier device attached to an untrusted platform obtains the guarantee that the boot process on the untrusted device is running untampered. The checksum function provides the guarantee to the verifier that SobTrA runs untampered by performing an optimized, self-checksumming calculation in a certain, upper-bounded timeframe.

We implemented a Cortex-A8 specific checksum function and showed that it is resistant against known attacks. Furthermore, we implemented a secure execution environment, preventing attacker interception by making sure that no exceptions can be triggered during the checksum calculation and replacing the exception vector table afterwards. Our prototype is able to run a software-based secure boot up to a Linux kernel. Experiments revealed that the approach is very robust in terms of timing, making it possible to clearly distinguish untampered and tampered execution even for very small overheads introduced by an attacker.

9. ACKNOWLEDGMENTS

Parts of this work were supported by the German Federal Ministry of Education and Research (BMBF) under grant 01BY1200A within the project *HIVE*.

10. REFERENCES

[1] W. Arbaugh, D. Farber, and J. Smith. A secure and reliable bootstrap architecture. In *Proceedings of the 1997 IEEE Symposium on Security and Privacy*, May 1997.

[2] ARM Limited. *ARM Cortex-A8 Technical Reference Manual*, May 2010.

[3] ARM Limited. *ARM Architecture Reference Manual – ARMv7-A and ARMv7-R edition*, July 2011.

[4] C. Castelluccia, A. Francillon, D. Perito, and C. Soriente. On the difficulty of software-based attestation of embedded devices. In *Proceedings of the 16th ACM conference on Computer and communications security*, CCS '09, 2009.

[5] R. W. Gardner, S. Garera, and A. D. Rubin. Detecting code alteration by creating a temporary memory bottleneck. *Trans. Info. For. Sec.*, 4:638–650, December 2009.

[6] J. T. Giffin, M. Christodorescu, and L. Kruger. Strengthening software self-checksumming via self-modifying code. In *Proceedings of the 21st Annual Computer Security Applications Conference*, pages 23–32, 2005.

[7] M. Jakobsson and K.-A. Johansson. Practical and secure software-based attestation. In *Workshop on Lightweight Security Privacy: Devices, Protocols and Applications (LightSec)*, pages 1–9, March 2011.

[8] R. Joshi, G. Nelson, and K. Randall. Denali: a goal-directed superoptimizer. In *Proceedings of the ACM SIGPLAN 2002 Conference on Programming language design and implementation*, PLDI '02, pages 304–314, 2002.

[9] R. Kennell and L. H. Jamieson. Establishing the genuinity of remote computer systems. In *Proceedings of the 12th conference on USENIX Security Symposium*, 2003.

[10] A. Klimov and A. Shamir. New cryptographic primitives based on multiword T-Functions. In B. Roy and W. Meier, editors, *Fast Software Encryption*, volume 3017 of *Lecture Notes in Computer Science*, pages 1–15. 2004.

[11] L. Martignoni, R. Paleari, and D. Bruschi. Conqueror: Tamper-proof code execution on legacy systems. In *Proceedings of the 7th international conference on Detection of intrusions and malware, and vulnerability assessment*, DIMVA'10, 2010.

[12] A. Perrig and L. V. Doorn. Refutation of "On the difficulty of software-based attestation of embedded devices".

[13] A. Seshadri. *A software primitive for externally-verifiable untampered execution and its applications to securing computing systems*. PhD thesis, Carnegie Mellon University, 2009.

[14] A. Seshadri, M. Luk, A. Perrig, L. van Doorn, and P. Khosla. SCUBA: Secure code update by attestation in sensor networks. In *Proceedings of the 5th ACM workshop on Wireless security*, WiSe '06, pages 85–94, 2006.

[15] A. Seshadri, M. Luk, E. Shi, A. Perrig, L. van Doorn, and P. Khosla. Pioneer: Verifying code integrity and enforcing untampered code execution on legacy systems. In *Proceedings of the twentieth ACM symposium on Operating systems principles*, SOSP '05, pages 1–16, 2005.

[16] A. Seshadri, A. Perrig, L. van Doorn, and P. Khosla. SWATT: Software-based attestation for embedded devices. In *Proceedings of the 2004 IEEE Symposium on Security and Privacy*, pages 272–282, 2004.

[17] U. Shankar, M. Chew, and J. D. Tygar. Side effects are not sufficient to authenticate software. In *Proceedings of the 13th conference on USENIX Security Symposium*, SSYM'04, 2004.

[18] G. Wurster, P. C. v. Oorschot, and A. Somayaji. A generic attack on checksumming-based software tamper resistance. In *Proceedings of the 2005 IEEE Symposium on Security and Privacy*, pages 127–138, 2005.

[19] Q. Yan, J. Han, Y. Li, R. H. Deng, and T. Li. A software-based root-of-trust primitive on multicore platforms. In *Proceedings of the 6th ACM Symposium on Information, Computer and Communications Security*, ASIACCS '11, 2011.

TrustID: Trustworthy Identities for Untrusted Mobile Devices

Julian Horsch, Konstantin Böttinger, Michael Weiß, Sascha Wessel,
and Frederic Stumpf
Fraunhofer AISEC
Garching near Munich, Germany
{firstname.lastname}@aisec.fraunhofer.de

ABSTRACT

Identity theft has deep impacts in today's mobile ubiquitous environments. At the same time, digital identities are usually still protected by simple passwords or other insufficient security mechanisms. In this paper, we present the TrustID architecture and protocols to improve this situation. Our architecture utilizes a Secure Element (SE) to store multiple context-specific identities securely in a mobile device, e.g., a smartphone. We introduce protocols for securely deriving identities from a strong root identity into the SE inside the smartphone as well as for using the newly derived IDs. Both protocols do not require a trustworthy smartphone operating system or a Trusted Execution Environment. In order to achieve this, our concept includes a secure combined PIN entry mechanism for user authentication, which prevents attacks even on a malicious device. To show the feasibility of our approach, we implemented a prototype running on a Samsung Galaxy SIII smartphone utilizing a microSD card SE. The German identity card nPA is used as root identity to derive context-specific identities.

Categories and Subject Descriptors

D.4.6 [**Operating Systems**]: Security and Protection

Keywords

Identity Derivation; Smartphone; Mobile Security; Combined PIN Entry; Secure Element; Identity Provider; Android; nPA

1. INTRODUCTION

In today's world characterized by personalized, Internet-driven services, every user possesses a multitude of digital identities for authentication to these services but also to physical entities. These identities are often presented in form of email addresses, user names or user identification numbers and secured by a diverse set of security mechanisms, e.g., passwords, Personal Identification Numbers (PINs), Transaction Authentication Numbers (TANs), and smart cards or other physical tokens in highly secure environments. The achieved security level of most of these mechanisms depends on how the user handles them. For example, the security of an identity protected by a password is only as strong as the password chosen by the user. Consequentially, identity theft is a widespread problem [8]. To address these issues, we propose the TrustID concept. Our four main contributions are:

1. An architecture for deriving and using context-specific IDs on mobile devices utilizing a Secure Element (SE) as credential store.

2. A protocol for secure ID *derivation* on a possibly unsecure or even malicious smartphone.

3. A protocol for secure ID *usage* on a possibly unsecure or even malicious smartphone covering several powerful use cases.

4. A secure combined PIN entry mechanism for user authentication *without* relying on a Trusted Execution Environment (TEE) in the smartphone or additional hardware like a trusted display/pinpad for the SE as opposed to, e.g., One-Time-Password (OTP) tokens.

In our concept, the user possesses *one* strong, long-term issued, generic root identity, called *RootID*. This RootID could, for instance, be a government-issued Electronic Identity Card (EIC). The user then uses this RootID to derive all kinds of different, context-specific IDs storing them in a certified SE in his off-the-shelf smartphone. The TrustID ID derivation protocol relies on a trusted third party, the Trusted Identity Provider (TIP), to decide about ID requests based on the information stored in the RootID. The derived IDs can then be used via all interfaces the smartphone provides, typically including Near Field Communication (NFC) but also the Internet, while the RootID remains at the user's home or some other secure place avoiding the risk of loss.

Moving the security basis away from the user towards highly secure SEs substantially increases overall security. Most users already own a smartphone and carry it with them, so its the most natural place to store the IDs the user needs on a daily basis. The certified SE can be included into the smartphone flexibly in different form factors, including embedded SEs, microSD cards and Universal Integrated Circuit Cards (UICCs). The concept also takes into consideration that there may be several different SE manufacturers who are allowed to produce SEs certified for the TrustID system. Nevertheless, using the user's smartphone, which is an untrusted and possibly malicious device, in a security relevant context requires some further security measures to be taken into consideration. We therefore propose a *secure combined PIN entry* mechanism, which allows to establish a secure channel between SE and RootID by using the corresponding secret PINs without the user entering them in clear via the smartphone's untrusted touchscreen. So the security of the ID derivation mechanism and the resulting ID does *not* rely on the security of the smartphone software stack, which is increasingly important since the past years show the growing relevance of smartphones as targets for diverse attacks [6, 1]. If the user loses his smartphone, he can use his RootID to revoke the IDs stored in the SE of the lost device. Our concept covers several use cases such as financial transactions, physical access control, car-sharing access to access control for online services.

This paper is organized as follows. In Section 2, we describe our attacker model. In Section 3, we give an overview of existing research results. Section 4 introduces the basic concept, architecture and the protocol for the TrustID ID derivation and usage. Aspects of our prototype implementation are discussed in Section 5. Section 6 evaluates our protocol regarding its security. We conclude in Section 7.

2. ATTACKER MODEL

The attacker has complete control over the entire network. On the smartphone, he is able to modify software, to run arbitrary programs, to read out RAM, and to eavesdrop bus systems. Attacks on the SE as well as the RootID are out-of-scope because these devices are hardened against software and hardware attacks. The attacker has no knowledge about the PINs protecting the SE and the RootID, but he might be able to gain knowledge of the combined PIN. Attacks on the TIP are also out-of-scope.

3. RELATED WORK

Leicher et al. [12] provide an OpenID based approach for mobile SSO across different devices. In contrast to our approach, their concept relies on the Mobile Network Operator (MNO) as root for the derivation of mobile identities and on a fully trusted mobile device.

Urien et al. [13] provide a mobile ID in form of an EAP-TLS smart card. Similar to our approach they store a key pair as identity credential in the smart card. For securing the communication, they use the TLS stack of those special smart cards to form secure channels between the different entities of their protocol. However, they do not scope a compromised smartphone in any case.

In [11], Hyppönen describes a protocol for deriving an ID from an identity issuer which is sending the credentials to the SE over an identity proxy (a mobile phone). Nevertheless, this approach does not deal with identity theft by the means of a relay attack as described in our security evaluation (see Section 6) or with a possible compromisation of the mobile device. Chen et al. [5] propose a mobile payment ID derived from the Citizen Digital Card (CDC), which is a governmental PKI-based ID card, onto an NFC smartphone.

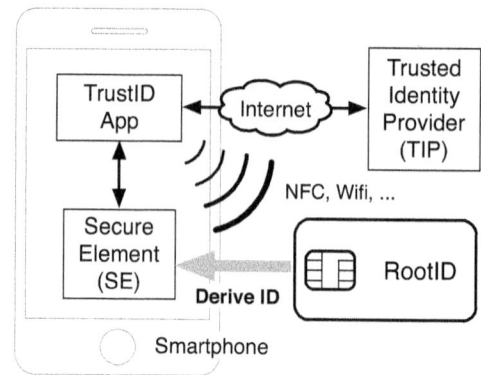

Figure 1: Overview of the TrustID system

This is similar to our scenario of ID derivation. However, their protocol relies on the MNO as trusted ID provider as he owns the SE used in their scenario (the SIM card). Further, the PIN for the CDC is entered in clear allowing an attacker compromising the smartphone to eavesdrop it.

Dmitrienko et al. [7] provide an approach for delegable access control utilizing NFC-enabled smartphones. Their system is not based on a RootID, but relies on users directly delegating their credentials to each other. In contrast to our approach where the smartphone can be completely untrusted, they rely on a large trusted computing base.

Summarizing, none of the previous contributions covers the full process of deriving multiple identities from a strong root identity employing a trusted identity provider, that might be integrated in a governmental PKI, while taking a compromised smartphone into account.

4. CONCEPT

The goal of the proposed TrustID architecture and protocol is to derive a context-specific identity from a RootID by interacting with a remote Trusted Identity Provider (TIP) and to store the derived ID into a SE inside a smartphone. An app on the smartphone acts as a hub and mediates the communication between the different entities without being able to discover any sensitive information. An *identity* in our concept basically consists of an asymmetric key pair and an associated certificate containing all additional information about the context and usage of the identity. The entities which are involved in the derivation process and their connections are depicted in the system overview in Figure 1. These entities are described in the following:

Smartphone. The smartphone mainly acts as a carrier for the SE and as runtime environment for the TrustID app providing the hardware interfaces necessary for the communication with the other entities (e.g., Wifi, NFC, SDIO) and with the user (via the touchscreen).

Secure Element. The SE (e.g., a microSD card or UICC) used in the TrustID protocol must be *certified*, i.e., must contain some key material for which the TIP is able to do a verification. This is discussed in detail in Section 4.3. This key material is *not* user-specific, but is used to provide a guarantee that the newly derived

ID is stored in an actual SE which matches the required security standards. Therefore, such SEs could be distributed/sold to the users without any personalization or pre-provisioning.

TrustID App. The TrustID app on the smartphone acts as a hub for all communication between the other entities and is responsible for presenting information to and getting input from the user via its User Interface (UI). In the TrustID protocols, all software on the smartphone can be untrusted because of the special PIN entry mechanism described in Section 4.3.

RootID. The RootID is some kind of long-term issued smart card, which securely stores the personal data of the user. The RootID must contain key material to authenticate itself towards the entity reading the data and to make sure that only authorized entities may read out its data. A typical example for RootIDs fulfilling these requirements are government-issued EICs like the German identity card nPA used in our prototype implementation (see Section 5).

Trusted Identity Provider. The TIP provides the backend of the system architecture and is connected to the smartphone through the Internet. In the ID derivation protocol, the TIP must decide if an identity request by a user is fulfilled based on the user's RootID and the SE in the user's smartphone. The TIP is also responsible for generating the certificate for the new ID.

4.1 Architecture

During ID derivation, several logical channels are established. Figure 2 shows the system architecture with named channels between the entities. We differentiate channels which conceptually directly connect two entities (solid lines) and channels which are established between two entities through a third TrustID entity (dashed lines):

RootID-Channel. This channel connects the TrustID app with the RootID. It is *unprotected* and is realized differently depending on the smartphone hardware and RootID form factor. For example, the channel could be established using an NFC connection to a contactless smart card RootID.

SE-Channel. This channel connects the TrustID app with the SE. It is *unprotected* and established differently depending on the SE form factor, e.g., via Secure Digital Input Output (SDIO) in case of a microSD card.

TIP-Channel. This channel connects the TrustID app with the TIP. The channel is established via the Internet and does *not* have to be protected, but can optionally use Transport Layer Security (TLS).

TIP-SE-Channel. This channel connects the TIP and the smartphone's SE. It is mutually authenticated and encrypted and established based on static asymmetric keys present in the involved entities.

RootID-SE-Channel. This channel connects the RootID and the smartphone's SE. Similar to the TIP-SE-Channel above, this channel is also mutually authenticated and encrypted but uses the PIN mechanism described in Section 4.3 to be established.

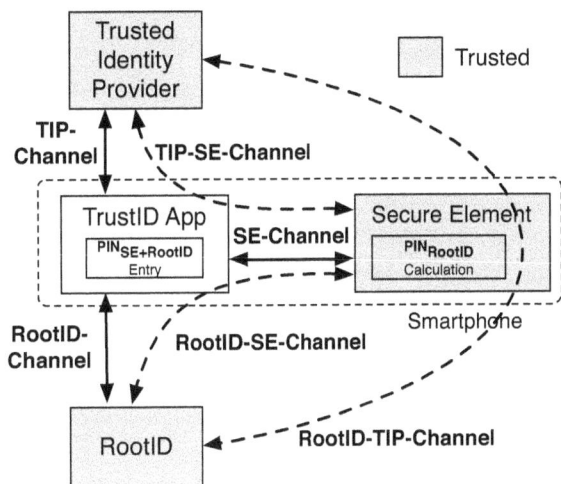

Figure 2: TrustID system architecture

RootID-TIP-Channel. This channel connects the RootID and the TIP. The channel is mutually authenticated and encrypted. It is established through the TIP-SE-Channel and the RootID-SE-Channel using the static key material in RootID and TIP. After this channel is established, any further communication between TIP and RootID is routed through this channel, which therefore replaces the two previous logical channels.

Attacks on these channels are discussed in the security evaluation in Section 6 after introducing the ID derivation protocol in detail in the next sections.

4.2 Protocol Prerequisites

As mentioned before, there are some prerequisites regarding the key material which has to be present on the entities to successfully run the TrustID protocol for ID derivation.

First, the **RootID** must contain an asymmetric key pair (e.g., ECC or RSA) SK_{RootID} (private), PK_{RootID} (public). For the public key PK_{RootID} the RootID additionally contains a certificate issued by the TIP or some other Certificate Authority (CA) which can be validated by the TIP depending on the used Public Key Infrastructure (PKI). Furthermore, the RootID contains the public key of the root of the PKI. In our concept description, the TIP is assumed to be the issuer of the certificate $Cert_{TIP}(PK_{RootID})$ as well as the root of the PKI to simplify the protocol discussion. Access to the RootID is protected by a PIN called PIN_{RootID}.

Second, the **SE** must contain key material quite similar to the one in the RootID, i.e., an asymmetric key pair (SK_{SE}, PK_{SE}), a certificate for the public key and the public key of the CA in charge. The certificate is issued by the manufacturer of the SE and vouches for a genuine and authentic SE. The SE contains a PIN called PIN_{SE} to be used in the ID derivation protocol and depending on the chosen usage protocol (see Section 4.4) an additional PIN_{Use} protecting usage of the derived IDs. Again, for simplicity, we use the TIP as CA but the PKI can be designed quite flexible. The only requirements regarding the overall PKI are:

- The TIP must be able to validate the certificates of both, the RootID and the SE.

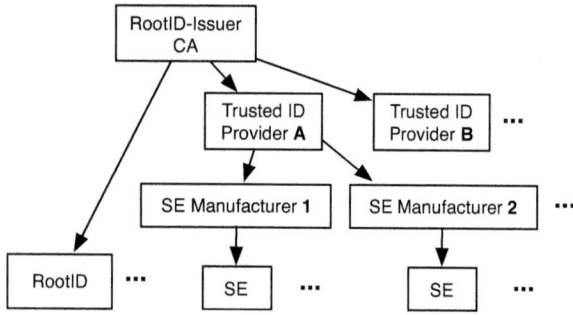

Figure 3: An example PKI for the TrustID system

- The TIP must be able to provide a certificate or a certificate chain which can be validated with the root CA keys contained in the SE and RootID (in our protocol description PK_{TIP} for both).

A simple example for a PKI is depicted in Figure 3. The depicted PKI allows for a system in which there are different TIPs, which are certified by the RootID issuer. The TIPs themselves certify different SE manufacturers.

4.3 Protocol

The real-life scenario for the TrustID protocol for ID derivation is the following: A user wants to store a context-specific identity in his smartphone, for example, some kind of virtual bank card, to get access to this specific service with his smartphone and without having to carry around his RootID and/or physical bank card. Therefore, the user starts the TrustID app on his smartphone, which he previously equipped with some certified SE (see Section 4.2), and generates the specific bank card request via the UI. This is where the TrustID ID derivation protocol starts. The protocol is depicted in Figure 4 and its single steps are described in the following. The key material prerequisites described in the previous section are also summarized in Figure 4 below each entity. At the end of the protocol, the new identity is stored securely in the certified SE inside the smartphone.

4.3.1 TIP-SE-Channel Establishment

In a first step, the SE and TIP establish the mutually authenticated and encrypted TIP-SE-Channel. The TIP-SE-Channel is established by using the static keys of both entities. With these, many different channel establishment protocols are possible, for example, a mutually authenticated certificate-based form of TLS. Since the SE is completely passive, all communication must be relayed by the smartphone and converted between the different transmission formats, for example, from Application Protocol Data Units (APDUs) to Hypertext Transfer Protocol (HTTP) requests and vice versa.

4.3.2 Secure Combined PIN Entry

A special PIN mechanism is used to establish the RootID-SE-Channel between RootID and SE. As described in Section 4.2, both the RootID and the SE each have a secret PIN (PIN_{RootID} and PIN_{SE}). These PINs are known to the user, who receives them together with the RootID/SE. Instead of entering one of the PINs directly via the touchscreen and

therefore exposing it to the possibly malicious software stack of the smartphone, the user has to do a simple calculation on both PINs to derive a *combined* PIN named $PIN_{SE+RootID}$. This calculation is denoted in Figure 4 as function f and takes PIN_{SE} and PIN_{RootID} as arguments:

$$PIN_{SE+RootID} = f(PIN_{SE}, PIN_{RootID})$$

The function should be chosen to be easily calculable by the user. The calculation must be invertible by the SE with the knowledge of PIN_{SE} in the next step. The function is therefore formally parameterized by PIN_{SE} resulting in the function $f_{PIN_{SE}}$ which only takes PIN_{RootID} as single argument. The SE receives the combined $PIN_{SE+RootID}$ and because of its knowledge about PIN_{SE} is able to calculate PIN_{RootID} with the inverse function $f_{PIN_{SE}}^{-1}$. To put it another way, only the SE intended to store the ID by the user is able to calculate the secret necessary to establish a channel to the RootID. After this calculation, both entities share a secret password in form of PIN_{RootID}, which never went through the possibly malicious software stack on the smartphone. This password is then used in the next step to establish the RootID-SE-Channel. The combined PIN entry binds the SE and RootID to each other for the protocol run preventing certain relay attacks as discussed in the evaluation in Section 6.

To make the PIN mechanism more clear, consider the following simple but realistic example for the PIN calculation function f:

$$f(x, y) := x + y$$
$$f_{PIN_{SE}}(x) := PIN_{SE} + x$$
$$f_{PIN_{SE}}^{-1}(y) := y - PIN_{SE}$$

In a concrete example with this specific PIN function, we assume $PIN_{SE} = 123456$ and $PIN_{RootID} = 345678$. The user uses the introduced function and calculates

$$PIN_{SE+RootID} = f_{PIN_{SE}}(345678) = 469134$$

and enters it through the untrusted touchscreen. The SE then calculates

$$PIN_{RootID} = f_{PIN_{SE}}^{-1}(469134) = 345678$$

to obtain the shared secret for the channel establishment with the RootID. This example also shows that the calculation to be done by the user does *not* have to be complicated.

Both, SE and RootID, must implement try counters for the PIN entry to prevent brute force attacks.

4.3.3 RootID-SE-Channel Establishment

After the secure combined PIN entry, the SE and RootID share a secret password PIN_{RootID} which they use in the next step to establish the secure RootID-SE-Channel. For that, a balanced Password-Authenticated Key Agreement (PAKE) protocol is used [3, 4, 10]. Such a protocol allows the two parties to derive a common cryptographic key based on a common human-memorable password. In our aforementioned example and implementation scenario where the RootID is the German ID card nPA, the PAKE protocol used is the Password Authenticated Connection Establishment (PACE) protocol [9], which is the standard way to establish a PIN based connection to the nPA. In this context, the SE in a way takes the role of an nPA terminal.

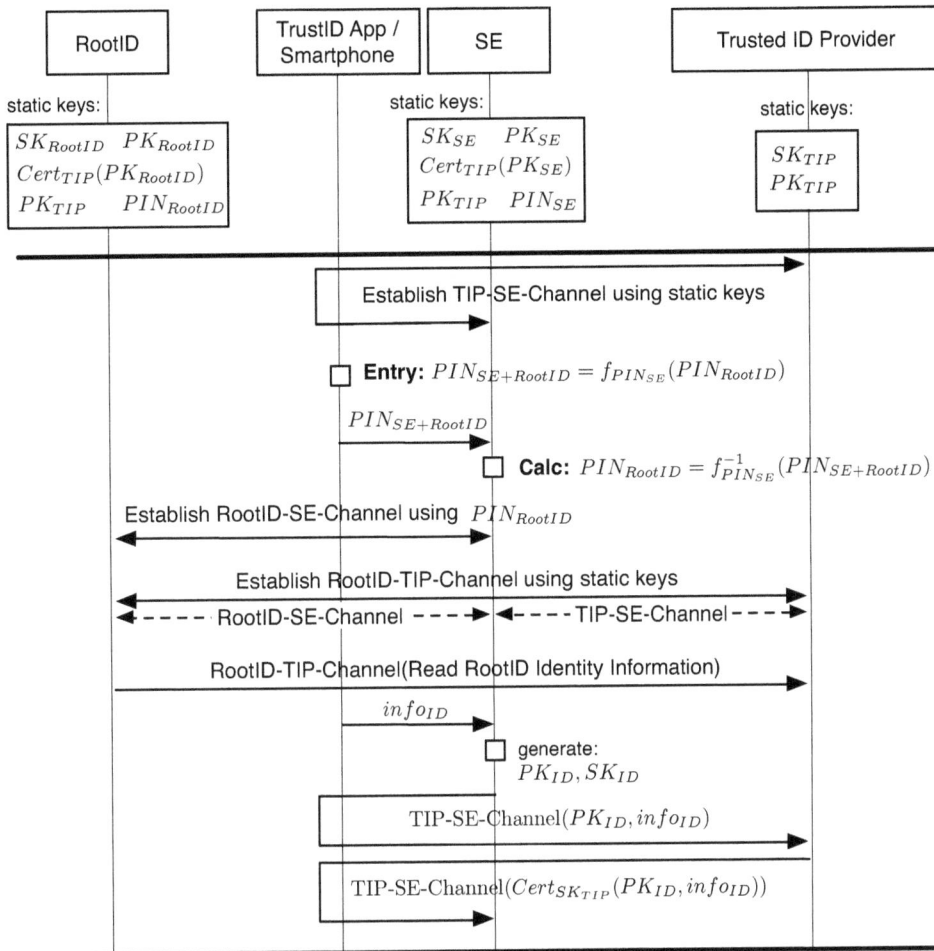

Figure 4: Protocol for the identity derivation

4.3.4 Read-out of the RootID Information

After the establishment of the RootID-SE-Channel and the TIP-SE-Channel, the RootID can be reached by the TIP going over the SE without data being sent unencrypted or unauthenticated at any point. The SE acts as a channel end-point for both channels and tunnels the communication accordingly. This tunnel is used for establishing another channel, the RootID-TIP-Channel which allows an end-to-end encrypted and mutually authenticated communication between RootID and TIP, i.e., without even the SE being able to eavesdrop information. Just as for the TIP-SE-Channel, the available key material in RootID and TIP allow for a certificate-based channel establishment protocol similar to TLS or the like. The newly set up RootID-TIP-Channel then replaces the two channels ending in the SE for all communication between RootID and TIP and is used to read the user's identity information stored in the RootID.

4.3.5 ID Generation, Validation and Transmission

As soon as the TIP has successfully read the RootID identity information, the derived ID generation is started. Therefore, the TrustID app on the smartphone encapsulates information regarding the identity requested by the user (via the UI) into an $info_{ID}$ data structure and sends it to the SE. The SE stores the $info_{ID}$ object and generates an new key pair (PK_{ID}, SK_{ID}) for the new ID. It is important that the key pair is generated directly on the SE to make sure that the private key for each ID does not *ever* leave the SE. Afterwards, the public key PK_{ID} is sent together with the $info_{ID}$ object encrypted and authenticated through the previously established TIP-SE-Channel to the TIP. The channel ensures that the TIP *only* accepts a public key for certification which was generated in the particular SE with which the protocol was previously initiated.

The TIP is now responsible for validating the ID request based on the information read from the RootID and the information to be contained in the new derived ID, i.e., the $info_{ID}$ object. The actual mechanism for the decision about granting or refusing an ID request is highly context-dependent and therefore not specified in the presented protocol. The TIP could, for example, consult a backend at a bank before granting a virtual bank card ID to a user.

If the TIP grants the request, it generates a certificate containing the public key for the newly derived ID as well as the $info_{ID}$ object. So the ID is always bound to the specific context it was created for. The certificate is then sent via the TIP-SE-Channel to the SE where it is stored together with the ID's key pair.

4.4 ID Usage

With the asymmetric key pair and the certificate for the public key including context-specific information ($info_{ID}$), the newly derived ID provides everything to be used in diverse, and application-specific ways. Basically, there are two major cases to be differentiated for a terminal using the derived ID: Either only the ID authenticates itself towards the terminal or the authentication is done mutually. In the first case, it is sufficient for the terminal to have access to the certificate chain by which the ID was certified to be able to validate the ID. In the second case, the terminal infrastructure must be included into the PKI (see Figure 3), so that every terminal gets an own certificate which can be validated by the SE using its pre-installed public root key, e.g., PK_{TIP} in our concept.

The IDs stored on the SE must be protected from unauthorized usage. Under our general assumption that the smartphone might be compromised, this protection can be provided using different PIN-based schemes. Note that it might also be possible to have no PIN protection for less security-critical identities and use cases where it is sufficient to have the smartphone as token without proving any knowledge (e.g., cafeteria micro-payments). We propose two different PIN-based schemes.

4.4.1 Basic Protection Scheme

In the first scheme, the usage of the IDs stored on the SE is protected by a *single* PIN, which we call PIN_{Use} in the following. This PIN is distinct from the PIN_{SE} used for the ID derivation. When an ID is to be used by a terminal, the user approves the usage by entering this PIN_{Use} on the *terminal* which is assumed to be trustworthy. The PIN_{Use} can then be used as shared secret for a PAKE protocol between SE and terminal like described previously for the ID derivation protocol. The untrusted smartphone is not able to gain knowledge about the PIN_{Use}.

4.4.2 Reverse Secure Combined PIN Entry

The first scheme requires the terminal to be fully trusted because it gains knowledge of the single PIN_{Use} necessary for unlimited use of all IDs stored in the SE. The second scheme allows to restrict this trust in the terminal by using a mechanism which we call *reverse secure combined PIN entry*. This mechanism is quite similar to the PIN entry mechanism described in the course of the ID derivation but reverses it. The steps are the following:

1. The user initiates the usage of an ID, e.g., by choosing the ID and putting the smartphone on a terminal reader. The terminal and/or the smartphone app send a usage request for the ID to the SE.

2. The SE generates a random *one-time valid PIN_{ID}*, calculates the previously introduced (see Section 4.3.2) function $f_{PIN_{SE}}^{-1}$ on this PIN to produce a combined PIN_{SE+ID} and returns it.

3. The combined PIN is presented to the user on the display of the smartphone. The user is able to reverse the calculation with the knowledge of the secret PIN_{SE} using $f_{PIN_{SE}}$.

4. The user enters the calculated PIN_{ID} on the terminal which is then able to use it in a PAKE protocol to establish a channel to the *specific* ID on the SE.

The first approach is quite easily usable requiring the user only to memorize an additional PIN_{Use} but requires the terminal to be more trustworthy than in the second approach. The second approach provides the improvement that the terminal only gains knowledge of a one-time valid shared secret. It furthermore restricts the access to only one specific ID. Nevertheless, the user *cannot* be sure that the used ID is the one he expects without any trust in either the terminal display or the smartphone display. As a partial solution to this problem, it could be required that both displays have to show which ID is about to be accessed. Furthermore, it must be ensured that an attacker might not gain access to the PIN_{SE+ID} displayed on the smartphone and the PIN_{ID} entered on the terminal *at the same time*. This would allow him to calculate the secret PIN_{SE} only known to the user and the SE. Both attacks require control over the terminal and the smartphone at the same time, significantly reducing their potential.

5. IMPLEMENTATION

Our prototype implementation uses the government-issued German ID card nPA as RootID, an Android smartphone running the TrustID App and a JavaCard-based SE in a microSD form factor in the corresponding slot of the smartphone. Due to the architecture necessary for the usage of the data stored in the nPA via the eID protocol [9], the TIP in the implementation consists of two distinct entities: The eID-Server and the actual TIP. In the following we discuss important aspects of the implementation regarding the different involved entities.

5.1 Trusted Identity Provider

As mentioned before, the TIP from the concept is divided in two distinct entities in the implementation. There is the actual TIP which is under our control and there is the eID-Server which is responsible for reading-out the nPA on behalf of our TIP. All communication is conducted via HTTP(s) requests/responses, which the app on the smartphone translates into APDUs to be sent to the SE or RootID and vice versa. The TLS protection on this layer is optional as the security of the communication is enforced by the TrustID protocol on top of it.

5.2 Applet on the SE

The applet in the prototype is running on a G&D Mobile Security Card SE 1.0. This SE provides the JavaCard API in version 2.2.1 and the applet is therefore programmed against this API version.

Main task of the applet is to store IDs and to provide functions to derive, manage and use them. An ID in the applet basically consists of an asymmetric RSA key pair (currently 2048 bit) and a certificate (X.509) issued by the TIP for the public key, which additionally contains information about the ID ($info_{ID}$) as X.509 extensions.

As a basic restriction of the current version of the prototype, the RootID-SE-Channel does not terminate in the JavaCard applet but directly in the TrustID Android app. This is mainly due to the fact that the JavaCard API of currently available microSD card SEs does *not* support the specific Elliptic Curve Cryptography (ECC) operations necessary for the PACE protocol channel establishment, which is the PAKE protocol to access the nPA. With an SE available supporting the required functionality, it would be necessary to port the related parts of the Android app into the SE applet to provide a complete implementation of the concept. Since the other parts of the prototype can be reused, this should only involve a moderate effort.

5.3 Android App

In the center of the implementation is the TrustID Android app. In the current prototype, the app is running on a Samsung Galaxy SIII (i9300) device with Cyanogenmod. The app provides a Graphical User Interface (GUI) which shows a list of IDs stored on the SE. The GUI allows to delete and activate the present IDs and to derive new ones. The usage of IDs is realized via the Card Emulation feature provided by the Cyanogenmod 10 release for the Galaxy SIII. This feature allows the smartphone to act as a contactless, i.e., NFC enabled, smart card while forwarding all incoming communication to software and vice versa. The TrustID app forwards this communication to the SE. This means that using one of the IDs stored on the SE is as easy as activating it and placing the smartphone on a reader.

The establishment of the secure channel between eID-Server and nPA is realized in the app using the open source library eIDClientCore [2].

Because of incompatibilities between the NFC hardware of the nPA and the Galaxy SIII, the prototype uses a so called *relay host* to enable their connection. An off-the-shelf smart card reader is connected to this relay host which reads the nPA and relays communication to the smartphone via wireless LAN.

The app listens for events indicating an NFC reader in reach and as soon as such an event is triggered provides a card emulation relay from this reader to the SE inside the smartphone. Therefore, it is only necessary to implement the ID usage functionality in the SE applet from where it can be directly used by a terminal reading the smartphone via card emulation.

6. SECURITY EVALUATION

In the following, we analyze the different channels and entities in the architecture for ID derivation (see Figure 2) regarding potential attacks and how the protocol prevents them. Security aspects for each **entity** are examined in the following based on our attacker model (see Section 2):

Trusted Identity Provider. This entity is assumed to be trusted and uncompromised and attacks against the backend are out of scope of the evaluation.

Secure Element and RootID. These entities are assumed to be trusted and unmodified. This is reasonable since they are distinct pieces of hardware hardened against software as well as physical attacks. Furthermore, both are protected by a PIN including a try counter.

TrustID App. This part of the system is assumed to be untrusted, i.e., may be maliciously modified. This must especially be considered in the evaluation with regards to user input/output.

We differentiate conceptually *direct* connection channels, i.e., the SE-Channel, the TIP-Channel and the RootID-Channel (solid lines in Figure 2), and the *indirect* connection channels, i.e., the TIP-SE-Channel, the RootID-SE-Channel

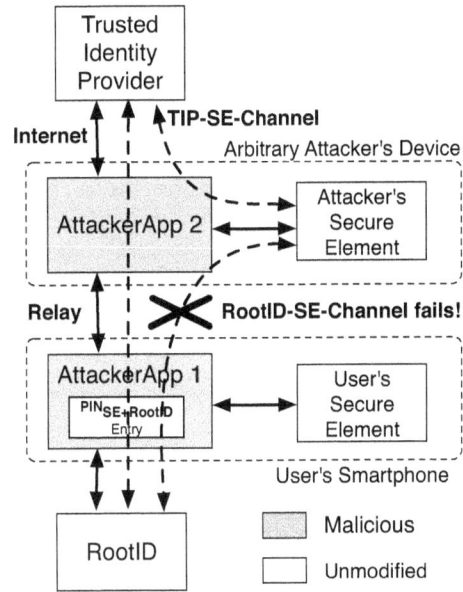

Figure 5: Relay attack and its prevention

and the RootID-TIP-Channel (dashed lines). Their security is evaluated in the following:

Direct Channels. All direct channels are unprotected, i.e., provide neither authentication nor encryption or integrity protection. They can more or less be thought of as physical connections and attacks are prevented by the secure channels on top of them.

TIP-SE-Channel. This channel is established using the static key material in a TLS-similar protocol. It is therefore protected against eavesdropping, manipulation and replay attacks. Since it is a remote channel via the Internet, the channel is implicitly relayed without introducing a security problem. With the authentication of the SE, the TIP can be sure that the channel ends in a *certified* SE but at this point there is *no* association to a specific user. This leads to the relay attack depicted in Figure 5. There, the attacker modifies the app on the user's smartphone to relay the communication remotely to an attacker's device also containing a certified SE. The goal of the attack is to have the user authenticate an ID derivation (with RootID and secret PINs) but storing the new ID in the attacker's SE. Since the TIP-SE-Channel is only guaranteed to be established with *any* certified SE, the attacker is able to set it up to his own SE. Still, the attack is prevented with the RootID-SE-Channel and the secure combined PIN entry as described in the following.

RootID-SE-Channel. The secure combined PIN entry mechanism (see Section 4.3.2) is used to establish the RootID-SE-Channel. This mechanism makes sure that the shared secret in form of the PIN_{RootID} can only be gained by the SE for which the user calculated the combined $PIN_{SE+RootID}$. This effectively binds a specific SE and RootID as intended by the user to each other for one protocol run. Since the attacker's SE, despite its knowledge of $PIN_{SE+RootID}$, is *not* able to calculate the shared secret, it cannot establish the RootID-SE-Channel. In other words, the RootID will not accept any connection attempt from the attacker's SE, effectively preventing the relay attack in Figure 5. By entering the combined PIN, the user furthermore guarantees the physical proximity of the three entities smartphone, SE and RootID, preventing also other relay attacks between these. Eavesdropping, replay and manipulation are prevented by using a secure PAKE protocol to establish the channel.

RootID-TIP-Channel. This channel is set up *through* the other secure channels using a TLS-similar, mutually authenticated certificate-based protocol. By establishing the channel through the RootID-SE-Channel and TIP-SE-Channel the different protocol steps are bound together, effectively preventing interleaving attacks.

The attacker might be able to modify the ID request generated by the user which would result in a different derived ID than intended by the user. Even if the attack is not detected by the TIP when validating the request against the RootID information, the wrongly derived ID would still *not* be under control of the attacker and safely stored in the user's SE. The attacker might be able to continously generate valid IDs on a compromised device containing a valid SE as soon as he gains knowledge of the $PIN_{SE+RootID}$. However, this attack is only possible as long as the RootID is in reach and, again, can be considered uncritical as the attacker does not gain control over the derived IDs. The attacker might also manipulate the displaying of IDs present on the SE, which we regard to be uncritical with the same argument as for the previous attacks. The same holds for all kinds of manipulations of communication data going through the app, including the $PIN_{SE+RootID}$.

7. CONCLUSION

In this paper, we introduced the TrustID architecture and protocol. Our approach allows for secure storage, derivation and usage of multiple context-specific identities on a possibly insecure or even malicious mobile device utilizing a SE as credential store. In the core of our concept, we introduced the secure combined PIN entry mechanism for user authentication, which does not rely on a trustworthy smartphone operating system or a TEE. Instead, the PIN to be entered is calculated by the user using a simple, invertible function on the secret PINs of his SE and RootID. Only the intended SE is then able to calculate the secret PIN necessary to establish a channel to the user's RootID and to proceed with the ID derivation. We also introduced a reverse secure combined PIN entry which can be used to provide access protection for the newly derived IDs even on a compromised smartphone.

We implemented a prototype running on a Samsung Galaxy SIII utilizing a microSD card SE. Identities can be derived from the German identity card nPA involving a Trusted Identity Provider connected through the Internet.

All in all, our approach provides a higher level of security than any pure software solution running on the application processor of a mobile device including TEE-based solutions are able to.

8. ACKNOWLEDGMENTS

This work was funded by the Bundesdruckerei GmbH.

9. REFERENCES

[1] A. J. Aviv, K. Gibson, E. Mossop, M. Blaze, and J. M. Smith. Smudge Attacks on Smartphone Touch Screens. In *WOOT'10: Proceedings of the 4th USENIX conference on Offensive technologies*. USENIX Association, Aug. 2010.

[2] BeID - Berlin electronic IDentity laboratory. eIDClientCore, July 2013. Retrieved July 19, 2013 from http://sar.informatik.hu-berlin.de/BeID-lab/eIDClientCore/.

[3] S. Bellovin and M. Merritt. Encrypted Key Exchange: Password-based Protocols Secure Against Dictionary Attacks. In *Research in Security and Privacy, 1992. Proceedings., 1992 IEEE Computer Society Symposium on*, pages 72–84, 1992.

[4] V. Boyko, P. MacKenzie, and S. Patel. Provably Secure Password-Authenticated Key Exchange Using Diffie-Hellman. In *Advances in Cryptology — EUROCRYPT 2000*, pages 156–171. Springer Berlin Heidelberg, May 2000.

[5] W.-D. Chen, K. E. Mayes, Y.-H. Lien, and J.-H. Chiu. NFC mobile payment with Citizen Digital Certificate. In *Next Generation Information Technology (ICNIT), 2011 The 2nd International Conference on*, pages 120–126, 2011.

[6] L. Davi, A. Dmitrienko, A.-R. Sadeghi, and M. Winandy. Privilege Escalation Attacks on Android. In *ISC'10: Proceedings of the 13th international conference on Information security*. Springer Berlin Heidelberg, Oct. 2010.

[7] A. Dmitrienko, A.-R. Sadeghi, S. Tamrakar, and C. Wachsmann. SmartTokens: Delegable Access Control with NFC-Enabled Smartphones. In *Trust and Trustworthy Computing*, volume 7344 of *Lecture Notes in Computer Science*, pages 219–238. Springer Berlin Heidelberg, 2012.

[8] A. Emigh. Online Identity Theft: Phishing Technology, Chokepoints and Countermeasures. *ITTC Report on Online Identity Theft Technology and Countermeasures*, Oct. 2005.

[9] Federal Office for Information Security (BSI). BSI TR-03110, Advanced Security Mechanisms for Machine Readable Travel Documents, Mar. 2012.

[10] O. Goldreich and Y. Lindell. Session-Key Generation Using Human Passwords Only. In *Advances in Cryptology — CRYPTO 2001*, pages 408–432. Springer Berlin Heidelberg, Aug. 2001.

[11] K. Hyppönen. An Open Mobile Identity Tool: An Architecture for Mobile Identity Management. In *EuroPKI '08: Proceedings of the 5th European PKI workshop on Public Key Infrastructure: Theory and Practice*. Springer Berlin Heidelberg, June 2008.

[12] A. Leicher, A. Schmidt, and Y. Shah. Smart OpenID: A Smart Card Based OpenID Protocol. In *Information Security and Privacy Research*, volume 376 of *IFIP Advances in Information and Communication Technology*, pages 75–86. Springer Berlin Heidelberg, 2012.

[13] P. Urien, E. Marie, and C. Kiennert. A New Convergent Identity System Based on EAP-TLS Smart Cards. In *Network and Information Systems Security (SAR-SSI), 2011 Conference on*, 2011.

Keystroke Biometrics: the User Perspective

Chee Meng Tey
DSO National Laboratories
tcheemen@dso.org.sg

Payas Gupta
New York University
payasgupta@nyu.edu

Kartik Muralidharan
Singapore Management
University
kartikm.2010@smu.edu.sg

Debin Gao
Singapore Management
University
dbgao@smu.edu.sg

ABSTRACT

Usability is an important aspect of security, because poor usability motivates users to find shortcuts that bypass the system. Existing studies on keystroke biometrics evaluate the usability issue in terms of the average false rejection rate (FRR). We show in this paper that such an approach underestimates the user impact in two ways. First, the FRR of keystroke biometrics changes for the worse under a range of common conditions such as background music, exercise and even game playing. In a user study involving 111 participants, the average penalties (increases) in FRR are 0.0360 and 0.0498, respectively, for two different classifiers. Second, presenting the FRR as an average obscures the fact that not everyone is suitable for keystroke biometrics deployment. For example, using a Monte Carlo simulation, we found that 30% of users would encounter an account lockout before their 50th authentication session (given a lockout policy of 3 attempts) if they are affected by external influences 50% of the time when authenticating.

Categories and Subject Descriptors

D.4.6 [**Software**]: OPERATING SYSTEMS—*Security and Protection, Authentication*; H.1.2 [**Information Systems**]: MODELS AND PRINCIPLES—*User / Machine Systems, Human factors*

Keywords

Authentication, Human Factors, Keystroke Biometrics

1. INTRODUCTION

Keystroke biometrics has a long history of research. Prior research has shown that typing patterns are unique to each individual and can be effectively used to identify and authenticate a user [1, 8, 15, 10, 9]. The advantages of keystroke

biometrics include low cost (no requirement for specialised hardware) and transparency of use [10].

However, being a form of behavioral biometrics, keystroke biometrics has lower accuracy when compared to physical biometrics due to the inherent variation in human behavior. Such accuracy is usually evaluated using the false acceptance rate (FAR), the proportion of anomalous attempts wrongly classified as legitimate, and false rejection rate (FRR), the proportion of legitimate attempts wrongly classified to be anomalous. In terms of FAR, a recent work by Tey et al. showed that typing patterns can be imitated [14], increasing the FAR to unacceptable levels and thereby challenging the uniqueness assumption. For FRR, prior research has suggested that typing patterns are not resistant against external influences. For example, Cho et al. and Hwang et al. showed that with active cooperation from participants, typing patterns can be influenced by artificial rhythms and cues [3, 12]. Khanna et al. showed that typing speed decreases under negative emotions and increases for positive emotions [6]. Banerjee et al. suggested that changes in posture may also influence the typing pattern [2].

In this paper, we investigate the usability of keystroke biometrics under various external influencing factors and conditions. We identify a list of common conditions that may affect user typing patterns and investigate the extent to which the FRR is affected. Prior work has studied selected factors with the aim of either improving typing consistency [3, 12], or inferring information about the external factor from the typing pattern [6].

We conduct a user study involving 111 participants and measure the change in FRR using the Scaled Manhattan classifier [1] and a bioinformatics based classifier [11]. We find that the extent of influence depends on both the classifier and the external condition. The detailed analysis on typing under different conditions can be found in Section 5.

We analyze the FRR and determine using a Monte Carlo simulation the frequency of account lockout when keystroke biometrics is used as the authentication technique. Our results show that keystroke biometrics deployment requires an adjustment in the lockout policy. This however introduces an undesirable trade-off in the FAR. We also show that not everyone is suitable for keystroke biometrics and envision that future research looks into novel ways to identify users who are not unsuitable. We suggest a change in direction from finding classifiers that have decent performance for all users, to finding one that works well for a majority.

2. BACKGROUND

In this section, we present the background of keystroke biometrics systems by briefly describing the two classifiers used in our experiments. We discuss the reasons why we choose these two classifiers in Section 3.

Keystroke biometrics systems collect information about the typing patterns of users and compare it against reference models in its database in order to perform identification or authentication. In order to build the reference models, users need to provide a certain number of training samples. In the literature, the number of samples collected varies from 8 to 400 [7]. In this paper, we choose a training sample size of 100. Given a test sample, the reference model produces a score which is compared against the model threshold to determine if the test sample should be accepted or rejected.

In the rest of this paper, given a set of n training vectors each of length l, we use the notation t_{ij} to denote the elements in the training set, where $1 \leq i \leq n$ identifies the training vector and $1 \leq j \leq l$ identifies the element within each vector.

2.1 Scaled Manhattan classifier

The Scaled Manhattan classifier [1] requires a mean vector $\bar{x}$ and an absolute deviation vector d. Each element in $\bar{x}$ and d is computed using the formulas:

$$\bar{x}_j = \frac{\sum_{i=1}^{n} t_{ij}}{n} \qquad d_j = \frac{\sum_{i=1}^{n} |t_{ij} - \bar{x}_j|}{n - 1}$$

Given a test vector y, the anomaly score s is computed using:

$$s = \sum_{j=1}^{l} \frac{|y_j - \bar{x}_j|}{d_j}$$

2.2 Bioinformatics based classifier

The bioinformatics based classifier [11] computes a motif vector using the following steps:

1. Computing a max vector m

$$m_j = \max_i t_{ij}$$

2. Mapping each vector in the training set t to a normalised vector u such that:

$$u_{ij} = \frac{t_{ij}}{m_{ij}}$$

3. Mapping each normalised vector u to a bin vector b such that: b_{ij}:

$$b_{ij} = \begin{cases} 0 & \text{if } 0 < u_{ij} \leq 0.05 \\ 1 & \text{if } 0.05 < u_{ij} \leq 0.10 \\ \cdots \\ 19 & \text{if } 0.95 < u_{ij} \leq 1.00 \end{cases}$$

4. Computing a position specific scoring matrix P with 20 rows and l columns from the set of bin vectors such that each element p_{kj} of P is given by:

$$p_{kj} = \frac{\text{count}_i(b_{ij} = k - 1)}{n}$$

where $1 \leq k \leq 20$ and $\text{count}_i(b_{ij} = k - 1)$ counts for all i the number of times b_{ij} equals to $k - 1$.

5. Computing a motif vector f such that:

$$f_j = \begin{cases} k & \text{if } \exists k : p_{kj} > 0.8 \\ -1 & \text{otherwise} \end{cases}$$

6. Counting the number of positive elements in f. If it is 21 or less, a new max vector m^* is computed such that:

$$m_j^* = \begin{cases} m_j \times 1.1 & \text{if } f_j < 0 \\ m_j & \text{otherwise} \end{cases}$$

Steps 2 to 6 are then repeated, substituting m^* for m, until the number of positive elements in f is more than 21. The last computed value of m is saved.

After obtaining the motif vector, to compute the anomaly score s for a test vector y, a bin vector y^* is obtained following steps 2 and 3. The score s is computed by comparing the differences between y^* and f element by element as follows:

$$s = \sum_{j=1}^{l} D(y_j^*, f_j) \quad \text{where} \quad D(\alpha, \beta) = \begin{cases} 0 & \text{if } \beta = -1 \\ 1 & \text{if } \beta \geq 0, \ \alpha = \beta \\ -1 & \text{if } \beta \geq 0, \ \alpha \neq \beta \end{cases}$$

2.3 Computation of threshold

Once an anomaly score is computed, a decision needs to be made to accept or reject the test sample. This requires a threshold parameter. For the Scaled Manhattan classifier, scores less than the threshold (close to the mean vector) are accepted. For the bioinformatics classifier, scores greater than the threshold (better match with motif vector) are accepted. In either case, the threshold defines a multidimensional boundary separating the acceptance space from the rejection space.

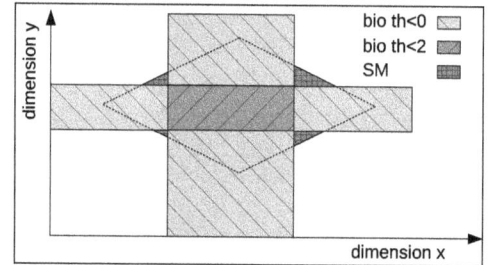

Figure 1: Comparison of classifier shapes

Figure 1 shows a possible arrangement of both classifiers that are trained on the same 2-d training set. Note that the centres of both shapes are not necessarily aligned. Any changes in typing pattern can be visualised as a shift on the diagram. Depending on the direction and magnitude of the shift, the resulting sample may be accepted by one classifier and rejected by the other. The Scaled Manhattan classifier is comparatively more vulnerable to shifts along the direction of the axes, while the bioinformatics based classifier is more vulnerable to shifts at 45° to the axes.

3. DESIGN CONSIDERATIONS AND APPROACH

High FRR results in usability problems because legitimate users may be unable to access the system or find it very frustrating to do so. This results in security problems, because it tempts users to bypass the system in ways that may compromise security. For example, users may simply leave their screens unlocked if the authentication process is inconvenient. For this reason, it is important to identify usability issues. This section documents the considerations that affect our measurement of usability and our experimental approach.

3.1 Feedback vs without feedback

In practical authentication scenarios, users know if the last login attempt succeeded or failed. The focus of this paper is to investigate the FRR after various user activities and under various conditions. To provide a more realistic evaluation, we decide to collect the data in our experiments with feedback.

We are interested to know the effects on FRR when feedback is provided. After enrolment, we plan for 2 sessions, one with feedback and one without. Comparing the FRR of these sessions allows us to determine if feedback affects the FRR, in which case existing evaluation methods may require changes to take this into account. The outcome is presented in Section 5.

3.2 Choice of conditions

There are a large number of possible activities and conditions that could potentially induce changes of FRR in authentication. In this section, we describe those that are chosen and the rationale.

3.2.1 Background music and noise

Background music occurs fairly commonly in certain workplaces or during celebratory periods. Certain users may prefer to work while listening to music. Certain environments may also be noisier in various circumstances. Prior research by Cho et al. and Hwang et al. showed that if a rhythmic music is played and users are instructed to actively follow the rhythm when typing, there is a change in their typing pattern [3, 12].

In our case, users are under passive influence. It is possible that a similar though reduced effect exists. For this experiment, we choose to play the fast paced 'The Dark Knight Rises' soundtrack by Hans Zimmer.

3.2.2 Low lighting and time pressure

Low lighting conditions arise in meeting rooms darkened for presentation or voluntary blackout events such as Earth Hour. For users who need to orientate their fingers by looking at the keyboard but who are not using a backlit keyboard, it may slowdown their typing.

Time pressure is a very common emotional condition of modern life that may affect the typing pattern. Prior research by Khanna et al. [6] showed that it is possible to infer changes in the emotion from the typing pattern. We ask in this paper whether the change in FRR is significant when there is a change in emotion due to time pressure. However, the inducement of time pressure needs to be done without causing the participants distress or causing them to type haphazardly. We display a ticking timer and inform the participants to complete their typing before the timer runs down, while offering a reward for the participant with the lowest FRR. Refer to Section 4.3 for the rationale of this reward.

The results from the low lighting and time pressure experiments also allow us to answer this question: during an emergency in a critical infrastructure environment, can an operator working under emergency backup lights and time pressure unlock his control station?

3.2.3 Plaster

A plaster applied around a finger is a common remedy for minor ailments. Although its occurrence may be rare, once applied, any effect on the typing pattern persists until the removal of plaster or the recovery of the underlying ailment. It is therefore interesting to evaluate its effect because existing evaluation methods are likely to exclude it.

3.2.4 Standing

We include standing because of past experience where it was observed to occur. Such a scenario may also arise in field work where standard office amenities are not expected to be replicated. It is known that posture affects typing pattern [2]. Our focus in this paper is the quantitative change.

3.2.5 Change of keyboard

Our emphasis is on the quantitative aspect of the change in FRR when there is a change of keyboard. This scenario is interesting because the outcome determines whether the keystroke biometrics database needs to be trained for different input devices. BYOD (Bring Your Own Device) developments, shared workstations, and even helpdesk technicians who may need login access to user devices are examples where a quantitative analysis is useful.

We include in our experiments only participants who are laptop users. Our experiments measure the change in FRR when they switch from the laptop keyboard to a standard external keyboard or an ergonomic keyboard.

3.2.6 Computer gaming and physical exercise

Both computer gaming and physical exercise are very common activities. Both induce emotional changes and possibly physical muscle strain. For our experiments, we look for participants who already have existing gaming or exercise habits. The experimental structure is designed to fit in with their routine rather than having the researchers dictate to them what they should do. For exercise in particular, we need to emphasise this point to the participants to avoid increasing the chance of injury.

For the gaming and exercise conditions, there is a possibility that the effect is long lasting and persists well beyond the end of the activity. We include an experiment to measure the FRR change after different rest periods.

3.3 Choice of userid and password

We choose as password the string `ths.ouR2` which had been shown to be more difficult to imitate [14]. This password also fits the complexity criteria in user environments and is in our opinion not atypical of actual user passwords. We choose `user1024` as the userid. We acknowledge the great diversity of userids in use. However, we have the constraint of choosing only one userid for all participants to avoid introducing the effect of typing difficulty into the sample data. We also need to avoid choosing a userid (e.g., based on a common name) that may be more familiar to some participants than others. The string `user1024` represents a good compromise in our opinion.

3.4 Choice of classifier

We compute the results using two classifiers. We choose the Scaled Manhattan classifier by Araujo [1] because it was identified as the best classifier (in terms of accuracy) in a survey by Killourhy and Maxion [7]. We choose as the second classifier, the bioinformatics based classifier by Revett [11], which was identified (in another survey) by Banerjee [2] as a classifier with good accuracy.

For experiments involving feedback, it is unrealistic to provide feedback from two classifiers at the same time. We choose arbitrarily to provide feedback for only the Scaled Manhattan classifier.

4. EXPERIMENT

In this section, we describe our experimental setup given the considerations discussed in Section 3. The basic idea of the experiments is to engage the participants in certain activities and conditions, and to measure the FRR of their authentication attempts. The whole study is divided into three sessions: s1, s2, and s3. s1 is conducted to build an anomaly dataset for training the classifier. s2 and s3 are conducted in a lab environment. s2 involves experiments that are unlikely to have any long-term effects on typing patterns while s3 involves experiments that *may* have long-term effects. Figure 2 shows the various stages of s2 and s3. Note that s2 and s3 are conducted on different days.

4.1 Participants and Setup

We recruit a total of 111 students in our tests. We receive IRB approval from our university, and compensate the participants for completion of the entire set of tasks. Table 4.1 summarises the participant demographics of our study.

Experiment	Male	Female
Background Noise	11	7
Low Light	16	7
Time Pressure	10	8
Plaster	9	8
Standing	14	4
Ergonomic KB	4	4
Standard External KB	6	3
Exercise with 45 min rest	14	4
Exercise with 15 min rest	11	5
Heavy Gamer with 45 min rest	16	4
Heavy Gamer with 15 min rest	11	7
Light Gamer with 45 min rest	9	9
Light Gamer with 15 min rest	9	12

Table 1: Demographics

4.2 s1: Anomaly dataset collection

s1 collects typing samples for the purpose of building an anomaly dataset. Each participant contributes 5 samples (without feedback of the classifier acceptance) for use as anomaly data for other participants. Each of them is required to type in a userid and password (provided by us) via our web interface. Participants are paid $4 for s1. Figure 3 shows the interface used.

This part of the study is designed to be conducted online. However, as some participants were unable to access the web interface due to technical glitches (e.g., browser compatibility), they completed s1 in a lab environment prior to the

start of s2. For these users, their typing patterns are excluded from the anomaly data set so as to ensure everyone uses a largely similar set of anomaly data. Out of 111 participants, 60 contributed 5 samples each for the anomaly data. Each of these participants' anomaly data-set contains 59×5 samples. The remaining 51 participants' anomaly data-set contains 60×5 samples.

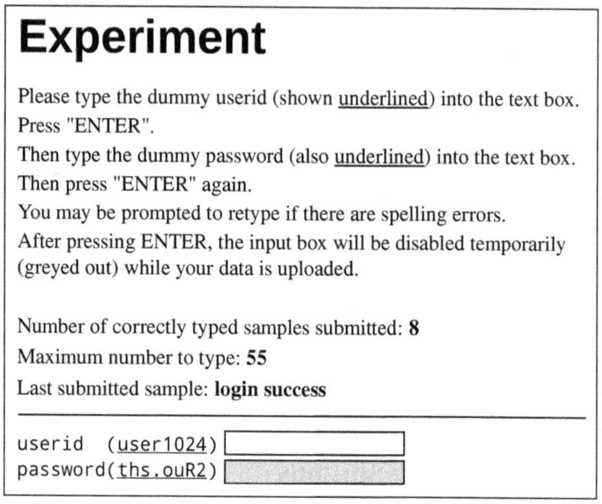

Experiment

Please type the dummy userid (shown underlined) into the text box. Press "ENTER".

Then type the dummy password (also underlined) into the text box. Then press "ENTER" again.

You may be prompted to retype if there are spelling errors.

After pressing ENTER, the input box will be disabled temporarily (greyed out) while your data is uploaded.

Number of correctly typed samples submitted: **8**

Maximum number to type: **55**

Last submitted sample: **login success**

```
userid  (user1024) [_____]
password(ths.ouR2) [_____]
```

Figure 3: User Interface for data collection

4.3 s2: Experiments with short-term effects

s2 is designed to investigate the effectiveness of keystroke biometrics under certain scenarios that we consider to have *short-term* effects. It is conducted in a lab environment post s1.

Participants are first required to answer a questionnaire capturing their emotional and physical state. This is followed by the creation of the training set whereby participants type 50 samples of the userid and password pair thrice with a gap of 10 minutes between each period. As discussed in Section 3, we design the session such that each collection period is short. We use the first 100 samples to train the classifier and the next 50 to calculate the FRR under no-feedback conditions, where there is no indication whether prior authentication attempts were successful.

Next, after a rest of 15 minutes, participants are asked to type 55 samples with feedback. We use the submitted samples to calculate the FRR, with feedback, for that user. This FRR is compared with the FRR (under no-feedback conditions) to observe the impact of feedback (if any) on a participant's FRR. We show the result of this evaluation in Section 5.

Finally, after another 15 minutes of rest, participants are asked to submit 55 samples under the following conditions: listening to fast music, with a plaster on the right index finger, using an ergonomic keyboard, using a standard external keyboard, under time pressure, under low light, and while standing (see Section 3.2).

Participants are encouraged to type the samples consistently and are in fact provided with a monetary incentive of $4 for doing so. The reason is that in practice, there is a natural penalty (account-lockout, repeated attempts) that discourages haphazard typing. This is missing in an experimental setting. The $4 incentive compensates for this.

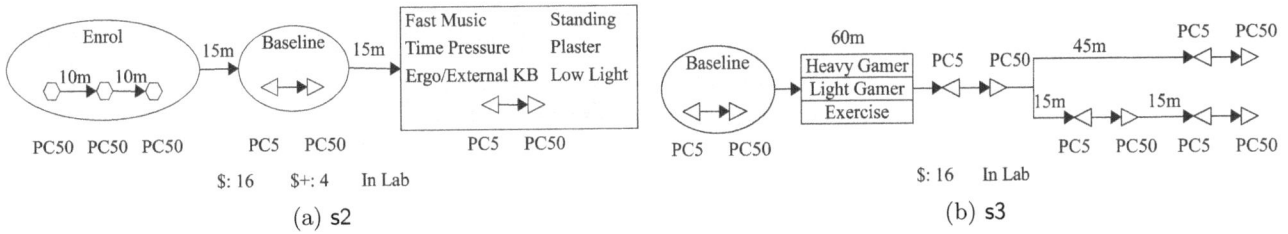

(a) s2

(b) s3

Figure 2: Experimental structure — PCn: Type userid and password n times, ◯: No feedback to user on the acceptance of their typing pattern (by the classifiers), ◁: Users are asked for their perception before providing the feedback, ▷: Feedback is provided to user, $: Amount paid for session, $+: amount paid as bonus for meeting certain criteria.

There is a possible risk of overcompensation that mask a worse FRR increase. However, the incentive provides certainty of the lower bound of the FRR increase.

At the end of s2, participants answer a questionnaire on the task experience. Note that samples with any typographical errors are not collected, but the count and order of such samples are recorded. Participants are required to retype whenever they make a typographical error.

4.4 s3: Experiments with long-term effects

The aim of s3 is to investigate the effectiveness of keystroke biometrics under scenarios that we consider to have relatively *long-term* effects. Similar to s2, participants first answer a questionnaire stating their emotional and physical states. We then collect the baseline typing pattern (55 samples) of each participant.

After the collection of baseline samples, participants are asked to perform the assigned activity (either playing a computer game or going to the gym). Each activity lasts for 60 minutes following which participants return to the lab to type 55 more samples as in s2.

After this sample collection, participants are divided into two groups. The first group is allowed to rest for 45 minutes following which 55 more typing-samples are collected. This is done to observe the effect of a long rest duration on the accuracy of their typing. Users are not allowed to use their smartphones or laptops during this rest period. They are, however, allowed to read magazines and other periodicals (provided by us) to pass time. This is to ensure that no typing is performed during the rest period, thereby minimising any undesirable influence on subsequent sample collection.

The second group is allowed to rest only for 15 minutes after which they are asked to type 55 samples. This cycle of a 15 minute rest followed by typing 55 samples is then repeated. This is done to observe the effect of intermittent rest on the accuracy of their typing. As in the first group, the participants do not perform any other typing. At the end of s3, participants answer a questionnaire on the task experience.

5. RESULTS

In this section, we present the results of our experiments. We omit the results for the experiments involving long term and intermittent rest at the end of s3. This is due to both the brevity of space and the inconclusive results for those experiments.

In our analysis, the significance level is computed using a paired student's t-test. Paired t-test is used because it indi-

cates (subject to a confidence level) whether there is a difference in the FRR with and without the environmental influences. Our null hypothesis is that there are no changes in FRR. The alternative hypothesis is that there are increases in FRR. A single-tailed test is used because we assume any changes in typing pattern increase the FRR. Subsequent results (see Figure 7) support this. The significance level follows a standard text book classification [5], where the descriptions 'highly significant', 'significant' and 'weakly significant' are used to describe p-values in the ranges of $[0, 0.01)$, $[0.01, 0.05)$, and $[0.05, 0.10)$, respectively. The criteria for pairing is based on the user.

5.1 Participant fatigue and feedback

In this section, we address concerns relating to participant fatigue and the provision of feedback that may affect the validity of our results.

5.1.1 Number of samples collected

First, we want to know whether the number of samples typed (55) is overwhelming and causes those typed later to be significantly different from those typed earlier. Figure 4 shows the relation between the average FRR for all participants and the sample index for the s2 baseline experiment.

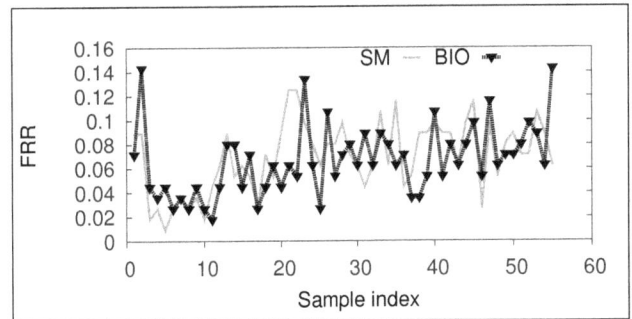

Figure 4: Effect of number of samples collected on the FRR

The coefficient of correlation between FRR and sample index are 0.4339 and 0.3994 for the Scaled Manhattan and bioinformatics classifier, respectively. This means that there is statistical support for the intuition that latter samples tend to have higher FRR than earlier samples. The slope of the regression lines through the two sets of data are, however, just 0.0007885 and 0.0007228, respectively. Therefore, the effect is not overwhelming. The time taken to collect 55 typing samples range from 3.5 min to 12.2 min, with an average of 5.3 min. The typing time is therefore short relative to the rest period.

5.1.2 *Feedback vs no feedback*

We compare for all participants the FRR of the samples collected without feedback with their session baseline which is collected with feedback. For the Scaled Manhattan classifier, the mean FRR of samples collected with feedback is 0.01106 higher than that without feedback. However, the difference is not statistically significant. On the other hand, the difference for the bioinformatics based classifier is 0.01427 and is highly significant.

If participants ignored the feedback, there should not be any significant differences. The results therefore suggest that users are not ignoring feedback and, surprisingly, are affected by it in a negative way. A possible explanation is that when users are trying hard to make sure they are typing "correctly", their typing pattern actually becomes slightly different from their enrolment pattern. This factor is not accounted for in existing literature and justifies our decision to collect typing samples with feedback.

5.2 Change of input devices

Table 2 shows the change in FRR when the input device is changed from the laptop keyboard to an external keyboard or an ergonomic keyboard. For both cases, the changes are large and highly significant. The Scaled Manhattan classifier is more adversely affected compared to the bioinformatics based classifier. Most people are unfamiliar with ergonomic keyboards and that has resulted in an extremely high FRR.

Exp	N	SM-B	SM-D	BIO-B	BIO-D
Ext. KB	9	0.1010	0.1697	0.0747	0.0889
Ergo. KB	8	0.0818	0.7500	0.0841	0.6182

Table 2: Effect of device factors on typing pattern. N: number of participants. SM-B: Baseline FRR (Scaled Manhattan). SM-D: Increase in FRR (Scaled Manhattan). BIO-B: Baseline FRR (Bioinformatics). BIO-D: Increase in FRR (Bioinformatics). All changes are highly significant.

It is clear from our results that patterns obtained using one keyboard should not be used to authenticate users when typing on a different type of keyboard. Given that in both home and corporate environments, owning multiple devices such as both a PC and a laptop is a common scenario, the results raise the question of how keystroke biometrics deployment should handle multiple input devices. A straightforward solution is to enrol the user multiple times, once for each device. However, it remains unclear whether a user can maintain a consistent typing pattern for each device when one is used only occasionally. We do not explore this issue in this paper and leave it as future work.

5.3 Effect of various conditions on FRR

Figure 5 summarises the effect of the conditions discussed in Section 3. We can see that other than the fast music experiment under the Scaled Manhattan classifier, all other conditions exhibit varying degrees of statistical significance. Different classifiers and groups of participants are affected differently by these conditions. The standing condition, plaster, and exercise are among the factors making

the larger differences, although such changes in FRR are not as big as those observed with the change in input devices.

The result for fast music is interesting. The change in FRR for the Scaled Manhattan classifier is minor and statistically insignificant. This contrasts with the one observed for the bioinformatics classifier. An explanation can be made based on a shape based interpretation of these two classifiers (see Section 2). Any changes in typing pattern corresponds to a multi-dimensional movement. It is therefore possible to move beyond the enclosure of one classifier region while remaining in the other classifier region.

Participants in the fast music experiment report that they type faster. Referring to Figure 1, this corresponds to a diagonal movement towards the approximate direction of the origin in a 2-d setting. The exact direction depends on the relative extent of movement in each dimension. This means that for the fast music experiments, the participants' typing pattern moved out of the bioinformatics region, but remained in the Scaled Manhattan region.

6. LOCKOUT AND ANNOYANCE

Even without keystroke biometrics, there is an FRR due to typing when users remember their passwords correctly, but type them wrongly. It is not a serious problem in practice because if a user makes typing errors on the initial tries, he can slow down and ensure the subsequent attempt is correct. With keystroke biometrics, such a strategy is no longer workable. If a user slows down, he increases the FRR due to keystroke biometrics. If he does not slow down, he increases the FRR due to typing mistakes. Implementing keystroke biometrics therefore increases the overall FRR of the system by more than just the keystroke biometrics FRR.

In this subsection, we investigate what the impact of this increase would be, in terms of both the likelihood of account lockout and the user reaction. To estimate the effect of the overall FRR on the user experience, we conducted a Monte Carlo simulation. We divide the users into groups based on the conditions shown in Figure 5. The simulation first picks a group, then a user within that group, both randomly. The overall FRR is computed for 2 cases: (a) baseline only, without any influence of the selected condition and (b) baseline + condition. The overall FRR takes into account both typing errors and keystroke biometrics error. The simulation computes, for each login session, the number of tries required to login.

Figure 6 shows the cumulative percentage of users who will encounter a lockout after a certain number of login sessions. For example, approximately 30% of users will encounter a lockout before their 50th authentication session if the lockout policy is 3 attempts and if, in 50% of the trials, they are under the influence of one of the conditions of Figure 5.

Figure 6 shows that keystroke biometrics is not for everyone. Even with a lockout policy of 5, approximately 10% of users will find keystroke biometrics very frustrating to use. This suggests that finding classifiers that work for all users is a difficult task. A possible alternative is to find classifiers that work well for the majority. The unsuitable minority requires an alternative login mechanism.

Figure 6 also shows that deployment of keystroke biometrics must come with an adjustment in lockout policy, but at a cost in security. Keystroke biometrics is considered as a security mechanism to enhance the security of weak password [10]. However, when the password is weak and the

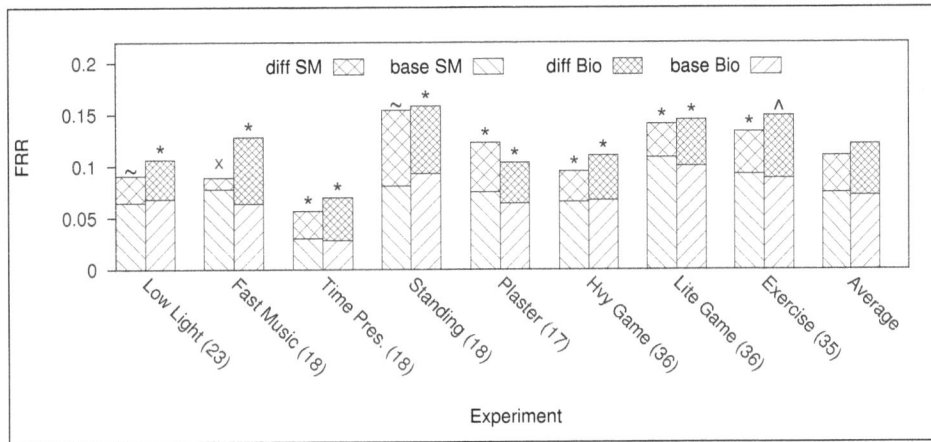

Figure 5: Effect of various conditions on typing pattern (baseline and increase in FRR). Numbers in brackets indicate the number of participants. ∧: highly significant. *: significant. ~: weakly significant. x: not significant.

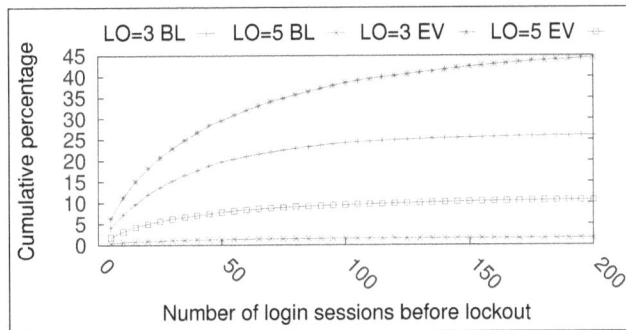

Figure 6: Number of authentication sessions before user gets lockout. LO: Lockout policy. BL: Baseline (no environmental factors). EV: Environmental factors in effect 50% of the time.

lockout is adjusted to 5, the added security may be modest. Table 3 shows the chance that an attacker can break into a system if he already knows the password. For an FAR value of 0.05, the overall FAR is 0.22622 if the attacker is allowed to make 5 attempts. In other words, approximately 1 in 4 such attempts will succeed.

	FAR			
Lockout Policy	0.001	0.01	0.02	0.05
1	0.00100	0.01000	0.02000	0.05000
2	0.00200	0.01990	0.03960	0.09750
3	0.00300	0.02970	0.05881	0.14263
4	0.00399	0.03940	0.07763	0.18549
5	0.00499	0.04901	0.09608	0.22622

Table 3: Chance of attacker success before lockout (detection).

Other than lockout, we are interested in possible user annoyance. We asked the participants for their reactions if, on average, they need to type their credentials multiple times before they can login. Table 4 summarises the responses.

Figure 7 shows the cumulative percentage of users who will encounter a login session in which they succeed but find very annoying. For example, more than 40% of users will

	2 tries	3 tries	4 tries	5 tries
Okay	37.62	5.94	0.99	0.00
Mildly annoying	51.49	51.49	16.83	3.96
Very annoying	10.89	42.57	82.18	96.04

Table 4: User response (%) to the number of tries require for authentication. E.g. 10.89% of users are very annoyed if they need 2 tries to login.

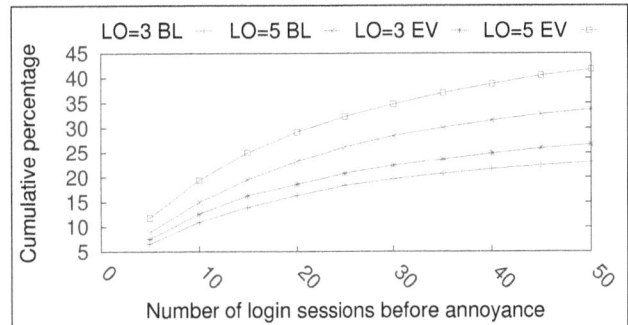

Figure 7: Number of authentication sessions before user encounters a very annoying one. LO: Lockout policy. BL: Baseline (no environmental factors). EV: Environmental factors in effect 50% of the time.

encounter an annoying session before their 50th authentication session if the lockout policy is 5 attempts and if, in 50% of the trials, they are under the influence of the conditions in Figure 5. The occurrence of annoyance is lower when the lockout policy is 3 because users get locked out before they have a chance to succeed (but feel annoyed). This shows that even after solving the lockout problem, keystroke biometrics still has to contend with user frustration over the multiple login attempts required.

7. LIMITATIONS

We discuss some limitations of our experiments in this section. In both sessions s2 and s3, we ask participants to abstain from exercise and gaming for the prior 24 hours, to avoid introducing any possible influence from these activities. We are dependent on the participants to observe these restrictions in good faith.

In our experiments, we collect the typing samples via a web based interface using participants' own laptop. The latter is because we want to ensure they are using a familiar keyboard layout. However, this also implies that the input devices come in a variety of OS and hardware. In particular, the timing granularity varies. For Windows XP systems, this can be up to 16 ms. In the literature, the timing granularity varies from 0.2 ms [7], 1 ms [1] and 10 ms [13, 4]. To ensure timings are collected accurately, we also exclude laptops which are overloaded with too many computationally intensive background processes.

In all our experiments, a single password is used. That password is chosen to be difficult to type, which unfortunately increases the chance of typing it wrongly, and in turn increases the FRR. If participants are to use an easier password, the number of typing errors should decrease. However, we believe our chosen password is more representative of those mandated by corporate security policies.

8. CONCLUSION

We find that various environmental factors such as playing computer games, exercise, lighting conditions, fast music, emotional pressure, and even the application of a plaster on one finger result in varying increase of FRR. Different users are also affected differently. Certain users are shown to be unsuitable for keystroke biometrics. This suggests that instead of a research direction that attempts to find classifiers that work for all users, a more practical approach may be to find users who have low baseline FRR and are tolerant towards environmental changes. This implies a hybrid approach where keystroke biometrics is implemented for only a subset of users, and is complemented by an alternative authentication mechanism.

Acknowledgment

This work was supported in part by Singapore Management University grant 13-C220-SMU-003.

9. REFERENCES

[1] L. Araujo, L. Sucupira, Jr., M. Lizarraga, L. Ling, and J. Yabu-Uti. User authentication through typing biometrics features. *Trans. Sig. Proc.*, 53(2):851–855, Feb. 2005.

[2] S. Banerjee and D. Woodard. Biometric Authentication and Identification using Keystroke Dynamics: A Survey. *Journal of Pattern Recognition Research*, 7:116–139, 2012.

[3] S. Cho, C. Han, D. H. Han, and H. il Kim. Web based keystroke dynamics identity verification using neural network. *Journal of Organizational Computing and Electronic Commerce*, 10:295–307, 2000.

[4] S. Haider, A. Abbas, and A. Zaidi. A multi-technique approach for user identification through keystroke dynamics. In *IEEE International Conference on Systems, Man and Cybernetics*, SMC 2000, pages 1336–1341, 2000.

[5] G. Keller and B. Warrack. *Statistics for management and economics*. Number v. 1 in International student edition: Wadsworth. Thomson/Brooks/Cole, 2003.

[6] P. Khanna and M.Sasikumar. Article: Recognising emotions from keyboard stroke pattern. *International Journal of Computer Applications*, 11(9):1–5, December 2010. Published By Foundation of Computer Science.

[7] K. Killourhy and R. Maxion. Comparing anomaly-detection algorithms for keystroke dynamics. In *Dependable Systems Networks, 2009. DSN '09. IEEE/IFIP International Conference on*, pages 125 –134, Jul 2009.

[8] K. S. Killourhy. *A Scientific Understanding of Keystroke Dynamics*. Dissertation, Carnegie Mellon University, 2012.

[9] F. Monrose and A. D. Rubin. Keystroke dynamics as a biometric for authentication. *Future Gener. Comput. Syst.*, 16(4):351–359, Feb 2000.

[10] A. Peacock, X. Ke, and M. Wilkerson. Typing Patterns: A Key to User Identification. *IEEE Security and Privacy*, 2(5):40–47, Sept. 2004.

[11] K. Revett. A bioinformatics based approach to user authentication via keystroke dynamics. *International Journal of Control, Automation and Systems*, 7:7–15, 2009.

[12] S. seob Hwang, H. joo Lee, and S. Cho. Improving authentication accuracy using artificial rhythms and cues for keystroke dynamics-based authentication. *Expert Systems with Applications*, 36(7):10649 – 10656, 2009.

[13] D. X. Song, D. Wagner, and X. Tian. Timing analysis of keystrokes and timing attacks on SSH. In *Proceedings of the 10th conference on USENIX Security Symposium - Volume 10*, SSYM'01, pages 25–25, Berkeley, CA, USA, 2001. USENIX Association.

[14] C. M. Tey, P. Gupta, and D. Gao. I can be You: Questioning the use of Keystroke Dynamics as Biometrics. In *Proceedings of NDSS*, San Diego, CA, Feb 2013.

[15] D. Umphress and G. Williams. Identity verification through keyboard characteristics. *International Journal of Man-Machine Studies*, 23(3):263–273, Sept. 1985.

Relationship-based Information Sharing in Cloud-based Decentralized Social Networks

Davide Alberto Albertini, Barbara Carminati
DISTA, Università degli Studi dell'Insubria
Via Mazzini 5, Varese, Italy
{davide.albertini, barbara.carminati}@uninsubria.it

ABSTRACT

Commercial OSNs have started to provide users with the ability to set their privacy settings for a more controlled information sharing. However, these settings do not prevent the social network manager to perform marketing research on user personal data, aiming, as example, at offering a personalized advertising to users. To cope with these requirements Decentralized Social Networks (DSNs) are emerged as a possible solution for moving users' personal data out from OSN realms. Unfortunately, it has been shown that DSNs have some limitations, in terms of usability and social features they offer. To overcome this problem, in this paper we extend the DSN framework so that users' data (e.g., resources and relationships) are securely stored in a public cloud data storage and shared according to relationship-based rules defined by owners, by at the same time supporting a privacy-preserving path finding. To this end, we make use of encryption techniques and we devise a new collaborative anonymization process. In the paper, besides presenting all the components of our framework, we analyze its security and present experiments showing the feasibility of the developed techniques.

Categories and Subject Descriptors

H.3.5 [**Information Storage and Retrieval**]: Online Information Services, Data Sharing, Web-based Services; K.6.5 [**Management of Computing and Information Systems**]: Security and Protection

Keywords

Online social network; Collaborative graph anonymization; Controlled information sharing; Privacy-preserving path finding.

1. INTRODUCTION

It is nowadays well accepted that in online social networks (OSN) information is released according to relationship-based

CODASPY'14, March 3–5, 2014, San Antonio, Texas, USA.
Copyright 2014 ACM 978-1-4503-2278-2/14/03 ...$15.00.
http://dx.doi.org/10.1145/2557547.2557574.

access rules (e.g., [7, 13]). In general, by means of these rules, information owner can pose conditions on the relationship(s) (e.g., on its type, depth, and possible trust value) the requestor has to have in order to be authorized to access owner's resources. Thus, by properly defining the privacy settings, users can control how their personal information is shared in the network. However the available privacy settings do not prevent the social network manager to perform marketing research on user personal data (e.g., Facebook, Google). The problem is exacerbated if we consider that some of the most known social networking sites have not been always transparent with respect to user privacy (see, for instance, [17] for a survey on these privacy concerns). Moreover, they showed their weaknesses in accidentally releasing user data (e.g., the Google cyber attack in 2009 [20] or Google glitches [29]).

All these reasons bring to observe that site-controlled privacy settings are not enough, but a more concrete solution is needed. As highlighted by Tim Berners-Lee *et al.* in [31], *Decentralized Social Networks (DSN)* are emerged as promising solution for moving users' personal data out from OSN realms. A DSN consists in a distributed system composed of multiple providers (federation) that run a social networking service. Each user can choose to store personal data on his/her own trusted provider inside the federation or to deploy his/her own provider on a private machine. However, it has been showed that few users are able to set up their own providers, as they prefer to subscribe to existing one. As example, the 70% of users of one of the most notable DSN, i.e., Diaspora, are subscribed at the same provider [4]. Moreover, DSN still needs to access the whole social graph in order to support several functionalities (e.g., users' wallboards, information sharing, group messaging). This requires users to expose information about their relationships to DSN manager. Several proposals have been presented in the context of DSN. Among these, Diaspora [16], Persona [2], SafeBook [9], PeerSon [8], Vegas [11], Vis-à-Vis [26] and DECENT [23]. All of them propose their own architecture for a decentralized OSN via P2P architecture or similar, but none of them solve the problem of a centralized management of relationship data. Moreover, in literature several solutions have been presented to hide data from OSN providers, such as Scramble! [3], FaceCloak [25], Lockr [27] or Trust&Share [12]. However, none of them moves out relationship data from OSN realms, leaving the providers the possibility to perform data mining on them.

For these reasons we believe that a stronger data protection paradigm should be integrated in Decentralized Social

Network. As a first step towards this direction, this paper proposes to extend the DSN architecture so that users' data (e.g., resources and relationships) are encrypted and stored in public cloud and released according to relationship-based rules defined by resources owners. In particular, the proposed extension requires that users encrypt their resources before uploading in the cloud. The adopted key management ensures that resources can be decrypted only by users for which it exists at least a relationship in the graph satisfying the corresponding access control rules. As described in the paper, the framework ensures that *neither the cloud nor the entities involved in the keys management are able to decrypt users' resources.*

Protecting the relationship information stored in the cloud requires a different approach. The literature offers several techniques for graph anonymization, where most of them anonymize the graph by either clustering nodes (e.g., [5, 10, 21]) or graph modification (e.g., [18, 22, 24]). However, all of them have been designed under two common assumptions. The first is that the anonymization process is carried out on the whole graph. Unfortunately, this cannot be applied in decentralized architectures. Indeed, in our scenario the anonymization process has to be carried out locally at user side, by exploiting only user local view. Moreover, existing solutions anonymize the graph by modifying its topology (i.e., adding/deleting edges). It is relevant to note that among these solutions Terzi *et al.* [18] proposed a graph anonymization technique only exploiting neighborhood information. However, similar to other solutions, the obtained anonymized topology is modified. This brings to a data loss that is not acceptable for a relationship-based access control.[1]

Given these strong requirements, we propose a *collaborative anonymization process that preserves the graph topology.* This is achieved by making use of polynomials to encode user contact lists. In the paper, we will show how polynomials are created and used to enforce a relationship-based information sharing. To the best of our knowledge, [6] is the only work proposing a collaboration among users for computing privacy-preserving operations over graphs, without editing their topology. Unfortunately these algorithms are suitable only to solve path-finding problem on path of length ≤ 2.

The paper is organized as follows. Section 2 presents the overall architecture of the cloud-based decentralized social network. The collaborative anonymization process is introduced in Section 3, whereas Section 4 illustrates the interactions among framework entities. A discussion on the security analysis is provided on Section 5. Section 6 presents some experiments showing the feasibility of the developed techniques, and Section 7 concludes the paper.

2. CLOUD-BASED DSN

In general, an OSN can be represented as undirected labeled graph $G=(V, E, RT)$, where: V represents the OSN users; E is the set of edges modeling direct connections between users in V; RT are the possible edge labels represent-

ing the type of relationship (e.g., friend, colleague, etc.). We say that u and v have a direct relationship of $RelType$, if there exists an edge $e \in E$ labelled with $RelType$; they have an indirect relationship of $RelType$ and depth n if there exists a path connecting u and v consisting only of n edges, all labelled with $RelType$. With reference to Figure 1, as example, node A is connected to G with direct friendship and to L with friendship of length 3.

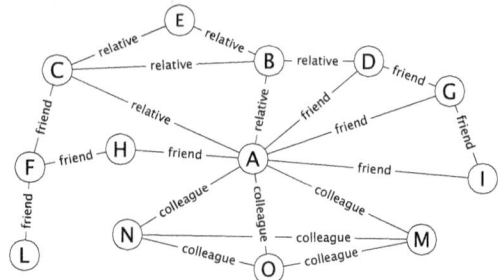

Figure 1: Example of social network graph

Given a resource rsc, its owner specifies a rule $\mathcal{R}$ according to which rsc has to be released in the OSN community. More precisely, inspired by access control models proposed for OSN (see, [7, 13, 14]), we assume that each rule states a set of conditions on the type and the depth of the relationship that the requestor has to have with the owner in order to access rsc. Formally, a rule $\mathcal{R}$ can be defined as a set of access conditions, each one in the form $ac = (RelType, MaxDepth)$. For simplicity, hereafter, we assume that access rules consist of a unique access condition ac, i.e., $\mathcal{R} = \{ac\}$.

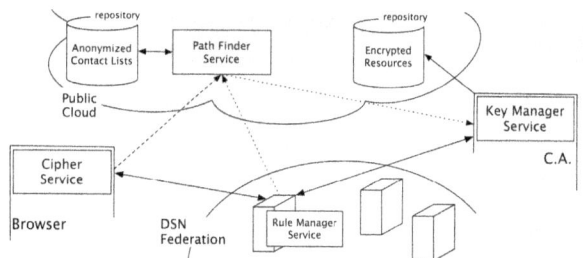

Figure 2: Cloud-based Decentralized Social Network

According to the proposed architecture (see Figure 2), resources to be shared are locally encrypted by owners and stored into cloud storage (i.e., *Encrypted Resources* repository in Figure 2).[2] Rule enforcement is carried out by releasing encryption keys only to requestors that satisfy at least one of the owner access rules. This enforcement requires the presence of two more entities: *Rule Manager Service* (*RMS*) to handle access control requests and *Key Manager Service* (*KMS*) for the keys management. As it will be discussed in Section 5, protocols regulating the resources release have been designed so that no one of *RMS* and *KMS* can decrypt owner resources as well as infer any information on owner relationships. This holds under the assumption that *RMS* and *KMS* do not collude together. In support of this assumption, we assume that *RMS* is implemented as a service in a DSN server; whereas *KMS* is an external trusted entity, whose role could be played by a Certificate Authority.

---

[1]In fact, adding a fake edge between existing nodes might create a new path satisfying some relationship-based rules, with the serious consequence of improper resource release. In contrast, deleting an edge might delete some real path making some rules no more satisfied and, as consequence, making the corresponding resource no more available to authorized users.

[2]In support of this, we assume that at the user is provided with the *Cipher Service* (*CS*) browser plugin, which is mainly in charge of owner's resources encryption and generation of anonymized owner's contact lists.

Moreover, to determine if a rule is satisfied, it is required to find those paths in the social network graph that connect owner to requestor. To protect relationship privacy, this path finding is carried out on anonymized data structures stored in the cloud (i.e., *Anonymized Contact Lists* (ACLs) in Figure 2). These data structures consist of an entry for each user storing, in a private way (i.e., as polynomials), the list of users that are connected with him/her at different depths. As described in Section 3, these data structures are computed by a collaborative anonymization process where each user sends an anonymized version of its direct contact list (i.e., a polynomial) that is then privately combined with other anonymized contact list at cloud side so as to obtain *ACLs*. This task is performed by the *Path Finder Service* (*PFS*) at cloud side.

3. COLLABORATIVE GRAPH ANONYMIZATION

The goal is to design an anonymization strategy such that given a requestor r and a rule $\mathcal{R} = (t, d)$ it is possible to verify if it exists a path of type t and length less or equal than d connecting the resource owner to r. In order to support this query, we define a set of anonymized data structures that organize users' contacts by relationship type and length of the connecting paths. More precisely, given a relationship type t and a user u, the proposed anonymized contact list $ACL_t^d(u)$ privately encodes identifiers of those users that are connected with u by a path of t type and length equal to d. Before presenting its definition, let us introduce some needed notations.

We assume that with each user is assigned a set of identifiers based on the types of the relationships he/she involved. More precisely, given a user $u \in V$, and a relationship type t, the unique type-based identifier for u is defined as $uid_u = h(id_u||t)$, where id_u is the unique identifier associated with u in the DSN realm.[3] Moreover, given a user $u \in V$, we denote with $CL_t^n(u) \subset V$ the set of users that have with u a relationship of type t and depth n. Hereafter, we denote with $UID_t^n(u) = \bigcup_{v \in CL_t^n(u)} \{uid_v\}$ the set containing all the identifiers of these users.

DEFINITION 3.1. *The* **Anonymized Contacts List** *for* $CL_t^n(u)$, *denoted as* $ACL_t^n(u)$, *is the set of coefficients of the polynomial* $P_{CL_t^n(u)}$ *of degree* $|CL_t^n(u)|$, *computed as follows:*

$$P_{CL_t^n(u)}(x) = \prod_{uid \in UID_t^n(u)} (x - uid). \qquad (3.1)$$

As such, $uid \in UID_t^n(u)$ *are all and the only possible roots of* $P_{CL_t^n(u)}$, *and* $P_{CL_t^n(u)}$ *results as a complete monic polynomial.*

EXAMPLE 3.1. *Based on social graph depicted in Figure 1, user A generates* $CL_{friend}^1(A) = \{D, G, H, I\}$, $CL_{relative}^1(A) = \{B, C\}$ *and* $CL_{colleague}^1(A) = \{M, N, O\}$. *According to Definition 3.1, the ACLs for user A are defined as the coefficients of the following polynomials:*

$$P_{CL_{friend}^1(A)}(x) = (x - h(id_D||friend)) \cdot (x - h(id_G||friend)) \cdot$$
$$\cdot (x - h(id_H||friend)) \cdot (x - h(id_I||friend))$$
$$P_{CL_{relative}^1(A)}(x) = (x - h(id_B||relative)) \cdot (x - h(id_C||relative))$$
$$P_{CL_{colleague}^1(A)}(x) = (x - h(id_M||colleague)) \cdot (x - h(id_N||colleague)) \cdot$$
$$\cdot (x - h(id_O||colleague))$$

Based on Definition 3.1, it is easy to verify if a node v satisfies an access rule $ac = (t, d)$ defined by user u. Indeed, it is required only to evaluate whether v's identifier, i.e., $h(id_v||t)$, is a root of at least a polynomial $P_{CL_t^n(u)}(x)$, with $n \leq d$. In contrast, under the assumption of a high degree of P it is hard to find all *uids* (see Section 5).

As Example 3.1 highlights, ACL_t^1 can be easily computed at user side. Unfortunately this does not hold for ACL_t^n with $n > 1$, since it requires to know *uids* of each indirectly connected users, whereas in this proposal we assume that users have only a local view (i.e., they only know their direct neighbors). To overcome this limitation, we propose a solution where *ACLs* for $n > 1$ are privately generated directly at cloud side by *PFS*.

The basic idea is that, given a certain $ACL_t^1(u)$ generated by u on his own, if v is a direct contact of type t for u,[4] then, for the same relationship type t, v's contacts at distance d have to be considered $(d+1)$-hops contacts of u and vice versa, for any $d > 1$. Thus, if $u \in CL_t^1(v)$, $\forall d > 1$, then $CL_t^d(u) \subseteq CL_t^{d+1}(v)$. As consequence, $ACL_t^d(v)$ has to contain *uids* encoded in $ACL_t^d(u)$ and $ACL_t^d(u)$ has to contain those which are encoded in $ACL_t^d(v)$.

To privately insert $ACL_t^d(v)$'s roots into $ACL_t^{d+1}(u)$, we exploit the polynomial property that, given $P(x)$ and $P'(x)$, the roots of the polynomial $Q(x) = P(x) \cdot P'(x)$ are all and only values in the union set of roots satisfying $P(x)$ and roots satisfying $P'(x)$.

As such, we assume that each time a anonymized contact list $ACL_t^1(u)$ for a new user u is received, *PFS* first verifies which of the already registered users, i.e., their uids, satisfy the new uploaded polynomial. That is, it determines the subset $S \subset V$ such that $\forall p \in V$, $P_{CL_t^1(u)}(uid_p) = 0 \iff p \in S$. Then, $\forall p \in S$: (1) it inserts the p's direct contacts into anonymized 2-hop contact list of u, that is, it stores into $ACL_t^2(u)$ the coefficients of polynomial resulting by the multiplication of $P_{CL_t^2(u)}(x) \cdot P_{CL_t^1(p)}(x)$; (2) it inserts the p's indirect contacts of distance n into anonymized $(n+1)$-hop contact list of u, i.e., $ACL_t^{n+1}(u)$, as coefficients of polynomial resulting by the multiplication of $P_{CL_t^{n+1}(u)}(x) \cdot P_{CL_t^n(p)}(x)$.

It is important to note that, step (2) could be performed for any n value. However, we limit this computation at threshold $MaxDepth$, which indeed constraints the maximum distance between two nodes in the anomyzed graph. As such, this value limits the length of the paths over which searches have to be performed. We believe this does not represent a limitation. Indeed, according to the small world property and other studies (e.g., [15]) we expect that every pair of users (u, v) is connected by a limited number of edges in the SN community.

EXAMPLE 3.2. *Let us consider the generation of ACL encoding a indirect friends list at 2-hops distance. Given* $P_{CL_{fr}^1(A)}(x)$ *of Example 3.1, the polynomial* $P_{CL_{fr}^2(A)}(x)$ *is*

---

[3]This relies on the assumption that inside DSN each user is uniquely identified by an unique *id*, which is true in each commercial OSN.

[4]That is, $uid_v = h(id_v||t)$ satisfies $P_{CL_t^1(u)}(x = uid_v) = 0$.

generated as follows: [5]

$$P_{CL^2_{fr}(A)}(x) = P_{CL^1_{fr}(D)}(x) \cdot P_{CL^1_{fr}(G)}(x) \cdot P_{CL^1_{fr}(H)}(x) \cdot P_{CL^1_{fr}(I)}(x) =$$
$$= [(x - uid_A) \cdot (x - uid_G)] \cdot$$
$$\cdot [(x - uid_A) \cdot (x - uid_D) \cdot (x - uid_I)] \cdot$$
$$\cdot [(x - uid_A) \cdot (x - uid_F)] \cdot$$
$$\cdot [(x - uid_A) \cdot (x - uid_G)] =$$
$$= (x - uid_A)^4 \cdot (x - uid_D) \cdot (x - uid_F) \cdot (x - uid_G)^2 \cdot (x - uid_I).$$

We assume that $ACLs$ are stored into a set of tables, one for each supported relationship type. More precisely, for each relationship type $t \in RT$, the corresponding $Table_t$ contains an entry for each user u storing into $MaxDepth$ columns the corresponding $ACL^n_t(u)$, with $1 \leq n \leq MaxDepth$.

4. RELATIONSHIP-BASED INFORMATION SHARING

Let us now introduce how the proposed framework enforces the relationship-based information sharing by illustrating protocols for resource upload and download. In doing that, we assume that communication between entities is transmitted over secure channels.[6] We assume that the public key of CS, K^+_{CS}, is known by RMS and KMS as it will be used to encipher messages directed to CS.

Resource Upload.

Given a resource rsc, before uploading it in the cloud, its owner, say user u, has to encrypt it using a symmetric key K_{rsc}. This key is computed as combination of two secrets, i.e. $K_{rsc} = \mathcal{F}(secret_u, secret_{rsc})$, which are separately generated by RMS and KMS.[7] These secrets are defined such that: $secret_u$ is uniquely associated with user u by RMS; $secret_{rsc}$ is uniquely associated with rsc by KMS.

Thus, before any upload, resource owner has to interact with RMS and KMS so as to retrieve the corresponding $secret_u$ and $secret_{rsc}$. The protocol underling this message exchange is represented in Table 1. Note that, as depicted also in Figure 2, CS communicates with KMS by means of RMS. Indeed, we adapted the structure of Needham-Schroeder protocol. As such, CS creates a message for RMS, by encapsulating inside it the message directed to KMS. Assuming that only KMS has the private key K^-_{KMS}, RMS cannot decrypt the encapsulated message, but just forward to KMS.

Thus, once the *secrets* are generated by RMS and KMS (messages 2, 4 in Table 1) and received by u (message 6 in Table 1, encrypted with CS public key), the user is able to compute K_{rsc}. Hence, u composes a message including the encrypted resource (to be transmitted to KMS) and the set of access control rules $\mathcal{R}_{rsc}$ that RMS has to store. As depicted, CS sends all messages to RMS, which then forwards nested encrypted messages to KMS. After the execution of

---

[5] Due to space constraint the label *'friend'* for relationship type is shortened as *'fr'*.

[6] If available and certificated, the CS uses the user's private-public key to encrypt messages; otherwise when a new CS instance is created, the KMS generates and certifies a couple of asymmetric keys $\langle K^+_{CS}, K^-_{CS} \rangle$ which are then communicated to the CS.

[7] Several $\mathcal{F}$ functions can be adopted. In actual implementation, we make use of XOR.

protocol depicted in Table 1, the cloud data storage service contains the encrypted resource, whereas RMS and KMS contain only resource metadata. In particular, KMS stores id_{rsc} and $secret_{rsc}$, whereas RMS saves id_{rsc} along with the resource access control rules $\mathcal{R}_{rsc}$.

1.	$CS \to RMS:$	$\{id_u, N_1, \{id_u, id_{rsc}, N_2\}_{K^+_{KMS}}\}_{K^+_{RMS}}$
2.	$RMS:$	Retrieve $secret_u$, if any, or generate a new one
3.	$RMS \to KMS:$	$\{id_u, id_{rsc}, N_2\}_{K^+_{KMS}}$
4.	$KMS:$	Compute new unique $secret_{rsc}$
5.	$KMS \to RMS:$	$\{secret_{rsc}, N_2 + 1\}_{K^+_{CS}}$
6.	$RMS \to CS:$	$\{secret_u, N_1 + 1, \ldots$ $\ldots \{secret_{rsc}, N_2 + 1\}_{K^+_{CS}}\}_{K^+_{CS}}$
7.	$CS:$	Compute $K_{rsc} = \mathcal{F}(secret_u, secret_{rsc})$
8.	$CS \to RMS:$	$\{id_u, N_1 + 2, id_{rsc}, \mathcal{R}_{rsc}, \{id_u, id_{rsc}, \{rsc\}_{K_{rsc}}, N_2 + 2\}_{K^+_{KMS}}\}_{K^+_{RMS}}$
9.	$RMS:$	Store $\mathcal{R}_{rsc}$
10.	$RMS \to KMS:$	$\{id_u, id_{rsc}, \{rsc\}_{K_{rsc}}, N_2 + 2\}_{K^+_{KMS}}$
11.	$KMS:$	Store $rsc_{K_{rsc}}$ in cloud storage service

Table 1: Resource upload protocol

Resource Download.

If a requestor req wishes to download and decrypt rsc, it sends a message to RMS with the corresponding ids (i.e., message 1 in Table 2). This retrieves the corresponding access rules $\mathcal{R}_{rsc}$, the id of rsc's owner (i.e., id_{own}). Then, assuming $\mathcal{R}_{rsc} = ac = (t, d)$, it inquires PFS to search for a path connecting the requestor to the owner, with all edges labeled with t and length less than d (i.e., messages 3-4 in Table 2). It is important to note that if PFS sends the yes/not answer back directly to RMS, this might bring to some information leakage. Indeed, for some particular access rules, knowing whether this is satisfied gives exact information on existing paths.

As example, let assume that A in Figure 1 has set up the rule $ac = (friend, 1)$ for a given resource. If D requests this resource, RMS will receive a positive answer from PFS, which makes RMS able to understand that between D and A there exists a direct friendship. In order to avoid this leakage PFS answers are sent only to KMS (i.e., message 5 in Table 2). Based on the answer, then KMS generates a *token* containing the $secret_{rsc}$ if the answer is a positive, i.e., there exists a path satisfying the rule, or a random number for negative answer. Together with the URL from which resource can be downloaded, the token is then encrypted with CS public key and send it to RMS (i.e., message 6 in Table 2).

1.	$CS \to RMS:$	$\{id_{req}, id_{rsc}, N_1\}_{K^+_{RMS}}$
2.	$RMS:$	Retrieve ac_{rsc} and id of rsc's owner, i.e., id_{own}
3.	$RMS \to PFS:$	$\{h(id_{own}||ac_{rsc}.type), h(id_{req}||ac_{rsc}.type), ar_{rsc}, \{id_{req}, id_{rsc}\}_{K^+_{KMS}}\}_{K^+_{PFS}}$
4.	$PFS:$	Check if path (own, req) fulfills ac_{rsc}
5.	$PFS \to KMS:$	$\{found, \{id_{req}, id_{rsc}\}_{K^+_{KMS}}\}_{K^+_{KMS}}$
6.	$KMS \to RMS:$	$\{token, URL_{rsc}\}_{K_{CS}^+}$ where $token = secret_{rsc}$ if $found$ is true, $token = random$ otherwise;
7.	$RMS \to CS:$	$\{secret_{own}, N_1 + 1, \{token, URL_{rsc}\}_{K^+_{CS}}\}_{K^+_{CS}}$
8.	$CS:$	Compute K_{rsc} with received *secrets*, then download and decrypt resource, if possible.

Table 2: Resource download protocol

The URL sent from KMS to CS is a temporarily valid URL provided by cloud storage service at KMS requests.

The rsc to be downloaded is reachable at this URL only for a small and fixed lapse of time, afterwards rsc is moved back to the private realm of the storage service, without any public access.[8] RMS adds $secret_{own}$ into the received message, encrypts with CS public key, and forwards it to CS (i.e., message 7 in Table 2). Then, user decrypts $secret_{own}$ and $token$ values, and generates $\mathcal{F}(secret_{own}, token)$, which returns the correct encryption key K_{rsc} only if the $token = secret_{rsc}$, that is, only if KMS receives positive answer from PFS, confirming the existence of a path satisfying the rule.

5. SECURITY ANALYSIS

Except of KMS, which is assumed to be trusted, the framework is evaluated in a honest-but-curios adversary model, as such CS, PFS, and RMS parties are assumed to properly follow the protocols, by trying at the same time to infer sensitive information.

5.1 Relationship-based resource sharing

Given a resource rsc owned by own, and the corresponding set of access rules $\mathcal{R}_{rsc}$, the framework has to ensure that a requestor $req \in V$ can access (i.e., decrypt) rsc if and only if at least an access condition $ac \in \mathcal{R}_{rsc}$ is satisfied, that is, if there exists at least a path connecting req and own whose relationship type and depth satisfy at least an access condition $ac_{rsc} \in \mathcal{R}_{rsc}$.

According the proposed architecture a user can access a resource rsc if it has the corresponding decryption key K_{rsc}. Let us show that secrets are distributed only to authorized users, i.e., users satisfying at least an access condition. Let assume that user req does not satisfy any of the access conditions in $\mathcal{R}_{rsc}$, but after the execution of protocol in Table 2, it received the correct secrets to compute K_{rsc}. Since req does not satisfy any rule and assuming that the protocol is fairly executed, at the end of execution req receives $secret_{own}$ and $token=random$ (see messages 6,7 in Table 2). This does not allow him to compute the encryption key $K_{rsc} \neq \mathcal{F}(secret_{own}, random)$. Under the assumption that $\mathcal{F}(\cdot, \cdot)$ is collusion-free $\mathcal{F}(secret_{own}, random) \neq \mathcal{F}(secret_{own}, secret_{rsc})$, as such a contradiction arises.

Note that the above statement considers only malicious internal users of DSN. For other attackers, the only way to access resources is to decrypt it. At this purpose an attacker has to obtain both the secrets. From Table 1, we can see that these $secrets$ are locally generated by RMS and KMS, and securely transmitted to CS in message 8 (or, similarly, in message 7 of Table 2). As such, to achieve $secret_{own}$, the message has to be decrypted with private key of requestor, whereas to access $secret_{rsc}$, two decryptions have to be performed. Under a honest-but-curios model we need to consider also the involved parties (i.e., PFS, and RMS, as KMS is trusted). However, the considerations made above for external attackers still hold, with the difference that RMS already knows $secret_{own}$. Moreover, it is not able to decrypt $\{secret_{rsc}, N_2+1\}_{K_{CS}^+}$ in message 5 of Table 1, hence it cannot retrieve $secret_{rsc}$ and build K_{rsc}.

Further relevant analysis is related to key reuse and resources update. Let suppose that a granted user req, fol-

lowing the protocol of Table 2, is authorized to download and decrypt rsc. Even if req knows the value of K_{rsc}, he cannot obtain the new URL value that is sent in message 6 of Table 2. Moreover, in case the resource or the corresponding access rule is changed, the framework considers the modified resource rsc' as a new resource, with the consequent generation of new $secret_{rsc'}$.

5.2 Relationship information leakage

According to the proposed framework, relationship information is stored at cloud side in the form of $ACLs$. As such, under the assumption that all messages are securely exchanged, we see only two ways to infer information on existing relationships: (1) inferring roots, i.e., $uids$, directly from ACLs, and (2) inferring information from the access request evaluation. Let see in more details both these two attacks.

5.2.1 Inference from ACLs

Tracing ACLs insertions. A first attack can be performed by PFS service. This service receives directly from users the $ACLs$ for their direct contacts, ACL^1. Then to built/update ACL^n with n$\geq$2, PFS tries all possible $uids$ for finding users with mutual friends, so as to propagate them in other $ACLs$. According to an honest-but-curious behavior, PFS could trace every computation result, obtaining thus roots/uids for each uploaded ACL^1. Having these uids, PFS could rebuild a set of graphs $\mathcal{G}=\bigcup_{t\in RT}\{G_t\}$. All these graphs are, topologically, subgraphs of the original graph G, except for their nodes' ids that are different from the one in G. Thus, under the assumption of a collusion-free $h(\cdot)$ function, PFS is not able to merge together the graphs in $\mathcal{G}$, since the same user appears in these graphs with different uids.

As firstly discussed in [1], a graph where only ids are anonymized (i.e., randomized) cannot provide enough privacy protection, as it can suffer of re-identification attacks. This kind of attack is possible under the assumption that the attacker knows the existence of given structures H, such as Hamiltonian graphs, in the actual graph. As such, since the graph topology is preserved, if the attacker finds H in a graph G_t, he/she can use this match to re-identify all nodes connected with that structure and, in turn, their contacts of relationship type t and so on. With respect to this attack, thus, we have to make two considerations. The first is that is hard for an attacker to identify these structures when the original structures can be split in more substructures. A further consideration is that, in order to perform the attack, that is, in order to search of a given structure in subgraphs G_t, if possible, the PFS has to know which structure it has to look for. This would require to access to some information of the real graph G, as example, by registering in the OSN (as in the attack in [1]) or by colluding with some existing OSN users. However, this is not possible under the assumption that PFS is curious but honest.

Direct uids computation from ACLs. This kind of attacks can be run: by an external entity that maliciously retrieved $Table_t$ from the cloud storage; by the cloud manager that gets malicious access to $Table_t$, under the assumption of untrusted public cloud. Given $ACLs$ tables, the attackers can try to follow two approaches: *solving polynomial* or extracting their roots by *brute force*. For both aspects, thus,

---

[8]Moving resources on temporary URL is a common approach used by several cloud storage services (e.g., Dropbox) to limit access at requested resources.

it's important to emphasize a common aspect of these approaches, that is the ground field over which the polynomials are built.

Solving polynomials. According to Definition 3.1, polynomials in $Table_t$ are generated such that they are in a complete monic form. This allows us to refer to the *Abel-Ruffini Theorem* that states that for equations with degree greater or equal than 5 there is no algebraic formula for root-finding. Note that we can reasonably assume that all our polynomials have a degree greater than 5, that is, all ACLs encode more than 5 contacts.[9]

Despite this, there exist both numerical and arithmetical ways for the polynomial root-finding problem [28]. But almost all of them are inefficient with high degree polynomials. For example, given a polynomial P of degree n, *Vincent-Akritas-Strzeboński* (*VAS*) method requires to compute at least n variable substitutions and transformations in a recursive approach. Furthermore, it is relevant to observe that polynomials in Definition 3.1 are similar to Wilkinson's polynomials [30], in that they are complete monic polynomial. As such, it also holds the Wilkinson property stating that root finding problem is generally ill-conditioned. Finally, since our polynomials are in the form $P(x) = \prod_{i=0}^{n}(x - a_i) \Rightarrow P(x) = \sum_{i=0}^{n} b_i x^{n-i}$, $b_0 = 1$, $b_n \neq 0$, the last coefficient b_n is defined as the multiplication of all the roots. As such, an alternative approach for root-finding requires to factorize b_n. Still, both root finding problem and integer factorization problem are well known to be hard problems. To the best of our knowledge, the most efficient ways to retrieve polynomial roots are the deterministic algorithms or randomized algorithms presented in [19], which have polynomial-time complexity. The required time, thus, may become really significant once the ground field over the problem is defined increases in space.

However, if an attacker exploits one of these techniques, the time and computational resources needed to retrieve the real graph make this kind of attack infeasible. Indeed, as previously discussed, retrieving roots is only the first step, that is, it only allows the attacker to find the set of anonymized graphs $\mathcal{G}$. Then the re-identification attack in [1] has to be performed. As such, we believe the time needed to carry out the overall re-identification attack is greater than the possible graph lifespan and utility time.

Brute force. To retrieve $uids$ from an ACL, attackers can have a brute force approach trying all possible $uids$ so as to verify which of them satisfy the ACL polynomial. A first thing to emphasize is that the time estimation for this attack highly depends on the dimension of the social network. More precisely, let assume that all edges have the same relationship type, as such all relationships are encoded in an unique table with an entry for each user in G. This brings to a scenario where the ACL table contains $|V| \cdot MaxDepth$ polynomials. In order to reconstruct the social graph it is enough to find the solutions for polynomials that encode users' direct contats, that is, $|V|$ polynomials. To retrieve direct contacts of a target user u, that is, to find the roots of polynomial $P_{CL^1(u)(x)}$ it is required, in the worst-case, $(|V| - 1) \cdot t_{eval}$, where V is set of users in G and t_{eval} is the time of polynomial evaluation. In fact, to solve a single polynomial out of $|V|$, the attacker has to evaluate such

polynomial with $|V| - 1$ possible $uids$. To reconstruct the whole graph, this process has to be repeated for every other user in V, without repetition. This brings to a time estimation of

$$\sum_{i=1}^{|V|-1} \left[(|V| - i) \cdot t_{eval} \right] = t_{eval} \sum_{i=1}^{|V|-1} (|V| - i) =$$

$$= t_{eval} \sum_{i=1}^{|V|-1} (i) = \frac{|V|(|V| - 1)}{2} t_{eval} \sim O(|V|^2) t_{eval}.$$

As example, in an OSN with $|V| = 1 \cdot 10^6$ and with $t_{eval} = 10ms$ (see Table 3), the attack requires $\sim 3.17 \cdot 10^2$ years. As such, we believe this attack is not feasible.

A final note holding for solving polynomials attack as well as for the brute force is about the ground field over which the polynomials are built. Indeed, $h(\cdot)$ has to be selected such to have a codomain large enough to contain, at least, $|V| \cdot |RT|$ different values. It is expected that $h(\cdot)$ generates up to 10^{12}, as example, which are then used for $uids$. Even though most of calculators may compute values up to $log_2(10^{12}) < 64$ bit, it is not true that they are able to perform a polynomial evaluation, e.g., during a brute force attack, since these operations imply several exponentiations.

5.2.2 Inference from access rule enforcement.

For some particular access rules, knowing if this is satisfied gives exact information on existing paths. To avoid this possible leakage, the resource download protocol has been designed such that neither KMS or RMS know both the query path and the answer. However, inference from access rule evaluation could be exploited by external attacker. As example, with reference to Figure 3, let's assume that an attacker wishes to know whether between u and v there exists a relationship of type t. The attacker has to: (1) create

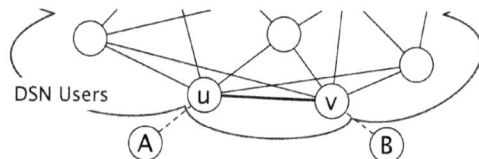

Figure 3: Inference Scenario Scheme

two fake social network users A and B; (2) A invites u to establish a new relationship, and B to v; (3) if both the relationships have been established, according to protocol in Table 1, A uploads a certain resource rsc with the following access rule $ac = (t, 3)$; (4) according to protocol in Table 2, B requests rsc: if the access is granted the attacker will know that between u and v it exists a direct relationship of type t.

Unfortunately this attack is possible as this information gain is intrinsic in the problem we are addressing (i.e., an information release regulated by existence of given relationships). However, there are some important considerations: (1) in order to accomplish the attack, both relationship requests have to be confirmed. This is less likely (i.e., half percentage) than to those attacks, like [1, 24] that assume to insert a subgraph H in G by connecting only a fake user with a real user; (2) with no clue on u and v, this attacks becomes really expensive. Indeed the attacker needs to successfully establish $2 \cdot |E| \cdot |RT|$ new relationships to discover

---

[9]For those polynomials with a lower degree, we can assume that CS adds some fake roots.

302

the whole graph topology. Moreover, in a real scenario, a OSN user confirms only a small percentage of relationship requests he/she receives from unknown people, and a refused relationship request cannot be replayed endlessly. Thus, a malicious entity needs an overwhelming effort to perform his attack.

6. EXPERIMENTAL EVALUATIONS

To evaluate the framework performance, we carried out several tests.[10] Each experiment ran exploiting Stanford SNAP datasets for Facebook.[11]

Our first experiment estimates the time required for the joining a new user to the anonymized graph.[12] As such, a parameter that greatly impacts this performance is the number of users that have been already registered in the graph. For this reason, the SNAP dataset has been split into two chunks of data: a $X\%$ of nodes for which the graph joining has to be performed, whereas the remaining are considered as already registered users. Experiments are carried out with 30% and 20% of nodes to be inserted, which is a collection of about 1200 and 800 adjacency lists, selected out of the dataset randomly. As reported in Figure 4, for each experiments users are organized according their coverage in the graph (i.e., x-axis). More precisely, the experiment is carried out as follows. (1) First, a new user u is randomly selected. (2) Then, it is computed the number of nodes that are connected with u with a path of $MaxDepth$ distance,[13] we refer to this value as $RelTree(u)_{MaxDepth}$. Based on this value, it is computed the coverage of u's relationships in SNAP graph G_{SNAP}, as $c = RelTree(u)_{MaxDepth}/|G_{SNAP}.V|$.[14] We limit the $MaxDepth$ value to 5.[15] (3) We then insert u in the anonymzed graph, tracking the time t required to complete the insertion procedure. The resulting couples $(coverage, t)$ are collected in Figure 4.

From the result we can infer that the time required to insert u, in its worst-case is:

$$t_{insert}(u) \sim MaxDepth \cdot \left(\frac{|N| \cdot (|N|+1)}{2} \cdot t_{eval} \cdot 2t_{mult} \right).$$

Moreover, assuming the time necessary to perform a polynomial evaluation (t_{eval}) and a multiplication between polynomials (t_{mult}) approximated with constant values, this time is $\sim O(|N|^2)$, where N is set of users that have been already successfully inserted before u.

---

[10]At this purpose, we set up Java classes to run the experiment exploiting $java.Math.BigInteger$ package for instantiating polynomials coefficients to overcome the limitation due to blown of values dimension; polynomials and users data are then stored in a MySQL database. The workstation used is an Intel Core 2 Quad Q6600 @ 2.40 GHz × 4, with 8GB RAM.

[11]http://snap.stanford.edu/data/index.html#socnets

[12]We recall that this implies that the new user u submits the anonymized list of its direct contacts, which is then elaborated by PFS to: (1) verify which of already registered users p are direct contacts of u; (2) propagate contacts of u in p's contact lists, and vice versa.

[13]The nodes are counted without repetition, since a certain node may be repeated at different depths

[14]Where $|G_{SNAP}.V|$ is the set of nodes in SNAP, which is about 4000.

[15]This value has been selected also based on SNAP Dataset statistics that point the value 4.7 as the *90-percentile effective longest shortest path*.

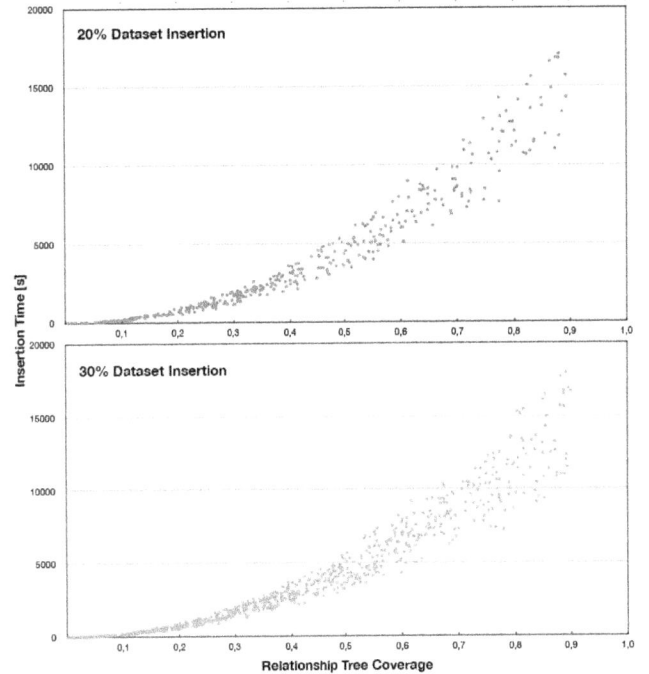

Figure 4: Time for new user insertion based on relationships coverage

To give more details on PFS performance, Table 3 presents the average time required for computing polynomial evaluations and multiplications during the user insertion. The values are divided, row by row, per depth d. These values may highlight how a polynomial evaluation requires generally short time, whereas a multiplication between polynomials requires more resources.

Level/depth	Polynomial Evaluation [ms]	Polynomial Multiplication [s]
1	10.777	20.072
2	498.921	110.972
3	1340.344	240.653
4	3207.567	305.899
5	6185.483	535.360

Table 3: Average time required for PFS operations

This result is encouraging, since we expect the system to perform much more polynomial evaluations than multiplications, in that we expect that a resource download should happen much more time than a user subscription in a legitimate scenario. Moreover, since an access control rule evaluation requires just a polynomial evaluation, Table 3 (i.e., the second column) represents also the average time for rule enforcement. At a final note, since users' relationships are grouped by their relationship types, the computational load of PFS due to multiplication is expected to be limited. Moreover this approach perfectly suits the cloud-based paradigm, because PFS can be replicated with small effort. Thus, a load-balancer entity may support PFS entities, and redirect requests to a non-locked service.

7. CONCLUSIONS

In this paper, we propose a DSN extension where users' personal data (i.e., digital resources, relationships) are securely stored in public cloud data storage and shared according to relationship-based rules defined by owners. We plan to extend the work reported in this paper along several directions. First, we plan to develop a prototype integrated with Facebook, so as to carry out a more extensive performance study. We also wish to extend the proposed privacy-preserving path finding so as to support more expressive access rules. As example, we intend to enforce also constraints on trust value of required relationships.

8. ACKNOWLEDGEMENTS

The research presented in this paper was partially funded by the European Office of Aerospace Research and Development (EOARD) and the Air Force for Scientific Research (ASFOR). The authors would like to thank the anonymous reviewers for their valuable comments and suggestions to improve the quality of the paper.

9. REFERENCES

[1] L. Backstrom, C. Dwork, J. Kleinberg. Wherefore art thou r3579x?: anonymized social networks, hidden patterns, and structural steganography. In Proc. *WWW*, 2007.

[2] R. Baden, A. Bender, N. Spring, B. Bhattacharjee, D. Starin. Persona: an online social network with user-defined privacy. In Proc. *ACM SIGCOMM*, 2009.

[3] F. Beato, I. Ion, S. Čapkun, B. Preneel, M. Langheinrich. For Some Eyes Only: Protecting Online Information Sharing.In Proc. *ACM CODASPY*, 2013.

[4] A. Bielenberg, L. Helm, A. Gentilucci, D. Stefanescu, H. Zhang. The Growth of Diaspora – A Decentralized Online Social Network in the Wild. In Proc. *IEEE INFOCOM*, 2012.

[5] S. Bhagat, G. Cormode, B. Krishnamurthy, D. Srivastava. Class-based graph anonymization for social network data. In Proc. *VLDB Endowment*, 2009.

[6] J. Brickell, V. Shmatikov. Privacy-Preserving graph algorithms in the semi-honest model. In Proc. *ASIACRYPT*, 2005.

[7] G. Bruns, P. W. L. Fong, I. Siahaan, M. Huth. Relationship-Based Access Control: Its Expression and Enforcement Through Hybrid Logic. In Proc. *ACM CODASPY*, 2012.

[8] S. Buchegger, D. Schiöberg, L. Vu, A. Datta. PeerSoN: P2P social networking: early experience and insights. In Proc. *ACM EuroSys*, 2009.

[9] L. A. Cutillo, R. Molva, M. Onen. Safebook: A distributed privacy-preserving Online Social Network. In Proc. *IEEE WoWMoM*, 2011.

[10] A. Campan, T. M. Truta. A clustering approach for data and structural anonymity in social networks. In Proc. *ACM PinKDD*, 2008.

[11] M. Dürr, M. Maier, F. Dorfmeister. Vegas - a secure and privacy-preserving peer-to-peer online social network. In Proc. *IEEE PASSAT*, 2012

[12] B. Carminati, E. Ferrari, J. Girardi. Trust&Share: Trusted Information Sharing in Online Social Networks. In Proc. *IEEE ICDE*, 2012.

[13] B. Carminati, E. Ferrari, A. Perego. Enforcing Access Control in Web-based Social Networks. In Proc. *ACM TISSEC*, 2009.

[14] B. Carminati, E. Ferrari, R. Heatherly, M. Kantarcioglu, B. Thuraisingham. A semantic web based framework for social network access control. In Proc. *ACM SACMAT*, 2009

[15] E. Y. Daraghmi, Y. S. Ming. Using graph theory to re-verify the small world theory in an online social network word. In Proc. *ACM iiWAS*, 2012.

[16] The Diaspora* Blog, online: *https://blog.diasporafoundation.org/*

[17] Electronic Privacy Information Center, Facebook Privacy. online: *http://epic.org/privacy/facebook/*

[18] D. Erdös, R. Germulla, E. Terzi. Reconstructing Graphs from Neighborhood Data. In Proc. *IEEE ICDM*, 2012.

[19] J. von zur Gathen, J. Gerhard. Modern Computer Algebra (3rd ed.). *Cambridge University Press*, 2013.

[20] Google official blog, A new approach to China. online: *http://googleblog.blogspot.com/2010/01/new-approach-to-china.html*. January 12, 2010.

[21] M. Hay, G. Miklau, D. Jensen, D. Towsley, P. Weis. Resisting structural re-identification in anonymized social networks. In Proc. *VLDB*, 2008.

[22] M. Hay, G. Miklau, D. Jensen, P. Weis, S. Srivastava. Anonymizing Social Networks. *Technical Report*, 2007.

[23] S. Jahid, S. Nilizadeh, P. Mittal, N. Borisov, A. Kapadia. DECENT: A Decentralized Architecture for Enforcing Privacy in Online Social Networks. In Proc. *IEEE SESOC*, 2012.

[24] K. Liu, E. Terzi. Towards identity anonymization on graphs. In Proc. *ACM SIGMOD*, 2008.

[25] W. Luo, Q. Xie, U. Hengartner. FaceCloak: An architecture for user privacy on social networking sites. In Proc. *ICCSE*, 2009.

[26] A. Shakimov, H. Lim, R. Cáceres, L. Cox, K. Li, D. Liu, A. Varshavsky. Vis-a-Vis: Privacy-Preserving Online Social Networking via Virtual Individual Servers. In Proc. *IEEE COMSNETS*, 2011.

[27] A, Tootoonchian, S. Saroiu, Y. Ganjali, A. Wolman. Lockr: better privacy for social networks. In Proc. *ACM CoNEXT*, 2009.

[28] S. A. Teukolsky, W. T. Vetterling, B. P. Flannery. Numerical Recipes: The Art of Scientific Computing (3rd ed.). *Cambridge University Press*, 2007.

[29] J. E. Vascellaro. Google discloses Privacy Glitch. online: *http://blogs.wsj.com/digits/2009/03/08/1214/*.

[30] J. H. Wilkinson. The evaluation of the zeros of ill-conditioned polynomials. Part I. *Numerische Mathematik 1*, 1959.

[31] C. A. Yeoung, I. Liccardi, K. Lu, O. Seneviratne, T. Berners-Lee. Decentralizarion: The Future of Online Social Networking. In Proc. *W3C Workshop on the Future of Social Networking*, 2009.

WebWinnow: Leveraging Exploit Kit Workflows to Detect Malicious URLs

Birhanu Eshete
Fondazione Bruno Kessler
Trento, TN, Italy
eshete@fbk.eu

V.N. Venkatakrishnan
Universtity of Illinois at Chicago
Chicago, IL, United States
venkat@uic.edu

ABSTRACT

Organized cybercrime on the Internet is proliferating due to exploit kits. Attacks launched through these kits include drive-by-downloads, spam and denial-of-service. In this paper, we tackle the problem of detecting whether a given URL is hosted by an exploit kit. Through an extensive analysis of the workflows of about 40 different exploit kits, we develop an approach that uses machine learning to detect whether a given URL is hosting an exploit kit. Central to our approach is the design of distinguishing features that are drawn from the analysis of attack-centric and self-defense behaviors of exploit kits. This design is based on observations drawn from exploit kits that we installed in a laboratory setting as well as live exploit kits that were hosted on the Web. We discuss the design and implementation of a system called WEBWINNOW that is based on this approach. Extensive experiments with real world malicious URLs reveal that WEBWINNOW is highly effective in the detection of malicious URLs hosted by exploit kits with very low false-positives.

Categories and Subject Descriptors

K.6.5 [**Security and Protection**]: Invasive Software

Keywords

Exploit Kits; malware; detection; machine learning

1. INTRODUCTION

Cybercrime has seen a proliferation in recent times. This has been largely due to development of criminal, for-profit, software infrastructure for conducting attacks on end-users. In this infrastructure, Exploit Kits occupy a central role as they facilitate the infection of users through browser compromises. An exploit kit is a piece of off-the-shelf software that can be licensed from the underground market, which when installed and configured on a web server, carries out a malicious campaign targeting innocent victims. Examples of attacks launched through these kits include drive-by-downloads, spam and denial-of-service. A website hosting an exploit kit is advertised through URLs disseminated through spam

links, search campaigns, social networks, web postings or website hijacking. Innocent victims that click on these URLs have their systems compromised through drive-by-download attacks, and the infected hosts are subsequently used for further criminal activities.

Given the role of exploit kits in cybercrime, it is a natural question to ask whether a given URL points to an exploit kit. This is a question that has significant implications for the safety of end-users on the Internet, given the proliferation of criminal activities in recent years. Therefore, identifying such exploit kit hosted URLs has the potential to be useful to a broad audience. For example, search engine vendors can use such detection techniques to prevent indexing of such URLs as they are usually accompanied with search term poisoning attacks. They also can pass on such blacklisted URLs to end users and to browser vendors, who can protect their customers from harmful infection. Anti-virus companies can also keep their signature datasets up-to-date by analyzing such URLs.

Previous work on detecting exploit kit hosted pages primarily relied on either looking for anomalous characteristics of the downloaded code [3, 11] or detect [9, 10] changes to the OS persistent state. The former is harder to define for new exploits included by the exploit kits (which are continuously updated), while the latter, involves the difficult issue of correct execution of malicious code.

This paper develops a new approach that uses machine learning to facilitate fast detection of exploit kit hosted pages. A unique characteristic of our approach is that it is drawn from an extensive analysis of the design and implementation of several available real-world exploit kits. This analysis is performed by installing the exploit kit software in a controlled environment, studying its source code, and by dynamic analysis through interaction with various browser personalities. In particular, we leverage on two sets of characteristics exhibited by all the exploit kits that we tested. The first set comes from their *attack-centric behavior*, that includes their methods for attacking browser clients (e.g., fingerprinting, obfuscation). The second set comes from their *self-defense behaviors*, i.e., those characteristics that are used to evade detection techniques. Based on our understanding of these two types of behaviors, we derive a set of features to train a classifier.

In addition, we augment the feature set obtained from our analysis with a set of features drawn from live exploit kits. Quite often, a real world deployment of an exploit kit (in terms of the number of redirections, domains traversed and similar customizations) often do not exhibit themselves when such kits are studied in a controlled setting. The set of features from locally deployed kits as well as from the live exploit kits, taken together, facilitate the training of a precise classifier that is used for detection.

Our system, WEBWINNOW, has a training phase and an actual detection phase. The training phase makes use of honeyclients that engage with locally installed kits and collect activity logs that are then used for training. In a similar fashion, we extract activity logs for live exploit kit URLs. During the detection phase, WEBWIN-NOW, when presented with a possibly malicious URL, interacts with the URL using a honeyclient, and classifies whether the URL is an exploit kit or not.

Analysis of URLs with exploit kits using a honeyclient infrastructure can be expensive from a resource standpoint. Past studies have recommended the use of search engines [6]. As a resource saving step, WEBWINNOW includes the use of a pre-filtering engine that was built based on our analysis of exploit kits. The pre-filtering engine scans a URL dataset and identifies those that are suspicious. These suspicious URLs are then forwarded to a honeyclient which then uses the classifier built for detection.

We perform an evaluation of WEBWINNOW over a dataset collected over a period of five months. Our dataset consists of a collection of Alexa top sites and publicly available malicious URL datasets. Our evaluation demonstrates a precise classifier yielding a true positive rate of 99.9% on a testing sample of malicious URLs.

This paper is organized as follows. Section 2 presents background on exploit kits. Section 3 presents a brief overview of our approach followed by a discussion of the choice of features for machine learning. Section 4 discusses the training of the classifier and the design of our training infrastructure. We discuss the detection phase in Section 5. A discussion of the implementation and evaluation appears in Section 6. Discussion of related work appears in Section 7. We conclude in Section 8.

2. BACKGROUND ON EXPLOIT KITS

Exploit kits are one of the most common methods used in cybercrime and their emergence has been well documented in recent work [4]. Cybercriminals target vulnerabilities in operating systems, web browsers, office software, and third-party plugins to infect victim machines. The advent of exploit kits dates back to 2006 when the MPack kit came in to picture for the first time [8].

A typical workflow in an exploit kit usually starts with a victim being lured to a URL (e.g., by clicking a link in a spam email) to visit a seemingly benign web page. After a series of redirections, the victim reaches a landing page. The kit then gathers identifying information of the victim in pursuit of vulnerabilities to exploit. At this stage, a kit analyzes the User-Agent information of the victim to identify the type and version number of the operating system, browser, and third-party plugins. If the exploit succeeds, a malicious payload (malware) is silently downloaded and executed on the victim's machine. In addition to delivering the exploit payload to the victim, the exploit kit also updates the infection statistics accessible to the kit administrator.

Exploit kits come with pre-written exploit code and they usually include installer scripts, a number of exploits, configuration details, administration features for the kit owner, and payload which includes botnets, fake anti-virus engine, and trojans. Exploit kits are sold (rented) in the underground marketplace and like legitimate software there are regular bug fixes, feature enhancements, customer support, end-user license agreements, and even competitions among the kit developers. Most exploit kits are written in PHP (some in C/C^{++}), use fingerprinting code, use extensive obfuscation, and use a number of third-party code (e.g., JavaScript and CSS). Examples of popular Exploit Kits include RedKit, CrimePack, CrimeBoss, Cool, Blackhole, SweetOrange, Eleanore, Fragus, NuclearPack, Sakura, NeoSploit, Siberia Private, and Styx.

According to the 2013 Internet Security Threat Report by Symantec [13], Blackhole had a share in 41% of all Web-based attacks in 2012. There was also the release of an updated version of the kit (Blackhole 2.0) hinting that its impact is likely to continue. An-other exploit kit is Sakura which took 22% of overall kit usage in 2012. The next 3 in the top 5 kits in 2012 are Phoenix (10%), Red-Kit (7%), and Nuclear (3%).

3. FEATURE DESIGN

In this section, we discuss how, based on our analysis of 38 distinct exploit kits, we derive distinguishing features based on which we train our classifiers for detection. Before discussing these details, we give an overview of our approach in WEBWINNOW.

In a nutshell, our approach is formulated as a machine learning based technique for the detection of malicious URLs hosted by exploit kits. At the core of our approach is that, based on the workflows of exploit kits, we leverage their *attack-centric* and *self-defense* behaviors to design distinguishing features based on which we train precise classifiers to detect malicious URLs. In this regard, our approach differs from systems (such as [3, 9]) that combine honeyclients and learning-based approaches to analyze the side-effects of malicious activities by inspecting pre-execution and post-execution snapshots of system properties. The following three steps summarize the pipeline of our approach:

- We first analyze source code and runtime behavior of exploit kits by installing them in a controlled setting. In addition, we probe live exploit kits on the Web to capture their activity and content they deliver to the client. By combining these observations, we identify attack-centric and self-defense mechanisms of exploit kits. Based on a careful examination of the attack-centric and self-defense behaviors, we then design features that are precise enough in distinguishing URLs hosted by exploit kits.

- Next, we extract these features from samples of (1) exploit kits we installed locally (2) live exploit kits and (3) non exploit kit URLs. Using the features, we train and evaluate learning algorithms from which we generate detection models. We discuss the training in detail in Section 4.

- Finally, given an unknown URL, we query the detection models to give the verdict as to whether the URL is an exploit kit URL or not. In Section 5, we describe the detection in detail.

Exploit kits manifest different characteristics in order to fulfill their major mission —to infect victim machines with malware. At the same time, we have observed that exploit kits have to do a great deal of self-defense to complicate the analysis task of detection systems. From an anonymous source, we were able to have access to the source code of 38 distinct exploit kits. With the purpose of leveraging these characteristics of exploit kits for detecting URLs linked with them, we analyzed these exploit kits. For these exploit kits, our analysis involved semi-automated source code inspection, installation, and then probing of the kits in a laboratory setting. For exploit kits hosted on the Web, as we do not have access to their source code, we relied on probing them in a contained environment. In the rest of this section, we describe how we take advantage of the attack-centric and self-defense behaviors of exploit kits to develop features we use to train our classifiers for detecting malicious URLs hosted by exploit kits.

3.1 Attack-Centric Behaviors

From the point of view of detecting malicious URLs that lead to exploit kits, we noticed that the attack chain of an exploit kit when it is visited by a victim client gives useful insights to characterize exploit kit behaviors. From our analysis, we identify the following four attack-centric behaviors of exploit kits.

3.1.1 Client Profiling

From our analysis, we noticed that an essential component in all exploit kits is the use of a fingerprinting routine in a form of obfuscated JavaScript code that is unpacked and executed on the client browser. Fingerprinting in most exploit kits has two components performed in the order –*identification* and then *validation*. Identification is about collecting the client profile which includes the type and version of the operating system, browser, and installed browser plugins. In particular, most exploit kits (34 out of 38) check the presence and version number of Acrobat Reader, Flash Player, and the Java WebStart plugin. All the 38 exploit kits we analyzed perform identification of the visiting client.

Validation involves further inspection of the client personality to check if the client is a real user as opposed to a bot. As per our analysis, 36 out of the 38 exploit kits perform validation with the exception of Eleonore and RDS which proceed to preparing the exploit based only on the identity of the client.

The crucial features we capture from client profiling are routines invoked when an obfuscated JavaScript is unpacked and executed on the client side. These are fingerprinting specific features manifesting themselves as routines from the common PluginDetect[1] library that is widely used by exploit kits to collect identifying information of the client. For example, de-obfuscation of the obfuscated JavaScript code used by exploit kits for fingerprinting consistently shows the occurrence of the flagship functions such as `getjavainfo.jar`, `pdpd()`, and `getversion()`. We confirmed the presence of these functions in 28 of the 38 exploit kits while the other 10 exploit kits used function aliases to wrap these functions. The feature *PluginDetect Routines* under the Interaction-Specific feature class in Table 1 is used to capture the unique number of these functions during client profiling.

3.1.2 Chain of Redirections

Live exploit kits we probed silently take clients through a chain of redirections to ultimately land them on the page that hosts the actual exploit. Depending on the remote resource they want to interact with (access), they use different redirect types. These include window-open, HTTP (with different status codes like HTTP 3XX), script source (mostly used to point to remote JavaScript), params (redirection based on URL parameters), applet (remote invocation of Java applet), JNLP (Java Network Launch Protocol invocation), iframe (specially hidden and small iframes as legitimate iframes are large enough to be visible), and HREF-based redirection. According to our observation when probing live exploit kits on the Web, we confirmed that exploit kits such as RedKit, SweetOrange, Blackhole, and Cool are particularly notorious in using complex redirection chains by combining these redirect methods.

3.1.3 Exploit Obfuscation

Except 2 exploit kits (BleedingLife and Cry217), all the rest (about 95%) of the exploit kits we analyzed obfuscate the malicious JavaScript code they use in client profiling, exploit preparation, and exploit delivery. Obfuscation renders static analysis techniques ineffective and further complicates the task of dynamic analysis. Usually, the obfuscation technique is one of the components to be revamped when a new version of an exploit kit is released. Because, by the time the kits are popular on the web, the obfuscation technique is likely to be uncovered and it is no more effective.

3.1.4 Allowing Additional Exploits

According to our analysis, 7 out of the 38 exploit kits allow uploading an additional exploit binary. To confirm the addition of new exploits, we first added a key-logger executable to CrimePack3.1.3 and Fragus1.0 exploit kits. Then, we visited the kits from a vulnerable client. In both cases, the key-logger executable was successfully downloaded to the client.

3.2 Self-Defense Behaviors

The primary purpose of exploit kits is to be effective in infecting victims with malware. However, to continuously infect victims, they need to escape detection techniques, for which they have to be armed with self-defense functionalities. In the following, we discuss six self-defense behaviors we observed in our analysis.

3.2.1 IP Blocking

In an attempt to escape from automated analysis techniques, almost all exploit kits we analyzed are equipped with IP blocking mechanisms against bots (e.g., GoogleBot) and IP addresses from ToR networks. About 87% of the exploit kits we analyzed have features to block IP addresses of known services from Anti-Virus companies or security researchers. The only exploit kits that do not use IP blocking are Bleeding Life, El Fiesta, NeoSploit, SEOSploit-Pack, and the Yes exploit kit.

3.2.2 Blacklist Lookup

Exploit kits check if their URL is blacklisted in one or more public blacklisting services. If so, the kit administrator changes the URL and the kit continues to operate until it is discovered and blacklisted again. In total, 6 of the 38 exploit kit in our analysis check their URL against one or more blacklists. CrimePack, for instance, has a feature that allows to lookup the kit URL in 8 major blacklists including the Google Safe Browsing service.

3.2.3 Signature Evasion

Anti-virus engines and Intrusion Detection Systems use string signatures to detect malicious content. Some exploit kits lookup the signature databases of online malware (virus) scanning services (such as virtest[2], virustotal[3]) so as to check if their signatures belong there. For example, the latest version of Blackhole (version 2.1.0) checks for its own signatures in *virtest* and *scan4you* online virus-scanning engines. The 5 exploit kits that check for their own signatures in online ant-virus engines are Adrenalin, Blackhole, Fragus, SpyEye, and ZeusKit.

3.2.4 Cloaking

We confirmed that 15 out of the 38 exploit kits use cloaking. When visited after a successful exploit delivery, most (13) of them respond with the HTTP 404 (page not found) error while a few (2) responded with a blank page with no content and/or action. There are two cases in which an exploit kit might use cloaking. One is up on failure to exploit a client either because the client turns out to be invulnerable or it is a bot. In this scenario, the kit responds with HTTP 404 error or redirects the client to a harmless page. Some exploit kits throw back to the client a random exploit just to try their chance (we noticed this in 0x88, Eleonore, Fragus, and Sava). The other case in which cloaking is used is when an already infected victim visits the exploit kit page. In this case, most exploit kits respond with HTTP 404 while some show a blank page.

---

[1] http://www.pinlady.net/PluginDetect/

[2] http://virtest.com
[3] http://virustotal.com

Aggregate-Behavioral:	Behavior
(1) Exploits	Attack
(2) Redirections	Attack
(3) Connections	Attack/Defense
(4) Locations	Attack/Defense
(5) Files	Attack/Defense
Interaction-Specific:	**Behavior**
(5) Window-Opens	Attack(redirect)
(7) HTTP Redirects	Attack(redirect)
(8) JNLP Redirects	Attack(redirect)
(9) Param Redirects	Attack(redirect)
(10) Script-SRC Redirects	Attack(redirect)
(11) Link Redirects	Attack(redirect)
(12) iFrame Redirects	Attack(redirect)
(13) Familiar Kit URLs	Defense (anti-robot)
(14) PluginDetect Routines	Attack(redirect)
(15) JavaWebStart Routines	Attack(redirect)
(16) URL Translation	Attack(redirect)
Connection-Specific:	**Behavior**
(17) ActiveX Attempts	Attack(obfuscation)
(18) HeapSpray Attempts	Attack(obfuscation)
(19) Unique Countries	Attack(redirect)
(20) Top Level Domains	Attack(redirect)
Content-Specific:	**Behavior**
(21) HTML	Defense(cloaking)
(22) CSS	Attack(obfuscation)
(23) JavaScript	Defense(obfuscation)
(24) JAR	Defense(obfuscation)
(25) Octet-Stream	Defense(obfuscation)
(26) Command	Defense(obfuscation)
(27) Plain Text	Defense(obfuscation)
(28) Compressed Content	Defense(obfuscation)
(29) XML	Defense(obfuscation)
(30) Portable Document	Defense(obfuscation)

Table 1: Features used in WEBWINNOW.

3.2.5 Blocking of Robots

We found the `robots.txt` file in 14 of the 38 exploit kits and in all the cases the kits disallow any indexing attempt. Search engine crawlers rely on the `robots.txt` file placed in the public directory of websites to check permission for indexing of web pages. Some exploit kits (e.g., CrimePack, Eleonore, Fragus, Nuke, Phoenix, Siberia) disallow indexing by blocking all bots. This is done in an attempt to escape from a more advanced analysis by search engines to filter-out (from their index) suspicious or malicious web pages. Although not all exploit kits block robots, our analysis shows that, when combined with attack-centric characteristics (e.g., client profiling, redirections), this behavior contributes to identify exploit kit URLs in practice.

3.2.6 Code Protection

Our analysis shows 3 distinct outcomes as to the code protection scheme used by exploit kits. About 8 (24%) use `IonCube`, about 5 (13%) use `ZendGuard`, and about 4 (10%) use custom code protection scheme (e.g., custom cryptography). The motivation in code protection is primarily to prevent code stealing while at the same time giving hard time for detection techniques that use code analysis. Despite these code protection mechanisms, source code is sometimes leaked. To combat source code leakage, some exploit kits (e.g., Blackhole) are shifting their "business model" to only rental —exploit-as-a-service paradigm.

3.3 Features

The features we draw from the attack-centric and self-defense behaviors of exploit kits are summarized in Table 1. We designed a total of 30 features of which 5 are *Aggregate-Behavioral*; 11 are *Interaction-Specific*; 4 are *Connection-Specific*; and 10 are *Content-Specific* features. Of all the the features, the interaction-specific features are the most discriminating features because we characterize fingerprinting and the various redirection attempts using fine-grained details of interaction types. In the following, we briefly describe these features. In Section 6, we evaluate the statistical significance of these features based on the training dataset.

3.3.1 Aggregate-Behavioral

These 5 generic features provide a course-grained characterization in terms of the number of known *exploits* (from `http://exploit-db.com`), aggregated count of *redirections*, total number of *connections* made to other destinations, total number of *locations* from which remote content is fetched, and total number of distinct *files* dropped on the client.

3.3.2 Interaction-Specific

In this class of features, 8 out of the 11 features have not been used by previous work. Only *HTTP Redirects*, *Script-SRC Redirects*, and *Link Redirects* have been used in previous work to detect malicious web pages. We noticed that these fine-grained redirection features are effective in identifying exploit kit URLs. Another particularly useful feature is the *PluginDetect Routines*, which counts the number of fingerprinting routines used by exploit kits.

3.3.3 Connection-Specific

The 4 features in this class are captured when connections are made to remote sources. They include *ActiveX* loading attempts (e.g., presence of Microsoft XMLHTTP ActiveX), *heap-spray* attempts (e.g., when the argument to the `eval()` function is too large), unique number of *countries* traversed and *Top Level Domains (TLDs)* involved in the connection. Such features are attributed to the strategy of cybercriminals to complicate the traceability of the exploit kit infrastructure (e.g., during take-down operations by law enforcement).

3.3.4 Content-Specific

We extract a total of 10 features from the content related activity logs. Some MIME-types (e.g., PDF, Shockwave file) are particularly attractive for exploit kit URLs as they target vulnerable plugins that render such file types. More precisely, we extract the the size of content delivered to the client for common MIME-types used on the web with emphasis on content-type used by exploit kits. In particular, these features include size of HTML, CSS, JavaScript, Octet-Stream (e.g., long byte pattern), command, plain text, compressed content (e.g., *. zip, *.gz, *.tar), XML, PDF, and Postscript content. Notice that where there is obfuscation these content-specific features are extracted after de-obfuscation so as to obtain feature values that can distinguish content delivered by exploit kits from content delivered by benign web sites.

4. TRAINING

We now present the training phase of WEBWINNOW by describing the training infrastructure for exploit kits we installed locally, live exploit kits on the Web, and non exploit kit URLs.

Based on the features derived from the behavioral characterization of exploit kits we described in the previous section, the goal of the training is to generate a model that is used to detect exploit kit URLs. To enrich our training set, we capture as much

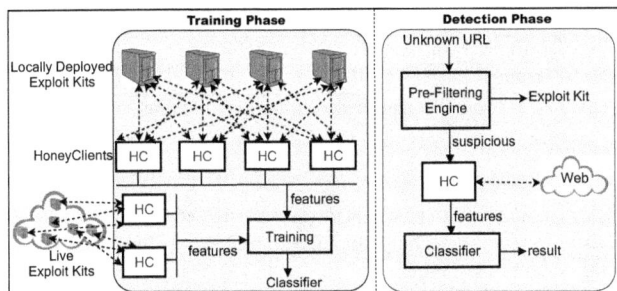

Figure 1: WEBWINNOW Training and detection pipeline.

activity-centric details as possible of both exploit kit and non exploit kit URLs in a contained environment. To this end, we divide the acquisition of our training dataset into three parts. The first part probes locally deployed exploit kits. The second part deals with probing of live exploit kit URLs. The third part involves probing of non-exploit kit URLs. In what follows, we describe these three contained probing steps in detail.

4.1 Locally Installed Exploit Kits

To inspect the attack-centric and self-defense behaviors of exploit kits, we installed exploit kits for which we were able to get the source code. The advantage of having locally installed exploit kits is twofold. First, it gives a deeper understanding of the operational mechanics of the exploit kits, specially how they orchestrate attacks. Second, it gives insights as to how the infection statistics is collected and the mechanisms that the exploit kits employ to evade detection techniques. In a virtualized environment with multiple exploit kits deployed on one side, we schedule honeyclients on the other side to visit the exploit kit URLs with a vulnerable user-agent personalities (details in Section 6.1). The honeyclients are directly pointed to and visit the landing page of the exploit kits so as to collect whatever the exploit kits throw back to the client.

More precisely, we collect HTML and CSS content, script loaded (mainly JavaScript), exploit payload dropped into the honeyclient, remote content fetched, and shell-code execution attempts, and more importantly the whole HTTP transaction. After a few seconds, we repeat the visit in order to compare the activity logs with the first visit. In most exploit kits, if the first visit succeeds in dropping an exploit payload, the subsequent visits from the same address of the honeyclient are usually served with benign-looking response or error codes.

4.2 Live Exploit Kits on the Web

For probing the activity log of live exploit kits on the Web, we rely on our data sources of live exploit kits in the wild. Given a live exploit kit URL at hand, we launch one of our honeyclients and probe the server to collect its activity logs with details similar to the exploit kits installed locally. The honeyclients we use for live exploit kits are separate from the ones we use for the locally installed kits. More importantly, we reset the honeyclients after collecting the activity logs of a given exploit kit before moving on to visit the next exploit kit URL.

An attentive reader might wonder about the distinction between the contained probing of locally installed and live exploit kits on the Web. There are two fundamental variations pertinent to the typical steps involved in exploit kit workflow we described in Section 2. In the first place, live exploit kits are engaged in a series of redirections before reaching the landing page while the locally installed ones are not. Secondly, compared to the versions of the kits we

deployed locally, we presume that live exploit kits are likely to be recent versions which give us a fresher insight of their workflow.

4.3 Non Exploit Kit URLs

For this class of URLs, we use publicly known benign URLs to monitor their execution activity using the same configuration of honeyclients used for locally installed exploit kits and live exploit kits. The difference in this case, however, is that we do not repeat the probing as we assume that these URLs have a fairly stable activity log apart from changes in page content and client-side code, which we do not analyze directly. We also use separate honeyclient instance to probe non exploit kit URLs to ensure sanity of logs.

4.4 Model Generation

To verify the exploit kit samples (of both locally installed and those live on the Web), we semi-automatically inspect the activity logs we collected to ensure that they drop into the honeyclient at least one exploit payload. Similarly, for non exploit kit samples, we manually check for the presence of suspicious samples that might arise due to compromised legitimate websites that might have been hijacked by cybercriminals and injected with an iframe leading to an exploit kit URL. After verifying the samples collected, we extract the 30 features described in the previous section. Finally, we label the samples as EK (Exploit Kit) for samples from locally installed and live kits on the Web or as NEK (Non-Exploit Kit) for those which are known to be benign.

Using the labeled samples, we use established supervised learning algorithms to train classifiers and evaluate them to decide which classifier to use for detection. The metrics to evaluate the classifiers is True Positive Rate (TPR) and False Positive Rate (FPR) on the training set using 10-fold cross validation. We used 3 tree-based learning algorithms namely: J48 Decision Tree, Random Tree, and Random Forest. In addition, we also used one stochastic learning algorithm (Bayes Network) and one function-based learning algorithm (Logistic Regression). Performance evaluation of these algorithms during training and testing is discussed in Section 6.

5. DETECTION

Given an unknown URL, to detect if it leads to an exploit kit site, WEBWINNOW's detection phase works as follows. If resource is a bottleneck, a pre-filtering step is invoked to check if the URL under examination can be quickly matched against pre-compiled rules based on URL anatomy of popular exploit kits. If not, the URL is directly analyzed using the learning-based classification. In the rest of this section, we discuss these two components of the detection in more detail.

5.1 Learning-Based Classification

Given an unknown URL, first a honeyclient probes the remote server the URL points to in order to collect activity logs from the beginning to the end of the interaction. From the transactions of the interaction, activity-centric features are extracted and an already trained model is queried to classify the URL as an exploit kit URL or not. The main assumption in the activity-centric characterization to distinguish exploit kit URLs from other types of URLs is the intrinsic workflow in exploit kits that involves client fingerprinting, series of redirections, attempts to deliver and then execute exploit payload, along with typical self-defense behaviors (e.g., cloaking).

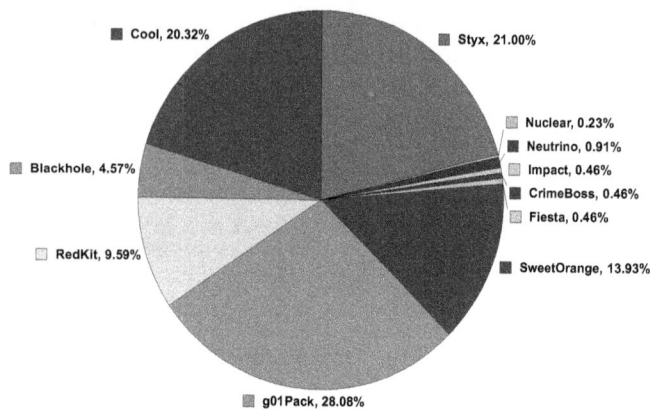

Figure 2: Distribution of live exploit kits probed.

Purpose	Non exploit kits	exploit kits	Total
Training	500	500	1000
Testing	1117	512	1629

Table 2: Dataset for training and testing.

5.2 Implementation Overview

To probe remote URLs, we use Thug[4], an open source honey-client written in Python. Thug is configured on a virtual machine image that we replicate as needed. We preferred using Thug because the level of granularity in the activity logs captured when probing a remote URL is suitably detailed for the workflow modeling in exploit kits.

Before probing exploit kit URLs, identifying parameters of the honeyclient personality such as user-agent string (e.g., browser type and version, operating system type and version), referrer, DOM events, and plugins are properly configured. We do this not only to simulate a realistic browsing behavior but also to maximize the chance of capturing the end-to-end infection chain that is orchestrated by exploit kits.

6. EVALUATION

This section discusses the evaluation of our approach in light of accuracy of the models generated, accuracy of classifiers on a separate test set, comparison of our approach with similar techniques, and analysis of false positives. More precisely, our evaluation is aimed at answering the following questions:

RQ$_1$: *Does workflow analysis of exploit kits and characterizing them with distinguishing features based on their attack-centric and self-defense behavior improve the detection accuracy of existing techniques in malicious web content detection?*

RQ$_2$: *Since client-side attacks such as drive-by-downloads are mostly initiated by exploit kits, can we build a mechanism to combat exploit kits in real time?*

RQ$_3$: *In modeling the dynamic behavior of exploit kits, can we leverage interaction of a potentially vulnerable client and an exploit kit server so as to build better models?*

6.1 Data Collection

To collect the dataset we use for our evaluation, we analyzed exploit kits in the period April-August 2013 for about 5 months in a contained environment. In this period, we scheduled the honeyclients to periodically visit and record the interactions involved with the exploit kits we installed locally. At the same time, we also probed on a daily basis live exploit kit URLs reported by online detection services and blacklists.

Using the locally installed exploit kits on the server side, we deployed 4 virtual machines as clients with the Thug honeyclient configured with Internet Explorer 6.0 on Windows XP SP 3 with plug-ins for Adobe Acrobat Reader (version 9.1.0), Java plugin (version

1.6.0.32), and Shockwave Flash (version 10.0.64.0). We noticed that most exploit kits check for such combination of browser, operating system, and plugins. As for the DOM events' configuration, we used the default which enables *load( )* and *mousemove( )* events.

With the same honeyclient configuration, for live exploit kits, we relied on the URLs reported as exploit kit URLs by the URL-Query[5] service. When we find these exploit kit sites live, we use our honeyclient to probe the URL and record the HTTP transaction. For each live exploit kit URL that succeeds in dropping an exploit binary to the honeyclient, we re-probe it after 10 seconds in case of different behavior (e.g., to check if it performs cloaking). It is important to note that collecting the execution dynamics of live exploit kits was not an easy task as exploit kits have a very short lifetime (usually less than 24 hours). This is because the kit owners relocate them once their URL is blacklisted. During the data collection, we frequently noticed that these URLs become unreachable in a matter of few minutes after they are publicly reported.

The data collection from live exploit kits involved 11kits on 500 exploit kits for which we semi-automatically verified the delivery of at least one exploit binary. Figure 2 shows the percentage distribution of each exploit kit in the collected dataset for training. In the top 3 are g01pack (28%), Styx (21%), and Cool (20%) comprising nearly 70% of the dataset followed by SweetOrange (14%), Red-Kit (10%), and Blackhole (5%). Interestingly, on June 26, 2013 McAfee released a report [12] that shows correlation with the high percentage of the Styx exploit kit in the data we collected.

6.2 Dataset

To train the classifier, we rely on samples collected from the execution dynamics of the exploit kits we installed and executed in a contained environment and exploit kit URLs that we probed on the Web and few others from [2, 14, 15, 17]. For non exploit kit samples, we used the Alexa top sites as we assume that these sites are less likely to host exploit kits. The collected dataset is divided into labeled training and testing set as shown in Table 2. The training set is used to train different classifiers and evaluate their performance while the testing set is used to evaluate the performance of the trained models on a dataset disjoint with the training set.

6.3 Setup

Training. Using the features collected on the training set, the WEKA machine learning suite [5] was used to train five supervised learning algorithms to derive detection models. The algorithms are: J48 Decision Tree, Random Tree, Random Forest, Bayes Network, and Logistic Regression. The training was done with 10-fold cross validation for all the algorithms.

Testing. On the testing set, the trained classifiers were independently ran and the classification results were analyzed for accuracy and false positives.

6.4 Results

6.4.1 Analysis of Features

Based on the training dataset we used in this work, we now discuss the significance of the features we presented in Section 3.

---

[4]https://github.com/buffer/thug

[5]http://urlquery.net

310

Classifier	TPR	FPR
J48 Decision Tree	100%	0.000
Random Tree	97.1%	0.029
Random Forest	99.8%	0.003
Bayes Network	100%	0.000
Logistic Regression	99.9%	0.001

Table 3: Performance of models on the training set.

Classifier	TPR	FPR
J48 Decision Tree	99.9%	0.001
Random Tree	89.9%	0.032
Random Forest	99.7%	0.002
Bayes Network	99.8%	0.003
Logistic Regression	99.4%	0.005

Table 4: Performance of classifiers on a separate testing set.

Aggregate-Behavioral. In the training set, the average number of redirections (of all types) for exploit kit URLs is 102 while for non exploit kit URLs is 82. On average, we found 1 exploit in the exploit kit dataset as opposed to zero in non exploit kit dataset. The average number of connections made to remote sources is 25 for exploit kit dataset while it is 20 in non exploit kits. These aggregate values of features, in fact, are fairly discriminative in putting apart exploit kit and non exploit kit URLs.

Interaction-Specific. While we observed an average of 1 JNLP-based redirection in exploit kit URLs, we could not come across even a single JNLP-based redirection attempt in non exploit kit URLs. The average number of HTTP 3XX redirections shows that the average is 5 in exploit kits compared to an average of 2 in non exploit kit dataset. One of the useful features in this class is the *PluginDetect Routines* with an average count of 2 for exploit kit dataset as opposed to zero for non exploit kit URLs.

Connection-Specific. Average number of ActiveX loading attempts is 4 for exploit kit dataset while it is 2 for non exploit kit dataset. Average number of unique countries traversed and TLDs involved is 4 and 3 respectively for exploit kit URLs. Whereas in non exploit kit dataset, it is 1 for both the countries and TLDs.

Content-Specific. On average, the size (in bytes) of plain text, HTML, CSS, and XML delivered by exploit kit URLs is less than content delivered by non exploit kit URLs. On the other hand, the average size of JavaScript, Octet-Stream, and portable document is greater in the case of exploit kit URLs. For instance, Octet-Stream average size in exploit kit dataset is 13 times that of non exploit kit octet-stream content. Similarly, the average JavaScript content delivered by exploit kit URLs is about 1.5 times bigger than JavaScript in non exploit kit URLs. These statistical variations are indicators of the discriminative power of these features in practice.

6.4.2 Accuracy of Models on the Training Set

The performance of the classifiers derived from our training set are shown in Table 3. We use the usual meanings of TPR (the percentage of correctly classified URLs for both labels), and FPR (the percentage of misclassified URLs for both labels). Using 10-fold cross validation, J48 Decision Tree and Bayes Network classifier have 100% TPR and 0% FPR. In fact, only the Random Tree classifier has the lowest TPR and the highest FPR (misclassification of 29 in 1000 URLs). Overall, the classifiers are quite precise which indicates the discriminative power of the features we derived by leveraging the attack-centric and self-defense behavior of exploit kits' workflow.

6.4.3 Accuracy of Classifiers on the Testing Set

Table 4 shows the accuracy of the classifiers on an independent test set. Overall, all the classifiers except Random Tree achieved above 99% accuracy with very low FPR. As shown in the results, the the classifiers are precise enough to correctly classify samples disjoint with the training set, which shows that our system is effective for realtime detection of exploit kit URLs.

6.4.4 Error Analysis

Here, using manual analysis, we reason out as to what caused the misclassification of URLs on the testing set.

The J48 Decision Tree classifier misclassified 2 exploit kit samples as non exploit kit URLs. One of these URLs is a file-sharing website from which users download content by interacting with the website and it has no redirections up on first encounter. However, when we manually clicked on the "Download" link, we witnessed 3 redirects to lead to a file to download. For the other URL, the (limited) data we had was not sufficient to infer a reason for the misclassification. The Random Tree classifier, misclassified 23 exploit kits as non exploit URLs. As shown in the results, this classifier was not as precise as the others. A manual inspection showed that the feature values for octet-stream and JavaScript content are less than the average size of these features for exploit kit URLs in the training set, which, we speculate, might have slightly skewed the classifier. The Random Forest classifier misclassified only 3 exploit kit URLs as non exploit kit URLs. In this case, 2 of the URLs span a single country and top-level domain, which is below the average feature value of 4 and 3 respectively for exploit kit URLs in the training set.

6.4.5 Comparison with Similar Systems

To compare our system with similar systems, we prepared a separate comparison set of 100 URLs reported to be linked with exploit kits by the URLQuery service at http://urlquery.net. We then submitted the dataset to WEBWINNOW and a public service, Wepawet [16], at about the same time. The results are summarized in Table 5. Overall, WEBWINNOW classified 31 URLs as exploit kits while Wepawet classified 19 as malicious and suspicious combined (2 and 17 respectively). Of the 31 URLs flagged as exploit kits by WEBWINNOW, Wepawet flagged 2 as malicious, 4 as suspicious, 23 as benign, and 2 as error. Manual analysis of the activity logs of these 31 URLs shows that they have dropped a binary payload to WEBWINNOW's honeyclient. We speculate that the large number of mismatch with Wepawet's output is probably attributed to the fact that it is a public service and the exploit kits might have blacklisted it to serve it with benign response. This mismatch partially confirmed with Wepawet's detailed reports for 7 of the URLs classified as benign to be pages with 404 (page not found) response.

Wepawet classified 67 URLs as benign and WEBWINNOW classified 63 as non exploit of which 33 URLs match the benign, and 12 URLs match the suspicious classification of Wepawet. WEBWINNOW was not able to finish the analysis of 6 URLs while Wepawet terminated with time-out error on 14 URLs. Overall, this experiment demonstrates the higher precision and accuracy of WEBWINNOW over existing tools in detecting malicious URLs hosted by exploit kits.

7. RELATED WORK

Kotov and Massacci [7] present a preliminary analysis of the source code of 30 different exploit kits. As per their analysis, the key strength of exploit kits is the functionalities to support the kit

Class	WebWinnow	Wepawet [16]
Benign	63	67
Malicious	31	19
Error	6	14

Table 5: Comparison summary.

owner to manage exploits, escape detection, and monitor traffic. On the other hand, they conclude that exploit kits use limited number of and unsophisticated vulnerabilities focusing on large volume of infection traffic to maximize the rate of successful infection of victims. One of the findings is that exploit kits have similar functionality, which also coincides with our preliminary analysis. Our motivation in this paper is to leverage exploit kit workflow in order to design a detection technique while the goal of the approach described in goal is to purely analyze and characterize exploit kits as software artifacts.

In another similar work, Allodi et.al [1] present, MalwareLab, an experience from a controlled experimental evaluation of resilience of 10 exploit kits with respect to changes in software configuration (e.g., browser personality of victims). As per the findings, there seem to be two types of exploit kits with regards to resilience to changes in software configuration. One type is those exploit kits designed to be effective for an extended period of time at the expense of lower infection rate. Another type is those exploit kits designed to be effective in infecting as many victims as possible within a very short period at the expense of low resilience. The contained analysis of exploit kits used in our work is similar to MalwareLab in some aspects such as the use of virtual machines and automation of execution when feasible. However, our goal is to have a deeper insight as to how the exploit kits function to perform attacks and to evade detection techniques.

Grier et.al [4] conducted a large-scale analysis on the emergence of "Exploit-as-a-Service" paradigm on the malware ecosystem by examining the current landscape of drive-by-downloads on the Internet. For the analysis, the authors analyze 77,000 malicious URLs from Google Safe Browsing and a crowd-sourced feed of blacklisted URLs known to lead to exploit kits. These URLs led to over 10,000 distinct executables. The results of contained execution of these binaries show about 32 families of malware (among which are the prominent ones) are carried around on the Web via drive-by-downloads supported by exploit kits (with Blackhole accounting for 29% of all malicious URLs). In addition, the authors also used passive DNS data to conclude that the infrastructure that hosts these exploit kits is short-lived (receives traffic only for about 2.5 hours). Although we did not measure the lifetime of exploit kits, we were also able to notice that they do not live long.

Honeyclient based detection systems (e.g., [3, 9]) rely on pre-execution and post-execution of the snapshot of the system properties to look for changes in system properties (e.g., new processes, strange memory allocation attempts, disk access attempts) to pinpoint malicious activity. In our approach, we take a different path by focusing on the actual execution and leverage it to derive distinguishing features to detect malicious URLs that host exploit kits.

8. CONCLUSION

Exploit kits are prevalent on the Internet and they contribute to a significant portion of web-based threats. Understanding how they function, attack victims, and evade detection systems is quite crucial in designing proactive techniques to detect them in real-time. In this paper, we leveraged the firsthand observation of the attack-centric and self-defense behavior of exploit kits to develop a machine learning approach that precisely detects malicious URLs hosted by exploit kits. Our evaluation shows that the classifiers we trained based on the features derived from the exploit kits' workflow perform very well with very low false positives.

Acknowledgments

This work was performed during the first author's visit to the University of Illinois at Chicago. This research was supported in part by U.S. National Science Foundation grants CNS-0845894 and CNS-1065537 and DGE-069311.

9. REFERENCES

[1] L. Allodi, V. Kotov, and F. Massacci. Malwarelab - experimentation with cybercrime attack tools. In *USENIX Workshop on Cyber Security Experimentation and Test (CSET)*, 2013.

[2] M. Blacklist. http://www.malwareblacklist.com/showMDL.php, June 2013.

[3] M. Cova, C. Kruegel, and G. Vigna. Detection and analysis of drive-by-download attacks and malicious javascript code. In *Proceedings of the 19th international conference on World wide web*, WWW '10, pages 281–290, 2010.

[4] C. Grier et al. Manufacturing Compromise: The Emergence of Exploit-as-a-Service. In *Proceedings of the 19th ACM Conference on Computer and Communication Security*, October 2012.

[5] M. Hall, E. Frank, G. Holmes, B. Pfahringer, P. Reutemann, and I. H. Witten. Weka 3: Data mining and open source machine learning software in java. http://www.cs.waikato.ac.nz/ml/weka/, July 2013.

[6] L. Invernizzi, S. Benvenuti, M. Cova, P. M. Comparetti, C. Kruegel, and G. Vigna. Evilseed: A guided approach to finding malicious web pages. In *Proceedings of the 2012 IEEE Symposium on Security and Privacy*, SP '12, 2012.

[7] V. Kotov and F. Massacci. Anatomy of exploit kits - preliminary analysis of exploit kits as software artefacts. In *ESSoS*, pages 181–196, 2013.

[8] R. Lemos. Mpack developer on automated infection kit. http://www.theregister.co.uk/2007/07/23/mpack_developer_interview/, July 2007.

[9] Y. min Wang, D. Beck, X. Jiang, R. Roussev, C. Verbowski, S. Chen, and S. King. Automated web patrol with strider honeymonkeys: Finding web sites that exploit browser vulnerabilities. In *In NDSS*, 2006.

[10] N. Provos, P. Mavrommatis, M. A. Rajab, and F. Monrose. All your iframes point to us. In *Proceedings of the 17th conference on Security symposium*, SS'08, Berkeley, CA, USA, 2008. USENIX Association.

[11] K. Rieck, T. Krueger, and A. Dewald. Cujo: efficient detection and prevention of drive-by-download attacks. In *Proceedings of the 26th Annual Computer Security Applications Conference*, ACSAC '10, 2010.

[12] S. Surgihalli and V. Krishnasamy. Styx exploit kit takes advantage of vulnerabilities. http://blogs.mcafee.com/mcafee-labs/styx-exploit-kit-takes-advantage_-of-vulnerabilities, June 2013.

[13] Symantec. Internet security threat report. http://www.symantec.com/content/en/us/enterprise/other_resources/b-istr_main_report_v18_2012_21291018.en-us.pdf, July 2013.

[14] S. E. Tracker. Spy eye tracker. https://spyeyetracker.abuse.ch/monitor.php?browse=binaries.

[15] Z. Tracker. Zues tracker. https://zeustracker.abuse.ch/monitor.php?browse=binaries.

[16] UCSB. Wepawet. http://wepawet.cs.ucsb.edu, Sep 2013.

[17] VxVault. Vx vault. http://vxvault.siri-urz.net/ViriList.php.

Privacy-Preserving Audit for Broker-Based Health Information Exchange

Se Eun Oh
University of Illinois at
Urbana-Champaign
seeunoh2@illinois.edu

Ji Young Chun
University of Illinois at
Urbana-Champaign
jychun@illinois.edu

Limin Jia
Carnegie Mellon University
liminjia@cmu.edu

Deepak Garg
Max Planck Institute for
Software Systems
dg@mpi-sws.org

Carl A. Gunter
University of Illinois at
Urbana-Champaign
cgunter@illinois.edu

Anupam Datta
Carnegie Mellon University
danupam@cmu.edu

ABSTRACT

Developments in health information technology have encouraged the establishment of distributed systems known as Health Information Exchanges (HIEs) to enable the sharing of patient records between institutions. In many cases, the parties running these exchanges wish to limit the amount of information they are responsible for holding because of sensitivities about patient information. Hence, there is an interest in broker-based HIEs that keep limited information in the exchange repositories. However, it is essential to audit these exchanges carefully due to risks of inappropriate data sharing. In this paper, we consider some of the requirements and present a design for auditing broker-based HIEs in a way that controls the information available in audit logs and regulates their release for investigations. Our approach is based on formal rules for audit and the use of Hierarchical Identity-Based Encryption (HIBE) to support staged release of data needed in audits and a balance between automated and manual reviews. We test our methodology via an extension of a standard for auditing HIEs called the Audit Trail and Node Authentication Profile (ATNA) protocol.

Categories and Subject Descriptors

F.4.1 [**Mathematical Logic and Formal Languages**]: Mathematical Logic—*Temporal logic*; D.4.6 [**Security and Protection**]: Cryptographic controls; K.4.1 [**Public Policy Issues**]: Privacy

Keywords

Audit; Health information technology; Formal logic; Hierarchical identity based encryption

1. INTRODUCTION

Broker systems enable organizations to index and share data securely by providing key infrastructure services. Such brokers provide an alternative to central repositories in which data is held as well as indexed by a central authority. The broker provides some level of indexing, provides for the transport of data, and supports security functions like authentication and audit, often without holding much of the key data itself except during its transport. These systems are of growing interest in the healthcare sector where efforts are being made internationally to take advantage of Electronic Health Records (EHRs), which enable institutions to represent medical data in standardized formats suited to inter-domain sharing. An advantage of the broker solution is that it limits the amount of information the broker needs to hold thus limiting risk and liability. For example, in the U.S. there are many nascent state-sponsored Health Information Exchange (HIE) systems where the state is reluctant to hold EMR data themselves because citizens have concerns about sharing their health data with government. Broker-based exchanges mitigate this concern while providing key benefits like the ability of healthcare providers to assemble patients' medical records quickly at the point of care.

Broker-based HIEs face a special problem with their access audit which aims to detect illegitimate accesses as part of general ongoing monitoring or specific investigations. The more audit data the HIE keeps the better it supports this function, but the more risk there is that the audit information itself will compromise privacy. Moreover, large numbers of transactions make it impossible to carry out manual audits at scale so there is a need for automation, which calls for keeping as much structured information as possible.

The goal of this paper is to explore the design space for privacy-preserving audit with automation supported by formal logical representation of audit policies. In particular, we develop a system in which Hierarchical Identity Based Encryption (HIBE) [11] is used in coordination with a logic-based audit algorithm [15] to limit the amount of information the auditor needs to know to carry out access audit. The system uses HIBE to encrypt sensitive data on the audit logs with a ranking of sensitivity. The auditor uses the audit algorithm to decide which portions of the log need to be decrypted to provide evidence of the audit decision. We use HIBE because it provides a convenient way to encrypt audit logs at a fine granularity (i.e., each event is encrypted using keys derived from the identifiers participating in that event) and limit the auditors to decrypt minimum-necessary data for audits. Since events occur frequently, but audits that require decryption of data are (presumed to be) rare, our framework provides an efficient audit procedure. We also explore the idea of extending the audit algorithm to provide understandable explanations for accesses rather than just claiming that an access can be proved consistent with or violate the policy. We design an audit architecture that augments an HIE using the ATNA [4] profile, a standard for auditing HIEs, and supports HIBE encryption of audit logs and an explanation-enabled audit procedure. A key feature of the design inspired by a pair of state HIEs (namely those for Maryland and Illinois) is the ability to combine the ATNA data with external documentation that is input to the audit algorithm. Our main contribution lies in the design and implementation of a practical system using this novel encryption and audit algorithm.

The rest of this paper is organized as follows. In Section 2, we provide background on HIE and HIBE. An overview of the architecture of our design is presented in Section 3. Next, we detail our hierarchical encryption algorithm (Section 4), the audit algorithm, and an example of using our infrastructure to audit accesses and produce explanations of the audit results (Section 5). We present our prototype implementation and evaluation results in Section 6. In the end, we discuss related work (Section 7) and conclude (Section 8).

2. BACKGROUND

Audit Standard for HIE. Because an HIE shares access to patient records to a broad community, it raises significant concerns about security and privacy [26]. To help address these concerns, the National Institute of Standards and Technology (NIST) recommends collecting and communicating audit logs about security-related events and data that should be gathered, consistent with applicable policy, as one of twelve services [23] to aid security and privacy protection for HIEs. The Audit Trail and Node Authentication (ATNA) Profile [4], is a standard developed by Integrating the Healthcare Environment (IHE) that provides an audit mechanism reflecting such security guidelines, with two strengths. First, it generates and keeps audit records in a centralized audit repository, which can be readily adapted to the typical HIE environment involving Cross Document Sharing (XDS) [4] and is compliant with HIPAA [3]. IHE stipulates that events defined in XDS.b [5] must be recorded in the audit trail. Second, the ATNA is compatible with diverse types of healthcare enterprises since it generates audit logs based on existing standards. In short, ATNA provides an infrastructure for auditing the HIE. However, it is still necessary to develop ways to stipulate policies and carry out the analysis of audit events on ATNA standard audit logs. Moreover, it may be necessary to work with external documentation that is not present in ATNA logs to achieve the overall goals of auditing the HIE. For instance, if one wishes to use billing records to confirm that an access to a record has been made to provide a (billed) service, then it may be desirable to integrate billing records into the underlying analytics engine rather than trying to make billing records a part of ATNA.

Hierarchical Identity Based Encryption. Hierarchical Identity Based Encryption (HIBE)[11, 24, 10] is a form of Identity Based Encryption (IBE) for hierarchical structures. IBE allows a sender to encrypt messages based on a receiver's identity, such as an e-mail address, before the receiver gets a secret decryption key from a Key Generation Center (KGC). The KGC generates a secret key to a user commensurate with the level of sensitivity of the data that the user needs to access. The private key will allow access at that level, or depth, in the hierarchy and at all lower levels and will also delegate authority to the holder of the private key to generate secret keys to users at lower levels. In other words, this is one-way access and delegation, so that a user at level k can generate a secret key for a user at any level lower than k, but lower level users can not use their secret keys to make secret keys for users at higher levels in the hierarchy. Upper level users who generate lower level keys are referred to as parents in the hierarchical structure. The HIBE system uses the following five algorithms.

HIBE.Setup : $(k, \mathsf{L}) \mapsto \{mk, \mathsf{Pub}\}$ takes security parameter k and maximum depth L, and outputs a master key mk and public parameters Pub.

HIBE.Extract : $(\mathsf{Pub}, mk, \mathsf{ID}) \mapsto sk_{\mathsf{ID}}$ takes the public parameters Pub, the master key mk and an identity $\mathsf{ID} = (id_1, ..., id_\ell)$ of depth $\ell(\leq \mathsf{L})$, and outputs a secret key sk_{ID} for the identity ID.

HIBE.Delegate : $(\mathsf{Pub}, sk_{\mathsf{ID}'}, \mathsf{ID}) \mapsto sk_{\mathsf{ID}}$ takes the public parameters Pub, a parent's secret key $sk_{\mathsf{ID}'}$ where the parent's identity $\mathsf{ID}' = (id_1, ..., id_{\ell'})$ of depth $\ell'(< \ell \leq \mathsf{L})$, and the child's identity $\mathsf{ID} = (id_1, ..., id_\ell)$ of depth ℓ. Then the algorithm outputs a secret key sk_{ID} for the identity ID.

HIBE.Encrypt$(\mathsf{Pub}, \mathsf{ID}, \mathsf{Msg}) \mapsto \mathsf{CT}$ takes the public parameters Pub, an identity ID and a message Msg, and outputs a ciphertext CT.

HIBE.Decrypt : $(\mathsf{Pub}, sk_{\mathsf{ID}}, \mathsf{CT}) \mapsto \mathsf{Msg}$ takes the public parameters Pub, a secret key sk_{ID} and a ciphertext CT, and outputs a message Msg.

In Section 4, we describe how to use HIBE for a workable system to encrypt, transmit, and store external documentation for later use by HIE auditors.

3. AUDIT ARCHITECTURE

Figure 1 shows a high-level schema of the HIE and our audit subsystem. As data is accessed in the HIE on a day-to-day basis, a significant amount of internal ATNA-based audit information is gathered by the HIE. This information includes data such as which specific user accessed a patient's Protected Health Information (PHI) and which specific pieces of the PHI were accessed. Individual healthcare organizations (HCOs) using the HIE offer supplementary audit logs (external documentation) such as patient registration (PR) and medical billing (BL). The prescription monitoring program (PMP) [2], a centralized repository managed by the state of Illinois, provides prescription details. Together, the three justify HCOs' medical providers' accesses to the HIE. During the audit information collection by the audit data processor (ADP), the identifier cross-reference manager (ID-CRM) matches each external party's internal patient ID, user ID and hospital ID with the HIE's IDs. However, because the HCOs may have privacy concerns about such information, we allow them (or ADP) to encrypt the sensitive information using HIBE. The information is decrypted by the audit subsystem only when it is necessary for an audit. We describe details for doing this in

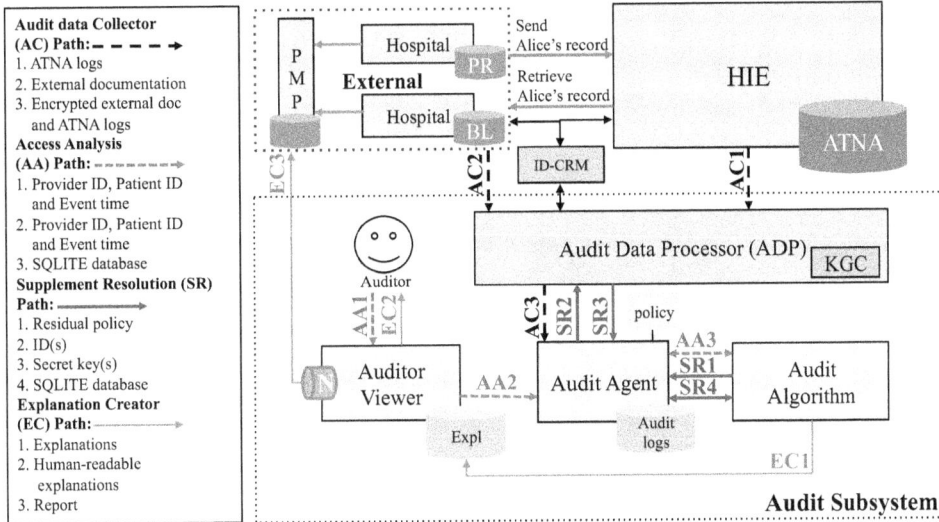

Figure 1: HIE Audit Infrastructure

Section 4. Our audit subsystem consists of four main components: (1) The ADP, which aggregates internal ATNA logs and external documentation from HCOs (called audit logs), encrypts external data and makes both available to the audit agent (path AC1 and AC2), (2) the audit agent, which is the main driver of remaining audit subsystem, (3) the audit algorithm, which is the core automation technology, and (4) an auditor viewer, which is the audit subsystem's interface for communicating with the auditor. The ADP contains the KGC for HIBE and must be trusted by the HCOs.

Access Analysis. The audit agent, which has the privacy policy relative to which audit is performed (represented in formal logic in our implementation), fetches relevant audit logs from the ADP (path AC3). The auditor sends a particular set of accesses of audit interest to the audit agent through the auditor viewer (paths AA1 and AA2). The audit agent passes the audit logs to the core audit algorithm in SQLite format (path AA3) along with the policy and the specific accesses of interest. The audit algorithm is designed to automatically check whether the specific access complies with the policy, if all relevant logs are available to it.

Supplement Resolution. Since some parts of the audit logs are encrypted, the audit algorithm may not be able to decide compliance or violation and return a residual policy (path SR1) which can be checked after the encrypted data has been decrypted (we describe the residual policy and its generation formally in Section 5).The audit agent determines what encrypted minimum information is needed to complete the audit by looking at the residual policy, and requests corresponding decryption keys from the ADP, more specifically the KGC (path SR2). Once the KGC returns the keys (path SR3), the audit agent decrypts the relevant external audit logs and sends the decrypted data to the audit algorithm as a SQLite database (path SR4). The ADP and the audit agent separately log the IDs whose keys were requested and the audit agent may additionally log the residual policies to facilitate a later audit on the audit process itself. The audit algorithm uses the newly available decrypted data to complete the audit.

Explanation Creator. The audit algorithm generates a formal explanation of why the access in question looks legitimate. This explanation is returned to the auditor viewer (path EC1), which then translates the explanation to human-readable form and returns it to the auditor (path EC2). If a policy violation is identified, the auditor viewer sends a notification with details of the audit log to the relevant HCOs (path EC3).

Our core audit algorithm (described in Section 5) is based on a prior algorithm called reduce, which can audit for policy violations even when some log information is missing [15]. Over this basic algorithm, we make two additional contributions. First, we extend reduce's output with explanations showing why a certain access satisfies or violates the policy. Second, we allow HCOs or the ADP to encrypt external audit logs in layers, through HIBE. This allows the audit agent to selectively decrypt minimum-necessary data, and facilitates any subsequent audit of the audit process and might increase the HCOs' confidence in the HIE. Use of HIBE (instead of conventional public-key cryptography) also allows the HCOs to encrypt data offline, without any interaction with the KGC.

4. HIERARCHICAL ENCRYPTION

In this section, we describe how we encrypt and decrypt external audit logs, specifically documentation, from the HCOs using HIBE for privacy protection during audits. There are various HIBE schemes that satisfy different properties and security goals. It is important to select a HIBE scheme with constant, small-size ciphertexts, e.g. [11], since such a scheme will optimize storage cost regardless of hierarchy depth. Even though privacy infringement investigations are rare in practice and encrypted sensitive data will seldom be decrypted, it must nonetheless be stored by the audit subsystem.

External Data Hierarchy and Identity. Suppose that the data in some external documentation $\mathcal{D}$ has been partitioned hierarchically into n degrees of sensitivity, resulting in data $\mathcal{D}_1, \ldots, \mathcal{D}_n$, where $\mathcal{D}_n$ is the data in the documentation

patient-id	HCO-id	date-of-bill	level1	level2	level3
eeb728473e1949a	Carle07RQ12	2013:09:08:10:18:41	$Enc_{ID_{1,1}}(\text{cs1010})$	$Enc_{ID_{1,2}}(\text{HEMOGLO...})$	$Enc_{ID_{1,3}}(73.8)$
d99486a44ca64cb	Provena01AV98	2013:09:17:02:48:29	$Enc_{ID_{2,1}}(\text{ra1010})$	$Enc_{ID_{2,2}}(\text{MCH,Auto...})$	$Enc_{ID_{2,3}}(279)$
42210b2417d74b1	NWM0329W2	2013:10:21:11:47:22	$Enc_{ID_{3,1}}(\text{pq1010})$	$Enc_{ID_{3,2}}(\text{PLATELET...})$	$Enc_{ID_{3,3}}(11.6)$

Table 1: observes-in-bill table

that is most sensitive, and $\mathcal{D}_1$ is the data that is the least sensitive. In our system, all data in $\mathcal{D}_n$ will be encrypted using an IBE identifier $ID_n = (id_1)$. We suggest this identifier be derived from non-sensitive descriptive information such as the HCO's identity, the patient's identity, degree of sensitivity, and time. Data in $\mathcal{D}_{n-1}$ will be assigned an identifier $ID_{n-1} = (id_1, id_2)$ and so on. Finally, data in $\mathcal{D}_1$ will be assigned an identifier $ID_1 = (id_1, ..., id_n)$. As an example, the billing table shown in Table 1 is hierarchically organized into 3 sensitivity levels. Information concerning observation result that a patient receives is level 3 sensitive (most sensitive), observation type is level 2 sensitive, and provider information is level 1 sensitive (least sensitive).

Billing Data Encryption. Table 1 shows encrypted patient observation information taken from illustrative medical bills. Consider data $\mathcal{D}$ that contains exactly the first row of the table. Within $\mathcal{D}$, data at the highest level of sensitivity, $\mathcal{D}_3(= 73.8)$, will be assigned identity $ID_3 = (id_1)$ which is the concatenation eeb728473e1949a || Carle07RQ12 || 2013:09:08:10:18:41 || level3 of non-sensitive identifying information. The identity of less sensitive data, $\mathcal{D}_2(=$ HEMOGLO...), is $ID_2 = (id_1, id_2)$, where $id_2 =$ level2. Finally, the identity of the least sensitive data $\mathcal{D}_1(=$ cs1010) is $ID_1 = (id_1, id_2, id_3)$, where $id_3 =$ level1. External documentation at each level of sensitivity ($\mathcal{D}_1, ..., \mathcal{D}_n$) is encrypted using the assigned identities ID_i ($1 \leq i \leq n$). For $i = 1$ to n, the ADP or the HCOs run HIBE.Encrypt(Pub, $ID_i, \mathcal{D}_i$) to get a corresponding ciphertext $Enc_{ID_i}(\mathcal{D}_i)$. For example, $Enc_{ID_{1,3}}(73.8)$ in Table 1 represents the encryption of the data $\mathcal{D}_3$. The corresponding HIBE encryption would be HIBE.Encrypt(Pub, $ID_{1,3}, 73.8$) where $ID_{1,3} = ID_3$.

This example is illustrative: All external documentation in our system is organized in tables and encrypted with HIBE. Identities used for encryption may have cell-, column- or table-granularity, depending on the nature of the documentation.

Issuance of Secret Keys and Decryption. When the audit algorithm requests encrypted data, the audit agent requests an appropriate secret key from the KGC for decryption. Assume that the audit agent needs the secret key corresponding to ID_k. To issue an appropriate secret key to the audit agent, the KGC runs HIBE.Extract(Pub, mk, ID_k) using its master key mk to get sk_{ID_k}. After receiving sk_{ID_k} from the KGC, the audit agent runs HIBE.Decrypt(Pub, $sk_{ID_k}, Enc_{ID_k}(\mathcal{D}_k)$) to obtain $\mathcal{D}_k$. If the audit agent needs additional information at any level k' that is lower than k, the audit agent runs HIBE.Delegate(Pub, $sk_{ID_k}, ID_{k'}$) to get a secret key $sk_{ID_{k'}}$, and then runs HIBE.Decrypt(Pub, $sk_{ID_{k'}}, Enc_{ID_{k'}}(\mathcal{D}_{k'})$) to get $\mathcal{D}_{k'}$. This does not require communication with the KGC.

5. AUDIT WITH EXPLANATIONS

Garg et al. [15] develop an algorithm for finding violations of a policy on system logs. Their algorithm takes into consideration incompleteness of information in logs. For example, if the policy carries the obligation "a notice must be sent in the next 30 days", then before the 30 day deadline is reached, the log may not contain enough information to decide whether or not this obligation is met. To account for incompleteness, the reduce algorithm uses a best-effort (but sound) approach; it checks as much of the policy as possible given the available log and returns a residual policy that captures policy conditions which could not be verified. When the missing information becomes available, the residual policy can be re-checked using the reduce algorithm itself. Here, we use reduce's support for incompleteness to audit iteratively; as iteration rounds progress, the audit algorithm decrypts increasingly sensitive, HIBE-encrypted external audit logs. This continues until either it is determined that there are no policy violations or relevant violations have been found. Thus, we limit the amount of external audit logs decrypted for audit.

It also helps audit to have an intuitive explanation of why a decision (policy violation or not) was made. For instance, it is helpful to know that a physician's access to a medical record in a hospital was allowed because the patient was referred to that hospital, or because that the patient visited that facility. Accordingly, we extend the reduce algorithm to also provide such an explanation.

5.1 Policy and Explanation Syntax

Following the prior work [15], we use a first-order logic as the policy specification language. We summarize the syntax of formulas and explanations in Figure 2. We write α to denote formulas and φ to denote generalized formulas, which are either formulas or audit decisions ($\top$ = no violation, $\bot$ = violation) coupled with explanations γ. Formulas include atomic predicates, true ($\top$), false ($\bot$), conjunctions ($\wedge$) and disjunctions ($\vee$) of formulas (denoted C and D, respectively), and first-order quantifiers ($\forall$ and $\exists$).

Here c denotes a restricted class of formulas, called guards, borrowed from [15]. They guarantee (statically) that the number of substitutions for x that makes c true is always finite. When guarded by a formula c, both universal and existential quantifiers can be handled easily. Readers may ignore the distinction between c and α for the purpose of understanding this section.

Each formula is annotated with a policy label, written ℓ. Labels have no semantic meaning except to establish a syntactic link between an explanation and the original formula from which the explanation was derived. The formula $\sigma \triangleright \varphi$ means that the substitution for free variables in φ is σ. This formula itself is not used for policy specification. It can appear in residual formulas output by our extended reduce algorithm.

An explanation γ corresponds to a sub-tree of labels of a formula's abstract syntax tree. An explanation is only meaningful relative to a formula. An explanation can be a single label, which points to a leaf position of the formula.

316

Conj clause	C	$::=$	$\bigwedge_i \varphi_i$
Disj clause	D	$::=$	$\bigvee_i \varphi_i$
Formula	α	$::=$	$\langle\ell\rangle P \mid \langle\ell\rangle\top \mid \langle\ell\rangle\bot \mid \langle\ell\rangle C \mid \langle\ell\rangle D$
			$\mid \langle\ell\rangle\forall\vec{x}.(c \supset \varphi) \mid \langle\ell\rangle\exists\vec{x}.(c \wedge \varphi)$
			$\mid \sigma \rhd \varphi$
Generalized form.	φ	$::=$	$\alpha \mid \texttt{expl}(\top,\gamma) \mid \texttt{expl}(\bot,\gamma)$
Explanation	γ	$::=$	$\ell \mid \ell \circ \gamma \mid \gamma_1 \oplus \gamma_2 \mid \sigma \rhd \gamma$

Figure 2: Syntax of formulas and explanations

A concatenated explanation $\ell \circ \gamma$ is an explanation for a formula labeled by ℓ at the root, where γ is, recursively, the explanation of the root's children. An explanation can also combine explanations from branches of a conjunction or disjunction (denoted $\gamma_1 \oplus \gamma_2$). Finally, an explanation can be guarded by a substitution σ (syntax: $\sigma \rhd \gamma$).

5.2 Extended Reduce Algorithm

The reduce algorithm, as presented in [15], takes as argument a policy formula α and an audit log $\mathcal{L}$ and returns a residual policy α', which may be $\top$ (no violation), $\bot$ (violation) or another formula called the residual formula (meaning that critical information is absent from the log; α' must be checked when more information is available). To extend reduce to generate explanations, we change it to take as input a policy represented as a generalized formula φ, a log $\mathcal{L}$ and, additionally, a substitution σ for free variables of φ. The output of our extended reduce algorithm is also a generalized formula. If the output is α, it means that some information necessary for audit is missing from the log, and α is the residual policy to be checked when that information becomes available. The output $\texttt{expl}(\top,\gamma)$ means that there is no policy violation and γ explains why that is the case. Similarly, the output $\texttt{expl}(\bot,\gamma)$ signals a policy violation justified by explanation γ.

We define a function simplify that takes a generalized formula and returns another generalized formula, in simpler form. The function simplify serves a dual purpose. First, it rewrites the original formula using basic rules of logic, e.g., it replaces $\varphi \wedge \top$ with φ. Second, and more importantly, if the input formula is equivalent to either $\top$ or $\bot$, it produces a succinct explanation of why that is the case by combining and selectively retaining explanations from the original formula. The output of simplify is either a residual policy formula α, or a binary answer ($\top$ or $\bot$) paired with an explanation γ.

We omit the detailed definitions of reduce and simplify; next, we demonstrate how the algorithm works.

5.3 Example Scenario

In this section, we present a simple audit scenario that illustrates reduce, simplify and HIBE.

Policy. Suppose a HIE's policy for data sharing is that a provider p_1 can send detailed information about a patient q to another provider p_2 if, within a year of such sharing, p_2 bills the insurance company for services provided to q at p_2. The encoding of a HIE's policy for data sharing is

Level 1 (least)	Level 2	Level 3 (most)
provider-id (p_2)	service-type (vl)	OBS-value(va)
INS-company (p)	INS-plan (c)	
	OBS-type (ty)	

Table 2: Sensitivity levels in the audit scenario

shown below. A provider p_1 can send a patient document m to a provider p_2 at time t ($\mathsf{send}(p_1, p_2, m, t)$), where (1) m describes patient q ($\mathsf{hasattrof}(m, q)$), (2) m includes detailed information ty and va about the patient, e.g., ty is the type of observation q is under and va is the result of the observation ($\mathsf{includes}(m, ty, va, t)$), (3) q is classified as type tp and provided with service vl at t ($\mathsf{patientInfo}(q, tp, vl, t)$), (4) p_2 works in organization o ($\mathsf{organization}(p_2, o, t)$), and (5) organization o records that patient q has an insurance plan p from company c at time t ($\mathsf{insuranceInfo}(q, p, c, t)$); then there should be a consequent patient medical bill of type b at time t' ($\mathsf{medical\text{-}bill}(q, b, t')$), t' should be within 365 days of the data sharing, the organization o should note that q has an insurance plan c with company p ($\mathsf{insurance}(q, p, c, o, t')$), and either the bill is from q's visit to p_2 or for an observation carried out by p_2 on q. Predicates $\mathsf{visits\text{-}in\text{-}bill}(q, p_2, vl, o, t')$ and $\mathsf{observes\text{-}in\text{-}bill}(q, p_2, ty, va, o, t')$ represent p_2's records of medical bills of the two specific types.

$\varphi_{pol} = \langle\texttt{DISC}\rangle$
$\forall p_1, p_2, m, q, t, ty, va, tp, vl, o, p, c$
  $\mathsf{send}(p_1, p_2, m, t) \wedge \mathsf{hasattrof}(m, q) \wedge$
  $\mathsf{includes}(m, ty, va, t) \wedge \mathsf{patientInfo}(q, tp, vl, t) \wedge$
  $\mathsf{organization}(p_2, o, t) \wedge \mathsf{insuranceInfo}(q, p, c, t)$
  $\supset \langle\texttt{AC}\rangle \exists t', b.\mathsf{medical\text{-}bill}(q, b, t') \wedge$
    $\langle\texttt{BLL}\rangle(\langle\texttt{time}\rangle\mathsf{timein}(t, t', t+365)$
      $\wedge\langle\texttt{INS}\rangle\mathsf{insurance}(q, p, c, o, t')$
      $\wedge\langle\texttt{DJ}\rangle(\langle\texttt{VST}\rangle(\langle\texttt{B}\rangle b = \text{visit-history} \wedge$
            $\langle\texttt{visit}\rangle\mathsf{visits\text{-}in\text{-}bill}(q, p_2, vl, o, t')))$
        $\vee(\langle\texttt{OBS}\rangle(\langle\texttt{B}\rangle b = \text{observation} \wedge$
            $\langle\texttt{obsv}\rangle\mathsf{observes\text{-}in\text{-}bill}(q, p_2, ty,$
                    $va, o, t')))))$

Audit Logs. The internal log contains information about all the predicates to the left of the implication in φ_{pol} as well as the predicate medical-bill. Predicates visits-in-bill and observes-in-bill record detailed information about patients' hospital visits, which are considered external documentations that belong to the hospital. Both external and internal logs are represented as database tables. Tables visits-in-bill and observes-in-bill are HIBE-encrypted according to levels shown in Table 2.

For illustration, we assume that the following substitution σ is the only one that satisfies the condition of the outermost universal quantification on the example log (here, terms like $P1$ starting with uppercase letters are constants):

$\sigma = p_1 \mapsto P1, p_2 \mapsto P2, m \mapsto M1, q \mapsto Q1, t \mapsto T1, ty \mapsto TY1,$
    $va \mapsto VA1, tp \mapsto TP1, vl \mapsto VL1, o \mapsto O1, p \mapsto PI, c \mapsto C1$

We further assume that $\mathsf{timein}(T1, T2, T1 + 365)$ and $\mathsf{timein}(T1, T3, T1 + 365)$ are true. Below are the (only) log entries about predicates to the right of $\supset$ in φ_{pol}.

  $\mathsf{medical\text{-}bill}(Q1, \text{visit-history}, O1, T2)$
  $\mathsf{medical\text{-}bill}(Q1, \text{observation}, O1, T3)$
  $\mathsf{visits\text{-}in\text{-}bill}(Q1, P2, VL1, O1, T2)$
  $\mathsf{observes\text{-}in\text{-}bill}(Q1, P2, TY2, VA2, O2, T3)$
  $\mathsf{insurance}(Q1, PI, C1, O1, T2)$

Reduce on Encrypted Data. In the initial phase of audit, the auditor does not possess decryption keys for external data. This poses no problem because reduce can handle log incompleteness; reduce treats the log incomplete in predicates like visits-in-bill, and simply returns such predicates in the residual output. The output of running reduce on φ_{pol} and the example log is shown in the next page.

$\varphi_{r1} = \langle\mathsf{DISC}\rangle\sigma\triangleright$
$\quad\langle\mathsf{AC}\rangle\sigma_1 \triangleright \langle\mathsf{BLL}\rangle$
$\quad(\langle\mathsf{time}\rangle\top\wedge \langle\mathsf{INS}\rangle\mathsf{insurance}(q,p,c,o,t')\wedge$
$\quad\langle\mathsf{DJ}\rangle(\langle\mathsf{VST}\rangle(\langle\mathsf{B}\rangle\top\wedge \langle\mathsf{visit}\rangle\mathsf{visits\text{-}in\text{-}bill}(q,p_2,vl,o,t'))$
$\quad\quad\vee\langle\mathsf{OBS}\rangle(\langle\mathsf{B}\rangle\bot\wedge$
$\quad\quad\quad\langle\mathsf{obsv}\rangle\mathsf{observes\text{-}in\text{-}bill}(q,p_2,ty,va,o,t')))$
$\quad\vee\sigma_2\triangleright\langle\mathsf{BLL}\rangle$
$\quad(\langle\mathsf{time}\rangle\top\wedge \langle\mathsf{INS}\rangle\mathsf{insurance}(q,p,c,o,t')\wedge$
$\quad\langle\mathsf{DJ}\rangle(\langle\mathsf{VST}\rangle(\langle\mathsf{B}\rangle\bot\wedge \langle\mathsf{visit}\rangle\mathsf{visits\text{-}in\text{-}bill}(q,p_2,vl,o,t'))$
$\quad\quad\vee\langle\mathsf{OBS}\rangle(\langle\mathsf{B}\rangle\top\wedge$
$\quad\quad\quad\langle\mathsf{obsv}\rangle\mathsf{observes\text{-}in\text{-}bill}(q,p_2,ty,va,o,t')))$

Here, $\begin{aligned}\sigma_1 &= t'\mapsto T2,\ b\mapsto visit\text{-}history\\ \sigma_2 &= t'\mapsto T3,\ b\mapsto observation\end{aligned}$

The existentially quantified variables t' and b in φ_{pol} have two possible substitutions, corresponding to the two entries in the medical-bill table. The residual formula hense contains a disjunction over these two possibilities.

Simplification. Next, we call simplify on φ_{r1} to condense as many explanations as possible. This yields:

$\varphi_{s1} = \langle\mathsf{DISC}\rangle\sigma\triangleright$
$\quad\langle\mathsf{AC}\rangle\sigma_1 \triangleright \langle\mathsf{BLL}\rangle$
$\quad(\mathsf{expl}(\top,\mathsf{time})\wedge \langle\mathsf{INS}\rangle\mathsf{insurance}(q,p,c,o,t')\wedge$
$\quad\langle\mathsf{DJ}\rangle(\langle\mathsf{VST}\rangle(\mathsf{expl}(\top,\mathsf{B})\wedge$
$\quad\quad\langle\mathsf{visit}\rangle\mathsf{visits\text{-}in\text{-}bill}(q,p_2,vl,o,t'))$
$\quad\quad\vee\mathsf{expl}(\bot,\mathsf{OBS}\circ\mathsf{B})))$
$\quad\vee\sigma_2\triangleright\langle\mathsf{BLL}\rangle$
$\quad(\mathsf{expl}(\bot,\mathsf{time})\wedge \langle\mathsf{INS}\rangle\mathsf{insurance}(q,p,c,o,t')\wedge$
$\quad\langle\mathsf{DJ}\rangle(\mathsf{expl}(\bot,\mathsf{VST}\circ\mathsf{B})$
$\quad\quad\vee\langle\mathsf{OBS}\rangle(\mathsf{expl}(\top,\mathsf{B})\wedge$
$\quad\quad\quad\langle\mathsf{obsv}\rangle\mathsf{observes\text{-}in\text{-}bill}(q,p_2,ty,va,o,t'))))$

Requesting Decryption Keys. To proceed further, we must decrypt the insurance table and either the observes-in-bill table or the visits-in-bill table. Since the maximum sensitivity level of entries in visits-in-bill is lower than that in observes-in-bill, the audit agent asks the KGC for keys at level 2 (the maximum level of visits-in-bill and insurance).[1] The KGC generates keys based on its master key mk and gives them to the audit agent. Both the KGC and the audit agent may log why the keys were generated (by recording the residual formula φ_{s1}) to aid a subsequent audit of this audit process. The audit agent then decrypts entries in those two tables and provides the formula φ_{s1} with the decrypted tables (added to the original log) to reduce. The output of reduce is the following formula φ_{d1}. Note that the clause guarded by σ_2 remains the same because even the extended log contains no information to reduce it.

$\varphi_{d1} =$
$\langle\mathsf{DISC}\rangle\sigma\triangleright$
$\langle\mathsf{AC}\rangle\sigma_1 \triangleright \langle\mathsf{BLL}\rangle$
$(\mathsf{expl}(\top,\mathsf{time})\wedge \mathsf{expl}(\top,\mathsf{INS})\wedge$
$\langle\mathsf{DJ}\rangle(\langle\mathsf{VST}\rangle(\mathsf{expl}(\top,\mathsf{B})\wedge\mathsf{expl}(\top,\mathsf{visit}))\vee\mathsf{expl}(\bot,\mathsf{OBS}\circ\mathsf{B})))$
$\vee\sigma_2\triangleright\langle\mathsf{BLL}\rangle$
$(\mathsf{expl}(\bot,\mathsf{time})\wedge \langle\mathsf{INS}\rangle\mathsf{insurance}(q,p,c,o,t')\wedge$
$\langle\mathsf{DJ}\rangle(\mathsf{expl}(\bot,\mathsf{VST}\circ\mathsf{B})$
$\quad\vee\langle\mathsf{OBS}\rangle(\mathsf{expl}(\top,\mathsf{B})\wedge$
$\quad\quad\langle\mathsf{obsv}\rangle\mathsf{observes\text{-}in\text{-}bill}(q,p_2,ty,va,o,t'))))$

---

[1] For simplicity, we assume here that the audit agents decrypts entire tables atomically. In practice, it could decrypt only specific rows of interest.

Simplification and Explanation. Finally, simplify is run on φ_{d1} to obtain the following output:

$\varphi_{s2} = \mathsf{expl}(\top, \mathsf{DISC}\circ\sigma \triangleright \mathsf{AC}\circ\sigma_1 \triangleright \langle\mathsf{BLL}\rangle\circ$
$\quad(\mathsf{time} \oplus \mathsf{INS} \oplus (\mathsf{DJ}\circ\mathsf{VST}\circ(\mathsf{B}\oplus\mathsf{visit}))))$

The result indicates that the log satisfies the policy. The reason is the following: (1) σ is the only substitution that makes the conditions associated with the action send true and (2) the conditions required for such a send (AC) under σ are true. The explanation of (2) is that there exists a substitution σ_1 that matches an entry in medical-bill and makes BLL true. More concretely, the time of the bill, the insurance information, and hospital's billing record of the patient all satisfy the policy constraints. In particular, the hospital's record shows that the patient visited the hospital (VST).

6. IMPLEMENTATION & EVALUATION

To validate our proposal, we implement the HIE (Figure 1) based on IHE Profile XDS.b[5]. It supports the sharing of patient clinical documents based on the HIE's document registry which keeps a patient document index and location where the documents are stored in. Based on these, the web-based document viewer looks for patient documents based on patient information. We implement a Java API to create ATNA-based XML logs [19] on top of HIE. We report our evaluation of HIBE key generation, decryption and the reduce algorithm based on a policy encoding the guidelines [6] of the U.S. Office of the National Coordinator (ONC) for Health Information Technology and a synthetic audit log. All experiments are performed on a machine with an Intel Core i7 2.3GHz processor and 1GB of memory, running Ubuntu 12.04. We use the Charm library [1] to implement the HIBE module. In particular, we use a symmetric curve with a 512-bit base field to initiate a group in the elliptic curve with bilinear pairings. For illustration purposes, we assume a maximum depth of three sensitivity levels in the hierarchy. To encrypt arbitrary messages with HIBE, we use a hybrid encryption scheme: we extract a session key after hashing [10] a random element from the message space of HIBE, encrypt messages with the session key via AES (CBC mode) symmetric encryption and encrypt the random element using HIBE [11].

Policy. According to the ONC, providers requesting a patient's IIHI (individually identifiable health information) by electronic means for treatment must verify a treatment relationship with a patient by attestation or artifacts such as patient registration, prescriptions, consults, and referrals. The top-level encoding of the policy is shown below and consists of a disjunction of six sub clauses, and at least one must be satisfied for each access. We omit the details of these clauses. φ_{pol}, shown in Section 5.3, is a simplified encoding of $\varphi_{Billing}$.

$\varphi_{ONC} = \forall p_1, p_2, m, q, t, ty, va, tp, vl, o, p, c$
$\quad\mathsf{send}(p_1,p_2,m,t)\wedge \mathsf{hasattrof}(m,q)\wedge$
$\quad\mathsf{includes}(m,ty,va,t)\wedge \mathsf{patientInfo}(q,tp,vl,t)\wedge$
$\quad\mathsf{organization}(p_2,o,t)\wedge \mathsf{insuranceInfo}(q,p,c,t)$
$\quad\supset\varphi_{Exception} \vee \varphi_{Billing} \vee \varphi_{Registration} \vee \varphi_{Prescription}$
$\quad\vee\varphi_{Referral} \vee \varphi_{Consult}$

Audit Logs. We generate synthetic data representing both external audit logs and internal ATNA logs. The generated ATNA log has a size of 5.7 MB, which represents

	Key Gen. (ms)	Session key Dec.(ms)	Message Dec.(ms)	Algorithm (ms)	Single access(ms)	Day (s)	Month (m)
Up to Level 3	17.73	20.76	0.06	42.6	81.15	6.57	3.26
Up to Level 2	11.73	13.73	0.04	41.3	66.80	5.41	2.68

Table 3: Consumption time for HIBE and reduce

9,644 accesses to HIE over 4 months (this realistic number is based on Johnson *et al.*'s data [18]). The external audit data has a size of 12 MB, and includes roughly 9,644 entries about patient registration, billing and referral. The external logs are encrypted using HIBE with three pre-defined sensitivity levels.

Evaluation Results. We evaluate the efficiency and scalability of both HIBE and the reduce algorithm. We use the audit scenario shown in Section 5.3 and break it into three phases. In the first phase, the auditor does not have any keys, and we measure the time reduce takes to generate a residual policy; in the second phase, we measure the time it takes the KGC to generate a decryption key given an ID, and the time it takes to decrypt relevant log data using the key (because our encryption is hybrid, the latter further splits into the time taken to decrypt the symmetric key, and the time take to decrypt the data using the symmetric key); in the third phase, we run reduce again and measure the time reduce takes to check the residual policy on the decrypted data. We run the audit scenario on two accesses, one requires a decryption key of level 2, and the other requires a decryption key of level 3. The size of messages encrypted up to level 2, shown in Table 3, is 416B including the session key and the size of messages encrypted up to level 3 is 580B including the session key. Table 3 summarizes our results. All numbers are averages of 20 trials (all have negligible standard deviations). The first column shows the time taken to generate HIBE decryption keys, the second column indicates the time needed to decrypt a session key with the HIBE key, the third column shows the time to decrypt a message using AES and the fourth column shows the total time consumed by reduce, which is derived by adding up the time for each iteration of reduce(before and after decryption). As can be seen, the total time is split almost evenly between reduce and the cryptographic operations for data at level 3 and is dominated by reduce for data at level 2. Johnson et al [18] report approximately 81 accesses per day in a typical HIE. Based on this number, we calculate the total time for auditing all accesses in a day and in a month to be 6.57/5.41 seconds (level 3/level 2) and 3.26/2.68 minutes, respectively. Since audit is an offline process, we consider these numbers practical.

Practical Issues in Deployment. Integrating our audit architecture into an actual distributed healthcare environment will require the HCOs to trust the security of the audit infrastructure. Our audit subsystem mitigates this concern to some extent, since data is stored encrypted and it is decrypted only when absolutely necessary and auditors never see log data unencrypted. However, in cases where human judgment is necessary, auditors may need access to unencrypted data. This raises concerns about auditor trustworthiness, but such concerns are orthogonal to our design and exist in all audit environments.

7. RELATED WORK

Audits in the Healthcare Domain. Previous works have envisaged a scientific and technical approach to audit the healthcare system. Gunter et al. [17] introduce access rules informed by probabilities (ARIP) to establish appropriate access rules for HCOs based on their work flows and social networks by analyzing audit logs and attributes of HCOs. However, their work is not feasible for infrastructure currently in place at HCOs, while our work is applicable to the real-world heterogeneous healthcare environment with IHE standard based audit infrastructure. In addition, Fabbri and LeFevre [13, 14] have proposed explanation-based auditing, which enables patients to review access to their health records with human interpretable explanations. They adopt a machine learning approach to automatically generate log explanation while we use the logic-based algorithm to identify the legitimacy of access based on the privacy policy. Gregg [16] builds an audit interface for the ATNA-based audit logs from a picture archiving and communications system (PACS). However, their work does not consider privacy.

Audit Log Encryption. We share the goal of previous encryptions of audit logs[12, 22, 27] to not only protect against malicious attackers, but also to limit exposure of private information in the log to an authorized auditor. Our approach is different from previous methods for encrypting audit logs because we supplement internal log information with external data, which we encrypt with HIBE, allowing auditors to access only the minimum necessary data. In doing so, our scheme creates an identity, a descriptive label, using terms that do not need to be encrypted, such as unidentifiable codes for patient, provider, and type and date of visit, for the audit log entry, allowing the auditor to find the log needed without the more cumbersome encrypted keyword approach previously used. In previous schemes, such as [27], the auditor has to match all encrypted keywords with a given trapdoor that contains those words. This makes it secure but extremely inefficient.

Algorithms for Policy Compliance Checking. We build on Garg et al.'s algorithm reduce for auditing policies over incomplete logs [15]. We inherit the policy language used by the reduce algorithm, which is a first-order logic that can encode first-order Linear Temporal Logic (LTL) formulas. Policies that are naturally specified in LTL can be easily translated to formulas in this logic. There has been much work on compliance checking of policies expressed in Linear Temporal Logic (LTL) [25, 7, 20, 9, 8, 21]. Most of the work focuses on runtime monitoring. In contrast, we assume that logs are recorded by audit agents, and post-hoc audit is applied to these logs. To our knowledge, reduce is the only policy-based log audit algorithm that can handle incomplete logs. We leverage reduce's capability to handle incomplete logs to integrate encrypted logs. We also extend reduce to generate explanations for the output of the algorithm.

8. CONCLUSIONS

We have proposed an audit infrastructure for broker-based HIE systems, that limits the information shared through HIE. The audit logs are encrypted with HIBE and stored in a centralized audit repository for effective HIE audit, and decrypted on a need-only basis by our audit subsystem. Our logic-based audit algorithm provides further evidence of the auditor's behavior, and thus increases the trustworthiness of the system. The initial performance evaluation of a prototype implementation shows that our proposed infrastructure is practical and scalable. As future work, we plan to implement the extended audit algorithm with explanations and investigate the possibility of combining audit and access control mechanisms in the HIEs.

Acknowledgements

This work was partially supported by NSF CNS 09-64392 (NSF EBAM) and HHS 90TR0003-01 (SHARPS). The views expressed are those of the authors only. We appreciated feedback on this work from Mark Chudzinski and Ivan Handler from the Office of Health Information Technology of the State of Illinois and from Mike Berry and Noam Arzt of HLN Consulting, LLC.

9. REFERENCES

[1] Charm: A tool for rapid cryptographic prototyping. http://www.charm-crypto.com.

[2] Illinois Prescription Monitoring Program. https://www.ilpmp.org/.

[3] HIPAA Security Series, 4 Security Standards: Technical Safeguards. Department of Health and Human Services USA, 2007.

[4] Integrating the healthcare enterprise volume 1 integration profiles. ACC, HIMSS and RSNA Integrating the Healthcare Enterprise, 2007.

[5] IHE IT Infrastructure Technical Framework Supplement 2007-2008 Cross-Enterprise Document Sharing-b (XDS.b). ACC, HIMSS and RSNA Integrating the Healthcare Enterprise, 2008.

[6] Privacy and Security Framework Requirements and Guidance for the State Health Information Exchange Cooperative Agreement Program. Office of the National Coordinator for Health Information Technology, 2012.

[7] F. Baader, A. Bauer, and M. Lippmann. Runtime verification using a temporal description logic. In *Proc. of FroCos*, 2009.

[8] H. Barringer, A. Goldberg, K. Havelund, and K. Sen. Rule-based runtime verification. In *Proc. of VMCAI*, 2004.

[9] D. A. Basin, F. Klaedtke, and S. Müller. Policy monitoring in first-order temporal logic. In *Proc. of CAV*, 2010.

[10] D. Boneh and X. Boyen. Efficient selective identity-based encryption without random oracles. *Journal of Cryptology*, 24(4):659–693, 2011.

[11] D. Boneh, X. Boyen, and E.-J. Goh. Hierarchical identity based encryption with constant size ciphertext. In *Advances in Cryptology–EUROCRYPT 2005*, pages 440–456. Springer, 2005.

[12] D. Davis, F. Monrose, and M. K. Reiter. Time-scoped searching of encrypted audit logs. In *Information and Communications Security*, pages 532–545. Springer, 2004.

[13] D. Fabbri and K. LeFevre. Explanation-based auditing. *Proc. VLDB Endowment*, 5(1), 2011.

[14] D. Fabbri and K. LeFevre. Explaining accesses to electronic medical records using diagnosis information. *Journal of the American Medical Informatics Association*, 20(1), 2013.

[15] D. Garg, L. Jia, and A. Datta. Policy auditing over incomplete logs: theory, implementation and applications. In *Proc. of CCS*, 2011.

[16] B. Gregg, H. D'Agostino, and E. Toledo. Creating an IHE ATNA-based audit repository. *Journal of Digital Imaging*, 2006.

[17] C. Gunter, D. Liebovitz, and B. Malin. Experience-based access management: A life-cycle framework for identity and access management systems. *Proc. of IEEE Security & Privacy*, 9(5), 2011.

[18] K. B. Johnson, K. M. Unertl, Q. Chen, N. M. Lorenzi, H. Nian, J. Bailey, and M. Frisse. Health information exchange usage in emergency departments and clinics: the who, what, and why. *Journal of the American Medical Informatics Association*, 18(5):690–7, 2011.

[19] G. Marshall. Security Audit and Access Accountability Message XML Data Definitions for Healthcare Applications. (September), 2004.

[20] G. Roşu and K. Havelund. Rewriting-based techniques for runtime verification. *Automated Software Engineering*, 12:151–197, 2005.

[21] M. Roger and J. Goubault-Larrecq. Log auditing through model-checking. In *Proc. of CSF*, 2001.

[22] B. Schneier and J. Kelsey. Secure audit logs to support computer forensics. *ACM Transactions on Information and System Security (TISSEC)*, 2(2):159–176, 1999.

[23] M. Scholl, K. Stine, K. Lin, and D. Steinberg. *Security Architecture Design Process for Health Information Exchanges (HIEs)*. 2010.

[24] J. H. Seo, T. Kobayashi, M. Ohkubo, and K. Suzuki. Anonymous hierarchical identity-based encryption with constant size ciphertexts. In *Public Key Cryptography–PKC 2009*, pages 215–234. Springer, 2009.

[25] P. Thati and G. Roşu. Monitoring algorithms for metric temporal logic specifications. *Electronic Notes in Theoretical Computer Science*, 113:145–162, 2005.

[26] J. R. Vest and L. D. Gamm. Health information exchange: persistent challenges and new strategies. *Journal of the American Medical Informatics Association*, 17(3):288–94, Jan. 2010.

[27] B. R. Waters, D. Balfanz, G. Durfee, and D. K. Smetters. Building an encrypted and searchable audit log. In *Proc. of NDSS*, 2004.

An Efficient Privacy-Preserving System for Monitoring Mobile Users: Making Searchable Encryption Practical

Gabriel Ghinita
University of Massachusetts, Boston
gabriel.ghinita@umb.edu

Razvan Rughinis
Politehnica University, Bucharest
razvan.rughinis@cs.pub.ro

ABSTRACT

Monitoring location updates from mobile users has important applications in several areas, ranging from public safety and national security to social networks and advertising. However, sensitive information can be derived from movement patterns, so protecting the privacy of mobile users is a major concern. Users may only be willing to disclose their locations when some condition is met, for instance in proximity of a disaster area, or when an event of interest occurs nearby. Currently, such functionality is achieved using *searchable encryption*. Such cryptographic primitives provide provable guarantees for privacy, and allow decryption only when the location satisfies some predicate. Nevertheless, they rely on expensive *pairing-based cryptography (PBC)*, and direct application to the domain of location updates leads to impractical solutions.

We propose secure and efficient techniques for private processing of location updates that complement the use of PBC and lead to significant gains in performance by reducing the amount of required pairing operations. We also implement two optimizations that further improve performance: materialization of results to expensive mathematical operations, and parallelization. Extensive experimental results show that the proposed techniques significantly improve performance compared to the baseline, and reduce the searchable encryption overhead to a level that is practical in a computing environment with reasonable resources, such as the cloud.

Categories and Subject Descriptors

H.2.8 [**Database Applications**]: Spatial databases and GIS

General Terms

Security, Experimentation

Keywords

Location Privacy, Pairing-based Cryptography

1. INTRODUCTION

Modern mobile devices with positioning capabilities (e.g., GPS) allow users to be informed about events that occur in their proximity. Several classes of applications benefit from the large-scale availability of location data, ranging from public safety and national security to social networks and advertising. One particular scenario of interest is that of *location-based alert systems*, where

mobile users wish to be immediately notified when their current location satisfies some condition, expressed as a spatial *search predicate*. For instance, in a public safety scenario, users want to be notified when they are getting close to a dangerous accident area. Alternatively, in the commercial domain, a user may want to be alerted when a retail store sales event is underway nearby.

The typical architecture of such a system uses a server that collects updates from the users and checks whether the alert condition is met. Such a service is provided by a commercial entity that is not fully trusted. Collection of user trajectories at a commercial site introduces serious privacy concerns, as sensitive personal information may be derived from a person's whereabouts [19, 16]. Therefore, protecting the privacy of users is a necessary feature of such a system, and the users must not report their exact locations to the server. Ideally, the only information that the server should be able to derive from the user updates is whether the conditions that the users subscribe to are satisfied or not. Various syntactic privacy models have been proposed [19, 15, 28, 17] that perform some sort of generalization of location before sharing, but these have been proven to be vulnerable, especially in the presence of background knowledge [16]. Furthermore, semantic privacy models such as differential privacy [13, 12, 10] are only suitable for releasing statistics, but not for processing privately individual updates.

Recently, several advanced encryption functions that allow evaluation of predicates on ciphertexts have been proposed [6, 24, 2]. These are broadly referred to as *searchable encryption* functions, since they allow the evaluation of certain types of queries without requiring decryption. Such encryption systems are asymmetric, i.e., they employ a secret key SK and a public key PK pair.

Figure 1 illustrates the envisioned system for location-based alerts using searchable encryption. The architecture has three types of entities: *(i)* the users, who send encrypted location updates using PK; *(ii)* a *trusted authority (TA)* which generates *tokens* for spatial search predicates using secret key SK; and *(iii) the server (S)* that collects updates from users and evaluates the predicates on the ciphertexts using the tokens. In practice, the TA may represent the public emergency department of a city, which is responsible for the safety of the citizens. The TA is trusted, but it does not have the necessary infrastructure to support a large-scale alert system, hence it outsources this service to S.

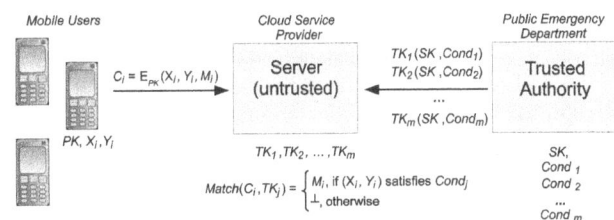

Figure 1: Location-based Alert System

However, S is a commercial entity that cannot be trusted with the user locations, so TA sets up a *SK/PK* pair, and distributes *PK* to the users. When an emergency occurs in a region (e.g., "Marina Bay block"), the TA creates a search token which is sent to S and matched against the ciphertexts received from users. The properties of searchable encryption guarantee that S is able to evaluate the predicate on the ciphertext (e.g., whether the user location is enclosed in the city block encoded by the search token) and learns only if the ciphertext matches or not, but no other information about user location is learnt by the server.

To understand search on encrypted data, it helps to consider each ciphertext as being composed of two parts: an encrypted index I and encrypted message M. M is the payload of the ciphertext, just the same as in the case of conventional encryption. The novel part about searchable encryption is the presence of index I, which is used for search, and can be seen as a parameter of the encryption function: $E_{PK}(I, M)$. When a user u_i constructs its update, it uses its current coordinates (X_i, Y_i) as index, and performs encryption as $E_{PK}((X_i, Y_i), M_i)$. At the server, if the index satisfies the predicate specified by a token, then the server is able to recover the message M_i from the user. However, this does not imply that S can find the exact user location, as M_i may contain information that is of other nature (e.g., an emergency contact number).

One prominent approach to searchable encryption called *Hidden Vector Encryption (HVE)* was proposed in [6]. The method allows queries on ciphertexts such as exact match, range and subset queries. HVE uses bilinear maps on groups of composite order [18] as mathematical foundation and makes extensive use of expensive operations such as bilinear maps pairings and exponentiations with large integers. As a result, HVE is very expensive and scales poorly. Later in Section 5, we show that in order to process the update from a single user only, it may take up to 100 seconds. Clearly, direct application of HVE for alert systems is not suitable.

In this paper, we propose secure and efficient techniques to support private location-based alert systems using searchable encryption. To the best of our knowledge, this is the first study of applying searchable encryption to the domain of private search with spatial predicates. Our specific contributions are:

i. We devise specific constructions that allow application of HVE to the problem of location-based alert systems with a reduced number of pairing operations, thus lowering the computational overhead of HVE.

ii. We develop optimizations based on reuse of expensive mathematical operation results and parallelization, which further reduce the HVE performance overhead.

iii. We perform an extensive experimental evaluation which shows that the proposed approach brings the overhead of searchable encryption to acceptable levels in a computing environment such as the cloud.

The rest of the paper is organized as follows: Section 2 overviews the proposed system and HVE. Section 3 presents the encoding techniques for efficient application of HVE, whereas Section 4 outlines the optimizations to reduce execution time. Section 5 contains the experimental evaluation results, followed by a survey of related research in Section 6. Finally, Section 7 concludes the paper and highlights directions for future work.

2. BACKGROUND

2.1 System and Privacy Model

Figure 2 illustrates the location-based alert system model, where a number of n users $\{u_1, \ldots, u_n\}$ move within a two-dimensional square unit space $[0, 1] \times [0, 1]$. Users continuously report their

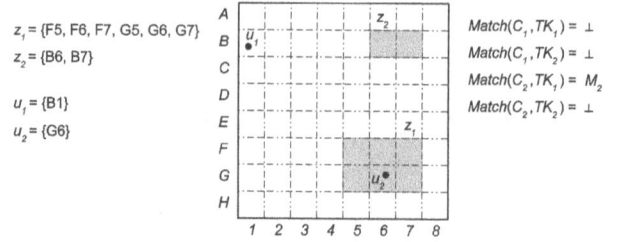

Figure 2: System Model ($n = 2$, $m = 2$, $d = 8$)

coordinates and wish to be notified when their location falls within any of m *alert zones* $\{z_1, \ldots, z_m\}$. Alert zones (or simply *zones*) are defined by a trusted authority, as detailed later in this section. For simplicity, we assume that the space is partitioned by a regular grid of size $d \times d$, and each alert zone covers a number of grid cells. The functional requirement of the system follows the spatial range query semantics, i.e., a user u must receive an alert corresponding to zone z if its location is *enclosed* by zone z.

The system architecture follows the model represented in Figure 1, and consists of three types of entities:

i. **Mobile Users** subscribe to the alert system and periodically submit encrypted location updates.

ii. The **Trusted Authority (TA)** is a trusted entity that decides which are the alert zones, and creates for each zone a search *token* that allows to check privately if a user location falls within the alert zone or not[1].

iii. The **Server (S)** is the provider of the alert system. It receives encrypted updates from users and search tokens from TA, and performs the predicate evaluation $Match$ to decide whether encrypted location $C_i (1 \leq i \leq n)$ falls within alert zone j represented by token $TK_j (1 \leq j \leq m)$. If the predicate holds, then $Match$ returns the message M_i encrypted by the user, otherwise it returns a void message ($\perp$).

The *privacy requirement* of the system dictates that the server must not learn any information about the user locations, other than what can be derived from the match outcome, i.e., whether the user is in a particular alert zone or not. In case of a successful match, the server S learns that user u is enclosed by zone z. In case of a non-match, the server S learns only that the user is outside the zone z, but no additional location information is disclosed. Note that, this model is applicable to many real-life scenarios, such as our motivating example in Section 1. For instance, users wish to keep their location private most of the time, but they want to be immediately notified if they enter a zone where their personal safety may be threatened. Furthermore, the extent of alert zones is typically small compared to the entire data domain, so the fact that S learns that u is *not* within the set of alert zones does not disclose significant information about u's location.

In practice, the TA role is played by an organization such as a city's public emergency department. Such an actor is trusted not to disclose SK and compromise user privacy, but at the same time does not have the technological infrastructure to monitor a large user population. Hence, the alert service is outsourced to a commercial entity, e.g., a cloud provider that plays the role of the server. The TA will issue alert zones to signal that certain areas of the city are affected by an emergency. In an alternate setting, the TA may be a national security agency which investigates potentially terrorist activities near a given location that it has information on. Cooperating civilians that are in the area may want to volunteer some

---

[1] Later in Section 3 we show how a single token can serve multiple zones, which increases performance.

attribute:

0	0	1	0	1	0

predicate:

0	0	*	0	1	*

(a) Match

attribute:

0	0	1	0	1	0

predicate:

*	*	0	0	1	*

(b) Non-Match

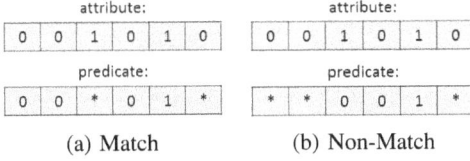

Figure 3: Predicate evaluation on ciphertexts with HVE

information, such as Wi-Fi packet traces captured by their devices. However, they do not want to disclose their location when they are outside the suspicious zone.

A private location-based alert system is also useful in social networks. A social network user u can create a SK/PK pair and distribute PK to its buddies. Next, u creates a token that represents his/her current location, e.g., a downtown restaurant. The network provider (e.g., Facebook), plays the role of the server: it monitors privately users, and sends the identifiers of buddies in the downtown area back to u. No information is gained by the server about locations of non-matching users.

Finally, we emphasize that the alert zones are *not* private. This is a reasonable assumption, since in practice the existence of emergency zones is public information that is broadly available. If it is important to protect the location of the zones, then a related flavor of HVE which protects token information can be used [2]. However, dealing with this scenario is outside the scope of this work.

2.2 Searchable Encryption with HVE

Hidden Vector Encryption (HVE) [6] is a searchable encryption system that supports predicates in the form of conjunctive equality, range and subset queries. Compared to earlier solutions ([3, 5]), HVE yields ciphertexts with considerably smaller length. Search on ciphertexts can be performed with respect to a number of *index attributes*. HVE represents an attribute as a bit vector (each element has value 0 or 1), and the search predicate as a *pattern* vector where each element can be 0, 1 or '*' that signifies a wildcard (or "don't care") value. Let l denote the HVE *width*, which is the bit length of the attribute, and consequently that of the search predicate. A predicate evaluates to $True$ for a ciphertext C if the attribute vector I used to encrypt C has the same values as the pattern vector of the predicate in all positions that are not '*' in the latter. Figure 3 illustrates the two cases of *Match* and *Non-Match* for HVE, whereas Algorithm 1 provides the matching pseudocode.

Algorithm 1: HVE_Match

Input : HVE index $I = [I_1 : I_l]$
Input : HVE token $T = [T_1 : T_l]$
Output: $True$ if I matches T, $False$ otherwise

if $\forall i \in [1 : l]$, $I_i = T_i$ or $T_i = *$ **then**
  return $True$
else
  return $False$

We provide additional mathematical background on HVE encryption and its operations in Appendix A.

3. PROPOSED SPATIAL HVE APPROACHES

In this section, we show how to use HVE for location-based alert systems. In Section 3.1 we outline a naive *baseline* technique which applies HVE in a straightforward manner to determine privately which users fall within one or more alert zones. The baseline leads to prohibitive costs, as shown by experiments in Section 5. To

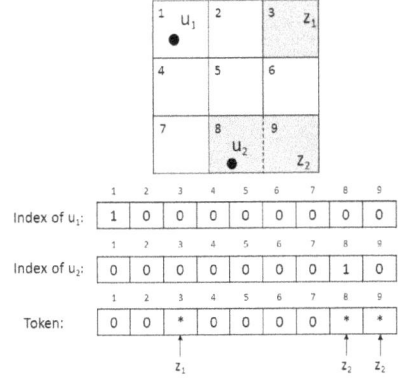

Figure 4: Naive Baseline Encoding

bring down the overhead of HVE, we propose in Section 3.2 a *hierarchical encoding* technique, which reduces the amount of cryptographic primitives required during search. Next, in Section 3.3 we further refine hierarchical encoding and devise the *Gray encoding*, which achieves superior computation savings.

3.1 Baseline Encoding

Recall that the data space is partitioned by a two-dimensional $d \times d$ regular grid. When a user reports its position, it sends to the server an encryption of the grid cell it is enclosed by. Similarly, the TA defines the alert zones as a set of grid cells. Each grid cell can be uniquely identified by a *cell identifier*, with values between 1 and d^2. Thus, the straightforward way to support searchable encryption for location-based alerts is to use an HVE with width $l = d^2$. The encoding of the HVE is performed as follows:

- When user u enclosed by grid cell i reports its location, it uses in the encryption process a bitmap index I of width d^2 where all the bits are set to '0' except bit i which is set to '1'.

- The TA creates a single token for search, which captures all the alert zones. The token is a bitmap with d^2 bits where all bits corresponding to cell identifiers that are included in an alert zone are set to '*'. All other bits are set to '0'.

- At the server (i.e., at query time), according to the rules for HVE query evaluation from Section 2.2, a user will be determined as a $Match$ if and only if the '1' bit in the encrypted location will correspond to a '*' entry in the token. This is equivalent to a subset query, and signifies that the user location is enclosed in some alert zone.

Consider the example in Figure 4, where $d = 3$. We have a number of nine grid cells, so the width of the HVE is $l = 9$. There are two alert zones: z_1 which consists of a single grid cell (3), and z_2 which spans two grid cells (8 and 9). Two users report their locations: u_1 enclosed by cell 1, and u_2 enclosed by cell 8. The index vectors of the two users are shown in the diagram. A single token is used to represent both alert zones, and a '*' is placed in the positions corresponding to the cells enclosed by the zones, namely 3, 8 and 9. The predicate evaluation for u_2 will return $Match$, as the position marked by '1' in the index of u_2 corresponds to a '*' in the token. Conversely, a *Non-Match* is returned for u_1, as the bit '1' in position 1 corresponds to a '0' in the token. Algorithm 2 provides the baseline encoding pseudocode.

As discussed in Appendix A, Eq. (1) from the query step executes two pairing operations and multiplies their results for every element in J, i.e., for every position that is not '*' in the token. Having a token with one position for each grid cell leads to high cost, so the naive encoding where the HVE width is equal to the

---
Algorithm 2: Baseline Encoding
---
p = ID of grid cell enclosing user u
A = set of grid cell IDs that make up the alert zone
User u: Set $I = [I_1 : I_{d^2}]$, $I_p = 1$ and $\forall i \neq p$, $I_i = 0$
User u: Send encrypted I to Server S
TA : Set $T = [T_1 : T_{d^2}]$, $T_i = *$ if $i \in A$ and $T_i = 0$
          otherwise
TA : Send encrypted T to Server S
Server: If $HVE\_Match(I, T) = True$, return $Match$
Server: Otherwise, return $NotMatch$

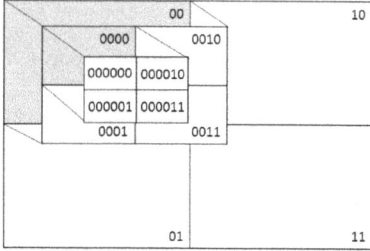

Figure 5: Hierarchical partitioning on three levels

number of cells is not appropriate. Furthermore, the sum of areas of all alert zones is relatively small compared to the entire dataspace, hence the number of '*' entries will be small, and the cardinality of set J will be large, increasing cost. Next, we propose two effective forms of encoding HVEs such that execution cost is reduced.

3.2 Hierarchical Encoding

The main problem of the baseline encoding is that the HVE width grows linearly with the grid cell count. We propose a technique that reduces the HVE width from d^2 to $2 \log d$, by using the binary representation of cell identifiers. However, in doing so, the representation of the search predicates (and thus, that of the tokens) becomes more complicated, since the advantage of the "bitmap-like" representation of the baseline is lost. To address this issue, we investigate how to aggregate representations of adjacent cells belonging to the same alert zone, in order to reduce the amount of tokens required. Aggregation is performed according to a hierarchical spatial structure, hence the name of *hierarchical encoding*.

We consider a logical organization of the grid cells into a quadtree-like structure[2] [29]. Figure 5 illustrates the space partitioning into four cells of equal size by using mediators on the Ox and Oy axes. Each of these four cells will have a 2-bit id: 00 for top left, 01 for bottom left, 10 for top right and 11 for bottom right. Next, each of these cells is partitioned recursively into four new cells, and the newly obtained 2-bit identifiers are concatenated as a suffix to the previous step identifiers. For simplicity, in this example we consider that the grid cell count is a power of 4, but any grid size can be accommodated in this model by using padding.

The diagram also shows how aggregation of cells from level j is performed into a larger cell at level $j + 1$ (in reverse direction of scoping). Note that, with the binary representation of identifiers, cell aggregation corresponds to binary minimization of a logical 'OR' expression composed of the terms that represent cell identifiers. As a result, instead of using a distinct token (i.e., HVE pattern) for each cell, we can use token aggregation and reduce the number of predicates that need to be tested. If two cells are in the same alert zone and their identifiers differ in just one bit, then a '*' can be used instead of that bit, similar to a wildcard in bi-

---
[2]Note that this is a logical structure, no physical index is required.

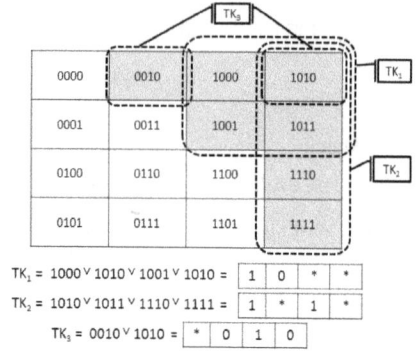

Figure 6: Hierarchical encoding and token aggregation

nary minimization. The newly obtained token is faster to generate and evaluate, because according to the operations described in Appendix A, only the positions in the pattern vector where the value is not '*' need to be considered (i.e., those in set J). Going one step further with minimization, if all of the four partitions belonging to the same quadtree node are in the same alert zone, then they can all be aggregated to the identifier of their parent. In our implementation, in order to generate HVE pattern vectors with aggregation, we use the binary expression minimization tool Espresso [26].

Consider for instance the example from Figure 6, where the alert zone is composed of seven cells. All four cells whose identifiers have prefix 10 are in the zone, hence they can all be aggregated to $TK_1 = 10**$. Also, cells on the last vertical line can be aggregated to $TK_2 = 1 * 1*$. Finally, cells 0010 and 1010 can be aggregated to $TK_3 = *010$. Note that, although these tokens overlap, this does not introduce a correctness problem at query (i.e., matching) time at the server. Furthermore, the monitoring server can evaluate them in order from the most general (highest number of '*'s) to the most specific one (lowest number of '*'s). If one token evaluates to a $Match$ on a particular (encrypted) user location, there is no need to evaluate the rest of the tokens, since it is clear that the user is in the alert zone. In addition, creating overlapping tokens helps if these tokens have more '*' symbols in their HVEs, because the cardinality of set J (Eq. (1) in Appendix A) decreases, hence query and token generation times decrease as well.

In summary, the hierarchical scheme works as follows:

Encryption. Users determine the binary identifier of the grid cell they are in, and create an HVE index I with that representation, having width $2 \log d$, where $d \times d$ is the grid size. The encryption is performed with respect to I. Since the grid parameters are public, the user can easily determine its enclosing cell and construct I.

Token Generation. For each alert zone z, the TA creates the set of binary representations of cell identifiers within the zone. Next, the TA computes the minimized binary expression equivalent to the logical 'OR' of all identifiers in the set. For each resulting term in the minimized expression, the TA creates a token, and the token will have a '*' symbol in each position that was reduced during the minimization. All tokens are sent to the server.

Query. For every user and alert zone, the server S performs matching as follows: S evaluates the encrypted user location against every token that represents the zone, in *decreasing* order of the number of '*' symbols in the token. In other words, tokens with a higher number of '*'s are considered first. If a $Match$ is obtained, then the remaining tokens for the zone are no longer considered. If a *Non-Match* is obtained for all tokens in the zone, then the server concludes that the user is not inside the zone.

Even though the number of tokens increases compared to the baseline, the width of each token is considerably smaller. In addition, the proportion of '*' symbols in a token is much higher for the hierarchical scheme, due to aggregation. Finally, considering tokens with a smaller J set first increases the chances of deciding on a $Match$ without having to consider all tokens of a zone. All these factors make the hierarchical encoding perform much faster than the baseline, as we show in Section 5. Algorithm 3 provides the hierarchical encoding pseudocode.

Algorithm 3: Hierarchical Encoding

---

p = ID of grid cell enclosing user u
A = set of grid cell IDs that make up the alert zone
User u: Set $I = [I_1 : I_{2\log_2 d}]$, s.t. $\forall i, I_i \in \{0,1\}$ and
$\qquad \sum_{i=1}^{2\log_2 d} I_i \cdot 2^{i-1} = p$
User u: Send encrypted I to Server S
TA : Create initial token set $TK = [TK_1 : TK_{2\log_2 d}]$,
$\qquad$ where $\forall a \in A, \exists T \in TK$ s.t. $\forall i, T_i \in \{0,1\}$ and
$\qquad \sum_{i=1}^{2\log_2 d} T_i \cdot 2^{i-1} = a$
TA : Reduce TK size by aggregating tokens within
$\qquad$ Hamming distance of 1
TA : Send encrypted TK to Server S
Server: If $\exists T \in TK$ s.t. $HVE\_Match(I,T) = True$,
$\qquad$ return $Match$; Else return $NotMatch$

3.3 Gray Encoding

The performance gain of the hierarchical technique comes from the ability to combine adjacent cells into a single search token with many '*' positions. In other words, the performance improves when the binary minimization of the logical 'OR' of cell identifiers is more effective. However, in some cases, no aggregation can be performed between two neighboring cells, as the Hamming distance between their identifiers is more than 1. As alert zones are composed of groups of neighboring cells, it is desirable to have small Hamming distance between adjacent cell identifiers. To improve the effectiveness of the binary minimization step, hence to increase the number of '*' values in search tokens, we represent cell identifiers using Gray codes [1]. This way, cell identifier values are assigned in such a manner that the Hamming distance between two adjacent cells is always 1, hence binary minimization is facilitated.

A one-dimensional Gray code vector is determined using the following recursive algorithm, where | represents the concatenation operator, and G_k is the vector of a Gray code instance at step k).

$$G_1 = (0,1)$$

$$G_k = (g_1, g_2, ... g_{2^k})$$

$$G_{k+1} = (0|g_1, 0|g_2, ..., 0|g_{2^k}, 1|g_{2^k}, ..., 1|g_2, 1|g_1)$$

For $k = 3$, the following Gray code vectors are obtained:

$$G_1 = (0,1)$$

$$G_2 = (00, 01, 11, 10)$$

$$G_3 = (000, 001, 011, 010, 110, 111, 101, 100)$$

Given a $d \times d$ grid, the length of the required Gray code necessary to represent all cells is $2^{\lceil log_2 d \rceil}$. We employ a Gray code instance independently for each of the two dimensions of the space, thus the identifier of a cell consist of the concatenation between the Gray code value for the y axis and the x axis values. Similar to hierarchical encoding, the scheme assumes a total number of cells that is a power of 4, but other cases can be handled by padding.

Figure 7 illustrates the advantage of using Gray encoding instead of hierarchical encoding for a 16-cell 4×4 grid. The alert zone

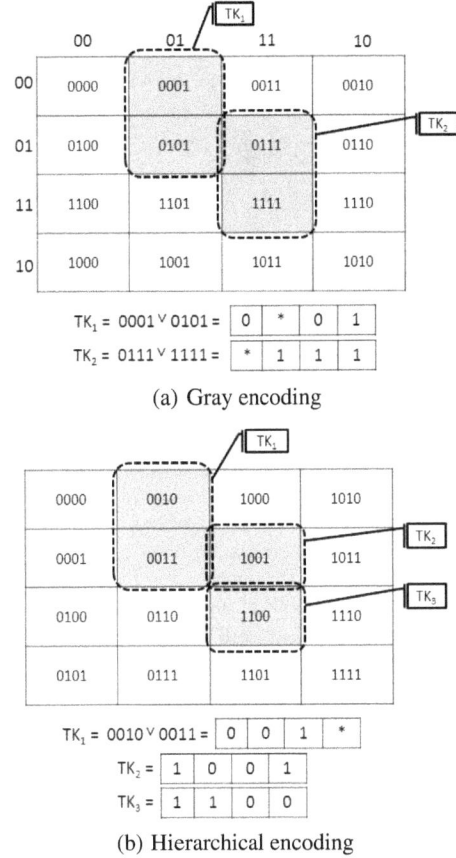

(a) Gray encoding

(b) Hierarchical encoding

Figure 7: Token Aggregation: Gray vs hierarchical encoding

consists of four cells. The two digits leading each row in the Gray encoding diagram (Figure 7(a)) mark the two-bit prefix shared by all the cell identifiers in that row. Conversely, the two digits on top of each column mark the two-bit suffix of all the cell identifiers in that column. Using binary minimization, the two tokens shown in the diagram are obtained, each of them having one '*' symbol. Figure 7(b) shows how the hierarchical encoding behaves for the same input. Due to the fact that moving from cell 1001 to 1100, or from 0011 to 1001 corresponds to a Hamming distance larger than 1, no aggregation is possible between these cell pairs. As a result, three tokens are necessary to represent this zone. Furthermore, two of these tokens have no '*' symbol, leading to more expensive evaluation. As we will show experimentally in Section 5, Gray encoding achieves more effective aggregation, especially in the case of skewed data (e.g., Gaussian distribution of alert zones).

The phases of encryption and query for the Gray encoding method are similar to their counterparts for the hierarchical encoding method of Section 3.2. The main difference is in the token generation phase, where the binary minimization is performed according to the Gray code cell identifier binary representation. As we show in the experimental evaluation in Section 5, using the Gray code representation can improve performance by achieving more effective binary minimization. This in turn results in either fewer tokens, or tokens with a larger proportion of '*' symbols.

4. PERFORMANCE OPTIMIZATIONS

4.1 Preprocessing mathematical operations

As discussed in Appendix A, the HVE mechanism involves a large number of exponentiations with very large integers which in-

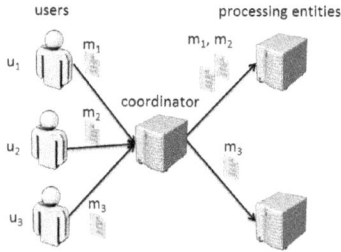

Figure 8: Parallel computation model

cur a significant computational cost. Fortunately, many of these exponentiations are performed on a common base. For example, if we take into consideration the encryption phase, in order to compute C' and C_0, A and V must be raised to the power of s. Even if s is chosen randomly for each run of this step, A and V depend on the public key, which remains unchanged for long periods of time (in commercial systems, re-keying can be done with frequency of once per year, or even less often). Furthermore, when computing $C_{i,1}$, because the index attributes consist of a vector of 0 and 1 values, the base of the power s can have only two values: H_i or $U_i \times H_i$. Because both of them depend only on the public key, these two exponentiations will always have a constant base. The same logic can be also applied to the exponentiations for token generation. By employing preprocessing on each of these fixed bases, the exponentiations become a lot faster. The preprocessing can be done offline, and the results used during online operation, leading to significant execution time savings.

When matching a token against an encrypted message, several pairing computations are performed. For a particular token, the values of K_0, $K_{i,1}$ and $K_{i,2}$ remain constant. When applying a pairing, Miller's algorithm is used [27]. Typically, for each such operation, it is required to compute several line equations. In [25] it is shown that effective preprocessing can be used as long as the first parameter is constant because the equations of the lines can be calculated and stored ahead of time. At runtime, the coordinates of a given point are substituted into these precomputed expressions. Since HVE requires symmetric elliptic curves, preprocessing can be also done for the second parameter. Preprocessed information is stored with each token and used by the server to improve the time of each pairing. Preprocessing each token must be done only when the tokens are generated at the trusted authority.

4.2 Parallelization

The server is monitoring a large number of users, and receives a large number of messages that must be matched against all tokens. This creates a considerable load on the server. However, we emphasize that the processing of a message from a user can be done independently from messages originating at other users. Furthermore, even for the same user, the matching for different alert zones are completely independent operations. This presents a great potential for parallelization. In fact, the problem is embarrassingly parallel, and significant execution time improvements can be obtained by using several CPUs for matching. Nowadays, even off-the-shelf desktop computers have multiple cores. Commercial cloud services typically have hundreds or thousands of CPUs available for computation. Due to the parallel nature of the problem, the speedup is expected to be close to linear, and the resulting system scales very well as the number of CPUs involved grows.

We consider a message-passing parallel computing paradigm, which is favored by the fact that only a small amount of data needs to be shared among distinct CPUs. A message-passing system can scale much easier to a large number of CPUs, without the need for

expensive hardware (as is the case for shared-memory machines). As programming environment, we chose the *Message Passing Interface (MPI)* which is a freely-available software. One master MPI process coordinates all other slave processes. The master process distributes to the slaves the search tokens. Then, as encrypted updates from users arrive, the master receives the requests and dispatches them to slaves. Load balancing can be easily implemented at the master level, which keeps track of the status of all slave processes. No communication is required between slave processes, and the master-slave communication is required only at the start and end of each task. Furthermore, distinct messages originating from the same user can be processed on different CPUs without any loss in correctness or performance (i.e., no state maintenance is required). After processing is done, if the token evaluated successfully, a response action can be taken by the processing CPU, or the event can be sent to a central server responsible only with handling what to do in case of a successful match.

Figure 8 illustrates the envisioned computing infrastructure. Users u_1, u_2 and u_3 send messages m_1, m_2 and m_3 to the coordinator. m_1 and m_2 are allocated to the first processing unit and m_3 to the second. As a result, the messages are processed in parallel, and the time between message generation and matching is reduced.

The infrastructure described above has a potential limitation in the case when a very small number of users subscribe to the system. If processing a message from a user is always finished before receiving messages from another, then only one single processing entity will be active at a time, whereas the others would idle. One solution could be to assign multiple CPUs to process the same message, but on different tokens. In order to do so, the central coordinator must broadcast the user message to each machine. Next, each processing unit will only perform matching with respect to a disjoint partition of the tokens. However, if one processing entity evaluates one token successfully, it will have to signal this event to other slaves, because there is no need to evaluate all other tokens for that particular zone. As a result, communication between the slaves becomes necessary, creating additional overhead and decreasing speedup. Nevertheless, an alert system is likely to have a large number of users, hence the architecture described in Figure 8 where each message is handled by a single CPU is sufficient.

5. EXPERIMENTAL EVALUATION

We implemented a C++ prototype of the proposed HVE-based location-based alert system and performance optimizations. We have used as dataset the city of Oldenburg, and generated user movements using Brinkhoff's *IAPG Network-based Generator of Moving Objects*[3] [7]. We generated alert zones within the boundaries of the dataset domain according to two distributions: uniform and Gaussian. We vary the percentage of space covered by alert zones compared to the entire dataspace extent from 2% to 6%, and we denote this parameter as *coverage*. We consider a regular grid partitioning the two-dimensional space with size ranging from 16 to 400. The HVE cryptographic functions were implemented using the Gnu MP library[4] and the Pairing-Based Cryptography library[5] from Stanford University. We use key lengths of 768, 1024 (default value), 1280 and 1536 bits. Throughout the experimental evaluation, we focus on the operations of encryption, token generation and query, and we do not consider the setup (key generation) phase. We have found that this phase always requires less than 2 seconds, and it is a one-time process, hence does not impact system performance. The experimental testbed consisted of a cluster with

---

[3] http://iapg.jade-hs.de/personen/brinkhoff/generator/

[4] Available online at http://gmplib.org/

[5] Available online at http://crypto.stanford.edu/pbc/

(a) Token generation   (b) Message encryption   (c) Query

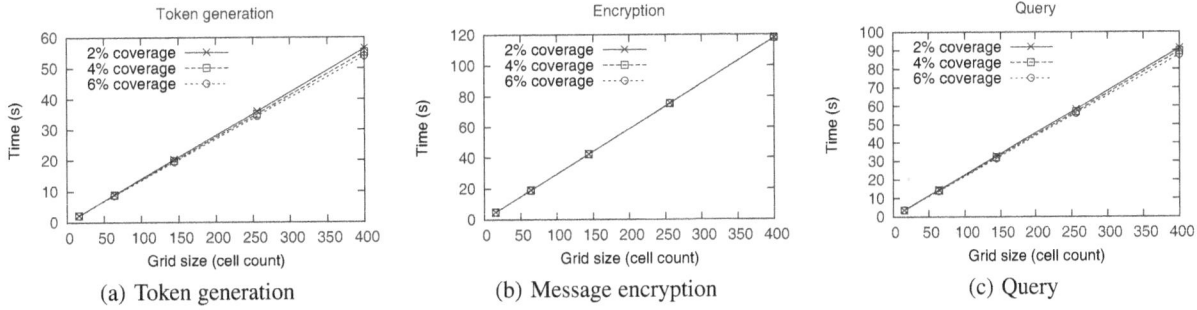

Figure 9: Baseline encoding results

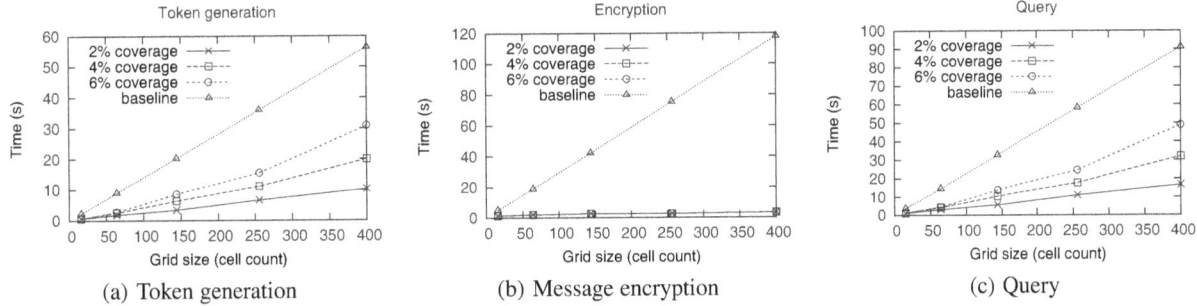

(a) Token generation   (b) Message encryption   (c) Query

Figure 10: Hierarchical encoding results on uniform data

8 machines, each having an Intel Xeon 2.53 GHz CPU and 32GB of RAM, running Red Hat Enterprise Linux and using a network connection of 10Gbps. For the parallel tests, we used as programming environment Open MPI 1.5.1.

5.1 Baseline Evaluation

We evaluate the performance of the baseline method introduced in Section 3.1, thus justifying our claim that direct application of searchable encryption to location-based alert systems is not practical. Figure 9 shows the execution time results obtained for token generation, encryption and query. The times presented are for a single operation, and present the average value obtained for a particular grid size and percentage of the area covered by alert zones (each percentage value has a different line in the graphs). First, we note that the coverage does not have a significant effect on the execution time, because the width of the HVE obtained is so large that the associated overhead overshadows the influence of the additional '*' symbols obtained as the area of alert zones grows. Second, it can be observed that the values obtained are very large, and clearly not acceptable in practice.

The token generation ranges from 10 to 60 seconds. Even though this is expensive, it can be argued that the TA does not execute this phase very often (only when a new alert zone occurs), hence its performance is not critical. However, encryption is very frequent, and it is executed at the resource-constrained mobile users. Even for moderate grid sizes, it takes 40 to 80 seconds to generate a single encrypted update! Furthermore, the time required at the server to process a single user update (i.e., perform matching against all alert zones) ranges between 30 and 60 seconds for moderate grid sizes, reaching as high as 100 seconds for the largest grid size.

5.2 Hierarchical and Gray Encoding

Next, we evaluate the hierarchical encoding performance against the baseline. Figures 10 and 11 show the comparison results for uniform and Gaussian alert zone distributions, respectively. Hierarchical encoding clearly outperforms the baseline, especially in terms of encryption time. The maximum time required for encryp-

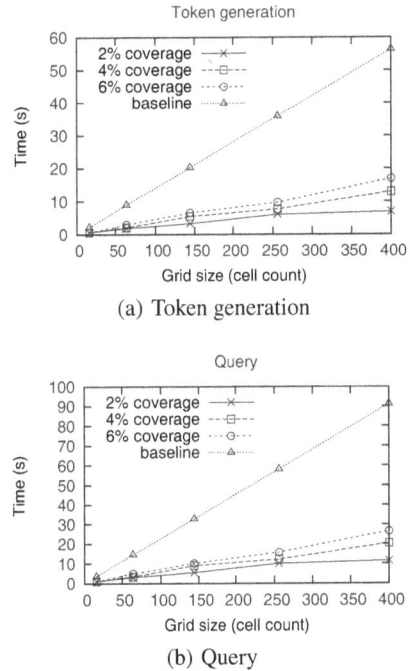

(a) Token generation

(b) Query

Figure 11: Hierarchical encoding results on Gaussian data

tion is 3 seconds, in contrast with 120 seconds for the baseline (Figure 9(b)). Recall that alert zones do not influence encryption, so a single line is present in Figure 10(b). Encryption is also independent of alert zone distribution, so we do not show encryption in Figure 11.

In terms of token generation and query time, the gain in performance is higher for the Gaussian distribution, since there is more potential for token aggregation. The reason is that minimization of binary expressions of cell identifiers is more effective when zones are clustered, which is likely to be the case in practice.

327

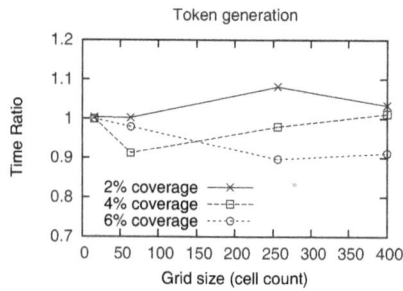

(a) Token generation

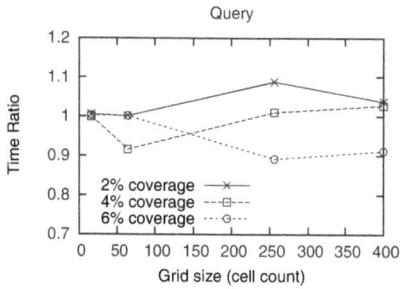

(b) Query

Figure 12: Gray vs. hierarchical encoding on uniform data

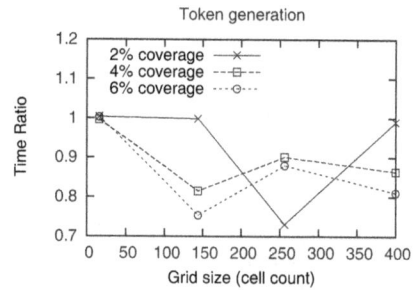

(a) Token generation

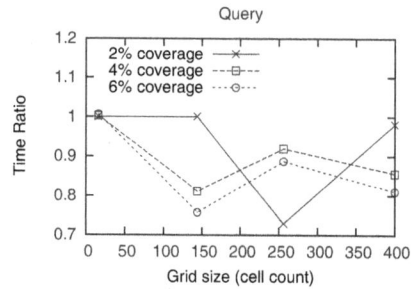

(b) Query

Figure 13: Gray vs. hierarchical encoding on Gaussian data

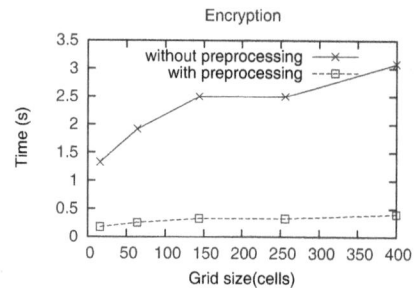

Figure 14: Encryption Time with preprocessing

As expected, execution time is higher for finer-grained grids. However, as opposed to the baseline, in the case of hierarchical encoding the coverage has a significant effect on token generation and query performance, as more alert zone cells translate into a larger number of tokens. Still, the variation with coverage is sublinear, due to the good effectiveness of the aggregation strategy employed (note how when coverage doubles from 2% to 4% for uniform data and largest grid size, the query time increases only 1.5 times). Although the absolute execution times are still high, hierarchical encoding significantly outperforms the baseline. Later in Section 5.3 we show how optimizations can be used to further cut down the performance overhead. For the rest of the experimental evaluation, we will omit the baseline results.

Next, we evaluate the effect of using Gray encoding on performance. Recall from Section 3.3 that using Gray codes provides better potential for aggregation, thus reducing the number of required tokens and/or increasing the proportion of '*' symbols in a token. Figures 12 and 13 present a comparison between the performance of the two encodings (since the encryption step is the same for hierarchical and Gray encodings, we omit that graph; the results are the same as in Figure 10(b)). For clarity, to keep the number of lines in the graph low, we present the ratio between the execution time of Gray divided by that of hierarchical encoding. Lower values of the ratio correspond to higher gains for the Gray encoding.

For uniform data, both encodings perform similarly, without a clear winner, due to the fact that the aggregation potential is equal in the two cases. On the other hand, for Gaussian data where alert zones are clustered, Gray encoding favors aggregation of cells. In practice, as alert zones are likely to be clustered, Gray can bring significant performance benefits, of up to 30%. The gain of Gray is higher as the coverage of alert zones increases, and there are more alternatives for cell aggregation.

5.3 Optimization Effect

In this section, we evaluate the performance of the proposed techniques when incorporating the performance optimizations dis-

cussed in Section 4. We show that, with the optimizations in place, the absolute cost of the proposed system for private location-based alerts can be brought down to a reasonable level, which can be practical in a commercial computing environment such as the cloud.

First, we show the effect of incorporating preprocessing to pre-compute and re-use some of the results to expensive mathematical operations, such as exponentiations with large numbers. Figure 14 presents the gain in encryption time (recall that encryption time is the same for hierarchical and Gray encoding, and is independent of alert zone distribution). The time is reduced to levels of at most half a second. For coarser-grained grids, this time is as low as 0.2 seconds. Recall that, having a low encryption time is very important, since this operation is performed at the mobile user device.

Figures 15 and 16 present the absolute token generation and query times for both proposed encoding techniques, and we choose the extreme values of the alert zone coverage scale, namely 2% and 6%. Token generation computation requirements range from half a second to 4 seconds. For Gaussian distribution of alert zones, which is more relevant for real-life scenarios, the time is lower, as aggregation is more effective. As expected, Gray slightly outperforms hierarchical encoding, especially for the Gaussian data. Also, as the coverage increases, more tokens are required to represent a zone, so the generation time increases. We believe that such times are reasonable in practice, especially since creation of alert zones is not a frequent event in the system operation. In terms of

328

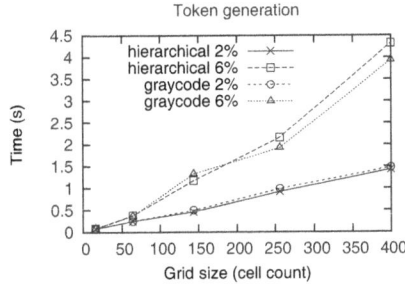

(a) Token generation

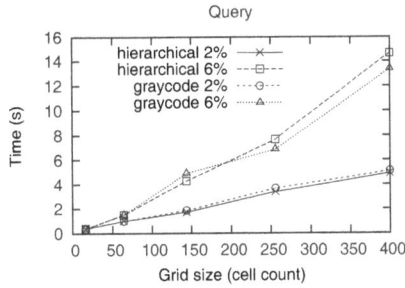

(b) Query

Figure 15: Effect of preprocessing on uniform data

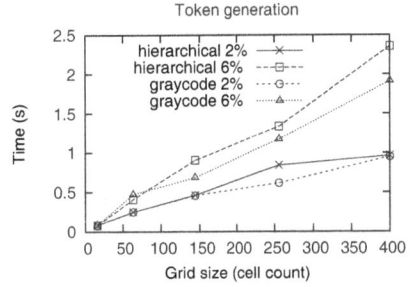

(a) Token generation

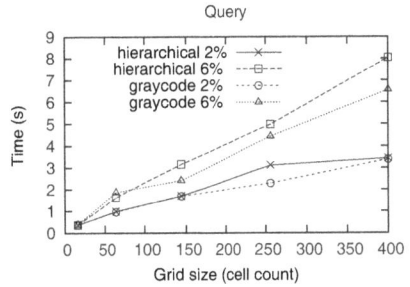

(b) Query

Figure 16: Effect of preprocessing on Gaussian data

querying (i.e., matching) at the server, the execution times are approximately cut in half compared to the non-optimized case (Figures 10 and 11). We remark a similar increasing trend in execution time as the grid size and coverage increase. The Gray encoding maintains its advantage, especially for Gaussian distribution of alert zones.

In Figure 17 we present the behavior of hierarchical encoding with preprocessing when the length of the encryption key is varied. We show results for two different grid granularities and coverage values, with Gaussian zone distribution. As expected, the performance decreases when key length increases. However, the 1024-bit setting, which according to industry standards is sufficient for securing individuals' information, does not incur a steep increase in performance overhead. Gray encoding results exhibit similar behavior.

Despite the gains of incorporating preprocessing, the absolute times for queries at the server are quite high. Given that an alert system is likely to serve a large number of users, scalability is a key concern. Reducing further the matching time is essential, so we use parallel processing to solve this problem. Figures 18 and 19 present the results when employing the parallel processing optimization. We used 2, 4 and 8 CPUs for computation. We considered both variable grid size for a fixed coverage of 6%, as well as variable coverage of alert zones for a fixed grid size of 250. The results show that a close-to-linear speedup can be obtained. For 8 CPUs for instance, the speedup is 7.3. This is a very encouraging outcome, and the query time is this way reduced to less than one second in the worst case. For median-scale settings of the grid size and coverage, we obtain absolute execution times of 0.15 seconds per query. We emphasize that, although we only had available 8 CPUs for testing, the problem studied is embarrassingly parallel in nature, so the availability of a larger number of CPUs is likely to lead to close-to-linear speedup values as well.

6. RELATED WORK

Location Privacy. The problem of location privacy has been extensively studied over the past decade, as it became clear that

mobile users' movement patterns can disclose sensitive information about individuals. A significant amount of research focused on the problem of private location-based queries, where users send their coordinates to obtain points of interest in their proximity. Some of the earlier work attempted to protect locations of real users by generating fake locations. For instance, in [23] the querying user sends to the server $k - 1$ fake locations to reduce the likelihood of identifying the actual user position. *SpaceTwist* [31] performs a multiple-round incremental range query protocol, based on a fake *anchor* location that hides the user coordinates. In [8], a random cloaking region that encloses the user is generated. However, the fake locations can be detected using various filtering techniques, which leaves the real users vulnerable.

A new direction of research started by [19] and continued by [14, 21, 28] relies on the concept of *Cloaking Regions (CRs)*. CR-based solutions implement the spatial k-anonymity (SKA) [21] paradigm. For each query, a trusted anonymizer service generates CRs that contain at least k *real* user locations. If the resulting CRs are *reciprocal* [21], SKA guarantees privacy for snapshots of user locations. However, supporting continuous queries [9] requires generating large-sized CRs. In [20, 11], the objective is to prevent the association between users and sensitive locations. Users define privacy profiles [11] that specify their sensitivity with respect to certain *feature types* (e.g., hospitals, bars, etc.), and every CRs must cover a diverse set of sensitive and non-sensitive features. In [22], the set of POI is first encoded according to a secret transformation by a trusted entity. A Hilbert-curve mapping (with secret parameters) transforms 2-D points to 1-D. Users (who know the transformation key) map their queries to 1D, and the processing is performed in the 1-D space. However, the mapping can decrease result accuracy, and the transformation may be vulnerable to reverse-engineering.

The problem with CR-based methods is that the underlying k-anonymity paradigm is vulnerable to background knowledge attacks. This is particularly a problem in the case of moving users, since trajectory information can be used to derive the identities behind reported locations. More recently, *differential privacy* [13], a

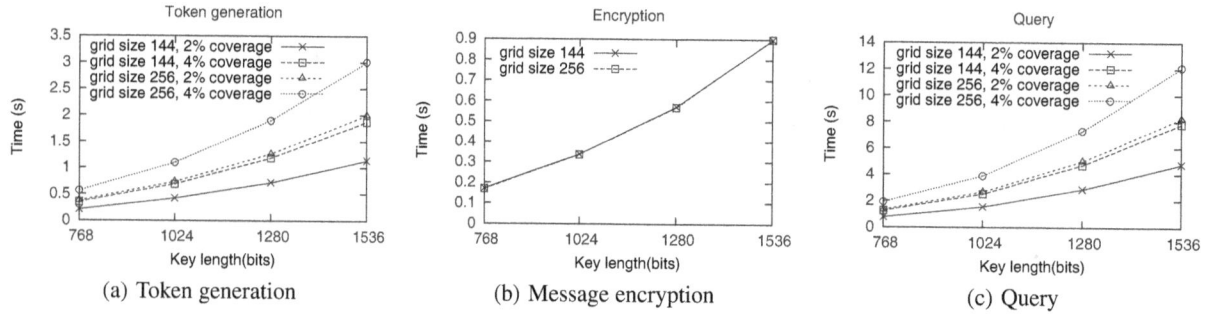

(a) Token generation   (b) Message encryption   (c) Query

Figure 17: Hierarchical encoding results for Variable Key Length, Gaussian data

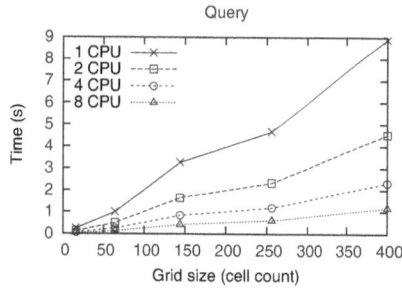

(a) Fixed area percentage

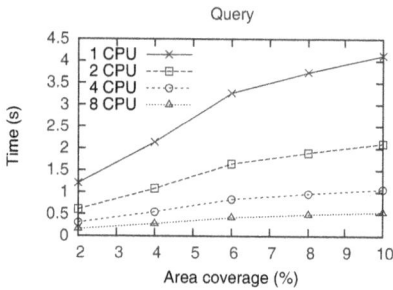

(b) Fixed grid size

Figure 18: Parralel results on uniform data

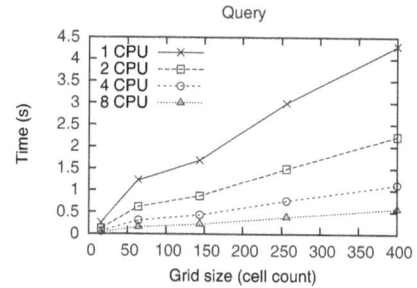

(a) Fixed area percentage

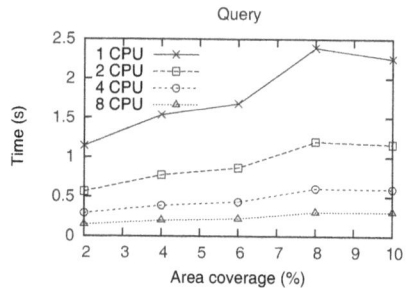

(b) Fixed grid size

Figure 19: Parralel results on Gaussian data

provably secure model for semantic privacy, has been used for spatial data in [10]. However, differential privacy is only suitable for aggregate releases of data, and cannot handle processing of individual updates, as required by an alert system.

Closer to our work, a Private Information Retrieval (PIR) protocol is proposed in [16] for nearest-neighbor queries. The protocol is provably secure, and also uses cryptography. However, it considers a 'pull-based' approach, and assumes that the user already knows the location s/he wants to retrieve points of interest from. In contrast, our focus is on a 'push-based' notification service, where the PIR solution cannot be applied since the user is not aware of where the alert zones are.

Searchable Encryption. One of the earliest works that coined the concept of searchable encryption was [30], which proposed provably secure cryptographic techniques for keyword search. Only exact matches of keywords were supported. Later in [5], the set of search predicates supported was extended to comparison queries. However, the resulting solution could not be easily extended to conjunctions of conditions, without a considerable increase in ciphertext and token size. The work in [6] further extended the set of supported predicates to subset queries, as well as conjunctions of equality, comparison and subset queries with small ciphertext and token size. The authors of [6] also introduced HVE,

which we employ as a building block in our solutions for private location-based alert systems. HVE protects the privacy of the encrypted messages received from users, but assumes that the token information (e.g., alert zones) is public. The more recent work in [2] extends HVE to also protect the tokens. However, the solution is more expensive.

7. CONCLUSION

In this paper, we proposed a provably-secure system for location-based alerts which uses searchable encryption. We introduced two alternate data encodings that allow the efficient application of cryptographic primitives for search on encrypted data (namely HVE), and we also devised performance optimizations that reduce the overhead of searchable encryption, which is notoriously expensive. To the best of our knowledge, this is the first attempt to use searchable encryption in the context of processing location data, and the experimental evaluation results show that searchable encryption can be made practical with careful system design and optimizations.

In future work, we plan to extend our solutions to more complex types of notification conditions. Currently, only range query semantics are supported, where a user is notified if its location falls within an alert zone. We will investigate techniques that also allow distance-based search predicates. In addition, we will research how to check conditions that depend on the locations of multiple users, and how to protect efficiently the privacy of alert zones as well.

Acknowledgments. This work has been supported by NSF award CNS-1111512.

8. REFERENCES

[1] J. R. Bitner, G. Ehrlich, and E. M. Reingold. Efficient generation of the binary reflected gray code and its applications. *Commun. ACM*, 19(9):517–521, Sept. 1976.

[2] C. Blundo, V. Iovino, and G. Persiano. Private-key hidden vector encryption with key confidentiality. In *Proceedings of the 8th International Conference on Cryptology and Network Security*, pages 259–277, 2009.

[3] D. Boneh, G. D. Crescenzo, R. Ostrovsky, and G. Persiano. Public key encryption with keyword search. In *EUROCRYPT 2004, volume 3027 of LNCS*, 2003.

[4] D. Boneh, E.-J. Goh, and K. Nissim. Evaluating 2-dnf formulas on ciphertexts. In *Proceedings of the Second international conference on Theory of Cryptography*, pages 325–341, 2005.

[5] D. Boneh, A. Sahai, and B. Waters. Fully collusion resistant traitor tracing with short ciphertexts and private keys. In *EUROCRYPT 2006, volume 4004 of LNCS*, pages 573–592, 2006.

[6] D. Boneh and B. Waters. Conjunctive, subset, and range queries on encrypted data. In *Proceedings of the 4th conference on Theory of cryptography*, pages 535–554, 2007.

[7] T. Brinkhoff. A Framework for Generating Network-based Moving Objects. *GeoInformatica*, 6(2):153–180, 2002.

[8] R. Cheng, Y. Zhang, E. Bertino, and S. Prahbakar. Preserving User Location Privacy in Mobile Data Management Infrastructures. In *Privacy Enhancing Technologies (PET)*, 2006.

[9] C.-Y. Chow and M. F. Mokbel. Enabling Private Continuous Queries for Revealed User Locations. In *SSTD*, pages 258–275, 2007.

[10] G. Cormode, C. Procopiuc, E. Shen, D. Srivastava, and T. Yu. Differentially private spatial decompositions. In *ICDE*, pages 20–31, 2012.

[11] M. Damiani, E. Bertino, and C. Silvestri. PROBE: an Obfuscation System for the Protection of Sensitive Location Information in LBS. Technical Report 2001-145, CERIAS, 2008.

[12] C. Dwork. Differential privacy in new settings. In *SODA*, pages 174–183, 2010.

[13] C. Dwork, F. McSherry, K. Nissim, and A. Smith. Calibrating noise to sensitivity in private data analysis. In *TCC*, pages 265–284, 2006.

[14] B. Gedik and L. Liu. Location Privacy in Mobile Systems: A Personalized Anonymization Model. In *Proc. of ICDCS*, pages 620–629, 2005.

[15] B. Gedik and L. Liu. Protecting Location Privacy with Personalized k-Anonymity: Architecture and Algorithms. *IEEE TMC*, 7(1):1–18, 2008.

[16] G. Ghinita, P. Kalnis, A. Khoshgozaran, C. Shahabi, and K. L. Tan. Private Queries in Location Based Services: Anonymizers are not Necessary. In *Proceedings of International Conference on Management of Data (ACM SIGMOD)*, 2008.

[17] G. Ghinita, P. Kalnis, and S. Skiadopoulos. PRIVE: Anonymous Location-based Queries in Distributed Mobile Systems. In *WWW*, 2007.

[18] O. Goldreich. The Foundations of Cryptography, Volume 2. *Cambridge University Press*, 2004.

[19] M. Gruteser and D. Grunwald. Anonymous Usage of Location-Based Services Through Spatial and Temporal Cloaking. In *USENIX MobiSys*, 2003.

[20] M. Gruteser and X. Liu. Protecting Privacy in Continuous Location-Tracking Applications. *IEEE Security and Privacy*, 2:28–34, 2004.

[21] P. Kalnis, G. Ghinita, K. Mouratidis, and D. Papadias. Preserving Location-based Identity Inference in Anonymous Spatial Queries. *IEEE TKDE*, 19(12), 2007.

[22] A. Khoshgozaran and C. Shahabi. Blind Evaluation of Nearest Neighbor Queries Using Space Transformation to Preserve Location Privacy. In *SSTD*, 2007.

[23] H. Kido, Y. Yanagisawa, and T. Satoh. An anonymous communication technique using dummies for location-based services. In *International Conference on Pervasive Services (ICPS)*, pages 88–97, 2005.

[24] Q. Liu, G. Wang, and J. Wu. Secure and privacy preserving keyword searching for cloud storage services. *J. Network Computing Applications*, 35(3):927–933, May 2012.

[25] B. Lynn. *On the Implementation of Pairing-Based Cryptography*. PhD thesis, Stanford University, 2007.

[26] P. McGeer, J. Sanghavi, R. Brayton, and A. S. Vincentelli. Espresso-signature: a new exact minimizer for logic functions. In *Proceedings of the 30th international Design Automation Conference*, pages 618–624, 1993.

[27] V. S. Miller. The weil pairing, and its efficient calculation. *J. Cryptol.*, 17(4):235–261, Sept. 2004.

[28] M. F. Mokbel, C.-Y. Chow, and W. G. Aref. The New Casper: Query Processing for Location Services without Compromising Privacy. In *VLDB*, 2006.

[29] H. Samet. The quadtree and related hierarchical data structures. *ACM Comput. Surv.*, 16(2):187–260, June 1984.

[30] D. X. Song, D. Wagner, and A. Perrig. Practical techniques for searches on encrypted data. In *IEEE Symposium on Security and Privacy*, 2000.

[31] M. L. Yiu, C. Jensen, X. Huang, and H. Lu. SpaceTwist: Managing the Trade-Offs Among Location Privacy, Query Performance, and Query Accuracy in Mobile Services. In *International Conference on Data Engineering (ICDE)*, pages 366–375, 2008.

APPENDIX

A. PRIMER ON HVE ENCRYPTION

HVE is built on top of a symmetrical bilinear map of composite order [4], which is a function $e : \mathbb{G} \times \mathbb{G} \to \mathbb{G}_T$ such that $\forall a, b \in G$ and $\forall u, v \in \mathbb{Z}$ it holds that $e(a^u, b^v) = e(a, b)^{uv}$. $\mathbb{G}$ and $\mathbb{G}_T$ are cyclic multiplicative groups of composite order $N = P \cdot Q$ where P and Q are large primes of equal bit length. We denote by $\mathbb{G}_p$, $\mathbb{G}_q$ the subgroups of $\mathbb{G}$ of orders P and Q, respectively. Let l denote the HVE *width*, which is the bit length of the attribute, and consequently that of the search predicate. HVE consists of the following phases:

Setup. The TA generates the public/secret (PK/SK) key pair and shares PK with the users. SK has the form:

$$SK = (g_q \in \mathbb{G}_q, \quad a \in \mathbb{Z}_p, \quad \forall i \in [1..l] : u_i, h_i, w_i, g, v \in \mathbb{G}_p)$$

To generate PK, the TA first chooses at random elements $R_{u,i}, R_{h,i}, R_{w,i} \in \mathbb{G}_q, \forall i \in [1..l]$ and $R_v \in \mathbb{G}_q$. Next, PK is determined as:

$$PK = (g_q, \quad V = vR_v, \quad A = e(g,v)^a,$$

$$\forall i \in [1..l] : U_i = u_i R_{u,i}, \quad H_i = h_i R_{h,i}, \quad W_i = w_i R_{w,i})$$

Encryption uses PK and takes as parameters index attribute I and message $M \in \mathbb{G}_T$. The following random elements are generated: $Z, Z_{i,1}, Z_{i,2} \in \mathbb{G}_g$ and $s \in \mathbb{Z}_n$. Then, the ciphertext is:

$$C = (C' = MA^s, \quad C_0 = V^s Z,$$

$$\forall i \in [1..l] : C_{i,1} = (U_i^{I_i} H_i)^s Z_{i,1}, \quad C_{i,2} = W_i^s Z_{i,2})$$

Token Generation. Using SK, and given a search predicate encoded as pattern vector I_*, the TA generates a search token TK as follows: let J be the set of all indices i where $I_*[i] \neq *$. TA randomly generates $r_{i,1}$ and $r_{i,2} \in \mathbb{Z}_p, \forall i \in J$. Then

$$TK = (I_*, K_0 = g^a \prod_{i \in J} (u_i^{I_*[i]} h_i)^{r_{i,1}} w_i^{r_{i,2}},$$

$$\forall i \in [1..l] : K_{i,1} = v^{r_{i,1}}, \quad K_{i,2} = v^{r_{i,2}})$$

Query is executed at the server, and evaluates if the predicate represented by TK holds for ciphertext C. The server attempts to determine the value of M as

$$M = C' / (e(C_0, K_0) / \prod_{i \in J} e(C_{i,1}, K_{i,1}) e(C_{i,2}, K_{i,2}) \quad (1)$$

If the index I based on which C was computed satisfies TK, then the actual value of M is returned, otherwise a special number which is not in the valid message domain (denoted by $\perp$) is obtained.

332

Is It Really You? User Identification Via Adaptive Behavior Fingerprinting

Paul Giura
AT&T Security Research
Center
New York, NY
paulgiura@att.com

Ilona Murynets
AT&T Security Research
Center
New York, NY
ilona@att.com

Roger Piqueras Jover
AT&T Security Research
Center
New York, NY
roger.jover@att.com

Yevgeniy Vahlis[*]
Bionym Inc
Toronto, ON Canada
yvahlis@bionym.com

ABSTRACT

The increased popularity of mobile devices widens opportunities for a user either to lose the device or to have the device stolen and compromised. At the same time, user interaction with a mobile device generates a unique set of features such as dialed numbers, timestamps of communication activities, contacted base stations, etc. This work proposes several methods to identify the user based on her communications history. Specifically, the proposed methods detect an abnormality based on the behavior fingerprint generated by a set of features from the network for each user session. We present an implementation of such methods that use features from real SMS, and voice call records from a major tier 1 cellular operator. This can potentially trigger a rapid reaction upon an unauthorized user gaining control of a lost or stolen terminal, preventing data compromise and device misuse. The proposed solution can also detect background malicious traffic originated by, for example, a malicious application running on the mobile device. Our experiments with annonymized data from 10,000 users, representing over 14 million SMS and voice call detail records, show that the proposed methods are scalable and can continuously identify millions of mobile users while preserving data privacy, and achieving low false positives and high misuse detection rates with low storage and computation overhead.

Categories and Subject Descriptors

C.2.0 [**Computer-Communication Networks**]: General—*security and protection*; D.4.6 [**Operating Systems**]: Security and Protection—*authentication, access controls*; K.6.5

---

[*]Dr. Vahlis participated in this work while being a member of the AT&T Security Research Center.

[**Management of Computing and Information Systems**]: Security and Protection—*authentication, unauthorized access*

Keywords

Identification; Behavior fingerprint; Mobile security

1. INTRODUCTION

Mobile devices, such as smartphones and tablets, are increasingly being lost or stolen due to their widespread use, tremendous popularity and price [8]. In turn, loss of a mobile device increases the likelihood of account misuse and stolen or compromised data, which calls for user identification schemes superior to traditional use of passwords, which are very often not strong enough [3].

In parallel, data theft and compromise are often also linked to a malware or trojan infection in a mobile terminal. There have been reports of malicious applications posting sensitive phone information, such as the IMSI (International Mobile Subscriber Identity) and the IMEI (International Mobile Equipment Identity), on remote servers [15]. Cell-phones are becoming the latest platform for malware spreading in data networks [10], with malicious applications constantly being reported in the media and industry [2,4,5,24].

Device misuse can potentially have an economic impact on the device user, which leads to customer dissatisfaction. This is the case of known instances of malware that send messages to premium rate numbers [1], with the resulting spike in the customer's monthly bill, or identity theft as a result of an unauthorized access to an email account through a stolen cell-phone [17]. Note that most user credentials, including online banking, can be reset via an email sent to the email account that an attacker could access in the case of compromising a lost or stolen device [27].

There are currently no means for rapid network-based detection of mobile device misbehavior, either originated by a piece of malware running in the background or as a result of misuse of the device after being lost/stolen. Most schemes addressing this problem rely on heavy processes running on the device, with the resulting limitations in terms of battery life impact and data storage. In the case of a lost or stolen mobile terminal, all preventive measures to avoid misuse or data compromise rely on a rapid reaction by the end user to, for example, change email passwords and, if necessary, contact the cellular provider to block the SIM (Subscriber Identity Module). In certain situations it might take a long time from the moment the device is lost until the user reports it. This would give a potential attacker plenty of time to compromise the device.

Cellular infrastructures need to provide means of network-based misuse detection independent - yet transparent - from the user that do not rely on any local computation or processing on the device. For example, if a cell-phone is lost or stolen at an airport prior to boarding a 14 hour intercontinental flight, the network should be able to independently detect and block any misbehavior originating from the stranded device. And eventually block the terminal if appropriate. Relying on the user reporting the incident would give the attacker 14 hours of time to compromise the device.

In this paper we tackle the problem of non-intrusive identification of a user that legitimately interacted with the device previously. In general there are several ways to identify a device user based on:

1) *what the user knows* (i.e. password, passphrase, etc.),
2) *what the user has* (i.e. biometrics, token, etc.),
3) *what the user does* (i.e. behavior, tasks patterns, etc.)
4) *who user knows* (i.e. user contacts).

This work focuses on finding a method that covers the last two categories: *what the user does* and *who the user knows*. More specifically, we analyze the network Call Detail Records (CDR) generated by the device in present and in the recent past, continuously extracting a behavior fingerprint for each time period under consideration (i.e. hour of day, day of week, etc). Then, for each new observation time window, we compute the distance, in a behavior fingerprint metric, between the current fingerprint sample and the one observed in the past. If the distance is larger than a threshold, that user is identified as illegitimate (not the one interacting with the device in the past). That triggers an alert sent that could be sent to the legitimate user on an alternate channel, or could be handled by the network operator which can potentially decide to block user access until her identification is confirmed. To the best of the author's knowledge, this is the first time that such an analysis on real data has been performed and shown to work.

The proposed methods are generic and can be applied to multiple attack scenarios. However, our solution is aimed to detect unauthorized access to user resources and to provide a detection mechanism in two possible scenarios: 1) stolen mobile devices (i.e. smart-phones, tablets, etc) and 2) mobile malware compromised devices. The same methods could be implemented on other portable computers and even desktop computers. The only difference would rely in the nature of the fingerprint features being extracted and processed. Note that the proposed system is not intended to detect a phone or tablet that is turned off after being lost or stolen, but for the case when the attacker does use the device. With this work we make the following key contributions:

- We formalize the problem of user identification based on behavior fingerprint and propose several methods to represent and compare user behavior in order to identify illegitimate users for different scenarios: normal different user, random attacker, informed attacker and compromised device.

- We implemented and tested seven possible user identification methods and reported the experiments with 10,000 users SMS and data calls from a tier-1 wireless carrier, representing over 14 million records. Our results show that in most cases the proposed methods can detect with over 90% accuracy most types of attacks within an hour with less than 5% false positives.

- We analyze the privacy properties of our method and show that in many cases, the information about raw user data that must be given to the identification system is minimal. In particular, privacy of contact information is always preserved, and even the communication pattern can be hidden to some degree.

The remainder of this paper is organized as follows. An overview of our methods is presented in Section 2. The behavior fingerprints extracted in each one of the methods under analysis are described in Section 3. Section 4 discusses the potential information leakage about each user profile from the information that we store. Our experimental results are summarized in Section 5 and related work is discussed in Section 6. Finally, the paper is concluded in Section 7.

2. METHOD OVERVIEW

2.1 Adversarial Model

Throughout this paper we consider the following adversarial models. In all cases, the goal of the adversary is to continue using the device for as long as possible while avoiding triggering the authentication mechanism.

2.1.1 User Swap

In this scenario we assume that an unsophisticated attacker has gained possession and control of the device. An unsophisticated attacker completely ignores the prior behavior of the user, and simply starts using the device as her own. The device usage behavior of the attacker in this case is independent from the behavior of the legitimate owner of the device. We believe that this scenario is applicable in many practical situations, where the attacker has gained possession of a device and has no familiarity with the legitimate owner as may be the case when the phone is lost or stolen by a pickpocket.

2.1.2 Informed Attacker

The second scenario that we consider is when the attacker knows the behavior pattern of the legitimate user, but is unable to fake certain activities. For example, the attacker can dial the same numbers as the owner, but is unlikely to be able to maintain a conversation for the same length of time because the person on the other end will recognize that the caller is not the owner of the device, and will refuse to continue the conversation. More precisely, the informed attacker generates events from a distribution which is a function of the real distribution of the owner behavior, but with an additional "noise" component which represents the actions taken by the adversary for her own purposes.

2.1.3 Compromised Device

In this scenario we assume the device is used in parallel by the legitimate user and a piece of malware or a trojan running in the background without the user knowledge. For

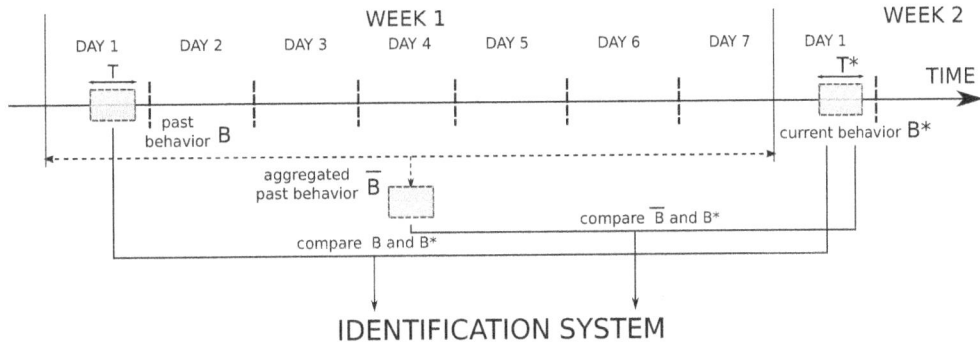

Figure 1: Schematic representation of a behavior based identification method.

example, the well known Android trojan GGTracker [1] attempts to dial or send SMS messages to premium numbers without user consent, incurring unexpected charges. In this scenario, the victim's device would be generating the exact same fingerprint as in the past, given the continued legitimate interaction of the user with the phone. In parallel, network traces would be created from the malicious connections that the malware or trojan operates. For our measurements, we generated adversarial events randomly according to what we believe is a reasonable distribution (described in detail in Section 5).

2.2 Problem Statement

In this section we focus on defining the behavior identification problem and identifying the properties of a robust and efficient solution. More formally, suppose that we have n different types of session (e.g., phone calls, SMS, data, etc), and that session of type i has m_i different features. For example, a feature in the "phone calls" session may correspond to a dialed number. We define user behavior over a period $T = [t_0, t_1]$ by a set of recorded sessions $\{S_1(T), \ldots, S_n(T)\}$, where each recorded session $S_i(T)$ is a subset of the features $f_{i,j}$ that were measured for the j-th feature of session type i, for a user during time period T. Then, given a user with behavior $S(T^*) = S_1(T^*), \ldots, S_n(T^*)$ over a period T^* we want to find an efficient, reliable and robust way to determine whether the same users' behavior recorded during another period T^* is *sufficiently similar* to the behavior during the period T. To do so we define two functions: $\rho(S(T))$ is some representation of the behavior $S(T)$ that is sufficient to compute a score, and $\beta(\rho(S(T^*)), \rho(S(T)))$ is a measure of similarity between behavior $S(T^*)$ and $S(T)$. To determine whether $S(T^*)$ is sufficiently close to $S(T)$, we check whether

$$|\beta(\rho(S(T)), \rho(S(T^*)))| \leq \varepsilon \qquad (1)$$

For some identification threshold $\varepsilon > 0$. Note that to perform the test, we must only store $\rho(S(T^*))$ and not the entire behavior record $S(T^*)$.

Besides being robust and accurate, the behavior fingerprint should preserve the privacy of the user behavior and should not reveal any information that can lead to the reconstruction of past user activity. A key challenge is to define the function ρ to retain enough information about the original recorded behavior to compute the score, while removing enough unneeded information to guarantee privacy.

Figure 1 shows an intuitive representation of how a behavior fingerprint method could be used by an identification system. The behavior fingerprint can be recorded for

a rolling time window T and sent to the identification system. Whenever an identification decision should be made, the current behavior fingerprint could be compared to the behavior recorded in the corresponding time window of the previous day, or the previous week day. If the difference is above the identification threshold then, based on the application, an action will be triggered. For example, in the case of mobile user behavior identification the system might react by requiring the user to identify herself using an alternate channel such as a web questionnaire or another factor of authentication.

3. BEHAVIOR FINGERPRINT

In this section we present the features used to generate the behavior fingerprint and three base methods to represent it along with the metrics to assess the behavior distance. The goal is to choose only methods that store fingerprints in encoded format so that they maintain the privacy of the user data even when the data is stored for longer periods of time in an adversarial environment. The aim behind considering privacy preservation using the suggested methods is to be compliant with the privacy regulations on the network providers. Having a privacy preserving identification system can also allow for the provision of such a service by a third party using the cellular network as a platform. We consider using the following three base methods to represent the set of features for each period of time: 1) a hash set , 2) a standard Bloom filter and 3) a counting Bloom filter. Starting from these three methods we experimented with other three derived combinations of them and reported the experimental results in Section 5.

3.1 Features

In general, a feature set should include measurable elements that have the potential to uniquely identify a user. For example, the set of numbers that the user calls on a regular basis, the duration of the calls with those numbers, the set of numbers that the user sends SMS to, base station identification numbers that serve the device, a list of URLs visited in the data transactions, a set of IP address that the device contacted, etc. However, for the scope of this paper we limited the feature set to the CDR records representing details from SMS and voice call transactions, used by most wireless carriers for billing. Thus, for each user, we consider a set of features containing data from the CDR records corresponding to the SMS and voice transactions within each observation time interval. Table 1 lists the set of features extracted from the CDRs. The left column represents the type of session, the center column contains the feature description and the right column lists the data type for that specific feature. In the next subsections we will describe the three methods to represent the set of features along with the metric used to compute the difference between any two sets of features.

Session	Feature	Type
SMS	# of outgoing msgs	int
	outgoing destinations	list
	SMS timestamps	list
	# of outgoing msgs for destination	list
	base station IDs	list
Voice	# of outgoing calls	int
	outgoing destinations	list
	call timestamps	list
	call duration for destination	list
	base station IDs	list

Table 1: Features for SMS and Voice sessions.

3.2 Hash Set

The first and most simplistic method to represent a set and be able to answer membership queries is to use a hash set. That is, instead of storing each element in the clear we use a one-way cryptographic hash function (e.g., SHA-1) [11] and store only a salted hash value of each element. For each user U and for each time T interval we store a set of hashes of the recorded feature values $S(T)$ together with a per-user nonce n_U that is generated once for each user. Specifically, let H be a cryptographic hash function. Then we define $\rho(S(T)) = \{H(f, n_U) | f \in S(T)\}$.

3.2.1 Jaccard Distance

To measure the distance between two hash sets S and S^*, we use the Jaccard distance, defined as follows:

$$J(S, S^*) = \frac{|S \cup S^*| - |S \cap S^*|}{|S \cup S^*|} \qquad (2)$$

With this method, all set membership queries have a precise answer. This comes at the expense of storing the same number of bits for each hash value of each feature in the set, regardless of the size of the element. Moreover, computation time for the Jaccard distance is linear in the size of the sets. This aspect becomes crucial when assessing the scalability of the fingerprinting method to hundreds of millions of users.

3.3 Standard Bloom Filter

A different more space efficient method to represent a set and support membership queries is to use a Bloom filter. A standard Bloom filter is a space-efficient probabilistic data structure used for representing a set in order to support membership queries. It was first introduced by Burton Bloom in 1970 [7]. A Bloom filter is identified by a bit array of size m with all the bits initially set to 0, and k independent hash functions with the range $\{1,\ldots,m\}$. When an element of a set is inserted into the Bloom filter, it is first hashed with all k hash functions and all the corresponding zero bits in the bit array are flipped to 1. If one of the corresponding hash functions bits is already set to 1, then a *collision* occurs and the bit is not changed. When an element is tested for membership in a set, the Bloom filter is queried as follows. First, the element is hashed with all k hash functions and all the corresponding bits in the bit array are checked. If all bits checked are 1 then we say the element was inserted in the Bloom filter with some probability, called the *false positives* rate, introduced because of the collisions in the insertion process. If at least one corresponding bit is 0 then we know precisely that the element was not inserted in the Bloom filter. Thus, a Bloom filter has no false negatives, and space-efficiency is achieved at the cost of a small probability of false positives. After inserting n elements in a Bloom filter, the false positives (FP) rate for subsequent membership queries is given by Equation 3.

$$FP = \left(1 - \left(1 - \frac{1}{m}\right)^{kn}\right)^k \approx (1 - e^{-kn/m})^k \qquad (3)$$

Our second method for representing the feature set is to use a Bloom filter for each time interval for each user. Because a Bloom filter can represent only a discrete set, from the feature set we generate a set of labels and insert them into the Bloom filter. The representation $\rho(S(T))$ is then simply the bit array of the Bloom filter and the hash functions.

3.3.1 Hamming Distance

We compute the difference between two Bloom filters corresponding to two different time intervals by using the Hamming distance [21]. Thus, for any two Bloom filters with their corresponding bit arrays B and B^* the Hamming distance is given by Equation 4:

$$H(B, B^*) = \sum_{i=1}^{m} B(i) \oplus B^*(i) \qquad (4)$$

where $B(i)$ represents the bit at index i for bit array B. Note that, unlike the Jaccard distance, the computation time for the Hamming distance is independent from the number of elements inserted in each Bloom filter and is dependent only on the size of the Bloom filter. Since standard Bloom filters can be represented as binary strings, computing the distance can be implemented as a simple XOR operation and a count of set bits.

3.4 Counting Bloom Filter

One limitation of using a standard Bloom filter is given by the fact that the insert operation is indempotent, that is, if the same element is inserted multiple times, the Bloom filter byte array will not change because of the way Bloom filter handles collisions. In many occasions knowing the number of times an element was inserted into a Bloom filter could be a useful feature. For example, a Bloom filter that stores phone numbers dialed by a user in a time interval will not show any difference if the user dials a number once or multiple times. The number of times a user calls a number could represent a feature that one might want to capture to define the usage pattern and user behavior.

In our method we use a variation of the standard Bloom filter, called *counting* Bloom filter [22], introduced for the first time in [14], that can capture the number of times an element was inserted into a Bloom filter. Essentially, a counting Bloom filter uses an array of counting bins rather than a single bit for each array position, representing the number of matches that are encountered for each corresponding position. Thus, there is a tradeoff between the storage savings achieved by the counting Bloom filter and the information stored in the filter. For instance, if the application requires counting bins with a maximum counter up to 255 then an array with bins of size 8 bits will suffice to represent the counters. However, this causes an increase in the storage by a factor of 8 compared to the space required for a standard Bloom filter. Another important property of a counting Bloom filter is the ability to remove elements from the Bloom filter by decrementing the counters corresponding to a given element. This property can also be used when inserting elements in overlapping time intervals. In this case, one can only insert the elements that are new in the new interval, and remove the elements that are no longer present. This avoids the need to re-insert every element into the Bloom filter.

The third method to represent the feature set is to use counting Bloom filters. Similar to inserting into the standard Bloom filter, we insert a set of labels derived from the set of features into the counting Bloom filter. The stored representation $\rho(S(T))$ is then the array of bins along with the definition of the hash functions used.

3.4.1 Euclidian Distance

We compute the difference between two counting Bloom filters corresponding to two different time intervals by using the Euclidian distance. Thus, for any two counting Bloom filters bin arrays CB and $CB*$ the Euclidian distance is given by Equation 5:

$$E(CB, CB^*) = \sqrt{\sum_{i=1}^{m}(CB(i) - CB^*(i))^2} \qquad (5)$$

where $CB(i)$ represents the value stored in the i-th bin of the bins array CB. Similarly to the case of standard Bloom filter, the computation time for the Euclidian distance is independent from the number of elements inserted in each counting Bloom filter and it is dependent only on the size of the bins array.

3.5 Contact-based Method

This section proposes a network-based method for behavior identification that improves the one in [26]. The idea is to compare statistical distributions of current and past user's communication activities. Let t_j and c_{t_j} represent a timestamp of a communication activity and a hash of a phone number contacted at time t_j, respectively. Then the pair (t_j, c_{t_j}) is the only information needed to analyze communication activity j.

The training period for this method has two steps. The first step makes the list $L^i = \cup_{t_j \in [\tau_0, \tau_1]} \{c_{t_j}\}$ of hashed phone numbers that user i contacts (calls and messages) during time period $[\tau_0, \tau_1]$. The second step monitors behavior of user i during time period $(\tau_1, \tau_2]$ and stores timestamps of user communications with existing and new contacts:

$$T_E^i = \cup_{t_j \in (\tau_1, \tau_2], c_t \in L^i} \{t_j\} \qquad (6)$$

and

$$T_N^i = \cup_{t_j \in (\tau_1, \tau_2], c_t \notin L^i} \{t_j\}, \qquad (7)$$

respectively. For user i, the further analysis uses the following three statistics:

(a) maximum number, M^i, of communications with new contacts per time interval, e.g. day, hour, 15 mins, etc.;

(b) α_1-percentile of the distribution of intervals between each two consecutive communications with existing contacts, p^i, where $75 \leq \alpha_1 \leq 100$; and

(c) α_2-percentile of the distribution of intervals between each two consecutive communications with new contacts, P^i, where $0 \leq \alpha_2 \leq 25$.

For each pair (t_k, c_k), the testing stage checks whether contact c_k is in the contact list L^i. If $c_j \notin L^i$ and the time elapsed since the last communication activity with any new contact is less than P^i, the alert score is raised. Also if the total number of communication events with new contacts exceeds M^i, the alert score is raised as well. In other words, the alert score is raised when a user communicates either with new contacts more frequently or with the existing contacts less frequently compared to the past communication history. Specifically, the alert score is raised whenever the time δ_t^e passed since the last communication with the existing contact exceeds p^i and there have been at least h communications with a new contact during this time (the last condition assures that the user is not simply inactive).

4. PRIVACY ANALYSIS

In this section we present an analysis of the privacy and information leakage of user data in our systems. Recall that for user behavior $S(T)$ during time period T, we must record $\rho_T = \rho(S(T))$ in order to later compute the similarity measure $\beta(\rho_T, \rho_{T^*})$ with some other time period T^*. We therefore concentrate on analyzing the information leakage from the stored representation ρ_T of the user data for the four different approaches that we described in Section 3. We consider each case separately. Below, we denote by $\rho_T(U)$ the representation of the recorded behavior for user U during time period T.

Hash sets.

In the hash set solution we store for each recorded feature f, a hash $H(f, n_U)$, where n_U is a random nonce generated for each user, and H is a cryptographic hash function. To analyze the privacy of the scheme we follow the common convention of modeling H as a random function (known as the random oracle model [6]). The representation ρ_T is therefore a set of random strings that is independently chosen for each user. Indeed, if H is random, then the values $H(f, n_U)$ and $H(f, n_{U'})$ are independently random as long as $n_U \neq n_{U'}$. This implies that, for example, one cannot determine whether the same feature appears in both $\rho_T(U)$ and $\rho_T(U')$. However, our representation does reveal whether the same feature f appears in two different time periods T and T' for the same user U. In fact, revealing this information is necessary to compute the Jaccard distance between $S(T)$ and $S(T')$. Additionally, $\rho_T(U)$ reveals the number of features that were recorded for user U during period T.

More formally, one can easily show that the representations of any two multi-user traces with the same feature counts per user are identically distributed, and therefore indistinguishable.

Bloom Filters.

A Bloom Filter is a concise and lossy representation of a set. Therefore, by storing the hash set in a Bloom Filter, we gain all the privacy benefits of the hash set, and in addition we remove a large amount of information due to the conciseness of the Bloom Filter representation. In our solution, we dynamically determine the size of the Bloom Filter for each user during the training period T^* to be an n-bit long array where $n = |S(T^*)|$ is the total number of recorded features. Consequently, we store n bits of information about a set of n features.

To determine the amount of information leakage about the underlying hash set, we must consider the entropy of the recorded features. Recall that an array of n bits has entropy at most n, and suppose that a feature has entropy γ and that all features are independent. Then, the amount of uncertainty left after exposing the Bloom Filter is $n(\gamma - 1)$. For example, for data of 10,000 users, we calculated the average entropy of CDR data to be roughly $\gamma n \approx 3.49n$. Therefore, an adversary that is given the Bloom Filter representation of the user behavior for the training period, has a probability of roughly $1/2^{3.49} \approx 8\%$ of correctly guessing a specific element of the hash set. We calculated the average number of CDR features for a customer is 44, and therefore in expectation the adversary will be able to recover roughly $1/2^{3.49} \cdot 44 \approx 4$ features from the hash set. For the elements that are recovered, we fall back to the basic privacy guarantees of the hash set as described above.

Counting Bloom Filters.

The analysis of privacy when counting Bloom Filters are used is very similar to the analysis for regular Bloom Filters. However, here each bucket is a counter instead of a bit. Suppose that each counter is represented by ℓ bits, then the amount of entropy left after exposing the counting array to the adversary is $\max\{0, n(\gamma - \ell)\}$. Unfortunately, for CDR data, this value is zero. Note that this does not mean that the user data is leaked, but rather that counting Bloom Filters may offer a privacy guarantee which is only as strong as the guarantee provided by the hash set representation[1].

Contact based method.

For the contact based solution, we must store hashed feature descriptions, as in the hash set representation. We additionally store the intervals between phone calls and messages made by the user, and the maximal number of communications with new contacts during the time period. However, if we set $\alpha_1 = 100$ and $\alpha_2 = 0$, we need only store the minimum and maximum intervals between communications to existing contacts. We then obtain essentially the same level of privacy as the hash set.

5. EXPERIMENTS

5.1 Data Set

The study presented in this paper uses 1 month of voice and text message communication data (April 2012) of over 10,000 post-paid cell-phone accounts. The data is obtained from more than 14 million anonymized Call Detail Records (CDR) of one of the major tier-1 cellular providers in the United States. CDRs are records that are logged each time a phone call or text message is sent over the network. In the

case where the two communicating entities are connected to the same provider, a duple of records is stored. The Mobile Originated (MO) record logs the data of the transmitting party, while the Mobile Terminated (MT) record stores information of the receiver. We use MO CDRs in this work.

Time	Transmission/Reception time and date
Orig	Originating number
Term	Terminating number
Call type	Mobile originated/terminated SMS/call
Duration	Duration of a voice call
LACCI	Location Area Code and Cell Id

Table 2: Call Detail Record Fields

Table 2 lists the CDR fields handled in our analysis. The originating and terminating phone numbers are completely anonymized. Each transaction is marked with a time stamp and we also record the Location Area Code and Cell Id (LACCI) of the base station that handled the traffic in the uplink (MO) or in the downlink (MT). The data is sampled across US population.

Attribute	Value
# of users	10,000
# of CDRs	14,874,731
duration of data	30 days
# of sessions	2
training data	14 days
testing data	16 days

Table 3: Data characteristics.

Data processing and anonymization

All the data utilized in this analysis is fully anonymized. No personal identifiers, such as phone numbers, are processed, substituting them for hashed values. The results presented in this paper do not include any details or information from the actual processed data, but just aggregated results on the performance of the algorithms *on* the anonymized data.

5.1.1 Training Data for Hash Set and Bloom Filter methods

We use the first 14 days of the original data as the training set for establishing the thresholds for each metric, and the remaining 16 days for generating the testing data. We assume there is no malicious activity in the training data.

5.1.2 Training Data for Contact based method

We use the first 9 days of the original data to make the list of contacts L^i and the following 5 days to store timestamps of user communications with existing and new contacts and compute the three statistics M^i, P^i and p^i and the remaining 16 days for generating the testing data.

5.1.3 Testing Data

We have generated several testing data sets in order to test our methods in different scenarios from the original data collected for the last 16 days, from day 15 to day 30.

Original data: The first testing set is represented by the original data collected from day 15 to day 30 of all data set. We use this data set to assess the False Positives rates, that represent instances when the user was required to authenticate with the system even though she was not supposed to. We will call this data set the original data and the remaining testing sets were generated from this data.

---

[1] This is a purely information theoretic property. We believe that in practice, it is unlikely that an adversary will be able to extract the entire hash set representation from the counting Bloom Filter.

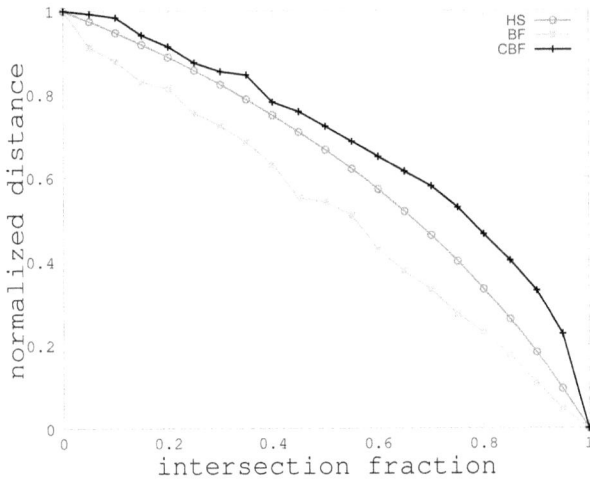

Figure 2: Normalized distance for random sets with variable intersection size.

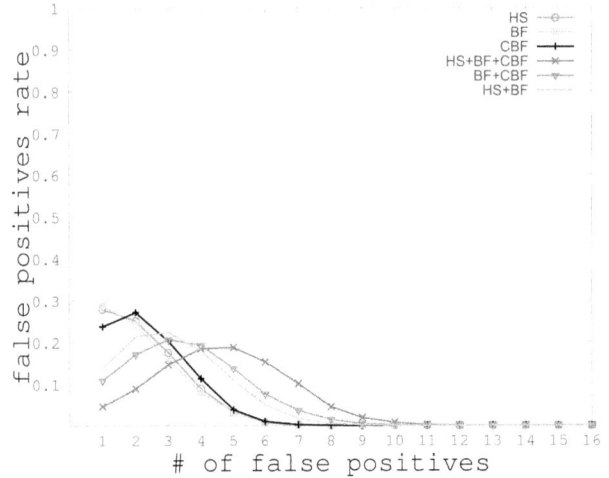

Figure 3: False positives for all methods.

Splicing data: The second testing data set was generated by swapping the original data between any random pairs of two users for the data from day 15 to day 30. This data set was used to test the detection rates when the device is used by an illegitimate normal user.

Random attacker data: Third testing data set was obtained from the original data by generating completely random communication activity for all users. This case was used to measure the detection rate for the cases when, for example, the device is stolen by an attacker that wants to get the most out of using the device in a short period of time. We assume the device connected to the same base stations.

Informed attacker data: Fourth testing data set was obtained from the original data by judiciously generating communication activity that is similar to the original activity. As such, for each testing day we simulated the case when a fraction of the SMS and voice calls, 10% in our experiments, were to the original numbers with the voice calls having zero duration. Note that if the attacker dials the contacts of the victim's phone, she will not be able to impersonate the victim. Therefore, the calls will be of zero duration or, at most, a couple of seconds if the attacker remains silent. We believed is reasonable to assume, an informed attacker cannot withstand a longer duration call with a victims contact in order to not be detected. We assume the device connected to the same base stations.

Malware communication data: This data set was generated to simulate a piece of malware communication activity. For this case we assumed the malware injects some random communication activity within the legitimate user activity. Thus, we generated a fraction of random communication activity, 50% in our experiments, on top of the original user activity. We assume the device connected to the same base stations.

5.2 Hash Set and Bloom Filter Methods

5.2.1 Feature Labels

For each session we consider a set of features that has the potential to uniquely identify a user behavior. For each feature of each session we derive a label that will represent the value of that feature in an encoded and discrete set of session features. Then we will use each of the first three

methods described in Section 3 to store the features sets for all sessions and to define the behavior fingerprint. Our behavior fingerprint design can accommodate any number of sessions but for the scope of this paper we are concerned to use features from the CDR records of SMS and voice calls that represent the SMS session and the voice session.

SMS Session: We consider the set of features and the corresponding labels listed in Table 4. For each day time window we generate a label with *zero*, *low* or *high* if the number of SMSes is either zero, smaller or larger than the average training data. For each destination, *dest*, we generate two labels, first with the destination itself and second with the destination concatenated with *high* or *low*, if the number of SMSes to that destination is smaller or larger than the average to that destination in the training data. From the timestamp of each communication activity we create a label from the destination concatenated with the corresponding day time shift. We partition the 24 hour day into three shifts, shift 1 from hour 0 to hour 8, shift 2 from hour 8 to hour 16 and shift 3 from hour 16 to hour 24. Finally, for each time window we create a label with the ID of each base station that the device contacted.

SMS Feature	Labels
# of outgoing msgs	zero, low, high
outgoing dsts w. counts	{dest} & ({dest}+low or {dest}+high)
day time shift	{dest}+1 or {dest}+2 or {dest}+3
list of base station IDs	{ID}

Table 4: SMS features and corresponding labels.

Voice Session: For the voice session we consider a similar set of features and we generate the labels in a similar way for number of outgoing destinations, day time shift and the list of base stations. However, for the voice session we take into account the duration of the voice calls and we generate the label *low* if the voice call has zero duration and *high* otherwise.

Voice Feature	Labels
# of outgoing voice calls	zero, low, high
outgoing dsts w. duration	{dest}, {dest}+low, {dest}+high
day time shift	{dest}+1 or {dest}+2 or {dest}+3
list of base station IDs	{ID}

Table 5: Voice features and corresponding labels.

5.2.2 Implementation, Parameters and Thresholds

We implemented the first three methods presented in Section 3 and several combinations of them. More specifically, we represent the behavior fingerprint using a hash set (HS), a Bloom filter (BF), a counting Bloom filter (CBF) as the base methods. From the base methods, we built other methods by using all three methods together (HS+BF+CBF), only standard Bloom filter and counting Bloom filter (BF+CBF), and hash set and standard Bloom filter (HS+BF).

We used the training data in order to decide on the parameters used and the identification threshold. For each user, we train on the first 14 days of communication activity (SMS and voice call) aggregated in daily slots, therefore 14 slots for training. When building the hash set we applied SHA-256 on each label generated from the data in each time window and we keep the first 128 bits as the hash value for each label.

For building the behavior fingerprints with Bloom filters we use two hash functions. We compute the SHA-256 on each label and then split it into two parts, each part representing a value of a hash function. We decide the size of the Bloom filters by choosing the size that has the potential to yield the most accurate distance between two Bloom filters and counting Bloom filters. We did so, by using Bloom filters to represent two generated sets of random elements that have a variable intersection size and observing the distance function. The size of each set is the average number of labels that we expect to get for each time window for all the users. Figure 2 shows, for each base method, how the distance between the fingerprints varies with the variation of the intersection size for the two random sets. The figure represents the results for using a Bloom filter size equal with the average number of elements inserted. That is, we use 1 bit to represent each label using a standard Bloom filter. We used 1 bin to represent each label in a counting Bloom filter for a total of 16 bits per element of storage for counters with maximum value of 65536 (2 bytes).

In the next step, we get the identification thresholds by computing the day maximum distance D_M, day minimum distance D_m between the fingerprint of the current time window and the fingerprint of the previous day, and the day maximum distance W_M and the day minimum distance W_m compared to the previous week day respectively for all the days in the training data in order to get the day distance variation interval $[D_m, D_M]$ and week variation interval $[W_m, W_M]$. For example for a day of Tuesday, we first get the fingerprint difference between Tuesday and Monday as well as the fingerprint between Tuesday and Tuesday from the previous week and then we compute the maximum and minimum differences among all the day and week distances for all the days.

5.2.3 False Positives

We tested the false positives rate by using the original data test set representing the last 16 days of user CDRs. For each day we compute the difference between the day fingerprint and the previous day and previous week day fingerprints into F_D and F_W respectively. In the analysis, we count a false positive when we obtain that both $F_D \notin [D_m, D_M]$ and $F_W \notin [W_m, W_M]$. More specifically, we count a false positive if the difference between the current day behavior fingerprint and the behavior fingerprint observed in the previous day and in the previous week day are not in the cor-

responding variation interval. Figures 3 shows the number of false positives that users get for the 16 days of original testing data. The y-axis represents the percentage of users, out of the total of 10,000 that have encountered the number of false positives on the x-axis, for each tested method. For example, the point (1, 0.22) represents that 22% or the users got exactly one false positive in the 16 days of testing data. For the derived methods, HS+BF+CBF, BF+CBF and HS+BF we count a false positive if the day fingerprint distance is not in the variation interval for each base method. By doing so we sum the probabilities of false positives for each method, resulting in larger false positives for derived methods than for the base methods. The figure shows that for the base methods the expected false positive rates for different number of false positives declines with the increase in the number of false positives. For derived methods the false positives rates are low for small numbers and climb up to 22% for 3,4 and 5 false positives in the 16 days of testing with original data.

5.2.4 Detection Rate

We tested the detection rate by using the generated splicing data, the random attacker data, the informed attacker data and the compromised device data for each method. We used the same training data as in the case of false positives testing in order to build the variation interval for each user behavior fingerprint. Figure 4 shows the detection results on splicing data. The x-axis represents the time window when the user was detected as not being the legitimate user, and the y-axis represents the percentage of users not detected for that window. For example the point (1, 0.98) on the HS+BF+CBF curve represents that 98% of the illegitimate users were detected as not being the legitimate users in the first testing time window. The derived method, HS+BF+CBF that combines all the base methods provides the best detection rate of more than 98% from the first testing day, for the splicing and random attacker cases shown in Figure 4 and Figure 5. Figure 6 and Figure 7 show the detection rates for informed attacker and compromised device. In these cases, as the behavior of the illegitimate users becomes more similar to the legitimate user behavior, the detection rate in the first time window starts to decrease to 87% and 45% respectively compared to the random attacker case. However, it increases significantly as more time windows are processed to identify the legitimate user with detection rates over 90% starting with time window 2 in the informed attacker case and time window 6 in the compromised device case.

Note that, because the counting Bloom filter retains more information and the detection rates for counting Bloom filter method are lower than those for standard Bloom filter, the results seem counter-intuitive. These results are explained by the use of Euclidean distance metric to compute the variation interval for counting Bloom filter which yields larger values than the Hamming distance for standard Bloom filter thus, larger variation intervals, hence lower detection rates.

If, in a real deployment each time window is shifted one hour these results show that the illegitimate user that exhibits a completely random network communication behavior can be identified with 98% accuracy in the first hour. Consequently, an informed attacker can be identified with 95% accuracy in the first 2 hours, and a compromised device with 90% accuracy within the first 6 hours. However,

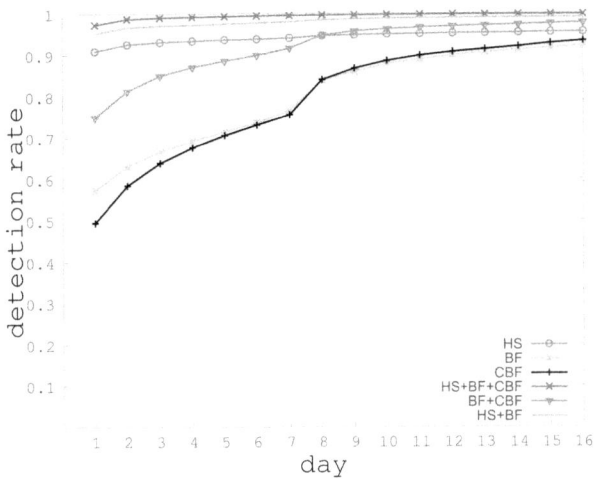

Figure 4: Detection rates for splicing.

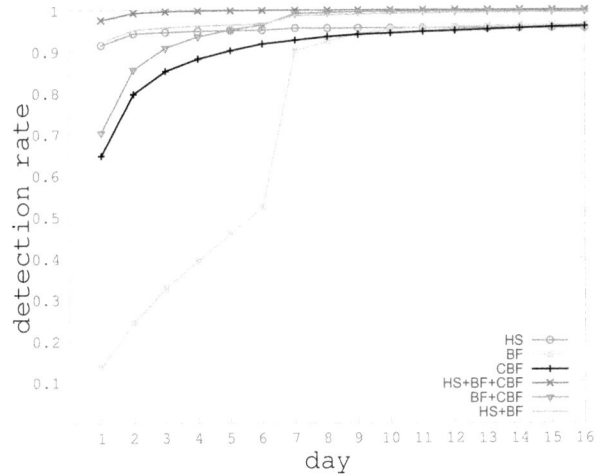

Figure 5: Detection rates for random attacker.

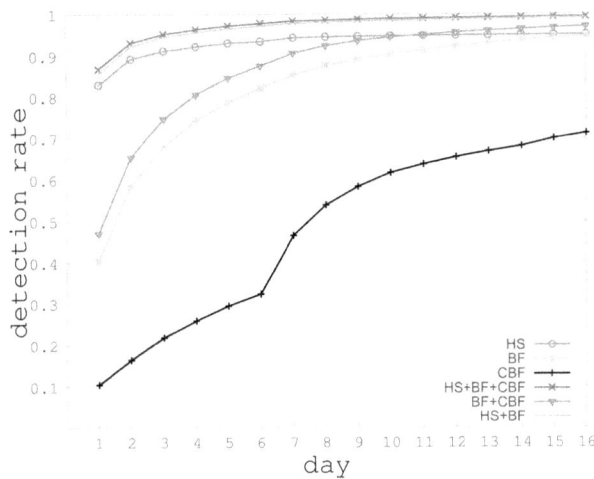

Figure 6: Detection rates for informed attacker.

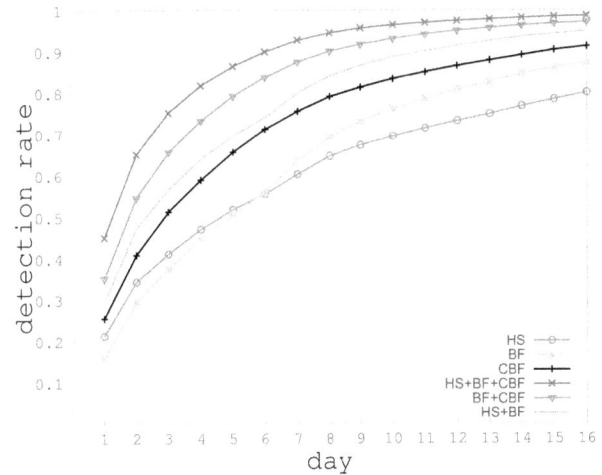

Figure 7: Detection rates for compromised device.

the results presented could be influenced by the parameters used such as Bloom filter sizes, the time window size, the amount of storage and computation available, etc. One could set the expected detection rate to be 99% and then be concerned on the higher number of false positives that could be mitigated by other means, by for example taking into account information other than the CDR records such as data call records, applications, communication content, etc. Nonetheless, our proposed methods could be used to represent other features as well, not only CDR records.

5.3 Contact-based Method Results

Since the contact-based method described in Section 3.5 uses statistical distributions of intervals between consecutive communication activities, it is effective only when the training set for each user contains at least a certain minimum number of events. To test the algorithm we consider only customers with at least 20 network activities (SMS or voice) to compute the probability distributions. This is opposed to hash set and Bloom filter methods, which can be used even when we have a few SMS or voice records available per customer at the training stage. To test this method we set $\alpha_1 = 90$ and $\alpha_2 = 25$.

As it can be seen in Figures 8 and 9, this method achieves very high detection rates in all the scenarios while still performing with acceptable false positive rate, always below 23% of users having one false positive in 16 days. The best detection rate is achieved for splicing, with just 95% of the users detected correctly. In the toughest scenario, a device compromised with malware, the method still achieves a very good result, with 1% users without false negatives.

5.4 Storage and Computation Requirements

The higher the detection rate a method has, the higher the storage and computation requirements. Specifically, the detection accuracy of each method is highly influenced by the information retained by its corresponding fingerprint representation. As such, the BF and CBF methods taken alone seem to provide the lowest detection performance, consistently lower than the hash set method. However, by combining the HS and BF methods into HS+BF seems to improve the HS method in all four scenarios. In other words, by adding an extra bit to the hash value per element for the Bloom filter representation has the potential to significantly improve the detection rate. In all but the compromised device experiments, the HS+BF method ranked the second

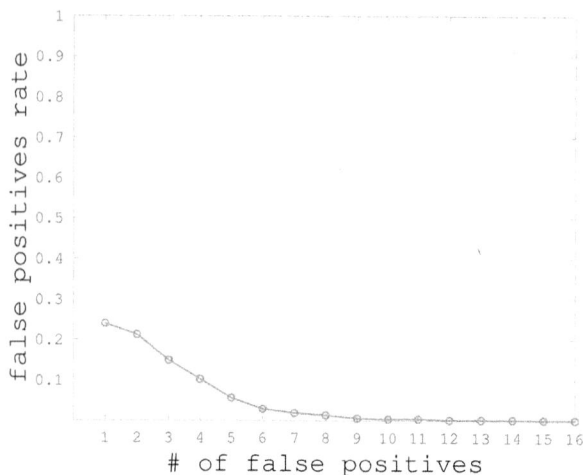

Figure 8: False positive rate for Contact-based Method.

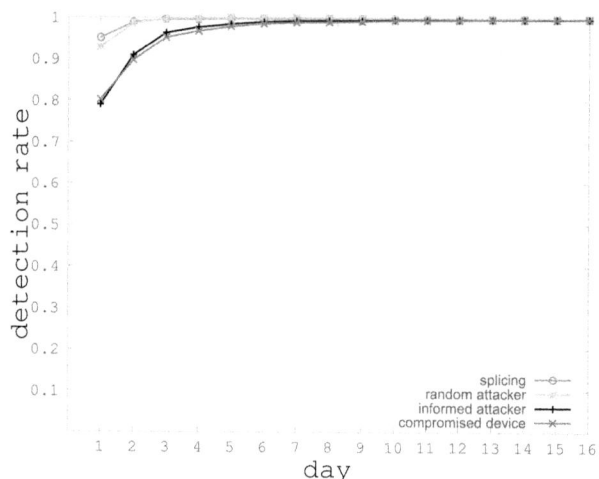

Figure 9: Detection rates for Contact-based Method.

best in terms of detection rate while increasing the storage requirements for the base HS method by a bit per element. Table 6 shows roughly how all the methods compare in terms of storage footprint, fingerprint construction and fingerprint testing.

Method	Storage (bits)	Construction	Testing
HS	128 x N	O(N)	O(N)
BF	N	O(N)	O(1)
CBF	16 x N	O(N)	O(1)
HS+BF+CBF	145 x N	O(N)	O(N)
BF+CBF	17 x N	O(N)	O(1)
HS+BF	129 x N	O(N)	O(N)
Contact-based	128 x N	O(N)	O(N)

Table 6: Storage and processing requirements as a function of the average number N of features for each time window.

Based on the amount of information retained, each method requires a different amount of storage. The standard Bloom filter requires the least while the method where all the sub-methods are combined requires the most storage. Constructing the behavior fingerprint requires roughly the same computational resources for all methods. However, the Bloom filter based methods, because they use the same fixed amount of storage for all time windows, require a constant number of operations when performing the fingerprint checking as compared to the other methods. In a real deployment, depending on the application and on the resource limitation, one could use the combination of HS+BF+CBF methods if the storage and computation requirements can be relaxed while the detection rate is high priority. On the other hand, if computation and storage are limited one could use BF+CBF and sacrifice from the accuracy of the detection but having lower false positives. Finally, if most of the entities to be monitored are active and have at least a certain number of transactions, one could use the Contact-based method that provides both low false positives and detection rates and reasonable storage requirements.

The implementation of the proposed methods can be highly parallelized and optimized based on the fingerprinting method used. For example, when using overlapping time windows, when computing the subsequent fingerprints, one can just discard the features that don't belong to the new time win-

dow and insert into the set representation only the new ones. In this way the fingerprint creating time might be reduces.

Finally, because user processing is independent from the rest of the computation for each user, all the users identification fingerprints could be processed in parallel in a separate thread. Moreover, with the increase popularity of distributed computing frameworks, such as MapReduce [12], the computation of data that belongs to million of users could be split and processed independently in parallel by different workers without the need to recombine the results as in the traditional MapReduce Implementation. However, the distributed computation aspect was not the main focus of our paper therefore we don't elaborate it here.

6. RELATED WORK

Several approaches exist in the literature to address the user management, user authentication and user identification problems for mobile terminals. In general, a user is identified on a device either based on something she knows (password), something she has (biometrics) or something she does (behavior analysis). Using passwords is the most common technique for user authentication in telecommunication systems. However, often users choose weak passwords consisting on simple words, short and simple sequences of numbers or easily available information about themselves (i.e. date of birth) [30]. Some solutions have been proposed aiming to protect all the passwords a user requires. A strengthened cryptographic hash function is used to compute secure passwords for arbitrarily many accounts while requiring the user to memorize only a single short password [18]. Biometrics is an alternative scheme for user authentication used in all kinds of applications and devices [25]. In this context, certain efforts aim to achieve highly accurate authentication systems by combining multiple biometric signatures [28]. Other schemes combine biometrics and behavior analysis. These are efficient authentication systems based on the fact that device usage varies significantly from person to person [13]. Implicit authentication systems have been proposed previously in the literature. These are transparent to the user, who is identified based on typing patterns [23] and keystroke dynamics [19]. The approach introduced in our paper resembles these in the sense that user identification is implicit and performed in a transparent way to the user.

Some recent work identifies users based on data from the sensors of a smart phone [20]. Following the same approach and proving its potential, the authors of [29] showed that user input on a smart phone can be inferred from measurement of the sensors on the device, such as the accelerometer and the gyroscope. One may assume that users prefer simple authentication schemes. Indeed, this would explain the frequency in which weak passwords are chosen. Surprisingly, the authors of [16] found that mobile users expect a transparent authentication that increases security and is performed continuously/periodically throughout the day. In this context, the authors of [26] present a method of implicit user authentication for mobile devices. However, in contrast to our methods, their approach is tested with data from just over 50 users and requires large storing of data in the device itself. Further, authentication schemes are also being proposed for different contexts other than mobile device access as it is the case presented in [9] for cloud access.

The major difference between our approach and most of the related methods is that in this work we are not focused on finding another method of authentication but rather a novel non-invasive robust, privacy preserving, accurate and network-based method of user identification that can work in conjunction with and confirm the authentication.

7. CONCLUSION

In this paper we introduce a set of methods to provide implicit and transparent user identification for mobile terminals. Based on the proposed networks, a cellular network can automatically detect device misuse as a result of a lost or stolen terminal or a piece of malicious software running in the background. This provides means for a rapid network-based detection and reaction that can potentially protect a mobile user from economic losses and identity theft.

As future work we intend to investigate using different combinations of contact-based method with the other methods, additional network feature sets and metrics to achieve lower false positive and higher detection rates. We seek to extend the recorded feature sets to the devices themselves and combine events on the device with events on the network. Moreover, we investigate using similar methods to identify users or entities of other devices or systems based on the past observed behavior.

Finally, because user data is very sensitive, an important direction is to design new metrics with very strong privacy guarantees that leak essentially no information about past user behavior, yet allow accurate identification. A promising direction is split the data among several servers, and rely on cryptographic techniques of secure computation to compute the identification outcomes.

8. REFERENCES

[1] GGTracker Android Trojan. http://goo.gl/apq7eV.

[2] Security Alert - SpamSoldier. The Lookout Blog, December 2012. http://goo.gl/7lkRM.

[3] The most common passwords used online in the last year revealed (and 'password' STILL tops the list). Daily Mail, October 2012. http://goo.gl/tN9Yhr.

[4] McAfee Threats Report: Second Quarter 2013. McAfee Labs, 2013. http://goo.gl/qJPh3e.

[5] C. Arthur. More than 50 android apps found infected with rootkit malware, March 2011. http://www.guardian.co.uk/technology/blog/2011/mar/02/android-market-apps-malware.

[6] M. Bellare and P. Rogaway. Random oracles are practical: a paradigm for designing efficient protocols. In *Proceedings of the 1st ACM conference on Computer and communications security*, CCS '93, pages 62–73, New York, NY, USA, 1993. ACM.

[7] B. H. Bloom. Space/time trade-offs in hash coding with allowable errors. *Commun. ACM*, 13:422–426, July 1970.

[8] B. Chen. Cellphone Thefts Grow, but the Industry Looks the Other Way. New York Times, May 2013. http://goo.gl/DWZwmV.

[9] R. Chow, M. Jakobsson, R. Masuoka, J. Molina, Y. Niu, E. Shi, and Z. Song. Authentication in the clouds: A framework and its application to mobile users. 2010.

[10] D. Dagon, T. Martin, and T. Starner. Mobile phones as computing devices: the viruses are coming! *IEEE Pervasive Computing*, 3(4):11 – 15, Oct 2004.

[11] C. De Canniere and C. Rechberger. Finding sha-1 characteristics: General results and applications. *Advances in Cryptology–ASIACRYPT 2006*, pages 1–20, 2006.

[12] J. Dean and S. Ghemawat. Mapreduce: simplified data processing on large clusters. In *Proceedings of the 6th conference on Symposium on Operarting Systems Design & Implementation - Volume 6*, pages 10–10, Berkeley, CA, USA, 2004. USENIX Association.

[13] H. Falaki, R. Mahajan, S. Kandula, D. Lymberopoulos, R. Govindan, and D. Estrin. Diversity in smartphone usage. In *Proceedings of the 8th international conference on Mobile systems, applications, and services*, pages 179–194. ACM, 2010.

[14] L. Fan, P. Cao, J. Almeida, and A. Z. Broder. Summary cache: a scalable wide-area web cache sharing protocol. *IEEE/ACM Trans. Netw.*, 8:281–293, June 2000.

[15] FortiBlog. Android droiddream uses two vulnerabilities, March 2011. http://blog.fortinet.com/android-droiddream-uses-two-vulnerabilities/.

[16] S. Furnell, N. Clarke, and S. Karatzouni. Beyond the pin: Enhancing user authentication for mobile devices. *Computer Fraud & Security*, 2008(8):12–17, 2008.

[17] C. Guo, H. Wang, and W. Zhu. Smart-phone attacks and defenses. In *HotNets III*, 2004.

[18] J. A. Halderman, B. Waters, and E. W. Felten. A convenient method for securely managing passwords. In *Proceedings of the 14th international conference on World Wide Web*, WWW '05, pages 471–479, New York, NY, USA, 2005. ACM.

[19] R. Joyce and G. Gupta. Identity authentication based on keystroke latencies. *Communications of the ACM*, 33(2):168–176, 1990.

[20] J. Kwapisz, G. Weiss, and S. Moore. Cell phone-based biometric identification. In *Biometrics: Theory Applications and Systems (BTAS), 2010 Fourth IEEE International Conference on*, pages 1–7. IEEE, 2010.

[21] J. H. v. Lint. *Introduction to Coding Theory*. Springer-Verlag New York, Inc., Secaucus, NJ, USA, 1982.

[22] M. Mitzenmacher. Compressed bloom filters. In *Proceedings of the twentieth annual ACM symposium on Principles of distributed computing*, PODC '01, pages 144–150, New York, NY, USA, 2001. ACM.

[23] M. Nisenson, I. Yariv, R. El-Yaniv, and R. Meir. Towards behaviometric security systems: Learning to identify a typist. *Knowledge Discovery in Databases: PKDD 2003*, pages 363–374, 2003.

[24] P. Pachal. Google removes 21 malware apps from android market, March 2011. http://www.pcmag.com/article2/0,2817,2381252,00.asp.

[25] S. Pankanti, R. Bolle, and A. Jain. Biometrics:the future of identification. *Computer*, 33(2):46 –49, feb 2000.

[26] E. Shi, Y. Niu, M. Jakobsson, and R. Chow. Implicit authentication through learning user behavior. 2010.

[27] R. Siciliano. Recycled, Lost, Stolen Phones, Equal Identity Theft. FinExtra, February 2009. http://goo.gl/OVgidl.

[28] R. Snelick, U. Uludag, A. Mink, M. Indovina, and A. Jain. Large-scale evaluation of multimodal biometric authentication using state-of-the-art systems. *Pattern Analysis and Machine Intelligence, IEEE Transactions on*, 27(3):450 –455, march 2005.

[29] Z. Xu, K. Bai, and S. Zhu. Taplogger: Inferring user inputs on smartphone touchscreens using on-board motion sensors. 2012.

[30] J. Yan, A. Blackwell, R. Anderson, and A. Grant. Password memorability and security: empirical results. *Security Privacy, IEEE*, 2(5):25 –31, sept.-oct. 2004.

Wiretap-proof: What They Hear is Not What You Speak, and What You Speak They Do Not Hear

Hemant Sengar
Technology Development
VoDaSec Solutions
Fairfax, VA
hsengar09@gmail.com

Haining Wang
Dept. of Computer Science
College of William and Mary
Williamsburg, VA
hnw@cs.wm.edu

Seyed Amir Iranmanesh
Dept. of Computer Science
College of William and Mary
Williamsburg, VA
sairan@cs.wm.edu

ABSTRACT

It has long been believed that once the voice media between caller and callee is captured or sniffed from the wire, either legally by law enforcement agencies or illegally by hackers through eavesdropping on communication channels, it is easy to listen into their conversation. In this paper, we show that this common perception is not always true. Our real-world experiments demonstrate that it is feasible to create a hidden telephonic conversation within an explicit telephone call. In particular, we propose a real-time *covert* communication channel within two-way media streams established between caller and callee. The real-time covert channel is created over the media stream that may possibly be monitored by eavesdroppers. However, the properly encoded media stream acts as a cover (or decoy) carrying bogus media such as an earlier recorded voice conversation. This spurious content will be heard if the media stream is intercepted and properly decoded. However, the calling and called parties protected by the covert communication channel can still directly talk to each other in privacy and real-time, just like any other normal phone calls. This work provides an additional security layer against media interception attacks, however it also exposes a serious security concern to CALEA (Communications Assistance for Law Enforcement Act) wiretapping and its infrastructure.

Categories and Subject Descriptors

C.2.0 [**Computer-Communication Networks**]: General—*Security and protection*

Keywords

Wiretapping, Media Eavesdropping, Covert Communication

1. INTRODUCTION

There are two kinds of eavesdroppers attempting to intercept voice media and listen into telephonic conversation. The first group belongs to illegal eavesdroppers who observe traffic (signaling, media or both) and try to learn who is calling whom and possibly the content of their communication. There are many examples of illegal interception of voice media. In January 2012, a trans-Atlantic call between the FBI and the UK's Scotland Yard in which operatives from the two law enforcement agencies discussed ongoing cases regarding a number of alleged hackers was intercepted, recorded by hackers and later uploaded on the web [20]. A few years ago, there was a Greek wiretapping case involving the illegal tapping of more than 100 mobile phones on the Vodafone Greece network, most of which belong to members of the Greek government and top-ranking civil servants [26]. In a corporate world, we can find many examples of illegal eavesdropping on CEOs or some other targets' phone calls attempting to learn about corporate strategies or financial information.

The second group of eavesdroppers belong to lawfully authorized surveillance, in which a target interception must be approved from the courts or a law enforcement agency. For example, there are recent examples of Illinois governor Rod Blagojevich's attempt of selling senate seat [29] and federal prosecutions of Raj Rajaratnam insider-trading case [28] using wiretapped telephone calls as crucial evidence. Lawfully authorized electronic surveillance is a critical tool used by law enforcement for investigative purposes and also for the prosecution of serious crimes. Most of the democratic countries in the world have electronic surveillance infrastructure and its associated rules and regulations in place. For example, the 1994 USA law for Communications Assistance for Law Enforcement Act (CALEA) requires telecommunication service providers to incorporate various capabilities for law enforcement wiretapping into their networks. These capabilities have been in place for many years in circuit-switched voice networks, i.e., public switched telephone networks (PSTN), to intercept and identify calling and called party information along with the communication content. Moreover, it is also required by the law that VoIP service providers must also be CALEA compliant and provide standard interfaces to their equipments for capturing call-related meta data (who is calling whom) and media content.

The focus of this paper lies in how to protect important information from falling into eavesdroppers' hands. In general, there are two methods – either make it indecipherable or hide in plain sight. The first method is known as encryption. The encrypted messages are secure against general prying eyes. However, plainly visible encrypted messages – no matter how unbreakable – will arouse suspicion, and may in themselves be incriminating in countries where encryption is illegal [30]. The second method is known as steganography, where a secret message is embedded within another cover message in such a way that an observer is not aware of anything unusual and does not have any suspicion. As today's computer and network technologies provide ready-made communication channels for steganography, it is believed that steganography has become a favorable communication channel for terrorists to conduct their activities [6, 10]. To date, steganography is used to hide bits and pieces of information by modifying cover medium's redundant bits. There are many commercial and open source software that can hide information in various types of digital media, such as images, audio, and text files, generally using their least significant bits (LSBs).

1.1 Existing Audio Steganography Methods

In audio steganography, tools such as S-Tools [2], MP3Stego [8], and Hide4PGP [11] employ standard embedding method of using LSB with WAV, MP3, and VOC audio file as cover media, respectively. The SteganRTP [16] tool also uses LSB, but it utilizes real-time media sessions as cover medium. For further improvement, Takahashi et al. [21] placed CELP-based codec (i.e., G.729) audio data within LSBs of G.711 generated audio. Similarly, Wang et al. [23] used Speex codec to hide compressed audio within LSBs of G.711 audio packets. As we note, there is a common thread running across all these audio steganography tools. This common thread is a well-known approach of using LSBs of cover media, because of its high capacity or throughput. Consequently, many methods and tools exist today to detect LSB-based covert channels [7, 19, 9, 24]. The other known audio steganography methods, such as spread spectrum, phase coding, and echo data hiding [14], are not very relevant to our work, as they cannot provide channel capacity high enough to hide real-time voice communication.

1.2 Challenges

To the best of our knowledge, except using LSBs, we are not aware of any other efforts of using audio steganography techniques in real-time communication channels to hide a real-time voice communication. It is mainly because of two reasons: (1) voice is time sensitive media and (2) its presentation requires at least several thousands bits of information per second. However, if we could show that it is possible to hide a telephonic conversation by creating a covert communication channel within another (i.e., cover) conversation, without using LSBs or any other previously known audio steganography methods, it will have profound effects on call monitoring and media interception. On one hand, it will provide a new security approach against illegal eavesdroppers; on the other hand, it will induce a serious security implication to CALEA and its infrastructure.

With the wide use of VoIP within enterprise networks, it is speculated that the confidential data (audio, image, text etc.) can be embedded and transmitted out of the networks via RTP streams. However, since LSB-based covert channels are easily detectable and have poor immunity to manipulation, the LSB-based methods have never been a serious threat. For example, it is well-known fact that such covert channels can be easily removed either by randomizing the LSBs or passing the audio stream through a transcoding process (e.g., converting 64 Kbps G.711 audio channel to 8 Kbps G.729 audio channel). None of the existing audio covert channels can survive after the transcoding process. In this paper, we attempt to develop a new method and experimentally demonstrate that even after transcoding, it is still feasible to recover and reconstruct the *lost* or *obfuscated* covert channel.

1.3 Contributions

In this paper, through real-world experiments, we demonstrate that it is feasible to create a real-time covert voice communication channel within an explicit and open media channel. We propose a new audio steganography method that is unique in several aspects:

(1) Waveform codec approach – in all previous approaches, compressed codecs such as G.729 (8Kbps) and Speex (2-44 Kbps) are used to hide audio within G.711 codec (64 Kbps) audio due mainly to low bandwidth requirement of compressed codecs (i.e., covert channel capacity is always lower than cover channel capacity). In our approach, we take a radically different approach by hiding 64 Kbps worth of information within another 64 Kbps G.711 encoded cover audio. (2) Cover audio sample replacements – in our approach, the cover and covert audio samples are interleaved with each other, a few of the cover audio samples are replaced with the covert audio samples, instead of modifying the bits of cover samples. (3) Reconstruction of imprecise waveform – at the receiver side, based on the limited number of covert audio samples, we discover all the missing samples and reconstruct a waveform that is approximate to the original one. (4) Transcoding process – as a sample-based approach, we can still recover the covert samples, even though the RTP stream may have undergone through the transcoding process reducing 64 Kbps G.711 stream to 8 Kbps G.729 stream. (5) Codebook-based approach – compared to LSB-based approaches, now peers have the flexibility to create their own private communication in many different ways, making the covert channel unpredictable and hard to decipher for eavesdroppers.

1.4 Brief Overview

Let's consider a two-party call where two audio streams between caller and callee undergo the encoding and decoding processes at the sender and receiver sides. At the sender side, the earlier recorded conversation is used as a cover media. Some of its samples are replaced with the samples that have some specific key characteristics of the real-time voice spoken over the microphone, and then the mixed samples are encoded, packetized and transmitted across the networks. At the receiver side, once the samples with the hidden voice characteristics and its time line (i.e., temporal relationship) are separated from the cover, the cover media is discarded. Using the received characteristic samples and its time information, we reconstruct the spoken words or phrases and then send it to the receiver-side speaker to play it out. Even if the properly decoded media is intercepted anywhere between caller and callee, it will still be very hard to guess or reconstruct the hidden communication. The intercepted media will be playing explicit spurious cover content only. Here we merely describe the one-way media stream operation, however, it should be noted that the same process is also be repeated in other direction to establish two-way media streams.

The remainder of the paper is structured as follows. In Section 2, we discuss the background of this work, including SIP-based IP telephony, CALEA, VoIP media stream, and conventional audio steganography methods. In Section 3, we describe our new real time voice steganography technique. In Sections 4 and 5, we present the encoding and decoding processes, respectively. In Section 6, we validate the efficacy of the proposed approach through real experiments. In Section 7, we survey related work. Finally, we conclude the paper in Section 8.

2. BACKGROUND

While the proposed approach of real-time voice steganography is general enough and applicable to both traditional PSTN and emerging VoIP telephony networks, our main focus is on VoIP networks. This is mainly due to two reasons: (1) VoIP networks provide a flexible platform to perform our proof of concept testing, and (2) our telephone sets are SIP-based softclients, in which we implement the modified approach of encoding and decoding of the media streams. However, it should be noted that the same method could also be implemented on smartphones and hardware-based analog phones.

2.1 SIP-based IP Telephony

The Session Initiation Protocol (SIP) [15], belonging to the application layer of the TCP/IP protocol stack, is used to set up, modify, and tear down multimedia sessions including telephone calls between two or more participants. SIP-based telecommunication architectures have two kinds of elements: end devices referred to as user agents (UAs) and SIP servers. Irrespective of being a software or hardware phone, UAs combine two sub-entities: the connection requester referred as the user agent client (UAC) and the connection request receiver referred to as the user agent server (UAS). Consequently, during a SIP session, both UAs switches back and forth between UAC and UAS functionalities. SIP messages consisting of request-response pairs are exchanged for call set up, from six kinds consisting of INVITE, ACK, BYE, CANCEL, REGISTER, and OPTIONS - each identified by a numeric code according in RFC 3261 [15].

2.2 Communications Assistance for Law Enforcement Act (CALEA)

The Communications Assistance for Law Enforcement Act (CALEA) is a United States wiretapping law passed in 1994 to regulate telecommunication compliance with lawful surveillance of digitally switched telephone networks. The objective of CALEA is to enhance the ability of law enforcement and intelligence agencies to conduct electronic surveillance. This requires that telecommunications carriers and manufacturers of telecommunications equipment modify and design their equipment, facilities, and services to ensure the built-in surveillance capabilities, allowing federal agencies to monitor all telephone, broadband Internet, and VoIP traffic in real-time [25].

The J-Standard (J-STD-025) defines the interfaces between a telecommunication service provider (TSP) and a Law Enforcement Agency (LEA) to assist the LEA in conducting lawfully authorized electronic surveillance. It is developed by a joint effort of Telecommunications Industry Association (TIA), the Alliance for Telecommunications Industry Solutions (ATIS), and various other industry organizations and interest groups. As a product of the traditional circuit-switched wireline and wireless telecommunications industry associations, the J-standard does not specifically address the requirements of other (competing) technologies such as Voice-over-IP (VoIP). However, J-standard serves as a guide to many other industry associations to develop their own specifications meeting their technical requirements.

Now we discuss how a VoIP service provider implements CALEA compliance. Here a VoIP target subscriber may call to another VoIP subscriber hosted by the same service provider or to an external number (call routed through PSTN networks). The session border controller (SBC) is an edge device between VoIP subscribers and the service provider's core network, and is used to exert control over the signaling and the media streams. The warrant for a particular target (i.e., a subscriber to be monitored) is provisioned on the SBC. The SBC uses directory number (DN) to match the target and intercept a call. The SBC provides intercepted call data events and replicated media for matching targets to the delivery function (DF), and then both content and target call data are relayed to the appropriate LEA's collection function (CF).

2.3 VoIP Media Stream

As a telephone subscriber talks over phone, the telephone device is responsible for capturing and transforming audio for transmis-

sion. The media capture process consists of capturing an uncompressed frame and transforming into a format suitable for encoder to generate a compressed frame. The compressed frames are packetized to create one or more (i.e., fragmented) RTP packets. The device may also participate in error correction and congestion control by adapting the transmitted media stream in response to feedback received from the other end.

Audio Capture: When a telephone caller speaks over phone, a device known as microphone responds to sound pressure. The microphone produces a time-varying electrical voltage proportional to the increase or decrease in local pressure that constitutes sound. This continuous time-varying voltage is an electric analog of the acoustic signal. The analog audio signals captured from the microphone are sampled, digitized and stored in a buffer. Once a fixed number of samples have been collected (i.e., a frame is formed), the buffer is made available to the application. The frame is not available to the application until the last sample is collected in the buffer. To avoid delays to the application, the buffer size is close to the frame duration.

Compression: The uncompressed audio data captured in the buffer is passed to encoder to produce compressed frames. Frames can be encoded in several ways depending on the compression algorithm used. Based on the negotiated codec choice between peers, state may be maintained between frames and is made available to the encoder along with each new frame of data. Some of the codecs produce fixed-size frames and some produce variable-size frames as their output.

RTP Packets: Now the frames are ready to be packetized as RTP packets before being transmitted over the network toward the other end, i.e., callee. The RTP packetization routine creates one or more RTP packets for a frame depending upon the maximum transmission unit (MTU) of the network. The packet header and payload are defined according to the used codec specification.

3. REAL-TIME VOICE STEGANOGRAPHY

From voice steganography perspective, it is a challenging task to hide a real-time voice communication within another real-time voice channel. The reason lies in three aspects. (1) *Capacity limitation*, the amount of information can be hidden in cover media is limited, but the voice channel requires at least several thousands of bits of information per second. Only the LSB-based approach is known to have the channel capacity of few thousands bits per second and therefore it is the most dominant method to hide various types of information, such as images, audio, and text. Except the LSB-based method, there is no other method that can achieve the high channel capacity or throughput. (2) *Time domain*, the hidden information has to be related with the time information, because at the receiver end we need to know what information has to be presented at what time. And finally, (3) *real-time presentation*, there are strict timing deadlines that must be met in terms presenting the data. The decoded hidden information must be presented within less than 150 ms at the other end[1]. Now we discuss how we solve these three limitations in our proposed approach while making the resulted covert channel harder to be detected.

3.1 Pulse Code Modulation

In telephony world the most commonly used voice codec is G.711. As a waveform codec, G.711 is an ITU-T standard for audio companding. Its formal name is Pulse code modulation (PCM) of voice frequencies. Non-uniform (logarithmic) quantization with 8 bits is

---

[1]The user perception of the voice quality starts deteriorating as the one-way latency exceeds 150 ms.

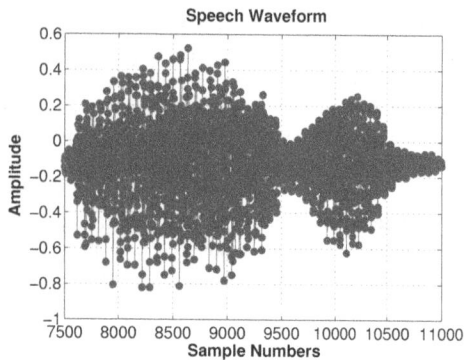

Figure 1: A Snapshot of Voice Utterance [8K Samples per Sec.]

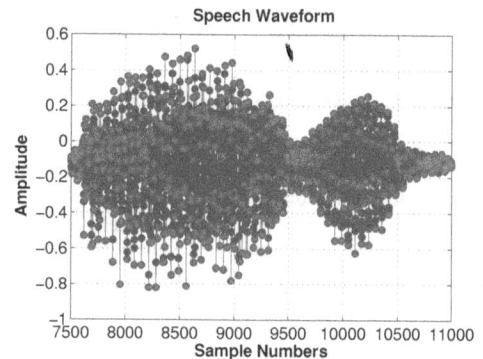

Figure 2: Local Maxima and Minima Data Points (Shown as Red ∗)

used to represent each sample, resulting in a bit rate of 64 kbit/s. There are two slightly different versions: $\mu - law$, which is used primarily in North America, and $A - law$, which is in use in most other countries outside North America.

The Pulse Code Modulation is based on the *Nyquist Frequency*. According to Nyquist Frequency, in order to recover all the Fourier components of a periodic waveform, it is necessary to use a sampling rate at least twice the highest waveform frequency. More formally:

- $x(t)$ is a band-limited signal with bandwidth f_h,

- $p(t)$ is a sampling signal consisting of pulses at internals $T_s = \frac{1}{f_s}$, where f_s is the sampling frequency,

- $x_s(t) = x(t)p(t)$ is the sampled signal,

then $x(t)$ can be recovered exactly from $x_s(t)$ if and only if $f_s \geq 2f_h$. If voice data is limited to frequencies below $4,000$ Hz ,then $8,000$ samples per second would be sufficient to completely characterize the voice signal. Based on this sampling theorem, speaker's utterances captured by the microphone are sampled as shown in Figure 1.

3.2 Capacity Limitation

The biggest challenge in audio steganography is to find a method that is not based on LSBs, but still can have channel capacity high enough to hide information worth of few thousands of bits per second. We know that according to Nyquist theorem $8,000$ samples per second would be sufficient to completely characterize the voice signal if its frequencies are limited below $4K$ Hz. However, the main question is *why do we need exact representation of the speech waveform, when an approximate representation is good enough to human ears?* Since we cannot carry $8,000$ samples worth of information in cover media, our goal is to find a method that can allow us to reconstruct a waveform similar to the original one using as few samples as possible, so that we can easily hide within the cover media.

As shown in Figure 2, we could use local maxima and minima sampling data points to characterize the whole speech waveform. During our experimentation, we find that using local maxima and minima data points can achieve $\approx 80 - 85\%$ reduction in the number of samples required to reconstruct the speech waveform. It should be noted that the reconstructed waveform from the limited number of sample data points will be an approximate representation of the original waveform. In the encoding process, we will show how to embed local maxima and minima data points within the cover media samples.

3.3 Time Domain

The second challenge is to attach time values with extrema data points, i.e., to relate maxima and minima data points to their time of occurrence. The knowledge of this temporal relationship is necessary if we would like to reconstruct the speech waveform at the receiver end. To address this problem, we work on the frame level representing 160 sample data points. Every 20 ms, the sender sends an RTP packet to the receiver with the payload of 160 samples. While these frames (hence RTP packets) are created for the cover media, we analyze the covert media frame for its maxima and minima values. The cover and covert frames are of same size (i.e., with the same number of samples). We detect the extrema occurrences and their corresponding indices within the covert frame. Then, at the same index position within the cover frame, we replace its sample with the covert extrema sample.

3.4 Real-Time Presentation

For an effective two-way communication, it is necessary that the sender's audio should be rendered at the receiver end within 150 ms. Since our encoding and decoding processes are at the individual packet level, we are able to present media to the receiver player device well below the threshold of 150 ms.

4. ENCODING PROCESS

In this section, we describe the role of telephony codebook and how the covert media is hidden within the cover media and transmitted to the other end (i.e., callee-side).

In cryptography, a codebook is a document used for implementing a code. A codebook contains a lookup table for coding and decoding; each word or phrase has one or more strings which replace it. The codebook shown in Figure 3 is a set of rules represented as code index. The two communicating parties select and agree upon a particular rule to create (encode) and decipher (decode) the covert communication channel. Although the code index selection process between peers is beyond the scope of the this work, it could still be selected either during the signaling (i.e., call setup) phase or out of band.

As shown in Figure 4, there are two media sources. The cover media is sourced from a pre-recorded .wav file and the covert media, i.e., the user's utterances, is originated from microphone device. Both audio sources are sampled at the rate of $8K$ samples per second. The samples are stored in their respective input buffers. When a fixed number of samples (e.g., 160 samples) are collected, they will be available to the encoding module. Before sending to the encoding module, we analyze the fixed-duration covert frame

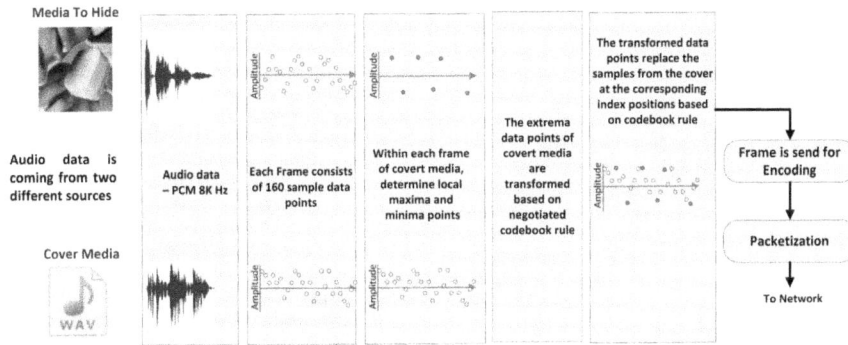

Figure 4: Encoding - Cover and Covert Media Samples are Interleaved Together

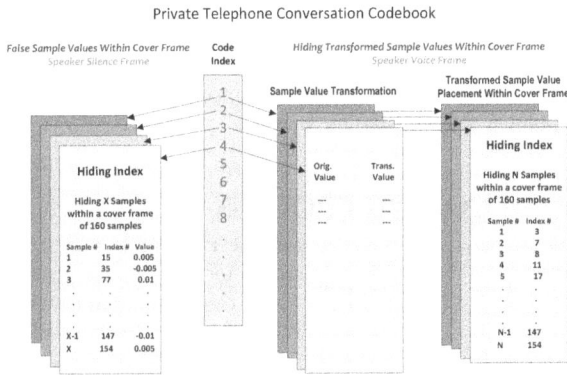

Figure 3: Telephone Codebook - Defines Rules as How the Samples of Covert Media are Transformed and also How to Interleave together with Cover Samples

to find local maxima and minima values and their corresponding index positions within 160 samples. Then, these extrema samples are transformed and replace the cover samples residing at the index positions as per selected codebook rule. It should be noted that the same cover media should not be reused for future communication. In the following, we briefly describe the encoding process in a step-by-step manner.

The codebook shown in Figure 3 is a document consists of a set of rules represented as code index. The codebook contains a lookup table for encoding and decoding. The two communicating parties select and agree upon a particular rule to create (encode) and decipher (decode) the covert communication channel. Although the code index selection process between peers is beyond the scope of the this work, it could still be selected either during the signaling (i.e., call setup) phase or out of band.

4.1 Determine Local Maxima and Minima

The user's speech utterances over microphone generate voiced and unvoiced speech in succession, separated by silence regions. Though in the silence region, there is no excitation supplied to the vocal tract (i.e., no speech output), still silence is an integral part of speech signal. To hide as much information as possible about the user's speech within the cover media, we treat each frame differently depending upon its relevance to the voice activity or how important it is in the reconstruction of the waveform at the receiver end. Now assume that for a particular covert frame of n $(= 160)$ samples, the values are $y_1, y_2, ..., y_n$. First we determine the maximum (y_{max}) and minimum (y_{min}) values of the samples within

the frame. If $y_{max} - y_{min} \leq 0.01$, it means that all the n samples of the frame are confined within a narrow band of 0.01 and we treat such a frame as silence without much voice activity. For silence covert frames, we do not determine local maxima and minima points; instead we choose X (very few, say 4-6) index positions within the cover frame and assign each one of them with a value as described in codebook rules (i.e., left side of Figure 3). Therefore, covert silence frames have insignificant impact on cover frames. For all the other covert frames with significant voice activity, we determine both local maxima and minima sample points.

Now assume that the value y_i is a local minimum if there exists a neighborhood y_{i-1}, y_i, and y_{i+1} with $y_i = \min\{y_{i-1}, y_i, y_{i+1}\}$. However, there are a large number of local minima points and therefore to filter out insignificant local minima points, we extend the neighborhood to y_j, $y_{j+1}, ..., y_i, y_{i+1}, ..., y_h$ with $j < i < h$ and consider only those y_i local minima points where $y_i = \min\{y_j, ..., y_h\}$, i.e., $y_i < y_k$ for $k = j, ..., i-1$ and $y_i < y_l$ for $l = (i+1), ..., h$. Similarly, we find y_i as a local maximum point in a list of sample values $y_1, y_2, ..., y_n$ if there exists a neighborhood y_j, $y_{j+1}, ..., y_i, y_{i+1}, ..., y_h$ with $j < i < h$ such that $y_i = \max\{y_j, ..., y_h\}$, i.e., $y_i > y_k$ for $k = j, ..., i-1$ and $y_i > y_l$ for $l = (i+1), ..., h$. In our experimentation, we find that the extrema value determination within the neighborhood of 3, 5, and 7 samples can achieve approximately 40%, 66%, and 82% reduction in the number of samples required to reconstruct the waveform, respectively.

4.2 Transform the Extrema Values

The local extrema values found in a covert frame are passed through a transformation process to modify its true value and scale down its range from $[+1.0, -1.0]$ to a much lower range of $[+0.1, -0.1]$ or $[+0.01, -0.01]$, with a reduction factor of 10 or 100, respectively. Now assume that $\mathbb{F}$ is a transformation function with Ψ as a desired reduction factor. Each code index has its own transformation function and reduction factor defined in the codebook rule (i.e., right side of Figure 3).

$$y_i \rightarrow [\mathbb{F}]_\Psi \rightarrow y_i' \quad \forall i, \text{ i.e., extrema indices}$$

Both the transformation functions and reduction factors are known to the receiver-side. Thus, based on the received transformed value y_i', its corresponding true value y_i can be recovered.

For example, in our experimentation this transformation operation is implemented as a three-step process: first, we determine the sign (positive or negative) of the extrema sample value; secondly, the absolute value of the sample is passed through the transformation function $\ln |y_i|$; and thirdly, the natural logarithm of the sample value is further reduced by a factor of $\Psi = 1000$ and then

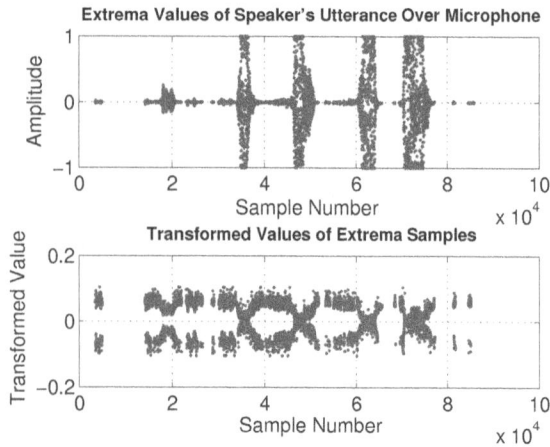

Figure 5: Transformation Operation on Extrema Sample

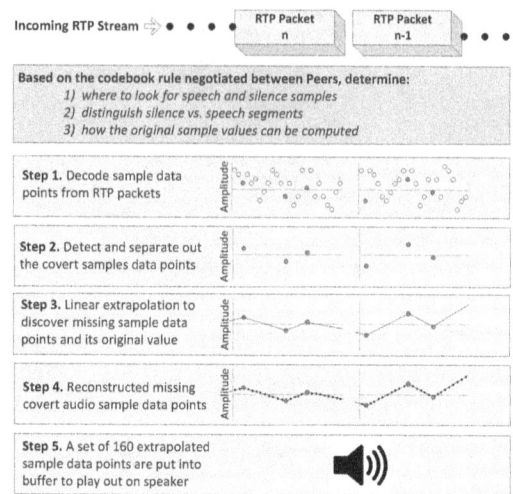

Figure 6: Decoding - Hidden Samples are Extracted and Extrapolated to Find Missing Samples

is assigned the same polarity as in the step one (i.e., $y_i' = \pm \ln |y_i|$ /1000). Figure 5 shows the transformation process where we apply the logarithm function and reduction factor on the original extrema samples, and thus transforming the true covert sample values before being transmitted within RTP payload.

The transformation process is applied on the extrema values mainly because of the following two reasons: (1) lower covert sample values will appear as a soft noise that can easily be hidden within the cover media's background noise when the cover media is intercepted and decoded by eavesdroppers; (2) even if a sample value is guessed, still it will be difficult to uncover the true value of the covert sample, making it very hard to reconstruct the covert samples and listen into the real content of a voice conversation. Therefore, the real communication remains private between two peers.

4.3 Determine Hiding Location

Now we need to determine some hiding locations and let the receiver-end be aware of them, so that the receiver can know exactly where to search for the hidden covert samples within a frame. There are many possibilities of selecting a hiding pattern. For example, as shown in Figure 3, these hiding locations can be selected as any arbitrary indexes within the frame. The codebook-based hiding locations achieve three features: first, it makes the implementation of decoding process very simple; secondly, it makes eavesdroppers exceedingly difficult to perform statistical analysis and find hiding patterns; and finally, by having the knowledge of hiding locations, we can still recover the covert sample values even if the RTP stream may have undergone through the transcoding process.

4.4 Swap Cover Samples

In this step we interleave both covert and cover samples together. The transformed extrema values of the covert media frame replace the samples of the cover media frame at the same corresponding indices based on the codebook rule negotiated between peers. If we assume that y_i' is an ith (e.g., say 5th) transformed covert sample, then after consulting the codebook rule as shown in Figure 3, we find that it will swap with the jth (e.g., 17th) sample Y_j of the cover frame, i.e., $Y_j \leftarrow y_i', \forall i$. Once the samples from the covert and cover media are interleaved together within a frame, they will be sent to the encoding process based on the codec negotiated during the initial call setup phase. The compressed audio data is packetized as RTP media packets and transmitted to the destination.

5. DECODING PROCESS

Once the G.711 encoded audio RTP stream arrives at the receiver side, the packets are validated for their correctness and the arrival time is also noted (for jitter, clock skew estimation etc.). Based on RTP time-stamps, these packets are ordered and added to an input queue. Then, the packets are extracted from the input queue and inserted into a source-specific playout buffer. The frames are held in the playout buffer for a period of time to smooth timing variations caused by the networks. In the very last processing stage, the frames are decompressed and rendered for users. Our decoding process is implemented at this stage, a set of processing steps are executed on the decompressed data to extract the hidden audio samples.

The decoding process is based on prior knowledge of what codebook rule is negotiated between peers. The codebook rule informs us as how to detect and distinguish covert samples from cover samples and also how to recover the original sample values from the received modified sample values. As shown in Figure 6, the decoding process can be described as a five step process. In the very first step, we get decompressed samples within a particular frame, say n^{th} time frame. In the second step, we detect and extract the hidden samples at particular index values (based on the codebook rule). The list of hiding indexes (i.e., the sample positions within a frame) for speech and silence is known between the sender and receiver. The received frame is checked for some particular index positions and their corresponding values to discover a pattern matching with the silence frame. If a pattern is found then the entire received frame is discarded and a new reconstructed frame of 160 samples[2] (all with 0.00 value) is put into play out buffer. Now assume that the nth time frame is a speech frame (i.e., a frame carrying covert speech samples). Following the codebook rule, we discover k data points (i, y_i'), where i is the index value and y_i' its corresponding value at i^{th} index. We maintain a list of $key - value$ pairs for all the discovered data points in the format $[i, y_i']$. It should be noted that the ith sample value may not be the true value of the hidden sample. The sender-side may have modified the true value by pass-

---

[2]Here we assume that each G.711 packet is worth of 20 ms audio with 160 samples. We can accommodate any changes in the packet size (such as 10 or 30 ms) if knowing the codec and its attributes negotiated between peers.

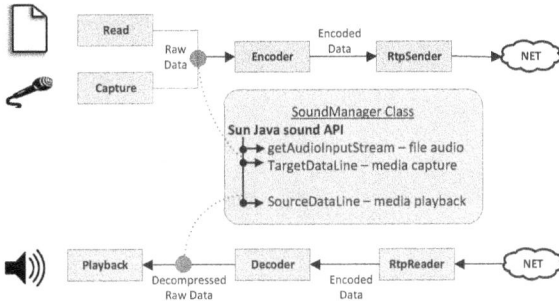

Figure 7: Encoding and Decoding Process Within a Java-based Peers SIP Client

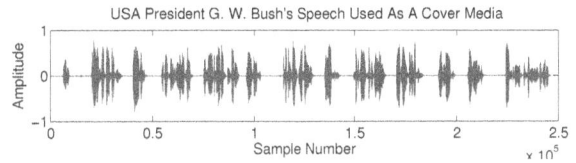

Figure 8: Cover Media

ing it through an operation known to the sender and receiver only. Therefore, at the receiver side knowing the modifying parameter (i.e., Ψ), and the transformation function (i.e., $\mathbb{F}$), we can extract the sample's original value $y_i \leftarrow y_i'$.

In the third step we apply linear extrapolation to recover missing samples. Using each pair of conjugate data points (such as i' and i), we calculate the slope ($m_i = \frac{y_i - y_{i'}}{i - i'}$) and intercept ($c_i = y_i - m_i * i$). In the fourth step, using the slope and intercept values, we estimate all the other missing samples between index i' and i. In this way, we can estimate $(i - i')$ samples for a domain of index values $[i', i)$. The third and fourth steps repeat for each pair of the conjugate data points in the list. In the fifth step, once 160 samples are estimated, we put them in device input buffer for playing.

6. EXPERIMENTAL EVALUATION

We implemented a prototype of the proposed wiretap-proof approach and deployed it in software-based phone clients. Then, we conducted a series of realistic experiments to validate its effectiveness. In our experimental testbed, two computers are used as the SIP-based telephones, and communicate with each other over IP networks. Their IP telephony service is provided by the same popular VoIP service provider. The service provider's SIP server and SBC are located in Greenville, SC. Both of the telephone endpoints i.e., the computers have 2.26 GHz Intel Core2Duo and 4 Gbytes of RAM, running Windows Vista OS and are connected to the Internet via cable modems. Both of the SIP clients are located in Aldie, VA, and the calls are routed through the Internet, while the service provider's network edge device (i.e., SBC) is located at 13 hops away with the average round trip time of 38 ms.

6.1 Softphone Implementation

Using the computer's audio system and microphone, a PC-based softphone, i.e., a software-based phone client, works as a regular telephone to place and answer phone calls. Our encoding and decoding processes are implemented with the publicly available open source Java-based SIP client known as *Peers* [1]. Throughout our implementation, we assume the following audio format:

```
// linear PCM 8kHz, 16 bits, mono, signed, little endian
audioFormat = new AudioFormat(8000, 16, 1, true, false);
```

For two-way communication, both encoding and decoding modules are implemented on a SIP client.

For the media handling, `IncomingRtpReader` and `Capture RtpSender` are included in Peers as the two main classes. The `IncomingRtpReader` is responsible for RTP depacketization, media decompression, and media playback; and `CaptureRtpRea der` is responsible for microphone capture, media encoding, and RTP packetization. However, for media processing, the whole me-

dia package relies on standard *Sun Java Sound API*. The Peer's `SoundManager` class implements its all interaction with the Java Sound API. Within this class, we have references for both *SourceDataLines* for media playback and *TargetDataLine* for media capture. Since our encoding and decoding processes are based on the raw data as shown in Figure 7, most of our software implementation is done within this class.

6.2 Experimental Results

In our experiments, for cover media we used both music clips and pre-recorded human conversation files, though in real life, it is preferable that caller should use his own earlier prerecorded telephone conversations. As an example, in Figure 8 we show a 30 sec. snippet of cover media source that is a pre-recorded speech of the former President G.W. Bush given in the eve of September 11th terrorist attack [22]. We selected this particular media file because it represents both silence and speech segments with the true nature of two-way communication (i.e., speech on and off periods).

The speaker's utterances over microphone are captured and sampled, and then the fixed size frames are created. Figure 9 (top) shows the extrema samples of the speaker's utterances *"Hello! How are you?"* over microphone within about 30 seconds call duration. It should be noted that the encoding process is per frame based, though the Figure shows the whole 30 seconds call duration. Figure 9 (bottom) shows how the extrema samples are transformed to some other values using a transformation function known to the receiver-side as well. For easy presentation, here we used $\ln |y_i| / 1000$ transformation operation to modify the true values of the extrema samples (i.e., y_i), although we could transform these samples in many different ways. The transformed values replace the cover media samples at the corresponding indices as indicated in the negotiated codebook rule during the call setup phase. In this way, we interleaved both covert and cover media samples together. The interleaved samples are packetized and transmitted over the Internet to the VoIP service provider, and then get relayed to the receiver-side phone.

The interleaved media packets can be captured by eavesdroppers between the caller and callee phones. We intercepted the me-

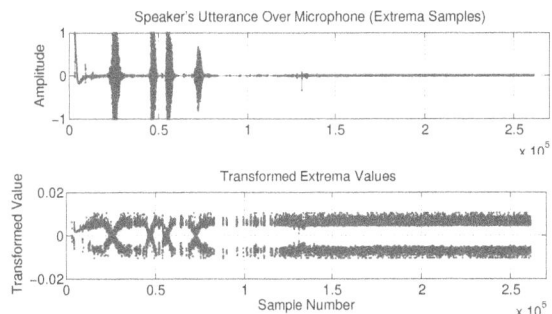

Figure 9: Original Extrema Samples (top) and its Transformed Values (bottom)

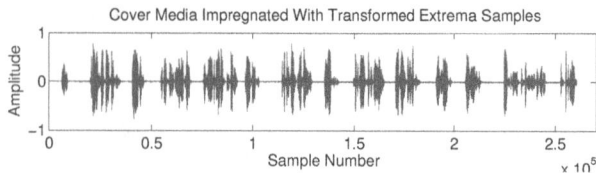

Figure 10: Cover Carrying Covert Media

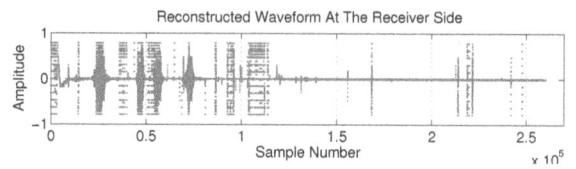

Figure 11: Reconstructed Audio Waveform from Discovered Covert Samples

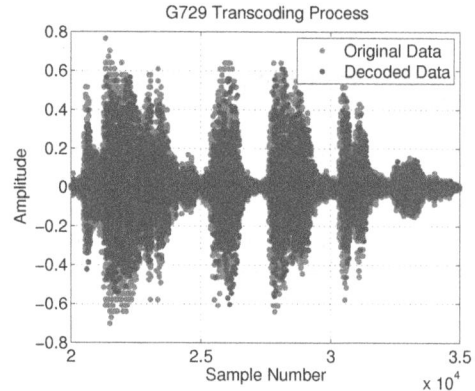

Figure 12: Sample Values Modified by Transcoding Process

dia packets at the SBC located at the edge of the VoIP service provider's network. The media packets are decoded and played using Wireshark tool. Figure 10 shows the intercepted media that is impregnated with covert samples. When we decode the audio, we are able to hear the cover media only.

Now our task is to measure the perceived audio quality. The Mean Opinion Score (MOS) is the most widely accepted measure of the perceived quality. However, it is generated by averaging the results of a set of standard, subjective tests where a number of listeners rate the heard audio quality. In our case, we are more interested in a quantitative measure based on algorithm. We used Perceptual Evaluation of speech (PESQ) [27], an International Telecommunication Union (ITU) standard. The algorithm estimates the perceived quality difference between the test and the original audio signal. The PESQ score is in the range of -0.5 to 4.5. For most cases, the audio signal with listening quality has a score between 1 to 4.5. In our experiments, we assumed the original cover media as a reference with the score of 4.5, and then we measured the perceived audio quality of interleaved audio signals. Based on experimental results, we found that the interleaved test audio signals have PESQ score of 1.7 to 2.3. The voice quality is high enough for human users to easily listen[3].

The analysis of received RTP stream is tabulated in Table 1 as experiment number 1. The media session duration is about 30 seconds, in which we captured 1635 RTP packets (one-way direction). We observed that the encoding process induces insignificant delay to individual packet departure time and the end point's perception of this call remains the same as any other normal calls.

Table 1: Analysis of RTP Stream (One Way)

Exp. Number	Total Packets	Max Jitter	Mean Jitter	Lost Packets	Sequence Error	PESQ Score
1	1635	3.10 ms	1.18 ms	0	0	1.75
2	2301	6.16 ms	1.08 ms	0	0	1.94
3	3346	1.97 ms	1.08 ms	0	0	2.18
4	6080	1.72 ms	0.95 ms	0	0	1.72
5	9107	2.68 ms	1.03 ms	0	0	1.89

At the receiver side, the decoding module of the softclient receives the decompressed samples from the interleaved media stream and tries to separate the covert samples from the cover media based on the already known hiding pattern. In our software implementation, during the speaker's silence period we are not able to detect the silence pattern precisely enough, resulting in false data points and thus introducing noise in the reconstructed audio signals. Both false and true discovered samples are reversely transformed to their original values, and all the missing samples are estimated using linear interpolation method. Figure 11 shows the reconstructed waveform based on the limited number of covert samples mixed with false samples. We performed quantitative measure of the perceived quality of the reconstructed audio signals. When we compared the

[3]Many compressed codecs have PESQ scores around 3.7.

speaker's utterances over the microphone to the receiver's perception as what is played out of the speaker, the PESQ score is 1.1 to 1.3. Thus, it still remains an audible quality even in the presence of false data points as noise.

6.3 Transcoding Scenario

During the initial growth and deployment, most of the VoIP service providers standardized on G.711 codec. It became a de facto codec choice because of its widespread use in telecommunication, low processing overhead, associated licensing cost, and high voice quality. However, G.711 requires a relatively high amount of bandwidth. In many cases where customers have limited upstream bandwidth (e.g., DSL deployments), they are forced to choose codecs requiring lower bandwidth such as G.729. Within VoIP networks, it is possible that individual end points (i.e., phones) may be using different codecs. The codec transcoding provides a way to change one codec format to others and vice versa, without making codec change on individual end points. Generally, transcoding is done at the edge of a service provider network on media gateways or session border controllers. Being proprietary in nature and involved licensing cost, we did not implement G.729 codec within Peers SIP clients. In our experiments, the G.711 audio stream was captured using wireshark tool and then the RTP payload raw data was transcoded to G.729 codec format using *VoiceAge Open G.729 Implementation* [4]. In order to recover the covert channel, we again transcode (or decode) the G.729 encoded raw data back to PCM format G.711 data. Figure 12 shows both the original G.711 RTP stream data points and the transformation to sample data point values after applying G.729 encoding and decoding processes.

Here we can clearly see as why the conventional audio steganography approaches do not survive the transcoding process. This is because almost all of the sample data points are modified to some new values. However, since our proposed approach is based on interleaving of the cover and covert media samples, it can preserve their relative magnitudes; therefore, it is still possible to reconstruct

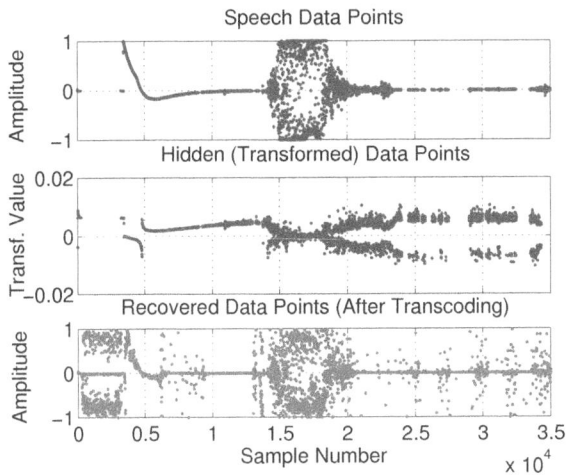

Figure 13: **Recovering Covert Data Points After Decoding** `G.729` **Audio**

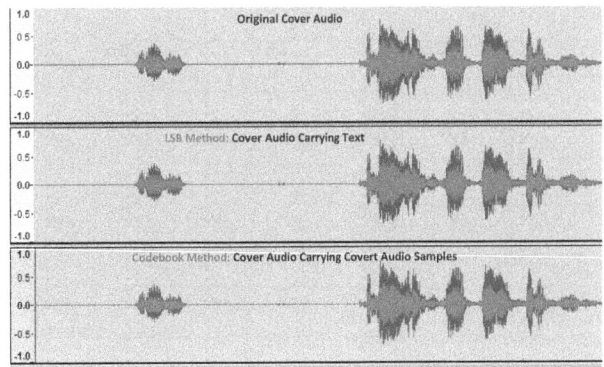

Figure 14: **Visual Waveform Comparison**

Table 2: Statistical Analysis of Samples

	Cover	LSB	Codebook
No of Samples	80,000	80,000	80,000
Mean	1.540e-05	1.538e-05	3.513e-04
Std Dev.	0.1090	0.1090	0.0999

the covert channel. The extrema data points of speaker's utterance *"Hello!"* over microphone is shown at the top part of Figure 13. The middle portion of Figure 13 shows the transformed values of the extrema samples that are interleaved with the cover samples. Later interleaved samples are encoded into `G.729` format. For covert channel recovery, we transcode it again back to `G.711` PCM data. Once the decoded data points are obtained from the `G.729` encoded audio, we apply the same procedure as described in Section 5. The lower part of Figure 13 shows the recovered covert samples. Because of the modified sample values, many of the hidden patterns meant to indicate silence segments were lost. These wrongly identified segments are treated as speech and when extrapolated to create missing samples cause noise.

6.4 Further Discussion

Since the proposed method does not use least significant bits of the samples or any previously known audio steganography methods, qualitatively our approach remains undetectable to current genre of LSB-based steganalysis tools. Now we discuss more intuitive approaches to identify and discover the presence of covert channel.

6.4.1 Visual Effect:

Since our approach is based on modifying whole samples, rather than bits, it seems that the proposed approach could be detected by examining the waveforms. We performed a set of experiments comparing both LSB-based methods and our proposed codebook-based sample replacement method. In the same cover media, we hide a line of text using Steghide [3] - a LSB-based tool and embed speaker's utterance *"Hello!"* using codebook-based sample replacement method, respectively. However, if we look at Figure 14, we cannot see any significant difference in the waveforms, and cannot guess there are different messages hidden in them.

6.4.2 Statistical Analysis:

To perform statistical analysis, we created 200 bins of equal size of 0.01 covering the sample value range of [-1.0, 1.0]. Figure 15 shows histograms and the distribution of bins for three separate cover medias. Based on the analysis results in Table 2, we can see that LSB-based media is almost identically distributed as the original cover media. The codebook-based method has higher mean compared to LSB-based media. However, it should be noted that

without the knowledge of original cover media, it is hard to differentiate and detect the presence of covert channel.

6.4.3 Voice Quality:

The voice quality of cover media is almost unaffected by LSB-based audio steganography. Within the 10 second cover media we hid two lines of text message, the PESQ score of LSB-based was still 4.48. By contrast, the proposed codebook-based sample replacement method has the PESQ score of about 2.0. When we hear intercepted media, there is always a soft-noise in the background. The untrained or casual ears cannot make any distinction, however algorithm-based quality monitoring tools can detect such noise easily. However, the fundamental question is *does the low voice quality mean presence of covert channel?* The short answer is "No", as voice quality also heavily depends upon the speaker's ambient environment. Moreover, even if we could guess the presence of covert channel, it is still very hard to find covert samples (i.e., hiding indexes within a frame) and its original value (i.e., transformation functions and its parameters) to reconstruct the waveform.

7. RELATED WORK

There are various malicious activities against telephony systems and their users. Most of these attacks are trying to exploit the insecure or poorly protected systems and to eavesdrop on unencrypted network traffic. Even the encrypted contents of VoIP traffic can be exposed by comparing packet size and interarrival times to language constructs [31, 32]. As VoIP has been increasingly adopted for communication in enterprises and organizations, the exfiltration of data by covert channels piggybacking on VoIP signaling and media sessions becomes a serious threat. Wojciech et al. [13] exploited free/unused protocol fields and used intentionally delayed audio packets to create a covert channel. Takhiro et al. [21] discussed various audio steganographic and watermarking techniques that may possible be used to create VoIP covert channels. Huang et al. [12] presented a novel high-capacity steganography algorithm for embedding data in the inactive frames of low bit rate audio streams encoded by `G.723.1` source codec.

The CALEA infrastructure is vulnerable to malicious attacks. Lawful interception requires the telephone service providers to al-

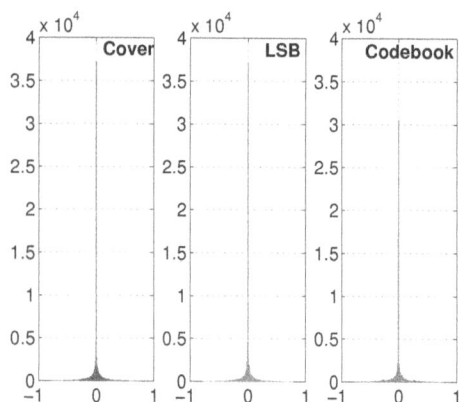

Figure 15: Statistical Analysis

low access to some particular target's call content and its related meta data. However, Sherr et al. [17] demonstrated the ability to prevent call audio from being recorded by injecting in-band signaling tones into a conversation. It is also possible that an attacker can overload the wiretapping system and prevent critical information to be logged [18]. Recently, Bates et al. [5] proposed an accountable wiretapping architecture that enhances wiretapping systems by adding tamper-evident records of wiretap events. However, our proposed work demonstrates that an attack can work in a very stealthy manner and then circumvent the existing accountable wiretapping infrastructure.

8. CONCLUSION

In this paper, we have presented a new audio steganography approach to create a real-time covert communication channel within another real-time media session. Our approach exploits the approximate audio signal construction to hide and recover voice information. Through real experiments, we have shown that even if we have only a few key characteristic samples of the waveform, a good approximate audio signal can still be recreated. By interleaving the cover and covert media samples, we can construct a real time covert voice channel and ensure two parties to have a regular phone conversion but in a secure and private fashion. Our study will expose a serious challenge to the media interception techniques used by law enforcement agencies. We hope our proposed wiretap-proof approach will motivate researchers and practitioners to further evaluate the security of the deployed interception systems and perform the vulnerability assessment of covert channels that could be created within media streams.

9. ACKNOWLEDGMENT

We would like to thank the VoDaSec team for their insightful feedback and comments. This work was partially supported by ARO grant W911NF-11-1-0149 and ONR grant N00014-13-1-0088. Any opinions, findings, and conclusions or recommendations expressed in this material are those of the authors and do not necessarily reflect the views of the funding agencies.

10. REFERENCES

[1] Peers Softphone. Website, http://peers.sourceforge.net/, 2013.

[2] S-Tools 4.0. Website, http://www.spychecker.com/program /stools.html, 2013.

[3] Steghide. Website, http://steghide.sourceforge.net/, 2013.

[4] VoiceAge – Open G.729. Website, http://www.voiceage.com/ openinit_g729.php, 2013.

[5] A. Bates, K. Butler, M. Sherr, C. Shields, and P. T. M. Blaze. Accountable Wiretapping -or- I know they can hear you now. In *NDSS*, 2012.

[6] D. McCullagh. Bin Laden: Steganography Master? Website, http://www.wired.com/politics/law/news/2001/02/41658? currentPage=all, 2012.

[7] O. Dabeer, K. Sullivan, U. Madhow, S. Chandrasekeran, and B. S. Manjunath. Detection of hiding in the least significant bit. In *In IEEE Trans. on Signal Processing*, pages 3046–3058, 2004.

[8] Fabien Petitcolas. mp3stego. Website, http://www.petitcolas .net/fabien/steganography/mp3stego/, 2013.

[9] J. Fridrich, M. Goljan, and R. Du. Reliable Detection of LSB Steganography in Color and Grayscale Images. *IEEE Multimedia*, 8:22–28, 2001.

[10] Gary C. Kessler. Steganography: Hiding Data Within Data. Website, http://www.garykessler.net/library/steganography .html, 2012.

[11] Heinz Repp. Hide4PGP. Website, http://www.heinz-repp.onli nehome.de/Hide4PGP.htm.

[12] Y. F. Huang, S. Tang, and J. Yuan. Steganography in Inactive Frames of VoIP Streams Encoded by Source Codec. *IEEE Transactions on Information Forensics and Security*, 6:296–306, 2011.

[13] W. Mazurczyk and K. Szczypiorski. Steganography of VoIP streams. *CoRR*, abs/0805.2938, 2008.

[14] N. Provos and P. Honeyman. Hide and seek: An introduction to steganography. *IEEE Security and Privacy*, 1(3):32–44, May-June 2003.

[15] J. Rosenberg, H. Schulzrinne, G. Camarillo, A. Johnston, J. Peterson, R. Sparks, M. Handley, and E. Schooler. SIP: Session Initiation Protocol. RFC 3261, IETF Network Working Group, 2002.

[16] l)ruid. DEFCON 15: Real-time Steganography with RTP. Website, http://www.youtube.com/watch?v=boTZ0ZAcF5I.

[17] M. Sherr, E. Cronin, S. Clark, and M. Blaze. Signaling Vulnerabilities in Wiretapping Systems. *IEEE Security & Privacy*, 3(6):13–25, 2005.

[18] M. Sherr, G. Shah, E. Cronin, S. Clark, and M. Blaze. Can they hear me now?: a security analysis of law enforcement wiretaps. In *ACM Conference on Computer and Communications Security*, 2009.

[19] K. Sullivan, O. Dabeer, U. Madhow, B. Manjunath, S. Chandrasekaran, and S. Chandrasekeran. LLRT Based Detection of LSB Hiding. In *In Proceedings of ICIP*, pages 497–500, 2003.

[20] T. Mogg . Anonymous hacks call between FBI and Scotland Yard about hackers. Website, http://www.digitaltrends.com/ international/anonymous-hacks-call-between-fbi-and-scotla nd-yard-about-hackers, 2012.

[21] T. Takahashi and W. Lee. An assessment of VoIP covert channel threats. In *SecureComm*, 2007.

[22] The Bots. The George W. Bush Public Domain Audio Archive. Website, http://www.thebots.net/GWBushSample Archive.htm, 2012.

[23] C. Wang and Q. Wu. Information Hiding in Real-Time VoIP Streams. *Proceedings of the Ninth IEEE International Symposium on Multimedia*, pages 255–262, 2007.

[24] A. Westfeld and A. Pfitzmann. Attacks on Steganographic Systems. In *Information Hiding*, pages 61–76, 1999.

[25] Wikipedia. CALEA. Website, http://en.wikipedia.org/wiki/Communications_Assistance_for_Law_Enforcement_Act, 2013.

[26] Wikipedia. Greek wiretapping case. Website, http://en.wikipedia.org/wiki/Greek_wiretapping_case_2004%E2%80%932005, 2013.

[27] Wikipedia. PESQ. Website, http://en.wikipedia.org/wiki/PESQ, 2013.

[28] Wikipedia. Raj Rajaratnam. Website, http://en.wikipedia.org/wiki/Raj_Rajaratnam, 2013.

[29] Wikipedia. Rod Blagojevich. Website, http://en.wikipedia.org/wiki/Rod_Blagojevich, 2013.

[30] Wikipedia. Steganography. Website, http://en.wikipedia.org/wiki/Steganography, 2013.

[31] C. V. Wright, L. Ballard, S. E. Coull, F. Monrose, and G. M. Masson. Spot Me if You Can: Uncovering Spoken Phrases in Encrypted VoIP Conversations. In *IEEE Symposium on Security and Privacy*, 2008.

[32] C. V. Wright, L. Ballard, S. E. Coull, F. Monrose, and G. M. Masson. Uncovering Spoken Phrases in Encrypted Voice over IP Conversations. *ACM Trans. Inf. Syst. Secur.*, 13(4):35, 2010.

Author Index

9 781450 331012